lonely planet

Mexico

D1052087

Baja California p700

**Copper Can
Northern M** p743

**Northern
Central
Highlands** p636

**Central
Pacific
Coast** p491

**Western
Central
Highlands** p576

**Around Mexico
City** p140

**Mexico
City** p62

Veracruz p203

Oaxaca p419

**Chiapas &
Tabasco** p347

**Yucatán
Peninsula** p254

THIS EDITION WRITTEN AND RESEARCHED BY

John Noble, Kate Armstrong, Stuart Butler, John Hecht, Anna Kaminski,
Tom Masters, Josephine Quintero, Brendan Sainsbury, Andy Symington,
Phillip Tang, Lucas Vidgen

Contents

PLAN YOUR TRIP

Welcome to Mexico 6
Mexico Map.............8
Mexico's Top 21........10
Need to Know 20
First Time Mexico...... 22
What's New 24
If You Like............. 25
Month by Month....... 30
Itineraries 34
Eat & Drink Like a Local........... 42
Exploring Mexico's Ancient Ruins 48
Travel with Children.... 54
Regions at a Glance.....57

ON THE ROAD

MEXICO CITY 62

AROUND MEXICO CITY 140
North of Mexico City ...141
Tepotzotlán 141
Tula................... 144
Teotihuacán........... 146
Pachuca 150
East of Mexico City ... 154
Puebla 154
Cholula................ 163
Popocatépetl & Iztaccíhuatl 166
Tlaxcala 167

Cacaxtla & Xochitécatl ...171
La Malinche............173
Huamantla.............173
Cantona 174
Cuetzalan.............174
Yohualichán............176
South of Mexico City...176
Tepoztlán..............176
Cuautla................ 180
Cuernavaca 182
Taxco 190
Parque Nacional Grutas de Cacahuamilpa 195
West of Mexico City...196

JUSTIN FOULKES /LONELY PLANET ©

Contents

Toluca 196
Nevado de Toluca 199
Valle de Bravo 199
Malinalco 201
Ixtapan de la Sal 202

VERACRUZ 203
Veracruz City 205
Central Veracruz 216
Central Coast 216
Xalapa 217
Córdoba 228
Fortín de las Flores 230
Coscomatepec 232

Orizaba 232
Pico de Orizaba 235
Northern Veracruz 236
Tuxpan 236
Papantla 238
El Tajín 240
Southeast Veracruz . . . 245
Tlacotalpan 245
Santiago Tuxtla 247
Tres Zapotes 248
San Andrés Tuxtla 248
Catemaco 250

Reserva de la
Biosfera Los Tuxtlas 252

**YUCATÁN
PENINSULA 254**
Quintana Roo 255
Cancún 255
Isla Mujeres 266
Isla Contoy 271
Isla Holbox 271
Puerto Morelos 273
Playa del Carmen 275
Isla Cozumel 279
Akumal 284
Tulum 286
Mahahual 294
Xcalak 295
Laguna Bacalar 296
Chetumal 297
Yucatán State 300
Mérida 301
Celestún 317
Dzibilchaltún 318
Progreso 319

Izamal 320
Chichén Itzá 322
Valladolid 328
Ek' Balam 331
Río Lagartos 332
Campeche State 333
Campeche 333
Edzná 339
Bolonchén de Rejón
& Xtacumbilxunaan 342
Balamkú 343
Calakmul 343
Chicanná 344
Becán 344
Xpujil 345
Río Bec 346
Hormiguero 346

**CHIAPAS
& TABASCO 347**
Chiapas 350
Tuxtla Gutiérrez 350
Chiapa de Corzo 355
San Cristóbal
de las Casas 358
Ocosingo 377
Toniná 378
Agua Azul & Misol-Ha . . . 379
Palenque 380
Bonampak, Yaxchilán
& the Carretera
Fronteriza 390
Comitán 400
El Soconusco
& Beaches 406
Tapachula 409
Tabasco 414
Villahermosa 414

SAN MIGUEL DE ALLENDE
P661

OAXACA......... 419
Oaxaca City......... 422
Valles Centrales 443
Monte Albán 443
Valle de Tlacolula....... 445
Valle de Zimatlán 449
Valle de Etla........... 451
Sierra Norte 452
Pueblos Mancomunados. .452
Western Oaxaca 454
Yanhuitlán, Coixtlahuaca
& Teposcolula 454
Oaxaca Coast 455
Puerto Escondido....... 456
Pochutla............. 469
Puerto Ángel 470
Zipolite............... 471
San Agustinillo 474
Mazunte............... 476
La Ventanilla 479
Bahías de Huatulco 480
Barra de la Cruz........ 487
**Isthmus
of Tehuantepec 487**
Salina Cruz 488
Tehuantepec 488
Juchitán.............. 488

CENTRAL PACIFIC
COAST 491
Mazatlán 493
Mexcaltitán 506
San Blas............. 507
Tepic................ 511
Chacala 512
San Francisco 514
Sayulita 515
Punta de Mita & Around ..517
Puerto Vallarta 518
Costalegre Beaches..... 534
Bahía de Navidad....... 535
Manzanillo............ 538
Boca de Pascuales...... 542
Michoacán Coast 543
Lázaro Cárdenas 546
Troncones 546
Ixtapa 548
Zihuatanejo........... 550
South of Ixtapa
& Zihuatanejo 559
Pie de la Cuesta 561
Acapulco 562
Costa Chica........... 574

WESTERN CENTRAL
HIGHLANDS 576
Guadalajara.......... 577
Tequila 601
Amatitán 601
Lago de Chapala....... 601
Zona de Montaña....... 605
Inland Colima State... 607
Colima 607
Inland Michoacán......612
Morelia............... 612
Reserva Mariposa
Monarca.............. 621
Angangueo 623
Zitácuaro............. 623
Pátzcuaro............. 624
Uruapan.............. 631
Angahuan 635

NORTHERN CENTRAL
HIGHLANDS 636
Querétaro State 638
Querétaro 638
Tequisquiapan......... 645
Northeast
Querétaro State 646
Guanajuato State..... 648
Guanajuato 648
León 658
Dolores Hidalgo 658
San Miguel de Allende... 661
Aguascalientes State ..673

PABLO GUZMAN/LONELY PLANET ©

SPIDER MONKEY

Contents

Aguascalientes 673

San Luis Potosí State . . 678

San Luis Potosí 678

Matehuala 684

Real de Catorce 684

La Huasteca Potosina . . . 689

Ciudad Valles 689

Rio Verde 691

Zacatecas State 691

Zacatecas 691

La Quemada 699

BAJA CALIFORNIA . . 700

Northern Baja 702

Tijuana 702

Playas de Rosarito 709

Ensenada 710

La Bufadora 714

Parque Nacional
Constitución de 1857 714

Mexicali 715

Southern Baja 716

Guerrero Negro 717

San Ignacio 718

Santa Rosalía 720

Mulegé 721

Loreto 723

La Paz 727

La Ventana 732

Los Barriles 733

Cabo Pulmo 733

Reserva de la Biosfera
Sierra de la Laguna 734

San José del Cabo 734

Los Cabos Corridor 737

Cabo San Lucas 737

Todos Santos 740

**COPPER CANYON &
NORTHERN
MEXICO 743**

**The Copper Canyon &
Ferrocarril Chihuahua
Pacífico 747**

Ferrocarril Chihuahua
Pacífico 749

El Fuerte 749

Cerocahui 752

Urique 753

Areponápuchi
(Posada Barrancas) 755

Parque de Aventura
Barrancas del Cobre 756

Divisadero 757

Creel 757

Batopilas 761

Northwest Mexico 764

Puerto Peñasco 765

Bahía de Kino 768

San Carlos 770

Álamos 771

Los Mochis 775

**Chihuahua &
Central North Mexico . . .777**

Chihuahua 777

Nuevo Casas Grandes &
Casas Grandes 783

Mata Ortiz 784

Hidalgo del Parral 784

Durango 786

Northeast Mexico 789

Saltillo 790

Parras 791

Cuatro Ciénegas 793

Monterrey 794

UNDERSTAND

Mexico Today 802

History 804

The Mexican
Way of Life 817

The Arts 821

The Mexican
Kitchen 830

Landscapes
& Wildlife 836

SURVIVAL GUIDE

Directory A–Z 846

Transportation 858

Language 865

Index 878

Map Legend 894

SPECIAL FEATURES

**Off the Beaten
Track: Mexico 40**

**Eat & Drink
Like a Local 42**

**Exploring Mexico's
Ancient Ruins 48**

**Chichén Itzá
3D Illustration 324**

Welcome to Mexico

Palm-fringed beaches, chili-spiced cuisine; steamy jungles, teeming cities; fiesta fireworks, Frida's angst: Mexico conjures up diverse, vivid dreams. And the reality lives up to the imagining.

An Outdoor Life

With steaming jungles, smoking, snow-capped volcanoes, cactus-strewn deserts and 10,000km of coast strung with sandy beaches and wildlife-rich lagoons, Mexico is an endless adventure for the senses and a place where life is lived largely in the open air. Take it easy dining alfresco beside a Pacific beach or strolling Guanajuato's colonial streets. Or get out and hike Oaxaca's mountain cloud forests or snorkel warm Caribbean reefs.

Art & Soul of a Nation

Mexico's pre-Hispanic civilizations built some of the world's great archaeological monuments, including Teotihuacán's towering pyramids and the exquisite Maya temples of Palenque. The Spanish colonial era left beautiful towns full of tree-shaded plazas and richly sculpted stone churches and mansions, while modern Mexico has seen a surge of great art from the likes of Diego Rivera and Frida Kahlo. Top-class museums and galleries document the country's fascinating history and its endless creative verve. Popular culture is just as vibrant, from the underground dance clubs and street art of Mexico City to the wonderful handicrafts of the indigenous population.

Travel for All

Travel in Mexico is what you make it and the country caters to all types of visitor. Stay in pampering resorts on the Riviera Maya, budget beach huts on the Pacific or colonial mansions in the highlands. Eat gourmet fusion food in chic city restaurants or equally delicious grandmothers' recipes at a busy market *comedor* (food stall). Getting from A to B is easy with comfortable buses running almost everywhere and an extensive domestic flight network.

Los Mexicanos

At the heart of your Mexican experience will be the Mexican people. A super-diverse crew, from Mexico City hipsters to the shy indigenous villagers of Chiapas, they're renowned for their love of color and frequent fiestas, but they're also philosophical folk, to whom timetables are less important than *simpatía* (empathy). You'll rarely find Mexicans less than courteous. They're more often positively charming, and know how to please guests. They might despair of ever being well governed, but they're fiercely proud of Mexico, their one-of-a-kind homeland with all its variety, tight-knit family networks, beautiful-ugly cities, deep-rooted traditions, unique agave-based liquors and sensationally tasty, chili-laden food.

Why I Love Mexico

By John Noble, Writer

I first felt Mexico's pull when reading, as a teenager, the barely credible story of Cortés and the Aztecs. My first visit was three months' backpacking from Ciudad Juárez to Ciudad Cuauhtémoc, and I found a kind of spiritual home in the misty, mysterious highlands of Chiapas. Since then I've wandered over most parts of Mexico on many trips and come to love its coasts, jungles, volcanoes and cities – and its superbly tasty food, spectacular ancient civilizations, inspired art and handicrafts and, most of all, its charming, hospitable, so very *real* people.

For more about our writers, see page 896

Above: Parroquia de San Miguel Arcángel (p662), San Miguel de Allende

Mexico

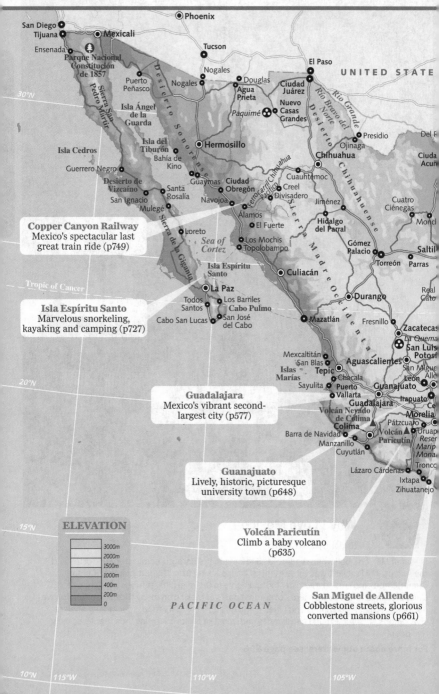

Copper Canyon Railway
Mexico's spectacular last
great train ride (p749)

Isla Espíritu Santo
Marvelous snorkeling,
kayaking and camping (p727)

Guadalajara
Mexico's vibrant second-
largest city (p577)

Guanajuato
Lively, historic, picturesque
university town (p648)

Volcán Paricutín
Climb a baby volcano
(p635)

San Miguel de Allende
Cobblestone streets, glorious
converted mansions (p661)

ELEVATION

| 3000m |
| 2000m |
| 1500m |
| 1000m |
| 400m |
| 200m |
| 0 |

PACIFIC OCEAN

N 0 — 300 km
0 — 150 miles

Fort Worth Dallas
OF AMERICA
Jackson
Montgomery
Baton Rouge
Tallahassee

Austin
Houston
San Antonio

edras Negras

evo
edo Laredo
McAllen
nterrey Reynosa Matamoros
Brownsville
Padre Island

Gulf of Mexico

25°N

Teotihuacán
The awesome Pyramids of
the Sun and Moon (p146)

Chichén Itzá
Simply spectacular ancient
Maya ruins (p322)

Mexico City
Mammoth, fascinating,
cultured metropolis (p62)

Tropic of Cancer

tehuala) Ciudad Victoria
Reserva de la Biosfera El Cielo
Tampico

eserva de la Biosfera Sierra Gorda

uerétaro
Pachuca

Mérida
Beautiful, cultured colonial
city (p301)

Ek'Balam
Río Lagartos
Progreso
Izamal
Tizimín
Mérida
Valladolid
Chichén Itzá
Uxmal

**Parque Nacional
Isla Contoy**
Isla Mujeres
Cancún
Puerto Morelos
Playa del Carmen
Isla Cozumel
Tulum

20°N

San Cristóbal de las Casas
Colonial charm and
Maya culture (p358)

Campeche

Felipe Carrillo Puerto
Reserva de la Biosfera Sian Ka'an

MEXICO CITY
Teotihuacán
Tlaxcala
Pico de Orizaba
Xalapa
Cardel
Veracruz
luca
ernavaca
Puebla
Taxco Cuautla
Popocatépetl
Córdoba
Orizaba
Tehuacán
Catemaco
Acayucan
Tlacotalpan
Santiago Tuxtla
Coatzacoalcos

Ciudad del Carmen

Reserva de la Biosfera Calakmul

Escárcega
Xpujil
Calakmul

Chetumal

Belize City
BELIZE

Chilpancingo
Acapulco
Pie de la Cuesta
erra Madre del Sur
Monte Albán
Oaxaca
Istmo de Tehuantepec
Juchitán
Tehuantepec
Tuxtla Gutiérrez
Villahermosa
Palenque
Ocosingo
Yaxchilán
San Cristóbal de las Casas
Comitán

Palenque
Exquisite Maya architecture
in jungle setting (p380)

Puerto Escondido
Pochutla
Puerto Ángel
Bahías de Huatulco
Tonalá
Reserva de la Biosfera La Encrucijada
Tapachula
Volcán Tacaná (4110m)

GUATEMALA
GUATEMALA CITY
SAN SALVADOR
EL SALVADOR

HONDURAS
TEGUCIGALPA

NICARAGUA

eserva Mariposa Monarca
Monarch butterflies in
their millions (p621)

Oaxaca Coast
Blissed-out beach-lovers'
nirvana (p455)

Oaxaca
Gorgeous handicrafts,
uniquely savory cuisine (p422)

100°W 95°W 90°W

Mississippi River
Río Usumacinta

Mexico's
Top 21

Peerless Palenque

1 Gather all your senses and dive head-first into the ancient Maya world at exquisite Palenque (p380), where pyramids rise above jungle treetops and furtive monkeys shriek and catapult themselves through dense canopies. Seek out the tomb of the mysterious Red Queen and her sarcophagus, wander the maze-like palace, gazing up at its iconic tower, then scale the stone staircase of the Templo de las Inscripciones, the lavish mausoleum of Pakal (Palenque's mightiest ruler), to survey the sprawling ruins from its summit.

Templo de las Inscripciones (p381)

Mexico City, Cultural Capital

2 The nation's long-standing political capital (p62) clearly stands at the forefront of Mexico's cultural scene as well. Remember that this is where many of the country's top muralists left behind their most important works, such as Diego Rivera's cinematic murals in the Palacio Nacional and the social-realism work of José Clemente Orozco in the Palacio de Bellas Artes. Art, music, dance and theater are everywhere – even a gondola ride along the ancient canals of Xochimilco wouldn't be complete without taking in a fervent mariachi ballad.

Monumento a la Independencia (p84)

BY: FER GREGORY/SHUTTERSTOCK ©

FITOPARDO.COM/GETTY IMAGES ©

The Pyramids of Teotihuacán

3 Once among Mesoamerica's greatest cities, Teotihuacán (p146) lies just an hour out of Mexico City. The immense Pirámide del Sol (Pyramid of the Sun) and Pirámide de la Luna (Pyramid of the Moon) dominate the remains of the metropolis, which even centuries after its collapse in the 8th century AD remained a pilgrimage site for Aztec royalty. Today it's a magnet for those who come to soak up the mystical energies that are believed to converge here. Pirámide del Sol (p147)

Oaxaca City

4 This highly individual southern city (p422) basks in bright upland light and captivates everyone with its deliciously inventive take on Mexican cuisine, gorgeous handicrafts, frequent colorful fiestas, handsome colonial architecture, booming arts scene and fine mezcals distilled in nearby villages. Within easy reach are the superb ancient Zapotec capital, Monte Albán, dozens of indigenous villages with busy craft markets, and the cool, forested hills of the Sierra Norte, perfect for hikers, mountain bikers and horseback riders. Oaxacan dessert stall

3

Mexico's Last Train Journey

5 The Ferrocarril Chihuahua Pacífico (Copper Canyon Railway; p749) remains one of Latin America's best rail trips. Trains climb from sea level at Los Mochis to Chihuahua's high desert plains via the sensational rocky landscapes of the Copper Canyon. Vistas from your window include alpine forests, subtropical valleys and glimpses of some of the world's deepest canyons. Alight at a photogenic stop for 15 minutes, or stay for days of exploring, hiking and biking.

Marvelous Mérida

6 The cultural capital (p301) of the Yucatán Peninsula, this large but manageable city has a beautifully maintained colonial heart. It's veined with narrow cobbled streets and dotted with sunny plazas, with a wealth of museums and galleries and some of the best food in the region. Just out of town are wildlife reserves, graceful haciendas (estates) and jungle-shrouded cenotes (sinkholes) to swim in. A little further afield, the little-visited Maya sites along the Ruta Puuc allow you to step back in time without the tour groups.

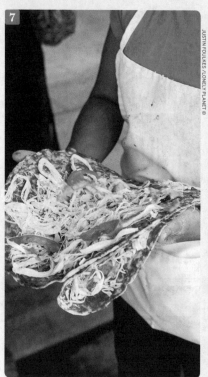

JUSTIN FOULKES /LONELY PLANET ©

Savor the Flavors

7 Mexican cuisine is like no other, and every part of the country has its own regional specialties, based on seasonal local ingredients and what's fresh on the day. For the tastiest travels, try local dishes from restaurants and busy market and street stalls – you'll lose count of the delicious culinary experiences you encounter. When it's time for fine dining, seek out some of the legion of creative contemporary chefs who concoct amazing flavor combinations from traditional and innovative ingredients. Street vendor with *tlayudas*

Shopping for Artisan Crafts

8 Mexico's infinitely varied *artesanías* (handicrafts) are today's successors to the beautiful costumes and ceramics of the pre-Hispanic nobility, and to the handcrafted clothes, baskets and pots of their humbler subjects. When browsing city stores, wandering through markets, or visiting artisans in their workshops to purchase textiles, silver and turquoise jewelry, ironwood carvings, bead-inlaid masks and more, the skill, creativity and color sense of potters, weavers, metalsmiths, carvers and leather workers delights the eye and tempts the pocket.

Relax on the Oaxaca Coast

9 After a few days on this 550km sequence of sandy Pacific beaches (p455) you'll be so relaxed you may not be able to leave. Head for the surf mecca and fishing port of Puerto Escondido, the low-key resort of Bahías de Huatulco, or the ultra-laid-back hangouts of Zipolite, San Agustinillo or Mazunte. Soak up the sun, eat good food, imbibe in easygoing beach bars and, when the mood takes you, have a swim, surf or snorkel, or board a boat to sight turtles, dolphins, whales, crocs or birdlife. Puerto Escondido (p456)

Magical San Cristóbal

10 Saunter the cobblestone streets of hill-ringed San Cristóbal de las Casas (p358), the high-altitude colonial city in the heart of indigenous Chiapas. A heady mix of modern and Maya, with cosmopolitan cafes and traditional culture, it's also a jumping-off point for Chiapas' natural attractions and fascinating Tzotzil and Tzeltal villages. Spend sunny days exploring its churches and bustling markets, or riding a horse through fragrant pine forest, and chilly evenings warmed by the fireplace of a cozy watering hole.

Chichén Itzá

11 There's a reason why this Maya site (p322) was declared one of the new Seven Wonders of the World – it is simply spectacular. From the imposing, monolithic El Castillo pyramid (where the shadow of the plumed serpent god Kukulcán creeps down the staircase during the spring and autumn equinoxes) to the Cenote Sagrado (Sacred Cenote) and curiously designed El Caracol, the legacy of Mayan astronomers will blow your mind. Cenote Sagrado (p326)

Huasteca Potosina, San Luis Potosí

12 Gorgeously green, lush Huasteca Potosina (p689), a subregion of San Luis Potosí, offers ruins, fascinating cave visits and wild and wet experiences. You can plunge into, boat to or ogle at a number of stunning waterfalls and rivers. Huastec culture is strong here: don't miss trying a local *zacahuil,* a massive *tamal.* The region is home to surrealist garden, Las Pozas, where gigantic Dalí-esque structures 'strut' their quirky stuff. Cascada de Tamul (p690)

Costa Maya

13 Do yourself a favor and get to this region while the going's still good. Unlike the overdeveloped Cancún and Riviera Maya, you can still find quiet fishing villages on the Costa Maya that put a premium on sustainable development, such as Mahahual (p294) and Xcalak (p295), both of which boast some of the best dive sites on the Caribbean coast. Then head inland for Laguna Bacalar (p296), a laid-back lakeside town known for its mesmerizing scenery, a 90m-deep cenote and an old Spanish fortress. Laguna Bacalar (p296)

JACOBO ZANELLA/GETTY IMAGES ©

WITOLD SKRYPCZAK/GETTY IMAGES ©

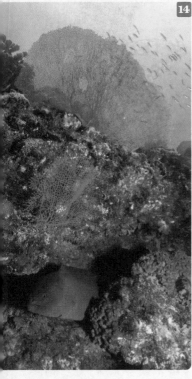

Cabo Pulmo

14 Rediscover the magic of old Baja by visiting the largely undeveloped east coast, discovering world-class diving off Cabo Pulmo (p733), the only coral reef on the west coast of North America and, at 71 sq km acres, one of the largest and most successful marine protected regions in the world. In this beautiful place you can see expect to see black coral bushes, schools of trigger fish, yellowfin tuna and snapper. Depending on the seasons and currents, you may also spy hammerhead sharks, huge manta rays and whale sharks.

Volcán Paricutín

15 As volcanoes go, Paricutín (p635) is still in its kindergarten years. Blasting out of a Michoacán maize field in 1943, it's one of the youngest volcanoes on Earth and the only one whose life cycle has been fully studied by scientists. Miraculously, Paricutín is also relatively easy to climb. Some rock hop across barren lava fields to bag the peak, others ride horses through hot black sand before dismounting for the final summit scramble. The goal's the same: a chance to stand atop a veritable geological marvel, viewing nature at its rawest.

Pico de Orizaba

16 Touch the sky high above Mexico on the gruelling climb to the 5611m summit of Pico de Orizaba (p235), the snow-capped highest mountain in the country. The trek is no walk in the park. You'll need the help of an experienced local trekking operator, clothing for extreme cold and a sense of adventure as big as the mountain itself. If this all sounds a bit extreme for you, enjoy any number of less-demanding trails on the peak's lower slopes.

GREG ELMS/GETTY IMAGES ©

Gregarious Guadalajara

17 Mexico's second-largest city (p577) dazzles despite being more a collection of pueblos than a great metropolis. This charmer gets under your skin with colonial buildings, lofty churches, labyrinthine markets, awesome public spaces and wonderful craft shopping in arty suburbs Tlaquepaque and Tonalá. The young and middle class party all weekend in smart bars and heaving dance clubs, and there's nowhere better in western Mexico to eat out, whether you're after local specialties such as spicy goat stew, or chic Mexican-French fusion cuisine.

Monarchs in their Millions

18 Canopies of golden-orange butterflies cover the forests and hill-sides in the Reserva Mariposa Monarca (Monarch Butterfly Reserve, p621), perhaps Mexico's most astonishing yearly natural phenomenon. It's the kind of annual event to plan your trip around – between November and March the migrant monarchs cover every surface, weighing down tree branches and changing the landscape into a permanent sunset as the butterflies winter far from the freezing Great Lakes during one of the planet's most spectacular migrations.

Espíritu Santo

19 Espíritu Santo (p727) island is spectacular in every way. Pink sandstone has been eroded by wind and waves into finger-like protrusions, each harboring a beautiful cove. And if this otherworldly beauty isn't enough then you can descend into the endless blue with whale sharks, dive the many colorful reefs, camp under a canopy of stunning stars, watch frolicking sea lions at their island colony and paddle your way along myriad azure bays.

Pacific Coastline

20 Running from the desert islands of Baja California to verdant coves backed by tropical mountains; from stretches of sand to mangrove-fringed lagoons teeming with birds, Mexico's Pacific coastline (p491) is stunning in its natural beauty. The primordial grandeur is punctuated by a series of resort towns – Mazatlán, Puerto Vallarta, Manzanillo, Ixtapa, Zihuatanejo, Acapulco – and world-class surf spots such as Barra de Nexpa, Boca de Pascuales, Troncones and Puerto Escondido, where clear barrels batter the shores. Acapulco (p562)

Guanajuato City

21 The glorious World Heritage–listed city of Guanajuato (p648) packs a huge amount into its narrow valley. The mining town turned colorful university city is a feast of plazas, museums, colonial mansions and pastel-hued houses. Snake your way along pedestrian alleyways, people-watch in squares, mingle with mariachi groups, or party hard at *estudiantinas* (traditional street parties) and in the many student bars. The underground tunnels – the town's major transportation routes – make for a particularly quirky way to get around.

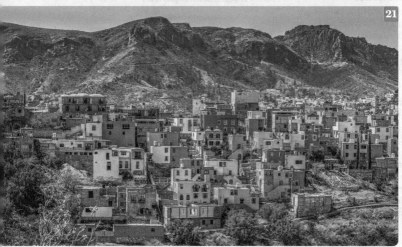

Need to Know

For more information, see Survival Guide (p845)

Currency
Peso (M$)

Language
Spanish; also about 70 indigenous languages.

Visas
All tourists must have a tourist permit, available on arrival. Some nationalities also need visas.

Money
ATMs and exchange offices widely available. Credit cards accepted in many midrange and top-end hotels.

Cell Phones
Many US and Canadian cellular carriers offer Mexico roaming deals. Mexican SIM cards can only be used in unlocked phones.

Time
Most of Mexico is on Hora del Centro (GMT/UTC minus six hours). Six northern and western states are on GMT/UTC minus seven or eight hours. Daylight savings applies in most of Mexico from April to October.

When to Go

Cabo San Lucas
GO Jan–Dec

Puerto Vallarta
GO Nov–May

Mexico City
GO Mar–Oct

Cancún
GO Nov–Aug

Oaxaca
GO Feb–Nov

Desert or semi-desert, dry climate
Warm to hot summers, mild winters
Tropical climate, wet & dry season
Tropical climate, rain year-round

High Season
(Dec–Apr)

➡ The driest months for most of Mexico, bringing winter escapees from colder countries.

➡ Christmas and Easter are Mexican holiday times, with transportation and coastal accommodations very busy.

Shoulder Season
(Jul & Aug)

➡ Vacation time for many Mexicans and foreigners. Hot almost everywhere and very wet on the Pacific coast. Accommodations prices go up in some popular areas.

Low Season
(May, Jun, Sep–Nov)

➡ May and June see peak temperatures in many areas.

➡ September is the heart of the hurricane season, which doesn't always bring hurricanes but does bring heavy rains on the Gulf and Pacific coasts.

Useful Websites

Mexico Cooks! (http://mexico cooks.typepad.com) Excellent blog on Mexican life.

Lonely Planet (www.lonely planet.com/mexico) Destination information, hotel bookings, traveler forum, videos and more.

México (www.visitmexico.com) Official tourism site with plenty of helpful ideas.

Planeta.com (www.planeta. com) Articles, listings, links, photos and more.

Geo-Mexico (http://geo-mexico. com) All sorts of informative and surprising stuff about Mexico.

Mexico Travel (http://gomexico. about.com) Travel news and info.

Important Numbers

Country code	52
Emergency	911
International access code	00
National tourist assistance (including emergencies)	088

Exchange Rates

Australia	A$1	M$11.90
Belize	BZ$1	M$8.29
Canada	C$1	M$12.38
Euro zone	€1	M$17.60
Guatemala	Q1	M$2.17
Japan	¥100	M$13.47
New Zealand	NZ$1	M$10.79
UK	UK£1	M$25.04
USA	US$1	M$16.56

For current exchange rates, see www.xe.com.

Daily Costs

**Budget:
Less than M$700**

➡ Hostel dorm bed: M$180; double room in budget hotel: M$350–600

➡ *Comida corrida* (fixed-price lunch) in economical restaurant: M$60–80

➡ 250km bus trip: M$220

**Midrange:
M$700–M$2000**

➡ Double room in midrange hotel: M$600–1200

➡ Good dinner with drinks: M$200–300

➡ Museum admission: M$10–70

➡ City taxi ride: M$30–60

➡ Hiking/rafting/mountain-biking day trip M$900–2000

**Top End:
More than M$2000**

➡ Double room in top-end hotel: M$1200–5000

➡ Fine dinner with drinks: M$300–500

➡ Personalized day tour: M$1500–2000

➡ Two-hour horseback ride: M$1000

Opening Hours

Where there are significant seasonal variations in opening hours, we provide hours for high season. Some hours may be shorter in shoulder and low seasons. Hours vary widely but the following are fairly typical.

Banks 9am-4pm Mon-Fri, 9am-1pm Sat

Stores/Shops 9am-8pm Mon-Sat (supermarkets and department stores 9am-10pm daily)

Restaurants 9am-11pm

Cafes 8am-10pm

Bars 1pm-midnight

Arriving in Mexico

Mexico City airport (p134) Authorized taxis, with ticket offices inside the airport, cost M$235 to central areas. Metrobús buses (M$30 plus M$10 for a smart card sold by machines inside the airport) serve some central areas. The metro (subway; M$5) operates from 5am (6am Saturday, 7am Sunday) to midnight; its Terminal Aérea station is 200m from the airport's Terminal 1.

Cancún airport (p265) Airport shuttles to downtown or the hotel zone cost around M$160 per person; taxis cost up to M$500. ADO buses run to downtown Cancún (M$64), Playa del Carmen and Mérida.

Getting Around

Bus Mexico's efficient, comfortable and reasonably priced bus network is generally the best option for moving around the country. On average you pay about M$1.10 per kilometer on 1st-class buses, covering around 75km per hour. Services are frequent on main routes.

Car A convenient option giving maximum independence. Roads are serviceable, with speeds generally slower than north of the border or in Europe. Rental rates start around M$600 per day, including basic insurance.

Air Over 60 cities are served by domestic flights, which are well worth considering for longer inter-city trips. Fares vary widely depending on the airline and how far in advance you pay.

For much more on **getting around**, see p860

First Time Mexico

For more information, see Survival Guide (p845)

Checklist

➡ Check that your passport is valid for at least six months beyond your stay in Mexico

➡ If flying, make sure you have a return ticket

➡ Organize travel insurance

➡ Make bookings (for accommodations, travel, restaurants)

➡ Inform your credit/debit card company

➡ Check if you can use your cell phone

➡ Get necessary immunizations well in advance

➡ Check your government's Mexico travel information

What to Pack

➡ International electrical adaptor (for non-North Americans)

➡ Swimming and beach gear

➡ Flashlight (torch)

➡ Driver's license (if driving)

➡ Sun hat and shades

➡ Sunscreen

➡ A waterproof garment

➡ Sturdy footwear

➡ Warm clothing

➡ Charcoal tablets to treat Montezuma's Revenge

➡ Phrasebook

Top Tips for Your Trip

➡ Expect the unfamiliar. If the strangeness of a foreign land starts to get to you, stay somewhere where you feel comfortable. International cuisine is available in almost any town.

➡ Get out of the cities and coastal resorts into the countryside and smaller towns and villages, where you'll see a side of Mexican life that many tourists miss.

➡ Try not to worry too much. Mexico's much-reported drug-gang violence happens mostly in a small number of places, chiefly in border towns, and tourists are rarely targeted. The country's most visited areas are little touched by the violence.

➡ Accept that things won't run like clockwork; live on zen time.

➡ Don't spread yourself too thin; pick a part of Mexico that you particularly want to explore.

What to Wear

In beach towns, shorts and short skirts are common; sleeveless tops are fine. Take some sleeves and long pants/skirts to protect against sun and mosquitoes, and for evenings or non-beach towns. Dress conservatively when visiting churches. Pack a sweater or warm jacket for cooler inland areas and air-conditioned buses or planes. A sun hat is essential; good, inexpensive ones are sold in Mexico.

Sleeping

Reserve accommodations for your first night in Mexico, if you're arriving somewhere at night, and if you're traveling during busy seasons.

Hotels These cover the spectrum, from basic budget establishments to chic boutique hotels and luxurious five-star resorts.

Hostels These exist in most places budget travelers congregate. Many have good facilities and often private rooms as well as dorms.

Cabañas Cabins and huts, mostly found at beach destinations, ranging from very basic to positively luxurious.

Camping & Hammocks In more budget-oriented beach spots, you can often sleep in a hammock or pitch a tent very cheaply.

Money

Plan on making cash purchases with pesos. Few businesses accept US dollars. It's easy to get pesos from ATMs using a major credit or debit card; all international airports have ATMs. Take a small reserve of cash (US dollars or, second-best, euros) to exchange at banks or *casas de cambio* (exchange offices) if ATMs prove unavailable. You can pay with major credit and debit cards at many airlines, midrange and top-end hotels, restaurants and stores.

Bargaining

It's worth asking if discount is available on room rates, especially if it's low season or you're staying more than two nights. In markets some haggling is expected. Unmetered taxis will often shave some pesos off their initial asking price.

Tipping

Many service workers depend on tips to supplement miserable wages.

Restaurants Tip 10% to 15% unless service is included in the check.

Hotels It's nice (though optional) to leave 5% to 10% of your room costs for those who keep it clean and tidy.

Taxis Drivers don't expect tips unless they provide some extra service.

Porters Airport and hotel porters usually get M$50 to M$100.

Attendants Car-parking and gas-station attendants expect M$5 to M$10.

Language

Mexico's main language is Spanish. Many Mexicans in the world of tourism also speak some English, often good English. In any accommodations catering to international travelers, you can get by with English. Still, it's useful and polite to know at least a few words of Spanish – Mexicans appreciate being greeted with *'Buenos días'* and appreciate you making the effort, even if they break into fluent English.

1 **Where can I buy handicrafts?**
¿Dónde se puede comprar artesanías?
don·de se pwe·de kom·prar ar·te·sa·nee·as

Star buys in Mexico are the regional handicrafts produced all over the country, mainly by the indigenous people.

2 **Which *antojitos* do you have?**
¿Qué antojitos tiene? ke an·to·khee·tos tye·ne

'Little whimsies' (snacks) can encompass anything – have an entire meal of them, eat a few as appetisers, or get one on the street for a quick bite.

3 **Not too spicy, please.**
No muy picoso, por favor. no mooy pee·ko·so por fa·vor

Not all food in Mexico is spicy, but beware – many dishes can be fierce indeed, so it may be a good idea to play it safe.

4 **Where can I find a *cantina* nearby?**
¿Dónde hay una cantina cerca de aquí?
don·de ai oo·na kan·tee·na ser·ka de a·kee

Ask locals about the classical Mexican venue for endless snacks, and often dancing as well.

5 **How do you say ... in your language?**
¿Cómo se dice ... en su lengua?
ko·mo se dee·se ... en su len·gwa

Numerous indigenous languages are spoken around Mexico, primarily Mayan languages and Náhuatl. People will appreciate it if you try to use their local language.

Etiquette

Mexicans are not huge sticklers for etiquette. Their natural warmth takes precedence.

Greetings *'Mucho gusto'* (roughly 'A great pleasure') is a polite thing to say when you're introduced to someone, accompanied by a handshake. If it's a woman and a man, the woman offers her hand first.

Pleasing people Mexicans love to hear that you're enjoying their country. They are slow to criticize or argue, expressing disagreement more by nuance than by blunt contradiction.

Visiting homes An invitation to a Mexican home is an honor for an outsider; you will be treated very hospitably. Take a small gift, such as flowers or something for the children.

What's New

Drinking Revolution

Mexicans' taste for alcoholic beverages from small-scale artisan producers is taking off big time. Dozens of micro- and nano-breweries are challenging the industrial beer giants with tasty ales, stouts and other *cervezas artesanales* (craft beers), available in most cities, especially in bars with a younger clientele. Also fashionable are quality artisan versions of the agave-based spirit mezcal, the capital of which is Oaxaca. Fashionable *mezcalerías* (bars specializing in mezcal) are sprouting like cacti after rain in Oaxaca, Mexico City and elsewhere.

Las Palmitas

Mexico's largest mural is a jigsaw puzzle of rainbow-painted houses, bringing a community spirit and a pop of color to a flagging neighborhood in Pachuca. (p151)

Acuario Inbursa

Mexico City's new aquarium is one of the world's biggest and showcases manta rays, piranhas and crocodiles, with sand shipped in from Florida and seawater from Veracruz. (p91)

Mazatlán–Durango Highway

This incredible new highway through the Sierra Madre Occidental is one of the most scenic drives imaginable and includes the Americas' highest bridge, the Puente Baluarte, which soars 402m above the valley floor. (p789)

Mercado Roma

Mexico City's Roma neighborhood has taken your local market and spun it into gourmet food-hall gold at this trendy hangout, bringing together top-notch nibbles and ingredients from around the capital and the globe. (p114)

Síijil Noh Há

The wooded grounds at this sublime ecotourism center near Felipe Carrillo Puerto, run by the local Maya community, overlook a quiet lake with a swimmable freshwater spring. (p293)

Museo de la Ballena

La Paz' well-designed new museum covers everything you could want to know about the gray whales that live and breed in the local waters. (p727)

Pasaje Rodríguez

This atmospheric arty alley reflects Tijuana's growing urban art scene. The vibrant graffiti-style murals are the perfect backdrop to the boho-style cafes, music bars, bookstores and craft shops. (p702)

For more recommendations and reviews, see lonelyplanet.com/Mexico

If You Like...

Beach Resorts

Puerto Vallarta Pacific resort and LGBT capital with dazzling beaches, stylish restaurants and hot nightlife. (p518)

Playa del Carmen The chicest, hippest resort on the Caribbean coast. (p275)

Zihuatanejo Combines a livable feel and characterfully intimate center with pleasant beaches and great nearby coastline. (p550)

Cancún North of the megaresorts you'll be pleasantly surprised to find Cancún's quiet side: Isla Blanca. (p255)

Cabo San Lucas Three main family-friendly beaches, excellent facilities, numerous bars and restaurants and water sports. (p737)

Mazatlán Attractively renovated colonial center, an old-time 1950s promenade and fun-in-the-sun beach-resort strip. (p493)

Bahía de Kino For the best stretch of sand in the north, head to these dazzling beaches. (p768)

Getaway Beaches

Oaxaca Coast International budget travelers make a beeline for blissed-out Mazunte, San Agustinillo and Zipolite. (p455)

Xcalak Timeless Caribbean coast with a wonderful barrier reef. (p295)

Playa Maruata Tranquil, low-budget Michoacán fishing village beloved by beach bums and sea turtles. (p544)

Barra de Potosí Palm-fringed white sands, calm waters and a lagoon full of birds and crocs. (p559)

Isla Holbox Escape the Riviera Maya and wander the sandy roads of this palm-fringed Gulf coast getaway. (p271)

Playa Tecolote Shallow waters, a pristine sandy beach and boat trips to Espíritu Santo. (p732)

Los Tuxtlas These mountain-backed beaches are the Gulf of Mexico's ultimate dropout spot. (p252)

Luxury Spas & Hotels

Casa Oaxaca Boutique Oaxaca hotel dedicated to art, with gorgeous contemporary rooms and a colonial patio. (p434)

Banyan Tree Cabo Marqués Asian-influenced seclusion at this exclusive coastal retreat near Acapulco. (p568)

Posada La Poza Pacific-side retreat at Todos Santos with lush gardens, saltwater pool and Jacuzzi and superb restaurant. (p741)

Present Moment Combine the relaxing Troncones beach vibe with yoga, art and luxury dining. (p547)

Bungalows Breakfast Inn Luxurious, hammock-hung Cabo San Lucas bungalows surrounding a pool, delicious breakfasts and superb service. (p738)

Pueblo Lindo A rooftop pool overlooks the white houses of Taxco scattered across the hills. (p194)

Siete Lunas Stroll through jungle from fashionable Sayulita to reach this romantic cliff-top retreat. (p516)

Hacienda de los Santos An almost unbelievably beautiful hotel in the colonial town of Álamos. (p773)

Amuleto Perched high over Zihuatanejo, this boutique retreat offers the ultimate de-stress. (p555)

Pyramids & Temples

Palenque Exquisite Maya temples backed by jungle-covered hills. (p381)

Chichén Itzá Vast Maya temple complex, its step-pyramid design testimony to the Maya's exceptional astronomy skills. (p322)

Uxmal Set in hilly Puuc, this large Maya site is a riot of fascinating carved-stone orna-mentation. (pictured right; p311)

Yaxchilán Impressive temples in a Chiapas jungle setting, reached only by river. (p396)

Monte Albán The ancient Zapotec capital sits on a peerless hilltop site outside Oaxaca. (p443)

Tulum These late Maya temples and pyramids sit right on a rugged stretch of Caribbean coast. (p286)

Calakmul High pyramids in a huge, remote Maya city, still largely hidden in protected rainforest. (p343)

Teotihuacán Massive Pyramids of the Sun and Moon, and mural-decked palaces in Mexico's biggest ancient city. (p146)

Tzintzuntzan Atmospheric Tarascan ruins with fantastic Lake Pátzcuaro views, few crowds and unusual rounded temples. (p631)

Edzná Marvel at the fine carvings at the Templo de Mascarones (Temple of Masks). (p339)

Historic Colonial Towns

Guanajuato The opulent mansions and winding streets of this university town squeeze into a picturesque valley. (p648)

San Miguel de Allende Artsy town of cobblestone streets and lovely stone architecture, with many foreign (mostly US) residents. (p661)

Oaxaca Gorgeous southern city with an indigenous flavor and stunning art and artisanry. (p422)

Zacatecas The magnificent cathedral in this former silver-mining city is the ultimate expression of colonial baroque. (p691)

Top: Uxmal archaeological site (p311)
Bottom: Cowboy boots, Mercado San Juan de Dios, Guadalajara (p596)

Mérida Even if you're not big on architecture, the stately mansions here never cease to impress. (p301)

Álamos Wander the cobbled streets of northern Mexico's colonial jewel. (p771)

Todos Santos This former cane-milling town has streets lined with handsome 19th-century brick-and-adobe haciendas. (p740)

Puebla Dense with restored colonial churches and mansions, sparkling with *azulejos* (painted ceramic tiles). (p154)

Morelia Unesco-listed since 1991, Morelia is anchored by one of Mexico's most spectacular cathedrals. (p612)

San Cristóbal de las Casas A very indigenous highland town with winding cobblestone streets and old churches aplenty. (p358)

Shopping

Mexico City Everything from craft stores to boutiques to fashion, flea and food markets. (p127)

San Miguel de Allende A mind-boggling array of folk art from all over Mexico. (p670)

Guadalajara The artisans' suburbs of Tlaquepaque and Tonalá are replete with classy ceramics, furniture and glass-ware. (p596)

Tepotzotlán Colorful beaded jaguar heads and animal forms made by the Huichol people. (p141)

Taxco One of the best places in Mexico for silverwork, especially jewelry. (p190)

Oaxaca (p440) prizes its black clay pottery, while **Puebla** (p161) is famous for colorful Talavera ceramics.

For the best woolen crafts and colorful textiles, head for **San Cristóbal de las Casas** (p371) and **Tuxtla Gutiérrez** . (p350)

León Buy your shoes, belts and bags at this leatherworks capital. (p658)

Mérida The one-stop shop for hammocks, *guayaberas* (men's shirts), *huipiles* (long, sleeveless tunics) and handicrafts. (p301)

Mexican Cuisine

Mexico City Unrivaled countrywide fare, from fusion restaurants serving *nueva cocina mexicana* to the world's best tacos. (p109)

Seafood Baja California's fish tacos, Veracruz' *huachinango a la veracruzana* and ceviche in Barra de Navidad.

Oaxaca Famed for its seven *moles* (chili-based sauces) and some of the country's best contemporary restaurants. (p436)

Cooking classes Prepare your own Mexican feasts under expert guidance in Oaxaca, Zihuatanejo, Tepoztlán and Tlaxcala.

Antojitos These ubiquitous 'little whims' made with *masa* (corn dough) include tacos, quesadillas, enchiladas and *tamales*.

Guadalajara Mexico's second city pitches forward-thinking fusion food against old staples such as *birria* (spicy-hot soup) and *tortas ahogadas* (chili-soaked pork sandwiches). (p591)

Baja Med Feast on Mexican-Mediterranean mélange cuisine in Tijuana (p702) and elsewhere in Baja California (p700).

Yucatán Peninsula Flavorful dishes rooted in Maya culture, such as *cochinita pibil* (slow-roasted pork.) (p254)

Coatepec Smell the coffee in the home of Mexican brew. (p224)

Museums & Galleries

Museo Nacional de Antropología Mexico City's National Anthropology Museum is chock-full of stupendous relics from pre-Hispanic Mexico. (p86)

Museo Frida Kahlo The poignant Mexico City home of the haunted artist. (p95)

Palacio Nacional Diego Rivera's famous Mexican history mural in Mexico City. (p70)

Museo Nacional de la Muerte All things related to death in this Aguascalientes museum, but far from macabre. (p673)

Museo de Antropología A superbly designed Xalapa space with a marvelous archaeological collection. (p218)

Museo de las Culturas de Oaxaca Excellent Oaxaca museum in a beautiful ex-monastery demonstrates continuities between pre-Hispanic and contemporary culture. (p426)

Museo Jumex One of Latin America's leading contemporary-art collections at this Mexico City museum. (p91)

Horno3 Outstanding Monterrey museum in the gigantic shell of a former blast furnace. (p797)

Gran Museo del Mundo Maya World-class museum in Mérida showcasing more than 1100 well-preserved Maya artifacts. (p301)

Museo de la Ballena Excellent La Paz museum featuring the California gray whale and related conservation efforts. (p727)

Hiking trail, Copper Canyon (p747)

Diving & Snorkeling

Mexico's Caribbean coast, with the world's second-largest barrier reef, is world famous for its abundant coral and tropical fish.

Banco Chinchorro Wreck-studded coral atoll off the southern end of the Caribbean coast. (p294)

Isla Cozumel Diving and snorkeling for all abilities at the island's 65 reefs. (p279)

Bahías de Huatulco A string of beautiful Pacific bays with several coral plates and more than 100 dive sites. (p482)

Xel-Há This eco-park on the Riviera Maya offers snorkeling in a natural aquarium. (p274)

Laguna de la Media Luna Has an underwater cave ideal for advanced diving. (p691)

Cabo Pulmo A magnificent coral reef and spectacular diving and snorkeling experiences. (p733)

Espíritu Santo Swim and snorkel with whale sharks, the world's biggest fish. (p727)

Surfing

Puerto Escondido The Mexican Pipeline beach break is world famous, but Puerto has intermediate and beginners' waves, too. (p457)

Boca de Pascuales Legendary hollow, hard-breaking barrels – strictly for experts. (p542)

Troncones A long, strong, world-class left-point break and some excellent beach breaks. (p546)

Sayulita Dependable, medium-sized waves, good for practicing or learning, with a mellow party vibe. (p515)

Ensenada There's a wonderful point break at San Miguel. (p710)

Barra de Nexpa One of several spots with healthy waves along the little-touched Michoacán coast. (p545)

San Blas For intermediates and beginners, with many beach and point breaks, and one of the world's longest waves. (p508)

Todos Santos The beaches surrounding this town offer some of the best swells in Baja. (p741)

Hiking, Mountain Biking & Horseback Riding

Copper Canyon Bike down incredible trails, hike through extraordinary landscapes, or let the horse take the strain. (p747)

Pueblos Mancomunados These Oaxacan mountain villages are linked by a scenic trail network. (p452)

Oaxaca Outstanding short- or long-distance rides with Horseback Mexico and, by bike, with Bicicletas Pedro Martínez. (p431)

Rancho El Charro Horse treks into jungle-covered mountains behind Puerto Vallarta. (p521)

Bici-Burro Great mountain-bike outings from San Miguel de Allende. (p665)

Real de Catorce Explore the desert hills on foot, bike or horse from this magical old silver town. (p684)

Parque Nacional Bahía de Loreto This beautiful national park is a world-class destination for a wide range of activities. (p724)

Pico de Orizaba Hikes in Mexico don't get more breathless or challenging than scaling the country's highest mountain. (p235)

Cañón del Sumidero Skip the bus and pedal 86km from San Cristóbal to this Chiapas landmark. (p357)

Wildlife

Whales Watch whales in Baja California's lagoons off Mazatlán (p493), Puerto Vallarta (p518) or Puerto Escondido (December to March). (p456)

Butterflies The trees in Michoacán's Reserva Mariposa Monarca turn orange in winter with millions of monarch butterflies. (p621)

Sea turtles Cuyutlán, Playa Colola, Playa Escobilla, Tecolutla and Xcacel-Xcacelito beaches are all major sea-turtle breeding grounds.

Birds Mexico's forests and coastal lagoons thrill bird-watchers. For flamingos head to Río Lagartos or Celestún.

Parque Nacional Sierra San Pedro Mártir Look for Caifornia condors circling above, and bobcats, deer and bighorn sheep at ground level. (p715)

Reserva de la Biosfera Los Tuxtlas Explore the Americas' northernmost tropical rainforests in this impressively diverse reserve. (p252)

Kayaking & Rafting

Sea of Cortez The islands and estuaries off Baja California's east coast are the stuff of kayakers' dreams. (p700)

Pacific Coast Kayak along the lagoons or islands off the Pacific Coast from Puerto Vallarta and Troncones. (p491)

Veracruz rafting Ride the white-water rapids plunging down from the Sierra Madre Oriental from Jalcomulco. (p226)

Oaxaca rafting Rivers near Bahías de Huatulco have waters suitable for everyone from beginners to experienced rafters. (p483)

Mulegé Enjoy the mangrove- and palm-lined Río Mulegé via a kayak or raft. (p722)

Lagos de Montebello Paddle around these turquoise Chiapas lagoons in a traditional wooden *cayuco* (canoe.) (p405)

Tequila & Mezcal

Oaxaca The world mezcal capital boasts atmospheric mezcal bars ranging from hip hangouts to connoisseurs' cantinas. (p438)

Bósforo Duck into this Mexico City hideaway for the finest mezcals in town. (p118)

Tequila Visit the distilleries of the Jalisco town that the drink is named after. (p602)

Expo Tequila A prime Tijuana place to taste and rate tequila from all over Mexico. (p703)

La Fundación Mezcalería Mérida bar pours organic mezcals with nightly live music. (p307)

Month by Month

TOP EVENTS

Día de Muertos, November

Carnaval, February

Día de la Independencia, September

Monarch butterfly season, February

Guelaguetza, July

January

It's warm in coastal and lowland areas, cool in the highlands and dry everywhere, attracting flocks of foreign tourists. The first week is Mexican holiday season, with transportation booked up and coastal resorts very busy.

🎎 Día de los Santos Reyes

January 6 (Three Kings' Day or Epiphany), rather than Christmas, is the day when Mexican children traditionally receive presents, commemorating the Three Kings' gifts for the baby Jesus. Mexicans eat *rosca de reyes,* a large oval sweetbread decorated with candied fruit.

🐦 Migratory Bird Season

January is the peak season for migratory birds along Mexico's Pacific coast. Lagoons and rivers at places such as Laguna Manialtepec and Lagunas de Chacahua are packed with fowl, and San Blas even holds an International Migratory Bird Festival. (p509)

🎎 Mérida Fest

Between January 5 and 28, Mérida celebrates its diverse culture with daily dance, music, theater, art, acrobatic shows and other cultural events. (p305)

February

Temperatures are marginally higher than in January, but it remains dry, making this a great month to be in Mexico, though it can still be cold in the north and at high altitudes.

🐦 Whale-Watching Season

Magnificent gray whales calve in bays and lagoons around Baja California from mid-December to mid-April. Whales can also be spotted along the whole Pacific coast during this period. Best months for Baja whale-watching are February and March.

🎎 Día de la Candelaria

Candlemas (February 2), commemorating the infant Jesus' presentation in the temple, is widely celebrated. In Tlacotalpan several days of festivities feature bull-running in the streets and a flotilla of boats following an image of the Virgin down the Río Papaloapan. (p246)

🎎 Carnaval

A big bash preceding the 47-day penance of Lent, Carnaval happens during the week leading up to Ash Wednesday (March 1, 2017; February 14, 2018). It's wildest in Veracruz, La Paz and Mazatlán, with parades and plenty of music, drinking, dancing, fireworks and fun.

🐦 Monarch Butterfly Season

From mid-November to March the forests of the Reserva Mariposa Monarca (Monarch Butterfly Reserve) turn bright orange as millions of large monarch butterflies winter here. The best time to watch them is on a warm, sunny afternoon in February. (p621)

March

It's getting steadily warmer all over Mexico, but it's still dry and the winter season for foreign tourism continues.

🎭 Festival de México

Mexico City's historic center hosts music, theater, dance and literary events featuring talent from Mexico and abroad – the capital's biggest cultural bash of the year. (p102)

🏃 Vernal Equinox

Visitors mob Chichén Itzá for the spring (March 20 to 21) and autumnal (September 21 to 22) equinoxes, when shadows resemble a serpent ascending or descending El Castillo pyramid. Almost the same effect happens for a week preceding and following each equinox. (p322)

🎭 Festival Internacional del Cine

Mexico's biggest film event of the year draws top international actors and directors to Guadalajara for 10 days each March, with more than 250 films screened to more than 100,000 viewers. (p587)

☆ Spring Break

US students get a week's break in late February or March (dates vary between colleges) and many head to Mexican resorts such as Cancún, Puerto Vallarta or Cabo San Lucas for days of over-the-top partying.

Top: Dancer, Mérida Fest
Bottom: Día de Muertos souvenirs (p33)

April

Temperatures continue to increase, but it stays dry. Semana Santa (Easter Week), which can be in March or April, is Mexico's major holiday week of the year, with tourist accommodations and transportation packed.

✷✸ Semana Santa

Semana Santa is the week from Palm Sunday to Easter Sunday (April 16, 2017; April 1, 2018). Good Friday sees solemn processions in many places, and enormous crowds attend a re-enactment of the Crucifixion in Iztapalapa, Mexico City. (p102)

✷✸ Feria de San Marcos

Millions of people attend the exhibitions, bullfights, cockfights, rodeos, concerts and other events of Mexico's biggest state fair, in Aguascalientes. It lasts about three weeks from mid-April, with the biggest parade on April 25. (p675)

May

Temperatures reach annual peaks in cities such as Mérida (average daily high 35°C), Guadalajara (31°C), Oaxaca (30°C) and Mexico City (26°C). It's low season for tourism, meaning cheaper accommodations prices.

✷✸ Feria de Morelia

This three-week fair sees regional dance performances, bullfights, agricultural and handicraft exhibitions, fireworks and plenty of partying in the Michoacán capital. (p616)

✷✸ Feria de Corpus Christi

Papantla's big bash features spectacular *voladores* (fliers) performances and indigenous dances, plus *charreadas* (Mexican rodeos), parades and bullfights. (p238)

✷✸ Expo Artesanal

Taking place at the Centro Cultural Tijuana, this superb arts-and-crafts festival (May 20 to 24) features handicrafts for sale from all over Mexico.

✷✸ Cinco de Mayo

Celebrating the battle on May 5 in 1862 when Mexican forces defeated French troops, the streets of Puebla, where the fighting happened, close for a huge parade of floats with the military, performers and dancers entertaining more than 20,000 people with re-enactments and celebrations. The following two weeks feature other events. (p158)

June

The rainy season begins, bringing heavy downpours in the southeast, in some places along the Pacific coast and in the central highlands. Tourist numbers and hotel prices remain low.

✷✸ Festival del Mole Poblano

Puebla celebrates its most famous contribution to Mexican cuisine, the chocolatey *mole poblano* sauce, in early June. (p158)

🏃 Surf's Up

Countless spots along the Pacific coast, including Puerto Escondido with its legendary Mexican Pipeline, enjoy superb swells from April/May to October/November. June to August generally see the biggest waves. Beginners can learn to surf almost year-round.

July

It's rainy in the southeast, central highlands and along the Pacific coast, but this is a summer vacation month for both foreigners and Mexicans, bringing busy times and higher prices at many tourist destinations.

✷✸ Guelaguetza

Oaxaca is thronged for this fantastically colorful feast of regional dance on the first two Mondays after July 16, with plenty of other celebratory events accompanying it. (p432)

🏃 Swimming with Whale Sharks

Massive whale sharks congregate to feed on plankton off Isla Contoy between mid-May and mid-September. The best time to swim with these gentle giants is mid-June to July.

August

The summer holiday season continues, as do the rains, although they're less intense in most areas. June to August are brutally hot in the north.

✺ Feria de Huamantla

Huamantla, east of Mexico City, lets rip over a few days and nights during its mid-August fair. On August 14 the streets are carpeted with flowers and colored sawdust. A few days later there's a Pamplona-esque running of the bulls. (p173)

✺ La Morisma

Zacatecas stages a spectacular mock battle with 10,000 participants, commemorating the triumph of the Christians over the Moors in old Spain, usually on the last weekend of August. (p695)

September

It's the height of the hurricane season on the Yucatán Peninsula and Mexico's coasts. It's also rainy in most places, with poor visibility for Caribbean divers.

✺ Día de la Independencia

On Independence Day (September 16) patriotic celebrations mark the anniversary of Miguel Hidalgo's 1810 call to rebellion against Spain, the Grito de Dolores. On the 15th, the Grito is repeated from every Mexican town hall, followed by fireworks. The biggest celebrations are in Mexico City. (p102)

October

Low season for tourism, with the possibility of hurricanes, but the rains ease off everywhere

except the Yucatán Peninsula.

✺ Festival Internacional Cervantino

Guanajuato's two- to three-week arts festival, dedicated to Spanish writer Miguel de Cervantes, is one of the biggest cultural happenings in Latin America, with performances by worldwide music, dance and theater groups. (p653)

✺ Festival Internacional de Música

This classical-music festival takes place in Morelia and is befitting of a city that is home to the oldest music conservatory in the Americas. Performances are held in various plazas, churches and theaters. (p616)

🏃 Copper Canyon Season

October, along with November and March, is one of the best months to visit northwest Mexico's spectacular canyon country, with temperatures not too hot at the bottom of the canyons, nor too cold at the top.

November

A quiet month. The weather is mostly dry and temperatures are subsiding. Snow tops the high peaks of the central volcanic belt.

✺ Día de Muertos

On the Day of the Dead (November 2) cemeteries come alive as families decorate graves and commune

with their dead, some holding all-night vigils. Special altars appear in homes and public buildings. Associated events start days before, notably around Pátzcuaro and Oaxaca.

✺ Feria de la Plata

Some of Mexico's best silverwork is on show during the week-long national silver fair in Taxco in late November or early December. *Charreadas,* concerts, dances and donkey races add to the fun. (p193)

December

A dry month almost everywhere, and as cool as it gets. International winter tourism gets going and the Christmas–New Year period is Mexican holiday time, with accommodations busy and prices high.

✺ Día de Nuestra Señora de Guadalupe

Several days of festivities throughout Mexico lead up to the feast day of the Virgin, the country's religious patron – the Day of Our Lady of Guadalupe (December 12). Millions converge on Mexico City's Basílica de Guadalupe. (p103)

✺ Christmas

Christmas is traditionally celebrated with a feast in the early hours of December 25, after midnight Mass. Pre- or post-Christmas events in some towns include *pastorelas* (nativity plays), as in Tepotzotlán and Pátzcuaro, and *posadas* (candlelit processions), as in Taxco.

Plan Your Trip
Itineraries

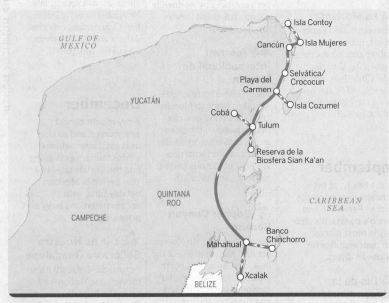

FLORIAN TROJER/GETTY IMAGES ©

Isla Contoy
Cancún — Isla Mujeres
Selvática/ Crococun
Playa del Carmen
Isla Cozumel
Cobá
Tulum
Reserva de la Biosfera Sian Ka'an

GULF OF MEXICO

YUCATÁN

QUINTANA ROO

CAMPECHE

CARIBBEAN SEA

Banco Chinchorro
Mahahual
Xcalak
BELIZE

10 DAYS Riviera Maya & Costa Maya Getaway

This journey showcases the best of Mexico's Caribbean coast, from the bustling beaches and nightlife of the Riviera Maya to the soporific charm of seaside villages along the Costa Maya. Some wonderfully scenic Maya ruins, caves and terrific diving and snorkeling add some action to a beach vacation.

Fly into Cancún and head straight for relaxed **Isla Mujeres'** beaches and snorkeling, taking a side trip to **Isla Contoy**, a national park with superlative bird-watching and, June to September, the chance to swim with whale sharks that congregate nearby.

Alternatively, opt for hip **Playa del Carmen**, with its own fine beaches, underwater activities and lively nightlife. 'Playa' is also the jumping-off point for the world-famous dive sites of **Isla Cozumel**. If you have kids, spend a day at the turtle farm on Isla Mujeres, one of the nearby 'eco-parks' such as **Selvática** with its 12 jungle zip-lines, or **Crococun** in Puerto

Maya ruins, Tulum (p286)

Morelos, an interactive zoo with crocodiles and wild monkeys. Next stop: **Tulum**, with one of Mexico's most perfect beaches and most spectacularly located Maya sites. Nearby are the pyramids and temples of **Cobá**, as well as the wildlife-rich Reserva de la Biosfera Sian Ka'an. South of Tulum the Costa Maya is less developed and less touristed than the Riviera Maya. Head to **Mahahual**, a laid-back village with snorkeling and diving at the coral atoll **Banco Chinchorro**, or the tiny fishing town of **Xcalak**, another excellent water-sports base. After three nights chilling at either of these, opt for a fourth night or, if you're worried that you missed out on **Cancún's** nightlife, spend your last night there.

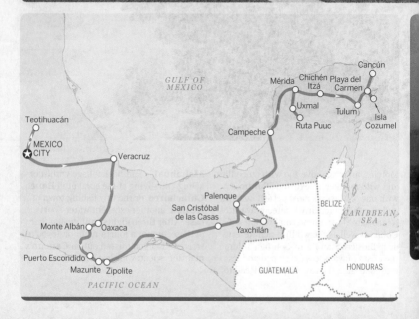

Beaches, Cities & Temples of Mexico's South

This classic journey leads south from Mexico's central heartland to its glorious Caribbean beaches, and gives a superb sampling of what makes the country so fascinating.

Start by exploring the exciting megalopolis of **Mexico City**, key to any understanding of the country. Take a side trip to the awesome pyramids at **Teotihuacán**, capital of ancient Mexico's biggest empire. Then head east to the fun-loving port city of **Veracruz**, before crossing the mountains southward to **Oaxaca**. This cultured colonial city, with Mexico's finest handicrafts, sits at the heart of a beautiful region with a large indigenous population. Don't miss the ancient Zapotec capital, **Monte Albán**, nearby.

Head to one of the relaxed beach spots on the Oaxaca coast, such as **Puerto Escondido**, **Mazunte** or **Zipolite**, for a few days' sun, surf and sand, before continuing east to **San Cristóbal de las Casas**, a beautiful highland town surrounded by intriguing indigenous villages. Move on to **Palenque**, perhaps the most stunning of all ancient Maya cities, with its backdrop of emerald-green jungle, and **Yaxchilán**, another marvelous Maya city, accessible only by river.

Head northeast to **Campeche**, an attractive mix of colonial city and bustling modern town, detouring to the ancient Maya city of **Calakmul** en route. Move on to colonial **Mérida**, the Yucatán Peninsula's lively cultural capital and the base for visiting the superb ruins of **Uxmal** and the **Ruta Puuc**. Next stop: **Chichén Itzá**, the most celebrated of all the Yucatán's Maya sites. From here it's on to **Tulum** on the Caribbean coast, another spectacular Maya site set beside a glorious beach. Finally make your way northward along the Riviera Maya to the hip beach town of **Playa del Carmen**, with a side trip to **Isla Cozumel** for world-class snorkeling and diving. End at Mexico's most popular and unabashed coastal resort, **Cancún**.

Top: Palenque archaeological site (p381)
Bottom: Cancún (p255)

10 DAYS Baja from Tip to Toe

The world's second-longest peninsula seems tailor-made for road tripping, with 1200km of road snaking through picturesque villages, along dramatic coastline and past otherworldly rock canyons. Baja's charms are further enhanced by its appealing colonial towns, world-class diving and some of the best fish tacos you'll ever taste.

Enjoy a full-on day of Mexican life-on-the-streets in **Tijuana** before heading south via the **Valle de Guadalupe** winery route, stopping to tour the vineyards and taste the terrific tipples. Then make a stop in **Ensenada** for great fish tacos and a stroll through the shopping streets before heading south via the Carretera Transpeninsular's spectacular desert scenery. If it's migration season (December to April), book a whale-watching tour at **Guerrero Negro**. Alternatively, continue south and detour to **Sierra de San Francisco** to view ancient petroglyphs in the local caves.

Further south, pass through San Ignacio and stop in **Mulegé** for a tranquil paddle in the cerulean **Sea of Cortez**. The highway then hugs the coast en route to **Loreto**, where you can spend a day or two discovering the artisan shops, great restaurants, historic architecture and 17th-century mission. Heading south again, the road passes several stunning beaches before ducking inland and leading you to the unspoiled charms of **La Paz**. Spend a day kayaking and snorkeling off the island of **Espíritu Santo**, or go swimming with whale sharks (October to March).

Next, stop at **Todos Santos**, a gorgeous little town with picturesque old sugar mills, before you hit wild **Cabo San Lucas**. Indulge in banana-boating, parasailing and other beach activities before hitting the bars, and don't forget to take a boat to **Land's End** for a glimpse of the magical stone arch. If you need a respite, head for **San José del Cabo**, Cabo's tamer twin, with its appealing colonial church, art galleries and a clutch of good restaurants, or go underwater for a closer glimpse of the reef at **Cabo Pulmo**.

Top: Tijuana (p702)
Bottom: Stand-up paddleboarding, Sea of Cortez

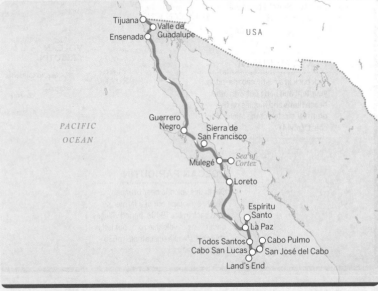

Off the Beaten Track: Mexico

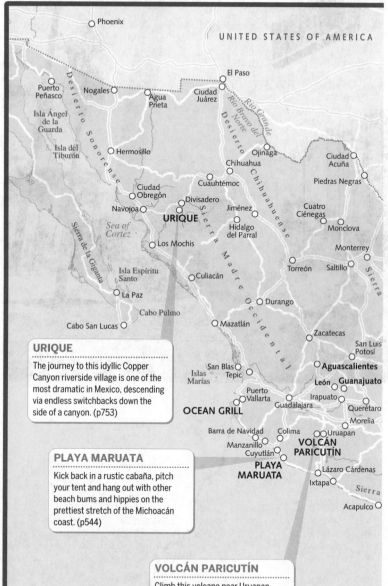

UNITED STATES OF AMERICA

Phoenix

El Paso

Puerto Peñasco

Nogales

Agua Prieta

Ciudad Juárez

Rio Bravo del Norte

Rio Grande

Isla Ángel de la Guarda

Desierto Sonorense

Ojinaga

Ciudad Acuña

Isla del Tiburón

Hermosillo

Chihuahua

Piedras Negras

Cuauhtémoc

Ciudad Obregón

Divisadero

URIQUE

Jiménez

Cuatro Ciénegas

Navojoa

Hidalgo del Parral

Monclova

Sea of Cortez

Los Mochis

Sierra Madre Occidental

Monterrey

Torreón

Saltillo

Sierra

Isla Espíritu Santo

Culiacán

La Paz

Durango

Cabo Pulmo

Mazatlán

Zacatecas

Cabo San Lucas

San Luis Potosí

San Blas

Aguascalientes

Islas Marías

Tepic

León **Guanajuato**

Puerto Vallarta

Irapuato

OCEAN GRILL

Guadalajara

Querétaro

Morelia

Barra de Navidad

Colima

Uruapan

Manzanillo

VOLCÁN PARICUTÍN

Cuyutlán

PLAYA MARUATA

Lázaro Cárdenas

Ixtapa

Sierra

Acapulco

URIQUE

The journey to this idyllic Copper Canyon riverside village is one of the most dramatic in Mexico, descending via endless switchbacks down the side of a canyon. (p753)

PLAYA MARUATA

Kick back in a rustic cabaña, pitch your tent and hang out with other beach bums and hippies on the prettiest stretch of the Michoacán coast. (p544)

VOLCÁN PARICUTÍN

Climb this volcano near Uruapan, which, exploding out of a farmer's field back in the 1940s, buried villages under tons of volcanic rock, but left a church's steeple unscathed. (p635)

PACIFIC

OCEAN

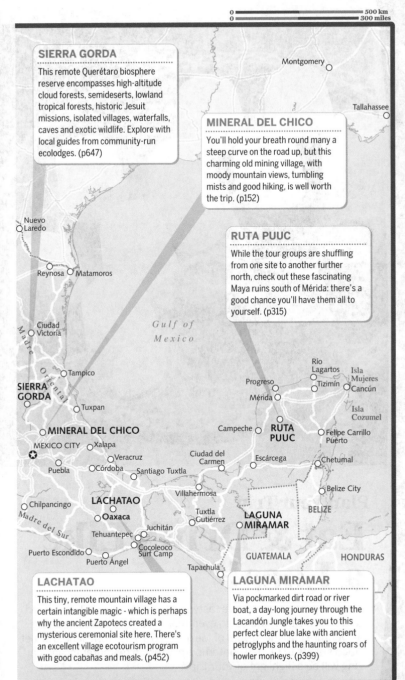

SIERRA GORDA

This remote Querétaro biosphere reserve encompasses high-altitude cloud forests, semideserts, lowland tropical forests, historic Jesuit missions, isolated villages, waterfalls, caves and exotic wildlife. Explore with local guides from community-run ecolodges. (p647)

MINERAL DEL CHICO

You'll hold your breath round many a steep curve on the road up, but this charming old mining village, with moody mountain views, tumbling mists and good hiking, is well worth the trip. (p152)

RUTA PUUC

While the tour groups are shuffling from one site to another further north, check out these fascinating Maya ruins south of Mérida: there's a good chance you'll have them all to yourself. (p315)

LACHATAO

This tiny, remote mountain village has a certain intangible magic - which is perhaps why the ancient Zapotecs created a mysterious ceremonial site here. There's an excellent village ecotourism program with good cabañas and meals. (p452)

LAGUNA MIRAMAR

Via pockmarked dirt road or river boat, a day-long journey through the Lacandón Jungle takes you to this perfect clear blue lake with ancient petroglyphs and the haunting roars of howler monkeys. (p399)

Oaxacan dessert

Plan Your Trip

Eat & Drink Like a Local

Mexican cuisine is far more tasty, fresh, varied, carefully prepared and creative than you could ever imagine before you start trying it. Venture into the flavors of Mexico, anywhere from simple street taco stands to refined contemporary fusion restaurants, and eating will be a highlight of your trip.

Must-Try Dishes

Traditional dishes that will leave you with the taste of Mexico:

Chiles en nogada

Chiles en nogada comprises green, white and red ingredients, the colors of the Mexican flag: poblano chili, stuffed with minced meat and flavored with spices, topped with a cream sauce and sprinkled with pomegranate seeds.

Tacos al pastor

One of the country's favorites, *tacos al pastor* ('in the style of the shepherd') is a corn tortilla filled with thinly sliced pork that's been cooked on a spit, and served with onion and cilantro (coriander).

Pozole

An historic dish, *pozole* is a soupy stew made of hominy corn, meat and vegetables, flavored with herbs. Toppings include lettuce, onion, radish and chili.

Food Experiences

Meals of a Lifetime

Quintonil (p115), Mexico City This contemporary gem showcases Mexican ingredients, paraded in multiple courses.

Pujol (p115), Mexico City A multiple-course tasting extravaganza of contemporary Mexican cuisine: reserve weeks ahead.

Ocean Grill (p529), Puerto Vallarta Stellar seafood lunches at a cliffside bistro reached by boat.

Allium (p592), Guadalajara Sleek new fine-dining competitor on the growing local gourmet circuit.

La Diferencia (p705), Tijuana Specializes in entomophagy – think innovative dishes using edible insects.

Nohoch Kay (p294), Mahahual Beautiful beach-front setting and scrumptious seafood.

Casa Oaxaca (p437), Oaxaca Magically combines Oaxacan and other flavors in delectably original ways.

Áperi (p669), San Miguel de Allende A cutting-edge, anything-goes experience enjoyed at the kitchen table.

Cheap Treats

Mexico has one of the world's great street-food cultures. All over the country, street stands, markets and small eateries dole out endless supplies of filling and nutritious snacks and light meals, morning, noon and night. The busiest stands usually have the tastiest offerings and freshest ingredients.

Foremost are the many varieties of *antojito* ('little whim'), light dishes using *masa* (corn dough). The quintessential *antojito* is the taco – meat, fish or vegetables wrapped in a tortilla (Mexico's ubiquitous corn or wheat-flour flatbread). Delicious varieties include *tacos al pastor* (with spit-cooked pork), *tacos de carne asada* (with grilled beef) and *tacos de pescado* (fish tacos, a favorite on the Pacific coast). There are many more types of *antojito* and an infinite variety of ingredients that can go into them. The most popular types include:

➡ *quesadillas* – a tortilla folded in half with a filling of cheese and/or other ingredients.

➡ *enchiladas* – lightly fried tortillas with fillings, and covered in a chili sauce.

➡ *tamales* – a wedge of *masa* mixed with lard, with stewed meat, fish or veggies in the middle, and steamed in corn husks or banana leaf.

Other common street foods:

➡ *tortas* – sandwiches (hot or cold) using a white bread roll.

➡ *elotes* – freshly steamed or grilled corn on the cob, usually coated in mayonnaise and often sprinkled with chili powder.

Dare to Try

Grasshoppers (*chapulines*) Fried with chili powder and garlic; they make a surprisingly munchable snack, especially accompanying a glass of mezcal. Plentiful in Oaxaca.

Corn fungus (*huitlacoche*) The black mold that grows on some cobs of corn (maize) has a truffle-like texture and has been considered a delicacy since pre-Hispanic times. Available during the mid-year rainy season at Mexico City's Mercado San Juan (p128) and as a sauce or stuffing ingredient at Axitla (p179), Tepoztlán.

Cow's-eye tacos (*tacos de ojos*) Yes that's right. Cows' eyes chopped up, steamed and put into tacos. Soft enough but not especially flavorsome and can be a bit greasy. Found at taco stands around the country and at Los Cocuyos (p110) restaurant in Mexico City.

Grubs and worms Ant larvae (*escamoles*) and maguey worms (*gusanos de maguey*) are seasonal fare from about March to June in the Puebla-Tlaxcala area. Elsewhere, at Onix (p618) in Morelia, you can wrap your tongue around scorpions.

Chilies for sale at a market

Local Specialties

Central Mexico

Guadalajara is famed for its *birria* (chili-spiced goat stew wrapped in agave leaves) and *tortas ahogadas* (drowned *tortas*) – sandwiches of *carnitas* (braised pork) and beans, soaked in a spicy sauce. In Tequila, the town that gave Mexico its most famous drink, you can visit distilleries, or even take the Tequila Express excursion train from Guadalajara. The city of Puebla has a proudly distinctive cuisine including perhaps Mexico's single most famous dish – *mole poblano,* a thick sauce of chilies, fruits, nuts, spices and chocolate, usually served over chicken.

Mexico City

The great melting pot of Mexican people and Mexican food, the capital has a vibrant street-food culture, with *antojitos* everywhere – at street stands, markets and thousands of taco stands. At the other end

---

COOKING CLASSES

Estela Silva's Mexican Home Cooking School (p170) Long-established school near Tlaxcala, focusing on local cuisine.

La Casa de los Sabores (p430) Classes in Oaxacan and other Mexican meals at one of the best schools in Oaxaca.

La Villa Bonita (p178) Courses of several days including accommodations, run by celebrated chef Ana García.

Little Mexican Cooking School (p273) Classes on the Riviera Maya, preparing menus from seven different Mexican regions.

Zihuatanejo Cooking School (p551) Highly recommended classes in local and national favorites.

Street stall vendors

of the culinary scale, top chefs create fantastic fusion dishes in ultra-contemporary restaurants melding haute-cuisine techniques with traditional Mexican ingredients, especially in the neighborhoods of Condesa, Roma and Polanco.

Oaxaca

This southern state is famed for its unique dishes. Greatest renown belongs to its many *moles* – rich, thick sauces made with chilies, spices, nuts and often tomatoes, that go over meats. Oaxaca is also the world capital of mezcal, a potent sipping liquor made from agave plants which is enjoying an upsurge in popularity.

Pacific Coast

Naturally, fresh fish and seafood are great here. *Pescado zarandeado* – fish grilled inside a wooden grill called a *zaranda* – is a specialty in the more northerly parts. Ceviches (marinated raw seafood cocktails) find a natural home in the hotter southern regions. Mazatlán, Sayulita, Puerto Vallarta and Zihuatanejo are all foodie havens, and Vallarta has attracted a good

number of international chefs to open gourmet fusion restaurants, which play a big part in its November Festival Gourmet International.

The North

Beef, from this region's extensive ranches, and seafood on the coast, are the specialties here. In Monterrey, the signature dish is *cabrito asado* (kid goat roasted on skewers over an open fire), best tried at El Rey del Cabrito (p799).

Yucatán Peninsula

Caribbean flavors and indigenous Maya recipes influence the cuisine of Mexico's southeast corner. The most famous dish is *cochinita pibil* – slow-cooked pork marinated in citrus juices and *achiote* (a spice made from red seeds) and traditionally roasted in a pit in the ground. A staple is the fiery *chile habanero* – habanero sauce goes well on *papadzules* (tacos stuffed with hard-boiled eggs and pumpkin-seed sauce). Don't miss *sopa de lima,* a soup made from turkey, lime and tortilla pieces.

Top: Ceviche

Bottom: Pasillo de Carnes Asadas (Grilled Meat Passage at Mercado 20 de Noviembre (p436), Oaxaca

How to Eat & Drink

When to Eat

Desayuno (breakfast) Usually served from 8:30am to 11am, it tends to be on the hearty side. Egg dishes are popular and some Mexicans down serious meaty platefuls.

Comida (lunch) The main meal of the day, usually served between 2pm and 4:30pm and comprising a soup or other starter, main course (typically meat, fish or seafood) and a small dessert. *Comida corrida*, also known as *menú del día*, is an inexpensive fixed-price lunch menu.

Cena (dinner) For Mexicans, dinner is a lighter meal than lunch and often not eaten till 9pm. Nearly all restaurants serving dinner open from as early as 7pm though, offering full menus for those who want them.

Snacks At almost any time of day you can grab an *antojito* or *torta* at a cafe or street or market stall. You can also get sandwiches (toasted) in some cafes.

Where to Eat

In general *restaurantes* (restaurants) have full, multi-course menus and a range of drinks to accompany meals, while *cafés* and *cafeterías* offer shorter menus of lighter dishes and their drinks may focus on coffee, tea and soft drinks. Other types of eatery:

➡ *comedor* – 'eating room'; usually refers to economical restaurants serving simple, straightforward meals

➡ *fonda* – small, frequently family-run eatery, often serving *comida corrida*

➡ *mercado* (market) – many Mexican markets have *comedor* sections where you sit on benches eating economical, home-style food cooked up on the spot

➡ *taquería* – stall or small eatery specializing in tacos

Menu Decoder

Our Food Glossary (p874) explans dishes you'll find on Mexican menus and the names of basic foods.

➡ *a la parrilla* – grilled on a barbecue grill

➡ *a la plancha* – grilled on a metal plate

➡ *al carbón* – cooked over open coals

➡ *aves* – poultry

Mole poblano (p831)

➡ *bebidas* – drinks

➡ *carnes* – meats

➡ *empanizado* – fried in breadcrumbs

➡ *ensalada* – salad

➡ *entradas* – starters

➡ *filete* – fillet

➡ *frito* – fried

➡ *huevos* – eggs

➡ *jugo* – juice

➡ *legumbres* – pulses

➡ *mariscos* – seafood (not fish)

➡ *menú de degustación* – tasting menu

➡ *mole* – rich, thick sauce, made with chilies, spices, nuts, often tomatoes and sometimes chocolate, that goes over meats

➡ *pescado* – fish

➡ *plato fuerte* – main dish

➡ *postre* – dessert

➡ *salsa* – sauce

➡ *sopa* – soup

➡ *verduras* – vegetables

Chichén Itzá (p322

Plan Your Trip

Exploring Mexico's Ancient Ruins

Mexico's ancient civilizations were the most sophisticated and formidable in North and Central America. These often highly organized societies didn't just build towering pyramids and sculpt beautiful temples; they could also read the heavens, do complicated mathematics and invent writing systems. Their sites are a national and global treasure and an experience not to be missed.

Where & When

Top Ten & Best Times To Visit

Most of Mexico's major pre-Hispanic sites are scattered around the center, south and southeast of the country. Here's our top 10, along with the best time of year to visit them. Most sites open daily 9am to 5pm (some close Monday). Arriving early means fewer visitors and lower temperatures.

Teotihuacán, central Mexico Year-round

Chichén Itzá, Yucatán Peninsula September to November

Uxmal, Yucatán Peninsula September to November

Palenque, Chiapas October to May

Monte Albán, Oaxaca October to May

Yaxchilán, Chiapas October to May

Calakmul, Yucatán Peninsula November to May

Tulum, Yucatán Peninsula November to June

El Tajín, Veracruz October to May

Templo Mayor, Mexico City Year-round

Mexico's Ancient Civilizations

Archaeologists have been uncovering Mexico's ancient ruins since the 19th century. Many impressive sites have been restored and made accessible to visitors, others have been explored in part, and thousands more remain untouched, buried beneath the earth or hidden in forests. The major civilizations were these:

Olmec Mexico's 'mother culture' was centered on the Gulf coast, from about 1200 BC to 400 BC. It's famed for the giant stone sculptures known as Olmec heads.

Teotihuacán Based in the city of the same name with its huge pyramids, 50km from Mexico City, the Teotihuacán civilization flourished in the first seven centuries AD, and ruled the largest of all ancient Mexican empires.

Maya The Maya, in southeast Mexico and neighboring Guatemala and Belize, flowered most brilliantly in numerous city-states between AD 250 and AD 900. They're famed for their exquisitely beautiful temples and stone sculptures. Maya culture lives on today among the indigenous population of these regions.

Toltec A name for the culture of a number of central Mexican city-states, from around AD 750 to AD 1150. The warrior sculptures of Tula are the most celebrated monuments.

Aztec With their capital at Tenochtitlán (now Mexico City) from AD 1325 to AD 1521, the Aztecs came to rule most of central Mexico from the Gulf coast to the Pacific. The best known Aztec site is the Templo Mayor in Mexico City.

Site Practicalities

➡ The most famous sites are often thronged with large numbers of visitors (arrive early). Others are hidden away on remote hilltops or shrouded in thick jungle, and can be the most exciting and rewarding to visit for those with an adventurous spirit.

➡ Admission to archaeological sites costs from nothing up to around M$220, depending on the site (only a handful of places, all in Yucatán state, cost more than M$70).

➡ Go protected against the sun and, at jungle sites, mosquitoes.

➡ Popular sites have facilities such as cafes or restaurants, bookstores, souvenir stores, audio guides in various languages and authorized (but not fixed-price) human guides.

➡ Little-visited sites may have no food or water available.

➡ Guided tours to many sites are available from nearby towns, but public transportation is usually available, too.

➡ Major sites are usually wheelchair accessible.

➡ Explanatory signs may be in Spanish only, or in Spanish and English, or in Spanish, English and a local indigenous language.

Resources

Colecciones Especiales Street View (www.inah.gob.mx/es/inah/322-colecciones-especiales-street-view) Take virtual tours of 27 sites in Google Street View.

Instituto Nacional de Antropología e Historia (www.inah.gob.mx) Mexico's National Institute of Anthropology and History administers 187 archaeological sites and 120 museums.

Mesoweb (www.mesoweb.com) A diverse resource on ancient Mexico, especially the Maya.

An Archaeological Guide to Central and Southern Mexico Joyce Kelly's book was published in 2001 and is still the best of its kind, covering 70 sites.

Top Museums

Some archaeological sites have their own museums, but there are also important city and regional museums that hold many of the most valuable and impressive pre-Hispanic artifacts and provide fascinating background on ancient Mexico.

Museo Nacional de Antropología (p86) The superb National Museum of Anthropology in Mexico City has sections devoted to all the important ancient civilizations, and includes such treasures as the famous Aztec sun stone and a replica of King Pakal's treasure-laden tomb from Palenque.

Museo de Antropología (p218) Mainly devoted to Gulf coast cultures, this excellent museum in Xalapa contains seven Olmec heads and other masterly sculptures among its 25,000-piece collection.

Tulum (p286)

Parque-Museo La Venta (p416) This outdoor museum-cum-zoo in Villahermosa holds several Olmec heads and other fine sculptures from the site of La Venta, moved here in the 1950s when La Venta was under threat from petroleum exploration.

Museo Maya de Cancún (p255) One of Mexico's most important collections of Maya artifacts, assembled from sites around the Yucatán Peninsula.

PRE-HISPANIC NUMBERS

Ancient Mexicans loved numbers. We've assembled some of our own:

8km of tunnels dug by archaeologists beneath Cholula's Tepanapa Pyramid

70m – the height of Teotihuacán's Pyramid of the Sun

100km – the length of the *sacbé* (stone-paved avenue) from Cobá to Yaxuna

120 mural-covered walls in Teotihuacán's Tetitla Palace

300 masks of Chaac, the rain god, at Kabah's Palace of Masks

15,000 ritual ball-game courts found in Mexico (so far)

20,000 human hearts ripped out for the re-dedication of Tenochtitlán's Templo Mayor in 1487

25 million – estimated population of Mexico at the time of the Spanish conquest (1521)

51

Mexico's Ruins

MAIN PRE-HISPANIC SITES

	SITE	PERIOD	DESCRIPTION
CENTRAL MEXICO	Teotihuacán (p146)	AD 0-700	Mexico's biggest ancient city, capital of the Teotihuacán empire
	Templo Mayor (p67)	AD 1375-1521	ceremonial center of the Aztec capital, Tenochtitlán
	Cholula (p163)	AD 0-1521	city & religious center
	Tula (p145)	AD 900-1150	major Toltec city
	Cantona (p174)	AD 600-1000	huge, well-preserved, little-visited city
	Tlatelolco (p98)	12th century -1521	site of main Aztec market & defeat of last Aztec emperor Cuauhtémoc
	Xochicalco (p186)	AD 600-1200	large, hilltop religious & commercial center
CHIAPAS	Palenque (p381)	100 BC-AD 740	beautiful major Maya city
	Yaxchilán (p397)	7th-9th centuries AD	Maya city
	Toniná (p378)	c AD 600-900	Maya temple complex
	Bonampak (p393)	8th century AD	Maya site
NORTHERN MEXICO	Paquimé (p784)	AD 900-1340	trading center linking central Mexico with northern desert cultures
OAXACA	Monte Albán (p443)	500 BC-AD 900	hilltop ceremonial center of Zapotec civilization
	Mitla (p448)	c AD 1300-1520	Zapotec religious center
	Yagul (p447)	AD 900-1400	Zapotec & Mixtec ceremonial center
VERACRUZ	El Tajín (p241)	AD 600-1200	town & ceremonial center of Classic Veracruz civilization
YUCATÁN PENINSULA	Chichén Itzá (p322)	2nd-14th centuries AD	large, well-restored Maya/Toltec city
	Uxmal (p311)	AD 600-900	Maya city
	Tulum (p286)	c AD 1200-1600	late Maya town & ceremonial center
	Calakmul (p343)	Approx 1st-9th centuries AD	huge, once very powerful Maya city, little restored
	Cobá (p291)	AD 600-1100	Maya city
	Kabah (p314)	AD 750-950	Maya city
	Ruta Puuc (p315)	AD 750-950	three Puuc Maya sites (Sayil, Xlapak, Labná)
	Edzná (p339)	600 BC-AD 1500	Maya city
	Becán (p344)	550 BC-AD 1000	large Maya site
	Xpuhil (p345)	Flourished 8th century AD	Maya settlement
	Ek' Balam (p331)	Approx AD 600-800	Maya city
	Dzibanché (p300)	200 BC-AD 1200	Maya city
	Kohunlich (p300)	AD 100-600	Maya city

HIGHLIGHTS	LOCATION/TRANSPORTATION
Pyramids of Sun and Moon, Calzada de los Muertos, palace murals	50km northeast of Mexico City; frequent buses
ceremonial pyramid	downtown Mexico City
world's widest pyramid	8km west of Puebla; frequent buses
stone pillars carved as warriors	80km north of Mexico City; 1km walk or taxi from Tula bus station
24 ball courts, unique street system	90km northeast of Puebla; taxi or *colectivo* from Oriental
Aztec temple-pyramid	northern Mexico City; trolleybus or metro
Pyramid of Quetzalcóatl	35km southwest of Cuernavaca; bus
exquisite temples with jungle backdrop	7km west of Palenque town; frequent combis
temples & other buildings in riverside jungle setting	beside Río Usumacinta, 15km northwest of Frontera Corozal; boat from Frontera Corozal
temples & pyramids on hillside	14km east of Ocosingo; combis from Ocosingo
superb, if weathered, frescoes	150km southeast of Palenque; van or bus to San Javier (140km), then taxi and van
adobe walls & buildings, clay macaw cages, rare geometric pottery	Casas Grandes village; bus or taxi from Nuevo Casas Grandes, 7km north
pyramids, observatory, panoramas	6km west of Oaxaca; bus
unique stone mosaics	46km southeast of Oaxaca; bus or *colectivo*
large ball court, rock 'fortress'	35km southeast of Oaxaca; bus or *colectivo* then 1.5km walk
rare niched pyramids, 17 ball courts, *voladores* ('fliers') performances	6km west of Papantla; bus or taxi
El Castillo 'calendar temple', Mexico's biggest ball court, El Caracol observatory, Platform of Skulls	117km east of Mérida, 2km east of Pisté village; buses from Mérida, Pisté & Valladolid
pyramids, palaces, riotous sculpture featuring masks of rain god Chaac	80km south of Mérida; buses from Mérida
temples & towers on Caribbean-side site	130km south of Cancún; taxi, walk or cycle from Tulum town
high pyramids with views over rainforest	60km south of Escárcega-Chetumal road; car, tour from Xpujil, Chicanná or Campeche, taxi from Xpujil or Escárcega
towering pyramids in jungle setting	50km northwest of Tulum; bus or *colectivo* from Tulum, or bus from Valladolid
Palace of Masks, with 300 Chaac masks	104km south of Mérida; car, or bus or tour from Mérida
palaces with elaborate columns & sculptures, including Chaac masks	around 120km south of Mérida; car, or bus or tour from Mérida
five-story pyramid-palace, Temple of Masks	53km southeast of Campeche; minibuses & shuttle service from Campeche
towered temples	8km west of Xpujil; taxi, tour or car
three-towered ancient 'skyscraper'	Xpujil town, 123km west of Chetumal; buses from Campeche & Escárcega, buses & *colectivos* from Chetumal
huge Acrópolis & high pyramid with unusual carving	23km north of Valladolid by taxi or *colectivo*
semiwild site with palaces & pyramids	68km west of Chetumal; car, taxi or tour from there or Xpujil
Temple of the Masks	56km west of Chetumal; car, taxi, or bus & 9km walk/ hitchhike

Plan Your Trip
Travel with Children

Best Regions for Kids

Yucatán Peninsula

Cancún, the Riviera Maya and nearby islands are geared to giving vacationers fun. The area is full of great beaches offering every imaginable aquatic activity, hotels designed to make life easy and attractions from jungle zip-lines to swimming in underwater rivers. Other parts of the peninsula are great if your kids will enjoy exploring Maya ruins.

Central Pacific Coast

The Pacific coast offers all conceivable types of fun in, on and under the ocean and lagoons, and a vast range of places to base yourself, from sophisticated Puerto Vallarta to easygoing Zihuatanejo and countless smaller spots where your time is just your family's and yours.

Mexico City

The capital keeps kids happy with a world-class aquarium, a hands-on children's museum, a first-rate zoo, dedicated kids' entertainment and activities, and parks and plazas full of space and fun.

The sights, sounds and colors of Mexico excite kids just as they do adults – and Mexicans love children, who are part and parcel of most aspects of life here. There are many child-friendly attractions and activities for kids of all ages, and with very few exceptions, children are welcomed at all accommodations and almost any cafe or restaurant.

Mexico for Kids

Eating

Children may be less keen to experiment with exciting Mexican flavors than their parents are, but Mexico has plenty of places serving up familiar international fare. Italian restaurants are plentiful, foods such as eggs, steaks, bread, rice and cheese are available everywhere, and fresh fruit is abundant. Simpler Mexican snacks such as quesadillas, burritos and tacos, or steaming corn cobs straight from a street cart, are good ways of trying out local flavors. Restaurant staff are accustomed to children and can usually provide high chairs or an extra plate for dish-sharing, or prepare something that's not on the menu, if requested.

Sleeping

Mexico has some excitingly different places to stay that will please most kids – anything beachside is a good start, and rustic *cabañas* (cabins) provide a sense of adventure (but choose one with good mosquito nets!). Many hotels have a rambling layout and open-air space – courtyards, pool areas, gardens. Beach hotels countrywide are geared to families.

Family rooms and accommodations with kitchens are widely available, and most hotels will put an extra bed or two in a room at little extra charge. Baby cots may not be available in budget accommodations. Most accommodations have wi-fi access, and in the midrange and top end there will often be child-friendly channels on the TV.

Our symbol 🏠 identifies places with particularly family-friendly facilities.

Getting Around

Try to do your traveling in smallish chunks of a few hours maximum. Many Mexican buses show nonstop movies, most of which are family-friendly and help distract kids from a dull trip. Children under 13 travel half-price on many long-distance buses, and if they're small enough to sit on your lap, they usually go for free. If you're traveling with a baby or toddler, consider investing in deluxe buses for the extra space and comfort.

Car rental and, on some routes, flying are alternatives to buses. If you want a car with a child safety seat, the major international rental firms are the most reliable providers.

In northern Mexico most kids love riding the 'Chepe' railway (Ferrocarril Chihuahua Pacífico or Copper Canyon Railway).

Children's Highlights

On & In the Water

Learn to surf Kids as young as five can take classes at many spots with gentler waves along the Pacific coast, including Mazatlán, Sayulita, Ixtapa, Puerto Escondido and San Agustinillo.

Spot turtles, dolphins and whales Boat trips head out from many places along the Pacific coast.

Snorkel tropical seas Many beaches on the Caribbean coast and islands, and some on the Pacific, provide calm waters and colorful marine life for beginners.

Ride a gondola Cruise ancient Aztec canals at Xochimilco, Mexico City (p92).

Multi-Adventure

Parque de Aventura Barrancas del Cobre (p756) Kids adore the Copper Canyon Adventure Park with its spine-tingling seven zip-lines carrying you halfway to the canyon floor from its lip at 2400m. There's rappelling, climbing and a cable car, too.

Selvática (p274) Award-winning zip-line circuit through the jungle near Puerto Morelos, with its own cenote (limestone sinkhole) for swimming.

Boca del Puma (p273) Zip-lining, horseback riding and a cenote to dip into, near Puerto Morelos.

Cobá (p291) This jungle-surrounded ancient Maya site near Tulum has pyramids, a zip-line and bicycles for pedaling around the network of trails.

Cuajimoloyas (p453) Horseback riding, mountain biking, hiking and a spectacular 1km zip-line in the mountains near Oaxaca.

Huana Coa Canopy (p496) Popular series of zip-lines in the forested hills near Mazatlán.

Animals

Acuario Inbursa (p91) This world-class mega-aquarium in Mexico City wows kids with manta rays, piranhas and crocodiles, while the Soumaya and Jumex museums just across the road will entertain the parents.

Baja whale-watching (p720) See massive gray whales and their calves off the coasts of Baja California – usually requires several hours in a boat, so best for older kids.

Zoológico de Chapultepec (p90) Mexico City's large zoo has a wide range of world creatures, including two pandas, in sizable enclosures.

Zoomat (p350) Tuxtla Gutiérrez' zoo has 180 species, all from the state of Chiapas, including several types of big cat.

Playa Escobilla (p469) See thousands of turtles crawl out of the ocean in a single night to lay eggs on this Oaxaca beach.

Crococun (☎998-850-37-19; www.crococun zoo.com; Hwy 307 Km 31, 3km north of Puerto Morelos; admission adult/child 6-12yr US$30/20; ☺9am-5pm) Interactive zoo in Puerto Morelos with crocodiles and wild monkeys.

Museums

Papalote Museo del Niño There are two of these fun, hands-on, children's museums – one in Mexico City (p90), one in Cuernavaca (p185). Good for kids up to about 11.

Museo Interactivo de Xalapa (www.mix.org. mx; Av Murillo Vidal 1735; adult/child M$70/50; ⊙9am-5pm Mon-Fri, 10am-7pm Sat & Sun; 📷) Themed rooms on science, ecology and art, and an IMAX cinema.

La Esquina: Museo del Juguete Popular Mexicano (p662) Stunning museum in San Miguel de Allende where kids can see what toys were like before the digital revolution!

Spectacles

Voladores (Fliers) This indigenous Totonac rite involves men climbing up a 30m-high pole then casting themselves off backward, attached only by ropes. Performed regularly at El Tajín (p242) and Mexico City's Museo Nacional de Antropología (p86).

Pirate Show (p336) Campeche recalls its pirate-battered past with Disney-esque spectaculars in an old city gate.

Folk dance Highly colorful, entertaining shows are given regularly by the Ballet Folklórico de México (p124) in Mexico City and Guelaguetza groups in Oaxaca, and at Mérida's Plaza Grande (p301).

Planning

➡ Bear in mind that few kids like traveling all the time. They're usually happier if they can settle into a place for a while, make friends and do some of the things they like doing back home.

➡ See a doctor about vaccinations at least one month – preferably two – before your trip.

➡ It's a good idea to book accommodations for at least the first couple of nights.

HEALTH & SAFETY

Children are more easily affected than adults by heat, disrupted sleep patterns, changes in altitude and strange food. Take care that they don't drink tap water, be careful to avoid sunburn, cover them up against insect bites and ensure you replace fluids if a child gets diarrhea.

Don't hesitate to go to a doctor if you think it may be necessary. In general, privately run hospitals and clinics in Mexico offer better facilities and care than public ones. Adequate travel insurance will cover the cost of private medical care.

➡ Diapers (nappies) and sunscreen are widely available, but you may not easily find wet wipes, other creams, baby foods or familiar medicines outside larger cities and tourist towns.

➡ Lonely Planet's *Travel with Children* has lots of practical advice on the subject, drawn from firsthand experience.

Documents for Under-18 Travelers

Mexican law requires Mexican minors (under-18s, including those with dual nationality) or foreign minors residing in Mexico, if departing from Mexico without a parent or legal guardian, to carry notarized written permission from a parent or guardian. There have been cases of other minors being asked to show consent forms, especially when leaving Mexico by land borders, even though the law does not require them to do so. The US embassy in Mexico therefore advises all minors traveling without both parents to carry notarized consent letters. Check with a Mexican consulate well in advance of travel on what needs to be done.

Regions at a Glance

Mexico City

Museums
Architecture
Food

Museum Mecca

You name it, Mexico City probably has a museum for it: from avant-garde art to pre-Hispanic artifacts and antique toys. Don't miss the world-class Museo Nacional de Antropología and Frida Kahlo's famed blue house.

Architectural Kaleidoscope

Few other cities in the world harbor cutting-edge contemporary structures, colonial palaces and pre-Hispanic ruins in one fell swoop. In the *centro histórico* alone, more than 1500 buildings are classified as historic monuments.

Culinary Melting Pot

The capital has fabulous eateries of many kinds and regional Mexican cuisine gets top billing. Everyone here seems to have an opinion on where you can find, say, the best Guerrero-style *pozole* (a hearty hominy, meat and veg soup) or the tastiest Yucatecan *cochinita pibil* (slow-roasted marinated pork).

p62

Around Mexico City

Food
Archaeological Sites
Small-Town Escapes

Regional Specialties

An incredible variety of indigenous ingredients and imported culinary influences combine in complex regional cuisines. Many towns have their own specialty, such as the pasties from the mining villages above Pachuca, or Puebla's famed *mole poblano*.

Ancient Architecture

Some of Mexico's most awe-inspiring ruins stand within a few hours' drive of the capital. Teotihuacán, with its stunning Pyramids of the Sun and Moon, is the most famous, but fascinating sites such as Cacaxtla, Xochitécatl, Xochicalco and Cantona can be explored in virtual solitude.

Pueblos Mágicos

With their leafy plazas, traditional crafts and gorgeous colonial edifices, remarkably well-preserved 'magical towns' such as Cuetzalan, Real del Monte, Malinalco and Valle de Bravo provide a perfect escape from the thick air and crowds of the capital.

p140

Veracruz

Archaeological Sites
Ecotourism
Food

Ancient Cultures

Several distinct pre-Hispanic cultures graced Mexico's Gulf coast, and all have left a weighty legacy. Examine the Classic Veracruz ruins of El Tajín with its curious niched pyramid and the magnificence of Totonac Zempoala, and see the genius of ancient sculptors in Xalapa's Museo de Antropología.

Going Green

A geographic anomaly of rugged volcanoes and unsullied rainforest, the Los Tuxtlas region is working hard to promote Mexico's green credentials with rustic accommodations, off-the-beaten-track hiking opportunities and a nascent tourist infrastructure.

Fish, Glorious Fish

Thanks to the state's 690km-long coastline, fish headlines most menus, in particular the spicy mélange known as *huachinango a la veracruzana* (Veracruz-style snapper). Lining up behind it are the distinctive *moles* of Xico and the gourmet coffee of Coatepec.

p203

Yucatán Peninsula

Diving & Snorkeling
Maya Ruins
Beaches

Into the Blue

With hundreds of kilometers of Caribbean coastline and the world's second-largest barrier reef, the region is a diver's and snorkeler's dream. Banco Chinchorro and Isla Cozumel are the superstars and Cancún's underwater sculpture garden provides another unique experience.

Oldies but Goodies

From world-famous Chichén Itzá to virtually unheard-of sites such as Ek' Balam, the Yucatán is dotted with spectacular pyramids and temples. Many have a resonating atmosphere that even the loudest tour groups can't diminish.

A Day at the Beach

Finding the right beach for you is simply a matter of hopping on a bus (or boat). From the debauchery of Cancún to lonely Costa Maya beaches such as Xcalak, the bleach-white sands and beautiful warm waters mustn't be missed.

p254

Chiapas & Tabasco

Indigenous Culture
Outdoor Adventure
Nature

Temples & Tradition

The world of the Maya lives on everywhere you turn here, from the preserved stone temples of Classic Maya civilization to the persistence of dramatic pre-Hispanic religious rituals and the intricate handwoven textiles and clothing still worn by many.

In Motion

Whether you're rappelling into a jungle sinkhole, bouncing over a stretch of white water in a rubber raft, or climbing a 4000m volcano, Chiapas has multiple ways to raise your adrenaline levels.

Birds & Beasts

Nesting turtles, roaring monkeys and flashes of rainbow plumage are standard fare in the jungles and on the misty mountains and sandy beaches of this biodiverse region that's full of rare and endangered wildlife.

p347

Oaxaca

Culture
Beaches
Outdoor Activities

Traditional & Cutting Edge

Oaxaca state is a cultural hub in so many senses, from Oaxaca City's vibrant arts scene to the distinctive Oaxacan cuisine and endlessly inventive handicrafts of the state's indigenous peoples. It all wraps up in a unique and proud Oaxacan regional identity.

Coast of Dreams

With 550km of sandy Pacific strands and wildlife-rich lagoons, Oaxaca's coastline has it all – the pumping surf of Puerto Escondido, the blissed-out traveler scene of Zipolite and Mazunte, and the resort attractions of low-key Bahías de Huatulco.

The Great Outdoors

Hike through the Sierra Norte's mountain forests, surf the Pacific swells, raft rivers from the hills to the sea, snorkel or dive the beautiful Huatulco bays, and spot whales, dolphins and turtles off the Pacific coast.

p419

Central Pacific Coast

Beaches
Food
Outdoor Activities

Surf & Sand

Conjure up the beach of your dreams and you'll find it here, whether wiggling your toes in the sand with margarita in hand, or chasing perfect waves along an endless ultramarine horizon.

Seafood Heaven

Sidle up to a beachside table at sunset, grab a cold beer and a fresh-cut lime and settle into a plateful of *pescado zarandeado* (char-broiled fish stuffed with vegetables and spices), *tiritas* (citrus-and-chili-marinated raw-fish slivers) or shrimp and red snapper cooked in a dozen different ways.

Natural Highs

Kayak across a lagoon at dawn, ride horses into the Sierra Madre, swim among flitting butterflies in a boulder-strewn river, watch pelicans and whales parade through the waves, or scan the nighttime sands for nesting mama turtles.

p491

Western Central Highlands

Food
Scenery
Culture

Culinary Feast

When Unesco listed Mexican cuisine as Intangible Cultural Heritage in 2010, it made special mention of Michoacán, whose food is often termed the 'soul food' of Mexico. Throw in *birria* (a spicy goat/lamb stew) from Jalisco washed down with local tequila, and you've got a veritable feast.

Volcanic Drama

Tiny Colima state packs a scenic punch with its dramatic twin volcanoes. For more glorious scenery don't miss the modern marvel of Volcán Paricutín in Michoacán.

Art & Crafts

The highlands groan with indigenous culture, most notably that of the thriving Purépecha people whose arts and crafts are sold around Pátzcuaro. You'll find superb art galleries and history museums in Guadalajara and Morelia and great shopping for arts and crafts in Tlaquepaque.

p576

Northern Central Highlands

Colonial Cities
Museums
Outdoor Adventures

Pedestrian Paradise

Cobblestone streets lined by gorgeous colonial stone mansions and churches make for fascinating exploration on foot. Towns and cities here are made for getting lost in – up narrow *callejones* (alleys) or down steep steps. You'll eventually end up on a pretty, laurel-tree-filled plaza.

Historic & Contemporary

Home to fascinating indigenous cultures and most of the silver that brought opulence to Mexico's colonial grandees, this region was also the birthplace of Mexican independence. Excellent museums highlight everything from historical heroes to contemporary art.

Natural Playground

An emerging adventure playground, this region offers the chance to rappel into giant sinkholes and snorkel inland lakes in the Huasteca Potosina, ride into deserts around Real de Catorce and search for macaws in Sierra Gorda caves.

p636

Baja California

Water Sports
Wine
Scenery

Surfing & Diving

Baja is a paradise for surfers of all levels, with beach, point and reef breaks up and down the Pacific coastline. Divers can do a two-tank dive in the Pacific and be in the natural aquarium of the Sea of Cortez in time for a night dive.

Ruta del Vino

The Valle de Guadalupe is producing the best wines in Mexico and this 'Napa Sur' is garnering international acclaim. Its Wine Route makes for a great day (or two) out.

Majestic Mountains, Tropical Paradise

Few places in the world have deserts just steps away from turquoise lagoons and high, pine-forested mountains just a couple of hours' drive inland. At every corner there are vistas that seem pulled from the pages of a vacation calendar.

p700

Copper Canyon & Northern Mexico

Outdoor Adventures
Colonial Towns
Museums

Great Outdoors

The north is all about topographical overload. An idyllic coastline, vast deserts, dramatic canyons and climates from alpine to subtropical all contribute to a wealth of wildlife and tantalizing hiking and biking options.

Charming Continuity

The gorgeous old towns of Álamos, with its wonderful hotels and restaurants, and Parras, with its longstanding viticulture, seduce visitors with the pull of bygone centuries.

From Sarapes to Steel

Monterrey's spectacular Parque Fundidora is replete with cultural interest, particularly the Horno3 museum devoted to steelmaking. In Saltillo you'll find museums focusing on the desert environment, *sarape* textiles and birdlife, while Chihuahua's impressive offerings include the former residence of Pancho Villa.

p743

On the Road

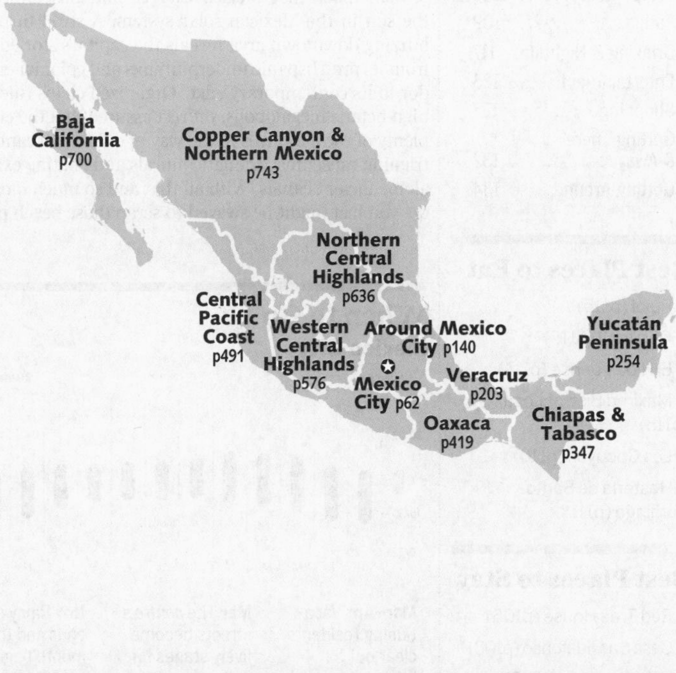

Baja California
p700

Copper Canyon & Northern Mexico
p743

Northern Central Highlands
p636

Central Pacific Coast
p491

Western Central Highlands
p576

Around Mexico City p140

Mexico City p62

Veracruz p203

Oaxaca p419

Yucatán Peninsula
p254

Chiapas & Tabasco
p347

Mexico City

🔖 55 / POP 22 MILLION / ELEV 2240M

Includes ➡

Sights 66
Activities 100
Courses 100
Tours 102
Festivals & Events . . .102
Sleeping 103
Eating 109
Drinking & Nightlife . . .117
Entertainment 123
Shopping 127
Getting There
& Away 132
Getting Around 134

Best Places to Eat

➡ Pujol (p115)

➡ Quintonil (p115)

➡ El Hidalguense (p114)

➡ Maximo Bistrot Local (p115)

➡ Los Cocuyos (p110)

➡ Hostería de Santo Domingo (p111)

Best Places to Stay

➡ Red Tree House (p106)

➡ Casa San Ildefonso (p103)

➡ Villa Condesa (p107)

➡ Casa Comtesse (p107)

➡ Chalet del Carmen (p109)

Why Go?

Much-maligned Mexico City is cleaning up its act these days. Revamped public spaces are springing back to life, the culinary scene is exploding and a cultural renaissance is flourishing. On top of all that, by largely managing to distance itself from the drug wars, the nation's capital remains a safe haven of sorts.

Remember that Mexico City is, and has always been, the sun in the Mexican solar system. A stroll through the buzzing downtown area reveals the capital's storied history, from its pre-Hispanic underpinnings and colonial-era splendor to its contemporary edge. Organized chaos rules in this high-octane megalopolis, yet rest assured that the city offers plenty of escape valves in the way of old-school cantinas, intriguing museums, dramatic murals and boating excursions along ancient canals. With all that and so much more going on, you just might be swayed to scrap those beach plans.

When to Go
Mexico City

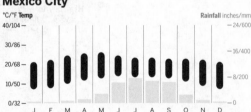

Mar–Apr Vacationing residents clear out for Easter, leaving the city remarkably calm.

Mar The *centro's* streets become lively stages for cultural events during the Festival de México.

Nov Rainy season ends and the month begins with colorful Day of the Dead festivities.

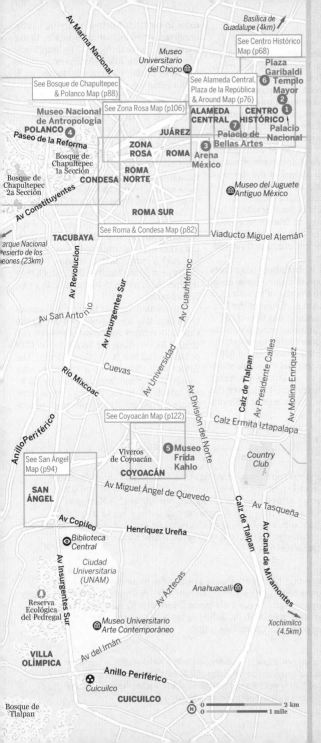

Mexico City Highlights

1 Studying Diego Rivera's tableau of Mexican history at **Palacio Nacional** (p70).

2 Marveling at Aztec ruins in the heart of downtown at **Templo Mayor** (p67).

3 Cheering on the masked heroes at the *lucha libre* (Mexican wrestling) bouts of **Arena México** (p127).

4 Gazing upon the Aztec sun stone and other superb pre-Hispanic relics at **Museo Nacional de Antropología** (p86).

5 Sharing Frida's pain at her birthplace, Casa Azul in Coyoacán, now home to the **Museo Frida Kahlo** (p95).

6 Singing along to mariachi ballads in the soulful **Plaza Garibaldi** (p74).

7 Feasting your eyes on colorful murals and folkloric dance performances at **Palacio de Bellas Artes** (p77).

History

Driving over the sea of asphalt that now covers this highland basin, you'd be hard-pressed to imagine that, a mere five centuries ago, it was filled by a chain of lakes. It would further stretch your powers to imagine that today's downtown was on an islet criss-crossed by canals, or that the communities who inhabited the island and the banks of Lago de Texcoco spoke a patchwork of languages that had as little to do with Spanish as Malay or Urdu. As their chronicles related, the Spaniards who arrived at the shores of that lake in the early 16th century were just as amazed to witness such a scene.

A loose federation of farming villages had evolved around Lago de Texcoco by approximately 200 BC. The biggest, Cuicuilco, was destroyed by a volcanic eruption three centuries later.

Breakthroughs in irrigation techniques and the development of a maize-based economy contributed to the rise of a civilization at Teotihuacán, 40km northeast of the lake. For centuries Teotihuacán was the capital of an empire whose influence extended as far as Guatemala. It was unable to sustain its burgeoning population, however, and fell in the 8th century to internal divisions, abandoned and left in ruins. Details are scarce as no written records were kept. Over the following centuries, power in central Mexico came to be divided between varying locally important cities, including Xochicalco to the south and Tula to the north. The latter's culture is known as Toltec (Artificers), a name coined by the later Aztecs, who looked back to the Toltec rulers with awe.

Aztec Mexico City

The Aztecs, or Mexica (meh-*shee*-kah), probably arrived in the Valle de México in the 13th century. A wandering tribe that claimed to have come from Aztlán, a mythical region in northwest Mexico, they acted as mercenary fighters for the Tepanecas, who resided on the lake's southern shore, and were allowed to settle on the inhospitable terrain of Chapultepec.

The tribe roamed the swampy fringes of the lake, finally reaching an island near the western shore around 1325. There, according to legend, they witnessed an eagle standing atop a cactus and devouring a snake (today seen on the Mexican flag), which they interpreted as a sign to stop and build a city, Tenochtitlán.

Tenochtitlán rapidly became a sophisticated city-state whose empire would, by the early 16th century, span most of modern-day central Mexico from the Pacific to the Gulf of Mexico and into far southern Mexico. The Aztecs built their city on a grid plan, with canals as thoroughfares and causeways to the lakeshore. In the marshier parts, they created raised gardens by piling up vegeta-

---

MEXICO CITY IN...

Two Days

Day one dawns and you find yourself standing in the **Zócalo** (p66), once the center of the Aztec universe. Explore the pre-Hispanic ruins at **Templo Mayor** (p67) then admire Diego Rivera's cinematic murals at **Palacio Nacional** (p70). Next, head south to **Xochimilco** (p92) and glide along ancient canals on a *trajinera* (gondola). Day two, delve into Mexico's past at **Museo Nacional de Antropología** (p86) and **Castillo de Chapultepec** (p87). Come nightfall, do tequila shots over mariachi music at **Plaza Garibaldi** (p74).

Four Days

With a couple more days, head out to the pyramids at **Teotihuacán** (p146). In the evening plug into the lively nightlife scene in **Roma** (p120) or **Condesa** (p119). Greet the new day with a stroll around **Alameda Central** (p78), making time to acquaint yourself with the **Palacio de Bellas Artes** (p77), then do some *artesanías* (handicrafts) shopping at **La Ciudadela** (p128).

One Week

Get to know the southern districts: visit **Museo Frida Kahlo** (p95) in Coyoacán and do dinner and mezcal sampling on the delightful **Jardín Centenario** (p96), or shop for quality crafts at San Ángel's **Bazar Sábado** (p130) market. Reserve Wednesday or Sunday evening for the **Ballet Folklórico de México** (p124).

tion and mud and planting willows. These *chinampas* (versions of which still exist at Xochimilco in southern Mexico City) gave three or four harvests yearly.

The Spanish arrived in 1519, fracturing Mexican civilization and turning native people into second-class citizens in just two years. When these invaders arrived, Tenochtitlán's population was between 200,000 and 300,000, while the entire Valle de México had perhaps 1.5 million inhabitants, making it one of the world's densest urban areas.

For a more complete account of the Spanish arrival, see p810.

Capital of Nueva España

So assiduously did the Spanish raze Tenochtitlán that only a handful of structures from the Aztec period remain visible today. Having wrecked the Aztec capital, they set about rebuilding it as their own. Conquistador Hernán Cortés hoped to preserve the arrangement whereby Tenochtitlán siphoned off the bounty of its vassal states.

Ravaged by disease, the Valle de México's population shrank drastically – from 1.5 million to under 100,000 within a century of the conquest. But the city emerged as the prosperous, elegant capital of Nueva España, with broad streets laid over the Aztec causeways and canals.

Building continued through the 17th century, but problems arose as the weighty colonial structures began sinking into the squishy lake bed. Furthermore, lacking natural drainage, the city suffered floods caused by the partial destruction in the 1520s of the Aztecs' canals. One torrential rain in 1629 left the city submerged for five years.

Urban conditions improved in the 18th century as plazas and avenues were installed, along with sewage and garbage-collection systems. This was Mexico City's gilded age.

Independence

On October 30, 1810, some 80,000 independence rebels, fresh from victory at Guanajuato, overpowered Spanish loyalist forces west of the capital. Unfortunately they were ill equipped to capitalize on this triumph and their leader, Miguel Hidalgo, chose not to advance on the city – a decision that cost Mexico 11 more years of fighting before independence was achieved.

Following the reform laws established by President Benito Juárez in 1859, monasteries and churches were appropriated by the government, then sold off, subdivided and

put to other uses. During his brief reign (1864–67), Emperor Maximilian laid out the Calzada del Emperador (today's Paseo de la Reforma) to connect Bosque de Chapultepec with the center.

Mexico City entered the modern age under the despotic Porfirio Díaz, who ruled Mexico for most of the years between 1876 and 1911. Díaz ushered in a construction boom, building Parisian-style mansions and theaters, while the city's wealthier residents escaped the center for newly minted neighborhoods to the west.

Modern Megalopolis

After Díaz fell in 1911, the Mexican Revolution brought war, hunger and disease to the streets of Mexico City. Following the Great Depression, a drive to industrialize attracted more money and people.

Mexico City continued to mushroom in the 1970s, as the rural poor sought economic refuge in its thriving industries, and the metropolitan-area population surged from 8.7 to 14.5 million. Unable to contain the new arrivals, Mexico City spread beyond the bounds of the Distrito Federal (DF; Federal District) and into the adjacent state of México. The result of such unbridled growth was some of the world's worst traffic and pollution. At last count, the Greater Mexico City area had more than 22 million inhabitants.

For seven decades, the federal government ruled the DF directly, with presidents appointing 'regents' to head notoriously corrupt administrations. Finally, in 1997, the DF gained political autonomy. In 2000 Andrés Manuel López Obrador, of the left-leaning PRD (Party of the Democratic Revolution), was elected mayor. *Capitalinos* (capital-city residents) approved of 'AMLO.' His initiatives included an ambitious makeover of the *centro histórico* and the construction of an overpass for the city's ring road.

While López Obrador was narrowly defeated in the presidential election of 2006 (an outcome he fiercely contested based on fraud allegations), his former police chief, Marcelo Ebrard, won a sweeping victory in Mexico City, consolidating the PRD's grip on the city government. The PRD has passed a flood of progressive initiatives, including same-sex marriage and the legalization of abortion and euthanasia. In 2012 Ebrard passed the reins to his former attorney general, Miguel Ángel Mancera, who won the Mexico City mayoral race with more than 60% of the vote. Mancera supports

MEXICO CITY HISTORY

a proposal to decriminalize and regulate marijuana consumption, a measure that is gaining traction in DF. In 2015 Mancera's government announced a major revamp of Avenida Chapultepec with new pedestrian (and, controversially, commercial) spaces, a sign of Mexico City's continual reinvention.

◉ Sights

You could spend months exploring all the museums, monuments, plazas, colonial buildings, monasteries, murals, galleries, archaeological sites, shrines and religious relics that this encyclopedia of a city has to offer – Mexico City shares billing with London for having the most museums of any city in the world.

Plan ahead as many museums close on Monday, while most waive their admission fees to residents on Sunday, thus attracting crowds.

The Distrito Federal comprises 16 *delegaciones* (boroughs), which are in turn subdivided into around 1800 *colonias* (neighborhoods). Though the vast urban expanse appears daunting, the main areas of interest to visitors are fairly well defined and easy to traverse.

Note that some major streets, such as Avenida Insurgentes, keep the same name for many kilometers, but the names (and numbering) of many lesser streets may switch every 10 blocks or so.

Often the easiest way to find an address is by asking for the nearest metro station. If you know the name of the *colonia*, you can locate streets at the Guia Roji website (www.guiaroji.com.mx).

Besides their regular names, many major streets are termed Eje (axis). The Eje system establishes a grid of priority roads across the city.

◉ Centro Histórico

Packed with magnificent buildings and absorbing museums, the 668-block area defined as the *centro histórico* is the obvious place to start your explorations. More than 1500 of its buildings are classified as historic or artistic monuments and it is on the Unesco World Heritage list. It also vibrates with modern-day street life and nightlife, and is a convenient area to stay.

Since 2000, money has been poured into upgrading the image and infrastructure of the *centro*. Streets have been repaved, buildings refurbished, lighting and traffic flow improved and security bolstered. New mu-

seums, restaurants and clubs have moved into the renovated structures, and festivals and cultural events are staged in the plazas, spurring a real downtown revival.

At the center of it all lies the massive Zócalo, downtown's main square, where pre-Hispanic ruins, imposing colonial-era buildings and large-scale murals convey Mexico City's storied past.

In true forward-looking, *chilango* (Mexico city inhabitants) style, the Zócalo, Plaza Tolsá and Gran Hotel opened themselves to international audiences when heavily featured in the James Bond *Spectre* film.

Zócalo   PLAZA
(Map p68; Plaza de la Constitución, Colonia Centro; Ⓜ Zócalo) The heart of Mexico City is the Plaza de la Constitución. Residents began calling it the Zócalo, meaning 'base,' in the 19th century, when plans for a major monument to independence went unrealized, leaving only the pedestal. Measuring 220m from north to south, and 240m from east to west, it's one of the world's largest city squares.

The ceremonial center of Aztec Tenochtitlán, known as the Teocalli, lay immediately northeast of the Zócalo. In the 1520s Cortés paved the plaza with stones from the ruins of the complex. In the 18th century the Zócalo was given over to a maze of market stalls until it was dismantled by General Santa Anna, who placed the unfinished monument in its center.

Today the Zócalo is home to the powers that be. On its east side is the Palacio Nacional (the presidential palace), on the north is the Catedral Metropolitana, and on the south are the city government offices. Jewelry shops and extravagant hotels line the arcade known as the Portal de Mercaderes on the plaza's west side.

As you emerge from metro Zócalo onto the vast central plaza, you may hear the booming of drums from the direction of the cathedral – the Aztec dancers are doing their thing. Wearing snakeskin loincloths, elaborately feathered headdresses and shell ankle bracelets, they move in a circle and chant in Náhuatl. At the center, engulfed in a cloud of fragrant copal smoke, drummers bang on the conga-like *huehuetl* (indigenous drum) and the barrel-shaped, slitted *teponaztli*.

Variously known as Danzantes Aztecas, Danza Chichimeca or Concheros, the dancers perform their ritual daily in the plaza. It is meant to evoke the Aztec *mitote*, a frenzied ceremony performed by preconquest

Mexicans at harvest times, although scant evidence exists that the dancers' moves bear any resemblance to those of their forebears.

The square has variously served as a forum for mass protests, free concerts, a human chessboard, a gallery of spooky Día de Muertos (Day of the Dead) altars and an ice-skating rink. It's even been a canvas for photo artist Spencer Tunick, who filled the square with 18,000 nude Mexicans in May 2007.

The huge Mexican flag flying in the middle of the Zócalo is ceremonially raised at 8am by soldiers of the Mexican army, then lowered at 6pm.

★ **Templo Mayor**   ARCHAEOLOGICAL SITE
(Map p68; ☑ 55-4040-5600; www.templomayor. inah.gob.mx; Seminario 8; M$59, audio guide M$80; ⊙ 9am-5pm Tue-Sun; M Zócalo) Before the Spaniards demolished it, the Teocalli of Tenochtitlán covered the site where the cathedral now stands, as well as the blocks to its north and east. It wasn't until 1978, after electricity workers happened on an eight-tonne stone-disc carving of the Aztec goddess Coyolxauhqui, that the decision was taken to demolish colonial buildings and excavate the Templo Mayor.

The temple is thought to be on the exact spot where the Aztecs saw their symbolic eagle perching on a cactus with a snake in its beak – the symbol of Mexico today. In Aztec belief this was, literally, the center of the universe.

Like other sacred buildings in Tenochtitlán, the temple was enlarged several times, with each rebuilding accompanied by the sacrifice of captured warriors. What we see today are sections of the temple's seven different phases. At the center is a platform dating from about 1400. On its southern half, a sacrificial stone stands in front of a shrine to Huizilopochtli, the Aztec war god. On the northern half is a chac-mool (a Maya reclining figure) before a shrine to the water god, Tláloc. By the time the Spanish arrived, a 40m-high double pyramid towered above this spot, with steep twin stairways climbing to shrines of the two gods.

The entrance to the temple site and museum is east of the cathedral, across the hectic **Plaza del Templo Mayor**. Authorized tour guides (with Sectur ID) offer their services by the entrance. Alternatively, rent an audio guide – available in English.

The on-site **Museo del Templo Mayor** (included in the site's admission price) houses a model of Tenochtitlán and artifacts from the site, and gives a good overview of Aztec, aka Mexica, civilization. Pride of place is given to the great wheel-like stone of Coyolxauhqui

MEXICO CITY FOR CHILDREN

As with elsewhere in Mexico, kids take center stage in the capital. Many theaters, including the **Centro Cultural del Bosque** (p124), stage children's plays and puppet shows on weekends and during school holidays. Animated movies are a staple at cinemas around town, though keep in mind that children's films are usually dubbed in Spanish.

Museums frequently organize hands-on activities for kids. The **Museo de la Secretaría de Hacienda y Crédito Público** (p74) often stages puppet shows on Sunday.

Mexico City's numerous parks and plazas are usually buzzing with kids' voices. **Bosque de Chapultepec** (p86) is the obvious destination, and then there are the **Papalote Museo del Niño** (p90), **La Feria** (p91), the **Zoológico de Chapultepec** (p90) and several lakes with rowboat rentals. In neighboring Polanco is the world-class aquarium **Acuario Inbursa** (p91). Also consider Condesa's **Parque México** (p85), where kids can rent bikes and where Sunday is family-activity day. **Plaza Hidalgo** (p96) in Coyoacán is another fun-filled spot with balloons, street mimes and cotton candy.

In **Xochimilco** (p92) kids will find riding the gondolas through the canals as magical as any theme park. Also in this part of town is the **Museo Dolores Olmedo** (p92), where peacocks and pre-Hispanic dogs occupy the gardens. Children's shows are performed in the patio on Saturday and Sunday at 1pm, and the museum offers workshops for children.

Another great option is the **Museo del Juguete Antiguo México** (p101), a fascinating toy museum with more than 60,000 collectibles on display.

For more on activities for children, see the 'Infantiles' section at the Conaculta website (www.mexicoescultura.com).

N

0   0.2 miles
0   400 m

Salón Los
Ángeles (660m)

Lerdo

Garibaldi

Garibaldi

Paseo de la Reforma

Dos de Abril

Santa Veracruz

Bellas
Artes

Bellas
Artes

Palacio de
Bellas
Artes 1

22

27

Centro Cultural
Universitario
Tlatelolco (800m);
Plaza de las Tres
Culturas (890m)

Tianguis Dominical
de la Lagunilla (270m)

Libertad

Rayón

Mercado Tepito

Lagunilla

Héroe de Granaditas

98

República de Costa Rica

Florida

Aztecas

República de Nicaragua

República de Ecuador

República de Paraguay

República de Brasil

República de Bolivia

República de Colombia

Metrobús República
de Argentina

República de Venezuela

Rodríguez Puebla

Santísima

Plaza
de Loreto

Calle del Carmen

San Ildefonso

37

Justo Sierra

5

República de
Argentina

44

31

Palacio
de la
Inquisición

Iglesia
de Santo
Domingo

Plaza
Santo
Domingo

Portales
de Santo
Domingo

28

República de Brasil

48

La Palma

Donceles

República de Honduras

Belisario Domínguez

Metrobús República
de Chile

República de Chile

56

Altuna

Comonfort

78

94

Allende

90

Incas

República de Perú

80

República de Cuba

83

50

Allende

Plaza
Garibaldi

Plaza
Montero

Plaza de la
Concepción

Plaza
Garibaldi 3 17

Plaza
Garibaldi

82

62

70

73

60

Plaza
Tolsá

69

Eje Central Lázaro Cárdenas

Palacio
Postal

Condesa

29

25

21

18

14

26

Tacuba

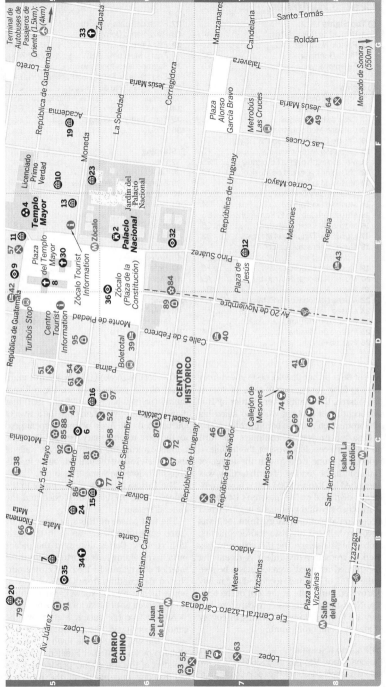

Centro Histórico

◎ **Top Sights**
1 Palacio de Bellas Artes..........................A4
2 Palacio Nacional E6
3 Plaza Garibaldi.......................................B2
4 Templo Mayor..E5

◎ **Sights**
5 Antiguo Colegio de San Ildefonso F4
6 Avenida Madero.....................................C5
7 Casa de los Azulejos..............................B5
8 Catedral Metropolitana.........................E5
9 Centro Cultural de España.....................E5
10 Ex Teresa Arte Actual.............................F5
11 Museo Archivo de la Fotografía.............E5
12 Museo de la Ciudad de México..............E7
13 Museo de la Secretaría de
     Hacienda y Crédito Público E5
14 Museo de la Tortura B4
15 Museo del Calzado El Borceguí B5
16 Museo del Estanquillo C5
17 Museo del Tequila y el Mezcal B2
18 Museo Interactivo de Economía
     (MIDE) C4
19 Museo José Luis Cuevas........................F5
20 Museo Nacional de Arquitectura A5
21 Museo Nacional de Arte........................B4
22 Museo Nacional de la Estampa A4
23 Museo Nacional de las Culturas............F5
24 Palacio de Iturbide................................B5
25 Palacio de Minería B4
26 Palacio Postal B4

27 Plaza de Santa Veracruz A4
28 Plaza Santo Domingo D4
29 Plaza Tolsá...B4
     Postal Museum............................(see 26)
30 Sagrario Metropolitano E5
31 Secretaría de Educación Pública E4
32 Suprema Corte de Justicia....................E6
33 Templo de la Santísima Trinidad G5
34 Templo de San Francisco B5
35 Torre Latinoamericana..........................B5
36 Zócalo E6

😴 **Sleeping**
37 Casa San Ildefonso F4
38 Chillout Flat...C5
39 Gran Hotel Ciudad de México D6
40 Hampton Inn & Suites...........................D7
41 Hostal Regina D8
42 Hostel Mundo Joven Catedral...............D5
43 Hotel Castropol E8
44 Hotel Catedral E4
45 Hotel Gillow...C5
46 Hotel Isabel...C7
47 Hotel Marlowe.......................................A5
48 Mexico City Hostel D4

🍴 **Eating**
49 Al Andalus F8
     Azul Histórico ....(see 97)
50 Café de Tacuba C4
51 Café El Popular......................................D5

(She of Bells on her Cheek), best viewed from the top-floor vantage point. She is shown decapitated, the result of her murder by Huizilopochtli, her brother, who also killed his 400 brothers en route to becoming top god.

Ongoing excavation continues to turn up major pieces. Just west of the temple, a monolithic stone carved with the image of Tlaltecuhtli, the goddess of earth fertility, was unearthed in October 2006 and is now prominently displayed on the museum's 1st floor.

Another key find was made in 2011 when a ceremonial platform dating from 1469 was uncovered. Based on historical documents, archaeologists believe the 15m structure was used to cremate Aztec rulers. A recent dig also turned up what archaeologists believe is the trunk of a sacred tree found at a newly discovered burial site at the foot of the temple. Now more than ever, researchers feel they are inching closer to the first discovery of an Aztec emperor's tomb.

★**Palacio Nacional**   PALACE
(National Palace; Map p68; ☑55-3688-1255; www.historia.palacionacional.info; Plaza de la Constitución;

◷10am-5pm; Ⓜ Zócalo) FREE Inside this grandiose colonial palace you'll see Diego Rivera murals (painted between 1929 and 1951) that depict Mexican civilization from the arrival of Quetzalcóatl (the Aztec plumed serpent god) to the post-revolutionary period. The nine murals covering the north and east walls of the first level above the patio chronicle indigenous life before the Spanish conquest.

The Palacio Nacional is also home to the offices of the president of Mexico and the Federal Treasury.

The first palace on this spot was built by Aztec emperor Moctezuma II in the early 16th century. Cortés destroyed the palace in 1521, rebuilding it as a fortress with three interior courtyards. In 1562 the crown purchased the building from Cortés' family to house the viceroys of Nueva España, a function it served until Mexican independence.

As you face the palace, high above the center door hangs the **Campana de Dolores**, the bell rung in the town of Dolores Hidalgo by Padre Miguel Hidalgo in 1810 at the start of the War of Independence. From the balcony underneath it, the president

52 Casino Español	C6
53 Coox Hanal	C8
54 El Cardenal	D5
55 El Huequito	A6
56 Hostería de Santo Domingo	D3
57 La Casa de las Sirenas	E5
58 La Casa del Pavo	C6
59 Los Cocuyos	B7
60 Los Girasoles	B4
61 Los Vegetarianos	D5
62 Mercado San Camilito	B2
63 Mi Fonda	A7
64 Restaurante Chon	F8

⊘ **Drinking & Nightlife**

65 Al Andar	C8
66 Bar La Ópera	B5
67 Bar Mancera	C6
68 Bar Oasis	B3
69 Café Jekemir	C8
Downtown Mexico	(see 97)
70 El Buen Tiempo	C4
71 Hostería La Bota	C8
72 La Faena	C6
73 La Purísima	C4
74 La Risa	C7
75 Las Duelistas	A7
Marrakech Salón	(see 70)
76 Mexicano	C8
77 Salón Corona	C6

⊙ **Entertainment**

78 Arena Coliseo	D3
79 Ballet Folklórico de México	A5
Centro Cultural de España	(see 9)
80 La Perla	C4
Palacio de Bellas Artes	(see 1)
81 Pasagüero + La Bipo	C5
82 Salón Tenampa	B2
83 Teatro de la Ciudad	C4
84 Ticketmaster Liverpool Centro	E6
Ticketmaster Mixup Centro	(see 16)
85 Zinco Jazz Club	C5

⊙ **Shopping**

86 American Bookstore	B5
87 Casasola Fotografía	C6
88 Dulcería de Celaya	C5
89 El Palacio de Hierro	D6
90 Galería Eugenio	C2
91 Gandhi	A5
92 Gandhi	C5
93 La Europea	A6
94 La Lagunilla	C1
Liverpool	(see 84)
95 Mumedi	D5
96 Plaza de la Computación y Electrónica	A7
97 Plaza Downtown Mexico	C6
98 Tepito	F1

delivers the *grito* (shout) – ¡Viva México! – on the evening of September 15 to commemorate independence.

Catedral Metropolitana CATHEDRAL
(Metropolitan Cathedral; Map p68; ☑ 55-5510-0440; www.catedralmetropolitanademexico.mx; Plaza de la Constitución; bell tower M$20; ⊙ cathedral 8am-8pm, bell tower 10:40am-6pm; Ⓜ Zócalo) One of Mexico City's most iconic structures, this cathedral is a monumental edifice: 109m long, 59m wide and 65m high. Started in 1573, it remained a work in progress during the entire colonial period, thus displaying a catalog of architectural styles, with successive generations of builders striving to incorporate the innovations of the day.

Original architect Claudio Arciniega modeled the building after Seville's seven-nave cathedral, but after running into difficulties with the spongy subsoil he scaled it down to a five-nave design of vaults on semicircular arches. The baroque portals facing the Zócalo, built in the 17th century, have two levels of columns and marble panels with bas-reliefs. The central panel shows the Assumption of the Virgin Mary, to whom the cathedral is dedicated. The upper levels of the towers, with unique bell-shaped tops, were added in the late 18th century. The exterior was completed in 1813, when architect Manuel Tolsá added the clock tower, topped by statues of Faith, Hope and Charity, and a great central dome.

The first thing you notice upon entering is the elaborately carved and gilded Altar de Perdón (Altar of Forgiveness). There's invariably a line of worshippers at the foot of the Señor del Veneno (Lord of the Poison), the dusky Christ figure on the right. Legend has it that the figure attained its color when it miraculously absorbed a dose of poison through its feet from the lips of a clergyman to whom an enemy had administered the lethal substance.

The cathedral's chief artistic treasure is the gilded 18th-century **Altar de los Reyes** (Altar of the Kings), behind the main altar. Fourteen richly decorated chapels line the two sides of the building, while intricately carved late-17th-century wooden choir stalls by Juan de Rojas occupy the central nave. Enormous painted panels by colonial masters Juan Correa and Cristóbal de

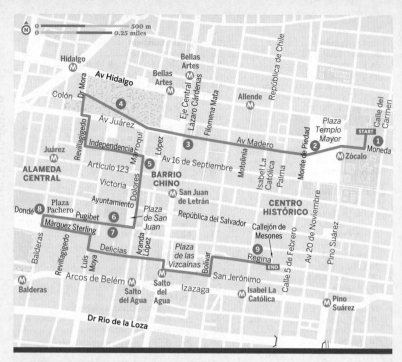

🏃 City Walk
Goin' Downtown

START EX TERESA ARTE ACTUAL
END REGINA CORRIDOR
LENGTH 5KM; THREE HOURS

Nothing beats wandering to fully appreciate the *centro's* rich history.

Kick things off in the slanted 17th-century **1 Ex Teresa Arte Actual** (p74) building. If there's one place that can put the sinking-city phenomenon into perspective, it's here.

As you cross the **2 Zócalo** (p66), one of the world's largest squares, stop and contemplate that the surrounding buildings sit atop Aztec temples. Some of the imposing colonial structures were built with materials from the pre-Hispanic ruins.

Continue west along bustling Avenida Madero to reach the **3 Torre Latinoamericana** (p75) skyscraper. To get a feel for just how far Mexico City's concave valley spans, take in the view from the observation deck.

Next spend time strolling **4 Alameda Central** (p78), downtown's newly reno-

vated park with fun fountains and a famous Diego Rivera mural at the west end.

Cut across Avenida Juárez to Calle Dolores and drop by **5 El Tío Pepe**, one of the city's oldest cantinas, for a beer or tequila.

Head south on Dolores to **6 Mercado San Juan** (p128), a 60-year-old market frequented by chefs and devout foodies. Look for **7 Gastrónomico San Juan** for wonderful deli treats and complimentary wine.

Exit the market on Pugibet and go west to Balderas to find **8 Centro de Artesanías la Ciudadela** (p128), a large crafts market with decent prices and great variety.

Return to the heart of downtown, walking east until you hit the **9 Regina corridor**, a happening pedestrian thoroughfare. Rest here at one of several sidewalk *mezcalerías*. If you prefer, cap off the walk at a nearby *pulque* joint on the corner of Mesones and Callejón de Mesones, a soulful spot that's been pouring the viscous fermented beverage for more than a century. *¡Salud!*

Villalpando cover the walls of the sacristy, the first component of the cathedral to be built.

Visitors may wander freely, though you're asked not to do so during Mass. A donation is requested to enter the sacristy or choir, where docents provide commentary, and you can climb the **bell tower**. Mexico City's archbishop conducts Mass at noon on Sundays.

Adjoining the east side of the cathedral is the 18th-century **Sagrario Metropolitano** (Map p68; ⊘8am-6:30pm). Originally built to house the archives and vestments of the archbishop, it is now the city's main parish church. Its front entrance and mirror-image eastern portal are superb examples of the ultradecorative Churrigueresque style.

Centro Cultural de España   CULTURAL CENTER
(Spanish Cultural Center; Map p68; www.ccemx. org; República de Guatemala 18; ⊘11am-9pm Tue-Sat, to 4pm Sun; Ⓜ Zócalo) ᴴᴿᴱᴱ Always has a variety of cutting-edge art exhibitions going on. In the basement you'll find the **Museo de Sitio**, an interesting museum with the remains of 'El Calmécac', a school where children of Aztec nobility received religious and military training during the reigns of Emperors Ahuízotl and Moctezuma II. It was built between 1486 and 1502.

Also in the museum are various artifacts unearthed as the cultural center was being expanded between 2006 and 2008, including several 2.4m-tall pre-Hispanic *almenas* (spiral-shaped decorative pieces), colonial-era ceramic objects and a weathered 20th-century handgun.

The cultural center's splendidly restored colonial building, which conquistador Hernán Cortés once awarded to his butler, has a cool terrace bar that stages live music and DJ sets Wednesday to Saturday from 10pm.

Museo Archivo de la Fotografía   MUSEUM
(Photographic Archive Museum; Map p68; ☑55-2616-7057; www.cultura.df.gob.mx/index. php/museo-archivo-de-la-fotografia; República de Guatemala 34; ⊘10am-6pm Tue-Sun; Ⓜ Zócalo) ᴴᴿᴱᴱ Occupying a 16th-century colonial building, the city's photo museum hosts exhibits focusing on all things Mexico City. Additionally, the museum has amassed a vast archive comprising a century's worth of urban images.

Plaza Tolsá   PLAZA
(Map p68; Ⓜ Bellas Artes) Several blocks west of the Zócalo is this handsome square, named after Manuel Tolsá, the illustrious

late-18th-century sculptor and architect who completed the Catedral Metropolitana. He also created the bronze equestrian statue of the Spanish king Carlos IV (who reigned from 1788 to 1808), which is the plaza's centerpiece. It originally stood in the Zócalo.

Unfortunately a botched restoration job using a nitric-acid solution recently left part of the statue's surface badly damaged. King Carlos rides in front of the **Museo Nacional de Arte** (National Art Museum; Map p68; ☑55-5130-3400; www.munal.gob.mx; Tacuba 8; M$37, free Sun; ⊘10am-5:30pm Tue-Sun; Ⓜ Bellas Artes). Built around 1900 in the style of an Italian Renaissance palace, the museum holds collections representing every school of Mexican art until the early 20th century. A highlight is the work of José María Velasco, depicting the Valle de México in the late 19th century.

Opposite is the **Palacio de Minería** (Palace of Mining; Map p68; ☑55-5623-2982; www. palaciomineria.unam.mx; Tacuba 5; tours M$30; ⊘tours 11am & 1pm Sat & Sun; Ⓜ Bellas Artes), where mining engineers were trained in the 19th century. Today it houses a branch of the national university's engineering department. A neoclassical masterpiece, the palace was designed by Tolsá and built between 1797 and 1813. Visits are by guided tour only. The palace contains four meteorites that struck northern Mexico, one weighing more than 14 tonnes. There's also a museum on Tolsá's life and work.

Palacio Postal   HISTORIC BUILDING
(Correo Mayor; Map p68; ☑55-5510-2999; www. palaciopostal.gob.mx; Tacuba 1; ⊘9am-6pm Mon-Fri, to 3:30pm Sat & Sun; ⍟; Ⓜ Bellas Artes) ᴴᴿᴱᴱ More than just Mexico City's central post office, this early-20th-century palace is an Italianate confection designed by the Palacio de Bellas Artes' original architect, Adamo Boari. The beige stone facade features baroque columns and carved filigree around the windows. Inside, the bronze railings on the monumental staircase were cast in Florence.

The small **Postal Museum** (Map p68; ⊘9am-6pm Tue-Fri, to 3pm Sat & Sun; Ⓜ Bellas Artes) ᴴᴿᴱᴱ, on the 1st floor, is where philatelists can ogle a design of the first stamp ever issued in Mexico.

Museo Interactivo de Economía (MIDE)   MUSEUM
(Interactive Museum of Economics; Map p68; ☑55-5130-4600; www.mide.org.mx; Tacuba 17; adult/child under 5yr M$70/free; ⊘9am-6pm Tue-

Sun; M Allende) The former hospital of the Bethlehemites religious order has been the home of this museum since 2006. A slew of hands-on exhibits is aimed at breaking down economic concepts. For coin connoisseurs, the highlight is the Banco de México's numismatic collection.

Museo de la Tortura   MUSEUM
(Museum of Torture; Map p68; ☑55-5521-4651; Tacuba 15; adult/child 7-13yr M$60/45; ⊙10am-6pm; M Allende) Displaying European torture instruments from the 14th to 19th centuries, including a metal-spiked interrogation chair and the menacing skull splitter, this museum has surefire appeal for the morbidly curious.

Museo de la Secretaría de Hacienda y Crédito Público   MUSEUM
(Finance Secretariat Museum; Map p68; ☑55-3668-1657; Moneda 4; ⊙10am-5pm Tue-Sun; M Zócalo) **FREE** Sure, the name is a tough sell (yay, let's go to the Finance Secretariat Museum!), but it's actually a very interesting place. The museum shows off works from its collection of more than 30,000 pieces of Mexican art, much of it contributed by painters and sculptors in lieu of paying taxes.

Built in the 16th century, the former colonial archbishop's palace also hosts a full program of cultural events (many free), from puppet shows to chamber music recitals. The building sits atop the Templo de Tezcatlipoca, a temple dedicated to an Aztec god often associated with night, death and change through conflict. You'll see the temple's stairs just off the renovated main patio.

★ Plaza Garibaldi   PLAZA
(Map p68; cnr Eje Central Lázaro Cárdenas & República de Honduras; mariachi song M$130-150; P; M Garibaldi) Every night the city's mariachi bands belt out heartfelt ballads in this festive square. Wearing silver-studded outfits, they toot their trumpets and tune their guitars until approached by someone who'll pay for a song. Also roaming Garibaldi are white-clad *son jarocho* groups, hailing from Veracruz, and *norteño* combos, who bang out northern-style folk tunes.

The notoriously seedy Garibaldi has had a makeover that includes heightened security, but it's still rough around the edges. The latest addition is the **Museo del Tequila y el Mezcal** (Map p68; www.mutemgaribaldi. mx; Plaza Garibaldi; M$50; ⊙1-10pm Sun-Wed, to 11:30pm Thu-Sat; M Garibaldi), which has exhibits explaining the origins and production processes of Mexico's two most popular distilled agave drinks. The tour ends with a tasting on a rooftop bar overlooking the plaza. An onsite store sells some decent, albeit overpriced, tequilas and mezcals.

Ex Teresa Arte Actual   MUSEUM
(Map p68; www.exteresa.bellasartes.gob.mx; Licenciado Verdad 8; ⊙10am-5pm; M Zócalo) **FREE** Mexico City was built atop a sloshy lake bed and it's sinking fast, as evidenced by this teetering former convent. The 17th-century building now serves as a museum for performance art, contemporary exhibits, concerts and the occasional movie screening.

Avenida Madero   STREET
(Map p68) This stately avenue west of the Zócalo boasts a veritable catalog of architectural styles.

Housed in a gorgeous neoclassical building two blocks from the square, **Museo del Estanquillo** (Map p68; ☑55-5521-3052; www. museodelestanquillo.com; Isabel La Católica 26; ⊙10am-6pm Wed-Mon; M Allende) **FREE** contains the vast pop-culture collection amassed over the decades by DF essayist and pack rat Carlos Monsiváis. The museum illustrates various phases in the capital's development by means of the numerous photos, paintings and movie posters from the collection.

Palacio de Iturbide (Palacio de Cultura Banamex; Map p68; ☑55-1226-0091; www.fomento culturalbanamex.org; Av Madero 17; ⊙10am-7pm; M Allende) **FREE**, with its late-18th-century baroque facade, is a few blocks west. Built for colonial nobility, in 1821 it became the residence of General Agustín Iturbide, a Mexican independence hero who was proclaimed emperor here in 1822. (He abdicated less than a year later, after General Santa Anna announced the birth of a republic.) It hosts exhibits drawn from the bank's extensive art collection.

Half a block past the pedestrian corridor Gante stands the amazing **Casa de los Azulejos** (House of Tiles; Map p68; ☑55-5512-9820; Av Madero 4; ⊙7am-1am; M Allende). Dating from 1596, it was built for the Condes (Counts) del Valle de Orizaba. Most of the tiles that adorn the outside walls were produced in China and shipped to Mexico on the Manila naos (Spanish galleons used until the early 19th century). The building now houses a Sanborns restaurant in a covered courtyard around a Moorish fountain. The staircase has a 1925 mural by Orozco.

Across the way, the **Templo de San Francisco** (Map p68; Av Madero 7; ⊙8am-8pm) is a remnant of the vast Franciscan monastery erected in the early 16th century over the site of Moctezuma's private zoo. In its heyday it extended two blocks south and east. The monastic complex was divvied up under the post-independence reform laws, and in 1949 it was returned to the Franciscan order in a deplorable state and subsequently restored. The elaborately carved doorway is a shining example of 18th-century baroque. Open-air art exhibitions are held in the adjoining atrium.

Rising alongside the monastery, the **Torre Latinoamericana** (Latin American Tower; Map p68; ☎ 55-5518-7423; http://torrelatinoamericana.com.mx; Eje Central Lázaro Cárdenas 2; adult/child M$80/60; ⊙9am-10pm; Ⓜ Bellas Artes) was Latin America's tallest building when constructed in 1956. Thanks to the deep-seated pylons that anchor the building, it has withstood several major earthquakes. If you want to learn more about the construction of the tower and downtown's centuries-long development, a museum on the 38th floor houses a permanent photo exhibition. Up above, views from the 41st-floor lounge bar and the 44th-floor observation deck are spectacular, smog permitting. Admission is free if you're just visiting the bar.

Museo Nacional de las Culturas MUSEUM (National Museum of Cultures; Map p68; ☎ 55-5512-7452; www.museodelasculturas.mx; Moneda 13; ⊙9am-5pm Tue-Sun; Ⓜ Zócalo) FREE Constructed in 1567 as the colonial mint, this renovated museum exhibits art, dress and handicrafts of the world's cultures, but there's no explanatory text in English.

Templo de la Santísima Trinidad CHURCH (Map p68; cnr Santísima & Zapata; Ⓜ Zócalo) The profusion of ornamental sculpture on the facade, including ghostly busts of the 12 apostles and a representation of Christ with his head in God's lap, is the main reason to visit the Church of the Holy Sacrament, five blocks east of the Zócalo as you walk along Calle Moneda.

Most of the carving was done by Lorenzo Rodríguez between 1755 and 1783.

Suprema Corte de Justicia MURAL (Supreme Court; Map p68; ☎ 55-4113-1000; Pino Suárez 2; ⊙9am-5pm Mon-Fri; Ⓜ Zócalo) FREE In 1940 muralist José Clemente Orozco painted four panels around the second level of the Supreme Court's central stairway, two dealing with the theme of justice.

A more contemporary take on the same subject, *La historia de la justicia en México* (The History of Justice in Mexico), by Rafael Cauduro, unfolds over three levels of the building's southwest stairwell.

Executed in his hyper-realist style, Cauduro's series (aka *The Seven Worst Crimes*) catalogs the horrors of state-sponsored crimes against the populace, including the ever-relevant torture-induced confession. On the southeast corner of the building's interior, Ismael Ramos Huitrón's *La busqueda de la justicia* (The Search for Justice) reflects on the Mexican people's constant struggle to obtain justice, as does the social realism work *La justicia* (Justice), by Japanese-Mexican artist Luis Nishizawa, on the northwest stairwell. On the first level of the main stairway, American artist George Biddle painted *La guerra y la paz* (War and Peace) shortly after WWII ended.

Photo ID required.

Museo de la Ciudad de México MUSEUM (Museum of Mexico City; Map p68; ☎ 55-5542-0083; www.cultura.df.gob.mx/index.php/museo-de-la-ciudad-de-mexico; Pino Suárez 30; M$28, Wed free; ⊙10am-6pm Tue-Sun; Ⓜ Pino Suárez) Formerly a palace of the Counts of Santiago de Calimaya, this 18th-century baroque edifice now houses a museum with exhibits focusing on city history and culture. Upstairs is the former studio of Joaquín Clausell, considered Mexico's foremost impressionist. The artist used the walls as a sketchbook during the three decades he worked here until his death in 1935.

Plaza Santo Domingo PLAZA (Map p68; cnr República de Venezuela & República de Brasil; 🚇 República de Argentina) Smaller and less hectic than nearby Zócalo, this plaza has long served as a base for scribes and printers. Descendants of those who did the paperwork for merchants using the customs building (now the Education Ministry) across the square, the scribes work on the west side beneath the **Portales de Santo Domingo**, aka Portales de Evangelistas.

To the north stands the maroon stone **Iglesia de Santo Domingo**, a beautiful baroque church dating from 1736. The three-tiered facade merits a close look: statues of St Francis and St Augustine stand in the niches alongside the doorway. The middle panel shows St Dominic de Guzmán receiving a staff and the Epistles from St Peter and

Alameda Central, Plaza de la República & Around

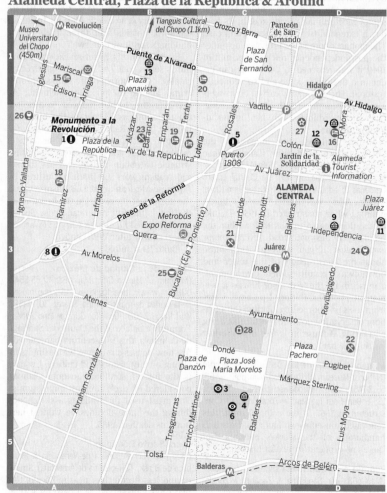

St Paul, respectively. At the top is a bas-relief of the Assumption of the Virgin Mary.

East of the church, the 18th-century **Palacio de la Inquisición** was headquarters of the Holy Inquisition in Mexico until Spain decreed its closure in 1812. Its official shield shows up at the top of the facade.

Secretaría de Educación Pública   MURAL
(Secretariat of Education; Map p68; ☏55-3601-1000; República de Brasil 31; ☉9am-3pm Mon-Fri; ◻República de Argentina) **FREE** The two front courtyards (on the opposite side of the building from the entrance off Plaza Santo

Domingo) here are lined with 120 fresco panels painted by Diego Rivera in the 1920s. Together they form a tableau of 'the very life of the people,' in the artist's words.

Each courtyard is thematically distinct: the one on the east end deals with labor, industry and agriculture, while the interior one depicts traditions and festivals. On the latter's top level is a series on proletarian and agrarian revolution, underneath a continuous red banner emblazoned with a Mexican *corrido* (folk song). A likeness of Frida Kahlo appears in the first panel as an arsenal worker.

A former Jesuit college built in the 16th century, San Ildefonso now hosts outstanding temporary art exhibitions.

Museo José Luis Cuevas MUSEUM
(Map p68; ☎ 55-5522-0156; www.museojoseluis cuevas.com.mx; Academia 13; M$20, Sun free; ⏱ 10am-6pm Tue-Sun; Ⓜ Zócalo) This museum showcases the works of artist Cuevas, a leader of the 1950s Ruptura movement, which broke with the politicized art of the post-revolutionary regime. Cuevas' *La Giganta*, an 8m-tall bronze female figure with some male features, dominates the central patio.

◉ Alameda Central & Around

Emblematic of the downtown renaissance, the rectangular park immediately northwest of the *centro histórico* holds a vital place in Mexico City's cultural life. Surrounded by historically significant buildings, the Alameda Central has been the focus of ambitious redevelopment over the past decade. In particular, the high-rise towers on the Plaza Juárez and adjacent new restaurants have transformed the zone south of the park, much of which was destroyed in the 1985 earthquake. Metro stations Bellas Artes and Hidalgo are located on the Alameda's east and west sides, respectively. The north–south Eje Central Lázaro Cárdenas passes just east of the park.

★Palacio de Bellas Artes ARTS CENTER
(Palace of Fine Arts; Map p68; ☎ 55-1000-4622; www.palacio.bellasartes.gob.mx; cnr Av Juárez & Eje Central Lázaro Cárdenas; museum M$49, Sun free; ⏱ 10am-6pm Tue-Sun; Ⓟ; Ⓜ Bellas Artes) Immense murals by world-famous Mexican artists dominate the top floors of this splendid white-marble palace, a concert hall and arts center commissioned by President Porfirio Díaz. Construction on the iconic building began in 1905 under Italian architect Adamo Boari, who favored neoclassical and art nouveau styles.

Complications arose as the heavy marble shell sank into the spongy subsoil, and then the Mexican Revolution intervened. Architect Federico Mariscal eventually finished the interior in the 1930s, utilizing the more modern art deco style.

On the 2nd floor are two early 1950s works by Rufino Tamayo: *México de hoy* (Mexico Today) and *Nacimiento de la nacionalidad* (Birth of Nationality), a symbolic

Antiguo Colegio de San Ildefonso MUSEUM
(Map p68; ☎ 55-5702-2834; www.sanildefonso. org.mx; Justo Sierra 16; adult/child under 12yr M$45/free, Tue free; ⏱ 10am-8pm Tue, to 6pm Wed-Sun; Ⓜ Zócalo) Diego Rivera, José Clemente Orozco and David Siqueiros painted murals here in the 1920s. Most of the work on the main patio is by Orozco; look for the portrait of Hernán Cortés and his lover La Malinche underneath the staircase. The amphitheater, off the lobby, holds Rivera's first mural, *La Creación*, undertaken on his return from Europe in 1923.

Alameda Central, Plaza de la República & Around

◎ **Top Sights**
1 Monumento a la Revolución A2

◎ **Sights**
2 Alameda Central E2
3 Biblioteca de México José
    Vasconcelos C4
4 Centro de la Imagen C5
5 El Caballito C2
6 La Ciudadela C5
7 Laboratorio de Arte Alameda D2
8 Monumento a Cristóbal Colón A3
    Monumento a la Revolución
    Observation Deck .... (see 1)
9 Museo de Arte Popular D3
10 Museo Franz Mayer E1
11 Museo Memoria y Tolerancia D3
12 Museo Mural Diego Rivera D2
    Museo Nacional de la
    Revolución .... (see 1)
13 Museo Nacional de San Carlos B1
    Paseo Cimentación .... (see 1)
14 Plaza Juárez E3

◎ **Sleeping**
15 Casa de los Amigos A1
16 Chaya D2
17 Hostel Suites DF B2
18 Palace Hotel A2
19 Plaza Revolución Hotel B2
20 Ramada Reforma C1

✖ **Eating**
21 El 123 .... C3
22 El Cuadrilátero D4
23 Gotan Restaurante B2

◎ **Drinking & Nightlife**
24 Bósforo D3
25 Café La Habana B3
26 Crisanta A2

◎ **Entertainment**
27 Cinemex Real D2

◎ **Shopping**
28 Centro de Artesanías La Ciudadela C4
29 Mercado San Juan E4

depiction of the creation of the *mestizo* (mixed ancestry) identity.

At the west end of the 3rd floor is Diego Rivera's famous *El hombre en el cruce de caminos* (Man at the Crossroads), originally commissioned for New York's Rockefeller Center. The Rockefellers had the original destroyed because of its anti-capitalist themes, but Rivera re-created it here in 1934.

On the north side are David Alfaro Siqueiros' three-part *La nueva democracia* (New Democracy) and Rivera's four-part *Carnaval de la vida mexicana* (Carnival of Mexican Life). To the east is José Clemente Orozco's *La katharsis* (Catharsis), depicting the conflict between humankind's 'social' and 'natural' aspects.

The 4th-floor **Museo Nacional de Arquitectura** (Map p68; ☑55-8647-5360; www.museonacionaldearquitectura.bellasartes.gob.mx; Av Juárez s/n; M$28, free Sun; ⊗10am-6pm Tue-Sun; Ⓜ Bellas Artes) features changing exhibits on contemporary architecture.

The recently renovated **Bellas Artes theater** (only available for viewing at performances) is itself a masterpiece, with a stained-glass curtain depicting the Valle de México. Based on a design by Mexican painter Gerardo Murillo (aka Dr Atl), it was assembled by New York jeweler Tiffany & Co from almost a million pieces of colored glass.

In addition, the palace stages outstanding temporary art exhibitions, seasonal opera and symphony performances and the Ballet Folklórico de México (p124).

Alameda Central   PARK
(Map p76; 🐾; Ⓜ Bellas Artes) Created in the late 1500s by mandate of then-viceroy Luis de Velasco, the Alameda took its name from the *álamos* (poplars) planted over its rectangular expanse. By the late 19th century the park was graced with European-style statuary and lit by gas lamps. It became the place to be seen for the city's elite.

Today the Alameda is a popular refuge, particularly on Sunday when families stroll its pathways and lovers snuggle on benches. The park was spruced up recently with dancing fountains, free wi-fi and well-manicured gardens rife with fragrant lavender plants.

Museo Mural Diego Rivera   MUSEUM
(Diego Rivera Mural Museum; Map p76; ☑55-5512-0754; www.museomuraldiegorivera.bellasartes.gob.mx; cnr Balderas & Colón; M$21, Sun free; ⊗10am-6pm Tue-Sun; Ⓜ Hidalgo) Home to one of Diego Rivera's most famous works, *Sueño de una tarde dominical en la Alameda Central* (Dream of a Sunday Afternoon in the Alameda Central), a 15m-long mural painted in 1947. Rivera imagined many of the figures who walked in the city from colonial times

onward, among them Hernán Cortés, Benito Juárez, Porfirio Díaz and Francisco Madero.

All are grouped around a *Catrina* (skeleton in pre-revolutionary women's garb). Rivera himself, as a pug-faced child, and Frida Kahlo stand beside the skeleton. Charts identify all the characters. The museum was built in 1986 to house the mural, after its original location, the Hotel del Prado, was wrecked by the 1985 earthquake.

Laboratorio de Arte Alameda   MUSEUM
(Alameda Art Laboratory; Map p76; ☑55-5510-2793; www.artealameda.bellasartes.gob.mx; Dr Mora 7; M$21, Sun free; ☉9am-5pm Tue-Sun; ⓂHidalgo) As is often the case with museums in the *centro,* the 17th-century former convent building that contains the Laboratorio de Arte Alameda is at least as interesting as its contents. Here you can catch installations by leading experimental artists from Mexico and abroad, with an emphasis on electronic and interactive media.

Plaza Juárez   PLAZA
(Map p76; ⓂBellas Artes) Representing the new face of the zone, the latest addition to the plaza is the **Museo Memoria y Tolerancia** (Memory & Tolerance Museum; Map p76; ☑55-5130-5555; www.myt.org.mx; Plaza Juárez 12; M$69, audio guide M$84; ☉9am-6pm Tue-Fri, 10am-7pm Sat & Sun; ⓂBellas Artes), a maze-like museum of 55 halls dedicated to preserving the memory of genocide victims. The multimedia exhibit chronicles crimes committed against humanity in Cambodia, Guatemala, Sudan, Rwanda and former Yugoslavia, as well as those perpetrated during the Holocaust.

Behind the fully restored **Templo de Corpus Christi**, which now holds the DF's archives, the plaza's centerpiece is a pair of Tetris-block towers by leading Mexican architect Ricardo Legorreta – the 24-story **Foreign Relations Secretariat** and the 23-story **Tribunales** building front a set of 1034 reddish pyramids in a broad pool, a collaboration between Legorreta and Spanish artist Vicente Rojo.

Museo de Arte Popular   MUSEUM
(Museum of Popular Art; Map p76; ☑55-5510-2201; www.map.df.gob.mx; cnr Independencia & Revillagigedo; adult/child under 13yr M$40/free, Sun free; ☉10am-6pm Tue & Thu-Sun, to 9pm Wed; ⓂJuárez) A major showcase for folk art. Contemporary crafts are thematically displayed from all over Mexico, including carnival masks from Chiapas, *alebrijes* (fanciful animal figures) from Oaxaca and trees of life from Puebla. The museum occupies the former fire department headquarters, itself an outstanding example of 1920s art deco by architect Vicente Mendiola. The ground-level shop sells quality handicrafts.

Museo Franz Mayer   MUSEUM
(Map p76; ☑55-5518-2266; www.franzmayer.org.mx; Av Hidalgo 45; M$45, Tue free; ☉10am-5pm Tue-Fri, to 7pm Sat & Sun; ⓂBellas Artes) Occupies the old hospice of the San Juan de Dios order, which under the brief reign of Maximilian became a halfway house for prostitutes. The museum is the fruit of the efforts of German-born Franz Mayer. Prospering as a financier in his adopted Mexico, Mayer amassed the collection of Mexican silver, ceramics and furniture now on display.

The exhibit halls open onto a sumptuous colonial patio, where you can grab a bite at the excellent Cloister Café.

Plaza de Santa Veracruz   PLAZA
(Map p68; ⓂBellas Artes) The sunken square north of the Alameda across Avenida Hidalgo is named for the slanting structure on the right, the **Iglesia de la Santa Veracruz**. Elaborately carved pillars flank the doorway of the 18th-century church.

Museo Nacional de la Estampa   MUSEUM
(MUNAE; Map p68; ☑55-5521-2244; www.museonacionaldelaestampa.bellasartes.gob.mx; Av Hidalgo 39; M$14, Sun free; ☉10am-6pm Tue-Sun; ⓂBellas Artes) Devoted to the graphic arts, this museum has thematic exhibits from its collection of more than 12,000 prints. The museum also does interesting temporary expositions that showcase works from Mexico and abroad.

La Ciudadela   CULTURAL CENTER
(Map p76; ⓂBalderas) The formidable compound now known as 'The Citadel' started off as a tobacco factory in the late 18th century, though it's best known as the scene of the Decena Trágica (Tragic Ten Days), the coup that brought down the Madero government in 1913. Today it's home to the **Biblioteca de México José Vasconcelos** (National Library; Map p76; ☑55-4155-0836; www.bibliotecademexico.gob.mx; Plaza de la Ciudadela 4; ☉8:30am-7:30pm; ⓂBalderas) **FREE**, which has holdings of more than 500,000 volumes and an extensive map collection. The central halls of the recently renovated building are given over to art exhibits.

Centro de la Imagen (Map p76; ☎55-4155-0850; http://centrodelaimagen.conaculta.gob.mx; Plaza de la Ciudadela 2; ☺noon-7pm Wed-Sun; Ⓜ Balderas) FREE, the city's photography museum, is at the Calle Balderas entrance. This innovatively designed space stages compelling exhibitions, often focusing on documentary views of Mexican life.

Across the plaza, inside the Centro de Artesanías La Ciudadela (p128), vendors offer a wide array of crafts from around Mexico, including black pottery from Oaxaca, guitars from Michoacán and silver jewelry from Taxco. Prices are generally fair, even before you bargain.

⦿ Plaza de la República & Around

Dominated by the copper-domed Monumento a la Revolución, you'll find this recently revamped plaza west of the Alameda Central. The grand art deco building northeast of the plaza is the Frontón de México, a now-defunct *jai-alai* (a squash-like game) arena.

★**Monumento a la Revolución** MONUMENT
(Map p76; www.mrm.mx; Plaza de la República; 🚇Plaza de la República) Originally meant to be a legislative chamber, construction of the Mon-

---

FRIDA & DIEGO

A century after Frida Kahlo's birth, and more than 50 years after Diego Rivera's death, the pair's fame and recognition are stronger than ever. In 2007 a retrospective of Kahlo's work at the Palacio de Bellas Artes attracted more than 440,000 visitors. Though attendance at the Rivera survey that followed was not so phenomenal, the show reminded visitors that the prolific muralist had been an international star in his own lifetime. The artists are inseparably linked in memory, and both artists were frequent subjects in each other's work.

Rivera first met Kahlo, 21 years his junior, while painting at the Escuela Nacional Preparatoria, where she was a student in the early 1920s. Rivera was already at the forefront of Mexican art, and his commission at the school was the first of many semi-propaganda murals on public buildings that he was to execute over three decades. He had already fathered children by two Russian women in Europe, and in 1922 he married 'Lupe' Marín in Mexico. She bore him two more children before their marriage broke up in 1928.

Kahlo was born in Coyoacán in 1907 to a Hungarian-Jewish father and Oaxacan mother. She contracted polio at age six, leaving her right leg permanently thinner than her left. In 1925 she was horribly injured in a trolley accident that broke her right leg, collarbone, pelvis and ribs. She made a miraculous recovery but suffered much pain thereafter. It was during convalescence that she began painting. Pain – physical and emotional – was to be a dominating theme of her art.

Kahlo and Rivera both moved in left-wing artistic circles, and they met again in 1928. They married the following year. Frida's mother thought Diego was too old, fat, communist and atheist for her daughter, describing the liaison as 'a union between an elephant and a dove.' Their relationship was definitely always a passionate love-hate affair. Rivera wrote: 'If I ever loved a woman, the more I loved her, the more I wanted to hurt her. Frida was only the most obvious victim of this disgusting trait.'

In 1934, after a spell in the US, the pair moved into a new home in San Ángel, now the **Museo Casa Estudio Diego Rivera y Frida Kahlo** (p93), with separate houses linked by an aerial walkway. After Kahlo discovered that Rivera had had an affair with her sister, Cristina, she divorced him in 1939, but they remarried the following year. She moved back into her childhood home, the Casa Azul (Blue House) in Coyoacán, and he stayed at San Ángel – a state of affairs that endured for the rest of their lives. Their relationship endured, too.

Despite the worldwide wave of Fridamania that followed the hit biopic *Frida* in 2002, Kahlo had only one exhibition in Mexico in her lifetime, in 1953. She arrived at the opening on a stretcher. Rivera said of the exhibition: 'Anyone who attended it could not but marvel at her great talent.' She died at the Blue House the following year. Rivera called it 'the most tragic day of my life... Too late I realized that the most wonderful part of my life had been my love for Frida.'

umento a la Revolución was interrupted by the Revolution, and there was talk of demolishing the building, but instead it was modified and given a new role. Unveiled in 1938, it contains the tombs of the revolutionary and post-revolutionary heroes Pancho Villa, Francisco Madero, Venustiano Carranza, Plutarco Elías Calles and Lázaro Cárdenas.

Both the monument and Plaza de la República on which it stands got a major makeover in 2010 to commemorate Mexico's centennial anniversary of the Revolution. Kids love frolicking in the plaza's geyser-like fountains, while at night the monument's renovated architectural features are highlighted by colorful lights.

The star attraction of the monument is the 65m-high **observation deck** (Map p76; ☑ 55-5592-2038; www.mrm.mx; Plaza de la República; adult/child under 13yr M$50/30, Wed free; ⊙ noon-8pm Mon-Thu, to 10pm Fri & Sat, from 10am Sun; ☐ Plaza de la República), accessed by a glass elevator. The vertigo-inducing lift opens to a spiraling staircase that ascends to a wide terrace with a panoramic view of the city.

Underlying the plaza and monument, the recently spruced-up **Museo Nacional de la Revolución** (National Museum of the Revolution; Map p76; ☑ 55-5546-2115; Plaza de la República; M$25, Sun free; ⊙ 9am-5pm Tue-Fri, to 6:30pm Sat & Sun) covers a 63-year period, from the implementation of the constitution guaranteeing human rights in 1857 to the installation of the post-revolutionary government in 1920. Explanatory text remains untranslated.

The monument also has an interesting basement art gallery, the **Paseo Cimentación** (Map p76; ☑ 55-5592-2038; admission package M$110; ⊙ noon-8pm Mon, Tue & Thu, to 6pm Wed, to 10pm Fri & Sat, 10am-8pm Sun), where you can check out temporary art exhibitions amid a labyrinth of gigantic steel beams that serve as the structure's foundation.

Museo Universitario del Chopo   MUSEUM
(☑ 55-5546-5484; www.chopo.unam.mx; Enrique González Martínez 10; M$30, Tue & Wed free; ⊙ 11am-7pm Tue-Sun; ☐ Revolución) You can't miss the prominent spires of this university-run museum. Parts of the old building, made of forged iron from Düsseldorf, were brought over in pieces and assembled in Mexico City around the turn of the 20th century. Chopo boasts wide, open spaces – ramps serve as showroom floors and high ceilings permit larger-than-life exhibits for contemporary art works. The museum also hosts modern dance performances and screens international and Mexican indie movies.

Museo Nacional de San Carlos   MUSEUM
(Map p76; ☑ 55-5566-8342; www.mnsancarlos. com; Puente de Alvarado 50; adult/child under 3yr M$35/free, Sun free; ⊙ 10am-6pm Tue-Sun; Ⓜ Revolución) Exhibits a formidable collection of European art from the 14th century to early 20th century, including works by Rubens and Goya. The unusual rotunda structure was designed by Manuel Tolsá in the late 18th century.

⊙ Paseo de la Reforma

Mexico City's grandest thoroughfare, known simply as 'Reforma,' traces a bold southwestern path from Tlatelolco to Bosque de Chapultepec, skirting the Alameda Central and Zona Rosa. Emperor Maximilian of Hapsburg laid out the boulevard to connect his castle on Chapultepec Hill with the old city center. After his execution, it was given its current name to commemorate the reform laws instituted by President Benito Juárez. Under the López Obrador administration, the avenue was smartly refurbished and its broad, statue-studded medians became a stage for book fairs and art exhibits. It is currently undergoing aggressive development, with office towers and new hotels springing up along its length.

Paseo de la Reforma links a series of monumental *glorietas* (traffic circles). A couple of blocks west of the Alameda Central is **El Caballito** (Map p76; Paseo de la Reforma s/n), a bright-yellow representation of a horse's head by the sculptor Sebastián. It commemorates another equestrian sculpture that stood here for 127 years and today fronts the Museo Nacional de Arte. A few blocks southwest is the **Monumento a Cristóbal Colón** (Map p76; Paseo de la Reforma s/n), an 1877 statue of Columbus gesturing toward the horizon.

Reforma's busy intersection with Avenida Insurgentes is marked by the **Monumento a Cuauhtémoc** (Map p106; Paseo de la Reforma), memorializing the last Aztec emperor. Two blocks northwest is the **Jardín del Arte**, site of a Sunday art market.

The **Centro Bursátil** (Map p106; Paseo de la Reforma s/n), an angular tower and mirror-ball ensemble housing the nation's Bolsa (stock exchange), marks the southern edge of the Colonia Cuauhtémoc. Continuing west past the US embassy, you will reach the symbol of Mexico City, the

Roma & Condesa

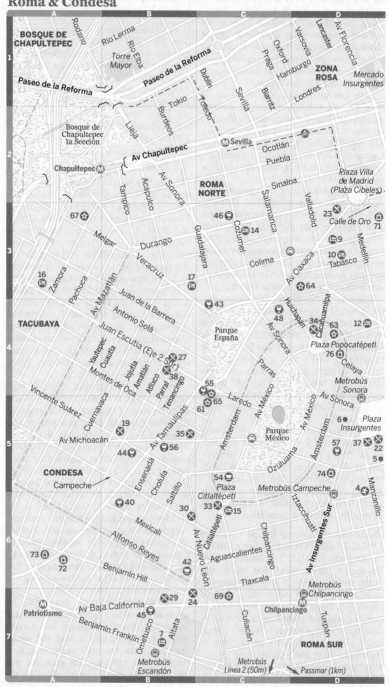

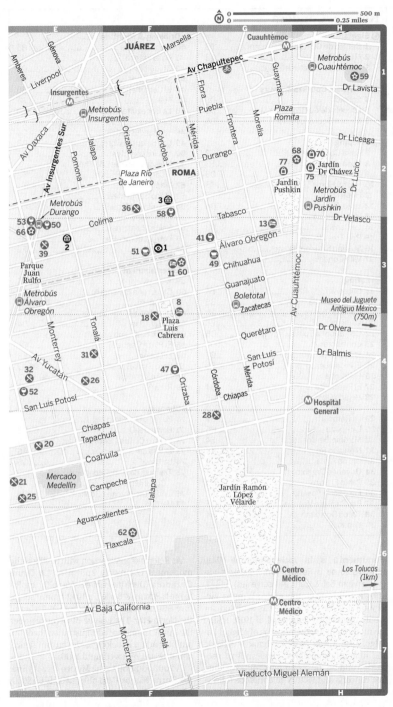

Roma & Condesa

◉ **Sights**
1 Centro de Cultura Casa Lamm	F3
2 MUCA Roma	E3
3 Museo del Objeto del Objeto	F2

⊕ **Activities, Courses & Tours**
4 Ecobici	D5
5 Escuela de Gastronomía Mexicana	D5
6 Mexico Soul & Essence	D5

⊟ **Sleeping**
7 Casa Comtesse	B7
8 Casa de la Condesa	F3
9 Hostel 333	D3
10 Hostel Home	D3
11 Hotel Milán	F3
12 Hotel Roosevelt	D4
13 Hotel Stanza	G3
14 La Casona	C3
15 Red Tree House	C6
16 Stayinn Barefoot Hostel	A3
17 Villa Condesa	B3

⊗ **Eating**
18 Cabrera 7	F4
19 Café La Gloria	B5
20 Cantina Riviera	E5
21 Ciénega	E5
22 Con Sabor a Tixtla	D5
23 Contramar	D3
24 El Califa	B7
25 El Hidalguense	E5
26 El Parnita	E4
27 El Pescadito	B4
28 Helado Obscuro	G5
La Capital	(see 30)
29 La Rambla	B7
30 Lampuga	B6
31 Maximo Bistrot Local	E4
32 Mercado Roma	E4
33 Ojo de Agua	C6
34 Orígenes Orgánicos	D4
35 Pablo El Erizo	B5
36 Panadería Rosetta	F2
37 Por Siempre Vegana Taquería	D5
38 Tacos Don Juan	B4
39 Yuban	E3

⊖ **Drinking & Nightlife**
40 Black Horse	B6
41 Casa Franca	G3
42 Chiquitito	B6
43 Condesa df	C4
44 El Centenario	B5
45 Felina	B7
46 La Bodeguita del Medio	C3
47 La Chicha	F4
48 La Clandestina	C4
49 Los Bisquets Obregón	G3
50 Los Insurgentes	E3
51 Maison Francaise de Thé Caravanserai	F3
52 Mama Rumba	E4
53 Mano Santa Mezcal	E3
54 Pastelería Maque	C5
55 Pata Negra	C4
56 Salón Malafama	B5
57 Tom's Leather Bar	D5
58 Traspatio	F2

⊙ **Entertainment**
59 Arena México	H1
60 Cafebrería El Péndulo	F3
61 Caradura	C5
62 Cine Tonalá	F6
63 El Bataclán	D4
64 El Imperial Club	D3
65 El Plaza Condesa	C4
66 El Under	E3
67 Foro Shakespeare	A3
68 Multiforo Alicia	H2
69 Ruta 61	C7

⊕ **Shopping**
70 Bazar de la Roma	H2
71 Bazar del Oro	D3
72 Centro Cultural Bella Época	A6
73 El Hijo del Santo	A6
74 La Naval	D5
75 Tianguis de Antigüedades de Cuauhtémoc	H2
76 Under the Volcano Books	D4
77 Vértigo	G2

Monumento a la Independencia (Map p106; Paseo de la Reforma s/n; ⊙ lookout visits 10am-1pm Sat & Sun; Ⓜ Insurgentes) FREE. Known as 'El Ángel,' this gilded Winged Victory on a 45m-high pillar was sculpted for the independence centennial of 1910. Inside the monument are the remains of Miguel Hidalgo, José María Morelos, Ignacio Allende and nine other notables. Thousands of people descend on the monument for occasional free concerts and victory celebrations following important Mexican soccer matches.

At Reforma's intersection with Sevilla is the monument commonly known as **La Diana Cazadora** (Diana the Huntress; Map p106; cnr Paseo de la Reforma & Sevilla), a 1942 bronze sculpture actually meant to represent the Archer of the North Star. The League of Decency under the Ávila Camacho administration had the sculptor add a loincloth to the buxom figure, and it wasn't removed until 1966.

A 2003 addition to the Mexico City skyline, the **Torre Mayor** (Map p106; ☎ 55-5283-8000; www.torremayor.com.mx; Paseo de la Reforma 505;

Ⓜ Chapultepec) stands like a sentinel before the gate to Bosque de Chapultepec. The earthquake-resistant structure, which soars 225m above the capital, is anchored below by 98 seismic-shock absorbers. Unfortunately the building's observation deck is permanently closed.

Across from the Torre Mayor is the **Torre BBVA Bancomer** (Bancomer Tower; Paseo de la Reforma s/n), a bank's 50-story skyscraper that became Mexico's tallest building upon its completion in 2015, with sky gardens every nine floors. Nearby, the 104m-high **Estela de Luz** (Pillar of Light; Map p106; Paseo de la Reforma s/n) was built to commemorate Mexico's bicentennial anniversary in 2010, though due to delays in construction and rampant overspending, the quartz-paneled light tower wasn't inaugurated until 2012. After eight former government officials were arrested in 2013 for misuse of public funds, it became known as the 'tower of corruption.' In the tower's basement you'll find the **Centro de Cultura Digital** (Map p106; www.centroculturadigital.mx; Estela de Luz; ⏰11am-7pm Tue-Sun; Ⓜ Chapultepec), a hit-and-miss cultural center with expositions focusing on digital technology.

Metro Hidalgo accesses Paseo de la Reforma at the Alameda end, while the Insurgentes and Sevilla stations provide the best approach from the Zona Rosa. On the Insurgentes metrobús route, the 'Reforma' and 'Hamburgo' stops lie north and south of the avenue respectively. Along Reforma itself, any westbound 'Auditorio' bus goes through the Bosque de Chapultepec, while 'Chapultepec' buses terminate at the east end of the park. In the opposite direction, 'I Verdes' and 'La Villa' buses head up Reforma to the Alameda Central and beyond. 'Zocalo' buses also run along Reforma.

◉ Zona Rosa

Wedged between Paseo de la Reforma and Avenida Chapultepec, the 'Pink Zone' was developed as an international playground and shopping district during the 1950s, when it enjoyed a cosmopolitan panache. Since then, however, the Zona Rosa has been in gradual decline and has lost ground to more fashionable neighborhoods such as Condesa and Roma. It's now a hodgepodge of touristy boutiques, strip clubs, discos and fast-food franchises. People-watching from its sidewalk cafes reveals a higher degree of diversity than elsewhere: it's one of the city's premier gay and lesbian districts and

an expat magnet, with a significant Korean population (and associated restaurants). The pedestrianised Calle Génova corridor gets constantly more polished with new yogurt cafes, gadget stores and student-filled bars in an attempt to keep the zone in the pink.

◉ Condesa

Colonia Condesa's striking architecture, palm-lined esplanades and joyful parks echo its origins as a haven for a newly emerging elite in the early 20th century. Mention 'La Condesa' today and most people think of it as a trendy area of informal restaurants, hip boutiques and hot nightspots. Fortunately much of the neighborhood's old flavor remains, especially for those willing to wander outside the valet-parking zones. Stroll the pedestrian medians along Ámsterdam, Avenida Tamaulipas or Avenida Mazatlán to admire art deco and California colonial-style buildings. The focus is the peaceful **Parque México**, the oval shape of which reflects its earlier use as a horse-racing track. Two blocks northwest is **Parque España**, which has a children's play area.

◉ Roma

Northeast of Condesa, Roma is a bohemian enclave inhabited by artists and writers. This is where Beat writers William S Burroughs and Jack Kerouac naturally gravitated during their 1950s sojourn in Mexico City. Built at the turn of the 20th century, the neighborhood is a showcase for Parisian-influenced architecture, which was favored by the Porfirio Díaz regime. Some of the most outstanding examples stand along Colima and Tabasco. When in Roma linger in the cafes and check out the art galleries and specialty shops along Colima. A stroll down Orizaba passes two lovely plazas – Río de Janeiro, with a statue replica of Michelangelo's David, and Luis Cabrera, which has beautiful fountains. On weekends inspect the **Tianguis de Antigüedades de Cuauhtémoc** (Map p82; cnr Av Cuauhtémoc & Dr Navarro; ⏰9am-5pm Sat & Sun), an antique market in a small park – walk to the eastern end of Álvaro Obregón, the Roma's main thoroughfare, then one block north along Avenida Cuauhtémoc.

Small, independent art galleries and museums are scattered around Roma. The website Arte Mexico (www.artemexico.org) has listings for Roma and elsewhere.

Museo del Objeto del Objeto   MUSEUM
(Museum of Objects; Map p82; www.elmodo.
mx/en; Colima 145; adult/child under 12yr M$50/
free; ⊙10am-6pm Tue-Sun; 🚇Durango) Packing
a collection of nearly 100,000 pieces, some
as old as the Mexican War of Independence
(1810), this two-story design museum tells
unique versions of Mexican history by com-
piling objects for thematic exhibits.

Centro de Cultura Casa Lamm   ARTS CENTER
(Map p82; ☑55-5511-0899; www.galeriacasa
lamm.com.mx; Álvaro Obregón 99; ⊙10am-6pm;
🚇Álvaro Obregón) **FREE** This cultural complex contains a gallery for contemporary
Mexican painting and photography as well
as an excellent art library.

MUCA Roma   MUSEUM
(Map p82; ☑55-5511-0925; www.mucaroma.
unam.mx; Tonalá 51; ⊙10am-8pm Tue-Sun;
🚇Durango) **FREE** Sponsored by Universidad
Nacional Autónoma de México (UNAM),
this university museum exhibits Mexican
and international contemporary art with
ties to science or new technology.

⊙ Bosque de Chapultepec

Chapultepec – Náhuatl for 'Hill of Grasshoppers' – served as a refuge for the wandering Aztecs before becoming a summer
residence for their noble class. It was the
nearest freshwater supply for Tenochtitlán.
In the 15th century Nezahualcóyotl, ruler of
nearby Texcoco, oversaw the construction of
an aqueduct to channel its waters over Lago
de Texcoco to the pre-Hispanic capital.

Today Mexico City's largest park, the
Bosque de Chapultepec covers more than
4 sq km, with lakes, a zoo and several excellent museums. It also remains an abode
of Mexico's high and mighty, containing the
current presidential residence, **Los Pinos**,
and a former imperial palace, the Castillo de
Chapultepec.

Sunday is the park's big day, as vendors line
the main paths and throngs of families come
to picnic, navigate the lake on rowboats and
crowd into the museums. Most of the major
attractions are in or near the eastern **1a Sección** (1st Section; Map p88; www.chapultepec.
org.mx/1ra-seccion-del-bosque-de-chapultepecec;
Bosque de Chapultepec; ⊙5am-6pm Tue-Sun;
Ⓜ Chapultepec), while a large amusement park
and children's museum dominate the 2da
Sección.

A pair of bronze lions overlooks the main
gate at Paseo de la Reforma and Lieja. Other
access points are opposite the Museo Tamayo, Museo Nacional de Antropología and by
metro Chapultepec. The fence along Paseo
de la Reforma serves as the **Galería Abierta
de las Rejas de Chapultepec**, an outdoor
photo gallery extending from the zoo entrance to the Museo Tamayo.

Chapultepec metro station is at the east
end of the Bosque de Chapultepec, near the
Monumento a los Niños Héroes and Castillo
de Chapultepec. Auditorio metro station is
on the north side of the park, 500m west of
the Museo Nacional de Antropología. 'Auditorio' buses travel along the length of Paseo
de la Reforma.

The 2da Sección of the Bosque de
Chapultepec lies west of the Periférico. To
get to the 2da Sección and La Feria amusement park from metro Chapultepec, find the
'Paradero' exit and catch a 'Feria' bus at the
top of the stairs. These depart continuously
and travel nonstop to the 2da Sección, dropping off riders at the Papalote Museo del
Niño and La Feria. In addition to family attractions, there's a pair of upscale lake-view
restaurants on Lago Mayor and Lago Menor.

★**Museo Nacional
de Antropología**   MUSEUM
(National Museum of Anthropology; Map p88;
☑55-5553-6381; www.mna.inah.gob.mx; cnr Paseo de la Reforma & Calz Gandhi; adult/child under
14yr M$64/free, audio guide M$75; ⊙9am-7pm
Tue-Sun; Ⓟ; ⓂAuditorio) This world-class
museum stands in an extension of the Bosque de Chapultepec. Its long, rectangular
courtyard is surrounded on three sides by
two-level display halls. The 12 ground-floor
salas (halls) are dedicated to pre-Hispanic
Mexico, while upper-level *salas* show how
Mexico's indigenous descendants live today,
with the contemporary cultures located directly above their ancestral civilizations.

Everything is superbly displayed, with
much explanatory text translated into English. At the entrance, you will find rentable
audio guides in English, and the starting
point for free guided tours (four daily except Sunday, one hour) in English, which
are worthwhile to make sense of Mexico's
complicated history. The vast museum offers
more than most people can absorb in a single visit. Here's a brief guide to the ground-
floor halls, proceeding counterclockwise
around the courtyard.

Culturas Indígenas de México Currently serves as a space for temporary exhibitions.

Introducción a la Antropología Introduces visitors to the field of anthropology.

Poblamiento de América Demonstrates how the hemisphere's earliest settlers got here and survived and prospered in their new environment.

Preclásico en el Altiplano Central Focuses on the pre-Classic period, treated here as running from approximately 2300 BC to AD 100, and the transition from a nomadic hunting life to a more settled farming existence in Mexico's central highlands.

Teotihuacán Displays models and objects from the Americas' first great and powerful state.

Los Toltecas y su Época Covers cultures of central Mexico from about AD 650 to 1250. On display is one of the four basalt warrior columns from Tula's Temple of Tlahuizcalpantecuhtli.

Mexica Devoted to the Mexica, aka Aztecs. Come here to see the famous sun stone, unearthed beneath the Zócalo in 1790, and other magnificent sculptures from the pantheon of Aztec deities.

Culturas de Oaxaca Displays the fine legacy of Oaxaca's Zapotec and Mixtec civilizations.

Culturas de la Costa del Golfo Spotlights the important civilizations along the Gulf of Mexico, including the Olmec, Totonac and Huastec. Stone carvings include two Olmec heads weighing in at almost 20 tonnes.

Maya Exhibits findings from southeast Mexico, Guatemala, Belize and Honduras. A full-scale replica of the tomb of King Pakal, discovered deep in the Templo de las Inscripciones at Palenque, is simply breathtaking.

Culturas del Occidente Profiles cultures of western Mexico.

Culturas del Norte Covers the Casas Grandes (Paquimé) site and other cultures from northern Mexico, and traces their links with indigenous groups of the US southwest.

In a clearing about 100m in front of the museum's entrance, indigenous Totonac people perform their spectacular *voladores* rite – 'flying' from a 20m-high pole – every 30 minutes.

Castillo de Chapultepec CASTLE
(Chapultepec Castle; Map p88; www.castillo dechapultepec.inah.gob.mx; Bosque de Chapultepec; ☺9am-5pm Tue-Sun; Ⓜ Chapultepec) A visible reminder of Mexico's bygone aristocracy, the 'castle' that stands atop Chapultepec Hill was begun in 1785 but not completed until after independence, when it became the national military academy. When Emperor Maximilian and Empress Carlota arrived in 1864, they refurbished it as their residence.

The castle sheltered Mexico's presidents until 1939 when President Lázaro Cárdenas converted it into the **Museo Nacional de Historia** (National History Museum; Map p88; ☎ 55-4040-5215; www.mnh.inah.gob.mx; adult/child under 13yr M$64/free; ☺9am-5pm Tue-Sun; Ⓜ Chapultepec).

Historical exhibits chronicle the period from the rise of colonial Nueva España to the Mexican Revolution. In addition to displaying such iconic objects as the sword wielded by José María Morelos in the Siege of Cuautla and the Virgin of Guadalupe banner borne by Miguel Hidalgo in his march for independence, the museum features a number of dramatic interpretations of Mexican history by leading muralists, including Juan O'Gorman's panoramic *Retablo de la independencia* (Panel of Independence).

The east end of the castle preserves the palace occupied by Maximilian and Carlota, with sumptuously furnished salons opening onto an exterior deck that affords sweeping city views. On the upper floor, Porfirio Díaz' opulent rooms surround a patio where a tower marks the top of Chapultepec Hill, 45m above street level.

To reach the castle, follow the road that curves up the hill behind the Monumento a los Niños Héroes. Alternatively, a trainlike vehicle (M$15 round trip) runs up every 15 minutes while the castle is open.

Back at ground level, follow the south side of the hill's base to find the formidable **Tribuna Monumental de las Águilas**, dedicated to Mexico's WWII veterans. On the left side of the monument, enter the **Audiorama**, a pebbly garden with body-contoured benches where you can enjoy opera or classical music.

Museo de Arte Moderno MUSEUM
(Museum of Modern Art; Map p88; ☎ 55-5211-8331; www.museoartemoderno.com; cnr Paseo

Bosque de Chapultepec & Polanco

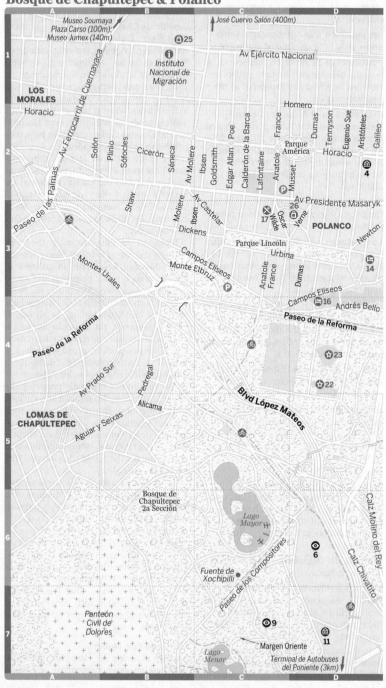

Museo Soumaya
Plaza Carso (100m);
Museo Jumex (140m)

José Cuervo Salón (400m)

25

Av Ejército Nacional

Instituto
Nacional de
Migración

LOS
MORALES

Horacio

Homero

Parque
América

Dumas
Tennyson
Eugenio Sue
Aristóteles
Galileo

Horacio

4

Solón
Plinio
Sófocles
Cicerón
Séneca
Av Molière
Ibsen
Goldsmith
Edgar Allan Poe
Calderón de la Barca
France
Anatole
Lafontaine
Musset

Av Ferrocarril de Cuernavaca

Paseo de las Palmas

Shaw

Molière
Ibsen
Av Castelar
Dickens

Av Presidente Masaryk

17

Oscar
Wilde
Verne
26

POLANCO

Newton

Parque Lincoln

Urbina

Anatole
France
Dumas

14

Montes Urales

Campos Elíseos
Monte Elbruz

Campos Elíseos

16

Andrés Bello

Paseo de la Reforma

Paseo de la Reforma

23

22

Av Prado Sur

Pedregal

Alicama

Blvd López Mateos

LOMAS DE
CHAPULTEPEC

Aguiar y Seixas

Bosque de
Chapultepec
2a Sección

Lago
Mayor

Calz Molino del Rey

Calz Chivatito

6

Fuente de
Xochipilli

Paseo de los Compositores

Panteón
Civil de
Dolores

9

11

Lago
Menor

Margen Oriente

Terminal de Autobuses
del Poniente (3km)

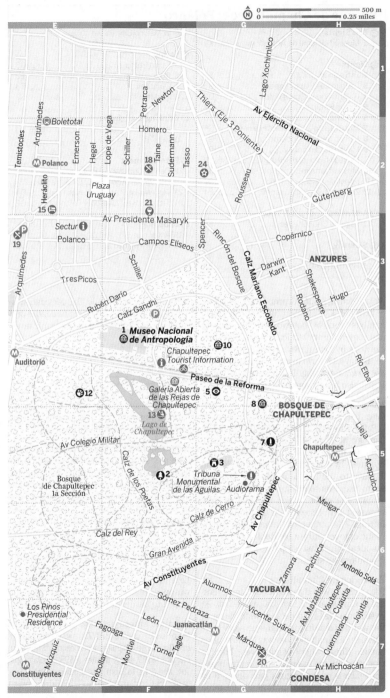

0   500 m
0   0.25 miles

E

Temistocles
Arquímedes
Boletotal
Emerson
Hegel
M Polanco
Heráclito
Plaza
Uruguay
15
Lope de Vega
Schiller
Petrarca
Homero
Taine
18
Sudermann
Tasso
24

F

Newton
Thiers (Eje 3 Poniente)

G

Lago Xochimilco
Av Ejército Nacional

H

1
2
Rousseau
Gutenberg
21
Av Presidente Masaryk
Sectur
Polanco
Campos Elíseos
Spencer
Rincón del Bosque
Copérnico
Darwin
Kant
Shakespeare
Rodano
Hugo
ANZURES
3
Tres Picos
Schiller
Rubén Darío
Calz Gandhi
1 **Museo Nacional de Antropología**
10
Chapultepec Tourist Information
M
Auditorio
12
5
Galería Abierta de las Rejas de Chapultepec
13
Lago de Chapultepec
8
BOSQUE DE CHAPULTEPEC
Río Elba
Calz Mariano Escobedo
4
Paseo de la Reforma
7
Chapultepec
Llela
M Chapultepec
Acapulco
5
Av Colegio Militar
Calz de los Poetas
2
3
Tribuna Monumental de las Águilas
Audiorama
Melgar
Bosque de Chapultepec 1a Sección
Calz de Cerro
Av Chapultepec
Calz del Rey
Gran Avenida
Av Constituyentes
Alumnos
TACUBAYA
Zamora
Pachuca
Antonio Solá
6
Los Pinos Presidential Residence
Fagoaga
León
Gómez Pedraza
Tornel
Tagle
Juanacatlán
M
Vicente Suárez
Márquez
20
Av Marzatlán
Yautepec
Cuautla
Cuernavaca
Jojutla
7
Muzquiz
Rebollar
Montiel
M Constituyentes
Av Michoacán
CONDESA

Bosque de Chapultepec & Polanco

⦿ **Top Sights**
1 Museo Nacional de Antropología F4

⦿ **Sights**
2 1a Sección F5
3 Castillo de Chapultepec G5
4 Galeria López Quiroga.........................D2
5 Jardín Botánico.....................................G4
6 La Feria..D6
7 Monumento a Los Niños Héroes.........G5
8 Museo de Arte Moderno G4
9 Museo Jardín del Agua.........................C7
   Museo Nacional de Historia..........(see 3)
10 Museo Tamayo G4
11 Papalote Museo del Niño D7
12 Zoológico de Chapultepec....................E4

⦿ **Activities, Courses & Tours**
13 Lago de Chapultepec F5

⦿ **Sleeping**
14 Casa Castelar..D3
15 Hábita Hotel E2

16 W Mexico City D4

⦿ **Eating**
17 Dulce Patria C3
18 Pujol..F2
19 Quintonil...E3
20 Taj Mahal..G7

⦿ **Drinking & Nightlife**
   Área..(see 15)
21 Big Red...F2

⦿ **Entertainment**
22 Centro Cultural del Bosque..................D4
   Lunario del Auditorio ....(see 23)
23 Ticketmaster Auditorio Nacional.........D4
24 Ticketmaster Liverpool Polanco G2

⦿ **Shopping**
25 Antara B1
26 Pasaje Polanco D3

de la Reforma & Calz Gandhi; M$25, Sun free; ⊙10:15am-5:30pm Tue-Sun; Ⓟ; ⓂChapultepec) Exhibits work by noteworthy 20th-century and contemporary Mexican artists, including canvases by Dr Atl, Rivera, Siqueiros, Orozco, Tamayo, O'Gorman and Frida Kahlo's *Las dos Fridas*, possibly her best-known painting. It also has temporary expositions.

Museo Tamayo MUSEUM
(Map p88; www.museotamayo.org; Paseo de la Reforma 51; M$21, Sun free; ⊙10am-6pm Tue-Sun; Ⓟ; ⓂAuditorio) A multilevel structure built to house international modern art, donated by Oaxaca-born painter Rufino Tamayo to the people of Mexico. The museum exhibits cutting-edge works from around the globe, which are thematically arranged with shows from the Tamayo collection. The renovated Tamayo has a new rustic-chic restaurant overlooking the park, an ideal breakfast stop before exploring Chapultepec's sights.

Zoológico de Chapultepec ZOO
(Map p88; www.chapultepec.df.gob.mx; Bosque de Chapultepec; ⊙9am-4:30pm Tue-Sun; ⓘ; ⓂAuditorio) FREE Home to a wide range of the world's creatures in large open-air enclosures, the Chapultepec zoo was the first place outside China where pandas were born in captivity. The zoo has two of these rare bears, descendants of the original pair donated by the People's Republic in 1975. Endangered

Mexican species include the Mexican gray wolf and the hairless xoloitzcuintle, the only surviving dog breed from pre-Hispanic times.

Jardín Botánico GARDENS
(Botanical Garden; Map p88; ☎55-5553-8114; Paseo de la Reforma s/n; ⊙10am-6pm Tue-Sun; ⓂChapultepec) FREE Highlighting Mexico's plant diversity, this 4-hectare complex is divided into sections that reflect the country's varied climatic zones. The garden also features a greenhouse full of rare orchids.

Monumento a Los Niños Héroes MONUMENT
(Map p88; Bosque de Chapultepec; ⓂChapultepec) The six marble columns marking the park's eastern entrance commemorate the 'boy heroes,' six young cadets who perished in battle. On September 13, 1847, 8000 US troops stormed Castillo de Chapultepec, which then housed the national military academy. Mexican General Santa Anna retreated before the onslaught, but the youths, aged 13 to 20, chose to defend the castle. Legend has it one of them, Juan Escutia, wrapped himself in a Mexican flag and leaped to his death rather than surrender.

Papalote Museo del Niño MUSEUM
(Map p88; ☎55-5237-1773; www.papalote.org. mx; Bosque de Chapultepec; museum M$129, planetarium M$99, IMAX theater M$99; ⊙9am-6pm Tue, Wed & Fri, to 11pm Thu, 10am-7pm Sat & Sun; Ⓟⓘ; ⓂConstituyentes) Your children won't

want to leave this innovative, hands-on museum. Here kids can put together a radio program, channel their inner mad scientist, join an archaeological dig and try out all kinds of technological gadgets and games. Little ones also get a kick out of the planetarium and IMAX theater.

La Feria AMUSEMENT PARK
(Map p88; ☑ 55-5230-2121; www.feriachapultepec. com.mx; Bosque de Chapultepec; all-access admission M$200; ☺ 8am-6pm Tue-Fri, 9:30am-8pm Sat & Sun; P ⓓ; Ⓜ Constituyentes) An old-fashioned amusement park with some hair-raising rides. The all-access Platino pass is good for everything, including La Feria's best roller coasters. Check the website for current opening times as they change throughout the month.

Museo Jardín del Agua MURAL
(Map p88; ☑ 55-5281-5382; Bosque de Chapultepec; M$24; ☺ 9am-6pm Tue-Sun; Ⓜ Constituyentes) Diego Rivera painted a series of murals for the inauguration of Cárcamo de Dolores, Chapultepec's waterworks facility built in the 1940s. Experimenting with waterproof paints, Rivera covered the collection tank, sluice gates and part of the pipeline with images of amphibious beings and workers involved in the project.

Hold on to your ticket as it includes entry to the nearby Natural History Museum (Museo de Historia Natural).

Outside the building, you can't miss another of Rivera's extraordinary works, **Fuente de Tláloc**, an oval pool inhabited by a huge mosaic-skinned sculpture of the Aztec god of water, rain and fertility. About 150m north is the beautiful **Fuente de Xochipilli**, dedicated to the Aztec 'flower prince,' with terraced fountains around a pyramid in the *talud-tablero* style typical of Teotihuacán.

◉ Polanco

The affluent neighborhood of Polanco, north of Bosque de Chapultepec, arose in the 1940s as a residential alternative for a burgeoning middle class anxious to escape the overcrowded *centro*. Metro Polanco is in the center of the neighborhood, while metro Auditorio lies at its southern edge.

Polanco is known as a Jewish enclave and also for its exclusive hotels, fine restaurants and designer stores along Avenida Presidente Masaryk. Some of the city's most prestigious museums and art galleries are here or in nearby Bosque de Chapultepec.

Museo Jumex MUSEUM
(www.fundacionjumex.org; Blvd Miguel de Cervantes Saavedra 303, Colonia Ampliación Granada; M$50, Sun free; ☺ 11am-8pm Tue-Sun; P) Built to house one of Latin America's leading contemporary art collections. Temporary exhibits draw on a collection of around 2600 pieces from renowned Mexican and international artists such as Gabriel Orozco, Francis Alys and Andy Warhol. 'Ejército Defensa' buses departing from metro Chapultepec leave you one block south of the museum at the corner of Avenida Ejército Nacional and Avenida Ferrocarril de Cuernavaca.

The museum's other location, north of Mexico City in Ecatepec, remains open with a focus on more experimental art. It's a bit of a trek from the city, but one that many art lovers have been willing to make over the years. See the website for directions.

Museo Soumaya Plaza Carso MUSEUM
(www.museosoumaya.org; Blvd Miguel de Cervantes Saavedra 303, Colonia Ampliación Granada; ☺ 10:30am-6:30pm) FREE Someone ought to tell Mexican billionaire Carlos Slim that bigger isn't always better. Named after his late wife, this six-story behemoth (plated with 16,000 aluminum hexagons) holds a large collection of sculptures by Frenchman Auguste Rodin and Catalan surrealist Salvador Dalí. The museum also contains worthy Rivera and Siqueiros murals and paintings by French impressionists, but there's too much filler.

To get here take an 'Ejército Defensa' bus from metro Chapultepec to the corner of Avenida Ejército Nacional and Avenida Ferrocarril de Cuernavaca, then walk one block north.

Acuario Inbursa AQUARIUM
(☑ 55-5395-4586; www.acuarioinbursa.com.mx; Blvd Miguel de Cervantes Saavedra 386; adult/child under 3yr M$135/free; ☺ 10am-6pm) Polanco's five-level aquarium showcases manta rays, piranhas, crocodiles and Carlos Slim's billions with sand shipped in from Florida and seawater from Veracruz. The price is steep for such a quick walk-through, though the lit-up *medusas* (jellyfish) will have kids hypnotised. Purchase tickets online to skip long queues.

Galeria López Quiroga GALLERY
(Map p88; www.lopezquiroga.com; Aristóteles 169; ☺ 10am-7pm Mon-Fri, to 2pm Sat; Ⓜ Polanco) FREE Specializes in sculptures, paintings

and photography by contemporary Latin American and Mexican artists, including works by Francisco Toledo, Rufino Tamayo and José Luis Cuevas.

⊙ Xochimilco & Around

Almost at the southern edge of DF, a network of canals flanked by gardens is a vivid reminder of the city's pre-Hispanic legacy. Remnants of the *chinampas* (raised fertile land where indigenous inhabitants grew their food), these 'floating gardens' are still in use today. Gliding along the canals in a fancifully decorated *trajinera* (gondola) is an alternately tranquil and festive experience. On weekends a fiesta atmosphere takes over as the waterways become jammed with boats carrying groups of families and friends. Local vendors and musicians hover alongside the partygoers, serving food and drink. Midweek, the mood is much calmer.

Xochimilco, Náhuatl for 'Place where Flowers Grow,' was an early target of Aztec hegemony, probably due to its inhabitants' farming skills. The Xochimilcas piled up vegetation and mud in the shallow waters of Lake Xochimilco, a southern offshoot of Lago de Texcoco, to make the fertile gardens known as *chinampas*, which later became an economic base of the Aztec empire. As the *chinampas* proliferated, much of the lake was transformed into a series of canals. Approximately 180km of these waterways remain today. The *chinampas* are still under cultivation, mainly for garden plants and flowers such as poinsettias and marigolds. Owing to its cultural and historical significance, Xochimilco was designated a Unesco World Heritage site in 1987.

Though the canals are definitely the main attraction, Xochimilco has plenty to see. East of **Jardín Juárez** (Xochimilco *centro's* main square) is the 16th-century **Parroquia de San Bernardino de Siena**, with elaborate gold-painted *retablos* (altarpieces) and a tree-studded atrium. South of the plaza, the bustling **Mercado de Xochimilco** covers two vast buildings: the one nearer the Jardín Juárez has fresh produce and an eating 'annex' for *tamales* (corn-based snacks with various fillings) and various prepared food; the other sells flowers, *chapulines* (grasshoppers), sweets and excellent *barbacoa* (savory barbecued mutton).

Xochimilco also boasts several visitor-friendly *pulquerías* (*pulque* bars), and

about 2km east of Jardín Juárez is one of the city's best art museums.

To reach Xochimilco, take metro line 2 to the Tasqueña station then follow the signs inside the station to the transfer point for the *tren ligero*, a light-rail system that extends to neighborhoods not reachable by metro. Xochimilco is the last stop. Upon exiting the station, turn left (north) and follow Avenida Morelos to the market, Jardín Juárez and the church. If you don't feel like walking, bicycle taxis will shuttle you to the *embarcaderos* (boat landings) for M$30.

Canals   HISTORIC SITE
(Xochimilco; boats per hr M$350, boat taxis one way per person M$20; P ♿; ℞ Xochimilco) Hundreds of colorful *trajineras* await passengers at the village's 10 *embarcaderos*. Nearest to the center are Belem, Salitre and San Cristóbal, about 400m east of the plaza, and Fernando Celada, 400m west of the plaza on Avenida Guadalupe Ramírez. On Saturdays and Sundays, 60-person *lanchas colectivas* (boat taxis) run between the Salitre and Nativitas *embarcaderos*.

Boats seat from 14 to 20 people, making large group outings relatively cheap. Before boarding the *trajinera*, you can buy beer, soft drinks and food from vendors at the *embarcaderos* if you fancy an on-board picnic while cruising.

Museo Dolores Olmedo   MUSEUM
(☎55-5555-1221; www.museodoloresolmedo.org.mx; Av México 5843; M$75, Tue free; ⊙10am-6pm Tue-Sun; ♿; ℞ La Noria) Possibly the most important Diego Rivera collection of all belongs to this museum, ensconced in a peaceful 17th-century hacienda. Dolores Olmedo, a socialite and patron of Rivera, resided here until her death in 2002. The museum's 144 Rivera works – including oils, watercolors and lithographs from various periods – are displayed alongside pre-Hispanic figurines and folk art.

Another room is reserved for Frida Kahlo's paintings. Outside the exhibit halls in the estate's gardens, you'll see peacocks and xoloitzcuintles.

To get here, from metro Tasqueña take the *tren ligero* to La Noria station. Leaving the station, turn left at the top of the steps and descend to the street. Upon reaching an intersection with a footbridge, take a sharp left, almost doubling back on your path, onto Antiguo Camino a Xochimilco. The museum is 300m down this street.

San Ángel

Settled by the Dominican order soon after the Spanish conquest, San Ángel, 12km southwest of the center, maintains its colonial splendor despite being engulfed by the metropolis. It's often associated with the big Saturday crafts market held alongside the Plaza San Jacinto. Though the main approach via Avenida Insurgentes is typically chaotic, wander westward to experience the old village's cobblestoned soul – it's a tranquil enclave of colonial mansions with massive wooden doors, potted geraniums behind window grills and bougainvillea spilling over stone walls.

La Bombilla station of the Avenida Insurgentes metrobús is about 500m east of the Plaza San Jacinto. Otherwise catch a bus from metro Miguel Ángel de Quevedo, 1km east, or from metro Barranca del Muerto, 1.5km north along Avenida Revolución.

Plaza San Jacinto   PLAZA
(Map p94; San Ángel Centro; 🚇La Bombilla) Every Saturday the Bazar Sábado brings masses of color and crowds of people to this square, 500m west of Avenida Insurgentes. **Museo Casa del Risco** (Map p94; ☎55-5616-2711; www.isidrofabela.com; Plaza San Jacinto 15; ⊙10am-5pm Tue-Sun; 🚇La Bombilla) **FREE** is midway along the plaza's north side. The elaborate fountain in the courtyard is a mad mosaic of Talavera tile and Chinese porcelain. Upstairs is a treasure trove of Mexican baroque and medieval European paintings. About 50m west of the plaza is the 16th-century **Iglesia de San Jacinto** (Map p94; ☎55-5616-2059; San Jacinto 18-Bis) and its peaceful gardens.

Museo Casa Estudio
Diego Rivera y Frida Kahlo   MUSEUM
(Diego Rivera & Frida Kahlo Studio Museum; Map p94; ☎55-5550-1518; www.estudiodiegorivera. bellasartes.gob.mx; cnr Diego Rivera & Av Altavista; OM$14, Sun free, camera use M$30; ⊙10am-6pm Tue-Sun; 🚇La Bombilla) If you saw the movie *Frida,* you'll recognize this museum, designed by Frida Kahlo and Diego Rivera's friend, architect and painter Juan O'Gorman. The artistic couple called this place home from 1934 to 1940 (Frida, Diego and O'Gorman each had their own separate house). Rivera's abode preserves his upstairs studio, while Frida's (the blue one) and O'Gorman's were cleared out for temporary exhibits.

Across the street is the San Ángel Inn. Now housing a prestigious restaurant, the former *pulque* hacienda is historically significant as the place where Pancho Villa and Emiliano Zapata agreed to divide control of the country in 1914.

It's a 2km walk or taxi ride from metrobús La Bombilla.

Museo de El Carmen   MUSEUM
(Map p94; ☎55-5550-4896; www.museodeel carmen.org; Av Revolución 4; adult/child under 13yr M$52/free, Sun free; ⊙10am-5pm Tue-Sun; 🚇La Bombilla) A storehouse of magnificent sacred art in a former school run by the Carmelite order. The collection includes oils by Mexican master Cristóbal de Villalpando, though the big draw is the collection of mummies in the crypt. Thought to be the bodies of 17th-century benefactors of the order, they were uncovered during the revolution by Zapatistas looking for buried treasure.

Museo de Arte Carrillo Gil   MUSEUM
(Map p94; ☎55-5550-6289; www.museodearte carrillogil.com; Av Revolución 1608; M$21, Sun free; ⊙10am-6pm Tue-Sun; 🚇Altavista) One of the city's first contemporary-art spaces, this museum was founded by Yucatecan businessman Álvaro Carrillo Gil to store a large collection he had amassed over many years. Long ramps in the building lead up to cutting-edge temporary exhibits and some of the lesser-known works by Diego Rivera, José Clemente Orozco and David Alfaro Siqueiros.

Jardín de la Bombilla   PARK
(Map p94; btwn Av de la Paz & Josefina Prior; 🚇La Bombilla) In this tropically abundant park spreading east of Avenida Insurgentes, paths encircle the **Monumento a Álvaro Obregón**, a monolithic shrine to the post-revolutionary Mexican president. The monument was built to house the revolutionary general's arm, lost in the 1915 Battle of Celaya, but the limb was cremated in 1989.

'La Bombilla' was the name of the restaurant where Obregón was assassinated in 1928. The killer, José de León Toral, was involved in the Cristero rebellion against the government's anti-church policies. In July the park explodes with color as the main venue for Feria de las Flores, a major flower festival.

Ciudad Universitaria

Two kilometers south of San Ángel, the **Ciudad Universitaria** (University City; www. unam.mx; 🚇Centro Cultural Universitario) is the

San Ángel

main campus of the Universidad Nacional Autónoma de México (UNAM). With about 330,000 students and 38,000 teachers, it's Latin America's largest university. Five former Mexican presidents are among its alumni, as is Carlos Slim, ranked the world's second-richest person in 2015.

Founded in 1551 as the Royal and Papal University of Mexico, UNAM is the second-oldest university in the Americas. It occupied various buildings in the center of town until the campus was transferred to its current location in the 1950s. Although it is a public university open to all, UNAM remains 'autonomous,' meaning the government may not interfere in its academic policies. It is Mexico's leading research institute and has long been a center of political dissent.

An architectural showpiece, UNAM was placed on Unesco's list of World Heritage sites in 2007. Most of the faculty buildings are scattered at the north end. As you enter

from Avenida Insurgentes, it's easy to spot the **Biblioteca Central** (Central Library), 10 stories high and covered with mosaics by Juan O'Gorman. The south wall, with two prominent zodiac wheels, covers colonial times, while the north wall deals with Aztec culture. **La Rectoría**, the administration building at the west end of the vast central lawn, has a vivid, three-dimensional Siqueiros mosaic on its south wall, showing students urged on by the people.

Across Avenida Insurgentes stands the **Estadio Olímpico**, built of volcanic stone for the 1968 Olympics. With seating for over 72,000, it's home to UNAM's Pumas soccer club, which competes in the national league's Primera División. Over the main entrance is Diego Rivera's sculpted mural on the theme of sports in Mexican history.

East of the university's main esplanade, the **Facultad de Medicina** (Faculty of Medicine) features an intriguing mosaic mural by

San Ángel

◎ Sights
1 Iglesia de San Jacinto...........................B3
2 Jardín de la Bombilla...........................C2
3 Monumento a Álvaro Obregón............C2
4 Museo Casa del Risco B3
5 Museo Casa Estudio Diego
  Rivera y Frida Kahlo......................... A1
6 Museo de Arte Carrillo Gil..................B2
7 Museo de El Carmen B2
8 Plaza San Jacinto................................B3

◎ Eating
9 Barbacoa de Santiago.........................B3
10 Cluny..B2
11 El Cardenal San Ángel.......................C2
12 Fonda San Ángel.................................B3
13 Montejo..C2
14 San Ángel Inn A2
15 Taberna del León A4

◎ Drinking & Nightlife
La Camelia .... (see 12)

◎ Entertainment
16 Centro Cultural Helénico B1
17 El Breve Espacio Mezcalería B3

◎ Shopping
18 Bazar Sábado B3
19 Gandhi..D2
20 Plaza Loreto...B4

Francisco Eppens on the theme of Mexico's *mestizaje* (blending of indigenous and European races.)

A second section of the campus, about 2km south, contains the **Centro Cultural Universitario**, a cultural center with five theaters, two cinemas, the delightful Azul y Oro restaurant and two excellent museums. To get to University City, take metrobús line 1 to the Centro Cultural Universitario (CCU) station, or go to metro Universidad and hop on the 'Pumabús,' a free on-campus bus. The Pumabús has limited service on weekends and holidays.

Museo Universitario Arte Contemporáneo MUSEUM
(MUAC; ☑ 55-5622-6972; www.muac.unam.mx; Av Insurgentes Sur 3000, Centro Cultural Universitario; adult/student Thu-Sat M$40/20, Wed & Sun M$20; ⊙10am-6pm Wed, Fri & Sun, to 8pm Thu & Sat; ℗; ⬚ Centro Cultural Universitario) Designed by veteran architect Teodoro González de León, the contemporary art museum's sloping, minimalist-style glass facade stands in stark contrast to the surrounding 1970s buildings.

Inside you'll find cutting-edge temporary exhibitions occupying nine spacious halls with impressive lighting and high ceilings. The modern works include paintings, audio installations, sculptures and multimedia art from Mexico and abroad.

Museo Universitario de Ciencias MUSEUM
(Universum; ☑ 55-5424-0694; www.universum. unam.mx; Circuito Cultural de Ciudad Universitaria s/n; adult/child M$70/60; ⊙9am-6pm Mon-Fri, from 10am Sat & Sun; ⬚ Centro Cultural Universitario) A huge science museum offering fun-filled attractions for kids, such as a planetarium and permanent exhibits that explore biodiversity, the human brain and much more. Nearby is the university sculpture garden, with a trail leading through volcanic fields past a dozen-or-so innovative pieces. The most formidable work is an enormous ring of concrete blocks by sculptor Mathias Goeritz.

◎ Coyoacán

Coyoacán ('Place of Coyotes' in the Náhuatl language), about 10km south of downtown, was Cortés' base after the fall of Tenochtitlán. Only in recent decades has urban sprawl overtaken the outlying village. Coyoacán retains its restful identity, with narrow colonial-era streets, cafes and a lively atmosphere. Once home to Leon Trotsky and Frida Kahlo (whose houses are now fascinating museums), it has a decidedly counter-cultural vibe, most evident on weekends, when assorted musicians, mimes and crafts markets draw large but relaxed crowds to Coyoacán's central plazas.

The nearest metro stations to central Coyoacán, 1.5km to 2km away, are Viveros, Coyoacán and General Anaya. If you don't fancy a walk, get off at Viveros station, walk south to Avenida Progreso and catch an eastbound 'Metro Gral Anaya' pesero (Mexico City name for a *colectivo*) to the market. Returning, 'Metro Viveros' peseros go west on Malintzin. 'Metro Coyoacán' and 'Metro Gral Anaya' peseros depart from the west side of Plaza Hidalgo.

San Ángel–bound peseros and buses head west on Avenida Miguel Ángel de Quevedo, five blocks south of Plaza Hidalgo.

★**Museo Frida Kahlo** MUSEUM
(Map p122; ☑ 55-5554-5999; www.museofrida kahlo.org.mx; Londres 247; adult Mon-Fri M$120, Sat & Sun M$140, student M$40, video guide M$70;

◎10am-5:45pm Tue & Thu-Sun, from 11am Wed; ⓂCoyoacán) Renowned Mexican artist Frida Kahlo was born in, and lived and died in, Casa Azul (Blue House), now a museum. Almost every visitor to Mexico City makes a pilgrimage here to gain a deeper understanding of the painter (and maybe to pick up a Frida handbag). Arrive early to avoid the crowds, especially on weekends.

Built by Frida's father Guillermo three years before her birth, the house is littered with mementos and personal belongings that evoke her long, often tempestuous relationship with husband Diego Rivera and the leftist intellectual circle they often entertained there. Kitchen implements, jewelry, outfits, photos and other objects from the artist's everyday life are interspersed with art, as well as a variety of pre-Hispanic pieces and Mexican crafts. The collection was greatly expanded in 2007 after the discovery of a cache of previously unseen items that had been stashed in the attic.

Kahlo's art expresses the anguish of her existence as well as her flirtation with socialist icons: portraits of Lenin and Mao hang around her bed and, in another painting, *Retrato de la familia* (Family Portrait), the artist's Hungarian-Oaxacan roots are fancifully entangled.

Plaza Hidalgo & Jardín Centenario   PLAZA
(Map p122) The focus of Coyoacán life, and the scene of most of the weekend fun, is its central plaza – actually two adjacent plazas: the **Jardín Centenario**, with the village's iconic coyotes frolicking in its central fountain; and the larger, cobblestoned **Plaza Hidalgo**, with a statue of the eponymous independence hero.

The **Casa de Cortés** (Map p122; ☑55-5484-4500; Jardín Hidalgo 1; ◎9am-7pm; ⓂCoyoacán), on the north side of Plaza Hidalgo, is where conquistador Cortés established Mexico's first municipal seat during the siege of Tenochtitlán, and later had the defeated emperor Cuauhtémoc tortured to make him divulge the location of Aztec treasure (the scene is depicted on a mural inside the chapel). Contrary to popular thought, Cortés never actually resided here. The building now houses Coyoacán's delegation offices.

The **Parroquia de San Juan Bautista** (Map p122; Plaza Hidalgo) and its adjacent former monastery dominate the south side of Plaza Hidalgo. First erected in 1592 by the Franciscans, the single-nave church has a lavishly ornamented interior, with painted scenes all over the vaulted ceiling. Be sure to inspect the cloister, featuring Tuscan columns and a checkerboard of carved relief panels in the corner of the ceilings.

Half a block east, the **Museo Nacional de Culturas Populares** (Map p122; ☑55-4155-0920; www.culturaspopularesindigenas.gob.mx; Av Hidalgo 289; M$13, Sun free; ◎10am-6pm Tue-Thu, to 8pm Fri-Sun; ⓂCoyoacán) stages innovative exhibitions on folk traditions, indigenous crafts and celebrations in its various courtyards and galleries.

★**Museo Casa de León Trotsky**   MUSEUM
(Map p122; ☑55-5658-8732; www.museocasadeleontrotsky.blogspot.mx; Av Río Churubusco 410; M$40; ◎10am-5pm Tue-Sun; ⓂCoyoacán) The Trotsky home, now a museum, remains much as it was on the day when a Stalin agent, a Catalan named Ramón Mercader, caught up with the revolutionary and smashed an ice ax into his skull. Memorabilia and biographical notes are displayed in buildings off the patio, where a tomb engraved with a hammer and sickle contains Trotsky's ashes.

Having come second to Stalin in the power struggle in the Soviet Union, Trotsky was expelled in 1929 and condemned to death in absentia. In 1937 he found refuge in Mexico. At first Trotsky and his wife, Natalia, lived in Frida Kahlo's Blue House, but after falling out with Kahlo and Rivera they moved a few streets northeast.

Bullet holes remain in the bedroom, the markings of a failed assassination attempt.

The entrance is at the rear of the old residence, facing Av Río Churubusco. Ask about free guided tours in English at the entrance.

Anahuacalli   MUSEUM
(Diego Rivera Anahuacalli Museum; ☑55-5617-4310; www.museoanahuacalli.org.mx; Calle Museo 150; adult/child under 16yr M$80/15; ◎11am-5pm Wed-Sun; ℗; ⓇXotepingo) Designed by Diego Rivera to house his collection of pre-Hispanic art, this museum is a temple-like structure of volcanic stone. The 'House of Anáhuac' (Aztec name for the Valle de México) also contains one of Rivera's studios and some of his work, including a study for *Man at the Crossroads,* the mural commissioned by the Rockefeller Center in 1934.

In November elaborate Day of the Dead offerings pay homage to the painter, and from April to early December the museum hosts free concerts at 1pm on Sundays, ranging from classical to regional folk music.

Anahuacalli is 3.5km south of Coyoacán. The ticket includes entry into both the Frida Kahlo Museum and Anahuacalli, and for M$130 also includes weekend round-trip transportation departing from the Casa Azul.

You can also take the *tren ligero* from metro Tasqueña to the Xotepingo station. Exit on the west side and walk 200m to División del Norte. Cross and continue 600m along Calle Museo.

Ex-Convento de Churubusco   HISTORIC BUILDING
(☑ 55-5604-0699; 20 de Agosto s/n, Colonia San Diego Churubusco; M General Anaya) This was the scene of a heroic military defeat on August 20, 1847. Mexican troops defended the former convent against US forces advancing from Veracruz in a dispute over the US annexation of Texas. The US invasion was but one example in a long history of foreign intervention in Mexico, as compellingly demonstrated in Churubusco's **Museo Nacional de las Intervenciones** (National Interventions Museum; ☑ 55-5604-0699; 20 de Agosto s/n; M$52, Sun free; ⊙ 9am-6pm Tue-Sun; M General Anaya).

The Mexicans fought off US forces until they ran out of ammunition and were beaten only after hand-to-hand fighting. Displays in the museum include an American map showing operations in 1847 and the plot by US ambassador Henry Lane Wilson to bring down the Madero government in 1913. Explanatory text is in Spanish.

The superbly restored exhibit rooms, bordered by original frescoes, surround a small cloister where numbered stations provided instructions for meditating monks. Leaving the museum, wander amid the monastery's old orchard, which now holds wonderful gardens.

The 17th-century former monastery stands within peaceful wooded grounds, 1.5km east of Plaza Hidalgo. To reach Churubusco from Coyoacán, catch an eastbound 'Metro General Anaya' bus from Carrillo Puerto, off Plaza Hidalgo. Otherwise, walk 500m west from the General Anaya metro station.

Viveros de Coyoacán   PARK
(☑ 55-5484-3524; www.viveroscoyoacan.gob.mx; Av Progreso 1; ⊙ 6am-6pm; M Viveros) A pleasant approach to Coyoacán's central plazas is through the Viveros de Coyoacán, the principal nurseries for Mexico City's parks and gardens. The 38.9-hectare swath of greenery, 1km west of central Coyoacán, is popular with joggers and great for a stroll, but watch out for belligerent squirrels!

From metro Viveros, walk south (right, as you face the fence) along Avenida Universidad and take the first left, Avenida Progreso.

Plaza Santa Catarina   PLAZA
(Map p122; M Viveros) About a block south of Coyoacán's nursery is Plaza Santa Catarina, with the modest, mustard-colored church that gives the square its name. Across the street, the **Centro Cultural Jesús Reyes Heroles** (Map p122; ☑ 55-5554-5324; Av Francisco Sosa 202; ⊙ 9am-8pm; M Viveros) is a colonial estate with a coffee shop and lovely grounds, where yuccas and jacarandas spring from carefully tended gardens.

◉ Cuicuilco

One of the oldest significant remnants of pre-Hispanic settlement within the DF, Cuicuilco echoes a civilization that stood on the shores of Lago de Xochimilco as far back as 800 BC. In its heyday in the 2nd century BC, the 'place of singing and dancing' counted as many as 40,000 inhabitants – at that time the Teotihuacán civilization was only just beginning to rise to importance. The site was abandoned a couple of centuries later, however, after an eruption of the nearby Xitle volcano covered most of the community in lava.

Zona Arqueológica Cuicuilco   ARCHAEOLOGICAL SITE
(www.inah.gob.mx; Av Insurgentes Sur s/n; ⊙ 9am-5pm; P; ☐ Villa Olímpica) FREE The principal structure is a huge circular platform of four levels, faced with volcanic stone blocks, which probably functioned as a ceremonial center. Set amid a park with sweeping views of the area and studded with cacti and shade trees, it makes a nice picnic spot. The site has a small museum containing skulls and artifacts discovered during excavations.

◉ Tlalpan

Tlalpan today is what Coyoacán used to be – an outlying village with a bohemian atmosphere coupled with some impressive colonial architecture. The municipal seat of Mexico City's largest *delegación*, Tlalpan sits at the foot of the southern Ajusco range and enjoys a cooler, moister climate. There are some fine restaurants along the arcades of the charismatic plaza. To get here take metrobús Línea 1 to Fuentes Brotantes and walk four blocks east to the main square.

La Jalisciense HISTORIC BUILDING
(Plaza de la Constitución 7; ⊙ noon-11:30pm Mon-Sat; 🚇 Fuentes Brotantes) This building opened its doors in 1870, making it arguably the oldest cantina in Mexico City – now that's a good reason to pop in and wet your whistle.

Museo de Historia de Tlalpán MUSEUM
(☑ 55-5485-9048; Plaza de la Constitución 10; ⊙ 2-8pm Mon-Fri, from noon Sat; 🚇 Fuentes Brotantes) **FREE** Hosts compelling contemporary art and historical exhibits in naturally lit galleries off the courtyard.

Casa Frisaac CULTURAL CENTER
(☑ 55-5485-3266; Plaza de la Constitución 1; ⊙ 8am-8pm; 🚇 Fuentes Brotantes) **FREE** This 19th-century estate, once the property of President Adolfo López Mateos, now houses an art gallery with temporary exhibits, and a small auditorium for concerts and dance performances.

Capilla de las Capuchinas Sacramentarias CHAPEL
(☑ 55-5573-2395; Av Hidalgo 43; M$200; ⊙ visiting hours 10-11:30am & 4-6pm Tue-Sun; 🚇 Fuentes Brotantes) There's a sublime simplicity about this chapel, located inside a convent for Capuchin nuns. Designed by modernist architect Luis Barragán in 1952, the austere altar, free of the usual iconography, consists only of a trio of gold panels. In the morning, light streams through a stained-glass window made by German-Mexican artist Mathias Goeritz. Visits by appointment only.

◉ Tlatelolco & Guadalupe

Plaza de las Tres Culturas HISTORIC SITE
(Plaza of the Three Cultures; ☑ 55-5583-0295; www.tlatelolco.inah.gob.mx; cnr Eje Central Lázaro Cárdenas & Flores Magón; ⊙ 8am-6pm; ℗; Ⓜ Tlatelolco) **FREE** So named because it symbolizes the fusion of pre-Hispanic and Spanish roots into the Mexican *mestizo* identity, this plaza displays the architectural legacy of three cultural facets: the Aztec pyramids of Tlatelolco, the 17th-century Spanish Templo de Santiago and the modern tower that houses the Centro Cultural Universitario.

Recent archaeological finds have altered long-held views about Tlatelolco's history. According to the conventional version, Tlatelolco was founded by an Aztec faction in the 14th century on a separate island in Lago de Texcoco and later conquered by the Aztecs of Tenochtitlán. But a pyramid excavated on the site in late 2007 actually predates the establishment of Tenochtitlán by as much as 200 years. All agree, however, that Tlatelolco was the scene of the largest public market in the Valle de México, connected by a causeway to Tenochtitlán's ceremonial center.

During the siege of the Aztec capital, Cortés defeated Tlatelolco's defenders, led by Cuauhtémoc. An inscription about the battle in the plaza translates as 'This was neither victory nor defeat. It was the sad birth of the *mestizo* people that is Mexico today.'

You can view the remains of Tlatelolco's main pyramid-temple and other Aztec buildings from a walkway around them. Tlatelolco's main temple was constructed in stages, with each of seven temples superimposed atop its predecessor. The double pyramid on view, one of the earliest stages, has twin staircases that supposedly ascended to temples dedicated to Tláloc and Huitzilopochtli. Numerous calendar glyphs are carved into the outer walls.

Recognizing the significance of the site, the Spanish erected the **Templo de Santiago** here in 1609, using stones from the Aztec structures as building materials. Just inside the main doors of this church is the **baptismal font of Juan Diego**.

Tlatelolco is also a symbol of modern troubles. On October 2, 1968, hundreds of student protesters were massacred here by government troops on the eve of the Mexico City Olympic Games. The weeks before the Olympics had been marked by a wave of protests against political corruption and authoritarianism, and president Gustavo Díaz Ordaz, anxious to present an image of stability to the world, was employing heavy-handed tactics to stop the unrest.

On that October day, helicopters hovered over the Plaza de las Tres Culturas and a massive police contingent cordoned off the protest zone. Suddenly shots rang out, apparently from the balcony that served as a speakers' platform. Police then opened fire on the demonstrators and mayhem ensued. A government-authorized account reported 20 protesters killed, though researchers and media reports estimate the real number is closer to 300.

The generally accepted theory, though there are many, is that the government staged the massacre, planting snipers on the balcony. To this day the incident still generates a massive protest march from Tlatelolco to the Zócalo on October 2.

Along Eje Central Lázaro Cárdenas, northbound trolleybuses pass right by the Plaza de las Tres Culturas.

Centro Cultural
Universitario Tlatelolco   MUSEUM

(☑55-5117-2818, ext 49646; www.tlatelolco.unam. mx; Flores Magón 1; adult/student M$30/15, Sun free; ⊙10am-6pm Tue-Sun; ⓂTlatelolco) The events that occurred before, during and after the 1968 massacre on Plaza de las Tres Culturas are chronicled in *Memorial del 68*, a compelling multimedia exhibit in the Centro Cultural Universitario Tlatelolco. The cultural center has two other outstanding permanent exhibits.

The shiny Museo de Sitio houses more than 400 objects unearthed at the archaeological site, such as pre-Hispanic offerings and ceramic artifacts. The interactive museum continues on the 2nd floor in the tower building across the way, where you can learn about colonial-era Tlatelolco and the area's flora and fauna. The tower's 3rd floor is home to the Colección Stavenhagen, an extraordinary collection of more than 500 pre-Hispanic clay and stone sculptures, including amusing animal figures and phallic works.

Basílica de Guadalupe   SHRINE

(www.virgendeguadalupe.org.mx; Plaza de las Américas 1; ⊙6am-9pm; ⓂLa Villa–Basílica) FREE A cult developed around this site after a Christian convert named Juan Diego claimed in December 1531 that the Virgin Mary appeared before him on the Cerro del Tepeyac (Tepeyac Hill). After numerous sightings, as the story goes, the lady's image was miraculously emblazoned on Diego's cloak, causing a bishop to believe the story and build a shrine in her honor.

Over the centuries Nuestra Señora de Guadalupe came to receive credit for all manner of miracles, hugely aiding the acceptance of Catholicism by Mexicans. Despite the protests of some clergy, who saw the cult as a form of idolatry (with the Virgin as a Christianized version of the Aztec goddess Tonantzin), in 1737 the Virgin was officially declared the patron of Mexico. Two centuries later she was named celestial patron of Latin America and empress of the Americas, and in 2002 Juan Diego was canonized by Pope John Paul II. Today the Virgin's shrines around the Cerro del Tepeyac (formerly an Aztec shrine site) are the most revered in Mexico, attracting thousands of pilgrims daily and hundreds of thousands

MEXICO CITY SIGHTS

WORTH A TRIP

PARQUE NACIONAL DESIERTO DE LOS LEONES

Cool, fragrant pine and oak forests dominate this 20-sq-km **national park** (☑55-5814-1171; http://desiertodelosleones.mx; ⊙ 6am-6pm) in the hills surrounding the Valle de México. Around 23km southwest of Mexico City and 800m higher, it makes for a fine escape from the carbon monoxide and concrete.

The name derives from the **Ex-Convento del Santo Desierto de Nuestra Señora del Carmen** (☑55-5814-1172; Camino al Desierto de los Leones; M$13; ⊙10am-5pm Tue-Sun), the 17th-century former Carmelite monastery within the park. The Carmelites called their isolated monasteries 'deserts' to commemorate Elijah, who lived as a recluse in the desert near Mt Carmel. The 'Leones' in the name may stem from the presence of wild cats in the area, but more likely it refers to José and Manuel de León, who once administered the monastery's finances.

The restored monastery has exhibition halls and a restaurant. Tours in Spanish are run by guides (garbed in cassock and sandals) who lead you through expansive gardens around the buildings and the patios within, as well as some underground passageways.

The rest of the park has extensive walking trails (robberies have been reported, so stick to the main paths). Next to El León Dorado restaurant, stairs lead down to a gorgeous picnic area with several small waterfalls and a duck pond.

Buses depart to the former *convento* from metro Viveros (in front of the 7-Eleven) at 7:30am Monday to Friday, or from Paradero las Palmas in San Ángel at 7:30am, noon and 3:30pm (also Monday to Friday). On Saturday and Sunday there are hourly departures from Paradero las Palmas and metro Viveros from 8am to 3:30pm. Be sure to ask the driver if the bus arrives as far as the *ex-convento* (some stop short in a mountain town called Santa Rosa).

on the days leading up to her feast day, December 12. Some pilgrims travel the last meters to the shrine on their knees.

Around 1700, to accommodate the faithful flock, the four-towered Basílica de Guadalupe was erected at the site of an earlier shrine. But by the 1970s, the old yellow-domed building proved inadequate to the task, so the new Basílica de Nuestra Señora de Guadalupe was built next door. Designed by Pedro Ramírez Vázquez, it is a vast, round, open-plan structure with a capacity of more than 40,000 people. The image of the Virgin, dressed in a green mantle trimmed with gold, hangs above and behind the basilica's main altar, where moving walkways bring visitors as close as possible.

The rear of the Antigua Basílica is now the **Museo de la Basílica de Guadalupe** (☑ 55-5577-6022; M$5; ☉ 10am-5:30pm Tue-Sun), which houses a fine collection of colonial art interpreting the miraculous vision.

Stairs behind the Antigua Basílica climb about 100m to the hilltop **Capilla del Cerrito** (Hill Chapel), where Juan Diego had his vision, then lead down the east side of the hill to the Parque de la Ofrenda, with gardens and waterfalls around a sculpted scene of the apparition. Continue on down to the baroque **Templo del Pocito**, a circular structure with a trio of tiled cupolas, built in 1787 to commemorate the miraculous appearance of a spring where the Virgen de Guadalupe had stood. From there the route leads back to the main plaza, re-entering it beside the 17th-century **Antigua Parroquia de Indios** (Parish of Indians).

To reach the Basílica de Guadalupe, take the metro to La Villa–Basílica station, then walk two blocks north along Calzada de Guadalupe, or you can take any 'Metro Hidalgo–La Villa' bus heading northeast on Paseo de la Reforma. To return downtown, walk to Calzada de los Misterios, a block west of Calzada de Guadalupe, and catch a southbound 'Auditorio' or 'Zócalo' bus.

🏃 Activities

Cycling

On Sunday mornings Paseo de la Reforma is closed to auto traffic from Bosque de Chapultepec to the Alameda Central, and you can join the legions of *chilangos* who happily skate or cycle down the avenue.

Bicitekas   CYCLING
(Map p106; http://bicitekas.org; ☉ departure time 9:30pm Wed) For an ambitious trek, this urban cycling group organizes rides departing from the Monumento a la Independencia Wednesday evenings. Groups of up to 200 cyclists ride to destinations such as Coyoacán and the northwestern suburb of Ciudad Satélite. Participants must be sufficiently robust to handle excursions of up to 40km. Helmets and rear lights are recommended.

Kayaking

Michmani   KAYAKING
(www.xochimilco.df.gob.mx/turismo/michmani_precios.html; Embarcadero Cuemanco, Xochimilco, off Anillo Periférico Sur; per hr M$50) Take in some of the quieter parts of the Xochimilco canals while kayaking, and do some bird-watching while you're at it. You'll spot ducks, egrets and herons, among many other migratory and endemic species, and you can also visit the many nurseries along the shores.

To get here, go to metro General Anaya and exit the station on the east side of Calzada de Tlalpan, then walk 50m north to catch a 'Tláhuac Paradero' pesero. Get off at the Embarcadero Cuemanco entrance and walk about 1km to Michmani, just beyond the *embarcadero*.

Lago de Chapultepec   KAYAKING
(Chapultepec Lake; Map p88; www.chapultepec.com.mx/visita.asp?Lugar=114; kayaks/paddleboats/rowboats per hr M$40/50/60; ☉ 9am-4:30pm Tue-Sun; Ⓜ Auditorio) Take a kayak, paddleboat or rowboat out for a spin with the ducks on Chapultepec Lake.

Ice-Skating

As part of a government program to bring fun recreational activities to the city's poorer inhabitants, a huge ice-skating rink is installed in the Zócalo during the Christmas holiday season. Ice-skates are loaned out free of charge, but the wait can be up to an hour.

💃 Courses

If you like to dance, learn a few great steps at the **Plaza de Danzón**, northwest of La Ciudadela, near metro Balderas. Couples crowd the plaza every Saturday afternoon to do the *danzón,* an elegant and complicated Cuban step that infiltrated Mexico in the 19th century. Lessons in *danzón* and other steps are given from 10am to 2:30pm and 4:30pm to 6pm; they cost M$30.

QUIRKY MEXICO CITY

Museo del Juguete Antiguo México (Antique Toy Museum; ☑ 55-5588-2100; www.museodeljuguete.mx; Dr Olvera 15, cnr Eje Central Lázaro Cárdenas; M$50; ⊙ 9am-6pm Mon-Fri, to 4pm Sat, 10am-4pm Sun; ℙ ♿; Ⓜ Obrera) Mexican-born Japanese collector Roberto Shimizu has amassed more than a million toys in his lifetime, and this museum showcases about 60,000 pieces, ranging from life-sized robots to tiny action figures. Shimizu himself designed many of the unique display cases from recycled objects.

Several blocks west of the museum, at Dr Garciadiego 157, the same owners run a cultural center that houses dozens of works by local graffiti muralists and Belgian street artist ROA. The museum staff will gladly show you around the cultural center if it's closed.

Patrick Miller (Map p106; ☑ 55-5511-5406; www.patrickmiller.com.mx; Mérida 17; M$30; ⊙ 10pm-3am Fri; Ⓜ Insurgentes) People-watching doesn't get any better than at this throbbing disco, founded by Mexico City DJ Patrick Miller. With a clientele ranging from black-clad '80s throwbacks to cross-dressers, the fun begins when dance circles open and regulars pull off moves that would make John Travolta proud.

La Faena (Map p68; ☑ 55-5510-4417; Venustiano Carranza 49B; ⊙ noon-midnight; ⎕ República del Salvador) This forgotten relic of a bar doubles as a bullfighting museum, with matadors in sequined outfits glaring within dusty cases, and bucolic canvases of grazing bulls.

Museo del Calzado El Borceguí (El Borceguí Shoe Museum; Map p68; ☑ 55-5510-0627; www.elborcegui.com.mx/museo.htm; Bolívar 27; ⊙ 10am-2pm & 3-6pm Mon-Fri, 10am-6pm Sat; Ⓜ Zócalo) At this shoe museum – and the oldest shoemaker in Mexico, since 1865 – there are over 2000 pieces of footwear on show, many from famous feet such as Mexican authors Carlos Fuentes and Elena Poniatowska, Louis XIV of France, Queen Elizabeth II, Magic Johnson's size 14½ basketball shoes and Neil Armstrong's lunar boots. Fashionistas and fetishists will delight at the styles organised by decades. Who doesn't want to see Japanese sandals made of rice hay?

Isla de las Muñecas (Embarcadero Cuemanco, Xochimilco; boat per hr M$350) For a truly surreal experience, head for Xochimilco and hire a gondola to the Island of the Dolls, where hundreds of creepy, decomposed dolls hang from trees. An island resident fished the playthings from the canals to mollify the spirit of a girl who had drowned nearby.

The best departure point for the four-hour round trip is Embarcadero Cuemanco. To get here, go to metro General Anaya and exit the station on the east side of Calzada de Tlalpan, then walk 50m north to catch a 'Tláhuac Paradero' pesero. Get off at the Embarcadero Cuemanco entrance.

Mercado de Sonora (cnr Fray Servando & Rosales, Colonia Merced Balbuena; ⊙ 10am-7pm; Ⓜ Merced) This place has all the ingredients for Mexican witchcraft. Aisles are crammed with stalls hawking potions, amulets, voodoo dolls and other esoterica. This is also the place for a *limpia* (spiritual cleansing), a ritual involving clouds of incense and a herbal brushing. Sadly some vendors at the market trade illegally in endangered animals. It's two blocks south of metro Merced.

Santa Muerte Altar (Alfarería, north of Mineros; ⊙ rosary service 5pm, first day of the month; Ⓜ Tepito) Often garbed in a sequined white gown, wearing a dark wig and clutching a scythe in her bony hand, the Saint Death figure bears an eerie resemblance to Mrs Bates from the film *Psycho*. The Santa Muerte is the object of a fast-growing cult in Mexico, particularly in Tepito, where many of her followers have lost faith in Catholicism. Enter the notoriously dangerous Tepito 'hood at your own risk; the safest day is the rosary service. It's three blocks north of metro Tepito.

Centro de Enseñanza Para Extranjeros LANGUAGE COURSE (Foreigners' Teaching Center; ☑ 55-5622-2470; www.cepe.unam.mx; Av Universidad 3002, Ciudad Universitaria; 6-week course M$7640; ⎕ Ciudad Universitaria) The national university offers six-week intensive language classes, meeting for three hours daily from Monday through Friday. Students who already speak Spanish may take content courses on Mexican art and culture.

Escuela de
Gastronomía Mexicana COOKING COURSE
(Map p82; 55-5264-2484; www.esgamex.
com; Coahuila 207; 3hr course incl ingredients
M$850-1000; Campeche) Learn how to cook
Mexican dishes from bilingual chefs. Popular classes inlcude *pozole* (hominy soup),
mole poblano (chicken in a chili and chocolate sauce) and *tamales*.

Tours

Turibús Circuito Turístico BUS TOUR
(55-5141-1360; www.turibus.com.mx; adult/
child 4-12yr M$140/70, themed tours M$100-800;
9am-9pm;) Red double-decker buses
run four *circuitos* (routes) across the city:
Centro (downtown), Sur (south, including
Frida Kahlo museum), Hipodromo (Polanco and Chapultepec) and Basílica (north).
Buses pass every hour or so and you can hop
off and on at any designated stop. All routes
stop on the west side of the cathedral. Fares
are slightly higher on Saturday and Sunday.
   Turibús also offers themed tours, including cantinas, *lucha libre*, palaces, museums
or food tasting. See the website for times.

Eat Mexico CULINARY
(US 917-930-7503, cell 55-43632896; www.
eatmexico.com; tours US$85-145) Bilingual
guides lead groups on three- to four-hour
themed walking tours. Choose between
street food, market fare, regional cuisine
or a nocturnal tacos and mezcal crawl. Eat
Mexico also does customized tours for specific culinary needs.

Mexico Soul & Essence CULINARY
(Map p82; 55-5564-8457, cell 55-29175408;
www.ruthincondechi.com; tours US$95-175, cook-
ing courses US$300) Customized culinary/
cultural excursions by Ruth Alegría, one
of the city's foremost food experts. She can
arrange dining outings, market tours and/
or specialized trips. She also offers an entertaining Mexican cooking course.

Journeys Beyond the Surface TOUR
(cell 55-17452380; www.travelmexicocity.com.
mx; group tours per person US$185-220) Person-
alized eight-hour walking tours on aspects
of the DF experience, with an off-the-beaten-
track attitude – for instance, you can do a
murals, graffiti and street art excursion. The
guides are well versed in history and anthropology if you choose to visit pre-Hispanic
and colonial-era sites.

Wayak TOUR
(55-5652-9331; www.wayak.mx; day trips per
person US$27-58, balloon rides incl ground trans-
portation US$175-250) Want a breath of fresh
air? This outfit does day trips to the colonial
town of Taxco, the pyramids of Teotihuacán
or, if you prefer, a balloon ride above the pyramids. See website for details.

Festivals & Events

Mexico City celebrates some unique local
events in addition to all the major nationwide festivals, which often take on a special
flavor in the capital.

Festival de México CULTURAL
(www.festival.org.mx; Mar) The *centro
histórico* hosts music, theater, dance and
culinary events featuring talent from Mexico and abroad – it's the city's biggest cultural
bash of the year.

Semana Santa RELIGIOUS
(Mar/Apr) The most evocative events of
Holy Week are in the Iztapalapa district,
9km southeast of the Zócalo, where a gruesome passion play is enacted on Good Friday.

Foundation of Tenochtitlán DANCE
(Aug; M Tlatelolco) Held on August 13 to celebrate the foundation of the Mexican capital, this is a major summit for Concheros
(Aztec dancers) on Plaza de las Tres Culturas
in Tlatelolco.

Grito de la Independencia FIREWORKS
(Sep; M Zócalo) On September 15, the eve
of Independence Day, thousands gather in
the Zócalo to hear the Mexican president's
version of the *Grito de Dolores* (Cry of Dolores), Hidalgo's famous call to rebellion
against the Spanish in 1810, from the central
balcony of the Palacio Nacional at 11pm. Afterwards, there's a fireworks display.

Día de Muertos CULTURAL
(Day of the Dead; Nov) In the lead-up to Day
of the Dead (November 1 and 2), elaborate *ofrendas* (altars) show up everywhere. Some of
the best are at Anahuacalli (p96), Museo
Dolores Olmedo (p92), the Zócalo (p66)
and in the neighborhood of San Andrés Mix-
quic (www.mixquic.com.mx) in the extreme
southeast of the Distrito Federal.

Fiesta de Santa Cecilia MUSIC
(Nov; M Garibaldi) The patron saint of musi-
cians is honored with special fervor at Plaza
Garibaldi on November 22.

Día de Nuestra Señora de Guadalupe
RELIGIOUS

(⊙Dec; Ⓜ La Villa-Basílica) At the Basílica de Guadalupe, the Day of Our Lady of Guadalupe caps 10 days of festivities that honor Mexico's religious patron. The number of pilgrims reaches millions by December 12, when groups of indigenous dancers perform nonstop on the basilica's broad plaza.

🛌 Sleeping

As a frequent destination for both Mexican and foreign visitors, the DF overflows with lodging options – everything from no-frills guesthouses to top-flight hotels. Some of the most reasonably priced places are in the *centro histórico*, while more luxurious accommodations, including branches of some major international chains, are concentrated in Polanco and the Zona Rosa. In the trendy Roma and Condesa neighborhoods, the offerings are mostly chic boutique hotels, with a few budget hostels. Midrange lodgings abound in the Alameda and Plaza de la República areas, though they tend to trade character for neutral modern comfort. (Note that places with the word *'garage'* on the sign generally cater to short-term trysting guests.)

🏠 Centro Histórico

For nonbusiness travelers, the historic center is the obvious place to stay. Ongoing renovations of its infrastructure and preservation of its numerous historic edifices have boosted the zone's appeal, and it remains one of the more affordable areas.

★ Casa San Ildefonso
HOSTEL $

(Map p68; ☑ 55-5789-1999; www.casasanildefonso.com; San Ildefonso 38; dm/d M$300/800, s/d without bathroom M$520/690, all incl breakfast; ⊛@🛜; Ⓜ Zócalo) A 19th-century building that most recently served as a storage facility for street vendors has been transformed into a cheerful hostel off a pedestrian thoroughfare. Unlike most downtown hostels, the high-ceiling dorms, private rooms and common areas here get wonderful sunlight. Guests have breakfast in a tranquil courtyard with a fountain, singing canaries and the gremlin-esque mascot Delfina.

Hostal Regina
HOSTEL $

(Map p68; ☑ 55-5709-4192; www.hostalcentrohistoricoregina.com; Calle 5 de Febrero 53; dm M$160-190, r without bathroom M$450, ste M$900,

all incl breakfast; ⊛@🛜; Ⓜ Isabel La Católica) Off the lively Regina corridor, this 18th-century historic building makes a great base to explore downtown. On offer are dorms with wooden floors and high ceilings, private rooms with shared bathrooms and a two-story 'suite' that comfortably sleeps four. Guests socialize on the rooftop bar.

Mexico City Hostel
HOSTEL $

(Map p68; ☑ 55-5512-3666; www.mexicocityhostel.com; República de Brasil 8; dm/d incl breakfast M$190/600, d without bathroom M$480; ⊛@🛜; Ⓜ Zócalo) Steps from the Zócalo, this colonial structure has been artfully restored, with original wood beams and stone walls as a backdrop for modern, energy-efficient facilities. Spacious dorms have four or six sturdy bunk beds on terracotta floors. Immaculate bathrooms trimmed with *azulejo* (painted ceramic tiles) amply serve around 100 occupants.

Hotel Castropol
BUSINESS HOTEL $

(Map p68; ☑ 55-5522-1920; http://hotelcastropol.com; Av Pino Suárez 58; s/tw/tr M$500/550/600; ⊛🛜) Minimalist, spacious rooms for peso watchers are hard to come by when the Zócalo is in sight at the end of the street. You not only get loads of cleanliness, marble and a flat-screen TV, but a handy budget restaurant, with the bar-filled Regina corridor kicking it nearby.

Hotel Isabel
HOTEL $

(Map p68; ☑ 55-5518-1213; www.hotel-isabel.com.mx; Isabel La Católica 63; s/d M$360/490, without bathroom M$250/360; ⊛@🛜; 🅿 República del Salvador) A longtime budget-traveler's favorite, the Isabel offers large, well-scrubbed rooms with old but sturdy furniture, high ceilings and great (if noisy) balconies, plus a hostel-like social scene. Remodeled rooms cost a touch more.

Hostel Mundo Joven Catedral
HOSTEL $

(Map p68; ☑ 55-5518-1726; http://mundojovenhostels.com; República de Guatemala 4; dm M$200, d with/without bathroom M$870/525, all incl breakfast; ⊛@🛜; Ⓜ Zócalo) Backpacker central, this HI affiliate is abuzz with a global rainbow of young travelers. Dorms are tidy and guests love the rooftop bar, but it's not the quietest of hostels. 'Quirky' bonuses include a free 10-minute massage.

Chillout Flat
B&B $$

(Map p68; ☑ 55-5510-2665; www.chilloutflat.com.mx; apt 102, Bolívar 8; s/d incl breakfast from

M$950/1000; ⊖@⊚; MAllende) Chill with other travelers in one of two downtown apartments that have been converted into colorful guesthouses with hardwood floors. Street-facing rooms in this lovely 1940s historic building recently got double-pane windows for noise reduction. Reservations a must.

Hotel Catedral
BUSINESS HOTEL **$$**
(Map p68; ✆55-5518-5232; www.hotelcatedral. com; Donceles 95; s/d/ste from M$910/1120/1255; P⊖@⊚; MZócalo) This comfortable lodging clearly benefits from its prime location in the heart of the *centro histórico*. Well-maintained rooms have flat-screens, desks, dark-wood furnishings and firm mattresses. For cityscape views, order a drink on the rooftop terrace.

Hotel Gillow
HOTEL **$$**
(Map p68; ✆55-5518-1440; www.hotelgillow.com; Isabel La Católica 17; s/d/ste M$800/860/1260; ⊖@⊚; MAllende) In this historic building with friendly, old-fashioned service, remodeled rooms are done up with faux-wood floors and flat-screen TVs. If available, request a double room with a private terrace.

Hampton Inn & Suites
HOTEL **$$$**
(Map p68; ✆55-8000-5000; www.hampton mexicocity.com; Calle 5 de Febrero 24; r/ste incl breakfast from US$119/139; ⊖✳@⊚; ⬚Isabel La Católica) This well-maintained historic gem underwent an elaborate makeover to preserve its facade and Talavera-tiled walls. Well-appointed rooms with contemporary furnishings surround a six-story atrium with a stained-glass ceiling. A good seafood restaurant shares the property.

Gran Hotel Ciudad de México
HOTEL **$$$**
(Map p68; ✆55-1083-7700; www.granhoteldela ciudaddemexico.com.mx; Av 16 de Septiembre 82; r/ ste incl breakfast from M$2134/3063; P⊖✳@⊚; MZócalo) The Gran Hotel flaunts the French art nouveau style of the pre-revolutionary era. Crowned by a stained-glass canopy crafted by Tiffany in 1908, the atrium is a fin de siècle fantasy of curved balconies, wrought iron elevators and chirping birds in giant cages. Rooms do not disappoint in comparison. Weekend brunch (M$250) is served on a terrace overlooking the Zócalo.

🛏 Alameda Central & Around

Like the *centro histórico*, this area continues to evolve with revitalised strips, though pockets of neglect are reminders of the 1985

earthquake that devastated the zone. By day the neighborhood bustles with shoppers, but after dark it quietens down considerably.

Hotel Marlowe
HOTEL **$$**
(Map p68; ✆55-5521-9540; www.hotelmarlowe .com.mx; Independencia 17; s/d/ste M$900/ 1050/1300; P⊖@⊚; MSan Juan de Letrán) The modern Marlowe stands across from Chinatown's pagoda gate. Grab a suite for a larger, brighter room with small balcony. Fitness freaks will appreciate the gym with a view.

Chaya
BOUTIQUE HOTEL **$$$**
(Map p76; ✆55-5512-9074; www.chayabnb.com; 3rd fl, Dr Mora 9; d/tw/ste US$119/155/226; ⊖⊚; MHidalgo) Like a secret at the edge of Alameda Central, diminutive Chaya nestles on the top floor of an exquisite art deco building. Rooms exude utilitarian chicness, making slabs of gray, wood and cream look good. Plush beds and terrific Mexican breakfasts add to the feeling of escape within the city.

Being so central brings occasional weekend noise from the park and bar below.

🛏 Plaza de la República & Around

Further away from the Zócalo, the area around the Monumento a la Revolución is awash with hotels, with a number of dives interspersed amid the business-class establishments. The semiresidential zone offers glimpses of neighborhood life.

Hostel Suites DF
HOSTEL **$**
(Map p76; ✆55-5535-8117; Terán 38; dm/d incl breakfast M$180/450; ⊖@⊚; ⬚Plaza de la República) Near the Monumento a la Revolución, this small HI-affiliated hostel offers pleasant common areas, dorms with in-room bathrooms and a great central location that leaves you within walking distance of downtown.

Casa de los Amigos
GUESTHOUSE **$**
(Map p76; ✆55-5705-0521; www.casadelosamigos .org; Mariscal 132; dm/s/d without bathroom M$100/150/250; ⊖@⊚; MRevolución) ✎ The Quaker-run Casa is a guesthouse popular with NGO workers, activists and researchers, but it welcomes walk-in travelers. Vegetarian breakfast (M$30) is served and guests can take yoga (M$10) or free weekly Spanish classes. You're not allowed to smoke or drink alcohol in the house. If you're interested in volunteer work, see the website for various options.

Plaza Revolución Hotel HOTEL $$

(Map p76; ☑55-5234-1910; www.hotelplaza revolucion.com; Terán 35; d/ste M$820/990; ⓅⓈ✻@☎; ⬚Plaza de la República) On a quiet street four blocks east of Plaza de la República, this glossy establishment is a stylish option in an area where cut-rate hotels are the norm. Modern rooms with wooden floors are done up in neutral colors and kept impeccably clean.

Palace Hotel HOTEL $$

(Map p76; ☑55-5566-2400; www.palace-hotel. com.mx; Ramírez 7; s/d/ste M$550/790/1110; ⓅⓈ@☎; ⬚Plaza de la República) Run by gregarious Asturians, the Palace has large, neatly maintained rooms, some with broad balconies giving terrific views down palm-lined Ramírez to the domed monument. Request a street-facing room if you want brighter digs. Cash-paying guests get substantial discounts.

Ramada Reforma HOTEL $$$

(Map p76; ☑55-5097-0277; www.ramadareforma .com; Puente de Alvarado 22; s/d incl breakfast from M$900/1800; ⓅⓈ✻@☎❄; ⓂHidalgo) Choose from refurbished 'standard' digs in this hotel's older section or pricier 'superior' rooms in the newer wing. A heated indoor pool awaits on the top floor. Just 1½ blocks from Reforma.

🏨 Zona Rosa & Around

Foreign businesspeople and tourists check in at the upscale hotels in this international commerce and nightlife area. Less-expensive establishments dot the quieter streets of Colonia Cuauhtémoc, north of Reforma, and Juárez, east of Insurgentes.

Capsule Hostel HOSTEL $

(Map p106; ☑55-5207-7903; Hamburgo 41; dm/d without bathroom M$250/500; Ⓢ☎) This poshtel is less Japanese capsule hotel and more boutique hospital ward (with equal cleanliness). Curtains wrap around the large dorm beds for ample privacy. Modern furnishings and surprising quiet rooms (request non-street side) provide an excellent budget option (finally) near the embassies and action of Zona Rosa.

Casa González GUESTHOUSE $$

(Map p106; ☑55-5514-3302; www.hotelcasagon zalez.com; Río Sena 69; s/d/ste M$730/871/1241; ⓅⓈ✻@☎; ⓂInsurgentes) A family-run operation for nearly a century, the Casa is a perennial hit with travelers seeking peace and quiet. Set around several flower-filled patios and semiprivate terraces, it's extraordinarily tranquil. Original portraits and landscapes decorate some rooms, apparently done by a guest in lieu of payment.

Hotel María Cristina HOTEL $$

(Map p106; ☑55-5703-1212; www.hotelmariacris tina.com.mx; Río Lerma 31; d/ste from M$850/1195; ⓅⓈ✻@☎; ⬚Reforma) Dating from the 1930s, this facsimile of an Andalucian estate makes an appealing retreat, particularly for the adjacent bar with patio seating. Though lacking the lobby's colonial splendor, rooms are generally bright and comfortable.

Hotel Bristol HOTEL $$

(Map p106; ☑55-5533-6060; www.hotelbristol .com.mx; Plaza Necaxa 17; d/ste M$985/1116; ⓅⓈ✻@☎; ⓂInsurgentes) A good-value option in the pleasant and central Cuauhtémoc neighborhood, the Bristol caters primarily to business travelers, offering carpeted rooms with soothing colors and an above-average restaurant.

Hotel Geneve HOTEL $$$

(Map p106; ☑55-5080-0800; www.hotelgeneve. com.mx; Londres 130; r incl breakfast M$2620, ste from M$3820; ⓅⓈ✻@☎; ⓂInsurgentes) This Zona Rosa institution strives to maintain a belle epoque ambience despite the globalized mishmash around it. The lobby exudes class, with dark wood paneling, oil canvases and high bookshelves. Rooms in the hotel's older rear section get a more pronounced colonial treatment, especially the 'vintage suites.'

Hotel Suites Amberes SUITES $$$

(Map p106; ☑55-5533-1306; www.suitesambres. com.mx; Amberes 64; d/tr/q M$2000/2500/2900; ⓅⓈ☎; ⓂInsurgentes) Sure to please families and small groups, the spacious suites here are basically large one- and two-bedroom apartments with fully equipped kitchens, dining rooms and sofa beds. Street-facing rooms have the added plus of balconies. On the top floor you'll find a sun deck, gym and sauna room.

Hotel Cityexpress BUSINESS HOTEL $$$

(Map p106; ☑55-1102-0280; www.cityexpress .com.mx; Havre 21; d/tw/ste incl breakfast M$1599/1693/1826; ⓅⓈ✻@☎; ⬚Hamburgo) The Cityexpress emphasizes comfort and functionality, but decor outshines the neutral-modern favored by most hotels in this price category.

Zona Rosa

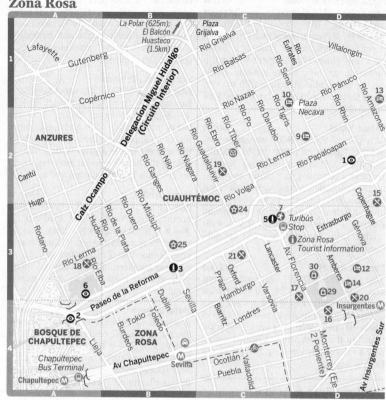

Condesa

Thanks to the recent appearance of several attractive lodgings, this neighborhood south of Bosque de Chapultepec makes an excellent base with plenty of after-hours restaurants, bars and cafes.

Stayinn Barefoot Hostel   HOSTEL $

(Map p82; ☎55-6286-3000; www.stayinnbarefoot.com; Juan Escutia 125; dm/d incl breakfast from M$250/750; ⊛🗠; Ⓜ Chapultepec) On the edge of Condesa, this artfully designed hostel is a breath of fresh air for a neighborhood lacking in budget accommodations. The cheerful lobby is done up in colorful mismatched tile floors and vintage furniture, while upstairs guests have use of a rooftop terrace. The Barefoot's welcoming mezcal bar seals the deal.

Hotel Roosevelt   HOTEL $$

(Map p82; ☎55-5208-6813; www.hotelroosevelt.com.mx; Av Insurgentes Sur 287, cnr Av Yucatán; d from M$770, ste M$1180; Ⓟ⊛🗠; 🚇 Álvaro Obregón) On the eastern limits of Condesa and within easy reach of the Cuban club district, this friendly if functional hotel should appeal to nocturnally inclined travelers. Most of the suites come with Jacuzzis and air-con.

★Red Tree House   B&B $$$

(Map p82; ☎55-5584-3829; www.theredtreehouse.com; Culiacán 6; s/d/ste incl breakfast from US$111/145/168; ⊛🗠; 🚇 Campeche) The area's first B&B has all the comforts of home, if your home happens to be decorated with exquisite taste. Each of the 17 bedrooms and suites is uniquely furnished, and the roomy penthouse has a private patio. Downstairs, guests have the run of a cozy living room and lovely rear garden, the domain of friendly pooch Abril.

Zona Rosa

◎ Sights

1 Centro Bursátil	D2
2 Centro de Cultura Digital	A4
Estela de Luz	(see 2)
3 La Diana Cazadora	B3
4 Monumento a Cuauhtémoc	F1
5 Monumento a la Independencia	C3
6 Torre Mayor	A3

◈ Activities, Courses & Tours

7 Bicitekas	C3

⊜ Sleeping

8 Capsule Hostel	E2
9 Casa González	D2
10 Hotel Bristol	C1
11 Hotel Cityexpress	E2
12 Hotel Geneve	D3
13 Hotel María Cristina	D1
14 Hotel Suites Amberes	D3

⊗ Eating

15 De Mar a Mar	D2
16 Fonda El Refugio	D4
17 King Falafel	D3
18 Primario	A3
19 Rokai	C2
20 Tezka	D3
21 Yug Vegetariano	C3

◉ Drinking & Nightlife

22 Buna 42	E4
23 Cantina Covadonga	E4
Nicho Bears & Bar	(see 17)

◉ Entertainment

24 Cinemex Casa de Arte	C3
25 Cinépolis Diana	B3
26 Patrick Miller	F3

⊕ Shopping

27 Fonart	F1
28 Jardín del Arte	E1
29 Mercado Insurgentes	D3
30 Plaza del Ángel	D3
31 Reforma 222	E2

The Red Tree also has five pleasant rooms in a house located a half-block away on Citlaltépetl.

★**Villa Condesa** BOUTIQUE HOTEL **$$$**
(Map p82; ☎55-5211-4892; www.villacondesa.
com.mx; Colima 428; r incl breakfast from US$155;
😊🛋; Ⓜ Chapultepec) You can say *adiós* to hectic Mexico City from the moment you set foot in the Villa's leafy lobby. The 14 rooms in this striking historic building combine classic touches (each has a piece of antique furniture) with the modern trappings of a first-rate hotel. Reservations required and children under 12 not allowed. Guests have free use of bicycles.

★**Casa Comtesse** B&B **$$$**
(Map p82; ☎55-5277-5418; www.casacomtesse.
com; Benjamín Franklin 197; r incl breakfast from M$1212; 🅿😊@🛋; 🚇 Escandón) Run by an amiable French owner, this 1940s historic building houses eight rooms adorned with tasteful art and furnishings and a parquet-floored dining area where guests mingle over breakfast. The Casa also has a graphic-arts gallery with interesting works by Mexican artists, and can arrange affordable tours to the Teotihuacán ruins.

🛏 Roma

Most of the places to stay in Roma are in the thick of things, with a slew of galleries, sidewalk cafes and bars within walking distance, and with party-central Condesa conveniently nearby, you'll find more than enough late-night distractions.

Hostel Home
HOSTEL $

(Map p82; ☑55-5511-1683; www.hostelhome. com.mx; Tabasco 303; dm incl breakfast M$190, r without bathroom M$500; ◉@☎; ◙Durango) Housed in a fine *porfiriato*-era building and managed by easygoing, English-speaking staff, this 20-bed hostel is on the narrow tree-lined Calle Tabasco, a gateway to the Roma neighborhood.

Hostel 333
HOSTEL $

(Map p82; ☑55-6840-6483; www.hostel333. com; Colima 333; dm incl breakfast M$170, d without bathroom M$500; @☎; ◙Durango) Guests revel in fiestas, barbecues and occasional gigs on a pleasant rooftop patio flanked by potted plants. Opt for standard-issue dorm rooms or private digs with shared bathroom.

Hotel Milán
HOTEL $$

(Map p82; ☑55-5584-0222; www.hotelmilan. com.mx; Álvaro Obregón 94; s/d M$575/605; P◉❄@☎; ◙Álvaro Obregón) Sitting on the main corridor of bohemian Roma, the Milán goes modern with minimalist decor and contemporary art in its lobby. In keeping with a recent makeover, upgraded rooms come with remodeled bathrooms.

Hotel Stanza
HOTEL $$

(Map p82; ☑55-5208-0052; www.stanzahotel. com; Álvaro Obregón 13; r/ste M$1040/1650; P◉❄@☎; ◙Jardín Pushkin) A business travelers' hotel at the east end of Álvaro Obregón, the Stanza has its own restaurant and gym and makes a cushy base in the heart of the hopping Roma neighborhood.

Casa de la Condesa
SUITES $$$

(Map p82; ☑55-5574-3186; www.extended staymexico.com; Plaza Luis Cabrera 16; ste incl breakfast from M$1500; ◉❄☎; ◙Álvaro Obregón) Right on the delightful Plaza Luis Cabrera, the Casa makes a tranquil base for visitors on an extended stay, offering 'suites' that are more like studio apartments with kitchens. See the website for weekly rates.

La Casona
BOUTIQUE HOTEL $$$

(Map p82; ☑55-5286-3001; www.hotellacasona. com.mx; Durango 280; r incl breakfast M$2618; ◉❄☎; ⓂSevilla) This stately mansion has been restored to its early-20th-century splendor to become one of the capital's most distinctive boutique hotels. Each of the 29 rooms is uniquely appointed to bring out its original charm.

🛏 Polanco

North of Bosque de Chapultepec, Polanco has excellent business and boutique hotel accommodations, but very little to offer if you're pinching pesos.

Casa Castelar
SUITES $$$

(Map p88; ☑55-5281-4990; www.casacastelar. com; Av Castelar 34; ste incl breakfast from US$119; ◉@☎; ⓂAuditorio) An affordable option by Polanco standards, the large comfy suites here give you plenty of bang for your buck. The recently remodeled Castelar has no common areas, but breakfast is served at your door. Chapultepec park's main sights are within walking distance.

Hábita Hotel
BOUTIQUE HOTEL $$$

(Map p88; ☑55-5282-3100; www.hotelnabita. com; Av Presidente Masaryk 201; d incl breakfast from US$221; P◉❄☎❄; ⓂPolanco) Architect Enrique Norten turned a functional apartment building into a smart boutique hotel. Decor in the 36 rooms is boldly minimalist and the most economical digs measure 20 sq meters (call them cozy or just plain small). The rooftop bar, called Área, is a hot nightspot.

W Mexico City
HOTEL $$$

(Map p88; ☑55-9138-1800; www.wmexicocity. com; Campos Elíseos 252; r from US$459 (Sun-Thu), US$272 (Fri & Sat); P◉❄@☎; ⓂAuditorio) One of the four sentinels opposite the Auditorio Nacional, this 25-floor business hotel is determined to break away from the stodginess of its neighbors. Cherry- and ebony-colored rooms feature silken hammocks hanging in the shower area. Rates drop considerably on Friday and Saturday.

🛏 Xochimilco

There's no better way to appreciate the natural wonders of Xochimilco's canals than to camp in the middle of it all.

Michmani
CAMPGROUND $

(☑55-5489-7773, cell 55-5591 4775; www. xochimilco.df.gob.mx; Embarcadero Cuemanco, off Anillo Periférico Sur; campsites per person incl tent M$150, cabin M$650; P) ✎ Ecotourism center Michmani arranges stays at La Llorona Cihuacoatl campground, which sits on a peaceful off-grid *chinampa*. The center rents tents, but you'll have to bring a sleeping bag, or you can stay in a tiny rustic cabin with two beds. Also available are barbecue grills and temascals (steam baths; M$250).

To get here, go to metro General Anaya and exit the station on the east side of Calzada de Tlalpan, then walk 50m north to catch a 'Tláhuac Paradero' pesero. Get off at the Embarcadero Cuemanco entrance and walk about 1km to Michmani, just beyond the *embarcadero*. From there a boat will take you to La Llorona.

Coyoacán & Ciudad Universitaria

The southern community has limited budget options and several appealing guesthouses. Check with the Coyoacán tourist office (p132) about short-term homestays.

El Cenote Azul — HOSTEL $
(55-5554-8730; Alfonso Pruneda 24, Colonia Copilco el Alto; dm M$250; M Copilco) This laid-back hostel near the UNAM campus has six neatly kept four- or two-bed rooms sharing three Talavera-tiled bathrooms. Monthly deals are available (M$2500). The downstairs bar of the same name is a popular hangout for university students. It's tucked away off Privada Ezequiel Ordoñes.

Hostal Cuija Coyoacán — HOSTEL $
(Map p122; 55-5659-9310; www.hostalcuija coyoacan.com; Berlín 268; dm/d incl breakfast M$240/750; M Coyoacán) This lizard-themed (for the roaming critters in the garden) HI hostel offers a clean and affordable base to check out Coyoacán's nearby sights. The house has pleasant common areas, but don't expect the smallish dorms and private rooms to wow you.

★ Chalet del Carmen — GUESTHOUSE $$
(Map p122; 55-5554-9572; www.chalet delcarmen.com; Guerrero 94; s/d/ste from M$877/1177/1477; M Coyoacán) Run by a friendly Coyoacán native and his Swiss wife, this ecofriendly house strikes a warm blend of Mexican and European aesthetics. On offer are five rooms and two suites with antique furnishings and brilliant natural lighting. Guests have use of a kitchen and bicycles. Reservations a must.

Hostal Frida — GUESTHOUSE $$
(Map p122; 55-5659-7005; www.hostalfrida byb.com; Mina 54; d/tr M$650/870; M Coyoacán) Don't let the 'hostal' tag fool you: this family-run place has well-appointed accommodations more along the lines of a guesthouse. Each of the six wooden-floored doubles occupies its own level in adjacent structures, and three come with kitchens. Wi-fi is fast.

Airport

Hotel Aeropuerto — HOTEL $$
(55-5785-5318; www.hotelaeropuerto.com.mx; Blvd Puerto Aéreo 380; d/tw M$640/770; M Terminal Aérea) Although there are several upscale hotels linked to the terminals, this affordable hotel across the street serves just fine for weary travelers. The only nonchain in the zone, it has helpful reception staff and neutral modern rooms, some overlooking the airport runway through soundproof windows.

Turn left outside the domestic terminal, and beyond the metro take a left onto Blvd Puerto Aéreo and cross via the pedestrian bridge.

Eating

The capital offers eateries for all tastes and budgets, from soulful taco stalls to gourmet restaurants. In recent years the city has emerged as a major destination for culinary travelers, as Mexican chefs win the sort of praise formerly reserved for their counterparts in New York and Paris. Even street food has been taken off the streets and dressed up for a growing trend of boutique food trucks, gourmet markets and converted buildings. Most of the hottest venues for contemporary cuisine show up in Roma, Condesa and Polanco.

Budget eaters will find literally thousands of restaurants and holes-in-the-wall serving *comida corrida* (set lunch) for as little as M$50. Market buildings are good places to look for these, while *tianguis* (street markets) customarily have eating areas offering tacos and quesadillas.

Certain items can be found all over town. In the evening, vendors roam the streets on bicycles selling hot *tamales,* their arrival heralded by nasal-toned recordings through cheap speakers. You'll know the *camote* (sweet potato) man is coming by the shrill steam whistle emitted from his cart, heard for blocks around.

Centro Histórico

The historic center is a great place to enjoy traditional Mexican dishes in elegant surroundings.

AROUND MEXICO ON A PLATE

The big city has long attracted opportunity seekers from all over the republic. Fortunately, these folks from Mérida, Chiapas, Jalisco and Guerrero strive to keep their traditions alive, first and foremost in the kitchen.

Con Sabor a Tixtla (Map p82; www.consaboratixtla.com; Chiapas 206, Colonia Roma; tacos M$25, mains M$85-135; ⊙1-6pm Mon & Tue, 10am-6pm Wed-Sun; ⊖♪; ▣Sonora) The home-cooked goodness of retired school teacher Enedina Bello González draws on two generations of family recipes from Tixtla, Guerrero. Specialties in this colorful Roma eatery include *pozole* (hominy soup) and *chiles rellenos tradicionales de Tixtla* (Tixtla-style stuffed chilies).

La Polar (☑55-5546-5066; www.lapolar.mx; Guillermo Prieto 129, Colonia San Rafael; birria M$120; ⊙7am-2am; ⊖; MNormal) Run by a family from Ocotlán, Jalisco, this boisterous beer hall has essentially one item on the menu: *birria,* a spiced goat stew. Spirits are raised further by mariachis and *norteño* combos who work the half-dozen salons here.

Coox Hanal (Map p68; ☑55-5709-3613; 2nd fl, Isabel La Católica 83, Colonia Centro; mains M$48-120; ⊙10:30am-6:30pm; ⊖☎; MIsabel La Católica) Started in 1953 by boxer Raúl Salazar from Mérida, this establishment prepares top-notch Yucatecan fare such as *poc chuc* (grilled pork marinated in orange juice) and *cochinita pibil* (pit-cooked pork). Then there's the obligatory four-alarm *habanero* salsa.

Los Tolucos (Hernández y Dávalos 40, cnr Bolívar, Colonia Algarín; pozoles M$64-79; ⊙10am-9pm; ⊖; MLázaro Cárdenas) Voted the best *pozole* in a Mexico City radio station contest. The Guerrero-style green *pozole* here has been drawing people from far and wide for more than four decades. The restaurant is three blocks east of metro Lázaro Cárdenas.

Tamales Chiapanecos María Geraldine (Map p122; ☑55-5608-8993; Plaza Hidalgo, Coyoacán; tamales M$35; ⊙10am-10pm Sat & Sun; MCoyoacán) At the passageway next to the San Juan Bautista church, look for these incredible *tamales* by Chiapas native doña María Geraldine. Wrapped in banana leaves, they're stuffed with ingredients such as olives, prunes and almonds, and laced with sublime salsas.

★ **Los Cocuyos** TAQUERÍA $
(Map p68; Bolívar 54; tacos M$10-15; ⊙10am-6am; MSan Juan de Letrán) *Suadero* (beef) tacos abound in the capital, but this place reigns supreme. Follow your nose to the bubbling vat of meats and go for the artery-choking *campechano,* a mixed beef and sausage taco. For the more adventurous eater, there are *ojo* (eye) or *lengua* (tongue) tacos.

Café El Popular CAFE $
(Map p68; ☑55-5518-6081; www.cafeelpopular.com.mx; Av 5 de Mayo 52; breakfast M$63; ⊙24hr; ⊖♪; MAllende) So popular was this tiny round-the-clock cafe that another more amply proportioned branch was opened next door. Fresh pastries, *café con leche* (coffee with milk) and good combination breakfasts are the main attractions.

Los Vegetarianos VEGETARIAN $
(Map p68; ☑55-5521-6880; Av Madero 56; set lunch M$75-95; ⊙8am-8pm; ⊖♪; MZócalo) De-spite its austere entrance, this is a lively upstairs restaurant where a pianist plinks out old favorites. The meatless menu includes a range of tasty variations on Mexican standards, such as *chile en nogada* (stuffed green chilies) filled with soymeat, and there are vegan options as well.

La Casa del Pavo SANDWICHES $
(Map p68; ☑55-5518-4282; Motolinía 40; tortas M$40; ⊙9am-9pm; ⊖; MAllende) Tasty *tortas de pavo* (turkey sandwiches) with avocado are served hot off the griddle at this old-school greasy spoon.

Mercado San Camilito MARKET $
(Map p68; Plaza Garibaldi; pozoles M$65-80; ⊙24hr; ⊖; MGaribaldi) This block-long building contains more than 70 kitchens preparing, among other items, Jalisco-style *pozole,* a broth brimming with hominy kernels and pork, served with garnishes such as radish and oregano – specify *maciza* (meat) if pig noses and ears fail to excite you.

★ **Hostería de Santo Domingo** MEXICAN $$
(Map p68; ☑ 55-5526-5276; www.hosteriade
santodomingo.mx; Belisario Domínguez 72; chile en
nogada M$220, mains M$80-250; ⊙ 9am-10:30pm
Mon-Sat, to 9pm Sun; ⊜ 🖰; 🖵 República de Chile)
Whipping up classic Mexican fare since
1860, Mexico City's oldest restaurant has a
festive atmosphere, enhanced by live piano
music. The menu offers numerous dishes,
but everyone comes here for the *chile en
nogada* (an enormous *poblano* chili pepper
stuffed with ground meat, dried fruit and
bathed in a creamy walnut sauce). Beware:
rumor has it the building is haunted.

Al Andalus MIDDLE EASTERN $$
(Map p68; ☑ 55-5522-2528; m_andalus171@
yahoo.com.mx; Mesones 171; shawarma M$80,
mains M$150-220; ⊙ 9am-6pm; 🖳 Pino
Suárez) In a superb colonial mansion in
the Merced textile district, Al Andalus caters to
the capital's substantial Lebanese community with old standbys such as shawarma,
kebab and falafel.

Café de Tacuba MEXICAN $$
(Map p68; ☑ 55-5518-4950; www.cafedetacuba.
com.mx; Tacuba 28; mains M$98-280, 4-course
lunches M$245; ⊙ 8am-11:30pm; ⊜ 🖰; 🖳 Allende)
Before the band there was the restaurant. Way
before. A fantasy of colored tiles, brass lamps
and oil paintings, this mainstay has served
antojitos (snacks such as tacos and *sopes* –
corn tortillas layered with beans, cheese and
other ingredients) since 1912. Lively *estudian-
tinas* (student musical groups) entertain the
dinner crowd Wednesday through Sunday.

Restaurante Chon MEXICAN $$
(Map p68; ☑ 55-5542-0873; Regina 160; appe-
tizers M$20-260, mains M$160-250; ⊙ 11am-7pm;
⊜ 🖰; 🖳 Pino Suárez) Pre-Hispanic fare is the
specialty of this cantina-style restaurant.
Sample *maguey* (agave) worms, *chapulines*
(grasshoppers) and *escamoles* (ant larvae).
Wash it all down with flavored *pulque* (a
fermented agave drink, aka 'the blood of the
gods'). Menu items such as crocodile and gar
are farm raised.

Casino Español SPANISH $$
(Map p68; ☑ 55-5521-8894; www.casinoespanol
demexico.com; Isabel La Católica 29; 4-course
lunches M$150; ⊙ 1-6pm Mon-Fri, restaurant
also 8am-noon daily; ⊜ 🖰; 🖳 Zócalo) The old
Spanish social center, housed in a fabu-
lous *porfiriato*-era building, has a popular
mesón (cantina-style eatery) downstairs,
where the courses keep coming, and an

elegant restaurant upstairs, which features
classic Spanish fare such as *paella valencia-
na* (paella Valencia-style).

★ **El Cardenal** MEXICAN $$$
(Map p68; ☑ 55-5521-8815; www.restaurante
elcardenal.com; Palma 23; breakfast M$72-90,
lunch & dinner M$130-250; ⊙ 8am-6:30pm; ⊜ 🖰;
🖳 Zócalo) Possibly the finest place in town
for a traditional meal, El Cardenal occupies
three floors of a Parisian-style mansion and
has a pianist playing sweetly in the background. Breakfast is a must, served with a
tray of just-baked sweet rolls and a pitcher
of frothy, semisweet chocolate. For lunch
the house specialty is the *pecho de ternera*
(oven-roasted veal breast).

The latest branch, **El Cardenal San Ángel** (Map p94; Av de la Paz 32; ⊙ 8am-6pm
Mon-Sat, from 9am Sun; 🖰; 🖳 La Bombilla), is in
the south.

Los Girasoles MEXICAN $$$
(Map p68; ☑ 55-5510-0630; www.restaurante
losgirasoles.com; Plaza Tolsá; mains M$175-239;
⊙ 8:30am-9pm Sun & Mon, to 10:30pm Tue-Sat;
⊜ 🖰; 🖳 Allende) This fine restaurant over-
looking the grand Plaza Tolsá boasts an
encyclopedic range of Mexican fare, from
pre-Hispanic-style ant larvae and grass-
hoppers to contemporary dishes such as
red snapper encrusted with *huanzontle*
flowers.

La Casa de las Sirenas MEXICAN $$$
(Map p68; ☑ 55-5704-3345; www.lacasadelas
sirenas.com.mx; República de Guatemala 32; mains
M$240-310; ⊙ 11am-11pm Mon-Sat, to 7pm Sun;
⊜ 🖰; 🖳 Zócalo) Housed in a 17th-century relic, Sirenas has a top-floor terrace that looks
toward the Zócalo via the Plaza del Templo
Mayor. It's an ideal perch to enjoy regional
dishes prepared with contemporary flair,
such as chicken bathed in pumpkin seed
mole (a type of chili sauce).

🍴 Alameda Central & Around

Though places on the immediate pe-
rimeter of the Alameda cater to tourists,
head down Luis Moya or along Ayuntamiento, south of the Alameda, for pockets
of the neighborhood's rustic heritage in
the form of *torta* (sandwich) stands and
chicken-soup vendors. Mexico City's modest
Barrio Chino (Chinatown) covers a single
paper-lantern-strung block of Calle Dolores,
one block south of the park, but its mediocre
restaurants are best avoided.

El Huequito
TAQUERÍA $

(Map p68; www.elhuequito.com.mx; Ayuntamiento 21; tacos al pastor M$16; ◷9:30am-10pm Mon-Sat, 10:30am-8:30pm Sun; 🚇Plaza San Juan) These old pros have been churning out delectable *tacos al pastor* (marinated pork roasted on a spit) since 1959. Several downtown Huequito branches offer the sit-down experience, but for some reason (the added touch of street grime, perhaps?) the tacos are better here at the original hole-in-the-wall location.

Mi Fonda
SPANISH $

(Map p68; ☎55-5521-0002; López 101; paella M$75; ◷11am-5pm Tue-Sun; ☺; 🚇Plaza San Juan) Working-class *chilangos* line up for their share of *paella valenciana*, made fresh daily and patiently ladled out by women in white bonnets. Jesús from Cantabria oversees the proceedings.

El Cuadrilátero
SANDWICHES $

(Map p76; ☎55-5510-2856; Luis Moya 73; tortas M$73-93; ◷7am-8pm Mon-Sat; ☺; 🚇Plaza San Juan) Owned by wrestler Super Astro, this *torta* joint features a shrine to *lucha libre* (Mexican wrestling) masks. The mother of all *tortas*, the 1.3kg cholesterol-packed Torta Gladiador (egg, sausage, bacon, beef, chicken and hot dog) is free if you can gobble it in 15 minutes – only 99 people have managed it in 23 years.

El 123
ASIAN $$

(Map p76; ☎55-5512-1772; www.123comidatienda.com; Artículo 123; mains M$80-135; ◷9am-9pm Sun-Wed, to 11pm Thu-Sat; ☺🛜✎; Ⓜ Juárez) Good Japanese, Thai and Vietnamese food like this is rare in the *centro*. Equally so, this cafe/restaurant/gift shop's cool antique-store design, which reveals its relationship to the sister Mog restaurants in Roma. The same dependable sushi, green curry and green-tea *mochi* (glutinous rice cake) ice creams stand out here. Cash only.

✖ Plaza de la República & Around

Gotan Restaurante
ARGENTINE $$

(Map p76; ☎55-5535-2136; Baranda 17, Colonia Tabacalera; mains M$69-199; ◷10am-8:30pm Mon-Fri; ☺🛜; 🚇Plaza de la República) One of the best and most authentic Argentine restaurants in town, owned by a kind Buenos Aires native and her Mexican husband. It's all about the details here: bread is baked daily and the meats and other key ingredients are imported from Argentina. Don't leave without trying the *postre de la nonna*, a delightful caramel custard.

✖ Zona Rosa & Around

While the Zona Rosa is packed with places to eat and drink, with few exceptions the area is dominated by uninspiring 'international' fare and fast-food franchises. North of Paseo de la Reforma, many new restaurants and bars are cropping up in the Colonia Cuauhtémoc.

Yug Vegetariano
VEGETARIAN $

(Map p106; ☎55-5333-3296; www.lovevegetariano.com; Varsovia 3; buffet lunches M$90, mains M$59-71; ◷7am-9pm Mon-Fri, 8:30am-8pm Sat & Sun; ☺🛜✎; Ⓜ Sevilla) The menu is tastebud heaven for vegetarians and vast enough for most carnivorous folk to find something they fancy. Choose from specialties such as squash-flower crepes, or go the lunch-buffet route.

King Falafel
MIDDLE EASTERN $

(Map p106; ☎55-5514-9030; Londres 178; falafel & salads M$65; ◷10am-7pm Mon-Fri, noon-6pm Sat; ☺🛜✎; Ⓜ Insurgentes) Run by an English-speaking Syrian Jew, this small eatery has a vegetarian-friendly menu of falafel in pita bread, mixed salads, tabbouleh and fresh hummus.

Primario
MEXICAN $$

(Map p106; ☎55-6840-7528; www.primariomx.com; Río Elba 31; mains M$80, menú del día M$150; ◷9am-6pm Mon-Sat; ☺🛜; Ⓜ Sevilla) This food truck turned modern Mexican restaurant still has the flavors right. Set menus are good, but it's worth squeezing in the standout starter – *gordita* of crab *al pibil* – before digging into a smoked marlin *tlayuda* (Mexican pizza).

Rokai
JAPANESE $$$

(Map p106; ☎55-5207-7543; Río Ebro 87, Colonia Cuauhtémoc; tasting menu lunch/dinner M$420/480; ◷1:30-5pm & 7-11pm Mon-Sat; ☺🛜; Ⓜ Insurgentes) Rokai takes Japanese food to a new level in Mexico City. Tokyo-born, Los Angeles-raised chef Hiroshi Kawahito recommends the 'omakase,' a changing tasting menu consisting of meticulously prepared dishes such as sushi and sashimi. Each course (there are nine for dinner) leaves you wanting more. As a rule, Kawahito only works with fresh fish and seafood.

Reserve ahead.

De Mar a Mar
SEAFOOD **$$$**

(Map p106; ☑55-5207-5730; www.demaramar. mx; Niza 13; mains M$160-260; ⊙1-10pm Mon-Sat, 11am-6pm Sun; ⊜☎; ⬚Hamburgo) One of the Zona Rosa's best restaurants, the menu here was designed by chef Eduardo Garcia, a rising star on the Mexico City culinary scene. All dishes, especially the ceviches and *tostadas* (baked or fried tortillas), stand out for their fresh ingredients, and dessert is a slice of heaven.

Fonda El Refugio
MEXICAN **$$$**

(Map p106; ☑55-5525-8128; www.fondaelrefugio. com; Liverpool 166; dishes M$120-240; ⊙1-10:30pm; ⊜☎✐; ⓂInsurgentes) Amid a collection of colorful pots and whimsical ceramic ornaments, the family-run *fonda* (inn), operating since 1954, serves Mexican favorites such as *mole poblano* (chicken in a chocolate-based sauce) and *chiles rellenos* (chilies stuffed with ground beef).

Tezka
INTERNATIONAL **$$$**

(Map p106; ☑55-9149-3000; www.tezka.com. mx; Amberes 78; mains M$219-440, tasting menu M$520; ⊙1-5pm & 8-11pm Mon-Fri, 1-6pm Sat & Sun; ⊜☎; ⓂInsurgentes) Specializing in contemporary Basque cuisine, Tezka ranks among Mexico City's finest restaurants. The regularly changing menu features elaborately prepared dishes such as rack of lamb, or you can dabble in the four-course tasting menu (two appetizers, a main dish and dessert).

✗ Condesa

La Condesa has dozens upon dozens of informal bistros and cafes – many with sidewalk tables – competing for business along several key streets. The neighborhood's restaurant zone is at the convergence of Michoacán, Vicente Suárez and Tamaulipas; many good establishments ring Parque México.

Tacos Don Juan
TAQUERÍA **$**

(Map p82; cnr Atlixco & Juan Escutia; tacos M$17-25; ⊙10am-5pm Mon-Fri, to 3pm Sat & Sun; ⊜; ⬚Campeche) A seriously good taco joint that's usually swarming with locals. The offerings vary daily: on Friday and Saturday it's all about the *carnitas* (deep-fried pork) and on Sunday you can rely on an old standby – *bistec con longaniza* (beef with sausage) topped with whole beans.

El Pescadito
SEAFOOD **$**

(Map p82; Atlixco 38; tacos M$30; ⊙11am-6pm Mon-Fri, from 10am Sat & Sun; ⬚Campeche) This bright-yellow taco joint is unmissable for the queue waiting for a (folding) seat. Nearly all nine fish/shrimp fillings are battered, Sonora style, for maximum crispy, juicy flavor. Pescadito's signature taco, *'quesotote'* – a chili stuffed with shrimp and cheese – is worth holding out for.

El Califa
TAQUERÍA **$**

(Map p82; ☑55-5271-7666; www.elcalifa.com. mx; Altata 22; tacos M$29-75; ⊙noon-4am; ⊜☎; ⓂChilpancingo) This popular taco shop puts its own spin on the classic snack, grilling slices of beef and tossing them on handmade tortillas. Tables are set with a palette of savory salsas. A favorite for best tacos around, though opening late helps.

Orígenes Orgánicos
ORGANIC **$$**

(Map p82; ☑55-5208-6678; www.origenes organicos.com; Plaza Popocatépetl 41A; mains M$113-181; ⊙8:30am-9:30pm Mon-Fri, 9am-6:30pm Sat & Sun; ⊜☎✐; ⬚Sonora) More than just a place to buy soy milk and certified organic produce, this store-cafe facing one of Condesa's loveliest plazas prepares tasty meals with an emphasis on seasonal, organic ingredients. Vegetarians and vegans have a glut of options.

Ojo de Agua
HEALTH FOOD **$$**

(Map p82; ☑55-6395-8000; cnr Citlaltépetl & Amsterdam; salads & sandwiches M$95-155; ⊙8am-10pm Mon-Thu, to 9pm Fri-Sun; ☎✐; ⓂChilpancingo) ✐ Missing those greens in Mexico City? Exciting salads with salmon steak or grilled apple and turkey keep this organic grocery-store cafe full of those who want to keep beautiful. The interesting juices and location next to a plaza and fountain are equally attractive.

Taj Mahal
INDIAN **$$**

(Map p88; www.tajmahaldf.com; Francisco Márquez 134; mains M$120-190; ⊙1-10pm Sun-Wed, to 11pm Thu-Sat; ⊜☎✐; ⓂJuanacatlán) A hard-working Bangladeshi man who used to roam the Condesa selling clothes out of a suitcase now has his own restaurant specializing in Indian cuisine. Vegetarians will find many options here, including garlic naan, vegetable biryani and flavored yogurt drinks.

Café La Gloria
FRENCH **$$**

(Map p82; ☑55-5211-4185; Vicente Suárez 41; mains M$95-190; ⊙noon-midnight Mon-Thu, to 1am Fri-Sun; ⊜☎✐; ⓂCampeche) A hip bistro in the heart of the zone, La Gloria remains a popular meeting place thanks to the reliably good salads, zesty pastas and quirky art on display.

La Rambla
STEAK $$

(Map p82; Ometusco s/n, btwn Av Baja California & Benjamín Hill; mains M$65-165; 1:30-9:30pm Mon-Thu, to 11:30pm Fri & Sat, 1-6pm Sun; Escandón) Owned by a Montevideo native, this intimate Uruguayan steakhouse grills tender cuts such as *milanesa de res* (breaded steak) and does vegetarian pizzas for nonmeat eaters, all at reasonable prices.

Lampuga
SEAFOOD $$$

(Map p82; 55-5286-1525; www.lampuga.com.mx; Ometusco 1, cnr Av Nuevo León; mains M$162-297; 1:30pm-2am Mon-Sat, to 6pm Sun; Chilpancingo) Fresh seafood is the focus at this appealing bistro. Tuna *tostadas* make great starters, as does the smoked marlin carpaccio. For a main course, have the catch of the day grilled over coals.

Pablo El Erizo
SEAFOOD $$$

(Map p82; www.pabloelerizo.com; Montes de Oca 6; mains M$160-230, tacos & appetizers M$75-150; 1-7pm Mon & Tue, to 10pm Wed-Sat; Campeche) Inspired by Baja California cuisine, this bistro has a knack for creating exceptional seafood dishes, such as seared tuna *tostadas* topped with crispy leek and Ensenada-style shrimp tacos.

La Capital
MEXICAN $$$

(Map p82; 55-5256-5159; Av Nuevo León 137; mains M$115-195; 1pm-midnight Mon-Wed, to 2am Thu-Sat, to 7pm Sun; Chilpancingo) Riding the latest 'cantina chic' (oxymoron?) wave, the Capital does traditional Mexican fare with a gourmet twist. Try the chili-encrusted tuna or the duck enchiladas.

Roma

Cantina Riviera
MEXICAN $

(Map p82; 55-5264-1552; Chiapas 174; tacos M$20-35; 1pm-2am; Sonora) A grand, converted cantina with rediscovered Mexican food and mezcal was bound to attract hipsters, justifiably. The golden *taco de lechón asado* (roast pork) and excellent *panuchos* (fried tortillas stuffed with beans and topped with pulled chicken) are favorites that make locals feel a cinematic nostalgia for old Mexico.

El Parnita
MEXICAN $

(Map p82; 55-5264-7551; www.elparnita.com; Av Yucatán 84; tacos M$25-38, tortas M$44-62; 1:30-6pm Tue-Sun; Sonora) What be-

gan as a small street stall has morphed into a see-and-be-seen restaurant in the Roma. This lunch-only establishment keeps it simple with a small menu of tried-and-true family recipes such as the *carmelita* (shrimp tacos with handmade tortillas) and the *viajero* (slow-cooked pork) taco. Reserve ahead for Saturday and Sunday.

Panadería Rosetta
BAKERY $

(Map p82; 55-5207-2976; Colima 179; bread M$20-45, baguettes M$24-75; 7am-8pm Mon-Sat, to 6pm Sun; Durango) Sublime sweet bread and baguettes are made fresh daily at this small bakery, with a bench for coffee and sandwiches, owned by chef Elena Reygadas, sister of award-winning Mexican filmmaker Carlos Reygadas.

Por Siempre Vegana Taquería
VEGAN $

(Map p82; cnr Manzanillo & Chiapas; tacos M$15; 6pm-midnight Mon-Sat; Sonora) Vegans can join in the street-food action with soy and gluten taco versions of *al pastor, loganiza* and chorizo. The late-night experience is complete with self-serve tubs of toppings – potato, *nopales* (cactus paddles), beans and salsas. There are also dairy-free cakes and Oaxacan ice cream.

Helado Obscuro
ICE CREAM $

(Map p82; 55-4444-4878; Córdoba 223; ice cream M$20-30; 11am-9pm Mon & Tue, to 10pm Wed-Sat, to 7pm Sun; Dr Márquez) Take a summery walk on the 'dark side' trying some alcohol-spiked ice cream. Concoctions with titillating names include the Mariachi en Bikini, with coconut milk, soursop and mezcal. Inventive flavors include tequila, wine, sake, whiskey cream and other tipples. Or go vanilla with dairy- and alcohol-free options. There is also a branch inside Mercado Roma (p114).

★ El Hidalguense
MEXICAN $$

(Map p82; 55-5564-0538; Campeche 155; mains M$75-220; 7am-6pm Fri-Sun; Campeche) Slow-cooked over aged oak wood in an underground pit, the Hidalgo-style *barbacoa* at this family-run eatery is off-the-charts delectable. Get things started with a rich consommé or *queso asado* (grilled cheese with herbs), then move on to the tacos. Top it off on a warm and fuzzy note, sampling the flavored *pulques*. Cash only.

Mercado Roma
MARKET $$

(Map p82; http://mercadoroma.com; Querétaro 225; snacks M$20-150; 9am-8pm Sun-Wed, to

11pm Thu-Sat; ✒; 🖳Sonora) Weekends at this gourmet food hall resemble a red-carpet event of well-to-do families and the best dressed (it has featured in top fashion mags). It is indeed an impressive, if cramped, space to meet, eat and drink. The nibbles are top-notch, representing a best-of from around town – Wagyu beef tacos, Mexican cheese, tapas, burrito-sushi, Vietnamese rolls and fine burgers.

The 'market' element brings fine ingredients to local pantries – spices, seafood, hams and hard-to-find items. Don't miss the Portuguese custard tarts, or the adjacent French bakery with Paris-good baguettes and pastries.

Cabrera 7   MEXICAN **$$**
(Map p82; ✒ 55-5264-4531; Plaza Luis Cabrera 7; mains M$139-247; ☉1-11pm Sun-Tue, to midnight Wed, to 2am Thu-Sat; ☕☎; 🖳Álvaro Obregón) The view here draws people as much as the food. Multiple spaces each have their own personality and occasion. The most impressive looks onto Plaza Luis Cabrera with its glittering fountain. A perfect accompaniment to incredible appetizers – *tacos baja* (hefty tempura prawns with a smoky mayo), or *cochinita pibil* (marinated pork) – that even outshine the mains.

Ciénega   COLOMBIAN **$$**
(Map p82; ✒ 55-5564-2255; Coahuila 200; mains M$100-130; ☉10am-7pm; ☕☎; 🖳Campeche) The background music of accordion-driven *vallenatos* (folk music) sets a feel-good mood at this popular Colombian comfort-food restaurant. Colombian expats go straight for the *sancocho* and *ajiaco* dishes, hearty stews just like *mamá* used to make.

★Maximo Bistrot Local   FUSION **$$$**
(Map p82; ✒ 55-5264-4291; www.maximobistrot. com.mx; Tonalá 133; mains M$170-350; ☉1-11pm Tue-Sat, to 7pm Sun; ☕) If there's one place that best represents Mexico City's exciting new culinary scene, it's Maximo Bistrot. The constantly changing menu, which draws on European and Mexican recipes, features fresh, seasonal ingredients. Best of all – the place is totally unpretentious. Owner/chef Eduardo García honed his cooking skills at Pujol (p115) under the tutelage of famed chef Enrique Olvera. Reservations a must.

Contramar   SEAFOOD **$$$**
(Map p82; ✒ 55-5514-9217; www.contramar. com.mx; Durango 200; appetizers M$105-225, mains M$205-300; ☉12:30-6:30pm Sun-Thu, to

8pm Fri & Sat; ☕☎; 🖳Durango) Seafood is the star attraction at this stylish dining hall with a seaside ambience. The specialty is tuna fillet Contramar-style – split, swabbed with red chili and parsley sauces and grilled to perfection. Also a standout is the tuna *tostada*, topped with crispy onions. Reservations recommended.

Yuban   MEXICAN **$$$**
(Map p82; www.yuban.mx; Colima 268; appetizers M$80-120, mains M$180-268; ☉1:30-11pm Tue-Thu, to 11:30pm Fri & Sat, to 6pm Sun; ☕☎; 🖳Durango) Savor the authentic flavors of Oaxaca, including exquisite *moles* and *tlayudas* (large tortillas folded over chorizo and cheese), *chapulin* tacos and some darn-good mezcals. An adjoining venue stages plays and screens Mexican indie flicks.

🍴 Bosque de Chapultepec & Polanco

Polanco is home to the signature restaurants of several of Mexico City's internationally hot chefs. Other places here present excellent regional cuisine from the Mexican coast.

★Pujol   MEXICAN **$$$**
(Map p88; ✒ 55-5545-4111; www.pujol.com.mx; Petrarca 254; menú degustación M$1495; ☉2-4pm & 6:30-11:30pm Mon-Sat; ☕; Ⓜ Polanco) Arguably Mexico's best gourmet restaurant, Pujol offers a contemporary take on classic Mexican dishes in a smartly minimalist setting. Famed chef Enrique Olvera regularly reinvents the menu, which is presented as a *menú degustación,* a multiple-course tasting extravaganza. It might take up to several weeks to get a table here, so reserve well ahead of time.

★Quintonil   MEXICAN **$$$**
(Map p88; ✒ 55-5280-1660; www.quintonil.com; Newton 55; mains M$395, menú degustación M$1100; ☉1-5pm & 7-11pm Mon-Sat; ☕☎) This contemporary innovator made the Top 50 Restaurants in the World list for creatively showcasing traditional Mexican dishes. Former Pujol chef Jorge Vallejo gives local, organic ingredients starring roles – which dazzle when Wagyu beef meets an opulent *pulque* and chile seco reduction; and elevate crab *tostadas* to a smoky revelation. It pays off, shining a spotlight on Mexico's culinary ascendancy.

Book weeks ahead.

Dulce Patria   MEXICAN $$$

(Map p88; ☑ 55-3300-3999; www.dulcepatria mexico.com; Anatole France 100; mains M$300-450; ⊘1:30-11:30pm Mon-Sat, to 5:30pm Sun; ⊝☏; ⓂPolanco) Cookbook author Martha Ortiz launched this restaurant several years ago after taking a brief sabbatical, and it certainly lives up to her high standards, in spite of some unfortunate interior-design choices. Reinvented traditional Mexican dishes such as *mole* enchiladas stuffed with plantain are deftly plated and delicious.

San Ángel

Barbacoa de Santiago   MEXICAN $

(Map p94; ☑ 55-5616-5983; Plaza San Jacinto 23; tacos & flautas M$30; ⊘9:30am-7pm Sun-Fri, 8:30am-7:30pm Sat; ⓆLa Bombilla) A quick and affordable *taquería* off the plaza, this place is known for its *barbacoa* and *flautas ahogadas* (fried rolled tacos dipped in a *chile pasilla* and *pulque* sauce).

Fonda San Ángel   MEXICAN $$

(Map p94; ☑ 55-5550-1942; www.fondasanangel. com.mx; Plaza San Jacinto 3; breakfast buffet M$185; ⊘9am-midnight Mon-Sat, to 7pm Sun; ⊝☏; ⓆLa Bombilla) On Saturday and Sunday, this attractive restaurant by the plaza does an abundant breakfast buffet with all kinds of egg dishes, pastries and freshly squeezed juices, plus great quesadillas.

Cluny   FRENCH $$

(Map p94; ☑ 55-5550-7350; www.cluny.com. mx; Av de la Paz 57; mains M$98-220, menu prix fixe M$220; ⊘12:30pm-midnight Mon-Sat, to 11pm Sun; ⊝☏; ⓆLa Bombilla) For unpretentious French cuisine, this bistro located in an open-air shopping center hits the spot. Quiches, salads, crepes, decadently delicious desserts and generous portions are the order of the day.

Taberna del León   MEXICAN $$$

(Map p94; ☑ 55-5616-2110; Altamirano 46; dishes M$195-395; ⊘1:30-11:30pm Mon-Wed, to midnight Thu-Sat, to 6pm Sun; ⊝☏; ⓆDr Gálvez) Chef Monica Patiño is one of the new breed of female stars stirring up traditional cuisine in innovative ways. Seafood is the specialty here, with the likes of *robalo a los tres chiles* (bass in three-pepper chili sauce) and corn blini with Norwegian salmon.

San Ángel Inn   MEXICAN $$$

(Map p94; ☑ 55-5616-1402; www.sanangelinn. com; Diego Rivera 50; breakfast M$74-120, lunch & dinner M$170-395; ⊘7am-1pm Mon-Fri, 8:30am-1pm Sat, to 10pm Sun; ⊝☏▨; ⓆAltavista) Classic Mexican meals are served in the garden and various elegant dining rooms of this historic estate next to the Museo Casa Estudio Diego Rivera y Frida Kahlo. On Saturday and Sunday mornings, the Inn provides activities for kids in the rear garden, meaning it's margarita time for mom and dad.

Montejo   YUCATECAN $$$

(Map p94; ☑ 55-5550-1366; Av de la Paz 16; mains M$155-275; ⊘1-10pm; ⊝☏; ⓆLa Bombilla) Along a cobbled street lined with restaurants, this inconspicuous Yucatecan establishment whips up regional favorites such as *sopa de lima* (lime soup), *cochinita pibil* and *papadzules* (tortillas stuffed with diced hard-boiled eggs and bathed in pumpkin-seed sauce).

Ciudad Universitaria

Azul y Oro   MEXICAN $$$

(☑ 55-5622-7135; www.azul.rest; Centro Cultural Universitario; mains M$150-300; ⊘1pm-1:30am Mon-Sat, to 6pm Sun; ⊝☏; ⓆCentro Cultural Universitario) Chef Ricardo Muñoz searches high and low in Mexico for traditional recipes and reinvents them to perfection. Fruits of his labor include *buñuelos rellenos de pato* (fried snacks filled with shredded duck and topped with *mole negro*) and *pescado tikin xic* (an elaborate grouper dish with plantain and tortilla strips). The latest branch by Muñoz is downtown at **Azul Histórico** (Map p68; ☑ 55-5510-1316; www.azul.rest; Isabel La Católica 30; M$150-300; ⊘9am-11:30pm Mon-Sat, to 9pm Sun; ⊝☏; ⓂZócalo).

Coyoacán

La Casa del Pan Papalotl   VEGETARIAN $

(Map p122; ☑ 55-3095-1767; www.casadelpan. com; Av México 25; breakfast M$95, lunch & dinner M$56-86; ⊘8am-10pm Mon-Fri, from 9am Sat & Sun; ⊝✐; ⓂCoyoacán) This hugely popular vegetarian restaurant draws a loyal breakfast crowd thanks to its organic egg dishes, *chilaquiles* (tortilla strips drenched in salsa) and fresh-made *pan* (bread). For lunch the lasagna with squash flower, mushrooms and poblano chili is a big hit.

Super Tacos Chupacabras   TAQUERÍA $

(Map p122; www.tacoschupacabras.com; cnr Avs Río Churubusco & México; tacos M$10; ⊘24hr; ⓂCoyoacán) Named after Mexico's mythical 'goat sucker' (a vampire-like creature), this famous *taquería* under a freeway overpass slings wonderful beef and sausage tacos. The specialty is the *'chupa,'* a mixed-meat taco that contains 127 secret ingredients, or so they say. Avail yourself of the grilled onions, *nopales,* whole beans and other tasty toppings.

Mercado de Antojitos
MARKET **$**

(Map p122; Higuera 6; pozoles M$60; ☺8am-11pm; ⊜; Ⓜ Coyoacán) Near Coyoacán's main plaza, this busy spot has all kinds of snacks, including deep-fried quesadillas, *pozoles* and *esquites* (boiled corn kernels served with a dollop of mayo). Look for the 'Pozole Estilo Michoacán' stall.

Churrería de Coyoacán
DESSERTS **$**

(Map p122; Allende 38; bag of 4 churros M$24; ☺8am-midnight Sun-Thu, 9am-1am Fri & Sat; Ⓜ Coyoacán) Here are Coyoacán's best deep-fried snacks. Get in line for a bag – chocolate-filled or straight up – then stroll over to Café El Jarocho (just next door) for coffee. Figure about three hours in the gym to work off these bad boys.

El Kiosko de Coyoacán
ICE CREAM **$**

(Map p122; Plaza Hidalgo 6; per scoop M$25; ☺9am-11pm Mon-Fri, to 12:30am Sat & Sun; ⊜; Ⓜ Coyoacán) This obligatory weekend stop has homemade ice cream and popsicles in flavors ranging from mango with chili to *maracuya* (passion fruit).

Corazón de Maguey
MEXICAN **$$$**

(Map p122; ☑55-5659-3165; www.corazonde maguey.com; Jardín Centenario 9A; mains M$159-299; ☺12:30pm-1am Sun-Wed, to 2am Thu-Sat; ⊜☎; Ⓜ Coyoacán) Adorned with old glass jugs used for transporting booze, this attractive restaurant does traditional Mexican fare that's typically prepared in mezcal-producing regions, such as stuffed *chile ancho* peppers from Queretaro, Oaxacan *tlayudas* (large folded tortillas) and beef tongue in red *mole,* hailing from Puebla. It's also a prime spot to sample some of Mexico's finest mezcals.

Los Danzantes
MEXICAN **$$$**

(Map p122; ☑55-5554-1213; www.losdanzantes. com; Jardín Centenario 12; mains M$199-365; ☺1:30pm-midnight Mon-Fri, 9am-2am Sat, 9am-10:30pm Sun; ⊜☎; Ⓜ Coyoacán) Los Danzantes puts a contemporary spin on traditional Mexican cuisine with dishes such as *huitlacoche* (trufflelike corn fungus) raviolis in *poblana* sauce, organic chicken in black *mole,* and *hoja santa* (Mexican pepperleaf) stuffed with

cheese and *chipotle* chili. You'll also find mezcal from its own famous distillery.

El Jardín del Pulpo
SEAFOOD **$$$**

(Map p122; cnr Allende & Malintzin; dishes M$170-220; ☺10am-6pm; ⊜; Ⓜ Coyoacán) Visitors descend on the communal tables at this market-corner place to devour shrimp tacos, fried whole fish, oyster cocktails and the namesake *pulpo* (octopus cooked in its own ink or in tequila).

🍴 Tlalpan

La Voragine
ITALIAN **$$**

(☑55-2976-0313; Madero 107, Colonia Tlalpan; mains M$80-120, pizzas M$135-245; ☺1pm-2am Tue-Sat, to midnight Sun; ☎☑; 🚇Fuentes Brotantes) Run by a fun-loving couple from New York and DF, this muraled pizzeria/bar prepares savory pizzas, exquisite manicotti and *fungi trifolati* (flambéed mushrooms in white-wine sauce). Or just drop in for a Mexican microbrew and enjoy the sunny patio upstairs. It's a half-block north of Tlalpan's main square.

🍴 Colonia del Valle & Around

Fonda Margarita
MEXICAN **$**

(☑55-5559-6358; www.fondamargarita.com; Adolfo Prieto 1354, Colonia Tlacoquemécatl del Valle; mains M$43-61; ☺5:30-11:30am Tue-Sun; ⊜☎; 🚇Parque Hundido) Possibly the capital's premier hangover-recovery spot, this humble eatery under a tin roof whips up batches of comfort food such as *longaniza en salsa verde* (sausage in green salsa) and *frijoles con huevo* (beans with egg). The *fonda* is beside Plaza Tlacoquemécatl, six blocks east of Avenida Insurgentes. There's usually a line to get in, but it moves fast.

🍷 Drinking & Nightlife

Cafes, bars and cantinas are all key social venues on the capital's landscape. The traditional watering holes are, of course, cantinas – no-nonsense places with simple tables, long polished bars and old-school waiters. A humbler kind of drinking establishment rooted in ancient Mexican tradition, *pulquerías* serve *pulque* (a pre-Hispanic, fermented alcoholic beverage). These places are lately experiencing a resurgence, with young *chilangos* rediscovering the joys of sharing a pitcher of the milky quaff. Another drink being taken back by Mexican youth is mezcal, the rustic mother of tequila.

Mexico City has banned smoking inside bars, though many establishments provide open-air smoking areas.

The capital's thriving club scene has become an obligatory stop on the international DJ circuit. To find out what's going on, pick up flyers at Condesa's Malafama (p120) billiard hall.

The city's many dance aficionados have a circuit of clubs and *salones de baile* (dance halls) to choose from. At many clubs it's customary to go in a group and share a bottle of rum or tequila (from around M$600, including mixers).

Centro Histórico

Hostería La Bota
BAR

(Map p68; ☑55-5709-9016; San Jerónimo 40; ⏰1pm-midnight Sun-Tue, to 2am Wed & Thu, to 3am Fri & Sat; ☎; Ⓜ Isabel La Católica) *Cerveza* (beer), mezcal cocktails, tapas and deliciously oily pizza are served amid a profusion of warped bullfighting bric-a-brac and recycled objects. A portion of your bar tab sponsors local art projects.

Salón Corona
BAR

(Map p68; ☑55-5512-5725; www.saloncorona. com.mx; Bolívar 24; ⏰10:30am-2am; Ⓜ Allende) Amiable staff serve up *tarros* (mugs) of light or dark *cerveza de barril* (draft beer) in this boisterous beer hall. It's a great place to get a taste of soccer-mad Mexico when a match is on TV, which is almost always.

Las Duelistas
PULQUERÍA

(Map p68; ☑55-1394-0958; Aranda 28; ⏰10am-9pm Mon-Sat; ☐ Plaza San Juan) Now graffitied with pre-Hispanic psychedelia, this classic

---

MEZCAL RENAISSANCE

In recent years the agave-based Mexican liquor mezcal, long thought of as just a poor rustic relative to tequila, has finally won the respect it deserves. Many bars around Mexico City now serve mezcal to the new breed of discerning aficionados.

La Clandestina (Map p82; Álvaro Obregón 298, Colonia Roma; ⏰6pm-2am Tue-Sat; ☐ Álvaro Obregón) Fashioned after a rural mom-and-pop shop, the Clandestina provides a detailed menu describing the elaboration process of the mezcals dispensed from jugs on high shelves. In true clandestine fashion, there's no sign outside, so look for the 'Casa Rey' frameshop sign left behind by the previous tenants.

Bósforo (Map p76; Luis Moya 31, cnr Independencia, Colonia Centro; ⏰6pm-2am Tue-Sat; Ⓜ Juárez) Blink and you might walk right past the friendliest neighborhood *mezcalería* in town. Behind the Bósforo's nondescript curtain await top-notch mezcals, an eclectic mix of music and surprisingly good bar grub.

Al Andar (Map p68; Regina 27, Colonia Centro; ⏰noon-1am; ☎; Ⓜ Isabel La Católica) Most of the late-night action at this tiny downtown bar spills out onto a convivial pedestrian thoroughfare. Choose from 25 varieties of quality mezcal while munching on *chapulines* (grasshoppers) and orange slices.

Mano Santa Mezcal (Map p82; ☑55-6585-4354; Av Insurgentes Sur 219; ⏰6pm-1am Tue & Wed, to 2am Thu-Sat, 2-10pm Sun; ☐ Durango) Often compared to having a drink at home because of the cheap, quality mezcal (or because you live in a designer-school laboratory), this small bar overflows with droves of the young and hip on weekends.

Alipús (www.alipus.com; Guadalupe Victoria 15, Colonia Tlalpan; ⏰1:30-10pm Mon & Tue, to 11pm Wed, to midnight Thu, to 1am Fri & Sat, noon-8pm Sun; ☐ Fuentes Brotantes) From the makers of the popular Oaxaca-based mezcal brands Alipús and Los Danzantes, this quaint bar in Tlalpan and the chic **Alipús Condesa** (☑55-5211-6845; www.alipus.com/alipuscondesa; Aguascalientes 232; ⏰1:30-11:30pm Mon-Thu, to 1am Fri & Sat, 2-8pm Sun) branch stock some of the finest mezcal in all of Mexico (ie Danzantes Pechuga Roja). The regional *antojitos* (snacks) are wonderful as well.

Mexicano (Map p68; Regina 27, Colonia Centro; ⏰11am-11pm Mon-Thu, to 1:30am Fri-Sat; Ⓜ Isabel La Católica) This rustic mezcal joint is a hangover waiting to happen. In addition to mezcal, Mexicano pours *pulque* and offers a good selection of microbrews. The '*puntas de madrecuixe*' mezcal from Oaxaca, which packs 78.8% alcohol by volume, will strip the enamel off your teeth.

pulquería has been rediscovered by young artists and musicians. Despite the new look, the *pulque* is still dispensed straight from the barrel in a variety of flavors.

Bar La Ópera
BAR

(Map p68; ☑55-5512-8959; www.barlaopera. com; Av 5 de Mayo 10; ☺1pm-midnight Mon-Sat, to 6pm Sun; Ⓜ Allende) With booths of dark walnut and an ornate copper-colored ceiling (said to have been punctured by Pancho Villa's bullet), this late-19th-century watering hole remains a bastion of tradition.

La Risa
PULQUERÍA

(Map p68; ☑55-5709-4963; Mesones 71; ☺noon-10pm Mon-Sat, to 7pm Sun; Ⓜ Isabel La Católica) University students squeeze into this intimate watering hole that has been pouring *pulque* since 1900. Be a sport and invite a struggling college kid to a mug.

Downtown Mexico
BAR

(Map p68; www.downtownmexico.com; Isabel La Católica 30; ☺10am-11pm Sun-Thu, to 2am Fri & Sat; ☏; Ⓜ Zócalo) The rooftop lounge bar at boutique hotel Downtown Mexico has become a popular spot to chill over drinks, and it's been known to host the occasional pool party with open bar and DJ sets.

Bar Mancera
BAR

(Map p68; ☑55-5521-9755; Venustiano Carranza 49; ☺2-10pm Mon-Thu, to 2am Fri & Sat; 🚇República del Salvador) More than a century old, this atmospheric gentlemen's salon seems preserved in amber, with ornate carved paneling and well-used domino tables.

Café Jekemir
CAFE

(Map p68; ☑55-5709-7086; www.cafejekemir. com; Isabel La Católica 88; ☺8am-9pm Mon-Sat; ☏; Ⓜ Isabel La Católica) Run by a family of coffee traders from Orizaba, this old distribution outlet, now transformed into a popular cafe, prepares good Veracruz coffee and Lebanese snacks.

Zona Rosa & Around

The Pink Zone, an international party center, boasts a high concentration of bars and clubs, and prices reflect its tourist orientation. Genova is holding out as the last bastion of cheap sports bars for students. Amberes is the hub of Zona Rosa's gay and lesbian bar scene.

Crisanta
BAR

(Map p76; ☑55-5535-6372; www.crisanta.mx; Av Plaza de la República 51; ☺9am-11pm Sun-Tue, to 2am Wed-Sat; ☏; 🚇Plaza de la República) A welcome sight in a nation where two breweries control about 98% of the market, Crisanta makes its own porter and sells Mexican and foreign craft beers. Jazz groups play twice a month on Friday and Saturday, and there's art on display in the back room. Antique furnishings and long wooden tables add character to the beer-hall atmosphere.

Café La Habana
CAFE

(Map p76; ☑55-5535-2620; Av Morelos 62; ☺7am-1am Mon-Sat, 8am-11pm Sun; ☏; 🚇Expo Reforma) This grand coffeehouse is a traditional haunt for writers and journalists, who linger for hours over a *café americano*. Legend has it that Fidel and Che plotted strategy here prior to the Cuban revolution.

Condesa

Condesa's bar scene continues to thrive, and new places are popping up (and shutting down) all the time. The most popular places are filled beyond capacity Thursday through Saturday evenings. The confluence of Avenidas Tamaulipas and Nuevo León has emerged as a major bar zone, earning it a reputation as a haven for *fresas* (literally 'strawberries'; a derogatory term for upper-class youth).

Pata Negra
BAR

(Map p82; ☑55-5211-5563; www.patanegra. com.mx; Av Tamaulipas 30; ☺1:30pm-2am; ☏; 🚇Campeche) Nominally a tapas bar, this oblong salon draws a friendly mix of 20-something *chilangos* and expats. Live Veracruz-style *son jarocho* bands perform on Saturday, while the program during the week usually features jazz, salsa or funk music.

Felina
COCKTAIL BAR

(Map p82; ☑55-5277-1917; Ometusco 87; ☺6pm-2am Tue-Sat; ☏; Ⓜ Chilpancingo) Long-standing Felina has come of age. Quiet confidence is felt in its low-level music, and in cocktails that don't rely on sweetness but leverage real ingredients, such as fresh juniper berries in the gin. Psychedelic wallpaper and vintage chairs give a nod to a 'funky' past, but times have changed, and the lounging crowd is well-dressed but oh so casual.

Black Horse
PUB

(Map p82; ☑55-5211-8740; www.caballonegro.com; Mexicali 85; ☺6pm-2am Tue-Sat; ☎; Ⓜ Patriotismo) Besides its draw as a preferred spot to catch televised soccer matches, this British pub boasts an international social scene and has excellent funk, jazz and indie-rock bands playing the back room.

El Centenario
CANTINA

(Map p82; ☑55-5553-5451; Vicente Suárez 42; ☺noon-1am Mon-Wed, to 2am Thu-Sat; ☎; Ⓜ Campeche) Laden with bullfighting memorabilia, this cantina is an enclave of tradition amid the modish restaurant zone.

Chiquitito
CAFE

(Map p82; www.chiquititocafe.com; Alfonso Reyes 232; ☺7:30am-7:30pm Mon-Sat; ☎; Ⓜ Chilpancingo) 🍴 Small in size, huge on Veracruz flavor. Coffee shops are everywhere in the Condesa but few have the know-how to bring out the best in their beans. The baristas at this hole-in-the-wall have it all figured out.

Salón Malafama
BAR

(Map p82; www.salonmalafama.com.mx; Av Michoacán 78; billiard table per hr M$100; ☺1pm-midnight Sun & Mon, to 1am Tue & Wed, to 2am Thu-Sat; ☎; Ⓜ Campeche) This sleek billiard hall doubles as a bar and gallery for photo exhibits. The well-maintained tables are frequented by both pool sharks and novices.

Condesa df
BAR

(Map p82; ☑55-5241-2600; www.condesadf.com; Veracruz 102; ☺2-11pm Sun-Wed, to 1am Thu-Sat; ☎; Ⓜ Chapultepec) The bar of the fashionable Condesa df hotel has become an essential stop on the Condesa circuit. Up on the roof, guests lounge on big-wheel wicker sofas and enjoy views of verdant Parque España across the way.

Pastelería Maque
CAFE

(Map p82; ☑55-2454-4662; www.maque.com.mx; Ozuluama 4; ☺11am-10pm; Ⓜ Campeche) Condesa sophisticates gather in the mornings and evenings at this Parisian-style cafe-bakery near Parque México. Waiters bring around trays of freshly baked croissants and *conchas* (round pastries sprinkled with sugar).

Roma

Cuban dance clubs abound in Roma, particularly near the intersection of Avenida Insurgentes and Medellín. Cocktail bars are sprinkled like glitter along Álvaro Obregón.

★ Traspatio
BAR

(Map p82; cnr Córdoba & Colima; ☺1pm-midnight Tue & Wed, to 2am Thu-Sat, to 10pm Sun; ☎; Ⓜ Durango) For the urban backyard barbecue experience, you'll love this open-air beer garden. It's a great little hideaway for chatting over *cerveza* or mezcal and munching on a *choripán* (grilled sausage on a roll) or a portobello mushroom burger.

La Chicha
BAR

(Map p82; ☑55-5574-6625; Orizaba 171; ☺1pm-midnight Mon-Wed, to 2am Thu-Sat; ☎; Ⓜ Jardín Pushkin) Mix one part Mexican vintage decor, one shot of rock vibe and throw in mezcal, tequila, beer and plenty of vegetarian snacks and you have the recipe for a bar full to its low-lit brim on weekends, yet still chilled enough for conversations. Part of a growing row of bars that shy away from the swankiness of Álvaro Obregón.

Casa Franca
COCKTAIL BAR

(Map p82; ☑55-5533-8754; ☺5pm-1am Tue & Wed, to 2am Thu-Sat; ☎; Ⓜ Jardín Pushkin) This upstairs bar is a labyrinth with more moods than a house party. The live jazz plays out in an intimate living room, while the corner balcony overlooking Álvaro Obregón captures that twinkle of Saturday night. The other (extremely) dark corners are made for lounging, sipping great cocktails and hand holding.

Los Insurgentes
PULQUERÍA

(Map p82; Av Insurgentes Sur 226; ☺2pm-1am Mon-Wed, 1pm-3am Thu-Sat; Ⓜ Durango) A testament to the city's booming *pulque* revival, this three-story *porfiriato*-era house may not please the purists, but unlike a traditional *pulquería*, here you get live music, DJ sets and other alcoholic drinks not called *pulque*.

Mama Rumba
DANCING

(Map p82; ☑55-5564-6920; www.mamarumba.com.mx; Querétaro 230; ☺9pm-3am Wed & Thu, 8pm-4am Fri & Sat; Ⓜ Sonora) Managed by a Havana native, Mama Rumba features contemporary salsa, with music by the house big band. If you'd like to take a class, dance instructors will get you started Wednesdays and Thursdays at 9pm and Fridays and Saturdays at 8pm. Mama Rumba has a larger branch in San Ángel at Plaza Loreto.

Cantina Covadonga
CANTINA

(Map p106; www.banquetescovadonga.com.mx; Puebla 121; ☺1pm-2am Mon-Wed, to 3am Thu & Fri; Ⓜ Insurgentes) Echoing with the sounds of clacking dominoes, the old Asturian social hall is a traditionally male enclave, though hipsters of both sexes have increasingly moved in on this hallowed ground.

La Bodeguita del Medio
BAR

(Map p82; ☑55-5553-0246; www.labodeguitadel medio.com.mx; Cozumel 37; ⊙1:30pm-2am Mon-Sat, to 12:30am Sun; Ⓜ Sevilla) The walls are tagged with verses and messages at this animated branch of the famous Havana joint. Have a mojito (a Cuban drink of rum, lime juice and mint leaves) and enjoy the excellent *son cubano* combos that perform here.

Buna 42
CAFE

(Map p106; ☑55-6724-5578; http://buna.mx; Orizaba 42; ⊙7am-9pm Mon-Fri, from 8am Sat & Sun; ⚲; Ⓜ Insurgentes) Contender for best coffee in DF, in a retro-chic space. Uses beans from across Mexico. Coffee snobs: go.

Los Bisquets Obregón
CAFE

(Map p82; ☑55-5584-2802; www.lbbo.com.mx; Álvaro Obregón 60; ⊙7am-midnight; ⚲; 🖥 Álvaro Obregón) *Chilango* families flock here for the *pan dulce* (sweet bread) and *café con leche*, dispensed from two pitchers, Veracruz-style.

Maison Francaise de Thé Caravanserai
TEAHOUSE

(Map p82; ☑55-5511-2877; www.caravanserai. com.mx; Orizaba 101; ⊙10am-10pm Mon-Sat, from noon Sun; ⚲; 🖥 Álvaro Obregón) This French-and 'Oriental'-style tearoom has more than 170 blends categorized by their intended use or effects. Visitors relax on comfortable sofas to enjoy their chosen brews, which are ceremoniously served on silver trays.

Polanco

Though not as cutting-edge as Roma and Condesa, this well-heeled neighborhood gets quite lively after dark.

Área
COCKTAIL BAR

(Map p88; ☑55-5282-3100; www.hotelhabita. com; Av Presidente Masaryk 201; ⊙7pm-2am Mon-Sat; ⚲; Ⓜ Polanco) Atop the Hábita Hotel, this open-air roof lounge does a brisk trade in exotic martinis, with sweeping city views as a backdrop and videos projected on the wall of a nearby building.

Big Red
BAR

(Map p88; ☑55-5255-5277; Av Presidente Masaryk 101; ⊙noon-10pm; ⚲; Ⓜ Polanco) A volume dealer with drinks reasonably priced by the ounce, plus whatever mixer you choose...

thus the place attracts a broader cross section of the populace than the usual Polanco *antro* (bar).

Xochimilco

Pulquería El Templo de Diana
PULQUERÍA

(☑55-5653-4657; Madero 17, cnr 5 de Mayo; ⊙10am-9pm; 🖥 Xochimilco) This classic *pulquería,* a block east of the main market, has a cheerful sawdust-on-the-floor vibe, with a mixed-age crowd enjoying giant mugs of the *maguey*-based beverage. Even a few females may pop in. Delivered daily from Hidalgo state, the *pulque* is expertly blended with flavorings such as Nescafé, *pistache* (pistachio) and *piñon* (pine nut).

Pulquería La Botijona
PULQUERÍA

(Av Morelos 109; ⊙10am-10pm; 🖥 Xochimilco) Possibly the cleanest *pulque* dispenser in town, this institutional green hall near the train station is a friendly, family-run establishment with big plastic pails of the traditional quaff lining the shelves.

San Ángel

La Camelia
BAR

(Map p94; ☑55-5615-5643; Madero 3; ⊙noon-8pm Sun-Thu, to 2am Fri & Sat; 🖥 La Bombilla) This restaurant-cantina has been drawing Mexican celebrities since 1931, as evidenced by the stars' photos on the walls. On Friday and Saturday karaoke nights, it's your time to shine with a rendition of, say, Michael Jackson or Madonna. Liquid courage comes in the form of tequila or *cerveza mexicana.*

Coyoacán

★ La Bipo
BAR

(Map p122; ☑55-5484-8230; Malintzin 155; ⊙1pm-midnight; ⚲; Ⓜ Coyoacán) This popular cantina plays up the kitschier elements of Mexican popular culture, with wall panels fashioned from plastic crates and sliced tin buckets as light shades. The menu, consisting of Mexican snacks, is hit and miss. DJs spin assorted tunes upstairs from Wednesday to Saturday.

Cantina La Coyoacana
CANTINA

(Map p122; Higuera 14; ⊙1pm-midnight Sun-Wed, to 2am Thu-Sat; ⚲; Ⓜ Coyoacán) Enter through swinging saloon doors and head to the open-air patio, where wailing mariachis do their thing in this traditional drinking establishment.

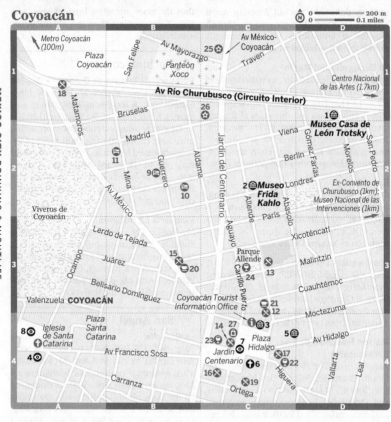

Coyoacán

◎ Top Sights

1 Museo Casa de León Trotsky D1
2 Museo Frida Kahlo C2

◎ Sights

3 Casa de Cortés C4
4 Centro Cultural Jesús Reyes
   Heroles A4
5 Museo Nacional de Culturas
   Populares C4
6 Parroquia de San Juan Bautista...........C4
7 Plaza Hidalgo & Jardín
   Centenario C4
8 Plaza Santa Catarina A4

🛏 Sleeping

9 Chalet del Carmen B2
10 Hostal Cuija Coyoacán B2
11 Hostal Frida..B2

✖ Eating

12 Churrería de Coyoacán C3
   Corazón de Maguey ....(see 23)

13 El Jardín del Pulpo................................C3
14 El Kiosko de Coyoacán C4
15 La Casa del Pan Papalotl B3
16 Los Danzantes......................................C4
17 Mercado de Antojitos............................C4
18 Super Tacos Chupacabras...................A1
19 Tamales Chiapanecos María
   Geraldine...C4

🍷 Drinking & Nightlife

20 Café El Jarocho B3
21 Café El Jarocho C3
22 Cantina La Coyoacana..........................C4
23 El Hijo del Cuervo C4
24 La Bipo C3

✪ Entertainment

25 Cineteca Nacional C1
26 Teatro Bar El Vicio C1

🛍 Shopping

27 Bazar Artesanal Mexicano C4

Café El Jarocho CAFE
(Map p122; ✆ 55-5658-5029; www.cafeeljarocho. com.mx; Cuauhtémoc 134; ⊙ 6:30am-1am Sun-Thu, to 2am Fri & Sat; Ⓜ Coyoacán) This immensely popular joint churns out coffee for long lines of java hounds. As there's no seating inside, people have their drink standing in the street or sitting on curbside benches. A **branch** (Map p122; Av México 25C) with seats is several blocks northwest of Jardín Centenario.

El Hijo del Cuervo BAR
(Map p122; ✆ 55-5658-7824; www.elhijodelcuervo. com.mx; Jardín Centenario 17; ⊙ 4pm-midnight Mon-Wed, 1pm-1:30am Thu, to 2am Fri & Sat, to 11:30pm Sun; Ⓜ Coyoacán) A Coyoacán institution, this stone-walled 'cultu-bar' on the Jardín Centenario is a longtime favorite on the local cultural scene. Jazz and rock groups perform on Tuesday, Wednesday and Thursday nights.

Tlatelolco & Around

Salón Los Ángeles DANCING
(✆ 55-5597-5181; www.salonlosangeles.mx; Lerdo 206, Colonia Guerrero; ⊙ 6-11pm Tue & 5-11pm Sun; Ⓜ Tlatelolco) Fans of dance-hall music shouldn't miss the outstanding orchestras or the graceful dancers who fill the vast floor of this atmospheric ballroom. The live music, consisting of salsa and *cumbia* (dance music originating in Colombia) on Sunday and swing and *danzón* on Tuesday, draws a mostly older crowd. It's located in the rough Colonia Guerrero, so take a taxi.

Two-hour dance classes are offered on Mondays at 6pm and Tuesdays at 4pm.

Colonia del Valle

Java junkies will make a special trip to this neighborhood just for the coffee – it's that good!

Passmar CAFE
(✆ 55-5669-1994; www.cafepassmar.com.mx; cnr Adolfo Prieto & Av Coyoacán, Mercado Lázaro Cárdenas; ⊙ 9am-7pm Mon-Sat; 🛜; 🚇 Amores) You'll be hard-pressed to find a place that takes a cup o' Joe more seriously than Passmar, and the proof is in the artful presentation of the cappuccino. You'll find the award-winning coffee in Mercado Lázaro Cárdenas, a block and a half southwest of metrobús Amores.

☆ Entertainment

There's so much going on in Mexico City on any given evening, it's hard to keep track. **Tiempo Libre** (www.tiempolibre.com.mx),

the city's comprehensive what's-on magazine, helps you sort it all out. It covers live music, theater, movies, dance, art and nightlife. Other useful publications with good websites are **La Semana de Frente** (www. frente.com.mx), **Donde Ir** (www.dondeir. com), **Chilango** (www.chilango.com) and Time Out Mexico (p131).

Ticketmaster sells tickets for all the major venues online, or visit any of its following branches: Auditorio Nacional (p125); **Liverpool Centro** (Map p68; Venustiano Carranza 92; ⊙ 11am-7pm; Ⓜ Zócalo); **Liverpool Polanco** (Map p88; Mariano Escobedo 425; ⊙ 11am-8pm; Ⓜ Polanco); **Mixup Centro** (Map p68; Av Madero 51; ⊙ 10am-9pm Mon-Sat, 11am-8pm Sun; Ⓜ Zócalo); and **Mixup Zona Rosa** (Génova 76; Ⓤ Insurgentes).

Cinemas

Mexico City is a banquet for movie-goers. Ticket prices run to around M$60 in commercial cinemas, with many places offering discounts on Wednesdays. Most movies are available in original languages with Spanish subtitles, except for children's fare. *El Universal* and *La Jornada* have daily listings.

Cineteca Nacional CINEMA
(Map p122; ✆ 55-4155-1200; www.cineteca nacional.net; Av México-Coyoacán 389, Colonia Xoco; 🛜; Ⓜ Coyoacán) Mexican and foreign indie movies are shown on 10 screens at the recently renovated Cineteca. In November the complex hosts the Muestra Internacional de Cine, an international film festival. From October to March you can catch free open-air screenings at dusk in the grass-covered rear garden. A film museum was under construction at last visit.

Cine Tonalá CINEMA
(Map p82; www.cinetonala.com; Tonalá 261; 🛜; 🚇 Campeche) A pleasant multipurpose venue for independent cinema, plays and concerts.

Cinépolis Diana CINEMA
(Map p106; ✆ 55-5511-3236; www.cinepolis.com. mx; Paseo de la Reforma 423; Ⓜ Sevilla) Commercial releases and international film-festival titles.

Cinemex Real CINEMA
(Map p76; ✆ 55-5257-6969; www.cinemex.com; Colón 17; Ⓜ Hidalgo) Screens mostly Hollywood movies and the occasional Mexican hit.

Cinemex Casa de Arte · CINEMA
(Cinemex Reforma; Map p106; ☑55-5257-6969; www.cinemex.com; Río Guadalquivir 104; Ⓜ Insurgentes) Primarily art-house flicks.

Filmoteca de la UNAM · CINEMA
(☑55-5704-6338; www.filmoteca.unam.mx; Av Insurgentes Sur 3000; ☐ Centro Cultural Universitario) Two cinemas at the Centro Cultural Universitario screen films from a collection of more than 43,000 titles.

Dance, Classical Music & Theater
Orchestral music, opera, ballet, contemporary dance and theater are all abundantly represented in the capital's numerous theaters. Museums, too, serve as (often free) performance venues, including the Museo de la Secretaría de Hacienda y Crédito Público (p74) and the Museo de la Ciudad de México (p75). The national arts council (Conaculta) provides a rundown of events on its website (www.mexicoescultura.com).

If your Spanish is up to it, you might like to sample Mexico City's lively theater scene. **Mejor Teatro** (www.mejorteatro.com.mx) covers the major venues.

Palacio de Bellas Artes · PERFORMING ARTS
(Map p68; www.bellasartes.gob.mx; Av Hidalgo 1; ☺box office 11am-7pm; Ⓜ Bellas Artes) The Orquesta Sinfónica Nacional and prestigious opera companies perform in Bellas Artes' ornate theater, while chamber groups appear in the recital halls. The venue is most famous, though, for the **Ballet Folklórico de México** (Map p68; www.balletfolklorico demexico.com.mx; ☺performances 8:30pm Wed, 9:30am & 9pm Sun; Ⓜ Bellas Artes), a two-hour festive blur of costumes, music and dance from all over Mexico.

Tickets are usually available on the day of the show, or from Ticketmaster.

Centro Cultural Universitario · PERFORMING ARTS
(☑55-5622-7003; www.cultura.unam.mx; Av Insurgentes Sur 3000; ☐ Centro Cultural Universitario) Ensconced in the woodsy southern section of the national university campus, Centro Cultural Universitario comprises five theaters, including the Sala Nezahualcóyotl, home of the UNAM Philharmonic; the Teatro Alarcón, a drama stage; and the Sala Miguel Covarrubias, a contemporary dance venue.

Centro Nacional de las Artes · PERFORMING ARTS
(CNA; ☑55-4155-0000; www.cenart.gob.mx; Av Río Churubusco 79, Colonia Country Club; ☎;

Ⓜ General Anaya) A sprawling cultural institute near Coyoacán that has many free events across the artistic spectrum, including contemporary dance, theater, art shows and classical concerts. To get here, exit metro General Anaya (Línea 2) on the east side of Calzada de Tlalpan, then walk north to the corner and turn right.

Centro Cultural del Bosque · PERFORMING ARTS
(Map p88; ☑55-5283-4600, ext 4408; www.ccb.bellasartes.gob.mx; cnr Paseo de la Reforma & Campo Marte, Colonia Chapultepec Polanco; ☺box office noon-3pm & 5-7pm Mon-Fri & prior to events; Ⓜ Auditorio) Behind the Auditorio Nacional, the Centro Cultural del Bosque features six theaters, including the Teatro de la Danza, dedicated to modern dance. On Saturday and Sunday afternoons, children's plays and puppet shows are often staged.

Foro Shakespeare · THEATER
(Map p82; ☑55-5553-4642; www.foroshakespeare.com; Zamora 7, Colonia Condesa; Ⓜ Chapultepec) A small independent theater with an eclectic program. Jazz ensembles perform Thursday night in the theater's restaurant-bar.

Centro Cultural Helénico · THEATER
(Map p94; ☑55-4155-0919; www.helenico.gob.mx; Av Revolución 1500, Colonia Guadalupe Inn; ☺box office 12:30-8:30pm; ☐ Altavista) This complex includes a 440-seat theater for major productions and a smaller cabaret-style venue for experimental plays.

Live Music
Mexico City's eclectic music offerings rock. On any given night, you can hear traditional Mexican, Cuban, jazz, electronica, garage punk and so on. Music sounds off everywhere: in concert halls, bars, museums – even on public transportation. Free gigs often take place at the Zócalo and Monumento a la Revolución. The 'conciertos' sections of **Tiempo Libre** (www.tiempolibre.com.mx) and **Ticketmaster** (www.ticketmaster.com.mx) include show listings.

The thriving mariachi music scene at Plaza Garibaldi (p74) gets going by about 8pm and stays busy until 3am.

The street market Tianguis Cultural del Chopo (p130) has a stage at its north end every Saturday afternoon for young and hungry metal and punk bands.

★ Centro Cultural de España · LIVE MUSIC
(Map p68; ☑55-5521-1925; www.ccemx.org; República de Guatemala 18; ☺10pm-2am Wed-Sat; Ⓜ Zó-

calo) **FREE** Young hipsters pack the terrace of this place each weekend for its excellent DJ and live-music sessions. Located directly behind the cathedral, the rebuilt colonial structure is usually quaking by midnight.

El Plaza Condesa
CONCERT VENUE

(Map p82; ☑55-5256-5381; www.elplaza.mx; Juan Escutia 4; 🚇Campeche) At the heart of the Condesa nightlife scene, this former movie theater now raises the curtain for pop and rock acts from Mexico and abroad.

Teatro de la Ciudad
CONCERT VENUE

(Map p68; ☑55-5130-5740, ext 2006; http://teatros.cultura.df.gob.mx; Donceles 36; ⊙box office 10am-3pm & 4-7pm; 🚇Allende) Built in 1918 and modeled after Milan's La Scala opera house, this lavishly restored 1300-seat hall gets some of the more interesting touring acts in music, dance and theater.

José Cuervo Salón
CONCERT VENUE

(☑55-5255-5322; www.ticketmaster.com.mx/jose-cuervo-salon-boletos-mexico/venue/163961; Lago Andrómaco 17, cnr Moliere, Colonia Ampliación Granada; ⊙box office 10am-6pm) A warehouse-sized venue for touring rock, world-music and salsa stars. With excellent sound, a wall-length bar and a dance floor for thousands, this is one of Mexico City's best concert halls. It's best reached by taxi.

Cafebrería El Péndulo
LIVE MUSIC

(Map p82; www.forodeltejedor.com; Álvaro Obregón 86; 🕿; 🚇Álvaro Obregón) Leading Mexican artists of varying musical genres play at this cafe-bookstore's rooftop venue. The adjoining open-air bar provides a nice atmosphere for hanging out after the show.

Ticketmaster
Auditorio Nacional
CONCERT VENUE

(Map p88; ☑55-9138-1350; Paseo de la Reforma 50, Bosque de Chapultepec; ⊙box office 10am-7pm Mon-Sat, 11am-6pm Sun; 🚇Auditorio) Major Mexican and visiting rock and pop artists take the stage at the 10,000-seat Auditorio Nacional. The adjoining **Lunario del Auditorio** (Map p88; www.lunario.com.mx; 🚇Auditorio) is a large club reserved mostly for jazz and folk acts.

★ Salón Tenampa
MARIACHIS

(Map p68; ☑55-5526-6176; Plaza Garibaldi 12; ⊙1pm-2am Sun-Thu, to 4am Fri & Sat; 🕿; 🚇Garibaldi) Graced with murals of the giants of Mexican song and enlivened by its own songsters, the Tenampa is a festive cantina on the north side of Plaza Garibaldi; a visit here is obligatory.

Multiforo Alicia
CONCERT VENUE

(Map p82; ☑55-5511-2100; www.facebook.com/pages/Multiforo-Alicia/244833642369; Av Cuauhtémoc 91A; 🚇Jardín Pushkin) Behind the graffiti-scrawled facade is Mexico City's premier indie-rock club. A suitably dark, seatless space, the Alicia stages mostly up-and-coming punk, surf and ska bands, who hawk their music at the store downstairs. See Alicia's Facebook page for show times.

El Imperial Club
CONCERT VENUE

(Map p82; ☑55-5525-1115; www.elimperial.tv; Álvaro Obregón 293, Colonia Roma; ⊙10pm-2:30am Tue & Wed, to 4am Thu-Sat; 🚇Sevilla) Mexican alternative-rock bands and the occasional imported act perform in this ornate two-story house with antique furnishings and vintage touches throughout.

Caradura
CONCERT VENUE

(Map p82; www.caradura.mx; 2nd fl, Av Nuevo León 73; ⊙9pm-2:30am Tue-Sat; 🚇Campeche) One of the best spots in town to exorcise your demons while rockin' out to garage, rockabilly and postpunk sounds.

Pasagüero + La Bipo
CONCERT VENUE

(Map p68; ☑55-5512-6624; Motolinía 33; ⊙10pm-3:30am Thu-Sat; 🕿; 🚇Allende) Some visionary developers took a historic building and transformed its stonewalled ground level into a restaurant-bar for various cultural happenings, especially rock and electronica gigs.

El Under
LIVE MUSIC

(Map p82; ☑55-5511-5475; www.theunder.org; Monterrey 80; ⊙9pm-5am Fri & Sat; 🚇Durango) At this underground-scene favorite, black-clad youths dance to the likes of Morrissey and Bauhaus on the old house's lower level, while upstairs local bands grind out everything from garage punk and rockabilly to death metal.

Zinco Jazz Club
JAZZ

(Map p68; ☑55-5512-3369; www.zincojazz.com; Motolinía 20; ⊙9pm-2am Wed-Sat; 🕿; 🚇Allende) A vital component in the *centro's* rebirth, Zinco is a subterranean supper club featuring local jazz and funk outfits as well as touring artists. The intimate basement room fills up fast when big-name acts take the stage.

Ruta 61
BLUES

(Map p82; ☑55-5211-7602; www.ruta61.com.mx; Av Baja California 281; ⊙7pm-1am Wed-Sat; 🚇Chilpancingo) This split-level venue stages electric blues artists in the Buddy Guy/Howlin' Wolf mold. About once a month

GAY & LESBIAN MEXICO CITY

Since the Distrito Federal (DF) assembly approved a same-sex marriage law (with the nation *then* the USA following suit), Mexico City has been seen as a bastion of tolerance in an otherwise conservative country. The city's mayor, Miguel Ángel Mancera, even declared to the world on Twitter that Mexico City is an LGBTTTI friendly city The longtime heart of gay life is the Zona Rosa – in particular Calle Amberes – yet many night owls prefer the downtown 'alternative' scene along República de Cuba. **GayCities** (www. mexicocity.gaycities.com) has useful information on gay-friendly hotels, bars and clubs. The Marcha de Orgullo Gay (Gay Pride) takes place one Saturday each June and sashays along Reforma from the Ángel to the Zócalo.

Marrakech Salón (Map p68; República de Cuba 18, Colonia Centro; ⏱7pm-2:30am Thu-Sat; Ⓜ Allende) Typical sights and sounds at this retro bar include bare-chested bartenders, bar-top dancing and festive music ranging from 1980s pop to hip-shaking *cumbias* (dance music from Colombia). It gets crowded and steamy, but no one seems to mind.

Nicho Bears & Bar (Map p106; www.bearmex.com; Londres 182, Zona Rosa; ⏱8pm-2:30am Thu-Sat; Ⓜ Insurgentes) Popular with 30-somethings, this Zona Rosa bear den has a slightly more sophisticated air than many of the bars lining the raucous gay strip on nearby Amberes.

La Purísima (Map p68; República de Cuba 17, Colonia Centro; ⏱7pm-2:30am Thu-Sat; Ⓜ Allende) Esentially two bars in one: dance the night away in a rip-roaring, garish disco downstairs, or head upstairs for mezcal, *pulque* and ironically bad/great music that hipsters like.

Bar Oasis (Map p68; ☑55-5521-9740; República de Cuba 2G, Colonia Centro; ⏱5pm-2am; Ⓜ Allende) This packed disco cuts across class lines, with both cowboys and businessmen dancing against a Day-Glo cityscape. Stick around past midnight Friday to Sunday for shows featuring lip-synching trannies.

El Buen Tiempo (Map p68; República de Cuba 21-C; ⏱6:30pm-2am) `FREE` Unique and wonderfully grungy, popular with ex/current *darks* (goths), punks and hipsters – gay and *buga* (straight). Expect to hear Midnight Oil, The Pixies, Morrissey, disco and '80s Mexican rock.

Tom's Leather Bar (Map p82; ☑55-5564-0728; www.toms-mexico.com; Av Insurgentes Sur 357, Colonia Condesa; ⏱9pm-3am Tue-Sun; 🛜; 🚇Campeche) For those who dare to get medieval, Tom's provides the props, with heraldic shields and candelabras highlighting a decidedly decadent decor and a notorious dark room that must be crossed to reach the bathroom. Bears, cubs and daddies wear the crown here, though less so on busy Tuesdays.

there's a direct-from-Chicago act, though you're more likely to see a local cover band.

El Balcón Huasteco LIVE MUSIC
(☑55-5341-6762; Sor Juana Inés de la Cruz 248, Colonia Agricultura; ⏱from 6:30pm Fri & Sat; Ⓜ Normal) This center for the preservation of the Huastec culture of Hidalgo and Veracruz stages performances by fiery trios and prepares snacks hailing from the region. Should you feel inspired, music and dance classes are offered. It's two blocks north of metro Normal.

El Breve Espacio Mezcalería LIVE MUSIC
(Map p94; www.elbreveespacio.mx; Frontera 4; ⏱10am-5:30pm Mon-Wed, to 2am Thu-Sat; 🛜; 🚇La Bombilla) Folk singers in the Silvio Rodríguez

mold take the stage at this temple of *trova* (troubadour-type folk music) near San Ángel's Plaza San Jacinto.

Cabaret

La Perla CABARET
(Map p68; ☑55-1997-7695; República de Cuba 44; ⏱showtimes 11pm & 1am Fri & Sat; 🚇República de Chile) Once a red-light venue, this cabaret has been reborn in the age of irony as a cradle of kitsch, with hilarious drag shows featuring traditional Mexican songstresses. Tickets go fast.

El Bataclán CABARET
(Map p82; ☑55-5511-7390; www.labodega. com.mx; Popocatépetl 25; ⏱9pm-2am Mon-Sat; 🚇Álvaro Obregón) A theater within a club (La

Bodega), this classic cabaret venue showcases some of Mexico's more offbeat performers. Afterwards, catch top-notch Cuban *son* combos over a rum-based mojito.

Teatro Bar El Vicio   CABARET
(Map p122; ☑ 55-5659-1139; www.lasreinaschulas. com; Madrid 13, Colonia del Carmen; ⊙9:30pm-2am Thu-Sun; Ⓜ Coyoacán) With liberal doses of politically and sexually irreverent comedy and a genre-bending musical program, this alternative cabaret is appropriately located in Frida Kahlo's old stomping ground.

Sports

Most of the daily newspapers have a generous sports section where you can find out who is kicking which ball where. True enthusiasts should look for **La Afición** (www. laaficion.com), a daily devoted to sports.

Corridas de toros (bullfights) take place on Sunday around 4pm (check website for specific times) at the **Plaza México** (☑ 55-5133-1939; www.lamexico.com; Augusto Rodin 241, Colonia Noche Buena; 🚇 Ciudad de los Deportes), one of the largest bullrings in the world, a few blocks west of Avenida Insurgentes. Bullfight season varies, but it usually runs from May to September and October to February.

The capital stages *fútbol* (soccer) matches in the national Primera División almost every weekend of the year. Mexico City has three teams: América, nicknamed Las Águilas (the Eagles); Las Pumas of UNAM; and Cruz Azul. There are two seasons: January to June and July to December, each ending in eight-team play-offs and a two-leg final to decide the champion. The biggest match of all is El Clásico, between América and Guadalajara, which fills the Estadio Azteca with 100,000 flag-waving fans. Get tickets in advance for this one.

Tickets to soccer matches (M$90 to M$650 for regular-season games) are usually available at the gate, or from Ticketmaster. There are several stadiums that host games.

Arena México   MEXICAN WRESTLING
(Map p82; ☑ 55-5588-0266; www.arenamexico. com.mx; Dr Lavista 197, Colonia Doctores; ⊙7:30pm Tue & 8:30pm Fri; 🚇 Cuauhtémoc) One of Mexico City's two wrestling venues, the 17,000-seat Arena México is taken over by a circus atmosphere each week, with flamboyant *luchadores* (wrestlers) such as Místico and Super Porky going at each other in tag teams or one-on-one. There are three or four bouts, building up to the headline match. Also check out the smaller **Arena Coliseo** (Map

p68; ☑ 55-5526-1687; www.cmll.com/arena_coliseo.htm; República de Perú 77; ⊙5pm Sun, except 3rd Sun of the month; 🚇 República de Chile).

Estadio Azteca   STADIUM
(☑ 55-5487-3309; www.esmas.com/estadioazteca; Calz de Tlalpan 3665; 🚇 Estadio Azteca) The country's biggest stadium (capacity 105,000) is home to the América soccer club. Games are played on weekend afternoons; check the website for kick-off times. Take the *tren ligero* from metro Tasqueña to the Estadio Azteca station.

Estadio Olímpico   STADIUM
(☑ 55-5325-9000; www.clubpumasunam.com; Av Insurgentes Sur 3000, Ciudad Universitaria; 🚇 CU) Home of the Pumas soccer team. To get here, go right after exiting metrobús station CU and look for the bus stop for free university transportation (called the Pumabús). 'Ruta 6' goes to Estadio Olímpico.

Estadio Azul   STADIUM
(☑ 55-5563-9040; www.cruz-azul.com.mx; Indiana 255, Colonia Nápoles; 🚇 Ciudad de los Deportes) This soccer stadium is next door to the Plaza México bullring.

Diablos Rojos   BASEBALL
(www.diablos.com.mx) Mexico City has one baseball team in the Liga Mexicana de Béisbol, the Diablos Rojos. During the regular season (April to July) it plays every other week at **Foro Sol** (http://www.diablos.com.mx/forosol.php; cnr Av Río Churubusco & Av Viaducto Río de la Piedad, Colonia Granjas México; 🚇 Ciudad Deportiva). From the metro, it's a five-minute walk to the ballpark. See the Diablos website for game times.

🔒 Shopping

Shopping can be a real joy in Mexico City, with *artesanías* (handicrafts) vendors, quirky shops and street markets competing for your disposable income.

Chilangos increasingly shop in modern malls with designer-clothing stores and Starbucks franchises, and more of these shrines to consumerism are popping up all the time. Among the more pleasant are **Plaza Loreto** (Map p94; cnr Av Revolución & Río de la Magdalena; ⊙11am-8pm; 🚇; 🚇 Dr Gálvez) in San Ángel; the open-air **Antara** (Map p88; www.antara.com.mx; Av Ejército Nacional 843B; ⊙11am-8pm; Ⓜ Polanco) in Polanco; and **Reforma 222** (Map p106; www.codigoreforma222.com.mx; Paseo de la Reforma 222; ⊙11am-9pm; Ⓜ Insurgentes) at the east end of the Zona Rosa.

Rare-book aficionados can dig up some gems in the used bookstores along Donceles in the *centro*. Books in English can be found in top-end hotels, major museums and some bookstores.

Mexico City's markets are worth visiting, not just for their varied contents but also for a glimpse of the frenetic business conducted within. In most neighborhoods you'll find a *tianguis* (street market) at least once a week, selling everything from fresh produce to clothing and antiques. *Tianguis* generally set up by 10am and break down around 5pm.

🛍 Centro Histórico & Around

Mexico City's smartest department-store chains, **El Palacio de Hierro** (Map p68; ☎ 55-5728-9905; www.palaciodehierro.com.mx; Av 20 de Noviembre 3; ⊙ 11am-9pm; Ⓜ Zócalo) and **Liverpool** (Map p68; ☎ 55-5262-9999; www.liverpool.com.mx; Venustiano Carranza 92; ⊙ 11am-9pm; Ⓜ Zócalo), both maintain their original 1930s stores downtown.

The streets around the Zócalo are lined with stores that specialize in everyday goods; you'll find plenty of shops selling similar items along the same street. To the west, used books show up on Donceles. Jewelry and gold outlets, as well as numismatics shops, are found along Palma, while opticians are east of the square on Avenida Madero. To the south, shoes are available on Avenida 20 de Noviembre, while along Bolívar, dozens of stores sell musical instruments. To the north, you'll find costume jewelry on República de Colombia and República de Venezuela.

Hundreds of computer stores huddle in the **Plaza de la Computación y Electrónica** (Map p68; www.plazadelatecnologia.com/mexico; Eje Central Lázaro Cárdenas 38; ⊙ 10am-6pm; Ⓜ San Juan de Letrán), south of Uruguay.

Centro de Artesanías
La Ciudadela   HANDICRAFTS
(Map p76; cnr Balderas & Dondé; ⊙ 10am-7pm Mon-Sat, to 6pm Sun; Ⓜ Balderas) A favorite destination for good stuff from all over Mexico. Worth seeking out are Oaxaca *alebrijes* (whimsical painted animals), guitars from Paracho and Huichol beadwork. Prices are generally fair, even before you bargain.

Mumedi   GIFTS
(Mexican Design Museum; Map p68; ☎ 55-5510-8609; www.mumedi.org; Av Madero 74; ⊙ 11am-9pm Mon, 8am-9pm Tue-Sun; 🛜; Ⓜ Zócalo) This design-museum gift shop sells interesting

pop-culture knickknacks, handbags and jewelry crafted mostly by local artisans.

Mercado San Juan   MARKET
(Map p76; www.mercadosanjuan.galeon.com; Pugibet 21; ⊙ 8am-5pm Mon-Sat, to 4pm Sun; 🖳 Plaza San Juan) Specializes in gourmet food items such as *huitlacoche* (trufflelike corn fungus) and rare fruit. Local chefs and foodies come here to score ingredients not available elsewhere in the city.

Plaza Downtown Mexico   MALL
(Map p68; Isabel La Católica 30; ⊙ 11am-8pm Mon-Sat, to 6pm Sun; Ⓜ Zócalo) Shops surrounding the central courtyard of a beautifully restored 18th-century colonial building sell crafts, ceramics, chocolate and clothes.

Casasola Fotografía   SOUVENIRS
(Map p68; www.casasolafoto.com; office 201, 2nd fl, Isabel La Católica 45; ⊙ 10am-7pm Mon-Fri, to 3pm Sat; 🖳 República del Salvador) Odds are you've probably seen this studio's world-famous revolution-era sepia photos. Items on sale include framed pictures, calendars, T-shirts and postcards. Photo ID required to enter the building.

La Europea   DRINK
(Map p68; ☎ 55-5512-6005; www.laeuropea.com.mx; Ayuntamiento 21; ⊙ 9am-8pm Mon-Sat, 11am-4pm Sun; 🖳 Plaza San Juan) Get reasonably priced tequila, mezcal and wine at this well-stocked liquor store.

Dulcería de Celaya   FOOD
(Map p68; ☎ 55-5521-1787; www.dulceriadecelaya.com; Av 5 de Mayo 39; ⊙ 10:30am-7:30pm; Ⓜ Allende) Candy store operating since 1874, with candied fruits and coconut-stuffed lemons. Worth a look just for the ornate building.

Galería Eugenio   HANDICRAFTS
(Map p68; ☎ 55-5529-2849; Allende 84; ⊙ 11am-5:30pm Mon-Sat; Ⓜ Garibaldi) Sells more than 4000 masks from all over the country; it's in the Lagunilla market area.

American Bookstore   BOOKS
(Map p68; ☎ 55-5512-0306; Bolívar 23; ⊙ 10am-6:30pm Mon-Fri, to 5:30pm Sat; Ⓜ Allende) Has novels and books on Mexico in English, plus Lonely Planet guides.

Gandhi   BOOKS
(www.gandhi.com.mx) Citywide chain with a voluminous range of texts on Mexico and Mexico City. Branches at **Avenida Madero** (Map p68; Av Madero 32; ⊙ 10am-9pm Mon-

Sat, 11am-8pm Sun; M Zócalo), **Bellas Artes** (Map p68; Av Juárez 4; ☉10am-9pm Mon-Sat, 11am-9pm Sun; M Bellas Artes) and **San Ángel** (Map p94; ☑55-2625-0606; Av Miguel Ángel de Quevedo 121; ☉10am-10pm; M Miguel Ángel de Quevedo). There are two outlets on the same block in San Ángel.

Tianguis Dominical de la Lagunilla MARKET
(cnr González Bocanegra & Paseo de la Reforma; ☉10am-6pm Sun; M Garibaldi) At this collector's oasis you can hunt for antiques, old souvenirs and bric-a-brac. Books and magazines are alongside La Lagunilla building.

La Lagunilla MARKET
(Map p68; cnr Rayón & Allende; ☉9am-8pm Mon-Sat, 10am-7pm Sun; M Garibaldi) This enormous complex comprises three buildings: building No 1 contains clothes and fabrics, No 2 has food and No 3 sells furniture.

Tepito MARKET
(Map p68; Héroe de Granaditas, Colonia Tepito; ☉10am-6pm Wed-Mon; M Lagunilla) The mother of all street markets is a maze of semipermanent stalls spreading east and north from La Lagunilla, with miles of clothes, pirated CDs, DVDs and electronics. Also known as a thieves' market for its smuggled goods and pickpockets. Enter crime-ridden Tepito at your own risk.

Zona Rosa & Around

★**Fonart** HANDICRAFTS
(www.fonart.gob.mx) This government-run crafts store sells quality wares from around Mexico, such as Olinalá-produced lacquered boxes and black pottery from Oaxaca. Branches at **Reforma** (Map p106; Paseo de la Reforma 116; ☉10am-7pm Mon-Fri, to 4pm Sat & Sun; M Reforma) and **Mixcoac** (Patriotismo 691; ☉10am-8pm Mon-Fri, to 7pm Sat, 11am-5pm Sun; M Mixcoac). Prices are fixed.

Mercado Insurgentes ARTS & CRAFTS
(Map p106; Londres 154; ☉10:30am-7:30pm Mon-Sat, to 4pm Sun; M Insurgentes) Packed with crafts – silver, pottery, leather, carved wooden figures – but you'll need to bargain to get sensible prices.

Plaza del Ángel ANTIQUES
(Map p106; www.antiguedadesmexico.com; Londres 161, btwn Amberes & Av Florencia; ☉9am-4pm Sat & Sun; M Insurgentes) Flea market within a mall of high-end antique shops selling silver jewelry, paintings, ornaments and furniture.

Jardín del Arte ARTS & CRAFTS
(Map p106; btwn Sullivan & Villalongín, Colonia San Rafael; ☉9am-5pm Sun; ⓡ Reforma) Local artists line the pathways of this park to sell their paintings while vendors hawk art supplies.

Condesa & Roma

Condesa presents an enticing array of trendy boutiques, quirky shops and gourmet food stores. In Roma much of the retail activity is along Álvaro Obregón and Colima.

Vértigo ARTS & CRAFTS
(Map p82; www.vertigogaleria.com; Colima 23; ☉noon-8pm Mon-Fri, to 7pm Sat, to 6pm Sun; ⓡ Jardín Pushkin) The store at this funky art gallery sells silk screens, graphic T-shirts and etchings made by popular Argentine illustrator Jorge Alderete. In addition to 'low brow' art shows, Vértigo stages acoustic music performances every so often.

La Naval DRINK
(Map p82; ☑55-5584-3500; www.lanaval.com.mx; Av Insurgentes Sur 373; ☉9am-9pm Mon-Sat, 11am-7pm Sun; ⓡ Campeche) Name your poison: this gourmet store stocks a tantalizing selection of mezcals and tequilas, as well as Cuban cigars.

Centro Cultural Bella Época BOOKS
(Map p82; ☑55-5276-7110; Av Tamaulipas 202, cnr Benjamín Hill, Colonia Condesa; ⓡ; M Patriotismo) One of the largest bookstores in Latin America; shelves of books, CDs and DVDs inside an impressive art deco cultural center.

Under the Volcano Books BOOKS
(Map p82; www.underthevolcanobooks.com; Celaya 25; ☉11am-7pm Mon-Fri, to 5pm Sat & Sun; ⓡ Sonora) Deals in buying and selling used English-language titles. An excellent selection and very good prices.

Bazar de la Roma ANTIQUES
(Map p82; Jardín Dr Chávez, Colonia Doctores; ☉10am-5pm Sat & Sun; ⓡ Jardín Pushkin) East of Avenida Cuauhtémoc, this market has used and antique items, large and small: books, beer trays, posters and furniture. A similar antiques and art market runs along Álvaro Obregón on the same days.

Bazar del Oro MARKET
(Map p82; Calle de Oro, Colonia Roma; ☉11am-7pm Sat & Sun; ⓡ Durango) This upscale street market between Avenida Insurgentes and Plaza Villa de Madrid has clothing, gifts and an excellent eating section.

El Hijo del Santo GIFTS

(Map p82; ☑55-5512-2186; www.elhijodelsanto. com.mx; Av Tamaulipas 219; ☺10am-9pm Mon-Sat; Ⓜ Patriotismo) Owned by wrestler El Hijo del Santo, this small specialty store sells (you guessed it) all things Santo. Among the offerings are kitschy portraits, hipster handbags and the ever-popular Santo mask.

🏠 Polanco

Polanco's Avenida Presidente Masaryk, aka the Rodeo Drive of Mexico, is lined with designer stores and other high-end retail establishments.

Pasaje Polanco SHOPPING CENTER

(Map p88; ☑55-5280-7976; Av Presidente Masaryk 360; ☺11am-8pm Mon-Sat, to 7pm Sun; Ⓜ Polanco) A classy complex flanked by sophisticated boutiques, specialty stores and a large crafts shop selling handbags, wrestling masks and Day of the Dead folk art.

🏠 San Ángel

Bazar Sábado ARTS & CRAFTS

(Map p94; ☑55-5616-0082; www.elbazaarsabado. com; Plaza San Jacinto 11; ☺10am-5:30pm Sat; 🚇 La Bombilla) The Saturday bazaar showcases some of Mexico's best handcrafted jewelry, woodwork, ceramics and textiles. Artists and artisans also display their work in Plaza San Jacinto itself and in adjacent Plaza Tenanitla.

🏠 Coyoacán

Bazar Artesanal Mexicano HANDICRAFTS

(Map p122; Carrillo Puerto 25; ☺11am-9pm Mon-Thu, 10am-11pm Fri-Sun; Ⓜ Coyoacán) Handmade jewelry, crafts and no shortage of touristy junk.

🏠 Other Neighborhoods

★Tianguis Cultural del Chopo MUSIC

(www.tianguisculturaldelchopo.freeiz.com; Calle Aldama s/n, Colonia Guerrero; ☺10am-5pm Sat; Ⓜ Buenavista) Gathering place for the city's various youth subcultures, with most of the vendor stalls selling clothes, DVDs and CDs. At the far end of the market is a concert stage for young-and-hungry bands. The main entrance is one block east of metro Buenavista.

Mercado de Jamaica MARKET

(cnr Guillermo Prieto & Congreso de la Unión, Colonia Jamaica; ☺24hr; Ⓜ Jamaica) Huge, colorful flower market, featuring both baroque floral arrangements and exotic blooms. It's one block south of metro Jamaica.

❶ Information

DANGERS & ANNOYANCES

Mexico City is generally portrayed as extremely crime ridden, so first-time visitors are often surprised at how safe it feels. Most of the narco-related violence that makes the news abroad happens in the northern and Pacific states, far from Mexico City. While crime rates remain significant in the capital, a few precautions greatly reduce any dangers.

Robberies happen most often in areas frequented by foreigners, including Plaza Garibaldi and the Zona Rosa. Be on your guard at the airport and bus stations. Crowded metro cars and buses are favorite haunts of pickpockets, so keep a close eye on your wallet and avoid carrying ATM cards or large amounts of cash. In case of robbery, don't resist – hand over your valuables rather than risk injury or death.

Statistically, traffic takes more lives in the capital than street crime. Always look both ways when crossing streets, as some one-way streets have bus lanes running counter to the traffic flow, and traffic on some divided streets runs in just one direction. Never assume that a green light means it's safe to cross, as cars may turn into your path – cross with other pedestrians.

Although not as prevalent as in the 1990s, taxi assaults still occur. Many victims have hailed a cab on the street and been robbed by armed accomplices of the driver. Taxis parked in front of nightclubs or restaurants should be avoided unless authorized by the management. Rather than hailing cabs, find a *sitio* (taxi stand) or request a radio taxi or Uber.

EMERGENCY

Agencia del Ministerio Público (☑55-5345-5382; Amberes 54; ☺24hr; Ⓜ Insurgentes) Report crime and get legal assistance. Has English-speaking staff to assist victims of crime.

Fire (☑068)

Police (☑066)

INTERNET ACCESS

Internet services are everywhere. Rates range from M$10 to M$30 per hour.

Plenty of cybercafes occupy the Insurgentes roundabout.

Centenario 4 (2nd fl, Jardín Centenario 4, Coyoacán; ☺8am-6pm Mon-Fri; Ⓜ Viveros)

Conecte Café (2nd fl, Génova 71, cnr Londres, Zona Rosa; ☺9:30am-3am Sun-Thu, to 6am Fri & Sat; Ⓜ Insurgentes)

Copy Land (Gante 12, Colonia Centro; ☺9am-7pm Mon-Fri, 10am-2pm Sat; Ⓜ Allende)

Esperanto (☑ 55-5512-4123; Independencia 66, Colonia Centro; ⊙ 8am-10pm Mon-Sat; Ⓜ Juárez)

Tecno Informática (☑ 55-5211-6784; Vicente Suárez 25, Colonia Condesa; ⊙ 10am-10pm Mon-Sat; Ⓜ Patriotismo)

MAPS

Mexico City tourist modules hand out color maps with enlargements of the *centro histórico*, Coyoacán and San Ángel. If you need more detail, pick up a Guía Roji (www.guiaroji.com.mx) *Ciudad de México* map (M$260). Find them at Sanborns stores and larger newsstands.

Inegi (Map p76; www.inegi.gob.mx) Centro (Map p76; ☑ 55-5130-7900; Balderas 71; ⊙ 9am-4pm Mon-Fri; Ⓜ Juárez); Colonia Mixcoac (Patriotismo 711, Colonia Mixcoac; ⊙ 9am-4pm Mon-Fri; Ⓜ Mixcoac) Mexico's national geographical institute publishes topographical maps covering the whole country (subject to availability). Headquarters are in Colonia Mixcoac.

MEDIA

English-language newspapers and magazines are sold at Sanborns stores and at **La Torre de Papel** (☑ 55-5512-9703; www.latorredepapel. com; Filomena Mata 6A, Colonia Centro; ⊙ 8am-6pm Mon-Fri, 9am-3pm Sat; Ⓜ Allende). Most major publications are sold at newsstands and have most of their content on their websites.

El Universal (www.eluniversal.com.mx) One of Mexico's oldest and biggest newspapers.

La Jornada (www.jornada.unam.mx) Newspaper known for its excellent cultural coverage and left-leaning news stories.

The News (www.thenews.com.mx) English-language national and world news coverage.

Tiempo Libre (www.tiempolibre.com.mx) The city's Spanish-language what's-on weekly is sold at newsstands everywhere.

Time Out Mexico (www.timeoutmexico.mx) A great source for dining, cultural and entertainment listings. Look for free copies in hotels, cafes, bars and nightclubs.

MEDICAL SERVICES

For recommendations for a doctor, dentist or hospital, call your embassy or **Sectur** (p132), the tourism ministry. A list of area hospitals and English-speaking physicians (with their credentials) is on the **US embassy website** (p849). A private doctor's consultation generally costs between M$500 and M$1200.

The pharmacies in **Sanborns** (www.sanborns. com.mx) stores are among the most reliable.

Cruz Roja (Red Cross; ☑ 065) For emergency medical attention.

Farmacia París (☑ 55-5709-3211; www. farmaciaparis.com; República del Salvador 97, Colonia Centro; ⊙ 8am-11pm Mon-Sat, 9am-9pm Sun; Ⓜ Isabel La Católica)

Farmacia San Pablo (☑ 55-5354-9000; www. farmaciasanpablo.com.mx; cnr Av Insurgentes Sur & Chihuahua, Colonia Roma; ⊙ 24hr; Ⓛ Álvaro Obregón) Delivery service around the clock.

Hospital ABC (American British Cowdray Hospital; ☑ 55-5230-8000, emergency 55-5230-8161; www.abchospital.com; Sur 136 No 116, Colonia Las Américas; Ⓜ Observatorio) English-speaking staff provide quality care.

Hospital Ángeles Clínica Londres (☑ 55-5229-8400, emergency 55-5229-8445; www. hospitalangelesclinicalondres.com; Durango 50, Colonia Roma; Ⓜ Cuauhtémoc) Hospital and medical clinic.

Médicor (☑ 55-5512-0431; www.medicor.com. mx; Independencia 66, Colonia Centro; ⊙ 9am-9pm Mon-Sat, to 7pm Sun; Ⓜ Juárez) For homeopathic remedies.

MONEY

Most banks and *casas de cambio* (exchange offices) change cash and traveler's checks, but some handle only euros and US or Canadian dollars. Rates vary, so check a few places. Mexico City is one of the few cities in the world where the exchange offices at the airport actually offer competitive rates. The greatest concentration of ATMs, banks and *casas de cambio* is on Paseo de la Reforma between the Monumento a Cristóbal Colón and the Monumento a la Independencia.

CCSole (www.ccsole.com.mx; Niza 11, Zona Rosa; ⊙ 9:30am-5:30pm Mon-Fri; Ⓜ Insurgentes) Deals in a wide variety of currencies.

Centro de Cambios y Divisas (☑ 55-5705-5656; www.ccd.com.mx; Paseo de la Reforma 87F; ⊙ 8:30am-7:30pm Mon-Fri, 9am-5pm Sat, 9:30am-2:30pm Sun; Ⓛ Reforma)

POST

The Mexican postal service's website (www. correosdemexico.com.mx) lists branches throughout the city.

Palacio Postal (Map p68; www.palacio postal.gob.mx; Tacuba 1; ⊙ 8am-8pm Mon-Fri, to 4pm Sat & Sun; Ⓜ Bellas Artes) The stamp windows, marked *estampillas,* at the city's main post office stay open beyond normal hours. Even if you don't need stamps, check out the sumptuous interior.

Post Office Cuauhtémoc Branch (Map p106; ☑ 55-5207-7666; Río Tiber 87; ⊙ 8am-7pm Mon-Fri, 9am-3pm Sat; Ⓜ Insurgentes)

Post Office Plaza de la República Branch (Map p76; Arriaga 11; ⊙ 8am-4pm Mon-Fri, 9am-1pm Sat; Ⓛ Plaza de la República)

TELEPHONE

There are thousands of Telmex card phones scattered around town. Pick up cards at shops or newsstands bearing the blue-and-yellow 'Ladatel' sign.

TOILETS

Use of the bathroom is free at some Sanborns stores, but otherwise M$5. Most market buildings have public toilets; just look for the 'WC' signs. Hygiene standards vary at these facilities, and a fee of M$3 to M$5 is usually charged. Toilet paper is dispensed by an attendant on request.

TOURIST INFORMATION

The National Tourism Secretariat, **Sectur** (Map p88; 🖉 55-5250-0151, US 800-482-9832; www.sectur.gob.mx; Av Masaryk 172, Bosques de Chapultepec), hands out brochures on the entire country, though you're better off at the tourism modules for up-to-date information about the capital.

The **Mexico City Tourism Secretariat** (🖉 800-008-90-90; www.mexicocity.gob.mx) has modules in key areas, including the airport and bus stations. Staff can answer your queries and distribute a map and practical guide. Staff members usually speak English. Most modules are open from 9am to 6pm daily.

Alameda Tourist Information (Map p76; cnr Av Juárez & Dr Mora, Colonia Centro; Ⓜ Hidalgo)

Basílica Tourist Information (🖉 55-5748-2085; Plaza de las Américas 1, Basílica de Guadalupe; ⊘ 9am-3pm Mon & Tue, to 6pm Wed-Sun; Ⓜ La Villa-Basilica) On the plaza's south side.

Centro Tourist Information (Map p68; 🖉 55-5518-1003; Monte de Piedad; Ⓜ Zócalo) Outside the Catedral Metropolitana.

Chapultepec Tourist Information (Map p88; Paseo de la Reforma; Ⓜ Auditorio) Near the Museo Nacional de Antropología.

Coyoacán Tourist Information Office (Map p122; 🖉 55-5658-0221; Jardín Hidalgo 1, Coyoacán; ⊘ 10am-8pm; Ⓜ Coyoacán) Inside the Casa de Cortés.

Nativitas Tourist Information (🖉 55-5653-5209; Xochimilco; ⊘ 9am-4pm Mon-Fri, to 5pm Sat & Sun; Ⓡ Xochimilco) At the Nativitas boat landing.

Xochimilco Tourist Information Office (🖉 55-5676-0810; www.xochimilco.df.gob. mx/turismo; Pino 36; ⊘ 8am-7pm Mon-Fri, 9am-6pm Sat & Sun; Ⓜ Xochimilco) Just off the Jardín Juárez.

Zócalo Tourist Information (Map p68; Templo Mayor; Ⓜ Zócalo) East of the Catedral Metropolitana.

Zona Rosa Tourist Information (Map p106; 🖉 55-5208-1030; cnr Paseo de la Reforma &

Av Florencia; Ⓜ Insurgentes) On the Zona Rosa side of Monumento a la Independencia.

TRAVEL AGENCIES

A number of hostels and hotels have an *agencia de viajes* on site or can recommend one nearby.

Mundo Joven (🖉 55-5482-8282; www.mundo joven.com) Airport (Sala E1, international arrivals, terminal 1; ⊘ 9am-8pm Mon-Fri, 10am-5pm Sat, to 2pm Sun; Ⓜ Terminal Aérea); Polanco (Eugenio Sue 342, cnr Homero; ⊘ 10am-7pm Mon-Fri, to 2pm Sat; Ⓜ Polanco); Zócalo (República de Guatemala 4, Zócalo; ⊘ 9am-7pm Mon-Fri, 10am-2pm Sat; Ⓜ Zócalo) Specializes in travel for students and teachers, with reasonable airfares from Mexico City. Issues ISIC, ITIC, IYTC and HI cards.

Turismo Zócalo (🖉 55-8596-9649; www. turismozocalo.com; 2nd fl, Palma 34, Colonia Centro; ⊘ 10am-7pm Mon-Fri, to 1pm Sat; Ⓜ Zócalo) Inside the Gran Plaza Ciudad de México mall. Also functions as a Boletotal outlet for bus bookings.

USEFUL WEBSITES

The following sites compile oodles of information on the capital.

Consejo Nacional Para la Cultura y las Artes (www.conaculta.gob.mx/cultura) Online arts and culture magazine that lists goings-on about town.

Secretaría de Cultura del Distrito Federal (www.cultura.df.gob.mx) Lists festivals, museums and cultural events.

Secretaría de Turismo (www.mexicocity.gob. mx) City tourism office's listings and practical information.

Sistema de Transporte Colectivo (www. metro.df.gob.mx) All about the Mexico City metro.

VISAS

Instituto Nacional de Migración (National Migration Institute; Map p88; 🖉 55-2581-0100; www.inm.gob.mx; Av Ejército Nacional 862; ⊘ 9am-1pm Mon-Fri) You'll need to come here if you want to extend a tourist permit, replace a lost one, or deal with other nonstandard immigration procedures. Catch the 'Ejercito' bus from metro Sevilla; it leaves you two blocks east of the office.

❶ Getting There & Away

AIR

Aeropuerto Internacional Benito Juárez (🖉 55-2482-2424; www.aicm.com.mx; Capitán Carlos León s/n, Colonia Peñón de los Baños; 🛜; Ⓜ Terminal Aérea) Mexico City's only passenger airport, and Latin America's largest, with an annual capacity of about 32 million passengers. The airport has two terminals, terminal 1 (the main terminal) and terminal 2 (located 3km from the main terminal). Carriers operating out of terminal 2 include Aeromar, Aeroméxico, Copa Airlines, Delta and Lan. All other airlines depart from terminal 1.

Red buses (M$12.50) run between the two terminals, making stops at *puerta* (door) 7 in terminal 1 and *puerta* 3 in terminal 2. The terminals also are connected by an *aerotrén*, a free monorail service for ticketed passengers only.

Both terminals have *casas de cambio* and peso-dispensing ATMs. Car-rental agencies and luggage lockers are in *salas* (hall) A and E2 of terminal 1.

Direct buses to Cuernavaca, Querétaro, Toluca, Puebla and Córdoba depart from platforms adjacent to *sala* E in terminal 1 and from *sala* D in terminal 2. Ticket counters in terminal 1 are on the upper level, off the food court. A pedestrian bridge off *sala* B leads to an ADO bus terminal with service to Acapulco and Veracruz.

More than 20 airlines provide international service to Mexico City. You can fly direct from more than 30 cities in the USA and Canada, half a dozen each in Europe, South America and Central America/Caribbean and from Tokyo. Seven different airlines connect the capital to about 50 cities within Mexico.

BUS

Mexico City has four long-distance bus terminals serving the four compass points: Terminal Norte (north), Terminal Oriente (called TAPO; east), Terminal Poniente (Observatorio; west) and Terminal Sur (south). All terminals have baggage-check services or lockers, as well as tourist-information modules, newsstands, card phones, internet, ATMs and snack bars.

There are also buses to nearby cities from the airport.

For trips of up to five hours, it usually suffices to go to the bus station, buy your ticket and go. For longer trips, many buses leave in the evening and tickets may well sell out earlier, so buy beforehand.

You can purchase advance tickets at **Oxxo** convenience stores throughout the city and **Boletotal** (✆ 55-5133-5133, 800-009-90-90; www.boletotal.mx), a booking agency for more than a dozen bus lines out of all four stations (a 10% surcharge is added to the cost of the ticket up to a maximum of M$50). Boletotal also offers purchase by phone with Visa or MasterCard. Boletotal branches:

Buenavista (Ticketbus; Buenavista 9, cnr Orozco y Berra; ⊘ 9am-2:30pm & 3:30-6:30pm Mon-Fri, to 2:30pm Sat; Ⓜ Revolución)

Polanco (Ticketbus; Map p88; cnr Homero & Arquímedes; ⊘ 9am-3pm & 4-6:30pm Mon-Fri, 9am-12:30pm Sat; Ⓜ Polanco)

Roma Norte (Ticketbus; Map p82; Mérida 156, cnr Zacatecas; ⊘ 9am-2:30pm & 3:30-6:45pm Mon-Fri, to 2:45pm Sat; Ⓜ Hospital General)

Zócalo (Turismo Zócalo; Map p68; 2nd fl, Palma 34, Colonia Centro, inside Gran Plaza Ciudad de México; ⊘ 10am-7pm Mon-Fri, to 1pm Sat; Ⓜ Zócalo)

Lines

Check schedules by visiting individual bus lines' websites.

ADO Group (✆ 800-702-80-00, 55-5133-2424; www.ado.com.mx) Includes ADO Platino (deluxe), ADO GL (executive), OCC (1st class), ADO (1st class) and AU (2nd class).

Autobuses Teotihuacán (✆ 55-5587-0501) Second class. No website.

Autovías (✆ 800-622-22-22; www.autovias.com.mx) First class.

Estrella Blanca Group (✆ 800-507-55-00, 55-5729-0807; www.estrellablanca.com.mx) Operates Futura, Costa Line and Elite (1st class).

Estrella de Oro (✆ 800-900-01-05, 55-5549-8520; www.estrelladeoro.com.mx) Executive and 1st class.

Estrella Roja (✆ 800-712-22-84, 55-5130-1800; www.estrellaroja.com.mx) First class.

ETN (✆ 800-800-03-86, 55-5089-9200; www.etn.com.mx) Includes ETN (deluxe) and Turistar (executive and deluxe).

Ómnibus de México (✆ 800-765-66-36, 55-5141-4300; www.odm.com.mx) First class.

Primera Plus (✆ 800-375-75-87; www.primeraplus.com.mx) Deluxe and 1st class.

Pullman de Morelos (✆ 800-624-03-60, 55-5549-3505; www.pullman.mx) Executive, deluxe and 1st class.

Terminals

Terminal de Autobuses del Norte (✆ 55-5587-1552; www.centraldelnorte.com.mx; Eje Central Lázaro Cárdenas 4907, Colonia Magdalena de las Salinas; Ⓜ Autobuses del Norte) The largest of the four bus terminals. Serves points north, including cities on the US border, plus some points west (Guadalajara, Puerto Vallarta), east (Puebla) and south (Acapulco, Oaxaca). Deluxe and 1st-class counters are mostly in the southern half of the terminal. Luggage-storage services are at the far south end and in the central passageway.

Terminal de Autobuses de Pasajeros de Oriente (TAPO; ✆ 55-5522-9381; Calz Zaragoza 200, Colonia Diez de Mayo; Ⓜ San Lázaro) For eastern and southeastern destinations, including Puebla, Veracruz, Yucatán, Oaxaca and Chiapas. Bus-line counters are arranged around a rotunda with a food court, internet terminals and ATMs. There's a left-luggage service in 'Túnel 1.'

Terminal de Autobuses del Poniente (Observatorio; ☑ 55-5271-0149; Av Sur 122, Colonia Real del Monte; Ⓜ Observatorio) The point for buses heading to Michoacán and shuttle services running to nearby Toluca. In addition, ETN offers service to Guadalajara.

Terminal de Autobuses del Sur (Tasqueña; ☑ 55-5689-9745; Av Tasqueña 1320, Colonia Campestre Churubusco; Ⓜ Tasqueña) Serves Tepoztlán, Cuernavaca, Taxco, Acapulco and other southern destinations, as well as Oaxaca, Huatulco and Ixtapa-Zihuatanejo. Estrella de Oro (Acapulco, Taxco) and Pullman de Morelos (Cuernavaca) counters are on the right side of the terminal, while OCC, Estrella Roja (Tepoztlán), ETN and Futura are on the left. In *sala* 3 you'll find luggage-storage service and ATMs.

CAR & MOTORCYCLE

Rental

Rental-car companies have offices at the airport, at bus stations and in the Zona Rosa area of the city. Rates generally start at about M$600 per day, but you can often do better by booking online. You can find a list of rental agencies online at the DF Tourism Secretariat website (www. mexicocity.gob.mx).

Avis (☑ 800-500-28-47, 55-5511-2228; www. avis.mx; Paseo de la Reforma 308; ⊘ 7am-10:30pm Mon-Fri, 8am-4pm Sat & Sun; Ⓜ Insurgentes)

Thrifty (☑ 55-5514-3404; www.thrifty.com; Paseo de la Reforma 322; Ⓜ Insurgentes)

Roadside Assistance

If you leave the city, the *Ángeles Verdes* (Green Angels) can provide highway assistance between 8am and 6pm. Just phone ☑ 078 and tell them your location.

Routes In & Out of the City

Whichever way you come into the city, once you're past the last *caseta* (toll booth) you enter a no-man's-land of poorly marked lanes and chaotic traffic. These *casetas* are also the points from which 'Hoy No Circula' rules (p138) take effect.

➡ **To Puebla** (east of DF), take the Viaducto Alemán (Río de la Piedad) east. From Roma and Zona Rosa, this is most conveniently accessed off Avenida Cuauhtémoc (Eje 1 Poniente). Immediately after crossing over the Viaducto – by the Liverpool department store – turn left for the access ramp. From the Zócalo take Viaducto Tlalpan to get onto Viaducto Alemán then follow signs to Calzada Zaragoza. This leads to the highway to Puebla, or for Puebla airport head north along Blvd Puerto Aéreo.

➡ **To Oaxaca or Veracruz**, also take the Viaducto Alemán to Calzada Zaragoza then follow the signs for Oaxaca until you join the Puebla highway.

➡ **To Querétaro** (north of DF), take Reforma from the Diana roundabout until you reach the Estela de Luz and turn right onto Calz Gral Mariano Escobedo. Keep right and look for the signs to take the ramp to Querétaro. Pass through the toll at Tepotzlán. Continue along for 200km. Take the exit toward Centro from Carretera México-Querétaro.

➡ **To Pachuca, Hidalgo and northern Veracruz** (north of DF), take Avenida Insurgentes north (also the route to Teotihuacán), which feeds into the highway.

➡ **To Cuernavaca** (south of DF), turn right (south) at the Zócalo onto Pino Suárez, which becomes Calzada Tlalpan. About 20km south, signs indicate a left exit for the *cuota* (toll highway) to Cuernavaca.

➡ **To Toluca** (west of DF), heading out of the city, take Paseo de la Reforma, which feeds right into the *cuota,* passing the high-rises of Santa Fe, to Toluca.

ⓘ Getting Around

Mexico City has an inexpensive, easy-to-use metro and an equally cheap and practical bus system plying all the main routes. Taxis are plentiful, but some are potentially hazardous.

TO/FROM THE AIRPORT

The metro is a cheap option for getting to the airport, though hauling luggage amid rush-hour crowds can be a Herculean task. Authorized taxis provide a painless, relatively inexpensive alternative, as does the metrobús.

Metro

➡ The airport metro station is Terminal Aérea, on Línea 5 (yellow). It's 200m from terminal 1: leave by the exit at the end of *sala* A (domestic arrivals) and continue past the taxi stand to the station.

➡ To the city center, follow signs for 'Dirección Politécnico.' At La Raza (seven stops away) change for Línea 3 (green) toward 'Dirección Universidad.' Metro Hidalgo, at the west end of the Alameda, is three stops south; it's also a transfer point for Línea 2 (blue) to the Zócalo.

➡ To get to the Zona Rosa from the airport, take Línea 5 to 'Pantitlán,' the end of the line. Change for Línea 1 (pink) and get off at metro Insurgentes.

➡ There is no convenient metro link to terminal 2, but red buses at the entrance of terminal 2 go to metro Hangares (Línea 5).

Taxi

➡ Safe and reliable *taxis autorizados* (authorized taxis) are controlled by a fixed-price ticket system.

➡ Purchase taxi tickets from booths located in *sala* E1 (international arrivals) as you exit customs, and by the *sala* A (domestic arrivals) exit.

» Fares are determined by zones. A ride to the Zócalo, Roma, Condesa or Zona Rosa costs M$235. One ticket is valid for up to four passengers. 'Sitio 300' taxis are the best.

» Porters may offer to take your ticket and luggage the few steps to the taxi, but hold on to the ticket and hand it to the driver. Drivers won't expect a tip for the ride, but will always welcome one.

Metrobús

» Línea 4 of the metrobús has luggage racks and on-board security cameras, making it a more comfortable option than the metro.

» Stops at *puerta* 7 in terminal 1 and *puerta* 3 in terminal 2. The ride costs M$30, plus you'll need to purchase a smart card (valid for all metrobús trips) for M$10 at machines inside the terminals. From terminal 1, it's about 45 minutes to reach the Zócalo.

» The line runs five blocks north of the Zócalo, along República de Venezuela and Belisario Domínguez, then it heads west along Avenida Hidalgo past metro Hidalgo. To return to the airport, catch it along Ayuntamiento or República del Salvador. See www.metrobus.df.gob.mx for more information.

TO/FROM THE BUS TERMINALS

The metro is the fastest and cheapest way to or from any bus terminal, but it's tricky to maneuver through crowded stations and cars. Taxis are an easier option – all terminals have ticket booths for secure *taxis autorizados*, with fares set by zone. A M$20 surcharge is applied from 9pm to 6am. An agent at the exit will assign you a cab.

Terminal Norte Metro Línea 5 (yellow) stops at Autobuses del Norte, just outside the terminal. To the city center, follow signs for 'Dirección Pantitlán,' then change at La Raza for Línea 3 (green) toward 'Dirección Universidad.' (The La Raza connection is a six-minute hike through a 'Tunnel of Science.') The taxi kiosk is in the central passageway; a cab for up to four people to the Zócalo, Roma or Condesa costs about M$135.

Terminal Oriente (TAPO) This bus terminal is next door to metro San Lázaro. To the city center or Zona Rosa, take Línea 1 (pink) toward 'Dirección Observatorio.' The authorized taxi booth is at the top (metro) end of the main passageway from the rotunda. The fare to the Zócalo is M$85; to the Zona Rosa, Roma or Condesa it's M$102.

Terminal Poniente Observatorio metro station, the eastern terminus of Línea 1 (pink), is a couple of minutes' walk across a busy street. A taxi ticket to Roma costs M$102, Condesa M$73 and the Zócalo M$135.

Terminal Sur It's a two-minute walk from metro Tasqueña, the southern terminus of Línea 2, which stops at the Zócalo. For the Zona Rosa, transfer at Pino Suárez and take Línea 1 to Insurgentes (Dirección Observatorio). Going to the terminal, take the 'Autobuses del Sur' exit, which leads upstairs to a footbridge. Descend the last staircase on the left then walk through a street market to reach the building. Authorized taxis from Terminal Sur cost M$140 to the *centro histórico* and M$152 to Condesa and Roma. Ticket booths are in *sala* 3.

BICYCLE

Bicycles can be a viable way to get around town and are often preferable to overcrowded, recklessly driven buses. Although careless drivers and potholes can make DF cycling an extreme sport, if you stay alert and keep off the major thoroughfares, it's manageable. The city government has encouraged bicycle use, with more bicycle-only lanes, and it's definitely catching on.

Bikes are loaned free from a module on the west side of the Catedral Metropolitana. You'll also find booths at Plaza Villa de Madrid in Roma, at the intersection of Mazatlán and Michoacán in Condesa, and several along Paseo de la Reforma, near the Monumento a la Independencia and Auditorio Nacional. Leave a passport or driver's license for three hours of riding time. The modules operate from 10:30am to 6pm Monday to Saturday, and 9:30am to 4:30pm on Sunday.

The Mexico City government rents commuter bikes through **Ecobici** (Map p82; ☑ 55-5005-2424; www.ecobici.df.gob.mx; Campeche 175; rentals 1/3/7 days M$90/180/300; ☺ 9am-6pm Mon-Fri, 10am-2pm Sat; ⛗ Campeche) to visitors on a daily and weekly basis. You'll need a Visa or MasterCard for the deposit and a passport or driver's license for ID. The bicycle share program works with smart cards and allows you to ride for up to 45 minutes between docking stations. To avoid paying a fine for exceeding 45 minutes, simply exchange the bike at a different station. Ecobici is a great option for exploring downtown, Roma and Condesa, neighborhoods with the greatest concentration of stations.

The *ciclovía* is an extensive bike trail that follows the old bed of the Cuernavaca railroad as far as the Morelos border. It extends from Avenida Ejército Nacional in Polanco through the Bosque de Chapultepec, skirting the Periférico freeway from La Feria to Avenida San Antonio, with several steep bridges passing over the freeways.

Another path follows Avenida Chapultepec along a protected median from Bosque de Chapultepec to the *centro histórico*, though a detour through the streets of Roma is ignored by motorists. A third route runs along Paseo de la Reforma from the Auditorio Nacional to downtown.

Every Sunday Paseo de la Reforma and several main downtown streets are closed off to traffic from 8am to 2pm and riders can enjoy a 26km *'ciclotón'* route that spans from Auditorio Nacional to the Basílica de Guadalupe.

BUSES FROM MEXICO CITY

DESTINATION	TERMINAL IN MEXICO CITY	BUS COMPANY	FARE (M$)	DURATION (HR)	FREQUENCY (DAILY)
Acapulco	Sur	Costa Line, Estrella de Oro	470-615	5	16
	Norte	Futura, Costa Line	470	5½-6	9
Bahías de Huatulco	Sur	OCC, Turistar	800-1018	15-15½	3
	Norte	OCC	800	16	4:45pm
Campeche	Oriente (TAPO)	ADO, ADO GL	1444-1742	16-18	6
	Norte	ADO	1444	17-18	2
Cancún	Oriente (TAPO)	ADO, ADO GL	1904-2160	24-27	5
Chetumal	Oriente (TAPO)	ADO	1556	19½-20	2
Chihuahua	Norte	Ómnibus de México	1605	18-19	7
Cuernavaca	Sur	Pullman de Morelos	105-115	1¼	frequent
Guadalajara	Norte	ETN, Primera Plus	635-825	6-7	frequent
	Poniente	ETN	760-825	6¼	4
Guanajuato	Norte	ETN, Primera Plus	528-630	5-5½	14
Matamoros	Norte	ETN, Futura	1150-1350	12½-13½	3
Mazatlán	Norte	Elite	1055-1114	13-16	13
Mérida	Oriente (TAPO)	ADO, ADO GL	1592-1882	19-20½	6
Monterrey	Norte	ETN, Futura	1035-1205	11-13	18
Morelia	Poniente	ETN	495	4-4¼	frequent
Nuevo Laredo	Norte	ETN, Futura, Turistar	1280-1465	15-15½	8
Oaxaca	Oriente (TAPO)	ADO, ADO GL, ADO Platino	560-945	6-6½	frequent
	Sur	ADO GL, OCC	628-700	6½	5
Palenque	Oriente (TAPO)	ADO	1170	12¾	6:10pm
Papantla	Norte	ADO	330	5-6	7
Pátzcuaro	Norte	Autovías, Primera Plus	393-497	5	7
	Poniente	Autovías	596	5	11
Puebla	Airport	Estrella Roja	220	2	every 40min
	Oriente (TAPO)	ADO, ADO GL, AU, Pullman de Morelos	150-192	2-2¼	frequent
Puerto Escondido	Sur	OCC, Turistar	915-1025	12-17½	2

DESTINATION	TERMINAL IN MEXICO CITY	BUS COMPANY	FARE (M$)	DURATION (HR)	FREQUENCY (DAILY)
Puerto Vallarta	Norte	ETN, Futura	962-1255	12-13½	5
Querétaro	Norte	ETN, Primera Plus	273-330	2¾-3	frequent
	Airport	Primera Plus	365	3	frequent
	Poniente	Primera Plus	273	3½-4	17
San Cristóbal de las Casas	Oriente (TAPO)	ADO GL, OCC	1256-1522	13-14	7
	Norte	OCC	1318	14-14½	4
San Luis Potosí	Norte	ETN, Primera Plus, Turistar	500-620	4½-5½	frequent
San Miguel de Allende	Norte	ETN, Primera Plus	394-475	3¼-4	7
Tapachula	Oriente (TAPO)	ADO GL, ADO Platino, OCC	1340-1834	16½-19½	11
Taxco	Sur	Pullman de Morelos	167	2½	4
Teotihuacán	Norte	Autobuses Teotihuacán	45	1	hourly 6am-9pm
Tepoztlán	Sur	OCC	113	1	frequent
Tijuana	Norte	Elite	1955	41	12
Toluca	Airport	TMT Caminante	147	1¾	hourly
	Poniente	ETN	75	1	frequent
Tuxtla Gutiérrez	Oriente (TAPO)	ADO, ADO GL, ADO Platino, OCC	1164-1670	11¾-12½	14
Uruapan	Poniente	Autovías, ETN	543-670	5¼-6	17
Veracruz	Oriente (TAPO)	ADO, ADO GL, ADO Platino, AU	420-720	5½-7¼	frequent
	Sur	ADO, ADO GL	664-748	5½-6¼	6
Villahermosa	Oriente (TAPO)	ADO, ADO GL, ADO Platino, AU	1002-1272	10-12¼	24
Xalapa	Oriente (TAPO)	ADO, ADO GL, ADO Platino, AU	294-604	4½-5	frequent
Zacatecas	Norte	Ómnibus de México	825	8	14
Zihuatanejo	Sur	Costa Line, Futura	665-735	9	4
	Poniente	Autovías	701	9	3

CAR & MOTORCYCLE

Touring Mexico City by car is strongly discouraged, unless you have a healthy reserve of patience. Even more than elsewhere in the country, traffic rules are seen as suggested behavior. Red lights may be run at will, no-turn signs are ignored and signals are seldom used. On occasion you may be hit with a questionable traffic fine. Nevertheless, you may want to rent a car here for travel outside the city. Avoid parking on the street whenever possible; most midrange and top-end hotels have guest garages. If you do park on the street, keep in mind that some neighborhoods, such as Cuauhtémoc, Roma and Polanco, have *parquímetros* (green parking meters usually located at the middle of the block). Feed them or your vehicle will be booted.

To help combat pollution, Mexico City operates its 'Hoy No Circula' (Don't Drive Today) program, banning many vehicles from being driven in the city between 5am and 10pm on one day each week. Additionally, vehicles nine years and older are prohibited from operating one Saturday a month. Exempted from restrictions are rental cars and vehicles with a *calcomanía de verificación* (emissions verification sticker), obtained under the city's vehicle-pollution assessment system.

For vehicles without the sticker (including foreign-registered ones), the last digit of the license-plate number determines the day when they cannot circulate. See the official website (http://hoynocirculacdmx.com, in Spanish) for more information.

Day	Prohibited last digit
Monday	5, 6
Tuesday	7, 8
Wednesday	3, 4
Thursday	1, 2
Friday	9, 0

METRO

The metro system (www.metro.df.gob.mx) offers the quickest way to get around Mexico City. Used by around 4.4 million passengers on an average weekday, it has 195 stations and more than 226km of track on 12 lines. Trains arrive every two to three minutes during rush hours. At M$5 a ride, it's one of the world's cheapest subways.

All lines operate from 5am to midnight weekdays, 6am to midnight Saturday and 7am to midnight Sunday and holidays. Platforms and cars can become alarmingly packed during rush hours (roughly 7:30am to 10am and 3pm to 8pm). At these times the forward cars are reserved for women and children, and men may not proceed beyond the '*Sólo Mujeres y Niños*' gate.

With such crowded conditions, it's not surprising that pickpocketing occurs, so watch your belongings.

The metro is easy to use. Lines are color-coded and each station is identified by a unique logo. Signs reading 'Dirección Pantitlán,' 'Dirección Universidad' and so on name the stations at the end of the lines. Check a map for the direction you want. Buy a rechargeable smart card for M$10 at any station and then add credit (the card also works for all metrobús lines). Additionally, the metro sells *boletos* (tickets) at the *taquilla* (ticket window). Feed the ticket into the turnstile and you're on your way. When changing trains, look for '*Correspondencia*' (Transfer) signs. Maps of the vicinity around each station are posted near the exits.

PESERO, METROBÚS & TROLLEYBÚS

Mexico City's thousands of buses and peseros operate from around 5am till 10pm daily, depending on the route. Electric trolleybuses generally run until 11:30pm. Only a few routes run all night, notably those along Paseo de la Reforma. This means you'll get anywhere by bus and/or metro during the day, but will probably have to take a few taxis after hours.

Pesero

Peseros (also called microbúses or combis) are gray-and-green minibuses operated by private firms. They follow fixed routes, often starting or ending at metro stations, and will stop at virtually any street corner. Route information is randomly displayed on cards attached to the windshield. Fares are M$4 for trips of up to 5km, and M$4.50 for 5km to 12km. Add 20% to all fares between 11pm and 6am. Municipally operated trolleybuses and full-sized cream-and-orange buses (labeled 'RTP') only pick up at bus stops. Fares are M$2 (M$4 for the express) regardless of distance traveled. Privately run green-and-yellow buses charge M$5.50 to M$6.

Metrobús

The metrobús is a wheelchair-accessible Volvo vehicle that stops at metro-style stations in the middle of the street, spaced at three- to four-block intervals. Access is by prepaid smart card, issued by machines for M$10 at the entrance to the platforms, and rides cost M$6. The rechargeable cards, which can also be used for the metro, are placed on a sensor device for entry. Most metrobús lines run from 5am to midnight. Línea (line) 1, the only metrobús route with 24-hour service, plies a dedicated lane along Avenida Insurgentes from metro Indios Verdes in northern DF down to the southern end of Tlalpan. Línea 2, which connects with Línea 1 at the Nuevo León station, runs west to east along Eje 4 Sur from metro Tacubaya to metro Tepalcates. Línea 3 operates on a north–south route from the Tenayuca station to Ethiopia, where you can transfer to

Línea 2. Línea 4 runs from metro Buenavista and cuts through the *centro histórico* to metro San Lázaro. The line also has an *'aeropuerto'* bus that goes to and from the airport for M$30.

Trolleybús

Trolleybuses follow a number of the key *ejes* (priority roads) throughout the rest of the city.

Routes

Here are some more useful routes:

➡ **Autobuses del Sur & Autobuses del Norte** (trolleybús) Eje Central Lázaro Cárdenas between north and south bus terminals (stops at Plaza de las Tres Culturas, Plaza Garibaldi, Bellas Artes/Alameda, metro Hidalgo).

➡ **Auditorio–La Villa** (metrobus Línea 7) Paseo de la Reforma between Auditorio Nacional and Basílica de Guadalupe (stops at Zona Rosa, Avenida Insurgentes, Alameda/metro Hidalgo, Plaza Garibaldi, Plaza de las Tres Culturas).

➡ **Metro Sevilla–Presidente Masaryk** (pesero) Between Colonia Roma and Polanco via Álvaro Obregón and Avenida Presidente Masaryk (stops at metro Niños Héroes, Avenida Insurgentes, metro Sevilla, Leibnitz).

➡ **Metro Tacubaya–Balderas–Escandón** (pesero) Between *centro histórico* and Condesa, westbound via Puebla, eastbound via Durango (stops at Plaza San Juan, metro Balderas, metro Insurgentes, Parque España, Avenida Michoacán).

TAXI

Mexico City has several classes of taxi. Cheapest are the cruising pink-and-white (or, being phased out, red-and-gold) street cabs, though they're not recommended due to the risk of assaults. If you must hail a cab off the street, check that it has actual taxi license plates: numbers are preceded with the letters A or B. Check that the number on them matches the number painted on the bodywork. Also look for the *carta de identificación* (called the *tarjetón*), a postcard-sized ID that should be displayed visibly inside the cab, and ensure that the driver matches the photo. If the cab you've hailed does not pass these tests, get another one.

UBER VS TAXIS

App-based, taxi-like service Uber (www.uber.com) has arrived in DF, to the despise of *taxistas* (taxi drivers) and the delight of many travelers, who prefer its comfortable vehicles, service, cashless system and often cheaper costs, especially for longer journeys such as to and from the airport. Order an Uber on your smartphone, pinpointing a pickup and destination on a map. The app records the details of every journey, driver and vehicle, making it safer than taxis. Many *chilangos* say they now go out at night more because of Uber.

In *libre* cabs (street cabs), fares are computed by *taxímetro* (meter), which should start at about M$9. The total cost of a 3km ride in moderate traffic – say, from the Zócalo to the Zona Rosa – should be M$30 to M$40. Between 11pm and 6am, add 20%.

Radio taxis, which come in many different colors, cost about three times as much as the others, but this extra cost adds an immeasurable degree of security. When you phone, the dispatcher will tell you the cab number and the type of car. If you have a smartphone or device, you can order a cab via the popular app Easy Taxi (http://easytaxi.com) or Uber (www.uber.com).

Maps in this chapter show the location of some key *sitios* (taxi stands) for radio taxis. Some reliable radio-taxi firms, available 24 hours, include the following:

Radio Maxi Seguridad (☑ 55-5768-8557, 55-5552-1376)

Sitio Parque México (Map p82; ☑ 55-5286-7164, 55-5286-7129)

Taxi-Mex (Map p82; ☑ 55-9171-8888; www.taximex.com.mx)

Taxis Radio Unión (☑ 55-5514-8074, 55-5514-7861; www.taxisradiounion.com.mx)

Around Mexico City

Includes ➡

Tepotzotlán 141
Tula 144
Teotihuacán. 146
Pachuca 150
Puebla 154
Cholula. 163
Tlaxcala 167
Cuetzalan. 174
Tepoztlán 176
Cuautla. 180
Cuernavaca 182
Taxco 190
Parque Nacional Grutas
de Cacahuamilpa 195
Toluca. 196
Malinalco 201

Best Places to Eat

➡ Las Ranas (p160)

➡ Restaurante y Cabañas San Diego (p154)

➡ La Sibarita (p179)

Best Places to Stay

➡ Hotel Mi Casita (p193)

➡ Hotel Hacienda de Cortés (p187)

➡ Posada del Tepozteco (p178)

Why Go?

With its daunting size and seemingly endless sprawl, the megalopolis of Mexico City might seem like a challenge to escape from, but even if you're in Mexico's capital for only a week, the ancient ruins, *pueblos mágicos* (magical villages) and stunning mountain landscape of the surrounding area should not be missed. Mexico City – like many capitals – has little in common with even its closest neighbors.

While many visitors to the region take a day trip to the awe-inspiring archaeological complex at Teotihuacán, the area offers much more – from the captivating colonial cities of Taxco, Puebla and Cuernavaca, to the eccentric small towns of Valle de Bravo and Tepoztlán. For those eager to taste some crisp, particulate-free mountain air, there are *pueblitos* (small towns) such as Cuetzalan and Real del Monte, the volcanic giants of Popocatépetl and Iztaccíhuatl, and the lesser-known ruins of Xochicalco and Cantona to visit.

When to Go
Puebla City

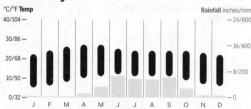

°C/°F Temp
40/104 —
30/86 —
20/68 —
10/50 —
0/32 —

Rainfall inches/mm
— 24/600
— 16/400
— 8/200
— 0

J F M A M J J A S O N D

May–Oct Rainy season; afternoon showers wash the air clean and bring wild mushrooms to the forests.

Sep The weeks before Independence Day are the time to taste the seasonal specialty *chiles en nogada*.

Nov–Apr Drier months; nominally cooler, making for pleasant daytime city exploration and casual hikes.

History

Long a cultural and economic crossroads, the region around present-day Mexico City has hosted a succession of important indigenous civilizations (notably the Teotihuacán, Toltec and Aztec). By the late 15th century, the Aztecs had managed to dominate all but one of central Mexico's states. Many archaeological sites and museums preserve remnants of this pre-Hispanic history – Puebla's Museo Amparo provides an excellent overview of the region's history and cultures.

Post-conquest, the Spanish transformed central Mexico, establishing ceramic industries at Puebla, mines at Taxco and Pachuca, and haciendas producing wheat, sugar and cattle throughout the region. The Catholic Church used the region as a base for its missionary activities and left a series of imposing churches and fortified monasteries. Today, most towns retain a central plaza surrounded by colonial buildings.

ⓘ Getting There & Around

The cities, towns and (to a lesser extent) even the villages around Mexico City enjoy excellent, often 1st-class, bus links to both the capital and each other. Even the very smallest backwaters have comfortable daily services to Mexico City and to the closest transportation hub. While airports also serve Puebla, Toluca, Cuernavaca and Pachuca, it's nearly always cheaper and easier to fly to Mexico City and travel onward from there. For all but the most obscure sights, traveling by bus is the easiest and most affordable option.

NORTH OF MEXICO CITY

The biggest attraction north of Mexico City is the extraordinary complex at Teotihuacán, once the largest metropolis in the Americas and one of Mexico's most spectacular pre-Hispanic sights. Further north, the well-preserved stone statues at Tula also draw visitors.

Far less visited, but equally impressive, are Parque Nacional El Chico and the mining village of Mineral del Chico – the perfect escape from the big city, with stunning views, wide-open spaces and friendly locals.

Pachuca, the fast-growing capital of dynamic Hidalgo state, has brightly painted houses, an attractive colonial center and a great line in Cornish pasties. From Pachuca, well-paved routes snake east and north to the Gulf coast, through spectacular country such as the fringes of the Sierra Madre Oriental mountain range and the coastal plain.

Tepotzotlán

🎵 55 / POP 38,000 / ELEV 2300M

This *pueblo mágico* is an easy day trip from Mexico City, but feels far from the chaotic streets of the capital, despite the fact that urban sprawl creeps closer to Tepotzotlán's colonial center every year.

◎ Sights

Museo Nacional del Virreinato MUSEUM (National Museum of the Viceregal Period; 🎵 55-5876-0245; www.virreinato.inah.gob.mx; Plaza Hidalgo 99; M$55; ⊙ 9am-6pm Tue-Sun) There's a very simple reason to visit this wonderful museum comprising the restored Jesuit **Iglesia de San Francisco Javier** and an adjacent **monastery**. Much of the folk art and fine art on display – silver chalices, pictures created from inlaid wood, porcelain, furniture and religious paintings and statues – comes from Mexico City cathedral's large collection, and the standard is very high.

Once a Jesuit college of indigenous languages, the complex dates from 1606. Diverse additions were made over the following 150 years, creating a showcase for the developing architectural styles of Nueva España.

Don't miss the **Capilla Doméstica**, with a Churrigueresque main altarpiece that boasts more mirrors than a carnival fun house. The facade is a phantasmagoric array of carved saints, angels, plants and people, while the interior walls and the Camarín del Virgen adjacent to the altar are swathed with gilded ornamentation.

★ Festivals & Events

Pastorelas RELIGIOUS
Tepotzotlán's highly regarded *pastorelas* (nativity plays) are performed inside the former monastery in the weeks leading up to Christmas. Tickets, which include Christmas dinner and piñata smashing, can be purchased at La Hostería del Convento de Tepotzotlán after November 1 or via Ticketmaster (🎵 55-5325-9000; www.ticketmaster.com.mx).

Around Mexico City Highlights

1 Enjoying a sunset drink on **Cuetzalan's** (p174) tiny *zócalo* amid the dramatic scenery of the Sierra Madre Oriental.

2 Being blown away by the spectacular pyramids at **Teotihuacán** (p146), or discovering some of central Mexico's most magnificent, lesser-known ancient sites at **Xochicalco** (p186) and **Cantona** (p174).

3 Wandering the steep cobblestone streets of **Taxco** (p190) and scoping out the city's famed silver shops.

4 Having a close encounter with Mexico's New Age culture in **Tepoztlán** (p141) and **Malinalco** (p201).

5 Feeling the mountain mists sweep over you in tiny **Mineral del Chico** (p152).

6 Admiring the impressive cathedral and many pretty, historic churches in **Puebla** (p154).

7 Climbing volcanic peaks such as **La Malinche** (p173), **Nevado de Toluca** (p199) or **Iztaccíhuatl** (p166).

8 Following in the footsteps of Mexico City's artists and high society and escaping to eternal spring in **Cuernavaca** (p182).

🛏 Sleeping

Tepotzotlán is geared toward day trippers, but there are a couple of good-value hotels.

Hotel Posada San José HOTEL **$**
(☑ 55-5876-0835; Plaza Virreinal 13; r M$350-500) Housed in a handsome colonial building on the south side of the *zócalo* (main plaza), this centrally located budget hotel has 12 small rooms. The rooms overlooking the plaza and those near the hotel's water pump are noisy, though cheaper.

Hotel Posada del Virrey HOTEL **$**
(☑ 55-5876-1864; Av Insurgentes 13; r with/without Jacuzzi M$600/400; 🅿 🛜) A short walk from the *zócalo*, this modern, motel-style posada (inn) is popular with weekenders. Rooms can be a bit dark but they're clean, quiet and have TVs.

🍴 Eating & Drinking

It's best to avoid the many almost indistinguishable, tourist-centric restaurants on the *zócalo*, where the food is mediocre and prices are high. A better option is to join the locals at the market behind the Palacio Municipal, where food stalls serve rich *pozole* (a thin stew of hominy, pork or chicken), *gorditas* (round masa cakes) and freshly squeezed juices all day long.

Comedor Vegetariano VEGETARIAN **$**
(☑ 55-5876-232; Plaza Tepotzotlán, Local A; comida corrida M$55; ⏰ 2-7pm Mon-Fri; 🍴) The yoga-instructor-owner-chef definitely sets the tranquil tone with her all-white outfits at this vegetarian restaurant in an inner courtyard. Set menus can include a simple salad, corn soup, sugar-free guava juice and natural yogurt with sunflower seeds. Tasty main dishes imitate meat favorites such as Veracruz-style 'fish' (from mushrooms) and gluten *milanesa* (Mexican schnitzel).

La Hostería del Convento de Tepotzotlán MEXICAN **$$**
(☑ 55-5876-0243; www.hosteriadelconvento.com. mx; Plaza Virreinal 1; mains M$120-175; ⏰ 10am-5pm) Housed within the monastery's bougainvillea-walled courtyard, La Hostería serves traditional brunch and lunch fare – hearty soups, young chicken with *manzano* chilies, and *cecina adobada* (Oaxacan-style chili-marinated pork) – to an elite clientele.

Los Molcajetes PUB
(Los Molca; Pensador Mexicano s/n; ⏰ 6pm-late Tue-Sun) Los Molca (as locals call it) feels homely with its yellow terrace walls, wild plants, hearty Mexican food and hodge-podge of paintings. Weekends get busy with students and older couples head-nodding (and sometimes spontaneously dancing) to pop hits and Mexican classics. Start off the night here with a *'cucaracha'* (cockroach), a potent shot of tequila and Kahlua.

❶ Getting There & Around

Tepotzotlán is on the Mexico City–Querétaro highway. From Mexico City's Terminal Norte, 2nd-class Autotransportes Valle del Mezquital (AVM) buses (M$41, 40 minutes) stop at the new Tepotzotlán bus terminal every 20 minutes en route to Tula. First-class *(directo)* buses stop every 40 minutes. From the station, catch a combi (M$7.50) or secure taxi (M$35) to the *zócalo* (Plaza Virreinal).

Tula

📞 773 / POP 27,000 / ELEV 2060M

A major city of the ancient, central Mexican culture widely known as Toltec, Tula is best known for its fearsome 4.5m-high stone warrior figures. Though less spectacular and far smaller than Teotihuacán, Tula is nonetheless fascinating and worth the effort of a day trip or overnight stay for those interested in ancient Mexican history.

The most attractive areas are the *zócalo* and Calle Quetzalcóatl, the pedestrianized street running north of the *zócalo* to a footbridge over the Tula river.

History

Tula was an important city from about AD 900 to 1150, reaching a peak population of 35,000. Aztec annals tell of a king called Topiltzin – fair-skinned, black-bearded and long-haired – who founded a Toltec capital in the 10th century. There's debate, however, about whether Tula was this capital.

The Toltecs were empire builders upon whom the Aztecs looked with awe, going so far as to claim them as royal ancestors. Topiltzin was supposedly a priest-king, dedicated to peaceful worship (the Toltecs sacrificed only animals) of the feathered serpent god Quetzalcóatl. Tula is known to have housed followers of the less-likable Tezcatlipoca (Smoking Mirror), god of warriors, witchcraft and life and death – worshipping Tezcatlipoca required human sacrifices. The story goes that Tezcatlipoca appeared in various guises in order to provoke Topiltzin.

As a naked chili-seller, he aroused the lust of Topiltzin's daughter and eventually married her. As an old man, he persuaded the teetotaling Topiltzin to get drunk.

The humiliated leader eventually left for the Gulf coast, where he set sail eastward on a raft of snakes, promising one day to return and reclaim his throne. (This myth caused the Aztec emperor Moctezuma much consternation when Hernán Cortés appeared on the Gulf coast in 1519.)

At Tula's height, its fertile land produced cacao and its artisans were famous for crafting volcanic glass obsidian. Then in 1170 the city was ransacked and went into decline. Neighboring tribes invaded and Tula was eventually destroyed by the Aztecs.

⊙ Sights

Zona Arqueológica   ARCHAEOLOGICAL SITE
(☑773-100-36-54; Carretera Tula-Iturbe Km 2; M$52, video use M$52; ☺9am-5pm) Two kilometers north of Tula's center, ruins of the main ancient ceremonial site are perched on a hilltop. The highlight is standing atop a pyramid, virtually face-to-face with Toltec warrior statues, with views over rolling countryside (and the industrial sprawl nearby). Throughout the near-shadeless site, explanatory signs are in English, Spanish and Náhuatl. Near the main museum and the entrance to the site, you'll find souvenir markets on the weekends. Both of the on-site museums are free with site admission.

The main **site museum**, displaying ceramics, metalwork, jewelry and large sculptures, is near the entrance, at the north side of the *zona* from downtown. Outside the museum is a small, well-signed (in Spanish) cacti **garden**.

From the museum, the first large structure you'll reach is the **Juego de Pelota No 1** (Ball Court No 1). Archaeologists believe its walls were decorated with sculpted panels that were removed under Aztec rule.

Climb to the top of **Pirámide B**, also known as the Temple of Quetzalcóatl or Tlahuizcalpantecuhtli (the Morning Star), to see up close the impressive remains of three columnar roof supports – which once depicted feathered serpents with their heads on the ground and their tails in the air. The four basalt warrior telamones (male figures used as supporting columns; known as 'Los Atlantes') at the top, and the four pillars behind, supported the temple's roof. Wearing headdresses, breastplates shaped like

butterflies and short skirts held in place by sun disks, the warriors hold spear throwers in their right hands and knives and incense bags in their left. The telamon on the left side is a replica of the original, now in Mexico City's Museo Nacional de Antropología. The columns behind the telamones depict crocodile heads (which symbolize the Earth), warriors, symbols of warrior orders, weapons and Quetzalcóatl's head.

On the pyramid's north wall are some of the carvings that once surrounded the structure. These show the symbols of the warrior orders: jaguars, coyotes, eagles eating hearts, and what may be a human head in Quetzalcóatl's mouth.

Now roofless, the **Gran Vestíbulo** (Great Vestibule) extends along the front of the pyramid, facing the plaza. The stone bench carved with warriors originally ran the length of the hall, possibly to seat priests and nobles observing ceremonies in the plaza.

Near the north side of Pirámide B is the **Coatepantli** (Serpent Wall), which is 40m long, 2.25m high and carved with geometric patterns and a row of snakes devouring human skeletons. Traces remain of the original bright colors with which most of Tula's structures were painted.

Immediately west of Pirámide B, the **Palacio Quemado** (Burned Palace) is a series of halls and courtyards with more low benches and relief carvings, one depicting a procession of nobles. It was probably used for ceremonies or reunion meetings.

On the far side of the plaza is a path leading to the **Sala de Orientación Guadalupe Mastache**, a small museum named after one of the archaeologists who pioneered excavations here. It includes large items taken from the site, including the huge feet of caryatids (female figures used as supporting columns) and a visual representation of how the site might have looked in its prime.

Catedral de San José   CATHEDRAL
(cnr Zaragoza & Calle 5 de Mayo) Tula's fortress-like cathedral, just off the *zócalo*, was part of the 16th-century monastery of San José. Inside, its vault ribs are decorated in gold.

⊨ Sleeping

Hotel Casablanca   BUSINESS HOTEL $
(☑773-732-11-86; www.casablancatula.com; Pasaje Hidalgo 11; s/d/tr M$400/440/550; ℗ ☎) This comfortable, practical business hotel is right in the heart of Tula, located at the end

of a narrow pedestrian street (look for the 'Milano' sign). Casablanca offers 36 rooms, all with cable TV, private bathroom and good wi-fi. Parking access is around back, via Avenida Zaragoza.

Hotel Tula HOTEL **$**

(☑773-732-50-10; cnr Manuel Rojo del Río & Xicoténcatl; d/tw/tr M$300/570/970; ☜) The large tiled rooms are sterile and the private bathrooms are basic, but beds are comfortable and clean and it's conveniently on the same street as the bus terminal for a quick stay to see the pyramids.

Hotel Cuellar BUSINESS HOTEL **$$**

(☑773-732-29-20; Calle 5 de Mayo 23; s/d/tr M$650/700/1000; ☒) You may be in Tula for the pyramids, but you can include a dip in the pool here in your city escape. The low ceilings, palm trees and ample parking might make you swear you're in an LA motel and not near the *zócalo*.

Hotel Real Catedral HOTEL **$$**

(☑773-732-08-13; www.realhoteles.com/real_cate dral; Av Zaragoza 106; r/ste incl breakfast M$632/927; P☒☜) A street back from the plaza, the Real Catedral has some luxurious perks (a small gym, in-room coffeemakers, hair dryers and safes) for the price. Many of the inside rooms lack natural light, but the suites offer balconies and street views. There's also a great selection of black-and-white photos of Tula in the lobby.

✖ Eating

Cocina Económica Las Cazuelas MEXICAN **$**

(Pasaje Hidalgo 129; menú del día M$45; ⊘7am-7pm Mon-Sat, to 6pm Sun; ☜) Come here for an excellent *menú del día* (menu of the day) that includes your choice of soup, main dishes such as *chiles rellenos* (cheese-filled chilis) and *milanesa*, and *agua* (water flavored with fresh fruit). The upstairs balcony, away from the kitchen, is cooler than the steamy, main dining room.

Mana VEGETARIAN **$**

(☑773-100-31-33; Pasaje Hidalgo 13; menú del día M$45, buffet M$65; ⊘8am-5pm Sun-Fri; ☑) This simple vegetarian restaurant serves a generous *menú del día* that includes wholewheat bread, vegetable soup and a pitcher of oat milk. There's also a selection of veggie burgers, *taquitos*, quesadillas, soups and salads. Everything's fresh, hearty and homemade.

❶ Getting There & Away

Tula's **bus depot** (Xicoténcatl 14) is a short walk from downtown. First-class **Ovnibus** (☑773-732-96-00; www.gvm.com.mx) buses travel to/from Mexico City's Terminal Norte (M$124, 1¾ hours, every 40 minutes) and direct to/from Pachuca (M$111, 1¼ hours, hourly). AVM runs 2nd-class buses to the same destinations every 15 minutes.

❶ Getting Around

If you arrive in Tula by bus, the easiest way to get around is on foot. To reach the *zócalo* (known locally as 'El Jardín') from the station, turn right on Xicoténcatl then immediately left on Rojo del Río and walk two blocks to Hidalgo. Take a right on Hidalgo, which dead-ends at Plaza de la Constitución and Jardín de Tula, Tula's main square.

To reach the Zona Arqueológica, continue right 200m along Calle Zaragoza until the bridge over the river and catch a *taxi colectivo* (M$7.50, 10 minutes) to the Oxxo store outside the *zona*. Return taxis also depart from here. The site's secondary, south entrance is locked and defunct.

Unfortunately, the town's bus station lacks an *empaque* (baggage check), which is problematic for day trippers traveling with luggage.

Teotihuacán

☑594 / ELEV 2300M

This complex of awesome pyramids, set amid what was once Mesoamerica's greatest city, is among the region's most visited destinations. The sprawling site compares to the ruins of the Yucatán and Chiapas for significance and anyone lucky enough to come here will be inspired by the astonishing technological might of the Teotihuacán (teh-oh-tee-wah-*kahn*) civilization.

Set 50km northeast of Mexico City, in a mountain-ringed offshoot of the Valle de México, Teotihuacán is known for its two massive pyramids, the Pirámide del Sol (Pyramid of the Sun) and the Pirámide de la Luna (Pyramid of the Moon), which dominate the remains of the metropolis.

Though ancient Teotihuacán covered more than 20 sq km, most of what can be seen today lies along nearly 2km of the Calzada de los Muertos. Buses arrive at a traffic circle by the southwest entrance (gate 1), while four other entrances are reached by the ring road around the site. There are parking lots and ticket booths at each entrance. Your ticket allows you to re-enter through any of them on the same day. The site museum is just inside the main east entrance (gate 5).

Exploring the site is fascinating, but rebuffing the indefatigable hawkers is exhausting. Crowds at the **ruins** (M$64; ⊘7am-5pm Tue-Sun) can be huge. They're thickest from 10am to 2pm, and are busiest on Sunday, holidays and around the vernal equinox; going early pays off. Due to the heat and altitude, it's best to take it easy while exploring the expansive ruins. Bring a hat and water – most visitors walk several kilometers, and the midday sun can be brutal. Afternoon rain showers are common from June to September. No big backpacks are permitted up the Pirámide del Sol, and children must be accompanied by adults. There's a M$45 fee for the use of a video camera, and parking costs an additional M$45.

History

Teotihuacán was Mexico's biggest ancient city and the capital of what was probably Mexico's largest pre-Hispanic empire. It was a major hub of migration for people from the south, with multi-ethnic groups segregated into neighborhoods. Studies involving DNA tests in 2015 theorize that it was these cultural and class tensions that led to Teo's downfall.

The city's grid plan was plotted in the early part of the 1st century AD, and the Pirámide del Sol was completed – over an earlier cave shrine – by AD 150. The rest of the city was developed between about AD 250 and 600. Social, environmental and economic factors hastened its decline and eventual collapse in the 8th century.

The city was divided into quarters by two great avenues that met near La Ciudadela (the Citadel). One of them, running roughly north–south, is the famous Calzada de los Muertos (Avenue of the Dead), so called because the later Aztecs believed the great buildings lining it were vast tombs, built by giants for Teotihuacán's first rulers. The major structures are typified by a *talud-tablero* style, in which the rising portions of stepped, pyramid-like buildings consist of both sloping *(talud)* and upright *(tablero)* sections. They were often covered in lime and colorfully painted. Most of the city was made up of residential compounds, some of which contained elegant frescoes.

Centuries after its fall, Teotihuacán remained a pilgrimage site for Aztec royalty, who believed that all of the gods had sacrificed themselves here to start the sun moving at the beginning of the 'fifth world,' inhabited by the Aztecs. It remains an important pilgrimage site: thousands of New Age devotees flock here each year to celebrate the vernal equinox (between March 19 and March 21) and to soak up the mystical energies believed to converge here.

◉ Sights

Pirámide del Sol
PYRAMID

The world's third-largest pyramid, surpassed in size only by Egypt's Cheops and the pyramid of Cholula, overshadows the east side of the Calzada de los Muertos. When Teotihuacán was at its height, the pyramid's plaster was painted bright red, which must have been a radiant sight at sunset. Clamber (carefully) up the pyramid's 248 steps – yes, we counted – for an inspiring overview of the ancient city.

The Aztec belief that the structure was dedicated to the sun god was validated in 1971, when archaeologists uncovered a 100m-long underground tunnel leading from the pyramid's west flank to a cave directly beneath its center, where they found religious artifacts. It's thought that the sun was worshipped here before the pyramid was built and that the city's ancient inhabitants traced the origins of life to this grotto.

The pyramid's base is 222m long on each side, and it's now just over 70m high. The pyramid was cobbled together around AD 100, from three million tonnes of stone, without the use of metal tools, pack animals or the wheel.

Pirámide de la Luna
PYRAMID

The Pyramid of the Moon, at the north end of the Calzada de los Muertos, is smaller than the Pirámide del Sol, but more gracefully proportioned. Completed around AD 300, its summit is nearly the same height as Pirámide del Sol because it's built on higher ground, and is worth scaling for perspective on the dominance of the larger pyramid. The **Plaza de la Luna**, just in front of the pyramid, is a handsome arrangement of 12 temple platforms.

Some experts attribute astronomical symbolism to the total number of 13 (made up of the 12 platforms plus the pyramid), a key number in the day-counting system of the Mesoamerican ritual calendar. The altar in the plaza's center is thought to have been the site of religious dancing.

Teotihuacán

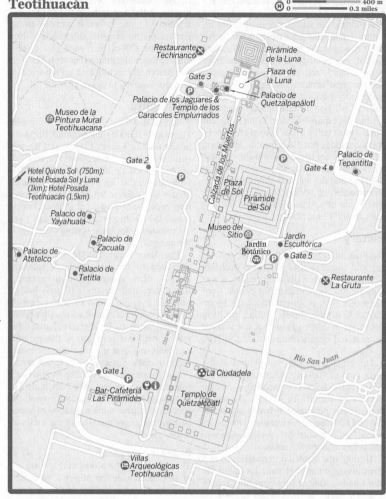

Calzada de los Muertos   RUIN

Centuries ago, the Calzada de los Muertos must have seemed absolutely incomparable to its inhabitants, who were able to see its buildings at their best. Gate 1 brings you to the avenue in front of La Ciudadela. For 2km heading north, the avenue is flanked by former palaces of Teotihuacán's elite and other major structures, such as the Pirámide del Sol. The Pirámide de la Luna looms large at the northern end.

Palacio de Quetzalpapálotl   PALACE

Off the Plaza de la Luna's southwest corner is the Palace of the Quetzal Butterfly,

thought to be the home of a high priest. The remains of bears, armadillos and other exotic animals were discovered here, showing that the area was used by the elite for cooking and rituals – not the kind of animals an average person would have eaten.

The **Palacio de los Jaguares** (Jaguar Palace) and **Templo de los Caracoles Emplumados** (Temple of the Plumed Conch Shells) are behind and below the Palacio de Quetzalpapálotl. The lower walls of several chambers off the patio of the Jaguar Palace display parts of murals showing the jaguar god blowing conch shells and praying to the rain god Tláloc. There are more complete murals in the Museo del Sitio.

The Templo de los Caracoles Emplumados, entered from the Palacio de los Jaguares' patio, is a now-subterranean structure of the 2nd or 3rd century. Carvings on what was its facade show large shells, possibly used as musical instruments.

La Ciudadela   RUIN
(Citadel) This expansive, square complex is believed to have been the residence of the city's supreme ruler. Four wide walls topped by 15 pyramids enclose a huge open space, with a major pyramid, the **Templo de Quetzalcóatl**, built around AD 250, to the east. Rooms here may have been the city's administrative center. Skeletal remains of 137 human victims have been found under and around this temple. DNA tests reveal they were brought from diverse parts of Mesoamerica to be sacrificed.

The four surviving steps of the Templo de Quetzacóatl's facade (there were originally seven) are adorned with striking carvings. In the *tablero* panels, the feathered serpent deity alternates with a two-fanged creature identified as the fire serpent, bearer of the sun on its daily journey across the sky. Imagine their eye sockets laid with glistening obsidian glass and the pyramid painted blue, as it once was. On the *talud* panels are side views of the plumed serpent. Some experts think the carvings depict war, while others interpret them as showing the creation of time.

Museo del Sitio   MUSEUM
(Museo de Teotihuacán; ☑594-958-20-81; ⊙9am-4:30pm) Lying just south of the Pirámide del Sol, Teotihuacán's site museum makes a refreshing stop midway through a visit to the historic complex. The museum has excellent displays of artifacts, fresco panels and a confronting display of real skeletons buried in the ground, demonstrating ancient local beliefs on death and the afterlife. Information is provided in English and Spanish.

Nearby are the **Jardín Escultórica** (a lovely sculpture garden with Teotihuacán artifacts), a botanic garden, public toilets, snack bar, picnic tables and a bookstore with designer gifts.

Palacio de Tepantitla   PALACE
This priest's residence, 500m northeast of the Pirámide del Sol, contains Teotihuacán's most famous fresco, the worn **Paradise of Tláloc**. The rain god Tláloc is shown attend-ed by priests, with people, animals and fish nearby. Above is the sinister portrait of the **Great Goddess of Teotihuacán**, thought to be a goddess of the darkness and war because she's often shown with jaguars, owls and spiders – underworld animals. Look for her fanged nosepiece and her shields adorned with spiderwebs.

Museo de la Pintura Mural
Teotihuacana   MUSEUM
(☑594-958-20-81; ⊙9am-4:30pm) This impressive museum showcases murals from Teotihuacán, as well as reconstructions of murals you'll see at the ruins. Admission is included in the site ticket.

Palacio de Tetitla & Palacio de
Atetelco   PALACE
A group of palaces lies west of Teotihuacán's main area, several hundred meters northwest of gate 1. Many of the murals, discovered in the 1940s, are well preserved or restored and perfectly intelligible. Inside the sprawling **Palacio de Tetitla**, 120 walls are graced with murals of Tláloc, jaguars, serpents and eagles. Some 400m west is the **Palacio de Atetelco**, whose vivid jaguar or coyote murals – a mixture of originals and restorations – are in the Patio Blanco in the northwest corner.

About 100m further northeast are **Palacio de Zacuala** and **Palacio de Yayahuala**, a pair of enormous walled compounds that probably served as communal living quarters. Separated by the original alleyways, the two structures are made up of numerous rooms and patios but few entryways.

🛏 Sleeping

The town of San Juan Teotihuacán, 2km from the archaeological zone, has a few good overnight options, which make sense if you want to start early at the site before the crowds arrive.

Hotel Posada Sol y Luna   HOTEL $
(☑594-956-23-71, 594-956-23-68; www.posada solyluna.com; Cantú 13, San Juan Teotihuacán; r/ste M$490/825; ℗ 🛜) At the east end of town, en route to the pyramids, this well-run hotel has 16 fine but unexciting carpeted rooms, all with TV and bathroom. Junior suites have rather ancient Jacuzzis in them – not worth paying extra for.

Hotel Posada Teotihuacán   HOTEL $
(☑594-956-04-60; Canteroco 5, San Juan Teotihuacán; s/d/tr M$180/250/330; ℗) The rooms

at this centrally located, family-run, budget posada are smallish but clean and all have a TV and private bathroom. There is only one individual and one triple room, so book ahead for these.

Hotel Quinto Sol
HOTEL $$

(☑ 594-956-18-81; www.hotelquintosol.com.mx; Av Hidalgo 26, San Juan Teotihuacán; d/tw/tr M$965/1050/1105; P@🛜🏊) There's a reason most tourist groups stay at the Quinto Sol when visiting the ruins at Teotihuacán. With its fine facilities – including a decent-size pool, large, well-appointed rooms, in-room security boxes and room service – this is one of the best-equipped hotels in town.

Villas Arqueológicas Teotihuacán
HOTEL $$$

(☑ 55-5836-9020; www.villasarqueologicas.com.mx; Periférico Sur s/n, Zona Arqueológica; r M$1250; P@🛜🏊) Just south of the Zona Arqueológica, this elegant hotel has a small gym, heated outdoor pool, a lit tennis court, playground and a spa with temascal (a traditional steam bath). There's also a refined Mexican restaurant. Wi-fi signal is only accessible in the lobby.

✖ Eating

Eating near the ruins is usually a pricey and disappointing experience. Touts can offer to drive you to and from their restaurant, only for you to find that their deals are not so great and that you're stuck without other nearby options. You're much better off bringing a picnic, though there are a couple of adequate restaurants worth seeking out. The most convenient is on the 3rd floor of the old museum building near gate 1, where the busy **Bar-Cafetería Las Pirámides** serves panoramic views of La Ciudadela.

★ Restaurante Techinanco
MEXICAN $$

(☑ 594-958-23-06; Zona Arqueológica ring road; mains M$90-120; ⊙ 9am-6pm) A short walk from gate 3, behind the Pirámide de la Luna, this homey restaurant serves excellent home cooking at comparatively reasonable prices. The small menu takes in local favorites from enchiladas to authentic homemade *moles* (chili-sauce dishes). Ask about the curative massages (from M$600) or call in advance for a temascal.

Restaurante La Gruta
MEXICAN $$$

(☑ 594-956-01-27; Zona Arqueológica ring road; mains M$220-420, menú del día M$220; ⊙ 11am-7pm) Set in a vast, cool cave a short distance from gate 5, this tourist-centric restaurant

is unapologetically gimmicky, yet the food, while pricey (go for the better-value *menú del día*), is surprisingly good and there's a 40-minute folkloric dance show on Saturdays at 3:30pm and Sundays at 3:30pm and 5:30pm. Reservations are a good idea.

❶ Information

Information Booth (☑ 594-956-02-76, reservations 594-958-20-81; www.inah.gob.mx; ⊙ 7am-6pm) Near the southwest entrance (gate 1) of Teotihuacán. Free Spanish-only site tours by authorized guides are available, with reservations.

❶ Getting There & Away

During daylight hours, Autobuses México–San Juan Teotihuacán runs buses from Mexico City's Terminal Norte to the ruins (M$44, one hour) every hour from 7am to 6pm. When entering the Terminal Norte, turn left and walk to the second-to-last desk on the concourse. Make sure your bus is headed for 'Los Pirámides,' not the nearby town of San Juan Teotihuacán (unless you are heading to accommodations in San Juan). There have been reports from readers of armed robberies on these buses. Check with the US State Department (www.travel.state.gov) for current warnings.

At the ruins, buses arrive and depart from near gate 1, also making stops at gates 2 and 3. Return buses are more frequent after 1pm. The last bus back to Mexico City leaves at 6pm; some terminate at Indios Verdes metro station, but most continue to Terminal Norte.

❶ Getting Around

To reach the pyramids from San Juan Teotihuacán, take a taxi (M$55) or any combi (M$12) labeled 'San Martín' departing from Avenida Hidalgo, beside the central plaza. Combis returning to San Juan stop on the main road outside gates 1, 2 and 3.

Pachuca

☑ 771 / POP 67,000 / ELEV 2425M

The unassuming capital of Hidalgo state is scattered over steep, wide hills and crowned with a massive Mexican flag and towering statue of Christ. Both the charming, brightly painted town center and the colorful jigsaw mural of homes in Palmitas are visible for kilometers around, although far-from-lovely urban sprawl has developed beyond the candy-box houses of the old town.

Even so, Pachuca is an underappreciated provincial capital, an excellent staging post for trips north and east into the dramatic Sierra Madre Oriental, or just to the nearby Mineral del Chico, and an appealing place to spend a couple of days away from the tourist bustle.

Silver was unearthed nearby as early as 1534, and Real del Monte's mines still produce quite a respectable amount of ore. Pachuca was also the gateway through which *fútbol* (soccer) entered Mexico, introduced in the 19th century by miners from Cornwall, England. The Cornish population also gave the town its signature dish, meat pastries known as pasties (and recognizable to any Brit as a Cornish pasty, albeit with some typically Mexican fillings).

The 40m-high **Reloj Monumental** (Clock Tower), built between 1904 and 1910 to commemorate the independence centennial, overshadows the north end of Pachuca's remodeled *zócalo,* Plaza de la Independencia, which is flanked by Avenida Matamoros on the east side and Avenida Allende on the west. Guerrero runs parallel to Avenida Allende, 100m to the west. Around 700m to the south, Guerrero and Avenida Matamoros converge at the modern Plaza Juárez.

◎ Sights

Cuartel del Arte CULTURAL CENTER
(cnr Hidalgo & Arista; ⊘10am-6pm Tue-Sun) FREE This gorgeous, sprawling cultural center is an oasis of calm at Pachuca's bustling heart. Formerly the Convento de San Francisco, the complex includes three excellent museums, an art gallery, a theater, a library and several lovely plazas. It's worth looking into the impressive (and still functioning) Parroquia de San Francisco church as well. From Plaza de la Independencia, walk two blocks east to Miguel Hidalgo and about 650m south to the corner of Hidalgo and Arista.

One highlight is the excellent **Museo Nacional de la Fotografía**, which displays early imaging technology and stunning selections from the 1.5 million photos in the National Institute of Anthropology and History (INAH) archives. The images – some by Europeans and Americans, many more by pioneering Mexican photojournalists such as Nacho López and Agustín Victor Casasola – provide a fascinating glimpse of Mexico from 1873 to the present.

Museo de Minería MUSEUM
(☑771-715-09-76; www.distritominero.com.mx; Mina 110; adult/student M$30/25; ⊘10am-6pm Tue-Sun) Pachuca's mining museum provides a good overview of the industry that shaped the region. Headlamps, miners' shrines and old mining maps are on display, and photos depict conditions in the shafts from the early years to the present. The museum also coordinates a *'ruta de turismo cultural minero'* (mining culture tourism route) in English, Spanish or French that visits several mining sites in the region. The museum is two blocks south and half a block east of the *zócalo.*

There's a M$25 charge to use a camera and a M$50 charge for the use of a video camera.

Las Palmitas MURAL
(cnr Palmitas & San Felipe de las Torres; ⊘24hr) FREE This jigsaw puzzle of rainbow-painted houses on a hillside makes up Mexico's largest mural. It took 14 months to paint, employing ex-gang members and bringing a community spirit to a once-sketchy neighborhood. The effect is striking and best viewed from the pedestran bridge over Río de las Avenidas, next to Sam's Club.

From the *centro,* walk about 10 minutes to the end of Avenida Revolución then one block south behind Plaza Bella.

◷ Tours

Tranvía Turistico TRAM
(☑771-718-71-20; www.tranviaturisticopachuca. com; adult/child M$60/50; ⊘11am-6pm Wed-Fri, 10:30am-6:30pm Sat & Sun) Motor-trolley tours depart hourly from the plaza's west side, traveling to 24 sites around the city, including the hilltop Cristo statue. The entire trip takes just over an hour.

⊨ Sleeping

Hotel América HOTEL $
(☑771-715-00-55; Victoria 203; s/d/tr M$280/300/400; P⊛) Bless América for bringing a straightforward, comfortable option to the center of Pachuca, at rates much lower than similar digs. Look for the eagle statues out front, at the corner of Allende and Victoria, a block southeast of the clock tower.

Hotel de los Baños HOTEL $$
(☑771-713-07-00; Av Matamoros 205; s/d/tr M$400/580/640; P@⊛) With its beautifully tiled old-world lobby, the Baños is Pachuca's most charming midrange hotel. All 55 rooms and bathrooms have been renovated yet retain antique accents such as wooden shutters. The hotel is located a block south of the clock tower. Wi-fi is patchy furthest from common areas.

Hotel Emily BUSINESS HOTEL $$$
(☑771-715-08-28, 800-501-63-39; www.hotelemily.
com.mx; Plaza Independencia; r/ste M$1279/1433;
P🐾@🛜) On the south side of the *zócalo*,
Emily has an excellent location, with bal-
conies overlooking the Reloj Monumental.
Rooms are modern and stylish, with flat-
screen TVs, laundry service and gym access.
The hotel restaurant has generic but surpris-
ingly tasty food in a sterile setting.

🍴 Eating & Drinking

Pachuca's famous regional specialty, *pastes*
(pasties), are available all over town, with
the tastiest at local joints rather than glossy
commercial stores. Baked in pizza ovens,
they contain a variety of fillings – the likes of
beans, pineapple and rice pudding – proba-
bly never imagined by the Cornish miners
who brought this English culinary tradition
to Mexico.

El Manzanillo BISTRO $
(http://elmanzanillo.com.mx; Guerrero 504; mains
M$65-150; ⊙9am-2am Mon-Sat, to noon Sun;
🐾🛜🅿) This modern, high-ceilinged bistro
is a sure bet. Whether it's a club sandwich
or Mexican classics such as enchiladas, the
food is spot on (even the seafood pasta!) and
the young weekend crowd are certain to be
fired up on mescal and craft beer at the at-
tached bar and courtyard. It's a block north
of the clock tower.

Pastes el Billar MEXICAN $
(cnr Ocampo & Zaragoza; pastes M$15; ⊙9am-
7pm Mon-Sat, to 6pm Sun; 🅿) Standout *pastes,*
from vegetarian *flor de calabaza* (zucchi-
ni flower) and *champiñon* (mushroom)
to *mole verde de pollo* (chicken in a spicy
pumpkin-seed sauce). It's on the east corner
of the *zócalo*.

Mina La Blanca Restaurant Bar MEXICAN $$
(☑771-715-18-96; www.restaurantlablanca.com.
mx; Av Matamoros 201; mains M$65-197; ⊙8am-
11pm) Pachuca's most famous restaurant, La
Blanca has been serving traditional *hidalguense* food, including *pastes* and a mean
caldo de hongo (mushroom soup), since
1953. The walls, adorned with black-and-
white photos and stained-glass windows
depicting industrial mining scenes, speak
of Pachuca's history. This is also a great
place to come for a low-key drink in the
evening.

Espresso Central LOUNGE
(Av Revolución 1008; ⊙8am-11pm; 🐾) In a stylish, two-story building constructed from
converted shipping containers, Espresso
Central has quality espressos, domestic
microbrews, decent wine, chai, crêpes and
bagels. At night the cafe and attached Black
Wolf bar become a hip nightspot, where Pachuca's cool kids and suit-wearers hang out
most nights of the week.

ℹ Information

ATMs are numerous around Plaza de la
Independencia.

Technopolis (Allende 502; per hr M$5; ⊙9am-
9pm Mon-Fri, from 10am Sat & Sun)

Tourist Module (☑771-715-14-11; www.
pachuca.gob.mx; Plaza de la Independencia;
⊙8:30am-6pm) Behind the clock tower; offers
very basic advice and colorful pamphlets about
surrounding towns.

ℹ Getting There & Away

Pachuca's **bus station** (☑771-713-34-47; Cam
Cueso) is 20 minutes' drive from downtown.
There's an ADO 1st-class bus service to/from
Mexico City's TAPO terminal (M$98, one hour 40
minutes, every half- or one hour) and Terminal
Norte (M$98, 1½ hours, every 10 minutes), as
well as Mexico City Airport (M$182, two hours,
hourly from 3am to 8pm), Poza Rica (M$234, 4½
hours, four daily) and Puebla (M$198, two hours,
every one to 1½ hours). Some routes have free
wi-fi. Buses also go frequently to and from Tula
and Querétaro.

Three scenic roads (Hwys 85, 105 and
130/132D) climb into the forested, often foggy,
Sierra Madre Oriental.

ℹ Getting Around

From the bus station car park, green-and-white
colectivos marked 'Centro' deposit passengers
at Plaza de la Constitución (M$7.50), a short
walk from the *zócalo*. In the reverse direction,
hop on a 'Central' *colectivo* along Avenida Allende. By taxi the trip costs M$35.

Around Pachuca

Mineral del Chico
☑771

You can take an easy and very lovely day
trip or weekend retreat from Pachuca to
the nearly 3000-hectare **Parque Nacional
El Chico** (www.parqueelchico.gob.mx), which
was established as a reserve in 1898, and the

charming old mining village **Mineral del Chico**, which is among the newest *pueblos mágicos* and outshines the much-larger Pachuca. The views are wonderful, the air is fresh and the mountains have some great hiking among spectacular rock formations and beautiful waterfalls. Most Mexicans who visit on the weekend hardly leave El Chico's cute main street – not surprising when the locals are this friendly, proving their motto *'pueblo chico, gente grande'* (small town, great people).

⊙ Sights & Activities

Colectivos marked 'Carboneras' (M$7.50) will drop you at the trailhead to the *mirador* (lookout) at **Peña del Cuervo**. From there, it's about a 25-minute walk.

Ask at local hotels or the park's **visitors center** (Centro de Visitantes; Carretera Pachuca–Mineral del Chico Km 7.5), a 10-minute drive from the village, for details about possible guided outdoor activities.

You can take an easy 1.5km self-guided walk to **Río del Milagro**, a small river dotted with abandoned mines and surrounded by trees. From the left of the church, walk downhill till the end, and continue left along the pathway until you reach the road and signs for the river. Walk carefully along the road and you will come to a path on your right down to the river with a valley vista. Bring warm clothes as the temperature can change in a snap in the afternoon.

A street back in most directions from the main street, Corona del Rosal will reveal views of the valley. A good spot is the maze of walkways behind the **Capilla del Calvario**, a rustic 19th-century chapel on Calvario, uphill from the church.

🛏 Sleeping & Eating

Mineral del Chico is an established weekend getaway, but it can feel like a ghost town during the week, when visitors may be hard-pressed to find an open place to eat after dark and even some hotels shut their doors. However, the available hotels often lower their prices and you'll have the trails and peaks almost entirely to yourself.

There are several **campgrounds** (campsites M$150, cabins M$400) with rudimentary facilities between Km 7 and Km 10 on Carretera Pachuca en route to Mineral del Chico.

Hospedaje El Chico   GUESTHOUSE **$**
(☎771-715-47-41; Corona del Rosal 1; r M$450-650; 📶) This small, 10-room homestay is a decent budget option, with clean if unexciting rooms. You'll have to ring the buzzer to get

AROUND MEXICO CITY AROUND PACHUCA

DON'T MISS

REAL DEL MONTE

This gorgeous mountain town is a tangle of houses, restaurants and pastie shops scattered across a pine-tree-carpeted hillside. The air is thin here, so don't be surprised if you find yourself with a mild case of altitude sickness, but it's also clean, crisp and can get cold and windy suddenly (bring a sweater, if not a coat).

Two kilometers past the Hwy 105 turnoff for Parque Nacional El Chico, Real del Monte (officially known as Mineral del Monte) was the scene of a miners' strike in 1776, commemorated as the first strike in the Americas. Most of the town was settled in the 19th century, after a British company commandeered the mines. Cornish-style cottages line many of the steep, cobbled streets.

Hotel Paraíso Real Hospedaje-Cafetería (☎771-797-02-20; www.hotelparaisoreal. com; d Sun-Thu M$500, Fri & Sat M$700; 🅿📶) has a friendly, family-run vibe and clean, modern rooms with tiled floors, cable TV and room service. There's an eclectic mix of rooms: some have low ceilings, while others have Jacuzzis (an additional M$100), balconies and views over town. Another good option with views over the town is **Hotel Real del Monte** (☎771-715-56-54; www.hotelesecoturisticos.com.mx; r Sun-Thu M$600, Fri & Sat M$700; 📶), an old 15-room hotel run by the same high-standards company that operates the two main hotels in nearby Mineral del Chico.

Second-class buses depart Pachuca's terminal for Real del Monte (M$9.50, 30 minutes, hourly). Combis (M$9.50, 15 minutes, every 30 minutes) leave from Avenida de la Raza, a block north of Plaza de la Constitución. Get off at the last stop, in the center of town, from where the last return bus to Pachuca departs at 9:15pm.

in. If El Chico appears to be closed midweek, ask next door at Casa Biseña. The same family owns both businesses.

Hotel El Paraíso
LODGE $$

(☑771-715-56-54; www.hoteleseoturisticos.com. mx; Carretera Pachuca s/n; r Sun-Thu M$950, Fri & Sat from M$1050; P) Nestled inside large, well-maintained grounds at the base of the mountain, with a fast-flowing stream running nearby, El Paraíso certainly has a location worthy of its name. The large, modern rooms lack individuality or charm, but they're very comfortable. A full-board option is available.

Hotel Posada del Amanecer
HOTEL $$

(☑771-715-56-54; www.hoteleseoturisticos. mx; Morelos 3; r Sun-Thu from M$750, Fri & Sat M$950; P) This 11-room adobe complex has spacious modern rooms with colonial touches on two levels beside a lovely patio. With no phones or TVs, it's a peaceful getaway. Children under 12 stay free. Massage, spa treatments and adventure activities such as rock climbing are offered for an extra fee.

Fonda el Fresno
MEXICAN $

(☑771-715-32-57; Corona del Rosal 10; set menu M$75; ⊙9am-9pm) This little bakery is more than a sweet place for a coffee. Out back, the grandparents make *sopa de papa* (potato soup) that zings with fresh parsley, vegetarian enchiladas (on request) with generous slices of avocado, and fresh *agua de melón* (cantaloupe juice drink). Streams of people come just for a taste bud–tweaking *cocol* (brown-sugar and caraway-seed bread triangle).

★Restaurante y Cabañas San Diego
SEAFOOD $$

(☑771-125-61-73; Carretera Pachuca s/n; mains M$100-120) Off the highway beside a rushing creek on the way into town (look for signs at the El Paraíso turnoff), San Diego is a true mountain escape. Head down to the wood fish shack, where you can watch trout being caught and prepared. The fish *a la mexicana,* stuffed with Oaxacan cheese, tomatoes, chilies and thick chunks of garlic, is excellent.

There are also two comfortable but rustic cabins available for rent, one smaller (up to four people, Sunday to Thursday M$650, Friday and Saturday M$750) than the other (up to 10 people, M$200 per person).

ⓘ Getting There & Away

From Avenida de la Raza, one block north of Plaza de la Constitución, in Pachuca, blue-and-white *colectivos* climb the winding roads up to Mineral del Chico (M$14.50, 40 minutes) every 20 minutes from 8am to 6pm. The last service back to Pachuca is at 7pm.

There's no direct transit service from Real del Monte, but those wanting to avoid a trip back to Pachuca to transfer *colectivos* can hire a taxi for about M$150.

EAST OF MEXICO CITY

The views get seriously dramatic as you head east from the capital, with the landscape peppered with the snowcapped, volcanic peaks of Popocatépetl, Iztaccíhuatl, La Malinche and Pico Orizaba – the country's highest summit. The rugged Cordillera Neovolcánica offers anything from invigorating alpine strolls to demanding technical climbs. Unpredictable Popocatépetl, however, remains off-limits due to volcanic activity.

The gorgeous colonial city of Puebla – Mexico's fifth-largest city – is the dominant regional center, a local transportation hub and a big tourist draw with its cathedral, rich culinary traditions, intriguing history and excellent museums. The surrounding state of Puebla is predominantly rural and home to approximately 500,000 indigenous people. This enduring presence provides the region with a rich handicraft legacy, with products including pottery, carved onyx and fine hand-woven and embroidered textiles.

Tlaxcala, the capital of the tiny state of the same name, has emerged as an attractive destination in its own right, with an exciting array of new restaurants, museums and boutique hotels. Far-flung Cuetzalan, meanwhile, is surrounded by lush, dramatic scenery and is among the most seemingly time-forgotten villages in the country.

Puebla

☑222 / POP 1.5 MILLION / ELEV 2160M

Once a bastion of conservatism, Catholicism and tradition, Puebla has come out of its colonial-era shell. The city retains a fantastically well-preserved center, a stunning cathedral and a wealth of beautiful churches, while younger *poblanos* (people from Puebla) are embracing the city's increasingly thriving art and nightlife scenes.

The city is well worth a visit, with 70 churches in the historic center alone, more than 1000 colonial buildings adorned with the *azulejos* (painted ceramic tiles) for which the city is famous, and a long culinary history that can be explored at any restaurant or food stall. For a city of its size, Puebla is far more relaxed and less gridlocked than you might expect.

History

Founded by Spanish settlers in 1531 as Ciudad de los Ángeles, with the aim of surpassing the nearby pre-Hispanic religious center of Cholula, the city became known as Puebla de los Ángeles (La Angelópolis) eight years later and quickly grew into an important Catholic center. Fine pottery had long been crafted from the local clay and after the colonists introduced new materials and techniques, Puebla pottery evolved as both an art and an industry. By the late 18th century, the city had emerged as a major producer of glass and textiles. With 50,000 residents by 1811, Puebla remained Mexico's second-biggest city until Guadalajara overtook it in the late 19th century.

In 1862, General Ignacio de Zaragoza fortified the Cerro de Guadalupe against the French invaders and on May 5 that year his 2000 men defeated a frontal attack by 6000, many of whom were handicapped by diarrhea. This rare Mexican military success is the reason for annual (and increasingly corporate-sponsored and drunken) celebrations in the USA, where the holiday is far more significant than in Mexico and hundreds of streets are named Cinco de Mayo. Few seem to remember that the following year the reinforced French took Puebla and occupied the city until 1867.

Modern Puebla still revolves around the city's old town, with the large, leafy *zócalo* and Mexico's tallest cathedral at its heart. The *centro histórico* is home to most of the attractions, hotels and restaurants of interest to international travelers. Most are within a few blocks of the main plaza.

The Zona Esmeralda, 2km west of the *zócalo,* is a stretch of Avenida Juárez with chichi boutiques, upscale restaurants and trendy nightclubs.

⊙ Sights

Zócalo   PLAZA
Puebla's central plaza was originally a marketplace where bullfights, theater and hangings occurred, before assuming its current arboretum-like appearance in 1854. The surrounding arcades date from the 16th century. The plaza fills with an entertaining mix of clowns, balloon hawkers, food vendors and people enjoying the free wi-fi on weekend evenings.

Catedral   CATHEDRAL
(cnr Avs 3 Oriente & 16 de Septiembre) Puebla's impressive cathedral, which appears on Mexico's M$500 bill, occupies the entire block south of the *zócalo*. Its architecture is a blend of severe Herreresque-Renaissance and early baroque styles. Construction began in 1550, but most of it took place under Bishop Juan de Palafox in the 1640s. At 69m, the towers are Mexico's tallest. The dazzling interior, the frescoes and the elaborately decorated side chapels are awe-inspiring, and most have bilingual signs explaining their history and significance.

Museo Amparo   MUSEUM
(☑222-229-38-50;   www.museoamparo.com; Calle 2 Sur 708; adult/student M$35/25, Mon free; ⊙10am-6pm Wed-Mon) This superb private museum, housed in two linked 16th- and 17th-century colonial buildings, is loaded with pre-Hispanic artifacts. Displayed with explanatory information sheets in English and Spanish, the collection is staggering. Notice the thematic continuity in Mexican design – the same motifs appear again and again on dozens of pieces. An example: the collection of pre-Hispanic cult skeleton heads are eerily similar to the candy skulls sold during Día de Muertos.

Templo de Santo Domingo   CHURCH
(cnr Avs 5 de Mayo & 4 Poniente) This fine Dominican church features a stunning **Capilla del Rosario** (Rosary Chapel), south of the main altar, which is the main reason to come here. Built between 1650 and 1690, it's heavy on gilded plaster and carved stone, with angels and cherubim seemingly materializing from behind every leaf. See if you can spot the heavenly orchestra. Outside the entrance, in the **Zona de Monumentos**, you'll often find sculpture exhibitions.

Casa de la Cultura   BUILDING
(☑222-232-12-27; Av 5 Oriente 5; ⊙10am-8pm) Occupying the entire block facing the south side of the cathedral, the former bishop's palace is a classic 17th-century brick-and-tile edifice that now houses government offices, the Casa de la Cultura and the State Tourist

Puebla

Office. Inside are art galleries, a bookstore and cinema, with a congenial cafe out back in the courtyard. Upstairs is the 1646 **Biblioteca Palafoxiana** (📞222-777-25-81; M$25, Sun free; ⏲10am-5pm Tue-Sun), the first public library in the Americas.

The library's gorgeous shelves – carved cedar and white pine – house thousands of rare books, including the 1493 *Nuremberg Chronicle* and one of the earliest New World dictionaries.

Iglesia de la Compañía   CHURCH

(cnr Av Palafox y Mendoza & Calle 4 Sur) This Jesuit church with a 1767 Churrigueresque facade is also called Espíritu Santo. Beneath the altar is a tomb said to be that of a 17th-century Asian princess who was sold into slavery in Mexico and later freed.

She was supposedly responsible for the colorful *china poblana* costume – a shawl, frilled blouse, embroidered skirt and gold and silver adornments. This costume be-

came a kind of 'peasant chic' in the 19th century. But 'china' (chee-nah) also meant 'maidservant,' and the style may have evolved from Spanish peasant costumes.

Next door is the 16th-century **Edificio Carolino** (cnr Av Palafox y Mendoza & Calle 4 Sur), now the main building of Universidad Autónoma de Puebla.

Museo del Ferrocarril   MUSEUM

(www.museoferrocarriles.org.mx; Calle 11 Norte 1005; adult/child M$12/free, Sun free; ⏲9am-5pm Tue-Sun; 👶) This excellent railway museum is housed in Puebla's former train station and the spacious grounds surrounding it, and has activities for kids. There are ancient steam-powered monsters through to relatively recent passenger carriages, and you can enter many of them. One carriage contains an excellent collection of photos of various derailments and other disasters that occurred during the 1920s and '30s.

Puebla

◎ Sights
Biblioteca Palafoxiana	(see 1)
1 Casa de la Cultura	C3
2 Catedral	C3
3 Edificio Carolino	D3
4 Iglesia de la Compañía	D3
5 Museo Amparo	C4
6 Museo Casa del Alfeñique	E3
7 Museo de la Revolución	D2
8 Museo José Luis Bello y González	C3
9 Templo de San Francisco	F3
10 Templo de Santo Domingo	C2
11 Zócalo	C3

◎ Activities, Courses & Tours
12 Turibus	C3

◎ Sleeping
13 Casona de la China Poblana	D3
14 El Sueño Hotel & Spa	C4
15 Gran Hotel San Agustín	B2
16 Hostal Casona Poblana	C4
17 Hostel Gente de Más	B2
18 Hotel Casa de la Palma Travel	D3
19 Hotel Colonial	D3
20 Hotel Mesón de San Sebastián	C4
21 Hotel Teresita	B3
22 Mesón Sacristía de la Compañía	D4
23 NH Puebla	B2

◎ Eating
24 Amalfi Pizzeria	D3
25 Antigua Churrería de Catedral	C3
26 El Mural de los Poblanos	C3
27 El Patio de las Ranas	C2
28 La Purificadora	F3
29 La Zanahoria	D4
30 Las Ranas	C2
31 Lola	D4
32 Mercado de Sabores Poblanos	A1
Restaurante Sacristía	(see 22)

◎ Drinking & Nightlife
33 A Go Go	E4
34 All Day Café	D4

◎ Entertainment
35 Celia's Cafe	D4

◎ Shopping
36 El Parián Crafts Market	E3
37 Talavera Uriarte	A1

Templo de San Francisco CHURCH
(Av 14 Oriente; ⊙8am-8pm) The north doorway of this church is a good example of 16th-century plateresque; the tower and fine brick-and-tile facade were added in the 18th century. In the north chapel is the mummified body of San Sebastián de Aparicio, a Spaniard who migrated to Mexico in 1533 and planned many of the country's roads before becoming a monk. Since he's now the patron saint of drivers, merchants and farm workers, his canonized corpse attracts a stream of worshippers.

Museo de la Revolución MUSEUM
(☎222-242-10-76; Av 6 Oriente 206; adult/student M$25/20, Sun free; ⊙10am-5pm Tue-Sun) This pockmarked 19th-century house was the scene of the first battle of the 1910 Revolution. The house retains its bullet holes and some revolutionary memorabilia, including a room dedicated to female insurgents.

Betrayed only two days before a planned uprising against the dictatorship of Porfirio Díaz, the Serdán family (Aquiles, Máximo, Carmen and Natalia) and 17 others fought 500 soldiers until only Aquiles, their leader, and Carmen were left alive. Aquiles, hidden under the floorboards, might have survived if the damp hadn't provoked a cough that gave him away. Both were subsequently killed.

Museo Casa del Alfeñique MUSEUM
(☎222-232-42-96; Av 4 Oriente 416; adult/student M$25/20, Sun free; ⏲10am-5pm Tue-Sun) This renovated colonial house is an outstanding example of the over-the-top 18th-century decorative style *alfeñique,* characterized by elaborate stucco ornamentation and named after a candy made from sugar and egg whites. The 1st floor details the Spanish conquest, including indigenous accounts in the form of drawings and murals. The 2nd floor houses a large collection of historic and religious paintings, local furniture and household paraphernalia, although all labeling is in Spanish only.

Museo José Luis Bello y González MUSEUM
(☎222-232-94-75; Av 3 Poniente 302; adult/student M$35/20, Sun free; ⏲10am-5pm Tue-Sun) This house is filled with the diverse art-and-crafts collection of the 19th-century industrialist Bello family who lived here. It's a treasure trove for fans of exquisite French, English, Japanese and Chinese porcelain and the museum's large collection of Puebla Talavera. The museum closes every January for maintenance.

Tours

Turibus BUS TOUR
(☎222-231-52-17; www.turibus.com.mx; Cholula tour adult/child M$180/95, centro tour adult/child M$80/45; ⏲Cholula tour 1pm, centro tour every 40min 10am-6pm) Operated by ADO bus lines, this four-hour tour gives an overview of the nearby town of Cholula, including the pyramid (admission is a separate cost). There is also a 1½-hour red double-decker-bus tour of Puebla's *centro histórico.* You can start either tour from the west side of the *zócalo* and buy tickets on board.

Festivals & Events

Feria de Puebla MUSIC
(⏲Apr-May) Starting in late April and ending in late May, this fair honors the state's achievements with cultural and music events.

Cinco de Mayo PARADE
(⏲May) The city's May 5 celebrations mark the day in 1862 when the Mexican army defeated the French. There is a huge parade and celebrations throughout the following fortnight.

Festival del Mole Poblano FOOD
(⏲Jun) In early June the city celebrates its most famous contribution to the culinary arts: *mole poblano,* a thick sauce of chilis, fruits, nuts, spices and chocolate.

Festival del Chile en Nogada FOOD
(⏲Aug) Leaving no culinary stone unturned, the city's savvy restaurateurs promote the country's 'patriotic recipe' – a chili stuffed with *picadillo* (a mix of ground meat and fruit) and topped in a luscious walnut cream sauce.

Día de Muertos CULTURAL
(⏲Oct) Puebla has jumped on the bandwagon, with a fortnight-long citywide cultural program starting in late October devoted to the Day of the Dead and including nighttime museum visits and viewings of *ofrendas* (altars).

Sleeping

Puebla's hotel scene is crowded and competitive, with a huge range of accommodations options for all budgets and new arrivals constantly stirring things up. Quite a few boutique three- and four-star hotels aimed at discerning travelers have kept standards high.

Many hotels in the city can be spotted some way off with illuminated 'H' signs over their entrance, although some of the newer generation don't advertise quite so directly. It's worth searching online for special last-minute, seasonal and weekend package rates. The Municipal Tourist Office on the *zócalo* hands out up-to-date flyers of budget hotels with prices.

Most colonial buildings have two types of room – interior and exterior – with the former often lacking windows and the latter frequently having windows or balconies exposed to a noisy street. Hotels that lack on-site parking often have an arrangement with nearby garages.

Hotel Teresita HOTEL **$**
(Hotel Teresa; ☎222-232-70-72; www.hotelteresita.com.mx; Av 3 Poniente 309; s/d/tr M$260/290/440; ⊜📶) Among the multiple dreary posadas near the *zócalo,* Hotel Teresita sparkles with modern rooms boasting private bathrooms. The trade-off is a tiny space, ancient TVs and internal-facing windows (with footfall noise), but crisp white sheets, comfy beds and thorough cleanliness make Teresita a bargain.

Hostel Gente de Más HOSTEL $

(☎ 222-232-31-36; www.gentedemashostel.com; Av 3 Poniente 713; dm/d/tr M$155/350/400; ☎) This fresh addition to Puebla's sleeping scene has 'poshtel' aspirations with arty, rustic touches to the former house. Bathrooms are tiny and noise travels easily along the long halls, but the rooms are clean and comfortable.

Gran Hotel San Agustín HOTEL $

(☎ 222-232-50-89; Av 3 Poniente 531; r/tw/tr/q incl breakfast M$280/380/440/490; P) This straightforward budget option is near the *centro histórico* and has clean rooms, a plant-filled courtyard with a small fountain and includes very basic breakfast. It's not the kind of place where you'll want to spend the day (the rooms are dark and unexciting), but it's a perfectly fine base for exploring the city on a budget.

Hostal Casona Poblana HOSTEL $

(☎ 222-246-03-83; Calle 16 de Septiembre 905; dm/d M$150/350; ☺☎) The rooms at this modern hostel have an openness, being built around a covered courtyard that is sociable without being party central. This setup means noise and cold travel easily, though wi-fi not so much. There is also a roof garden and small kitchen. Look for the large 'Hostal' banner out front.

Hotel Casa de la Palma Travel BOUTIQUE HOTEL $$

(☎ 222-232-23-42; http://casadelapalmapuebla. com/travel; Av 3 Oriente 213; d/tw M$600/800; ☎) Palma Travel is surrounded by great places to eat and drink in the historic center and boasts massive rooms, minimally decorated in colonial furniture and Talavera. Throw in bathrooms decked out with earthy marble floors and you get a lot of luxury for the asking price. Staff speak English and French.

Hotel Colonial HOTEL $$

(☎ 222-246-46-12, 800-013-00-00; www.colonial. com.mx; Calle 4 Sur 105; s/d/tr M$740/840/940; P☎) Once part of a 17th-century Jesuit monastery and existing as a hotel in various forms since the mid-19th century, Colonial exudes heritage from its many gorgeously furnished rooms (half with colonial decor, half modern). There's a good restaurant and a fantastic 1890 gilt elevator. An unbeatable vibe and location despite occasional live-music and street noise.

Hotel Mesón de San Sebastián BOUTIQUE HOTEL $$

(☎ 222-242-65-23; www.mesonsansebastian.com; Av 9 Oriente 6; d/ste incl breakfast M$790/1300; ☎) This elegant boutique hotel has a colorful courtyard, accommodating staff who speak English, and garners praise for being family friendly. Each of the 17 rooms are individually decorated and named after a saint. All rooms have TV, phone, safe, minibar and antique furnishings. During quiet periods the hotel offers discounts.

El Sueño Hotel & Spa BOUTIQUE HOTEL $$$

(☎ 222-232-64-89, 222-232-64-23; www.elsueno-hotel.com; Av 9 Oriente 12; ste incl breakfast M$1750-3000; P❋☎) An oasis of minimalist chic amid the colonial bustle of Puebla's old town, Sueño's 20 rooms are sleek, high-ceilinged and thematically decorated. Each is inspired by a different female Mexican artist. There's a hot tub and sauna, plasma TVs in the rooms and a martini bar in the lobby. Rooms are discounted on Sundays.

Mesón Sacristía de la Compañía BOUTIQUE HOTEL $$$

(☎ 222-242-45-13; www.mexicoboutiquehotels.com/ mesonsacristia; Calle 6 Sur 304; ste incl breakfast M$1600-2000; P☎) With eight rooms set around a bright, kitschy, pink courtyard, this small inn feels like the home of an eccentric grandmother. The junior suites are actually just standard rooms, while the two master suites are bigger and more worthy of the title. The downstairs restaurant, which serves aromatic US-style breakfasts and refined *poblano* cuisine, gets rave reviews from guests.

Casona de la China Poblana LUXURY HOTEL $$$

(☎ 222-242-56-21; www.casonadelachinapoblana. com; cnr Calle 4 Norte & Av Palafox y Mendoza; ste M$2107-3821; P) This elegant boutique hotel is stunning and knows it. Shamelessly dubbing itself Puebla's 'most exclusive hotel,' China Poblana has massive, gorgeous suites decorated in a mixture of styles, a lovely courtyard and La Cocina de la China Poblana restaurant.

NH Puebla BUSINESS HOTEL $$$

(☎ 222-309-19-19, 800-726-05-28; www.nh-hotels. com; Calle 5 Sur 105; r/ste US$89/157; P❋☎☒) Attracting both business travelers and pleasure seekers, NH is modern and offers good service without being stuffy. The rooms are large and contemporary, with extremely comfortable beds, good views and access to the rooftop bar and a small pool and gym.

✖ Eating

Puebla's culinary heritage, of which *poblanos* are rightly proud, can be explored in a range of eateries throughout the city, from humble street-side food stalls to elegant colonial-style restaurants. However, given the city's renown as a culinary center, it's surprising how few truly excellent high-end restaurants there are.

★ La Zanahoria   VEGETARIAN $

(222-232-48-13; Av 5 Oriente 206; mains M$22-62, set meals M$60, daily buffet adult/child M$84/47 Mon-Thu, M$99/52 Fri-Sun; ⊘7am-9pm; ☺ ☎ ⚲ ☝) This (entirely meat-free) godsend for vegetarians is an excellent place for lunch, and is moments from the *zócalo*. The drawcard is the popular daily buffet from 1pm to 6pm in the spacious interior colonial courtyard. It features more than 20 dishes, salads and desserts, such as soy-meat lasagna, *chilaquiles* and Middle Eastern tabbouleh.

The extensive à la carte menu includes everything from veggie hamburgers to *nopales rellenos* (stuffed cactus paddles). In the front of the restaurant is the express service area (including a juice bar and a health-food snack shop).

★ Las Ranas   TAQUERÍA $

(222-242-47-34; Av 2 Poniente 102; tacos & tortas M$9-30; ⊘noon-9:15pm) This local institution is *the* place to try one of Puebla's great dishes: the *taco árabe*. Unbelievably moist *al pastor* (shepherd-style) pork is marinated and spit-grilled then rolled in fresh, slightly charred Middle Eastern–style flatbread. This restaurant and the annex across the street, **El Patio de las Ranas** (Av 2 Poniente 205; tacos & tortas M$9-30; ⊘noon-9:15pm), are perpetually full but worth the wait for the unforgettable tacos.

Mercado de Sabores Poblanos   MARKET $

(Av 4 Poniente, btwn 11 & 13 Norte) The 6570-sq-meter Mercado de Sabores Poblanos is a thrilling complement to Puebla's food scene. A sparkling food court serves local specialties such as *cemitas* (a style of sandwich/burger unique to Puebla), *pipián verde* (green pumpkin-seed sauce) and *tacos árabes* (Arabic taco) from 130-odd vendors.

Lola   CAFE $

(222-246-09-66; Calle 3 Oriente 407; snacks M$50-80; ⊘10am-9pm Tue-Sat, to 8pm Sun) The hip Puebla vibe radiates strongly at this leafy corner of artsy stalls and Talavera-clad antique stores. The scatter of outdoor tables at the cafe/bar is perfect for people-watching and listening to the live musicians often playing, day and night, while scoffing the especially good burritos, substantial salads or beer.

Antigua Churreria de Catedral   CAFE $

(cnr Calles 5 Oriente & 2 Sur; churros M$3; ⊘9am-midnight) There's always a hungry queue for these delicious, crispy *churros* (doughnutlike fritters). Half the fun is the spectacle of watching them being made behind the glass.

El Mural de los Poblanos   MEXICAN $$

(222-242-05-03; www.elmuraldelospoblanos.com; Av 16 de Septiembre 506; mains M$140-240; ⊘8am-11pm Sun-Thu, to 11:30pm Fri & Sat) Set back from the street in a gorgeous, plant-filled colonial

---

PUEBLA'S SEASONAL TREATS

Justly famous for its incredible cuisine, Puebla also offers an array of seasonal, local delicacies that adventurous eaters should not miss.

Escamoles (March to June) – Ant larvae; looks like rice and is usually sautéed in butter.

Gusanos de maguey (April to May) – Worms that inhabit the maguey plant, typically fried in a drunken chili and *pulque* (a low-alcohol brew made from the maguey plant) sauce.

Huitlacoche (June to October) – Inky-black corn fungus with an enchanting, earthy flavor. Sometimes spelled *cuitlacoche*.

Chiles en nogada (July to September) – Green chilies stuffed with *picadillo* (a mix of ground meat and dried fruit), covered with a creamy walnut sauce and sprinkled with red pomegranate seeds.

Chapulines (October to November) – Grasshoppers purged of digestive matter then dried, smoked or fried in lime and chili powder.

courtyard, El Mural de los Poblanos serves excellent, traditional *poblano* dishes in an elegant setting. The house specialty is five kinds of *mole*. Other favorites include the smoky goat-cheese-stuffed ancho *chile relleno* (dried *poblano* chili) and the trilogy of *cemitas*.

Reservations are a good idea on busy Friday and Saturday nights and holidays.

Amalfi Pizzeria
PIZZA **$$**

(📞222-403-77-97; Av 3 Oriente 207B; pizzas M$140-170; ⊗1-9:45pm Sun-Thu, to 11pm Fri & Sat) It's easy to see why this excellent wood-oven pizzeria – with dim lighting, terracotta walls and beamed ceilings – is a popular date spot. In addition to a wide selection of fine, thin-crust pizzas, there's decent wine and Italian classics such as caprese salads and pasta. Because the dining room is small, a reservation wouldn't hurt.

Restaurante Sacristía
MEXICAN **$$**

(📞222-242-45-13; Calle 6 Sur 304; mains M$115-175; ⊗9am-10:30pm Mon-Sat, to 6pm Sun) Set in the delightful colonial patio of Mesón Sacristía de la Compañía hotel, this is an elegant place for a meal of authentic *mole* and creative twists on rich *poblano* cuisine, or a cocktail or coffee in the intimate Confesionario bar. Live piano and violin soloists (and flower petals by request) lend a romantic ambience most nights from around 9pm.

If you like what you taste, inquire about the small-group cooking classes.

La Purificadora
INTERNATIONAL **$$$**

(www.lapurificadora.com; Callejón de la 10 Norte 802, Paseo San Francisco, Barrio El Alto; mains M$155-250) The restaurant at La Purificadora, one of Puebla's chicest boutique hotels, is set in a spare, loft-like space with unfinished walls and long, narrow wood-plank tables. The menu tends more toward the indulgent and elaborate, with dishes such as jumbo shrimp with chipotle hollandaise or a cassoulet of Mennonite asadero cheese, dehydrated tomato and confit of onion.

🍷 Drinking & Nightlife

During the day students pack the sidewalk tables along the pedestrian-only block of Avenida 3 Oriente, near the university. At night, mariachis lurk around Callejón de los Sapos – Calle 6 Sur between Avenidas 3 and 7 Oriente – but they're being crowded out by the bars on nearby Plazuela de los Sapos.

These rowdy watering holes are packed on weekend nights, when many of them become live-music venues.

A Go Go
LOUNGE

(Av 3 Oriente 603; 📞) A young crowd hangs out at this arty venue, decorated with graffiti murals and '50s wallpaper. Live bands and DJs play in the cavernous bar, while the spacious courtyard has a summery buzz that is fueled by the cheap, creative cocktails and good-sized bar food late into the evening.

All Day Café
CAFE

(📞222-242-44-54; Av 7 Oriente) This cafe-bar, a student hangout just off Plazuela de los Sapos, is housed in a bright courtyard and turns into a club in the evenings. It serves a range of sandwiches (M$45 to M$60), sushi (M$60), pastries, coffees and cocktails all day long, just as the name suggests.

Celia's Cafe
LIVE MUSIC

(Av 5 Oriente 608; ⊗9am-10:30pm Wed-Fri, to 11:30pm Sat) Try before you buy at this sprawling bar/restaurant. Every *mole poblano* (Mexico's most famous dish), coffee and tequila shot is served up in (purchasable) Talavera-ware whipped up in Celia's own studio. From 8pm musicians add old-world romance to the *poblano* decor with live piano, *trova* (troubadour-type folk music) or *bohemia* (love songs).

🛍 Shopping

Puebla has plenty of shops selling the colorful, hand-painted ceramics known as Talavera. There are several good stores on Plazuela de los Sapos and the streets around it. Designs reveal Asian, Spanish-Arabic and Mexican indigenous influences. Bigger pieces are expensive, delicate and difficult to transport.

A number of shops along Avenida 6 Oriente, to the east of Avenida 5 de Mayo, sell traditional handmade Puebla sweets such as *camotes* (candied sweet-potato sticks) and *jamoncillos* (bars of pumpkin-seed paste).

For quirky antique stores, head to Callejón de los Sapos, around the corner of Avenida 5 Oriente and Calle 6 Sur. Most shops open from 10am through to 7pm. On Saturday and Sunday, there is a lively outdoor antiques market here and at the Plazuela de los Sapos from 11am to 5pm.

Talavera Uriarte CERAMICS
(✆ 222-232-15-98; www.uriartetalavera.com.mx; Av 4 Poniente 911; ◷ 9am-7pm Mon-Fri, 10am-6pm Sat, 10am-5pm Sun) Unlike most of Puebla's Talavera shops, Uriarte still makes its pottery on site. The showroom displays a gorgeous selection of high-quality, intricately painted pieces. Founded in 1824, the company is now owned by a Canadian expat. Factory tours are offered 10am to 1pm Monday through Friday.

El Parián Crafts Market HANDICRAFTS
(Plaza Parián) Browse local Talavera, onyx and trees of life, as well as the types of leather, jewelry and textiles that you'll find in other cities. Some of the work is shoddy, but there's also some quality handiwork and prices are reasonable.

Information

EMERGENCY
Tourist Police (✆ 800-903-92-00)

INTERNET ACCESS
There are several places to get online along Calle 2 Sur. Most charge M$5 to M$10 per hour.

MEDICAL SERVICES
Cruz Roja (Red Cross; ✆ 222-235-86-31) Gives emergency medical attention.
Hospital UPAEP (✆ 222-229-81-34; Av 5 Poniente 715)

MONEY
ATMs are plentiful throughout the city, but mostly on Avenida Reforma near the *zócalo*, where banks have exchange and traveler's check facilities.

POST
Main Post Office (✆ 222-232-64-48; Av 16 de Septiembre s/n)

TOURIST INFORMATION
Municipal Tourist Office (✆ 222-404-50-47, 222-404-50-08; Portal Hidalgo 14; ◷ 9am-8pm Mon-Fri, to 3pm Sun) English- and French-speaking office with free maps, use of internet-connected PCs and excellent information about what's on.
State Tourist Office (✆ 222-246-20-44; Av 5 Oriente 3; ◷ 8am-8pm Mon-Sat, 9am-2pm Sun) Information for destinations outside of Puebla. In the Casa de Cultura building, facing cathedral yard.

🛈 Getting There & Away

AIR
Puebla's international airport, **Aeropuerto Hermanos Serdán** (✆ 222-232-00-32; www.aeropuerto-puebla.es.tl), has patchy service and closes whenever there is volcanic ash in the air. The **Toluca airport** (p198) is likely a better option. There are, however, several domestic Volaris flights. The airport is 22km west of Puebla, off Hwy 190.

BUS
Puebla's full-service **Central de Autobuses de Puebla** (CAPU; ✆ 222-249-72-11; www.capu.com.mx; Blvd Norte 4222) is 4km north of the *zócalo* and 1.5km off the autopista.

From Mexico City and towns to the west, most buses to and from Puebla use the capital's TAPO station, though some travel to Terminal Norte or Terminal Sur in Tasqueña. The trip takes about two hours.

Both **ADO** (www.ado.com.mx) and **Estrella Roja** (ER; ✆ 800-712-22-84; www.estrellaroja.com.mx) travel frequently between the two cities, operating both 1st-class and wi-fi-enabled deluxe buses.

From CAPU, there are buses at least once a day to almost everywhere to the south and east.

Frequent 'Cholula' *colectivos* (M$7.50, 30 minutes) leave from Avenida 6 Poniente, near the corner with Calle 13 Norte.

CAR & MOTORCYCLE
Puebla is 123km east of Mexico City by Hwy 150D. Traveling east of Puebla, 150D continues to Orizaba (negotiating a cloudy, winding 22km descent from the 2385m-high Cumbres de Maltrata en route), Córdoba and Veracruz.

BUSES FROM PUEBLA

DESTINATION	FARE (M$)	DURATION (HR)	FREQUENCY (DAILY)
Cuetzalan	190	3½	4
Mexico City (TAPO or Tasqueña)	150-192	2-2½	50
Oaxaca	430-508	4-4½	6
Veracruz	352-424	3½	28

ⓘ Getting Around

Most hotels and places of interest are within walking distance of Puebla's *zócalo*. At the CAPU bus station, buy a ticket at the kiosk for an **authorized taxi** (www.taxisautorizadoscapu.com) to the city center (M$55). Alternatively, follow signs for 'Autobuses Urbanos' and catch combi 51 (M$6) to the corner of Avenida 4 and Blvd 5 de Mayo, three blocks east of the *zócalo*. The ride takes 15 to 20 minutes. From the city center to the bus station, catch any northbound 'CAPU' *colectivo* from the same corner, or along Calle 9 Sur. All city buses and *colectivos* cost M$6.

Call **Radio Taxi** (☏ 222-243-70-59) for secure taxi service within the city – a good idea if you're traveling alone or going out at night.

Cholula

☏ 222 / POP 120,000 / ELEV 2170M

Though it's almost a suburb of Puebla these days, Cholula is far different in its history and relaxed daytime ambience. Owing to its large student population, the town has a surprisingly vibrant nightlife and some decent restaurants and accommodations options within a short walk of the huge *zócalo*.

Cholula is also home to the widest pyramid ever built (yes, wider than any in Egypt) – the Pirámide Tepanapa. Despite this claim to fame, the town's ruins are largely ignored because, unlike those of Teotihuacán or Tula, the shrubbery-covered pyramid has been so badly neglected over the centuries that it's virtually unrecognizable as a human-made structure.

History

Between around AD 1 and 600, Cholula grew into an important religious center, while powerful Teotihuacán flourished 100km to the northwest. Around AD 600, Cholula fell to the Olmeca-Xicallanca, who built nearby Cacaxtla. Some time between AD 900 and 1300 the Toltecs and/or Chichimecs took over and it later fell under Aztec dominance. There was also artistic influence from the Mixtecs to the south.

By 1519 Cholula's population had reached 100,000 and the Pirámide Tepanapa was already overgrown. Cortés, having befriended the neighboring Tlaxcalans, traveled here at the request of the Aztec ruler Moctezuma, but it was a trap and Aztec warriors had set an ambush. The Tlaxcalans tipped off Cortés about the plot and the Spanish struck first. Within a day they killed 6000 Cholulans before the city was looted by the Tlaxcalans.

Cortés vowed to build a church here for every day of the year, or one on top of every pagan temple, depending on which legend you prefer. Today there are 39 churches – far from 365 but still plenty for a small city.

The Spanish developed nearby Puebla to overshadow the old pagan center and Cholula never regained its importance, especially after a severe plague in the 1540s decimated its indigenous population.

◉ Sights

Zona Arqueológica PYRAMID

(☏ 222-235-97-20; M$52; ⊘9am-6pm Tue-Sun) The **Pirámide Tepanapa**, located two blocks to the southeast of Cholula's central plaza, looks more like a hill than a pyramid and has a domed church on top so it's tough to miss. The town's big drawcard is no letdown with kilometers of tunnels veining the inside of the structure. The Zona Arqueológica comprises the excavated areas around the pyramid and the tunnels underneath.

The church grounds on the peak are worth the trip alone for panoramic views across Cholula to the volcanoes and Puebla.

Visitors enter via the tunnel on the north side, which takes you on a spooky route through the center of the pyramid. Several pyramids were built on top of each other during various reconstructions, and more than 8km of tunnels have been dug beneath the pyramid by archaeologists to penetrate each stage, with 800m accessible to visitors. You can see earlier layers of the building from the access tunnel, which is a few hundred meters long.

The access tunnel emerges on the east side of the pyramid, from where you can follow a path around to the **Patio de los Altares** on the south side. Ringed by platforms and unique diagonal stairways, this plaza was the main approach to the pyramid. Three large stone slabs on its east, north and west sides are carved in the Veracruz interlocking scroll design. At its south end is an Aztec-style altar in a pit, dating from shortly before the Spanish conquest. On the mound's west side is a reconstructed section of the latest pyramid, with two earlier exposed layers.

Rather than following the path south, you can head straight up the stairs to the brightly decorated **Santuario de Nuestra Señora de los Remedios** that tops Pirámide Tepanapa and looks down upon the Patio de los Altares. It's a classic symbol of conquest,

Cholula

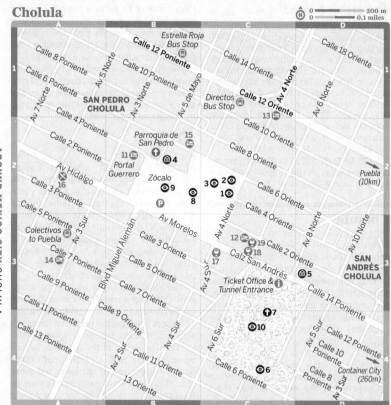

though possibly an inadvertent one as the church may have been built before the Spanish realized the mound contained a pagan temple. You can climb to the church for free on a path starting near the northwest corner of the pyramid.

The small **Museo de Sitio de Cholula** (Calz San Andrés), across the road from the ticket office and down some steps, provides the best introduction to the site, with a cutaway model of the pyramid mound showing the various superimposed structures. Admission is included in the site ticket.

Zócalo   PLAZA

(Plaza de la Concordia) The **Ex-Convento de San Gabriel**, facing the east side of Cholula's huge *zócalo* (in San Pedro, not to be confused with Zócalo de San Andrés to the east), includes a tiny but interesting **Franciscan library** and three fine churches, all of which will appeal to travelers interested in antique books and early religious

and Franciscan history. On the left, as you face the ex-convent from the *zócalo,* is the Arabic-style **Capilla Real**, which has 49 domes and dates from 1540.

In the middle is the 19th-century **Capilla de la Tercera Orden**, and on the right is the **Templo de San Gabriel**, founded in 1530 on the site of a pyramid.

Museo de la Ciudad de Cholula   MUSEUM

(Casa del Caballero Águila; cnr Av 5 de Mayo & Calle 4 Oriente; M$20, Sun free; ⊙9am-3pm Thu-Tue) This excellent museum is housed in a fantastically restored colonial building on the *zócalo*. The small but strong collection includes ceramics and jewelry from the Pirámide Tepanapa, as well as later colonial paintings and sculptures. And most interestingly of all, you can watch through a glass wall as museum employees painstakingly restore smashed ceramics and repair jewelry.

Cholula

⊙ **Sights**
1 Capilla de la Tercera Orden................C2
2 Capilla Real...C2
3 Ex-Convento de San Gabriel..............C2
4 Museo de la Ciudad de Cholula..........B2
5 Museo de Sitio de Cholula..................D3
6 Patio de los Altares........................... C4
7 Santuario de Nuestra Señora de
   los Remedios..................................... C4
8 Templo de San Gabriel.......................B2
9 Zócalo..B2
10 Zona Arqueológica C4

🛏 **Sleeping**
11 Casa Calli..B2
12 Estrella de Belem................................C3
13 Hostal de San Pedro...........................C1
14 Hotel La Quinta Luna...........................A3
15 Hotel Real de Naturales B2

🍴 **Eating**
16 La Casa de Frida A2

🍷 **Drinking & Nightlife**
17 Bar Reforma C3
18 La Lunita C3
19 Maaema C3

🎭 Festivals & Events

Shrove Tuesday   HISTORICAL
(☉ Feb) Masked Carnaval dancers re-enact a battle between French and Mexican forces in Huejotzingo, 14km northwest of Cholula, off Hwy 190.

Quetzalcóatl Ritual   CULTURAL
On both the spring (late March) and fall (late September) equinoxes, this pre-Hispanic ritual is re-enacted with poetry, sacrificial dances, firework displays and music performed on traditional instruments at the pyramid.

Festival de la Virgen de los Remedios   DANCE
(☉ Sep) Perhaps the most important Cholulan holiday of the year, this festival is celebrated the week of September 1. There are traditional dances daily atop the Pirámide Tepanapa. Cholula's regional feria is held during the following weeks.

🛏 Sleeping

With a clutch of good-value hotels and a couple of boutique favorites, Cholula makes an attractive alternative to staying in Puebla for those who prefer a laid-back pace.

Hotel Real de Naturales   BUSINESS HOTEL $
(☎222-247-60-70; www.hotelrealdenaturales.com; Calle 6 Oriente 7; d/tr/q M$550/650/750, ste M$950-1000; [P][🛜][❄]) This 45-room hotel was built in the colonial style to blend into the surrounding architectural landscape and it succeeds with its shady courtyards, tile baths, tasteful black-and-white photography and elegant archways. Its central location and many considered details make it an excellent bargain for the price.

Casa Calli   BOUTIQUE HOTEL $
(☎222-261-56-07; www.hotelcasacalli.com; Portal Guerrero 11; d/tw/tr M$590/720/840; [P][🛜][❄]) Right on the *zócalo,* this hotel contains 40 stylishly minimalist rooms, an attractive pool and an Italian restaurant-bar in the lobby. Prices are reasonable and weekend spa packages are available (from M$1980). Rooms are discounted slightly in quiet periods Sunday to Thursday.

Hostal de San Pedro   HOSTEL $
(☎222-178-04-95; www.hostaldesanpedro.com; Calle 6 Norte 1203; dm/d/tw/tr incl breakfast M$170/450/500/600; [P][♿][@][🛜]) The only true hostel in Cholula is a quick stroll from the *zócalo* and has clean, comfy beds in a quiet location. Upstairs rooms are built around a sunny terrace where you could easily pass an afternoon. If you end up staying even longer, there are long-term deals with laundry use.

★ Estrella de Belem   LUXURY HOTEL $$$
(☎222-261-19-25; www.estrelladebelem.com.mx; Calle 2 Oriente 410; r incl breakfast M$2000-2500; [P][✳][🛜][❄]) This beautiful hotel has just six rooms, each with gorgeous, thoughtful touches such as radiant-heat floors, noise-blocking windows, bathtubs and LCD TVs. The master suites are especially luxurious, with fireplaces and Jacuzzis. Common areas include a lovely, grassy courtyard and a small, rooftop swimming pool that has views over the town. No children under 12.

Hotel La Quinta Luna   LUXURY HOTEL $$$
(☎222-247-89-15; www.laquintaluna.com; Av 3 Sur 702; r incl breakfast M$2050, ste M$2550-4175; [P][🛜]) This rarefied hotel is popular with a wealthy weekender crowd. The seven stylish rooms occupy a thick-walled 17th-century mansion set around a charming garden and are a gorgeous mix of colonial antiques, plush bedding, flat-screen TVs and contemporary art. Meetings with the featured *poblano* artists are happily arranged.

There's a great library and the excellent restaurant is open to nonguests who reserve.

✖ Eating & Drinking

La Casa de Frida
MEXICAN $$

(☑222-178-23-03; Miguel Hidalgo 109; mains M$80-225, weekend buffet M$115; ⊙9:30am-6pm Sun-Thu, to 10pm Fri & Sat; ☎☑♨) This cavernous gem gives a nod to Frida Kahlo's home in Mexico City. Mexican handicrafts (plus the artist-owner's murals) are splashed throughout the courtyard, Mexican musicians croon on one side and excellent flame-grilled steaks sizzle on the other. Service is excellent, there is a kids' playroom and the *pipián verde* (chicken in a spiced pepita sauce) is exceptionally complex.

La Lunita
CANTINA

(☑222-247-00-11; www.lalunita.com; cnr Avs Morelos & 6 Norte 419) In the pyramid's shadow, this raucous, family-run bar has been in business since 1939. Painted in bright colors and decorated with an assortment of old advertising posters and knickknacks, La Lunita looks just like the movie version of a Mexican cantina. It's popular with locals who come for its broad-ranging menu (mains M$69 to M$162), live music, football on TV and plentiful drinks.

Maaema
CLUB

(Av 6 Norte 1; ⊙2pm-midnight Sun-Thu, to 3am Fri & Sat; ☎) It's easy to strike up a conversation with the casual, young crowd at this busy restaurant-club, with its recycled furniture. Chat about the bicycle stools, sewing-machine tables or sawn-in-half bathtub sofas. Then admire the roof-garden view of the church atop Pirámide Tepanapa, lit like a golden beacon, while the electro plays. The veggie burgers and bar food aren't bad either.

Container City
BAR

(www.containercity.com.mx; cnr Calle 12 Oriente & Av 2 Sur) This collection of trendy bars, restaurants, clubs and shops is hopping at night. Set in revamped and stacked former shipping containers in eastern Cholula, it's the hangout of choice for the city's fashionistas and hipsters.

Bar Reforma
CANTINA

(cnr Avs 4 Norte & Morelos; ⊙6pm-12:30am Mon-Sat) Attached to Hotel Reforma, Cholula's oldest drinking spot is a classic, corner abode with swinging doors and plastic flowers, specializing in iceless margaritas

and freshly prepared sangrias. After 9pm it's popular with the university pre-clubbing crowd.

ℹ Getting There & Away

Frequent *colectivos* to Puebla (M$7.50, every 20 minutes) leave from the corner of Calles 5 Poniente and 3 Sur, while larger *directos*, or buses (M$8, every 30 minutes), leave from the corner of Calles 2 Norte and 12 Oriente. Buses and *colectivos* stop two or three blocks north of the *zócalo*. The trip takes 20 to 40 minutes, depending on how *directo* they go.

Popocatépetl & Iztaccíhuatl

Mexico's second- and third-highest peaks, volcanoes Popocatépetl (po-po-ka-*teh*-pet-l; 5452m) and Iztaccíhuatl (iss-ta-*see*-wat-l; 5220m) form the eastern rim of the Valle de México, about 40km west of Puebla and 70km southeast of Mexico City. While the craterless Iztaccíhuatl is dormant, Popocatépetl (Náhuatl for 'Smoking Mountain,' also called Don Goyo and Popo) is very active and its summit has been off-limits for the last decade. Legend has it that Iztaccíhuatl resembles a sleeping woman who died with grief for Popocatépetl, who returned from war to find her gone and is still now explosively angry for his loss. Between 1994 and 2001, Popo's major bursts of activity triggered evacuations of 16 villages and warnings to the 30 million people who live within striking distance of the crater. In 2013, 2015 and again in 2016, explosions catapulted ash into the sky, disrupting domestic and US flights to and from airports in Mexico City and Toluca.

Mexico's **Centro Nacional de Prevención de Desastres** (National Disaster Prevention Center; ☑24hr hotline 55-5205-1036; www.cenapred.gob.mx) monitors volcanic activity through variations in gas emissions and seismic intensity. Though almost entirely in Spanish, the website posts daily webcam photo captures and updates on conditions.

Historically, Popo has been relatively tranquil, with most activity occurring in the cooler winter months when ice expands and cracks the solidified lava around the crater rim. The last really big blast occurred over 1000 years ago, and volcanologists estimate that there's a 10% chance of one in the near future. In recent years the only danger to visitors has been air quality. The air can feel heavily polluted when there is volcanic activity, so asthmatics and people with breathing difficulties should check pollution levels before they head outdoors, and drink plenty of water. The good news is that the fetching Iztaccíhuatl (White Woman), 20km north of Popo from summit to summit, remains open to climbers.

🏃 Activities

Hiking & Climbing

Izta's highest peak is **El Pecho** (5220m). All routes require a night on the mountain and there's a shelter hut between the staging point at La Joya, the main southern trailhead, and Las Rodillas, one of Itza's lesser peaks, that can be used during an ascent of El Pecho. On average, it takes at least five hours to reach the hut from La Joya, then another six hours from the hut to El Pecho, and six hours back to the base.

Before making the ascent, climbers must contact the **Parque Nacional Iztaccíhuatl-Popocatépetl** (☑597-978-38-29; http://iztapo po.conanp.gob.mx; Plaza de la Constitución 9B, Amecameca; ☉7am-9pm) office, located on the southeast side of Amecameca's *zócalo*, to register. All visitors must pay the M$30.50 per-day park-entrance fee. The park's website also offers excellent maps and a handy downloadable English-language climbing guide.

About 24km up from Amecameca, there are lower-altitude trails through pine forests and grassy meadows near Paso de Cortés, the trailhead that leads to breathtaking glimpses of nearby peaks. La Joya is another 4km from Paso de Cortés. *Colectivos* departing from Amecameca's plaza for Paso de Cortés cost M$80. From the national park office, taxis will take groups to La Joya (40 minutes) for a negotiable M$300.

Basic shelter with electricity is available at the **Altzomoni Lodge** (beds per person M$30.50), roughly halfway between Paso de Cortés and La Joya. You must reserve in advance at the park office and bring bedding, warm clothes and drinking water.

Climate & Conditions

It can be windy and well below freezing any time of year on Izta's upper slopes, and it's nearly always below freezing near the summit at night. Ice and snow are fixtures here; the average snow line is 4200m. The ideal months for ascents are November to February, when there is hard snowpack for crampons. The rainy season (April to October) brings with it the threat of whiteouts, thunderstorms and avalanches.

Anyone can be affected by altitude problems, including life-threatening altitude sickness. Even Paso de Cortés is at a level where you should know the symptoms.

Guides

Iztaccíhuatl should be attempted *only* by experienced climbers. Because of hidden crevices on the ice-covered upper slopes, a guide is advisable. Besides the following reader recommendations, the national park office may have suggestions.

Livingston Monteverde (www.tierra dentro.com), who is based in Tlaxcala, is a founding member of the Mexican Mountain Guide Association, and has 25 years of climbing experience. He speaks fluent English, basic French and some Hebrew and Italian.

Mario Andrade (☑55-1826-2146; mountain up@hotmail.com) is an authorized, English-speaking guide, based in Mexico City, who has led many Izta climbs. His fee is US$350 for one person; less per person for groups. The cost includes round-trip transportation from Mexico City, lodging, mountain meals and rope usage.

Tlaxcala

☑246 / POP 90,000 / ELEV 2250M

The capital of Mexico's smallest state is unhurried and unself-conscious, with a compact colonial downtown defined by grand government buildings, imposing churches and one of the country's more stunning central plazas. Despite its small stature, Tlaxcala is neither timid nor parochial. With a large student population, good restaurants and bars and a handful of excellent museums, the city has a surprisingly vibrant cultural life. Because there's no single attraction that puts Tlaxcala on tourist itineraries, it remains largely undiscovered, despite its location less than two hours' drive from Mexico City.

Two large central plazas converge at the corner of Avenidas Independencia and Muñoz. The northern one, which is surrounded by colonial buildings, is the *zócalo* called Plaza de la Constitución. The southern square is Plaza Xicohténcatl. Traveling by bus you'll arrive a 10-minute walk from the *zócalo* at the city's hilltop station.

Tlaxcala

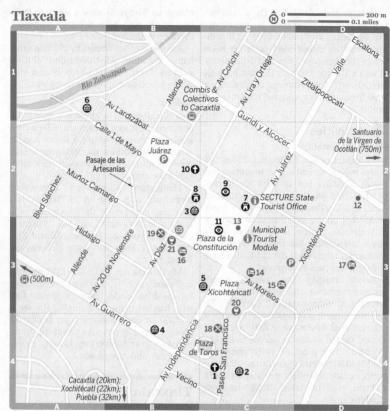

History

In the last centuries before the Spanish conquest, numerous small warrior kingdoms (*señoríos*) arose in and around Tlaxcala. Some of them formed a loose federation that remained independent of the Aztec empire as it spread from the Valle de México in the 15th century. The most important kingdom seems to have been Tizatlán, now in ruins on the northeast edge of Tlaxcala.

When the Spanish arrived in 1519, the Tlaxcalans fought fiercely at first but ultimately became Cortés' staunchest allies against the Aztecs (with the exception of one chief, Xicoténcatl the Younger, who tried to rouse his people against the Spanish and is now a Mexican hero). In 1527 Tlaxcala became the seat of the first bishopric in Nueva España, but a plague in the 1540s devastated the population and the town has played only a supporting role ever since.

Sights

Museo de Arte de Tlaxcala MUSEUM
(246-462-15-10; Plaza de la Constitución 21; adult/student/under 12yr M$25/12.50/free, Sun free; 10am-6pm Tue-Sun) This fantastic contemporary-art museum houses an excellent cache of early Frida Kahlo paintings that have been returned to the museum after several years on loan to other museums around the world. Both the museum's main building on the *zócalo* and the smaller **branch** (Avenida Guerrero 15) FREE hold some interesting temporary exhibits and a good permanent collection of modern Mexican art.

Plaza de la Constitución PLAZA
(Plaza de la Constitución) It's easy to pass an afternoon reading or just people-watching in Tlaxcala's shady, spacious *zócalo*. The 16th-century **Palacio Municipa**, a former grain storehouse, and the **Palacio de**

Tlaxcala

◉ Sights
1 Capilla Abierta...............................C4
Casa de Artesanías......................(see 6)
2 Ex-Convento Franciscano de
la Asunción C4
3 Museo de Arte de Tlaxcala B2
4 Museo de Arte de Tlaxcala B4
5 Museo de la Memoria.....................C3
Museo Regional de
Tlaxcala ....(see 2)
6 Museo Vivo de Artes y
Tradiciones Populares A1
7 Palacio de Gobierno C2
8 Palacio de Justicia B2
9 Palacio Municipal..........................C2
10 Parroquia de San José B2
11 Plaza de la Constitución C3

⊕ Activities, Courses & Tours
12 México Viejo....................................D2
13 Tranvía El Tlaxcalteca....................C3

⬤ Sleeping
14 Hostería de Xicohténcatl...............C3
15 Hotel Minatzín................................C3
16 Hotel Posada San Francisco.........B3
17 Posada La Casona de Cortés.........D3

⊗ Eating
18 Fonda del Convento.......................C4
19 Jaque's...B3

◉ Drinking & Nightlife
20 Pulquería Tía Yola.........................C3
21 Vinos y Piedra................................B3

AROUND MEXICO CITY TLAXCALA

Gobierno occupy most of its north side. Inside the latter there are vivid murals of Tlaxcala's history by Desiderio Hernández Xochitiotzin. Off the *zócalo's* northwest corner is the orange-stucco and blue-tile **Parroquia de San José.** As elsewhere in the *centro histórico,* bilingual signs explain the significance of the church and its many fountains.

The 16th-century building on the plaza's northwest side is the **Palacio de Justicia,** the former Capilla Real de Indios, built for the use of indigenous nobles. The handsome mortar bas-reliefs around its doorway include the seal of Castilla y León and a two-headed eagle, symbol of the Hapsburg monarchs who ruled Spain in the 16th and 17th centuries.

Museo Vivo de Artes y Tradiciones Populares MUSEUM
(☑246-462-23-37; Blvd Sánchez 1; ⊙10am-6pm Tue-Sun) **FREE** This popular arts museum has displays on Tlaxcalan village life, weaving and *pulque*-making, sometimes with demonstrations. Artisans serve as guides to the more than 3000 artifacts on display. The cafe and handicrafts next door at the **Casa de Artesanías** (http://artesanias.tlaxcala.gob.mx) are also worth a look.

Museo de la Memoria MUSEUM
(☑246-466-07-92; Av Independencia 3; adult/student M$20/10; ⊙10am-5pm) This modern history museum looks at folklore through a multimedia lens and has well-presented exhibits on indigenous government, agriculture and contemporary festivals. Explanations are only in Spanish.

Santuario de la Virgen de Ocotlán CHURCH
(Hidalgo 1, Ocotlán; ⊙8am-7pm) One of Mexico's most spectacular churches is an important pilgrimage site for those who believe the Virgin appeared here in 1541 – her image stands on the main altar in memory of the apparition. The classic Churrigueresque facade features white stucco 'wedding cake' decorations contrasting with plain red tiles. During the 18th century, indigenous artist Francisco Miguel spent 25 years decorating the altarpieces and the chapel beside the main altar.

Visible from most of town, the hilltop church is 1km northeast of the *zócalo.* Walk north from the *zócalo* on Avenida Juárez/Avenida Independencia for three blocks then turn right onto Zitlalpopocatl. Alternatively, 'Ocotlán' *colectivos* travel the same route.

Ex-Convento Franciscano de la Asunción HISTORIC BUILDING
This former monastery is up a shaded path from the southeast corner of Plaza Xicohténcatl. Built between 1537 and 1540, it was one of Mexico's earliest monasteries and its church – the city's cathedral – has a beautiful Moorish-style wooden ceiling.

Just below the monastery, beside the 19th-century Plaza de Toros (bullring), is a **capilla abierta** (open chapel) with three unique Moorish-style arches. One of the entrances is locked, but you can access the *capilla* from other entry points.

Museo Regional de Tlaxcala (☑246-462-02-62; ⊙10am-6pm) **FREE**, housed within the monastery building, has a large collection of religious paintings and sculptures and some pre-Hispanic artifacts from nearby archaeological sites.

 Courses

**Estela Silva's Mexican
Home Cooking School**   COOKING COURSE
(📞246-468-09-78; www.mexicanhomecooking.com)
Learn to cook *poblano* cuisine with Señora
Estela Silva and her sous-chef husband, Jon
Jarvis, in the couple's Talavera-tiled kitchen
in Tlacochcalco, 10km south of Tlaxcala. The
English-Spanish bilingual course includes
all meals plus lodging in private rooms with
fireplaces (transportation to/from the school
can be arranged). An all-inclusive, six-night/
five-day course is US$1798, but shorter stays
can be arranged.

☞ Tours

Tranvía El Tlaxcalteca   BUS TOUR
(📞246-458-53-24; Plaza de la Constitución, Portal Hidalgo 6; adult/child M$65/55; ☺every 2hr
10am-7pm) This motorized streetcar visits 33
downtown sights with Spanish narration.
No reservations necessary.

✰✰ Festivals & Events

Virgen de Ocotlán   RELIGIOUS
(☺May) On the third Monday in May, the
figure of the Virgen de Ocotlán is carried
from its hilltop perch at Santuario de La
Virgen de Ocotlán to neighboring churches,
attracting equal numbers of onlookers and
believers. Throughout the month, processions commemorating the miracle attract
pilgrims from around the country.

Nacional de Danza Folklórica   DANCE
(☺Sep) This vibrant celebration brings
dancers from around the country to Tlaxcala's Teatro Xicohténcatl during the last week
of September.

Fiesta de Todos los Santos   CULTURAL
(☺Oct-Nov) Tlaxcala's Fiesta de Todos los
Santos draws people from around the state
between late October and mid-November,
when *charrería* (horsemanship), bullfights
and other rodeo-inspired pageantry take
center stage. The festival kicks off with a
pamplonada (running of the bulls) and includes Día de Muertos activities.

🛌 Sleeping

Hostería de Xicohténcatl   GUESTHOUSE $
(📞246-466-33-22; Portal Hidalgo 10; s/d/tr
M$400/450/600, ste M$650-1200; 🅿🛜) Half of
the 16 rooms at this straightforward budget
hostería are large, multiroom suites with
kitchens, making it a bargain for families,

groups or those in town for an extended
stay. The *hostería* is clean, if a bit sterile, and
the location – right on Plaza Xicohténcatl –
is excellent.

**★Posada La
Casona de Cortés**   BOUTIQUE HOTEL $$
(📞246-462-20-42; http://lacasonadecortes.com.
mx; Av Lardizábal 6; r from M$775, ste M$995;
🅿🛜) Set around a lush courtyard with
fruit trees and a fountain, this affordable
boutique hotel seems almost too good to
be true. The rooms, which have firm beds,
tiled floors and high-pressure showers, are
decorated with Mexican *artesanías* (handi-
crafts). The bar has a working 1950s jukebox
and a roof deck with views of church stee-
ples and volcanic peaks.

Hotel Minatzín   BOUTIQUE HOTEL $$
(📞246-462-04-40; Xicohténcatl 6; d/tw/ste
M$600/900/1300; 🅿❄🛜) This converted co-
lonial house has stone tiling, is light, bright
and airy and makes a fine match with Tlaxcala's nearby *zócalo*. All five spacious rooms
have 3D TVs and feel more indulgent, and
the beds much plusher, than the price suggests. The suite sleeps four.

Hotel Posada San Francisco   LUXURY HOTEL $$$
(📞246-144-55-55;http://hotelsanfranciscotlaxcala.
mx; Plaza de la Constitución 17; r M$1544, ste
M$1995-2940; 🅿❄🛜) The bullfighter-
themed bar at this hotel is the kind of place
you'd expect to find a famous author swill-
ing fine tequila – check out the stained-
glass ceiling in the lobby, the pool and the
patio restaurant. While the building evokes
17th-century grandeur, rooms are modern.

🍴 Eating & Drinking

For a small city, Tlaxcala has an impressive
number – and diversity – of good restau-
rants. The eastern side of the *zócalo* is over-
run by underwhelming sidewalk cafes, but
there are better options on the south side
and on nearby Plaza Xicohténcatl. Tlaxca-
la's Mercado Emilio Sánchez Piedras is one
of the most pleasant markets around. To
get there from Parroquia de San José, walk
seven minutes along Avenida Lira y Ortega
until the corner with Escalona.

Jaque's   MEXICAN $
(Muñoz Camargo 2; mains M$45-85, menú del
día M$45; ☺8am-6:30pm; 🛜) It's just a few
steps from the *zócalo,* but the Mexican fare
is much better here, plus you still have the
white tablecloths and bay windows peering

down on the street. The *pechuga a la diabla* (chicken schnitzel stuffed with panela cheese in a spicy tomato sauce) is as devilishly good as the name susgests.

Fonda del Convento   MEXICAN **$$**
(☑246-462-07-65; Paseo de San Francisco 1; mains M$99-149; ☺8am-8pm) This unassuming home-style restaurant has been a local favorite for four decades. The menu focuses on traditional Tlaxcalteca cuisine, including *gusanos* (maguey worms), *escamoles* (ant larvae), *mole poblano*, rabbit in *pulque* and a family-recipe *pipián* (green pumpkin-seed sauce).

Pulquería Tía Yola   PULQUERÍA
(☑246-462-73-09; Plaza Xicohténcatl 7; ☺10am-9pm) Sip one of a dozen-or-so flavors of house-made *pulque* in a stone courtyard decorated with Día de Muertos figurines and mosaics of Aztec gods. The sidewalk tables along the plaza are a prime location for weekend people-watching.

Vinos y Piedra   WINE BAR
(☑246-466-21-57; Plaza de la Constitución 19; ☺7:30am-11:30pm Sun-Thu, to 1am Fri & Sat) This wine bar is complete with spittoons at each table, a basement wine cellar (visible through a section of see-through floor) and domestic and imported *vinos*. This hangout for Tlaxcala's elite serves tapas (M$45 to M$85) with an emphasis on highfalutin dishes such as grapes rolled in blue cheese. Breakfasts include *chapatas* (Mexican sandwiches) with shrimp and hummus.

The sidewalk tables are great for an evening drink.

ⓘ Information

Several banks on Avenida Juárez, near the tourist office, exchange dollars and have ATMs. There is also an ATM inside the bus terminal. Internet cafes are plentiful.

Farmacia Cristo Rey (Av Lardizábal 15; ☺24hr) Around-the-clock pharmacy.
Hospital General (☑246-462-35-55; Corregidora s/n)
Police (☑246-464-52-57)
Post Office (cnr Avs Muñoz & Díaz)
SECTURE State Tourist Office (☑246-465-09-60; www.tlaxcala.gob.mx/turismo; cnr Avs Juárez & Lardizábal; ☺9am-7pm Mon-Fri, 10am-6pm Sat) The English-speaking staff are eager to sing Tlaxcala's praises and equip travelers with colorful bird's-eye-view maps and a handful of brochures. They're also found at the tourist module (Portal Hidalgo 6; ☺9am-

7pm) – no English spoken – on the east side of the *zócalo*.

ⓘ Getting There & Away

Tlaxcala's bus terminal sits on a hill 1km west of the central plaza. For Mexico City's TAPO terminal, **ATAH** (☑246-466-00-87) runs 1st-class buses (M$136, two hours, every 30 minutes). Frequent 2nd-class Verde buses go to Puebla (M$22). Taxis between the station and downtown cost M$35.

ⓘ Getting Around

Most *colectivos* (M$5) passing the bus terminal are heading into town, although it takes just 10 minutes to walk. Exit the terminal, turn right down the hill till you hit Avenida Guerrero then turn right past the towering steps of Escalinata de Héroes. To reach the terminal from the center, catch a blue-and-white *colectivo* on the east side of Blvd Sánchez.

Cacaxtla & Xochitécatl

These sister sites, about 20km southwest of Tlaxcala and 32km northwest of Puebla, are among Mexico's most intriguing.

Cacaxtla (ca-*casht*-la) is one of Mexico's most impressive ancient ruins with its many high-quality, vividly painted depictions of daily life. Rather than being relegated to a museum collection, these works – including frescoes of a nearly life-size jaguar and eagle warriors engaged in battle – are on display within the site itself. Located atop a scrubby hill with wide views of the surrounding countryside, the ruins were discovered in 1975 when men from the nearby village of San Miguel del Milagro, looking for a reputedly valuable cache of relics, dug a tunnel and uncovered a mural.

The much older ruins at Xochitécatl (so-chi-*teh*-catl), 2km away and accessible from Cacaxtla on foot, include an exceptionally wide pyramid as well as a circular one. A German archaeologist led the first systematic exploration of the site in 1969, but it wasn't until 1994 that it was opened to the public.

History

Cacaxtla was the capital of a group of Olmeca-Xicallanca, or Putún Maya, who arrived in central Mexico as early as AD 450. After the decline of Cholula (which they probably helped bring about) in around AD 600, they became the chief power in southern Tlaxcala and the Puebla valley. Cacaxtla peaked from AD 650 to 950 and was abandoned by AD 1000 in the face of possibly Chichimec newcomers.

Atop a higher hill, the ruins of Xochitécatl predate Christ by a millennium. Just who first occupied the spot is a matter of dispute, but experts agree that whereas Cacaxtla primarily served as living quarters for the ruling class, Xochitécatl was chiefly used for gory Quecholli ceremonies honoring Mixcoatl, god of the hunt. That isn't to say Cacaxtla didn't hold similar ceremonies – the discovery of the skeletal remains of hundreds of mutilated children attest to Cacaxtla's bloody past.

◉ Sights

Cacaxtla ARCHAEOLOGICAL SITE

(☑ 246-416-00-00; Circuito Perimetral s/n, San Miguel del Milagro; admission incl Xochitécatl & museums M$62; ⊙ 9am-5:30pm; P) The large murals at Cacxtla are on display among the ruins themselves. They evoke a real sense of history where it happened and are worth seeing before they, unfortunately, continue to fade into history. The main attraction is a natural platform, 200m long and 25m high, called the **Gran Basamento** (Great Base), now sheltered under an expansive metal roof. Here stood Cacaxtla's main civic and religious buildings and the residences of its ruling priestly classes.

Starting at the parking lot opposite the site entrance, it's a 200m walk to the ticket office, museum and restaurant. From the ticket office it's another 600m downhill to the top of the entry stairs to the Gran Basamento in the **Plaza Norte**.

From here the path winds clockwise around the ruins until you reach the **murals**, many of which clearly show Maya influence among the symbols from the Mexican highlands. This combination of styles in a mural is unique to Cacaxtla.

Before reaching the first mural you'll come to a small patio, of which the main feature is an **altar** fronted by a small square pit, in which numerous human remains were discovered. Just beyond the altar you'll find the **Templo de Venus**, which contains two anthropomorphic sculptures – a man and a woman – in blue, wearing jaguar-skin skirts. The temple's name is attributed to the appearance of numerous half-stars around the female figure which are associated with Earth's sister planet, Venus.

On the opposite side of the path, away from the Plaza Norte, the **Templo Rojo** contains four murals, only one of which is visible. Its vivid imagery is dominated by a row of corn and cacao crops whose husks contain human heads.

Facing the north side of Plaza Norte is the long **Mural de la Batalla** (Battle Mural), dating from before AD 700. It shows two warrior groups, one wearing jaguar skins and the other bird feathers, engaged in ferocious battle. The Olmeca-Xicallanca (the jaguar warriors with round shields) are clearly repelling invading Huastecs (the bird warriors with jade ornaments and deformed skulls).

Beyond the Mural de la Batalla, turn left and climb the steps to see the second major **mural group**, behind a fence to your right. The two main murals (c AD 750) show a figure in a jaguar costume and a black-painted figure in a bird costume (believed to be the Olmeca-Xicallanca priest-governor) standing atop a plumed serpent.

Xochitécatl ARCHAEOLOGICAL SITE

(☑ 246-416-00-00; Circuito Perimetral s/n, San Miguel del Milagro; admission incl Cacaxtla & museums M$62; ⊙ 9am-5:30pm; P) Because of its outline and the materials used, archaeologists believe the circular **Pirámide de la Espiral** was built between 1000 and 800 BC. Its form and hilltop location suggest it may have been used as an astronomical observation post, or as a temple to Ehécatl, the wind god. From here the path passes three other pyramids.

The **Basamento de los Volcanes**, which is all that remains of the first pyramid, is the base of the Pirámide de los Volcanes and it's made of materials from two periods. Cut square stones were placed over the original stones, visible in some areas, and then stuccoed over. In an interesting twist, the colored stones used to build Tlaxcala's municipal palace appear to have come from this site.

The **Pirámide de la Serpiente** gets its name from a large piece of carved stone with a snake head at one end. Its most impressive feature is the huge pot found at its center, carved from a single boulder, which was hauled from another region. Researchers surmise it was used to hold water.

Experts speculate that rituals honoring the fertility god were held at the **Pirámide de las Flores**, due to the discovery of several sculptures and the remains of 30 sacrificed infants. Near the pyramid's base – Latin

America's fourth-widest – is a pool carved from a massive rock, where the infants were believed to have been washed before being killed.

🏳 Tours

México Viejo   TOUR

(✆ 246-466-85-83; http://mexicoviejotours.com; Interior 2, Guridi y Alcocer 50, Tlaxcala; adult/child M$570/390; ⊘ depart 10am, return 3pm) A guided tour of the history of the site, this is a good option for travelers short on time.

❶ Getting There & Away

Considering how close the archaeological zone is to Mexico City, Tlaxcala and Puebla – it's roughly smack in the middle of the three cities – getting to and from Cacaxtla-Xochitécatl on public transit is inconvenient and time-consuming.

Cacaxtla is 1.5km uphill from a back road between San Martín Texmelucan (near Hwy 150D) and Hwy 119, the secondary road between Tlaxcala and Puebla. To reach the site from Tlaxcala, catch a 'San Miguel del Milagro' *colectivo* from the corner of Escalona and Sánchez Piedras, which will drop you off about 500m from Cacaxtla.

From Puebla, Flecha Azul buses go direct from the CAPU terminal to the town of Nativitas, about 3km east of Cacaxtla. From there, catch a 'Zona Arqueológica' *colectivo* to the site.

Between Cacaxtla and Xochitécatl, taxis (M$60) are available on weekends, or walk the 2km (about 25 minutes).

La Malinche

The long, sweeping slopes of this dormant 4460m volcano, named after Cortés' indigenous interpreter and lover, dominate the skyline northeast of Puebla.

The main route to the volcano is Hwy 136; turn southwest at the 'Centro Vacacional Malintzi' sign. Before you reach the center, you must register at the entrance of the **Parque Nacional La Malintzi**. La Malinche, Mexico's fifth-tallest peak, is snowcapped only a few weeks each year, typically in May.

Centro Vacacional IMSS Malintzi (✆ 55-5238-2701; http://centrosvacacionales.imss.gob. mx; campsites M$60, cabins up to 6 people M$865-1278, up to 9 people M$1360; [P]), operated by the Mexican Social Security Institute, has 50 cabins, including rustic and 'luxury' options, at a frosty 3333m. The family-oriented resort has woodsy grounds and fine views of the peak. The remodeled cabins are basic, but include TV, fireplace, hot water and kitchen

with refrigerator. It gets crowded from Friday to Sunday, but is quiet midweek. Those not staying can park here for M$40. Prices are about M$100 higher on weekends and holidays.

Beyond the vacation center, the road becomes impassable by car. It's about 1km by footpath to a ridge, from where it's an arduous five-hour round-trip hike to the top. Hikers should take precautions against altitude sickness.

Huamantla

✆ 247 / POP 52,000 / ELEV 2500M

Huamantla has invested greatly in its downtown area, gussying up its colonial city center and renovating its charming *zócalo*. With La Malinche looming over town, this is a pleasant base camp for exploring the surrounding countryside, once you get past its sprawling suburbs.

Huamantla sees a few sleepless nights during its annual **feria** in August. The day before the Feast of the Assumption (August 15), locals blanket the town's streets with elaborate carpets of flowers and colored sawdust. The following Saturday, there's a running of the bulls, similar to that in Pamplona – but more dangerous since the uncastrated males charge from two directions. During the feria, rates double and rooms are reserved well in advance. If everything is full, seek out a room in Puebla or Tlaxcala.

◉ Sights

Museo de Títere   MUSEUM

(✆ 247-472-10-33; Parque Juárez 15; adult/student & senior/child M$20/10/5, Sun free; ⊘ 10am-6pm Tue-Sat, to 3pm Sun) The national puppet museum displays dolls and marionettes from all around the world in a fantastic new building on the *zócalo*. It's a fun stop for the young and young at heart.

🛏 Sleeping & Eating

Hotel Centenario   HOTEL $

(✆ 247-472-05-87; Juárez Norte 209; r M$380-550, ste M$700; [P] @ 🛜) Just a short walk from the *zócalo*, Hotel Centenario has 33 bright-pink, spacious rooms with new bathrooms and wi-fi access. The staff are helpful and there's a good coffee shop in the lobby.

★**Hacienda Soltepec**   HISTORIC HOTEL $$

(✆ 247-472-14-66; www.haciendasoltepec.com; Carretera Huamantla-Puebla Km 3; d/ste Sun-Thu

M$890/1090, Fri & Sat M$1090/1290; P 🛜 🐕)
Just outside of town, this gorgeous renovated hacienda is a former movie set (María Félix stayed here for months while filming one of her classics) with views of Malinche, horse stables, tennis courts and a fantastic in-house restaurant. Its own *pulque* brewery is also open for visits on Saturday and Sunday.

La Casa de los Magueyes MEXICAN $$
(📞 247-472-28-63; Reforma Sur 202; mains M$95-165; ⊘ 9am-10pm Mon-Sat, to 6pm Sun) A wonderful home-style restaurant that serves regional dishes made with seasonal ingredients such as *maguey* buds and wild mushrooms.

🛈 Getting There & Away

Oro and Suriano have frequent services from Puebla. ATAH runs buses from Tlaxcala's main station every seven minutes (M$18). The bus doesn't always stop at a station, so be sure to tell the driver you're going to Huamantla *centro* to avoid missing the town entirely.

Cantona

Given its isolation, a good distance from any town of significance, the vast and incredibly well-preserved Mesoamerican city of **Cantona** (M$41; ⊘ 9am-7pm) is virtually unknown to travelers. With 24 ball courts discovered, this is now believed to have been the biggest single urban center in Mesoamerica, stretched over 12 sq km in an ethereal lava-bed landscape dotted with cacti and yucca and enjoying incredible views of Pico de Orizaba to the south.

The site was inhabited from AD 600 to 1000 and is of interest for two main reasons. Unlike most other Mesoamerican cities, no mortar was used to build it, meaning all the stones are simply held in place by their weight. It's also unique in its design sophistication – all parts of the city are linked by an extensive network of raised roads connecting some 3000 residences. There are several small pyramids and an elaborate **acropolis** at the city's center. With good information panels in English and an access road, Cantona is now being promoted as a tourist attraction. The **Museo de Sitio de Cantona** (📞 276-596-53-07; adult/student M$45/free, Sun free; ⊘ 9am-5pm Tue-Sun) is a modern, well-organized on-site museum displaying 598 pre-Hispanic objects from

the inhabitants of Cantona, with a large showcase of volcanic obsidian, including a 2000-year-old obsidian dagger used for human sacrifice. The focus is on how the people of the region once lived, really bringing it to life with cooking implements and the reconstruction of a thatched hut. The information panels are unfortunately only in Spanish for now.

From Oriental, which is the nearest decent-sized town, Grupo Salazar covered pickup-truck *colectivos* leave every 20 minutes from the corner of Carretera Federal Puebla-Teziutlan and 8 Poniente for Cantona (M$35, 45 minutes). The trucks have 'Tepeyahualco' on their windshield. Tell the driver your destination when you board.

Otherwise, taxis to the site are M$150 or more for a round trip. If you have your own transportation, visiting Cantona makes for a good side trip en route to Cuetzalan.

Cuetzalan

📞 233 / POP 6000 / ELEV 980M
One of the most exhilarating trips in the region, the gorgeous drive to Cuetzalan is an adventure in itself. Beyond the Zaragoza turnoff, the road becomes dramatic, snaking up hills and around hairpin bends and offering breathtaking views. At the end of it all is the remote, humid town of Cuetzalan (Place of the Quetzals). A striking village built on a precipitous slope, Cuetzalan is famed for its vibrant festivals and Sunday *tianguis* (weekly street markets) that attract scores of indigenous people in traditional dress. On the clearest days you can see all the way from the hilltops to the Gulf coast, 70km away, as the quetzal flies.

Three structures rise above Cuetzalan's skyline: the plaza's freestanding **clock tower**, the Gothic spire of the **Parroquia de San Francisco** and, to the west, the tower of the **French Gothic Santuario de Guadalupe**, with its highly unusual decorative rows of *los jarritos* (clay vases).

⊙ Sights

Las Brisas & Cascada del Salto WATERFALL
About 5km northeast of town, there's a pair of lovely waterfalls. The natural swimming pools beneath the falls are enticing – bring your bathing kit. Rickshaw mototaxis will deposit you at the trailhead and await your return.

★ Festivals & Events

Feria del Café y del Huipil　　CULTURAL
(☉Oct) For several lively days around October 4, Cuetzalan celebrates both its patron saint, St Francis of Assisi, and the start of the coffee harvest with the Festival of Coffee and Huipiles. It features hearty drinking, traditional quetzal dancing and airborne *voladores* (literally 'fliers'), the Totonac ritual in which men, suspended by their ankles, whirl around a tall pole.

The *voladores,* whose tradition was recognized as an Intangible Cultural Heritage by Unesco in 2009, perform for tourists (and tips) several times a day on weekends. It's a remarkable, not-to-miss performance.

⌂ Sleeping

Posada Jaqueline　　GUESTHOUSE $
(☏233-331-03-54; Calle 2 de Abril 2; s/d M$200/250; 🖥) Jaqueline's 20 basic but clean rooms, overlooking the uphill side of the *zócalo,* are one of Cuetzalan's best-value options with cable TV and 24-hour hot water. Some upstairs rooms share a balcony and have views over the town.

Tosepan Kali　　LODGE $$
(☏233-331-09-25; www.tosepankali.com; Km 1.5 de la Carretera Cuetzalan, San Miguel Tzinacapan; s/d/tr/q incl breakfast M$350/700/1050/1400; 🅿🖥🏊) 🍴 High on a hill midway between Cuetzalan and the nearby town of San Miguel Tzinacapan, Tosepan Kali looks like a treehouse nestled in dense foliage. Constructed largely of bamboo and stone and collecting rainwater, this beautiful ecohotel – its name means 'our house' in Náhuatl – is the work of a local indigenous cooperative and includes a large pool with valley views.

Taselotzin　　LODGE $$
(☏233-331-04-80; www.taselotzin.mex.tl; Yoloxóchitl, Barrio Zacatipan; dm/s/d/tr M$165/370/620/825, cabins for up to 4 people M$1210; 🅿🖥) Just outside Cuetzalan, this lodge is run by an association of Nahua craftswomen who campaign for fair trade. The 10-room hotel offers traditional massages and a restaurant that serves local dishes. Follow the right-hand fork past the turnoff to the Puebla road; watch for an inconspicuous sign on the right-hand side, about 300m downhill.

Hotel La Casa de la Piedra　　BOUTIQUE HOTEL $$
(☏233-331-00-30; www.lacasadepiedra.com; García 11; r M$880-960, ste M$1970; 🅿🖥🏊) All 16 rooms in this renovated-yet-rustic former coffee-processing warehouse have picture windows and refinished wooden floors. Upstairs, the two-level suites accommodate up to four people and offer expansive views of the valley. Downstairs rooms have tiled bathrooms, rough stone walls and one or two beds.

Hotel Posada Cuetzalan　　HOTEL $$
(☏233-331-01-54; www.posadacuetzalan.com; Zaragoza 12; s/d/tr/q M$655/913/1085/1220; 🅿🖥🏊) This handsome hotel, 100m uphill from the *zócalo,* has three large courtyards full of chirping birds, a swimming pool, a good restaurant featuring local fruit liqueurs and 36 well-kept rooms with tropical colors, tiled floors, lots of lightly stained wood and cable TV. There's wi-fi in the front rooms near the office.

✗ Eating & Drinking

Regional specialties, sold at many roadside stands, include fruit wines, smoked meats and herbal liqueurs.

Restaurante Yoloxóchitl　　MEXICAN $
(☏233-331-03-35; Calle 2 de Abril No 1; mains M$40-65; 🖥) Beautifully decorated with plants, antiques and ancient jukeboxes, Yoloxóchitl has views over the cathedral and a selection of salads, *antojitos* (tortilla-based snacks) and meat dishes, as well as wild mushrooms pickled in chipotle chili.

La Terraza　　SEAFOOD $$
(☏233-331-04-16; Hidalgo 33; mains M$80-150, breakfasts M$58; ☉8am-10pm) This family-run restaurant, decorated with photos of the town's annual festivities, is extremely popular with locals for its large selection of breakfasts, *mariscos* (seafood), quesadillas, *platillos de la región* and crawfish (in season).

Bar El Calate　　BAR
(☏233-331-05-66; Morelos 9B) On the west side of the *zócalo,* this is *the* place to sip homemade hooch. There are 36 flavors, including liquors infused with coffee, limes, berries – you name it. Try the all-curing *yolixpán,* which is a local herbal liquor with an anis flavor.

🛍 Shopping

Centro de Desarrollo Artesanal Matachiuj　　ARTS & CRAFTS
(Hidalgo 917; ☉9am-7pm Wed-Mon) This fair-trade market has a range of quality weavings and other crafts that come with the benefit

of meeting the producer, as many wares are made on-site by local artisans.

ⓘ Information

On the east side of the *zócalo*, there's a semi-helpful **tourist office** (☏ 233-331-05-27; Plaza Celestino Gasca s/n; ☺ 9am-9pm) with much-needed town maps and help with accommodations. Next door, Santander has an ATM.

ⓘ Getting There & Away

From 6am to 6pm, Vía runs between Puebla and Cuetzalan (M$190, 3½ hours, hourly). It pays to check road conditions and buy your return bus tickets in advance during the rainy season. Primera Plus runs six (seven on Friday) buses a day, starting at 4am, between Cuetzalan and Mexico City's TAPO bus station (M$350, six hours). The last bus to TAPO leaves at 3:50pm. There are additional services on Sundays.

ⓘ Getting Around

On the town's steep streets, three-wheeled mototaxis (from M$25 or about M$100 an hour) offer rides with a thrill. Covered pickup trucks provide transportation (M$8) to nearby *pueblitos*.

Yohualichán

About 8km northeast of Cuetzalan, the last 2km along a steep cobblestone road, this ceremonial **pre-Hispanic site** (M$35; ☺ 9am-5:30pm) has niche pyramids similar to El Tajín's that are in varying states of ruin. The site is impressive and well worth a visit, not least for the great views from this side of the valley. The entrance is adjacent to Yohualichán's church and town plaza. To get here, ask at the tourist office for a *camión* (truck) passing by the pyramids.

SOUTH OF MEXICO CITY

A host of great destinations sit south of the Mexican capital, including mystical Tepoztlán, breathtaking Taxco and the superb complex of caves at Grutas de Cacahuamilpa. The main road south from Mexico City, Hwy 95D, climbs from the smog-choked Valle de México into refreshing pine forests above 3000m and then descends to Cuernavaca, 'the city of eternal spring,' a long-time popular escape from Mexico City and a home-away-from-home for many North Americans and *chilangos* (Mexico City inhabitants) who own second houses here.

The state of Morelos, which encompasses Cuernavaca and Tepoztlán, is one of Mexico's smallest and most densely populated. Valleys at different elevations have a variety of microclimates, and many fruits, grains and vegetables have been cultivated here since pre-Hispanic times. The archaeological sites at Tepoztlán and Xochicalco show signs of the agricultural Tlahuica civilization and the Aztecs who subjugated them. During the colonial era, most of the region was controlled by a few families, including descendants of Cortés. You can visit their palaces and haciendas, along with 16th-century churches and monasteries. Unsurprisingly, the *campesinos* (peasants) of Morelos were fervent supporters of the Mexican Revolution, and local lad Emiliano Zapata is the state's hero. Those with an interest in the peasant revolutionary leader should head to Cuautla, the first city that Zapata conquered, and 6km further south to Aneneculico, where he was born.

The mountainous state of Guerrero boasts utter gems such as the silver-mining tourist mecca Taxco, one of the best-preserved colonial towns in Mexico.

Tepoztlán

☏ 739 / POP 14,000 / ELEV 1700M

A weekend trip from the capital to Tepoztlán rarely disappoints. This beautifully situated small town with a well-preserved historic center surrounded by soaring jagged cliffs is just 80km south of Mexico City. As the birthplace of Quetzalcóatl, the omnipotent serpent god of the Aztecs over 1200 years ago (according to Mesoamerican legend), Tepoztlán is a major Náhuatl center and a mecca for New Agers who believe the area has a creative energy.

This *pueblo mágico* boasts an impressive pyramid, a great crafts market and a host of charming restaurants and hotels. It also retains indigenous traditions, with some elders still speaking Náhuatl and younger generations learning it in school, making it a rarity among the towns ringing the Mexican capital.

Everything in Tepoztlán is easily accessible on foot, except the cliff-top Pirámide de Tepozteco, a 2.5km strenuous hike away. Street names change in the center of town; eg Avenida 5 de Mayo becomes Avenida Tepozteco north of the *zócalo*.

◎ Sights

Pirámide de Tepozteco
PYRAMID

(M$47, Sun free; ⊙9am-5pm) The main sight in town is this 10m-high pyramid perched atop a sheer cliff at the end of a very steep paved path that begins at the end of Avenida Tepozteco. Built in honor of Tepoztécatl, the Aztec god of harvest, fertility and *pulque,* the pyramid is more impressive for its location than actual size. At the top, depending on haze levels, the serenity and the panorama of the valley make the hike worthwhile.

Spotting the plentiful coati (raccoon-like animal) there is also a bonus.

Tepotzteco is actually some 400m above the town. Be warned that the path is tough, so head off early to beat the heat and wear decent shoes. The 2.5km walk is not recommended to anyone not physically fit. A store at the peak sells refreshments, but you should bring water with you anyway. Video-camera use is M$47. The hike itself is free, but to get close to the pyramid (and the view) you must pay the admission fee.

Ex-Convento Domínico
de la Natividad
CHURCH

This monastery, situated east of the *zócalo,* and the attached church were built by Dominican priests between 1560 and 1588. The plateresque church facade has Dominican seals interspersed with indigenous symbols, floral designs and various figures, including the sun, moon and stars, animals, angels and the Virgin Mary. Upstairs, various cells house a bookstore, galleries and a regional history museum.

The monastery's arched entryway is adorned with an elaborate seed mural of pre-Hispanic history and symbolism. Every year during the first week of September, local artists sow a new mural from 60 varieties of seeds.

Museo de Arte Prehispánico
Carlos Pellicer
MUSEUM

(☑739-395-10-98; Pablo González 2; M$10; ⊙10am-6pm Tue-Sun) Behind the Dominican church, this archaeology museum has a small but interesting collection of pieces from around the country, donated by Tabascan poet Carlos Pellicer Cámara. The objects on display, a mix of human and animal figures, are lively and vibrant. The stone fragments depicting a pair of rabbits – the symbol for Ometochtli, the leader of the 400 rabbit gods of drunkenness – were discovered at the Tepozteco pyramid site.

AROUND MEXICO CITY TEPOZTLÁN

Tepoztlán

◎ Sights
1	Ex-Convento Domínico de la Natividad	B3
2	Museo de Arte Prehispánico Carlos Pellicer	B3

🛏 Sleeping
3	Hotel Posada Ali	B1
4	Posada del Tepozteco	A3
5	Posada Nican Mo Calli	B1

🍴 Eating
6	El Brujo	A2
7	El Ciruelo	B2
8	El Mango Biergarten-Restaurante	B3
9	El Tlecuil	A3
	La Sibarita	(see 4)
10	Los Buenos Tiempos	A3
11	Los Colorines	A2
12	Tepoznieves	A3

Courses

La Villa Bonita
COOKING COURSE

(📞777-233-58-05; www.lavillabonita.com; Aniceto Villamar 150, Colonia Tierra Blanca; weekend course incl 2 nights accommodations US$754-1102) On a hillside above town, this cooking school is the project of Ana García, one of Mexico's most celebrated chefs. García's course earns rave reviews from students. The six guest rooms have French doors opening onto a gorgeous patio overlooking the Tepoztlán valley, with a swimming pool carved out of volcanic rock. Check the website for longer packages.

✯ Festivals & Events

Tepoztlán is a hyper-festive place, with many Christian feasts superimposed on pagan celebrations. With eight *barrios* (neighborhoods) and an equal number of patron saints, there always seems to be some excuse for fireworks.

Carnaval
DANCE

During the five days preceding Ash Wednesday (46 days before Easter Sunday), Carnaval features the colorful dances of the Huehuenches and Chinelos with feather headdresses and beautifully embroidered costumes.

Fiesta del Templo
RELIGIOUS

(☺Sep) On September 7 an all-night celebration goes off on Tepozteco hill near the pyramid, with copious consumption of *pulque* in honor of Tepoztécatl. The following day is the Fiesta del Templo, a Catholic celebration featuring theater performances in Náhuatl.

The holiday was first intended to coincide with – and perhaps supplant – the pagan festival, but the *pulque* drinkers get a jump on it by starting the night before.

⌂ Sleeping

Tepoztlán has a range of good accommodations options, but as a small town with lots of visitors, it can sometimes be hard to find a room during festivals and on weekends. If you can't find a room, keep your eyes peeled for private homes offering weekend rooms, marked with *hospedaje económico* signs.

Posada Nican Mo Calli
HOTEL $$

(📞739-395-31-52; www.hotelnican.com; Netzahualcóyotl 4A; r M$1150, ste M$1250-2200; 🅿🛜🏊) With brightly painted public areas, a heated pool, stylish rooms (some with balconies and great mountain views) and plenty of animals hanging around, Nican Mo Calli is just right for a romantic weekend away and one of the best options in town. Rates discounted 20% Sunday to Thursday.

Hotel Posada Ali
GUESTHOUSE $$

(📞739-395-19-71; www.posadaali.com; Netzahualcóyotl 2C; d Sun-Thu M$500, Fri & Sat M$800; 🅿🛜🏊) Ali has a mix of 20 comfortable rooms, from the small, darker and more affordable rooms on the lower floors to the larger rooms upstairs. There's a *frontón* (jai alai) ball court and a small pool where you can have drinks served to you. The roof garden has lounge chairs for calming mountain views.

Light sleepers may not like the nearby church bells ringing throughout the night.

Posada del Valle
RESORT $$

(📞739-395-05-21; www.posadadelvalle.com.mx; Camino a Mextitla 5; r Sun-Thu M$950, Fri & Sat M$1450, spa package M$3240; 🅿🏊) Located east of town this hotel-spa has quiet, romantic rooms (no children under 16) and a good Argentine restaurant. Spa packages include two nights' accommodations, breakfast, massages and a visit to the temascal. It's 2km down Avenida Revolución 1910 – just follow the signs for the final 100m to the hotel.

★Posada del Tepozteco
LUXURY HOTEL $$$

(📞739-395-00-10; www.posadadeltepozteco.com; Paraíso 3; d/tw M$1650/1850, ste M$2100-2900; 🅿@🛜🏊) This refined hotel was built as a hillside mansion in the 1930s. The 20 rooms are airy and individually decorated, most boasting magnificent views over town, and share a wonderful garden and pool. The guest book contains famous names, including Angelina Jolie, who stayed in room 5 when she dropped by. Rates are discounted up to 30% during the week.

✗ Eating & Drinking

This small town is hopping on weekends, when cafes and bars fill up with enthusiastic visitors. Unfortunately for those visiting midweek, many of the best spots are only open Friday to Sunday.

El Tlecuil
VEGAN $

(Mercado Municpial de Tepoztlán s/n; snacks M$25; ☺9am-9pm) Only in Tepotzlán does the traditionally chaotic market hide a stall with vegan pre-Hispanic food. Mainly this means croquette taste bombs wrapped up as tacos. Flavor highlights include *siete semillas* (mixed sunflower, pepita and other seeds) and an inventive apple hash.

El Brujo BAKERY $

(Av 5 de Mayo; breakfasts M$65-95; ⊙9am-9pm; 🖉) This wonderful bakery-restaurant on the town's main drag is the best bet for a full breakfast, with excellent omelettes and Mexican standards such as *chilaquiles* – strips of fried corn tortillas, bathed in sauce. It also has great coffee and fantastic desserts. Just looking at the cake case is likely to start you salivating.

Los Buenos Tiempos BAKERY $

(🖉739-395-05-19; Av Revolución 1910 No 14B; pastries M$8-35) Head here for the best pastries around – the smell drifting over the *zócalo* alone will probably bring you on autopilot. There's also good coffee and a lively social scene, and it's a great place to buy a pastry breakfast to take up to the pyramid with you.

Tepoznieves ICE CREAM $

(Av Revolución 1910 s/n; scoops M$10-25) A homegrown ice-cream emporium, Tepoznieves serves some 100 heavenly flavors, including exotic scoops such as cactus and pineapple-chili. There are several branches across town.

Los Colorines MEXICAN $$

(🖉739-395-01-98; Av Tepozteco 13; mains M$52-126; ⊙9am-9pm; 🖉🖮) Inside the pink exterior of this buzzing restaurant, the hearty Mexican fare bubbles away in *cazuelas* (clay pots) and tastes fresh and traditional – try the regional *chiles rellenos* or *huauzontle* (broccoli-like flower buds). Eating here is a joy for the piñatas, spaciousness and the sense of being at a fiesta at grandma's colorful ranch. Cash only.

La Sombra del Sabino CAFE $$

(🖉739-395-03-69; www.lasombradelsabino.com. mx; Av Revolución 1910 No 45; mains M$135-160; ⊙10am-7pm Wed-Sun; 🖘) This 'literary cafe' and bookstore serves coffee, tea, wine or beer and simple fare – pastries, sandwiches and salads – in a contemplative garden setting. La Sombra del Sabino also hosts readings and events and sells a small selection of English-language books.

**El Mango
Biergarten-Restaurante** GERMAN $$

(🖉739-395-22-53; www.elmango.org; Campesinos 7; mains M$65-145; ⊙2-9pm Fri-Sun) Craving goulash, spaetzle, bratwurst and hearty, freshly baked bread? This German-run beer garden, just down the hill from the *zócalo*, serves genuine German food. To wash it down, Mango's beer list includes both imported European beers and domestic, artisanal *cerveza*. There's live jazz and blues on weekends. See the website for an event calendar.

Axitla MEXICAN $$

(🖉739-395-05-19; Av Tepozteco; breakfast M$50-110, mains M$80-165; ⊙10am-7pm Wed-Sun; 🖉) This Swiss Family Robinson–style sprawling treehouse, just off the pathway to the archaeological site, is set amid thick forest. There's a good selection of breakfasts available and a wide-ranging Mexican and international menu, including chicken breast stuffed with *huitlacoche* in chipotle sauce, sweet and sour ribs and quail.

★**La Sibarita** MEXICAN $$$

(🖉777-101-16-00; www.posadadeltepozteco.com. mx; Posada del Tepozteco, Paraíso 3; mains M$200-300; ⊙8:30am-10pm Sun-Thu, to 11pm Fri & Sat; 🖘) High on a hill above town, the restaurant at Posada del Tepozteco has gorgeous views of the valley below. With surreal cliffs and a pyramid overhead, the restaurant's setting is striking. The menu features dishes such as chicken breast stuffed with goat cheese, *róbalo* (snook) carpaccio in vinaigrette and rose-petal *nieve* (sorbet), all paired with imported wines.

El Ciruelo INTERNATIONAL $$$

(🖉777-219-37-20; www.elciruelo.com.mx; Zaragoza 17; mains M$120-230; ⊙1-6:30pm Sun-Thu, to 10:30pm Fri & Sat; 🖮) Set in a courtyard with views of the cliffs and pyramid, this long-standing favorite serves an impressive upscale menu of dishes from *camarones al curry* (curried shrimp) and *salmón chileno a la mantequilla* (Chilean salmon in butter sauce) to good pizzas, salads and international dishes, though prices seem a bit inflated. Saturdays and Sundays have special play areas for kids.

🛍 **Shopping**

Tepoz has a fantastic, atmospheric daily **market** that convenes on the *zócalo*. It's at its fullest on Wednesday and Sunday. As well as the daily fruit, vegetable, clothing and crafts on sale, on Saturday and Sunday stalls around the *zócalo* sell a wide selection of handicrafts.

ℹ Information

On the west side of the plaza, Bancomer and HSBC have ATMs. There are several internet cafes scattered around town.

ℹ Getting There & Around

Don't confuse Tepoztlán with Tepotzotlán to the north of Mexico City.

ADO/OCC (www.ado.com.mx; Av 5 de Mayo 35) runs 1st-class buses mainly to/from Mexico City's Terminal Sur (M$116, one hour, every 20 to 30 minutes 5am to 8pm), but also to Terminal Norte (M$120, 1¾ hours, two daily) and direct to/from Mexico City's airport ($171, 1½ hours, three daily).

Ometochtli direct buses run to Cuernavaca (M$22, 45 minutes) every 20 minutes 6am to 9pm. They leave from the Ometochtli station, on the hill leading out of town on the Cuernavaca–Tepoztlán road (at the west end of 5 de Mayo). Unfortunately, this route has become notorious lately for accidents and robberies on the bus, sometimes armed and violent. It is safer to take a secure taxi (M$100 to M$150) or go via Mexico City's Terminal Sur.

ADO/OCC buses to Cuautla (M$22, 45 minutes) depart frequently from the Hwy 115D tollbooth just outside town.

Cuautla

☑735 / POP 154,000 / ELEV 1300M

Cuautla (*kwout*-la) has none of Tepoztlán's scenic beauty, or the architectural merit of Cuernavaca, but it does have sulfur springs that have attracted people for centuries, as well as serious revolutionary credentials.

Cuautla was a base for one of Mexico's first leaders in the independence struggle, José María Morelos y Pavón, until he was forced to leave when the royalist army besieged the town in 1812. A century later it became a center of support for Emiliano Zapata's revolutionary army. However, if Mexican history and *balnearios* (bathing places) aren't your thing, there's not much for you here – modern Cuautla is a perfectly pleasant town, but there's little to see and do aside from the above.

The two main plazas are Plaza Fuerte de Galeana, better known as the Alameda (a favorite haunt of mariachis-for-hire at weekends), and the *zócalo*.

⊙ Sights

Ex-Convento de San Diego   HISTORIC BUILDING
(Batalla 19 de Febrero s/n) In 1911 presidential candidate Francisco Madero embraced Emiliano Zapata at Cuautla's old train station in the Ex-Convento de San Diego. Steam enthusiasts will want to come on Saturday, when Mexico's only steam-powered train fires up for short rides from 4pm to 9pm. The Ex-Convento is now home to Cuautla's **tourist office** (**☑**735-352-52-21; ⊙9am-8pm).

Museo Histórico del Oriente   MUSEUM
(**☑**735-352-83-31; Callejón del Castigo 3; M$39, Sun free; ⊙10am-5pm Tue-Sun) The former residence of José María Morelos houses the Museo Histórico del Oriente. Each room here covers a different historical period with displays of pre-Hispanic pottery, good maps and early photos of Cuautla and Zapata. The Mexican War of Independence rebel leader's remains lie beneath the imposing **Zapata monument** in the middle of Plazuela Revolución del Sur.

☆ Activities

Balnearios (Thermal Baths)

Cuautla's best-known *balneario* is the riverside **Agua Hedionda** (Stinky Water; **☑**735-352-00-44; www.aguahedionda.mx; end of Av Progreso; adult/child M$75/40; ⊙9am-5:30pm). Waterfalls replenish two lake-sized pools with sulfur-scented tepid water. Take an 'Agua Hedionda' bus (M$6) from Plazuela Revolución del Sur. There's a two-for-the-price-of-one deal on Thursdays.

Other *balnearios* worth visiting include **El Almeal** (http://balnearioelalmeal.com.mx; Hernández; adult/child M$50/30, campsites per person M$60; ⊙9am-6pm) and the nicer **Los Limones** (Gabriel Teppa 14; adult/child M$65/45; ⊙8:30am-6pm). Both places are served by the same spring (no sulfur) and have extensive shaded picnic grounds. Prices are reduced by M$10 Monday to Friday. Children under 3 free.

🛌 Sleeping & Eating

Hotel Defensa del Agua   HOTEL **$**
(**☑**735-352-16-79; Defensa del Agua 34; d/tr/q Sun-Thu M$200/300/480, Fri & Sat M$300/480/560; **P🛱📶❄**) This modern, clean hotel is set out in a motel style with a small pool and spacious rooms with TV, phone and fan. There's a very handy Italian Coffee Company branch in the building for breakfast. Avoid rooms with windows facing the noisy street.

Hotel & Spa Villasor   RESORT **$$**
(**☑**735-303-55-03; Av Progreso; s/d/ste M$490/630/1050; **P❄📶❄**) Out of town and

¡QUE VIVA ZAPATA!

A peasant leader from Morelos state, Emiliano Zapata (1879–1919) was among the most radical of Mexico's revolutionaries, fighting for the return of hacienda land to the peasants with the cry '*¡Tierra y libertad!*' (Land and freedom!). The Zapatista movement was at odds with both the conservative supporters of the old regime and their liberal opponents. In November 1911 Zapata disseminated his *Plan de Ayala*, calling for restoration of all land to the peasants. After winning numerous battles against government troops in central Mexico (some in association with Pancho Villa), he was ambushed and killed in 1919.

Ruta de Zapata

In Anenecuilco, 6km south of Cuautla, what's left of the adobe cottage where Zapata was born (on August 8, 1879) is now the **Museo de la Lucha para la Tierra** (Museo y Casa de Emiliano Zapata; cnr Av Zapata & Ayuntamiento; admission M$35; ⊘10am-5pm), with a rousing mural of Zapata's life story.

About 20km south is the **Ex-Hacienda de San Juan Chinameca** (Cárdenas s/n; ⊘9:30am-5pm) FREE (in the town of the same name), where in 1919 Zapata was lured into a fatal trap by Colonel Jesús Guajardo, following the orders of President Venustiano Carranza, who was eager to dispose of the rebel leader and consolidate the post-revolutionary government. Pretending to defect to the revolutionary forces, Guajardo set up a meeting with Zapata, who arrived at Chinameca accompanied by a guerrilla escort. Guajardo's men gunned down the general before he crossed the abandoned hacienda's threshold.

The hacienda has a small and, unfortunately, horribly maintained museum with a meager collection of photos and newspaper reproductions. But there's a statue of Zapata astride a rearing horse at the entrance, where you can still see the bullet holes where the revolutionary died and where old men gather to celebrate their fallen hero.

From Chinameca head 20km northwest to Tlaltizapán, the site of the excellent **Cuartel General de Zapata** (Guerrero 2; ⊘10am-6pm Tue-Sun) FREE, the main barracks of the revolutionary forces. Here you can see Zapata's rifle (the trigger retains his fingerprints), the bed where he slept and the outfit he was wearing at the time of his death (riddled with bullet holes and stained with blood).

Though it's possible to do this route via *colectivo* (yellow 'Chinameca' combis traveling to Anenecuilco and Chinameca leave from the corner of Garduño and Matamoros in Cuautla every 10 minutes), it can be an all-day ordeal. The Morelos state tourism office in Cuernavaca arranges tours of the route.

---

located opposite the Agua Hedionda baths, this modern place has a large pool and comfortable rooms equipped with phone, fan and cable TV. With its own spa treatments, Villasor is the best option for relaxation, but it's not convenient for those without transportation.

Alameda   DINER $
(cnr Los Bravos & Ferrara; breakfasts M$50-90; ⊘7:30am-7:30pm; 🅿) Situated between the *zócalo* and Plaza Alameda, this bright, tropical-hued fast-food diner serves excellent breakfasts, including large, tasty omelettes and a dazzling array of freshly squeezed fruit juices. For lunch, it has a full range of hamburgers, *tortas* and sandwiches, including many vegetarian options.

Las Golondrinas   MEXICAN $$
(☎735-354-13-50; www.restaurantelasgolondrinas.com; Catalán 19A; mains M$85-135; ⊘8am-10pm) Set in a 17th-century building filled with plants and koi ponds, Golondrinas offers an attractive atmosphere and excellent service. House specialties include a range of *molcajetes* (spicy stews cooked in a large stone mortar). Light breakfasts include egg-white omelettes.

🛈 Getting There & Away

OCC (☎800-702-80-00; www.ado.com.mx) has 1st-class buses to Mexico City's Terminal Sur (M$116, two hours, every 15 minutes). Across the street, **Pullman de Morelos** (☎735-352-73-71; www.pullman.com.mx) travels to Tepoztlán (M$20, 45 minutes, every 20 minutes).

Cuernavaca

📍 777 / POP 339,000 / ELEV 1480M

There's always been a formidable glamour surrounding Cuernavaca (kwehr-nah-*vah*-kah), the capital of Morelos state. With its vast, gated haciendas and sprawling estates, it has traditionally attracted high-society visitors year-round for its warmth, clean air and attractive architecture.

Today this tradition continues, even though urban sprawl has put a decisive end to the clean air and you're more likely to see vacationing North Americans and college students studying Spanish on month-long courses than meet international royalty or great artists in the street.

History

The first settlers to the valleys of modern Morelos are believed to have arrived in 1500 BC. In the centuries between AD 200 and 900 they organized a highly productive agricultural society and developed Xochicalco and other large constructions throughout the region. Later, the dominant Mexica (Aztecs) called them Tlahuica, which means 'people who work the land.' In 1379 a Mexica warlord conquered Cuauhnáhuac, subdued the Tlahuica and exacted an annual tribute that included 16,000 pieces of *amate* (bark paper) and 20,000 bushels of corn. The tributes payable by the subject states were set out in a register the Spanish later called the Códice Mendocino, in which Cuauhnáhuac was represented by a three-branch tree. This symbol now graces Cuernavaca's coat of arms.

The Mexica lord's successor married the daughter of the Cuauhnáhuac leader, and from this marriage was born Moctezuma I Ilhuicamina, the 15th-century Aztec king, who was a predecessor to Moctezuma II Xocoyotzin, encountered by Cortés. Under the Aztecs, the Tlahuica traded extensively and prospered. Their city was a learning and religious center, and archaeological remains suggest they had a considerable knowledge of astronomy.

When the Spanish arrived the Tlahuica were fiercely loyal to the Aztecs. In April 1521 they were finally overcome and Cortés torched the city. Soon the city became known as Cuernavaca, a more Spanish-friendly version of its original appellation.

In 1529 Cortés received his belated reward from the Spanish crown when he was named Marqués del Valle de Oaxaca, with an estate that covered 22 towns, including Cuernavaca, and 23,000 indigenous Mexicans. After he introduced sugar cane and new farming methods, Cuernavaca became a Spanish agricultural center, as it had been for the Aztecs. Cortés' descendants dominated the area for nearly 300 years.

With its salubrious climate, rural surroundings and colonial elite, Cuernavaca became a refuge for the rich and powerful in the 1700s and 1800s, including José de la Borda, the 18th-century Taxco silver magnate. Borda's lavish home was later a retreat for Emperor Maximilian and Empress Carlota. Cuernavaca has also attracted many artists and achieved literary fame as the setting for Malcolm Lowry's 1947 novel *Under the Volcano*.

⊙ Sights & Activities

Plaza de Armas PLAZA
(Zócalo; Gutenberg) Cuernavaca's *zócalo*, Plaza de Armas, is flanked on the east by the Palacio de Cortés, on the west by the **Palacio de Gobierno** and on the northeast and south by restaurants and roving bands of mariachis. It's the only main plaza in Mexico without a church, chapel, convent or cathedral overlooking it.

Although you can't enter the Palacio de Gobierno, it is a nice spot to contemplate some attractive architecture and enjoy the music.

Jardín Juárez GARDENS
(Guerrero) Adjoining the northwest corner of the Plaza de Armas is the Jardín Juárez, where the central gazebo (designed by tower specialist Gustave Eiffel) houses juice and sandwich stands. Live-band concerts on Thursday and Sunday evenings start at 6pm. Roving vendors sell balloons, ice cream and corn on the cob under the trees, which fill up with legions of cacophonous grackles at dusk.

Even more entertaining are the guitar trios who warm up their voices and instruments before heading to the cafes across the street to serenade willing patrons. You can request a ballad or two for around M$75.

Palacio de Cortés HISTORIC BUILDING
Cortés' imposing medieval-style fortress stands opposite the southeast end of the Plaza de Armas. This two-story stone palace was built on the base of the city pyramid that Cortés destroyed after taking Cuauhnáhuac. The base is still visible from various points

on the ground floor. The palace houses the excellent **Museo Regional Cuauhnáhuac** (M$46, Sun free; ⊙9am-6pm Tue-Sun, last ticket 5:30pm), which has two floors of exhibits highlighting Mexican cultures and history. On the upstairs balcony is a fascinating mural by Diego Rivera.

The mural was commissioned in the mid-1920s by Dwight Morrow, the US ambassador to Mexico. Flowing from right to left, scenes from the conquest through to the 1910 Revolution emphasize the cruelty, oppression and violence that have characterized Mexican history.

While upstairs covers events from the Spanish conquest to the present, the ground floor exhibits focus on pre-Hispanic cultures, including the local Tlahuica and their relationship with the Aztec empire. Most labeling is in Spanish only, with a few well-translated exceptions.

Cortés resided here until he turned tail for Spain in 1541. The palace remained with Cortés' family for most of the next century, but by the 18th century it was being used as a prison. During the Porfirio Díaz era it became government offices.

Recinto de la Catedral
CHURCH

(www.catedraldecuernavaca.org; Hidalgo 17; ⊙7:30am-8pm) Cuernavaca's cathedral stands in a large high-walled *recinto* (compound); the entrance gate is on Hidalgo. The cathedral was built in a grand, fortress-like style in an effort to impress, intimidate and defend against the natives. Franciscans started work on what was one of Mexico's earliest Christian missions in 1526, using indigenous labor and stones from the rubble of Cuauhnáhuac. The first structure was the **Capilla Abierta de San José**, an open chapel on the cathedral's west side.

The cathedral itself, the **Templo de la Asunción de María**, is plain and solid, with an unembellished facade. The side door, which faces north to the compound's entrance, shows a mixture of indigenous and European features – the skull and crossbones above it is a symbol of the Franciscan order. Inside are frescoes rediscovered early in the 20th century. Cuernavaca was a center for Franciscan missionary activities in Asia and the frescoes – said to show the persecution of Christian missionaries in Japan – were supposedly painted in the 17th century by a Japanese convert to Christianity.

The cathedral compound also holds two smaller churches. On the right as you enter is the **Templo de la Tercera Orden de San Francisco**. Its exterior was carved in 18th-century baroque style by indigenous artisans and its interior has ornate, gilded decorations. On the left as you enter is the 19th-century **Capilla del Carmen**, where believers seek cures for illness.

Museo Robert Brady
MUSEUM

(☑777-316-85-54; www.bradymuseum.org; Netzahualcóyotl 4; M$40; ⊙10am-6pm Tue-Sun) Let's face it, who wouldn't want to be independently wealthy and spend their life traveling around the world collecting art for their lavish Mexican mansion? If that option isn't open to you, visit this museum – easily Cuernavaca's best – and live vicariously. The one-time home of American artist and collector Robert Brady (1928–86), the museum, which is housed in the Casa de la Torre, is a wonderful place to spend time appreciating the exquisite taste of one man.

Originally part of the monastery within the Recinto de la Catedral, the house is a stunning testament to a man who knew what he liked. Brady lived in Cuernavaca for 24 years after a spell in Venice, but his collections range from Papua New Guinea and India to Haiti and South America. Every room, including the two gorgeous bathrooms and kitchen, is bedecked in paintings, carvings, textiles, antiques and folk arts from all corners of the Earth. Among the treasures are works by well-known Mexican artists, including Rivera, Tamayo, Kahlo and Covarrubias, as well as Brady's own paintings (check out his spot-on portrait of his friend Peggy Guggenheim). The gardens are lovely too, with a very tempting (but off-limits) swimming pool in one of them and a little cafe in the other.

Classic and contemporary films are shown in the museum's courtyard every Wednesday at 6pm for a M$25 donation. Movies are in their original language with Spanish subtitles.

MMAPO
MUSEUM

(Museo Morelense de Arte Popular; ☑777-318-62-00; Hidalgo 239; ⊙10am-5pm Tue-Sun) FREE An excellent addition to Cuernavaca, this bright and inviting museum showcases handicrafts from Morelos, including lifesize *chinelos* (costumed dancers with upturned chins from Morelos). Most of the

AROUND MEXICO CITY CUERNAVACA

Cuernavaca

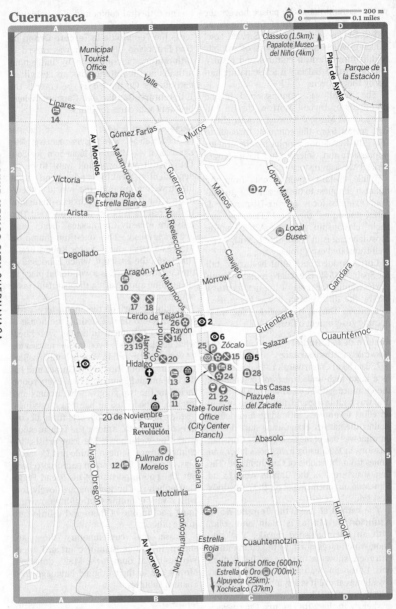

pieces are displayed out in the open, not behind glass, so you can get close and admire the handiwork. The attached store sells quality pieces that you won't see in your average craft market.

Jardín Borda
GARDENS

(☎777-318-82-50; Av Morelos 271; adult/child M$30/15, Sun free; ☺10am-5:30pm Tue-Sun) Beside the 1784 **Parroquia de Guadalupe**, this extravagant property, inspired by Versailles, features gardens formally laid out in a series

Cuernavaca

⊙ Sights
1 Jardín Borda A4
2 Jardín Juárez C4
3 MMAPO B4
  Museo Regional
    Cuauhnáhuac ....(see 5)
4 Museo Robert Brady B4
5 Palacio de Cortés................................. C4
6 Plaza de Armas C4
7 Recinto de la Catedral........................ B4

⊜ Sleeping
8 Hostería del Sol.................................... C4
9 Hotel Antigua Posada.......................... C6
10 Hotel Colonial B3
11 Hotel Juárez B4
12 Hotel Laam B5
13 Hotel Las Hortensias........................... B4
14 Las Mañanitas A1

⊗ Eating
15 Casa Hidalgo C4

16 Emiliano's B4
17 La India Bonita...................................... B3
18 La Maga Café B3
19 L'arrosoir d'Arthur................................ B4
   Restaurant Las Mañanitas............(see 14)
20 Trattoria Marco Polo............................ B4

⊝ Drinking & Nightlife
21 El Romántico C4
22 La Plazuela C4

⊕ Entertainment
23 Cine Teatro Morelos B4
24 Face to Face.. C4
25 Los Arcos.. C4
26 Teatro Ocampo..................................... B4

⊚ Shopping
27 Mercado Adolfo López Mateos C2
28 Mercado de Artesanías y Plata.............C4

of terraces with paths, steps and fountains. Duck into the house to get an idea of how Mexico's 19th-century aristocracy lived. In typical colonial style, the buildings are arranged around courtyards. In one wing, the **Museo de Sitio** has exhibits on daily life during the empire period and original documents with the signatures of Morelos, Juárez and Maximilian.

The property was designed in 1783 for Manuel de la Borda as an addition to the stately residence built by his father, José de la Borda. From 1866, Emperor Maximilian and Empress Carlota entertained their courtiers here and used the house as a summer residence.

Several romantic paintings in the Sala Manuel M Ponce, a recital hall near the entrance of the house, show scenes of the garden in Maximilian's time. One of the most famous paintings depicts Maximilian in the garden with La India Bonita, the 'pretty Indian' who later became his lover. Originally there was a botanical collection to show off, with hundreds of varieties of ornamental plants and fruit trees. Because of a water shortage, the baroque-style fountains now operate only on weekends.

Papalote Museo del Niño MUSEUM
(Av Vicente Guerrero 205; M$50, group of 4 M$165; ☺10am-5pm Tue-Sun; ⊞) Built as part of a land deal with the city, this excellent children's museum has an odd location in a

shopping center beside a Costco, about 4km north of downtown, but for travelers with children it's well worth seeking out. Geared toward education, technology and play, the museum includes a large Lego exhibit, musical elements and lots of bright colors. There's an IMAX in the same complex and discounts for families and groups.

🎓 Courses

Cuernavaca is a well-established center for studying Spanish at all levels and has dozens of language schools. As such, standards are high, teaching is usually very thorough and prices competitive (generally M$2500 to M$5000 per week, plus fees and housing). The best schools offer small-group or individual instruction at all levels with four to five hours per day of intensive instruction, plus a couple of hours' conversation practice. Classes begin each Monday and most schools recommend a minimum enrollment of four weeks.

With so many teaching styles and options, prospective students should research the choices carefully. Contact the tourist office for an extensive list of schools.

🎉 Festivals & Events

Carnaval CARNIVAL
(☺Feb/Mar) Over the five days leading up to Ash Wednesday, Cuernavaca's colorful Carnaval celebrations feature parades and art

WORTH A TRIP

XOCHICALCO

Atop a desolate plateau with views for kilometers around, **Xochicalco** (☎777-379-74-16; admission M$59; ⏱9am-6pm, last ticket 5pm) is a relatively easy day trip from Cuernavaca that shouldn't be missed. Large enough to make the journey worthwhile, but not so well known as to be overrun with tourists, this exceptional site is one of the most impressive in the region.

A Unesco World Heritage site and one of central Mexico's most important archaeological sites, Xochicalco (so-chee-*cal*-co) is Náhuatl for 'place of the house of flowers.' The collection of white stone ruins, many still to be excavated, covers approximately 10 sq km. They represent the various cultures – Tlahuica, Toltec, Olmec, Zapotec, Mixtec and Aztec – for which Xochicalco was a commercial, cultural and religious center. When Teotihuacán began to weaken around AD 650 to 700, Xochicalco began to rise in importance, achieving its peak between AD 650 and 900, with far-reaching cultural and commercial relations. Around AD 650 Zapotec, Maya and Gulf coast spiritual leaders convened here to correlate their respective calendars. Xochicalco remained an important center until around 1200, when its excessive growth precipitated a demise similar to that of Teotihuacán.

The site's most famous monument is the **Pirámide de Quetzalcóatl**. Archaeologists have surmised from its well-preserved bas-reliefs that astronomer-priests met here at the beginning and end of each 52-year cycle of the pre-Hispanic calendar. Site signs are in English and Spanish, but information at the excellent, ecologically sensitive **museum**, situated 200m from the ruins, is in Spanish only.

From October through May, the site sometimes offers a nighttime **light show** (☎for reservations 737-374-30-90; xochicalco.mor@inah.gob.mx; M$7) on Friday and Saturday nights. It's quite a spectacle, but call ahead because the shows are not regular.

From Cuernavaca's market, *colectivos* with 'Xochi' on their windshield (M$14) depart every 30 minutes for the site entrance. Larger buses from the Pullman de Morelos terminal make the same trip, directly, but only on Saturday and Sunday. On arrival you'll need to walk to the museum to buy tickets. The last return *colectivo* leaves around 6pm. Alternatively, take a taxi (M$30) from the site to the nearby town of Alpuyeca, where there are frequent *colectivos* back to Cuernavaca.

exhibits, plus street performances by Tepoztlán's Chinelo dancers.

Feria de la Primavera   CULTURAL
(⏱Mar-Apr) From late March to early April, the city's Spring Fair includes cultural and artistic events, plus concerts and a beautiful exhibit of the city's spring flowers.

🛏 Sleeping

Some of the best boutique hotels in the country are here, aimed squarely at weekend refugees from the capital. Budget hotels tend to be simple and spare, while midrange hotels are few and far between. The town fills up with visitors from Mexico City at weekends and holidays, when prices rise significantly at many hotels.

Hotel Las Hortensias   HOTEL $
(☎777-318-52-65; www.hotelhortensias.com; Hidalgo 13; s/d/tw M$300/390/440; ☜) Cheap and central, Las Hortensias has small,

sparse rooms, a lush garden and staff who seem to constantly be cleaning. Street-side rooms are noisy, so bring earplugs, or ask for one of the darker interior rooms.

Hotel Colonial   HOTEL $
(☎777-318-64-14; Aragón y León 19; s/d/tw/tr M$280/380/420/560; ☜) While basic, this relaxed budget hotel is excellent value. There's a garden at its center, cable TV, a free water cooler and decorative floors. The upstairs rooms with balconies and tall ceilings are best.

Hotel Juárez   HOTEL $
(☎777-314-02-19; Netzahualcóyotl 19; r M$350; Ⓟ☜☒) The rooms at this well-located hotel are large and airy but have tired beds. To compensate, a breezy terrace overlooks a large grassy backyard, an attractive swimming pool and Cuernavaca's clay-tiled rooftops. It's nothing fancy, but it's a good budget option, especially for a dip in the water.

Hostería del Sol   GUESTHOUSE **$$**
(☑ 777-318-32-41; Callejón de la Bolsa del Diablo; d/ste M$650/850, d/tr without bathroom M$450/550; ☀) This well-located charmer is spotlessly clean, including the spacious bathrooms shared by half of the six rooms. All rooms are beautifully decorated in traditional blue-and-yellow tones. The biggest negatives – no wi-fi and all windows face the distant bars of Plazuela del Zacate, which can get rowdy on weekends. It's best to ring ahead, although staff don't speak English.

Hotel Antigua Posada   HOTEL **$$**
(☑ 777-310-21-79; www.hotelantiguaposada.com.mx; Galeana 69; r incl breakfast M$850-1000, ste incl breakfast M$1150-1300; P ☎ ☀) This exclusive little hideaway is a short walk from the center of town and boasts just 11 rooms behind its unpromising exterior. But once inside there's a lovely courtyard and great service. The rooms are gorgeous, complete with wooden beams and rustic touches.

Hotel Laam   BUSINESS HOTEL **$$**
(☑ 777-314-44-11; www.laamhotel.com.mx; Av Morelos 239; r M$960-1520; P ☎ ☀) With a motel feel and comfortable, if sterile, rooms (some with huge terraces), this slick hotel is good value. Set back from the road, giving it distance from street noise, Hotel Laam comes with a tiled swimming pool and well-tended grounds.

★**Hotel Hacienda de Cortés**   HISTORIC HOTEL **$$$**
(☑ 777-315-88-44, 800-220-76-97; www.hotelhaciendadecortes.com.mx; Plaza Kennedy 90; d M$2375, ste M$2968-6060; P ☎ ☀) Built in the 16th century by Martín Cortés (successor to Hernán Cortés as Marqués del Valle de Oaxaca), this former sugar mill was renovated in 1980 and boasts 23 rooms of various levels of luxury, each with its own private garden and terrace. There's also a swimming pool built around old stone columns, a gym and an excellent restaurant.

It's approximately 4km southeast of the center of town.

Las Mañanitas   LUXURY HOTEL **$$$**
(☑ 777-362-00-00; www.lasmananitas.com.mx; Linares 107; ste incl breakfast Sun-Thu from M$4069, Fri & Sat from M$5135; P ❄ ☎ ☀) If you're really out to impress someone, book a room at this stunning place. It's a destination hotel – you may not want to leave the whole weekend – so the fact that it's not in the center of town isn't too important. The large rooms are beautifully understated, many with terraces overlooking the gardens, full of peacocks and a heated pool.

✕ Eating

Cuernavaca is a great food town with a few excellent high-end restaurants and plenty of good cafes. There are, however, surprisingly few enticing midrange options.

Emiliano's   MEXICAN **$**
(Rayon 5; mains M$28-80, menú del día M$40-60) Quiz any local on their favorite place to eat and you'll be directed to the thatched roof of Emiliano's. Complex *mole* and other Mexican sure things, such as stuffed chilies, are only enhanced with tortillas you can watch being handmade. Add breakfast and you'll be here all day.

La India Bonita   MEXICAN **$$**
(☑ 777-318-69-67; www.laindiabonita.com; Morrow 115; mains M$99-209; ⊙ 8am-9:30pm) Set in a lush courtyard, Cuernavaca's oldest restaurant also has some of its best traditional Mexican food – from *brocheta al mezcal* (skewered meats marinated in mezcal) to *chile en nogada* (*poblano* pepper in walnut sauce) – with the occasional enticing twist. India Bonita operates a tasty bakery-cafe next door.

L'arrosoir d'Arthur   FRENCH **$$**
(Calle Juan Ruiz de Alarcón 13; mains M$140-180, menú del día M$110; ⊙ 9am-midnight Thu-Tue, from 1pm Wed; ☎) As much a hangout and nightspot as a restaurant, this French-owned place in a loft space downtown has excellent, affordable French dishes (crepes, cassolette, chicken in mustard sauce), good cocktails and wines. On weekends, the chilled, European vibe gets more energetic with live music, theater, dance and poetry events.

La Maga Café   MEXICAN **$$**
(Morrow 9; buffet M$99; ⊙ 1-5pm Mon-Sat; ☎ ✐) The colorful buffet at La Maga features multitudes of glazed pots filled with salads, pastas, fruit, vegetables, and daily specials such as glistening *pollo en adobo* (chicken marinated in chili and herbs) and *tortas de elote* (cheesy corn croquettes). There are great vegetarian options and a community vibe, sometimes with live music. Arrive early to nab a window seat.

Trattoria Marco Polo   PIZZA **$$**
(☑ 777-318-40-32; Hidalgo 30; pizzas M$73-183; ⊙ 1-10:30pm Sun-Thu, to midnight Fri & Sat; ✐)

Italian dishes, including a broad range of excellent, thin-crust pizzas, and an attractive setting just across from the cathedral make this a decent option for reasonably priced international fare.

★ **Restaurante**
Hacienda de Cortés　　　INTERNATIONAL **$$$**
(☑ 800-220-76-97, 777-315-88-44; www.hotelhacien dadecortes.com.mx; Plaza Kennedy 90; mains M$105-320; ☺ 7am-11pm; ☻ 🗑 🏊) Situated within Hotel Hacienda de Cortés, this elegant but unpretentious hotel restaurant serves an excellent selection of salads and delicious international dishes, including a fantastic vegetarian lasagna, tuna in almond sauce with risotto, and well-prepared Angus steaks. The dining room is spectacular, with massive vines climbing the walls and wrought-iron chandeliers overhead.

Restaurant Las Mañanitas　　　FRENCH **$$$**
(www.lasmananitas.com.mx; Linares 107; breakfasts M$105-285, mains M$265-500; ☺ 8am-11pm) The restaurant and bar of Cuernavaca's most famous hotel, Las Mañanitas, is a luxurious splurge, open to all. The expansive menu has a heavy French accent, with dishes such as entrecôte Bourguignon and sumptuous desserts. Reserve a table inside the mansion or on the terrace, where you can watch wildlife wander among modern garden sculptures.

Casa Hidalgo　　　MEXICAN **$$$**
(☑ 777-312-27-49; www.casahidalgo.com; Jardín de los Héroes 6; mains M$135-215, menú del día M$215; ☺ 8am-11pm Sun-Thu, to midnight Fri & Sat) Directly opposite the Palacio de Cortés, with a great terrace and upstairs balcony, this popular restaurant attracts a well-heeled crowd of local socialites and wealthy visitors. The menu is eclectic – try cold mango-agave soup with jicama, or *tlaxcalteca* chicken breast stuffed with cheese and roasted *poblano* pepper with three salsas: squash blossom, spinach and chipotle.

🍷 **Drinking & Nightlife**

There's a buzzing nightlife in Cuernavaca, supported by a year-round student population that keeps nightspots busy every night of the week. Plazuela del Zacate and the adjacent alley Las Casas have a good mix of rowdy and laid-back bars – all open around sunset and staying open until the last patron leaves. There are no cover charges and almost every downtown bar offers two-for-one drink specials most nights of the week.

The more upmarket clubs impose a modest cover charge, but women are usually let in for free. Some clubs enforce dress codes and trendier places post style police at the door. Things really get going after 11pm.

El Romántico　　　BAR
(Plazuela del Zacate; ☺ 11am-midnight) This small bar has very functional leatherette tables and isn't especially romantic. The real attraction is very cheap beer and cocktails and a jubilant crowd.

Classico　　　CLUB
(☑ 777-316-49-02; Av Teopanzolco 503; ☺ 11pm-late Fri & Sat) Classico is an upscale, indoor-outdoor club for Cuerna's hipster elite. Dress to impress.

La Plazuela　　　DJ
(Las Casas) This is the home of pumping house and techno clubs with that tell-tale accordion of Mexican *norteño* thrown into the mix.

☆ **Entertainment**

Hanging around the central plazas is a popular activity, especially on Sunday evenings, when open-air concerts are often staged. There are often recitals at Jardín Borda (p184) on Thursday nights, too.

If your *español* is up to it, sample Cuernavaca's theater scene.

Cine Teatro Morelos　　　CINEMA
(☑ 777-318-10-50; Av Morelos 188; tickets from M$25; 🎬) Morelos' state theater hosts quality film series, plays and dance performances. There's a full schedule posted out front and a bookstore and cafe inside.

Teatro Ocampo　　　THEATER
(☑ 777-318-63-85; Jardín Juárez 2) Near Jardín Juárez, this theater stages contemporary plays. A calendar of cultural events is posted at its entrance.

Los Arcos　　　DANCE
(Jardín de los Héroes 4; minimum consumption M$60; ☺ salsa 9:30-11:30pm Thu, Fri & Sun) Come here to dance salsa, not on a stage but around the tables of families having dinner on the terrace, with crowds of appreciative onlookers. The live band's carnival beats can be heard from the other side of the plaza and have a magnetic effect on your swiveling hips.

Face to Face　　　GAY
(Plazuela del Zacate) The crowd at this gay club is a mix of students and older locals.

It's quiet during the week, but picks up pace from Thursday through the weekend when drag acts such as Frida Ciccone perform and the venue is showered in frenetic laser lights.

The entrance, opposite neighboring bar El Romántico, is nondescript and easy to miss – look for the doorperson on a stool.

Shopping

There are some good quality *guayaberas* (men's appliqued shirts), *huipiles* (long, sleeveless tunics) and upmarket souvenirs in the plaza opposite the cathedral and along the same street.

Mercado de Artesanías y Plata HANDICRAFTS
(Handicrafts & Silver Market; ⊙10am-8pm daily) This relaxed market has handicrafts such as coconut lamps and hand-painted ceramics, found all over Mexico, as well as a plethora of handmade *chinelo* dolls with upturned beards, a specialty of Morelos. It's a shady place to browse and prices are reasonable. To find the market, look for the huge statue of Morelos, the man himself, at the entrance.

Mercado Adolfo López Mateos MARKET
(Adolfo López Mateos; ⊙8am-6pm daily) A sprawling, semi-covered market selling fresh produce and other wares, Mercado Adolfo López Mateos bursts with the smells of fruit, meat, flowers and smoked chilies.

ℹ Information

EMERGENCY
Ambulance (☑777-311-85-02)
Tourist Police (☑800-903-92-00)

INTERNET ACCESS
There's internet access at the Futura and Estrella Blanca bus station and internet cafes all over town.

MEDICAL SERVICES
Cruz Roja (Red Cross; ☑777-315-35-05)

Hospital Inovamed (☑777-311-24-82; Cuauhtémoc 305) A private hospital in Colonia Lomas de la Selva, 1km north of town.

POST
Main Post Office (Plaza de Armas; ⊙8am-7pm Mon-Fri, 9am-3pm Sat)

TOURIST INFORMATION
There's an information booth in the cathedral, at the north end of the *zócalo* (9am to 6pm daily) and other kiosks around town, including at most bus stations. Ask for maps.
Municipal Tourist Office (☑777-329-44-04; www.cuernavaca.gob.mx/turismo; Av Morelos 278; ⊙9am-6pm) Also has a tourist police office.
State Tourist Office (☑777-314-38-81, 777-314-38-72, 800-987-82-24; www.morelos turistico.com; Av Morelos Sur 187; ⊙9am-6pm) This excellent tourist office has a wealth of brochures, maps and information. Also has a city center (☑777-314-39-20; www.morelos turistico.com; Hidalgo 5; ⊙9am-6pm) branch.

ℹ Getting There & Away

Hwy 95D (the Mexico City–Acapulco toll road) skirts the city's east side. If you're driving from the north, take the Cuernavaca exit and cross to Hwy 95 (where you'll see a statue of Zapata on horseback). Hwy 95 becomes Blvd Zapata then Avenida Morelos as you descend south into town. From Avenida Matamoros (still traveling south) the Avenida Morelos is one way, northbound only. To reach the center, veer left down Matamoros.

BUS
Cuernavaca's main-line bus companies operate separate long-distance terminals.

The Estella Roja depot has departures to Toluca (M$200, three hours), at 6:45pm, and Cuautla. The Pullman de Morelos depot is the most conveniently located station and has buses to Mexico City Airport and the Mexico City southern terminal. The Flecha Roja terminal has buses to Puebla (M$260, three hours, three to four daily), Taxco, Tepoztlán, Tepotzotlán and Puebla.

BUSES FROM CUERNAVACA

DESTINATION	FARE (M$)	DURATION (HR)	FREQUENCY (DAILY)
Cuautla	62	1½	28
Mexico City	94-135	1½	40
Mexico City airport	150	2	24
Taxco	90	1¾	13
Tepoztlán	21	½	28

Estrella de Oro (EDO; ☑777-312-30-55; www.estrelladeoro.com.mx; Av Morelos Sur 812)

Estrella Roja (ER; ☑777-318-59-34; www.estrellaroja.com.mx; cnr Galeana & Cuauhtemotzin)

Flecha Roja & Estrella Blanca (FR & EB; ☑777-312-26-26; www.estrellablanca.com.mx; Av Morelos 503, btwn Arista & Victoria) Futura, Costa Line and executive ETN services leave from here as well.

Pullman de Morelos (PDM; ☑777-318-09-07; www.pullman.com.mx; cnr Calles Abasolo & Netzahualcóyotl)

CAR & MOTORCYCLE

Cuernavaca is 89km south of Mexico City, a 1½-hour drive on Hwy 95 or a one-hour trip on Hwy 95D. Both roads continue south to Acapulco – Hwy 95 detours through Taxco; Hwy 95D is more direct and much faster.

ⓘ Getting Around

You can walk to most places of interest in central Cuernavaca. Local buses (M$6.50) advertise their destinations on their windshields. Many local buses, and those to nearby towns, leave from the southern corner of the city's labyrinthine market, Mercado Adolfo López Mateos. Taxis to most places in town cost the base fare of M$35. There have been reports of robberies on local buses in Cuernavaca, so exercise caution if you must use them.

The bus depots are in walking distance of the zócalo, except the Estrella de Oro bus terminal, 1km south (downhill) of the center, which is reachable on Ruta 17 or 20 down Galeana. In the other direction, catch any bus heading up Avenida Morelos. Ruta 17 and 20 buses head up Avenida Morelos and stop within one block of the Pullman de Morelos terminal at Casino de la Selva.

Taxco

☑762 / POP 53,000 / ELEV 1800M

The first sight of Taxco (tahss-ko) across the steep valley as you approach it from the north is enough to take your breath away. Scattered down a precipitous hillside surrounded by dramatic mountains and cliffs, its perfectly preserved colonial architecture and the twin belfries of its baroque masterpiece, Templo de Santa Prisca, make for one of the most beguiling views anywhere in the central highlands.

Taxco, 160km southwest of Mexico City, has ridden waves of boom and bust associated with the fantastically wealthy silver deposits discovered here in the 16th century and then repeatedly until the early 20th century. With its silver now almost depleted, the town has fallen back on tourism to sustain it. As such, it's a rare example of preservation-centric development in Mexico. Unlike many colonial-era towns, Taxco has not been engulfed by industrial suburbs, and its status as a national historical monument means that even new buildings must conform to the old in scale, style and materials.

The downside of this embrace of the past is that the town sometimes feels like a museum piece that's given itself over to visitors, who flood Taxco at weekends and during festivals. Despite this, Taxco is a striking small city and one of the best weekend trips from the capital.

While one of the joys of Taxco is getting lost while aimlessly wandering the pretty streets, it's actually a very easy place to find your way around. The twin belfries of Santa Prisca make the best landmark, situated as they are on the zócalo, Plaza Borda. Nearly all of the town's streets are one way, with the main road, Avenida de los Plateros, being the only major two-way street. This is where both bus stations are located and is the road for entering and leaving the town. The basic colectivo route is a counterclockwise loop going north on Avenida de los Plateros and south through the center of town.

History

Taxco was called Tlachco (Ball-Playing Place) by the Aztecs, who dominated the region from 1440 until the Spanish arrived. The colonial city was founded by Rodrigo de Castañeda in 1529, with a mandate from Hernán Cortés. Among the town's first Spanish residents were three miners, Juan de Cabra, Juan Salcedo and Diego de Nava, and the carpenter Pedro Muriel. In 1531, they established the first Spanish mine in North America.

The Spaniards came searching for tin, which they found in small quantities, but by 1534 they had discovered tremendous lodes of silver. That year the Hacienda El Chorrillo was built, complete with water wheel, smelter and aqueduct – the remains of the latter form the old arches (Los Arcos) over Hwy 95 at the north end of town.

The prospectors quickly depleted the first silver veins and fled Taxco. Further quantities of ore were not discovered until 1743. Don José de la Borda, who had arrived in 1716 from France at the age of 16 to work with his miner brother, accidentally unearthed one of the region's richest veins. According to the legend, Borda was riding near where the Templo de Santa Prisca now stands when his horse stumbled, dislodged a stone and exposed the precious metal.

Borda went on to introduce new techniques of draining and repairing mines, and he reportedly treated his indigenous workers better than most colonial mine owners. The Templo de Santa Prisca was the devout Borda's gift to Taxco. His success attracted more prospectors, and new silver veins were found and played out. With most of the silver gone, Taxco became a quiet town with a dwindling population and economy.

In 1929 a US architect and professor named William (Guillermo) Spratling arrived and, at the suggestion of the then US ambassador Dwight Morrow, set up a silver workshop as a way to rejuvenate the town. (Another version has it that Spratling was writing a book and resorted to the silver business because his publisher went bust. A third has it that Spratling had a notion to create jewelry that synthesized pre-Hispanic motifs with art deco modernism.) The workshop evolved into a factory, and Spratling's apprentices began establishing their own shops. Today Taxco is home to hundreds of silver shops, many producing for export.

◉ Sights & Activities

Templo de Santa Prisca   CHURCH

(Plaza Borda 1) The icon of Taxco, Santa Prisca is one of Mexico's most beautiful and striking pieces of baroque architecture. Its standout feature (best viewed side-on) is the contrast between its belfries, with their elaborate Churrigueresque facade, and the far more simple, constrained and elegant nave. The rose-colored stone used on the facade is extraordinarily beautiful in sunlight – look for the oval bas-relief depiction of Christ's baptism above the doorway. Inside, the intricately sculpted, gold-covered altarpieces are equally fine Churrigueresque specimens.

Santa Prisca was a labor of love for town hero José de la Borda. The local Catholic hierarchy allowed the silver magnate to donate this church to Taxco on the condition that he mortgage his mansion and other assets to guarantee its completion. The project nearly bankrupted him, but the risk produced an extraordinary legacy. It was designed by Spanish architects Juan Caballero and Diego Durán, and was constructed between 1751 and 1758.

Museo Guillermo Spratling   MUSEUM

(🖉 762-622-16-60; Delgado 1; M$35; ⊙ 9am-6pm Mon-Sat) This very well laid-out three-story history and archaeology museum is off an alley behind Templo de Santa Prisca. It contains a small but excellent collection of pre-Hispanic jewelry, art, pottery and sculpture from US silversmith William Spratling's private collection. The phallic cult pieces are a particular eye-opener. On the basement floor there are examples of Spratling's designs using pre-Hispanic motifs. The top floor hosts occasional temporary exhibits.

Museo de Arte Virreinal   MUSEUM

(🖉 762-622-55-01; Ruiz de Alarcón 12; adult/student M$20/15; ⊙ 10am-6pm Tue-Sun) This charming, rather ragtag religious-art museum is housed in a wonderful old house. It hosts a small but well-displayed collection of art, which is labeled in English and Spanish. The most interesting exhibit describes restoration work on Santa Prisca, during which some fabulous material (including tapestries, woodwork altarpieces and rich decorative fabrics) was discovered in the basement of the house. There is also an interesting display on the Manila Galleons, which pioneered trade between the Americas and the Far East.

The Museo de Arte Virreinal is often referred to as Casa Humboldt, even though the famous German explorer and naturalist Friedrich Heinrich Alexander von Humboldt slept here for only one night in 1803.

Casa Borda   BUILDING

(🖉 762-622-66-34; Centro Cultural Taxco, Plaza Borda; ⊙ 10am-6pm Tue-Sun) FREE Built by José de la Borda in 1759, the Casa Borda serves as a cultural center hosting experimental theater and exhibiting contemporary sculpture, painting and photography by Guerrero artists. The building, however, is the main attraction. Due to the unevenness of the terrain, the rear window looks out on a precipitous four-story drop, even though the entrance is on the ground floor.

Teleférico   CABLE CAR

(one way/round trip adult M$65/85, child M$50/65; ⊙ 8am-7pm) From the north end of Taxco, near Los Arcos, a Swiss-made gondola ascends 173m to the Hotel Monte Taxco resort, affording fantastic views of Taxco and the surrounding mountains. To find the entrance, walk uphill from the south side of

Taxco

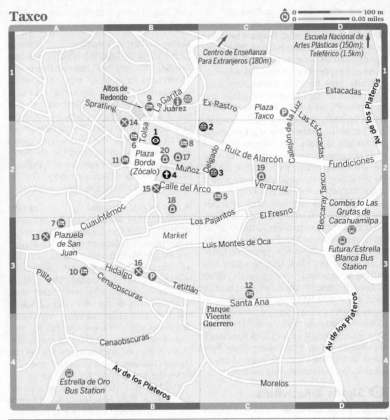

Taxco

◉ Sights
1 Casa Borda	B2
2 Museo de Arte Virreinal	C2
3 Museo Guillermo Spratling	C2
4 Templo de Santa Prisca	B2

⌂ Sleeping
5 Hostel Casa Taxco	C2
6 Hotel Agua Escondida	B2
7 Hotel Casa Grande	A3
8 Hotel Emilia	B2
9 Hotel Mi Casita	B1
10 Hotel Santa Prisca	A3
11 Posada Los Balcones	B2

12 Pueblo Lindo	C3

⊗ Eating
13 Hostería Bar El Adobe	A3
14 La Hacienda de Taxco	B2
La Sushería	(see 8)
15 Pizza Pazza	B2
16 Restaurante Santa Fe	B3

🛍 Shopping
17 EBA Elena Ballesteros	B2
18 Mercado de Artesanías Plata	B2
19 Nuestro México Artesanias	C2
20 Patio de las Artesanías	B2

Los Arcos and turn right through the Escuela Nacional de Artes Plásticas gate.

🎓 Courses

Taxco's cosy mountain atmosphere and relative safety makes it a popular place for foreigners, especially Americans, to study Spanish and silverwork.

Centro de Enseñanza Para Extranjeros
LANGUAGE

(CEPE; ☎762-622-34-10; www.cepe.unam.mx; Ex Hacienda El Chorrillo s/n; courses from M$2942 per month) This branch of Mexico City's Universidad Nacional Autónoma de México offers intensive Spanish-language courses in the atmospheric Ex-Hacienda El Chorrillo. The art school next door (www.enap.unam.mx) offers workshops in painting and jewelry from US$1200.

✦ Festivals & Events

Be sure to reserve your hotel in advance if your visit coincides with one of Taxco's annual festivals. Check exact dates of movable feasts with the tourist office.

Fiestas de Santa Prisca & San Sebastián   RELIGIOUS
(☺ Jan) Taxco's patron saints are honored on January 18 (Santa Prisca) and January 20 (San Sebastián), when locals parade by the Templo de Santa Prisca for an annual blessing, with their pets and farm animals in tow.

Jornadas Alarconianas   ARTS
This summertime cultural festival, honoring Taxco-born playwright Juan Ruiz de Alarcón, presents concerts and dance performances by internationally renowned performing artists.

Día del Jumil   FOOD
(☺ Nov) The Monday after the Day of the Dead (November 2), locals celebrate the *jumil* – the edible beetle said to represent the giving of life and energy to Taxco residents for another year. Many families camp on the Cerro de Huixteco (above town) over the preceding weekend, and townsfolk climb the hill to collect *jumiles* and share food and camaraderie.

Feria de la Plata   CRAFTS
(☺ Nov/Dec) The week-long national silver fair convenes in late November or early December. Craft competitions are held and some of Mexico's best silverwork is on display. Other festivities include rodeos, concerts, dances and burro races.

Las Posadas   CULTURAL
(☺ Dec) From December 16 to 24, nightly candlelit processions fill Taxco's streets with door-to-door singing. Children are dressed up to resemble biblical characters. At the end of the night, they attack piñatas.

🛏 Sleeping

Taxco has a wealth of hotels, from large four- and five-star resorts to charming family-run posadas. During holiday weekends, when the hordes arrive from Mexico City, it's a good idea to reserve ahead.

Earplugs are also a good idea. Owing to the innumerable Volkswagen taxis that serve as transportation in this, the steepest of hill towns, street noise is a problem nearly everywhere.

Hotel Casa Grande   HOTEL $
(☎ 762-622-09-69; www.hotelcasagrandetaxco. com.mx; Plazuela de San Juan 7; s with/without bathroom M$330/210, d M$515/330, tr M$600/400; 🖥) Its excellent location and hypnotic terrace views over the *plazuela* make Casa Grande an attractive budget option, but bring your earplugs as the music from the restaurant-bar La Concha Nostra goes late into the night, especially on weekends.

Hostel Casa Taxco   HOSTEL $
(☎ 762-622-70-37; www.hostelcasataxco.mx; Veracruz 5; dm/d M$200/550; 🖥) You know Taxco is getting with the times when you lay eyes on this beautiful converted house with its artisanal tiles and furnishings – it's almost a poshtel. The dorms only have two or four beds, and there's the calm vibe of a colonial home. There's also an open-plan kitchen and a roof terrace with cathedral views.

Posada Los Balcones   HOTEL $
(☎ 762-622-02-50; Plazuela de los Gallos 5; s/d M$300/500; 🖥) As its name suggests, many of the 15 rooms at this straightforward hotel have small balconies overlooking the boisterous narrow street below. Just moments from Santa Prisca, Los Balcones is centrally located. Every spacious room has its own bathroom and TV.

★ Hotel Mi Casita   INN $$
(☎ 762-627-17-77; www.hotelmicasita.com; Altos de Redondo 1; s/d/tr/ste incl breakfast M$600/750/850/950; 🖥@🖥) This elegant colonial home run by a family of jewelry designers boasts 12 beautifully and individually decorated rooms just moments from the *zócalo,* with wraparound balconies giving views over the cathedral. The comfortable rooms feature original hand-painted bathroom tiles, three with Talavera bathtubs, some with private terraces and all with fans.

Hotel Santa Prisca   HOTEL $$
(☎ 762-622-00-80; Cenaobscuras 1; r M$480-780, ste M$780-970; 🅿🖥) The 31-room Santa Prisca has traditional Mexican decor and a welcoming courtyard garden. It has a great

AROUND MEXICO CITY TAXCO

location too, right in the thick of things. Rooms are smallish, but most have breezy private balconies. All have two beds, and newer, sunnier rooms cost a bit more. The parking lot is reached through a tunnel at the hotel's uphill end.

Hotel Agua Escondida   BUSINESS HOTEL $$
(✆762-622-07-36, 800-504-03-11; www.aguaescondida.com; Plaza Borda 4; r/ste M$1150/1650; P@🛜🌊) Facing the *zócalo,* Hotel Agua Escondida is popular with visiting silver importers and has two swimming pools, a spa and a cafe-bar on a high terrace with unmatchable views of Santa Prisca. The 60 comfortable, remodeled rooms have colonial furnishings and are sometimes discounted during the week. Rooms with balconies overlooking the street suffer from traffic noise.

Hotel Emilia   HOTEL $$
(✆762-622-13-90; www.hotelemilia.com.mx; Ruiz de Alarcón 7; d/tr M$850/950; 🛜🌊) All 14 rooms are spotlessly clean and have beautiful tiled bathrooms. Owned by a family of famous silver workers, this intimate hotel has colonial charm and includes free use of the pools at nearby Hotel Agua Escondida. Sadly, it's in an especially noisy location – ask for a room at the back, but don't miss the views from the rooftop terrace.

Pueblo Lindo   HOTEL $$$
(✆762-622-34-81; www.pueblolindo.com.mx; Hidalgo 30; r & ste incl breakfast M$1290-2190; P@🛜🌊) This luxurious hotel manages to balance style and substance, embracing a modern Mexican-inspired aesthetic with bright colors and wooden furnishings. There's a bar-lounge and excellent service. The rooftop pool has fantastic views over Taxco, as do many of the rooms.

✗ Eating

Many of the best spots in town to grab a bite are also good places for a drink.

La Sushería   JAPANESE $
(Ruiz de Alarcón 7; sushi M$55-90; ⊙1-11pm; 🛜🍴) This sushi restaurant in the lobby of Hotel Emilia reflects modern Taxco with its designer furniture but casual vibe. The sushi is fresh and finished nicely with the green-tea ice cream – heaven in a cocktail glass. If you're here on a date or a business lunch, the slick booths are the perfect place to impress.

Restaurante Santa Fe   MEXICAN $
(✆762-622-11-70; Hidalgo 2; mains M$65-100; ⊙8am-9:30pm) In business for over 50 years, Santa Fe is a favorite among locals for its fairly priced traditional fare such as *conejo en chile ajo* (rabbit in garlic and chili). The walls are plastered with patron photos and some excellent black-and-white shots of ye-olde Taxco. The three-course *menú de hoy* is a bargain at M$80, especially for dinner.

Pizza Pazza   PIZZA $$
(Arco 1; pizzas M$99-195; ⊙11am-1am) This is a perfect place to take in the town's scenery – the buzzing *zócalo,* Santa Prisca, twinkling white mountain homes in the background and Taxco's statue of Jesus are all visible from the roof terrace. These features make the thin-crust pizzas seem closer to heaven than they probably are, but nobody seems to mind.

La Hacienda de Taxco   MEXICAN $$
(✆762-622-11-66; Plaza Borda 4; mains M$75-170; ⊙7:30am-10:30pm; 👶) Offering an extensive menu of traditional Mexican dishes (including house-made jam in the morning and a 20-ingredient, house-made *mole* in the afternoon), La Hacienda also has considerate touches, like the option of egg-white-only breakfasts, vegetarian dishes and child-sized portions.

Hostería Bar El Adobe   MEXICAN $$
(✆762-622-14-16; Plazuela de San Juan 13; mains M$55-175; ⊙8am-11pm) This place doesn't have the *zócalo* views, but the interior is charmingly decorated with black-and-white photos of everyone from Pancho Villa to Elvis. Plus the cute balcony tables are more private. On weekends, there's *pozole* (M$65), live *trova* music on Saturday night and a buffet (M$125) on Sunday.

🛍 Shopping

Patio de las Artesanías   JEWELRY
(Plaza Borda) If you are looking for silver, there are several shops to wander through in the Patio de las Artesanías building.

EBA Elena Ballesteros   JEWELRY
(✆762-622-37-67; www.ebaplata.com; Muñoz 4) EBA Elena Ballesteros has creative, well-crafted silver designs.

Mercado de Artesanías Plata   JEWELRY
(⊙11am-8pm) For quantity rather than quality, trawl the vast, haphazardly displayed

BUSES FROM TAXCO

DESTINATION	FARE (M$)	DURATION (HR)	FREQUENCY (DAILY)
Acapulco	240-260	4-5	7 EDO & from Futura terminal
Cuernavaca	75	1½	5 EDO
	90	1½	12 from Futura terminal
Mexico City (Terminal Sur)	187	2½	4 EDO
	185	2½	5 from Futura terminal

masses of rings, chains and pendants at the Mercado de Artesanías Plata. You can haggle for good prices here, even if you have to search hard for something unique.

Nuestro México Artesanías HANDICRAFTS
(☑762-622-09-76; Veracruz 8; ⊗10am-6pm) Treasure hunters will love fossicking in this storehouse of handicrafts from across Mexico. Most of the favorite souvenirs are here – coconut masks, papier-mâché devils, flying cherubs, fish wind chimes and, yes, silver. The prices are marked and close to what you pay on the street outside.

ℹ Information

Several banks around the main plazas and bus stations have ATMs. There are card phones near Plaza Borda and quieter ones in nicer hotel lobbies.

Cruz Roja (Red Cross; ☑065)
Hospital General (☑762-622-93-00)
Police (☑762-622-10-17)
Post Office (Palacio Municipal, Juárez 10)
Tourist Module (cnr Juárez & Plazuela del Exconvento; ⊗9am-8pm) Tourism office next to the post office with maps and good information. Note that the tourism kiosk in the main plaza mostly exists to hand out brochures and push tours.

ℹ Getting There & Away

The shared **Futura/Estrella Blanca terminal** (Avenida de los Plateros) offers luggage storage. The Estrella de Oro (EDO) terminal is at the south end of town. The Futura bus to Mexico City runs mostly on the hour, but after the 9am departure, the next is at noon then 2pm.

For more frequent bus services to the coast, take a shared taxi (M$24) from in front of the bus station to the nearby town of Iguala, about 30 minutes away.

ℹ Getting Around

Apart from walking, combis (white Volkswagen minibuses) and taxis are the best way to navigate Taxco's steep and narrow cobbled streets.

Combis (M$6) are frequent and operate from 7am to 8pm. 'Zócalo' combis depart from Plaza Borda, travel down Cuauhtémoc to Plazuela de San Juan then head down the hill on Hidalgo. They turn right at Morelos, left at Avenida de los Plateros and go north, passing the Futura bus station, until La Garita, where they turn left and return to the zócalo. 'Arcos/Zócalo' combis follow the same route except that they continue past La Garita to Los Arcos, where they do a U-turn and head back to La Garita. Combis marked 'PM' (for Pedro Martín) go to the southern end of town from Plaza Borda, past the Estrella de Oro bus station. Taxis cost M$25 to M$35 for trips around town.

Parque Nacional Grutas de Cacahuamilpa

One of central Mexico's most stunning natural sights, the **Cacahuamilpa caverns** (☑721-104-01-56; http://cacahuamilpa.conanp. gob.mx; admission with guide adult/child M$75/50; ⊗10am-7pm; ℙ) are a must-see for anyone visiting Taxco or Cuernavaca. The scale of the caves is hard to imagine, with vast chambers up to 82m high leading 1.2km beneath the mountainside, inside of which are mind-blowing stalactites and stalagmites.

Unfortunately, individual access to the (perfectly safe) pathway through the caves is not allowed. Instead, visitors are allocated free guides who lead large group tours (departures each hour on the hour), with constant stops to point out shapes (Santa Claus, a kneeling child, a gorilla) in the rock. At the end of the hour-long tour, you can wander back to the entrance – with the lights now off – at your own pace. Most guides do not speak English.

From the cave exit it's possible to follow a steep path for 15 minutes to the fast-flowing **Río Dos Bocas**. There are spectacular views year-round and tranquil pools for swimming during the dry season. Bring bug spray.

Weekends are often very crowded, with long lines and large group tours – making midweek a more pleasant time for a visit. There are restaurants, snacks and souvenir stores near the entrance. Between the entrance and the caves, it's possible to take a short zipline (M$70) across the treetops, or you can just walk the 150m around. The last ticket for the caverns is sold at 5pm.

❶ Getting There & Away

To reach the caves, take an Estrella Roja 'Grutas' bus from the Futura bus terminal on Avenida de los Plateros in Taxco (M$34, 40 minutes, every 40 minutes) or taxi (M$180). Buses deposit you at the crossroad where the road splits off to Cuernavaca. From there, walk 350m downhill to the park's visitors center. Return buses leave from the same crossroad (every 40 minutes, last bus 8pm).

WEST OF MEXICO CITY

The area to the west of Mexico City is dominated by the large industrial and administrative city of Toluca, the capital of the state of Mexico. While pleasant, Toluca has little to recommend it to travelers and most bypass it en route to the area's two wonderful small-town, colonial gems. Malinalco is a sleepy and remote village with some fascinating pre-Hispanic ruins perched above it, and Valle de Bravo, a cosmopolitan getaway favored by Mexico's elite, is located on the shores of a large, artificial reservoir a dramatic two-hour drive west of Toluca. The countryside surrounding Toluca itself is scenic, with pine forests, rivers and a huge extinct volcano, Nevado de Toluca.

Toluca

📞 722 / POP 490,000 / ELEV 2660M

Like many colonial Mexican cities, Toluca's development has created a ring of urban sprawl around what remains a very picturesque old town. The traffic problems alone can be enough to dampen the city's appeal, but those who make time to visit will find Toluca a pleasant, if bustling, small city. It's an enjoyable place to spend a day exploring

attractive plazas, lively shopping arcades, art galleries and museums.

Toluca was an indigenous settlement from at least the 13th century. The Spanish founded the modern city in the 16th century after defeating the resident Aztecs and Matlazincas, and it became part of Hernán Cortés' expansive domain, the Marquesado del Valle de Oaxaca. Since 1830 it's been the capital of Mexico state, which surrounds the Distrito Federal on three sides, like an upside-down U.

The main road from Mexico City becomes Paseo Tollocan on Toluca's eastern edge, before bearing southwest and becoming a ring road around the city center's southern edge. Toluca's bus station and the huge Mercado Juárez are 2km southeast of the center, off Paseo Tollocan.

The vast Plaza de los Mártires, with the cathedral and Palacio de Gobierno, marks the town center. Most of the action, however, is concentrated a block south in the pedestrian precinct ringed by archways *(los arcos)*. Shady Parque Alameda is three blocks west along Hidalgo.

◉ Sights

The 19th-century **Portal Madero**, running 250m along Avenida Hidalgo, is lively, as is the commercial arcade along the pedestrian street to the east, which attracts mariachis after 9pm. A block north, the large, open expanse of **Plaza de los Mártires** is surrounded by fine old government buildings; the 19th-century **cathedral** and the 18th-century **Templo de la Santa Veracruz** are on its south side. On Plaza Garibay's north side is the 18th-century **Templo del Carmen**.

Museo de Antropología e História   MUSEUM
(📞722-274-12-00; Blvd Reyes Heroles 302; adult/child M$10/5, Sun free; ◷9am-6pm Mon-Sat, to 3pm Sun) This standout museum presents exhibits on the state's history from prehistoric times to the 20th century, with a good collection of pre-Hispanic artifacts. It also traces pre-Hispanic cultural influences up to the modern day in tools, clothing, textiles and religion. Nearly all of the labels are only in Spanish.

★**Cosmovitral Jardín Botánico**   GARDENS
(Cosmic Stained-Glass Window Botanical Garden; 📞722-214-67-85; cnr Juárez & Lerdo de Tejada; adult/child M$10/5; ◷9am-6pm Tue-Sun) At the northeast end of Plaza Garibay, the

stunning and unique Cosmovitral Jardín Botánico was built in 1909 as a market. The building now houses 3500 sq meters of lovely gardens, lit through 48 stained-glass panels by the Tolucan artist Leopoldo Flores.

Centro Cultural Mexiquense MUSEUM
(State of Mexico Cultural Center; ☑722-274-12-00; Blvd Reyes Heroles 302; adult/child M$10/5, Sun free; ☺10am-6pm Mon-Sat, to 3pm Sun) This large cultural center, 4.5km west of the city center, houses three good museums (which all keep the same hours). It's no must-see, but still a worthwhile diversion for visitors interested in local arts and crafts, local archaeology and modern art.

From downtown you can take a cab (M$40), though it's easy to take one of the plentiful *colectivos* from outside the Mercado Juárez – just look for 'Centro Cultural' on its destination board. The circuitous ride takes 20 minutes.

Get off by the large grass roundabout near the Monterrey University Toluca campus, cross to the opposite side and the museum complex is through the gate and down the road.

Museo de Culturas Populares MUSEUM
(☑722-274-12-00; Blvd Reyes Heroles 302; adult/child M$10/5; ☺9am-6pm Mon-Sat) This museum has a wonderfully varied collection of Mexico's traditional arts and crafts, with some astounding 'trees of life' from Metepec, whimsical Day of the Dead figures and a fine display of *charro* (cowboy) gear. There are also mosaics, traditional rugs, a loft and a gift shop.

Museo de Arte Moderno MUSEUM
(☑722-274-12-00; Blvd Reyes Heroles 302; adult/child M$10/5, Sun free; ☺10am-6pm Mon-Sat, to 3pm Sun) Traces the development of Mexican art from the late-19th-century Academia de San Carlos to the Nueva Plástica and includes paintings by Tamayo, Orozco and many others. There's an impressive spherical mural of people fighting against slavery, which makes up part of the building itself, as well as exhibits of challenging pieces of contemporary art.

Museo de Bellas Artes MUSEUM
(☑722-215-53-29; Degollado 102; adult/child M$10/5; ☺10am-6pm Tue-Sun) The ex-convent buildings adjacent to the Templo del Carmen, on the north side of Plaza Garibay, house Toluca's Museo de Bellas Artes, which exhibits paintings from the colonial period to the early 20th century.

🕝 Tours

Tranvía TRAM
(☑722-330-50-52; www.tranviatoluca.com; adult/child M$60/30; ☺ departs hourly 11am-5pm) This motorized trolley leaves from the cathedral and visits two dozen sites in the city in 50 minutes.

🛏 Sleeping

Hotel Colonial INN **$**
(☑722-215-97-00; Hidalgo Oriente 103; s/d/tr M$350/400/500; ☑🖹) The rooms overlooking the busy main road are the best, but also the loudest, at this well-run and excellent-value hotel. The impressive lobby and friendly staff are other good reasons to come here. Rates include free parking nearby in a lot on Juárez. Popular with groups, so call ahead.

Hotel Maya HOTEL **$**
(☑722-214-48-00; Hidalgo 413; r with/without bathroom M$270/220; 🖹) The extremely central location of this one-grandma-run posada makes a handy, if no-frills, base for a quick visit of Toluca's sights. If street noise bothers you, choose a darker interior room.

Hotel Don Simón BUSINESS HOTEL **$$**
(☑722-213-26-96; www.hoteldonsimon.com; Matamoros 202; d/tr M$800/1000; ☑@🖹) The rooms at Don Simón are immaculately clean and bright, if a little heavy on the brown furnishings of yesteryear, which continue into the attached restaurant. It's a definite winner for value in central Toluca – the staff are friendly, the street is quiet and it's just a short walk to Cosmovitral.

Fiesta Inn Toluca Centro BUSINESS HOTEL **$$$**
(☑722-167-89-00; www.fiestainn.com; Allende Sur 124; r/ste M$1249/2849; ☑@🖹) This modern, sleek, 85-room Fiesta Inn (formerly the Gran Hotel) has airy, comfortable rooms, a small gym and a cafe-bar-restaurant in the lobby. There's a second Fiesta Inn near the airport.

🍴 Eating & Drinking

Toluqueños take snacking and sweets very seriously and you can join them in the arcades around Plaza Fray Andrés de Castro. Other stalls sell candied fruit and *jamoncillos* (pumpkin-seed *pastes*), and *mostachones* (sweets made of burned milk).

Most eateries in the center are open from around 8am to 9pm.

★ La Gloria
Chocolatería y Pan 1876 CAFE $
(Quintana Roo; snacks M$10-35; ⊘11am-11pm) You'll probably be the only foreigner at this wonderful, friendly, family-run cafe. It serves a tempting menu of local cuisine, from *tacos al pastor* (spicy pork tacos) to delicious *sermones* (sandwiches) stuffed with oven-baked pork or shredded chicken bathed in *mole poblano*.

Arte Café Libros ETC CAFE $
(☑722-213-87-32; Independencia 101, upstairs; baguettes M$35-80; ⊘9am-6pm Mon-Fri; ⊛) The name sums it up nicely – art by local artists, fresh coffee and baguettes on the terrace and plenty of books to browse or buy. The ETC would be the live music, film festivals and odds and ends for sale such as T-shirts, healing herbs and jewelry. Closed weekends unless there is an event on.

Hostería Las Ramblas MEXICAN $$
(☑722-215-54-88; Calle 20 de Noviembre 107D; mains M$110-180; ⊘9am-8pm; ✍) On a pedestrian mall, this atmospheric restaurant feels like a throwback to the 1950s, with white tablecloths and retro decor. Attentive waiters serve full breakfasts, including excellent vegetarian options such as the *omelette campesino* – panela cheese, *rajas* (poblano) chili and zucchini – and a variety of lunch and dinner mains such as *mole verde* and *conejo al ajillo* (liberally garlicked rabbit).

🛍 Shopping

Casart ARTS & CRAFTS
(Casa de Artesanía; Aldama 102; ⊘10am-6pm Tue-Sun) This downtown location of Casart – the state organization promoting local crafts – is fantastic both for its beautiful home, set around a courtyard, and its wonderful selection of quality arts and crafts. Prices are fixed and therefore higher than you might be able to get haggling in markets for an inferior product (for the best prices, go directly to the source).

ℹ Information

There are banks with ATMs near Portal Madero.

City Tourist Office (☑722-384-11-00, ext 104; www.toluca.gob.mx/turismo; Plaza Fray Andrés de Castro, Edificio B, Local 6, Planta Baja)

Cruz Roja (Red Cross; ☑722-217-33-33)

State Tourist Office (☑722-212-59-98; www.edomexico.gob.mx; cnr Urawa & Paseo Tollocan) Inconveniently located 2km southeast of the center, but with English-speaking staff and good maps.

Tourist Information Kiosk (Palacio Municipal) Helpful kiosk with free city map.

ℹ Getting There & Away

The modern, efficient and low-stress **Aeropuerto Internacional de Toluca** (☑722-279-28-00; www.vuelatoluca.com) is an excellent alternative to Mexico City's massive and intimidating airport. Conveniently located off Hwy 15, about 10km from downtown, the airport is adjacent to the industrial zone and a group of business-friendly chain hotels.

Toluca is the hub for budget airline **Interjet** (www.interjet.com.mx), which offers flights to Las Vegas and all over Mexico.

Spirit Airlines (☑800-772-7117; www.spirit.com) and **Volaris** (☑800-122-80-00; www.volaris.com.mx) also offer international service. They fly travelers between Toluca and several cities in the United States, including Los Angeles, Chicago, Las Vegas, Houston, San Francisco, Seattle, Newark, Miami, New York and Atlanta.

Europcar (www.europcar.com), **Dollar** (www.dollar.com) and **Alamo** (www.alamo.com) all have rental-car offices at the airport.

There are frequent buses from the airport to both Mexico City (M$115 Interjet Shuttlebus to Polanco, Reforma or WTC) and the capital's Aeropuerto Internacional (M$153 Caminante

BUSES FROM TOLUCA

DESTINATION	FARE (M$)	DURATION (HR)	FREQUENCY (DAILY)
Cuernavaca	71	2	24
Mexico City (Poniente)	50-70	1	40
Morelia	330	2	14
Taxco	91	3	7
Valle de Bravo	85	2¼	10
Zihuatanejo	641	9	3

Shuttlebus), which take an hour or two, depending on traffic. Interjet also shuttles to Cuernavaca (M$232). An authorised taxi from the airport to downtown Toluca costs about M$25 and takes 20 to 30 minutes.

Toluca's **bus station** (Berriozábal 101) is 2km southeast of the center. Ticket offices for many destinations are on the platforms or at the gate entrances, and it's fair to say it can be a confusing place. Look for monitors at gate entrances that reveal which gates sell which destination.

❶ Getting Around

Large 'Centro' buses go from outside Toluca's bus station to the town center (M$8, 20 minutes) along Lerdo de Tejada and by Plaza de los Mártires. From Juárez in the center, 'Terminal' buses go to the bus station. Taxis from the bus station to the city center cost around M$40.

Nevado de Toluca

Among the highest peaks in the region, the long-extinct volcano Nevado de Toluca (also known as Xinantécatl) is Mexico's fourth-tallest peak. Nevado has two summits on the crater rim. The lower summit, Pico del Aguila (4620m), is closer to the parking area and is the more common day hike. The main or highest summit is called Pico del Fraile (4704m) and requires an additional three to four hours of hike time.

The earlier you reach the summit, the better the chance of clear views. The crater contains two lakes, El Sol and La Luna. The summit area can be snowy from November to March, and is sometimes good for cross-country skiing, but the **Parque Nacional Nevado de Toluca** is closed during the heaviest snowfalls. On October 1, 2013 the Mexican government redesignated the national park a *zona protegida* (protected area), legalising and legitimising the unregulated mining activity that had been going on there. Most people still continue to call it a national park.

From the park entrance a road winds 3.5km up to the **main gate** (Carretera Temascaltpec Km 18, San Antonio Acahualco; per vehicle M$20, per camioneta M$40; ☺10am-5pm); last entry is at 3pm. From there it's a 17km drive along an unsurfaced road up to the crater. Dress warmly – it gets chilly up top.

Just beyond the gate, **Posada Familiar** (☏722-214-37-86; campsite/dm M$85/150) offers basic lodging at a heavily used refuge

with shared hot showers, a kitchen (without utensils) and a common area with a fireplace. Bring extra blankets. On Saturday and Sunday, food is served at stalls around Parque de los Venados and at the gate near the summit. Midweek, bring your own food and water.

From Toluca, taxis will take you to the trailhead for upwards of M$250, or there and back (including time for a look around) for a negotiable M$500. Be sure to hire a newer taxi; the road up is very rough and dusty. Most international car-rental companies also have offices in Toluca.

Mario Andrade (☏55-1826-2146; mountain up@hotmail.com; transportation, 1 meal & park entrance US$200) leads one-day climbs and also guides climbers on Izta ascents.

Valle de Bravo

☏726 / POP 28,000 / ELEV 1800M

With one of the loveliest colonial centers in central Mexico, the *pueblo mágico* of Valle de Bravo is an utter charmer and a wonderful spot for an escape from Mexico City. A long, winding and occasionally stunning mountain road runs the 85km west from Toluca, taking you to the shores of Lago Avandaro – this is an artificial lake, the result of the construction of a hydroelectric station.

The setting here is reminiscent of the northern Italian lakes, with thickly wooded, mist-clad hills and red terracotta roofing used throughout the town. Valle, as it's known, is famous for being the weekend retreat of choice for the capital's well-connected upper classes. The views at the lakeside are stunning, but the beguiling and largely intact colonial center is arguably the real draw here. Boating on the lake is very popular as well, as are hiking and camping in the hills around the town. Valle is set up well for visitors. There's a tourist-info kiosk on the wharf and essential services, including ATMs and internet cafes, are found around the main plaza, which is a 10-minute walk uphill from the waterfront.

In late October or early November, the week-long **Festival de las Almas**, an international arts and culture extravaganza, brings in music and dance troupes from all over Europe and Latin America.

🛏 Sleeping

For a small town, this popular weekend escape from Mexico City has a good selection of budget posadas and midrange hotels. The most affordable options are within two blocks of the bus station.

★Hotel San José   HOTEL $

(☏726-262-09-72;   http://sanjosevalle.com.mx; Callejón San José 103; d M$400-500; 🛜) This converted ranch-style hotel is just a block from the zócalo, but hidden down an alley away from the noise, with a small garden where you can admire the view of the hills. Huge rooms have extremely comfortable beds, and light-filled bathrooms with luxury trimmings – heavy shower curtains and plush bath rugs. Most have kitchenettes. The biggest steal in Valle.

Posada Familiar Los Girasoles   GUESTHOUSE $

(☏726-262-29-67; Plaza Independencia 1; s & d M$450, tr M$500, q M$600-750) The nine-room Girasoles has an enviable location on the zócalo. It has spacious and spotlessly clean rooms, complete with rustic touches and a warm, family-run feeling. Expect to be asked where you're from and shown photos of former guests (all 'friends') who have stayed here.

Hotel Casanueva   BOUTIQUE HOTEL $$

(☏726-262-17-66; Villagrán 100; s/d/ste Fri & Sat M$890/1100/1500, Sun-Thu M$715/880/1200; 🛜) Set on the west side of the zócalo, the Casanueva has individually designed rooms decorated with tasteful arts and crafts. The most stylish option downtown, the hotel's suite, which sleeps four, is especially lovely. Some rooms have private balconies over the square.

Rodavento   RESORT $$$

(☏726-251-41-82; www.hotelrodavento.com; Carretera Valle de Bravo-Los Saucos Km 3.5; ste from M$2500; 🅿❄🛜🐕) Set on a sprawling property outside of Valle, this rustic-luxe hotel distinguishes itself with its natural design – using earth tones, traditional wood stoves and sliding glass doors opening onto the forest, gardens and a private lake. It also offers special activities for kids.

🍴 Eating

There are scores of restaurants and cafes along the wharf and around the zócalo; many are only open from Friday to Sunday. If there ever was a time to try esquite (lime and chili-flavored corn in a cup) from street stalls, this is it. Villagrán, on the west side of the zócalo, has very clean food stands.

Las Palomas   MEXICAN $

(cnr Calle 16 de Septiembre & El Vergel; mains M$60-120, menú del día M$65; ⏱9am-9pm; 🐕🍴♿) Late into the evening, the children are bright eyed and high on the fresh hot churros at this family-friendly restaurant, a block north of the cathedral. The large open space isn't just for families – couples come for the sharp vinaigrette alcachofas (artichokes), which play nicely with the creamy salmon.

Restaurante Paraíso   FISH $$

(☏726-262-47-31; Fray Gregorio Jiménez de la Cuenca s/n; mains M$75-160; ⏱8am-10pm) Has fantastic lake views and a sprawling menu of seafood specialties, plus excellent and imaginatively prepared local trout. Come early and watch the sunset from the rooftop patio.

Soleado   FUSION $$

(☏726-262-58-31; Pagaza 314; mains M$95-175; ⏱1-10pm Sat-Thu, to midnight Fri, closed Mon; 🛜🍴♿) Soleado calls itself cocina del mundo and indeed there is a dish and a dessert from many a 'kitchen of the world' on offer. Admittedly, most dishes, from Indian curry to Italian veg lasagna, have a (tasty) Mexican twist. The low-lit restaurant with lofty views is a great place for groups, with dishes to please all tastes.

ℹ Information

Tourist Information Stand (zócalo east side; ⏱9am-5pm) Staff speak a bit of English, give directions and have free maps and tour brochures.

ℹ Getting There & Away

Considering the hordes of tourists who descend on Valle each weekend, transportation options are relatively few. Most visitors are affluent Mexicans, who come by car.

Autobuses Mexico-Toluca-Zinacantepec y Ramales runs hourly 2nd-class directos from early morning to late afternoon between Mexico City's Terminal Poniente and Valle de Bravo's small bus terminal on Calle 16 de Septiembre (M$182, 2¼ hours). For a scenic ride ask for the southern, 'Los Saucos' route, which travels along Hwy 134 and through a national park. If driving, that's the route to take as well.

There is no direct bus between Malinalco and Valle de Bravo. You have to travel via Toluca (M$75) or Mexico City.

Malinalco

📋 714 / POP 7000 / ELEV 1740M

Set in a valley of dramatic cliffs and ancient ruins, this *pueblo mágico* continues its transformation into the next Tepoztlán. Weekends see crowds, but still far fewer than those that descend on more easily accessible weekend escapes. The drive to Malinalco is one of the most enjoyable to be had in the area, with dramatic scenery lining the road south of Toluca.

There are already a clutch of hippie stores, a handful of international restaurants and, it seems, a surprising number of boutique hotels. The town is far from fully developed, though, and it's almost unnervingly quiet midweek, when it can still be a challenge to find a decent place to eat outside of the *zócalo*.

The village itself has a charming colonial core set around a well-preserved convent and two central plazas, which sit side by side. In the larger plaza, the **tourist module** (www.malinalco.net; ☯ 9am-4pm Mon-Fri, to 5pm Sat & Sun) offers limited help and there's an ATM on Hidalgo, on the convent's north side. **Cyber Malinalco** (Hidalgo 104; per hr M$11) offers reasonably priced internet access.

◉ Sights

Aztec Temples   ARCHAEOLOGICAL SITE
(Av Progreso s/n; M$52; ☯ 9am-6pm Tue-Sun, last entry 5pm) An invigorating 358-step hike up the mountainside above Malinalco takes you to one of the country's few reasonably well-preserved temples, from where there are stunning views of the valley and beyond. The site is fascinating and includes *El paraíso de los guerreros* (a mural that once covered an entire wall), depicting fallen warriors becoming deities and living in paradise. From the main square follow signs to the *zona arqueológica,* which take you up the hillside on a well-maintained, signed footpath.

The Aztecs conquered the region in 1476 and were busy building a ritual center here when they were conquered by the Spanish. **El Cuauhcalli** (Temple of the Eagle and Jaguar Knight, where sons of Aztec nobles were initiated into warrior orders) survived because it was hewn from the mountainside

itself. The entrance is carved in the form of a fanged serpent.

Temple IV, located on the far side of the site, continues to baffle archaeologists. As the room is positioned to allow the first rays of sunlight to hit it at dawn, there has been speculation that this place was part of a Mexican sun cult, a solar calendar, or a meeting place for nobles – or some combination of these.

Situated near the site entrance, the **Museo Universitario Dr Luis Mario Schneider** (📋 714 147-12-88; M$10; ☯ 10am-4pm Tue-Sun) explores the region's history and archaeology in a beautiful, modern museum space.

Augustinian Convent   CHURCH
(☯ 9am-6pm) A well-restored 16th-century convent, fronted by a tranquil tree-lined yard, faces the central plaza. Impressive frescoes fashioned from herb- and flower-based paint adorn its cloister.

☞ Tours

Tour Gastronómico Prehispánico   CULINARY
(📋 cell 55-55091411; aplegaspi@prodigy.net.mx) This pre-Hispanic food tour includes a visit to the market, a cooking class using traditional utensils and methods, and a three-course meal.

🛏 Sleeping

This small town has an inordinate number of hotel rooms, but reservations remain a good idea. Because Malinalco is geared toward weekend visitors, you'll have no trouble finding a room Sunday to Thursday nights, though some of the nicer hotels aren't open for walk-ins (or at all) midweek.

El Asoleadero   HOTEL $
(📋 714-147-01-84; cnr Aldama & Comercio; r M$500, with kitchen M$700; 🅿 🖥 ☀) Just uphill from Malinalco's main drag, El Asoleadero offers spacious, modern and airy rooms with stunning views of the *pueblito* and surrounding cliffs. You can enjoy the million-peso vista from the courtyard's small pool with a cold beer from the lobby.

Hotel Santa Mónica   GUESTHOUSE $
(📋 714-147-00-31; Hidalgo 109; r M$350; 🖥) Just a few steps from the *zócalo* and en route to the archaeological zone, this is the best ultra-budget option, with clean, if shabby, rooms (all with private bathroom and TV) scattered around a simple courtyard. Expect

rooster wake-up calls at dawn. Prices are even lower midweek.

Casa Navacoyan BOUTIQUE HOTEL **$$$**
(☑714-147-04-11; www.casanavacoyan.mx; Prolangación Calle Pirul 62; ste incl breakfast from M$2084; P❖⏦✦) This gorgeous hotel on the outskirts of town has just six rooms, each decorated in a sort of upscale, home-style aesthetic, like staying at your wealthy aunt's house in the country. The immaculately groomed yard is the real attraction, with palm trees, a gorgeous pool and views of Malinalco's famed hills and cliffs.

✖ Eating

Perhaps surprisingly for such a small town, Malinalco has a few very good restaurants. Unfortunately for those visiting midweek though, most of the better options (on Avenida Hidalgo and around the *zócalo*) are only open Thursday through Sunday.

Mari Mali MEXICAN **$**
(Av Juárez 4; mains M$55-80, menú del día M$70; ☺10am-6pm Fri-Wed; ❖✦) The only casual, classy and clean place serving set-menu breakfasts and lunches midweek. Mexican classics such as enchiladas and *pozole* make it on the menu, as does a better-than-it-sounds *guayaba* (guava) jelly. The fruit sellers outside are a colorful bonus.

★ Los Placeres INTERNATIONAL **$$**
(☑714-147-08-55; Plaza Principal s/n; mains M$75-190; ☺2-7pm Thu, 2-10pm Fri, 9:30am-10pm Sat, 9:30am to 5pm Sun; ✦✦) This artsy restaurant on Malinalco's *zócalo* serves international fare (Nicoise salad or chicken curry), alongside creative takes on traditional Mexican dishes, such as omelettes with *poblano* sauce, trout with *ancho* chilies or fondue *al tequila*. There are elaborate murals, tile-mosaic tabletops and the likes of Robert Johnson on the sound system.

El Puente de Má-Li INTERNATIONAL **$$**
(☑714-147-17-43; Hidalgo 22; mains M$145-260; ☺1-6pm Tue-Thu, to 11pm Fri & Sat, 9am-6pm Sun) After the tiny bridge as you leave the *zócalo* for the ruins, this atmospheric restaurant is set around a colonial dining room and a great back garden where you can try a selection of *antojitos*, pastas, soups and steaks.

❶ Getting There & Away

Most public transportation to Malinalco goes via Tenancingo. **Águila** (☑800-224-84-52; www.autobusesaguila.com.mx), however, runs two buses each afternoon (4:20pm and 6:20pm), with an additional service Saturday and Sunday (8:45am) from Mexico City's Terminal Poniente (M$98, two hours). If you can't wait, Águila also runs twice an hour between Terminal Poniente and Tenancingo (M$90, two hours, every 30 minutes).

From Tenancingo, take the *colectivo* (M$12, 30 minutes) or taxi (M$65) to Malinalco. Águila buses do not have toilets on board. The weekend-only direct bus from Malinalco to Terminal Poniente runs at 3:50pm and 5:10pm from outside the Santander bank on Hidalgo.

From gate 6 of Toluca's bus station, take a Flecha Roja bus to Tenango (M$30, 1½ hours, every 10 minutes), and from outside the Elektra store take a *colectivo* to Malinalco (M$14, 35 minutes).

Though the distances are short, traveling from Malinalco to Cuernavaca can take hours. It is, however, possible to hire a taxi (M$165, about one hour) and travel between the two towns via the incredibly scenic trip through Puente Caporal–Palpan–Miacatlán to the town of Alpuyeca, near the Xochicalco ruins. From there it's easy to flag one of the frequent buses traveling along Hwy 95, and continue either north (to Cuernavaca and Mexico City) or south (to Taxco and the coast).

Ixtapan de la Sal

☑721 / POP 18,000 / ELEV 1880M

Ixtapan is known throughout Mexico for its curative waters, which have attracted visitors since the town was founded centuries ago by indigenous travelers from the Pacific coast who were amazed to discover salt water inland while on their way to Tenochtitlán. Despite its long history, there's not much to see here and the only reason to stop is to visit **Ixtapan Parque Acuático** (☑800-493-27-26; www.parqueixtapan.com; adult/child Fri-Sun M$220/free, Mon-Thu M$95/free; ⏰spa 8am-7pm, aquatic park 9am-6pm), a sprawling water park mixing curative thermal-water pools with waterfalls, water slides, a wave pool and a miniature railway. There's a range of hotels in town.

Águila buses run from Toluca (M$41, one hour, every 20 minutes) and Taxco (M$51, 1¼ hours, every 45 minutes).

Veracruz

Includes ➡

Veracruz City....... 205
Xalapa 217
Córdoba........... 228
Orizaba........... 232
Tuxpan 236
Papantla.......... 238
El Tajín 240
Tlacotalpan........ 245
Catemaco 250
Reserva de la Biosfera
Los Tuxtlas........ 252

Best Places to Eat

➡ El Brou (p222)

➡ Emilio Bistrot (p212)

➡ Villa Rica Mocambo (p213)

➡ Marrón Cocina Galería (p235)

Best Places to Stay

➡ Mesón del Alférez Xalapa (p221)

➡ Hotel Posada Doña Lala (p246)

➡ Casa Real del Café (p225)

➡ Hotel del Río (p234)

Why Go?

Taking up much of Mexico's Gulf coastline, the long and diverse state of Veracruz is where the Spanish conquest of the Aztecs began. It was also the cradle of the aptly named Veracruz Mesoamerican culture at El Tajín and is home to Mexico's highest peak – soaring, snowcapped Orizaba.

As a destination, it's routinely overlooked by travelers, and while it's true that the beaches are better in the Yucatán and the colonial towns can be more impressive in Mexico's central and western Highlands, Veracruz has a steady supply of charms in both categories. It also lays claim to the World Heritage site of colonial Tlacotalpan, the inspiring Biosphere Reserve of Los Tuxtlas and some gorgeous *pueblos mágicos* (magical villages), including hilly Papantla, cobbled Coscomatepec and the coffee-growing center of Xico.

Its biggest attraction, however, is its quietness. Wherever you go here, you'll find yourself well off the beaten path, with discoveries just waiting to be made.

When to Go
Veracruz City

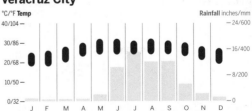

°C/°F Temp — Rainfall inches/mm

Oct Cheap prices, bearable temperatures and barely another tourist in sight.

Feb & Mar The Veracruz Carnaval kicks off the biggest party on Mexico's eastern coast.

Nov–Feb Peak tourist season for non-Mexicans with less rain and balmy temperatures.

Veracruz Highlights

1 Deciphering a triumvirate of Mesoamerican cultures in Xalapa's architecturally magnificent **Museo de Antropología** (p218).

2 Marveling at the many colors of colonial **Tlacotalpan** (p245), perhaps Mexico's least known World Heritage site.

3 Imagining past glories at the extensive ruins of **El Tajín** (p241).

4 Taking a boat across Laguna de Sontecomapan for fresh fish on the beach at **La Barra** (p253).

5 Sipping gourmet coffee in the cloud forest–encased towns of **Coatepec** (p224) or **Xico** (p226).

6 Standing breathless atop the summit of Mexico's highest mountain, magnificent **Pico de Orizaba** (p235).

7 Watching grown men fly at a one-of-a-kind *voladores* (fliers) ceremony in **Papantla** (p239).

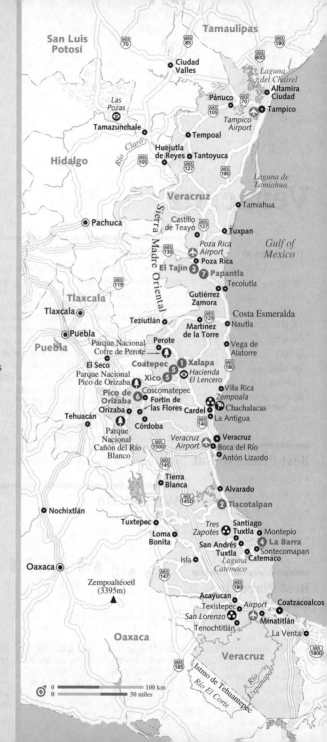

History

The Olmecs, Mesoamerica's earliest known civilization, built their first great center around 1200 BC at San Lorenzo in southern Veracruz state. In 900 BC, the city was violently destroyed, but Olmec culture lingered for several centuries at Tres Zapotes. During the Classic period (AD 250–900), the Gulf coast developed another distinctive culture, known as the Classic Veracruz civilization. Its most important center was El Tajín, which was at its peak between AD 600 and 900. In the post-Classic period the Totonacs established themselves in the region south of Tuxpan. North of Tuxpan, the Huastec civilization flourished from AD 800 to 1200. During this time, the warlike Toltecs also moved into the Gulf coast area. In the mid-15th century, the Aztecs took over most of the Totonac and Huastec areas, exacting tributes of goods and sacrificial victims, and subduing revolts.

When Hernán Cortés arrived in April 1519, he made Zempoala's Totonacs his first allies against the Aztecs by vowing to protect them against reprisals. Cortés set up his first settlement, Villa Rica de la Vera Cruz (Rich Town of the True Cross), and by 1523 all the Gulf coast was in Spanish hands. Forced slavery, newly introduced diseases and the ravages of war severely reduced indigenous populations.

Veracruz harbor became an essential trade and communications link with Spain and was vital for anyone trying to rule Mexico, but the climate, tropical diseases and pirate threats inhibited the growth of Spanish settlements.

Under dictator Porfirio Díaz, Mexico's first railway linked Veracruz to Mexico City in 1872, stimulating industrial development. In 1901, oil was discovered in the Tampico area, and by the 1920s, the region was producing a quarter of the world's oil. In the 1980s, the Gulf coast still held well over half of Mexico's reserves and refining capacity. Today, the region is not as large a player as it used to be, but is still a significant contributor to Mexico's oil economy.

ⓘ Information

DANGERS & ANNOYANCES

Mexico's infamous drug war migrated to Veracruz in early 2011 with nasty gang wars claiming lives in Veracruz City, Boca del Río and Xalapa. At its peak, 35 victims of drug violence were unceremoniously dumped on the street in Veracruz City. This resulted in the dismissal of the entire city police force by the central government on the basis that it had become so infiltrated by the Zetas drug cartel that it was no longer fit for purpose. Things have quietened down since then and, despite some understandably bad press, the state remains relatively safe for travelers, with incidents of drug-related crime against foreign tourists very rare indeed.

The biggest risk to most travelers is petty theft in cheap hotel rooms and pickpocketing in crowded market areas, especially in big cities. Hurricanes threaten between June and November; check out the **US National Hurricane Center website** (www.nhc.noaa.gov) for the latest. Mosquitoes in coastal regions can carry dengue fever, especially in central and southeastern Veracruz.

VERACRUZ CITY

☏ 229 / POP 568,000

Veracruz, like all great port cities, is an unholy mélange of grime, romance and melted-down cultures. Conceived in 1519, this is Mexico's oldest European-founded settlement, but, usurped by subsequent inland cities, it's neither its most historic, nor its most visually striking. Countless sackings by the French, Spanish and North Americans have siphoned off the prettiest buildings, leaving a motley patchwork of working docks and questionable hybrid architecture, punctuated by the odd stray colonial masterpiece. But Veracruz' beauty is in its grit rather than its grandiosity. A carefree spirit reigns in the *zócalo* (main square) most evenings, where the primary preoccupation is who to cajole into a *danzón* (traditional couples dance).

History

Hernán Cortés arrived at the site of present-day Veracruz on Good Friday, April 21, 1519, and began his siege of Mexico. By 1521 he had crushed the Aztec empire.

Veracruz provided Mexico's main gateway to the outside world for 400 years. Invaders and pirates, incoming and outgoing rulers, settlers, silver and slaves – all came and went, making Veracruz a linchpin in Mexico's history. In 1569, English sailor Francis Drake survived a massive Spanish sea attack here. In 1683, vicious Frenchman Laurent de Gaff and his 600 men held Veracruz' 5000 inhabitants captive, killing escapees, looting, drinking and raping. Soon after, they left much richer.

Under bombardment from a French fleet in the Pastry War, General Antonio López de Santa Anna was forced to flee Veracruz in 1838, wearing nothing but his underwear. But the general managed to respond heroically, expelling the invaders. When Winfield Scott's army attacked Veracruz during the Mexican-American War, more than 1000 Mexicans died before the city surrendered.

In 1861, Benito Juárez announced that Mexico couldn't pay its debts to Spain, France and Britain. The British and Spanish planned only to take over Veracruz' customhouse, but retreated on seeing that Frenchman Napoleon III sought to conquer Mexico. After Napoleon III's five-year intervention ended, Veracruz experienced revitalization. Mexico's first railway was built between Veracruz and Mexico City in 1872, and foreign investment poured into the city.

US troops occupied Veracruz in 1914, halting a delivery of German arms to dictator Victoriano Huerta. Later in the Revolution, Veracruz was briefly the capital of the reformist Constitutionalist faction led by Venustiano Carranza.

Today, Veracruz is an important deep-water port, handling exports, manufacturing and petrochemical industries. Tourism, particularly from the domestic sector, is another large income earner.

⊙ Sights

★ Zócalo
PLAZA

Any exploration of Veracruz has to begin in its *zócalo* (also called the Plaza de Armas and Plaza Lerdo), the city's unofficial outdoor 'stage' where inspired organized events overlap with the day-to-day improvization of Mexican life. The handsome public space is framed on three sides by *portales* (arcades), the 17th-century **Palacio Municipal**, and an 18th-century **cathedral**. The level of activity accelerates throughout the day until the evening, when the *zócalo* becomes thick with music, entertainers, merrymakers and bystanders.

★ Museo Histórico Naval
MUSEUM

(☑229-931-40-78; Arista 418; adult M$30, children under 6yr free; ⊙10am-5pm Tue-Sun) Occupying a former naval academy, the Museo

---

THE FOUNDING OF VERACRUZ – MARKS I, II AND III

There is an intriguing murkiness about the first Spanish settlement on mainland America north of Panama.

Popular myth suggests that Hernán Cortés was the first European to arrive in the Veracruz area, but, in truth, fellow Spaniard Juan de Grijalva beat him to it by about six months. Grijalva docked on the Isla de Sacrificios (a short way offshore of Veracruz) in late 1518, where he found evidence of human sacrifice and spent 10 days trading with Mesoamerican natives.

Cortés' more famous flotilla arrived via the Yucatán coast in 1519, and quickly set up a temporary camp on a beach opposite the island of San Juan de Ulúa, on the site of present-day Veracruz. However, a real city wasn't established here for another 80 years. Instead, Cortés and his men quickly abandoned their malaria-ridden camp and trekked 40km north to the Totonac settlement of Zempoala, where they were courted by the corpulent chief, Xicomecoatl, with whom they made a cynical alliance against the Aztecs. Xicomecoatl sent Cortés' entourage 30km further north to the city of Quiahuiztlán with 400 Zempoala-hired porters, where they were met by a population of 15,000 curious citizens. With their ships already docked on the adjacent coast, Cortés was determined to cut legal ties with Diego Velázquez, his overseer in Cuba, and decided to found a town near Quiahuiztlán, declaring himself the legal *adelantado* (governor). Christened Villa Rica de la Vera Cruz (Veracruz Mk I), it consisted of little more than a fort, a chapel and some barracks but, small as it was, it was the first recorded European-founded settlement in North America. Around 1524, due to its limitations as a port, the town was moved south to La Antigua (Veracruz Mk II) and sited several kilometers inland on the banks of the Río Antigua, where small ships could be docked. But as the Spanish empire grew, Antigua's river location made it less practical for larger ships, meaning supplies had to be hauled overland to San Juan de Ulúa, where they often fell prey to smugglers. As a result, around 1599, Veracruz was moved for a third time back to the site of the original encampment on the coast opposite San Juan de Ulúa.

PASEO DEL MALECÓN & BOULEVARD

Veracruz' harbor is a busy oil port with rigs off the coast. While this is unlikely to please tourists' tropical beach holiday desires, it does somehow add to the gritty romanticism of the waterfront walk on the *malecón* (harbor boardwalk). Start at the rows of vendor stalls at the Mercado de Artesanías, which sell a kaleidoscope of souvenirs. Here you'll pass the high-rise **Pemex building** (Paseo del Malecón), which is an early example of modern Mexican architecture and has some interesting murals.

Heading south, the *malecón* becomes a wide pedestrian walkway called the *bulevar* (pronounced 'boo-ley-bar'). Following the coast, it stretches south for roughly 8km and along the way it passes lighthouse piers, statues of famous government figures, and monuments to the city's defenders and sailors who died at sea. Two notable statues are the **statue of the Spanish emigrant** (Paseo del Malecón), celebrating Veracruz' role as a disembarkation point for immigrants, and the **statue of Alexander Von Humboldt** (Blvd Camacho), the German naturalist/explorer who visited the area in 1803–04 and collected important information about the flora and indigenous cultures. All these statues are found within a few hundred meters of one and other close to the port and city center.

Two blocks inland from the *malecón* is the 1998 **Altar a la Patria** (Av 16 de Septiembre), an obelisk marking the buried remains of those who defended Veracruz during its numerous conflicts.

Histórico Naval has had a recent overhaul and some of the dusty old exhibits have become exciting, interactive displays that offer a titanic lesson in Mexico's maritime heritage. Highlights include the ship simulator and the chance to (sort of) pilot a helicopter. There are also exhibits focusing on the US attacks on Veracruz in 1847 and 1914. The in-house cafe offers a place for a quiet rest.

The big drawback for non-Spanish speakers is that most of the displays are only in Spanish.

Museo de la Ciudad de Veracruz   MUSEUM
(Veracruz City Museum; ☑ 229-931-63-55; Av Zaragoza 397; ⊙ 10am-7pm Tue-Fri, 10am-6pm Sat, 10am-3pm Sun) FREE Worth a visit for the charming colonial-era building alone, the Museo de la Ciudad de Veracruz does a good job of recounting the city's history from the pre-Hispanic era, and also gives a feel for the essence of this proud and lively city through explanations of its music, diverse ethnic roots and politics. There is some labeling in English, and plenty of models and dioramas to boot.

The attractive courtyard often hosts cultural experiences such as dance shows, Día de Muertos events and more.

San Juan de Ulúa   FORTRESS, MUSEUM
(☑ 229-938-51-51; adult/student & child M$52/free; ⊙ 9am-4:30pm Tue-Sun) The city's colonial fortress has been almost swallowed up by the modern port, and you have to squint to pick it out amid the container ships and cranes across the harbor. The central part of the fortress was a prison, and a notoriously inhumane one, during the Porfirio Díaz regime. Today, San Juan de Ulúa is an empty ruin of passageways, battlements, bridges and stairways undergoing lengthy renovations. Guided tours are available in Spanish and, quite often, in English.

The fort was originally built on an island that's since been connected to the mainland by a causeway. The earliest fortifications date from 1565 and a young Francis Drake got his comeuppance here in a violent battle in 1569. During the colonial period, the fort and island became the main entry point for Spanish newcomers to Mexico.

To get here, you can take a taxi (M$50) or, weather permitting, a *lancha* (boat taxi; M$30) from the *malecón* (beach promenade).

Entry is free on Sundays.

Baluarte de Santiago   FORTRESS, MUSEUM
(☑ 229-931-10-59; Canal s/n; adult/child M$52/free; ⊙ 10am-4:30pm Tue-Sun) Until 1880, Veracruz was a walled city surrounded by mighty medieval defenses. The Baluarte de Santiago, the only surviving fort of nine, was built in 1526 beside what was then the waterfront. Slowly crumbling, it looks very out of place standing alone on the backstreets of the old town. It's not really worth paying the entry fee to go inside, despite the exhibit of pre-Hispanic gold jewelry that was discovered nearby. You can walk around the outside battlements for free.

It's also sometimes known as El Polvorín.

Veracruz

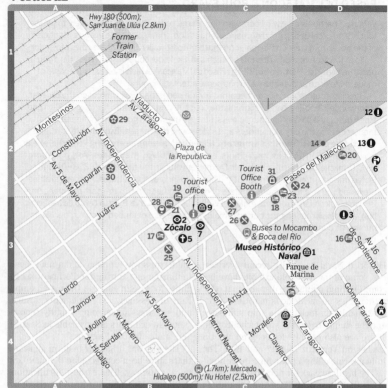

Acuario de Veracruz
AQUARIUM

(☏229-931-10-20; www.acuariodeveracruz.com; Blvd Camacho s/n; adult/child M$120/65, shark feeding M$440/240; ◷10am-7pm Mon-Thu, 10am-7:30pm Fri-Sun) One of Veracruz' biggest attractions and allegedly the best of its kind in Latin America, this aquarium still falls a long way short of similar establishments in the rest of the world. Situated 2km south of the center in a small generic mall on the waterfront, its centerpiece is a large doughnut-shaped tank filled with sharks, rays and turtles that glide around visitors. Brave visitors can don diving gear and enter the shark tank and feed the toothy fish (rather you than us!).

The aquarium also contains a dolphinarium and a manatee exhibit. Aquarium authorities claim they are aiding dolphin and manatee conservation and research, but animal welfare groups around the world claim that such exhibits are cruel.

Fototeca
ARTS CENTER

(☏229-932-87-67; Callejón El Portal de Miranda 9; ◷9am-1pm & 2-7pm Tue-Sun) FREE On the southeast side of the *zócalo*, this small arts center has rotating photographic and video exhibitions. It's spread over three floors of a restored colonial building, though sometimes only the ground floor is operating.

Faro Carranza
LIGHTHOUSE

(Paseo del Malecón) Facing the waterfront on the *malecón*, Faro Carranza comprises a lighthouse and navy offices guarded by a large **statue of Venustiano Carranza**. It was here that the 1917 Mexican Constitution was drafted. Every Monday morning the Mexican navy goes through an elaborate parade ceremony in front of the building.

Museo Agustín Lara
MUSEUM

(☏229-937-02-09; Ruíz Cortines s/n, Boca del Río; adult/student M$20/10; ◷10am-2:30pm & 4-6pm

0 ——— 200 m
0 ——— 0.1 miles

Veracruz Harbor

Veracruz

◎ Top Sights
1 Museo Histórico Naval D3
2 Zócalo B3

◎ Sights
3 Altar a la Patria D3
4 Baluarte de Santiago D4
5 Cathedral B3
6 Faro Carranza D2
7 Fototeca C3
8 Museo de la Ciudad de Veracruz C4
9 Palacio Municipal C3
10 Pemex Building E2
11 Statue of Alexander Von
   Humboldt E2
12 Statue of the Spanish Emigrant D2
13 Statue Venustiano Carranza D2

◯ Activities, Courses & Tours
   Amphibian .... (see 19)
14 Harbor Tours D2
15 Scubaver F4

◯ Sleeping
16 El Faro D3
17 Gran Hotel Diligencias B3
18 Hawaii Hotel C3
19 Hotel Colonial B2
20 Hotel Emporio D2
21 Hotel Imperial B3
22 Mesón del Mar C3
23 Ruíz Milán Hotel C2

⊗ Eating
24 Gran Café de la Parroquia D2
25 Gran Café del Portal B3
   Los Canarios .... (see 20)
26 Mariscos Tano C3
27 Nieves del Malecón C3

◯ Drinking & Nightlife
   Bar El Estribo .... (see 17)
28 Bar Prendes B3

◯ Entertainment
29 Las Barricas B2
30 Teatro Principal Francisco Javier
   Clavijero B2

◯ Shopping
   Libros y Arte Fototeca .... (see 7)
31 Mercado de Artesanías C2

Tue-Fri, 10am-4pm Sat & Sun) A monument to one of Veracruz' most famous musical icons, this museum displays a range of Agustín Lara's personal belongings, furniture and memorabilia in the musician's old city residence. It is situated just off Blvd Camacho, 4km south of the city center.

🏊 Activities

Diving & Snorkeling

You wouldn't expect lucid diving right near such an oil-rigged city, but Veracruz has some pretty good options (including at least one accessible wreck) on the reefs near the offshore islands. Visibility is best in May.

Scubaver   DIVING
(☎ 229-932-39-94; www.scubaver.net; Hernández y Hernández 563; 2 dives M$900) This friendly and centrally located outfit is used to dealing with foreigners.

Veracruz Adventures   DIVING, SNORKELING
(☎ 229-931-53-58; www.veracruzadventures.com; Blvd Camacho 681A; beginner dives from M$990) Dive school offering quality equipment, and diving and snorkeling excursions from the Veracruz area. Guides speak English.

BEACHES & LAGOONS

Inseparable from the *jarocho* (Veracruz) identity is the beach. You'll find pleasant stretches of beach all the way down through Boca del Río. As a rule of thumb, the further from the oil rigs the better, but locals can be seen enjoying them all.

Alternatively, you can find *lanchas* (M$100 Monday to Thursday and M$130 Friday to Sunday) by the aquarium that will take you to **Cancuncito**, a sandbar off the coast touted as the best beach in Veracruz, with light sand and clear water. Another part of the *lancha* beat is the **Isla de Sacrificios**, an island once used for Totonac human sacrifice and later as a leprosy colony. It's now part of a protected nature and marine reserve called **Parque Marino Nacional Sistema Arrecifal Veracruzano**. Sometimes, when tourism is low, *lanchas* aren't to be found, but harbor-tour boats stop there on some tours.

Some 11km from the center, the gritty, off-shoot town of **Boca del Río** has a smattering of brightly colored seafood restaurants overlooking the mouth of the river on Blvd Camacho. *Lanchas* offering boat tours to mangrove forests leave from here. Over the bridge, the coastal road continues about 8km further down the coast from Boca del Río to **Mandinga**, known for its seafood (especially *langostinos bicolores* – two-colored prawns), where you can hire a boat (from the *zona de restaurantes*) to take you around mangrove lagoons rich with wildlife.

Mundosubmarino   DIVING
(☑ 229-980-63-74; www.mundosubmarino.com. mx; Blvd Camacho 3549; beginner dives from M$950) Recommended operator offering day and night dives, plus a range of courses and excursions.

Courses

Language
Immersion School   LANGUAGE COURSE
(☑ 229-931-47-16; www.veracruzspanish.com; Alacio Pérez 61; per week from US$650) This laid-back, North American–owned school offers Spanish courses which focus on learning about the city and its culture. Class sizes are limited to just two people, so you'll get extremely high levels of personal attention, and there's far more than usual included in weekly packages, from immersive trips into the city, to ecotourism and scuba-diving options. Prices are per person and include accommodations, classes and food.

Tours

Amphibian   ADVENTURE
(☑ 229-931-09-97; www.amphibianveracruz.com; Hotel Colonial lobby, Lerdo 117; per person from M$450) In addition to offering activity-based tours, Amphibian also conducts diving and snorkeling trips, rafting expedeitions to nearby rivers, rappelling, and sightseeing excursions.

Aventura Extrema   ADVENTURE
(☑ 229-202-65-57; www.aventuraextrema.com) Offers rappelling, horseback riding, rafting and hiking around Veracruz.

Harbor Tours   BOAT
(☑ 229-935-94-17; www.asdic.com.mx; adult/child from M$90/50; ⊙ 9am-6pm) Boats from the *malecón* offer 45-minute tours of the harbor, plus a variety of other excursions.

Festivals & Events

Carnaval   CARNIVAL
Veracruz erupts into a nine-day party before Ash Wednesday in February or March. Flamboyant parades wind through the city daily, beginning with one devoted to the 'burning of bad humor' and ending with the 'funeral of Juan Carnaval.' Throw in fireworks, dances, salsa and samba music, handicrafts, folklore shows and children's parades, and it adds up to be one of Mexico's greatest fiestas. See the tourist office (p215) for a program of events.

Sleeping

Hotel prices vary greatly according to demand and can shift from day to day at busy times (mid-July to mid-September, Carnaval, Semana Santa, Christmas and New Year). Book in advance for these times and be aware that prices may increase by 10% to 40%. Out of season there are big savings to be made. When choosing where to stay, bear in mind that while it's entertaining, the *zócalo* can be loud at night.

Oyster Hostel
HOSTEL $

(✆ 229-931-06-76; Xicotencatl 1076 Col. Flores Magon; incl breakfast dm from M$150, d M$390; ❄ 🛜) Smart, bright, clean and well-run, with an often fun-loving crowd in residence and clued-up management, the Oyster Hostel is currently the best backpackers in town. The breakfast spread is unusually good for this price band and it's close to the waterfront and walking distance to many of the town's sights. Dorms have a maximum of six beds.

Nu Hotel
HOTEL $

(✆ 229-937-09-17; www.nuhotel.com.mx; Av La Fragua 1066; s/d M$500/550; P ⊖ ❄ 🛜) The Nu has pitched itself amid the scruffy next-to-bus-station hovels and declared war. It's no contest really, especially at these prices. Savor the clean, minimalist-chic rooms; young, casual staff; and cool downstairs cafe. The only real drawback is the location, 3km south of the *zócalo,* which isn't really handy for anything – except the buses, of course.

El Faro
HOTEL $

(✆ 229-931-65-38; Av 16 de Septiembre 223; r M$350-400, q M$550; ❄ 🛜) This no-frills place is a central budget option, just a short wander from the seafront. Room prices go up depending on the size and number of beds, and the cheaper ones can be very dark, with no natural daylight. That said, it's clean, safe and in the heart of the city.

The receptionist speaks excellent English.

Counter Culture Party Hostel
HOSTEL $

(✆ 229-260-25-73, 299-242-60-31; Xicoténcatl 1835, btwn Enríquez & Pérez; dm/r from M$175/$330; ❄ 🛜) If good times and chilled vibes matter more than cleanliness and order, then the Party Hostel is *the* place to come in Veracruz. With no curfew and cheap beer available from the bar, it's all about boozy fun here. There are bus excursions to nightspots every Thursday, Friday and Saturday night, while communal dinners ensure you'll make friends very quickly.

★ Mesón del Mar
BOUTIQUE HOTEL $$

(✆ 229-932-50-43; www.mesondelmar.com.mx; Morales 543; r from M$500; ❄ 🛜) This colonial charmer boasts friendly staff, well cared for rooms with tall ceilings (many have mezzanines with extra sleeping spaces) and buckets of local atmosphere. Balconies, beautifully tiled bathrooms, ceiling fans

and wooden furniture all add to the mix, and while calling it a boutique hotel may be slightly overstating the case, this is certainly Veracruz' best midrange option.

Hawaii Hotel
HOTEL $$

(✆ 229-989-88-88; www.hawaiihotel.com.mx; Paseo del Malecón 458; s/d/tr M$700/800/1000; P ❄ 🛜 ❄) Who knows why it's called the Hawaii Hotel? The 30-room hotel looks more like the prow of a boat, with a marble and white decor inside. However, it's the best value on the *malecón,* and some of the spacious, sunlight-filled rooms have marvelous views. Extras such as hairdryers and fridges make for a comfortable stay.

Hotel Imperial
HISTORIC HOTEL $$

(✆ 229-931-34-70, 229-932-12-04; www.hotelimperialveracruz.com; Lerdo 153; r/ste from M$600/900; ⊖ ❄ 🛜 ❄) Claiming to be the oldest hotel in the Americas, the Imperial has been open nonstop since 1793. And while its ornate public areas (check out the elevator!) will certainly please colonial history buffs, everything else about the place is a bit of a letdown and rather shabby.

Hotel Colonial
HOTEL $$

(✆ 229-932-01-93; www.hcolonial.com.mx; Lerdo 117; r M$595-960; P ❄ 🛜 ❄) Dated and confusingly sprawling, the Colonial continues to rest on its main laurel – a central *zócalo* location. With a curious blend of colonial and 1970s styles splashed in terracotta-orange paint, the artex-wallpapered rooms are somewhat musty, but have all the basic comforts you need, and some have great views.

Not surprisingly given the location, the rooms can be noisy, but the hotel has so many nooks and crannies that it's easy to secure a more tranquil escape at the back.

Ruíz Milán Hotel
HOTEL $$

(✆ 229-932-37-77; www.ruizmilan.com; cnr Paseo del Malecón & Gómez Farías; r/ste from M$750/$840; P ❄ 🛜) This aging, but smartened up property on the *malecón* offers decent value, comfortable rooms and friendly staff who work hard to make guests feel welcome. Rooms are spacious and have been gradually improved by management, and yet deals (as low as M$500 per night) can still be had in low season.

★ Hotel Emporio
LUXURY HOTEL $$$

(✆ 229-932-00-20; www.hotelesemporio.com/veracruz; Paseo del Malecón 244; r from M$1873; P ⊖ ❄ 🛜 ❄) Hands down the best hotel in

Veracruz. The whole place is shot through with arty touches and the rooms are spacious, each with their own large balcony and beautifully appointed bathroom. There's also three pools, a gym, a cocktail bar and a dynamite location on the liveliest stretch of the *malecón,* with the historic Gran Café de la Parroquia (p213) next door.

Out of season deals can see prices drop 40% on the listed rack rates.

Gran Hotel Diligencias   LUXURY HOTEL **$$$**
(☑800-505-55-95, 229-923-02-80; www.gran hoteldiligencias.com; Av Independencia 1115; r from M$1340; 🅿❄❅🛜💱) The fanciest option on the *zócalo* has a smart lobby full of fresh flowers and abuzz with livery-clad bellhops. Upstairs the huge rooms deliver solid old-fashioned elegance, if not personality, though touches such as coffeemakers and remodeled bathrooms sweeten the deal. You'll find more atmosphere downstairs in the adjoining El Estribo Bar and Villa Rica restaurant.

✖ Eating

Two main factors strongly influence Veracruz cooking: its location by the ocean and its role as a port. The first factor means there's an abundance of seafood. The second has made it a melting pot for various foreign cultures and dishes.

Using seafood and the pre-Hispanic diet of beans, corn and squash as a base, the local cuisine has absorbed Spanish and Afro-Caribbean influences over the last five centuries to create such genre-blending dishes as *huachinango a la veracruzana* (red snapper in a spicy tomato sauce), *arroz a la tumbada* (a kind of paella-like soup) and *pollo encacahuatado* (chicken in a peanut sauce). Excellent seafood can be procured anywhere, but the condensed strip of *palapas* (thatched-roof shelters) on the *malecón* just south of the aquarium has made it their (sometimes expensive) specialty.

The *zócalo* cafes under the ever-lively, music-filled *portales* are popular spots for drinks and food. They all offer the same tasty, price-hiked varieties. Cheaper and better alternatives nearby include an array of late-night restaurants with outdoor seating on Molina and Avenida Zaragoza (mains M$40 to M$60). You can also join *jarochos* (inhabitants of Veracruz) in the mazes of **Mercado Hidalgo** (⊙8am-3pm Mon-Fri), where you can find nooks that serve cheap, delectable local favorites like *cocteles de mariscos* (seafood

cocktails), *mondongo* (prepared cow stomach) and delicious *moles.*

Mariscos Tano   SEAFOOD **$**
(Molina 20; meals M$35-100; ⊙9am-10pm) A rehearsal room for a trio of *jarocho* musicians, Tano, which has been in business since 1967, is crammed with faded 1970s photos of the owner posing with Vegas girls. While cleanliness might leave a little to be desired and the food, while tasty, is certainly not haute cuisine, there's a real salt-of-the-sea Veracruz atmosphere with a *son* (folk music) soundtrack.

Nieves del Malecón   ICE CREAM **$**
(☑229-931-70-99; www.nievesdelmalecon.com; Av Zaragoza 286; scoops from M$20; ⊙8am-midnight) *Jarochos* prefer sorbets *(nieves)* over ice cream and this is one of the town's sorbet favorites, sandwiched between the *malecón* and the *zócalo.* Loquacious 'callers' stand outside drumming up business, competing with a rival place (with its own 'callers') directly across the street. Try the delicious mamey (apple) flavor, or opt for the Veracruz staple, vanilla.

★Emilio Bistrot   SEAFOOD **$$**
(☑229-931-13-06; Av 16 de Septiembre 1394; mains M$100-200; ⊙1:30-6:30pm Sun-Mon, 1:30-10:30pm Tue & Wed, 1:30pm-midnight Thu-Sat) Little known (for the moment anyway) by tourists, Emilio's is adored by locals who enjoy the clean, contemporary yet intimate feel of the place and creative dishes that mix Mexican, Italian (although to be honest the pasta isn't great) and old Spanish flavors. Highlights are Galician-style octopus tacos, the ceviche and sweet-tooth pleasing desserts.

Bistro Marti   FRENCH **$$**
(☑229-213-95-73; Calle Magallanes 213; lunch menu from M$95, mains M$100-200; ⊙1-11:30pm Tue-Fri, 5pm-midnight Sat, 1-7pm Sun) This highly regarded French restaurant, with just a hint of Italian to it, serves a seasonally changing menu that can be loaded with treats, such as delicately presented scallops or classic mussels in white wine sauce, as well as more unusual items such as cheese soup. The setting manages to be romantic, modern and cozy all at once.

Los Canarios   SPANISH, MEXICAN **$$**
(☑229-989-33-00; Paseo del Malecón 224; meals M$75-270; ⊙1-11pm; ❄🍴) With large windows overlooking the *malecón,* it's hard to

resist this fancy place in the super-smart Hotel Emporio. Slink inside and reacquaint yourself with à la mode Spanish cooking, mixed, of course, with a few Mexican inflections. The paella's excellent, the breaded chicken is unusually succulent, and the service doesn't miss a beat.

The hungry should watch out for the seafood buffet (M$250) served all day Friday to Sunday.

Gran Café del Portal   INTERNATIONAL **$$**

(☑229-931-27-59; Av Independencia 1187; mains M$60-190, menu from M$100; ☉7am-midnight; ☎) This smart and impressively decorated place just off the *zócalo* is actually quite relaxed despite its surface formality. Indeed, service can be positively laid-back, though the deft aim of the coffee/milk-pouring waiters is as precise as any you'll find in Veracruz. Full meals are available, as well as the mainstays of milky coffee and sweet pastries.

★**Villa Rica Mocambo**   SEAFOOD **$$$**

(☑229-922-21-13; www.villaricamocambo.com. mx; Calz Mocambo 527, Boca del Río; mains M$160-350; ☉11am-10pm Sun-Wed, to midnight Thu-Sat) For those on short itineraries, there aren't many reasons to make the pilgrimage to Boca del Río. But food – and this restaurant in particular – could swing it. Fish is the all-encompassing ingredient, from charcoal-grilled octopus to stuffed sea bass, and the beachside service is attentive. More than a few people say it serves the best seafood in Veracruz.

Mardel   ARGENTINIAN **$$$**

(☑229-937-56-42; www.mardel.com.mx; Blvd Camacho 2632; mains M$120-350; ☉7am-11pm Mon-Sat, 8am-11pm Sun; ☎) Owned by a retired Argentine football player, this upscale restaurant has a great seafront position and specializes in rib-eye steaks. There are also Mexican and Spanish influences on the extensive menu, but regulars advise sticking to the staple: a perfectly cooked slab of cow. The TVs showing sports can be a distraction or a delight, depending on your point of view.

 Drinking & Nightlife

The *portales* cafes are drinking strongholds. But head south some distance on the *malecón* and you'll find the majority of the city's fast-paced and ever-changing nightlife.

Bar El Estribo   BAR

(☑229-923-02-80; Av Independencia 1115; ☉9am-late) For close on two hundred years the highbrow Bar El Estribo, which is a part of the Gran Hotel Diligencia, has been keeping the good people of Veracruz lubricated. Smartly turned out waiters serve up a wide selection of drinks and snacks.

Bar Prendes   BAR

(Lerdo; ☉9am-late) For a front-row seat for whatever's happening in the *zócalo* on any given night, look no further than Prendes; its trendy modern furniture occupies a prize slice of real estate under the *portales*. Beers come in long tubes with taps at the bottom for groups.

GRAN CAFÉ DE LA PARROQUIA

To say that Veracruz' greatest 'sight' is a cafe might seem like a slur on this grizzled port city's reputation, but walk into the **Gran Café de la Parroquia** (☑229-932-25-84; www. laparroquia.com; Gómez Farías 34; mains M$40-180; ☉6am-midnight) – over two centuries old – and the penny will quickly drop. With its immense but un-showy interior, the Parroquia pulls in anything from 2000 to 4000 customers a day, and every facet of Veracruz' diverse personality is on show here. Patrons hold court, make noise and, more significantly, tap their spoons on their coffee glasses. The spoon-tapping – a Parroquia tradition dating from the 1890s – is to attract the attention of the ultra-professional waiters. Gliding like ballet dancers between the tables, they carry two huge steaming jugs, one filled with coffee and the other with hot milk. The de rigueur drink in the Parroquia is *lechero*, a milky coffee brought to your table as an espresso measure in the bottom of a glass. Tap your spoon on the glass rim and – hey presto – a white-jacketed waiter quickly appears, extends his jug high in the air, and fills your glass with scientific precision.

The Parroquia has inspired some spin-offs in recent years (including one right next door which some people confuse with the original), but none come close to matching the atmosphere and spirit of the original on Veracruz' Paseo del Malecón. It also serves meals but they're pretty so-so.

DANZÓN DAYS

It's hard to wander far in Veracruz without stumbling into a plaza-full of romantic *jarochos* indulging in the city's favorite pastime, the *danzón*. An elegant tropical dance, it melds influences of the French contradance with the rhythms of African slaves.

As with most Latin American dances, the *danzón* has its roots in Cuba. It was purportedly 'invented' in 1879 by popular band leader Miguel Failde, who showcased his catchy dance composition *Las Alturas de Simpson* in the port city of Matanzas. Elegant and purely instrumental in its early days, the *danzón* required dancers to circulate in couples rather than groups, a move which scandalized white polite society of the era. By the time the dance arrived in Mexico, brought by Cuban immigrants in the 1890s, it had become more complex, expanding on its peculiar syncopated rhythm, and adding other instruments such as the conga to form an *orquesta típica*.

Though the *danzón* faded in popularity in Cuba in the 1940s and '50s with the arrival of the *mambo* and the *chachachá,* in Mexico it continued to flourish. Indeed, since the 1990s the *danzón* has undergone a huge revival in Veracruz, particularly among mature citizens. The bastion of the dance is the *zócalo* on Friday and Saturday evenings, and if you hang out on the square for long it's quite probable that someone will whisk you off your feet and make you join in (which can be something of a mixed blessing).

Entertainment

Of course, there are always marimbas and mariachis on the *zócalo*. And the coastline boulevard is known as *la barra más grande del mundo* (the biggest bar in the world), *barra* referring both to the sandbar and the drinks bar. During holiday times, it's an outdoor party with live music and dancing in the streets. Many venues line Blvd Camacho.

Teatro Principal
Francisco Javier Clavijero THEATER
(☑ 229-200-22-47; Emparán 166) This theater has a long history and has had many incarnations. It moved here in 1819 and adopted its current architectural style (French neo-classical with some tremendous mosaics) in 1902. The latest refurb was in 2011. Plays, musicals and classical concerts are performed here.

Las Barricas LIVE MUSIC, CLUB
(Constitución 72; cover Fri, Sat & for live music M$50-120; ⊙2pm-4am Mon-Sat) This *jarocho*-recommended live-music venue and club plays a variety of music: reggaeton, salsa, pop, rock etc. It's on the small side, so expect to be packed in with the raucous, jovial crowd, especially on weekends.

La Casona de la Condesa CLUB
(Blvd Camacho 1520; cover Fri & Sat M$30-60; ⊙10pm-5am Tue-Sun) La Casona attracts an older (ie not teenage) crowd and offers solid live music at night, and at other times even hosts occasional art exhibitions. It is situated close to the seafront, 5km south from the city center on Blvd Camacho.

Shopping

Avenida Independencia is the city's main shopping thoroughfare. Souvenirs are best procured at the Mercado de Artesanías on the *malecón*. You can buy cheap bottles of vanilla here and good-quality coffee. Jewelry – especially silver – is also economical and sometimes engraved with interesting Aztec/Maya motifs.

Mercado de Artesanías MARKET
(Paseo del Malecón) Souvenir city populates 30-plus tiny adjacent booths that line the stretch of the *malecón* closest to the *zócalo*, selling everything from T-shirts to vanilla.

Libros y Arte Fototeca BOOKS
(☑229-934-22-33; Callejón El Portal de Miranda 9; ⊙10am-1pm & 2-7pm Tue-Sun) Inside the Fototeca building on the corner of the *zócalo,* this place has good regional and international selections.

Information

There's a cluster of banks with ATMs a block north of the *zócalo;* ATMs are generally widely available throughout the city. Most banks change US dollars, and some change euros as well.

Card phones proliferate around the *zócalo*.

There's a 24-hour facility in the 2nd-class terminal of the bus station.

Ambulance, Fire & Police (☑066)

Beneficencia Española (☎229-262-23-00; www.benever.com.mx; Av 16 de Septiembre 955) A hospital that can offer general medical services to visitors to Mexico.

Hospital Regional (☎229-931-29-23; Av 20 de Noviembre 1074) General hospital.

Post Office (Plaza de la República 213) A five-minute walk north of the *zócalo*.

Tourist office (☎229-922-95-33; http://veracruz.mx; Palacio Municipal; ◷8am-3pm) Has helpful staff and plenty of maps and brochures. There's another small booth (cnr Paseo del Malecón & Arista; ◷9am-9pm) at the far western end of the Mercado de Artesanías.

ⓘ Getting There & Away

AIR

Veracruz International Airport (VER; www.asur.com.mx) is 18km southwest of the center, near Hwy 140. Frequent flights to Monterrey, Villahermosa, Mérida, Cancún and Mexico City are offered by Aeroméxico (www.aeromexico.com), Aeromar (www.aeromar.com.mx) and MAYair (www.mayair.com.mx), in addition to a handful of other national airlines. Direct flights to/from Houston are offered by United (www.united.com.)

BUS

Veracruz is a major hub, with good services up and down the coast and inland along the Córdoba–Puebla–Mexico City corridor. Buses to and from Mexico City can be heavily booked at holiday times.

Bus Station (Av Díaz Mirón, btwn Tuero Molina & Orizaba) The bus station is located 3km south of the *zócalo* and has ATMs. The 1st-class/deluxe area is in the part of the station closest to Calle Orizaba. For more frequent, slightly cheaper and slower 2nd-class services, enter on the other side from Avenida Lafragua. There's a 24-hour luggage room here.

CAR & MOTORCYCLE

Local and international car-rental agencies have desks at Veracruz airport. There are also some other agencies scattered around town. Rates start at M$350 per day.

ⓘ Getting Around

Veracruz airport is small, modern and well organized, with a cafe and several shops. There's no bus service to or from town; official taxis cost M$250 to the *zócalo*. You must buy a ticket upfront from a booth in the arrivals hall, which helps to avoid being ripped off. Going the other way, just M$120 is the going rate, but agree on a price before you get in.

To get downtown from the 1st-class bus station, take a bus marked 'Díaz Mirón y Madero' (M$10). It will head to Parque Zamora then up Avenida Madero. For the *zócalo*, get off on the corner of Avenida Madero and Lerdo and turn right. Returning to the bus stations, pick up the same bus going south on Avenida 5 de Mayo. Booths in the 1st- and 2nd-class stations sell taxi tickets to the center (*zócalo* area; M$40 to M$45). In the tourist office, you can get a summary sheet of official taxi-ride costs, which

BUSES FROM VERACRUZ CITY

Daily first-class ADO departures from Veracruz.

Buses also go to Campeche, Cancún, Chetumal, Matamoros, Mérida, Nuevo Laredo and Salina Cruz.

DESTINATION	FARE (M$)	DURATION (HR)	FREQUENCY (DAILY)
Catemaco	180	3½	hourly
Córdoba	132-146	1½	frequent
Mexico City	420-620	5½-6	frequent
Oaxaca	590	7½	4
Orizaba	160-170	2½	frequent
Papantla	256	4	3
Puebla	328-424	3½-4	12
San Andrés Tuxtla	164	3	6
Santiago Tuxtla	168	2½	12
Tampico	594	8½	5
Tuxpan	334	5	frequent
Villahermosa	540-618	7½	frequent
Xalapa	from 128	2	frequent

is helpful for guarding against tourist price inflation.

Buses marked 'Mocambo-Boca del Río' (M$10 to Boca del Río) leave regularly from the corner of Avenida Zaragoza and Serdán, near the *zócalo;* they go via Parque Zamora and Blvd Camacho to Playa Mocambo (20 minutes) and on to Boca del Río (30 minutes). AU buses also go there from the 2nd-class station.

CENTRAL VERACRUZ

Curvy Hwy 180 follows the coast past dark-sand beaches to Cardel, where Hwy 140 branches west to Xalapa, the state capital. Charming mountain towns sprinkle the inland volcanic ranges, which are laced with dramatic river gorges. From Veracruz, Hwy 150D heads southwest to Córdoba, Fortín de las Flores and Orizaba, on the edge of the Sierra Madre.

Central Coast

The beaches north of the city of Veracruz are a popular Mexican vacation spot, and the area also boasts the impressive Zempoala ruins.

Zempoala

✓ 296 / POP 9400

The impressive pre-Hispanic Totonac town of Zempoala (or Cempoala) is little visited by non-Mexican tourists, but well rewards the minor effort of getting to it. It's 42km north of Veracruz and 4km west of Hwy 180 in modern Zempoala. The turnoff is by a Pemex station 7km north of Cardel. There's a *voladores* pole and performances are enacted sporadically – normally during Semana Santa and holidays. Zempoala is most easily reached through Cardel – take a bus marked 'Zempoala' (M$12) from beside Hotel Cardel, or a taxi (M$70).

History

Zempoala became a major Totonac center after about AD 1200 and fell to the Aztecs in the mid-15th century. The 30,000-person town had defensive walls, underground water and drainage pipes. As Hernán Cortés approached the town, one of his scouts reported that the buildings were made of silver – but it was only white paint shining in the sun.

Zempoala's chief – a corpulent fellow nicknamed *el cacique gordo* (the fat chief) by the Spanish – struck an alliance with Cortés for protection against the Aztecs. But his hospitality didn't stop the Spanish from smashing statues of his gods and lecturing his people on the virtues of Christianity. It was at Zempoala in 1520 that Cortés defeated the expedition sent by Cuba's Spanish governor to arrest him.

A smallpox epidemic in 1575–77 decimated Zempoala and most of the survivors moved to Xalapa. By the 17th century the town was abandoned. The present town dates from 1832. Townsfolk fled from here in 1955 during category 5 Hurricane Janet, which caused further damage to the ruins.

◉ Sights

Zempoala
Archaeological Site   ARCHAEOLOGICAL SITE
(M$52; ⊙9am-6pm) The Zempoala (Cempoala) Archaeological Site is a quiet and fairly impressive site, with a lovely mountain backdrop. The monuments at the site have undergone extensive renovation works. Although this makes it easier to see what everything once was, it has erased any real sense of romance from the place. Most of the buildings are faced with smooth, rounded, riverbed stones, but many were originally plastered and painted. A typical feature is battlement-like 'teeth' called *almenas.*

There are four Spanish-speaking guides at the site who give explanations for free (tips recommended). Roberto del Moral Moreno is the only one who knows some English. He charges approximately M$100 per tour. The small site **museum** has some interesting clay figurines, polychrome plates and obsidian flints; it's best to check it out first.

The **Templo Mayor** (Main Temple), uncovered in 1972, is an 11m-high pyramid with a wide staircase ascending to the remains of a shrine. When they first encountered Zempoala, Cortés and his men lodged in **Las Chimeneas**, whose hollow columns were thought to be chimneys – hence the name.

The circle of stones in the middle of the site is the **Circulo de los Guerreros**, where lone captured soldiers battled against groups of local warriors. Few won.

There are two main structures on the west side. One is known as the **Templo del**

Sol and has two stairways climbing its front side in typical Toltec-Aztec style. The sun god was called Tonatiun and sacrifices were offered to him here on the **Piedra de Sacrificios**. The 'fat chief,' officially known as Xicomacatl, sat facing the macabre spectacle on the appropriately large **altar**.

To its north, the second structure is the **Templo de la Luna**, with a structure similar to Aztec temples to the wind god, Ehecatl.

East of Las Chimeneas is **Las Caritas** (Little Heads), named for niches that once held several small pottery heads.

Another large temple to the wind god, known as the **Templo Dios del Aire**, is in the town itself – go back south on the site entrance road, cross the main road in town and then go around the corner to the right. The ancient temple, with its characteristic circular shape, is beside an intersection.

🛈 Getting There & Away

The bus from Cardel (M$15) drops you right outside the entrance to the archaeological site.

La Antigua

🚍 296 / POP 990

The city of Veracruz' second incarnation (1525–99) reveals little of its past identity with its languid grid of sleepy, cobbled streets and moss-covered ruins. People still live here, but it's a backwater these days, albeit a pleasant one, and worth a detour for its historical significance and good seafood.

A Spanish settlement was established here in 1525, and it's rumored that this is where conquistador Cortés moored his boats to a ceiba tree. The tree – gnarly and gigantic – is still standing. The eye-catching ruined building, half-strangled by tree roots and vines, is a 16th-century custom house, sometimes erroneously called the 'Casa de Cortés.' The tiny walled Ermita del Rosario church, probably dating from 1523, is considered to be the oldest in the Americas.

Lanchas will motor you along the pleasant Río Antigua for around M$50 to M$100 per person, depending on how many people want to go.

Along the river there's a cluster of seafood restaurants. At the end of the row, adjacent to a pedestrian-only suspension bridge, the celebrated **Las Delicias Marinas** (🚍296-971-60-38; Río Huitzilapan waterfront; mains M$90-200; ⏰10:30am-7:30pm)

serves exquisite fresh and saltwater fish that could emulate anything in Veracruz. The charcoal-grilled octopus has to be tasted to be believed. There's music and dance entertainment here at weekends.

Colectivo taxis charge M$6 to M$10 from the village to the highway 1km away, where buses to Veracruz and Cardel pass every 15 minutes or so. Flag down the driver just north of the toll booth.

Xalapa

🚍 228 / POP 425,000 / ELEV 1427M

Familiar to the world primarily due to the super hot, green chili that was named after it, Xalapa (also spelled Jalapa, but always pronounced ha-*la*-pa) is actually about as different to the fiery jalapeño pepper as can be – unlike sweaty coastal Veracruz city, Xalapa's highland location makes it temperate and often quite cloudy. Coolness defines the city in other ways too: this is Mexico in an Afghan coat with a heavy literary tome under its arm, thanks to a large alternative and student population. The city is lively at night and has a thriving cultural scene (it has its own branch of the Hay Festival of Literature & the Arts, for example). Most people are surprised to learn that it's Xalapa and not Veracruz city that's the state capital.

Xalapa is a traffic-asphyxiated place, whose unattractive urban sprawl gives way to a far more alluring state, full of well-kept parks, bustling pedestrian streets and colonial architecture. The superb anthropological museum is the main pull for visitors here, but the gargantuan pre-Hispanic relics are supplemented by hip bars, weighty bookstores and a superb array of quality coffee joints, making this one of Mexico's most enjoyable state capitals.

History

Founded by Totonacs in the early 1200s, Xalapa was part of the Aztec empire when Hernán Cortés and his men passed through in 1519. Because of its appealing climate and location, Spain strategically placed a monastery here to proselytize to the indigenous population. By the 17th century it had evolved into a commercial axis and meeting hub. Today Xalapa is still a commercial center for coffee, tobacco and flowers.

Xalapa

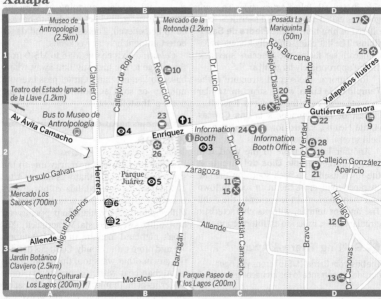

◉ Sights

★ **Museo de Antropología** MUSEUM
(☏228-815-09-20; Av Xalapa s/n; adult/student M$50/25, audio guide M$23; ☺9am-5pm Tue-Sun) Set in spacious gardens on the west side of Avenida Xalapa, 4km northwest of the center, the building that encases this remarkable museum (containing Mexico's second-finest archaeological collection) is a work of art in its own right – a series of interconnecting galleries that fall like a regal staircase down the side of a lush hill. Viewing archaeological treasures has rarely been this pleasurable. As there's so much to see, allow yourself a good chunk of time to visit.

The exhibits' scale and breadth rival the museum's intricate layout. Three key Gulf coast pre-Hispanic civilizations are represented – namely the Olmecs, the Totonacs and the Huastecs – and the exhibits are presented chronologically within their sections, with clearly labeled explanations in Spanish. Laminated English information sheets are attached to the wall at the entrance to each new room, but a good audio guide in English (bring ID to leave as collateral) explains the most important items in detail. Several spaces concentrate on the Olmec culture from southern Veracruz, from which comes the most celebrated piece, the sculpture *El señor de las Limas*. There's also an array of fine work associated with the pre-Hispanic ball game.

There's a small cafe on the upper floor and a truly excellent bookstore, while the walk back up the hill through the beautifully kept garden is a delight.

To get there, take a 'Camacho-Tesorería' bus (M$8) from the corner of Enríquez and Parque Juárez. To return, take a bus marked 'Centro.' A taxi costs M$30.

Parque Juárez PLAZA
Xalapa's centrally located main square feels like a terrace, with its south side overlooking the valley below and the snowcapped cone of Pico de Orizaba beckoning in the distance. Greener and better kept than most other plazas in Mexico, you'll find monkey puzzle trees and manicured hedges among the shoe-shiners, balloon sellers and wandering minstrels.

On the plaza's north side is the 1855 neoclassical **Palacio Municipal** (Av Enríquez) and on the east side is the **Palacio de Gobierno** (Parque Juárez), the seat of Veracruz' state government. The Palacio de Gobierno has a fine mural by Mario Orozco Rivera depicting the history of justice above the stairway near the eastern entrance on Enríquez.

Parroquia de San José (200m);
Galería de Arte Contemporáneo (500m);
Central de Autobuses de Xalapa (2.3km);
Azteca (2:8km)

Xalapa

◎ Sights
1 Catedral Metropolitana......................B2
2 Museo Casa de Xalapa.......................B3
3 Palacio de Gobierno C2
4 Palacio Municipal.............................B2
5 Parque Juárez B2
6 Pinacoteca Diego Rivera....................B3

⊕ Activities, Courses & Tours
7 Escuela para Estudiantes
    Extranjeros E1
8 Veraventuras..................................F2

⊟ Sleeping
9 Hostal de la Niebla..........................D2
10 Hotel Limón B1
11 Mesón del Alférez Xalapa C2
12 Posada Casa Regia..........................D3
13 Posada del Cafeto...........................D3

✕ Eating
14 El Brou.......................................E1
15 La Candela...................................C2
16 La Fonda.....................................C2
17 Piacevole Bistro D1
18 Plazoleta E2

○ Drinking & Nightlife
19 Angelo Casa de Té D2
20 Café Cali C1
21 Cubanías.....................................D2
22 Espresso 58 ....D2
23 Gran Café de la Parroquia B2
24 Jugos California C2

✪ Entertainment
25 Centro Recreativo Xalapeño D1
26 El Ágora......................................B2
27 Tierra Luna F3

⊙ Shopping
28 Café Colón D2

Catedral Metropolitana CATHEDRAL
(cnr Enríquez & Revolución) An unfinished masterpiece, Xalapa's cathedral lacks a second tower but still impresses with its scale and grandiosity. Moreover, rather than compensating for its steep hillside position, the architecture makes full use of it to inspire awe as you enter, forcing you to raise your head to see the altar and giant crucifix centerpiece. A mélange of neo-Gothic and baroque, the church contains the remains of St Rafael Guízar y Valencia, beatified by Pope John Paul II in 1995.

Parque Paseo de los Lagos PARK
(Zona Universitaria) ◢ Xalapans escape the monstrous traffic just south of Parque Juárez in this serendipitous park which has 3km of delightful lakeside paths, most commonly used for jogging (and making out). At its northern end is the **Centro Cultural Los Lagos** (☎228-812-12-99; Paseo de los Lagos s/n), a lovely cultural center; check out the bulletin board to find out about cultural events and drop-in dance or yoga classes.

Pinacoteca Diego Rivera GALLERY
(☎228-818-18-19; Herrera 5; ⊙10am-7pm Tue-Sat) FREE Tucked beneath the west side of the plaza, this small gallery houses a modest collection of Rivera's works, as well as

pieces from other Mexican artists. There's excellent coffee to be had at the Jarocho-style Café outside.

Parque Ecológico Macuiltépetl PARK
(⊙5am-7pm) Atop a hill north of the city, this 40-hectare park is actually the heavily wooded cap of an extinct volcano. Spiraling to the top, the park's paths are a treasure for the city's robust fraternity of joggers, and provide expansive views of Xalapa and the surrounding area.

Museo Casa de Xalapa MUSEUM
(☎228-841-98-02; Herrera 7; ⊙10am-7pm Tue-Sun) FREE For a quick exposé of Xalapan history, head to this museum in an old colonial

house close to Parque Juárez. It's small, but lovingly put together.

Galería de Arte Contemporáneo
GALLERY

(☑tel, info 228-817-03-86; Xalapeños Ilustres 135; ⊙9am-6pm Tue-Sun) FREE The town's contemporary art gallery is in a renovated colonial building 1km east of the center. Showing an interesting range of temporary exhibitions and some ceramics, there's also a small movie theater that screens art-house films, mostly for free.

Parroquia de San José
CHURCH

(cnr Xalapeños Ilustres & Arieta) In the learned San José quarter, this church dates from 1770 and confirms Xalapa's penchant for asymmetrical one-towered religious edifices. Architecturally, it displays an unusual blend of baroque and Mudejar styles, including some horseshoe arches. Directly behind is the Mercado Alcalde y García, a covered market spiced up with some cool cafe-restaurants in the lower levels.

Jardín Botánico Clavijero
PARK

(Antigua Carretera a Coatepec Km 2.5; ⊙9am-5pm) Southwest of the town center, this attractive park has an expansive collection of subtropical and cloud-forest plants. The pines are particularly prolific.

🏃 Activities

Local tour operators offer cultural trips to outlying towns and archaeological sites, and also provide easygoing sports-oriented outdoor excursions such as hiking, rafting and rappelling.

Bird-Watching
BIRD-WATCHING

(☑228-818-18-94; straub_robert@yahoo.com) Local bird-watching guide Robert Straub, a

---

VERACRUZ' MESOAMERICAN CULTURES

Several pre-Hispanic cultures inhabited Mexico's central Gulf coast. Here's a brief who's who.

Olmec Often referred to as the 'mother culture' of the civilizations that followed, the Olmecs invented many of Mesoamerica's cultural hallmarks, including colossal stone heads carved from basalt boulders, the legendary Mesoamerican ball game and the macabre practice of human sacrifice. As early agriculturists, they emerged in southern Veracruz and Tabasco in the regional centers of San Lorenzo (35km southeast of Acayucan), La Venta (in present-day Tabasco) and, later, Tres Zapotes. Their culture flourished from around 1200–900 BC in San Lorenzo and from about 800–400 BC in La Venta.

Classic Veracruz The Classic period (AD 250–900) saw the rise of a number of statelets with a shared culture, together known as the Classic Veracruz civilization. The artistic hallmark of Classic Veracruz is a style of abstract carving featuring pairs of curved and interwoven parallel lines. This civilization was particularly obsessed with the ball game; its most important center, El Tajín, which flourished from about AD 600 to 900, contains 17 ball courts.

Totonac The Gulf coast's most colorful culture flowered between AD 800 and 1200 on the thin coastal strip between Zempoala and Papantla. Calling their land Totonacapan, the Totonacs built great cities such as Zempoala and Quiahuiztlán where they practiced weaving and embroidery, and farmed the land for maize, squash, cotton and vanilla. Though big proponents of the Mesoamerican ball game, the Totonacs also concocted more lasting legacies such as the *voladores* (fliers) rite, which still survives today. Despite aiding the Spanish in their quest to defeat the Aztecs, Totonacapan quickly fell to smallpox and Spanish treachery after the 1520s. Currently there are still around 244,000 native Totonac speakers, mainly in northern Veracruz and the Sierra Norte de Puebla.

Huastec Native to the far north of Veracruz state, the ancient Huastecs spoke a language related to Maya. Historical evidence suggests that they migrated north from the Yucatán Peninsula around 1000 BC. Industrious cotton farmers and painters of elaborate pottery, the Huastecs were also known for their musical prowess; *huapango*, played by a trio of two guitars and a violin, has made notable contributions to mariachi music. Huastec culture reached its zenith between AD 800 and 1200. The language has survived into modern times and still lists approximately 145,000 speakers.

member of COAX (a conservation-minded bird-watching club), offers tours in the area, or can hook up birders with experienced local guides if he is busy. Straub authored a bird-watching guide to Veracruz, *Guía de Sitios* – proceeds go to Pronatura, a conservation nonprofit.

Courses

Escuela para Estudiantes Extranjeros
LANGUAGE COURSE

(School for Foreign Students; ☑228-817-86-87; www.uv.mx/eee; Gutiérrez Zamora 25; courses from US$220, plus registration fee US$100) The Universidad Veracruzana's Escuela para Estudiantes Extranjeros offers short-term, accredited programs on the Spanish and Náhuatl languages and on Mexican culture and history. Most students chose to stay in one of the homestay programs organised by the univeristy.

Tours

Veraventuras
ADVENTURE

(☑228-818-97-79; www.veraventuras.com) Offers rafting excursions, camping trips and many other activities, including trips to nearby hot springs.

Sleeping

Xalapa is blessed with some charming places to stay, many of which have low prices and lots of colonial attitude.

Posada del Cafeto
HISTORIC HOTEL $

(☑228-817-00-23; www.pradodelrio.com; Dr Canovas 8; r incl breakfast from M$525; @☎) There's lots of traditional Mexican character to the honey yellow Posada del Cafeto, which is centrally located but on a quiet side street. The dual inner patios with their finely sculpted stairways and arches create a kind of 'secret garden' feel. Rooms are spacious, individually decorated and very comfortable. Breakfast is served in a cute on-site cafe.

Hostal de la Niebla
HOSTEL $

(☑228-817-21-74; www.delaniebla.com; Gutiérrez Zamora 24; dm/s/d incl breakfast M$170/360/360; P☎) Something of a mirage in these climes, this modern Scandinavian-style hostel is no half-baked nod to the backpacker market. Rather, it's a spotless, well-organized, community-oriented accommodations featuring airy rooms with decks and terraces. There's access to lockers and a kitchen. Accommodations are in either six-bed dorms or large private rooms.

Posada Casa Regia
HOTEL $

(☑228-812-05-91; www.posadacasaregia.com.mx; Hidalgo 12; s/d M$380/430; P☎) Pleasant and colorful, this small hotel lures you in with its fancy plant- and tile-filled lobby, though the inward-facing rooms are rather less exciting. Parking costs M$100 per night.

Hotel Limón
HOTEL $

(☑228-817-22-04; Revolución 8; s/d M$180/240; ☎) The term 'dusty jewel' could have been invented with the Hotel Limón in mind. The 'dusty' part refers to the rooms, which are perfectly adequate but crying out for a refurb. The 'jewel' is the blue-tiled courtyard, seemingly inherited from richer past owners. An economical option for the unfussy, it's also very central (just steps from the cathedral).

★Mesón del Alférez Xalapa
HISTORIC HOTEL $$

(☑228-818-01-13; www.pradodelrio.com; Sebastián Camacho 2; r incl breakfast M$678, ste incl breakfast from M$831; ❋☎) This gorgeous place right in the center of town manages to get it all just right. It's a quiet, classy, colonial-style retreat from the roaring traffic outside, with beautiful split-level rooms (beds upstairs, living room below), flower-filled greenery and the best breakfast in town in its refined La Candela restaurant. A bargain.

Colombe Hotel Boutique
BOUTIQUE HOTEL $$

(☑228-818-89-89; www.colombehotel.com; Calle Vista Hermosa 16; d from M$885, ste M$2260; P❋≋) A short way out of the city center, this small hotel has rooms that are liberally doused in gaudy paint and decorations. All differ from one another and range from the Río, which is a bit like sleeping inside a technicolor rainbow, to the mellow tones of the Aqua room and the local flavored Suite México.

Add to all this a good swimming pool, a cozy bar and restaurant, and helpful staff, and you'd already be looking at a winnner but there's the price – an absolute bargain.

Posada La Mariquinta
GUESTHOUSE $$

(☑228-818-11-58; www.lamariquinta.xalapa.net; Alfaro 12; s/d from M$580/720, ste M$720-1150; P⊜☎) This plant-filled guesthouse is set in an 18th-century colonial residence with rooms arranged around a lovely garden. The rooms could perhaps do with a little more pizzazz, but it's quiet, friendly and stuffed with art, antiques and general curiosities.

The best of these can be found in the fabulous library-cum-reception room with its old books and furniture.

Eating

Stylish cafes and restaurants abound in Xalapa, many offering interesting regional menus and vegetarian choices. Callejón González Aparicio, between Primo Verdad and Mata, is an alley loaded with hip international eateries and even hipper crowds. One local specialty worth trying is *chiles rellenos* (stuffed peppers).

La Fonda
MEXICAN $

(☑ 228-818-72-82; Callejón Diamante 1; dishes M$50-100; ⊗ 8am-5:30pm) A microcosm of the Xalapa eating experience, La Fonda invites you to squeeze past the tortilla-making señorita at the door and climb upstairs, where the mural-festooned interior gives onto a narrow plant-adorned balcony overlooking the main street. The menu juxtaposes formidable *mole* with *chileatole de pollo* (chicken soup with little floating cobs of corn).

Plazoleta
MEXICAN $

(☑ 228-165-56-00; Gutiérrez Zamora 46; dishes M$45-120; ⊗ 8:30am-11pm Mon-Sat, 9:30am-11pm Sun; ♿) This popular cafeteria has street-view seating as well as tables placed around trees and vines in a courtyard. There's a climbing frame out back to keep kids happy, while its good value all-you-can-eat buffet (M$50 per person) will please lovers of quantity not quality. As well as traditional Mexican food, there's an extensive coffee menu and fresh fruit juices on tap.

Mercado de la Rotonda
MARKET $

(Revolución s/n; ⊗ 7am-6pm) Located at the north end of Revolución, this untouristed market has numerous orderly eateries offering delicious regional food on the cheap.

★ El Brou
MEDITERRANEAN $$

(☑ 228-165-49-94; Soto 13; mains M$70-150; ⊗ 9am-5pm; ♠♪) Housed in a delightful high-ceilinged colonial lounge, El Brou gets it right on all counts. The varied menu offers a delicious and arty take on Mediterranean and Mexican cuisine, and the modern touches to its traditional decor give it a chic look and feel. It only serves lunch so settle in for a long and memorable one.

★ La Candela
MEXICAN $$

(☑ 228-818-01-13; www.pradodelrio.com; Sebastián Camacho 2; mains M$70-160; ⊗ 8am-3:30pm; ♠) Hidden downstairs in the Mesón del Alférez Xalapa, this brightly decorated place attracts a crowd of loyal regulars who come for the inventive Mexican cuisine and great steaks at lunchtime, but it's the breakfasts, which are accepted by nearly all Xalapeños as being the best in town, that really please hungry tummies.

Piacevole Bistro
PIZZA $$

(☑ 228-186-59-23; Insurgentes 3; mains M$70-150; ⊗ 7-11pm Mon-Sat; ♠) You may have to fight to get a seat at this excellent pizzeria and wine bar (there are only half-a-dozen tables), but it's well worth the effort. The formula is winningly simple: handmade pasta and pizza, some excellent Mexican wines (yes, these exist), cool decor and an animated clientele. There are plans to expand, and delivery is available.

Vinissimo Xalapa
INTERNATIONAL $$$

(☑ 228-812-91-13; www.vinissimo.com.mx; Av Araucarias 501; mains around M$200; ⊗ 2pm-midnight Mon-Sat) Elegant, but not pretentious, the Vinissimo Xalapa offers outstanding 'alta cocina' dishes created with imagination and fresh market produce. The often-changing menu takes its risottos and pastas from Italy, duck, foie-gras and snails from France and seafood flavors from the wild coastline of Spanish Galicia. There's a comprehensive wine list and the staff are attentive.

It's a 10-minute cab ride east of the city center.

Drinking

★ Café Cali
CAFE

(www.cafecali.com.mx; Callejón Diamante 23A; breakfasts M$170; ⊗ 9am-11pm) The enticing smell of roasting coffee beans wafts down the alleyway and seems to envelop the entire block surrounding the wonderful Café Cali. The interior of the cafe is classic bohemia and the coffees and cakes pure bliss.

Gran Café de la Parroquia
CAFE

(☑ 228-812-31-75; www.laparroquiadeveracruz.com; Enríquez s/n; mains M$40-140; ⊗ 6am-midnight) A cousin to the renowned branch in Veracruz city, the Gran Café is a fine place for a morning coffee and breakfast but it lacks the atmosphere and sense of history of the Veracruz original.

Espresso 58
CAFE

(Primo Verdad 7; coffee M$13-25; ⊘7:30am-11pm; 🔊) A sleek cafe that attracts loquacious student debaters and those who just want to be glued to their smart phones. The in-house Café Mahal coffee (locally grown, of course) is *muy rico* and the baristas are charming.

Jugos California
JUICE BAR

(☑228-817-22-71; Enríquez 26; juices M$20-40; ⊘7am-9:30pm) Besides *antojitos* (typical Mexican snacks), this place serves fantastic volcano-like fruit salads, delicious juice combos, smoothies and even chocolate soy shakes.

Angelo Casa de Té
CAFE

(☑228-841-08-39; Primo Verdad 21A; tea from M$10; ⊘8am-9pm) The shelves at this cute little place are lined with tins of different kinds of tea, the walls are adorned in pictures of tea-pickers and fields the world over, and it has good chocolate and homemade cookies to tuck into.

Cubanías
BAR

(Callejón González Aparicio; ⊘5pm-1:30am; 🔊) Veracruz' Cuban influences rise to the surface in this boisterous bar, with mojitos, beer and – should you be peckish – large Cuban sandwiches on offer. It guards the entrance to Callejón González Aparicio and live music rocks up later on.

☆ Entertainment

Being a university town, Xalapa has a vivacious nightlife. The loudest buzz can be found in jam-packed Callejón González Aparicio, the covered alley off Primo Verdad filled with trendy bars.

★ Tierra Luna
PERFORMING ARTS

(☑228-812-13-01; http://tierraluna.com.mx; Rayón 18; ⊘9am-10pm Mon-Thu, 9am-2am Fri & Sat; 🔊) A sanctuary for arty types, the historic high-ceilinged Tierra Luna provides a changing roster of poetry readings, theater performances and music gigs. It also serves tasty cafe fare (mains M$50 to M$90), including a breakfast menu and a range of alcoholic drinks. There's a small bookstore and a craft store too.

Centro Recreativo Xalapeño
ARTS CENTER

(☑228-195-82-24; Xalapeños Ilustres 31; ⊘9am-8pm) On bookish Xalapeños Ilustres, this cultural center is the font of pretty much everything that passes for 'art' in Xalapa. Jam sessions, tango classes, art expos, sculpture competitions and Cine Francés all kick off here; keep your eye on the poster board or check out the Facebook page for upcoming events.

The building is an attractive 19th-century colonial gem with a courtyard and small cafe (Luna Negra).

El Ágora
ARTS CENTER

(☑228-818-57-30; www.agora.xalapa.net; Parque Juárez; ⊘10am-10pm Tue-Sun, 9am-6pm Mon; 🔊) A busy and sleekly modern arts center with a cinema, theater, gallery, bookstore and cafe.

Teatro del Estado Ignacio de la Llave
THEATER

(☑228-818-43-52; cnr Llave & Av Ávila Camacho; ⊘from 8pm) The impressive state theater hosts both the Orquesta Sinfónica de Xalapa and the Ballet Folklórico of the Universidad Veracruzana. It is situated 1.5km northwest of Parque Juárez, up Avenida Ávila Camacho.

🛍 Shopping

An epicenter of Xalapa's alternative culture is Callejón Diamante, an alley lined with boutiques and street vendors selling cheap jewelry, incense and paraphernalia. Bookstores line Xalapeños Ilustres. Xalapa is *the* place to get your hair braided or your back tattooed.

Café Colón
FOOD & DRINK

(Primo Verdad 15) ✐ Old-school coffee roasters will grind Coatepec's best in front of your eyes in this aromatic store. It sells for around M$150 per kilo.

ℹ Information

A **tourist information booth** (www.xalapa. gob.mx; Palacio Municipal; ⊘9am-8pm) in the Palacio Municipal has helpful info and maps. There's another larger **office** (Enríquez; ⊘9am-8pm) nearby.

There are banks with 24-hour ATMs along Enríquez and Gutiérrez Zamora.

Centro de Especialidades Médicas (☑228-814-45-00; www.cemev.gob.mx; Ruíz Cortines 2903) Excellent medical care.

Post Office (cnr Gutiérrez Zamora & Diego Leño)

Xalapa Mio (www.xalapamio.com) Official tourist office site.

Xalapa Tourist Network (www.xalapa.net) General tourist information site about things to see and do in and around the city.

❶ Getting There & Away

Xalapa is a transportation hub with excellent connections throughout the state and beyond.

BUS

Xalapa's modern and well-organized bus station, the **Central de Autobuses de Xalapa** (CAXA; Av 20 de Noviembre), is 2km east of the center and has an ATM, cafes and telephones. Second-class buses for Xico and Coatepec regularly leave from Mercado Los Sauces, about 1km west of the center on Circuito Presidentes. First-class services are offered by ADO and good 2nd-class services by AU.

Buses to Jalcomulco leave from the **Azteca bus station** (Niños Héroes 85), a couple of kilometers north of the center.

CAR & MOTORCYCLE

Xalapa is famous for its traffic-choked streets, and driving here can be a challenging prospect; just negotiating the sprawling suburbs to find the center can be difficult as signage is poor.

Hwy 140 to Puebla is narrow and winding until Perote; the Xalapa–Veracruz highway is very fast and smooth. Going to the northern Gulf coast, it's quickest to go to Cardel, then north on Hwy 180.

❶ Getting Around

For buses from CAXA to the center, follow signs to the taxi stand, then continue downhill to the main Avenida 20 de Noviembre. The bus stop is to the right. Any bus marked 'Centro' will pass within a block or two of Parque Juárez (M$10). For a taxi to the center, you have to buy a ticket in the bus station (M$35 to M$45). To return to the bus station, take the 'Camacho-CAXA-SEC' bus from Avenida Ávila Camacho or Hidalgo.

Around Xalapa

The dramatic landscapes around Xalapa, with rivers, gorges and waterfalls, cradle some charming mountain towns and worthwhile places.

Hacienda El Lencero

Almost as old as New Spain itself, this former posada (inn) was initiated in 1525 by Juan Lencero, a soldier loyal to Hernán Cortés, and served as a resting place for tired travelers toiling between a newly Europeanized Mexico City and the coast. Today it is the **Museo Ex-Hacienda El Lencero** (☑228-820-02-70; Carretera Xalapa-Veracruz Km 10; adult/child M$40/30; ⊗10am-5pm Tue-Sun), incorporating a superbly restored house furnished with antiques, along with some delightful gardens embellished with a lake and a 500-year-old fig tree.

To get to the estate, travel 12km southeast of Xalapa on the Veracruz highway, and then turn down a signposted road branching off to the right for a few kilometers. From Xalapa, catch one of the regular 'Miradores' buses (M$12) from the Plaza Cristal shopping center.

Coatepec

☑228 / POP 53,600 / ELEV 1200M

Waking up and smelling the coffee has rarely been this epiphanic. Cradled in the Sierra Madre foothills, Coatepec's coffee production has long been its raison d'être, a fact that will become instantly clear as soon as you step off the bus and inhale. The settlement

BUSES FROM XALAPA

The daily ADO services listed in the table leave from CAXA.

Destinations also served by ADO include Acayucan, Campeche, Cancún, Catemaco, Córdoba, Mérida, Orizaba and Poza Rica.

DESTINATION	FARE (M$)	DURATION (HR)	FREQUENCY (DAILY)
Cardel	74-82	1	18
Mexico City (TAPO)	294-380	4½	6
Papantla	276	4	14
Puebla	208	2½	15
Tampico	624	9½	3
Veracruz	128-166	2	frequent
Veracruz airport	332	1½	6
Villahermosa	658	8½	6

dates from 1701 and coffee has been grown in the surrounding cloud forests for almost as long. The crop has brought wealth to the town; Coatepec – which lies a mere 15km south of Xalapa – is adorned with rich gaudily painted colonial buildings. In 2006 it was nominated as a *pueblo mágico* by the Mexican government. It makes a laid-back alternative to nearby Xalapa.

In late September, Coatepec vivaciously celebrates its patron saint, San Jerónimo, making it an excellent time to visit.

◉ Sights

Parque Miguel Hidalgo   PLAZA
Coatepec's main square is green and bereft of the worst of the town's traffic. In its center stands a glorious *glorieta* (bandstand) that doubles up as a cafe. Set back from the road on the eastern side is the unashamedly baroque Parroquia de San Jerónimo, named after the city's patron saint.

Cerro de las Culebras   VIEWPOINT
Cerro de las Culebras (Snake Hill; Coatepec in the Náhuatl language) is easily accessible from the town center. The walk takes you up cobbled steps to a lookout tower with a white statue of Christ on top. From here there are magnificent city and mountain views. To get there, walk three blocks west from the main plaza on Lerdo, then north all the way up Independencia.

Museo y Jardín
de Orquideas   MUSEUM, GARDENS
(Aldama 20; ⊙10am-5pm Wed-Sun) FREE Coatepec's humid cloud forests support numerous species of orchid and an amiable local *señora* has collected many of them for this museum/garden a few blocks from the main square. Displays highlight both cultivation and conservation techniques. Reserve 30 minutes to see the full gamut.

Museo El Cafétal Apan   MUSEUM
(www.elcafe-tal.com; Carretera Coatepec-Las Trancas Km 4; M$40; ⊙9am-5pm) ✐ If you want to learn a bit more about the history of coffee in the region, visit this museum that displays antique coffee-making tools. There are hands-on demonstrations showing how coffee is produced, and also coffee tastings. It's a bit out of town; a taxi will cost M$40.

Cascada Bola de Oro   WATERFALL
The nearest waterfall to town is in the environs of a well-known Coatepec coffee *finca*

(estate), which also has various trails and a natural swimming pool. To get there follow Calle 5 de Mayo north to a bridge, continue north on Calle Prieto and then turn left into Calle Altamirano. After passing the last shop, hang a right, cross a bridge and turn left onto a path. The tourist office dispenses useful maps.

🛏 Sleeping

Ashram Coatepec   HOSTEL $
(☎228-816-10-55; www.ashramdecoatepec.org; Mina 100; dm or campsite M$100; P🐾) On the outskirts of town, this ashram has yoga, meditation (sessions in both take place on Monday, Wednesday and Friday) and walking trails through its lush grounds. The immaculate treatment of the gorgeous meditation and yoga spaces isn't replicated in the dormitories, but it's a cheap enough place to hang your hat. All food here is vegetarian.

★ Casa Real del Café   HISTORIC HOTEL $$
(☎228-816-63-17; www.casarealdelcafe.com.mx; Gutiérrez Zamora 58; r incl breakfast from M$1050; P🐾🛜) This colonial-style hotel is owned by local coffee farmers whose aromatic products fortuitously find their way into the onsite Antiguo Beneficio cafe. Split-level rooms offer historic luxury with dark wood and gorgeously tiled bathrooms, while the communal courtyard sports reclining chairs, a spa and a reading room with, in case you're short of reading material, the complete *Encyclopedia Britannica*.

Hotel Mesón del
Alférez Coatepec   BOUTIQUE HOTEL $$
(☎228-816-67-44; www.pradodelrio.com; Jiménez del Campillo 47; incl breakfast d from M$840, ste from M$1094; 🐾❄🛜) Behind the mustard yellow walls of this old town house lies a secret courtyard with a dominating fountain and a jungle of flowers. Surrounding this lies a web of rooms filled with heavy timber furnishings, polished floors, wood beam ceilings and colonial accents. It's a gorgeous place to stay with helpful staff, but some rooms can be a bit dark.

An excellent breakfast is included.

Posada de Coatepec   HISTORIC HOTEL $$$
(☎228-816-05-44; www.posadacoatepec.com.mx; Hidalgo 9; d incl breakfast from M$1435; P🐾♿) Coatepec's hallmark hotel is in a resplendent colonial-era building; the central courtyard is overflowing with plants and features a gurgling fountain. It boasts a pool, exhibits

JALCOMULCO – RAFTING ADVENTURES

Surrounded by lush ravines and just 30km southeast of Xalapa, this town hugs the Río Antigua (known as the Río Pescados) and is very picturesque. The area is rich with caves and luscious swimming spots, but it's most famous for its rapids, which accommodate white-water enthusiasts from the beginner through to the more advanced.

There are a number of tour operators offering local activities. Those recommended include **Aventuras Sin Límites** (☑279-832-35-80; www.raftingsinlimite.com; Zaragoza 58, Jalcomulco), **Huitzilapan Expediciones** (☑279-832-36-10; www.huitzilapanexpediciones.com.mx; Juárez 52, Jalcomulco; activities per day from M$680) and **México Verde** (☑800-362-88-00; www.mexicoverde.com; Carretera Tuzamapan-Jalcomulco Km 4; trips from M$660), which has its own resort on the road coming into town from the northwest.

There are buses (M$30) to Jalcomulco from Xalapa at the Azteca bus terminal, as well as buses from Cardel.

from local artists, tranquil gardens and a full-sized antique coach parked in the lobby. The rooms are large, but rather on the dark and musty side, as is typical with colonial mansions.

Given this, it's a little overpriced, but its impressive public areas can't be beaten for atmosphere.

✖ Eating

Casa Coffino CAFE, INTERNATIONAL $
(Jiménez del Campillo 17; snacks M$50-120; ⊗8am-10pm; 🐕) An interesting cafe encased in a head-turning art nouveau–style building a block from the plaza. Coffino's specialty is its own rich coffee (called Café de Altura), but it also serves light food, cakes and smoothies in a beautiful flower-filled courtyard.

★ Café Santa Cruz MEXICAN $$
(☑228-200-40-59; Zamora 24; mains M$90-140; ⊗1-10pm) From the outside, this blushing terracotta building resembles a country farmhouse, but the tiny dining room (there's only a handful of tables) is all light, modern and very relaxed. The folk who work here serve memorable Mexican gourmet dishes, imaginative salads and, wait for it, red and green pepper cheesecake. Highly original and almost reason enough to visit Coatepec.

🍷 Drinking & Entertainment

★ El Café de Avelino CAFE
(Aldama 6; ⊗noon-5pm) The best coffee in Coatepec (no mean feat!) comes from a cafe with two tables and four chairs (five if you count the owner's) occupying the lobby of the magnificent Mansión de los Azulejos (House of Tiles). Owner Avelino Hernández – known locally as the *Poeta del Café* (coffee poet) – brews minor miracles from

his Coatepec, Cosailton, Xico and Teocelo brands.

You can buy the beans for M$200 per kilo.

El Kiosko CAFE
(Parque Hidalgo; ⊗8am-7pm) Small alfresco cafe selling java out of the old *glorieta* in the center of the plaza.

🛍 Shopping

La Misión SOUVENIRS, ACCESSORIES
(Aldama 6; ⊗9am-7pm) In this shop you'll find carefully selected local items such as organic coffee, essential oils, *maguey* honey and soy milk.

ℹ Information

There's a helpful **tourist office** (☑228-816-04-34; Palacio Municipal s/n; ⊗9am-2pm & 4-7pm Mon-Fri, 9:30am-6:30pm Sat & Sun) in the Palacio Municipal on Parque Hidalgo.

ℹ Getting There & Away

Regular buses (M$10) arrive from Xalapa's CAXA and Los Sauces terminals, or a taxi is M$80 to M$100. Buses for Xico (M$9) leave from Constitución between Aldama and Juárez. The ADO **bus station** (5 de Mayo s/n) serves Puebla and Mexico City.

Xico

☑228 / POP 18,600 / ELEV 1300M
Slowly emerging from Coatepec's shadow, quieter and hillier Xico is, arguably, a far more beguiling place, and in 2011 joined the ranks of Mexico's government-sanctioned *pueblos mágicos*. Just 8km away from Coatepec, Xico attracts devotees of *mole* and handicrafts rather than coffee, while its cobbled streets and varied colonial

architecture make it an increasingly popular weekend retreat. Within Mexico the town is best known for its annual Fiesta de Santa Magdalena, held each July and famous for a running of the bulls à la Pamplona in Spain.

⊙ Sights

If you ask at the tourist office, they might be able to organize a coffee farm tour.

Cascada de Texolo WATERFALL
It's a pleasant, signposted 3km walk from Xico and past an ex-hacienda to the narrow, plunging 80m Cascada de Texolo and the Cascada de la Monja (Waterfall of the Nun). It's a luxurious place to take a dip, and '80s movie fans should look out: the former cascade featured in *Romancing the Stone* (1984); the said 'stone' was hidden behind it.

Museo del Vestido MUSEUM
(Parroquia, cnr Av Hidalgo & Juárez; M$10; ⊙3-7:30pm Tue-Sun) An esoteric, niche museum displaying a revolving collection of St María Magdalena's past festival dresses, dating from 1910.

Casa-Museo Totomoxtle MUSEUM
(cnr Aldama & Juárez; ⊙10am-4pm) FREE A small museum highlighting the town's peculiar artisanal pastime of making intricate and detailed figures from *hojas de maiz* (maize leaves). Only in Xico! Opening hours can be flexible.

✸ Festivals & Events

Fiesta de Santa Magdalena RELIGIOUS
The mother of all festivals takes place in Xico between July 15 and 24. Gigantic floral arches are raised, and streets are artistically decorated with carpets of colored sawdust in preparation for the saint's procession. The Magdalena statue in the Parroquia de Santa María Magdalena (located at the end of Avenida Hidalgo) is clothed in a different elaborate dress each day for 30 days around the fiesta. A running of the bulls takes place through the streets on July 22.

⊟ Sleeping & Eating

Posada los Naranjos HOTEL $
(☑228-153-54-54; Av Hidalgo 193; r from M$350; P🛜) With just nine rooms and right in the center of town, this no-frills place is a decent budget option. Rooms are clean and simple, and there's a pleasant cafe here too. It's a short amble down Xico's main street from the church. If you stay here you'll get to hear the beautiful dawn chorus of the church bell.

★**Las Magdalenas** BOUTIQUE HOTEL $$
(☑228-813-03-14; www.lasmagdalenas.com.mx; Hidalgo 123; r incl breakfast M$1490-1590; P🛜) This gorgeous colonial house has been impressively transformed into an outstanding boutique hotel. It boasts a fabulous garden full of flowers, common areas dripping in regal decoration and split-level rooms that are surprisingly light and modern for such an old-world setting. All round this place is a winner.

Hotel Paraje Coyopolan HOTEL $$
(☑228-813-12-66; www.coyopolan.com; Venustiano Carranza Sur s/n; r incl breakfast from M$685; P🛜) It's all about retina-burning bright colors and lively Mexican design at this OK place right on the river just outside the town. The hotel arranges hiking, canyoning and rappelling in the surrounding mountains and canyons, making it a great base for outdoor activities. The on-site restaurant also serves regional food and there's occasional live music.

Restaurante Mesón Xiqueño MEXICAN $$
(☑228-813-07-81; Av Hidalgo 148; meals M$50-150; ⊙9am-9pm) Near the corner with Calle Carranza is Mesón Xiqueño, Xico's best known restaurant. Here you can try the famous local *mole* (a complex mix of chocolate, banana, apple, chili, sucrose and numerous secret ingredients), served in a number of different ways, while dining at one of the tables spread out over the lovely courtyard.

🛍 Shopping

Derivados Acamalin Productos Xiquenial Artesanías FOOD
(Av Hidalgo 150; ⊙9am-7pm) Xico's trademark *mole* can be procured at Derivados Acamalin Productos Xiquenial Artesanías. Also sells organic coffee.

ℹ Information

Tourist Office (☑228-813-16-18; Av Hidalgo 76; ⊙9am-6pm) The small tourist office is encased in the Casa de la Cultura and is a friendly source of information for the town and its surroundings.

ⓘ Getting There & Away

From Xalapa, take a bus to Xico (M$18) from Los Sauces terminal. From Coatepec, Xico buses (M$10) frequently leave from Constitución, one block southeast of the main plaza.

Córdoba

📞 271 / POP 140,000 / ELEV 924M

Mention you're going to Córdoba to a coastal dweller and you may well get a sarcastic eye roll. *Cordobeses* are often seen as haughtier and less modest than their more down-to-earth *jarocho* brethren, though 'urbane' would be a kinder description.

Not to be confused with its famous namesakes in Spain and Argentina, Córdoba, Veracruz, has an illustrious history and a justifiable sense of civic pride; the contract that sealed Mexico's independence was signed here in 1821. The city itself was originally founded in 1618 as a staging post between Mexico City and the coast, with the purpose of protecting the Spanish crown's interests from the local slave rebellion, led by Gaspar Yanga, that was strong in the area.

As an overnight stop, Córdoba trumps other central Veracruz cities such as Orizaba and Fortín de las Flores on the strength of its main plaza. It's a 24-hour live 'show,' where theater-goers in high heels dodge hungry pigeons and grandpas moonlight as marimba players. Watching over it all is an impressive baroque cathedral, easily the most resplendent in the state.

Be aware that Córdoba has a complicated system of street numbering – a map from your hotel or the tourist office will be a big help.

◉ Sights

Most of Córdoba's sights ring its main plaza, Parque de 21 de Mayo, which is a sight in itself.

★ Parque de 21 de Mayo   PLAZA

You don't come to Córdoba's main plaza to tick off a list of 'sights.' You come here to live life. The square vies with Veracruz city's as the region's most jazzy and vibrant. It's far larger than the port city's plaza, though a seemingly unending line of musicians makes up for any lack of intimacy. Opposite the cathedral on the square's west side is the splendiferous Palacio Municipal, replete with a memorable Diego Rivera interior mural.

Ex-Hotel Zevallos   HISTORIC BUILDING

(Parque de 21 de Mayo) Built in 1687, this is the former home of the *condes* (counts) of Zevallos. It's on the northeast side of Parque de 21 de Mayo, behind the *portales*. Plaques in the courtyard record that Juan O'Donojú and Agustín de Iturbide met here on August 24, 1821, and agreed on the terms for Mexico's independence. They also concurred that a Mexican, not a European, should be head of state. The building is now full of restaurants and cafes.

Catedral de la Inmaculada
Concepción   CATHEDRAL

(Parque de 21 de Mayo) Dating from 1688, this blue baroque cathedral has an elaborate facade flanked by twin bell towers. The interior is surprisingly ornate for Mexico, with gold-leaf detailing and marble floors. The chapel features candlelit statues with altars, such as a gruesome Jesus on the cross and an eerily despairing Virgen de la Soledad. The mixture of glitz and gore is a visual metaphor for a disturbing historical dichotomy: the richness of the conquistadors and the misery that the indigenous people endured.

Museo de Antropología   MUSEUM

(Calle 3, btwn Avs 3 & 5; ⊙9am-5pm Mon-Fri) **FREE** This museum, which is a part of the city university, has a modest but interesting collection of artifacts including a fine Aztec ball-court marker and some Olmec figurines. There's also a replica of the magnificent statue of *El señor de las Limas* that resides in Xalapa's Museo de Antropología (p218). You'll find it just off the main square, opposite the Centro Cultural Municipal.

Parque Ecológico Paso Coyol   PARK

(📞271-714-20-84; cnr Calle 6 & Av 19, Bella Vista; M$2) 🐾 Formerly a 4-hectare abandoned lot overrun by 'delinquents,' this eco-conscious park is now patronized by *cordobeses*, who run and walk trails that snake around gardens punctuated with exercise stations. Your meager entrance fee pays for both *campesinos* (country people) and biologists alike to maintain the place. Follow Calle 3 south from the plaza for 1.5km. The street changes name, weaves through a suburb and bottoms out at the park.

🎊 Festivals & Events

Good Friday   RELIGIOUS

On the evening of Good Friday, Córdoba marks Jesus' crucifixion with a procession of silence, in which thousands of residents walk through the streets behind an altar of the Virgin. Everyone holds a lit candle, no one utters a word and the church bells are strangely quiet.

🛏 Sleeping

Hotel Palacio
HOTEL $

(☎271-712-21-88; www.hotelpalaciocordoba.com.mx; cnr Calle 2 & Av 3; s/d incl breakfast M$490/540; P❄🛜) The best budget option in Córdoba is this large place with a smart, bright lobby and rather less impressive, characterless rooms, only some of which have air-con. However, it's just a block from the plaza and has its own underground car park, so it's fine for an overnight stay.

Hotel Mansur
HOTEL $$

(☎271-712-60-00; www.hotelmansur.com.mx; Av 1 No 301, cnr Calle 3; r incl breakfast from M$662; P❄🛜) Claiming five stories of prime viewing space above Córdoba's main plaza, the Mansur, with its vast balconies equipped with thick wooden chairs, makes you feel as if you're part of the 'show' going on below. The old-world lobby has lots of wood and silver-framed mirrors, but the rooms themselves, while perfectly decent, are somewhat on the dull side.

There's no price hike for rooms at the front, so request one of these if you relish a view and one at the back if all you desire is peace and quiet (quiet being a relative term in Mexico).

Hotel Layfer
HOTEL $$

(☎271-714-05-05; www.hoteleslayfer.com; Av 5 No 908, btwn Calles 9 & 11; s/d M$735/895; P❄🛜≋) Definitely Córdoba's fanciest hotel (if not necessarily its best value), the Layfer has modern, and not wildly exciting, rooms arranged around a central swimming pool. Mileage is added with a wide array of extras including complimentary body-care products, a bar, gym, restaurant and games room.

Hotel Bello
HOTEL $$

(☎271-712-81-22; www.hotelbello.com/cordoba; cnr Av 2 & Calle 5; s/d/tr M$550/650/690; P❄@🛜) Brightly painted in yellow and thus hard to miss, this modern hotel is spotless and well located just moments from the main square. The rooms are fresh, some with great views toward Pico de Orizaba, and the staff are affable. Go for the top-floor balcony rooms.

🍴 Eating

Córdoba has a lively eating scene with plenty of choice. For a cheap meal, try the little eateries on Avenida 5 in between Calles 1 and 2.

Calufe Café
CAFE $

(Calle 3 No 212, btwn Avs 4 & 2; coffee from M$10; ⊘8am-9pm Sun-Wed, to midnight Thu-Sat; 🛜) If only all cafes could be like this. Calufe occupies the interior of an agreeably peeling colonial mansion with eclectic nooks arranged around a dimly lit plant-filled courtyard. Guitar and vocal duos provide a melancholy musical backdrop in the evenings. Calufe sells its own blend of coffee, along with melt-in-the-mouth coffee cake and other diet-busting snacks.

★ Roof Garden Restaurant
MEXICAN $$

(☎271-716-41-42; Av 9 Bis, btwn Calles 26 & 28; mains M$50-150; ⊘9:30am-11pm) Creatively crafted and presented contemporary Mexican cooking with flashes of inspiration from a sun-soaked Mediterranean, this informal, plant-filled and cheery little restaurant out in the western reaches of the city is arguably the best place to eat in Córdoba. Alongside modern takes on Mexican classics there's a range of pastas, multi-layer burgers and good coffee.

Crepas y Carnes Los 30s
MEXICAN $$

(☎271-712-33-79; www.crepasycarneslos30s.com; Av 9, btwn Calles 20 & 22; crepes M$100, mains M$90-250; ⊘1:30pm-midnight Sun-Wed, 12:30pm-1am Thu-Sat; 🛜) A sprawling and hugely popular place amid a long stretch of restaurants along Av 9. Terming itself 'cocina del barrio' (cookery of the quarter), it has a colonial feel, and its walls are decked with art and old photographs. The crepes are excellent and range from the savory to the very sweet. There's also pizza, fish, pasta and various grills on the extensive menu.

El Balcón del Zevallos
PARRILLA, MEXICAN $$$

(Av 1 No 101, cnr Calle 1; mains M$100-200; ⊘5pm-midnight Mon-Thu, from 1pm Fri-Sun) The upper floor of the beautiful former Hotel Zevallos claims the prize for Córdoba's most famous restaurant. It has a refined inner sanctum, a balcony overlooking the plaza, an extensive wine list (the usual Spanish and Chilean suspects), and good meat dishes cooked *a la parrilla* (on the barbecue) at your table. Service is sharp but not overly officious.

BUSES FROM CÓRDOBA

Deluxe and first-class buses from Córdoba.

DESTINATION	FARE (M$)	DURATION (HR)	FREQUENCY (DAILY)
Fortín	15	½	frequent
Mexico City (TAPO)	340-390	5	frequent
Oaxaca	460	6½	3
Orizaba	36	¾	frequent
Puebla	202-242	3	frequent
Veracruz	132-146	1½	frequent
Xalapa	216	3	hourly

ℹ️ Information

Banks around the Plaza de Armas have 24-hour ATMs.

Hospital Covadonga (☎ 271-714-55-20; www.corporativodehospitales.com.mx; Av 7 No 1610; ☺ 24hr) Urgent medical care at all hours.

Tourist Office (☎ 271-712-43-44; Centro Cultural Municipal, Av 3, cnr Calle 3; ☺ 8:30am-4pm & 6-7:30pm Mon-Fri, 10am-2pm Sat & Sun) Helpful staff offer maps and information. Volunteers sometimes give tours of the city.

ℹ️ Getting There & Around

BUS

Córdoba's **bus station** (Av Privada 4), which has deluxe, 1st-class and 2nd-class services, is 2.5km southeast of the plaza. To get to the town center from the station, take a local bus marked 'Centro' or buy a taxi ticket (M$30). To Fortín de las Flores and Orizaba, it's more convenient to take a local bus from the corner of Avenida 11 and Calle 3 than to go out to the Córdoba bus station.

CAR & MOTORCYCLE

Córdoba, Fortín de las Flores and Orizaba are linked by toll Hwy 150D, the route that most buses take, and by the much slower Hwy 150. A scenic back road goes through the hills from Fortín, via Huatusco, to Xalapa.

Fortín de las Flores

☎ 271 / POP 21,000 / ELEV 970M

With a name like this, it's perhaps appropriate that flowers and lush greenery are all around in this attractive little town, which is a center for cut-flower cultivation and has nurseries and private gardens surrounding it. Though it's a peaceful weekend retreat for Mexico City's middle class, those from further afield might find it better day-trip fodder from bases in Córdoba or Orizaba. Fortín's annual flower festival runs for a week in late April or early May.

🏃 Activities

Barranca de Metlac   HIKING

🖉 Fortín's most striking feature is this deep jungle-fringed ravine, carved out by the Río Metlac. Spanning it is the **Puente de Metlac**, the highest rail bridge in North America, measuring 131m high by 90m long. Alongside it sits a slightly older and marginally lower road bridge. The original rail bridge, the Puente de San Miguel, sits a couple of kilometers north. Built in 1873, it sweeps across the canyon in an unusual curve. The Barranca hides some excellent hikes.

For the quickest access, head west from the center of Fortín down Avenida 1 which turns into the Fortín Viejo road. This quiet road bends steeply downhill for about 2km to join another busier road. Pass over the river here, turn immediately right and follow a dirt forest road north alongside the river to **El Corazón** (Fortín de las Flores; M$15), a basic facility with a weathered swimming pool and a snack-shack. Past the pool and to the left-hand side of an electricity plant, a pathway leads you to a huge staircase (440 steps) up to the Metlac road bridge for vertiginous and verdant views. To get back to Fortín, cross the bridge and cut back along the path that forks to the right at its eastern side.

A 6km stretch of old railway line to the north of the Puente de Metlac has been converted into a Vía Verde for walkers and cyclists. This beautiful juxtaposition of nature and 19th-century engineering includes seven tunnels, two stations, a bridge house ruin and the original 1873 bridge.

Cecila Rábago CULTURAL TOUR

([✓] cell 271-1202030; cecirabago@hotmail.com; 1-4 people per day from M$1200) A well-established, bilingual tour guide in the area, Cecila's an expert on history and sites in the Fortín-Córdoba–Orizaba area. A firecracker of a lady, she can offer tours of the city and organic coffee plantations, take you on all-day hiking excursions off the tourist track, and many other things in between.

🛌 Sleeping

Hotel Fortín de las Flores HOTEL $$

([✓] 271-713-00-55; Av 2, btwn Calles 5 & 7; d/ste from M$561/793; [P][❄][🛜][🏊]) Attractive gardens and a pool offset the austerity in evidence elsewhere at this long-established and very ordinary central option. Rooms are pleasantly tiled, have antique, and very noisy, air-con units and good bathrooms, while the pool has super views toward Pico de Orizaba. The whole place has a not-unpleasant faded-glory-hacienda feel about it. Skip the breakfast.

⭐Hotel Posada Loma HOTEL $$$

([✓] 271-713-06-58; www.posadaloma.com; Carretera Córdoba-Fortín Km 333; s/d incl breakfast from M$1560/1755, bungalows sleeping 4 incl breakfast M$5071; [P][😊][❄][🛜][🏊]) 🅿 For a (somewhat overpriced) treat, head to this place 1km outside the center of Fortín on the road to Córdoba. Initial impressions may not suggest a garden oasis, but drive up the hill and that's exactly what you get. The rooms are spacious, with private terraces, tasteful wooden furniture and big fireplaces for the winter months.

The real reason to come here though is for the grounds; a marvel of greenhouses, orchid collections, flower-filled gardens, terraces and a pool. The renowned breakfast in its restaurant – with exotic fresh-juice blends and spectacular views of Pico de Orizaba – is unbeatable, as is the flora tour by its friendly and knowledgeable owner, Lolis Álvarez.

Eating

A number of cafes and restaurants surround the main plaza.

Kiosko Café MEXICAN $

(Av 3, btwn Calles 1 & 3; mains M$50-100; ⊙ 7:30am-11:30pm; 🛜) Smack in the middle of the main plaza, this cafe enjoys unmatched real estate. Formerly the library, it now serves coffee, fresh juices and simple meals in the sunshine. The *sopa azteca* (spicy tortilla soup) is excellent.

El Fogon MEXICAN $$

([✓] 271-713-13-39; Calle 5 Nta 607A; mains M$100-150; ⊙ 10am-10pm Tue-Sun) There's a tropical vibe to this open-sided, thatch-roofed restaurant surrounded by big leafed plants (there's also a more formal indoor dining area). It's known across town for its hearty steaks and other meat-based Mexican dishes.

ℹ️ Information

Tourist Office ([✓] 271-713-06-02; Palacio Municipal; ⊙ 8am-4pm Mon-Fri) You'll find the small but helpful tourist office in the Palacio Municipal, upstairs on the right-hand side. Town maps are available here.

ℹ️ Getting There & Away

In Fortín, local bus services arrive and depart from Calle 1 Oriente, on the northeast corner of the plaza. Frequent 2nd-class buses go to Córdoba and Coscomatepec. The ADO **bus station** (cnr Av 2 & Calle 6) has 1st-class bus departures. The 2nd-class bus to Orizaba goes through the gorgeous countryside but is more crowded and slower.

VERACRUZ FORTÍN DE LAS FLORES

BUSES FROM FORTÍN DE LAS FLORES

First-class bus departures from the ADO bus station.

DESTINATION	FARE (M$)	DURATION (HR)	FREQUENCY (DAILY)
Córdoba	15	½	8
Mexico City (TAPO)	382	4½	3
Orizaba	28	½	10
Veracruz	160	2	4
Xalapa	220	3½	4

Coscomatepec

📞 272 / POP 15,000 / ELEV 1588M

Easily one of Veracruz state's most enchanting towns, tongue-twister Coscomatepec (simply Cosco to anyone living there) is likely to work its magic on you quickly and irreversibly. Set amid the foothills of Pico de Orizaba, which towers in the distance when the clouds part, the steep, cobbled colonial streets and the charming main square all look like a film set for old Mexico. Shops selling intricate handmade saddles, leather goods, quality cigars and delicious bread all draw visitors, while a clutch of good hotels highlight the town's growing reputation as a weekend getaway from Veracruz, Xalapa and Mexico City.

💿 Sights & Activities

You can take tours through the famous bakery, cigar factory and saddle shops. These are arranged through the **tourist office** (📞272-737-04-80; www.vivecosco.com; cnr Amez & Argüelles s/n; ☺9am-4pm Mon-Fri) in the Plaza Municipal. They also provide information on a variety of activities, such as hiking, rappelling, horseback riding, zip-lining and rock climbing in the area, which is rich with caves, rivers, old bridges and waterfalls.

If you're a climber (with your own equipment) or a hiker, and want someone to show you cool places, call experienced, bilingual local climbing and hiking guide **Edson Escamilla** (📞273-105-13-43, cell 273-737-04-81; x_on56@hotmail.com; per person per day plus tip M$300-600). He's awfully nice and shows people around locally, as well as leading climbs to Pico de Orizaba.

The town is famous for its incredibly ornate artisanal saddles and horse tack, and if you need to tart up your steed then there are a couple of places selling the full range of gear in and around the main square. One such place is **Proyecciones Artesanales** (📞273-737-00-67; www.talabarteriaproarte.com.mx; Av Guadalupe Victoria 8). For Coscomatepec's famous bread head to **La Fama** (Guerrero 6; ☺6am-7pm); it's been baking since 1924.

🛏 Sleeping & Eating

The restaurant scene in Coscomatepec is pretty unimpressive, but there are a couple of cheap and cheerful local places in the town center.

Plaza Real HOTEL $

(📞273-737-00-96; http://hotelplazarealcosco.com; Av Bravo cnr López Rayón; d/tw M$449/549; 🛜) One block to the east of the main square, this hotel has plenty of Mexican flavor and a couple of quirks, such as the owner drives his SUV into the lobby to park it overnight. But it's a solid and good-value choice, with spacious, pleasantly painted rooms and sunflower tiled basins.

It can be somewhat noisy in the evenings here, as the rooms surround an atrium where sound travels impressively. Do try to get a room at the front of the building, as these are the only ones with natural light.

Posada del Emperador HISTORIC HOTEL $$

(📞272-737-15-20; www.laposadadelemperador.com; cnr Av Juárez (Calle 2) & Domínguez (Av 3); r incl breakfast from M$720; ❋🛜❋) The Emperador wins over all but the most unromantic with its beautiful historical decor, antique furniture, four-poster beds, exquisite views and a plant-filled interior. The hotel also boasts an extensive spa with massage, hot tubs, pool and temascal (a pre-Hispanic steam bath), as well as wonderful valley views from the restaurant and terrace. There's even a small chapel.

Fated Hapsburg emperor Maximilian apparently stopped here in the 1860s (hence the name) before his date with destiny and a firing squad.

ℹ Getting There & Away

From Fortín, Coscomatepec is a one-hour bus ride (M$20); a taxi costs around M$70. Regular buses also connect to Córdoba. The **bus terminal** (Miguel Lerdo de Tejada btwn Reforma & Gutiérrez Zamora) is five minutes' walk northeast of the main plaza.

Orizaba

📞272 / POP 121,000 / ELEV 1219M

Orizaba manages to surprise you. At first sight it's a workaday medium-sized Mexican town, but it quickly turns out to be one of the more appealing towns in Veracruz and is home to several idiosyncratic sights, a pleasant old colonial center, some lovely parks and a gorgeous riverside walk. It's also within easy reach of Mexico's highest mountain, the magnificent Pico de Orizaba, and a new cable car has made accessing this dormant volcano easier than ever before. The most striking sight in the town itself is Gustave Eiffel's unique art nouveau Palacio de Hierro (Iron Palace), while the most revealing is the excellent art museum, home to the second-largest Diego Rivera collection in Mexico.

Orizaba was founded by the Spanish to guard the Veracruz–Mexico City road. An industrial center in the late 19th century, its factories were early centers of the unrest that led to the unseating of dictator Porfirio Díaz. In 1898, a Scotsman running a local steel factory founded Mexico's first soccer team, called Orizaba Athletic Club. Today the city has a big brewery and is home to cement, textile and chemical industries.

⊙ Sights

★ Palacio de Hierro   MUSEUM
(Parque Castillo; ⊘9am-7pm) **FREE** The 'Iron Palace' is Orizaba's fanciful art nouveau landmark. The palace's interior has been converted into half a dozen small museums. Most notable are the Museo de la Cerveza, tracking Orizaba's beer industry; the Museo de Fútbol (soccer); the Museo de Presidentes y Banderas with info on *every* Mexican president as well as a whole load of flags; and the Museo Interactivo with a small planetarium and some science exhibits, including a bed of nails you can lie on.

Also on-site are the Museo de Geográfico de Orizaba (geography of the Orizaba area) and Museo de las Raíces de Orizaba (archaeological artifacts).

Alexandre Gustave Eiffel, a master of metallurgy who gave his name to the Eiffel Tower and engineered the Statue of Liberty's framework, designed this pavilion, which was built in Paris. Orizaba's mayor, eager to acquire an impressive European-style Palacio Municipal, bought it in 1892. Piece by piece it was shipped, then reassembled in Orizaba.

★ Teleférico de Orizaba   CABLE CAR
(Sur 4, btwn Calles Poniente 3 & Poniente 5; Mon-Fri M$30, Sat, Sun & holidays M$50; ⊘9am-6pm Mon-Fri, 9am-7pm Sat, Sun & holidays) Orizaba's newest attraction (opened in 2014) is this cable car, which rattles and sways visitors from its riverside site across from the Palacio Municipal right up to the top of the Cerro del Borrego hill for incredible views over the city and easy access to hiking routes. It takes just five minutes to travel nearly 1km and climb some 320m. Vertigo sufferers will probably just have to ask people to describe the view to them!

It's a fab excursion and once you reach the top of the Cerro del Borrego you'll find signed walking trails and an 'eco-park,' which has picnic areas, a small military museum, playgrounds and, between 1pm and 6pm on weekends, a re-creation of a military battle that took place here in the late 19th century.

Museo de Arte del Estado   MUSEUM
(State Art Museum; ☑272-724-32-00; cnr Av Oriente 4 & Sur 25; M$15; ⊘10am-7pm Tue-Sun) Orizaba's wonderful Museo de Arte del Estado is housed in a gorgeously restored colonial building dating from 1776. The museum is divided into rooms that include Mexico's second-most-important permanent Diego Rivera collection with 33 of his original works. There are also contemporary works by regional artists. Guides give complimentary tours in Spanish. The museum is frustratingly situated a good 2km east of Parque Castillo.

Parque Castillo   PLAZA
Smaller than your average Mexican city plaza, Parque Castillo is bereft of the normally standard Palacio Municipal (town hall), which sits several blocks away on Av Colón Poniente. Instead, it is watched over by the eclectic Palacio de Hierro and a 17th-century parish church, the Catedral de San Miguel Arcángel. On the south side is the neoclassical and still-functioning Teatro Ignacio de la Llave (1875), font of opera, ballet and classical music concerts.

Parque Alameda   PARK
(Av Poniente 2 & Sur 10; ⊛) About 1km west of the center, Parque Alameda is either a very large plaza or a very small park, depending on your expectations. What it doesn't lack is activity. Aside from the obligatory statues of dead heroes, you'll find an outdoor gym, a bandstand, food carts, shoe-shiners and a kids playground, including a huge jungle of bouncy castles and air-filled slides. Practically the whole city rolls in at weekends after Sunday Mass.

🏃 Activities

Río Orizaba   WALKING, OUTDOORS
Unusually for a Mexican city, Orizaba has an unbroken collection of pleasant paths bordering its clean eponymous river. There are 13 bridges along the way, including a suspension bridge and the arched Puente La Borda, dating from 1776. A good starting

VERACRUZ ORIZABA

point is off Poniente 8, about 600m north-west of the Palacio de Hierro. From here you can head north to the Puente Tlachichilico or south to Puente La Borda.

If as you walk you hear a deep growl that sounds suspiciously like a tiger, don't run away. There's an unexpected collection of cages along the walkway containing monkeys, parrots, crocodiles, lamas and, yes, even a tiger.

Adventure Tours ADVENTURE TOUR
A number of adventure tour operators are based in Orizaba. They can arrange various outdoor activities in nearby hills, mountains and canyons, including climbs partway up Pico de Orizaba. Highlights of the area include the gorgeous Cañón de la Carbonera near Nogales and the Cascada de Popócatl near Tequila. Recommended operators include **Alberto Gochicoa** (☑cell 272-103-73-44) and **Erick Carrera** (☑cell 272-134-55-71).

🛏 Sleeping

Higher-end options are on the Avenida Oriente 6 traffic strip. Low-end choices are near the center.

★ Hotel del Río HOTEL $
(☑272-726-66-25; http://hoteldelrio.tripod.com; Av Poniente 8 No 315, btwn Calles Norte 5 & Norte 7; r from M$300; P❄🖥) A very pleasant place for an exceptional price make this a surefire winner. It has an attractive location right by the Río Orizaba, simple modern rooms in an old building, and a congenial, bilingual owner. It might not be as flowery and fancy as some hotels in Veracruz state, but it's certainly among the best value.

Hotel Posada del Viajero HOTEL $
(☑272-726-33-20; Madero Norte 242; s/d M$180/249; P🖥) This narrow, central hotel doesn't look overly appealing from the outside, but it's unusually good value, and is run by a helpful and friendly family that keeps the place clean and tidy. Another plus is that there's a strong wi-fi signal in the rooms, which is rare for a budget hotel in Mexico.

Hotel Plaza Palacio HOTEL $
(☑272-725-99-23; Poniente 2 2-Bis; s/d/tr M$335/400/460; 🖥) You can't get more central than this place; the windows look directly onto the Palacio de Hierro. It's nothing special architecturally and the

rooms are clean but not particularly characterful. But you do get cable TV and a fan, as well as having the town right on your doorstep.

Gran Hotel de France HISTORIC HOTEL $$
(☑272-725-23-11; Av Oriente 6 No 186, btwn Calles Sur 5 & Sur 6; d incl breakfast from M$770; P😊❄) This historic late-19th-century building offers so much potential. It has a splendid, high-ceilinged patio with *azulejos* tiles, hanging plants and a fountain. However, the rooms are rather dark and drab, and the colonial atmosphere suffers somewhat from the *telenovelas* blaring from various TV sets in the lobby.

Hotel Mision Orizaba BOUTIQUE HOTEL $$$
(☑272-106-92-94; www.hotelesmision.com.mx; Oriente 6 No 64, btwn Calles Sur 9 & Sur 11; d from M$1065; P❄🖥🏊) Officially the smartest place in town, this recently revamped place has comfortable if surprisingly plain rooms set around a courtyard and a tiny swimming pool. There are some thoughtful touches to the rooms such as fresh flowers, writing desks and coffee machines. Plus the staff are very helpful.

🍴 Eating & Drinking

In sedate Orizaba many restaurants close early. Head to the plaza for noteworthy Orizaban snacks including *garnachas* (open tortillas with chicken, onion and tomato salsa) and filled *pambazos* (soft white bread rolls dipped in pepper sauce).

★ Gran Café de Orizaba CAFE $
(☑272-724-44-75; www.grancafedeorizaba.com; Palacio de Hierro, cnr Av Poniente 2 & Madero; snacks M$35-70; ⊙8am-10:30pm; 🖥) How often in Mexico can you sit back and enjoy a coffee and cake on the balcony of a regal cafe, inside an iron palace designed by Gustave Eiffel? Exactly – but this is your chance. The delightful decor, smart staff and selection of sandwiches, crepes and cake make this an obvious place to break up your exploration of Orizaba.

El Interior CAFE $
(Cnr Av 4 & Calle Sur 9; snacks M$40-70; ⊙9am-8:30pm) Books, coffee and art. This small literary cafe connected to a book and craft store is just what we wish all bookstores were like! El Interior is handily sandwiched between Parque Castillo and the Museo Arte del Estado.

La Pergola
MEXICAN $

(cnr Av Oriente 8 & Sur 7; mains M$50-100; ⊙7am-10pm) There are actually two Pergolas, both near the main drive-by of Avenida Oriente 6. Which you choose is a toss-up; both offer no-nonsense Mexican food and the breakfasts in particular receive a communal 'thumbs-up' from local opinion.

★ Marrón Cocina Galería
ITALIAN $$

(☑272-724-01-39; Oriente 4 1265 ; mains M$60-120; ⊙2-11pm Tue-Thu & Sun, 2pm-midnight Fri & Sat) With buckets for lampshades, sunflowers on the tables and rough painted wooden furnishings, this cool and very good Italian restaurant has an easy, informal and convivial atmosphere. The menu runs through all the classic Italian dishes (as well as some Mexican ones), but it's probably best loved by locals for its crunchy, thin pizzas.

El Churrasco Casa de Asados
STEAK $$

(☑272-725-28-83; Poniente 7 No 314, btwn Calle Sur 4 & Calle Sur 6; mains M$70-120, buffet men/women/children M$159/119/80; ⊙1-11pm Mon-Thu, 1pm-midnight Fri & Sat, 1-8pm Sun) Not a place that will appeal to vegetarians. This is a through and through steakhouse where a trolley is rolled up to your table covered in different cuts of meat from which you make your choice. It's then taken away and expertly sizzled up and served with a salad (see vegetarians, you're not totally overlooked!).

It also has a buffet with rather sexist pricing!

❶ Information

Banks with ATMs are on Avenida Oriente 2, a block south of the plaza.

Hospital Orizaba (☑272-725-50-19; www.corporativodehospitales.com.mx; Sur 5 No 398) Hospital

Tourist Office (☑272-728-91-36; www.orizaba.travel; Palacio de Hierro; ⊙9am-7pm) Has enthusiastic staff and plenty of brochures. City maps cost M$10.

❶ Getting There & Around

BUS

Local buses from Fortín and Córdoba stop four blocks north and six blocks east of the town center, around Avenida Oriente 9 and Norte 14. The AU 2nd-class bus station is at Zaragoza Poniente 425, northwest of the center.

The modern 1st-class **bus station** (cnr Av Oriente 6 & Sur 13) handles all ADO, ADO GL and deluxe UNO services.

CAR & MOTORCYCLE

Toll Hwy 150D, which bypasses central Orizaba, goes east to Córdoba and west, via a spectacular ascent, to Puebla (160km). Toll-free Hwy 150 runs east to Córdoba and Veracruz (150km) and southwest to Tehuacán, 65km away over the hair-raising Cumbres de Acultzingo.

Pico de Orizaba

At a cloud-scraping and breathless 5611m, the snowcapped Pico de Orizaba is Mexico's tallest mountain and it dominates the horizons for miles around. Called Citlaltépetl (Star Mountain) in the Náhuatl language, the views from the summit of this massive dormant volcano take in the mountains of Popocatépetl, Iztaccíhuatl and La Malinche to the west and the Gulf of Mexico to the east. You might imagine then that thoughts

VERACRUZ PICO DE ORIZABA

BUSES FROM ORIZABA

Daily first-class buses.

DESTINATION	FARE (M$)	DURATION (HR)	FREQUENCY (DAILY)
Córdoba	36	¾	every 30min
Fortín de las Flores	28	½	hourly
Mexico City (TAPO)	320-370	4	frequent
Mexico City (Terminal Norte)	370	4	3
Oaxaca	430	5	2
Puebla	188-228	2	frequent
Veracruz	160-170	2½	frequent
Xalapa	230	4	7

of scaling this monster would tempt tourists from far and wide, but you'd be wrong. The only higher peaks in North America are Mt McKinley in Alaska and Mt Logan in Canada and that should give you a clue as to why so few people summit the mountain. It is, put simply, a serious undertaking and is only really suitable for experienced high-altitude trekkers prepared for extreme cold and possible altitude sickness.

Anyone climbing the mountain should be well-equipped and all but the most experienced will need a guide. There are a number of recommended guide companies from the US, but the only local one is **Servimont** (☑245-451-50-19; www.servimont.com.mx; Ortega 1A, Tlachichuca), a climber-owned outfit passed down through the Reyes family. As the longest-running operation in the area, it also acts as a Red Cross rescue facility. It's based in the small town of Tlachichuca (2600m), which is a common starting point for expeditions. Book your expedition with Servimont two to four months in advance and allow four to seven days to acclimatize, summit and return. Do not attempt to rush up this mountain because altitude sickness, which at these heights can be deadly, is a very real concern. If you experience any kind of headaches, descend until the pain disappears.

Mexico's Volcanoes by RJ Secor offers some good info, and topographical maps can be mail-ordered way ahead of time or bought in person from **Inegi** (www.inegi.gob.mx) offices in Veracruz or Xalapa. The best climbing period is October to March, with the most popular time being December and January.

Hostel accommodations at Servimont's base camp (which is a former soap factory adorned with interesting mountaineering antiques) are included in your climbing package. Those not traveling with Servimont can stay at the friendly, family-run **Hotel Citlaltépetl** (☑245-451-51-69; makina_ tropikal@hotmail.com; Morelos 102, Tlachichuca; s/d/tr M$150/280/390) in Tlachichuca. To get here from Orizaba, catch a bus from the 1st-class terminal to Ciudad Serdán (M$50, two hours), then another to Tlachichuca (M$16, one hour).

NORTHERN VERACRUZ

The northern half of Veracruz state, between the coast and southern fringes of the Sierra Madre Oriental, mainly consists of lush rolling pastureland. Laguna de Tamiahua is the region's largest wetland, while the Gulf has some fine isolated (though sometimes polluted) beaches. The major attraction is El Tajín archaeological site, but even this attracts a fraction of the visitor numbers of more popular parts of Mexico. Beyond El Tajín you'll most likely be one of the only tourists around and constanty greeted with big-hearted smiles.

Tuxpan

☑783 / POP 85,000

Tuxpan (sometimes spelled Túxpam), 300km north of Veracruz and 190km south of Tampico, is a steamy fishing town and minor oil port. If you pass through, you can enjoy excellent seafood, take a trip across the broad Río Tuxpan to visit a little museum devoted to Cuban-Mexican friendship, or join vacationing Mexicans on Playa Norte, the beach 12km to the east. The town itself is no great beauty, but is well set up for overnighting travelers passing through.

◎ Sights & Activities

Museo de la
Amistad México-Cuba   MUSEUM
(Mexican-Cuban Friendship Museum; Obregón s/n; ◎9am-8pm) **FREE** Completely refurbished in 2014, the Mexican-Cuban Friendship Museum is filled with displays on José Martí, pictures of Che Guevara and Castro, and other memorabilia. To get to the museum, take a boat (M$5) across the river from the quay near the ADO bus station, walk several blocks south to Obregón, then turn right. The museum is at the western end of Obregón, on the river. Cuban-themed cultural events happen here on Friday nights.

On November 25, 1956, the errant lawyer-turned-revolutionary, Fidel Castro, set sail from the Río Tuxpan with 82 poorly equipped soldiers to start an uprising in Cuba. The sailing was made possible thanks to an encounter in Mexico City between Castro and Antonio del Conde Pontones (aka 'El Cuate'). On meeting Castro for the first time, Pontones, a legal arms dealer, was immediately taken by the Cuban's strong personality and agreed to help him obtain guns and a boat. To smooth the process he bought a house on the south side of the Río Tuxpan, where he moored the boat and allowed Fidel to meet in secret. Today that house is the Museo de la Amistad México-Cuba.

Playa Norte
BEACH

Tuxpan's beach, 12km east of town, is a wide strip stretching 20km north from the Río Tuxpan's mouth. *Palapa* restaurants make it a chilled-out place to eat cheap seafood and take a break from the city. Flag down the local buses marked 'Playa' (M$8, 25 minutes); they leave regularly from the south side of Blvd Reyes Heroles by the river quay and drop you at the south end of the beach.

Paseos Turísticos Negretti
BOAT TOUR, DIVING

(☑ 783-835-45-62; www.turismonegretti.mx; Recrea s/n) A local tour operator that organizes diving (M$2000 per eight-person group, not including equipment), fishing (M$400 per boat per hour), boat trips to nearby mangroves (M$550 for two hours), kayaking (M$100 per person) and water-skiing (M$300 for 30 minutes). It has an office on the south side of the Río Tuxpan where the cross-river ferry docks.

🛏 Sleeping

As a popular holiday spot for Mexicans, there's a wide range of hotels in Tuxpan including a number of smart business chain hotels.

Hotel Reforma
HOTEL $$

(☑ 783-834-11-46; http://hotel-reforma.com.mx; Av Juárez 25, btwn Garizurieta & Ortega; s/d M$835/935; Ⓟ❄🛜) The grand exterior of the Reforma leads into a smart atrium lobby with a small waterfall and some 98 comfortable if rather functional rooms. They include flat-screen TVs and relentless brown carpeting. There's a smart restaurant downstairs.

Hotel Florida
HOTEL $$

(☑ 783-834-02-22; www.hotel-florida.com.mx; Av Juárez 23, btwn Morelos & Garizurieta; incl breakfast s M$700-780, d M$800-880; Ⓟ⊖❄🛜) The centrally located Florida, opposite the Palacio Municipal, has friendly staff, a continental breakfast, spacious rooms with big windows and views over, well nothing in particular, and communal decks above bustling (read noisy) Avenida Juárez. Check out your room before you commit to one because there's quite a difference between them all, even if prices are the same.

🍴 Eating

Parque Reforma (the town's main plaza) is a block back from the *malecón* on Juárez, and is flanked by restaurants and cheap eateries. For the best seafood, locals will direct you downriver to a strip of *palapas* in the fishing community of La Mata; it's 6km east of the center, at the mouth of the Laguna de Tampamachoco. There are more *palapas* at Playa Norte.

El Mejicano
MEXICAN $

(Parque Reforma, cnr Morelos & Corregidora; mains M$50-100; ⊙7am-midnight; 🛜) This friendly, popular place has a cafeteria feel and gets busy mid-afternoon with local office workers coming for a cheap and delicious lunch. Try the chicken tacos and wash them down with a cool *agua de jamaica* (hibiscus iced tea). Service comes with good intentions but can be on the slow side.

ℹ Information

Staff at Tuxpan's simple **tourist booth** (☑ 783-110-28-11; http://tuxpan.com.mx; Palacio Municipal; ⊙9am-7pm Mon-Fri, 10am-2pm Sat) have vast reserves of enthusiasm: you'll go away overloaded with maps and brochures. Plenty of ATMs can be found on Avenida Juárez.

VERACRUZ TUXPAN

BUSES FROM TUXPAN

First-class departures from the ADO station.

DESTINATION	FARE (M$)	DURATION (HR)	FREQUENCY (DAILY)
Mexico City (Terminal Norte)	370-406	4-4½	7
Papantla	78	2	hourly
Poza Rica	40	1	frequent
Veracruz	334	6	hourly
Villahermosa	868	13	4
Xalapa	358	6	8

❶ Getting There & Around

Most 1st-class buses leaving Tuxpan are *de paso* (passing through). Booking a seat in advance might be a good idea. There are several bus terminals, but the 1st-class ADO **bus station** (cnr Rodríguez & Av Juárez) is the most convenient from the center.

There is a M$5 ferry service across the river at various points between Guerrero and Parque Reforma.

Papantla

📞 784 / POP 53,500 / ELEV 196M

Spread across a succession of wooded hills, the solidly indigenous city of Papantla has a history, look and feel that stares firmly back in time to a pre-Hispanic or, more precisely, Totonac period of grandeur. Predating the Spanish conquest, the city was founded around AD 1230. Traditionally a launching pad for people visiting the nearby ruins of El Tajín, Papantla has carved its own niche in recent years, stressing its indigenous heritage and promoting its central position in the world's best vanilla-growing region. You'll see Totonacs wearing traditional clothing here – the men in loose white shirts and trousers, the women in embroidered blouses and *quechquémitls* (traditional capes). Meanwhile *voladores* 'fly' and local artisans peddle handicrafts in the attractive main square.

◉ Sights

Zócalo
PLAZA

Officially called Parque Téllez, Papantla's *zócalo* is terraced into the hillside below the Iglesia de la Asunción. Wedged beneath the cathedral and facing the square is a symbolic 50m-long relief mural. Depicting Totonac and Veracruz history, it was designed by Papantla artist Teodoro Cano in 1979. A serpent stretches along the mural, bizarrely linking a pre-Hispanic stone carver, El Tajín's Pirámide de los Nichos, and an oil rig.

Iglesia de Nuestra Señora
de la Asunción
CHURCH

(Zócalo) Overlooking the *zócalo* from its high platform, this church is notable for its large cedar doors and quartet of indoor canvases by a Jalisco artist. Begun in 1570 by the Franciscans, it was added to in stages over the subsequent centuries; the bell tower wasn't completed until 1875.

Outside stands a 30m-high *voladores* pole. Ritualistic performances normally take place every two hours between 11am and 7pm Monday to Saturday. During low season (October to April), performances can be seen at 9am, noon, 4pm and 7pm Friday to Sunday.

Museo de la Ciudad
Teodoro Cano
MUSEUM

(Curti s/n; M$40; ⊙8am-8pm Mon-Sat)
Legendary Paplanta artist Teodoro Cano (b 1932) was once a student of Mexican art giant Diego Rivera. This small museum displays a handful of Cano's fine paintings, an alluring combination of both dark and ebullient scenes that are drawn almost exclusively from Totonac culture. The Totonac theme extends to the museum's other artifacts, including photos and traditional clothing displays. It's small, but immensely satisfying. A modern on-site auditorium hosts regular cultural events.

Volador Monument
MONUMENT

(Callejón Centenario s/n) At the top of the hill towers Papantla's *volador* monument, a 1988 statue by Teodoro Cano, portraying a musician playing his pipe and preparing for the four fliers to launch. To reach the monument, take Calle Centenario heading uphill from the southwest corner of the cathedral yard, before turning left into steep Callejón Centenario.

Casa de la Cultura
ARTS CENTER

(Pino Suárez s/n; ⊙10am-2pm Mon-Sat) The Casa de la Cultura hosts art classes and has a display of local artwork on the top floor.

⚐ Tours

Gaudencio Simbrón
FISHING

(📞783-842-01-21, 784-121-96-54; per day M$400) Guide Gaudencio Simbrón is more commonly known as *el de la ropa típica* (the guy who wears traditional clothes), because he sports Totonac costume. He works through Hotel Tajín and can guide you through El Tajín, Papantla and its environs.

✸ Festivals & Events

Feria de Corpus Christi
CULTURAL

The fantastic Feria de Corpus Christi, in late May and early June, is the big annual event in Papantla. As well as the bullfights, parades and *charreadas* (Mexican rodeos) that are usual in Mexico, Papantla celebrates its Totonac cultural heritage with spectacular indigenous dances. The main procession is on the first Sunday when *voladores* fly in elaborate ceremonies several times a day.

Festival de Vainilla   FOOD

A major celebration in Papantla, the Vanilla Festival on June 18 features indigenous dancers, gastronomic delights sold in street stalls, and all manner of vanilla products.

🛏 Sleeping

Papantla has a decidedly uninspiriing selection of places to stay. However, prices are low and rooms are at least clean!

Hotel Tajín   HOTEL $$

(📞784-842-01-21; www.hoteltajin.com.mx; cnr Núñez & Domínguez 104; s/d/tr M$645/725/847, ste from M$1018; 🅿️❄️🛰️🎱) So what if the interior is a little dated and worn; the Tajín is an intrinsic part of the Papantla experience with a prime edge-of-*zócalo* location and an Italianate pool and on-site cafe. It's not a fancy hotel by any means but the whole place oozes character, even if its 62 rooms range from the cozy to the ho-hum.

It's just off the *zócalo;* if you're facing the chuch, follow the road beneath it to the left.

Hotel Provincia Express   HOTEL $$

(📞784-842-16-45; provinciaexpress_papantla@hotmail.com; Enríquez 103; r incl breakfast from M$550; ❄️🛰️) This welcoming hotel is on the *zócalo,* facing the church across the square. There are 20 rooms in two categories – the spacious, bright and pleasant ones looking out across the main square (an extra M$70 each) or the rather cell-like, dark ones with smelly toilets elsewhere.

Needless to say, it's well worth paying the extra M$70 for the rooms facing the square; ask for rooms 1 to 6. Skip the breakfast.

🍴 Eating

Papantla's *zócalo* is home to a good selection of local restaurants and cafes. Mercado Juárez, at the southwest corner of the plaza opposite the cathedral, has stalls that sell cheap, fresh regional food.

Café Catedral   BAKERY, CAFE $

(cnr Domínguez & Curato; ⊙8am-10pm) The town's best coffeehouse (ask any local) doubles as a bakery. Grab a cake, muffin or *pan dulce* (sweet bread) from one of the display cases, sit at a cheap cafe table, and wait for the chief *señora* to come round with an old-fashioned tin jug to fill up your cup.

Everyone seems to know everyone else here, and local gossip bounces off the walls.

★ Plaza Pardo   MEXICAN $$

(📞784-842-00-59; 1st fl, Enríquez 105; mains M$75-130; ⊙7:30am-11:30pm; 🛰️) There's no place better to absorb the atmosphere of Papantla than the Plaza Pardo's delightful

---

PAPANTLA'S VOLADORES: BUNGEE JUMPING PIONEERS

The idea of launching yourself head first from a great height with only a rope tied around your ankles for support is popularly thought to have been conceived by bungee jumping New Zealanders in the 1980s. But in truth, Papantla's Totonac *voladores* (fliers) have been flinging themselves off 30m-high wooden poles (with zero safety equipment) for centuries. Indeed, so old is this rather bizarre yet mystic tradition, no one is quite sure how or when it started.

The rite begins with five men in elaborate ceremonial clothing climbing to the top of the pole. Four of them sit on the edges of a small frame at the top and rotate the frame to twist the ropes around the pole. The fifth man dances on the platform above them while playing a *chirimía*, a small drum with a flute attached. When he stops playing, the others fall backward. Arms outstretched, they revolve gracefully around the pole and descend to the ground, upside down, as their ropes unwind.

One interpretation of the ceremony is that it's a fertility rite and the fliers make invocations to the four corners of the universe. It's also noted that each flier circles the pole 13 times, giving a total of 52 revolutions. The number 52 is not only the number of weeks in the modern year but also was an important number in pre-Hispanic Mexico, which had two calendars, one corresponding to the 365-day solar year, the other to a ritual year of 260 days. The calendars coincided every 52 solar years.

Voladores ceremonies are best observed at El Tajín, outside Papantla's cathedral, and occasionally at Zempoala.

balcony overlooking the *zócalo*. While the interior is perfectly pleasant, it's a big step down in romance and views. The menu offers a large range of *antojitos,* fish and meats, all cooked in inventive ways.

Highlights are the octopus cooked in its ink and the passion fruit cheesecake – do NOT miss that!

Naku Restaurante Papanteco   MEXICAN **$$**
(☑784-842-31-12; Colegio Militar s/n; mains M$70-130; ☺8am-8pm Sun-Thu, 8am-10pm Fri & Sat) This restaurant, a couple of kilometres northeast of town, has traditionally dressed wait staff serving supposedly authentic Totonac cuisine (though we suspect/hope they've removed some of the less savory items that people probably ate back then...) The garden setting is nice, the food very tasty and the bread is baked in a big mud-clay oven.

Restaurante la Parroquia   INTERNATIONAL **$$**
(Hotel Tajín, Núñez 104; mains M$75-140; ☺8am-10pm; ☎) This air-conditioned hotel bar-restaurant has an extensive international menu. There's also a short wine list (M$80 to M$140), and it serves cocktails made with locally produced vanilla extract. The hotel also contains a cafe.

Shopping

Here in Mexico's leading vanilla-growing center, you'll find quality vanilla extract, vanilla pods and *figuras* (pods woven into the shapes of flowers, insects or crucifixes). There's a good artisan store on the southwest corner of the *zócalo*. You'll also encounter traditional Totonac clothing and handmade baskets.

❶ Information

The helpful **tourist office** (☑784-842-90-16; www.municipiopapantla.com; Reforma 100; ☺8am-6pm Mon-Fri) is inside the Palacio Municipal on the *zócalo*. It's a bit hidden; enter by the main door and ask the security guard for directions. There's a small kiosk outside the Palacio Municipal that's staffed at weekends too, and which has helpful maps of the town center and the surrounding region.

You'll find two banks with ATMs on Enríquez, just east of the *zócalo*. The post office is four blocks northwest of the plaza.

❶ Getting There & Away

A few long-distance buses leave from Papantla's quaint ADO **bus station** (cnr Juárez & Venustiano Carranza), a short, steep walk from the center. Taxis from the ADO to the center are M$20. You can make bus reservations online or at the ticket counter just east of the plaza. At the 2nd-class **bus station** (cnr 20 de Noviembre & Olivo), just off the plaza by the Pemex station, Transportes Papantla (TP) serves the coastal towns to the south and has slightly less expensive buses to Poza Rica and Tuxpan.

El Tajín

This wonderfully evocative, and under visited, ancient city was 'rediscovered' accidentally by an officious Spaniard looking for illegal tobacco plantations in 1785. Today, El Tajín paints a bold contemporary picture. Its pyramids and temples burst off a plain surrounded by low, verdant hills 6km west of Papantla. These extensive ruins are the most impressive reminder of Classic Veracruz civilization. If you're sensible, you'll try and come as late in the day as possible in order to catch the reddening sky, bubbling clouds and reflective calm (assuming your

BUSES FROM PAPANTLA

First-class ADO services.

DESTINATION	FARE (M$)	DURATION (HR)	FREQUENCY (DAILY)
Mexico City (Terminal Norte)	330	4½	6
Poza Rica	28	¾	frequent
Tampico	384	5½	2
Tuxpan	78	2	hourly
Veracruz	256	4	6
Xalapa	276	4	8

visit doesn't coincide with that of a tour bus) of the site shortly before closing.

Probably founded in AD 100, El Tajín (the name is Totonac for 'thunder,' 'lightning' or 'hurricane') reached its zenith as a city and ceremonial center between AD 600 and 900. Around 1230 the site was abandoned, possibly after a fire and attacks by Chichimecs. Quickly engulfed by the jungle, it lay unknown to the Spanish until 1785.

Among El Tajín's special features are rows of square niches on the sides of buildings, numerous ball courts and sculptures depicting human sacrifice connected with the ball game. Archaeologist José García Payón believed that El Tajín's niches and stone mosaics symbolized day and night, light and dark, and life and death in a universe composed of dualities, though many are skeptical of this interpretation.

◉ Sights

The **El Tajín site** (M$64; ⊙9am-5pm) covers an area of about 10 sq km. To see everything, you'll walk a few kilometers over a couple of hours. There's little shade and it can get blazingly hot, so come early or late. Most buildings and carvings have some sort of labeling in English and Spanish, but many of the information boards are weathered and hard to read, meaning that if you want to understand the site in detail, a guided tour will be a great help. A multilingual guide service is available for M$250 per hour for one to six people. Do drop in to the on-site museum at the entrance (included in your ticket price) to see an excellent model of the site and some impressive relics and handicrafts discovered here.

Bordering the parking lot are stalls selling food and handicrafts. The visitors center has a restaurant, a left-luggage room, an information desk and souvenir shops. Those seeking more information should look for the book *Tajín: Mystery and Beauty,* by Leonardo Zaleta, sometimes available in several languages in the souvenir shops.

Plaza Menor · PLAZA

Beyond the Plaza del Arroyo in the south of the site flanked by pyramids on four sides, is the Plaza Menor (Lesser Plaza), part of El Tajín's main ceremonial center and possible marketplace, with a low platform in the middle. All of the structures around this plaza were probably topped by small temples,

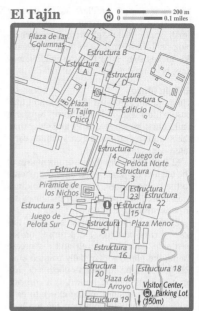

some decorated with red or blue paint, traces of which remain.

Juego de Pelota Sur · BALL COURT

Some 17 ball courts have been found at El Tajín. The Juego de Pelota Sur (Southern Ball Court) dates from about 1150 and is the most famous of the courts, owing to the six relief carvings on its walls which depict various aspects of the ball game ritual.

The panel on the northeast corner is the easiest to make out: in the center, three ball-players perform a ritual post-game sacrifice with one player ready to plunge a knife into the chest of another, whose arms are held by the third player. Death gods and a presiding figure look on. The other panels depict various scenes of ceremonial drinking of *pulque* (a milky, low-alcohol brew made from the *maguey* plant).

The Juego de Pelota de las Pinturas (Ball Court of the Paintings), to one side of the Pirámide de los Nichos, is so called as it has two very impressively preserved red and blue geometric friezes on its north-facing side.

Pirámide de los Nichos · PYRAMID

El Tajín's most emblematic structure, the beautifully proportioned Pyramid of the

Niches, is just off the Plaza Menor. The six lower levels, each surrounded by rows of small square niches, climb to 18m. Archaeologists believe that there were originally 365 niches, suggesting that the building may have been used as a kind of calendar.

El Tajín Chico   STRUCTURES

The path north toward Plaza El Tajín Chico passes the Juego de Pelota Norte (Northern Ball Court), which is smaller and older than the southern court and bears fainter carvings on its sides.

El Tajín Chico was the government area of the ancient city and would have been home to the ruling classes. Many of the buildings at El Tajín Chico have geometric stone mosaic patterns known as 'Greco' (Greek).

Edificio I, probably once a palace, has some terrific carvings. Estructura C, on the east side, with three levels and a staircase facing the plaza, was initially painted blue. Estructura A, on the plaza's north side, has an arch construction known as a corbeled arch, with two sides jutting closer to each other until they are joined at the top by a single slab, which is typical of Maya architecture. Its presence here is yet another oddity in the jigsaw puzzle of pre-Hispanic cultures.

Northwest of Plaza El Tajín Chico is the unreconstructed Plaza de las Columnas (Plaza of the Columns), one of the site's most important structures. It originally housed a large open patio and adjoining buildings stretching over the hillside. Some wonderful reassembled carved columns are displayed in the museum.

★ Voladores
Performances   INDIGENOUS CULTURE

A 30m high *voladores* pole stands outside the entrance to the ruins. Totonacs perform the *voladores* rite (which was traditionally carried out only once a year) three times per day beside the visitor center. Before they start, a performer in Totonac regalia requests donations (around M$20 per person should suffice) from the audience.

❶ Getting There & Away

Frequent buses come from Poza Rica. From Papantla, buses (M$15) marked 'Pirámides Tajín' leave every 20 minutes or so from Calle 16 de Septiembre, directly behind Hotel Tajín. The site is 300m from the highway – buses drop you off near the market, before the entrance to Tajín.

Taxis to/from Papantla cost M$70. There are usually one or two waiting outside the ruins.

South of Papantla

Hwy 180 runs near the coast for most of the 230km between Papantla and Veracruz. Highlights include a turtle conservation project, the sparkling Costa Esmeralda and Quiahuiztlán, a stunning, out-of-the-way Totonac site. The area is bereft of tourists during low season.

Tecolutla
📞 766 / POP 4600

This lazy seaside town, with a reasonable strip of sand and a slew of seafood restaurants and cheap hotels nearby, passes for one of Veracruz' more pleasant beachfronts. Cancún this most definitely isn't. Instead, the place is as dead as a doornail midweek when it's not a holiday, though in high summer and during Semana Santa it's a different story. There are banks and ATMs on the plaza.

🏃 Activities

★ Grupo Ecologista Vida
Milenaria   VOLUNTEERING

(📞 766-846-04-67; www.vidamilenaria.org.mx; Niños Héroes 1; donation required) ✐ This small turtle conservation place (a short walk from the center where Niños Héroes hits the ocean) is run by Fernando Manzano Cervantes, known locally as 'Papá Tortuga.' In addition to educating the public, he has been effectively protecting and releasing green and Kemp's ridley turtles here for over 35 years. Visitors are welcome to look at the hatchlings.

If you stop by, think about buying a trinket souvenir because this is a privately funded show. Volunteers are especially needed here in April and May, when patrolling beaches (35km worth) and collecting the turtle eggs is imperative (when possible the eggs are left in their original nest site but at others time they're reburied in a safer area). Most of the patrolling is done at night between 10pm and 6am. Camping and the use of kitchen and bathroom facilities is free to volunteers.

The highest number of turtles are released in June, but in late October you can join hundreds of locals in celebrating the release of the baby turtles in the Festival de Las Tortugas.

Boat Trips
BOAT TOUR

(per group M$350-450) Walk toward the Río Tecolutla on Emilio Carranza and you'll hit the *embarcadero* (pier), where boats will take you fishing or through dense mangrove forests rich with wildlife, including pelicans.

🛏 Sleeping

Hotels abound in this tourist-reliant town. Smarter options are outside the town itself, but there are plenty of cheap hotels near the plaza, and nicer ones toward the ocean.

Aqua Inn Hotel
HOTEL $$

(☑766-846-03-58; www.tecolutla.com.mx/aquainn cnr Aldama & Av Obregón; r from M$800; P ❄ 🛜 ⛱) This modern place in the middle of town and a short walk from the water has clean, functional rooms, all with cable TV. There's a small rooftop pool, and a cool cafe and restaurant. Prices drop steeply outside high season, making it a bargain during off-peak times.

★ Hotel Azúcar
BOUTIQUE HOTEL $$$

(☑232-321-06-78; www.hotelazucar.com; Carretera Federal Nautla-Poza Rica Km 83.5; r incl breakfast from US$136; P ❄ 🛜 ⛱) Not in Tecolutla itself, this impressive beach-side design hotel goes for the minimalist zen look. The rooms are scorching white with rustic chic decor, gorgeous whitewashed public areas topped in thatch, a sumptuous pool, impressive spa and a sublimely laid-back restaurant.

Hotel Santa Luisa Finca-Resort
RESORT $$$

(☑766-845-01-54; www.fincasantaluisa.com.mx; Carr Fed Gutiérrez Zamora; s/d incl breakfast from M$1050/1300; P ❄ 🛜 ⛱) While this hotel isn't on the beach, it can boast a riverside setting surrounded by dangly palm trees and tropical flowers. The rooms have summer bright decor and big windows from which to lap up the river view. Staff are helpful, the pool enticing and the restaurant serves good seafood. It's a short drive west of town.

🍴 Eating

Unless you hate fresh, inexpensive seafood, you'll enjoy the high-quality fare on offer in Tecolutla. On the beach, all the *palapa* places sell cold beer, while vendors hawk seafood cocktails. There are numerous eateries along the walk from the plaza to the beach on Avenida Obregón.

El Cotarro
SEAFOOD $

(Av Obregón s/n; mains M$40-90; ⊙8am-10pm) It may not keep up with the kitschy sea-themed decor of most of its neighbors, but El Cotarro's food is fresh and inexpensive. The *mojarra al ajo* is a freshly caught tilapia drenched in garlic.

Porteño Café
CAFE $

(cnr Aldama & Av Obregón; ⊙8am-11pm) This handy town center place, which lives inside the Aqua Inn, serves *antojitos* and panini as well as good coffee.

ℹ Getting There & Away

Tecolutla is 41km east of Papantla. There are regular 2nd-class Transportes Papantla buses between Tecolutla and Papantla (M$40) that arrive and depart from outside the church in Avenida Obregón, one block west of the main plaza. There is also a small but swanky 1st-class ADO **bus station** (cnr Abasolo & Ahumada) a few blocks from the main plaza. Many buses to and from Tecolutla have to transfer through Gutiérrez Zamora. ADO offers services to some major cities including Mexico City's Terminal Norte (M$358), as well as services to Poza Rica (M$88) and Papantla (M$56.)

Costa Esmeralda & Around

The Emerald Coast stretches roughly between La Guadalupe and Nautla, and its waters, more accurately described as semi-precious, lap the grayish-blond sands, which are a huge draw for Mexican holidaymakers. With so many other postcard pretty tropical beaches in Mexico this is a stretch of coastline that will probably have limited appeal to foreign travelers, not least because the main coastal road runs directly behind the beaches for much of their length, and development has been haphazard.

That said, it's a raging summer spot where small waves splash onto 20km of beaches, and Mexican families descend en masse to enjoy fresh fish, cold beer and swimming. The rest of the year, especially midweek, it's tranquil and a good match for beach lovers and crowd haters. You can throw down cash for upscale digs, or do it on the cheap. Advertised and unadvertised campgrounds proliferate.

At the mouth of the Río Filobobos (known as Río Bobos and famous for its rapids), head southwest of Nautla on Hwy 131 and you'll hit **Tlapacoyan**, where a handful of rafting companies are based, and where the waterfall Cascada de Encanto provides a gorgeous swimming spot. **Aventura Extrema** (📞229-202-65-57; www.aventuraextrema. com.mx; rafting packages from M$750) has facilities near Tlapacoyan and offers one- to three-day packages including food, accommodations or camping, and various other adventure activities. A highlight of Bobos rafting is the two riverside archaeological sites, **Caujilote** and **Vega de la Peña**, which most companies stop to visit.

Five kilometers south of Nautla is **Hotel Istirinchá** (📞235-317-42-01; www.istirincha. com.mx; Hwy 180 Km 102; r M$850-1250, ste M$1550; 🅿✳🛜🌊), a hard-to-classify resort/eco-hotel with some genuine green credentials. Once a tract of deforested land used for cattle grazing, the 70-hectare site has been transformed since it was bought in 1999 by a private owner intent on returning it to its natural jungle-like habitat. There's a lagoon for kayaking, an isolated driftwood-covered beach, trails through pines and palm trees, and (less 'eco') a collection of caged animals such as toucans and crocodiles. The organized activities, including horseback riding and cycling, are a little tame, but it's a lovely place to wander. Rooms are comfortable but do suffer from the damp a bit. There's also a restaurant and pool. Turtles nest on the beach from June to August. You'll see signs at the entrance on the highway and it's about a 20-minute walk to the hotel from where the bus leaves you.

To get to any coastal location on Costa Esmeralda, take a nondirect bus on Hwy 180 and tell the driver where you want to stop.

Punta Villa Rica & Around

Between Nautla and Veracruz, the coast is remarkably wild and unexplored, despite its weighty historical significance. The only blemish is Mexico's sole nuclear power station, on Laguna Verde, about 80km north of Veracruz port on Hwy 180. It's been in operation since 1989.

👁 Sights & Activities

Villa Rica   VILLAGE

Standing in this tiny dusty fishing village 69km north of modern-day Veracruz, it's hard to believe you're gazing at the site of the first European-founded settlement north of Panama in mainland America.

These days the historic settlement hardly merits a label on most maps, though there's a smattering of houses here, along with a small hotel, a couple of rustic restaurants and the weed-covered foundations of some buildings constructed by Cortés and his men soon after their arrival.

Never properly consolidated, the 'Veracruz that once was,' founded as Villa Rica de la Vera Cruz in 1519, lasted only until 1524 when it was moved to present-day La Antigua. There's a small and attractive curved beach, and you can trace it around past some dunes and across an isthmus to reach the Cerro de la Cantera, a rocky outcrop famed for its plunging *quebraditas* (ravines).

Villa Rica is about 1km east of the main Hwy 180. Ask any bus driver on the Cardel–Nautla run to stop at the entrance road to the Quiahuiztlán ruins. From here it's an easy walk to the village.

⭐**Quiahuiztlán**   ARCHAEOLOGICAL SITE
(M$36, Sun free; ⏰9am-5pm) Perched like a mini–Machu Picchu on a plateau beneath a horn-shaped mountain (the Cerro de Metates), Quiahuiztlán (place of the rains) is a pre-Hispanic Totonac town and necropolis. Counting 15,000 inhabitants at the time of Cortés' arrival in 1519, its history before that is sketchy, although there was certainly a settlement here by AD 800. Enjoying a commanding view of the Gulf coast, the now-deserted site has two pyramids, more than 70 tombs and some carved monuments.

Rock climbers revere the precipitous Cerro de Metates (with routes graded 5.6 to 5.8) that rises behind. It's a pleasant 3km walk up a winding paved road to the part of the site that overlooks the ocean. From here you can experience the sacred Totonac ruins in solitude and amid nature, unlike more touristed ruins. The first question most of the sporadic visitors to these amazing Totonac ruins ask is: why, given its historic importance and stunning setting, is there no one else here? Alas, there's no logical answer. Rather it's best just to relish the tranquillity and keep mum. If you want to arrive by a Hwy 180 bus, have the driver drop you at the Quiahuiztlán turnoff.

⭐**EcoGuías La Mancha**   OUTDOORS
(📞296-100-11-63; www.ecoturismolamancha.com; La Mancha-Actopan, Carretera Federal Cardel-

Nautla Km 31; campsites own/borrowed tent M$60/100, cabañas per person/entire M$150/1200) 🖉 All hail this progressive association of locals that has developed a homespun, grass-roots environment education center. The facilities, located 1km from the beach, offer interpretive walks, bird-watching excursions, apiary tours, horseback riding and kayak tours where you can see mangroves and wildlife. Accommodations are rustic (eight-person cabins or rent-a-tents), but it's a great off-the-beaten-path choice that supports the local community. From the La Mancha eastbound turnoff on Hwy 180, it's 1km down the road. Bring repellent.

🛏 Sleeping & Eating

Rustic accommodations are available at EcoGuías La Mancha. All the eating options can be found on Villa Rica's compact main drag, which leads from the main coastal road to the beach.

Villas Arcon   HOTEL **$$**
(📞296-964-91-72; www.villasarcon.com; Villa Rica; s/d M$700/850; 🅿✳🛜🗙) At the entrance to Villa Rica, this attractively set low-rise resort hotel offers spotless and well-loved rooms that allow you to live in some comfort while getting in touch with Mexico's gritty essence. The rooms surround a pool and it's a short walk through the village to the beach.

Restaurant Miriam   SEAFOOD **$**
(Villa Rica; mains M$50-120; ⊙10am-7pm) Friendly Miriam and her extended family serve up delicious seafood dishes to order, in what is essentially an extension of their living room. Be warned, when she offers you her *picantísimo* (spiciest) dish, she's not kidding!

Restaurante Totonacapan   SEAFOOD **$**
(Villa Rica; mains M$60-120; ⊙noon-8pm) The jovial proprietor often calls innocent bystanders over to this alfresco thatched-roof affair, the last structure on the town's main road and just where the beach begins. The food is ocean-fresh fish and shrimp.

SOUTHEAST VERACRUZ

Southeast Veracruz is arguably the most beautiful part of the state, and yet tourism is still on a very modest scale. Here you'll find languorous wetlands, volcano-dappled rainforest, breathtaking lakes and the superb Reserva de la Biosfera Los Tuxtlas, a well-run biosphere reserve that will appeal to anyone wanting to get off the beaten track. As part of the former heartland of ancient Olmec culture, the area is laden with archaeological sites, not to mention Tlacotalpan, a Unesco World Heritage site that will enchant anyone lucky enough to head this way.

Tlacotalpan

📘288 / POP 7600
Possibly the finest Unesco World Heritage town that no one's ever heard of, Tlacotalpan is a near-perfect identikit of early-19th-century colonial architecture, completely unblemished by modern interferences, save for a light (by Mexican standards) smattering of traffic. The color palette is extraordinary here; the lucid sunsets over the adjacent Río Papaloapan add subtle oranges and yellows to the rainbow of colonial houses, bringing to mind a Havana where the houses haven't been allowed to decay.

Once an important river port, Tlacotalpan has changed little since the 1820s. The town, Unesco-listed in 1998, was hit by devastating floods in September 2010 which inundated 500 historic buildings and prompted the evacuation of 8500 people. The recovery has been remarkable, with only a high watermark drawn onto a wall on Calle Alegre to show how disastrous the flooding was.

⊙ Sights & Activities

While Tlacotalpan does have a couple of small museums and other such 'classic' tourist sights, this is the kind of town where you'll have a magical time just by simply walking the streets and taking in the colors and atmosphere. Tlacotalpan has two plazas, Hidalgo and Zaragoza, which are directly adjacent to each other. Together they harbor equally magnificent churches; the light blue **Capilla o Santuario de la Candelaria** dating from 1779 and furnished with local coral stone, and the neoclassical **Iglesia San Cristóbal**, begun in 1812 and gorgeously painted in blue and white.

Be sure to take a stroll by the riverside and down Cházaro, which starts from the Palacio Municipal and has wall-to-wall, whacky-colored, colonial-style houses and buildings with columns, tiles and high arches.

Museo Salvador Ferrando
MUSEUM

(Alegre 6; M$20; ⊙11am-6pm Tue-Sat, 12:30-7pm Sun) The Ferrando, named for a Tlacotalpan artist, is the best of Tlacotalpan's handful of mini-museums. It displays assorted artifacts, furniture, paintings and other knickknacks within a charming old colonial mansion.

Casa Museo Agustín Lara
MUSEUM

(Beltrán 6; M$20; ⊙10am-6pm Mon-Sat) This museum features memorabilia of *tlacotalpeño* Agustín Lara (1900–70), a legendary musician, composer and Casanova. Its appeal is perhaps greater to Mexicans than it is to foreign tourists.

Villin Montalio
GALLERY

(5 de Mayo 53; ⊙9am-6pm Mon-Sat) Tlacotalpan is well known for its locally made cedar furniture. Drop by this office/workshop to see it being made, and to see some of the finished products on display as well.

Mini-Zoológico Museo
MUSEUM

(Av Carranza 25; ⊙10am-5pm Mon-Sat) Lovers of the utterly bizarre should hotfoot it to the home of Don Pío Barrán. He keeps several enormous crocodiles and a range of artifacts, including a locally excavated mastodon tooth and a sword that supposedly belonged to Porfirio Díaz. A donation is expected (M$15 to M$20 should suffice).

Boat Rides
BOAT TOUR

(hour-long ride M$300) If you walk the *malecón* near the restaurants, you're bound to run into a *lanchero* (boatman) offering to whisk you down the scenic river for an hour-long boat ride to see a nearby lagoon. It's not the Amazon, but it's a lovely way to spend a late afternoon.

🎊 Festivals & Events

Día de la Candelaria
RELIGIOUS

In late January and early February, Tlacotalpan's huge Candelaria festival features bull-running in the streets. An image of the Virgin is also floated down the river, followed by a flotilla of small boats.

🛏 Sleeping

Prices triple or quadruple during the Candelaria holiday, during which reservations, made weeks ahead of time, are essential.

★ Hotel Posada Doña Lala
HISTORIC HOTEL $$

(☑288-884-24-55; http://hoteldonalala.mx; Av Carranza 11; s/d/ste M$650/750/1000; P🖥❄) 🖥) With its sun-bleach pink facade looking toward the river, Doña Lala is a gorgeous colonial-style hotel with spacious rooms and high ceilings that manages to be effortlessly elegant without being over the top. We'd go so far as to say it's one of our favorite hotels in Veracruz. For great views try and get a room overlooking the square.

There's an excellent restaurant downstairs and even an indoor pool to enjoy.

Casa de la Luz
GUESTHOUSE $$

(☑288-884-23-31; www.casadelaluz-mexico.com; Aguirre 15; r/ste M$550/800; ❄🖥) Once the home of the town's midwife, this old whitewashed house has been beautifully looked after by its friendly expat owner, Bill. He welcomes guests into his home and goes to extraordinary lengths to ensure they're happy and well looked after during their stay. There are two rooms available: one standard double, and one suite with two double beds.

There's also an apartment, which can be rented for longer stays.

Hotel Casa del Río
HOTEL $$

(☑288-884-29-47; www.casadelrio.com.mx; Cházaro 39; r/ste M$850/1100; 🖥❄🖥) Creating modern, stylish, minimalist rooms in a colonial mansion is definitely a challenge, but the Hotel Casa del Río does a good job of it with its nine spacious offerings. Its best feature is definitely the terrace overlooking the river. Oh, and the breakfast. We liked that a lot!

Hotel Doña Juana
GUESTHOUSE $$

(☑288-884-34-80; http://hoteldonajuana.com; Juan Enríquez 32; r from M$550; ❄🖥) This is a modern multi-layered building that has small, but very well-kept rooms. The ample use of terracotta colors and statement art make it stand out from many similarly priced places, as do the helpful, smiling staff.

🍴 Eating

The riverside is lined by fish restaurants that operate from lunchtime to sunset each day, serving up the catch of the day.

Rokala
MEXICAN $$

(Plaza Zaragoza; mains M$80-155; ⊙6pm-1am; 🖥) With its unbeatable position under the colonial arches on the Plaza Zaragoza, this friendly place with alfresco dining buzzes year-round. Mains range from fresh fish and prawns plucked from the river to meat grills and typical *antojitos*. For atmosphere alone it's a clear winner, but the food itself is only average. Remember to slap on some mosquito repellent if eating here in the evening.

Restaurant Doña Lala　　MEXICAN **$$**
(Av Carranza 11; mains M$75-160; ⊘7am-10pm; 🛜) Easily the smartest eating option in town, this place inside the hotel of the same name has a friendly staff and is patronized by a crowd of local eccentrics who vie for the best seats on its terrace. The wide-ranging selection of Mexican dishes won't disappoint and the locally caught seafood (especially the prawns) is sensational.

☆ Entertainment

Tlacotalpan is surprisingly lively at night for such a small town. Indeed, at weekends, you may need earplugs to sleep. Bars around Plaza Zaragoza and along Avenida Carranza spill out into the streets, music is loud and the party goes on into the wee hours. More formal gatherings convene in the gorgeous French-style **Teatro Netzahualcóyotl** (Av Carranza).

ℹ Information

There's an ATM in one side of Hotel Posada Doña Lala, near the plaza.
Tourist Office (www.tlacotalpan-turismo.gob. mx/turismo.html; Alegre & Lerdo de Tejada; ⊘9am-3pm Mon-Fri) Right off Plaza Hidalgo. The office has helpful maps.

ℹ Getting There & Around

Hwy 175 runs from Tlacotalpan up the Papaloapan valley to Tuxtepec, then twists and turns over the mountains to Oaxaca (320km). ADO, whose riverside station is situated outside the Mercado Municipal, three blocks east of the center, offers services to Mexico City (M$638), Puebla (M$496), Xalapa (M$252) and San Andrés Tuxtla (M$92).

Wonderfully flat, Tlacotalpan is a perfect spot for bike riding. You can arrange bike hire through **Bici Cletando** (📞288-100-46-86; per hr M$30), which rents bikes from a stand outside the Iglesia La Candelaria on Plaza Zaragoza.

Santiago Tuxtla

📞294 / POP 15,000 / ELEV 180M
Santiago centers on a lovely, verdant main plaza – one of the state's prettiest – and is surrounded by the rolling green foothills of the volcanic Sierra de los Tuxtlas. It's far more laid-back and a touch more charming than its built-up neighbor San Andrés, with its plaza strewn with ladies arm-in-arm, couples lip-to-lip and shoes getting vigorously shined. It's not on the tourist track per se, but it has a couple of interesting sights that make it worth a visit.

All buses arrive and depart near the junction of Morelos and the highway. To get to the center, continue down Morelos, then turn right into Ayuntamiento, which leads to the main plaza, a few blocks away.

⊙ Sights

Olmec Head　　MONUMENT
(Plaza Olmeca) Dominating the main plaza, this stone monolith is known as the 'Cobata head,' after the estate where it was found. Thought to be a very late Olmec production, it's the biggest known Olmec head, weighing in at 40 tonnes, and is unique in that its eyes are closed.

Museo Tuxteco　　MUSEUM
(📞294-947-10-76; Ayuntamiento; M$42; ⊘9am-5pm Tue-Sun) This museum on the main plaza exhibits artifacts such as Olmec stone carvings, including a colossal head, a monkey-faced *hacha* (axe) with obsidian eyes, and a Tres Zapotes altar replica. There's also an interesting Spanish colonial room, with impressive suits of armor and a bust of poor Cuauhtémoc, the last Aztec emperor. Sadly, there's no labeling in English.

★⁕ Festivals & Events

Santiago celebrates the festivals of San Juan (June 24) and Santiago Apóstol (June 25) with processions and dances, including the *Lisere*s, in which the participants wear jaguar costumes.

The week before Christmas is also a time of huge festivity.

⌂ Sleeping & Eating

★ **Mesón de Santiago**　　HOTEL **$$**
(📞294-947-16-70; www.mesonsantiago.com.mx; 5 de Mayo No 8; d from M$760; 🅿❄🛜⊞) With a fresh white interior and a well-preserved colonial exterior, this fantastic place right on the main plaza is unexpected in such a quiet and little-visited place. The peaceful courtyard is immaculate and has a small pool. Rooms are tastefully decorated, with deeply burnished wood furniture, beautifully tiled bathrooms and domed staircases.

VERACRUZ SANTIAGO TUXTLA

BUSES FROM SANTIAGO TUXTLA

First-class buses.

DESTINATION	FARE (M$)	DURATION (HR)	FREQUENCY (DAILY)
Córdoba	264	3½	3
Mexico City	550-646	8	3
Puebla	380-512	5½	2
San Andrés Tuxtla	36-44	½	frequent
Tlacotalpan	76	1	4
Veracruz	168	2½	frequent
Villahermosa	374	5½	1 Fri, Sun & Mon
Xalapa	278	4½	3

Restaurant Colonial   MEXICAN **$**
(Hwy 180; mains M$60-120; ⊗8am-8pm) This
is the smartest place in town (OK, that's
not saying a huge amount), where you'll
find *cocina típica* with a focus on seafood
and grilled meat. It's just a little up the hill
from the ADO bus station (in the direction
of Veracruz), on the main road through the
town.

❶ Getting There & Around

All local and regional buses and *colectivos taxis*
to San Andrés Tuxtla are frequent and stop at
the junction of Morales and Hwy 180. A private
taxi between the towns is M$70. Frequent 2nd-
class buses also go to Catemaco, Veracruz,
Acayucan and Tlacotalpan.

While the TLT and AU stops are just down Morelos, there's an ADO bus station on the highway
itself, at the corner with Morelos.

Tres Zapotes

📞 294 / POP 3500

The important late-Olmec center of Tres
Zapotes is now just a series of mounds in
cornfields. However, interesting artifacts are
displayed at the museum in the town of Tres
Zapotes, 23km west of Santiago Tuxtla. The
trip to this tiny town is well worthwhile if
you're interested in archaeology. And if old
stones aren't your thing, then a visit offers a
great chance to get seriously off the beaten
track.

Tres Zapotes was occupied for over 2000
years, from around 1200 BC to AD 1000. It
was probably first inhabited while the great
Olmec center of La Venta (Tabasco) still
flourished. After the destruction of La Venta
(about 400 BC), the city carried on in what
archaeologists call an 'epi-Olmec' phase –
the period during which the Olmec culture

dwindled, as other civilizations (notably
Izapa and Maya) came to the fore. Most
finds are from this later period.

The small **Museo de Tres Zapotes**
(M$35; ⊗9am-5pm Tue-Sun) notably has the
1.5m Tres Zapotes head, an Olmec head dating from about 100 BC. The biggest piece,
Stela A, depicts three human figures in the
mouth of a jaguar. Other pieces include a
sculpture of what may have been a captive
with hands tied behind his back, and the upturned face of a woman carved into a throne
or altar. The museum attendant is happy to
answer questions in Spanish or give a tour
(tipping is appreciated).

The road to Tres Zapotes goes southwest
from Santiago Tuxtla; a 'Zona Arqueológica'
sign points the way from Hwy 180. Eight
kilometers down this road, you fork right
onto a paved stretch for the last 15km to
Tres Zapotes. It comes out at a T-junction,
from where you go left then left again to
reach the museum. From Santiago Tuxtla
there are 2nd-class buses (M$30) and tax-
is (M$30/120 *colectivo*/private). Taxis leave
from the Sitio Puente Real, on the far side of
the pedestrian bridge at the foot of Zaragoza
(the street going downhill beside the Santiago Tuxtla museum).

San Andrés Tuxtla

📞 294 / POP 62,000 / ELEV 300M

Like a lot of modern towns, San Andrés puts
function before beauty. The busy service
center of the Las Tuxtlas region is best used
for bus connections and link-ups to its more
enticing peripheral sights, including a volcano and a giant waterfall. Cigar aficionados
will definitely want to visit, as San Andrés is
Mexico's cigar capital. The center of town is

orderly and attractive, with a soaring orange and yellow tiled church on the main plaza.

◉ Sights & Activities

Salto de Eyipantla · WATERFALL
(M$10) Twelve kilometers southeast of San Andrés, a 244-step staircase leads down to the spectacular Salto de Eyipantla, a 50m-high, 40m-wide waterfall. To avoid the steps (and a soaking), you can also enjoy it from a *mirador* (lookout). Part of Mel Gibson's movie *Apocalypto* was filmed here.

Follow Hwy 180 east for 4km to Sihuapan, then turn right to Eyipantla. Frequent TLT buses (M$12) make the trip from San Andrés, leaving from the corner of Cabada and 5 de Mayo, near the market. Car park 'guardians' will ask for money to watch your car and we've received reports that if you don't pay up they'll simply vandalize it while you're gone.

Santa Clara Cigar Factory · CIGAR FACTORY
(☎294-947-99-06; Blvd 5 de Febrero No 10; ☺8:30am-3pm) FREE Watch and inhale as the *puros* are speedily rolled by hand at this cigar factory, on the highway, a block or so away from the bus station. Cigars of assorted shapes and sizes, including the monstrous Magnum, are available at factory prices, and the 50 *torcedores* employed here (together rolling an amazing 10,000 *puros* a day) are happy to demonstrate their technique.

Laguna Encantada · LAKE
The 'Enchanted Lagoon' occupies a small volcanic crater 3.5km northeast of San Andrés in jungle-like terrain. A dirt road goes there, but no buses do. Some locals advise not walking by the lake alone as muggings have occurred in the past; check with the guides at the nearby Yambigapan homestay for updates.

Cerro de Venado · NATURE RESERVE
(M$5) 🏃 This 23-hectare reserve, which was created in 2009 with the planting of thousands of trees, is 2.5km from Laguna Encantada on the road to Ruíz Cortines. There are 500 steps up to a 650m hill with fabulous views of the town, lake and mountains.

🛏 Sleeping & Eating

San Andrés doesn't have a lot of choice, but you'll be comfortable.

Hotel Posada San Martín · HOTEL $$
(☎294-942-10-36; Av Juárez 304; s/d/tr M$488/575/660; P❊🖥❄) Midway between the main road and the main plaza, this hacienda-style posada is a fabulous deal and a very unexpected find. It has a pool set in a peaceful garden and antiques scattered about its public areas. The rooms are spacious, clean and all have charmingly tiled sinks.

Hotel del Parque · HOTEL $$
(☎294-942-01-98; www.hoteldelparque.com; Madero 5; s/d/ste M$600/700/1200; P❊🖥) San Andrés' main central option is clean, modern and has a busy cafe on the ground floor where locals love to drink coffee and gossip. Some rooms have lovely views of the cathedral and, although bathrooms are rather pokey and on the old side, this is a good, if bland, choice.

Yambigapan · MEXICAN $
(Hotel Posada San Martín, Av Juárez 304; mains M$50-80; ☺7:30am-8pm; 🖥) Inside Hotel Posada San Martín, the town's nicest hotel, you'll find this small, cozy restaurant, serving exceptionally tasty and interesting local dishes whipped up by the talented *doña* Amelia. If you like her food (which you certainly will), then sign up to one of her informal cookery classes (Spanish only; price negotiable).

VERACRUZ SAN ANDRÉS TUXTLA

BUSES FROM SAN ANDRÉS TUXTLA
The services listed run from ADO.

DESTINATION	FARE (M$)	DURATION (HR)	FREQUENCY (DAILY)
Córdoba	272	3½	3
Mexico City	624	8	3
Puebla	360-518	6½	2
Santiago Tuxtla	36-44	⅓	hourly
Tlacotalpan	92	1½	3
Veracruz	164	3	hourly
Xalapa	284	5	2

ⓘ Information

The tiny **tourist office** (Madero 1; ⊙ 8:30am-3:30pm) inside the Palacio Municipal is on the west side of the main plaza. A Banamex (with ATM) is on the south side; the market is three blocks west.

ⓘ Getting There & Around

San Andrés is the transportation center for Los Tuxtlas, with fairly good bus services in every direction. First-class buses with ADO and 2nd-class with AU depart from their respective stations on Juárez just off the Santiago Tuxtla–Catemaco highway, and about a 10-minute walk from the center. Rickety but regular 2nd-class TLT buses are often the quickest way of getting to local destinations. They leave from a block north of the market and skirt the north side of town on 5 de Febrero (Hwy 180). Frequent *colectivos taxis* to Catemaco and Santiago also leave from the market – they're speedier than the bus but cost a fraction more.

Catemaco

🖉 294 / POP 28,000 / ELEV 340M

Sleepy Catemaco is an unlikely traveler hotspot, and yet it's the obvious base for exploring Reserva de la Biosfera Los Tuxtlas. Small and not a little scruffy, it's reminiscent of a dusty backpacker destination from the 1980s, but without a significant number of backpackers. With a long tradition of shamans who will exorcise your nasty spirits, a gorgeous lakeside setting and alluring natural sights branching out in all directions, Catemaco is somewhere anyone getting to know the region will want to pass through.

◉ Sights & Activities

Laguna Catemaco   LAKE

🖉 Catemaco sits on the shore of the 16km-long Laguna Catemaco, which is ringed by volcanic hills and is actually a lake and not a lagoon. East of town are a few modest gray-sand beaches where you can take a dip in cloudy water.

Basílica del Carmen   CHURCH

Catemaco's main church was named a basilica (ie a church with special ceremonial rights) in 1961, due primarily to its position as a pilgrimage site for the Virgen del Carmen. It's said she appeared to a fisherman in a cave by Laguna Catemaco in 1664, in conjunction with a volcanic eruption. A statue of the virgin resides in the church and is venerated on her feast day every July 16.

The intricate interior and haunting stained glass of the church belie its modernity; the current building only dates from 1953, though it looks at least a century older.

🛌 Sleeping

Hotel Acuario   HOTEL $

(🖉 294-943-04-18; cnr Boettinger & Carranza; r from M$300; P🖥) This friendly budget option has 25 clean rooms just off the *zócalo*. It's well kept, though plain and fan-cooled. Some rooms have balconies and views – try for one of these, as those at the back lack natural daylight. Cable TV is a bonus.

Hotel Los Arcos   HOTEL $$

(🖉 294-943-00-03; www.arcoshotel.com.mx; Madero 7; s/d from M$600/850; P🖥🖥🖥) This is the smartest option in the town itself. Centrally located, it's a friendly, well-run place

---

THE WITCHING HOUR

On the first Friday in March each year, hundreds of *brujos* (shamans), witches and healers from all over Mexico descend on Catemaco to perform a mass cleansing ceremony. The event is designed to rid them of the previous year's negative energies, though in recent years the whole occasion has become more commercial than supernatural. Floods of Mexicans also head into town at this time to grab a shamanic consultation or *limpia* (cleansing), and eat, drink and be merry in a bizarre mix of otherworldly fervor and hedonistic indulgence.

Witchcraft traditions in this part of Veracruz go back centuries, mixing ancient indigenous beliefs, Spanish medieval traditions and voodoo practices from West Africa. Many of these *brujos* multitask as medicine men or women (using both traditional herbs and modern pharmaceuticals), shrinks and black magicians, casting evil spells on enemies of their clients. If you want to arrange a consultation, contact a tour agency, or ask along the *malecón*.

Catemaco

with small rooms with desks. Each room has its own semi-private outdoor space and seating area. There's cable TV and even a (very) small pool.

Hotel La Finca RESORT **$$$**
(☑294-947-97-00; www.lafinca.mx; Hwy 180 Km 47; r from M$1500; P☻❋🛜🖵) This friendly resort on the lakeshore, some 2km west of the town, is rather dated and pricey (discounts out of season), but it's the most comfortable place to stay in Catemaco. Rooms have large, lake-view balconies, and a pool with slides and a hot tub. It's a deal outside peak seasons, if seclusion from town is pleasing to you.

It provides *lancha* (motorboat) and spa services.

✖ Eating & Drinking

The lake provides the specialties here: *tegogolo* (a snail, reputed to be an aphrodisiac, eaten with chili, tomato, onion and lime) sold by street vendors, and *chipalchole* (shrimp or crab-claw soup). Many similar restaurants serving fresh fish line the *malecón*.

La Casa de Los Tesoros CAFE **$**
(Aldama 4; mains M$30-100; ⊙9am-9pm; 🛜) Creative in every way. This very popular hippie-styled place is part cafe-restaurant, part gallery and part arty gift shop, selling locally produced handicrafts. It's renowned among locals for its breakfasts and in particular for the gut-busting build your own omelettes. There's also a good range of herbal teas.

Catemaco

◎ Sights
1 Basílica del Carmen............................C2

🛏 Sleeping
2 Hotel Acuario...B1
3 Hotel Los Arcos....................................B2

✖ Eating
4 La Casa de Los Tesoros......................C2
5 La Ola..B2

🍸 Drinking & Nightlife
6 La Panga...A2

La Ola SEAFOOD, MEXICAN **$$**
(Paseo del Malecón s/n; dishes M$75-140; ⊙11am-9pm; 🛜) A vast waterfront restaurant on the *malecón,* serving all the seafood you could want, including reasonable *pargo* (red snapper), *a la veracruzana* (spicy sauce) or *empanizado* (in breadcrumbs).

La Panga BAR
(Paseo del Malecón s/n; mains M$85-160; ⊙9am-2am, restaurant to 7pm) This bar-restaurant, literally floating on the lake with its own boardwalk, is an idyllic place to lean back, sip *cerveza* and grab a bite to eat while the sun disappears beyond the lake and the rolling hills.

ℹ Information

Catemaco slopes gently down toward the lake. A **tourist office** (☑434-943-00-16; Municipalidad; ⊙9am-3pm & 4-9pm Mon-Fri) on the north side of the *zócalo* is extremely helpful, though no English is spoken. It provides high-quality maps of the surrounding region.

BUSES FROM CATEMACO

ADO's first-class bus services.

DESTINATION	FARE (M$)	DURATION (HR)	FREQUENCY (DAILY)
Mexico City	580-674	9½	3
Puebla	534	7	4
Santiago Tuxtla	44	1	frequent
San Andrés Tuxtla	32	½	frequent
Veracruz	180	3½	7
Xalapa	316	5½	2

❶ Getting There & Away

ADO and AU buses operate from a lakeside **bus terminal** (cnr Paseo del Malecón & Revolución). Local 2nd-class TLT buses run from a bus station 700m west of the plaza by the highway junction and are a bit cheaper and more frequent than the 1st-class buses. *Colectivo* taxis arrive and depart from El Cerrito, a small hill about 400m to the west of the plaza on Carranza.

To arrive at communities surrounding the lake and toward the coast, take inexpensive *piratas*. They leave from a corner five blocks north of the bus station.

Reserva de la Biosfera Los Tuxtlas

The various nature reserves around Catemaco were conglomerated in 2006 into this Biosphere Reserve under Unesco protection. This unique volcanic region, rising 1680m above the coastal plains of southern Veracruz, lies 160km east of the Cordillera Neovolcánica, making it something of an ecological anomaly. Its complex vegetation is considered the northernmost limit of rainforest in the Americas. Despite its many charms, the region receives few international visitors and has little tourism infrastructure. This all makes it a wonderful area to explore for those with a love of nature and the offbeat.

Laguna Catemaco

To explore Laguna Catemaco, there are *lancheros* along the *malecón* offering boat trips. Boats can be paid for *colectivo* (ie per place) or can be hired for up to six people. Expect to pay M$100 *colectivo* or M$400 for a private *lancha* for an hour's boat trip. You can visit several islands on the lake; on the largest, Isla Tenaspi, Olmec sculptures have been discovered. Isla de los Changos (Monkey Island) shelters red-cheeked monkeys,

originally from Thailand. They belong to the Universidad Veracruzana, which acquired them for research.

On the northeast shore of the lake, the Reserva Ecológica de Nanciyaga (☑294-943-01-99; www.nanciyaga.com; Carretera Catemaco-Coyame; ⊙cabin reservations 9am-2pm & 4-6pm Mon-Fri, 9am-2pm Sat ; Ⓟ) ✎ is a kind of reserve within a reserve and pushes an indigenous theme in a small tract of rainforest. The grounds are replete with a temascal, an ancient planetarium and Olmec-themed decorations and replicas. Day visitors are welcome. One night's lodging (M$1730 for two people with meals) in solar-powered rustic cabins includes a mineral mud bath, a massage, a guided walk and the use of kayaks. You have to walk to the bathrooms (torches provided), so it's not for everyone, but it provides an incredible experience for those who want to be very close to nature. Arrive by *pirata* (M$10), taxi (M$80) or boat (M$50 per person; hire in Catemaco).

Follow the lake's eastern shore along the dirt road another 8km and you can earn a bit more luxury at the meditative Prashanti Tebanca (☑294-107-79-98; www.prashanti.com.mx; r M$1100-2500; Ⓟ❋ⓈⓈ). It's a rather more comfortable version of Nanciyaga with a *nuevo*-Buddhist vibe, although one that's rather overpriced for what it offers. Numerous boat and jeep tours can be organized here.

Laguna de Sontecomapan

In the town of Sontecomapan, 15km north of Catemaco, there are some lagoon-side restaurants and the idyllic Pozo de los Enanos (Well of the Dwarves) swimming hole, where local youths launch, Tarzanlike, from ropes into the water. You can catch a *lancha* from Sontecomapan to anywhere else on the

Los Tuxtlas

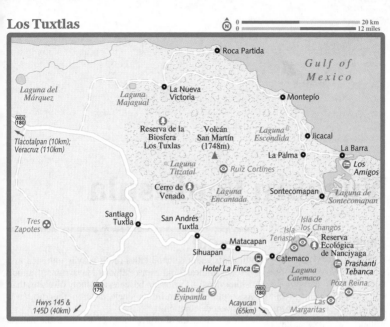

lake. Taxis from Catemaco cost M$60, or a *pirata* M$20.

Los Amigos (229-690-34-08; www.losamigos.com.mx; incl breakfast dm M$270, cabañas 2 people M$580, 6 people M$1200-1700) is a well-run, peaceful retreat close to where the *laguna* enters the ocean. The fantastic *cabañas* tucked into the verdant hillside have lovely balconies sporting hammocks and spectacular views of the bay. There are nature trails to a beautiful lookout, kayak rentals and a restaurant. The boat ride there from Sontecomapan is about 15 to 30 minutes.

The Coast

The small fishing village of **La Barra**, with its pleasant beaches and seafood restaurants, can be reached by a *lancha* from Sontecomapan (M$500 including a tour of the mangroves on the way), or via a side road going east from La Palma, 8km north of Sontecomapan. Do not miss a lunch of *sierra* fish cooked simply in soy sauce, garlic, salt and butter, and enjoyed in one of the simple restaurants on the (usually deserted) sea-facing beach.

Northwest of La Barra is the tiny beach town of **Jicacal**. You can access Jicacal from a rough road that forks east from the main road. Delectable, fresh-from-the-line seafood is available in restaurants there. The dirt road to the left, right before you hit Jicacal, will lead you 10 minutes down a gorgeous wreck of a road to a moldering relic of a hotel. From there, you'll find a path leading to a long set of crumbling stairs going to **Playa Escondida** (Hidden Beach), which earns its name; during the work week in the low season, you'll probably have the gorgeous blond sands and turquoise waters to yourself. For our money, this is probably the single best beach in the whole state.

Yucatán Peninsula

Includes ➡

Cancún............255
Isla Mujeres........ 266
Isla Holbox..........271
Playa del Carmen....275
Isla Cozumel 279
Tulum 286
Chetumal..........297
Mérida 301
Celestún............317
Chichén Itzá 322
Valladolid.......... 328
Campeche........ 333
Xpujil 345

Best Places to Eat

➡ Nohoch Kay (p294)

➡ Kiosco Verde (p263)

➡ Yerba Buena del Sisal (p331)

➡ Wayan'e (p307)

➡ Taquería Honorio (p289)

➡ Restaurante Xel-Ha (p298)

Best Swimming & Diving Spots

➡ Banco Chinchorro (p294)

➡ Isla Cozumel (p279)

➡ Laguna Bacalar (p296)

➡ Cenote Xlacah (p319)

➡ Hacienda San Lorenzo Oxman (p330)

Why Go?

With intriguing colonial cities (both heavily touristed and virtually unheard of), world-famous Maya ruins, tranquil fishing villages, Caribbean beaches, and more dive sites than you could ever cram into a single vacation, the Yucatán is one sweet destination.

Despite patches of overzealous development, the natural beauty of the Yucatán abides. Limestone sinkholes, ideal for swimming and diving, abound on the peninsula, while fascinating outdoor activities await in wildlife-rich nature reserves.

Around here, the past is the present and the present is the past. You'll witness it in the towering temples of the Maya, Toltecs and Itzáes, in the cobblestone streets of colonial centers, and in the culture of the Maya themselves, quietly maintaining their traditions as the centuries tick by.

When to Go
Playa del Carmen

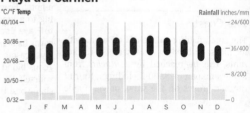

Jan & Feb Mérida fest in January and Carnaval in February take place with relatively cool climes.

May & Jun The summer's hot and June is a good time to swim with whale sharks.

Sep–Nov Low-season discounts galore; pleasant November weather for the Day of the Dead.

History

The Maya – accomplished astronomers and mathematicians, and architects of some of the grandest monuments ever known – created their first settlements in what is now Guatemala as early as 2400 BC. Over the centuries, Maya civilization expanded steadily northward, and by AD 550 great Maya city-states were established in southern Yucatán. In the 10th century, the great cities of southern Yucatán slowly dissolved, as attention shifted northward to new power centers such as Chichén Itzá.

The last of the great Maya capitals, Mayapán, started to collapse around 1440, when the Xiu Maya and the Cocom Maya began a violent and protracted struggle for power. In 1540, Spanish conquistador Francisco de Montejo the Younger (son of legendary conquistador Francisco de Montejo the Elder) utilized the tensions between the still-feuding Maya sects to conquer the area. The Spaniards allied themselves with the Xiu against the Cocom, finally defeating the Cocom and gaining the Xiu as reluctant converts to Christianity.

Francisco de Montejo the Younger, along with his father and cousin (named...you guessed it, Francisco de Montejo), founded Mérida in 1542 and within four years brought most of the Yucatán Peninsula under Spanish rule. The Spaniards divided the Maya lands into large estates where the indigenous people were put to work as indentured servants.

When Mexico won its independence from Spain in 1821, the new Mexican government used the Yucatecan territory to create huge plantations for the cultivation of tobacco, sugarcane and *henequén* (agave rope fiber). The Maya, though legally free, were enslaved in debt peonage to the rich landowners.

In 1847 the Maya rose up in a massive revolt against the Spanish. This was the beginning of the War of the Castes. Finally, in 1901, after more than 50 years of sporadic, but often intense, violence, a tentative peace was reached. However, it would be another 30 years before the territory of Quintana Roo came under official government control. To this day some Maya do not recognize its sovereignty.

The mass development of Cancún in the early 1970s led to hundreds of kilometers of beachfront property along the Caribbean coast being sold off to commercial interests, displacing many small fishing communities. While many indigenous people still eke out a living by subsistence agriculture or fishing, large numbers now work in the construction and service industries. Some individuals and communities, often with outside encouragement, are having a go at ecotourism, opening their lands to tourists or working as guides.

QUINTANA ROO

You'd think that solitude would be in short supply in Quintana Roo (pronounced 'kin-tah-nah *roh*'), one of Mexico's most visited states. But even in gringo-friendly Cancún, you can still find quiet slices of paradise.

There are glaring-white beaches stretching all the way from Cancún to the Belizean border, unassuming Caribbean islands protected by the barrier reef, and impressive Maya sites throughout this long-arching sliver of limestone, salt and sea.

The high season for Quintana Roo is basically December to April. Prices (and crowds) peak from mid-December to mid-January, late February to early March (the US spring break) and a week on either side of Easter.

Cancún

📞 998 / POP 630,000

Cancún is a tale of two cities. There's the glitzy hotel zone with its famous white-sand beaches, unabashed party scene and sophisticated seafood restaurants. Then there's the actual city itself, which gives you a taste of local flavor at, say, a neighborhood taco joint or at the undeveloped beaches of Isla Blanca, just north of downtown.

That's what keeps Cancún interesting. Had your fill of raucous discos in the hotel zone? Escape to a downtown salsa club. Tired of lounging around the pool in Ciudad Cancún? Simply hop on a bus and head for the sapphire waters of the hotel zone.

◎ Sights & Activities

⭐ **Museo Maya de Cancún**   MUSEUM

(Maya Museum; Map p258; www.inah.gob.mx; Blvd Kukulcán Km 16.5; M$64; ◉9am-6pm Tue-Sun; 🚍R-1) Holding one of the Yucatán's most important collections of Maya artifacts, this modern museum is a welcome sight in a city known more for its party scene than cultural attractions. On display are some 400 pieces found at key sites in and around the peninsula, ranging from sculptures to ceramics and jewelry. One of the three halls shows temporary Maya-themed exhibits.

0 — 100 km
0 — 60 miles
N

Progres[o]
Sisal
Dzibilchalt[ún]
Reserva de la Biosfera Ría Celestún
Kinchil
Méri[da]
Celestún 3
MEX 281
U[xmal]
Maxcanú
MEX
Bécal
Uxma[l]
La Costa
Santa Cruz
Calkiní
K[abah]
Hecelchakán
Tenabo
Bolonchén de Rejón
CAMPECHE
MEX 180
San Antonio Cayal
Hopel[chén]
Edzná
Pich
Dzibal[...]
Champotón
Gulf of Mexico
Bahía de Campeche
MEX 180
Sabancuy
MEX 261
Campeche
Isla del Carmen
Puerto Real
Ciudad del Carmen
Laguna de Términos
Zacatal
Escárcega
MEX 186
Balamku
Conhuas
Chicanná
Frontera
MEX 180
Tabasco
Hormig[...]
MEX 186
Candelaria
Calakmul
Reserva [de] la Biosf[era] Calakm[ul]
Jonutla
Río Candelaria
Ciudad Pemex
Catazajá
Emiliano Zapata
MEX 186
Chiapas
Parque Nacional El Mirador-Dos Lagunas-Río Azul
GUATEMALA

Yucatán Peninsula Highlights

1 Chilling on the soft sands of the Costa Maya fishing village **Mahahual** (p294) and diving at **Banco Chinchorro** (p294).

2 Taking in the glorious colonial architecture in cultural capital **Mérida** (p301).

3 Beach-bumming and flamingo-watching in **Celestún** (p317).

4 Finding out why they named **Chichén Itzá** (p322) one of the 'seven modern wonders of the world,' or why **Ek' Balam** (p331) should have made the list.

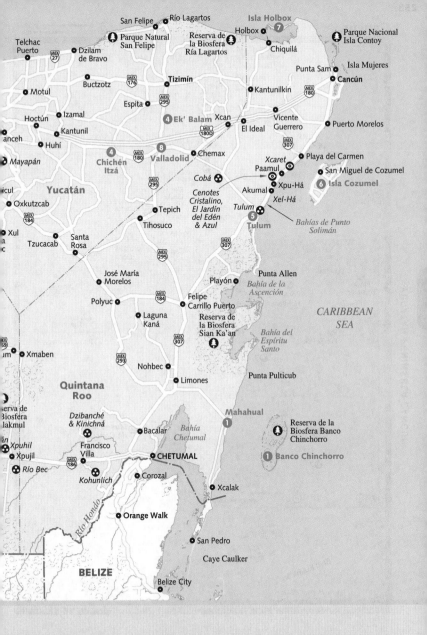

5 Marveling at Maya ruins dramatically situated on a cliff in **Tulum** (p286), then going for a swim down below.

6 Plunging into some of the world's best diving sites at **Isla Cozumel** (p279).

7 Getting up close and personal with the whale sharks off **Isla Holbox** (p271).

8 Taking a dip in crystal clear cenotes in and around colonial city **Valladolid** (p328).

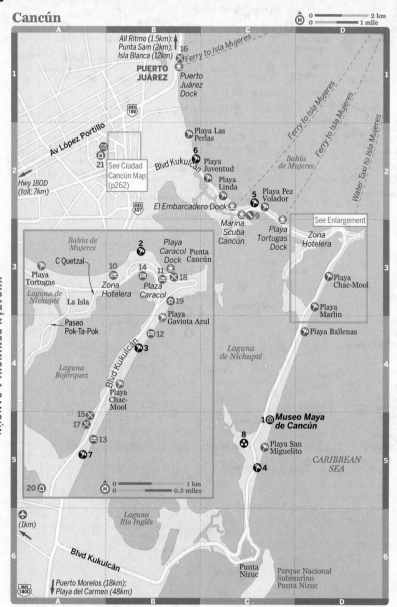

0 ____ 2 km
0 ____ 1 mile

All Ritmo (1.5km);
Punta Sam (2km);
Isla Blanca (12km)

PUERTO JUÁREZ

Ferry to Isla Mujeres

16

Puerto Juárez Dock

MEX 180

Av López Portillo

Playa Las Perlas

6

Blvd Kukulcán

Playa Juventud

21

See Ciudad Cancún Map (p262)

Hwy 180D (toll; 7km)

MEX 307

Playa Linda

El Embarcadero Dock

5 Playa Pez Volador

9

Bahía de Mujeres

Ferry to Isla Mujeres

Water Taxi to Isla Mujeres

Marina Scuba Cancún

Playa Tortugas Dock

See Enlargement

Zona Hotelera

Bahía de Mujeres

2

C Quetzal

Playa Tortugas

10

Zona Hotelera

14

11

18

Plaza Caracol

Playa Caracol Dock

Punta Cancún

Playa Chac-Mool

Laguna de Nichupté

La Isla

Paseo Pok-Ta-Pok

19

Playa Gaviota Azul

12

3

Playa Marlin

Laguna Bojórquez

Blvd Kukulcán

Playa Ballenas

Laguna de Nichupté

Playa Chac-Mool

15

17

13

7

20

0 ____ 1 km
0 ____ 0.5 miles

1 **Museo Maya de Cancún**

8

Playa San Miguelito

4

CARIBBEAN SEA

Laguna Río Inglés

(1km)

Blvd Kukulcán

Puerto Morelos (18km);
Playa del Carmen (48km)

MEX 180D

Punta Nizuc

Parque Nacional Submarino Punta Nizuc

Cancún's original anthropology museum shut down in 2006 due to structural damage from hurricanes. This time around, the new museum features hurricane-resistant reinforced glass. The price of admission includes access to the adjoining San Miguelito archaeological site.

San Miguelito
ARCHAEOLOGICAL SITE

(Map p258; ☎998-885-38-43; www.inah.gob.mx; Blvd Kukulcán Km 16.5; M$64; ⊙9am-4:30pm;

Cancún

◎ **Top Sights**
1 Museo Maya de Cancún......................C5

◎ **Sights**
2 Playa Caracol..B3
3 Playa Chac-Mool....................................B4
4 Playa Delfines...C5
5 Playa Langosta..C2
6 Playa Las Perlas.....................................B2
7 Playa Marlin..A5
San Miguelito.....................................(see 1)
8 Zona Arqueológica El Rey.....................C5

◎ **Activities, Courses & Tours**
Asterix...(see 9)
9 Scuba Cancún...C2

◎ **Sleeping**
10 Beachscape Kin Ha Villas &
Suites..B3
11 Hostal Mayapan.....................................B3

12 Hostel Natura..B4
13 Me by Melia...A5
14 Suites Costa Blanca...............................B3

◎ **Eating**
15 El Fish Fritanga......................................A5
16 Kiosco Verde..B1
17 La Habichuela Sunset............................A5
18 Mocambo..B3
Surfin' Burrito...................................(see 12)

◎ **Drinking & Nightlife**
Rose Bar..(see 13)

◎ **Entertainment**
19 Coco Bongo..B3

◎ **Shopping**
20 La Europea...A5
21 Mercado 28...A2

YUCATÁN PENINSULA CANCÚN

🖳R-1) Cancún's newest archaeological site opened in 2012 and contains more than a dozen restored Maya structures inhabited between 1200 and 1550, prior to the arrival of the conquistadors. A path from the Museo Maya leads to remains of houses, a palace with 17 columns and the site's tallest structure: the 8m-high Pirámide (Pyramid), which was rebuilt three times. Access to the ruins is included in the entrance fee to the Museo Maya.

Zona Arqueológica El Rey ARCHAEOLOGICAL SITE
(Map p258; Blvd Kukulcán Km 18; M$47; ⊘8am-4:30pm; 🖳R-1) In the Zona Arqueológica El Rey, on the west side of Blvd Kukulcán, there's a small temple and several ceremonial platforms. The site gets its name from a sculpture excavated here of a noble, possibly a *rey* (king), wearing an elaborate headdress. El Rey, which flourished from AD 1200 to 1500, and nearby San Miguelito were communities dedicated to maritime trade and fishing.

All Ritmo AMUSEMENT PARK
(www.allritmocancun.com/en/waterpark; Puerto Juárez-Punta Sam Hwy Km 1.5; adult M$295-310, child 5-12yr M$247-260; ⊘10am-7pm Wed-Mon) Little ones can splish and splash to their heart's content at this water park, which also has mini-golf and shuffleboard. The turnoff is 2km north of the Ultramar ferry terminal. 'Punta Sam' *colectivos* on Avenida Tulum (opposite the bus terminal) will drop you at the turnoff, and it's a short walk from there.

Beaches

Under Mexican law, you have the right to walk and swim on every beach in the country. In practice, it is difficult to approach many stretches of beach without walking through the lobby of a hotel, particularly in the Zona Hotelera. However, you'll usually be able to cross the lobby without problems and proceed to the beach.

If you'd like to see what Cancún looked like before the development boom, a dirt road north of Ciudad Cancun's Punta Sam leads to **Isla Blanca**, where you'll find a gorgeous stretch of secluded white-sand beach. About 10km from Punta Sam you'll reach beach club and cabins **Cabañas Playa Blanca** (☑cell 998-2139131; Isla Blanca; beach club M$30, cabins M$500-1000; ℗) with a sublime coast overlooking Isla Mujeres.

The Zona Hotelera beaches' Km markers on Blvd Kukulcán get bigger as you go from north to south.

Playa Las Perlas BEACH
(Map p258; Km 2.5) A small beach with a great kids' playground, bathrooms and free *palapa*-topped tables. Free parking. Access from north side of the Holiday Inn.

Playa Langosta BEACH
(Map p258; Km 5) In the middle of the north end of Zona Hotelera, Playa Langosta is a gem of a place for swimming. Facing Bahía de Mujeres, the beach is coated with Cancún's signature powdered coral sand and the waters are quite shallow, making it good for

snorkeling. If you've had enough of the water there are lots of beach restaurants and bars.

Playa Caracol
BEACH

(Map p258; Km 8.7) Next to the Isla Mujeres ferry dock, this tiny stretch of sand is probably the least inviting, but you can head left when you hit the water to get to the lovely beach 'belonging' to the Hotel Riu. No parking.

Playa Chac-Mool
BEACH

(Map p258; Km 9.5) With no parking, this is one of the quieter beaches with a lifeguard on duty. No food but there are stores and restaurants near the access, opposite Señor Frogs.

Playa Marlin
BEACH

(Map p258; Km 12.5) A long, lovely stretch of sand with lifeguards on duty and deck chairs, umbrellas and tables for rent. There's no food, but there is an Oxxo out on Blvd Kukulcán, north of the Kukulcán Plaza where the beach access is.

Playa Delfines
BEACH

(Map p258; Km 17.5) Delfines is about the only beach with a public car park; unfortunately, its sand is coarser and darker than the exquisite fine sand of the more northerly beaches. On the upside, the beach has great views, there are some nearby Maya ruins to check out and, as the last beach along the boulevard, it is rarely crowded. Heed the signs regarding swimming conditions as undertows are common here.

Water Activities

There's no shortage of dive shops and specialized tour operators offering water activities, including reef and cenote dives, fishing trips and snorkeling.

★ Museo
Subacuático de Arte
DIVING, SNORKELING

(MUSA Underwater Museum; www.musacancun. com; snorkeling tour US$41.50, 1-tank dive US$64.50) ✐ Built to divert divers away from deteriorating coral reefs, this one-of-a-kind aquatic museum features more than 500 life-size sculptures in the waters of Cancún and Isla Mujeres. The artificial reefs are submerged at depths of 4m and 8m, making them ideal for snorkelers and first-time divers. Organize dives through diving outfits; Scuba Cancún is recommended.

Scuba Cancún
DIVING

(Map p258; ☎ 998-849-75-08; www.scubacancun. com.mx; Blvd Kukulcán Km 5.2; 1-/2-tank dives US$62/77, equipment rental extra) A family-owned and PADI-certified dive operation with many years of experience, Scuba Cancún was the city's first dive shop. It offers a variety of snorkeling, fishing and diving expeditions (including cenote and night dives). It also runs snorkeling and diving trips to the underwater sculpture museum, aka MUSA.

☞ Tours

Isla Contoy, an uninhabited island that receives only 200 visitors a day, is a delight for birding and snorkeling. It's home to more than 170 bird species.

Asterix
TOUR

(Map p258; ☎ 998-886-42-70; www.contoytours. com; Blvd Kukulcán Km 5.2; adult/child 5-12yr US$109/63; ☺ tours 9am-5pm Tue, Thu & Sat) Tours to Isla Contoy depart from **Marina Scuba Cancún** (Map p258). They include guide, breakfast, lunch, open bar and snorkeling gear.

Hostel Mundo Joven
TOUR

(Map p262; ☎ 998-271-47-40; www.mundojoven. com; Av Uxmal 25; ☺ 10am-7pm Mon-Fri, to 2pm Sat; ☒ R-1) Drop by this excellent downtown travel agency to hook up tours to uninhabited Isla Contoy or for excursions to the Maya ruins of Chichén Itzá and Tulum.

🛏 Sleeping

Cancún is made up of two very distinct areas: the downtown area, Ciudad Cancún, which is on the mainland, and Isla Cancún, a sandy spit of an island usually referred to as the Zona Hotelera (Hotel Zone).

🛏 Downtown

Downtown has numerous budget digs and some appealing small hotels. The main north–south thoroughfare is Avenida Tulum, an avenue lined with banks, shopping

---

BEACH SAFETY

A system of colored pennants warns beachgoers of potential swimming dangers:

Blue Normal, safe conditions.

Yellow Use caution; changeable conditions.

Red Unsafe conditions; use a swimming pool instead.

centers and restaurants. The beach is just a taxi or bus ride away.

Mezcal Hostel
HOSTEL $

(Map p262; ✆cell 998-1259502; www.mezcal hostel.com; Mero 12; dm/r incl breakfast US$14/45; 🌐❄️🛜🛗; 🖥️R-1) Any place with mezcal in its name must be good, or so the logic goes. In this case, it is indeed all good at the Mezcal Hostel, which occupies a beautiful two-story house in a quiet residential area. Private rooms and dorms are kept very clean and weekly Sunday barbecue parties are perfect for sipping smoky mezcal.

Hostel Ka'beh
HOSTEL $

(Map p262; ✆988-892-79-02; www.cancun hostel.hostel.com; Alcatraces 45; incl breakfast dm from M$250, r M$700; 🌐❄️🛜; 🖥️R-1) A good central option just off the buzzing Parque de las Palapas, this small hostel has a lived-in feel that goes hand in hand with the relaxed vibe. Expect many social activities at night, most organized around food and drink.

★Hotel El Rey del Caribe
HOTEL $$

(Map p262; ✆998-884-20-28; www.elrey delcaribe.com; Av Uxmal 24; s/d incl breakfast M$900/983; 🌐❄️🛜🛗; 🖥️R-1) 🌿 El Rey is a true ecotel – they recycle, employ solar collectors and cisterns, use gray water on the gardens, and have some rooms with composting toilets. This beautiful spot has a swimming pool and Jacuzzi in a jungly courtyard that's home to a small family of *tlacuaches* (opossums). All rooms have a fully equipped kitchenette, comfortable beds and fridges.

Cancún International Suites
HOTEL $$

(Map p262; ✆998-884-17-71; www.cancuninter nationalsuites.com; Gladiolas 16, cnr Alcatraces; r/ste M$1100/2000; 🌐❄️🛜; 🖥️R-1) Colonial-style rooms and suites in this remodeled hotel are comfortable and quiet and the location is great – right off Parque de las Palapas and conveniently close to downtown's restaurant and bar zone.

Náder Hotel & Suites
HOTEL $$

(Map p262; ✆998-884-15-84; www.suitesnader cancun.com; Av Náder 5; d/ste incl breakfast US$54/75; 🌐❄️🛜; 🖥️R-1) The Náder caters to business travelers but it's also a hit with families thanks to its ample rooms and suites with large common areas and kitchens. Even the 'standard' setup here gets you digs with some serious elbow room.

🛏️ Zona Hotelera

Blvd Kukulcán leaves Ciudad Cancún and goes eastward to the Zona Hotelera, home to many restaurants, bars and hotels. Big chain hotels dominate the strip, but there are some affordable options.

Hostal Mayapan
HOSTEL $

(Map p258; ✆998-883-32-27; www.hostalmaya pan.com; Blvd Kukulcán Km 8.5; dm M$180-235, r M$850, incl breakfast; 🌐❄️@🛜; 🖥️R-1) Located in an abandoned mall, this is a great budget spot in the Zona Hotelera. Thanks to its location just 30m from the beach, it's one of our favorite hostels in town. The rooms are superclean and there's a little hangout area in an atrium upstairs (the old food court?.)

Hostel Natura
HOSTEL $$

(Map p258; ✆998-883-08-87; www.hostelnatura cancun.com; Blvd Kukulcán Km 9.5; dm US$26-27, r US$60; 🌐❄️🛜; 🖥️R-1) Up above a health food restaurant of the same name, this new hostel offers private rooms with lagoon views and somewhat cramped dorms, offset by the airy rooftop common area. The party zone is close by.

Suites Costa Blanca
HOTEL $$

(Map p258; ✆998-883-08-88; www.suites costablanca.com; Blvd Kukulcán Km 8.5; r from M$950; 🌐❄️🛜; 🖥️R-1) A rare midrange option in the Zona Hotelera, which in and of itself makes this a great find. The hotel claims to offer 'Mediterranean-style' suites, but they're really just large (somewhat outdated) rooms with sitting areas and small balconies.

Beachscape Kin Ha Villas & Suites
HOTEL $$$

(Map p258; ✆998-891-54-00; www.beachscape. com.mx; Blvd Kukulcán Km 8.5; r from US$138; 🅿️🌐❄️@🛜🛗; 🖥️R-1) A good family spot, Beachscape offers a babysitting service, a play area for kids and a swimmable beach with calm waters. You'll never need to leave the hotel's grounds (though we think you should), as there are bars, markets, travel agencies and more on the premises. All rooms feature a balcony and two double beds or one king-sized bed.

The price listed is for the European plan, but you can arrange an all-inclusive stay.

Me by Melia
LUXURY HOTEL $$$

(Map p258; ✆998-881-25-00; www.mebymelia. com; Blvd Kukulcán Km 12; d all-inclusive from M$6550; 🅿️🌐❄️@🛜🛗; 🖥️R-1) 'Enough about

Ciudad Cancún

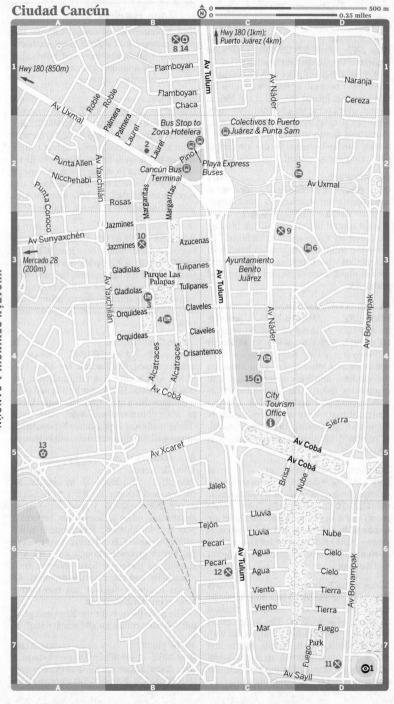

Ciudad Cancún

◉ Sights
1 Plaza de Toros D7

◉ Activities, Courses & Tours
2 Hostel Mundo Joven B2

◉ Sleeping
3 Cancún International Suites B3
4 Hostel Ka'beh B4
5 Hotel El Rey del Caribe D2
6 Mezcal Hostel D3
7 Náder Hotel & Suites C4

◉ Eating
8 El Paisano del 23 .... B1
9 El Tigre y El Toro C3
10 La Habichuela B3
11 La Playita D7
12 Los de Pescado C6

◉ Entertainment
13 Grand Mambo Café A5

◉ Shopping
14 Mercado 23 .... B1
15 Mercado Municipal Ki-Huic C4

you, let's talk about me!' That's the philosophy at this ubermodern, expressionist-inspired hotel. It won't suit everyone, but if you prefer clean lines over standard Cancún baroque, it's the place for you. Only half the rooms have ocean views, and it just ain't worth it to pay this much and not have a view of the Caribbean blue.

✖ Eating

In the downtown area, Mercados 23 and 28, and Parque de las Palapas all have food stalls. In general, you'll find more economical options in Ciudad Cancún than the Zona Hotelera.

Los de Pescado   SEAFOOD $
(Map p262; www.losdepescado.com; Av Tulum 32; tacos & tostadas M$27-29, ceviche M$86-129, burritos M$39-43; ⊙10am-6pm; ☻; ☐R-27) It's easy to order at a place where you have only four choices: ceviche (seafood marinated in lemon or lime juice, garlic and seasonings), tacos, *tostadas* (fried tortilla) or burritos. Try the fish and shrimp tacos with fixings from the salad station and you'll understand why locals dig this spot.

El Paisano del 23   MEXICAN $
(Map p262; cnr Cedro & Cericote, Mercado 23; tortas M$35; ⊙6am-4pm; ☐R-1) A local favorite

for more than 40 years, the *paisano* ('fellow countryman' – it's the owner's nickname) marinates *pierna* (pork leg) in red wine and then slow cooks it. The *tortas* (sandwiches) go fast, especially on weekends.

★ Kiosco Verde   SEAFOOD $$
(Map p258; www.restaurant-kiosco-verde.blog spot.mx; Av López Portillo s/n, Puerto Juárez; mains M$80-140; ⊙noon-7pm Wed-Mon; ☻☎) The Green Kiosk just might be the most underrated seafood restaurant in all of Cancún. It began in 1974 as a grocery store and now it serves elaborate fresh fish and seafood dishes, such as coconut-encrusted shrimp and succulent grilled whole fish. Don't leave without trying the Mexican craft beers or mezcal.

To get here, catch a northbound 'Puerto Juárez' *colectivo* along Avenida Tulum, opposite the bus station.

Surfin' Burrito   MEXICAN $$
(Map p258; www.facebook.com/thesurfinburrito; Blvd Kukulcán Km 9.5; burritos M$62-119; ⊙24hr; ☻; ☐R-1) Always a crowd-pleaser on the strip, where cheap eats come few and far between, this small joint prepares beef, shrimp, fish and vegetarian burritos with your choice of tasty fixings. It's open 24/7 and makes jumbo margaritas, making it a popular late-night haunt.

El Fish Fritanga   SEAFOOD $$
(Map p258; www.elfishfritanga.com; Blvd Kukulcán Km 12.6; mains M$132-265, tacos M$23-28; ⊙11am-11pm; ☻☎; ☐R-1) With plastic tables set under little *palapa* huts (shelter with a thatched, palm-leaf roof and open sides) on a sandy floor, this is one of the Zona Hotelera's back-to-basics places. Good-value seafood, killer 1L mojitos and a great place for sunset drinks overlooking the lagoon. If you need to go even further back to basics, they run a cut-price taco stand out front.

Va q' Va   SEAFOOD $$
(www.vaqva.com.mx; Calle 107, btwn Av Leona Vicario & Niños Héroes; mains M$80-160; ⊙10am-7pm; ☻) The fish and seafood are pretty good here but the real draw is the festive atmosphere, plus you get to enjoy a meal in a working-class neighborhood far removed from the tourist center. It's worth the trip just for the marimba music and *Clamato micheladas* (beer with Clamato juice – a tomato and clam cocktail mix – lime and salt).

It's best reached by taxi.

La Playita
SEAFOOD $$

(Map p262; Av Bonampak 60; mains M$90-170; ⊙11am-2am; ⊜🛜; 🚇R-27) Beat the heat with refreshing, light dishes such as seafood cocktails and ceviche *tostadas*. To drink, try the 'frozen *miche*,' a beer-based cocktail best described as a brain freeze waiting to happen. The daily drink specials and outdoor seating make this one of downtown's most popular bars.

El Tigre y El Toro
ITALIAN $$$

(Map p262; Av Náder 64; mains M$105-180; ⊙6pm-midnight; ⊜🛜🖊; 🚇R-1) Gourmet thin-crust pizza and homemade pastas are served in a pebbly candlelit garden at El Tigre y El Toro ('tiger' and 'bull' are the owners' nicknames). Many locals rank this as Cancún's *numero uno* pizza joint.

La Habichuela
FUSION $$$

(Map p262; 🖊998-884-31-58; www.lahabichuela. com; Margaritas 25; mains M$190-315, cocobichuela M$525; ⊙1pm-midnight; ⊜🛜; 🚇R-1) This elegant restaurant has a lovely courtyard dining area, just off Parque de las Palapas. The specialty is the *cocobichuela* (shrimp and lobster in curry sauce served inside a coconut with tropical fruit), but almost anything on the menu is delicious. The seafood ceviche and *tapas al ajillo* (assorted seafood accented with garlic) are mouthwatering. **La Habichuela Sunset** (Map p258; 🖊998-840-62-80; Blvd Kukulcán Km 12.6; mains M$250-400; ⊙noon-midnight; 🛜; 🚇R-1), the restaurant's slightly pricier Zona Hotelera branch, affords a gorgeous lagoon view.

Mocambo
SEAFOOD $$$

(Map p258; 🖊998-883-03-98; www.mocambo cancun.mx; Blvd Kukulcán Km 9.5; mains M$150-355; ⊙noon-11pm; ⊜🛜; 🚇R-1) Definitely one of the best spots in the Zona Hotelera, the *palapa*-covered Mocambo sits right on the ocean and serves up excellent seafood dishes such as grouper and a savory seafood paella. There's live music Tuesday through Sunday nights.

🍸 Drinking & Nightlife

For a very local night out in the downtown area, check out the bars around the base of the **Plaza de Toros** (Bullring; Map p262; cnr Avs Bonampak & Sayil).

The club scene in the Zona Hotelera is young, loud and booze-oriented – the kind that often has an MC urging women to display body parts to hooting and hollering crowds. The big dance clubs charge around M$1100 to M$1300 admission, which includes open-bar privileges. Most don't get hopping much before midnight.

A number of clubs are clustered along the northwest-bound side of Blvd Kukulcán, all within easy stumbling distance of one another.

Rose Bar
BAR

(Map p258; Blvd Kukulcán Km 12, in Me by Melia; ⊙4pm-midnight Sun-Fri, to 3am Sat; 🛜; 🚇R-1) In hipster hotel Me by Melia, Rose Bar has a more relaxed, chilled-out vibe than some of the raucous clubs in the party zone. DJs spin tunes on the bar's open-air deck on Saturday, and on Thursday at 9pm there's a short burlesque show.

Coco Bongo
CLUB

(Map p258; 🖊998-883-50-61; www.cocobongo. com.mx; Blvd Kukulcán Km 9.5, Forum Mall; ⊙10pm-5am; 🚇R-1) This is the spot where spring-breakers go wild, and it tends to be happening just about any day of the year. Dancing is interspersed with live acts featuring celebrity impersonators and acrobats throughout the night.

☆ Entertainment

★ Grand Mambo Café
CLUB

(Map p262; 🖊998-884-45-36; www.mambocafe. com.mx; cnr Avs Xcaret & Tankah, in Plaza Hong Kong; ⊙10:30pm-5am Wed-Sat; 🚇R-2) The large floor at this happening club is the perfect place to practice those Latin dance steps you've been working on. Live groups play Cuban salsa and other tropical styles.

🛍 Shopping

Locals head to either **Mercado 28** (Mercado Veintiocho; Map p258; cnr Avs Xel-Há & Sunyaxchén; ⊙6am-7pm) or **Mercado 23** (Map p262; Av Tulum s/n; ⊙6am-7pm; 🚇R-1) for clothes, shoes, inexpensive food stalls and so on. Of the two, Mercado 23 is the least frequented by tourists. If you're looking for a place *without* corny T-shirts, this is where to go.

Mercado Municipal Ki-Huic
MARKET

(Map p262; Av Tulum s/n; ⊙9am-9pm; 🚇R-1) This warren of stalls and shops carries a wide variety of souvenirs and handicrafts.

La Europea
DRINK

(Map p258; www.laeuropea.com.mx; Blvd Kukulcán Km 12.5; ⊙10am-9pm Mon-Sat, 11am-7pm Sun;

R-1) A gourmet liquor store with reasonable prices, knowledgeable staff and the best booze selection in town, including top-shelf tequilas and mezcals. Most airlines allow you to travel with up to 3L of alcohol, but check first. *¡Salud!*

ℹ️ Information

EMERGENCY

Cruz Roja (Red Cross; ☎ 065)
Police (☎ 066; Blvd Kukulcán Km 12.5; R-1)
Tourist Police (☎ 998-885-22-77)

IMMIGRATION

Instituto Nacional de Migración (Immigration Office; ☎ 998-881-35-60; cnr Av Náder 1 & Av Uxmal; ☉ 9am-1pm Mon-Fri) Go here to replace lost immigration forms.

MEDICAL SERVICES

Hospital Playa Med (☎ 998-140-52-58; Av Náder 13, cnr Av Uxmal; ☉ 24hr; R-1) Modern facility with 24-hour assistance.

MONEY

There are several banks with ATMs on Avenida Tulum, between Avenidas Cobá and Uxmal.

POST

Main Post Office (Map p258; cnr Avs Xel-Há & Sunyaxchén; ☉ 8am-4pm Mon-Fri, 9am-12:30pm Sat) Downtown at the edge of Mercado 28. You can also post mail in the red postal boxes sprinkled around town.

TOURIST INFORMATION

City Tourism Office (Map p262; ☎ 998-887-33-79; cnr Avs Cobá & Náder; ☉ 9am-4pm Mon-Fri) City tourist office with ample supplies of printed material and knowledgeable staff.

ℹ️ Getting There & Away

AIR

Aeropuerto Internacional de Cancún (CUN; ☎ 998-848-7200; www.asur.com.mx; Carretera Cancún-Chetumal, Km 22; ⬆), about 8km south of the city center, is the busiest airport in southeast Mexico. It has ATMs, money exchange and rental cars.

Cancún is served by many direct international flights and by connecting flights from Mexico City. Low-cost domestic carriers fly from Mexico City to Cancún and they have international routes as well. MayAir flies prop planes to Cozumel and Mérida.

Interjet (☎ 998-892-02-78; www.interjet.com; Av Xcaret 35, Plaza Hollywood) Flies direct to Miami and Havana.

MayAir (☎ USA 414-755-2527, toll-free Mexico 800-962-92-47; www.mayair.com.mx)

VivaAerobus (☎ 81-8215-0150; www.vivaaerobus.com; Hwy 307 Km 22, Cancún airport) Nonstop to Houston.

YUCATÁN PENINSULA CANCÚN

BUSES FROM CANCÚN

DESTINATION	FARE (M$)	DURATION (HR)	FREQUENCY (DAILY)
Chetumal	354-456	5½-6	frequent
Chichén Itzá	135-258	3-4	14
Chiquilá	114	3½-4	3
Felipe Carrillo Puerto	186-248	3½-4	3
Mérida	300-578	4-4½	frequent
Mexico City	1928	27	1 to Terminal Norte; 6:30pm
Mexico City (TAPO)	1904-2160	24½-28	4
Palenque	876-1040	13-13½	3
Playa del Carmen	34-60	1-1½	frequent ADO & Playa Express
Puerto Morelos	22-24	½-¾	frequent ADO & Playa Express
Ticul	220	8½	frequent
Tizimín	130	3	3
Tulum	116-130	2½	frequent
Valladolid	150-158	2-2¼	8
Villahermosa	550-1480	12¾-14½	frequent

Volaris (☑ 55-1102-8000; www.volaris.com; Hwy 307 Km 22, Cancún airport) Service to Mexico City.

BOAT

Ferries from Cancún to Isla Mujeres leave from several docks around Cancún. For information about departure points and fares, see www.granpuerto.com.mx.

BUS & TAXI

Cancún's **bus terminal** (Map p262; cnr Avs Uxmal & Tulum) occupies the wedge formed where Avenidas Uxmal and Tulum meet. Across Calle Pino from the bus terminal is **Playa Express** (Map p262; Calle Pino), which runs air-conditioned shuttles down the coast to Playa del Carmen every 10 minutes until early evening, stopping at major towns and points of interest. ADO covers the same ground and beyond with its 1st-class service.

CAR

Rental-car agencies have facilities at the airport and La Isla Shopping Village in the Zona Hotelera. An economy-sized vehicle with liability insurance runs about M$500 per day.

Avis (☑ 800-288-88-88, 998-176-80-30; www.avis.com.mx; Blvd Kukulcán Km 12.5, Centro Comercial La Isla)

National (☑ 998-881-8760; www.nationalcar.com; Cancún airport)

ⓘ Getting Around

TO/FROM THE AIRPORT

Frequent ADO buses go to Ciudad Cancún (M$64) between 7:40am and 12:30am. They depart from outside the terminals. Once in town, the buses travel up Avenida Tulum to the bus terminal on the corner of Avenida Uxmal. Going to the airport from Ciudad Cancún, the same ADO airport buses (Aeropuerto Centro) leave regularly from the bus station. ADO also offers

---

COSTA VS RIVIERA

Traveling through the coastal region of Quintana Roo you're likely to see two phrases bandied about by the tourist industry – the Costa Maya and the Riviera Maya. While they're occasionally used interchangeably, they are in fact two distinct regions. The Costa Maya is about 100km of beachfront spanning from Xcalak in the south to Reserva de la Biosfera Sian Ka'an in the north. The Riviera Maya begins at the northern boundary of the Costa Maya and stretches north to Cancún.

---

bus service out of the airport to Playa del Carmen and Mérida.

Airport shuttle vans Green Line and Super Shuttle run to and from Ciudad Cancún and the Zona Hotelera for about M$160 per person.

BUS

To reach the Zona Hotelera from downtown, catch any bus with 'R1,' 'R2,' 'Hoteles' or 'Zona Hotelera' displayed on the windshield. These buses travel along Avenida Tulum toward Avenida Cobá, then eastward on Avenida Cobá.

To reach Puerto Juárez and the Isla Mujeres ferries, you can either take a northbound 'Punta Sam' or 'Puerto Juárez' **colectivo** (Map p262) from a bus stop on Avenida Tulum (across from the ADO terminal), or you can catch an R-1 'Puerto Juárez' bus.

TAXI

Cancún's taxis don't have meters. Fares are set for given journeys, but always agree on a price before getting in. From downtown, you'll pay around M$130 to Punta Cancún, and M$70 to Puerto Juárez. Hourly and daily rates run about M$240 and M$2000 respectively.

Isla Mujeres

☑ 998 / POP 16,000

Some people plan their vacation around Cancún and pencil in Isla Mujeres as a side trip. But Isla Mujeres is a destination in its own right, and it's generally quieter and more affordable than what you get across the bay.

Sure, there's quite a few ticky-tack tourist shops, but folks still get around by golf cart. As for the crushed-coral beaches and turquoise-blue waters, well, you really just have to see them for yourself.

There's just enough here to keep you entertained: snorkel or scuba dive, visit a turtle farm, or just put on the sunglasses and open that book you've been dying to finish.

⊙ Sights & Activities

Isla Mujeres Turtle Farm   FARM
(Isla Mujeres Tortugranja; ☑ 998-888-07-05; Carretera Sac Bajo Km 5; M$30; ⊙ 9am-5pm; ⓓ) ⌖
Although they're endangered, sea turtles are still killed throughout Latin America for their eggs and meat. In the 1980s, efforts by a local fisherman led to the founding of this *tortugranja* (turtle farm), 5km south of town, which safeguards breeding grounds and protects eggs.

If you're coming from the bus stop, bear right at the 'Y' just beyond Hacienda Mun daca's parking lot (the turn is marked by a tiny sign). The farm is easily reached from town by taxi (M$60).

Museo Capitán Dulché MUSEUM, BEACH
(www.capitandulche.com; Carretera a Garrafón Km 4.5; M$65; ⊘10:30am-6:30pm; P) And you thought Isla Mujeres had no culture. Here you get not only a maritime museum detailing the island's naval history but also one of the best beach clubs in town – and we're not just saying that because of the cool boat bar.

Punta Sur VIEWPOINT, GARDENS
(ruins M$30) At the island's southernmost point you'll find a lighthouse, a sculpture garden and the worn remains of a temple dedicated to Ixchel, Maya goddess of the moon and fertility. Various hurricanes have pummeled the ruins over time and there's now little to see other than the sculpture garden, the sea and Cancún in the distance. Taxis from town cost about M$105.

Beaches

Playa Norte BEACH
`FREE` Once you reach Playa Norte, the island's main beach, you won't want to leave. Its warm, shallow waters are the color of blue raspberry syrup and the beach is crushed coral. Unlike most of the island's east coast, Playa Norte is safe for swimming and the water is only chest deep even far from shore.

Playa Garrafón BEACH
Head to this beach for excellent snorkeling. It's 6.5km from the tourist center. A cab costs M$100.

Diving, Snorkeling & Bird-Watching

Within a short boat ride of the island are a handful of lovely dives, such as **Barracuda**, **La Bandera**, **El Jigueo**, **Ultrafreeze** and **Arrecife Manchones.** You can expect to see sea turtles, rays and barracuda, along with a wide array of hard and soft corals.

Snorkeling with whale sharks just off Isla Contoy is the latest craze. The season runs from mid-June through September. Folks at local dive shops can arrange your trip.

Also popular are bird-watching tours to Isla Contoy, an uninhabited island with more than 170 bird species.

Sea Hawk Divers DIVING
(☑998-877-02-96; www.seahawkislamujeres.com; Carlos Lazo s/n; 1-/2-tank dives incl equipment

Isla Mujeres

US$70/85, resort course US$95, whale-shark tour US$125) Offers reef dives, resort courses, fishing trips and whale-shark snorkeling tours. Rents rooms, too.

Fisherman's Cooperative TOUR
(☑cell 998-1534883; cnr Av Rueda Medina & Madero; snorkeling incl lunch M$350, Isla Contoy tours M$1000, whale-shark tour M$1400; ⊘office 8am-8pm) The local fisherman's cooperative offers snorkeling tours to various sites, including Isla Contoy, the reef off Playa Garrafón, and does whale-shark outings as well.

Isla Mujeres Town

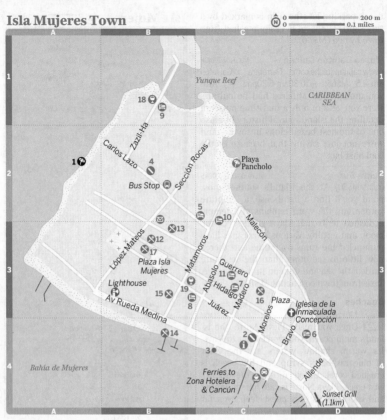

Isla Mujeres Town

Sights
1 Playa Norte A2

Activities, Courses & Tours
2 Aqua Adventures Eco Divers C4
3 Fisherman's Cooperative..................... C4
4 Sea Hawk Divers B2

Sleeping
5 Apartments Trinchan C2
6 Casa El Pío.. D4
7 Hotel Belmar C3
8 Hotel Kinich.. B3
9 Hotel Villa Kiin.....................................B1
10 Poc-Na Hostel C2

11 Xbulu-Ha Hotel C3

Eating
12 Lola Valentina B3
13 Mercado Municipal B3
14 Mininos B4
15 Olivia B3
16 Pita Amore C3
17 Rooster Café.. B3

Drinking & Nightlife
18 Fenix Lounge B1
Poc-Na Hostel ....(see 10)
19 T&T Tropical Paradise B3

Aqua Adventures Eco Divers　　DIVING
(📞998-236-43-16; www.diveislamujeres.com; Juárez 1, cnr Morelos; 2-tank dives incl equipment US$90; whale-shark tour US$125; ⏰8:30am-7pm Mon-Sat, 10am-6pm Sun) Great for snorkeling with whale sharks and has 15 sites for reef dives.

🛏 Sleeping

★ **Poc-Na Hostel**　　HOSTEL $
(📞998-877-00-90; www.pocna.com; Matamoros 15; incl breakfast dm with fan/air-con M$155/195, d with/without bathroom M$430/370, camping

per person M$110; ⊖ ✳ 🛜) You can't beat this hostel's common areas. For starters, it's right on a lovely palm-shaded beach, home to one of the town's most happening beach bars at night – and you can also pitch a tent if you bring your own. Guests can chill in a cool *palapa* lobby bar, where breakfast is served and local bands play nightly.

Apartments Trinchan   APARTMENT $
(☎ 998-877-08-56, cell 998-1666967; atrinchan@prodigy.net.mx; Carlos Lazo 46; r with fan/air-con M$400/450, apt with fan/air-con M$450/500; ⊖ ✳ 🛜) Since it has no website, you'll have to take our word for it when we say this is one of the best budget deals in town – and the beach is right around the corner. If it's available, opt for one of the large apartments with full kitchen.

Hotel Kinich   BOUTIQUE HOTEL $$
(☎ 998-888-09-09; www.islamujereskinich.com; Juárez 20; r/ste incl breakfast M$1200/1800; ⊖ ✳ 🛜) Boutique Hotel Kinich gives you plenty of bang for your buck in low season, when rates drop by about 40%, and even in high season the huge rooms with balconies are still a pretty good deal, especially the family-friendly suites.

Xbulu-Ha Hotel   HOTEL $$
(☎ 998-877-17-83; www.islamujeres.biz; Guerrero 4; d/tr/ste from M$700/820/980; ⊖ ✳ 🛜) Quite a bargain, especially if you're traveling with a small group or family. Some of the standard and deluxe rooms here can accommodate three to four people, as can the larger suites, which come with kitchenette.

Hotel Belmar   HOTEL $$
(☎ 998-877-04-30; www.hotelbelmarisla.com; Av Hidalgo 110; d/ste M$1100/1600; ⊖ ✳ 🛜) Run by the same friendly family that owns the pizza joint downstairs, Belmar offers comfy, well-kept rooms with tiled floors and (some) balconies. Prices span four distinct seasons.

Hotel Villa Kiin   HOTEL $$$
(☎ 998-877-10-24; www.villakiin.com; Zazil-Ha 129; incl breakfast r from M$1530, bungalows from M$1955; ⊖ ✳ 🛜) With one of the safest beaches for swimming, and recently remodeled rooms, Villa Kiin remains one of the island's premier hotels. You can opt for a room with new furniture, rocking chairs and ocean views (from some), or you can stay in a bungalow. The bungalows sit right on a beach with hammocks.

Casa El Pío   BOUTIQUE HOTEL $$$
(www.casaelpio.com; Hidalgo 3; r US$95-113; ⊖ ✳ 🛜 🏊) Book a room well in advance if you want to stay at this small – and very popular – boutique hotel. One of the five rooms has an ocean view, as does the rooftop terrace, and all rooms have handcrafted wood furnishings, fantastic photographs of the island and many other interesting design details. Online reservations only (there's no phone).

✗ Eating

For cheap eats, drop by the **Mercado Municipal** (Guerrero s/n, btwn López Mateos & Matamoros; mains M$35-100; ⊙ 7am-5pm).

Pita Amore   MEDITERRANEAN $
(Guerrero s/n, btwn Morelos & Madero; sandwiches M$35-45; ⊙ 12:30-10pm Mon-Sat, 6-10pm Sun; ⊖ 🛜 🗲) This unassuming shack does just three varieties of pita sandwiches and does them extremely well. The chicken, beef and vegetarian pitas are the creation of a New York Culinary Institute alum. The secret lies in the homemade sauces and outstanding pita bread, which comes from a Lebanese bakery in Mérida.

Rooster Café   CAFE $$
(Hidalgo s/n; breakfasts M$77-125; ⊙ 7am-3pm; ⊖ 🛜) The undeniable king of the breakfast providers on the island is this cute little cafe with a couple of tables out front and blasting air-con inside. The menu covers the classics and throws in a couple of inventive twists, all served up with excellent coffee and attentive service.

Mininos   SEAFOOD $$
(Av Rueda Medina s/n; mains M$90-170; ⊙ 10am-9pm) A colorfully painted *palapa* restaurant with a sand floor, Mininos dishes up tasty garlic shrimp, fried whole fish and octopus, as well as delicious seafood soups. It's popular with locals and tourists alike.

Mango Café   BREAKFAST $$
(Payo Obispo 725, Colonia Meterológico; mains M$85-125; ⊙ 7am-3pm; ⊖ 🛜) See the south side of town and drop by Mango Café for some self-serve coffee and a hearty Caribbean-inspired breakfast. The hot items here are coconut French toast and eggs Benedict in a curry hollandaise sauce. It's a short bike or cab ride away, about 3km south of the ferry terminal.

★ Olivia
MEDITERRANEAN **$$$**

(☑998-877-17-65; www.olivia-isla-mujeres.com; Matamoros; mains M$120-235; ☺5-9:30pm Tue-Sat; ☻☎) This delightful Israeli-run restaurant makes everything from scratch, from Moroccan-style fish served on a bed of couscous to chicken shawarmas wrapped in fresh-baked pita bread. Ask for a candlelit table out back in the garden. Olivia closes from mid-September to mid-October. Reservations recommended.

Lola Valentina
FUSION **$$$**

(Av Hidalgo s/n; mains M$125-275; ☺8am-1pm & 5-10pm; ☻☎✐) Overlooking the quieter north side of the restaurant strip, Lola does excellent Mexican fusion with dishes along the line of Thai-style shrimp tacos. Also on the menu are several vegan, gluten-free items such as a quinoa, rice and potato burrito wrap.

🍸 Drinking & Entertainment

★ T&T Tropical Paradise
LOUNGE

(www.facebook.com/tropicalparadiseislamujeres; Matamoros 20; ☺5am-2pm) You gotta love a place with sand floors – and unlike some of the nearby bars, T&T dares to play music from the 21st century!

Poc-Na Hostel
BAR

(www.pocna.com; Matamoros 26; ☺7pm-3am; ☎) Has a lobby bar with nightly live music and a beachfront bar with bonfires and more hippies than all the magic buses in the world. It's a scene, and an entertaining one at that.

Fenix Lounge
BAR

(☑998-274-00-73; www.fenixisla.com; Zazil-Ha 118; ☺11:30am-10pm Tue-Sat, to 8pm Sun; ☎) A waterfront *palapa* bar where you can go for a swim in calm waters, enjoy excellent cocktails like the spicy mango margarita and groove to live music on weekends.

ℹ Information

Hospital Integral Isla Mujeres (☑998-877-17-92; Guerrero, btwn Madero & Morelos) Doctors available 24/7.

HSBC (cnr Av Rueda Medina & Morelos)

Post Office (☑998-877-00-85; cnr Guerrero & López Mateos; ☺9am-5pm Mon-Fri, to noon Sat)

Tourist Information Office (☑998-877-03-07; direcciondeturismo@hotmail.com; Av Rueda Medina 130, btwn Madero & Morelos; ☺9am-4pm Mon-Fri) Offers a number of brochures. Some staff members speak English.

ℹ Getting There & Away

There are several points of embarkation from Cancún to reach Isla Mujeres. Most people cross on Ultramar passenger ferries. The R-1 'Ultramar' city bus in Cancún serves all Zona Hotelera departure points and Puerto Juárez, in Ciudad Cancún. Daily parking fees in and around the terminals cost between M$50 and M$100.

If you're on a tight budget, it's cheaper to leave from Puerto Juárez. For more ferry info, see www.granpuerto.com.mx.

ℹ Getting Around

BICYCLE

Cycling is a great way to get around the island. A number of shops rent bikes for about M$150 per day.

Rentadora Fiesta (Av Rueda Medina s/n, btwn Morelos & Bravo; per hr/day M$50/150; ☺8am-5pm) Rents mountain bikes and beach cruisers.

BUS & TAXI

A local bus (there's just one) departs from behind the market or from the ferry dock, and heads along Avenida Rueda Medina. You can get to the entrance of Hacienda Mundaca, within 300m of the Turtle Farm (Tortugranja), and as far south as Playa Lancheros (1.5km north of Playa Garrafón). It's a cheap ride, but expect long waits.

Taxi rates are set by the municipal government and posted at the taxi base just south of the passenger ferry dock.

PASSENGER FERRIES FROM CANCÚN TO ISLA MUJERES

DEPARTS FROM	FARE (M$)	DURATION (MIN)	FREQUENCY (DAILY)
El Embarcadero	230	25	6
Playa Caracol	230	25	6
Playa Tortugas	230	25	8
Puerto Juárez	78	25	frequent

SCOOTER & GOLF CART

Many people find golf carts a good way to get around the island, and convoys of them can be seen tooling down the roads.

Scooters are also available but inspect them carefully before renting. Costs vary, and are sometimes jacked up in high season, but they generally start at about M$250 per day.

Mega Ciro's (☑998-877-05-68; Av Guerrero 11; incl gas & insurance scooter per 8hr M$250, golf cart per 24hr M$650; ☺9am-5pm) Scooters and golf carts get good maintenance here.

Isla Contoy

Spectacular **Isla Contoy** (☑998-234-99-05; contoy@conanp.gob.mx) is a bird-lover's delight: an uninhabited national park and sanctuary that is an easy day trip from Cancún and from Isla Mujeres. About 800m at its widest point and more than 8.5km long, it has dense foliage that provides ideal shelter for more than 170 bird species, including brown pelicans, olive cormorants, turkey birds, brown boobies and frigates, as well as being a good place to see red flamingos, snowy egrets and white herons.

Whale sharks are often sighted north of Contoy between June and September. In an effort to preserve the park's pristine natural areas, only 200 visitors are allowed access each day. Bring binoculars, mosquito repellent and sunblock.

🛈 Getting There & Away

Daily visits to Contoy are offered by the **Fisherman's Cooperative Booth** (p267) on Isla Mujeres. The trip includes a light breakfast, lunch (with fish caught en route), snorkeling (gear provided) and beverages.

Isla Holbox

☑984 / POP 1500

Isn't life great when it's low-fi and low-rise? That's the attitude on friendly Isla Holbox (hol-bosh) with its sandy streets, colorful Caribbean buildings, and lazing, sun-drunk dogs. Holbox is a welcome refuge for anyone looking to just get away from it all ('all' likely meaning the hubbub of Cancún).

The island is about 30km long and from 500m to 2km wide, with seemingly endless beaches, tranquil waters and a galaxy of shells in various shapes and colors. Lying within the Yum Balam reserve, Holbox is home to more than 150 bird species, including roseate spoonbills, pelicans, herons, ibis and flamingos. In summer, whale sharks congregate nearby, and snorkeling with the gentle giants is unquestionably the island's biggest tourist draw.

Golf carts are big here, but walking to the town square from the dock takes less than 10 minutes and the beach is just a few blocks away from the square. Nobody uses street names, but just so you know, it's Avenida Tiburón Ballena that connects the town with the ferry dock.

🛏 Sleeping

Most upscale accommodations are scattered along the beachfront on the island's northern shore in what locals call the Zona Hotelera, while budget and midrange options are near the town square.

Hostel Tribu HOSTEL $
(☑984-875-25-07; www.tribuhostel.com; Av Pedro Joaquín Coldwell; dm/r from M$170/550; ☺❄☎) With so many activities available here (from salsa lessons to yoga and kayaking), it doesn't take long to settle in with the tribe. Six-bed dorms and private rooms are clean, colorful and cheerful. Tribu also has a book exchange and a bar that stages weekly jam sessions. From the plaza, it's one block north and two blocks west.

Casa Lupita HOTEL $$
(☑984-875-20-17; casalupita@sihoteles.net; Calle Palomino; r/ste M$800/1500; ☺❄☎) A great midrange option on the east side of the plaza, the spacious rooms catch good breezes and the suites have private balconies overlooking the action on the square.

Hotel Casa Barbara HOTEL $$
(☑984-875-23-02; reservas@hotelcasabarbara. mx; Av Tiburón Ballena s/n; r incl breakfast M$1092; ☺❄☎❅) A very comfortable hotel with a swimming pool surrounded by a verdant garden. Rooms are decked out with rustic furnishings and cushy beds, and most have porches overlooking the garden. It's halfway between the ferry dock and the beach.

★Casa Takywara HOTEL $$$
(☑984-875-22-55; www.casatakywara.com; Paseo Carey s/n; r incl breakfast US$132-165; ☺❄☎) Out on the quiet western end of town, this beautiful waterfront hotel stands out for its striking architecture and stylishly decorated rooms with kitchenettes and sea-view balconies. It's built next to a patch of protected

A GAME OF DOMINOES – SWIM WITH THE WHALE SHARKS

Between June and late August, massive whale sharks congregate around Isla Holbox to feed on plankton. They are the largest fish in the world, weighing up to 15 tonnes and extending as long as 15m from gaping mouth to arching tail. Locals call them dominoes because of their speckled skin.

The best time to track these gentle giants is in July and August, but that also happens to be shoulder season, when you can get up to two dozen boats rotating around a single whale shark. It's unpleasant for both shark and swimmer, so think twice about taking a tour during this season. The alternative is going in June, but you risk not spotting any whale sharks.

The World Wildlife Fund has been working with the local community since 2003 to develop responsible practices for visiting the whale sharks, trying to balance the economic boon of these tours with the environmental imperatives of protecting a threatened species.

When swimming with the whale shark only three swimmers (including your guide) are allowed in the water at a time. You are not allowed to touch the fish, and are required to wear either a life jacket or wet suit to ensure you do not dive below the shark.

wetland where you'll hear the song of chirping cicadas. Rates drop considerably during the low season. It's 1km west of Avenida Tiburón Ballena.

✖ Eating

Taco Cueto
MEXICAN $

(Av Pedro Joaquín Coldwell, btwn Av Tiburón Ballena & Esmedregal; tacos M$14-23, burritos M$79-115; ◷ 6pm-12:30am; ☻) Tired of seafood? Head to this taco joint for good *arrachera* (flank steak) and *al pastor* (marinated pork) tacos and burritos. There are even a few vegetarian options for noncarnivores. It's northeast of the plaza.

Limoncito
BREAKFAST $

(Av Damero s/n; breakfast M$60-80; ◷ 8:30am-9pm; ☻) This colorful little *palapa*-covered restaurant on the square slings excellent Mexican breakfasts. The *motuleños* (eggs in tomato sauce served with fried plantain, ham and peas) is a local favorite, as are the enchiladas.

Las Panchas
MEXICAN $$

(Morelos s/n, btwn Avs Damero & Pedro Joaquín Coldwell; antojitos M$24-36, mains M$90-150; ◷ 7:30am-11:30am & 1-6pm; ☻) Ask just about anyone in town where to go for good, cheap eats and they'll probably point to Las Panchas, where you can get delicious Yucatecan *antojitos* (snacks) such as *chaya* (tree spinach) *tamales, panuchos* and *salbutes* (fried tortillas with tasty toppings).

Edelyn Pizzería & Restaurant
PIZZA $$

(Plaza Principal; pizzas M$100-190, pizzas with lobster topping M$300-450; ◷ noon-11:30pm; ☻) We would be remiss if we didn't mention the self-proclaimed creators of Holbox's famous

lobster pizza, but locals say you can find much better pies with the coveted lobster topping elsewhere in town (hint: one is right across the square).

El Chapulím
MEXICAN $$$

(Tiburón Ballena s/n; M$220-250; ◷ 7pm till the food runs out Mon-Sat; ☻) 'No menu, always fresh' is the motto at this Mexican bistro. El Chapulím doesn't take reservations and the kitchen closes when the food runs out, usually around 10pm or so. Since fresh is the operative word here, chef Erik Winckelmann comes to your table usually offering some type of fish or seafood creation.

Los Peleones
FUSION $$$

(Av Tiburón Ballena s/n; mains M$140-250; ◷ 4-11pm; ☻☏) Mexico meets Argentina at this small, wrestling-themed restaurant overlooking the town square. The homemade pasta is excellent – try the portobello raviolis in gorgonzola sauce.

Viva Zapata
SEAFOOD $$$

(Av Damero s/n, just off plaza's northwest end; mains M$100-270; ◷ 11am-11:30pm; ☻) You really shouldn't leave the island without trying the mixed seafood platter here (order for two or ask for a single portion if traveling solo). It's a wonderful feast usually consisting of grilled lobster tail, fish, crab and other fresh shellfish, or you can opt for the surf-and-turf option.

❶ Information

Bancomer has an ATM on the 2nd story of the Alcaldía on the plaza. Sometimes it runs out of money and many places don't take plastic, so bring plenty of cash.

ℹ Getting There & Around

Ferries run to Holbox from the port town of Chiquilá, usually from 6am to 9pm (M$80 one-way). It takes about 25 minutes to reach the island.

Buses from the terminal in Cancún (M$86, 3½ hours) leave for Chiquilá at 7:50am, 10:10am and 12:50pm. Alternatively, you have the option of taking a taxi from Cancún for about US$100.

If you're driving, your vehicle will be safe in the Chiquilá parking lot for M$50 per 12 hours.

Holbox's sand streets see few autos, but golf carts have become ubiquitous – still, consider using your walking shoes instead. Golf-cart taxis cost M$30 in town and M$80 out to Punta Coco.

Rentadora El Brother (☑ 984-875-20-18; Av Tiburón Ballena s/n, north of plaza; cart per hr/day M$150/800; ⊙ 9am-5pm) See the Brother if you want to rent a golf cart.

Puerto Morelos

☑ 998 / POP 9200

Halfway between Cancún and Playa del Carmen, Puerto Morelos retains its quiet, small-town feel despite the building boom north and south of town. While the village offers enough restaurants and bars to keep you entertained by night, it's really the shallow Caribbean waters that draw visitors here. Another reason to come is to hit the artisans' market, one block south of the plaza's west corner. There's an ATM on the plaza.

◉ Sights & Activities

Jardín Botánico Dr Alfredo Barrera Marín GARDENS
(Jardín Botánico Yaax Che; ☑ 998-206-92-33; Hwy 307 Km 320; adult/child 3-10yr M$120/50; ⊙ 8am-4pm Mon-Sat; ☀) One of the largest botanical gardens in Mexico, this 65-hectare reserve has about 2km of trails and sections dedicated to epiphytes (orchids and bromeliads), palms, ferns, succulents (cacti and their relatives) and plants used in traditional Maya medicine. The garden also holds a large animal population, including the only coastal troops of spider monkeys left in the region.

It's 1.3km south of the Puerto Morelos turnoff.

Aquanauts DIVING
(☑ 998-206-93-65; www.aquanautsdiveadventures. com; Hotel Hacienda Morelos, Av Melgar s/n; 1-/2-tank reef dives US$70/90, snorkeling US$30; ⊙ office 8am-4pm Mon-Sat) Runs many interesting tours, including drift diving, cenote and shipwreck dives, and lionfish hunting. The dive shop is one block south of the plaza, in Hotel Hacienda Morelos.

Boca del Puma SWIMMING
(☑ cell 998-2412855; www.bocadelpuma.com; Ruta de los Cenotes Km 16; cenote admission adult/child 5-14yr US$12/7; ⊙ 9am-5pm; ☀) For chilling cenote action, check out the ecopark Boca del Puma, 16km west of Puerto Morelos. Other activities available include zip-lining and ATVs.

☙ Courses

Little Mexican Cooking School COOKING COURSE
(☑ 998-251-80-60; www.thelittlemexicancooking school.com; Av Rojo Gómez 768, cnr Lázaro Cárdenas; per class US$128; ⊙ 10am-3:30pm Tue-Fri) Ever wonder how to cook delicious regional Mexican cuisine? Here's your chance. During this six-hour course you'll learn all about ingredients used in Mexican cooking and how to prepare at least seven dishes. See website to book a class.

Puerto Morelos Language Center LANGUAGE COURSE
(☑ 998-871-01-62; www.puertomorelosspanish center.com; Niños Héroes 46; classes per hour/week US$25/200, homestay per day US$45-60) In addition to hourly and weekly classes of 20 hours, the language center also offers an immersion program with the option of living with a Mexican host family. The school doubles as a travel agency if you're looking to hook up tours and activities.

⌕ Sleeping

Hotel Sevilla HOTEL $
(☑ 998-206-90-81; pm.h.sevilla@gmail.com; Av Niños Héroes 29; d from M$500; ☖✳☏) The Spanish-run Sevilla is really nothing special but it's one of the only budget options in town during high season. The best bet is the rooftop rooms, which get good natural light and afford partial views of Puerto Morelos.

Posada El Moro HOTEL $$
(☑ 998-206-90-05; www.posadaelmoro.com; Av Rojo Gómez s/n; r incl breakfast US$69-79, ste US$105-117; ℗☖✳☏☀) A well-run property, with cheery geraniums in the halls and courtyard. Some rooms have kitchenettes, all have couches that fold out into futons, and there's a small pool in a tropical garden. Prices drop substantially in low season. It's northwest of the plaza.

Casitas Kinsol GUESTHOUSE **$$**

(✆ 998-206-91-52; www.casitas-kinsol.com; Av Zetina Gazca Lote 18; r from US$49; ❂ 🛜) Great for people who want to see what life's like on the other side of town (yes, there are signs of life west of the highway!). Kinsol offers eight *palapa*-style huts with beautiful design details such as Talavera tile sinks and handcrafted furnishings. It's a peaceful spot where even the dogs and cats get along. It's 3km west of town.

Casa Caribe B&B **$$$**

(✆ 998-251-80-60; www.casacaribepuertomorelos.com; Av Rojo Goméz 768; r M$1610; ❂❄🛜) Just follow your nose to Casa Caribe, an elegantly decorated B&B that shares its lovely grounds with the Little Mexican Cooking School. Rooms have sweeping beach views from private balconies, and though only one comes with air-con, all five get fantastic sea breezes. Your breakfast is a creation of the culinary school, so you know it will be good.

✖ Eating

There are a number of attractive little beachside eateries – go for a wander along the attractive *malecón* (esplanade) and see which one grabs your fancy.

Le Café d'Amancia CAFE **$**

(Av Rojo Gómez s/n; sandwiches & bagels M$35-85; ☉7am-2pm & 5-10pm Tue-Sun; ❂🛜✍) Right on the plaza, this is a spotlessly clean place with a pleasing ambience. It serves bagels, sandwiches, pies, good strong coffee, and fruit and veggie *licuados* (milkshakes).

El Nicho BREAKFAST **$$**

(www.elnicho.com.mx; Av Tulum s/n, cnr Av Rojo Gómez; breakfast M$55-105, lunch M$75-150; ☉7am-2pm Fri-Wed; ❂🛜✍) Puerto Morelos' best and most popular breakfast spot, El Nicho serves organic egg dishes, eggs Benedict, *chilaquiles* (fried tortilla strips in salsa) with chicken, and organic coffee from Chiapas. Vegetarians will find many good options here.

THE RIVIERA FUN PARKS

Given the scale of tourism in Riviera Maya, it should come as no surprise that theme parks are a huge draw. Some may find these places too Disney-like, others will see them as simply a fun day out, especially when traveling with kids.

It's worth mentioning that some parks offer an optional swim-with-dolphins activity, and though it may seem like a lovely idea, animal welfare groups suggest interaction with dolphins and other sea mammals held in captivity creates stress for these creatures.

Selvática (✆ 998-847-45-81; www.selvatica.com.mx; Ruta de los Cenotes Km 19; canopy tour incl hotel pick-up adult/child 3-11yr US$99/49; ☉tour times 9am, 10:30am, noon & 1:30pm; ⊞) Inland from Puerto Morelos, this adventure outfit only runs prearranged tours. Come for adrenaline-pumping zip-lining, swimming in a cenote and more. Check the website for age restrictions for each tour.

Xplor (✆ 984-803-44-03; www.xplor.travel; all-inclusive adult/child 5-11yr M$1904/952; ☉9am-5pm; ⊞) This large park 6km south of Playa del Carmen features circuits that take you zip-lining, rafting, driving amphibious jeeps, swimming in an underground river and hiking through caverns.

Aktun Chen (✆ toll-free 800-099-07-58; www.aktun-chen.com; Hwy 307 Km 107; full tour incl lunch adult/child US$110/88; ☉9:30am-5:30pm Mon-Sat; ⊞) Forty kilometers south of Playa del Carmen, this small park features a 585m-long cave, a 12m-deep cenote, 10 zip-lines and a small zoo.

Xcaret (✆ 984-206-00-38; www.xcaret.com; Hwy Chetumal-Puerto Juárez Km 282; adult/child 5-12yr from M$1584/792; ☉9am-9pm; ⊞) One of the originals in the area, with loads of nature-based activities and stuff for grown-ups like a Mexican wine cellar and day spa. It's 6km south of Playa del Carmen.

Xel-Há (✆ 984-803-44-03, toll-free 855-326-26-96; www.xelha.com; Hwy Chetumal-Puerto Juárez Km 240; adult/child 5-11yr from M$1424/712; ☉9am-6pm; ⊞) Billing itself as a natural outdoor aquarium, Xel-Há is built around an inlet 13km north of Tulum. There are lots of water-based activities on offer, including a river tour and snorkeling.

★ Al Chimichurri

STEAK $$$

(☑998-252-46-66; Av Rojo Gómez s/n; mains M$115-320; ☺5-11pm Tue-Sun; ☻) You definitely can't go wrong with the fresh pasta and wood-fired pizza here, but this Uruguayan grill is best known for its steaks. The star cuts are a *Flintstones*-size rib eye, tender flank steak and filet mignon in home-made beef gravy. It's just south of the plaza.

🛍 Shopping

Alma Libre Books & Gifts   BOOKS, CRAFTS

(www.almalibrebooks.com; Av Tulum; ☺10am-6pm mid-Nov–late Apr) Has more than 20,000 new and used books. The friendly owners are a great resource for information about the area, as is the website, which has vacation rental listings and a monthly newsletter. The store also carries art from the Yucatán, gift items and local gourmet food products.

❶ Getting There & Away

Playa Express and ADO buses that travel between Cancún and Playa del Carmen drop you on the highway. Buses and Playa Express vans from Cancún's ADO terminal cost M$22 to M$24. If you're arriving at the Cancún airport, there are frequent bus departures from there to Puerto Morelos for M$90.

Taxis are usually waiting at the turnoff to shuttle people into town for M$25; cabs parked at the plaza will take you back to the highway.

Playa del Carmen

☑984 / POP 150,000

Sitting coolly on the lee side of Cozumel, Playa del Carmen's beaches are the places to see and be seen by vacationing Europeans and North Americans. The waters aren't as clear as those of Cancún or Cozumel, and the beach sands aren't quite as champagne-powder perfect as they are further north, but Playa (as it's locally known) makes up for that with its thriving nightlife and diverse culinary scene.

With daily cruise-ship visitors, Playa is starting to feel like a mass-tourism destination, but it retains its European chic, and you only need to head several blocks west of the haughty pedestrian strip on Quinta Avenida (5 Avenida) to catch glimpses of the nontouristy side of things.

◉ Sights & Activities

Beaches

Playa's lovely white-sand beaches are much more accessible than Cancún's: just head down to the ocean, stretch out and enjoy. Numerous restaurants and bars front the beach in the tourist zone.

If crowds aren't your thing, head north of Calle 38, where a few scrawny palms serve for shade. Here the beach extends for uncrowded kilometers, but be extra careful with your belongings, as thefts are a possibility.

About 3km south of the ferry terminal, you'll find a refreshingly quiet stretch of beach that sees relatively few visitors.

Diving & Snorkeling

In addition to great ocean diving, most outfits offer cenote dives. Prices are similar at most shops: two-tank dives (M$1700), cenote dives (M$2500), snorkeling (M$750), whale-shark tours (M$2700) and open-water certification (M$7200).

Phocea Mexico   DIVING

(☑984-873-12-10; www.phocea-mexico.com; Calle 10 s/n; ☺8am-6pm) French, English and Spanish are spoken at Phocea Mexico. The shop does dives with bull sharks from November to March.

Scuba Playa   DIVING

(☑984-803-31-23; www.scubaplaya.com; Calle 10 s/n; ☺7:30am-9pm) A PADI five-star instructor development dive resort, with technical diving courses available.

⛶ Courses

International House   LANGUAGE COURSE

(☑984-803-33-88; www.ihrivieramaya.com; Calle 14 No 141; per week US$230, r US$36, homestay incl breakfast US$33) Offers 20 hours of Spanish class per week. You can stay in residence-hall rooms (even if you're not taking classes), but the best way to learn a language is to take advantage of the school's homestays with Mexican host families.

Playalingua del Caribe   LANGUAGE COURSE

(☑984-873-38-76; www.playalingua.com; Calle 20 s/n; 1 week without/with homestay US$245/455, hourly class US$23) Offers 20-hour-per-week classes as well as homestays. It also has optional classes in Maya language, Mexican cooking and salsa dancing.

Playa del Carmen

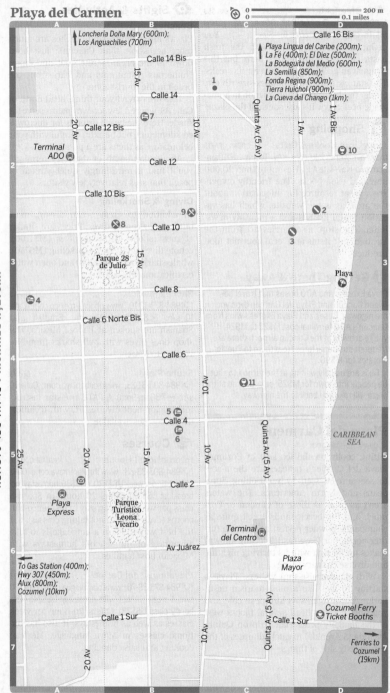

YUCATÁN PENINSULA PLAYA DEL CARMEN

0 — 200 m
0 — 0.1 miles

Loncheria Doña Mary (600m);
Los Anguachiles (700m)

Calle 16 Bis

Calle 14 Bis

Calle 14

Playa Lingua del Caribe (200m);
La Fé (400m); El Diez (500m);
La Bodeguita del Medio (600m);
La Semilla (850m);
Fonda Regina (900m);
Tierra Huichol (900m);
La Cueva del Chango (1km);

1

7

15 Av

20 Av

Calle 12 Bis

Terminal
ADO

10 Av

Quinta Av (5 Av)

1 Av

1 Av Bis

10

Calle 12

2

Calle 10 Bis

9

2

8

Calle 10

3

Parque 28
de Julio

15 Av

Playa

Calle 8

4

Calle 6 Norte Bis

Calle 6

10 Av

11

5
Calle 4

6

CARIBBEAN
SEA

25 Av

20 Av

15 Av

Quinta Av (5 Av)

Calle 2

Playa
Express

Parque
Turístico
Leona
Vicario

Av Juárez

Terminal
del Centro

To Gas Station (400m);
Hwy 307 (450m);
Alux (800m);
Cozumel (10km)

Plaza
Mayor

Calle 1 Sur

Quinta (5 Av)

Calle 1 Sur

10 Av

Cozumel Ferry
Ticket Booths

Ferries to
Cozumel
(19km)

20 Av

Playa del Carmen

⊕ **Activities, Courses & Tours**
1 International House	C1
2 Phocea Mexico	D2
3 Scuba Playa	C3

🛏 **Sleeping**
4 Hostel Playa	A3
5 Hotel Barrio Latino	B5
6 Hotel Casa Tucán	B5
7 Hotel Playa del Karma	B1

🍴 **Eating**
| 8 Kaxapa Factory | B3 |
| 9 La Famiglia | B2 |

🍷 **Drinking & Nightlife**
| 10 Blue Parrot Club | D2 |
| 11 Playa 69 | C4 |

👉 Tours

Alltournative   ADVENTURE TOUR
(☑984-803-99-99; www.alltournative.com; Hwy
307 Km 287) Alltournative's packages include
zip-lining, rappelling and kayaking, often
combined with visits to archaeological sites.
It also takes you to nearby Maya villages for
an 'authentic' experience that could easily
be had on your own. The office is out of the
way; you're better off calling or reserving
online.

🛏 Sleeping

Hostel Playa   HOSTEL $
(☑984-803-32-77; www.hostelplaya.com.mx; Calle
8 s/n; dm/d/tr incl breakfast M$200/490/735;
🅿🕑🛜) This place was made for mingling
with its central common area, a cool garden spot and a rooftop terrace. The private
rooms are simple but decent enough, and
the staff is extremely helpful and has great
suggestions on what to see and do.

⭐**Hotel Playa del Karma**   BOUTIQUE HOTEL $$
(☑984-803-02-72; www.hotelplayadelkarma.com;
15 Av, btwn Calles 12 & 14; r from M$1084; 🅿🕑
🌀🛜🌊) The closest you're going to get to the
jungle in this town, rooms here face a lush
courtyard with a small pool. All rooms have
air-con and TV, and some come with kitch-
enette, sitting area and sweet little porches
with hammocks. The hotel arranges tours to
nearby ruins and diving sites.

Hotel Barrio Latino   HOTEL $$
(☑984-873-23-84; www.hotelbarriolatino.com;
Calle 4 s/n; r incl breakfast M$1200; 🕑🌀@🛜)
Offers 18 clean, colorful rooms with good

ventilation, ceiling fans or air-con, tiled
floors, bathrooms and hammocks (in addition to beds). The place is often full and the
front gate often locked. Discounted rates are
available for extended stays, and the prices
drop precipitously in low season. Guests get
to make free international calls.

Hotel Casa Tucán   HOTEL $$
(☑984-873-02-83; www.casatucan.de; Calle 4 s/n;
r with fan/air-con US$60/80, ste US$100; 🅿🕑
🌀🛜🌊) This German-run hotel is a warren
of 30 rooms of several types. Rooms have
fans or air-con, a couple have kitchenettes,
and some come with a minibar. The Casa
has a pleasant tropical garden (that draws in
a lot of mosquitoes) and a cafe serving good,
affordable food.

La Semilla   B&B $$$
(☑984-147-32-34; www.hotellasemilla.com; Calle
38 Norte s/n; r incl breakfast from US$238;
🕑🌀🛜) Smallish rustic-chic rooms here are
attractively adorned with vintage objects
purchased from flea markets and haciendas. At night guests mingle in a lush candlelit garden over complimentary wine or
beer, and upstairs breakfast is served in an
open-air loft space decorated with antique
furniture.

🍴 Eating

You should head out of the tourist zone to
find cheap, quality eats. There are also cheap
food stands on 10 Avenida between Calles 8
and 10.

Lonchería Doña Mary   YUCATECAN $
(Calle 28 s/n, cnr 30 Av; snacks M$10-35, soups
M$30-50; ⏰6pm-1:30am; 🕑) You'll probably
have to wait for a table at this popular eatery and service can be slow. But it's worth
the wait when you try Mary's Yucatecan
comfort food. All dishes are prepared with
chicken: *tamales, panuchos* (fried tortilla
with refried beans and toppings), *salb-
utes* (same as *panuchos* sans beans) and a
hearty chicken soup, just like ma used to
make.

Kaxapa Factory   SOUTH AMERICAN $
(www.kaxapafactory.com; Calle 10 s/n; mains
M$50-90; ⏰10am-10pm Tue-Sun; 🕑🌀🛜) The
specialty at this Venezuelan restaurant on
the park is *arepas,* a delicious corn flatbread stuffed with your choice of shredded
beef, chicken or beans and plantains. There
are many vegetarian and gluten-free options
here and the refreshing fresh-made juices

go nicely with just about anything on the menu.

La Cueva del Chango
MEXICAN $$

(www.lacuevadelchango.com; Calle 38 s/n, btwn Quinta Av & the beach; breakfast M$76-90, lunch & dinner M$136-172; ⊙8am-11pm Mon-Sat, to 2pm Sun; ☺☎) You're in for a real treat when you visit the 'Monkey's Cave,' a Mexican restaurant known for its fresh and natural ingredients. Grab a table in a jungly *palapa* setting or enjoy the verdant garden out back. For breakfast, try the *chilaquiles* with *xcatic* chili; for dinner, go for the shrimp in chili *pasilla* with cacao and fried plantain.

Los Aguachiles
SEAFOOD $$

(Calle 34 s/n, btwn Avs 25 & 30; tostadas M$39-43, mains M$99-160; ⊙noon-7:30pm; ☺☎) Done up in Mexican cantina style yet with one big difference: the menu – consisting of tacos, *tostadas* and the like – was designed by a chef. So yeah, good luck finding artfully prepared tuna *tostadas* in any of the neighborhood watering holes.

La Famiglia
ITALIAN $$$

(www.facebook.com/lafamigliapdc; 10 Av s/n; mains M$140-250; ⊙4-11:30pm Tue-Sun; ☺☎) Pay a visit to the family and enjoy superb wood-fired pizza and handmade pastas, raviolis and gnocchi. Playa is a magnet for Italian restaurants, but this definitely ranks among the best of them.

🍷 Drinking & Nightlife

The party generally starts on Quinta Avenida then heads down to the beach clubs.

> **WORTH A TRIP**

CRISTALINO CENOTE

On the west side of the highway, 23km south of Playa del Carmen, is a series of wonderful cenotes. Among these is **Cristalino Cenote** (Hwy 307 s/n; adult/child 3-10yr M$100/60; ⊙8am-6pm), just south of the Barceló Maya Resort. It's easily accessible, only about 70m from the entrance gate, which is just off the highway. Two more sinkholes, **Azul** and **El Jardín del Edén**, sit just south of Cristalino along the highway. But Cristalino is the best of the three, as you can dive there (or just launch yourself off the rocks into the water below).

La Bodeguita del Medio
DANCING

(www.labodeguitadelmedio.com.mx; Quinta Av s/n; ⊙1:30pm-2am; ☎) The writing is literally on the walls, and on the lampshades, and pretty much everywhere at this Cuban restaurant-bar. After a few mojitos you'll be dancing the night away to live *cubana* music. Get there at 7:30pm for free salsa lessons.

La Fé
BAR

(cnr Quinta Av & Calle 26; ⊙10am-2pm; ☎) Caters to a young hipster crowd with its affordable *cubetazos* (bottled beer served in buckets) and DJ nights Wednesday through Sunday.

Playa 69
GAY

(www.rivieramayagay.com; alley off Quinta Av, btwn Calles 4 & 6; ⊙9pm-5am Tue-Sun) This gay dance club proudly features foreign strippers from such far-flung places as Australia and Brazil, and it stages weekend drag queen shows.

Blue Parrot Club
DANCE

(☑cell 984-1862515; www.facebook.com/blue parrotplaya; Calle 12 s/n; ⊙10am-5am) This is the Blue Parrot Suites' immensely popular open-sided *palapa* beachfront bar with swing chairs, a giant outdoor dance floor and lots of sand. The bar stages live music or DJs and features a nightly fire-dancing show.

ℹ Information

Banamex (cnr Calle 12 & 10 Av)

Post Office (cnr 20 Av & Calle 2; ⊙9am-4pm Mon-Fri, to noon Sat)

ℹ Getting There & Away

BOAT

Ferries depart frequently to Cozumel from Calle 1 Sur, where you'll find three companies with ticket booths. Barcos Caribe is the cheapest of the bunch. Transcaribe, south of Playa, runs car ferries to Cozumel.

Barcos Caribe (www.barcoscaribe.com; one-way fare adult/child 5-12yr M$135/70)

Mexico Waterjets (www.mexicowaterjets.com; one-way fare adult/child 6-11yr M$162/96)

Ultramar (www.granpuerto.com.mx; one-way fare adult/child 6-11yr M$163/97)

BUS

Playa has two bus terminals, but each sells tickets and provides information for at least some of the other's departures. Playa Express shuttle buses are a quicker way to head as far north as Cancún.

Terminal ADO (www.ado.com.mx; 20 Av s/n, cnr Calle 12) The Terminal ADO is where most 1st-class bus lines arrive and depart.

BUSES FROM PLAYA DEL CARMEN

DESTINATION	FARE (M$)	DURATION (HR)	FREQUENCY (DAILY)
Cancún	48-60	1¼	frequent
Cancún international airport	156	1	frequent
Chetumal	266-382	4¼-5	13
Chichén Itzá	135-282	4	7:30am (2nd-class), 8am, 2:30pm (2nd-class)
Cobá	84-120	2	11 (1st- & 2nd-class)
Mérida	408-450	4¼-5¾	frequent
Palenque	812-972	11½-12	3
San Cristóbal de las Casas	1010-1218	17-17½	3
Tulum	54-62	1	frequent
Valladolid	186	2¾	6

Terminal del Centro (Quinta Av s/n, cnr Av Juárez) All 2nd-class bus lines (including Mayab) are serviced at the old bus station, Terminal del Centro.

Playa Express (Calle 2 Norte) Offers quick, frequent service to Puerto Morelos for M$22 and downtown Cancún for M$34.

COLECTIVO

Colectivos to Tulum & Cancún (Calle 2, cnr 20 Av) *Colectivos* depart from Calle 2 as soon as they fill (about every 15 minutes) from 4am to midnight. They will stop anywhere along the highway between Playa and Tulum, charging a minimum of M$20. Luggage space is limited, but they're great for day trips. From the same spot, you can grab a *colectivo* to Cancún (M$34).

Isla Cozumel

📞 987 / POP 79,000

Cozumel is too resilient, too proud to let itself become just another cheesy cruise-ship destination. Leaving the tourist area – and the gringo-friendly souvenir shops behind – you still see an island of quiet cool and genuine authenticity. Garages still have shrines to the Virgin, there's a spirited Caribbean pathos, and of course there are some tourist things to do – such as diving down to some of the best reefs in the world, hanging in the pleasant town square and exploring the island's less-visited windswept shore.

History

Maya settlement on Cozumel dates from AD 300. During the post-Classic period, Cozumel flourished as a trade center and, more importantly, a ceremonial site. Every Maya woman living on the Yucatán Peninsula and beyond was expected to make at least one pilgrimage here to pay tribute to Ixchel (the goddess of fertility and the moon) at a temple erected in her honor. Archaeologists believe this temple was at San Gervasio, a bit north of the island's geographical center.

⊙ Sights

After checking out the Museo de la Isla de Cozumel in San Miguel, rent a vehicle or take a taxi to see the rest of the island; cyclists will need to brave the regular strong winds on the island.

Museo de la Isla de Cozumel   MUSEUM
(📞 987-872-14-34; www.cozumelparks.com; Av Melgar s/n; M$60; ⊙9am-4pm Mon-Sat) The Museo de la Isla de Cozumel presents a clear and detailed picture of the island's flora, fauna, geography, geology and ancient Maya history. Thoughtful and detailed signs in English and Spanish accompany the exhibits. It's a good place to learn about coral before hitting the water, and it's one not to miss before you leave the island.

Parque Punta Sur   NATURE RESERVE
(📞 987-872-40-14; www.cozumelparks.com; Carretera Costera Sur Km 27; adult/child 3-11yr M$210/120; ⊙9am-4pm Mon-Sat) For the price of admission to this ecotouristic park, you can visit a lighthouse, a small nautical museum and a Maya ruin. About 10 minutes away by car is an observation tower where you can see migratory birds and possibly crocodiles. The park area

YUCATÁN PENINSULA ISLA COZUMEL

Isla Cozumel

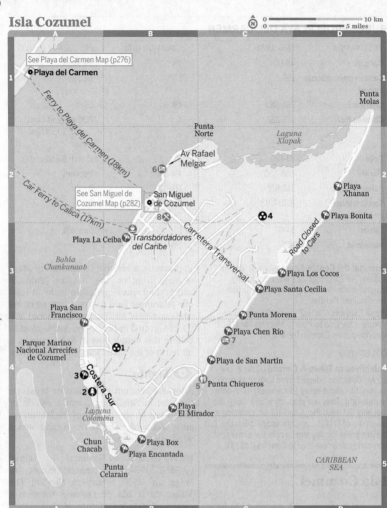

Isla Cozumel

⊙ Sights
1 El Cedral.. B4
2 Parque Punta Sur A4
3 Playa Palancar.. A4
4 San Gervasio Ruins............................... C2

❸ Activities, Courses & Tours
5 Playa Bonita Surfboard Rental C4

⊟ Sleeping
6 Hotel B Cozumel..................................... B2
7 Ventanas al Mar...................................... C4

✗ Eating
8 Camarón Dorado..................................... B2

offers a beach with a shallow reef, a restaurant and three midday boat tours to Laguna Colombia. You'll need your own vehicle or a taxi (M$300 one way) to get here.

El Cedral ARCHAEOLOGICAL SITE

(☺24hr) FREE This Maya ruin, a fertility temple, is the oldest on the island. It's the size of a small house and has no ornamentation. El

Cedral is thought to have been an important ceremonial site; the small church standing next to the tiny ruin today is evidence that the site still has religious significance for locals.

San Gervasio Ruins
ARCHAEOLOGICAL SITE

(www.cozumelparks.com; Carretera Traversal Km 7; M$125; ⊙8am-3:45pm; P) This overpriced Maya complex is Cozumel's only preserved ruin. San Gervasio is thought to have been the location of the sanctuary of Ixchel, goddess of fertility, and thus an important pilgrimage site at which Maya women – in particular prospective mothers – worshipped. But its structures are small and crude, and the clay idols of Ixchel were long ago destroyed by the Spaniards.

Beaches

The best beaches are on the southwest coast, facing the lagoon, but most have been snapped up by resorts and are hard to access.

The eastern shoreline is the wildest part of the island and presents some beautiful seascapes and many small blowholes (there's a bunch around Km 30.5). Swimming is dangerous on most of the east coast because of riptides and undertows. At Playa Chen Río, just past El Pescador restaurant at Km 42, there's a swimmable saltwater pool.

At Punta Chiqueros, near Km 37, a restaurant rents bodyboards and longboards.

Playa Palancar
BEACH

(Carretera Costera Sur Km 19; snorkel-gear rental M$130) About 17km south of town, Palancar is a great beach to visit during the week when the crowds thin out. It has a beach club renting snorkel gear and there's a restaurant. Near the beach, Arrecife Palancar (Palancar Reef) has some excellent diving (it's known as Palancar Gardens), as well as fine snorkeling (Palancar Shallows).

Punta Molas
RUIN

FREE Head to the far northeast of the island and you'll find yourself at the deserted lighthouse of Punta Molas. But take a 4WD, as this point isn't the easiest to reach. You'll want to fill up that gas tank and be prepared – there isn't much traffic around here to flag down for help. Once in the vicinity, you'll find some fairly good beaches and some minor ruins. The best camping spot along the road is at the lovely Playa Bonita.

Activities

Cozumel and its surrounding reefs are among the world's most popular diving spots. The sites have fantastic year-round visibility (commonly 30m or more) and a jaw-droppingly impressive variety of marine life that can be observed while drift diving. Among the best spots are Santa Rosa Wall, Punta Sur Reef, Colombia Shallows and Palancar Gardens.

Prices are usually quoted in US dollars. Expect to pay between US$80 to US$100 for a two-tank dive (equipment included) or introductory course. PADI open-water certification costs US$350 to US$400.

The best snorkeling sites are reached by boat. Most snorkeling-only outfits in downtown go to one of three stretches of reef nearby, all accessible from the beach. If you go with a dive outfit instead, you can often get to better spots, such as Palancar Reef or the adjacent Colombia Shallows, near the island's southern end.

Deep Blue
DIVING

(☑987-872-56-53; www.deepbluecozumel.com; Calle Salas 200; 2-tank dives incl equipment US$100, snorkeling incl gear US$57; ⊙7am-9pm) This PADI and National Association of Underwater Instructors (NAUI) operation has knowledgeable staff, state-of-the-art gear and fast boats that give you a chance to get more dives out of a day. A snorkeling outing visits three sites.

Playa Bonita Surfboard Rental
SURFING

(Carretera Coastal Oriente Km 37; per day bodyboard/surfboard M$120/480) Hit the surf on a bodyboard or longboard at Punta Chiqueros. Playa Bonita restaurant, at Km 37, rents them with proof of ID.

🛏 Sleeping

★Hostelito
HOSTEL $

(☑987-869-81-57; www.hostelcozumel.com; Av 10 Norte s/n, btwn Av Juárez & Calle 2 Norte; dm without/with air-con M$180/195, d M$550, ste from M$600; ❀✸🕙) Stay in a fan-cooled or air-conditioned dorm room, or check out the recently remodeled rooms and suites, which have been significantly improved with new beds and furnishings. The pleasant open-air kitchen and rooftop sundeck are great for hanging out and exchanging diving stories.

Hotel Mary Carmen
HOTEL $$

(☑987-872-05-81; www.hotelmarycarmen.com.mx; Av 5 Sur 132; d M$790; ❀✸🕙) Mary Carmen's lobby seems a bit odd in a design sense with its mix of antiques and mismatched modern furnishings, but it definitely ain't boring. Clean, colorful rooms overlook a central

San Miguel de Cozumel

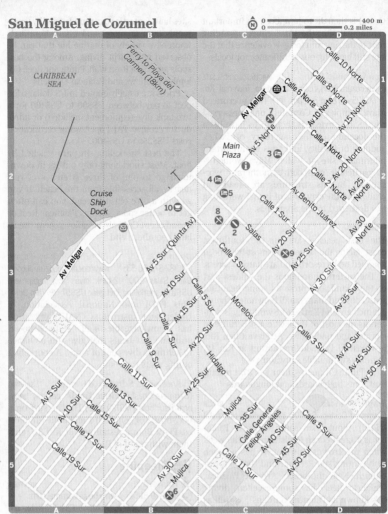

courtyard where the owner keeps more than a dozen turtles, so watch your step! It's just a short walk from the ferry terminal.

Suites Colonial Cozumel
HOTEL **$$**

(☎USA 877-228-6747, toll-free 800-227-26-39; www.suitescolonial.com; Av 5 Sur, btwn Calles 1 Sur & Salas; r/ste incl breakfast US$59/68; ☺❄☞) Down a passageway off Avenida 5 Sur, this place has lovely 'studios' (rooms with cable TV, fridge and lots of varnished-wood touches) and nice, one-bedroom suites with kitchenettes. A complimentary breakfast buffet is served around the corner at sister property Casa Mexicana.

Ventanas al Mar
HOTEL **$$$**

(☎984-267-22-37; www.ventanasalmarcozumel.com; Carretera Costera Oriente Km 43.5; r/ste incl breakfast from US$115/175; ☒☺☞☒) ☞ Notable as it's the only windward hotel on the island, Ventanas al Mar might be right for you if you are looking to get away from it all (*way* away from it all). The rooms have great ocean views and the constant wind will lull you to sleep – or drive you crazy if you're a light sleeper.

★ Hotel B Cozumel
BOUTIQUE HOTEL **$$$**

(☎987-872-03-00; www.hotelbcozumel.com; Carretera Playa San Juan Km 2.5; r US$120-160, ste

San Miguel de Cozumel

⊙ Sights
1 Museo de la Isla de Cozumel C1

⊙ Activities, Courses & Tours
2 Deep Blue C2

⊙ Sleeping
3 Hostelito C2
4 Hotel Mary Carmen C2
5 Suites Colonial Cozumel C2

⊗ Eating
6 Cha Cha's Kitchen B5
7 Kinta C1
8 La Choza C2
9 Mercado Municipal C3

⊙ Drinking & Nightlife
10 El Coffee Cozumel................................B2

US$170; ➌✦⬡✉) The place to B and B seen, this hip hotel on the north shore may not have that sand beach you're after, but just wait till you get a look at the azure infinity pool, saltwater pool and oceanfront hot tub. Rooms here are fashioned with recycled objects, and bikes are available to hit the town.

It's about 3km north of the ferry terminal.

🍴 Eating & Drinking

Cheapest of all eating places are the little market *loncherías* (lunch stalls) next to the **Mercado Municipal** (Calle Salas s/n, btwn Avs 20 & 25 Sur; snacks & mains M$25-80; ⊙8am-5pm).

Camarón Dorado   SEAFOOD $
(www.facebook.com/camaron.dorado; cnr Av Juárez & Calle 105 Sur; tortas M$33-38, tacos M$17-28; ⊙7am-3pm Tue-Sun; ➌✦) If you're headed to the windward side of the island or just want to see a different aspect of Cozumel, drop by the Camarón Dorado for a superb *torta de camaron capeado* (battered shrimp on a roll). Be warned: these bad boys are highly addictive. It's 2.5km southeast of the ferry terminal.

La Choza   MEXICAN $$
(☎987-872-09-58; Av 10 Sur 216; breakfast M$52-70, lunch & dinner M$96-180, set menu M$115; ⊙7am-10pm; ➌✦) An excellent and popular restaurant specializing in regional Mexican cuisine, with classics like chicken in *mole poblano* (a sauce of chilies, fruits, nuts, spices and chocolate). All mains come with soup. La Choza also offers a *comida corrida* (set menu) for the lunch crowd.

Cha Cha's Kitchen   INTERNATIONAL $$
(☎cell 987-5642525; www.facebook.com/chachas kitchen; Calle Mujíca s/n, btwn Calles 15 Sur & 17 Sur; soups & salads M$35-100, mains M$95-110; ⊙noon-4pm Mon-Thu; ➌) A mom-and-daughter team from Minnesota whip up everything from gringo comfort food to Mexican fu-

sion and vegan dishes out of their Cozumel home-turned-restaurant. The changing menu usually features a main dish, soup, salad and dessert, and believe us when we say you shouldn't skip dessert.

Kinta   MEXICAN $$$
(☎987-869-05-44; www.kintarestaurante.com; Av 5 Norte; mains M$170-215; ⊙5:30-11pm Tue-Sun; ➌✦) Putting a gourmet twist on Mexican classics, this chic bistro is one of the best restaurants on the island. The shrimp-and-scallop enchiladas dish is a tried-and-true favorite, and for dessert treat yourself to a *budín de la abuelita,* aka granny's pudding.

El Coffee Cozumel   CAFE
(cnr Calle 3 Sur & Av Melgar; mains M$63-89; ⊙7am-11pm) A tempting array of fresh-baked goods and organic coffee from the Mexican highlands make this place popular with locals and visitors alike. Pies are baked fresh daily.

ℹ Information

There are ATMs, banks and internet joints on the plaza.

Post Office (cnr Calle 7 Sur & Av Melgar; ⊙9am-4:30pm Mon-Sat)

Tourist Information Office (☎987-869-02-11; 2nd fl, Av 5 Sur s/n, Plaza del Sol; ⊙8am-3pm Mon-Fri) Pick up maps and travel brochures here.

ℹ Getting There & Away

AIR

Cozumel's **airport** (☎987-872-20-81; www.asur. com.mx; Blvd Aeropuerto Cozumel s/n) is 3km northeast of town; follow the signs along Avenida Melgar. Some airlines fly direct from the USA; European flights are usually routed via the USA or Mexico City. Domestic carriers Interjet and MayAir serve Cozumel.

Interjet (☎800-011-23-45, USA 866-285-95-25; www.interjet.com) Flies direct to Mexico City.

EXPLORE MORE SOUTH OF PLAYA DEL CARMEN

South of Playa del Carmen are several worthwhile coastal villages. These areas tend toward upscale tourism, and offer spectacular diving, snorkeling and some amazing beaches. Here are a few of our faves:

Punta Venado Eco-Park (☑ 984-879-39-98; www.puntavenadoadventures.com; Hwy 307 Km 278, Punta Venado; horseback riding per person US$90; ☺ 9am-5pm) About 15km south of Playa del Carmen, this is a great spot for horseback riding.

Paamul The secluded beach makes this area popular with visiting RV travelers, sea turtles and divers alike. **Paamul Hotel** (☑ 984-875-10-50; www.paamul.com; Hwy 307 Km 85; ste from US$175, cabañas from US$120, campsites per person US$13; P ✿ ☎) offers lodgings and diving services. It's 17km south of Playa.

Xpu-Há This is a sugar-sweet beach area 38km south of Playa del Carmen.

Tankah A few kilometers south of the Hwy 307 turnoff for Punta Solimán you'll find this cozy beach community. Visit www.tankah.com for info.

Xcacel-Xcacelito Just 3km north of Xel-Há, this is the state's most important turtle-nesting beach. Volunteer with turtles through **Fauna y Cultura de México** (p857) or just check out the lovely cenote and snorkeling found here.

Bahías de Punta Solimán These beautiful bays have stylish private houses for rent – www.locogringo.com has a good offering.

MayAir (☑ 987-872-36-09; www.mayair.com. mx) Service to Cancún with continuing flight to Mérida.

BOAT

Passenger ferries operated by **México Waterjets** (www.mexicowaterjets.com) and **Ultramar** (www.granpuerto.com.mx) run to Cozumel from Playa del Carmen (one-way M$155, hourly 6am to 9pm). See websites for schedules.

To transport a vehicle to Cozumel, Transbordadores del Caribe operates ferries out of the Calica car ferry terminal, 10km south of Playa del Carmen.

❶ Getting Around

TO/FROM THE AIRPORT

Frequent shared shuttle vans run from the airport into town (M$57), to hotels on the island's north end (M$96) and to the south side (M$97 to M$140). To return to the airport in a taxi, expect to pay M$85 from town.

BICYCLE

A bicycle can be a great way to get to the northern and southern beaches on the west side of flat Cozumel. The completely separate bicycle-scooter lane on the Chankanaab Hwy sees a good deal of car traffic from confused tourists and impatient cab drivers, so be careful.

Shark Rider (☑ 987-120-02-31; Av 5 Norte s/n, btwn Av Juárez & Calle 2 Norte; per day bikes M$100-150, scooters M$250; ☺ 8am-7pm) In addition to scooters you can rent beach cruis-

ers, mountain bikes and racing bikes here. It's on an alley off Avenida 5 Norte.

CAR & MOTORCYCLE

Car rentals start at M$400 with liability insurance *(daños a terceros)* included, but be sure to ask that the price includes the coverage.

Shark Rider (p284) offers scooters, as do many other places in town. There is a helmet law, and it is enforced.

Rentadora Isis (☑ 987-872-33-67; www. rentadoraisis.com.mx; Av 5 Norte, btwn Calles 2 Norte & 4 Norte; scooter/car per day incl liability insurance US$20/35; ☺ 8am-6:30pm) A fairly no-nonsense place with cars in good shape, Rentadora Isis' Cozumel branch rents convertible VW Beetles and scooters with little seasonal variation in prices.

TAXI

Fares are around M$35 (in town), M$80 (to the Zona Hotelera) and M$1000 for a day trip around the island. Fares are posted just outside the ferry terminal.

Akumal

☑ 984/POP 1400

Famous for its beautiful beach and large, swimmable lagoon, Akumal (Place of the Turtles) does indeed see turtles come ashore to lay their eggs from May to November, even though resort development has encroached on some of their nesting grounds. Akumal is one of the Yucatán Peninsula's oldest resort areas and consists primarily of pricey hotels, condominiums and residential developments (occupied mostly by North Americans) on nearly 5km of wide beach bordering four consecutive bays. Most sights and facilities are reached by taking the first turnoff, Playa Akumal, as you come south on the highway.

◉ Sights & Activities

Although increasing population is taking its toll on the reefs that parallel Akumal, diving remains the area's primary attraction.

Centro Ecológico Akumal   MUSEUM
(☑ 984-875-90-95; www.facebook.com/cea.akumal; 4-week volunteer program incl lodging from US$360; Ⓟ) ✈️ FREE) To learn more about the area's ecology, check out this center's small museum on the east side of the road at the town's entrance, where there are several exhibits on reef and turtle ecology. And for those aged over 21, it offers a four-week volunteer program focused on protection, conservation and research of female sea turtles, their nests and hatchlings.

Laguna Yal-Kú   SWIMMING
(adult/child 4-12yr M$218/155, snorkel gear M$78; ⊙9am-5pm; 🐾) Laguna Yal-Kú is a beautiful lagoon 2km north of the Playa Akumal entrance. The rocky lagoon, without a doubt

one of the region's highlights, runs about 500m from its beginning to the sea. It is home to large schools of brightly colored fish, and the occasional visiting turtle.

Akumal Dive Shop   DIVING
(☑ 984-875-90-32; www.akumaldiveshop.com; 1-/2-tank dive M$700/1120, fishing per boat M$2520-3800, snorkeling M$300, catamaran M$630-1330; ⊙8am-5pm) Dive trips and deepsea fishing excursions are offered by Akumal Dive Shop, at the town entrance. It also does snorkeling trips to the reef and remote beaches, and it rents catamarans.

🛏️ Sleeping

You'll find a bunch of holiday houses for rent on www.akumalvacations.com.

Hotel Maria José   HOTEL $
(☑ cell 984-1194530; r M$500; ❄️🌐) There's not much joy for budget travelers in Akumal, but across the highway in Akumal Pueblo (about a 10-minute walk or short taxi ride from the beach), this family-run place offers rather sparse but clean rooms.

★ Que Onda   HOTEL $$$
(☑ 984-875-91-01; www.facebook.com/queonda akumal; Caleta Yalkú Lote 97; s/d/q US$90/110/150; ❄️🌐🏊) Relatively affordable by Akumal standards, Que Onda has quiet, pleasant rooms overlooking a lush garden with a

YUCATÁN PENINSULA AKUMAL

RESPONSIBLE DIVING

Please consider the following tips when diving to help preserve the ecology and beauty of reefs:

➡ Avoid touching or standing on living marine organisms, or dragging equipment across the reef. Polyps can be damaged by even the gentlest contact. If you must hold on to the reef, touch only exposed rock.

➡ Be conscious of your fins. Even without contact, the surge from fin strokes near the reef can damage delicate organisms. Take care not to kick up clouds of sand, which can smother organisms.

➡ Practice and maintain proper buoyancy control. Major damage can be done by divers descending too fast and colliding with the reef.

➡ Take great care in underwater caves. Spend as little time within them as possible, as your air bubbles may be caught within the roof and thereby leave organisms high and dry. Take turns to inspect the interior of a small cave.

➡ Resist the temptation to collect or buy corals or shells, or to loot marine archaeological sites (mainly shipwrecks).

➡ Ensure that you take home all your rubbish and any litter you may find as well. Plastics in particular are a serious threat to marine life.

➡ Do not feed fish.

➡ Minimize your disturbance of marine animals. *Never* ride on the backs of turtles.

large pool and one of the best restaurants in town. A large two-story room sleeps four people.

✖ Eating & Drinking

At the town's entrance, hit **Lonchería Aku-malito** (sandwiches M$30-55; mains M$70-135; ⊙7am-9pm) for cheap Mexican eats.

Turtle Bay Café & Bakery CAFE **$$**
(www.turtlebaycafe.com; Plaza Ukana 1; mains M$85-165; ⊙7am-9pm; ⊜🛜📝) A appealing breakfast spot, this appealing cafe slings a wide variety of gringo comfort food ranging from breakfast burritos to eggs Benedict. The lunch and dinner menus include sourdough flat-bread pizzas, burgers and tasty fish and seafood options, such as blackened grouper tacos. It's near the town entrance.

La Buena Vida BAR
(www.labuenavidarestaurant.com; Coast road Lote 35; ⊙11am-11pm; 🛜) A popular beachside restaurant-bar with sand floors, swings, roaming musicians and a drinks menu with gimmicky cocktail names such as 'The Viagra,' which offers you 'a stiff one.' The restaurant (mains M$100 to M$240) is very good here.

❶ Getting There & Away

Most 2nd-class buses and *colectivos* traveling between Tulum and Playa del Carmen will drop you on the highway, from where it's about 500m to the entrance of town.

Tulum

☑984 / POP 28,000

Tulum's spectacular coastline – with all its confectioner-sugar sands, jade-green water and balmy breezes – makes it one of the top beaches in Mexico. Where else can you get all that and a dramatically situated Maya ruin? There's also excellent cave and cavern diving nearby, swimmable cenotes and a variety of lodgings and restaurants to fit every budget.

Some may be put off by the fact that the town center, where the affordable eats and sleeps are found, sits right on the highway, making the main drag feel more like a truck stop than a tropical paradise. But you can always head down to the coast and find that tranquil beachside bungalow.

History

Most archaeologists believe that Tulum was occupied during the late post-Classic period (AD 1200–1521) and that it was an important port town during its heyday. The Maya sailed up and down this coast, maintaining trading routes all the way down into Belize. When Juan de Grijalva sailed past in 1518, he was amazed by the sight of the walled city, its buildings painted a gleaming red, blue and yellow and a ceremonial fire flaming atop its seaside watchtower.

The ramparts that surround three sides of Tulum (the fourth side being the sea) leave little question as to its strategic function as a fortress. Several meters thick and 3m to 5m high, the walls protected the city during a period of considerable strife between Maya city-states. Not all of Tulum was situated within the walls. The vast majority of the city's residents lived outside them; the civic-ceremonial buildings and palaces likely housed Tulum's ruling class.

The city was abandoned about 75 years after the Spanish conquest. It was one of the last of the ancient cities to be abandoned; most others had been given back to nature long before the arrival of the Spanish. But Maya pilgrims continued to visit over the years, and indigenous refugees from the War of the Castes took shelter here from time to time.

'Tulum' is Maya for 'wall,' though its residents called it Zama (Dawn). The name Tulum was apparently applied by explorers during the early 20th century.

◉ Sights

Tulum Ruins ARCHAEOLOGICAL SITE
(www.inah.gob.mx; Hwy 307 Km 230; M$64, parking M$50-100, tours from M$644; ⊙8am-5pm; 🅿) The ruins of Tulum preside over a rugged coastline, a strip of brilliant beach and green-and-turquoise waters that'll leave you floored. It's true the extents and structures are of a modest scale and the late post-Classic design is inferior to those of earlier, more grandiose projects – but wow, those Maya occupants must have felt pretty smug each sunrise.

Tulum is a prime destination for large tour groups. To best enjoy the ruins without feeling like part of the herd, you should visit them early in the morning. A M$20 train takes you to the ticket booth from the entrance, or just hoof the 500m. You'll find cheaper parking just east of the main parking lot, along the old entrance road. There's a less-used southern foot entrance from the beach road.

Exploring the Ruins

Visitors are required to follow a prescribed route around the ruins. From the ticket booth, head north along nearly half the length of Tulum's enormous **wall**, which measures approximately 380m south to north and 170m along its sides. The **tower** at the corner, once thought to be a guard post, is now believed by some to have been a type of shrine. Rounding the corner, you enter the site through a breach in the north wall.

Once inside, head east toward the **Casa del Cenote**, named for the small pool at its southern base. A small tomb was found in the *casa*. Walk south toward the bluff holding the **Templo del Dios del Viento** (Temple of the Wind God) – roped off at the time of research – which provides the best views of El Castillo juxtaposed with the sea below.

Below the Wind God's hangout is a lovely little stretch of **beach** (also roped off). Next, head west to **Estructura 25**, which has some interesting columns on its raised platform and, above the main doorway (on the south side), a beautiful stucco frieze of the Descending God. Also known as the Diving God, this upside-down, part-human figure appears elsewhere at Tulum, as well as at several other east-coast sites and Cobá. It may be related to the Maya's reverence for bees (and honey), perhaps a stylized representation of a bee sipping nectar from a flower.

South of Estructura 25 is **El Palacio**, notable for its ornamentation, with X-shaped figures lined up above the eaves. From here, head east back toward the water and skirt the outside edge of the central temple complex (keeping it to your right). Along the back are some good views of the sea. Heading inland again on the south side, you can enter the complex through a corbeled archway past the restored **Templo de la Estela** (Temple of the Stela), also known as the Temple of the Initial Series. Stela 1, now in the British Museum, was found here. It was inscribed with the Maya date corresponding to AD 564 (the 'initial series' of Maya hieroglyphs in an inscription gives its date). At first this confused archaeologists, who believed Tulum had been settled several hundred years later than this date. It's now thought that Stela 1 was brought to Tulum from Tankah, a set-

Tulum Ruins

⊕ N 0 ▬▬▬ 50 m

Tower
Entrance
Gate
Casa del Cenote
Parking (700m); Toilets (700m); Hwy 307 (800m); Tulum (3km)
Minitemples
Templo del Dios del Viento
Estructura 25
Beach
Estela 2
Templo del Dios Descendente
El Palacio
Estructura 20
Oratorio
El Castillo
Tickets
Exit
Templo de las Pinturas
Templo de la Estela
(No Public Vehicle Access)
Plataforma de la Danza
Archway
Beach
Guard Tower Gate
Muralla Fortificada
Gate
CARIBBEAN SEA

tlement 4km to the north dating from the Classic period.

At the heart of the complex you can admire Tulum's tallest building, a watchtower appropriately named **El Castillo** (The Castle) by the Spaniards. Note the Descending God in the middle of its facade, and the Toltec-style 'Kukulcánes' (plumed serpents) at the corners, echoing those at Chichén Itzá. To the Castillo's north is the small, lopsided **Templo del Dios Descendente**, named for the relief figure above the door. South of the Castillo you'll find steps leading down to a (usually very crowded) beach, where you can go for a swim.

After some beach time, heading west toward the exit will take you to the two-story **Templo de las Pinturas**, constructed in several stages around AD 1400 to 1450. Its decoration was among the most elaborate at Tulum and included relief masks and colored murals on an inner wall. The murals have been partially restored, but are nearly impossible to make out. This monument might have been the last built by the Maya before the Spanish conquest and, with its columns, carvings and two-story construction, it's probably the most interesting structure at the site.

Tulum

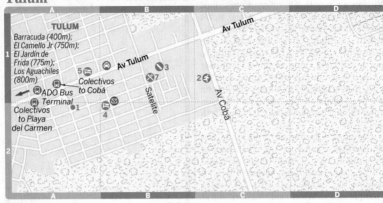

Activities

Snorkeling or swimming right from the beach is possible and fun, but be careful of boat traffic. Cave and cavern diving in nearby cenotes is a big draw for diving enthusiasts, but should always be done with a professional dive shop.

I Bike Tulum
BICYCLE RENTAL

(📞 984-802-55-18; www.ibiketulum.com; Av Cobá Sur s/n, cnr Venus; bicycle per day M$100, scooter per day incl insurance M$500; ⊙9am-5:30pm Mon-Sat) Rents a bike with lock and helmet, or if you prefer, a scooter.

Xibalba Dive Center
DIVING

(📞 984-871-29-53; www.xibalbadivecenter.com; Andromeda 7, btwn Libra Sur & Geminis Sur; 1-/2-tank dive US$85/140) One of the best dive shops in Tulum, Xibalba is known for its safety-first approach to diving. The center specializes in cave and cavern diving, but it also does ocean dives. Xibalba doubles as a hotel and offers attractive packages combining lodging, diving and cave-diving classes.

Tours

Community Tours Sian Ka'an
ECOTOUR

(📞 984-871-22-02, cell 984-1140750; Osiris Sur s/n, cnr Sol Oriente; tours per person US$75-129; ⊙7am-8pm) 🌿 This outfit runs various excursions to the magnificent Reserva de la Biosfera Sian Ka'an, which include kayaking in canals, bird-watching or visiting Maya ruins. Community Tours is a sustainable tourism project run by locals from Maya communities.

Sleeping

Tulum Pueblo

The town center, referred to as Tulum Pueblo, straddles the highway (called Avenida Tulum through town) southwest of the Cobá junction. It's at least 3km to the beach from here, but transportation options are plentiful. If you want sand and surf at your doorstep, head for the Zona Hotelera.

El Jardín de Frida
HOSTEL $

(📞 984-871-28-16; www.fridastulum.com; Av Tulum s/n, Tulum Pueblo, btwn Av Kukulcán & Chemuyil; dm/r/ste incl breakfast M$200/850/1200; 🅿️😊🛜) 🌿 The main house, dorms and private rooms are painted in colorful Mexican pop-art style at this ecohostel. All rooms are fan-cooled with the exception of the suites, which come with optional air-con. The mixed dorms are clean and cheerful, and the hostel has a fun little bar area.

★ L'Hotelito
HOTEL $$

(📞 984-160-02-29; www.hotelitotulum.com; Av Tulum s/n; d incl breakfast US$60; 😊❄️@🛜) Wooden boardwalks pass through a jungle-like side patio to generous, breezy rooms at this character-packed, Italian-run hotel. The attached restaurant does good breakfasts, too. Two rooms upstairs come with wide balconies, but they also catch more street noise from the main strip down below.

Hotel Kin-Ha
HOTEL $$

(📞 984-871-23-21; www.hotelkinha.com; Orión Sur s/n, btwn Sol & Venus; d with fan/air-con US$70/83; 🅿️😊❄️🛜) A small Italian-run hotel with

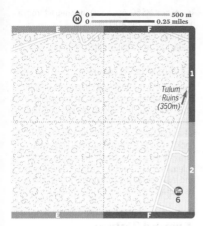

Tulum

⊕ Activities, Courses & Tours
1 Community Tours Sian Ka'an.............A2
2 I Bike Tulum C1
3 Xibalba Dive Center..............................B1

⊜ Sleeping
4 Hotel Kin-Ha B2
5 L'Hotelito...A1
6 Zazil-Kin F2

⊗ Eating
7 Taquería Honorio.................................B1

pleasant rooms surrounding a small court-yard with hammocks. The location is ideal – the bus stop for *colectivos* going to the beach and ruins is right around the corner. Guests are allowed to use Kin-Ha's sister property facilities on the beach.

⊨ Zona Hotelera

From the highway at the Cobá junction, a road leads about 3km to the coastal road servicing the Zona Hotelera. This string of waterfront lodgings extends more than 10km south of the ruins, and the road eventually enters the Reserva de la Biosfera Sian Ka'an.

Cenote Encantado   CAMPGROUND **$**
(☑ cell 984-1425930; www.cenoteencantado.com; Carretera Tulum-Boca Paila Km 10.5; tents per person M$290; ⊜) A rare budget option near the beach, this new-agey spot gets its name from a pretty cenote right in the camp-ground's backyard. Guests here stay in large furnished tents with beds, rugs and night-stands. It's not in front of the beach, but you can walk or bike there.

You can swim or snorkel in the cenote, but watch out for crocs! It's 6.5km south of the T-junction, near the Reserva de la Bios-fera Sian Ka'an entrance.

Zazil-Kin   CABAÑAS **$$**
(☎ 984-124-00-82; www.hotelzazilkintulum.com; Carretera Tulum-Boca Paila Km 0.47; cabañas M$1050, without bathroom M$750, r from M$1550; ⓟ⊜❄🛜) About a 10-minute walk from the ruins, this popular place resembles a little Smurf village with its dozens of painted *cabañas*. Zazil-Kin also has more expensive

air-conditioned, double-occupancy rooms, some of which can be a bit musty. If you opt for the bare-bones *cabañas,* electricity is available from 7am to 7pm. Bring insect repellent, you'll need it!

**★ Hotel La
Posada Del Sol**   BOUTIQUE HOTEL **$$$**
(☑ cell 984-1348874; www.laposadadelsol.com; Carretera Tulum-Boca Paila Km 3.5; r incl breakfast US$179; ⊜🛜) ⌖ Employing recycled objects found on the property after a hurricane, Posa-da Del Sol stands out for its naturally beauti-ful architecture. The solar- and wind-powered hotel has no air-con, but rooms catch a nice ocean breeze and just wait till you see the many wonderful design details. The beach here is pretty darn sweet, too.

✗ Eating

Most restaurants are located in Tulum Pueb-lo. In the Zona Hotelera, head to one of the hotels for good eats.

★ Taquería Honorio   TAQUERÍA **$**
(Satélite Sur s/n; tacos M$13, tortas M$28; ⊕ 5:30am-1:30pm Tue-Sun; ⊜) It began as a street stall and became such a hit that it's now a taco joint with a proper roof over-head. Yucatecan classics like *relleno negro* (shredded turkey in dark sauce) and *co-chinita* (pulled pork in annatto marinade) are served on handmade tortillas and *tortas.* You should definitely eat here.

Los Aguachiles   SEAFOOD **$$**
(☎ 984-802-54-82; Av Tulum s/n, cnr Palenque; to-stadas M$40-43, mains M$70-175; ⊕ noon-7:30pm; ⊜🛜) If you skipped this place while in Playa del Carmen, here's another chance. Fish ta-cos and tuna *tostadas* go down oh-so-nicely with a *michelada* (beer, lime and Clamato juice) in this airy cantina-style restaurant at the south end of town.

Barracuda
SEAFOOD **$$**
(www.facebook.com/barracudatulum1; Av Tulum; mains M$80-180; ⊙noon-9:30pm Tue-Sun; ⊜ 🔊) A very popular seafood eatery known for its *parillada de mariscos,* a large platter (for two people) with grilled fish, shrimp, lobster, octopus and squid.

Puro Corazón
MEXICAN **$$$**
(☑cell 984-1151197; www.purocorazontulum. wordpress.com; Carretera Tulum-Boca Paila Km 5.5; appetizers M$95-150, mains M$195-250; ⊙10:30am-10pm Tue-Sun; ⊜ 🔊 ☑) Reasonably priced by Zona Hotelera standards, and with its nightly live music and excellent cocktails, Puro Corazón is an inviting spot to spend an evening. Everything on the menu is prepared with a gourmet twist.

Posada Margherita
ITALIAN **$$$**
(☑cell 984-8018493; www.posadamargherita.com; Carretera Tulum-Boca Paila Km 7; mains M$80-250; ⊙7am-9:30pm; ⊜) This hotel's restaurant is candlelit at night, making it a beautiful, romantic place to dine. The fantastic food, including pasta, is made fresh daily and consists mostly of organic ingredients. The wines and house mezcal are excellent. It's 3km south of the T-junction.

❶ Information

Tulum Pueblo has numerous currency-exchange booths, ATMs and banks, and a **post office** (cnr Orión & Sol; ⊙8am-4pm Mon-Fri, to noon Sat).

❶ Getting There & Away

Tulum's bus terminal is centrally located on the town's main strip. *Colectivos* leave from Avenida Tulum for **Playa del Carmen** (M$40, 45 minutes), and for **Felipe Carrillo Puerto** (Av Tulum s/n; M$50, one hour) they depart from a block south of the ADO terminal.

ADO Bus Terminal (www.ado.com.mx; Av Tulum s/n, btwn Calles Alfa & Júpiter)

❶ Getting Around

Colectivos to the beach (M$10) run frequently from a bus stop on the corner of Venus and Orión from 6am to 7:30pm. You can also catch *colectivos* from there to the ruins.

Bicycles and scooters can be a good way to go back and forth between the town and beach.

Taxi fares are fixed from the taxi stands in Tulum Pueblo. They charge M$70 to the ruins and M$70 to M$150 from town to the Zona Hotelera.

Around Tulum

Gran Cenote

Gran Cenote
SWIMMING
(Hwy 109 s/n; M$150, snorkeling gear M$80, diving M$200; ⊙8am-5pm) About 4km west of Tulum is Gran (Grand) Cenote, a worthwhile stop on the highway between Tulum and the Cobá ruins, especially if it's a hot day. You can snorkel among small fish and see underwater formations in the caverns if you bring your own scuba gear. A cab from Tulum costs M$60 one way, or it's an easy bike ride.

Cobá
☑984 / POP 1300
Though not as large as some of the more famous ruins, Cobá is 'cool' because you feel like you're in an Indiana Jones flick. It's set deep in the jungle and many of the ruins

BUSES FROM TULUM

DESTINATION	FARE (M$)	DURATION (HR)	FREQUENCY (DAILY)
Cancún	92-130	2	frequent
Chetumal	174-268	3¼-4	frequent
Chichén Itzá	190	2½-2¾	9am, 2:45pm
Cobá	66	1	10:11am
Felipe Carrillo Puerto	54-92	1¼	frequent, consider taking a *colectivo*
Laguna Bacalar	180	3	8:33pm
Mahahual	240	2½	9am, 5:45pm
Mérida	206-298	4-5	frequent
Playa del Carmen	38-62	1	frequent
Valladolid	84-108	2	frequent

are yet to be excavated. Walk or bike along ancient *sacbés* (stone-paved avenues), climb up vine-covered mounds, and ascend to the top of Nohoch Mul for a spectacular view of the surrounding jungle.

History

Cobá was settled much earlier than nearby Chichén Itzá and Tulum, and construction reached its peak between AD 800 and 1100. Archaeologists believe that this city once covered an area of 50 sq km and held a population of 40,000 Maya.

Cobá's architecture is a curiosity: its towering pyramids and stelae resemble the architecture of Tikal, which is several hundred kilometers away, rather than the much nearer sites of Chichén Itzá and the northern Yucatán Peninsula. Some archaeologists theorize that an alliance with Tikal was made through marriage, to facilitate trade between the Guatemalan and Yucatecan Maya. Stelae appear to depict female rulers from Tikal holding ceremonial bars and flaunting their power by standing on captives. These Tikal royal females, when married to Cobá's royalty, may have brought architects and artisans with them.

Archaeologists are also baffled by the extensive network of *sacbés* in this region, with Cobá as the hub. The longest runs nearly 100km, from the base of Cobá's great pyramid Nohoch Mul to the Maya settlement of Yaxuna. In all, some 40 *sacbés* passed through Cobá, parts of the huge astronomical 'time machine' that was evident in every Maya city.

◉ Sights

Cobá Ruins   ARCHAEOLOGICAL SITE
(www.inah.gob.mx; M$64, guides M$500, bike rentals M$45, parking M$50; ⊙8am-5pm; Ⓟ) The archaeological site entrance, at the end of the road on the southeast corner of Laguna Cobá, has a parking lot with surrounding eateries and snack stands. Be prepared to walk several kilometers on paths, depending on how much you want to see. If you arrive after 11am, you'll feel a bit like a sheep in a flock.

A short distance inside, at the Grupo Cobá, there is a concession renting bicycles. These can only be ridden within the site, and are useful if you really want to get around the further reaches; also they're a great way to catch a breeze and cool off. If the site is crowded, however, it's probably best to walk. Pedicabs are another popular option for those who are tired or have limited mobility. Bring insect repellent.

➡ Grupo Cobá

The most prominent structure in the Grupo Cobá is **La Iglesia** (the Church). It's an enormous pyramid; if you were allowed to climb it, you could see the surrounding lakes (which look lovely from above on a clear day) and the Nohoch Mul pyramid. To reach it, walk just under 100m along the main path from the entrance and turn right.

Take the time to explore Grupo Cobá; it has a couple of corbeled-vault passages you can walk through. Near its northern edge, on the way back to the main path and the bicycle concession, is a very well-restored *juego de pelota* (ball court).

➡ Grupo Macanxoc

As you head for Grupo Macanxoc you'll see interesting flora along the 1km-long trail. At the end of the path stands a group of restored stelae that bore reliefs of royal women who are thought to have come from Tikal. You'll find the path to Macanxoc about 200m beyond the *juego de pelota*.

➡ Grupo de las Pinturas

The temple at Grupo de las Pinturas (Paintings Group) bears traces of glyphs and frescoes above its door and remnants of richly colored plaster inside. You approach the temple from the southeast. Leave by the trail at the northwest (opposite the temple steps) to see two stelae. The first of these is 20m along, beneath a *palapa*. Here, a regal figure stands over two others, one of them kneeling with his hands bound behind him. Sacrificial captives lie beneath the feet of a ruler at the base. You'll need to use your imagination, as this and most of the other stelae here are quite worn. Continue along the path past another badly weathered stela and a small temple to rejoin a path leading to the next group of structures.

➡ Grupo Nohoch Mul

Nohoch Mul (Big Mound) is also known as the Great Pyramid, which sounds a lot better than Big Mound. It reaches a height of 42m, making it the second-tallest Maya structure on the Yucatán Peninsula. Calakmul's Estructura II, at 45m, is the tallest. Climbing the old steps can be scary for some. Two diving gods are carved over the doorway of the temple at the top (built in the post-Classic period, AD 1100–1450), similar to sculptures at Tulum.

The view from up top is over many square kilometers of flat scrubby forest, with glimpses of lake. The trail to Grupo Nohoch Mul takes you past several interesting sights along the way. Northeast of the Grupo de las Pinturas turnoff you'll reach one of Cobá's two **juego de pelota** courts. Look at the ground in the center of the court to spot a carved stone skull (the winner or loser of the ball game?) and the carved relief of a jaguar.

After the ball court, the track bends between piles of stones – a ruined temple – and you reach a junction of sorts. Turn right (east) and head to the structure called **Xaibé**. This is a tidy, semicircular stepped building, almost fully restored. Its name means 'the Crossroads,' as it marks the juncture of four separate *sacbés*. Going north from here takes you past **Templo 10** and **Stela 20**. The exquisitely carved stela – worn, but not nearly so badly as the others – bears the date AD 730 and a familiar theme: a ruler standing imperiously over two captives. In front of it is a modern line drawing depicting the original details.

🏃 Activities

Cenotes Choo-Ha, Tamcach-Ha & Multún-Ha
SWIMMING

(admission per cenote M$55; ⊘8am-6pm) About 6km south of the town of Cobá, on the road to Chan Chen, you'll find a series of three locally administered cenotes: Choo-Ha, Tamcach-Ha and Multún-Ha. These cavern-like cenotes are nice spots to cool off with a swim, or a snorkel if you bring your own gear.

Bicycle Rental
BICYCLE RENTAL

(per day M$50; ⊘8am-5pm) To hit the cenotes south of town, you can rent a bike at this place on the main drag, next to Restaurant La Pirámide. Hotel Sac-Be rents bicycles, too.

🍴 Sleeping & Eating

Hotel Sac-Be
HOTEL $

(☑cell 984-1443006; www.hotelsacbe.com; dm M$150, d/tr M$550/650; P🐕❄) The best budget digs in town. Clean and friendly, the Sac-Be is actually two sister properties on the main strip heading into Cobá. It offers dorms with air-conditioning, in-room bathrooms and private rooms can sleep four people.

Hacienda Cobá
HOTEL $$$

(☑cell 998-2270168; www.haciendacoba.com; Av 1 Principal Lote 114; d incl breakfast US$75; P🐕📶) Hacienda-style rooms with rustic furniture sit in a pleasant jungle setting with lots of chirping birdies and the occasional spider monkey sightings. It's about 200m south of the Hwy 109 turnoff to Cobá and 2.5km from

the ruins, so you'll either need a car or be willing to walk or cab it into town.

Restaurant Ki-Jamal
MEXICAN $$

(mains M$70-160, lunch buffet M$170; ⊘8am-5pm; 🐕📶) 🍴 Owned by the Maya community, Ki-Jamal (which means tasty food in Maya) does indeed do some tasty traditional dishes and there's a lunch buffet as well. It's a pleasant spot for a meal when there are no tour buses around. It's in the ruins parking lot.

Restaurant La Pirámide
MEXICAN $$

(mains M$70-150; ⊘8am-5pm; 🐕📶) At the end of the town's main drag, by the lake, this restaurant is pretty touristy but does decent Yucatecan fare like *cochinita* and *pollo pibil* (achiote-flavored chicken or pork). The open-air setup allows for nice views.

ℹ Getting There & Away

Most buses serving Cobá go to the ruins to drop off passengers at a bus station; some only go as far as Hotel El Bocadito, which also serves as a bus station. Buses run six times daily between Tulum and Cobá (M$50 to M$68, 45 minutes). Buses also go to Valladolid (M$60 to M$70, 45 minutes) and Chichén Itzá (M$120, 1½ hours).

Day trippers from Tulum can reach Cobá by taking **colectivos** (M$50) that depart from Avenida Tulum and Calle Osiris.

The road from Cobá to Chemax is arrow-straight and in good shape. If you're driving to Valladolid or Chichén Itzá this is the way to go.

Tulum to Punta Allen

Punta Allen sits at the end of a narrow spit of land that stretches south nearly 40km from its start below Tulum. There are some charming beaches along this coast, with plenty of privacy, and most of the spit is within the protected Reserva de la Biosfera Sian Ka'an. You'll need a vehicle or bike to explore Sian Ka'an; intrepid travelers will find remote coastal camping sites. The road can be a real muffler-buster between gradings, especially when holes are filled with water from recent rains, making it difficult to gauge their depth.

◉ Sights & Activities

Reserva de la Biosfera Sian Ka'an
NATURE RESERVE

(Sian Ka'an Biosphere Reserve) Sian Ka'an (Where the Sky Begins) is home to a small population of spider and howler monkeys, American crocodiles, Central American tapirs, four turtle species, giant land crabs, more than 330

THE TALKING CROSS

In the small town of Felipe Carrillo Puerto you'll find one of the oddest tourist attractions in the region: the Shrine to the Talking Cross. The story goes like this: in 1849, when the War of the Castes turned against them, the Maya of the northern Yucatán Peninsula made their way to Carrillo Puerto seeking refuge. Regrouping, they were ready to sally forth again in 1850 when a 'miracle' occurred. A wooden cross erected at a cenote on the western edge of the town began to 'talk,' exhorting the Maya to continue the struggle against the Spanish and promising victory. The talking was believed to be done by a ventriloquist working with a religious leader, but the people looked upon it as the authentic voice of their aspirations.

The oracle guided the Maya in battle for more than eight years, until their great victory, conquering the fortress at Bacalar. Carrillo Puerto today remains a center of Maya pride. The talking cross has been returned to its shrine, the **Santuario de la Cruz Parlante** (cnr Calles 69 & 60; ⊙5:30am-9pm), and Maya from around the region still come to visit it, more for what it represents in the Maya people's struggle against inequality and injustice than for any supposed miraculous properties. Crowds gather here especially on May 3, the Day of the Holy Cross.

Felipe Carrillo is just off the main highway (95km south of Tulum) and has frequent bus connections with Cancún, Tulum and Chetumal. Should you choose to stay, **Hotel Esquivel** (☑983-834-03-44; www.hotelesquivel.blogspot.com; Calle 63 s/n, btwn Calles 66 & 68; d with fan/air-con M$500/570, ste M$670; P❄❀🖥📶🏊) is a good option near the plaza. About 8km south of town you can go kayaking at **Síijil Noh Há** (☑984-834-05-25; siijil nohhankp@gmail.com; off Hwy 307, Laguna Ocom turnoff; M$15, kayaks M$50, cabañas M$250; ⊙7am-7pm) 🖉, a gorgeous lakeside ecotourism center.

bird species (including roseate spoonbills and some flamingos), manatees and some 400 fish species, plus a wide array of plant life.

About 10km south of the reserve entrance is the visitors center, where you'll find a watchtower that provides tremendous bird's-eye views of the lagoon.

There are no hiking trails through the heart of the reserve; it's best explored with a professional guide.

Punta Allen

☑984 / POP 470

The fishing town of Javier Rojo Gómez is more commonly referred to as Punta Allen, the name of the point 2km south. This is truly the end of the road.

The area is known primarily for its catch-and-release bonefishing; tarpon and snook are very popular sport fish as well. Cooperatives in town offer fishing trips, dolphin-watching outings and snorkeling expeditions.

There are no ATMs or internet cafes in town. Electricity generally works between 10am to 2pm and 7pm to midnight.

🛏 Sleeping & Eating

The best places to eat in town are the beach-front restaurants.

Hotel Costa del Sol   BUNGALOW $$
(☑cell 984-8025387; caribejew@gmail.com; camp-sites per person M$125, r M$900-1200; P❀📶) At the entrance to town, this laid-back spot has quaint fan-cooled bungalows and rooms right on the beach. If you bring your own tent, you can camp on the sand.

Fisherman Fishing Lodge   SEAFOOD $$
(☑984-107-35-02; www.fishermanlodge.net; south of the dock; mains M$120-195, lobster M$250; ⊙8am-10pm; ❀📶) Serves breakfast meals fit for a hearty angler's appetite and a varied lunch and dinner menu featuring pizza and fresh lobster. Offers lodging-and-fishing package deals (rooms from M$800) and welcomes nonfisherfolk, too.

Muelle Viejo   SEAFOOD $$
(mains M$70-150; ⊙noon-9pm Tue-Sun) Overlooking a dock where fishers bring in the daily catch, this colorful beach house serves fresh seafood cocktails, decent fried fish dishes and lobster when it's in season.

❶ Getting There & Away

A rental car or scooter is the only way to reach Punta Allen, but prepare for 5km/h to 10km/h speeds and more than a few transmission-grinding bumps. Or you can always bike it if you're up for the long ride.

Mahahual

☑983 / POP 920

Mahahual prides itself on its sustainable approach to tourism, so imagine locals' reactions when a cruise-ship dock was built in the early 2000s. Yet aside from the tacky souvenir shops and gringo-friendly bars on the north side of town, the south side retains much of its charm as a laid-back Caribbean beach town. What's more, there's great diving and snorkeling here, and there's just enough nightlife along the beachfront *malecón* to keep you entertained. There's an ATM in town but bring cash in case it runs out of money.

◉ Sights & Activities

Mahahual Beach   BEACH
The beach right off Mahahual's beautiful *malecón* has great sand, plus water so shallow you can swim out a good 100m.

Banco Chinchorro   DIVE SITE
Divers won't want to miss the reefs and underwater fantasy worlds of the Banco Chinchorro, the largest coral atoll in the northern hemisphere. Some 45km long and up to 14km wide, Chinchorro's western edge lies about 30km off the coast, and dozens of ships have fallen victim to its barely submerged ring of coral.

The atoll and its surrounding waters were made a biosphere reserve (Reserva de la Biosfera Banco Chinchorro) to protect them from depredation. But the reserve lacks the personnel needed to patrol such a large area, and many abuses go undetected.

Most dives here go to a maximum of 30m, as there are no decompression chambers for miles. And with a ban on wreck dives recently lifted, there are plenty of shipwreck sites worth exploring. Along the way there are coral walls and canyons, rays, turtles, giant sponges, grouper, tangs, eels and, in some spots, reef, tiger and hammerhead sharks.

There's good snorkeling as well, including *40 Cannons*, a wooden ship in 5m to 6m of water. Looters have taken all but about 25 of the cannons, and it can only be visited in ideal conditions.

Mahahual Dive Centre   DIVING
(☑983-102-09-92, cell 983-1367693; www.mahahualdivecentre.com; Huachinango Km 0.7, cnr Cazón; 2-/3-tank dives M$2450/2850, snorkeling M$1650) Does trips to nearby sites as well as Banco Chinchorro and the fishing village of Punta Herrero.

Doctor Dive   DIVING
(☑cell 983-1036013; www.doctordive.com; Av Mahahual s/n, cnr Coronado; 2-tank dive/snorkeling incl equipment US$100/30; ☺8am-9pm) In addition to scuba and snorkeling excursions, the Doctor runs spearfishing outings for lionfish, an invasive species with no known predators in the Caribbean region. Lionfish ceviche, anyone? It's actually quite good.

⏏ Sleeping & Eating

Addresses are given as distances from the military checkpoint at the north entrance to town. There are more than a dozen restaurants along the *malecón*.

Hostal Jardín Mahahual   HOTEL $
(☑983-834-57-22; www.facebook.com/hostal.jardin; Sardina s/n, cnr Rubia; dm M$130, r with/without air-con M$620/450; ☻❄☎) For the price, this is a surprisingly stylish little hostel with five private rooms and an eight-bed coed dorm. Rooms are spotless and the dorms are the best in town by far. It's set back two blocks from the beach, near Calle Rubia.

★Posada Pachamama   HOTEL $$
(☑983-834-57-62; www.posadapachamama.net; Huachinango s/n; r from M$700, q M$1200; ℗☻❄☎) Rooms at the Pachamama (which means Mother Earth in Inca) range from small interior singles and doubles with ocean views to more ample digs that sleep four. It has a good on-site restaurant and the staff are very knowledgeable about local activities.

Ko'ox Quinto Sole   BOUTIQUE HOTEL $$$
(☑983-834-59-42; www.kooxquintosoleboutiquehotel.com; Carretera Mahahual-Xcalak Km 0.35; r M$1775-2500, ste M$3200-3500; ℗☻❄☎) One of the fanciest hotels in town, the spacious rooms here have heavenly beds and private balconies (some with Jacuzzi). It's on a quiet beach north of the boardwalk and 350m south of the lighthouse at town's entrance.

★Nohoch Kay   SEAFOOD $$
(Big Fish; cnr Malecón & Cazón; mains M$125-160, platter per person M$300; ☺1-9:30pm; ☻) Nohoch Kay, aka the Big Fish, definitely lives up to its name. Don't miss this Mexican-owned restaurant, where they prepare succulent whole fish in a garlic and white-wine sauce, or opt for the surf-and-turf platter, which includes lobster, steak, octopus and shrimp.

Fernando's 100% Agave   MEXICAN $$
(Malecón, btwn Calles Martillo & Coronado; mains M$110-180; ☺2-10pm Tue-Sun; ☻) With its new

smaller boardwalk location, Fernando's feels more intimate now. The restaurant-bar offers up fish and seafood dishes prepared with sauces ranging from sweet coconut-mango to spicy red. After dinner – or before – try a smooth-tasting Siete Leguas tequila.

Getting There & Around

There's no official bus terminal in Mahahual. At last visit, liquor store Solo Chelas (at Calles Huachinango and Cherna) sold tickets for a daily ADO northbound bus, which departs at 5pm for Tulum (M$240, three hours), Playa del Carmen (M$310, four hours) and Cancún (M$370, five hours).

Shuttle vans leave hourly from 5:45am to 6:45pm to Chetumal (M$88, 2½ hours), Laguna Bacalar (M$55, two hours) and Limones (M$50, one hour), where you can catch frequent northbound buses. The terminal is on the corner of Calles Sardina and Cherna.

Xcalak

📞 983 / POP 380

The rickety wooden houses, beached fishing launches and lazy gliding pelicans make this tiny town plopped in the middle of nowhere a perfect escape. Blessed by virtue of its remoteness and the Chinchorro atoll (preventing the creation of a cruise-ship port), Xcalak may yet escape the development boom.

Today, there are no signs of Xcalak getting a bank, grocery store or gas station anytime soon, so stock up before you come.

Sights & Activities

The mangrove swamps stretching inland from the coastal road hide some large lagoons and form tunnels that invite kayakers to explore. There's a remote Maya ruin on the western side of the lagoon. Your hotelier can tell you how to get there.

XTC Dive Center
DIVING

(www.xtcdivecenter.com; Coast road Km 0.3; 2-tank dives to Banco Chinchorro US$110, snorkeling trips US$45-75, PADI certification US$529, rooms US$45-60) XTC is the one-stop shop for all your needs. It offers dive and snorkel trips to the wondrous barrier reef offshore, and to Banco Chinchorro. It also rents diving equipment, provides PADI open-water certification, and operates fishing and bird-watching tours. Additionally, XTC rents three nice, affordable rooms and has a good restaurant-bar.

It's 300m north of town.

Sleeping

With the exception of the 'downtown' Caracol Caribe, most hotels are found on the old coastal road leading north from town. Addresses are expressed in kilometers north along the coast from town.

Casa Carolina
HOTEL $$$

(📞 USA 678-630-7080; www.casacarolina.net; Coast road Km 2.5; r incl breakfast US$120; 🖥) Bright, cheery yellow Casa Carolina has four rooms with large, hammock-equipped balconies facing the sea. Each has a kitchen with fridge, and the bathrooms try to outdo one another with their beautiful Talavera tilework. Use of kayaks, snorkel gear and bicycles is included.

Hotel Tierra Maya
HOTEL $$$

(📞 USA 330-735-3072; www.tierramaya.net; Coast road Km 2; r US$107-119, ste US$179; 🅿😊) A modern beachfront hotel has six lovely rooms (three quite large), each tastefully appointed with many architectural details. Each of the rooms has a balcony facing the sea; the bigger rooms even have small refrigerators.

Eating

The most reliable eats in town (in terms of opening hours) can be found at the Coral Bar & Grill, attached to XTC Dive Center.

Toby's
SEAFOOD $$

(mains M$85-165; ⊙11am-8:30pm Mon-Sat; 😊🖥) On the main drag, the friendly chitchat and well-prepared fish and seafood dishes make this a popular expat spot. Try the coconut shrimp or lionfish and you'll know why.

Costa de Cocos
INTERNATIONAL $$

(www.costadecocos.com; Coast road Km 1; breakfast US$5-6, lunch & dinner US$5-19; ⊙7am-8:30pm; 😊🖥) This fishing lodge's restaurant-bar is one of the better options in town. It serves both American- and Mexican-style breakfasts and does fish tacos for the lunch and dinner crowd. The bar produces its own craft whiskey and has pale ale on tap.

Getting There & Around

Buses to Chetumal (and Limones, where you can grab northbound buses) leave at 5am and 2pm; they stop on the coast road behind the lighthouse.

Driving from Limones, turn right (south) after 55km and follow signs to Xcalak (another 60km).

The coastal road from Xcalak to Mahahual often closes during rainy season.

You can charter a boat at XTC Dive Center for US$300 (min five people) to San Pedro, Belize.

Laguna Bacalar

♫ 983 / POP 11,000

Laguna Bacalar comes as a surprise in this region of scrubby jungle. More than 60km long, this crystal-clear lake offers opportunities for camping, swimming, kayaking and simply lazing around.

It's noted mostly for its large cenote, old Spanish fortress and popular *balnearios* (swimming grounds). There's not a lot else going on, but that's why people like it here. Around the town plaza, you'll find an ATM, a taxi stand and a tourist information office.

◉ Sights & Activities

Fortress FORTRESS
(cnr Av 3 & Calle 22; M$67; ⊙ 9am-7pm Tue-Sun) The fortress above the lagoon was built to protect citizens from raids by pirates and the local indigenous population. It also served as an important outpost for the Spanish in the Caste War. In 1859 it was seized by Maya rebels, who held the fort until Quintana Roo was finally conquered by Mexican troops in 1901.

Today, with formidable cannons still on its ramparts, the fortress remains an imposing sight. It houses a museum exhibiting colonial armaments and uniforms from the 17th and 18th centuries.

Cenote Azul SWIMMING
(Hwy 307 Km 34; adult/child under 10yr M$10/free; ⊙ 10am-6pm) **FREE** Close to the south end of the *costera* (coast highway), about 3km south of Bacalar's city center, is this 90m-deep natural pool with an on-site bar and restaurant. It's 200m east of Hwy 307; many buses will drop you nearby. You can rent kayaks here.

Balneario SWIMMING
(Av Costera s/n, cnr Calle 14; ⊙ 9am-5pm) **FREE** This beautiful public swimming spot lies several blocks south of the fort, along Avenida Costera. Parking costs M$10.

⛏ Sleeping & Eating

Hostal Pata de Perro HOSTEL $
(♫ 984-834-20-62; www.patadeperrobacalar.com; Calle 22 No 63; d from M$510, ste M$750-1560; ☻❊☎) This adults-only hostel on the square houses immaculate rooms, ranging from three-bed setups with shared bathrooms to ample suites with kitchenettes and private bathrooms. Your detail-oriented hosts, Veronica and Alejandro, go out of their way to make sure you have a pleasant stay. Curiously, the 'dog's paw' doesn't accept pets.

Amigo's Hotel Bacalar HOTEL $$
(♫ 983-107-92-34; www.bacalar.net; Av Costera s/n; d M$900; ☐☻❊@☎) Right on the lake and about 500m south of the fort, this ideally located property has five spacious guest rooms with king-size beds, hammocks, satellite TV, terraces and a *palapa*-covered common area with a lake view.

Casa Caracol HOTEL $$$
(♫ 983-834-30-14; www.hotel-caracol.com; Av Costera 609; r US$136; ☐☻☎) If you're looking for creature comforts such as air-con and TV, this place isn't for you. If you want a sublime place to relax, Casa Caracol delivers big time. Five *cabañas* overlook a lush garden and a lakeshore full of stromatolites (rock formations with ancient fossil remains) that date back more than 3 billion years.

Kayaks, paddleboards and bicycles are available. There's a three-night minimum stay during high season.

Orizaba MEXICAN $
(Av 7, btwn Calles 24 & 26; breakfast M$30-50, set menu M$60; ⊙ 8am-4pm; ☻) Highly recommended by locals and expats alike, this place prepares breakfast and a set menu of homestyle Mexican favorites such as *poc-chuc* (grilled pork) in a casual setting.

★ La Playita SEAFOOD $$
(www.laplayitabacalar.com; Av Costera 765, cnr Calle 26; mains M$104-159; ⊙ 2-10pm Tue-Sun; ☻☎) A sign outside reads, 'Eat, drink and swim': that pretty much sums it up. Fish and seafood dishes are tasty, albeit on the smallish side, but the Alipús mezcal and fine swimming certainly make up for that. A large rubber tree, which provides shade in the pebbly garden, was nearly uprooted in 2007 when Hurricane Dean pummeled the coast.

ⓘ Getting There & Away

Buses don't enter town; however, taxis and most combis will drop you at the town square. Buses arrive at the Bacalar's ADO terminal on Hwy 307, near Calle 30. From there it's about a 10-block walk southeast to the main square.

From the ADO station, buses go to Cancún, Mahahual, Xcalak, Tulum and other destinations.

If you're driving from the north and want to reach the town and fort, take the first Bacalar exit and continue several blocks before turning left (east) down the hill. From Chetumal, head west to catch Hwy 307 north; after 25km on the highway you'll reach the signed right turn for Cenote Azul and Avenida Costera, aka Avenida 1.

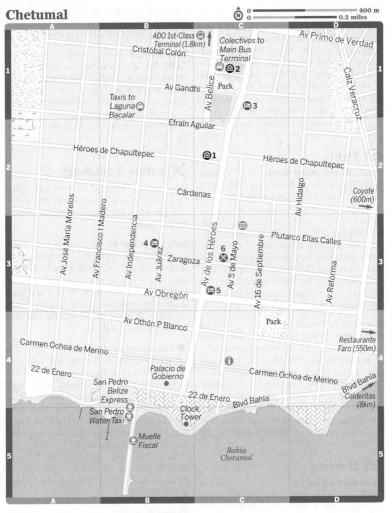

Chetumal

Chetumal

📱 983 / POP 150,000

The capital city of Quintana Roo, Chetumal is a relatively quiet place going about its daily paces. The bayside esplanade hosts carnivals and events, and the modern Maya museum is interesting (though a bit short on artifacts). Impressive Maya ruins, amazing jungle and the border to neighboring Belize are all close by. Though sightings are rare (there are no tours), manatees can sometimes be seen in the rather muddy bay or nearby mangrove shores.

Chetumal

◎ Sights
1 Museo de la Ciudad C2
2 Museo de la Cultura Maya C1

🛏 Sleeping
3 Capital Plaza C1
4 Hotel Grand Marlon B3
5 Hotel Palma Real C3

🍴 Eating
6 Café Los Milagros C3

History

Before the Spanish conquest, Chetumal was a Maya port, but the town was not officially 'settled' until 1898, when Spanish troops moved in to put a stop to the illegal trade in arms and lumber by descendants of the War of the Castes rebels. Dubbed Payo Obispo, the town changed its name to Chetumal in 1936. In 1955, Hurricane Janet virtually obliterated downtown, but the city was rebuilt to a grand plan with a grid of wide boulevards.

◉ Sights

Museo de la Cultura Maya   MUSEUM
(☑ 983-832-68-38; Av de los Héroes 68, cnr Av Gandhi; M$69; ◷ 9am-7pm Tue-Sun) The Museo de la Cultura Maya is the city's claim to cultural fame – a bold showpiece beautifully conceived and executed, though regrettably short on artifacts. It's organized into three levels, mirroring Maya cosmology. The main floor represents this world; the upper floor the heavens; and the lower floor Xibalbá, the underworld. The various exhibits cover all of the Mayab (lands of the Maya).

Museo de la Ciudad   MUSEUM
(Local History Museum; Héroes de Chapultepec, cnr Av de los Héroes; adult/child under 13yr M$26/13; ◷ 9am-7pm Tue-Sun) The Museo de la Ciudad is small but neatly done, displaying historic photos, military artifacts and old-time household items (even some vintage telephones and a TV). At last visit, the museum was adding two new rooms and interactive exhibits to bring it up to speed with the 21st century.

🛏 Sleeping

Hotel Palma Real   HOTEL $
(☑ 983-833-09-63; www.palmarealchetumal.com; Av Obregón 193; d M$500; P ⊛ ❄ 🎧) Unlike many of the budget hotels in town, rooms here get plenty of natural light and they're spacious, too. The only drawback is that it straddles a busy intersection, but traffic usually quiets down at a reasonable hour.

Hotel Grand Marlon   HOTEL $$
(☑ 983-285-32-79; www.hotelesmarlon.com; Av Juárez 88, btwn Zaragoza & Plutarco Elías Calles; r/ste from M$700/930; P ⊛ ❄ 🎧 🏊) With modern facilities and a pool area complete with Astroturf and a lukewarm Jacuzzi, the 'Grand' almost achieves 'hip boutique' status. The simple, stylish rooms are an excellent deal. Or, save a few hundred pesos by heading across the street to the plain ol' Marlon, its sister hotel, but don't say we didn't warn you about the noisy air-con units.

Capital Plaza   HOTEL $$$
(☑ 983-835-04-00; www.capitalplaza.mx; Av de los Héroes 171, cnr Av Gandhi; d M$1200, ste M$1600-2600; P ⊛ ❄ 🎧 🏊) One of the fanciest hotels in town, comfortable rooms overlook a courtyard with a swimming pool surrounded by tropical gardens, a restaurant and bar. The Maya sun mirror in the lobby adds interesting flair.

🍴 Eating & Drinking

Near the ADO 2nd-class terminal, you'll find a row of small, simple eateries serves cheap meals at the Mercado Ignacio Manuel Altamirano.

Café Los Milagros   CAFE $
(☑ 983-832-44-33; Zaragoza s/n; breakfast M$45-110, lunch M$26-92; ◷ 7am-6pm Mon-Fri, 7am-1pm Sat & Sun; ⊖ 🎧) Serves great espresso and food outdoors. A favorite with Chetumal's student and intellectual set, it's a good spot to chat with locals or while away the time with a game of dominoes.

★ Restaurante Xel-Ha   SEAFOOD $$
(☑ 983-285-02-87; Av Yucatán s/n, Calderitas; mains M$120-200; ◷ 11am-8pm; ⊖) For some of the best fresh fish around, head about 8km north of Chetumal to the fishing village of Calderitas, where you'll find this classic bayside seafood restaurant. The fried whole fish, usually *boquinete* (hogfish), is cooked just right and deftly plated.

To get here, head north on Blvd Bahía to Avenida Yucatán. Or take a 'Calderitas' bus from the Museo de la Cultura Maya. You can also cycle here.

Restaurante Faro   STEAK $$$
(www.facebook.com/rest.faro; Blvd Bahía 54, btwn Av Othón Blanco & Heróico Colegio Militar; breakfast M$65-79, lunch & dinner M$175-229; ◷ 8am-1pm Mon, to 11:30pm Tue-Thu & Sun, to 12:30am Fri & Sat; ⊖ 🎧) With indoor and outdoor seating overlooking the bay, the Faro offers reasonably priced breakfasts and a bay view. The steakhouse's lunch and dinner menu includes choice beef cuts, fish, seafood dishes and an array of salads.

ℹ Information

There are several banks and ATMs around town, including an ATM inside the bus terminal.

Cruz Roja (Red Cross; ☏ 065; cnr Avs Independencia & Héroes de Chapultepec; ☺24hr) For medical emergencies.

Post Office (☏ 983-832-98-47; cnr Plutarco Elías Calles & Av 5 de Mayo; ☺8am-7pm Mon-Fri, to 2pm Sat)

Tourist Information Office (☏ 983-833-24-65; Av 5 de Mayo 21, cnr Ochoa de Merino; ☺8:30am-4:30pm Mon-Fri) Has brochures and a well-meaning staff.

❶ Getting There & Away

AIR

Chetumal's small airport is roughly 2km northwest of the city center along Avenida Obregón. It's served by domestic carrier **Interjet** (☏ 800-011-23-45; www.interjet.com).

BOAT

Belize-bound ferries depart from the **muelle fiscal** (Dock; Blvd Bahía).

San Pedro Belize Express (☏ 983-832-16-48; www.belizewatertaxi.com; Av Blvd Bahía s/n, Muelle Fiscal) Boat transportation to Belize City, Caye Caulker and San Pedro.

San Pedro Water Taxi (www.sanpedrowatertaxi.com; Blvd Bahía s/n, Muelle Fiscal; one-way to San Pedro/Caye Caulker US$60/65) Runs water taxis to San Pedro and Caye Caulker, in Belize.

BUS

The ADO 1st-class bus terminal is about 2km north of the center, just west of the intersection of Avenidas Insurgentes and Belice. Services are provided by ADO and OCC, among other lines.

The ADO 2nd-class terminal, just west of the Museo de la Cultura Maya, is a good place to get info. Caribe, Sur and Mayab buses leave from here.

Beilze-bound buses depart from the Nuevo Mercado Lázaro Cárdenas, on Calzada Veracruz at Confederación Nacional Campesina Campeche (also called Segundo Circuito), about 10 blocks north of Avenida Primo de Verdad. Bus line San Juan departs from the Ist-class terminal to Flores, Guatemala for Tikal. Tickets can be purchased at the Mi Escape booth.

Departures listed below leave from the 1st-class terminal, unless noted otherwise.

BUSES FROM CHETUMAL

DESTINATION	FARE (M$)	DURATION (HR)	FREQUENCY (DAILY)
Bacalar	30-32	¾	frequent; 2nd-class, minibus terminal
Belize City, Belize	150	4-4½	frequent; Nuevo Mercado Lázaro Cárdenas
Campeche	283-440	6-7	3; 1st- & 2nd-class
Cancún	235-354	5½-6½	frequent
Corozal, Belize	30-50	1	frequent; Nuevo Mercado Lázaro Cárdenas
Escárcega	232-288	4	9
Felipe Carrillo Puerto	128	2½-3	5; 1st- & 2nd-class
Flores, Guatemala (for Tikal)	450	7½-8	7am
Mahahual	80-128	2½-3½	3; 1st- & 2nd-class
Mérida	444	5½-6	4
Orange Walk, Belize	75	2¼	frequent; Nuevo Mercado Lázaro Cárdenas
Palenque	356-602	6½-7½	5
Tulum	179-268	3¼-4	11
Valladolid	202	5½	3; 2nd-class
Veracruz	1070	17	6:30pm
Villahermosa	580	8¼-9	7
Xcalak	100	4-4½	5:40am & 4:10pm from 2nd-class
Xpujil	118-140	2-3	5

TAXI

City cabs charge about M$20 for short trips. Taxis on Avenida Independencia (between Efraín Aguilar and Avenida Gandhi) charge M$40 per person for Laguna Bacalar.

ⓘ Getting Around

Most places in Chetumal's tourist zone are within walking distance. To reach the main bus terminal from the center, catch a *colectivo* from the corner of Avenidas Belice and Cristóbal Colón, in front of the 2nd-class bus station. Ask to be left at the *glorieta* at Avenida Insurgentes. Head left (west) to reach the terminal.

You'll also find Calderitas buses departing from the same corner.

West of Chetumal

The Maya archaeological sites of Dzibanché, Kinichná and Kohunlich are well worth checking out and you'll never have to deal with large crowds! All three can be reached by car from Chetumal.

◉ Sights

Dzibanché & Kinichná ARCHAEOLOGICAL SITE
(combined admission M$46; ◷ 8am-5pm) Though a chore to get to, these sites are definitely worth a visit for their secluded, semiwild nature. Dzibanché (meaning 'writing on wood') was a major city extending more than 40 sq km, and on the road to it you pass huge mounds covered in trees. There are a number of excavated palaces and pyramids, but the site itself is not completely excavated.

A little further down the road, Kinichná is a hilltop site whose partially excavated acropolis affords panoramic views of the countryside. The road between the two is poorly signposted. If you're driving, keep veering left. You'll see the hill – keep moving toward it.

Kohunlich ARCHAEOLOGICAL SITE
(M$62, guide M$300; ◷ 8am-5pm) The archaeological site sits on a carpeted green. The ruins, dating from both the late pre-Classic (AD 100–200) and the early Classic (AD 300–600) periods, are famous for the great **Templo de los Mascarones** (Temple of the Masks), a pyramid-like structure with a central stairway flanked by huge, 3m-high stucco masks of the sun god.

A few hundred meters southwest of Plaza Merwin are the **27 Escalones** (27 Steps), which are the remains of an extensive residential area.

The hydraulic engineering used at Kohunlich was a great achievement; 90,000 of the site's 210,000 sq meters were cut to channel rainwater into Kohunlich's once enormous reservoir.

🛏 Sleeping

Explorean LUXURY HOTEL $$$
(☎ 800-504-50-00; www.explorean.com; Km 5.65; r from M$7921; ❋ @ ⚲ ☒) Halfway along the entrance road to the site is the super-deluxe Explorean which ticks all the boxes – infinity pool, hushed, sophisticated ambience, staff in flowing white uniforms etc. Cabins (more like small houses) are cool and comfortably furnished. Activities such as tours of the ruins and night kayaking are included in the price.

ⓘ Getting There & Away

The turnoff for Dzibanché and Kinichná is 44km west of Chetumal, off Hwy 186. The ruins are 24km northeast along a paved road (to reach the site, turn right about 2.5km after the town of Morocoy).

The turnoff to Kohunlich is 3km west of the Dzibanché turnoff along Hwy 186; from the junction, a road runs for 8.5km to the ruins.

The sites are best reached by car.

YUCATÁN STATE

Sitting regally on the northern tip of the peninsula, Yucatán state sees less mass tourism than its flashy neighbor, Quintana Roo. It is sophisticated and savvy, and the perfect spot for travelers more interested in cultural exploration than beach life. Sure, there are a few nice beaches in Celestún and Progreso, but most people come to this area to explore the ancient Maya sites peppered throughout the region, like the Ruta Puuc, which will take you to four or five ruins in just a day.

Visitors also come to experience the past and present in the cloistered corners of colonial cities, to visit *henequén* haciendas (vast estates that produced agave plant fibers, used to make rope) lost to time or restored by caring hands to old glory, and to discover the energy, spirit and subtle contrasts of this authentic corner of southeastern Mexico.

Mérida

⏱ 999 / POP 830,000

Since the Spanish conquest, Mérida has been the cultural capital of the peninsula. It is a town steeped in colonial history, with narrow streets, broad central plazas and the region's best museums. It's also a perfect place from which to kick off your adventure into the rest of Yucatán state. There are cheap eats, good hostels and hotels, thriving markets and events happening just about every night in the downtown area. It's best to visit Mérida during the cooler months, from November to February.

Long popular with European travelers looking to go beyond the hubbub of Quintana Roo's resort towns, Mérida is not an 'undiscovered Mexican gem' like some of the tourist brochures claim. Simply put, it's a tourist town, but a tourist town too big to feel like a tourist trap. And as the capital of Yucatán state, Mérida is also the cultural crossroads of the region, and there's something just a smidge elitist about Mérida: the people who live here have a beautiful town, and they know it.

History

Francisco de Montejo the Younger founded a Spanish colony at Campeche, about 160km to the southwest, in 1540. From this base he took advantage of political dissension among the Maya people, conquering T'ho (now Mérida) in 1542. By the decade's end, Yucatán was mostly under Spanish colonial rule.

When Montejo's conquistadors entered T'ho, they found a major Maya settlement of lime-mortared stone that reminded them of the Roman architecture in Mérida, Spain. They promptly renamed the city and proceeded to build it into the regional capital, dismantling the Maya structures and using the materials to construct a cathedral and other stately buildings. Mérida took its colonial orders directly from Spain, not from Mexico City, and Yucatán has had a distinct cultural and political identity ever since.

During the War of the Castes, only Mérida and Campeche were able to hold out against the rebel forces. On the brink of surrender, the ruling class in Mérida was saved by reinforcements sent from central Mexico in exchange for Mérida's agreement to take orders from Mexico City.

Mérida today is the peninsula's center of commerce and culture, a bustling city that has benefited greatly from the *maquiladoras* (manufacturing plants) that opened in the 1980s and '90s and the tourism industry that picked up during those decades.

◉ Sights & Activities

On Sunday mornings Calle 60 and part of the Paseo de Montejo is closed off to traffic as people take to the streets biking, skating and dog walking. Bikes can be rented at **Bici Mérida** (⏱ cell 999-2873538; Paseo de Montejo s/n, btwn Calles 45 & 47; per hr M$30; ⊙ 8am-9pm Mon-Fri, to 6pm Sat, 7am-2pm Sun; 🚻 R-2).

★ **Gran Museo del Mundo Maya** MUSEUM
(Calle 60 Nte No 299E; M$150; ⊙ 8am-5pm Wed-Mon, light & sound show 8:30pm; 🅿; 🚻 R-2) A world-class museum celebrating Maya culture, the Gran Museo houses a permanent collection of more than 1100 remarkably well-preserved artifacts, including a reclining chac-mool sculpture from Chichén Itzá and a cool underworld figure unearthed at Ek' Balam (check out homeboy's punk-rock skull belt and reptile headdress). If you're planning on visiting the area's ruins, drop by here first for some context and an up-close look at some of the fascinating pieces found at the sites.

Inaugurated in 2012, the contemporary building was designed in the form of a ceiba, a sacred tree believed by the Maya to connect the living with the underworld and the heavens above. On a wall outside, the museum offers a free light-and-sound show at night.

You'll find it about 12km north of downtown on the road to Progreso. Public transportation running along Calle 60 will leave you at the museum's entrance.

Plaza Grande PLAZA
FREE One of the nicest plazas in Mexico, where huge laurel trees shade the park's benches and wide sidewalks. It was the religious and social center of ancient T'ho; under the Spanish it was the Plaza de Armas, the parade ground, laid out by Francisco de Montejo (the Younger).

Casa de Montejo MUSEUM
(MuseoCasaMontejo; www.casasdeculturabanamex. com/museocasamontejo; Calle 63 No 506, Palacio de Montejo; ⊙ 10am-7pm Mon-Sat, to 2pm Sun) **FREE** Casa de Montejo is on the south side of the Plaza Grande and dates from 1549. It originally housed soldiers but was soon converted into a mansion that served members of the Montejo family until 1970. Today it

YUCATÁN PENINSULA MÉRIDA

Mérida

YUCATÁN PENINSULA MÉRIDA

Fiesta Americana (700m);
Taquería Nuevo San Fernando (1km);
La Tradición (1.3km)

Calle 43

Calle 45

Calle 47

Calle 74A

Calle 74

Calle 49

Calle 72

Calle 47A

Parque
Santa
Ana
32
33

Calle 49
35

Calle 66

Calle 70

Calle 68

Calle 64

Calle 62

Calle 60

Calle 58

Calle 51
26
Calle 51
16
36
41

Calle 53
Calle 53
28
9
30 24 15
25

23
Calle 55
Calle 55

Calle 57
Calle 57
31
11

Parque de
Santiago

Parque Zoológico
del Centenario
(950m)

Calle 59
39
27
3
Parque
de la Madre
State
Tourist
Office
Parque
Hidalgo
7
19

Calle 61
29
37
City
Tourist
Office
8
10
2
5
38
20
1

14
Calle 65

40
Calle 64
Calle 62

Progreso
Bus Terminal

Calle 67
Calle 67

(10km)

Terminal
de Segunda
Clase

Calle 69

Parque de
San Juan
Parque de
San Juan

CAME Bus
Terminal

Airport
Bus Stop

Calle 71

Calle 69

Hamacas
El Aguacate (150m)

Mérida

◎ Sights
1 Casa de Montejo C6
2 Catedral de San Ildefonso D5
3 Iglesia de Jesús D5
4 Iglesia La Mejorada.............................F5
5 Museo de Arte Contemporáneo.........D5
6 Museo de Arte Popular de
    Yucatán F5
7 Palacio de Gobierno C5
8 Palacio Municipal................................C5
9 Parque Santa Lucía D4
10 Plaza Grande......................................C5
11 Teatro Peón Contreras D4

☺ Activities, Courses & Tours
12 Bici Mérida.. E2
   Historic Center Tours................. (see 8)
13 Instituto Benjamín Franklin E5
14 Los Dos..B6
   Nómadas Hostel .... (see 26)
15 Turitransmérida..................................D4

🛌 Sleeping
16 Art Apart Hostel.................................D3
17 Casa Ana B&B....................................F4
18 Casa Isabel...E4
19 Gran Hotel..D5
20 Hostal Zócalo......................................C5
21 Hotel del Peregrino.............................E3
22 Hotel La Piazzetta F5
23 Hotel Medio Mundo.............................C4
24 Hotel Santa Lucía D4
25 Luz en Yucatán D4
26 Nómadas Hostel C3

✗ Eating
27 Amaro..C5
28 Apoala...D4
29 La Casa de Frida B5
30 La Chaya Maya D4
31 La Chaya Maya C4
32 La Socorrito D2
   Lo Que Hay.............................. (see 23)
33 Manjar Blanco.....................................D2

🍷 Drinking & Nightlife
34 La Fundación Mezcalería E4
35 La Negrita...D2
36 Orgánico..D3

✪ Entertainment
37 Centro Cultural Olimpo C5

🛍 Shopping
38 Casa de las Artesanías.......................B5
39 Guayaberas Jack C5
40 Hamacas Mérida C6
41 Tejón Rojo D3

YUCATÁN PENINSULA MÉRIDA

houses a bank and museum with a permanent exhibition of renovated Victorian, neorococo and neorenaissance furnishings of the historic building.

Outside, take a close look at the facade, where triumphant conquistadors with halberds stand on the heads of generic barbarians (though they're not Maya, the association is inescapable). Typical of the symbolism in colonial statuary, the vanquished are rendered much smaller than the victors; works on various churches throughout the region feature big priests towering over or in front of small indigenous people. Also gazing across the plaza from the facade are busts of Montejo the Elder, his wife and his daughter.

Museo de Arte Contemporáneo   MUSEUM
(Macay; ☑ 999-928-32-36; www.macay.org; Pasaje de la Revolución s/n, btwn Calles 58 & 60; ☺10am-6pm Wed-Mon) FREE Housed in the former archbishop's palace, the attractive Museo de Arte Contemporáneo holds permanent exhibitions of Yucatán's most famous painters and sculptors, as well as revolving exhibitions of contemporary art from Mexico and abroad.

Catedral de San Ildefonso   CATHEDRAL
(Calle 60 s/n; ☺6am-7pm) FREE On the site of a former Maya temple is Mérida's hulking, severe cathedral, begun in 1561 and completed in 1598. Some of the stone from the Maya temple was used in its construction. The massive crucifix behind the altar is **Cristo de la Unidad** (Christ of Unity), a symbol of reconciliation between those of Spanish and Maya heritage.

To the right over the south door is a painting of Tutul Xiu, *cacique* (indigenous chief) of the town of Maní paying his respects to his ally Francisco de Montejo at T'ho. (De Montejo and Xiu jointly defeated the Cocomes; Xiu converted to Christianity, and his descendants still live in Mérida.)

In the small chapel to the left of the altar is Mérida's most famous religious artifact, a statue called **Cristo de las Ampollas** (Christ of the Blisters). Legend says the statue was carved from a tree that was hit by lightning and burned for an entire night without charring. It is also said to be the only object to have survived the fiery destruction of the church in the town of Ichmul (though it was blackened and blistered from the heat). The statue was moved to the Mérida cathedral in 1645.

Other than these items, the cathedral's interior is largely plain, its rich decoration having been stripped away by angry peasants at the height of anticlerical fervor during the Mexican Revolution.

Palacio de Gobierno   MURALS
(Calle 61 s/n; ☺8am-8pm) FREE Built in 1892, the Palacio de Gobierno houses the state of Yucatán's executive government offices (and a tourist office). Have a look inside at the murals and oil paintings by local artist Fernando Castro Pacheco. Completed in the late 1970s, they portray a symbolic history of the Maya and their interaction with the Spaniards.

Museo de Arte Popular de Yucatán   MUSEUM
(Yucatán Museum of Popular Art; Calle 50A No 487; ☺10am-5pm Tue-Sat, to 3pm Sun) FREE In a building built in 1906, the Museo de Arte Popular de Yucatán has a small rotating exhibition downstairs that features pop art from around Mexico. The permanent exhibition upstairs gives you an idea of how locals embroider *huipiles* (long, woven, white sleeveless tunics with intricate, colorful embroidery) and explains traditional techniques used to make ceramics. Watch out for jaguars drinking toilet water!

Palacio Municipal   HISTORIC BUILDING
(City Hall; Calle 62 s/n) FREE Originally built in 1542, Mérida's Palacio Municipal was twice refurbished, in the 1730s and the 1850s.

◉ Calle 60

Calle 60 is one of Mérida's most historic streets. The downtown portion of Calle 60 is closed off to traffic Thursday through Sunday nights, making for a nice stroll.

Parque Santa Lucía   PARK
(cnr Calles 60 & 55) The pretty little Parque Santa Lucía has arcades on the north and west sides; this was where travelers would get on or off the stagecoaches that linked towns and villages with the provincial capital. Today it's a popular restaurant area and venue for **Serentas Yucatecas** (Yucatacen Serenades), a free weekly concert on Thursday at 9pm.

Iglesia de Jesús   CHURCH
(Calle 60 s/n) The 17th-century Iglesia de Jesús is also called Iglesia de la Tercera Orden. Built by Jesuits in 1618, this is the sole surviving edifice from a complex of buildings that once filled the entire city block.

The church was built from the stones of a destroyed Maya temple that once occupied the same site. On the west wall facing Parque Hidalgo, look closely and you can see two stones still bearing Maya carvings.

Teatro Peón Contreras THEATER
(www.sinfonicadeyucatan.com.mx; cnr Calles 60 & 57) The enormous Teatro Peón Contreras was built between 1900 and 1908, during Mérida's *henequén* heyday. It boasts a main staircase of Carrara marble, a dome with faded frescoes by Italian artists, and various paintings and murals throughout the building. The **Yucatán Symphony Orchestra** performs here Friday at 9pm and Sunday at noon throughout most of the year. See the website for more information.

Tours

For night bike tours, head to Parque de Santa Ana (Calles 60 and 47) on Wednesday at 9pm. See www.cicloturixes.org for more info.

Historic Center Tours WALKING TOUR
(999-942-00-00; www.merida.gob.mx/turismo; Calle 62 s/n, Plaza Grande; walking tours 9:30am Mon-Sat) FREE The city tourist office runs free guided walking tours of the historic center departing daily from the Palacio Municipal. You can also rent audio guides here for M$80 if you prefer to go it alone.

Turitransmérida TOUR
(999-924-11-99; www.turitransmerida.com.mx; Calle 55, btwn Calles 60 & 62; 8am-7pm Mon-Fri, to 1pm Sat, to 10am Sun) Turitransmérida does group tours to sites around Mérida, including Celestún, Chichén Itzá, Uxmal and Kabah, the Ruta Puuc and Izamal.

Courses

Los Dos COOKING COURSE
(www.los-dos.com; Calle 68 No 517; 1-day courses & tours US$185-210) Run by US-educated chef David Sterling, this cooking school offers a wide variety of courses and tours with a focus on flavors of the Yucatán. A morning street-eats tour visits popular stalls and markets.

Instituto Benjamín Franklin LANGUAGE COURSE
(999-928-00-97; www.benjaminfranklin.com. mx; Calle 57 No 474A; per hr/4-week course US$12/720) This nonprofit teaches intensive Spanish-language and content courses on Mexican history for advanced students.

PASEO DE MONTEJO

Paseo de Montejo, which runs parallel to Calles 56 and 58, was an attempt by Mérida's 19th-century city planners to create a wide boulevard similar to the Paseo de la Reforma in Mexico City or the Champs-Élysées in Paris. Europe's architectural and social influence can be seen along the Paseo in the fine mansions built by wealthy families around the end of the 19th century.

Festivals & Events

Mérida Fest CULTURAL
(www.merida.gob.mx/festival; Jan) This cultural event held throughout most of January celebrates the founding of the city with art exhibits, concerts, theater and book presentations at various venues.

Carnaval RELIGIOUS
(Feb/Mar) Prior to Lent, in February or March, Carnaval features colorful floats, dancers in costumes and nonstop festivities. It's celebrated with greater vigor in Mérida than anywhere else in Yucatán state.

Primavera Cultural MUSIC
(www.culturayucatan.com; May/Jun) A month-long event usually in May or June, it celebrates *trova* (troubadour-type folk music) and just about any other music genre you can imagine.

Toh Bird Festival FESTIVAL
(Festival de las Aves Toh; www.festivalavesyucatan. com; Nov) Holds various events throughout the year, culminating with a 'bird-a-thon' (bird-counting competition) in late November. Based in Mérida.

Sleeping

Nómadas Hostel HOSTEL $
(999-924-52-23; www.nomadastravel.com; Calle 62 No 433; dm from M$169, d M$450, without bathroom M$390; P※@🖥🏊) One of Mérida's best hostels; there are mixed and women's dorms, as well as private rooms. Guests have use of a fully equipped kitchen with fridge, as well as showers and hand-laundry facilities. It even has free salsa and cooking classes, and an amazing pool out back. See the hostel's website for various tours available to nearby ruins.

Hostal Zócalo
HOSTEL $

(☑999-930-95-62; hostalzocalo@yahoo.com; Calle 63 No 508; dm M$175, r M$450, without bathroom M$350, all incl breakfast; ☻@🛜) A great location in a beautiful old colonial building makes this hostel unique. It has firm beds and the big breakfast buffet gets rave reviews. The staff is friendly enough; however, the service comes up short at times.

Art Apart Hostel
HOSTEL $

(☑999-923-24-63; www.artaparthostel.com; Calle 60 No 456A; dm with fan/air-con M$135/160, r with fan/air-con M$400/550; ☻❄🛜🏊) It's like stepping into a museum at this funky hostel, where you'll find oddball art in every nook and cranny, including the gardens, hallways and pool area. Dorms and rooms vary, some are fairly simple, but all have original artwork. The previous owner was an eccentric collector who was much better at buying than selling the pieces.

Hotel Santa Lucía
HOTEL $

(☑999-928-26-72; www.hotelsantalucia.com.mx; Calle 55 No 508; s/d/tr M$450/540/600; P☻❄🛜🏊) Across from the park of the same name, this centrally located hotel is clean, secure and popular. The pool is small but clean, and the rooms have TV, phone and just so-so mattresses.

★Luz en Yucatán
BOUTIQUE HOTEL $$

(☑999-924-00-35; www.luzenyucatan.com; Calle 55 No 499; r US$59-79, ste US$59-79, apt US$69-150; P☻❄🛜🏊) While many much blander hotels are loudly claiming to be 'boutique,' this one is quietly ticking all the boxes – individually decorated rooms, fabulous common areas and a wonderful pool-patio area out back. The house it offers for rent across the road, which sleeps seven people and has a hot tub, is just as good, if not better.

Hotel La Piazzetta
HOTEL $$

(☑999-923-39-09; www.hotellapiazzettamerida. com; Calle 50A No 493, btwn Calles 57 & 59; d incl breakfast M$850; P☻❄🛜) Off a quiet side street overlooking Parque de la Mejorada, this friendly little place has just four rooms with views of the park or the pleasant patio area. Each of the well-appointed rooms contains memorabilia from the owners' world travels. Free bike loans are available and at last visit an on-site restaurant was being built.

Hotel del Peregrino
HOTEL $$

(☑999-924-30-07; www.hoteldelperegrino.com; Calle 51 No 488, btwn Calles 54 & 56; r incl breakfast M$895; ☻❄@🛜) After a recent colonial-style makeover the new-look Peregrino is sporting restored tile floors, Talavera tile sinks and some modern creature comforts, such as Netflix service (because cable TV is so '90s). Breakfast is served in a patio downstairs and upstairs you can relax in the hotel's rooftop hot tub.

Casa Ana B&B
B&B $$

(☑999-924-00-05; www.casaana.com; Calle 52 No 469; r incl breakfast from US$50; ☻❄🛜🏊) Casa Ana is an intimate escape and one of the best deals in town. It has a small natural-bottom pool and a cozy overgrown garden complete with Cuban tobacco plants (memories of home for the Cuban owners, no doubt). The rooms are spotless and have Mexican hammocks and (whew) mosquito screens.

Gran Hotel
HOTEL $$

(☑999-923-69-63; www.granhoteldemerida.com; Calle 60 No 496; s/d M$695/925; P☻❄🛜) This was indeed a grand hotel when built in 1901. Most rooms in this old-timer got a recent makeover; several still have the same old period furnishings and faded carpets. Despite the wear, they retain many elegant and delightful decorative flourishes.

★Casa Isabel
B&B $$$

(☑999-286-73-16; robertdstix@gmail.com; Calle 54 No 476; r incl breakfast US$80-100; ☻❄🛜🏊) The former residence and architectural work of Manuel Cantón (the architect who designed Mérida's iconic Palacio Cantón), this glorious *porfiriato*-era mansion has been passionately restored to regain its splendor of old. On offer are just two rooms: one a cozy setup near the pool area, the other a street-facing room with high ceilings and pretty tile floors.

The hosts, an amiable American and Iranian couple, love animals so feel free to bring Fluffy. Formerly Casa Esperanza.

Hotel Medio Mundo
HOTEL $$$

(☑999-924-54-72; www.hotelmediomundo.com; Calle 55 No 533; d incl breakfast US$80-90; ☻❄🛜🏊) This former private residence has been completely remodeled and painted in lovely colors. Its ample, simply furnished rooms have super-comfortable beds, beautiful tiled sinks and plenty of natural light. One of the two courtyards has a swimming pool, the other a fountain, and there's a good on-site vegan restaurant. The well-traveled, charming hosts make their guests feel at home.

✖ Eating & Drinking

Don't miss 'Mérida en Domingo,' an all-day food and crafts market on the main plaza every Sunday. It's a great place to sample regional cuisine.

★ Wayan'e   TAQUERÍA $

(cnr Calles 59 & 46; tacos M$11-15, tortas M$18-25; ☺7am-2:30pm Mon-Sat; ⊜) Popular for its *castacan* (fried pork belly), Wayan'e (meaning 'here it is' in Maya) is one of Mérida's premier breakfast spots. Vegetarians will find options here, such as the *huevo con ix-katic* (egg with chili) taco and fresh juices. But if you eat meat, it's all about the greasy goodness of the *castacan torta*.

La Socorrito   YUCATECAN $

(Calle 47, btwn Calles 58 & 60; tortas M$17; ☺7am-2pm; ▣R-2) These old pros have been slow-cooking *cochinita* in underground pits for more than six decades. You'll find this delightful hole-in-the-wall on the plaza side of the Mercado de Santa Ana.

Manjar Blanco   MEXICAN $$

(Calle 47, btwn Calles 58 & 60; mains M$75-140; ☺8am-6pm; ⊜🕾; ▣R-2) This family-run restaurant puts a gourmet twist on regional favorites. The *tortillitas tropicales* (fried plantains with smoked pork) are delicious, and sweet tooths will love the namesake *manjar blanco* (a coconut-cream dessert).

La Chaya Maya   MEXICAN $$

(www.lachayamaya.com; Calle 55 No 510; mains M$67-178; ☺1-10pm Mon-Sat, 8am-10pm Sun; ⊜🕾) Popular with locals and tourists alike, this restaurant has opened a new location in a lovely downtown colonial building. Consider La Chaya your introduction to classic Yucatecan fare like *relleno negro* (black turkey stew) or *cochinita pibil* (slow-cooked pork). The **original location** (cnr Calles 62 & 57; ☺from 7am daily) opens for breakfast.

La Casa de Frida   MEXICAN $$

(✆999-928-23-11; www.lacasadefrida.com.mx; Calle 61 No 526A; mains M$130-190; ☺6-10pm Mon-Sat; ⊜) Go here for delicious duck in *mole* sauce or another well-prepared Mexican classic, *chile en nogada* (stuffed poblano chili). Don't be surprised if pet bunny Coco hops into the dining area to greet you. No rabbit on the menu here.

Amaro   INTERNATIONAL $$

(✆999-928-24-51; www.restauranteamaro.com; Calle 59 No 507; mains M$99-235; ☺11am-2am;

⊜🕾☑) This romantic dining spot (especially at night, when there are performing *trova* acts) is in the courtyard of the house where Andrés Quintana Roo – poet, statesman and drafter of Mexico's Declaration of Independence – was born in 1787. The menu includes Yucatecan dishes, such as annatto-marinated chicken, and a variety of vegetarian and continental dishes.

Apoala   MEXICAN $$$

(✆999-923-19-79; Calle 60 No 471, Parque Santa Lucía; mains M$135-260; ⊜🕾) Drawing on traditional recipes from Oaxaca, which much like the Yucatán is known for its extraordinary regional cuisine, Apoala reinvents popular dishes such as *enmoladas* (stuffed tortillas in a rich *mole* sauce) and *tlayudas* (a large folded tortilla with sliced beef, black beans and Oaxaca cheese).

Eureka   ITALIAN $$$

(✆999-926-26-94; www.facebook.com/eureka cucinaitaliana#_=_; Av Rotary Internacional 117, cnr Calle 52; mains M$120-240; ☺1-11pm Tue-Sat, to 6pm Sat; ⊜🕾☑) Many locals consider this to be the best Italian food in town – and that's no small feat in a city known for excellent *cucina italiana*. The signature dish of Chef Fabrizio Di Stazio is the *riccioli eureka*, freshmade pasta in white ragu sauce with mushrooms and an aromatic hint of truffle.

Lo Que Hay   VEGAN $$$

(www.hotelmediomundo.com; Calle 55 No 53; 3-course dinners M$160; ☺7-10pm; ⊜🕾☑) Even nonvegans usually give an enthusiastic thumbs up to this dinner-only restaurant, where three-course vegan meals are served in a serene courtyard. The changing menu ranges from Mexican and international cuisine to raw vegan, and it includes a drink and dessert. Lo Que Hay is in the Hotel Medio Mundo and it welcomes nonguests.

★ La Fundación Mezcalería   BAR

(www.facebook.com/lafundacion; Calle 56 No 465; ☺8pm-3am Wed-Sat; 🕾) A popular bicyclists' hangout, especially on Wednesday, this retro-styled bar with nightly live music has an excellent selection of organic mezcals and an atmosphere conducive to knocking 'em back. Careful though: this stuff packs a mean punch.

La Negrita   DANCING

(www.lanegritacantina.com; Calle 62 s/n, cnr Calle 49; ☺noon-10pm; 🕾) If the live music here doesn't inspire you to get a tropical groove on, it's just a matter of time before the mojitos and mezcals have you dancing the night away. The rear garden makes a nice spot to catch a breather and chat with locals. Groups go on after 5pm from Wednesday to Sunday.

Slavia BAR
(cnr Paseo de Montejo & Calle 29; ⊘7pm-2am Tue-Sat) Jam-packed with Indian knickknacks, Slavia serves up fusion food and drinks in a casual environment, while adjoining bar Cubaro does mojitos (rum and mint cocktails) and DJ sessions on a deck overlooking Merida's iconic Monumento a la Patria.

Orgánico CAFE
(Calle 53 No 502, btwn Calles 60 & 62; coffee M$20-42; ⊘8am-4pm Mon, to 11pm Tue-Sat; 🛜) Java junkies will love this place's organic coffee, which is prepared with beans from the highlands of Chiapas, Veracruz and Guerrero. Hungry? You'll find good vegetarian options here.

☆ Entertainment

Every Thursday night at 9pm Parque Santa Lucía (p304) hosts Serenatas Yucatecas, a free concert featuring traditional Yucatecan serenades. On Sunday evenings you'll find concerts and dance performances on Plaza Grande. See www.yucatantoday.com for monthly event listings.

Centro Cultural Olimpo CONCERT VENUE
(☑999-924-00-00, ext 80152; www.merida.gob. mx/capitalcultural; cnr Calles 62 & 61) Offers something nearly every night: films, concerts, art installations, you name it.

🛍 Shopping

Mérida is a fine place for buying Yucatecan handicrafts. Purchases to consider include hammocks and traditional Maya clothing, such as colorful, embroidered *huipiles,* panama hats and wonderfully comfortable *guayaberas* (thin-fabric shirts with pockets and appliquéd designs).

Casa de las Artesanías HANDICRAFTS
(☑999-928-66-76; www.artesanias.yucatan.gob. mx; Calle 63 s/n, btwn Calles 64 & 66; ⊘8:30am-9pm Mon-Sat, 10am-5pm Sun) One place to start looking for handicrafts is this government-supported market for local artisans. Prices are fixed.

Guayaberas Jack CLOTHING
(www.guayaberasjack.com.mx; Calle 59 No 507A; ⊘10am-8:30pm Mon-Sat, to 2:30pm Sun) The *guayabera* is the classic Mérida shirt, but in buying the wrong one you run the risk of looking like a waiter. Drop into this famous shop to avoid getting asked for the bill.

Hamacas Mérida HANDICRAFTS
(☑999-924-04-40; www.hamacasmerida.com.mx; Calle 65 No 510, btwn Calles 62 & 64; ⊘9am-7pm Mon-Fri, to 2pm Sat) Has a large catalog with all kinds of sizes, shapes and colors, plus it ships worldwide.

Tejón Rojo SOUVENIRS
(www.tejonrojo.com; Calle 53 No 503; ⊘noon-9pm) A great little shop that sells trendy graphic T-shirts and an assortment of Mexican pop-culture souvenirs, including coffee mugs, jewelry, handbags and wrestling masks.

❶ Information

Banks and ATMs are found throughout the city.
City Tourist Office (☑999-942-00-00, ext 80119; www.merida.gob.mx/turismo; Calle 62, Plaza Grande; ⊘8am-8pm) Right on the main plaza, it is staffed with helpful English speakers. Here you can hook up free walking tours of the city, which depart daily at 9:30am, and you can rent audio guides for M$80.
Clínica de Mérida (☑999-942-18-00; www. clinicademerida.com.mx; Av Itzáes 242, cnr Calle 25; ⊘24hr; 🚍 R-49) Good private clinic with laboratory and 24-hour emergency service.
Emergency (☑066)
Post Office (☑999-928-54-04; Calle 53 No 469, btwn Calles 52 & 54; ⊘8am-7pm Mon-Fri, to 3pm Sat)
State Tourist Office (☑999-930-31-01; www. yucatan.travel; Calle 61 s/n, Plaza Grande; ⊘8am-8pm) In the entrance to the Palacio de Gobierno. There's usually an English speaker on hand.

❶ Getting There & Away

AIR
Aeropuerto Internacional de Mérida (Mérida International Airport; ☑999-940-60-90; www. asur.com.mx; Hwy 180 Km 4.5; 🚍 R-79) Mérida's airport is a 10km, 20-minute ride southwest of the Plaza Grande off Hwy 180 (Avenida de los Itzáes). It has car-rental desks, an ATM, currency-exchange service and a tourist information booth.

Domestic Airlines
Most international flights to Mérida make connections through Mexico City. Nonstop international services are provided by Aeroméxico and United Airlines. Several low-cost domestic carriers fly there as well.

Aeroméxico (☑ toll-free 800-021-40-00; www.aeromexico.com) Flies direct from Miami.

Interjet (☑ in USA 866-285-9525, toll-free 800-011-23-45; www.interjet.com) Serves Mexico City, where you can catch connecting flights to New York, Miami and Houston.

Mayair (☑ toll-free 800-962-92-47; www.mayair.com.mx) Runs prop planes to Cancún that continue on to Cozumel.

VivaAerobus (☑ in USA 888-935-98-48, toll-free 818-215-01-50; www.vivaaerobus.com) Service to Mexico City and Monterrey.

Volaris (☑ in Mexico City 55-1102-8000, in USA 866-988-3527; www.volaris.com) Direct to Mexico City and Monterrey.

BUS

Mérida is the bus transportation hub of the Yucatán Peninsula. Take care with your bags on night buses and those serving popular tourist destinations (especially 2nd-class buses); there have been reports of theft on some routes.

There are a number of bus terminals. See www.ado.com.mx for more info.

CAME Bus Terminal (☑ 999-920-44-44; Calle 70 s/n, btwn Calles 69 & 71) Aka the 'Terminal de

BUSES FROM MÉRIDA

DESTINATION	FARE (M$)	DURATION (HR)	FREQUENCY (DAILY)
Campeche	202-254	2½-3	frequent
Cancún	198-440	4½-6½	frequent: CAME & Terminal de Segunda Clase
Celestún	56	2½	frequent; Noreste terminal
Chetumal	444	6	4
Chichén Itzá	80-144	1½-2	frequent; CAME & Noreste terminal
Escárcega	258	4-4½	4; Terminal de Segunda Clase
Felipe Carrillo Puerto	200	6	frequent; Terminal de Segunda Clase
Izamal	27	1½	frequent; Noreste terminal
Mayapán	25	1½	hourly; Noreste terminal
Mexico City	1582-1882	20	7
Palenque	544-576	7½-10	4
Playa del Carmen	408-450	4-6	frequent
Progreso	19	1	frequent; Progreso bus terminal
Río Lagartos/San Felipe	142-196	3½	3; Noreste terminal
Ruta Puuc (round trip; 30min at each site)	179	8-8½	8am; Terminal de Segunda Clase
Ticul	50-76	1¾	frequent; Terminal de Segunda Clase
Tizimín	105-110	2	frequent; Noreste terminal
Tulum	298	4	4
Uxmal	55	1½	5; Terminal de Segunda Clase
Valladolid	95-178	2½-3	frequent

Primera Clase,' Mérida's main bus terminal has (mostly 1st-class) buses – including ADO, OCC and ADO GL – to points around the Yucatán Peninsula and faraway places such as Mexico City.

Fiesta Americana Bus Terminal (☎ 999-924-83-91; cnr Calle 60 & Av Colón; 🚍 R-2) A small 1st-class terminal on the west side of the Fiesta Americana hotel complex servicing guests of the luxury hotels on Avenida Colón, north of the city center. ADO buses run between here and Cancún, Playa del Carmen, Villahermosa and Ciudad del Carmen.

Noreste Bus Terminal (cnr Calles 67 & 50) Noreste, Sur and Oriente bus lines use this terminal. Destinations served from here include many small towns in the northeast part of the peninsula, including Tizimín and Río Lagartos; Cancún and points along the way; and small towns south and west of Mérida, such as Celestún, Ticul, Ruinas de Mayapán and Oxkutzcab.

Parque de San Juan (Calle 69, btwn Calles 62 & 64) From all around the square and church, combis (vans and minibuses) depart for Muna, Oxkutzcab, Tekax, Ticul and other points.

Progreso Bus Terminal (☎ 999-928-39-65; Calle 62 No 524) There's a separate terminal with buses leaving for the northern beach town of Progreso (M\$19, every 10 minutes).

Terminal de Segunda Clase (TAME; Calle 69) Aka TAME (Terminal de Autobuses de Segunda Clase), this terminal is just around the corner from the CAME bus terminal. ADO, Mayab, Oriente, Sur, TRT and ATS run mostly 2nd-class buses to points in the state and around the peninsula, including Felipe Carrillo Puerto and Ticul.

CAR

The most flexible way to tour the many archaeological sites around Mérida is to travel with a rental car. Assume you will pay M\$450 to M\$500 per day (tax and insurance included) for short-term rental of an economy-sized vehicle. Getting around Mérida's sprawling tangle of one-way streets is better done on foot or bus.

Several agencies have branches at the airport and on Calle 60, between Calles 55 and 57. You'll get the best deal by booking online.

Easy Way (☎ 999-930-95-00; www.easyway rentacar-yucatan.com; Calle 60 No 484, btwn Calles 55 & 57; ☉ 7am-11pm)

National (☎ 999-923-24-93; www.nationalcar. com; Calle 60 No 486F, btwn Calles 55 & 57; ☉ 7am-10pm)

ⓘ Getting Around

TO/FROM THE AIRPORT

Two taxi companies provide speedy service between the airport and downtown, charging M\$200 per carload (same price for hotel pick-up).

A city bus labeled 'Aviación 79' (M\$7) travels between the main road of the airport entrance (the bus does not enter the airport) and the city center every 15 to 30 minutes until 9pm, with occasional service until 11pm. The best place to catch the same bus to the airport is at Parque San Juan, from the corner of Calles 62 and 69.

BUS

Most parts of Mérida that you'll want to visit are within 10 blocks of the Plaza Grande. Given the slow speed of city traffic, travel on foot is often the fastest way to get around.

City buses are cheap at M\$7, but routes can be confusing. Merida.transpublico.com provides detailed maps of the routes.

To travel between the Plaza Grande and the upscale neighborhoods to the north along Paseo de Montejo, catch the R-2 'Hyatt' or 'Tecnológico' line along Calle 60. To return to the city center, catch any bus heading south on Paseo de Montejo displaying the same signs and/or 'Centro.'

TAXI

More and more taxis in town are using meters these days. If you get one with no meter, be sure to agree on a price before getting in. For getting around downtown and to the bus terminals, M\$20 to M\$50 is fair. Taxi stands can be found at most of the barrio parks.

Radio Taxímetro del Volante (☎ 999-928-30-35) For 24-hour radio taxi service.

South of Mérida

There's a lot to do and see south of Mérida. The major draws are the old *henequén* plantations, some still used for cultivating leaves, and the well-preserved Maya ruins like Uxmal and the lesser-known sites along the Ruta Puuc.

Uxmal

☎ 997

Uxmal was an important city, and its dominance extended to the nearby towns of Sayil, Kabah, Xlapak and Labná. Although Uxmal means 'Thrice Built' in Maya, it was actually constructed five times.

That a sizable population flourished in this dry area is yet more testament to the engineering skills of the Maya, who built a series of reservoirs and *chultunes* (cisterns) lined with lime mortar to catch and hold water during the dry season. First settled in about AD 600, Uxmal was influ-

South of Mérida

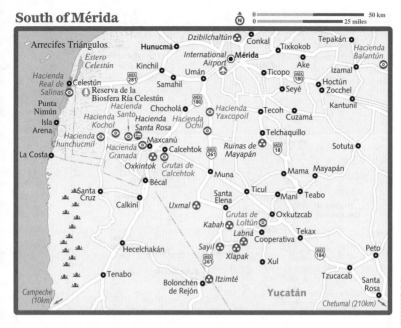

enced by highland Mexico in its architecture, most likely through contact fostered by trade. This influence is reflected in the town's serpent imagery, phallic symbols and columns. The well-proportioned Puuc architecture, with its intricate, geometric mosaics sweeping across the upper parts of elongated facades, was also strongly influenced by the slightly earlier Río Bec and Chenes styles.

The scarcity of water in the region meant that Chaac, the rain god or sky serpent, was supreme in importance. His image is ubiquitous at the site, in the form of stucco masks protruding from facades and cornices. There is much speculation as to why Uxmal was largely abandoned in about AD 900; one theory is that drought conditions may have reached such proportions that the inhabitants had to relocate. Later, the Xiu dynasty, which had controlled Uxmal for several hundred years, moved their seat of power to near present-day Maní, launching a rebellion against the kingdom of Mayapán, which had usurped much of the power in the region.

Rediscovered by archaeologists in the 19th century, Uxmal was first excavated in 1929 by Frans Blom. Although the site has been restored, much is yet to be discovered.

⊙ Sights

Uxmal Ruins
ARCHAEOLOGICAL SITE

(Hwy 261 Km 78; adult/child under 13yr M$203/free, light & sound show M$83, parking M$30, guides M$700; ☺ site 8am-5pm, light & sound show 8pm Apr-Oct & 7pm Nov-Mar; 🅿) Pronounced oosh-mahl, Uxmal is one impressive set of ruins, easily ranking among the top Maya archaeological sites. It is a large site with some fascinating structures in good condition and bearing a riot of ornamentation. Adding to its appeal is Uxmal's setting in the hilly Puuc region, which lent its name to the architectural patterns in this area.

Puuc means 'hills,' and these, rising up to about 100m, are the first relief from the flat northern and western portions of the peninsula. For an additional cost, Uxmal projects a nightly light-and-sound show. It's in Spanish but there are audio translators available.

➡ Casa del Adivino

(Pirámide del Adivino) As you approach Uxmal, the Casa del Adivino comes into view. This temple (the name translates as 'Magician's House'), 35m high, was built in an unusual oval shape. What you see is a restored version of the temple's fifth incarnation, consisting of round stones held rudely together with lots of cement. Four earlier temples were completely covered in the final rebuild

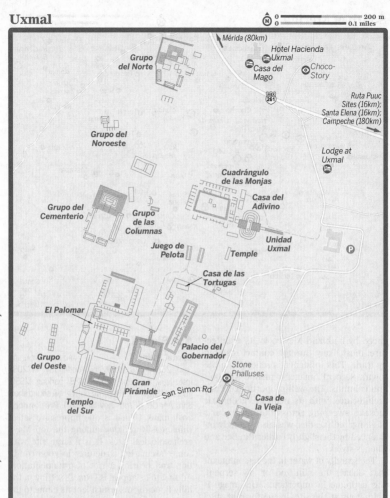

ing by the Maya, except for the high doorway on the west side, which remains from the fourth temple.

➡ Cuadrángulo de las Monjas

The 74-room, sprawling Nuns' Quadrangle is directly west of the Casa del Adivino. Archaeologists guess variously that it was a military academy, royal school or palace complex. The long-nosed face of Chaac appears everywhere on the facades of the four separate temples that form the quadrangle. The northern temple, the grandest of the four, was built first, followed by the southern, then the eastern and finally the western.

➡ Casa de las Tortugas

The House of the Turtles, which you'll find south of the Juego de Pelota (Ball Court), is named for the turtles carved on the cornice. The Maya associated turtles with the rain god, Chaac. According to Maya myth, when the people suffered from drought, so did the turtles, and both prayed to Chaac to send rain.

The frieze of short columns, or 'rolled mats,' that runs around the temple below the turtles is characteristic of the Puuc style.

➡ Palacio del Gobernador

The Governor's Palace, with its magnificent facade nearly 100m long, is arguably the most impressive structure at Uxmal. The buildings have walls filled with rubble, faced with cement and then covered in a thin veneer of limestone squares; the lower part of the facade is plain, the upper part festooned with stylized Chaac faces and geometric designs, often lattice-like or fretted.

Other elements of Puuc style are decorated cornices, rows of half-columns (as in the Casa de las Tortugas) and round columns in doorways (as in the palace at Sayil).

Researchers recently discovered some 150 species of medicinal plants growing on the east side of the palace. Due to the high concentration of plants growing there it's believed they were cultivated by the Maya to treat stomach infections, snake bites and many other ailments.

➡ Gran Pirámide

The 30m-high, nine-tiered pyramid has been restored only on its northern side. Archaeologists theorize that the quadrangle at its summit was largely destroyed in order to construct another pyramid above it. That work, for reasons unknown, was never completed. At the top are some stucco carvings of Chaac, birds and flowers.

➡ El Palomar

West of the Gran Pirámide sits a structure whose roofcomb is latticed with a pattern reminiscent of the Moorish pigeon houses built into walls in Spain and northern Africa – hence the building's name, which means the Dovecote or Pigeon House. Honeycombed triangular 'belfries' sit on top of a building that was once part of a quadrangle.

➡ Casa de la Vieja

Off the southeast corner of the Palacio del Gobernador's platform is a small complex, now largely rubble, known as the Casa de la Vieja (Old Woman's House). In front of it is a small *palapa* (thatch-roof shelter) that covers several large phalluses carved from stone.

🛏 Sleeping & Eating

There is no town at Uxmal, just a cluster of hotels. More services can be found in Santa Elena, 16km away, or in Ticul, 30km to the east. Next to Hotel Hacienda Uxmal you'll find an interesting **chocolate museum** (www.choco-storymexico.com; Hwy 261 Km 78, near Hotel Hacienda Uxmal; adult/child 6-12yr M$120/90; ⊙9am-7:30pm).

Casa del Mago   HOTEL **$$**

(✆997-976-20-13; www.casadelmago.com; Hwy 261 Km 78; r incl breakfast US$57; 🅿❄🖥) The only midrange option in Uxmal, Casa del Mago consists of four basic rooms with red-tile floors and ceiling fans. Guests have use of the adjoining, sister property's pool. These are the cheapest rooms in town so book ahead.

Lodge at Uxmal   LUXURY HOTEL **$$$**

(✆in USA 877-240-5864, toll-free 800-719-54-65; www.mayaland.com; Hwy 261 Km 78; r from M$1600; 🅿❄🖥🏊) Rooms could be nicer for the price, but you can't beat the easy access to the ruins and the pool certainly adds value. Some of the more expensive rooms have Jacuzzis. We don't suppose Stephens and Catherwood enjoyed such luxury when they passed through the area in the late 1830s.

Hotel Hacienda Uxmal   HISTORIC HOTEL **$$$**

(✆in USA 877-240-58-64, toll-free 800-719-54-65; www.mayaland.com; Hwy 261 Km 78; r from US$104; 🅿❄🖥🏊) This Mayaland Resort is 500m from the ruins. It housed the archaeologists who explored and restored Uxmal. Wide, tiled verandas, high ceilings, great bathrooms and a beautiful swimming pool make this a very comfortable place to stay. There are even rocking chairs to help you kick back after a hard day of exploring.

ℹ Getting There & Away

Uxmal is 80km from Mérida. Departures (M$56, 1½ hours, four daily) on the Sur bus line leave from Mérida's 2nd-class terminal. But going back to Mérida, passing buses may be full. If you get stuck, a taxi to nearby Santa Elena costs M$150 to M$200.

Tours offered by **Nómadas Hostel** (✆999-924-52-23; www.nomadastravel.com; Calle 62 No 433; tours to Celestún/Chichén Itzá/Uxmal & Kabah M$695/475/475) in Mérida are always a good option, or rent a car and visit other ruins in the area.

Santa Elena

✆997 / POP 3800

Originally called Nohcacab, the town known as Santa Elena today was virtually razed in 1847 in the War of the Castes. *'Ele-na'* means burnt houses in Maya. The Mexican government changed the name to Santa Elena in a bold PR stunt.

Santa Elena makes a great base to explore the nearby ruins of Uxmal, Kabah and those along the Ruta Puuc, so it's best to rent a car.

◉ Sights

Santa Elena Museum
MUSEUM

(M$10; ⊗9am-6:30pm) This small museum perched on a hill is dedicated to a gruesome find – 18th-century child mummies found buried beneath the adjoining cathedral. There are also some *henequén*-related exhibits.

🛏 Sleeping & Eating

★Pickled Onion
B&B $$

(☑cell 997-1117922; www.thepickledonionyucatan.com; Hwy 261, Santa Elena; r incl breakfast from US$40; P⊜⊚⊠) Offers the chance to stay in a modern adobe-walled hut with lovely tiled floors and bathrooms. The recently renovated rooms keep you cool with *palapa* roofs, and all come with coffee makers and mosquito netting. We love the pool and surrounding gardens, and the excellent restaurant does food to go if you want to picnic while visiting nearby ruins.

The Pickled Onion is on the south end of town, off Hwy 261.

Nueva Altia
B&B $$

(☑cell 998-2190176; Hwy 261 Km 159; d incl breakfast US$49; P⊜⊚) 𝒫 If you're looking for some peace and quiet, this is *the* place. Geometrically designed to get nice cross breezes, the spiral-shaped bungalows were inspired by ancient Maya architecture. If you've got time, the caretaker will gladly show you around parts of the 13-hectare property and tell you about the unearthed Maya ruins tucked away on the wooded grounds.

The ecohotel runs on solar energy. The turnoff is 1km south of Santa Elena, then head 800m east down a dirt road.

Restaurant El Chac-Mool
MEXICAN $$

(☑997-978-51-17; www.facebook.com/chacmool uxmal; Calle 18 No 211B, Santa Elena; mains M$70-110; ⊗9am-10pm; ⊜⊚) Off Hwy 261 at the southern entrance to Santa Elena, Restaurant El Chac-Mool is a friendly place serving Yucatecan food that includes a hearty vegetarian plate of rice, beans and fried bananas. It doubles as a hotel, too.

Kabah

Kabah (AD 750 to 950) was once the most important city in the region. Its ruins straddle Hwy 261, about 100km south of Mérida. It's easiest to reach the site by car, or from Mérida you can take a weekly Oriente bus (M$179, Sunday at 8am) that makes stops at Kabah, Uxmal and three Ruta Puuc ruins. The bus leaves from the Terminal de Segunda Clase (TAME) on Calle 69.

◉ Sights

Kabah
ARCHAEOLOGICAL SITE

(Hwy 261; M$47, guides M$450; ⊗8am-5pm) On entering, head right to climb the stairs of **El Palacio de los Mascarones** (Palace of the Masks). Standing in front of it is the Altar de los Glifos, whose immediate area is littered with many stones carved with glyphs. The palace's facade is an amazing sight, covered in nearly 300 masks of Chaac, the rain god or sky serpent. Most of their huge noses are broken off; the best intact beaks are at the building's south end.

These noses may have given the palace its modern Maya name, Codz Poop (Rolled Mat; it's pronounced more like 'Codes Pope' than some Elizabethan curse).

When you've had your fill of noses, head north and around to the back of the Poop to check out the two restored **atlantes** (an *atlas* – plural *'atlantes'* – is a male figure used as a supporting column). These are especially interesting, as they're some of the very few 3D human figures you'll see at the main Maya sites. One is headless and the other wears a jaguar mask atop his head.

Descend the steps near the *atlantes* and turn left, passing the small **Pirámide de los Mascarones**, to reach the plaza containing **El Palacio**. The palace's broad facade has several doorways, two of which have a column in the center. These columned doorways and the groups of decorative *columnillas* (little columns) on the upper part of the facade are characteristic of the Puuc architectural style.

Steps on the north side of El Palacio's plaza put you on a path leading about 200m through the jungle to the **Templo de las Columnas**, which has more rows of decorative columns on the upper part of its facade. At last visit, access to the temple was closed due to restoration.

West of El Palacio, across the highway, a path leads up the slope and passes to the south of a high mound of stones that was once the **Gran Pirámide** (Great Pyramid). The path curves to the right and comes to a large restored **monumental arch**. It's said that the *sacbé*, or cobbled and elevated ceremonial road, leading from here goes through the jungle all the way to Uxmal, terminating at a smaller arch; in the other

SACRED WATERS

Cenotes (limestone sinkholes) are a special feature of the Yucatán Peninsula. There are over 6000 of them in the region and debate continues as to why there are so many in the area. Many attribute it to the impact of the Chicxulub meteor some 65 million years ago and it's a compelling theory – looking at a map of known cenotes, there are none in the near vicinity of the impact site and a huge proliferation beginning at a radius of about 100km. What is generally agreed is that cenotes are formed when the limestone bedrock forming the roof of an underground cavern collapses, exposing the groundwater underneath.

Cenotes are, for the most part, connected to the network of underground rivers that runs beneath the entire peninsula, which is every cave diver's dream setup. An entire industry has grown around cenote diving and, alongside dinosaur and human remains, divers have discovered many valuable items from Maya times. It's believed that cenotes were used for human sacrifice (an offering to the gods) during the pre-Hispanic era.

That cenotes were sacred to the Maya is no surprise – rivers and lakes are rare in the Yucatán Peninsula and any freshwater source was bound to take on a heightened significance. Caves also had a special meaning, as they were seen as the gateway to Xibalbá, the underworld.

History and geology aside, cenotes also make for fantastic swimming holes. There's nothing like slipping into those cool, crystal-clear waters in the middle of the jungle on a steamy Yucatán day. Before plunging into a cenote make sure you're not using sunblock, lotions, perfumes, insect repellent or other products that pollute the water system.

direction it goes to Labná. Once, all of the Yucatán Peninsula was connected by these marvelous 'white roads' of rough limestone.

At present nothing of the *sacbé* is visible, and the rest of the area west of the highway is a maze of unmarked, overgrown paths leading off into the jungle.

Ruta Puuc

The Ruta Puuc (Puuc Route) meanders through rolling hills dotted with seldom-visited Maya ruins sitting in dense forests. From Hwy 261, a road branches off to the east (5km south of Kabah) and winds past the ruins of Sayil, Xlapak and Labná, eventually leading to the Grutas de Loltún (a large cave system). The sites offer some marvelous architectural detail and a deeper acquaintance with the Puuc Maya civilization.

◉ Sights

Sayil   ARCHAEOLOGICAL SITE
(Ruta Puuc; M\$47; ☺8am-5pm) Sayil is best known for El Palacio, the huge three-tiered building that has an 85m-long facade and is reminiscent of the Minoan palace on Crete. The distinctive columns of Puuc architecture are used here often, either as supports for the lintels, as decoration between doorways or as a frieze above them, alternating with stylized Chaac masks and 'descending gods.'

Taking the path south from the palace for about 400m and bearing left, you come to the temple named **El Mirador**, whose rooster-like roofcomb was once painted a bright red. About 100m beyond El Mirador, beneath a protective *palapa,* is a stela bearing the relief of a fertility god with an enormous phallus, now sadly weathered.

Grupo Sur is a bit further, and offers beautiful jungle-covered ruins with tree roots twisting through the walls.

The ruins of Sayil are 4.5km from the junction of the Ruta Puuc with Hwy 261.

Xlapak   ARCHAEOLOGICAL SITE
(Ruta Puuc; ☺8am-5pm) FREE The ornate *palacio* at Xlapak (shla-pak), also spelled Xlapac, is quite a bit smaller than those at nearby Kabah and Sayil, measuring only about 20m in length. It's decorated with the inevitable Chaac masks, columns and colonnettes and fretted geometric latticework of the Puuc style. The building is interesting and on a bit of a lean.

Plenty of motmots brighten up the surrounding forests. The name Xlapak means 'Old Walls' in Maya and was a general term among local people for ancient ruins.

Xlapak is about 10km east of the Ruta Puuc junction with Hwy 261.

Labná   ARCHAEOLOGICAL SITE
(Ruta Puuc; M\$47; ☺8am-5pm; P) This is *the* Ruta Puuc site not to miss. Archaeologists

believe that, at one point in the 9th century, some 3000 Maya lived at Labná. To support such numbers in these arid hills, water was collected in *chultunes* (cisterns); there were some 60 *chultunes* in and around the city; several are still visible. **El Palacio**, the first building you come to, is one of the longest in the Puuc region, and much of its decorative carving is in good shape.

On the west corner of the main structure's facade, straight in from the big tree near the center of the complex, is a serpent's head with a human face peering out from between its jaws, the symbol of the planet Venus. Toward the hill from this is an impressive Chaac mask, and nearby is the lower half of a human figure (possibly a ballplayer) in loincloth and leggings.

The lower level has several more well-preserved Chaac masks, and the upper level contains a large *chultun* that still holds water. The view of the site and the hills beyond from there is impressive.

Labná is best known for **El Arco**, a magnificent arch once part of a building that separated two quadrangular courtyards. It now appears to be a gate joining two small plazas. The corbeled structure, 3m wide and 6m high, is well preserved, and the reliefs decorating its upper facade are exuberantly Puuc in style.

Flanking the west side of the arch are carved *na* with multitiered roofs. Also on these walls, the remains of the building that adjoined the arch, are lattice patterns atop a serpentine design. Archaeologists believe a high roofcomb once sat over the fine arch and its flanking rooms.

Standing on the opposite side of the arch and separated from it by the *sacbé* is a pyramid known as **El Mirador**, topped by a temple. The pyramid itself is largely stone rubble. The temple, with its 5m-high roofcomb, is well positioned to be a lookout, thus its name.

Labná is 14km east of the Ruta Puuc junction with Hwy 261.

ⓘ Getting There & Away

To visit the Ruta Puuc sites, you can take a weekly Oriente bus (M$179, Sunday at 8am) that makes stops at all three ruins, plus Kabah and Uxmal. The bus leaves from the Terminal de Segunda Clase (TAME) in Mérida on Calle 69. Turitransmérida (p305) does Ruta Puuc tours on a more regular basis.

Grutas de Loltún

One of the largest dry-cave systems on the Yucatán Peninsula, the **Grutas de Loltún** (Loltún Caverns; adult/child under 13yr M$117/free, parking M$22; ⊙ tours 9:30am, 11am, 12:30pm, 2pm, 3pm & 4pm; 🚹) provided a treasure trove of data for archaeologists studying the Maya. The name means 'stone flower' in Maya; carbon dating of artifacts found here reveals that the caves were used by humans 2200 years ago. Chest-high murals of hands, faces, animals and geometric motifs were apparent as recently as 25 years ago, but so many people have touched them that scarcely a trace remains, though some handprints have been restored.

A few pots are displayed in a niche, and an impressive bas-relief, El Guerrero, guards the entrance. Other than that, you'll mostly see illuminated limestone formations.

To explore the labyrinth, you must take a scheduled guided tour, usually in Spanish but sometimes in English if the group warrants it. The services of the guides are included in the admission price, though they expect a tip afterward (M$50 per person is fair). Tours last about one hour and 20 minutes, with lots of lengthy stops. Some guides' presentations are long on legends (and jokes about disappearing mothers-in-law) and short on geological and historical information.

ⓘ Getting There & Away

About 15km north and east of Labná, a sign points left to the Grutas de Loltún, 5km further northeast.

Colectivos to Oxkutzcab (osh-kootz-kahb; M$55, 1½ hours, frequent) depart from Calle 67A in Mérida, aside Parque San Juan. Loltún is 7km southwest of Oxkutzcab, where you can catch *colectivos* (M$15) to the caves from Calle 51 (in front of the market).

Renting a car is the best option for reaching the Grutas.

Ruinas de Mayapán

Though far less impressive than many Maya sites, **Mayapán** (M$39; ⊙ 8am-5pm) is historically significant – it was one of the last major dynasties in the region and established itself as the center of Maya civilization from 1200 to 1440. The site's main attractions are clustered in a compact core, and visitors usually have the place to themselves. It is one of few sites where you can ascend to the top of the pyramid.

The city of Mayapán was large, with a population estimated to be around 12,000; it covered 4 sq km, all surrounded by a great defensive wall. More than 3500 buildings, 20 cenotes and traces of the city wall were mapped by archaeologists working in the 1950s and in 1962. The late Post-classic workmanship is inferior to that of the great age of Maya art.

Among the structures that have been restored is the **Castillo de Kukulcán**, a climbable pyramid with fresco fragments around its base and, at its rear side, friezes depicting decapitated warriors. The reddish color is still faintly visible. The **Templo Redondo** (Round Temple) is vaguely reminiscent of El Caracol at Chichén Itzá.

These ruins are some 50km southeast of Mérida. Don't confuse the ruins of Mayapán with the Maya village of the same name, which is about 40km southeast of the ruins, past the town of Teabo.

ℹ Getting There & Away

The Ruinas de Mayapán are just off Hwy 184, a few kilometers southwest of the town of Telchaquillo. Second-class buses to Telchaquillo (M$25, 1½ hours, hourly) run from the Noreste bus terminal in Mérida. They'll let you off near the entrance to the ruins and pick you up on your way back. You may want to consider renting a car to get here.

Celestún

📞 988 / POP 6800

Celestún is a sleepy sun-scorched fishing village that moves at a turtle's pace – and that's how locals like it. There's a pretty little square in the center of town and you'll encounter some nice beaches, but the real draw here is the Reserva de la Biosfera Ría Celestún, a wildlife sanctuary abounding in waterfowl, with flamingos as the star attraction.

⊙ Sights & Activities

Reserva de la Biosfera Ría
Celestún   WILDLIFE RESERVE
The 591-sq-km Reserva de la Biosfera Ría Celestún is home to a huge variety of animals and birdlife, including a large flamingo colony. You can see flamingos (via boat tours) year-round in Celestún, but they're usually out in full force from November to mid-March.

Morning is the best time of day, though from 5pm onward the birds tend to concentrate in one area after the day's feeding, which can make for good viewing.

🧭 Tours

Flamingo tours are Celestún's main draw. Trips from the beach last 2½ hours and begin with a ride along the coast for several kilometers, during which you can expect to see egrets, herons, cormorants, sandpipers and many other bird species. The boat then turns into the mouth of the *ría* (estuary).

Continuing up the *ría* takes you under the highway bridge where other boat tours begin and beyond which lie the flamingos. Depending on the tide, the hour, the season and climate conditions, you may see hundreds or thousands of the colorful birds. In addition to taking you to the flamingos, the captain will wend through a 200m mangrove tunnel and visit freshwater springs welling into the saltwater of the estuary, where you can take a refreshing dip.

Tours from the bridge run 1½ hours and tend to be better organized than those departing from the beach. Expect to pay around M$210 to M$230 per passenger. Prices can be slightly higher departing from the beach.

With either the bridge or beach option, your captain may or may not speak English.

★ Nature Tour   BOAT TOUR
(📱cell 999-2660422, cell 988-9676130; henry dzib@hotmail.com; per boat incl guide M$1910) 🚤 Brothers and naturalists Alex and Henry Dzib, Celestún's foremost experts on the area's wildlife, offer custom-made tours to watch flamingos, crocodiles, dolphins and a variety of birds. They also do fly-fishing trips.

Flamingo Tour   BIRD-WATCHING
(Hwy 281 s/n; per boat M$1260, per person M$230) Motorboats for bird-watching tours depart from the beach at Calle 11 (outside Restaurant Celestún) and from a dock at the town's entrance, just under the bridge. Tours from the bridge are more organized and you'll have a better chance of finding a knowledgeable English-speaking guide there. During the trip, you'll see flamingos, Bird Island, a mangrove tunnel and a spring.

🛌 Sleeping

The hotels are all on the beach road. More upscale accommodations are found heading north out of town.

Villas del Mar
HOTEL $

(📱 cell 999-9691111; www.villasdelmar.com.mx; Calle 12 s/n, btwn Calles 23 & 25; r without/with air-con M$500/600; 🅿🌀❄) If you're looking for comfort, this hotel with modern colonial-style rooms clearly has the upper hand on the other budget hotels in town. An added plus are the free kayaks, and for an additional cost the hotel offers coastal horseback-riding tours. The drawbacks: there's no wi-fi and the beach is generally cleaner on the north side of town.

Hotel Flamingo Plaza
HOTEL $$

(📱 988-916-21-33; drivan2011@hotmail.com; Calle 12 No 67C; r M$700; 🅿🌀❄🛜🏊) Family-run hotel on the beach with a pool overlooking the coast. Weathered sinks and showers could use some maintenance but the place is kept clean. It's 800m north of Calle 11.

★ Casa de Celeste Vida
GUESTHOUSE $$$

(📱 988-916-25-36; www.hotelcelestevida.com; Calle 12 No 49E; r/apt US$95/130; 🅿🌀🛜) This friendly Canadian-owned place offers comfortably decked-out rooms with kitchens and an apartment that sleeps four – all with water views and the beach at your doorstep. Kayak and bike use are free for guests. The hosts are happy to arrange flamingo tours, or if you prefer, a nighttime crocodile excursion. It's 1.5km north of Calle 11.

🍴 Eating

Beachfront restaurants usually close at around 7pm.

El Palmar
TAQUERÍA $

(Calle 13 s/n; tacos M$10-15; ⏰7pm-3am; 🌀) The only eating option in town that keeps late hours. The spit-roasted tacos al pastor (marinated pork) and arrachera (flank steak) tacos provide a welcome break from the fish and seafood routine.

Restaurant Los Pampanos
SEAFOOD $$

(Calle 12 s/n; mains M$90-140, lobster M$250; ⏰11am-7pm; 🌀) A tranquil joint on the beach, north of Calle 11, this is a great spot for afternoon margaritas on the sand. Try the fresh lobster or a fish fillet stuffed to the brim with shellfish.

Dolphin
BREAKFAST $$

(Calle 12 No 104, cnr Calle 13; mains M$50-98; ⏰8:30am-1pm Wed-Mon, 6-10pm Fri & Sat; 🌀🛜) An excellent breakfast spot at Hotel Gutiérrez; full breakfasts include coffee, juice, fresh-made bread, marmalade and some mighty fine egg dishes. Dolphin opens on Friday and Saturday night for dinner with menu items such as curry dishes, salads and tortas.

ⓘ Information

Don't plan on using high-speed internet here. There's an ATM in the Super Willy's supermarket on the plaza, but bring some cash anyway – it's been known to dry up.

ⓘ Getting There & Away

Frequent buses head for Celestún (M$56, 2½ hours) from Mérida's Noreste bus terminal. The route terminates at Celestún's plaza, a block inland from Calle 12.

There are also colectivos on the plaza that will take you to downtown Mérida for M$40.

By car from Mérida, the best route to Celestún is via the new road out of Umán.

Dzibilchaltún

Dzibilchaltún
ARCHAEOLOGICAL SITE

(Place of Inscribed Flat Stones; adult/child under 12yr M$132/free, parking M$20; ⏰site 8am-5pm, museum 9am-4pm Tue-Sun; 🅿) Lying about 17km due north of central Mérida, Dzibilchaltún was the longest continuously utilized Maya administrative and ceremonial city, serving the Maya from around 1500 BC until the European conquest in the 1540s. At the height of its greatness, Dzibilchaltún covered 15 sq km. Some 8400 structures were mapped by archaeologists in the 1960s; few of these have been excavated. Aside from the ruins, the site offers a lovely, swimmable cenote and a Maya museum.

In some ways it's unimpressive if you've already seen larger places, such as Chichén Itzá or Uxmal, but twice a year humble Dzibilchaltún shines. At sunrise on the equinoxes (approximately March 20 and September 22), the sun aligns directly with the main door of the Templo de las Siete Muñecas (Temple of the Seven Dolls), which got its name from seven grotesque dolls discovered here during excavations. As the sun rises, the temple doors glow, then 'light up' as the sun passes behind. It also casts a cool square beam on the crumbled wall behind. Many who have seen both feel the sunrise here is more spectacular than Chichén Itzá's famous snake, and is well worth getting up at the crack of dawn to witness.

Enter the site along a nature trail that terminates at the modern, air-conditioned **Museo del Pueblo Maya**, featuring artifacts from throughout the Maya regions of Mexico, including some superb colonial-era religious carvings and other pieces. Exhibits explaining both ancient and modern Maya daily life are labeled in Spanish and English. Beyond the museum, a path leads to the central plaza, where you'll find an open chapel that dates from early Spanish times (1590–1600).

The **Cenote Xlacah** is more than 40m deep and a fine spot for a swim after exploring the ruins. In 1958 a National Geographic Society diving expedition recovered more than 30,000 Maya artifacts, many of ritual significance, from the cenote. The most interesting of these are now on display in the site's museum. South of the cenote is **Estructura 44** – at 130m it's one of the longest Maya structures in existence.

Chablekal-bound *colectivos* depart frequently from Calle 58 (between Calles 57 and 59) in Mérida. They'll drop you about 750m from the site's entrance.

Progreso

📱969 / POP 54,000

If Mérida's heat has you dying for a quick beach fix, or if you want to see the longest pier (6.5km) in Mexico, head to Progreso (also known as Puerto Progreso). The beach is long and, as with other Gulf beaches, the water is murky; visibility even on calm days rarely exceeds 5m. Winds can hit here full force in the afternoon and can blow well into the night, especially from December to March when *los nortes* (northern winds) kick up. *Méridanos* come in droves on weekends, especially during the Mexican holiday period of July and August. During that time it can be difficult to find a room with a view and, sadly, you'll see more litter on the beach. Once or twice a week the streets flood with cruise-ship tourists, but the place can feel empty on off nights, which makes a refreshing change.

🏊 Activities

El Corchito SWIMMING
(Hwy 27 s/n, cnr Calle 46; M$25; ☺9am-5pm) Take a refreshing dip in one of three freshwater swimming holes surrounded by mangroves at nature reserve El Corchito. Motorboats take visitors across a canal to the reserve. El Corchito is home to iguanas, boa constrictors, small crocs, raccoons and a band of coatis. The coons and coatis are skilled food thieves, something to consider if you bring lunch.

🛏 Sleeping & Eating

Hostal Zócalo Beach HOSTEL **$**
(📱969-103-02-94; www.facebook.com/hostalzo calobeach; Calle 21 s/n, cnr Calle 54; dm M$150, r M$400-450, all incl breakfast; ☺) This 1920s art deco mansion houses the most colorful lodging in town. Previously it served as a boarding house and long before the building existed, the property was a pirates' base camp. The eccentric owner insists that a pirate ghost roams the hallways and it has signaled to him that a booty is buried under the house.

Playa Linda Hotel HOTEL **$$**
(📱969-103-92-14; www.playalindayucatan.com; Calle 76 s/n, btwn Calles 19 & 21; r/ste from M$600/900; ☺❄🤙) Rooms go fast at this hotel on the boardwalk, so book ahead. Comfy standard rooms are decked out with contemporary dark-wood furnishings, while suites come with kitchenettes and beachfront balconies. Walls can be a bit thin in some rooms; avoid those near the staircase and upgrade to a 'studio.' The rooftop view of the pier and coastline is spectacular.

Flamingo's SEAFOOD **$$**
(Calle 19 s/n, cnr Calle 72; mains M$95-200; ☺7:30am-midnight; ☺🤙) A longtime local favorite on the boardwalk, Flamingo's fries up a tasty *pescado boquinete al mojo de ajo* (a whole hogfish cooked with garlic). Free

---

THE OTHER BIG BANG

In the small town of Chicxulub, just outside Progreso, is a small plaque dedicated to arguably the biggest event in planet Earth's history. Here, about 65 million years ago, a meteor smashed into the peninsula, which according to scientists led to a catastrophic change in the climate and the extinction of the dinosaurs.

There's not much to see here apart from the plaque, but if you're into visiting sites of historical importance, you could hardly find a bigger one than this.

YUCATÁN PENINSULA PROGRESO

DIY: EXPLORE THE BACK ROADS SOUTH OF MÉRIDA

There are numerous attractions worth seeing as you travel south from Mérida. Here are a few of our favorites.

Hacienda Yaxcopoil (☎cell 999-9001193; www.yaxcopoil.com; Hwy 261 Km 186; museum admission M$75; ⊘8am-6pm Mon-Sat, 9am-5pm Sun; P) A vast estate that grew and processed *henequén* (agave plant fibers); many of its numerous French Renaissance–style buildings have undergone picturesque restorations.

Hacienda Ochil (☎999-924-74-65; www.haciendaochil.com; Hwy 261 Mérida–Muna Km 175; M$30; ⊘10am-6pm; P ⊞) Provides a fascinating, though basic, look at how *henequén* was grown and processed.

Grutas de Calcehtok (Grutas de X'Pukil; ☎cell 999-2627292; off Hwy 184; 1hr tour M$100; ⊘8am-8pm; P ⊞) These caves are said by some to comprise the longest dry-cave system on the Yucatán Peninsula.

Oxkintok (www.inah.gob.mx; M$47, guides M$550; ⊘8am-5pm; P) Inscriptions found at this site contain some of the oldest known dates in the Yucatán, and indicate that the city was inhabited from the pre-Classic to the post-Classic period (300 BC to AD 1500).

Cenotes de Cuzamá (☎cell 999-9261577; admission 1-4 people M$300; ⊘8am-4pm) Three kilometers east of the town of Cuzamá, accessed from the small village of Chunkanan, are three amazing limestone sinkholes, visited by horse-drawn rail cart, in the grounds of an old *henequén* hacienda.

snacks are served while you're waiting for the main dish.

Elio al Mare　　　　　　　　ITALIAN $$$
(Calle 21 No 60, btwn Calles 38 & 40; mains M$150-300; ⊘1-10pm; ☺) Far removed from the cruise-ship crowd, this Italian-owned beachfront *ristorante* prepares fresh fish, seafood and pasta dishes and possibly the best bread in town. Cap off the meal with a glass of wine on the deck, which catches ocean breezes.

❶ Getting There & Away

Progreso is 33km north of Mérida, along a highway that's basically a continuation of Paseo de Montejo.

The bus station on Calle 29 has frequent Mérida-bound buses and there are also *colectivos* (M$16) to Mérida departing from the corner of Calles 80 and 29.

To get to Progreso from Mérida, go to the Progreso Bus Terminal (p310) or catch a *colectivo* one block east of the terminal on Calle 60.

Izamal

☎988 / POP 26,000
Just under 70km east of Mérida, Izamal is a quiet, colonial gem of a town, nicknamed La Ciudad Amarilla (the Yellow City) for the golden paint that brightens the walls of the downtown buildings. It is easily explored on foot and makes a great day trip from Mérida.

In ancient times, Izamal was a center for the worship of the supreme Maya god, Itzamná, and the local sun god, Kinich-Kakmó. A dozen temple pyramids were devoted to these or other gods. It was probably these bold expressions of Maya religiosity that provoked the Spaniards to build the enormous Franciscan monastery that stands today at the heart of this town.

◉ Sights

Convento de
San Antonio de Padua　　　MONASTERY
(Calle 31 s/n; admission free, sound & light show adult/child under 13yr M$94/free, museum M$5; ⊘6am-8pm, sound & light show 8:30pm Mon-Sat, museum 9am-5pm Mon-Fri) When the Spaniards conquered Izamal, they destroyed the major Maya temple, the Ppapp-Hol-Chac pyramid, and in 1533 began to build from its stones one of the first monasteries in the western hemisphere. Work on the Convento de San Antonio de Padua was finished in 1561. Under the monastery's arcades, look for building stones with an unmistakable maze-like design; these were clearly taken from the earlier Maya temple. There's a **sound-and-light show** here six nights a week.

The monastery's principal church is the **Santuario de la Virgen de Izamal**, which is approached by a ramp from the main square. The ramp leads into the **Atrium**, a huge arcaded courtyard in which the **fiesta of the Virgin of Izamal** takes place each August 15.

At some point the 16th-century **frescoes** beside the entrance of the sanctuary were completely painted over. For years they lay concealed under a thin layer of whitewash until a maintenance worker who was cleaning the walls discovered them.

The church's original altarpiece was destroyed by a fire believed to have been started by a fallen candle. Its replacement, impressively gilded, was built in the 1940s. In the niches at the stations of the cross are some superb small figures.

In the small courtyard to the left of the church, look up and toward the Atrium to see the original sundial projecting from the roof's edge. A small **museum** at the back commemorates Pope John Paul II's 1993 visit to the monastery. He brought with him a silver crown for the statue of the patron saint of Yucatán, the Virgin of Izamal.

The monastery's front entrance faces west; it's flanked by Calles 31 and 33 on the north and south, respectively, and Calles 28 and 30 on the east and west.

Kinich-Kakmó ARCHAEOLOGICAL SITE
(Calle 27 s/n, btwn Calles 26B & 28; ⊙8am-5pm) **FREE** Three of the town's original 12 Maya pyramids have been partially restored. The largest (and the third largest in Yucatán) is the 34m-high Kinich-Kakmó, three blocks north of the monastery. Legend has it that a deity in the form of a blazing macaw would swoop down from the heavens to collect offerings left here.

🛏 Sleeping & Eating

Several *loncherías* (snack bars) occupy spaces in the market on the convent's southwest side.

Hotel Casa Colonial HOTEL $
(☑988-954-02-72; hotelcasacolonial@hotmail.com; Calle 31 No 331, cnr Calle 36; ⊕❋🛜) A clean and spacious option compared to some of the other more run-down and cramped budget hotels in town. Some rooms come with dining tables, microwaves and mini-fridges.

★**Hacienda Hotel Santo Domingo** HOTEL $$
(☑cell 988-9676136; www.izamalhotel.com; Calle 18, btwn Calles 33 & 35; r M$900-1290, ste M$1390-1890, campsites M$150-250; ⓟ⊕🛜🏊) Set on a 13-hectare property with lush gardens, walking trails, a pool and *palapa* restaurant, this serene spot will most definitely win over nature lovers. It's also that rare place with accommodations for all budgets, from affordable camping and midrange options to very attractive suites, some with natural stone sinks and showers. It's five blocks from the monastery.

★**Kinich** MEXICAN $$
(Calle 27 No 299, btwn Calles 28 & 30; mains M$65-190; ⊙10am-10pm; ⊕🛜) Sure, it's touristy, but this is fresh, handmade Yucatecan cuisine at its finest. The *papadzules kinich* – rolled tortillas stuffed with diced egg and topped with pumpkin-seed sauce and smoky sausage – is a delightful house specialty. Kinich is also famous for its *dzic de venado*, a shredded venison dish.

❶ Getting There & Away

Buses run out of Izamal's **Oriente Bus Terminal** (☑988-954-01-07; Calle 32 s/n, cnr Calle 31A) and the nearby **Terminal del Centro** (www.autobusescentro.com; Calle 33, cnr Calle 30).

BUSES FROM IZAMAL

DESTINATION	FARE (M$)	DURATION (HR)	FREQUENCY (DAILY)
Cancún	160	5	5
Chichén Itzá	67	1½-2	3; Terminal del Centro; transfer in Hoctún
Dzilam de Bravo	39	1½	2; Terminal del Centro
Mérida	27	1½	frequent
Tizimín	85	2½	3
Valladolid	59	2	3

YUCATÁN PENINSULA IZAMAL

Chichén Itzá

♪ 985 / POP 5500

History

Most archaeologists agree that the first major settlement at Chichén Itzá, during the late Classic period, was pure Maya. In about the 9th century, the city was largely abandoned, for reasons unknown. It was resettled around the late 10th century, and some Mayanists believe that shortly thereafter it was invaded by the Toltecs.

Toltec culture was fused with that of the Maya, incorporating the Toltec cult of Quetzalcóatl (Kukulcán, in Maya). Throughout the city, you will see images of both Chaac, the Maya rain god, and Quetzalcóatl, the plumed serpent.

The substantial fusion of highland central Mexican and Puuc architectural styles makes Chichén unique among the Yucatán Peninsula's ruins. The fabulous El Castillo and the Plataforma de Venus are outstanding architectural works, built during the height of Toltec cultural input.

The warlike Toltecs contributed more than their architectural skills to the Maya. They elevated human sacrifice to a near obsession, and there are numerous carvings of the bloody ritual in Chichén demonstrating this. After a Maya leader moved his political capital to Mayapán, while keeping Chichén as his religious capital, Chichén Itzá fell into decline. The city was finally abandoned – this time for good – in the 14th century, but the once-great city remained the site of Maya pilgrimages for many years.

◉ Sights

Ik Kil Parque Eco-Arqueológico   CENOTE
(♪985-851-00-02; cenote_ikkil@hotmail.com; Hwy 180 Km 122; adult/child under 12yr M$70/35; ⊗8am-5pm; P⛲) About 2.5km east of the western entrance of the Chichén Itzá ruins, a cenote has been developed into a divine swimming spot. Small cascades of water plunge from the high limestone roof, which is ringed by greenery. Arrive no later than 11am to beat the tour groups.

Grutas de Balankanché   CAVE
(Hwy 180 Km 126; adult/child under 13yr M$117/free; ⊗9am-4pm; P) In 1959 a guide to the Chichén Itzá ruins was exploring a cave on his day off when he came upon a narrow passageway. He followed the passageway

for 300m, meandering through a series of caverns. In each, perched on mounds amid scores of glistening stalactites, were hundreds of ceremonial treasures the Maya had placed there 800 years earlier. Among the discovered objects were *ritual metates* and *manos* (grinding stones), incense burners and pots.

In the years following the discovery, the ancient ceremonial objects were removed and studied. Eventually most of them were returned to the caves, and placed exactly where they had been found.

Outside the caves, you'll find a good botanical garden (displaying native flora with information on the medicinal and other uses of the trees and plants) and a tiny museum. The museum features large photographs taken during the exploration of the caves, and descriptions (in English, Spanish and French) of the Maya religion and the offerings found in the caves. Also on display is text about modern-day Maya ceremonies called Ch'a Chaac, which continue to be held in all the villages on the Yucatán Peninsula during times of drought and consist mostly of praying and making numerous offerings of food to rain god Chaac.

Compulsory 45-minute tours (minimum six people, maximum 30) have melodramatic, not-very-informative recorded narration that is nearly impossible to make out, but if you'd like it in a particular language, English is at 11am, 1pm and 3pm; Spanish is at 9am, noon, 2pm and 4pm; and French is at 10am.

Be warned that the cave is unusually hot, and ventilation is poor in its further reaches. The lack of oxygen (especially after a few groups have already passed through) makes it difficult to draw a full breath until you're outside again.

The turnoff for the caverns is 6km east of Chichén Itzá on the highway to Valladolid. Second-class buses heading east from Pisté toward Valladolid will drop you at the Balankanché road. The entrance to the caves is 350m north of the highway.

Chichén Itzá   ARCHAEOLOGICAL SITE
(Mouth of the Well of the Itzáes; www.chichenitza.inah.gob.mx; off Hwy 180, Pisté; adult/child under 13yr M$220/free; guided tours M$750; ⊗8am-5pm Tue-Sun; P) The most famous and best restored of the Yucatán Maya sites, Chichén Itzá, while tremendously overcrowded – every gawker and his or her grandmother is trying to check off the new seven wonders of the world – will still impress even the most

jaded visitor. Many mysteries of the Maya astronomical calendar are made clear when one understands the design of the 'time temples' here. Other than a few minor passageways, climbing on the structures is not allowed.

At the vernal and autumnal equinoxes (around March 20 and September 22), the morning and afternoon sun produces a light-and-shadow illusion of the serpent ascending or descending the side of El Castillo's staircase. The site is mobbed on these dates, however, making it difficult to see, and after the spectacle, parts of the site are sometimes closed to the public. The illusion is almost as good in the week preceding and following each equinox (and draws much smaller crowds), and is re-created nightly in the light-and-sound show year-round. Some find the spectacle fascinating, others think it's overrated. Either way, if you're in the area around the equinox and you've got your own car, it's easy to wake up early for Dzibilchaltún's (see p318) fiery sunrise and then make it to Chichén Itzá by midafternoon, catching both spectacles on the same day.

The heat, humidity and crowds in Chichén Itzá can be fierce; try to explore the site either early in the morning or late in the afternoon.

The 45-minute light-and-sound show begins each evening at 8pm in summer and 7pm in winter. At last visit, tickets were free, but the show was only open to guests of participating hotels registered at www.nochesdekukulkan.com. By the time you're reading this the show may be open to the general public at an additional cost.

◉ Exploring the Ruins

El Castillo
ARCHAEOLOGICAL SITE

Entering Chichén Itzá, El Castillo (aka the Pyramid of Kukulcán) rises before you in all its grandeur. The first temple here was pre-Toltec, built around AD 800, but the present 25m-high structure, built over the old one, has the plumed serpent sculpted along the stairways and Toltec warriors represented in the doorway carvings at the top of the temple. You won't see the carvings, however, as ascending the pyramid was prohibited after a woman fell to her death in 2006.

The structure is actually a massive Maya calendar formed in stone. Each of El Castillo's nine levels is divided in two by a staircase, making 18 separate terraces that commemorate the 18 20-day months of the

Maya Vague Year. The four stairways have 91 steps each; add the top platform and the total is 365, the number of days in the year. On each facade of the pyramid are 52 flat panels, which are reminders of the 52 years in the Maya calendar round.

To top it off, during the spring and autumn equinoxes, light and shadow form a series of triangles on the side of the north staircase that mimic the creep of a serpent (note the carved serpent's heads flanking the bottom of the staircase).

The older pyramid inside El Castillo has a red jaguar throne with inlaid eyes and spots of jade; also lying behind the screen is a chac-mool (Maya sacrificial stone sculpture). The entrance to **El Túnel**, the passage up to the throne, is at the base of El Castillo's north side. You can't go in, though.

Researchers in 2015 learned that the pyramid most likely sits atop a 20m-deep cenote, which puts the structure at greater risk of collapsing.

Gran Juego de Pelota
ARCHAEOLOGICAL SITE

The great ball court, the largest and most impressive in Mexico, is only one of the city's eight courts, indicative of the importance the games held here. The court, to the left of the visitors center, is flanked by temples at either end and is bounded by towering parallel walls with stone rings cemented up high. Along the walls of the ball court are stone reliefs, including scenes of decapitations of players.

There is evidence that the ball game may have changed over the years. Some carvings show players with padding on their elbows and knees, and it is thought that they played a soccer-like game with a hard rubber ball, with the use of hands forbidden. Other carvings show players wielding bats; it appears that if a player hit the ball through one of the stone hoops, his team was declared the winner. It may be that during the Toltec period, the losing captain, and perhaps his teammates as well, were sacrificed (and you thought your dad was hard on you in Little League).

The court exhibits some interesting acoustics: a conversation at one end can be heard 135m away at the other, and a clap produces multiple loud echoes.

Templo del Barbado
ARCHAEOLOGICAL SITE

The structure at the ball court's north end, called the Temple of the Bearded Man after a carving inside it, has finely sculpted pillars and reliefs of flowers, birds and trees.

Chichén Itzá

It doesn't take long to realize why the Maya site of Chichén Itzá is one of Mexico's most popular tourist draws. Approaching the grounds from the main entrance, the striking castle pyramid **El Castillo** ❶ jumps right out at you – and the wow factor never lets up.

It's easy to tackle Chichén Itzá in one day. Within a stone's throw of the castle, you'll find the Maya world's largest **ball court** ❷ alongside eerie carvings of skulls and heart-devouring eagles at the Temple of Jaguars and the Platform of Skulls. On the other (eastern) side are the highly adorned **Group of a Thousand Columns** ❸ and the **Temple of Warriors** ❹. A short walk north of the castle leads to the gaping **Sacred Cenote** ❺, an important pilgrimage site. On the other side of El Castillo, you'll find giant stone serpents watching over the High Priest's Grave, aka El Osario. Further south, marvel at the spiral-domed **Observatory** ❻, the imposing Nunnery and Akab-Dzib, one of the oldest ruins.

Roaming the 47-hectare site, it's fun to consider that at its height Chichén Itzá was home to an estimated 90,000 inhabitants and spanned approximately 30 sq km. So essentially you're looking at just a small part of a once-great city.

El Caracol
Observatory
Today they'd probably just use a website, but back in the day priests would stand from the dome of the circular observatory to announce the latest rituals and celebrations.

Edificio de
las Monjas
(Nunnery)

❻

Akab-Dzib

Entrance

Grupo de las Mil Columnas
Group of a Thousand Columns
Not unlike a hall of fame exhibit, the pillars surrounding the temple reveal carvings of gods, dignitaries and celebrated warriors.

THE LOWDOWN

» **Arrive** at 8am and you'll have a good three hours or so before the tour-bus madness begins. Early birds escape the merchants, too.

» **Remember** that Chichén Itzá is the name of the site; the actual town where it's located is called Pisté.

El Castillo
The Castle
Even this mighty pyramid can't bear the stress of a million visitors ascending its stairs each year. No climbing allowed, but the ground-level view doesn't disappoint.

Gran Juego de Pelota
Great Ball Court
How is it possible to hear someone talk from one end of this long, open-air court to the other? To this day, the acoustics remain a mystery.

Entrance

Parking Lot

Visitors Center

Templo de los Jaguares (Temple of Jaguars)

Tumba del Gran Sacerdote (High Priest's Grave)

Plataforma de los Cráneos (Platform of Skulls)

Cenote Sagrado
Sacred Cenote
Diving expeditions have turned up hundreds of valuable artifacts dredged from the cenote (limestone sinkhole), not to mention human bones of sacrificial victims who were forced to jump into the eternal underworld.

Templo de los Guerreros
Temple of Warriors
The Maya associated warriors with eagles and jaguars, as depicted in the temple's friezes. The revered jaguar, in particular, was a symbol of strength and agility.

Chichén Itzá

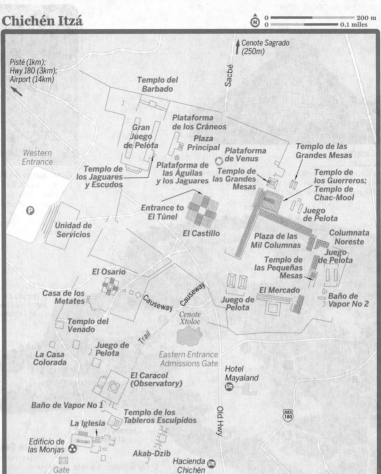

Plataforma
de los Cráneos
ARCHAEOLOGICAL SITE

The Platform of Skulls (Tzompantli in Náhuatl, a Maya dialect) is between the Templo de los Jaguares y Escudos and El Castillo. You can't mistake it, because the T-shaped platform is festooned with carved skulls and eagles tearing open the chests of men to eat their hearts. In ancient days this platform was used to display the heads of sacrificial victims.

Plataforma de las Águilas
y los Jaguares
ARCHAEOLOGICAL SITE

Adjacent to the Platform of Skulls, the carvings on the Platform of the Eagles and Jaguars depict those animals gruesomely grabbing human hearts in their claws. It is thought that this platform was part of a temple dedicated to the military legions responsible for capturing sacrificial victims.

Cenote Sagrado
ARCHAEOLOGICAL SITE

From the Platform of Skulls, a 400m rough stone *sacbé* runs north (a five-minute walk) to the huge sunken well that gave this city its name. The Sacred Cenote is an awesome natural well, some 60m in diameter and 35m deep. The walls between the summit and the water's surface are ensnared in tangled vines and other vegetation.

Grupo de las Mil Columnas   RUIN

Comprising the Templo de los Guerreros (Temple of the Warriors), the Templo de Chac-Mool (Temple of Chac-Mool) and the Baño de Vapor (Sweat House or Steam Bath), this group, behind El Castillo, takes its name (Group of the Thousand Columns) from the forest of pillars stretching south and east.

El Osario   ARCHAEOLOGICAL SITE

The Ossuary, otherwise known as the Bonehouse or the **Tumba del Gran Sacerdote** (High Priest's Grave), is a ruined pyramid to the southwest of El Castillo. As with most of the buildings in this southern section, the architecture is more Puuc than Toltec. It's notable for the beautiful serpent heads at the base of its staircases.

A square shaft at the top of the structure leads into a cave below that was used as a burial chamber; seven tombs with human remains were discovered inside.

El Caracol   ARCHAEOLOGICAL SITE

Called El Caracol (The Snail) by the Spaniards for its interior spiral staircase, this **observatory**, to the south of the Ossuary, is one of the most fascinating and important of all Chichén Itzá's buildings (but, alas, you can't enter it). Its circular design resembles some central highlands structures, although, surprisingly, not those of Toltec Tula.

In a fusion of architectural styles and religious imagery, there are Maya Chaac rain-god masks over four external doors facing the cardinal points. The windows in the observatory's dome are aligned with the appearance of certain stars at specific dates. From the dome the priests decreed the times for rituals, celebrations, corn-planting and harvests.

Edificio de las Monjas   ARCHAEOLOGICAL SITE

Thought by archaeologists to have been a palace for Maya royalty, the so-called Edificio de las Monjas (Nunnery), with its myriad rooms, resembled a European convent to the conquistadors, hence their name for the building. The building's dimensions are imposing: its base is 60m long, 30m wide and 20m high.

The construction is Maya rather than Toltec, although a Toltec sacrificial stone stands in front. A smaller adjoining building to the east, known as **La Iglesia** (The Church), is covered almost entirely with carvings. On the far side at the back there are some passageways that are still open,

leading a short way into the labyrinth inside. They are dank and slippery, they smell of bat urine, and it's easy to twist an ankle as you go, but Indiana Jones wannabes will think it's totally cool.

Akab-Dzib   ARCHAEOLOGICAL SITE

East of the Nunnery, the Puuc-style Akab-Dzib is thought by some archaeologists to be the most ancient structure excavated here. The central chambers date from the 2nd century. The name means 'Obscure Writing' in Maya and refers to the south-side annex door, whose lintel depicts a priest with a vase etched with hieroglyphics that cannot be translated.

🛏 Sleeping

Most of Chichén's lodgings, restaurants and services are ranged along 1km of highway in the village of Pisté, to the western side of the ruins. It's 1.5km from the ruins' main entrance to the first hotel in Pisté. Hwy 180 is known as Calle 15A as it passes through Pisté.

Pirámide Inn   HOTEL $

(☑ 985-851-01-15; www.piramideinn.com; Calle 15 No 30; campsites per person M$50, r M$500; P ⊕ ❄ 🛜 ☀) Campers can pitch a tent or hang a hammock under a *palapa,* enjoy the inn's pool, have use of tepid showers and watch satellite TV in the lobby. Campers also have use of clean shared toilet facilities and a safe place to stow gear. The spacious rooms have decent bathrooms and two spring-me-to-the-moon double beds.

Hotel Chichén Itzá   HOTEL $$

(☑ 985-851-00-22, in USA 800-235-4079; www.mayaland.com; Calle 15 No 45; r/ste M$980/1360; P ⊕ ❄ 🛜 ☀) On the west side of Pisté, this hotel has 42 pleasant rooms with tiled floors and old-style brick-tiled ceilings. Rooms in the upper range face the pool and the landscaped grounds, and all have firm beds and minibars. Parents may bring two kids under 13 for free.

Hotel Dolores Alba   HOTEL $$

(☑ 985-858-15-55; www.doloresalba.com; Hwy 180 Km 122; r incl breakfast M$1000; P ⊕ ❄ 🛜 ☀) A good midrange option with substantial online discounts and kids will dig the hotel's two pools (one has a rock bottom). Semi-rustic rooms here won't wow you, but they're comfy enough. Dolores Alba offers transportation to Chichén Itzá, but you're on your own getting back. It's 2.5km east of Chichén Itzá's eastern entrance and 5km from town.

Hacienda Chichén
RESORT $$$

(☑ 999-920-84-07, in USA 877-631-00-45; www.haciendachichen.com; Zona Hotelera Km 120; d from M$2460; P❂✳📶☎) About 300m from the Chichén Itzá entrance, this resort sits on the well-manicured grounds of a 16th-century hacienda with an elegant main house and towering ceiba trees. The archaeologists who excavated Chichén during the 1920s lived here in bungalows, which have been refurbished and augmented with new ones. Monthly activities on offer include Maya cooking classes and bird-watching.

✕ Eating

The highway through Pisté is lined with more than 20 eateries, large and small.

Cocina Económica Fabiola
MEXICAN $

(Calle 15 s/n; mains M$30-60; ⊘7am-10pm; ☻) For a good, honest, cheap meal hit this humble little place at the end of the strip of eateries opposite the church. The *sopa de lima* (lime soup) and *pollo yucateco* (Yucatecan chicken) come highly recommended.

Las Mestizas
MEXICAN $$

(Calle 15 s/n; mains M$70-100; ⊘8am-10pm; ☻📶) *The* place to go in town if you're craving decent Yucatecan fare. There's indoor and outdoor seating – depending on the time of day, an outdoor table may mean you'll be getting tour-bus fumes to go with that *cochinita*.

❶ Getting There & Away

Oriente has ticket offices near the east and west sides of Pisté, and 2nd-class buses passing through town stop almost anywhere along the way. Many 1st-class buses only hit the ruins and the west side of town, close to the toll highway.

Shared vans to Valladolid (M$30, 40 minutes) pass through town regularly.

❶ Getting Around

Buses to Pisté generally stop at the plaza; you can make the hot walk to and from the ruins in 20 to 30 minutes. There is a taxi stand near the west end of town; the prices are M$35 to the ruins, M$70 to Cenote Ik Kil and M$140 to Grutas de Balankanché.

During Chichén Itzá's opening hours, 1st- and 2nd-class buses serve the ruins (check with the driver), and they will take passengers from town when there's room. The 2nd-class buses will also leave you near Cenote Ik Kil and the Grutas de Balankanché. If you plan to see the ruins and then head directly to another city by 1st-class bus, buy your bus ticket at the visitors center before hitting the ruins, for a better chance of getting a seat.

Valladolid
☑ 985 / POP 74,000

Yucatán's third-largest city is known for its quiet streets and sun-splashed pastel walls. It's worth staying here for a few days or even a week, as the provincial town makes a great hub for visits to Río Lagartos, Chichén Itzá, Ek' Balam and a number of beautiful nearby cenotes. The city resides at that magic point where there's plenty to do, yet it still feels small, manageable and affordable.

History

Valladolid has seen its fair share of turmoil and revolt over the years. The first Spanish settlement was founded in 1543 near the Chouac-Ha lagoon, some 50km from the coast, but it was too hot and there were way too many mosquitoes for Francisco de Montejo, nephew of Montejo the Elder, and his merry band of conquerors. So they upped and moved their city to the Maya ceremonial center of Zací (sah-*see*), where they faced heavy resistance from the local Maya. Eventually the Elder's son, Montejo the Younger,

BUSES FROM CHICHÉN ITZÁ

DESTINATION	FARE (M$)	DURATION (HR)	FREQUENCY (DAILY)
Cancún	137-258	3-4½	9
Cobá	69	2	1; 7:30am
Mérida	78-144	1¾-2½	frequent
Playa del Carmen	135-282	3½-4	2; 7:30am, 4:30pm
Tulum	100-190	2½-3	3
Valladolid	30	1	8

Valladolid

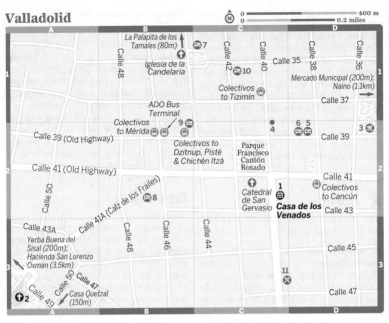

Valladolid

◉ Top Sights
1 Casa de los Venados C2

◉ Sights
Convento de Sisal .... (see 2)
2 Templo de San Bernardino A3

◆ Activities, Courses & Tours
3 Cenote Zací D2
4 Rudy Tours C2

◉ Sleeping
5 Casa Marlene D2
6 Casa Tía Micha D2
7 Hostel La Candelaria C1
8 Hotel Tunich-Beh B2
9 Hotel Zací B2
10 La Aurora C1

⊗ Eating
11 Conato 1910 .... C3

took the town. The Spanish conquerors, in typical fashion, ripped down the town and laid out a new city following the classic colonial plan.

During much of the colonial era, Valladolid's physical isolation from Mérida kept it relatively autonomous from royal rule, and the Maya of the area suffered brutal exploitation, which continued after Mexican independence. Barred from entering many areas of the city, the Maya made Valladolid one of their first points of attack following the outbreak of the War of the Castes in 1847 in Tepich, not far south on the border with Quintana Roo. After a two-month siege, the city's defenders were finally overcome.

◉ Sights

★ Casa de los Venados
MUSEUM
(☎ 985-856-22-89; www.casadelosvenados.com; Calle 40 No 204, btwn Calles 41 & 43; admission by donation; ⊙ tours 10am or by appointment) Featuring over 3000 pieces of museum-quality Mexican folk art, this private collection is unique in that objects are presented in a house, in the context that they were originally designed for, instead of being roped off in glass cases. The tour (in English or Spanish) brushes on the origins of some of the more important pieces and the story of the award-winning restored colonial mansion that houses them.

Templo de San Bernardino
CHURCH

(Church of San Bernardino; cnr Calles 49 & 51; admission Mon-Sat M$30, Sun free; ⊙9am-7pm) The Templo de San Bernardino and the adjacent **Convento de Sisal** are about 700m southwest of the plaza. They were constructed between 1552 and 1560 to serve as fortress and church. The church's charming decoration includes beautiful rose-colored walls, arches, some recently uncovered 16th-century frescoes and a small image of the Virgin on the altar. These are about the only original items remaining; the grand wooden *retablo* (altarpiece) dates from the 19th century.

✦ Activities

There are several cenotes around Valladolid that are well worth visiting.

★ Hacienda San Lorenzo Oxman
SWIMMING

(off Calle 54; M$30; ⊙9am-6pm) Once a *henequén* plantation and a refuge for Caste War insurgents in the mid-19th century, today the hacienda's main draw is a gorgeous cenote that's far less crowded than other sinkholes in and around Valladolid, especially if you visit Monday through Thursday.

To get there by bike or car, take Calle 41A (Calzada de los Frailes) past the Templo de San Bernardino along Calle 54A, turn right on Avenida de los Frailes, then hang a left on Calle 54 and head about 3km southwest. A taxi to the hacienda costs about M$70.

Cenote X'Kekén
SWIMMING

(Cenote Dzitnup; admission 1/2 cenotes M$60/90; ⊙8:30am-5:20pm) One of two cenotes at Dzitnup (recently renamed X'Kekén Jungle Park), X'Kekén is a massive limestone formation with stalactites hanging from its ceiling. The pool is artificially lit and very swimmable. Here you can also take a dip in cenote Samulá, a lovely cavern pool with *álamo* roots stretching down many meters.

Pedaling a rented bicycle to the cenotes takes about 20 minutes. By bike from the town center take Calle 41A (Calzada de los Frailes), a street lined with colonial architecture. Go one block past the Templo de San Bernardino along Calle 54A, then make a right on Calle 49, which becomes Avenida de los Frailes and hits the old highway. Follow the *ciclopista* (bike path) paralleling the road to Mérida for about 3km, then turn left at the sign for Dzitnup and continue for just under 2km.

Shared *colectivos* depart for Dzitnup (M$20) from Calle 44, between Calles 41 and 43.

Cenote Zací
SWIMMING

(www.cenotezaci.com.mx; Calle 36 s/n, btwn Calles 37 & 39; adult/child 3-11yr M$25/20; ⊙9am-6pm) Among the region's several underground cenotes is Cenote Zací, set downtown in a park that also holds a restaurant and souvenir shops. People swim in this open-air swimming hole, and while it's pleasant enough, don't expect crystalline waters. Look in the water for catfish or overhead for a colony of bats.

🛌 Sleeping

Hotel Zací
HOTEL $

(☑985-856-21-67; www.hotelzaci.com.mx; Calle 44 No 191; d M$595; P❋❄🐕❄) Conveniently located one block west of the bus station and a block east of the main plaza, rooms here get the colonial treatment, as does the lobby with its handsome antique furniture. The Zací also runs a 'more austere' budget hotel across the street but we much prefer this one, where you get a pool out back.

★ La Aurora
HOTEL $$

(☑985-856-12-19; www.hotellaaurora.com; Calle 42 No 192; d M$640; P❋❄🐕❄) If only more economical hotels were like the colonial-style Aurora. Well-appointed rooms overlook a pretty courtyard with a pool and potted plants, and the kicker is the rooftop Jacuzzi and bar. If possible, avoid the noisier street-facing rooms.

Hotel Tunich-Beh
B&B $$

(☑985-856-22-22; www.tunichbeh.com; Calle 41A, btwn Calles 46 & 48; d incl breakfast from M$950; P❋❋🐕❄) At this great old house lovingly converted into a hotel, well-equipped rooms surround a swimming pool and there are some nice *palapa*-shaded common areas for kicking back. The staff is very helpful and there are bikes available to ride to nearby cenotes.

Casa Tía Micha
BOUTIQUE HOTEL $$$

(☑985-856-04-99; www.casatiamicha.com; Calle 39 No 197; r incl breakfast from US$115; P❋❋🐕❄) The corridor and rear garden are beautifully lit at night in this family-run boutique hotel just off the plaza. Some of the tastefully adorned colonial-style rooms have king-size beds, and the upstairs suite comes with a Jacuzzi. If the Tía is booked, on the same block you'll find sister property **Casa Marlene** (☑985-856-04-99; Calle 39 No 193).

Eating

★ Yerba Buena del Sisal   MEXICAN $
(☑985-856-14-06; www.facebook.com/yerbabuenadelsisal; Calle 54A No 217; mains M$60-80; ☺8am-5pm Tue-Sun; ☻🖧🍴) Wonderfully healthy and delicious dishes are served in a peaceful garden. Tortilla chips and three delectable salsas come to the table while you look over the menu, which offers many great vegetarian and mostly organic dishes, ie the delightful *tacos maculum* (made with handmade corn tortillas, beans, cheese and aromatic Mexican pepper leaf).

If you're craving meat, try the *tacos de carne ahumada* (smoked pork tacos).

Conato 1910   MEXICAN $$
(Calle 40 No 226; mains M$60-130; ☺5pm-midnight Wed-Mon; ☻🖧🍴) A meeting spot for revolutionaries in the early 20th century, this historic building now houses one of the best restaurants in town in an atmospheric setting with muraled walls. The vegetarian-friendly menu features a wide variety of options, such as salads and pastas, and there are also excellent chicken and beef dishes.

ℹ Getting There & Away

BUS
Valladolid's main bus terminal is the convenient **ADO bus terminal** (www.ado.com.mx; cnr Calles 39 & 46).

COLECTIVO
Often faster than 2nd-class buses are the *colectivos* that depart as soon as their seats are filled. Most operate from 7am to 7pm.

Direct services run to Mérida (near the ADO bus terminal; M$110, two hours) and **Cancún** (p255; one block east of the plaza; M$170, two hours); confirm they're nonstop. *Colectivos* for Pisté and Chichén Itzá (M$30, one hour) leave north of the ADO bus terminal; for **Tizimín** (Calle 40, btwn Calles 35 & 37; M$40, 40 minutes) from Calle 40 between Calles 35 and 37; and for **Ek' Balam** (p331; M$50) take a 'Santa Rita' *colectivo* from Calle 44, between Calles 35 and 37.

ℹ Getting Around

Bicycles are a great way to see the town and get out to the cenotes. You can hire them from **Hostel La Candelaria** (☑985-856-22-67; www.hostelvalladolidyucatan.com; Calle 35 No 201F; dm/r incl breakfast M$160/440; ☻@🖧) or **Rudy Tours** (☑985-856-20-29, cell 985-1131565; roesro27@hotmail.com; Calle 40, btwn Calles 37 & 39; tours M$300, bike per hr M$20; ☺10am-6pm).

Ek' Balam

◉ Sights

Ek' Balam   ARCHAEOLOGICAL SITE
(adult/child under 13yr M$181/free, guide M$600; ☺8am-5pm) The fascinating ruined city of Ek' Balam reached its peak in the 8th century, before being suddenly abandoned. Vegetation still covers much of the archaeological site, but excavations and restoration continue to add to the sights, including an interesting ziggurat-like structure near the entrance, as well as a fine arch and a ball court. Most impressive is the gargantuan Acrópolis, whose well-restored base is 160m long and holds a 'gallery' – actually a series of separate chambers.

BUSES FROM VALLADOLID

DESTINATION	FARE (M$)	DURATION (HR)	FREQUENCY (DAILY)
Cancún	102-186	2½-3½	frequent
Chichén Itzá/Pisté	27-84	¾	frequent
Chiquilá (for Isla Holbox)	105	4	1; 3am
Cobá	48-114	1	5
Izamal	55	2½	1; 12:50pm
Mérida	102-178	2-3½	frequent
Playa del Carmen	186	2½-3	frequent
Tizimín	27	1	frequent
Tulum	108	1½-2	9

Built atop the base of the Acrópolis is Ek' Balam's massive main pyramid, reaching a height of 32m and sporting a gaping jaguar mouth. Below the mouth are stucco skulls, while above and to the right sits an amazingly expressive figure. On the right side stand unusual winged human figures (some call them Maya angels, although a much more likely explanation is that they are shaman or medicine men).

The turnoff for the archaeological site is 17km north of Valladolid, and the ruins are another 6km east from the turnoff.

From the Ek' Balam entrance you can visit the **X'Canché Cenote** (M$30), a 1.5km walk – or you can rent a bicycle (M$70). Also available at this ecotourist center are zipline tours and cabin rentals.

🛏 Sleeping & Eating

⭐ **Genesis Eco-Oasis**   GUESTHOUSE $$
(✆cell 985-1010277; www.genesisretreat.com; Ek' Balam pueblo; d from M$919, without bathroom M$685, incl breakfast; @ 🕮) 🏊 The Genesis Eco-Retreat offers B&B intimacy in a quiet, ecofriendly setting. This is a true ecotel: gray water is used for landscaping, some rooms are naturally cooled and there's even an entire wall made out of plastic bottles. The place is postcard-beautiful – there's a chilling swimming pool and a temascal (pre-Hispanic steam bath) on-site – and it offers delicious veggie meals.

The hotel is sometimes closed between September and early October. Reservations required.

❶ Getting There & Away

Colectivos (M$50) to Ek' Balam depart from Calle 44, between Calles 35 and 37, in Valladolid.

Río Lagartos

📞 986 / POP 3400

With the largest and most spectacular flamingo colony in Mexico, Río Lagartos definitely warrants a trip. Situated 103km north of Valladolid and 52km north of Tizimín, this fishing village lies within the Reserva de la Biosfera Ría Lagartos. The mangrove-lined estuary is also home to snowy egrets, tiger herons, snowy white ibis, hundreds of other bird species and the crocodiles that gave the town its name (Alligator River) – Spanish explorers mistook the inlet for a river and the crocs for alligators. The best months for

viewing flamingos are from April through September.

The Maya knew the place as Holkobén and used it as a rest stop on their way to the nearby lagoons (Las Coloradas), from which they extracted salt. (Salt continues to be extracted today, on a much vaster scale.) Intrepid travelers can head east of town past Las Coloradas on a coastal dirt road all the way to the small town of El Cuyo.

The road into town is the north–south Calle 10, which ends at the waterfront Calle 13. There's no bank or ATM in town, so bring lots of cash.

👉 Tours

⭐ **Río Lagartos Adventures**   BOAT TOUR
(✆cell 986-1008390; www.riolagartosadventures. com; Calle 19 No 134; per boat 2hr M$1200, fly-fishing from M$2200) This outfit run by local expert Diego Núñez Martínez does various water and land expeditions, including flamingo- and crocodile-watching, snorkeling to Isla Cerritos, fly-fishing and excursions designed for photography. Diego is a licensed English-speaking guide with training as a naturalist and is up to date on the area's fauna and flora, which includes some 400 bird species.

He organizes the tours out of Ria Maya Restaurante.

Ismael Navarro   BOAT TOUR
(✆986-862-00-00, cell 986-8665216; riolaga@hot mail.com; Calle 9; per boat 2hr M$1000, fly-fishing M$3500) A licensed naturalist worth seeking out for a tour of the local flora and fauna. Besides the flamingo and fly-fishing outings, Ismael takes shorebird tours along the mudflats in winter. You'll find him and his partner, captain 'Chino Mosca,' at Balneario Chiquilá, a restaurant and swimming hole on the east end of Calle 9.

🛏 Sleeping & Eating

Punta Ponto Hotel   HOTEL $
(✆986-862-05-09; www.hotelpuntaponto.com; Calle 9 No 140, cnr Calle 19; r incl breakfast M$450-700; P ✺ ❄ 🛜) One of the best deals in town and your kind host, Roger, is a great source of information. Two rooms have balconies with estuary views, and the breezy, open-air common spaces seal the deal.

El Perico Marinero   HOTEL $$
(✆986-862-00-58; www.elpericomarinero.com; Calle 9, near Calle 19; d incl breakfast M$600-700; ❄) Business must be booming at the Perico's waterfront seafood restaurant just down the

road. Río Lagarto's newest hotel offers seven pleasant rooms, some with estuary vistas, rocking chairs and handmade wood furnishings, and all come with excellent beds.

Restaurant y Posada Macumba SEAFOOD $$
(☑ 986-862-00-92; www.restaurantmacumba.com; Calle 16 No 102, cnr Calle 11; mains M$85-135; ☺8am-8pm; ☻☎) One of the best restaurants in town specializing in fresh fish and seafood. Upstairs the waterfront Macumba has four smallish rooms (M$400 to M$500) with funky Caribbean design details. The panoramic view of the penthouse (M$700) makes it a screaming deal.

❶ Getting There & Away

Several Noreste buses run daily between Tizimín (M$36 to M$46, one hour and 15 minutes), Mérida (M$142 to M$196, three to four hours) and San Felipe (M$8, 20 minutes). The bus station is on Calle 19, between Calles 6 and 8. Noreste serves Valladolid and Cancún, but you'll need to transfer in Tizimín.Campeche state is home to vast stretches of tangled jungle, some of the region's least visited and most imposing Maya ruins, forgotten pastoral villages, bird-choked coastal lagoons and an inspiring colonial-era capital city. It's the least touristed of the Yucatán states, and it exudes a laid-back, provincial charm. The massive restored Edzná archaeological site is probably the best-known sight, but this is also the wildest corner of the peninsula, and the Reserva de la Biosfera Calakmul is Mexico's largest. Beyond the cacophonous roar of the howlers and hiccupping frogs rise more massive ruined Maya cities, such as Calakmul and Becán. Along the coast, the Laguna de Términos is a prime location for bird-watching expeditions.

CAMPECHE STATE

Campeche state is home to vast stretches of tangled jungle, some of the region's least visited and most imposing Maya ruins, forgotten pastoral villages, bird-choked coastal lagoons and an inspiring colonial-era capital city. It's the least touristed of the Yucatán states, and it exudes a laid-back, provincial charm. The massive restored Edzná archaeological site is probably the best-known sight, but this is also the wildest corner of the peninsula, and the Reserva de la Biosfera Calakmul is Mexico's largest. Beyond the cacophonous roar of the howlers and hiccupping frogs rise more massive ruined Maya cities, such as Calakmul and Becán. Along the coast, the Laguna de Términos is a prime location for bird-watching expeditions.

Campeche
☑981 / POP 220,400
Campeche is like a colonial fairyland. The walled city center is a tight enclave of perfectly restored pastel-colored buildings, narrow cobblestone streets, fortified ramparts and well-preserved mansions from the 18th and 19th centuries. Added to Unesco's list of World Heritage sites in 1999, the state capital has been so painstakingly restored you'll wonder if it's real. Nearly 2000 historic buildings have been renovated, but beyond the walls lies a typical Mexican provincial capital, complete with a frenetic market, a quiet *malecón* and old fishing docks.

Besides the numerous mansions built by wealthy Spanish families during Campeche's heyday, two segments of the city's famous wall have also survived, as have seven of the *baluartes* (bastions or bulwarks) that were built into it.

History

The Spanish first set their sights on Campeche – then a Maya trading village called Ah Kim Pech (Lord Sun Sheep-Tick) – in 1517, but resistance by the local Maya prevented the Spaniards from fully conquering the region for nearly a quarter of a century. A Spanish outpost was founded in 1531 but quickly abandoned due to Maya hostility. By 1540, however, the conquistadors had gained sufficient control, under the leadership of Francisco de Montejo the Younger, to found a permanent settlement, which they named Villa de San Francisco de Campeche.

The city emerged as the major port for the Yucatán Peninsula, but it faced regular pirate attacks. After a particularly appalling assault in 1663 left the city in ruins, the king of Spain ordered construction of Campeche's famous walls, putting an end to the periodic carnage. Today the economy of the city is largely driven by fishing and, increasingly, tourism, which to some extent has funded the downtown area's renovation.

❂ Sights & Activities
Plaza Principal
Shaded by spreading carob trees, and ringed by tiled benches with broad footpaths radiating from a belle époque kiosk,

Campeche

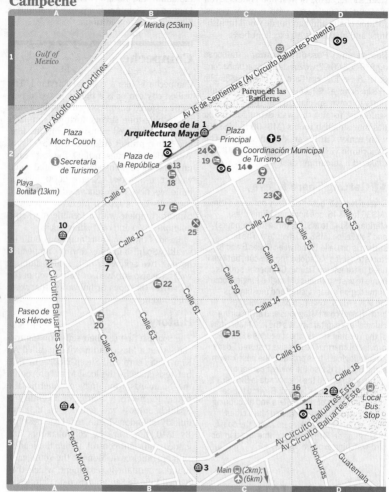

Campeche's appealingly modest central square started life in 1531 as a military camp. Over the years it became the focus of the town's civic, political and religious activities, and it remains the core of public life. The plaza is seen at its best on weekend evenings, when it's closed to traffic and concerts are staged.

A popular path for joggers, cyclists, strolling friends and cooing sweethearts, the *malecón*, Campeche's waterfront promenade, makes for a breezy sunrise ramble or sunset bike ride.

Centro Cultural
Casa Número 6
CULTURAL CENTER

(Calle 57 No 6; M$20, audio guide M$15; ⊙ 9am-9pm) During the prerevolutionary era, when this mansion was occupied by an upper-class *campechano* family, Número 6 was a prestigious plaza address. Wandering the premises, you'll get an idea of how the city's high society lived back then. The front sitting room is furnished with Cuban-style pieces of the period. Inside are exhibition spaces, a pleasant back patio and a gift shop.

tiles, the Ex-Templo de San José is a wonder to behold; note the lighthouse, complete with weather vane, atop the right spire. Built in the early 18th century by Jesuits who ran it as an institute of higher learning until they were booted out of Spanish domains in 1767, it now serves as an exhibition space.

Forts & Bastions

After a particularly blistering pirate attack in 1663, the remaining inhabitants of Campeche set about erecting protective walls around their city. Built largely by indigenous labor with limestone extracted from nearby caves, the barrier took more than 50 years to complete. Stretching over 2km around the urban core and rising to a height of 8m, the hexagonal wall was linked by eight bastions. The seven that remain display a treasure trove of historical paraphernalia. You can climb atop the bulwarks and stroll sections of the wall for sweeping views of the port.

Puerta del Mar　　　　　　　　GATE
(Sea Gate; cnr Calles 8 & 59) FREE The Puerta del Mar provided access from the sea, opening onto a wharf where small craft delivered goods from ships anchored further out. The shallow waters were later reclaimed, so the gate is now several blocks from the waterfront.

★**Museo de la
Arquitectura Maya**　　　　　　MUSEUM
(Calle 8; M$39; ◎9am-5:30pm Tue-Sun) The Baluarte de Nuestra Señora de la Soledad, designed to protect the Puerta del Mar, contains the fascinating Museo de la Arquitectura Maya, the one must-see museum in Campeche. It provides an excellent overview of the sites around Campeche state and the key architectural styles associated with them. Five halls display stelae taken from various sites, accompanied by graphic representations of their carved inscriptions with brief commentaries in flawless English.

Museo de la Ciudad　　　　　MUSEUM
(Calle 8; M$35; ◎9am-8pm) Named after Spain's King Carlos II, the Baluarte de San Carlos houses the Museo de la Ciudad. This small but worthwhile museum chronologically illustrates the city's tempestuous history via well-displayed objects: specimens of dyewood, muskets, a figurehead from a ship's prow and the like. The dungeon downstairs alludes to the building's use as a military prison during the 1700s.

YUCATÁN PENINSULA CAMPECHE

Catedral de Nuestra Señora
de la Purísima Concepción　　CATHEDRAL
(Calle 55; ◎6:30am-9pm) FREE Dominating Plaza Principal's east side is the two-towered cathedral. The limestone structure has stood on this spot for more than three centuries, and it still fills beyond capacity most Sundays. Statues of Sts Peter and Paul occupy niches in the baroque facade; the sober, single-nave interior is lined with colonial-era paintings.

Ex-Templo de San José　HISTORIC BUILDING
(former San José Church; cnr Calles 10 & 63; ◎10am-8pm) Faced with blue-and-yellow

Campeche

◉ Top Sights
1 Museo de la Arquitectura Maya C2

◎ Sights
2 Baluarte de San Francisco D4
3 Baluarte de San Juan C5
4 Baluarte de Santa Rosa A5
5 Catedral de Nuestra Señora de la
  Purísima Concepción C2
6 Centro Cultural Casa Número 6 .... C2
7 Ex-Templo de San José B3
8 Galería y Museo de Arte Popular E4
9 Jardín Botánico Xmuch Haltún D1
10 Museo de la Ciudad A3
11 Puerta de Tierra D5
12 Puerta del Mar B2

◔ Activities, Courses & Tours
13 Kankabi' Ok B2
14 Tranvía de la Ciudad C2

⊝ Sleeping
15 H177 Hotel C4
16 Hacienda Puerta Campeche D4
17 Hotel América B3
18 Hotel Boutique Casa Don
  Gustavo B2
19 Hotel Campeche C2
20 Hotel Francis Drake A4
21 Hotel Guarandocha Inn C3
22 Hotel López B3

✖ Eating
23 Café La Parroquia C2
24 El Bastión de Campeche C2
25 Luz de Luna B3
26 Mercado Principal E4

⊝ Drinking & Nightlife
27 La Casa Vieja C2

⊙ Entertainment
Puerta de Tierra .... (see 11)

Baluarte de Santa Rosa   HISTORIC BUILDING
(cnr Calle 14 & Av Circuito Baluartes Sur; ⊙9am-3pm) FREE The Baluarte de Santa Rosa has some pirate-themed woodcuts and information on the city's forts.

Baluarte de San Juan   HISTORIC BUILDING
(Calle 18; ⊙8am-7:30pm Tue-Sun) FREE The Baluarte de San Juan is the smallest of the seven bulwarks. On its south side you can see the bell that was rung to alert the population in times of danger.

Puerta de Tierra   GATE
(Land Gate; Calle 18; M$15; ⊙9am-6pm) The Puerta de Tierra, on the eastern side of the town wall, was opened in 1732 as the principal ingress from the suburbs. It is now the venue for a sound-and-light show.

Baluarte de San Francisco   HISTORIC BUILDING
(Calle 18) FREE Once the primary defensive bastion for the adjacent Puerta de la Tierra, the Baluarte de San Francisco now houses a small cultural center.

Galería y Museo de Arte Popular   MUSEUM
(Museum & Gallery of Folk Art; cnr Avs Circuito Baluartes Este & Circuito Baluartes Nte; ⊙9am-9pm) FREE Directly behind Iglesia de San Juan de Dios is the **Baluarte de San Pedro**. Carved in stone above the entry is the symbol of San Pedro: two keys to heaven and the papal tiara. Climb the steep ramp to the roof and look between the battlements to see San Juan's cupola. Downstairs, the Galería y Museo de Arte Popular displays beautiful indigenous handicrafts.

Jardín Botánico Xmuch Haltún   GARDENS
(cnr Calles 8 & 49; adult/child aged 3-12yr M$10/5; ⊙8am-9pm) Inside the Baluarte de Santiago, this small botanic garden houses a range of indigenous and non-native plants. It makes for a peaceful, leafy respite when the sun gets particularly brutal.

Fuerte Museo San José del Alto   FORT
(Calle Francisco Morazán; M$43; ⊙8am-5pm Tue-Sun; ℗) Built in the late 18th century, this neatly restored fort (with drawbridge and moat) sits atop Cerro de Bellavista. Inside, a **museum** illustrates the port's maritime history through models, weaponry and other paraphernalia, including a beautiful ebony rudder carved in the shape of a hound.

To get here, catch a 'Bellavista Josefa' or 'Morelos' bus from the market; some might also be marked 'San Jose del Alto'. You might have to walk a bit from where the bus drops you. Taxis cost around M$50.

Museo Arqueológico de Campeche & Fuerte de San Miguel   MUSEUM, FORT
(Campeche Archaeological Museum; Av Escénica s/n; M$46; ⊙8:30am-5pm Tue-Sun; ℗) Campeche's largest colonial fort, facing the Gulf of Mexico some 4km southwest of the city center, is now home to the excellent Museo Arqueológico de Campeche. Here you can

admire findings from the sites of Calakmul and Edzná, and from Isla de Jaina, an island north of town once used as a burial site for Maya aristocracy.

To get here take a bus or *combi* (minibus; marked 'Lerma') from the market. Ask the driver to let you off at the access road (just say 'Fuerte de San Miguel'), then hike 300m up the hill. Taxis cost M$50.

Stunning jade jewelry and exquisite vases, masks and plates are thematically arranged in 10 exhibit halls. The star attractions are the jade burial masks from Calakmul. Also displayed are stelae, seashell necklaces and clay figurines.

Equipped with a dry moat and working drawbridge, the fort itself is a thing of beauty. The roof deck, ringed by 20 cannons, affords wonderful harbor views.

🎧 Tours

Tranvía de la Ciudad TOUR
(tours adult/child 11yr & under M$100/30; ⊙ hourly 9am-noon & 5-8pm) Daily bilingual tours by *tranvía* (trolley) depart from Calle 10 beside the Plaza Principal, lasting 45 minutes. They cover Campeche's historical center, traditional neighborhoods and part of the *malecón*. Occasionally, another trolley called *El Guapo* goes to Fuerte de San Miguel and Fuerte de San José, though they don't leave enough time to visit the forts' museums. Check schedules at the ticket kiosk in the Plaza Principal.

Kankabi' Ok TOUR
(✍ 981-811-27-92; www.kankabiok.com; Calle 59 No 3; ⊙ 9am-8pm Mon-Sat, 10am-2pm Sun) Offers city tours, trips to archaeological sites such as Edzná, Chenes and the Ruta Puc. Also rents bikes and does ecotourism and beach trips.

🛏 Sleeping

The streets in the historic center (which is where you will want to stay) follow a numbered sequence: inland-oriented streets have odd numbers and cross-streets even numbers.

Hotel Guarandocha Inn HOTEL $
(✍ 981-811-66-58; rool_2111@hotmail.com; Calle 55, btwn Calles 12 & 14; incl breakfast d M$460-550, tr M$670; ❋ @ 🛜) One of the better options in town is at this modest but pleasant hotel. Rooms are nice and spacious, and the newer ones upstairs are brighter and more open (and cost a bit more). A very simple breakfast is included.

Hotel Campeche HOTEL $
(✍ 981-816-51-83; hotelcampeche@hotmail.com; Calle 57, btwn Calles 8 & 10; s/d with fan M$280/320, with air-con M$370/450; ❋ 🛜) Not much in the way of frills here, but the plaza-side location and big rooms in this classically crumbling building are about the best budget bet in town. A couple of rooms have little balconies looking out over the plaza.

★ Hotel López HOTEL $$
(✍ 981-816-33-44; www.hotellopezcampeche.com. mx; Calle 12 No 189; s/d/ste M$650/720/980; ❋ 🛜 🏊) This elegant hotel is one of Campeche's best midrange options. Small but modern and comfortably appointed rooms open onto curvy art deco balconies around oval courtyards and pleasant greenery. Bring your swimsuit for the lovely pool out back.

Hotel América HOTEL $$
(✍ 981-816-45-76; www.hotelamericacampeche. com; Calle 10 No 252; s/d M$550/680; P ❋ @ 🛜) A large central hotel, the América is a good midrange choice. The highlight here is a pretty courtyard restaurant with tables and umbrellas – don't worry, the music dies down at night. Nearly 50 large, clean rooms are located in the surrounding arcaded corridors and can vary widely, so check out a few if you don't like what you first see.

Hotel Francis Drake HOTEL $$
(✍ 981-811-56-26; www.hotelfrancisdrake.com; Calle 12 No 207; s/d M$860/950, ste from M$1050; ❋ 🛜) A somewhat baroque lobby leads to cool, fresh rooms with a sprinkling of tasteful decoration. Bathrooms and balconies are tiny, but the rooms are huge (other hotels would call them suites) with king-sized beds and separate sitting areas.

H177 Hotel HOTEL $$
(✍ 981-816-44-63; Calle 14 No 177; s/d M$900/1250; ❋ 🛜) With its slick and trendy lines, this hotel is different from anything else in traditional Campeche. It boasts 24 spacious and modern-styled rooms decked out in strong natural colors, and the bathrooms have glass-walled showers. There's also a Jacuzzi, and breakfast is included. Ask for a discount in low season.

**Hotel Boutique
Casa Don Gustavo** BOUTIQUE HOTEL $$$
(✍ 981-816-80-90; www.casadongustavo.com; Calle 59 No 4; r/ste from M$2200/2600; P ❋ 🛜 🏊) Just 10 rooms decorated with antique furniture (and huge modern bathrooms), though

everything is so perfectly museumlike it's almost hard to relax. Give it a shot at the small pool with hammocks nearby, or try the rooftop Jacuzzi. Colorful tiled hallways line an outdoor courtyard, and there's a restaurant too. Call or check the website for promotions.

Hacienda Puerta Campeche
BOUTIQUE HOTEL $$$

(☑981-816-75-08; www.luxurycollection.com; Calle 59 No 71; r from M$4258; P❈@🛜🐾) This beautiful boutique hotel has 15 suites with high ceilings and separate lounges. Perfectly manicured gardens and grassy lawns offer peace, while the partly covered pool has nearby hammocks that are fit for a Maya king. It also runs a restored luxury hacienda 26km outside the city, on the way to the Edzná ruins.

✖ Eating & Drinking

The emblematic *campechano* dish is *pan de cazón* – a tortilla sandwich filled with minced shark meat and beans and smothered in tomato sauce. Wash one down with an *horchata de coco* (rice and coconut drink) and you'll be livin' *la vida local*.

Calle 59 is partly closed off to traffic, and a little dining precinct is blossoming, with outdoor seating and wandering musicians, making it a lovely place to eat or enjoy a few drinks once the sun goes down.

Café La Parroquia
MEXICAN $

(☑981-816-25-30; Calle 55 No 8; mains M$60-170, lunch specials M$80; ☺24hr) Open 24 hours, this casual restaurant appeals to both locals and foreigners with its wide-ranging menu and attentive staff. Order everything from fried chicken to grilled pork to turkey soup, plus regional specialties and seafood dishes like *ceviche*. Tonnes of drinks make it all go down easy, and don't miss the creamy flan for dessert.

★ Luz de Luna
INTERNATIONAL $$

(☑981-811-06-24; Calle 59 No 6; mains M$90-150; ☺8am-10pm Mon-Sat) Carved, painted tables and folksy decor add a creative atmosphere to this popular restaurant on a pedestrian street. The menu choices are equally interesting – try the shrimp salad, chicken fajitas, flank steak or vegetarian burritos. There are plenty of breakfast options as well, especially omelettes.

El Bastión de Campeche
MEXICAN $$

(Calle 57 No 24; mains M$100-180; ☺6:30pm-midnight) Don't let the drab exterior fool you – this plazaside stalwart serves up some good *campechano* dishes. Cool off with a chaya juice before tucking in to a chicken breast stuffed with *cochinita pibil* – as delicious and decadent as it sounds.

La Casa Vieja
BAR, RESTAURANT

(Calle 10 No 319A; ☺8:30am-12:30am) There's no better setting for an evening cocktail than La Casa Vieja's colonnaded balcony overlooking the Plaza Principal. Look for the stairs next to the McDonald's ice-cream counter.

☆ Entertainment

There's invariably someone performing on the Plaza Principal every Saturday and Sunday evening from around 6:30pm. For Campeche's hottest dance bars and clubs, head 1km south from the city center along the *malecón,* past the Torres del Cristal skyscraper.

Incidents from Campeche's pirate past are re-enacted several nights a week in the **Puerta de Tierra** (adult/child 4-10 yr M$50/25; ☺8pm Thu-Sun), in a Disney-esque extravaganza with lots of cannon blasts and flashing lights.

ℹ Information

Campeche has numerous banks with ATMs, open 8am to 4pm Monday to Friday, 9am to 2pm Saturday.

Central Post Office (cnr Av 16 de Septiembre & Calle 53; ☺8:30am-4pm Mon-Fri, 8-11:30am Sat)

Cruz Roja (Red Cross; ☑981-815-24-11; cnr Av Las Palmas & Ah Kim Pech) Medical services; some 3km northeast of downtown.

Hospital Dr Manuel Campos (☑981-811-17-09; Av Circuito Baluartes Nte, btwn Calles 14 & 16)

Secretaría de Turismo (☑981-127-33-00; www.campeche.travel; Plaza Moch-Couoh; ☺8am-9pm Mon-Fri, to 8pm Sat & Sun) Good information on the city and Campeche state.

ℹ Getting There & Away

AIR

The airport is 6km southeast of the center.

Aeroméxico (☑Mexico 55-5133-4000; www.aeromexico.com) flies to Mexico City at least twice daily. Regular flights are also offered by low-cost

BUSES FROM CAMPECHE

DESTINATION	FARE (M$)	DURATION (HR)	FREQUENCY (DAILY)
Cancún	578-698	7hr	7 buses
Chetumal	440	6hr	2pm
Mérida (via Bécal)	200-254	2½hr	half-hourly ADO & ADO GL
Mérida (via Uxmal)	150-195	4½hr	5 daily
Mexico City	1444-1742	17hr	8 buses
Palenque	384	6hr	3 buses
San Cristóbal de Las Casas	548	9hr	10:15pm ADO
Villahermosa	356-572	6hr	frequent
Xpujil	314	5hr	2pm ADO

carriers **Interjet** (☑ Mexico 55-1102-5555, toll-free USA 866-285-9525; www.interjet.com).

BUS

Campeche's **main bus terminal** (☑ 981-811-99-10; Av Patricio Trueba 237), usually called the ADO or 1st-class terminal, is about 2.5km south of Plaza Principal via Avenida Central. Buses provide 1st-class and deluxe services to major cities as well as 2nd-class services to Sabancuy (M$102), Hecelchakán (M$62), Candelaria (M$188) and points in Tabasco. To get to the new terminal, catch any 'Las Flores,' 'Solidaridad' or 'Casa de Justicia' bus by the post office.

The **2nd-class terminal** (☑ 981-811-99-10; Av Gobernadores 289), often referred to as the 'old ADO' station, is east of the Mercado Principal. Second-class buses to Hopelchén (M$62), Bolonchén, Xpujil and Bécal (M$61) depart from here. To reach the 2nd-class terminal, catch a 'Terminal Sur' or 'Ex-ADO' bus from the post office.

To get to Edzná (M$40, one hour), catch a Valle Edzná *colectivo* from Calle Chihuahua near the corner of Calle Nicaragua, by the Mercado Principal. They leave every half hour from 7am to 7pm.

CAR

If you're heading for Edzná or taking the long route to Mérida or the fast toll road going south, take Calle 61 to Avenida Central and follow signs for the airport and either Edzná or the *cuota* (toll road). For the non-toll route south, just head down the *malecón*. For the short route to Mérida, go north on the *malecón*.

Arriving in Campeche from the south via the *cuota*, just turn left at the roundabout signed for the *universidad*, then turn right up the *malecón* when you hit the coast, and you will arrive instantly oriented.

Easy Way Rent a Car (☑ 981-811-22-36; www.campechecarrental.com; Calle 59, btwn Calles 8 & 10; ⊗ 8:30am-9:30pm Mon-Sat) In addition to some outlets at the airport, several car rental agencies can be found downtown including Easy Way. Rates are generally higher than in Mérida or Cancún.

ⓘ Getting Around

Local buses leave from the Mercado Principal or across Avenida Circuito Baluartes from the market. Most go at least partway around the Circuito before heading to their final destinations. The flat fare is M$6.

Taxis charge between M$30 and M$60 for rides within the city – prices go up at night. Tickets for authorized taxis from the airport to the center (M$120) are sold from a booth in the terminal.

Consider renting a bicycle for a ride along the *malecón* or through the streets of the Centro Histórico. **Kankabi' Ok** (p337) has a decent selection of bikes.

Drivers should note that even-numbered streets in the Centro Histórico take priority, as indicated by the red (stop) or black (go) arrows at every intersection.

AROUND CAMPECHE

Edzná

The closest major ruins to Campeche are about 53km to the southeast. **Edzná** (M$48; ⊗ 8am-5pm) once covered more than 17 sq km and was inhabited from approximately 600 BC to the 15th century AD. Most of the visible carvings date from AD 550 to 810.

1. Mérida (p301)
An elegant colonial town, Mérida is the cultural capital of the region.

2. Scuba diving in a cenote
Crystal clear water offers the opportunity to swim through underground rock formations.

3. Cenote near Valladolid (p328)
It's possible to visit, and swim in, a number of stunning cenotes within easy distance of this charming city.

4. Becán, Campeche (p344)
One of the largest and most elaborate Maya sites, surrounded by lush forest.

Though it's a long way from such Puuc Hills sites as Uxmal and Kabah, some of the architecture here has elements of the Puuc style. What led to Edzná's decline and gradual abandonment remains a mystery.

Beyond the entrance is a *palapa* protecting carvings and stelae from the elements. A path from here leads about 400m through vegetation to the zone's big draw, the **Plaza Principal** (follow the signs for the Gran Acrópolis), which is 160m long, 100m wide and surrounded by temples. On your right as you enter from the north is the **Nohochná** (Big House), a massive, elongated structure that was topped by four long halls probably used for administrative tasks, such as the collecting of tributes and the dispensing of justice. The built-in benches facing the main plaza were designed for spectators to view theatrical and ritual events.

Across the plaza is the **Gran Acrópolis**, a raised platform holding several structures, including Edzná's major temple, the 31m-high **Edificio de los Cinco Pisos** (Five-Story Building). It rises five levels from its vast base to the roofcomb and contains many vaulted rooms. A great central staircase of 65 steps goes right to the top. Some of the weathered carvings of masks, serpents and jaguar heads that formerly adorned each level are now in the *palapa* near the ticket office.

The current structure is the last of four remodels, and was done primarily in the Puuc architectural style. Scholars generally agree that this temple is a hybrid of a pyramid and a palace. The impressive roofcomb is a clear reference to the sacred buildings at Tikal in Guatemala.

In the Pequeña Acrópolis, to the south of the main plaza, is the *palapa*-protected **Templo de Mascarones** (Temple of Masks), which features carved portrayals of the sun god, Kinich-Ahau. The central motif is the head of a Maya man whose face has been modified to give him the appearance of a jaguar.

🛈 Getting There & Away

From Campeche, minibuses (M$40, one hour) leave from Calle Chihuahua every half hour from 7am to 7pm.

Kankabi' Ok (p337) in Campeche provides guided tours of Edzná (including transportation) for M$820 per person.

Leaving the site by car, you can either go north on Hwy 120 to pick up Hwy 261 east to Hopelchén, or alternatively head toward Dzibalchén and the Chenes site of Hochob by going south to Pich, then east to Chencoh, 54km from Edzná over a decent but little-used road.

Bolonchén de Rejón & Xtacumbilxunaan

Heading east from Campeche, you'll reach San Antonio Cayal, then Hopelchén (with a Pemex gas station), where Hwy 261 turns north. After 34km, the town of **Bolonchén de Rejón** appears out of the lush countryside. This small outpost is famous for its festival of Santa Cruz, held each year on May 3.

Bolonchén de Rejón is close to the **Grutas de Xtacumbilxunaan** (M$65; ⏱10am–5pm Tue-Sun; ♿), pronounced 'Grutas de *shtaa*-koom-beel-shoo-*nahn*' (go on, give it a shot), about 3km south of town. Lighted steps lead down to a barely visible cenote, beyond which a passage leads 100m deeper into the bedrock, bedecked with stalactites and stalagmites. Be aware that the wooden ladder is for demonstration purposes only, to show how the Maya used to descend to

---

DIY: EXPLORE MORE OF CAMPECHE

Leave the beaten track and head out into the less-explored corners of Campeche. Here are some ideas to get you started.

Chenes sites Northeastern Campeche state is dotted with more than 30 sites in the distinct Chenes style, recognizable by the monster motifs around doorways in the center of long, low buildings of three sections, and by temples atop pyramidal bases.

Laguna de Términos The largest lagoon in the Gulf of Mexico area, the Laguna de Términos comprises a network of estuaries, dunes, swamps and ponds that together form a uniquely important coastal habitat.

Bécal While on the surface Bécal may look like a somnolent *campechano* town, underneath a multitude is laboring away at the traditional craft of hat making.

the cave floor. Doing so yourself would be very foolish. Sur buses traveling between Hopelchén and Mérida will drop you at the cave entrance. In addition, *colectivos* depart for Bolonchén from the north side of Hopelchén's plaza, passing near the caves. Check with the driver for return times.

Hwy 261 continues north into Yucatán state to Uxmal, with a side road leading to the ruins along the Ruta Puuc.

SOUTH OF CAMPECHE

The southern part of the peninsular region – now bordering modern-day Guatemala – was the earliest established, longest inhabited and most densely populated territory in the Maya world. Here you will find the most ancient and most architecturally elaborate archaeological sites on the peninsula. Heading south from Campeche, you'll reach Escárcega, where Hwy 186 cuts due east across southern-central Campeche state and on to Chetumal in Quintana Roo – a 273km ride. This route passes several fascinating Maya sites and goes through the ecologically diverse Reserva de la Biosfera Calakmul.

The largest settlement between Escárcega and Chetumal is Xpujil. Situated on Hwy 186 about 2km west of the Campeche–Quintana Roo border, Xpujil is a great place from which to stage your exploration of the region. The only gas station in the same stretch is about 5km east of Xpujil.

The predominant architectural styles of the region's archaeological sites are Río Bec and Chenes. The former is characterized by long, low buildings that look like they're divided into sections, each with a huge serpent or monster-mouth door. The facades are decorated with smaller masks, geometric designs (with many X forms) and columns. At the corners of the buildings are tall, solid towers with extremely small, steep, nonfunctional steps, topped by small false temples. Many of these towers have roofcombs. The Chenes architectural style shares most of these characteristics, except for the towers.

Balamkú

Discovered in 1990, **Balamkú** (Temple of the Jaguar; M$36; ⊙8am-5pm) is 60km west of Xpujil (88km east of Escárcega). This small site's attractions are its frescoes and an exquisite, ornate stucco frieze. Amazingly, much original color is still visible on both the frescoes and the frieze. You'll notice toads dominate the designs at Balamkú. These amphibians, not only at home on land and in water, were considered to move easily between this world and the next. The toad was a revered spirit guide who helped humans navigate between earth and the underworld.

The frescoes are open to public viewing, but the frieze is housed in a locked building. The caretaker will open the door – a tip is appreciated.

A taxi from Xpujil to Balamkú costs M$900 (round trip including two hours' waiting time).

Calakmul

In 1931, US botanist Cyrus Lundell became the first outsider to 'discover' **Calakmul** (M$48; road maintance fee per car M$50 plus per person M$30, park fee M$56; ⊙8am-5pm), which means 'Adjacent Mounds.' Mayanists consider Calakmul to be a site of vital archaeological significance. The site bears comparison in size and historical significance to Tikal in Guatemala, its chief rival for hegemony over the southern lowlands during the Classic era.

From about AD 250 to 695, Calakmul was the leading city in a vast region known as the Kingdom of the Serpent's Head. Its perpetual rival was Tikal, and its decline began with the power struggles and internal conflicts that followed the defeat of Calakmul's king Garra de Jaguar (Jaguar Paw).

As at Tikal, there are indications that construction occurred over a period of more than a millennium. Beneath Edificio VII, archaeologists discovered a burial crypt with some 2000 pieces of jade, and tombs continue to yield spectacular jade burial masks; many of these objects are on display in Campeche city's Museo Arqueológico (p336). Dotted around the site are at least 120 carved stelae, though many are eroded.

So far, only a fraction of Calakmul's 100-sq-km expanse has been cleared, and few of its 6500 buildings have been consolidated, let alone restored; however, exploration and restoration are ongoing.

Lying at the heart of the vast Reserva de la Biosfera Calakmul, the ruins are surrounded by rainforest, which is best viewed from the top of one of the several pyramids.

YUCATÁN PENINSULA BALAMKÚ

VISITING CALAKMUL

Calakmul is *big* – you could easily spend a few hours wandering around the site and if you stop to look at details, take photos and climb temples, this could stretch to a couple more. If all that activity is likely to get you peckish, pack some snacks and water – the nearest eats are 40km away.

There are over 250 bird species living in the reserve, and you are likely to see ocellated turkeys, parrots and toucans. Other wildlife protected by the reserve includes jaguars, spider monkeys, pumas, ocelots and white-lipped peccaries.

Twenty kilometers down the access road is the ultramodern **Museo del Centro de Comunicación y Cultura** (⊘7am-3pm) **FREE**, which showcases fossil finds from the region and some ceramics from Calakmul, and has a small botanical garden featuring plants traditionally used by the Maya for food and medicine.

🛏 Sleeping & Eating

Comedor & Cabañas La Selva CABIN $
(☑983-733-87-06; Hwy 186 Km 95; campsite M$50, cabins M$300-600; ⊘restaurant 6am-10pm) Simple, friendly open *palapa* restaurant (set meals M$90) with nearby grassy camping sites. Ask about their very basic and rustic *cabañas* (cabins), within the nearby village of Conhuás. Look for the restaurant near the entrance to the Balamkú ruins.

Hotel Puerta Calakmul HOTEL $$$
(☑998-892-26-24; www.puertacalakmul.com.mx; Hwy 186 Km 98; cabañas from M$2620; P🛇❄) This upscale jungle lodge is 700m from the highway turnoff. The 15 spacious bungalows are nice though not luxurious, all come with mosquito nets and overhead fans. There's a decent, screened-in restaurant where you can dine from 7am to 9:30pm (mains M$120 to M$300), plus a small pool. Wi-fi in main building only.

ℹ Getting There & Away

Kankabi' Ok (p337) in Campeche and **Río Bec Dreams** (p344) near Chicanná run tours to Calakmul.

If you are driving, the turnoff to Calakmul is 56km west of Xpujil, and the site is 60km south of the highway at the end of a decent paved road.

A cab to Calakmul from Xpujil costs M$900 to M$1000, including a couple of hours' waiting time.

Chicanná

Aptly named 'House of the Snake's Jaws,' this **archaeological site** (M$43; ⊘8am-5pm) is best known for the remarkably well-preserved doorway on Estructura 11, featuring a hideous fanged visage. Buried in the jungle 11km west of Xpujil and 400m south of Hwy 186, Chicanná is a mixture of Chenes and Río Bec architectural styles. The city attained its peak during the late Classic period, from AD 550 to 700, as a sort of elite suburb of Becán.

Río Bec Dreams (www.riobecdreams.com; Hwy 186 Km 142; cabañas for two M$620-1300, extra person M$180; P🛇) provides unquestionably the best accommodations in the area. This Canadian-run jungle lodge has thatched-roof 'jungalows' sharing a bathhouse, and *cabañas* with private bathrooms in the woods. Environmentally sound facilities include composting toilets, rainwater collection devices and solar electricity.

A taxi from Xpujil to Chicanná costs around M$400 (round trip including one hour waiting time).

Becán

Eight kilometers west of Xpujil, this archaeological **site** (M$48; ⊘8am-5pm) is perched atop a rock outcrop, encircled by a 2km moat that snakes its way around the entire city to protect it from attack. Becán (literally 'path of the snake') is also the Maya word for 'canyon' or 'moat.' Seven causeways crossed the moat, providing access to the city. Becán was occupied from 550 BC until AD 1000.

This is among the largest and most elaborate sites in the area. The first thing you'll come to is a plaza. If you walk while keeping it to your left, you'll pass through a rock-walled passageway and beneath a corbeled arch. You will soon reach a huge twin-towered temple with cylindrical columns at the top of a flight of stairs. This is Estructura VIII, dating from about AD 600 to 730. The view from the top of this temple has become partially obscured by the trees, but on a clear day you can still see structures at the Xpuhil ruins to the east.

Northwest of Estructura VIII is Plaza Central, ringed by 30m-high Estructura IX (the tallest building at the site) and the more interesting Estructura X. In early 2001, at X's far south side, a stucco mask still bearing some red paint was uncovered. It is enclosed in a wooden shelter with a window for viewing.

In the jungle to the west are more ruins, including the Plaza Oeste, which is surrounded by low buildings and a ball court. Much of this area is still being excavated and restored, so it's only intermittently open to the public.

Loop back east, through the passageway again, to the plaza; cross it diagonally to the right, climbing a stone staircase to the Plaza Sureste. Around this plaza are Estructuras I through IV; a circular altar (Estructura IIIA) lies on the east side. Estructura I has the two towers typical of the Río Bec style. To exit, you can go around the plaza counterclockwise and descend the stone staircase on the southeast side, or go down the southwest side and head left.

A taxi from Xpujil to Becán costs around M$400 (round trip including one hour waiting time).

XPUJIL

983 / POP 4000

The hamlet of Xpujil (pronounced 'shpu-heel') lies at the junction of Hwy 186 (which runs east to Chetumal and west to Chiapas) and Hwy 269, which runs north to meet Hwy 261 at Hopelchén, a short hop from Campeche. A good base from which to explore the area's sites, Xpujil is growing rapidly in the anticipation of a tourist boom. However, it still has no bank or laundry, and the nearest gas station is 5km east of town. Several restaurants, a couple of hotels and a taxi stand are near the bus depot.

From the junction, the ruins of Xpuhil are less than 1km west, Becán is 8km west, Chicanná is 11.5km west, Balamkú is 60km west and the Calakmul ruins are 120km southwest.

Sights

Xpuhil ARCHAEOLOGICAL SITE

(M$43; ⊙8am-5pm) On the west edge of town, the ruins of Xpuhil are a striking example of the Río Bec style. The three towers (rather than the usual two) of Estructura I rise above

a dozen vaulted rooms. The 53m central tower is the best preserved. With its banded tiers and impractically steep stairways leading up to a temple that displays traces of a zoomorphic mask, it gives you a good idea of what the other two towers must have looked like in Xpuhil's 8th-century heyday. Go around back to see a fierce jaguar mask embedded in the wall below the temple.

Tours

Servidores Turísticos Calakmul ECOTOUR

(983-871-60-64; www.ecoturismocalakmul.com; Carretera Escárcega-Chetumal, Km 153; ⊙9am-2pm & 3-7pm Mon-Sat) Servidores Turísticos Calakmul, around 200m east of the Xpujil junction, provides ecotours led by trained guides from nearby communities. In addition to tours of Maya sites in the area, it offers nature walks, plant identification, bird-watching and horseback riding tours, photo safaris and rural tourism experiences such as visits to beekeepers and organic farms. On one popular excursion you can observe millions of bats emerging from a cenote. One-day tours to Calakmul for up to 12 people cost M$900. It also rents bikes for M$150 a day. Look for head honchos Fernando and Leticia at the office or the Yaax'che campground along the road to Calakmul.

Sleeping

There are rustic hotels in town, and more accommodations in Zoh-Laguna, 10km north of Xpujil.

Hotel Calakmul HOTEL $

(983-871-60-29; www.hotelcalakmul.com.mx; Av Calakmul No 70; cabañas M$400; r from M$650; P ❄ 🛜 ≋) At the west end of town, about 350m west of the stoplight, is this large hotel. It has 27 small, tiled rooms with tiny bathrooms and little sitting areas out front. The six so-called 'cabañas,' near the parking lot, are tiny shacks set too close together and sharing outside bathrooms – a very odd combination with the more modern hotel. With luck they'll just tear them down to make more room around the new pool. There's a good restaurant on the premises (open 6am to midnight, mains M$60 to M$120).

Hotel Victoria HOTEL $

(983-871-60-27; Hwy 186; r with fan/air-con M$250/350; P ❄ @) The best of a clutch of fairly nondescript hotels around the main intersection, this one has large, clean rooms and a reasonable on-site restaurant.

Cabañas Mercedes
CABIN **$**

(☑ cell 983-114-97-69; Calle Zapote s/n; cabañas s/d M$250/300) Fifteen basic bungalows with mosquito nets, ceiling fans and open-shower bathrooms can be found at this rustic place. Decent meals are served in the thatched-roof restaurant (mains from M$80). Don Antonio is the well-informed host who knows about the area's ruins.

Eating

Aside from the hotel restaurants, there are various greasy spoons clustered around the bus station and roadside taquerías toward the Xpuhil ruins.

Concha del Caribe
MEXICAN **$**

(Hwy 186; mains M$80-130; ⊘ 7am-10pm) Opposite the bus terminal, this is a good choice for seafood, meat and snacks, washed down with an ice-cold *agua de jamaica* (hibiscus tea).

❶ Getting There & Around

No buses originate in Xpujil, so you just have to hope there's a vacant seat on one passing through. The **bus terminal** (☑ 983-871-60-27; Hwy 186) is just east of the Xpujil junction, on the north side of the highway. You can hire a taxi in town to take you to Zoh-Laguna for around M$80.

There are also taxi *colectivos* to Chetumal (M$120 per person, 1½ hours).

To reach Becán, Hormiguero, Calakmul or other sites you will need to book a tour or hire a cab. The taxi stand is on the north side of the junction.

SOUTH OF XPUJIL

Río Bec

Southeast of Xpujil, you can explore a series of remote Maya sites at Río Bec. You're best off hiring a guide with a 4WD truck; it's possible to arrange this in Xpujil or at the Ejido 20 de Noviembre (a collective farm located roughly 28km southeast of Xpujil). The going rate is around M$1000 per person, per day. A taxi from Xpujil would be the other option, although depending on road conditions, drivers may be reluctant to go. Alternatively, check with Río Bec Dreams (p344) near Chicanná.

Hormiguero

Spanish for 'anthill,' **Hormiguero** (⊘ 8am-5pm) **FREE** is an ancient site, with some buildings dating as far back as AD 50; however, the city flourished during the late Classic period. It has one of the most impressive buildings in the region. Entering the site, you will see the 50m-long Estructura II, which has a giant Chenes-style monster-mouth doorway with much of its decoration in good condition. Also check out Estructura V, 60m to the north.

Hormiguero is reached by heading 14km south from Xpujil junction, then turning right and heading another 8km west on a shoddily paved road. Taking a cab from Xpujil to Hormiguero will cost you around M$420.

Chiapas & Tabasco

Includes ➜

Tuxtla Gutiérrez 350
Chiapa de Corzo. . . . 355
San Cristóbal
de las Casas 358
Toniná. 378
Palenque 380
Bonampak, Yaxchilán
& the Carretera
Fronteriza 390
Comitán 400
Tapachula 409
Villahermosa 414

Why Go?

Chilly pine-forest highlands, sultry rainforest jungles and attractive colonial cities exist side by side within Mexico's southernmost states, a region awash with the legacy of Spanish rule and the remnants of ancient Maya civilization. Palenque and Yaxchilán are evocative vestiges of powerful Maya kingdoms, and the presence of modern Maya is a constant reminder of the region's rich and uninterrupted history. The colonial hubs of San Cristóbal de las Casas and Chiapa de Corzo give way to sandbar beaches and fertile plots of coffee and cacao in the Soconusco, and for outdoor adventurers, excursions to Laguna Miramar and the Cañón del Sumidero are unmissable.

Nature lovers willing to venture off the beaten track will swoon over the frothy cascades and exotic animals of the Lacandón Jungle and the El Triunfo reserve.

Best Hidden Waterfalls

➜ Las Nubes (p398)

➜ Cascada de las Golondrinas (p392)

➜ El Aguacero (p355)

➜ Tapijulapa (p417)

➜ El Chiflón (p402)

Best Places to Stay

➜ Casa Mexicana (p409)

➜ Hostal Tres Central (p351)

➜ Madre Sal (p407)

➜ La Joya Hotel (p367)

➜ Hotel Nak'am Secreto (p400)

When to Go
San Cristóbal de las Casas

Jan Fiesta Grande de Enero in Chiapa de Corzo, and San Juan Chamula's change of *cargo*-holders.

Jun–Nov Nesting season for sea turtles along the beaches of the Pacific coast.

Nov–Apr The driest months, though evenings in San Cristóbal are chilly November to February.

Chiapas & Tabasco Highlights

❶ Scaling the jungly hills and soaring Maya temples of **Palenque** (p380).

❷ Strolling the high-altitude cobblestone streets of **San Cristóbal de las Casas** (p358).

❸ Cruising through the waterway and sheer high rock cliffs of the spectacular **Cañón del Sumidero** (p357).

❹ Spending a few splendid days hiking and relaxing at pristine mountain-ringed **Laguna Miramar** (p399).

❺ Exploring the towering mangroves and watching for nesting turtles at **Madre Sal** (p407).

❻ Flitting between the sapphire and emerald lakes of **Lagos de Montebello** (p404).

❼ Wandering amid the roar of howler monkeys at the riverside Maya ruins of **Yaxchilán** (p397).

❽ Playing under the spray of **El Aguacero** (p355) and cooling off in a deep river canyon.

CHIAPAS

History

Low-lying, jungle-covered eastern Chiapas gave rise to some of the most splendid and powerful city-states of Maya civilization. During the Classic period (approximately AD 250–900), places such as Palenque, Yaxchilán and Toniná were the centers of power, though dozens of lesser Maya powers – including Bonampak, Comalcalco and Chinkultic – prospered in eastern Chiapas and Tabasco during this time, as Maya culture reached its peak of artistic and intellectual achievement. The ancestors of many of the distinctive indigenous groups of highland Chiapas today appear to have migrated to that region from the lowlands after the Classic Maya collapse around AD 900.

Central Chiapas was brought under Spanish control by the 1528 expedition of Diego de Mazariegos, and outlying areas were subdued in the 1530s and '40s, though Spain never gained full control of the Lacandón Jungle. New diseases arrived with the Spaniards, and an epidemic in 1544 killed about half of Chiapas' indigenous population. Chiapas was ineffectively administered from Guatemala for most of the colonial era, with little check on the colonists' excesses against its indigenous people, though some church figures, particularly Bartolomé de Las Casas (1474–1566), the first bishop of Chiapas, did fight for indigenous rights.

In 1822 a newly independent Mexico unsuccessfully attempted to annex Spain's former Central American provinces (including Chiapas), but in 1824 Chiapas opted (by a referendum) to join Mexico rather than the United Provinces of Central America. From then on, a succession of governors appointed by Mexico City, along with local landowners, maintained an almost feudal control over Chiapas.

Periodic uprisings bore witness to bad government, but the world took little notice until January 1, 1994, when Zapatista rebels suddenly and briefly occupied San Cristóbal de las Casas and nearby towns by military force. The rebel movement, with a firm and committed support base among disenchanted indigenous settlers in eastern Chiapas, quickly retreated to remote jungle bases to campaign for democratic change and indigenous rights. The Zapatistas have failed to win any significant concessions at the national level, although increased government funding steered toward Chiapas did result in noticeable improvements in the state's infrastructure, the development of tourist facilities and a growing urban middle class.

ⓘ Getting There & Around

Bus links within the region and to other states are very good; for regional routes, minibuses, combis and *colectivo* taxis are a speedier (though less spacious) alternative.

There aren't lots of car-rental options in Chiapas. Tuxtla Gutiérrez has a number of agencies both at the airport and in town, but otherwise it's pretty thin. San Cristóbal has one rental company, and there are a few in Tapachula. The only other convenient place to rent is Villahermosa, Tabasco.

Tuxtla Gutiérrez

✔ 961 / POP 550,000 / ELEV 530M

In Chiapas, Tuxtla Gutiérrez is as close to a big city as you're going to get. A busy modern metropolis and transportation hub, the state capital doesn't overwhelm with style, though it makes up for it with lots of amenities and nightlife. Most travelers pass through either the shiny modern airport or the bus station on the way to somewhere else, but it's a comfortable, worthwhile and warm place to spend a day or two.

A few blocks west of the Jardín de la Marimba, Avenida Central becomes Blvd Belisario Domínguez; many of the Tuxtla's best hotels and restaurants are strung along this road, as well as the city's big-box megastores.

◉ Sights

Zoológico Miguel Álvarez del Toro   ZOO
(Zoomat; www.zoomat.chiapas.gob.mx; Calz Cerro Hueco s/n; adult/child M$60/20, adult before 10am Wed-Sun M$30, Tue free; ⊘8:30am-4:30pm Tue-Sun) Chiapas, with its huge range of natural environments, has the highest concentration of animal species in North America, including several varieties of big cat, 1200 butterfly species and more than 600 birds. About 180 of these species, many of them in danger of extinction, are found in relatively spacious enclosures at Tuxtla's excellent zoo. Beasts you'll see here include ocelots, jaguars, pumas, tapirs, red macaws, toucans, snakes, spider monkeys and three species of crocodile.

Most interpretive materials are in both English and Spanish. To get to the zoo take a Ruta 60 'Zoológico' *colectivo* (M$8, 20 minutes) from the corner of 1a Calle Oriente Sur and 7a Avenida Sur Oriente. A taxi from the center costs around M$55.

Museo de la Marimba
MUSEUM

(9a Calle Poniente Norte; M$10, Sun free; ⊙ 10am-9pm Tue-Sun) On the Jardín de la Marimba, this small museum showcases 100 years of this ubiquitous instrument, with both antique and modern models on display and a photo exhibition of the most revered marimba performers.

Plaza Cívica
PLAZA

Bustling and broad, Tuxtla's main plaza occupies two blocks flanked by an untidy array of concrete government and commercial structures. At its southern end, across Avenida Central, you'll find nice hill views in front of the whitewashed modern **Catedral de San Marcos**. The cathedral's clock tower tinkles out a tune on the hour to accompany a kitsch merry-go-round of apostles' images, which emerges from its upper levels.

Museo del Café
MUSEUM

(www.museodelcafe.chiapas.gob.mx; 2a Calle Oriente Norte 236; adult/child M$10/5; ⊙ 9am-5pm Mon-Sat) Operated by the state government, this small museum contains exhibits (descriptions in Spanish only) on the cultivation and processing of everyone's favorite bean. The rooms are pleasantly air-conditioned and visitors receive a cup of brew to savor in the building's pretty courtyard.

Parque Madero
PARK

The park's **Museo Regional de Chiapas** (☏ 961-613-43-75; Calz de los Hombres Ilustres; M$48; ⊙ 9am-6pm Tue-Sun), an imposing modern building, has a sampling of lesser archaeological pieces from Chiapas' many sites, and a slightly more interesting history section, running from the Spanish conquest to the revolution, all in Spanish only.

Parque Madero also contains the lush oasis of the **Jardín Botánico** FREE and a low-key children's theme park.

Take a Ruta 3 or 20 *colectivo* from 6a Av Norte Poniente.

🧭 Tours

Transporte Panorámico Cañón del Sumidero
TOUR

(☏ cell 961-1663740) Daily bus tours leave from Tuxtla's Jardín de la Marimba at 9:30am and 1pm if a minimum of five people show up. Three tours are available: viewing the canyon from above at five *miradores*

JARDÍN DE LA MARIMBA

To take your *paseo* (stroll) with the locals, stop by this leafy plaza in the evening. It's located eight blocks west of Plaza Cívica, and the whole city seems to turn out here for the free nightly marimba concerts (6pm to 9pm), especially at weekends. Couples of all ages dance around the central bandstand, and the scores of sidewalk cafes – which stay open until at least 10pm or 11pm – serve some of the best coffee in town.

(lookout points; M$150, 2½ hours), a *lancha* (motorboat) trip with return transportation (M$390, 4½ hours) and an all-day *miradores* and *lancha* trip (M$450, morning departure only). Call a day beforehand to confirm departures.

Private regional tours also available.

🛏 Sleeping

Good budget hotels cluster in the city center, while most midrange and luxury hotels – primarily big international chains – are strung out along Avenida Central Poniente and Blvd Belisario Domínguez west of the center. The larger hotels offer sizable online and weekend discounts.

★Hostal Tres Central
HOSTEL $

(☏ 961-611-36-74; www.facebook.com/TresCentral; Calle Central Norte 393; dm M$150, r with/without bathroom M$573/375; P ❄ ✳ @ 🛜) Tuxtla's one and only hostel is a stylish Ikea-esque respite with ubercomfortable beds in either four-person dorms or spacious two-bed privates (those with shared bathroom have a shower and sink in the room). The rooftop terrace views of the surrounding hills can't be beat. No kitchen facilities, though there is an on-site cafe/bar.

Hotel Catedral
HOTEL $

(☏ 961-613-08-24; www.hotel-catedral.net; 1a Av Norte Oriente 367; s/d M$350/400, with air-con M$450/500; P ❄ ✳ 🛜) A friendly family-run place, this excellent budget option has neat, superclean rooms with dark wood furniture and ceiling fans. It also has comfortable hall couches. Pass on the noisier downstairs rooms off the lobby. Free drinking water and morning coffee.

CHIAPAS & TABASCO TUXTLA GUTIÉRREZ

Tuxtla Gutiérrez

Hotel del Carmen
HOTEL **$$**

(☎961-612-30-84; www.hoteldelcarmen.net; 2a Av Sur Poniente 826; r M$700, incl breakfast M$740; ❄🛜) This hotel is an excellent midrange option in a great spot between the old and new parts of town. Rooms are large and charmingly simple and there's a good restaurant on-site.

Hotel Santa María
HOTEL **$$**

(☎961-614-65-77; hotelsantamariatuxtla@hotmail. com; 8a Calle Poniente Norte 160; r M$480-700; P❄🛜) Situated on the pretty Jardín de la Marimba and near a number of good coffeehouses, this small hotel has slightly aging rooms featuring folksy decorations and decent bathrooms with mosaic tiling.

Hotel María Eugenia
HOTEL **$$**

(☎961-613-37-67; www.mariaeugenia.com.mx; Av Central Oriente 507; s/d M$960/1050, d Fri & Sat M$575; P❄@🛜) A good full-service option in the center, its 83 airy, bright and spacious rooms have either a king-sized bed or two double beds, and many have great views.

Hilton Garden Inn
HOTEL **$$$**

(☎961-617-18-00; www.tuxtlagutierrez.hgi.com; cnr Blvds Belisario Domínguez & Los Castillos; r/ ste M$1460/1770; P❄❄@🛜) The luxurious 167-room Hilton sits in a commercial area 2.5km west of the Jardín de la Marimba. Gadget-lovers will appreciate the Mp3 player/alarm clock, adjustable pillow-top mattresses and internet-ready televisions, and style fans will groove on the rainforest showerheads and Herman Miller chairs.

✗ Eating

Lots of upscale and international chain options are west of the center, along Blvd Belisario Domínguez, and a number of enjoyable cafes cluster in the center around the Jardín de la Marimba.

Tuxtla Gutiérrez

◎ Sights

1 Catedral de San Marcos C3
2 Jardín Botánico......................................F1
3 Jardín de la Marimba..........................A2
4 Museo de la Marimba..........................A2
5 Museo del Café....................................D2
6 Museo Regional de Chiapas F1
7 Parque Madero.....................................F1
8 Plaza Cívica..C2

◎ Activities, Courses & Tours

9 Transporte Panorámico Cañón
   del Sumidero A2

◎ Sleeping

10 Hostal Tres Central C2
11 Hotel Catedral D2
12 Hotel del Carmen...............................A3
13 Hotel María Eugenia D3
14 Hotel Santa María A2

◎ Eating

15 Cafetería del Parque...........................A2
16 Horno Mágico.....................................D3
17 Las Pichanchas E3
18 Restaurante La Casona C3

2:30-10:30pm Sun; 🛜) Thin-crust wood-fired pizza, washed down with craft beer in *Tuxtla*? Yep – this is the most frequently recommended pizzeria in town, for a reason. The atmosphere's just right, prices are reasonable and there's occasional live music.

Las Pichanchas CHIAPANECO **$$**
(www.laspichanchas.com.mx; Av Central Oriente 837; mains M$120-180; ☺noon-midnight; 😊🚐) This courtyard restaurant specializes in Chiapas food with live marimba music and, from 8:30pm to 10pm every night, a show of colorful traditional Chiapas dances that whips up quite a party atmosphere. Try the tasty *tamales* or *pechuga jacuané* (chicken breast stuffed with beans in a *hoja santa* sauce), and leave room for *chimbos*, a dessert made from egg yolks and cinnamon.

Ring the bell over the table to order the signature Pumpo drink.

❶ Information

There's an ATM at the departure level of the airport.

Banorte (Av Central Oriente, btwn 2a & 3a Calle Oriente Sur; ☺9am-5pm Mon-Fri, to 2pm Sat) Changes dollars.

Post Office (2a Calle Oriente Norte 227; ☺8am-5pm Mon-Fri, 10am-2pm Sat) In the Palacio Federal.

★**Restaurante La Casona** MEXICAN **$**
(1a Av Sur Poniente 134; breakfast M$40-70, mains M$60-95; ☺7am-10pm; 😊) Beyond the stately carved wooden doors is a dramatic tableclothed dining room with high ceilings and interior arches in a century-old building. Dine on regional dishes such as *pollo juchi* (fried chicken with pickled vegetables and potatoes) or *tasajo en salsa de chirmol* (sliced beef in tomato sauce) and listen to marimba performances from 2pm to 6pm.

Horno Mágico BAKERY, CAFE **$**
(2a Calle Oriente Norte 116; pastries around M$30; ☺8:30am-10pm; 😊) A new outpost of the San Cristóbal fave, with tasty fresh croissants and pastries and an air-conditioned upstairs for sipping espresso. Live music some nights.

Florentina Pizza PIZZERIA **$$**
(12a Poniente Norte 174; mains from M$110; ☺5pm-midnight Tue-Fri, 2:30pm-12:30am Sat,

Municipal Tourism Office (9a Calle Poniente Norte; ⊙ 9am-2pm & 4-8pm) Inside the Museo de la Marimba.

Secretaría de Turismo (☑ 961-617-05-50, 800-280-35-00; www.turismochiapas.gob.mx; ⊙ 8am-4pm Mon-Fri, 9am-1pm Sat) The main state tourism office has a toll-free phone number for Chiapas information; English speakers rarely available.

Scotiabank (cnr Ave Central Oriente & 4a Calle Oriente; ⊙ 8:30am-4pm Mon-Fri)

ℹ Getting There & Away

AIR

Tuxtla's small and gleaming **Aeropuerto Ángel Albino Corzo** (☑ 961-153-60-68; www.chiapas aero.com; Sarabia s/n) is 35km southeast of the city center and 18km south of Chiapa de Corzo. Aeroméxico (www.aeromexico.com), Interjet (www.interjet.com.mx) and Volaris (www.volaris. mx) have nonstop services to Mexico City. Aerotucán (www.aerotucan.com.mx) has direct flights to Oaxaca, while VivaAerobus (www. vivaaerobus.com.mx) has services to Cancún, Guadalajara and Monterrey.

BUS, COLECTIVO & COMBI

Free wi-fi and a huge contiguous supermarket are bonuses of the modern **OCC terminal** (☑ 961-125-15-80, ext 2433; 5a Av Norte Poniente 318). It's about 2.5km northwest of the Jardín de la Marimba and houses all the 1st-class and deluxe buses and the 2nd-class Rápidos del Sur line. OCC and ADO tickets can also be purchased at **Boletotal** (1a Av Norte Poniente 944; ⊙ 8am-10pm Mon-Fri, 10am-6pm Sat & Sun), alongside the Jardín de la Marimba. More 2nd-class buses and combis depart from the **Terminal de Transporte Tuxtla** (cnr 9a Av Sur Oriente & 13a Calle Oriente Sur), with frequent departures for destinations including San Cristóbal, Ocosingo and Ocozocoautla.

For Chiapa de Corzo (M$15, 45 minutes), combis leave every few minutes between 5am and 10:30pm from 1a Avenida Sur Oriente.

To San Cristóbal

For San Cristóbal de las Casas (M$50, one hour), minibuses and combis are faster and more frequent (every 10 minutes) than the bus.

Corazón de María (13a Calle Oriente Sur) Combis depart from a storefront near Av Central Oriente; services 4am to 9pm.

Ómnibus de Chiapas (cnr 15a Calle Oriente Sur & 4a Av Sur Oriente) Comfortable minibuses (called 'sprinters'); departures 5am to 10pm.

CAR & MOTORCYCLE

In addition to companies at the airport, in-town rental agencies include an **Alamo** (www.alamo. com; 5a Av Norte Poniente 2260), near the OCC bus station, and **Europcar** (www.europcar.com; Blvd Belisario Domínguez 2075).

ℹ Getting Around

TO/FROM THE AIRPORT

From the airport, prepay taxis (one to three passengers) meet all flights and go to central Tuxtla (M$230, 40 minutes), Chiapa de Corzo (M$270, 30 minutes) and San Cristóbal (M$650 private or M$220 shared, one hour). OCC runs minibuses directly from the terminal to San Cristóbal (M$210) at 9am, 10am, 1pm, 3:30pm, 4pm and 8:30pm, though the schedule is subject to change.

Monarca Viajes (☑ cell 961-1328191; monarcaviajes@hotmail.com) does door-to-

BUSES FROM TUXTLA GUTIÉRREZ

DESTINATION	FARE (M$)	DURATION (HR)	FREQUENCY (DAILY)
Cancún	1130-1340	17-20	5
Comitán	100	3	frequent
Mérida	856-1376	13-14	5
Mexico City (TAPO & Norte)	1164-1418	11½-12	11
Oaxaca	644	10	9:30pm
Palenque	262-320	6-6½	6
Puerto Escondido	578	11-12	2
San Cristóbal de las Casas	52-64	1¼	frequent
Tapachula	394-446	4½-6	frequent
Tonalá	144-216	2-2½	frequent
Villahermosa	336-434	4-5	12

door transfers between town and the airport for M$300 (one to three passengers); reserve in advance.

BUS, COLECTIVO & COMBI

A biodiesel bus service called ConejoBus (M$6; ☺ 5am-11pm) plies Blvd Belisario Domínguez–Avenida Central; you'll need a prepaid card (M$5 from the Palacio de Gobierno on the Parque Central) to ride. For other areas, consult www.tuxmapa.com.mx for local combi routes. Taxi rides within the city cost M$40 to M$50.

West of Tuxtla Gutiérrez

Consider renting a car in Tuxtla to hit both the Sima de las Cotorras and El Aguacero, though tour agencies in both Tuxtla and San Cristóbal can organize day trips here. To get there independently, you'll need to travel via Ocozocoautla (also called Coita); from Tuxtla's Terminal de Transporte Tuxtla, take the minibus with a pineapple on its side (M$15, 30 minutes). A number of tour agencies in San Cristóbal offer rafting, climbing and hiking expeditions into the incredible Río La Venta canyon, one of the most beautiful and least visited natural attractions of Chiapas.

Sima de las Cotorras

The **Sima de las Cotorras** (Abyss of the Parrots; www.simaecoturismo.com; adult/child under 10yr M$20/free; ☺6am-7pm)) is a dramatic 160m-wide sinkhole that punches 140m down into the earth. At sunrise, a green cloud of screeching parrots spirals out for the day, trickling back before dusk. With binoculars you can see a series of red pre-Hispanic rock paintings that decorate one side of the cliff face, and you can also hike or rappel down inside this intriguing subterranean hole.

Lodging (☑cell 968-1178081; d/tr/6-person cabañas M$400/600/1000; ℗☺) and campsites are available (the spacious six-person, two-room *cabañas* (cabins) are well worth the extra cost), and there is a good **restaurant** perched on the edge of the sinkole, which serves scrumptious *tamales* and handmade tortillas.

From the last stop in Ocozocoautla (Coita), located on Hwy 190 right at the signed turnoff for the Sima, take a taxi (around M$300, 50 minutes). Three daily Piedra Parada *colectivos* (M$13) also leave from this stop, but let you off 4km before

the Sima. Driving from Tuxtla, it's reasonably well signed all the way. Go all the way through Ocozocoautla, turning right at the minibus terminal (there's a blue turnoff sign here, but it's not visible coming from this direction), go 3.5km north, then 12km on a good dirt road.

El Aguacero

Forget the gym – the 724 well-built steps to this **cascade** (www.cascadaelaguacero.com; M$25; ☺7am-5pm) will suffice as your daily workout. Plunging into the sheer Río La Venta canyon, El Aguacero is a gorgeous series of frothy stair-steps that tumble and spray. In dryer months (usually December through May), you can stroll along sandy riverbed beaches to the waterfall. When the water's high, it's a half-hour hike from the staircase along a shady jungle trail.

The entrance fee allows you access to the parking facilities, restrooms and showers. Camping and hammock space (also with showers) are available, and there is a restaurant as well as a small *comedor* (food stall), usually serving quesadillas.

From Ocozocoautla (Coita), *colectivos* to El Gavilán/Las Cruces can drop you off at the highway turnoff, and it's a 3km walk down to the entrance. If the stairs up from the river leave you in a heap, management charges around M$70 per vanload to drive you back up or M$200 for a ride to or from Ocozocoautla. Drivers should look for the turnoff sign about 15km west of Ocozocoautla.

Chiapa de Corzo

🌐961 / POP 45,000 / ELEV 450M

An overlooked jewel set 12km east of Tuxtla Gutiérrez on the way to San Cristóbal, Chiapa de Corzo is a small and attractive colonial town with an easygoing, provincial air. Set on the north bank of the broad Río Grijalva, it's the main starting point for trips into the Cañón del Sumidero.

Chiapa de Corzo has been occupied almost continuously since about 1200 BC. Before the Spaniards arrived, the warlike Chiapa tribe had their capital, Nandalumí, a couple of kilometers downstream, on the opposite bank of the Grijalva. When Diego de Mazariegos invaded the area in 1528, the Chiapa hurled themselves by the hundreds to their death in the canyon rather than surrender.

Mazariegos founded a settlement called Chiapa de Los Indios here, but quickly shifted his base to San Cristóbal de las Casas, where he found the climate and indigenous inhabitants more manageable.

◉ Sights

The *embarcadero* (jetty) for Cañón del Sumidero boat trips is two blocks south of the plaza down 5 de Febrero. Look for the road lined with vendors.

Plaza
PLAZA

Impressive arcades frame three sides of the plaza, and a beefy tree called La Pochota buckles the sidewalk with its centuries-old roots. Venerated by the indigenous people who founded the town, it's the oldest ceiba tree along the Río Grijalva. But the focal point of the plaza is La Pila (also called the Fuente Colonial), a handsome brick fountain completed in 1562 in Mudejar-Gothic style. It's said to resemble the Spanish crown.

Templo de Santo Domingo de Guzmán
CHURCH

(Mexicanidad Chiapaneca 10) The large Templo de Santo Domingo de Guzmán, one block south of the main plaza, was built in the late 16th century by the Dominican order. Its adjoining convent is now the **Centro Cultural** (☑997-616-00-55; Mexicanidad Chiapaneca 10; ⊙10am-5pm Tue-Sun) FREE, home to an exposition of the wood and lino prints of talented Chiapa-born Franco Lázaro Gómez (1922–49), as well as the Museo de la Laca, which is dedicated to the local craft specialty: lacquered gourds. The museum holds pieces dating back to 1606.

Chiapa de Corzo Archaeological Site
ARCHAEOLOGICAL SITE

(Av Hidalgo, Barrio Benito Juárez; ⊙8am-4:30pm) FREE On a trade route between the Pacific and the Gulf, the sprawling Chiapa de Corzo settlement had close ties to neighboring Maya and Olmec cultures. At its peak, it counted about 200 structures, but was abandoned around AD 500. After years of excavation, three Zoque pyramid structures are now on view here, 1.5km east of the main plaza. These visible structures were built between 1600 and 1800 years ago, but sit on mounds dating back as far as 750 BC.

Though the guarded ruins receive few visitors, it's worth an hour to climb around the deserted temples and marvel at the big-sky countryside. Recent excavation of one nearby mound (not open to the public) unearthed the oldest known pyramid tomb in Mesoamerica and new evidence linking it to Olmec centers such as La Venta.

The site entrance is near the Nestlé plant and the old highway (on the road that goes to La Topada de la Flor), but the site isn't signed from the road. Taxis charge about M$150 round trip from the plaza with an hour of wait time.

✦ Festivals & Events

Fiesta Grande de Enero
CULTURAL

Held for a week in mid-January, this is one of Mexico's liveliest and most extraordinary festivals, including nightly dances involving cross-dressing young men, known as Las Chuntá. Women don the highly colorful, beautifully embroidered *chiapaneca* dress, and blond-wigged, mask-toting *Parachicos* (impersonating conquistadors) parade on a number of days. A canoe battle and fireworks extravaganza follow on the final evening.

🛏 Sleeping

Posada Rocio
HOTEL $

(☑961-616-02-04; Zaragoza 347; s/d from M$300/360; ⊛) Just off the main plaza, this humble little setup ticks all the budget-hotel boxes with its decent-sized, clean rooms, friendly management and a good location.

Hotel La Ceiba
HOTEL $$

(☑961-616-03-89; www.laceibahotel.com; Av Domingo Ruíz 300; r/tr M$780/1030; P⊛❄☏⊛) The most upscale place in town (though the rooms are quite simple), La Ceiba has a full-service spa and restaurant, an inviting pool, a lush garden and 87 well-kept air-conditioned rooms with cable TV. It's two blocks west of the main plaza.

Hotel Santiago
HOTEL $$

(☑cell 961-1531049; www.hoteldesantiago.com; López s/n; r M$653; ⊛) Down by the port, this medium-sized hotel has plenty of colonial stylings from the outside but very few on the inside. Rooms are arranged around a central patio/ lightwell and are big, comfortable and simple. It's a quiet spot (except in festival time of course) despite its central location. If you're here in low season definitely ask for a discount.

Eating

Restaurants on the *embarcadero* have near-identical, and equally overpriced, menus. The river views are nice, though battling marimba players tend to amp up the noise level. The market (southeast of the plaza) is your best bet for an inexpensive meal. *Tascalate* (a sweet concoction of ground cacao, pine nuts, toasted corn, cinnamon and annatto) can be found on most menus, and many shops sell the drink powder.

Restaurant Los Corredores   CHIAPANECO $
(Madero 35; mains M$80-150; ⊘8am-6:30pm; 🖐) Facing the southwest corner of the main plaza, Los Corredores does a bit of everything: good breakfasts, reasonably priced fish plates and a few local specialties including *pepita con tasajo* (beef with a spicy pumpkin-seed sauce). It displays a fascinating collection of historical town photos.

**Restaurant Jardines
de Chiapa**   CHIAPANECO $$
(www.restaurantesjardines.com.mx; Madero 395; mains M$95-180; ⊘9am-6pm; 🖐) Not too far from the main plaza, this large place is set around a garden patio with atmospheric brick columns. The long menu includes tasty *cochinito al horno* (oven-baked pork).

Ombaba   INTERNATIONAL $$
(Victorico Grajales s/n; mains M$90-160; ⊘1-11pm Tue-Sun) Doing a little bit of everything (and a very good job of it), this newish restaurant claims to be a steakhouse, but also has very good seafood and traditional dishes on offer. A few craft beers, a good wine list and a selection of fresh juices make up the drinks menu.

ℹ Information

The **state tourism office** (☑961-616-10-13; 5 de Febrero s/n; ⊘8am-4pm Mon-Fri, 9am-1pm Sat) is in the Municipal building in front of the main plaza. You'll also find ATMs around the plaza.

ℹ Getting There & Away

Combis from Tuxtla Gutiérrez (M$11, 45 minutes) leave frequently from 1a Avenida Sur Oriente (between Calles 5a and 7a Oriente Sur) between 5am and 10:30pm. They arrive (and return to Tuxtla) from the north side of the main plaza.

There's no direct transportation between San Cristóbal and the center of Chiapa de Corzo. From San Cristóbal, catch a Tuxtla-bound combi and ask to be let off at the Chiapa de Corzo stop on the highway (M$35, 30 minutes). From there, cross the highway and flag down a combi (M$6) to the plaza. From Chiapa de Corzo to San Cristóbal, catch a combi from the plaza back to the highway and then flag down a combi heading to San Cristóbal. You'll rarely wait more than a few minutes for a connecting combi in either direction.

DON'T MISS

CAÑÓN DEL SUMIDERO

The Sumidero Canyon is a spectacular fissure in the earth, found north of Tuxtla Gutiérrez. In 1981 the Chicoasén hydroelectric dam was completed at its northern end, damming the Río Grijalva, which flows through the canyon, and creating a 25km-long reservoir. Traveling between Tuxtla and Chiapa de Corzo, the road crosses the Grijalva just south of the canyon mouth.

The most impressive way to see the canyon is from a **lancha** (motorboat; return trip M$210; ⊘8am-4pm) that speeds between the canyon's towering rock walls. It's about a two-hour return trip, starting at either Chiapa de Corzo or the Embarcadero Cahuaré, 5km north of Chiapa along the road to Tuxtla. You'll rarely have to wait more than half an hour for a boat to fill up. Bring a drink, something to shield you from the sun and, if there's any chance of bad weather, some warm clothing or a waterproof jacket.

It's about 35km from Chiapa de Corzo to the dam. Soon after you pass under Hwy 190, the canyon walls tower an amazing 800m above you. Along the way you'll see a variety of birds – herons, cormorants, vultures, kingfishers – plus probably a crocodile or two. The boat operators will point out a few odd formations of rock and vegetation, including one cliff face covered in thick hanging moss, resembling a giant Christmas tree. *Lanchas* sometimes have to plow through a sheen of floating plastic garbage when wet-season rains wash in trash from Tuxtla Gutiérrez.

San Cristóbal de las Casas

📍 967 / POP 170,000 / ELEV 1940M

Set in a gorgeous highland valley surrounded by pine forest, the colonial city of San Cristóbal (cris-*toh*-bal) has been a popular travelers' destination for decades. It's a pleasure to explore San Cristóbal's cobbled streets and markets, soaking up the unique ambience and the wonderfully clear highland light. This medium-sized city also boasts a comfortable blend of city and countryside, with restored century-old houses giving way to grazing animals and fields of corn.

Surrounded by dozens of traditional Tzotzil and Tzeltal villages, San Cristóbal is at the heart of one of the most deeply rooted indigenous areas in Mexico. A great base for local and regional exploration, it's a place where ancient customs coexist with modern luxuries.

The city is a hot spot for sympathizers (and some opponents) of the Zapatista rebels, and a central location for organizations working with Chiapas' indigenous people. In addition to a solid tourist infrastructure and a dynamic population of artsy and politically progressive foreigners and Mexicans, San Cristóbal also has a great selection of accommodations and a cosmopolitan array of cafes, bars and restaurants.

History

Diego de Mazariegos founded San Cristóbal as the Spanish regional base in 1528. Its Spanish citizens made fortunes from wheat, while the indigenous people lost their lands and suffered diseases, taxes and forced labor. The church afforded some protection against colonist excesses. Dominican monks reached Chiapas in 1545, and made San Cristóbal their main base. The town is now named after one of them, Bartolomé de Las Casas, who was appointed bishop of Chiapas and became the most prominent Spanish defender of indigenous people in colonial times. In modern times Bishop Samuel Ruiz, who passed away in 2011, followed in Las Casas' footsteps, defending the oppressed indigenous people and earning the hostility of the Chiapas establishment.

San Cristóbal was the state capital of Chiapas from 1824 to 1892, but remained relatively isolated until the 1970s, when tourism began to influence its economy. Recent decades have seen an influx of indigenous villagers into the 'Cinturón de Miseria' (Belt of Misery), a series of impoverished, violence-ridden, makeshift colonies around San Cristóbal's *periférico* (ring road). Many of these people are here because they have been expelled from Chamula and other communities as a result of internal politico-religious conflicts. Most of the craft sellers

CHIAPAS & TABASCO SAN CRISTÓBAL DE LAS CASAS

SAN CRISTÓBAL IN...

Two Days

Start the day inhaling the rich aroma of a locally roasted cup of **Chiapan coffee** and then limber up with a **yoga class**. Put on some comfortable walking shoes and explore the colonial churches of **Templo de Santo Domingo** (p363) and the **cathedral** (p363), and then get lofty, climbing the twin hills of **Cerro de San Cristóbal** and **Cerro de Guadalupe** (p367) to survey the city.

Spend the second day visiting the traditional indigenous villages of **San Lorenzo Zinacantán** (p375) and **San Juan Chamula** (p374) by horseback or bicycle, and in the evening drop by a **cinema** to catch a movie on local history or current events.

Four Days

With more time, build on the itinerary above and refresh your sagging Spanish with a few days of **language classes**. You can dig deeper into the local culture with visits to the **Museo de la Medicina Maya** (p359) and the ethno-history landmark of **Na Bolom** (p359).

Browse for the best of local *artesanías* at **women's weaving cooperatives** and the paper- and book-making workshop of **Taller Leñateros** (p371). Jaunt out of town to gawk at the trippy cave formations at the **Grutas de San Cristóbal** (p376). Linger over cocktails and snacks at a convivial bar and groove to the music at **Café Bar Revolucion** (p370).

around Santo Domingo church and the underage hawkers around town come from the Cinturón de Miseria.

San Cristóbal was catapulted into the international limelight on January 1, 1994, when the Zapatista rebels selected it as one of four places from which to launch their revolution, seizing and sacking government offices in the town before being driven out within a few days by the Mexican army. Political and social tensions remain, but San Cristóbal continues to attract travelers, real estate investment and a growing middle class.

San Cristóbal and Los Altos de Chiapas – the state's central highlands, mostly 2000m to 3000m high – have a temperate climate. Daytime temperatures are usually warm, but evenings can get very cold between November and February, when you'll want a good jacket to ward off chill.

⊙ Sights

San Cristóbal is very walkable, with straight streets rambling up and down several gentle hills. Heading east from Plaza 31 de Marzo, Real de Guadalupe has a pedestrian-only section with a concentration of places to stay and eat. Another pedestrian mall, the Andador Turístico, runs up Hidalgo and Avenida 20 de Noviembre.

★**Na Bolom**   HISTORIC BUILDING
(www.na-bolom.org; Guerrero 33; M$40, with tour M$50; ⊙7am-7pm) An atmospheric museum-research center, Na Bolom for many years was the home of Swiss anthropologist and photographer Gertrude Duby-Blom (Trudy Blom; 1901–93) and her Danish archaeologist husband Frans Blom (1893–1963). Na Bolom means 'Jaguar House' in the Tzotzil language (as well as being a play on its former owners' name). It's full of photographs, archaeological and anthropological relics and books.

The house tour provides a revealing insight into the lives of the Bloms and the Chiapas of half a century and more ago – though the picture presented of the Lacandones does dwell more on their past than their present. The Bloms bought the 19th-century house in 1950, and while Frans explored and surveyed ancient Maya sites all over Chiapas (including Palenque, Toniná and Chinkultic), Trudy studied, photographed and fought to protect the scattered Lacandón people of eastern Chiapas and their jungle environment.

DON'T MISS

CENTRO DE TEXTILES DEL MUNDO MAYA

Upstairs inside the Ex-Convento de Santo Domingo, this excellent **museum** (Calz Lázaro Cárdenas; admission M$52; ⊙9am-6pm Tue-Sun) showcases over 500 examples of handwoven textiles from throughout Mexico and Central America. Two permanent exhibition rooms display *huipiles* (sleeveless tunics) – including a 1000-year-old relic fashioned from tree bark. Videos show how materials and clothes are created, and there are some explanations in English. Admission is bundled with the **Museo de los Altos de Chiapas** (p363).

Since Trudy's death, Na Bolom has continued the thrust of the Bloms' work, with the house operating as a museum and research center for the study and support of Chiapas' indigenous cultures and natural environment, and as a center for community and environmental programs in indigenous areas. The library of more than 9000 books and documents here is a major resource on the Maya.

Na Bolom also offers guest rooms (p367) and meals made with organic vegetables grown in its garden.

★**Museo de la Medicina Maya**   MUSEUM
(Av Salomón González Blanco 10; M$20; ⊙10am-6pm Mon-Fri, to 4pm Sat & Sun) This award-winning museum on the northern edge of town introduces the system of traditional medicine used by many indigenous people in the Chiapas highlands. Exhibits include displays of a ritual scene inside a church and a midwife assisting at a birth, a dated video about the work of traditional midwives and a new display about the issue of native plants and corporate biopiracy.

The museum is run by Organización de Médicos Indígenas del Estado de Chíapas (Omiech), a group of 600 indigenous healers, midwives, herbalists and prayer specialists. Traditional Maya medicine is a matter of praying to the spirit of the earth, listening to the voice of the blood and expelling bad spirits from the soul, with the aid of candles, bones, pine needles, herbs and the occasional chicken sacrifice. Information is available in English,

San Cristóbal de las Casas

400 m
0.2 miles

Museo de la Medicina Maya (400m)

Río Amarillo

Combis to San Juan Chamula

Honduras

Colombia

Real de Mexicanos

Brasil

Venezuela

Argentina

Canada

Natutours (300m)

Río Amarillo

Puente Tiboli

Caminero 47

Mercado Municipal

Combis to Zinacantán

Combis to San Juan Chamula

Robledo

Diaz Ordaz

Bermudas

Tonalá

Diagonal Arriaga

Utrilla

Utrilla

Calz Lazaro Cardenas

Av 16 de Septiembre

Escuadrón 201

Av 5 de Mayo

Av 12 de Octubre

Plaza

Centro de Textiles del Mundo Maya

81

12

13

19

34

76

28

32

27

46

33

9

72

44

29

36

23

15

Tercera Calle

Segunda Calle

Primera Calle

Dugelay

Chiapa de Corzo

Colón

Colón

Comitán

Tapachula

Yajalon

Dr. Navarro

Av 20 de Noviembre

Calle 28 de Agosto

Calle 1 de Marzo

Av 5 de Mayo

Calle 5 de Febrero

43

19

Calz Roberta

Calz Franz Blom

Na Bolom

2

41

Guerrero

Huixtla

Cintalapa

Ejército Nacional

Belisario Domínguez

Paniagua

MA Flores

Colón

Real de Guadalupe

Isabel La Católica

Ejército Nacional

Real de Guadalupe

Cerro de Guadalupe (150m)

7

22

82

55

79

40

56

CHIAPAS & TABASCO

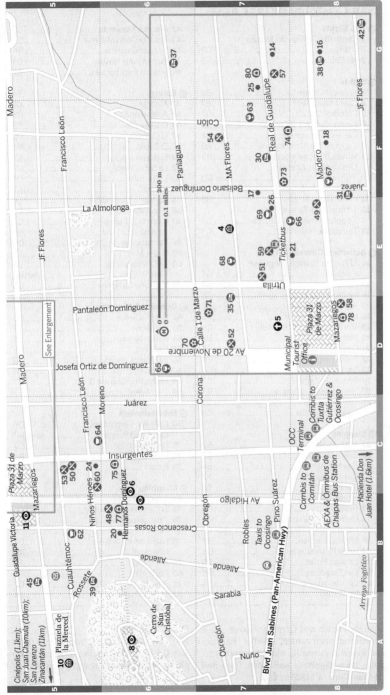

San Cristóbal de las Casas

⊚ Top Sights
1 Centro de Textiles del Mundo
  Maya C3
2 Na Bolom F3

⊚ Sights
3 Arco del Carmen B6
4 Café Museo Café.. E7
5 Catedral.. D7
6 Centro Cultural El Carmen C6
7 Cerro de Guadalupe G4
8 Cerro de San Cristóbal A6
9 Museo Bichos e Insectos B3
  Museo de los Altos de
  Chiapas .... (see 12)
10 Museo del Ámbar de Chiapas A5
11 Plaza 31 de Marzo B5
12 Templo & Ex-Convento de
  Santo Domingo de Guzmán C3
13 Templo de la Caridad C3

⊙ Activities, Courses & Tours
14 El Puente Spanish Language
  School.. G7
15 Explora A4
16 Instituto de Lenguas Jovel..................... G8
17 Jaguar Adventours F7
18 La Casa en el Árbol F8
19 Marcosapata o En Bici Tours C3
20 Nichim Tours B6
21 Otisa E8
22 Petra Vertical.. F4
23 SendaSur B4
24 Shaktipat Yoga C5
25 Tienda de Experiencias G7
26 Trotamundos... B4
  Viajes Chincultik.......................... (see 30)

⊜ Sleeping
27 Anthara Hotel B2
28 Bela's B&B C3
29 Casa de Alma.. B4
30 Casa Margarita... F7
31 Docecuartos F8
32 Hostal Akumal B3
33 Hotel b'o.. B3
34 Hotel Casa Mexicana............................... C4
35 Hotel Diego de Mazariegos D7
36 Hotel El Paraíso B4
37 Hotel Posada Jovel G6
38 La Joya Hotel G8
39 Las Escaleras.. B5
40 Le Gite del Sol.. E4
41 Na Bolom F3

42 Parador Margarita.................................... G8
43 Posada Corto Maltese D3
44 Posada Ganesha....................................... B4
45 Puerta Vieja Hostel.................................. B5
46 Rossco Backpackers B2

⊗ Eating
47 Alebrije C1
48 Anabanana B6
49 Crustaceos E8
50 El Caldero C5
  El Eden ....(see 36)
51 El Horno Mágico E7
52 La Salsa Verde.. D7
53 La Tertulia C5
54 Mumo F7
55 No Name Quesadillas E4
56 Pierre Restaurant Francés..................... E4
57 Pizzería El Punto....................................... G7
  Restaurante LUM ....(see 33)
58 Sensaciones de Chiapas D8
59 Super Más E7
60 Te Quiero Verde.. C5
  TierrAdentro.....................................(see 69)
61 Trattoria La Nonna................................... C3

⊜ Drinking & Nightlife
62 Café La Selva B5
63 Cocoliche F7
64 Kakao Natura C5
65 La Ruina D6
66 La Viña de Bacco E8
67 Latino's F8
68 Mezcalería Gusana Grela E7
69 TierrAdentro E7

⊛ Entertainment
70 Cafe Bar Revolución................................ D6
  Cinema El Puente ....(see 14)
71 Dada Club D7
72 El Paliacate B4
73 Kinoki F7

⊜ Shopping
74 Abuelita Books F7
75 El Camino de los Altos C6
76 J'pas Joloviletik....................................... C3
77 La Pared... B6
78 Lágrimas de la Selva D8
  Meltzanel ....(see 34)
79 Nemi Zapata.. E4
80 Poshería.. G7
81 Sna Jolobil C2
82 Taller Leñateros.. E4

Spanish, French and German. Also on-site is a medicinal plant garden, a herbal pharmacy and a *casa de curación*, where treatments are done. It's a 20-minute walk north from Real de Guadalupe or M$25 by taxi.

Plaza 31 de Marzo PLAZA

The leafy main plaza is a fine place to take in San Cristóbal's unhurried highland atmosphere. Shoe-shiners, newspaper sellers and *ambulantes* (mobile street vendors) gather around the elaborate iron bandstand.

The Hotel Santa Clara, on the plaza's southeast corner, was built by Diego de Mazariegos, the Spanish conqueror of Chiapas. His coat of arms is engraved above the main portal. The building is a rare secular example of plateresque style in Mexico.

Catedral   CATHEDRAL
(Plaza 31 de Marzo) On the north side of the plaza, the cathedral was begun in 1528 but wasn't completed until 1815 because of several natural disasters. Sure enough, new earthquakes struck in 1816 and also 1847, causing considerable damage, but it was restored again from 1920 to 1922. The gold-leaf interior has five gilded altarpieces featuring 18th-century paintings by Miguel Cabrera.

Templo & Ex-Convento de Santo Domingo de Guzmán   CHURCH
(Utrilla; ⊘6:30am-2pm & 4-8pm) FREE Located just north of the center of town, the 16th-century Templo de Santo Domingo is San Cristóbal's most beautiful church, especially when its facade catches the late-afternoon sun. This baroque frontage, with outstanding filigree stucco work, was added in the 17th century and includes the double-headed Hapsburg eagle, then the symbol of the Spanish monarchy. The interior is lavishly gilded, especially the ornate pulpit.

On the western side, the attached former monastery contains a regional museum and an excellent Maya textile museum (p359). Around Santo Domingo and the neighboring **Templo de la Caridad** (built in 1712), Chamulan women and bohemian types from around Mexico conduct a colorful daily crafts market. The weavers' showroom of Sna Jolobil (p371) is now in a separate light-filled building on the northwest section of the grounds.

Museo de los Altos de Chiapas   MUSEUM
(Calz Lázaro Cárdenas s/n; M$52; ⊘9am-6pm Tue-Sun) One of two museums inside the Ex-Convento de Santo Domingo, which is located on the western side of the Templo de Santo Domingo, this museum has several impressive archaeological relics – including stelae from Chincultik – as well as exhibits on the Spanish conquest and evangelization of the region. Admission is bundled with Centro de Textiles del Mundo Maya (p359).

Museo del Ámbar de Chiapas   MUSEUM
(www.museodelambar.com.mx; Plazuela de la Merced; M$20; ⊘10am-2pm & 4-8pm Tue-Sun) Chiapas amber – fossilized pine resin, around 30 million years old – is known for its clarity and diverse colors. Most is mined around Simojovel, north of San Cristóbal. This museum explains all things amber (with information sheets in English, French, German, Japanese and Italian), and displays and sells some exquisitely carved items and insect-embedded pieces. Note that a number of nearby jewelry shops have appropriated the museum's name, but this is the only place around that's housed in an ex-convent – you can't miss it.

Arco del Carmen   GATE
The Arco del Carmen, at the southern end of the Andador Turístico on Hidalgo, dates from the late 17th century and was once the city's gateway.

Centro Cultural El Carmen   BUILDING
(Hermanos Domínguez s/n; ⊘9am-2pm & 4-8pm Mon-Fri) FREE The ex-convent, just east of the Arco del Carmen, is a wonderful colonial building, with a large, peaceful garden. It's now the Centro Cultural El Carmen, hosting art and photography exhibitions and the occasional musical event.

Café Museo Café   MUSEUM
(MA Flores 10; M$30; ⊘8am-10pm Mon-Sat, to 8pm Sat & Sun) This combined cafe and coffee museum is a venture of Coopcafé, a grouping of more than 17,000 small-scale, mainly indigenous, Chiapas coffee growers. The museum covers the history of coffee and its cultivation in Chiapas, from highly exploitative beginnings to the community-based indigenous coffee production that's increasingly well marketed today. The information is translated into English. You can taste some of that flavorful organic coffee in the cafe.

Museo Bichos e Insectos   MUSEUM
(www.museodebichos.com; 16 de Sepiembre 23; admission M$35; ⊘10:30am-2pm & 4-8pm Mon-Fri, 11am-6pm Sat & Sun; ⊛) A small museum but still home to over 2000 insects (only a few of them are alive, and very few of the mounted ones are labeled). Check out old wasp nests, huge beetles, leaf insects, spiders, crickets, butterflies and dragonflies. Live insects and other creepy crawlies include scorpions, beetles and centipedes; you can hold a tarantula too.

THE ZAPATISTAS

On January 1, 1994, the day the North American Free Trade Agreement (Nafta) was implemented, a previously unknown leftist guerrilla army emerged from the forests to occupy San Cristóbal de las Casas and other towns in Chiapas. The Ejército Zapatista de Liberación Nacional (EZLN; Zapatista National Liberation Army) linked antiglobalization rhetoric with Mexican revolutionary slogans, declaring that they aimed to both overturn the oligarchy's centuries-old hold on land, resources and power, and improve the wretched living standards of Mexico's indigenous people.

The Mexican army evicted the Zapatistas within days, and the rebels retreated to the fringes of the Lacandón Jungle to wage a propaganda war, mainly fought via the internet. The Zapatistas' balaclava-clad, pipe-puffing Subcomandante Marcos (a former university professor named Rafael Guillén) rapidly became a cult figure. High-profile conventions against neoliberalism were held, international supporters flocked to Zapatista headquarters at La Realidad, and Zapatista-aligned peasants took over hundreds of farms and ranches in Chiapas.

A set of accords on indigenous rights and autonomy was negotiated between the Zapatistas and the Mexican government but never ratified, and tension and killings escalated in Chiapas through the 1990s. According to Amnesty International, the paramilitary groups responsible for a massacre in Acteal in 1997 were armed by the authories. By 1999 an estimated 21,000 villagers had fled their homes after a campaign of intimidation.

After a high-profile Zapatista media campaign, La Otra Campaña (The Other Campaign), during Mexico's 2006 presidential election, the EZLN has mostly remained dormant, with only the occasional conference and mobilization, its political influence slight outside its own enclaves. The movement still maintains five regional 'Juntas de Buen Gobierno' (Committees of Good Government) and many autonomous communities, though some former supporters have grown disillusioned and many have left the movement.

Further background is available in *The Zapatista Reader*, an anthology of writers from Octavio Paz and Gabriel García Márquez to Marcos himself, and Bill Weinberg's *Homage to Chiapas: The New Indigenous Struggles in Mexico*.

Courses

Several good language schools offer instruction in Spanish, with flexibility to meet most level and schedule requirements. Weekly rates given below are for three hours' tuition five days a week, but many variations (classes only, hourly instruction, homestays etc) are available.

La Casa en el Árbol LANGUAGE COURSE
(☎967-674-52-72; www.lacasaenelarbol.org; Madero 29; classes per week from M$1200, homestay & meals per week M$1625) The 'Tree House' is an enthusiastic, socially committed school that teaches Tseltal and Tsotsil. It offers lots of out-of-school activities and is also a base for volunteer programs. Mexican cooking classes are also available.

Instituto de Lenguas Jovel LANGUAGE COURSE
(☎967-678-40-69; www.institutojovel.com; Madero 45; individual/group classes per week US$215/140, homestay per week from US$98) Instituto Jovel is professional and friendly, and has a top-class reputation among students. Most tui-

tion is one-on-one, and it has a beautiful location. Classes in Mexican cooking and salsa dancing are offered too.

El Puente Spanish Language School LANGUAGE COURSE
(☎967-678-37-23; infoelpuente@gmail.com; Real de Guadalupe 55; individual/group classes per week $US160/140, with homestay & meals US$250/230) Housed in the Centro Cultural El Puente, which also has a vegetarian cafe, a cinema and gallery. Classes are offered for any period, starting from one day.

Shaktipat Yoga YOGA
(☎cell 967-130-33-66; http://shaktipatyoga.com.mx; Niños Héroes 2; class M$50) A studio in the healing arts complex of Casa Luz with multilingual vinyasa, ashtanga and hatha yoga classes. Multiclass discounts.

Tours

Agencies in San Cristóbal (open approximately 8am to 9pm) offer a variety of tours, often with guides who speak English,

French or Italian, though many offer transportation only. Typical daytrips run to Chiapa de Corzo and Cañón del Sumidero (from M$400, six to seven hours), Lagos de Montebello and El Chiflón waterfalls (M$450, nine to 10 hours) and Palenque, Agua Azul and Misol-Ha (M$550, 14 hours). All prices are per person (usually with a minimum of four people).

Nichim Tours   ADVENTURE TOUR
(☑967-678-35-20; www.nichimtours.com.mx; Hermanos Domínguez 15) Full-service agency offering adventurous tours to the Selva El Ocote, as well as regional day trips to amber mines and workshops, and indigenous markets. Multilingual guides.

Natutours   OUTDOORS
(☑967-678-12-95; www.natutours.com.mx; Calle 28 de Agosto 4; ⊙9am-4pm Mon-Sat) 🌿 Specializes in ecotourism (including intriguing tree climbing outings), jungle treks, cultural tourism and also holds workshops to promote recycling and sustainable use in the region.

SendaSur   ECOTOUR
(☑967-678-39-09; www.sendasur.com.mx; 5 de Febrero 29; ⊙9am-2pm & 4-7pm Mon-Fri, 9am-noon Sat) 🌿 A partner-based ecotourism network in Chiapas, SendaSur that can help with independent travel and reservations in the Lacandón and El Ocote jungle regions.

Petra Vertical   ADVENTURE TOUR
(☑967-631-51-73; www.petravertical.com; Isabel La Católica 9b) Regional climbing, rappeling and rafting excursions, with destinations including the Sima de las Cotorras, El Aguacero, the Cañon de la Venta, and the Chorreadero waterfall and cave system near Chiapa de Corzo. Also organizes walking trips from San Cristóbal to the Arcotete river cave and the Huitepec reserve.

Explora   ADVENTURE TOUR
(☑967-631-74-98; www.ecochiapas.com; Calle 1 de Marzo 30; ⊙9:30am-2pm & 4-8pm Mon-Fri, 9:30am-2pm Sat) Adventure trips to the Lacandón Jungle, including multiday river kayaking and rafting.

Viajes Chincultik   TOUR
(☑967-678-09-57; www.tourshotel.com.mx; Casa Margarita, Real de Guadalupe 34; ⊙9am-7pm Mon-Fri, to 2pm Sat) Regional tours and transfers at good prices.

Tienda de Experiencias   TOUR, BUS TOUR
(☑967-631-57-32; www.tiendadeexperiencias.mx; Real de Guadalupe 40A) Offers small group tours to artisan cooperatives, scuba/snuba diving in cenotes and other eclectic 'experiences.' Its Jungle Connection hop-on/hop-off bus route circles the Lacandón.

Jaguar Adventours   CYCLING
(☑967-631-50-62; www.adventours.mx; Belisario Domínguez 8A; bicycle rentals per hour/day M$40/M$200; ⊙9am-2:30pm & 3:30-8pm Mon-Sat, 9am-2:30pm Sun) Does bicycle tours to Chamula and Zincantán (M$700), plus longer expeditions. Prices start at M$450 per person. Also rents quality mountain bikes with helmet and lock.

Marcosapata o En Bici Tours CYCLING, HIKING
(☑967-141-72-16; http://marcosapata1.wordpress.com) Offers tailored hiking tours (M$250) and bike tours visiting San Lorenzo Zinacantán, San Juan Chamula and Rancho Nuevo (M$250 to M$300) or the Cañon del Sumidero (M$500). Speaks English and French. Ask for Marco Antonio Morales at the clothing store at Utrilla 18.

Otisa   TOUR
(☑967-678-19-33; www.otisatravel.com; Real de Guadalupe 3C) Major operator that does all the standard tours.

Trotamundos   TOUR
(☑967-678-70-21; Real de Guadalupe 26C) Regional transportation, Tuxtla airport transfers and trips to Laguna Miramar.

★ Festivals & Events

Semana Santa   RELIGIOUS
The Crucifixion is acted out on Good Friday in the Barrio de Mexicanos, northwest of town.

Feria de la Primavera y de la Paz   CULTURAL
(Spring & Peace Fair) Easter Sunday is the start of the weeklong town fair, with parades, musical events and bullfights.

**Festival Internacional
Cervantino Barroco**   ART
(www.conecultachiapas.gob.mx) In late October, this free weeklong cultural program keeps things hopping with world-class music, dance and theater.

⌂ Sleeping

San Cristóbal has a wealth of budget accommodations, but also a number of appealing and atmospheric midrange hotels, often set in colonial or 19th-century mansions, along with a smattering of top-end luxury. The high seasons here are during Semana Santa and the following week, and the months of July and August, plus the Día de Muertos and Christmas–New Year holidays. Most prices dip at least 20% outside high season.

Real de Guadalupe Area

Le Gite del Sol HOTEL $
(967-631-60-12; www.legitedelsol.com; Madero 82; s/d M$340/440, without bathroom M$240/305; @🐾) A bountiful breakfast complements simple rooms with floors of radiant sunflower yellow and bathrooms that look a bit like oversized shower stalls, or pleasant rooms with shared facilities in a newer location across the street. French and English spoken, and kitchen facilities available.

Casa Margarita HOTEL $$
(967-678-09-57; www.tourshotel.com.mx; Real de Guadalupe 34; s/d incl breakfast M$680/800; P🐾) This popular and well-run travelers' haunt offers tastefully presented, impeccably clean rooms with reading lights.

West of Plaza 31 de Marzo

Puerta Vieja Hostel HOSTEL $
(967-631-43-35; www.puertaviejahostel.com; Mazariegos 23; incl breakfast dm M$120, r with/without bathroom M$390/320; 🐾) A spacious hostel in a high-ceilinged colonial building with a large garden, kitchen, temascal (pre-Hispanic steam bath) and sheltered interior courtyard, its dorms (one for women only) are a good size, and the rooftop ones have fab views. Private rooms have one queen and a bunk bed. Room and board exchanges are available for a minimum one month volunteer commitment.

Hostal Akumal HOSTEL $
(cell 967-1161120; Calle 16 de Sepiembre 33; dm/s/d incl breakfast M$120/210/420; 🐾) Friendly, live-in owners, a decent location and a big free breakfast (a prominent sign quite rightly states 'Continental breakfast is not real breakfast') are some of the winning points at this centrally located hostel. There's a roaring fireplace in the lounge for chilly nights, a funky courtyard hangout area and the rooms and dorms are adequate, if nothing exciting.

Posada Ganesha GUESTHOUSE $
(967-678-02-12; www.posadaganesha.com; Calle 28 de Agosto 23; dm/s/d without bathroom incl breakfast M$190/320/500; 🐾🐾) An incense-infused posada trimmed in Indian fabrics, this is a friendly and vibrant place to rest your head, with a simple guest kitchen and a pleasant lounge area. The free-standing *cabaña* room is especially nice. Yoga sessions twice daily Monday to Friday.

Hotel b¨o BOUTIQUE HOTEL $$$
(967-678-15-15; www.hotelbo.mx; Av 5 de Mayo 38; r from M$3885, ste M$4965; P🐾@🐾) San Cristóbal meets Miami Beach in a boutique hotel that breaks the traditional colonial-architecture barrier with super-modern, trendy lines and unique, artsy touches. The large rooms and suites are very elegant and boast glass-tile bathrooms with ceiling showers, while the flowery gardens host fine water features.

Las Escaleras BOUTIQUE HOTEL $$$
(967-678-81-81; www.lasescalerashotel.com; Isauro Rossette 4; r M$1992-2816; 🐾) Sophisticated, charming and oozing with character, this hilltop retreat isn't for the leg-weary (there are even more stairs than the name implies) but if you're looking for style, it's one of the best options in town.

Casa de Alma BOUTIQUE HOTEL $$$
(967-674-77-84; www.casadealma.mx; 16 de Septiembre 24; ste from M$4570; 🐾) Offering just the right mix of colonial charm and modern comforts, the huge suites here boast fantastic views, stylish decor and private terraces and balconies.

Hotel El Paraíso HOTEL $$$
(967-678-00-85; www.hotelposadaparaiso.com; Calle 5 de Febrero 19; s/d/tr M$1270/1605/1950; 🐾🐾) Combining colonial style with a boutique-hotel feel, El Paraíso has a bright wood-pillared patio, a stunning garden sitting area and loads of character. The high-ceilinged rooms are not huge, but all have natural light, and several are bilevel with an extra bed upstairs. The in-house restaurant, L'Eden, is excellent.

South of Plaza 31 de Marzo

Docecuartos HOTEL $$
(967-678-10-53; Benito Juárez 1; r from M$1250; 🐾) Set around a charming courtyard, there are indeed only 12 rooms here, which adds to the intimate feel but makes booking a

necessity pretty much any time of year. The rooms themselves are gorgeoulsy decked out, with just the right balance of colonial stateliness, indigenous color and modern amenity, and the supercentral location gets a big thumbs up.

Parador Margarita HOTEL $$
(☑967-116-01-64; www.tourshotel.com.mx; JF Flores 39; s/d/tr incl breakfast M$820/958/1434; P🖥) Rooms along a pretty courtyard here sport one king- or two queen-sized beds, and some include details like fireplaces, stained glass windows and bathroom skylights. Other pluses include in-room heaters and a pleasant back patio overlooking a large lawn.

Hacienda Don Juan Hotel HOTEL $$
(☑967-674-71-27; www.hotelhaciendadonjuan.mx; Prolongacion Insurgentes 162; r from M$690; ✳🖥) A fair hike to the south of town, this large hotel wins points for its eclectic folk decorations, lush and rambling grounds and friendly service. Rooms are generously proportioned – most have fireplaces and some look out over the gardens.

★La Joya Hotel B&B $$$
(☑967-631-48-32; www.lajoyahotelsancristobal. com; Madero 43A; r incl breakfast US$160-205; P😊@🖥) A visual feast, offering five rooms ripped from a high-end design magazine, with exquisite cabinetry, enormous bathrooms and antiques curated from the owners' world travels. Fireplace sitting areas and heaters grace each room, and a rooftop terrace beckons with hill views. Attentive service includes afternoon snacks, bedtime tea, and a specially prepared light dinner for late international arrivals.

🛏 North of Plaza 31 de Marzo

Rossco Backpackers HOSTEL $
(☑967-674-05-25; www.backpackershostel.com. mx; Real de Mexicanos 16; incl breakfast dm M$180-220, d/tr M$550/800; P😊@🖥) Rossco Backpackers is a friendly, sociable and well-run hostel with good dorm rooms (one for women only), a guest kitchen, a movie-watching loft and a grassy garden. Private upstairs rooms have nice skylights. A free night's stay if you arrive by bicycle or motorcycle!

Posada Corto Maltese GUESTHOUSE $
(☑967-674-08-48; www.posadacortomaltese.com; Ejército Nacional 12; dm M$120, s/d/tr without bathroom M$250/350/450; 😊🖥) A simple place, its enormous fruit-tree garden buzzes with

TWO VIEWPOINTS
....
Want to take in the best views in town? Well, you'll have to work for them, because at this altitude the stairs up these hills can be punishing. The **Cerro de San Cristóbal** (off Hermanos Dominguez) and **Cerro de Guadalupe** (off Real de Guadalupe) lord over the town from the west and east, respectively, and churches crown both lookouts. The Iglesia de Guadalupe becomes a hot spot for religious devotees around the Día de la Virgen de Guadalupe. These areas are not considered safe at night.

hummingbirds and roaming chickens (buy eggs and cook them in the guest kitchen) and includes a kids' treehouse and a brick oven. It's a respite for folks who treasure green space in the city. Discounts for longer stays available.

Anthara Hotel HOTEL $$
(☑967-674-77-32; www.antharahotel.com; Real de Mexicanos 7; d M$900-1000; 😊🖥) 🎐 Solar-heated hot water and heated floors distinguish this three-floor hotel centered around a small garden courtyard. Rooms have dark wood furniture and large closets, though bathrooms aren't particularly ample. Snag 301 for choice mountain views.

Hotel Posada Jovel HOTEL $$
(☑967-678-17-34; www.hoteljovel.com; Paniagua 28; posada s/d/tr M$500/550/700, posada per person without bathroom M$130, hotel s/d M$800/1000; P✳🖥) Most rooms in the economical 'posada' building are basic and OK; those below can be musty and some share bathrooms. For more comfort, head to the 'hotel' section across the street. Here, rooms surrounding a pretty garden are larger and more brightly decorated, come with cable TV and access a wonderful terrace with views. Restaurant available.

Na Bolom HOTEL $$$
(☑967-678-14-18; www.nabolom.org; Guerrero 33; r/ste incl breakfast M$1395/2387; P😊🖥) This famous museum/research institute (p359), about 1km from Plaza 31 de Marzo, has 16 stylish (though not necessarily luxurious) guest rooms, all loaded with character and all but two with log fires. Meals are served in the house's stately dining room. Room rates include a house tour.

Bela's B&B B&B $$$
(☏ 967-678-92-92; www.belasbandb.com; Dr Navarro 2; incl breakfast s/d M$1280/1540, without bathroom M$770/1030; ⓟ♨🛜🍽) A dreamy oasis in the center of town, this tranquil dog-friendly B&B will seduce you with its lush garden, electric blankets, towel dryers and on-site massages. The five comfortable rooms are trimmed in traditional local fabrics and some of them have lovely mountain views. There is a three-day minimum stay.

Hotel Casa Mexicana HOTEL $$$
(☏ 967-678-06-98; www.hotelcasamexicana.com; Calle 28 de Agosto 1; r/ste from M$1600/$2200; ⓟ♨🏠🛜) A gallery as well as a charming colonial hotel, the stylish and inviting Casa Mexicana displays modern art alongside traditional fabrics and solid-wood pillars and furnishings. The main patio is filled with a lush tropical garden and the 54 attractive rooms are equipped with cable TV; you'll find a restaurant, bar and sauna.

Hotel Diego de Mazariegos HOTEL $$$
(☏ 967-678-08-33; www.diegodemazariegos.com; Calle 5 de Febrero 2; r M$1350, ste M$1700-2100; ⓟ🛜) This classy, long-established hotel occupies two 18th-century mansions built around beautiful, wide courtyards. The 76 rooms are large and decked out with traditional fabrics and fittings, but also have modern comforts including cable TV. Some have fireplaces, and the suites have spa tubs.

✖ Eating

The foodie jackpot of Chiapas, San Cristóbal has more tantalizing food options than any other place in the state. If you can verbalize a culinary craving, chances are some restaurant exists here to fulfill it. Vegetarians are embarrassingly spoiled for choice. ¡Provecho!

✖ Real de Guadalupe Area

Self-caterers can stock up at the centrally located **Super Más** (Real de Guadalupe 22; ⊙8am-10pm) market, and there are a number of fruit and vegetable shops on Dugelay where the pedestrianized section of Real de Guadalupe ends.

★TierrAdentro MEXICAN $
(Real de Guadalupe 24; set menu M$55-130; ⊙8am-11pm; ♨🛜🍽) A popular gathering center for political progressives and coffee-swigging, laptop-toting locals (not

that they're mutually exclusive), this large indoor courtyard restaurant, cafe and pizzeria is a comfortable place to while away the hours. It's run by Zapatista supporters, who hold frequent cultural events and conferences on local issues.

El Horno Mágico BAKERY $
(Utrilla 7; bread & pastries M$20-40; ⊙8am-9pm) For picnic fixings or a tasty snack, scoop up some crusty French breads (the pecan is divine), chocolate croissants or a savory pastry.

Pizzería El Punto PIZZERIA $$
(Real de Guadalupe 47; pizzas M$100-160; ⊙noon-11pm; ♨🍽) Forget the cardboard crap that passes for pizza in some parts, these crispy pies are the best in town, bar none. The central branch of this excellent pizzeria has a full bar, swanky black and red decor and a lovely balcony overlooking Real de Guadalupe.

Crustaceos SEAFOOD $$
(Madero 22; mains M$100-150; ⊙noon-8pm; 🛜) Seriously good seafood, including the perennial favorites: ceviche and garlic-marinated shrimp. The atmosphere's very laid back and things can get a bit rowdy, especially when there are two-for-one beers on offer.

Pierre Restaurant Francés FRENCH $$
(Real de Guadalupe 73; mains M$110-420; ⊙1:30-10pm; ♨🍽) Everything – including pasta, butter, cheese and bread – is made from scratch at this scrumptious French restaurant with a seasonal menu. A few favorites include duck ravioli with wild mushrooms, *verduras salteadas en hojaldra* (vegetable pastry) and the dessert tarts. Vegetarian mains as well.

✖ West of Plaza 31 de Marzo

★Restaurante LUM MEXICAN $$
(Hotel b'o, Av 5 de Mayo 38; mains M$110-200; ⊙7am-11pm) This swanky indoor-outdoor restaurant which serves up the regional cuisines of Chiapas, Veracruz and the Yucatán is in San Cristóbal's first designer hotel. Custom-made lamps, reflecting pools and walls of geometrically stacked firewood create a funky contemporary ambience.

El Eden MEXICAN, INTERNATIONAL $$
(Hotel El Paraíso, Calle 5 de Febrero 19; mains M$82-180; ⊙7am-11pm; ♨🍽) This quality restaurant's tempting European and Mex-

ican menu includes *fondue suiza* (Swiss fondue), *sopa azteca* (tortilla, chili, onion and herb base topped with shredded chicken, fresh cheese, lime, avocado and coriander) and succulent meat dishes, all served around a cozy fireplace or out in the leafy courtyard. There's a good-sized wine list too, which includes French and Spanish vintages.

South of Plaza 31 de Marzo

Te Quiero Verde   VEGETARIAN $
(Niños Heroes 4; mains from M$56; ⊙noon-9pm Wed-Mon; 🎵🍴) If you've ever doubted that a vegan burger can be truly tasty, you need to get down here. The soups and salads are OK too, but the burgers steal the show.

La Tertulia   CAFE $
(Cuathémoc 2; breakfasts around M$38; ⊙9:30am-5pm Sun & Mon, to 10pm Tue-Sat) One of the coolest cafes in town also does great breakfasts, yummy salads and a passable pizza, all served up with ooh-la-la presentation in pleasingly boho surrounds. A little on-site gift store selling local produce and souvenirs rounds out the picture.

Anabanana   MEXICAN $
(Av Hidalgo 9; mains M$30-90; ⊙10am-6pm Mon-Sat; 🍴) This long-time *tortas* (sandwiches) and juice joint on a pedestrian street is a cute and good-value choice for typical Mexican food and no-frills international options. Great for people-watching, plus good breakfasts.

El Caldero   MEXICAN $
(Insurgentes 5; soups from M$68; ⊙11am-10pm; 🍴) Simple, friendly little El Caldero specializes in delicious, filling Mexican soups – *pozole* (shredded pork in broth), *mondongo* (tripe), *caldo* (broth) – with avocados, tortillas and various salsas. One vegetarian option too.

Sensaciones de Chiapas   MEXICAN $$
(Plaza 31 de Marzo 10A; mains M$80-130; ⊙8am-midnight) Inside the Hotel Ciudad Real, this is a great place to try authentic Chiapas cuisine including *chipilín* (a leafy green legume) soup, quesadilla de Cochinita, a great range of *mole* (chili sauce) dishes and the house specialty: chicken thighs stuffed with cheese, ham and other goodies. Occasional live marimba bands accompany your meal.

🍴 North of Plaza 31 de Marzo

★No Name Quesadillas   MEXICAN $
(Paniagua 49B; quesadillas M$35; ⊙8-10:30pm Thu-Tue; 🍴) A sweet couple sells gourmet quesadillas and flavored *atoles* (sweet, corn-based hot drinks) at this signless storefront with romantic courtyard seating. The menu changes daily: vegetarian Sunday through Tuesday, seafood Thursday, meat on Friday – pretty cheeky in this mostly Catholic country – and a mixed bag on Saturday.

Get a gander at ingredients like wild mushrooms, crunchy seasonal ants, squash flowers and spicy chorizo, and line up early before the food sells out.

Alebrije   MEXICAN $
(Caminero 4; mains M$35-70; ⊙8am-6pm Mon-Sat) A fun, economical and busy *cocina popular* (popular kitchen) across from the Mercado Municipal, Alebrije serves freshly prepared food like *enfrijoladas con pollo* (tortillas with bean sauce, cheese and chicken), *chilaquiles* (tortilla strips drenched in salsa) and *pollo con verduras* (chicken and vegetables) to a dedicated local clientele.

Mumo   INTERNATIONAL $$
(MA Flores 16; mains M$80-160; ⊙12:30-11pm Tue-Sun) This tiny 10-seater is well loved throughout the city, both for its eclectic decorations and the loving care that goes into each plate. Bread, salad dressings and ice cream are all made in-house and the build-your-own salads (choose from 20 ingredients) are well worth a mention. Live music and guest chefs Thursday nights.

La Salsa Verde   TAQUERÍA $$
(Av 20 de Noviembre 7; 5 tacos M$60-120; ⊙8am-midnight; 🍴🎵) Meat sizzles on the open-air grill and TVs blare at this taco institution (more than 30 years in business), with tables of families and clubgoers packed into its two large dining rooms.

Trattoria La Nonna   ITALIAN $$
(Dr Navarro 10; mains M$135-180; ⊙2-10pm Mon & Wed-Sat, 2-4:30pm Sun; 🍴) This mother-and-daughter-run Italian eatery specializes in ravioli, handmade fresh every day. Depending on what's in season, expect fillings of sea bass with eggplant, four cheese with walnut and arugula, or rabbit with rosemary and green olive. The sauces are divine – don't miss the mango, chipotle and gorgonzola if it's around.

🍷 Drinking & Nightlife

The aroma of roasted highland-grown coffee beans wafts through the streets of San Cristóbal, and a strong dose is never far away. Along with the Café Museo Café (p363), try **Café La Selva** (Crescencio Rosas 9; ⊗8:30am-11pm; 🐾) or **TierrAdentro** (Real de Guadalupe 24; ⊗7:30am-1am; 🐾) for the good stuff – organic, indigenous-grown and delicious.

Cocoliche   COCKTAIL BAR

(Colón 3; ⊗noon-midnight; 🐾) By day Cocoliche is a bohemian international restaurant (mains M$75 to M$120), but in the evening its mismatched Chinese lanterns and wall of funky posters set the scene for hanging out with friends over boozy *licuados* (milkshakes). Jostle for a sofa near the fireplace on chilly nights, and check out the nightly Latin jazz and salsa, and occasional theater events at 9pm.

La Viña de Bacco   WINE BAR

(🖉967-119-19-85; Real de Guadalupe 7; ⊗2pm-midnight Mon-Sat) At San Cristóbal's first wine bar, chatty patrons spill out onto the street, a pedestrian block off the main drag. It's a convivial place, pouring a large selection of Mexican options (among others), starting at a reasonable M$25 per glass. A free tapa with every glass of wine.

Mezcalería Gusana Grela   MEZCALERÍA

(MA Flores 2; ⊗7pm-3am Mon-Sat) Wedge yourself in at one of a handful of tables and try some of the dozen or so artisanal mezcals (M$40 to M$50) from Oaxaca, many which are fruit-infused.

Kakao Natura   CAFE

(Moreno 2A; ⊗8am-10pm) For something different, melt into a hot chocolate at this *chocolatería*. The dozen or so varieties of artisanal chocolates (M$9 each) make fine gifts – if you can resist eating them yourself.

La Ruina   CLUB

(Calle 28 de Agosto 13; ⊗10pm-late Wed-Sat) Everyone drifts here after hours to dance the rest of the night away in a diminutive wooden building with full bar and cheap beer. Work it to a fun mix of *cumbia* (dance music originating from Colombia), hip-hop, dub step, reggae and salsa.

Latino's   CLUB

(🖉967-678-99-27; Madero 23; Fri & Sat M$50; ⊗8pm-3am Mon-Sat) A bright restaurant and dance spot where the city's *salseros* (salsa musicians) gather to groove. A salsa/*merengue/cumbia/bachata* band plays at 11pm Thursday through Saturday.

☆ Entertainment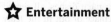

Most live-music venues are free, and clubs generally enforce the no-smoking law.

★ Cafe Bar Revolución   LIVE MUSIC

(www.elrevo.com; Calle 1 de Marzo 11; ⊗1pm-1am) There's always something fun at Revolución, with two live bands nightly (at 9pm and 11pm) and an eclectic lineup of salsa, rock, blues, jazz and reggae. Dance downstairs or order a mojito or caipirinha and chat in the quieter upstairs *tapanco* (attic).

El Paliacate   ARTS CENTER

(Av 5 de Mayo 20; ⊗6-11pm Tue-Sat) An alternative cultural space with a small restaurant and a bar serving wine, beer and artisan mezcal, El Paliacate's main stage hosts music events including rock en Tzotzil, *son jarocho* (a type of folk music) and experimental bands, plus the occasional documentary film or theater presentation. There's bike parking inside and chill-out rooms upstairs.

Dada Club   JAZZ

(🖉967-631-75-61; www.dadaclubjazz.net; Calle 1 de Marzo 6A; ⊗7pm-1am Thu-Sun; 🐾) Deep red walls and flickering flame lamps set the backdrop for the best jazz and blues in town. An intimate balcony hovers beside the stage, where live music runs from 9:30pm to midnight.

☆ Cinema

San Cristóbal is a fine place to immerse yourself in Mexican and Latin American cinema, political documentaries and art-house movies. West of the center, the **Cinépolis** (www.cinepolis.com; adjacent to the Chedraui) multiplex pays first-run flicks for M$60; the cinemas listed here charge M$30.

Kinoki   CINEMA

(🖉967-678-50-46; http://forokinoki.blogspot.com; Belisario Domínguez 5A; ⊗1-11:30pm; 🐾) With a beautiful upstairs space and terrace, this art gallery and tea salon screens two films nightly at 6:30pm and 8:30pm. Private cinema rooms available with over 3500 movies on hand.

Cinema El Puente CINEMA
(☎ 967-678-37-23; Centro Cultural El Puente, Real de Guadalupe 55; ⊘ Mon-Sat) Screenings at 6pm and 8pm.

 Shopping

Real de Guadalupe and the Andador Turístico have some upscale craft shops, but the busy daily crafts market around Santo Domingo and La Caridad churches is also a good place to check out. In addition to textiles, another Chiapas specialty is amber, sold in numerous jewelry shops. When buying amber, beware of plastic imitations: the real thing is never cold and never heavy, and when rubbed should produce static electricity and a resiny smell.

Taller Leñateros ARTS & CRAFTS
(www.tallerlenateros.com; Paniagua 54; ⊘ 8:30am-5pm Mon-Fri, to noon Sat) 🖉 A society of Maya artists, the 'Woodlanders' Workshop' crafts exquisite handmade books, posters and fine-art prints from recycled paper infused with local plants, using images inspired by traditional folk art. It's an open workshop, so you can watch the art in progress.

Poshería DRINK
(Real de Guadalupe 46A; ⊘ 10am-9pm) Pick up a bottle of artisanal *pox* (pronounced 'posh'; alcohol made from sugarcane) infused with honey, chocolate or fruits like *nanche* (a sweet, yellow fruit). Definitely not what the common folk are drinking, since bottles sell for M$50 to M$200 and the alcohol content averages only about 14%.

Meltzanel CLOTHING
(Calle 28 de Agosto 3; ⊘ 9am-2pm & 4-8pm Mon-Fri, 10am-8pm Sat) Modern designs fashioned from traditional Maya textiles.

Abuelita Books BOOKS
(Colón 2; ⊘ noon-6pm, closed Wed & Sun; 🛜) A great place for a leisurely browse over homemade brownies, hot coffee or a steamy tea; come here to replenish your reading material from an excellent selection of new and used books in English (other languages also available). Free English movies on Thursday nights.

Nemi Zapata HANDICRAFTS
(www.nemizapata.com; MA Flores 57; ⊘ 9am-7pm Mon-Fri, 9:30am-3:30pm Sat) 🖉 A fair-trade store that sells products made by Zapatista communities: weavings, embroidery, coffee and honey, as well as Ejército Zapatista de Libéracion Nacional (EZLN; Zapatista National Liberation Army) cards, posters and books.

Lágrimas de la Selva JEWELRY
(Plaza 31 de Marzo; ⊘ 10am-9pm Mon-Sat, noon-9pm Sun) A lovely jewelry store where you can watch jewelers work with amber.

INDIGENOUS WOMEN'S WEAVING COOPERATIVES

The outstanding indigenous *artesanías* (handicrafts, folk arts) of the Chiapas highlands are textiles such as *huipiles* (sleeveless tunics), blouses and blankets, and Tzotzil weavers are some of the most skilled and inventive in Mexico.

J'pas Joloviletik (Utrilla 43; ⊘ 9am-2pm & 4-7pm Mon-Fri, plus some Sat & Sun) A 30-year-old cooperative, J'pas Joloviletik – the name means 'those that weave' in Tzotzil – is comprised of 184 women from 12 communities, and they have a spacious shop on the east side of the Templo de Santo Domingo.

Sna Jolobil (snajolobil@gmail.com; Calz Lázaro Cárdenas s/n; ⊘ 9am-2pm & 4-7pm Mon-Sat) Next to the Templo de Santo Domingo, Sna Jolobil – Tzotzil for 'The Weaver's House' – exhibits and sells some of the very best *huipiles*, blouses, skirts, rugs and other woven items, with prices ranging from a few dollars for small items to thousands for the best *huipiles* (the fruit of many months' work).

A cooperative of 800 weavers from the Chiapas highlands, it was founded in the 1970s to foster the important indigenous art of backstrap-loom weaving, and has revived many half-forgotten techniques and designs.

El Camino de los Altos (http://elcaminodelosaltos.blogspot.com; Insurgentes 19; ⊘ 10am-3pm & 4-8pm Mon-Sat) Creators of the exquisite furnishings inside the Hotel b¨o, El Camino de los Altos is a collaboration of French textile designers and 130 Maya weavers.

La Pared BOOKS
(Av Hidalgo 13B; ⊙10:30am-8:30pm Tue-Sat, noon-7pm Sun) New and used books in English and other languages.

❶ Information

IMMIGRATION

Instituto Nacional de Migración (☑967-678-02-92; Diagonal Hermanos Paniagua 28; ⊙9am-1pm Mon-Fri) On a corner with the Pan-American Hwy, 1.2km west of the OCC bus station.

MEDICAL SERVICES

Dr Luis José Sevilla (☑967-678-16-26, cell 967-1061028; Calle del Sol 12; ⊙6am-10pm) Speaks English and Italian; can make house calls. Located west of the center near the Periférico.

Hospital de la Mujer (☑967-678-07-70; Insurgentes 24) General hospital with emergency facilities.

MONEY

Most banks require your passport if you want to change cash, though they only change money Monday through Friday. There are also handy ATMs at the OCC bus station and on the southern side of the Plaza 31 de Marzo.

Banamex (Insurgentes btwn Niños Héroes & Cuauhtémoc; ⊙9am-4pm Mon-Sat) Has an ATM; exchanges dollars.

Banco Azteca (Plaza 31 de Marzo; ⊙9am-8pm) Hidden in the back of the Elektra furniture store; exchanges dollars and euros. Dollar exchange limited to USD$300 daily per person.

Lacantún Money Exchange (Real de Guadalupe 12A; ⊙9am-9pm Mon-Sat, 9am-2pm & 4-7pm Sun) Open outside bank hours but rates are worse.

POST

Main Post Office (Allende 3; ⊙8am-4pm Mon-Fri, 8am-2pm Sat)

TELEPHONE

Lada Ahorro (Av 20 de Noviembre btwn Calle 28 de Agosto & Escuadrón 201; ⊙9am-9pm) Inexpensive international calls.

TOURIST INFORMATION

Municipal Tourist Office (☑967-678-06-65; Palacio Municipal, Plaza 31 de Marzo; ⊙9am-9pm) Staff are generally knowledgeable about the San Cristóbal area; English spoken.

❶ Getting There & Away

A fast toll autopista (M$56 for cars) zips to San Cristóbal from Chiapa de Corzo. Follow the highways signs that say 'cuota' (toll).

BUSES FROM SAN CRISTÓBAL DE LAS CASAS

DESTINATION	FARE (M$)	DURATION (HR)	FREQUENCY (DAILY)
Campeche	548	10	6:20pm
Cancún	700-1242	18-19	3 OCC, 1 AEXA
Ciudad Cuauhtémoc (Guatemalan border)	132	3¼	3
Comitán	64	1¾	Frequent OCC & colectivos
Mérida	778	12¾	6:20pm
Mexico City (TAPO & Norte)	1240-1560	13-14	13
Oaxaca	604-726	11-12	3
Ocosingo	52-88	2	7 OCC, 3 AEXA, frequent colectivos
Palenque	122-248	5	6 OCC, 3 AEXA
Pochutla	584	11-12	2
Puerto Escondido	668	12½-13	2
Tuxtla Gutiérrez	52	1-1¼	Frequent OCC; 4 AEXA
Tuxtla Gutiérrez airport (Ángel Albino Corzo)	210	1½	8
Villahermosa	402	5½-7	10am

AIR

San Cristóbal's airport has no regular passenger flights; the main airport serving town is at Tuxtla Gutiérrez. Eight daily direct OCC minibuses (M$210) run to the Tuxtla airport from San Cristóbal's main bus terminal; book airport-bound tickets in advance, and consult www.ticketbus.com.mx for schedules to/from 'Ángel Albino Corzo Aeropuerto.'

A number of tour agencies run shuttles to the Tuxtla airport for around M$280 per person.

Taxis Jovel (☑ 967-678-23-53; Pan-American Hwy at Allende) Taxis Jovel picks up passengers for the airport, charging M$520 per carload (M$65 colectivo); reserve a day beforehand.

BUS & COLECTIVO

The Pan-American Hwy (Hwy 190, Blvd Juan Sabines, 'El Bulevar') runs through the southern part of town, and nearly all transportation terminals are on it or nearby. From the OCC bus terminal, it's six blocks north up Insurgentes to the central square, Plaza 31 de Marzo.

The main 1st-class **OCC terminal** (☑ 967-678-02-91; cnr Pan-American Hwy & Insurgentes) is also used by ADO and UNO 1st-class and deluxe buses, plus some 2nd-class buses. Tickets can also be purchased at **Ticketbus** (☑ 967-678-85-03; Real de Guadalupe 16; ☉ 7:30am-10pm) in the center of town. AEXA buses and Ómnibus de Chiapas minibuses share a terminal across the street from the OCC terminal.

All colectivo vans (combis) and taxis have depots on the Pan-American Hwy a block or so from the OCC terminal. They generally run from 5am until 9pm and leave when full. Colectivo taxis to Tuxtla, Comitán and Ocosingo are available 24 hours; if you don't want to wait for it to fill, you must pay for the empty seats.

For Tuxtla Gutiérrez, comfortable Ómnibus de Chiapas 'sprinter' minibuses (M$50) are the best bet; they leave every 10 minutes.

For Guatemala, most agencies offer a daily van service to Quetzaltenango (M$390, eight hours), Panajachel (M$390, 10 hours) and Antigua (M$500, 12 hours); Viajes Chincultik is slightly cheaper, and also has van service to Guatemala City and Chichicastenango. Otherwise, go to Ciudad Cuauhtémoc and pick up onward transportation from the Guatemala side.

CAR & MOTORCYCLE

San Cristóbal's only car-rental company **Optima** (☑ 967-674-54-09; optimacar1@hotmail.com; Mazariegos 39) rents manual transmission cars. Rates vary wildly depending on the season and demand. Sizable discounts are given for payment in cash. Drivers must be 25 or older and have a credit card.

AMATENANGO DEL VALLE

The women of this Tzeltal village by the Pan-American Hwy, 37km southeast of San Cristóbal, are renowned potters. Pottery here is still fired by a pre-Hispanic method, building a wood fire around the pieces rather than putting them in a kiln. Amatenango children find a ready tourist market with animalitos – little pottery animal figures that are inexpensive but fragile. If you visit the village, expect to be surrounded within minutes by young animalito sellers. From San Cristóbal, take a Comitán-bound bus or combi.

❶ Getting Around

To self-propel, **Jaguar Adventours** (p365) rents good-quality mountain bikes.

Combis (M$8) go up Crescencio Rosas from the Pan-American Hwy to the town center.

Croozy Scooters (☑ cell 967-683-22-23; Belisario Domínguez 7; scooters per 3hr/day M$300/450, motorcycles per 3hr/day M$400/540; ☉ 10am-6pm) rents well-maintained Italika CS 125cc scooters and 150cc motorcycles. The price includes a free tank of fuel, maps, locks and helmets; passport and M$500 deposit required.

Taxis cost M$30 within town and M$34 at night.

Around San Cristóbal

The inhabitants of the beautiful Chiapas highlands are descended from the ancient Maya and maintain some unique customs, costumes and beliefs.

Markets and festivals often give the most interesting insight into indigenous life, and there are lots of them. Weekly markets at the villages are nearly always on Sunday. Proceedings start as early as dawn, and wind down by lunchtime. Occasions like Carnaval (late February/early March), for which San Juan Chamula is particularly famous, Semana Santa, and Día de Muertos (November 2) are celebrated almost everywhere.

During the day, walking or riding by horse or bicycle along the main roads to San Juan Chamula and San Lorenzo Zinacantán should not be risky; however, it's not wise to wander into unfrequented areas or down isolated tracks.

Around San Cristóbal de las Casas

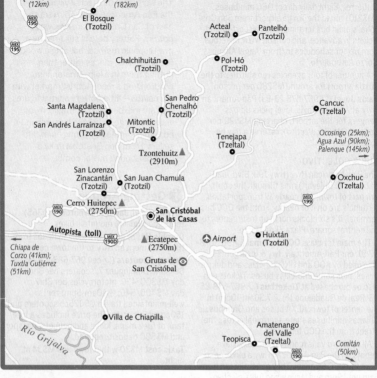

Tours

Exploring the region with a good guide can open up doors and give you a feel for indigenous life and customs you could never gain alone. All San Cristóbal agencies offer four- or five-hour trips to local villages, usually San Juan Chamula and San Lorenzo Zinacantán, for about M$200, or four- or five-hour guided horseback rides to San Juan Chamula for the same price. Don't take anything too valuable with you; thefts have occurred in the past.

Alex & Raúl Tours   CULTURAL TOUR
(📱 967-678-91-41; www.alexyraultours.wordpress. com; per person M$240) This outfit runs enjoyable and informative minibus tours in English, French or Spanish. Raúl and/or a colleague wait at the wooden cross in front of San Cristóbal's cathedral from 8:45am to 9:30am daily, going to San Juan Chamula and Zinacantán. Trips to Tenejapa,

San Andrés Larraínzar or Amatenango del Valle can also be arranged for a minimum of four people.

ℹ Getting There & Away

Transportation to most villages goes from points around the Mercado Municipal in San Cristóbal. Combis to San Juan Chamula (M$15) leave from spots on Calle Honduras and Utrilla frequently; for Zinacantán, combis (M$18) and *colectivo* taxis (M$20) go at least hourly, from a yard off Robledo. Transportation runs from before daybreak to around dusk.

San Juan Chamula

POP 3300 / ELEV 2200M

The Chamulans are a fiercely independent Tzotzil group. Their main village, San Juan Chamula, 10km northwest of San Cristóbal, is the center for some unique religious practices – although conflicts between adherents of traditional Chamulan Catholicism and converts to evangelical, Pentecostal and other branches of Christianity have resulted in the expulsion of many thousands of Chamulans from their villages in the past couple of decades. Here, as in other places in Mexico and Central America, rejection of Catholicism was also in part a political rejection of the long-standing supremacy of the Catholic mestizo majority. In San Juan Chamula, evangelicalism is associated with the Zapatista movement. Most of the evangelical exiles now inhabit the shantytowns around San Cristóbal.

Chamulan men wear loose homespun tunics of white wool (sometimes, in cool weather, thicker black wool), but *cargo*-holders – those with important religious and ceremonial duties – wear a sleeveless black tunic and a white scarf on the head. Chamulan women wear fairly plain white or blue blouses and/or shawls and woolen skirts.

Outsiders can visit San Juan Chamula, but a big sign at the entrance to the village strictly forbids photography inside the village church or at rituals. Do *not* ignore these restrictions; the community takes them very seriously. Nearby, around the shell of an older church, is the village graveyard. Though it's no longer practiced, traditionally black crosses were for people who died old, white for the young, and blue for others.

Sunday is the weekly market, when people from the hills stream into the village to shop, trade and visit the main church. A corresponding number of tourist buses also stream in, so you might prefer to come another day (though due to local superstitions, there are fewer worshippers on Wednesdays).

✨ Festivals & Events

Carnaval   CARNIVAL
During Carnaval, groups of minstrels stroll along the roads in tall, pointed hats with long, colored tassels, strumming guitars and chanting. Much *pox*, an alcoholic drink made from sugarcane, is drunk. Festivities also mark the five 'lost' days of the ancient Long Count calendar, which divided time into 20-day periods (18 of these make 360 days, leaving five to complete a year).

Fiesta de San Juan Bautista   RELIGIOUS
Up to 20,000 people gather to dance and drink on June 24.

Change of Cargo-Holders   CULTURAL
The annual rotation of the honored (but expensive) community leadership positions known as *cargos;* December 30 to January 1.

San Lorenzo Zinacantán
POP 3900 / ELEV 2558M
The orderly village of San Lorenzo Zinacantán, about 11km northwest of San Cristóbal, is the main village of the Zinacantán municipality (population 36,000). Zinacantán people, like Chamulans, are Tzotzil. The men wear distinctive pink tunics embroidered with flower motifs and may sport flat, round, ribboned palm hats. Women wear pink or purple shawls over richly embroidered blouses.

The people of Zinacantán are great flower growers. They have a particular love for the geranium, which – along with pine branches – is offered in rituals for a wide range of benefits.

> **DON'T MISS**
>
> ### TEMPLO DE SAN JUAN
>
> Standing beside the main plaza, Chamula's main church is a ghostly white, with a vividly painted arch of green and blue. Inside the darkened sanctuary, hundreds of flickering candles, clouds of copal incense, and worshippers kneeling with their faces to the pine-needle-carpeted floor make a powerful impression. Chamulans revere San Juan Bautista (St John the Baptist) above Christ, and his image occupies a more important place in the church.
>
> You must obtain tickets (M$20) at the **tourist office** (⊘ 7am-6pm) beside the plaza before entering.
>
> Chanting *curanderos* (literally 'curers'; medicine men or women) may be rubbing patients' bodies with eggs or bones, and worshippers often drink soft drinks (burps are believed to expel evil spirits) or copious amounts of *pox* (alcohol made from sugarcane). Images of saints are surrounded with mirrors and dressed in holy garments.

INDIGENOUS PEOPLES OF CHIAPAS

Of the 4.8 million people of Chiapas, approximately a quarter are indigenous, with language being the key ethnic identifier. Each of the eight principal groups has its own language, beliefs and customs, a cultural variety that makes Chiapas one of the most fascinating states in Mexico.

Travelers to the area around San Cristóbal are most likely to encounter the Tzotziles and the Tzeltales. Their traditional religious life is nominally Catholic, but integrates pre-Hispanic elements. Most people live in the hills outside the villages, which are primarily market and ceremonial centers.

Tzotzil and Tzeltal clothing is among the most varied, colorful and elaborately worked in Mexico. It not only identifies wearers' villages but also continues ancient Maya traditions. Many of the seemingly abstract designs on these costumes are in fact stylized snakes, frogs, butterflies, birds, saints and other beings. Some motifs have religious-magical functions: scorpions, for example, can be a symbolic request for rain, since they are believed to attract lightning.

The Lacandones dwelled deep in the Lacandón Jungle and largely avoided contact with the outside world until the 1950s. They now number less than 1000 and mostly live in three main settlements in that same region (Lacanjá Chansayab, Metzabok and Nahá), with low-key tourism being one of their major means of support. Lacandones are readily recognizable in their white tunics and long black hair cut in a fringe. Most Lacandones have now abandoned their traditional animist religion in favor of Presbyterian or evangelical forms of Christianity.

Traditionally treated as second-class citizens, indigenous groups mostly live on the least productive land in the state, with the least amount of government services or infrastructure. Many indigenous communities rely on subsistence farming and have no running water or electricity, and it was frustration over lack of political power and their historical mistreatment that fueled the Zapatista rebellion, putting a spotlight on the region's distinct inequities.

Today, long-standing indigenous ways of life are challenged both by evangelical Christianity – opposed to many traditional animist-Catholic practices and the abuse of alcohol in religious rituals – and by the Zapatista movement, which rejects traditional leadership hierarchies and is raising the rights and profile of women. Many highland indigenous people have emigrated to the Lacandón Jungle to clear new land, or to Mexican and US cities in search of work.

Despite all obstacles, indigenous identities and self-respect survive. Indigenous people may be suspicious of outsiders, and may resent interference in their religious observances or other aspects of their life, but if treated with due respect they are likely to respond in kind.

The huge central **Iglesia de San Lorenzo** (M$15) was rebuilt following a fire in 1975. Photography is banned in the church and churchyard.

A small market is held on Sundays until noon, and during fiesta times. The most important celebrations are for **La Virgen de La Candelaria** (⊘ Aug 7-11) and **San Sebastián** (⊘ Jan 19-22).

Grutas de San Cristóbal

The entrance to this long **cavern** (M$23, parking M$10; ⊘ 8am-4:30pm) is situated in pine woods 9km southeast of San Cris-

tóbal, a five-minute walk south of the Pan-American Hwy. The first 350m or so of the cave is lit and open for viewing, with a concrete walkway threading through a dazzling chasm of stalagmites and stalactites. An extensive army base surrounds the caves, but visitors are still welcome. Horseback riding is available from the parking area, where you'll also find some *comedores* (food stalls).

To get here, take a Teopisca-bound combi (M$20) from the Pan-American Hwy, about 150m southeast of the OCC bus station in San Cristóbal, and ask for 'Las Grutas'.

Ocosingo

919 / POP 42,000 / ELEV 900M

A respite from both the steamy lowland jungle and the chilly highlands, the bustling regional market town of Ocosingo sits in a gorgeous and broad temperate valley midway between San Cristóbal and Palenque. The impressive Maya ruins of Toniná are just a few kilometers away.

There's not a great deal to make a traveler linger here, but the market area along Avenida 2 Sur Oriente, three to five blocks east (downhill) from the central plaza, is the busiest part of town and worth checking out. The **Tianguis Campesino** (Peasants' Market; cnr Av 2 Sur Oriente & Calle 5 Sur Oriente; ☺6am-5pm) is for the area's small-scale food producers to sell their goods direct; only women are allowed to trade here, and it's a colorful sight, with most of the traders in traditional dress.

The valleys known as Las Cañadas de Ocosingo, between Ocosingo and the Reserva de la Biosfera Montes Azules to the southeast, form one of the strongest bastions of support for the Zapatistas, and Ocosingo saw the bloodiest fighting during the 1994 uprising, with about 50 rebels killed here by the Mexican army.

Ocosingo spreads east (downhill) from Hwy 199. Avenida Central runs down from the highway to the broad central plaza, overlooked from its east end by the Templo de San Jacinto. Some hotels, restaurants and services are along Calle Central Norte, running off the north side of the plaza.

🛏 Sleeping

Hotel Central   HOTEL $
(☎919-673-00-24; cnr Av Central & Calle Central; s/d M$330/370, air-con extra M$100; ⓟ❋❄🛜) Fronting the plaza, the comfortable Hotel Central has ample rooms with cable TV and fan, and a great terrace. Ask for one of the upstairs rooms; corner room 12 is especially bright and breezy.

Hospedaje Esmeralda   GUESTHOUSE $
(☎919-673-00-14; rosi_esmeralda@hotmail.com; Calle Central Norte 14; s/d without bathroom M$200/220; ⓟ🛜) This small guesthouse has five adequate rooms, all with bright indigenous bedcovers and fans. There's a restaurant (mains M$70 to M$100), and the owners – who know the area inside out – are happy to give information to nonguests

if you buy a drink or meal. It also offers horseback-riding excursions (M$350, two hours) in the countryside outside Ocosingo.

🍴 Eating

Restaurant Los Rosales   MEXICAN, BREAKFAST $
(Hotel Margarita, Calle Central Norte 19; breakfast M$60-80, mains M$80-130; ☺7am-11pm; 🛜) With a wall of windows looking out over the rooftops to views of never-ending green mountains, this upstairs eatery makes a pleasant place to plot your day.

Rahsa   MEXICAN $$
(3a Sur Oriente 26; mains M$80-130; ☺7am-10pm Mon-Sat, noon-8pm Sun; 🛜) A step above most of the fairly workaday restaurants on offer in Ocosingo, Rahsa combines contemporary techniques with traditional recipes to very good effect. The atmosphere is cozy (no blasting music – yay!) and the service can be slow, but the food is worth the wait.

Las Delicias   MEXICAN, BREAKFAST $$
(Av Central 5; mains M$85-140; ☺7am-11pm; ⊜🛜) On the plaza-facing veranda of the Hotel Central, this restaurant has big portions and good breakfasts (from M$45).

🛍 Shopping

Fábrica de Quesos Santa Rosa   FOOD
(☎919-673-00-09; 1a Calle Oriente Norte 11; ☺8am-2pm & 4-8pm Mon-Sat, 8am-2pm Sun) Ocosingo is known for its *queso amarillo* (yellow cheese). There are nine main types sold by this cheesemaker, including 'de bola,' which comes in 1kg balls with an edible wax coating and a crumbly, whole-fat center. Free factory tours available during business hours.

ℹ Information

The plaza's a free wi-fi hotspot, and internet cafes there charge M$10 per hour. **Santander**

ℹ TAKING PHOTOS

It's important to be respectful of local customs in this part of Mexico. Indigenous villages are often extremely close-knit, and their people can be suspicious of outsiders and particularly sensitive about having their photo taken. In some villages cameras are, at best, tolerated – and sometimes not even that. You may put yourself in physical danger by taking photos without permission. If in any doubt, ask first.

BUSES FROM OCOSINGO

DESTINATION	FARE (M$)	DURATION (HR)	FREQUENCY (DAILY)
Palenque	76-138	2½	6 OCC, 3 AEXA; very frequent *colectivos*
San Cristóbal de las Casas	52-88	2¼	6 OCC, 5 AEXA; very frequent *colectivos*
Tuxtla Gutiérrez	116-212	3½	5 OCC, 5 AEXA

(cnr Calle Central Norte & Av 1a Norte; ◉9am-4pm Mon-Fri, 10am-2pm Sat) and the plazaside **Banamex** (Av Central; ◉9am-4pm Mon-Fri) both exchange dollars and have ATMs. Santander changes euros too.

The **Municipal Tourism Office** (◉8am-4pm Mon-Fri), with a kiosk on the plaza and a ground-floor office in the plaza-front Palacio Municipal, has regional and city maps, though you're better off getting actual information at Hospedaje Esmeralda.

❶ Getting There & Away

Ocosingo's **OCC bus terminal** (☑919-673-04-31) is on Hwy 199, 600m west of the plaza; the 1st-class **AEXA bus terminal** (☑cell 919-1140679; www.autobusesaexa.com.mx) is across the road. In addition to San Cristóbal, Tuxtla Gutiérrez and Palenque, buses from the OCC terminal also go to Campeche, Cancún, Mérida and Villahermosa. The main *colectivo* terminal is across the street from AEXA.

A walled lot behind the market is the terminus for trucks to Nahá (M$50, 2½ hours, 11am and noon departures) and Laguna Miramar.

Toniná

◉ Sights

Toniná   ARCHAEOLOGICAL SITE
(☑919-108-22-39; M$46; ◉8am-5pm) The towering ceremonial core of Toniná, overlooking a pastoral valley 14km east of Ocosingo, comprises one of the Maya world's most imposing temple complexes. This was the city that brought mighty Palenque to its knees.

The year AD 688 saw the inauguration of the Snake Skull–Jaguar Claw dynasty, with ambitious new rulers bent on controlling the region. Palenque was their rival state, and when Toniná captured the Palenque ruler K'an Joy Chitam II in 711, it's likely that he had his head lopped off here.

Toniná became known as the Place of the Celestial Captives, because its chambers held the captured rulers of Palenque and other Maya cities, who were destined to be ransomed for large sums or decapitated. A recurring image in Toniná sculpture is of captives before decapitation, thrown to the ground with their hands tied.

To enter the site, follow the road from the entrance and **site museum** (◉closed Mon), which details Toniná's history (in Spanish) and contains most of the best artifacts. The road turns into a footpath, crosses a stream and climbs to the broad, flat Gran Plaza. At the south end of the Gran Plaza is the **Templo de la Guerra Cósmica** (Temple of Cosmic War), with five altars in front of it. Off one side of the plaza is a **ball court**, inaugurated around AD 780 under the rule of the female regent Smoking Mirror. A decapitation altar stands cheerfully beside it. In 2011 archaeologists discovered two life-size stone sculptures of captive warriors inscribed as being from Copán (in Honduras), confirming that Maya kingdom's wartime alliance with Palenque.

To the north rises the ceremonial core of Toniná, a hillside terraced into a number of platforms, rising 80m above the Gran Plaza. At the right-hand end of the steps, rising from the first to the second platform, is the entry to a ritual labyrinth of passages.

Higher up on the right-hand side is the Palacio de las Grecas y de la Guerra (Palace of the Grecas and War). The *grecas* are a band of geometrical decoration forming a zigzag x-shape, possibly representing Quetzalcóatl. To its right is a rambling series of chambers, passages and stairways, believed to have been Toniná's administrative headquarters.

Higher again is Toniná's most remarkable sculpture, the **Mural de las Cuatro Eras** (Mural of the Four Eras). Created between AD 790 and 840, this stucco relief of four panels – the first, from the left end, has been lost – represents the four suns, or four eras of human history. The people of Toniná believed themselves to be living in the fourth sun – that of winter, the direction north, mirrors and the end of human life. At the center of each panel is the upside-down head of a decapitated prisoner. Blood spurting from the prisoner's neck forms a ring of feathers and, at the same time, a sun. In one panel, a dancing skeleton holds a decapitated head. To the left of the head is a lord of the underworld, resembling an enormous rodent.

Up the next set of steps is the seventh level, with remains of four temples. Behind the second temple from the left, more steps descend into the very narrow Tumba de Treinta Metros (Thirty-Meter Tomb), an impossibly slim passageway that's definitely not for the claustrophobic!

Above here is the acropolis, the abode of Toniná's rulers and site of its eight most important temples – four on each of the two levels. The right-hand temple on the lower level, the **Templo del Monstruo de la Tierra** (Temple of the Earth Monster), has Toniná's best-preserved roof-comb, built around AD 713.

On the topmost level, the tallest temple, the Templo del Espejo Humeante (Temple of the Smoking Mirror), was built by Zots-Choj, who took the throne in AD 842. In that era of the fourth sun and the direction north, Zots-Choj had to raise this, Toniná's northernmost temple, highest of all, which necessitated a large, artificial northeast extension of the hill.

❶ Getting There & Away

Combis to Toniná (M$16) leave from a roofed depot just behind Ocosingo's Tianguis Campesino every 30 minutes. The last one returns around 5:30pm. A taxi costs around M$130.

Agua Azul & Misol-Ha

These spectacular water attractions – the thundering cascades of Agua Azul and the 35m jungle waterfall of Misol-Ha – are both short detours off the Ocosingo–Palenque road. During the rainy season, they lose part of their beauty as the water gets murky, though the power of the waterfalls is magnified.

Both are most easily visited on an organized day tour from Palenque, though it's possible, for about the same price, to go independently. One reason to visit on your own is to spend more time at Misol-Ha, which is usually a shorter tour stop. Agua Azul is especially built-up and crowded with vendors.

◉ Sights

Agua Azul   WATERFALL
(M$40) Agua Azul is a breathtaking sight, with its powerful and dazzling white waterfalls thundering into turquoise (outside rainy season) pools surrounded by verdant jungle. On holidays and weekends the place is packed; at other times you'll have few companions. The temptation to swim is great, but take extreme care, as people do drown here. The current is deceptively fast, the power of the falls obvious, and there are many submerged hazards like rocks and dead trees.

If you're in decent shape, keep walking upstream – the crowds thin out the further up you go.

The turnoff for Agua Azul is halfway between Ocosingo and Palenque, some 60km from each. A paved road leads 4.5km down to Agua Azul from Hwy 199. A well-made stone and concrete path with steps runs 700m up beside the falls from the parking area, which is packed with food and souvenir stalls. Basic lodging is also available.

Unfortunately, theft isn't uncommon, so don't bring valuables, keep an eye on your belongings and stick to the main paved trail.

Misol-Ha   WATERFALL
(total M$35) Just 20km south of Palenque, spectacular Misol-Ha cascades approximately 35m into a wonderful wide pool surrounded by lush tropical vegetation. It's a sublime place for a dip when the fall is not excessively pumped up by wet-season rains. A path behind the main fall leads into a cave, which allows you to experience the power of the water close up. Misol-Ha is 1.5km off Hwy 199 and the turnoff is signposted, and two separate *ejidos* (communal landholdings) charge admission.

🛏 Sleeping & Eating

Centro Turístico Ejidal
Cascada de Misol-Ha   CABIN $
(☑ 916-345-12-10; www.misol-ha.com; d/tr M$330/450, f with kitchen M$580-700; ☺ restaurant 7am-7pm, to 10pm high season; ℗☺) Has great wooden cabins among the trees near the waterfall, with fans, hot-water bathrooms and mosquito netting, plus a good open-air restaurant (mains M$80 to M$160). Nighttime swims are dreamy.

ℹ Getting There & Away

Most Palenque travel agencies offer daily Misol-Ha and Agua Azul trips. Trips cost around M$350 including admission fees, and last six or seven hours, spending 30 to 60 minutes at Misol-Ha and two to three hours at Agua Azul. Trips can also be organized to deposit you in San Cristóbal afterward for an additional M$120.

To visit the sites independently from Palenque, negotiate a taxi or take an Ocosingo-bound combi from 5a Poniente Sur to the *cruceros* (turnoffs). At Agua Azul (M$40), *camionetas* (pickup trucks) run down to the entrance. There's no regular transportation in from the Misol-Ha highway junction (M$28), but it's a pretty 1.5km pastoral walk.

Palenque

🌙 916 / POP 43,000 / ELEV 80M

Deservedly one of the top destinations of Chiapas, the soaring jungle-swathed temples of Palenque are a national treasure and one of the best examples of Maya architecture in Mexico. Modern Palenque town, a few kilometers to the east, is a sweaty, humdrum place without much appeal except as a jumping-off point for the ruins and a place to find internet access. Many prefer to base themselves at one of the forest hideouts along the road between the town and the ruins, including the funky travelers' hangout of El Panchán.

History

The name Palenque (Palisade) is Spanish and has no relation to the city's ancient name, which may have been Lakamha (Big Water). Palenque was first occupied around 100 BC, and flourished from around AD 630 to around 740. The city rose to prominence under the ruler Pakal, who reigned from AD 615 to 683. Archaeologists have determined that Pakal is represented by hieroglyphics of sun and shield, and he is also referred to as Escudo Solar (Sun Shield). He lived to the then-incredible age of 80.

During Pakal's reign, many plazas and buildings, including the superlative Templo de las Inscripciones (Pakal's own mausoleum), were constructed in Palenque. The structures were characterized by mansard roofs and very fine stucco bas-reliefs.

Pakal's son Kan B'alam II (r 684–702), who is represented in hieroglyphics by the jaguar and the serpent (and is also called Jaguar Serpent II), continued Palenque's expansion and artistic development. He presided over the construction of the Grupo de las Cruces temples, placing sizable narrative stone steles within each.

During Kan B'alam II's reign, Palenque extended its zone of control to the Río Usumacinta, but was challenged by the rival Maya city of Toniná, 65km south. Kan B'alam's brother and successor, K'an Joy Chitam II (Precious Peccary), was captured by forces from Toniná in 711, and probably executed there. Palenque enjoyed a resurgence between 722 and 736, however, under Ahkal Mo' Nahb' III (Turtle Macaw Lake), who added many substantial buildings.

After AD 900, Palenque was largely abandoned. In an area that receives the heaviest rainfall in Mexico, the ruins were soon overgrown, and the city remained unknown to the Western world until 1746, when Maya hunters revealed the existence of a jungle palace to a Spanish priest named Antonio de Solís. Later explorers claimed Palenque was capital of an Atlantis-like civilization. The eccentric Count de Waldeck, who in his 60s lived atop one of the pyramids for two years (1831–33), even published a book with fanciful neoclassical drawings that made the city resemble a great Mediterranean civilization.

It was not until 1837, when John L Stephens, an amateur archaeology enthusiast from New York, reached Palenque with artist Frederick Catherwood, that the site was insightfully investigated. Another century passed before Alberto Ruz Lhuillier, the tireless Mexican archaeologist, uncovered Pakal's hidden crypt in 1952. Today it continues to yield fascinating and beautiful secrets – most recently, a succession of sculptures and frescoes in the Acrópolis del Sur area, which have vastly expanded our knowledge of Palenque's history.

Frans Blom, the mid-20th-century investigator, remarked: 'The first visit to Palenque is immensely impressive. When one has lived there for some time this ruined city becomes an obsession.' It is certainly not hard to understand why.

◎ Sights

Hwy 199 meets Palenque's main street, Avenida Juárez, at the **Glorieta de la Cabeza Maya** (Maya Head Statue; Map p384), a roundabout with a large statue of a Maya chieftain's head, at the west end of the town. The new main ADO bus station is here, and Juárez heads 1km east from this intersection to the central square, **El Parque** (Map p384).

A few hundred meters south of the Maya head, the paved road to the Palenque ruins, 7.5km away, diverges west off Hwy 199. This road passes the site museum after about 6.5km, then winds on about 1km further uphill to the **main entrance to the ruins** (Map p382).

Palenque Ruins   ARCHAEOLOGICAL SITE
(Map p382; M$51; ⊙8am-5pm, last entry 4:30pm) Ancient Palenque stands at the precise point where the first hills rise out of the Gulf coast plain, and the dense jungle covering these hills forms an evocative backdrop to Palenque's exquisite Maya architecture. Hundreds of ruined buildings are spread over 15 sq km, but only a fairly compact central area has been excavated. Everything you see here was built without metal tools, pack animals or the wheel.

As you explore the ruins, try to picture the gray stone edifices as they would have been at the peak of Palenque's power: painted blood red with elaborate blue and yellow stucco details. The forest around these temples is still home to howler monkeys, toucans and ocelots. The ruins and surrounding forests form a national park, the Parque Nacional Palenque, for which you must pay a separate M$27 admission fee at Km 4.5 on the road to the ruins.

Palenque sees more than 1000 visitors on an average day, and visitation spikes in the summer holiday season. Opening time is a good time to visit, when it's cooler and not too crowded, and morning mist may still be wrapping the temples in a picturesque haze. Refreshments, hats and souvenirs are available outside the main entrance. Vendors line many of the paths through the ruins.

Official site guides are available by the entrance. Two Maya guide associations offer informative two-hour **tours** for up to seven people, which cost M$880 in Spanish or M$1020 in English, French, German or Italian. French, German and Italian speakers may have to wait a bit longer as there are fewer guides available.

Most visitors take a combi or taxi to the ruins' main (upper) entrance, see the major structures and then walk downhill to the museum, visiting minor ruins along the way.

Combis to the ruins (M$24 each way) run about every 10 minutes during daylight hours. In town, look for 'Ruinas' combis anywhere on Juárez west of Allende. They will

also pick you up or drop you off anywhere along the town–ruins road.

Be aware that the mushrooms sold by locals along the road to the ruins from about May to November are the hallucinogenic variety.

➡ Templo de las Inscripciones Group

As you walk in from the entrance, passing to the south of the overgrown **Templo XI** (Map p382), the vegetation suddenly peels away to reveal many of Palenque's most magnificent buildings in one sublime vista. A line of temples rises in front of the jungle on your right, culminating in the Templo de las Inscripciones about 100m ahead; El Palacio, with its trademark tower, stands to the left of the Templo de las Inscripciones; and the Grupo de las Cruces rises in the distance beneath a thick jungle backdrop.

The first temple on your right is Templo XII, called the **Templo de la Calavera** (Temple of the Skull; Map p382) for the relief sculpture of a rabbit or deer skull at the foot of one of its pillars. The second temple has little interest. Third is **Templo XIII** (Map p382), containing a tomb of a female dignitary, whose remains were found colored red (as a result of treatment with cinnabar) when unearthed in 1994. You can look into the **Tumba de la Reina Roja** (Tomb of the Red Queen) and see her sarcophagus. With the skeleton were found a malachite mask and about 1000 pieces of jade. Based on DNA tests and resemblances to Pakal's tomb next door, the theory is that the 'queen' buried here was his wife Tz'ak-b'u Ajaw. The **tomb of Alberto Ruz Lhuillier** (Map p382), who discovered Pakal's tomb in 1952, lies under the trees in front of Templo XIII.

Palenque Ruins

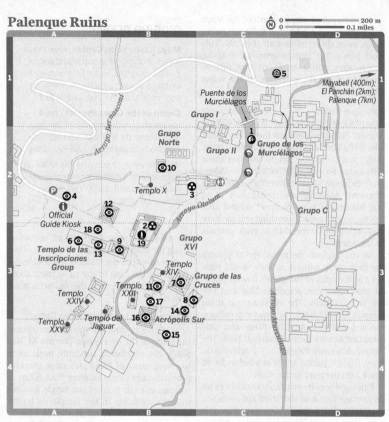

0 _____ 200 m
0 _____ 0.1 miles

Mayabell (400m);
El Panchán (2km);
Palenque (7km)

Palenque Ruins

◎ Sights

1 Baño de la Reina	C2
2 El Palacio	B3
3 Juego de Pelota	B2
4 Main (Upper) Entrance	A2
5 Museo de Sitio	C1
6 Templo de la Calavera	A3
7 Templo de la Cruz	B3
8 Templo de la Cruz Foliada	B3
9 Templo de las Inscripciones	B3
10 Templo del Conde	B2
11 Templo del Sol	B3
12 Templo XI	B2
13 Templo XIII	A3
14 Templo XVII	B3
15 Templo XIX	B4
16 Templo XX	B3
17 Templo XXI	B3
18 Tomb of Alberto Ruz Lhuillier	A3
19 Tower	B3

The **Templo de las Inscripciones** (Temple of the Inscriptions; Map p382), perhaps the most celebrated burial monument in the Americas, is the tallest and most stately of Palenque's buildings. Constructed on eight levels, the Templo de las Inscripciones has a central front staircase rising 25m to a series of small rooms. The tall roofcomb that once crowned it is long gone, but between the front doorways are stucco panels with reliefs of noble figures. On the interior rear wall are three panels with the long Maya inscription, recounting the history of Palenque and this building, for which Mexican archaeologist Alberto Ruz Lhuillier named the temple. From the top, interior stairs lead down into the tomb of Pakal (now closed to visitors indefinitely, to avoid further damage to its murals from the humidity inevitably exuded by visitors). Pakal's jewel-bedecked skeleton and jade mosaic death mask were removed from the tomb to Mexico City, and the tomb was re-created in the Museo Nacional de Antropología. The priceless death mask was stolen in an elaborate heist in 1985 (though recovered a few years afterward), but the carved stone sarcophagus lid remains in the closed tomb – you can see a replica in the site museum.

➡ El Palacio

(Map p382) Diagonally opposite the Templo de las Inscripciones is El Palacio, a large structure divided into four main courtyards, with a maze of corridors and rooms. Built and modified piecemeal over 400 years from the 5th century on, it was probably the residence of Palenque's rulers.

Its **tower** (Map p382), built in the 8th century by Ahkal Mo' Nahb' III and restored in 1955, has remnants of fine stucco reliefs on the walls, but you're not allowed to climb up inside it. Archaeologists believe the tower was constructed so that Maya royalty and priests could observe the sun falling directly into the Templo de las Inscripciones during the winter solstice.

The northeastern courtyard, the **Patio de los Cautivos** (Patio of the Captives), contains a collection of relief sculptures that seem disproportionately large for their setting; the theory is that they represent conquered rulers and were brought from elsewhere.

In the southern part of the complex, the extensive subterranean bathrooms included six toilets and a couple of sweat baths.

➡ Grupo de las Cruces

Pakal's son, Kan B'alam II, was a prolific builder, and soon after the death of his father started designing the temples of the Grupo de las Cruces (Group of the Crosses). All three main pyramid-shaped structures surround a plaza southeast of the Templo de las Inscripciones. They were all dedicated in AD 692 as a spiritual focal point for Palenque's triad of patron deities. The 'cross' carvings in some buildings here symbolize the ceiba tree, which in Maya belief held up the universe.

The **Templo del Sol** (Temple of the Sun; Map p382), on the west side of the plaza, has the best-preserved roofcomb at Palenque. Carvings inside, commemorating Kan B'alam's birth in AD 635 and accession in 684, show him facing his father. Some view this beautiful building as sure proof that Palenque's ancient architects were inspired by the local hallucinogenic mushrooms. Make up your own mind!

Steep steps climb to the **Templo de la Cruz** (Temple of the Cross; Map p382), the largest and most elegantly proportioned in this group. The stone tablet in the central sanctuary shows the lord of the underworld smoking tobacco on the right and Kan B'alam in full royal attire on the left. Behind is a reproduction of a panel depicting Kan B'alam's accession.

On the **Templo de la Cruz Foliada** (Temple of the Foliated Cross; Map p382), the corbel arches are fully exposed, revealing how Palenque's architects designed these buildings. A well-preserved inscribed tablet shows a king (probably Pakal) with a sun shield emblazoned on his chest, corn growing from his shoulder blades, and the sacred quetzal bird on his head.

➡ Acrópolis Sur

In the jungle south of the Grupo de las Cruces is the **Southern Acropolis**, where archaeologists have made some terrific finds in recent excavations. You may find part of the area roped off. The Acrópolis Sur appears to have been constructed as an extension of the Grupo de las Cruces, with both groups set around what was probably a single long open space.

Templo XVII (Map p382), between the Cruces group and the Acrópolis Sur, contains a reproduction carved panel depicting Kan B'alam, standing with a spear, with a bound captive kneeling before him (the original is in the site museum).

In 1999, in **Templo XIX** (Map p382), archaeologists made the most important Palenque find for decades: an 8th-century limestone platform with stunning carvings of seated figures and lengthy hieroglyphic texts that detail Palenque's origins. A reproduction has been placed inside Templo XIX. The central figure on the long south side of the platform is the ruler Ahkal Mo' Nahb' III, who was responsible for several of the buildings of the Acrópolis Sur, just as the Grupo de las Cruces was created by Kan B'alam II. Also on view is a wonderful reproduction of a tall stucco relief of U Pakal, the son of Ahkal Mo' Nahb'.

Also discovered in 1999, **Templo XX** (Map p382) contains a red frescoed tomb built in 540 that is currently Palenque's most active dig. Archaeologists began restoration work inside the tomb in 2012, and now believe that it might be the final resting place of K'uk B'alam I, an ancestor of Pakal.

Palenque

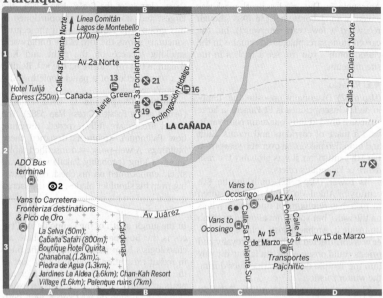

In 2002 archaeologists found in **Templo XXI** (Map p382) a throne with very fine carvings depicting Ahkal Mo' Nahb', along with his ancestor the great Pakal, and his son U Pakal.

➡ Grupo Norte

North of El Palacio is a **Juego de Pelota** (Ball Court; Map p382) and the handsome buildings of the Northern Group. Crazy Count de Waldeck lived in the so-called **Templo del Conde** (Temple of the Count; Map p382), constructed in AD 647.

➡ Palenque Northeastern Groups

East of the Grupo Norte, the main path crosses Arroyo Otolum. Some 70m beyond the stream, a right fork will take you to **Grupo C**, a set of jungle-covered buildings and plazas thought to have been lived in from about AD 750 to 800.

If you stay on the main path, you'll descend some steep steps to a group of low, elongated buildings, probably occupied residentially from around AD 770 to 850. The path goes alongside the Arroyo Otolum, which here tumbles down a series of small falls forming natural bathing pools known as the **Baño de la Reina** (Queen's Bath; Map p382). Unfortunately, you can't bathe here anymore.

The path then continues to another residential quarter, the **Grupo de los Murciélagos** (Bat Group), and then crosses the **Puente de los Murciélagos**, a footbridge across Arroyo Otolum.

Across the bridge and a bit further downstream, a path goes west to **Grupo 1** and **Grupo 2**, a short walk uphill. These ruins, only partly uncovered, are in a beautiful jungle setting. The main path continues downriver to the road, where the museum is a short distance along to the right.

Museo de Sitio   MUSEUM
(Map p382; Carretera Palenque-Ruinas Km 7; with ruins ticket free; ⊙9am-4:30pm Tue-Sun) Palenque's site museum is worth a wander, displaying finds from the site and interpreting, in English and Spanish, Palenque's history. Highlights include a blissfully air-conditioned room displaying a copy of the lid of Pakal's sarcophagus (depicting his rebirth as the maize god, encircled by serpents, mythical monsters and glyphs recounting his reign) and finds from Templo XXI. Entry to the sarcophagus room permitted every half hour.

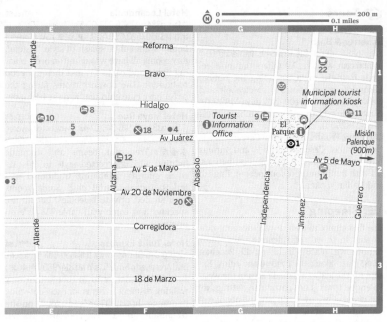

Palenque

◎ Sights

| 1 El Parque | H2 |
| 2 Glorieta de la Cabeza Maya | A2 |

⊕ Activities, Courses & Tours

3 Servicios Turísticos de Palenque	E2
4 Transportador Turística Scherrer & Barb	F2
5 Turística Maya Chiapas	E2
6 Viajes Kukulcán	C3
7 Viajes Misol-Ha	D2

⊜ Sleeping

8 Hostal San Miguel	E1
9 Hotel Chan-Kah Centro	G1
10 Hotel Lacandonia	E1
11 Hotel Lacroix	H1

12 Hotel Maya Rue	F2
13 Hotel Maya Tulipanes	B1
14 Hotel Palenque	H2
15 Hotel Xibalba	B2
16 Yaxkin	B1

⊗ Eating

17 Abarrotes Monterrey	D2
18 Aluxes	F2
Café Jade	(see 16)
19 El Huachinango Feliz	B1
20 Restaurant Las Tinajas	F2
21 Restaurant Maya Cañada	B1

⊜ Drinking & Nightlife

| 22 Italian Coffee Company | H1 |

El Panchán   NEIGHBORHOOD
(www.elpanchan.com; Carretera Palenque-Ruinas Km 4.5) Just off the road to the ruins, El Panchán is a legendary travelers' hangout, set in a patch of dense rainforest. It's the epicenter of Palenque's alternative scene and home to a bohemian bunch of Mexican and foreign residents and wanderers. Once farmed as ranchland, the area has been reforested by the remarkable Morales family, some of whom are among the leading archaeological experts on Palenque. El Panchán has several (mostly rustic) places to stay, a couple of restaurants, a set of sinuous streams rippling their way through every part of the property, nightly entertainment (and daily drumming practice), a meditation temple, a temascal and a constant stream of interesting visitors from all over the world.

Tours

Transportador Turística Scherrer & Barb
TOUR

(Map p384; ✆cell 916-1033649; fermerida_69@hotmail.com; Av Juárez 13) Offers the most eclectic tours in town, including the remote Lacandón communities of Metzabok and Nahá (day trip M$1400, two days M$2500), Guatemala's Piedras Negras archaeological site (M$2500), and cool day trips off the Carretera Fronteriza like the Cascada de las Golondrinas, Cascada Welib-já and various bird-watching and kayaking destinations. All with a minimum of four people; English and Italian spoken.

🛏 Sleeping

The first choice to make is whether you want to stay in or out of Palenque town. Most out-of-town places, including El Panchán (p385), are along the road to the ruins. Except for the leafy La Cañada area in the west, Palenque town is not particularly attractive, but if you stay here you'll have plenty of restaurants and services nearby.

Prices given here are for the high season, which is mid-July to mid-August, mid-December to early January, and Semana Santa. Rates drop by up to 35% at other times.

🛏 In Town

Yaxkin
HOSTEL $

(Map p384; ✆916-345-01-02; www.hostalyaxkin.com; Prolongación Hidalgo 1; dm M$162, d with/without bathroom M$472/342, r with air-con & bathroom M$586; ⓟ⊜✹@❋) Channeling laid-back El Panchán from pretty La Cañada, this former disco has been revamped into a modern hostel with a guest kitchen, ping-pong table, multiple lounges and a swank restaurant/bar and cafe. Rooms without air-con are monastic but funky. The fan-cooled dorms (one for women only) and private rooms with air-con feel more pleasant and comfortable.

Hostal San Miguel
HOTEL $

(Map p384; ✆916-345-01-52; hostalmiguel1@hotmail.com; Hidalgo 43; dm M$150, s/d with fan M$250/380, with air-con M$380/510; ⊜✹❋) Who doesn't love a hotel with towel animals? A quiet and clean economical choice; rooms have good light and views from the upper floors. Dark two- and four-bed dorms don't have hot water or air-con, and all air-con rooms have two queen beds.

Hotel Lacandonia
HOTEL $$

(Map p384; ✆916-345-00-57; Allende 77; s/d/tr/q M$550/620/750/810; ⓟ✹❋) A modern hotel with a subtle splash of style. Tasteful, airy rooms all have wrought-iron beds, reading lights and cable TV, and there's a good restaurant. The upstairs rooms facing the street have cute balconies and the best light.

Hotel Maya Rue
HOTEL $$

(Map p384; ✆916-345-07-43; www.hotelmayarue palenque.com; Aldama s/n; r/tr M$750/900; ✹@❋) Tree-trunk beams and dramatic lighting add unexpected style to this 12-room offering combining traditional materials and industrial chic. Some rooms have shaded private balconies, but all are spacious and come with cable TV. Cafe on premises.

Hotel Tulijá Express
HOTEL $$

(✆916-345-01-04; www.tulijahotelpalenque.com; Blvd Aeropuerto Km 0.5; s/d M$814/980; ✹❋❋) Just on the edge of town (but within easy walking distance), this is an excellent-value midrange hotel. There's a good on-site restaurant, and a great pool area. It's not bursting with character, but is a solid choice nonetheless.

Hotel Lacroix
HOTEL $$

(Map p384; ✆916-345-15-35; www.lacroixhotel.wordpress.com; Hidalgo 10; r M$800-950; ⓟ⊜✹❋❋) This well-tended, family-friendly 16-room hotel near El Parque sports tasteful sponge-painted peach rooms – upper ones with small balconies – and attractive murals. There's a large pool with a tinted translucent roof, a casual restaurant and superfriendly service.

Hotel Chan-Kah Centro
HOTEL $$

(Map p384; ✆916-345-03-18; Av Juárez 2; s/d M$680/890; ⊜✹@❋) In the center and right on the park, this classy place has 17 air-conditioned and stone-adorned rooms with terraces and a park-view restaurant. The corner rooms are best. Wi-fi is in the restaurant only.

Hotel Xibalba
HOTEL $$

(Map p384; ✆916-345-04-11; www.hotelxibalba.com; Merle Green 9, La Cañada; s/d M$650/800; ⓟ✹@❋) Located in the tranquil neighborhood of La Cañada, this midrange hotel offers 35 pleasant, clean and tiled rooms with cable TV. There's a definite Maya theme here, with rock-accented architectural details, pastel colors and a replica of the lid from Pakal's sarcophagus on display. Restaurant on premises.

Hotel Palenque
HOTEL $$

(Map p384; ☑ 916-345-01-03; www.hotelpalenque. com.mx; Av 5 de Mayo 15; s/d incl breakfast from M$647/867; [P][❄][🛜][🏊]) All 28 rooms here are plain but very clean, and most have two queen beds. The upstairs rooms – off a breezy wide walkway – have gorgeous hill views. The fruit-tree garden, pretty terrace bar with pool and the restaurant are all pleasant spots to relax.

Hotel Maya Tulipanes
HOTEL $$$

(Map p384; ☑ 916-345-02-01, 800-714-47-10; www.mayatulipanes.com.mx; Cañada 6, La Cañada; r/tr M$1450/1600; [P][➡][❄][@][🛜][🏊]) Entered through a muraled foyer, this La Cañada hotel has large, comfortable, air-conditioned rooms with two wrought-iron double beds and minimalist decor. It's designed around a pretty garden with a small pool and a restaurant. Contact for discounts.

Misión Palenque
HOTEL $$$

(☑ 916-345-02-41; www.hotelmisionpalenque.com; Periférico Oriente s/n; s/d M$1100/1680; [P][❄][🛜][🏊]) Set on lush grounds just to the east of the center, this 207-room behemoth has all the trimmings you'd expect; supercomfy rooms, fabulous gardens and pool area, a good on-site restaurant and ultra-attentive staff.

🏘 Outside Town

While Palenque town hosts traffic and commerce, the surrounding area, especially between town and the ruins, offers some magical spots where howler monkeys romp in the tree canopy and unseen animals chirp after dark. The compound of El Panchán (p385) is a traveler favorite, with low-key budget *cabañas* nestled in the stream-crossed jungle. Frequent daytime combis between town and the ruins will drop you off and pick you up anywhere along this road.

Margarita & Ed Cabañas
GUESTHOUSE $

(☑ 916-348-69-90; www.margaritaandedcabanas. blogspot.com; Carreterra Palenque-Ruinas Km 4.5, El Panchán; cabañas M$285, r with fan M$320-410, s/d with air-con M$480/570; [P][❄]) With the most spotless digs in the jungle, Margarita has welcomed travelers to her exceptionally homey place for decades. Bright, clean and cheerful rooms have good mosquito netting, and the more rustic screened *cabañas* are

well kept too, with reading lights and private bathrooms. There's free drinking water, a book exchange, and a lovely newer building with superspacious rooms.

Chato's Cabañas
CABAÑAS $

(☑ cell 916-1092829; www.elpanchan.com; El Panchán; s/d/tr M$250/320/440; [P]) Dotted around the Panchán jungle, Chato's wood and concrete cabins have sponge-painted walls, decorative window bars, fans and well-screened windows, and some include nice little porches.

El Jaguar
CABAÑAS $

(☑ cell 916-1192829; www.elpanchan.com; El Panchán; campsites per person M$40, dm/s/d M$100/170/300; [P]) Formerly known as Rakshita's, the no-frills Jaguar is a psychedelic fantasy of colorful murals and DIY construction. Dorm mosquito netting and ground-level room security are iffy; the two-story units are pretty groovy. All have hot water and fans.

Jungle Palace
CABAÑAS $

(☑ cell 916-1147420; www.elpanchan.com; El Panchán; s/d M$220/270, without bathroom M$130/160) A basic option in El Panchán, the Jungle Palace offers rudimentary though well-screened and secure cabins with fans and hot water; some units back onto a stream. The best are freestanding, while others share walls and have somewhat less privacy.

Mayabell
HOTEL, CAMPGROUND $$

(☑ 916-341-69-77; www.mayabell.com.mx; Carretera Palenque-Ruinas Km 6; campsites per person M$75, vehicle site with hookups M$210, cabañas without bathroom M$320, r with fan/air-con M$820/1100; [P][❄][🛜][🏊]) With a sprawling jungleside pool frequented by monkeys, this spacious grassy campground has tons of clean and comfortable sleeping options, plus an enjoyable restaurant. Rooms with air-con are very homey and comfortable; those with fan are more basic, as are the shared bathrooms.

It's just 400m from Palenque's site museum, but being inside the national park means you will have to pay the M$27 park entry fee if you arrive between 7am and 8pm.

Cabaña Safari
CABAÑAS $$

(☑ 916-345-00-26; www.hotelcabanasafari.com; Carretera Palenque-Ruinas Km 1; campsites per person with/without gear M$170/120, d bungalows without bathroom M$300, r/tr M$990/1100; 回※常호) Comfort and connectivity aren't sacrificed at these jungly *palapa*-roofed *cabañas* with air-con, private porches, flat-screen TV and in-room wi-fi. Rocks, tree branches and wall murals give personality to the spacious (including some two-level) air-con rooms; three circular fan-cooled bungalows are teeny tiny. There's a plunge pool, temascal and full restaurant, plus a paintball course in the works.

★ Boutique Hotel
Quinta Chanabnal   BOUTIQUE HOTEL $$$
(☎916-345-53-20; www.quintachanabnal.com; Carretera Palenque-Ruinas Km 2.2; r US$210, ste US$340-462; 回※常호) The Maya-inspired architecture and impeccable service at this decadent boutique hotel will leave you swooning. Enter through heavy wood doors (carved by local artisans) into spacious stone-floor suites that contain majestically draped four-poster beds and cavernous bathrooms. Water features on the premises include a creek, a small lagoon and a multitiered swimming pool.

Massages, a temascal and a fine restaurant are available. The Italian owner, a Maya expert, also speaks German, French, English and Spanish.

Jardines La Aldea   HOTEL $$$
(☎916-345-16-93; www.hotellaaldea.net; Carretera Palenque-Ruinas Km 2.8; r M$1300-1500; 回※常호) The four-star Aldea has 33 large, beautiful and bright *palapa*-roofed rooms set amidst lovely grounds. Each room has an outside terrace with hammock. It's a stylish place, with a peaceful hilltop restaurant and a wonderful pool area. There are no TVs, making it an ideal place to get away from it all.

Piedra de Agua   BOUTIQUE HOTEL $$$
(☎916-345-08-42; www.palenque.piedradeagua.com; Carretera Palenque-Ruinas Km 2.5; r US$130; 回호常호) Spare off-white-and-wood minimalism marks this new designer *cabaña* compound that pampers guests with oodles of bath products, plush robes, private terrace tubs and hammocks outside every room, but no air-con. Breakfast, a bar and massages are available, though the lap pool and Jacuzzi are the most popular amenities.

Chan-Kah Resort Village   RESORT $$$
(☎916-345-11-34; www.chan-kah.com.mx; Carretera Palenque-Ruinas Km 3; r/ste M$1436/3464; 回호※@常호) Swimmers will go woozy contemplating the Chan-Kah's stupendous 70m stone-lined swimming pool in lush jungle gardens. A large quality resort on the road to the ruins, it has handsome well-spaced wood-and-stone cottages with generous bathrooms, ceiling fans, terrace and air-con. It's rarely busy, except when tour groups block-book the place.

✗ Eating

Palenque is definitely not the gastronomic capital of Mexico. There's a decent variety of restaurants, though some are laughably overpriced. A number of inexpensive stands and sit-down spots can be found near the AEXA bus terminal and on the east side of El Parque in front of the church.

★ Don Mucho's   MEXICAN, INTERNATIONAL $
(Carretera Palenque-Ruinas Km 4.5, El Panchán; mains M$60-150; ⊙7am-11pm) The hot spot of El Panchán, popular Don Mucho's provides great-value meals in a jungly setting, with a candlelit ambience at night. Busy waiters bring pasta, fish, meat, plenty of *antojitos* (typical Mexican snacks), and pizzas (cooked in a purpose-built Italian-designed wood-fired oven) that are some of the finest this side of Naples.

Live music – usually *andina*, *cumbia* or Cuban – starts around 8pm Friday through Sunday (at 9:30pm other nights), plus there's a rousing fire-dancing show most nights at 11pm.

Café Jade   MEXICAN, CHIAPANECO $
(Map p384; Prolongación Hidalgo 1; breakfast M$42-68, mains M$53-90; ⊙7am-11pm; ➤🖭) A chill indoor/outdoor spot on the ground floor of the Yaxkin hostel, with long sofa seating at tree-plank tables. Good for breakfast, Chiapan specialities and chicken dishes.

Abarrotes Monterrey   SUPERMARKET $
(Map p384; Av 5 de Mayo; ⊙7am-9pm) The largest supermarket in the center, but no fresh produce.

★ Restaurant Las Tinajas   MEXICAN $$
(Map p384; cnr Av 20 de Noviembre & Abasolo; mains M$85-130; ⊙7am-11pm; ➤) It doesn't take long to figure out why this place is always busy. It slings enormous portions of excellent home-style food – enough to keep you (and possibly another person) fueled up for hours. *Pollo a la veracruzana* (chicken in a tomato, olives and onion sauce) and

camarones al guajillo (shrimp with a not-too-hot type of chili) are both delicious, as is the house salsa.

La Selva MEXICAN $$
(☑916-345-03-63; Hwy 199; mains M$85-220; ⊙11:30am-11:00pm; ☻) Palenque's most upscale restaurant serves up well-prepared steaks, seafood, salads and *antojitos* under an enormous *palapa* roof, with jungle-themed stained-glass panels brightening one wall. Try the *pigua* (freshwater lobster) when it's available in the fall. Reserve ahead in high season.

El Huachinango Feliz SEAFOOD $$
(Map p384; Hidalgo s/n; mains M$90-160; ⊙9am-11pm) Popular, atmospheric restaurant in the leafy La Cañada neighborhood. It has an attractive front patio with tables and umbrellas, and there's also an upstairs covered terrace. Seafood is the specialty here: order seafood soup, seafood cocktails, grilled fish or shrimp served 10 different ways. The service is slooow but the food is worth the wait.

Restaurant Maya Cañada MEXICAN $$
(Map p384; Merle Green s/n; breakfast M$85-110, mains M$85-200; ⊙7am-11pm; ☻☎) This relatively upmarket and professionally run restaurant in the shady La Cañada area serves fine steaks, regional specialties and terrific seafood kebabs. It's open to the air and has a cool upstairs terrace.

🍷 Drinking & Nightlife

Palenque doesn't have much of a nightlife scene. In the evenings you'll often spot more travelers waiting for a night bus than out on the town. Along the ruins road, you can listen to live music at Mayabell, and Don Mucho's has hip-swinging live ensembles plus fire dancers performing nightly. In town, the **Aluxes** (Map p384; Av Juárez 49; ⊙3pm-midnight; ☻) restaurant serves interesting cocktails and has live *trova* (troubadour-type folk music) Friday through Sunday from 9pm on; some options can also be found by poking around La Cañada. Bars in the center tend toward the unsavory.

Italian Coffee Company CAFE
(Map p384; cnr Jiménez & Reforma; ⊙8am-11pm; ☎) Weary traveler, welcome to air-conditioned nirvana.

ℹ PALENQUE BUS WARNING

It's best to travel the winding stretch of road between Palenque and San Cristóbal during daylight, as highway holdups – though by no means common – do occasionally occur. There have also been recent reports of thefts on the night bus from Mérida. When taking buses along these routes, consider stowing valuables in the checked luggage compartment.

ℹ Information

IMMIGRATION
Instituto Nacional de Migración (⊙24hr) The immigration office is about 1.5km north of town on Hwy 199; hail a *colectivo* taxi (M$9) that's headed in that direction.

MEDICAL SERVICES
Clínica Palenque (Velasco Suárez 33; ⊙8:30am-1:30pm & 5-9pm) Dr Alfonso Martínez speaks English.

MONEY
Both of the below banks change dollars and euros (bring a copy of your passport).
Banco Azteca (Av Juárez, btwn Allende & Aldama; ⊙9am-9pm)
Bancomer (Av Juárez 96; ⊙8:30am-4pm Mon-Fri) Also has an ATM.

POST
Post Office (Map p384; Independencia s/n; ⊙8am-8:30pm Mon-Fri, to noon Sat)

TOURS
Numerous travel agencies in Palenque offer transportation packages to Agua Azul and Misol-Ha, to Bonampak, Yaxchilán and Lacanjá Chansayab, and to Flores, Guatemala. Agencies, mostly open from around 8am to 9pm daily, include **Servicios Turísticos de Palenque** (Map p384; ☑916-345-13-40; www.stpalenque.com; Av 5 de Mayo), **Turística Maya Chiapas** (Map p384; ☑916-345-07-98; turis_maya@hotmail.com; Av Juárez 123), **Viajes Kukulcán** (Map p384; ☑916-345-15-06; www.kukulcantravel.com; Av Juárez 8) and **Viajes Misol-Ha** (Map p384; ☑916-345-22-71; Av Juárez 148).

TOURIST INFORMATION
Municipal tourist information kiosk (Map p384; El Parque; ⊙9am-2pm & 6-9pm Mon-Fri)
Tourist Information Office (Map p384; cnr Av Juárez & Abasolo; ⊙9am-8pm Mon-Sat,

BUSES FROM PALENQUE

DESTINATION	FARE (M$)	DURATION (HR)	FREQUENCY (DAILY)
Campeche	382	5-5½	5 ADO
Cancún	630-1040	12-13½	6 ADO
Mérida	576	8	5 ADO
Mexico City (1 TAPO & 1 Norte)	1108-1308	13½	2 ADO
Oaxaca	856	15	ADO at 2:35pm
Ocosingo	76-138	2½	11 ADO, 5 AEXA, very frequent vans
San Cristóbal de las Casas	122-206	5	12 ADO, 5 AEXA
Tulum	524-844	10-11	6 ADO
Tuxtla Gutiérrez	186-324	6½	11 ADO, 5 AEXA
Villahermosa	150-174	2½	frequent ADO & AEXA
Villahermosa airport	278	2¼	5 ADO

to 1pm Sun) The state tourism office's help center has the most reliable town, regional and transportation information, as well as maps. The regional office (☎ 916-345-03-56; ☺ 8am-4pm Mon-Fri), outside the center, can answer questions by phone.

ⓘ Getting There & Away

AIR

In 2014 Palenque's long-deserted **airport** (☎ 916-345-16-92) finally opened to commercial flights. Interjet has twice-weekly service to Mexico City, and Ka'an Air does short hops to Tuxtla Gutiérrez with plans to fly to Santa Elena (Guatemala), the gateway to Tikal. Otherwise, the closest major airport is Villahermosa; ADO runs a direct airport service (M$278) in comfortable minibuses.

BUS

In a spacious location behind the Maya head statue, **ADO** (Map p384; ☎ 916-345-13-44) has the main bus terminal, with deluxe and 1st-class services, an ATM and left-luggage facilities; it's also used by OCC (1st class). It's a good idea to buy your outward bus ticket a day in advance.

AEXA (Map p384; ☎ 916-345-26-30; www.autobusesaexa.com.mx; Av Juárez 159), with 1st-class buses, and Cardesa (2nd class) is about 300m east on Avenida Juárez.

COLECTIVOS

Vans to Ocosingo (M$55) wait on Calle 5a Poniente Sur and leave when full.

Many combis for destinations along the Carretera Fronteriza (including Lacanjá Chansayab, Bonampak, Yaxchilán and Benemérito de las Américas) and for Pico de Oro leave from an outdoor *colectivo* **terminal** (Map p384) just south of the ADO bus station.

ⓘ Getting Around

Taxis charge M$55 (up to M$70 at night) to El Panchán or Mayabell, and M$60 to the ruins. Combis (M$25) from the center ply the ruins road until dark. **Radio Taxis Santo Domingo** (☎ 916-345-01-26) has on-call service.

Bonampak, Yaxchilán & the Carretera Fronteriza

The ancient Maya cities of Bonampak and Yaxchilán, southeast of Palenque, are easily accessible thanks to the Carretera Fronteriza (Hwy 307), a good paved road running parallel to the Mexico–Guatemala border, all the way from Palenque to the Lagos de Montebello, around the fringe of the Lacandón Jungle. Nights here are wonderfully quiet, the sky screaming with stars and the ground twinkling with fireflies. Bonampak, famous for its frescoes, is 152km by road from Palenque; the bigger and more important Yaxchilán, with a peerless jungle setting beside the broad and swift Río Usumacinta, is 173km by road, then about 22km by boat.

The Carretera Fronteriza is the main thoroughfare connecting a number of excellent ecotourism projects, dreamy waterfalls, Lacandón villages and lesser-known archaeological ruins. It's also the main route from Chiapas to Guatemala's northern Petén region (home of several major Maya sites, including mighty Tikal) via the town of Frontera Corozal. Phones in this region usually have satellite service or Guatemala-based numbers.

☞ Tours

Organized tours can be helpful in this region if you have limited time and aren't driving. Always check package inclusions and exclusions, so you can plan your meals and park fees. Following are the standard tours (including entry fees and some meals) per person offered by Palenque travel agencies:

➡ Bonampak and Yaxchilán day trips (M$750 to M$1000) usually include two meals and transportation in an air-conditioned van – a good deal since independent transportation to both is time-consuming and tours include the Bonampak transportation fee; two-day trips (M$1450 to M$1600) include an overnight stay at Lacanjá Chansayab.

➡ Transportation to Flores, Guatemala Transportation (M$450 to M$600, 10 to 11 hours) is by van to Frontera Corozal, river launch up the Usumacinta to Bethel in Guatemala, and public bus on to Flores.

➡ Flores via Bonampak and Yaxchilán (M$1320 to M$1580) with an overnight in Lacanjá Chansayab.

In Palenque, Transportador Turística Scherrer & Barb (p386) organizes more off-the-beaten-path trips to the region, including the Lacandón villages of Nahá and Metzabok and waterfalls in the area; San Cristóbal-based SendaSur (p365) can help with reservations for independent travelers.

❶ Information

DANGERS & ANNOYANCES

Drug and human trafficking are facts of life in this border region, and the Carretera Fronteriza more or less encircles the main area of Zapatista

---

❶ HORA DE DIOS

This part of Mexico tends to ignore daylight saving time, as do *colectivo* companies that originate in cities like Comitán and Palenque that service the region. From April through October, check your watch against the company's to double-check transportation schedules. If they're using 'God's time,' you'll be departing an hour later than the official 'government time.'

---

rebel activity and support, so expect numerous military checkpoints along the road and from this area to Palenque and Comitán. These checkpoints generally increase security for travelers, but don't tempt easy theft by leaving money or valuables unattended during stops. For your own security, it's best to be off the Carretera Fronteriza before dusk. For similar reasons, all border crossings with Guatemala are places you should aim to get through early in the day.

In the rainy months of September and October, rivers are usually too swollen for safe swimming.

Don't forget insect repellent.

❶ Getting There & Away

From Palenque, Autotransporte Chamoán runs vans run to Frontera Corozal (M$130, 2½ to three hours, every 40 minutes from 4am to 5pm), leaving from the outdoor *colectivo* terminal near the Maya head statue and south of the bus station. Use them for visits to Bonampak and Lancanjá Chansayab, because upon request they'll stop at the junction closest to the ruins, known as Crucero Bonampak (M$95, two hours), instead of the San Javier stop on the highway.

Línea Comitán Lagos de Montebello (☑ 916-345-12-60; Velasco Suárez btwn Calles 6a & 7a Poniente Norte), west of Palenque market, runs hourly vans to Benemérito de las Américas (M$115) 10 times daily (3:30am to 2:45pm), with most continuing around the Carretera Fronteriza to the Lagos de Montebello (M$285, seven hours to Tziscao) and Comitán (M$290, eight hours).

Both companies stop at San Javier (M$73, two hours), the turnoff for Lacanjá Chansayab and Bonampak, 140km from Palenque, and at Crucero Corozal (M$94, 2½ hours), the intersection for Frontera Corozal. For Cascada Welib-Já and Nueva Palestina, take any Carretera Fronteriza–bound combi from Palenque.

Gas stations along the Carretera Fronteriza are limited. From Palenque to Comitán (via the Chajul cutoff road) you'll find them in Chancalá and Benemérito only, but plenty of entrepreneurial locals sell reasonably priced gasoline from large plastic containers. Look for homemade '*Se vende gasolina*' signs.

Palenque to Bonampak

❂ Sights

Cascada Welib-Já　　　　　WATERFALL
(M$30; ☺8am-7pm) Thirty kilometers from Palenque, these 25m-high curtains of water aren't the most dramatic water features in the area, but the turquoise river pools make excellent swimming spots. Amenities include a cross-river zip-line (M$50) and a

simple restaurant. From Palenque, take a combi to the well-signed highway entrance (M$38, 30 minutes); it's a 700m walk in.

Cascada de las Golondrinas   WATERFALL
(Nueva Palestina; M$25; ⊘restaurant 9am-4pm) A lovely water feature tucked 10km off the highway, two rivers cascade dramatically from a high point of 35m and you can swim in clear blue water during the dry season. A wooden boardwalk crosses the outflow, and at dusk hundreds of swallows duck in to bed down in a cave beneath the falls, streaming out at dawn.

You can camp here (campsite M$60), in lovely shady spots with basic facilities. From Palenque, take a combi to the turnoff for Nueva Palestina (M$55, two hours), where taxis charge M$130 one way to the falls. Arrange a return pickup. Drivers should go 9km toward Nueva Palestina to the signed turnoff; the falls are another 1km in.

Plan de Ayutla   ARCHAEOLOGICAL SITE
(near Nueva Palestina; ⊘8am-5pm) FREE The remote Maya ruins of Plan de Ayutla sit on an evocatively overgrown site, with buildings in various states of excavation and abandonment. From the dirt lot under dense tree canopy, follow a winding path up the rise to the North Acropolis, one of three constructed on natural hills. Visitors can explore a maze of interconnected rooms over four levels of the former residential palace complex.

The most significant building in this acropolis is Structure 13, a dramatically vaulted structure with an exterior decorated with unique stepped apron moldings. It was here that archaeologists recently discovered an astronomical observatory with two upper rooms containing window channels aligned in order to view the winter solstice and the solar zenith.

Plan de Ayutla was inhabited between 150 BC and AD 1000 and is believed to have been a regional seat of power between 250 BC and AD 700. Based on its size and features (including its ball court – at 65m long the largest in the upper Río Usumacinta region), archaeologists have two theories about the site's history. One hypothesis is that it was the city of Sak T'zi' (White Dog), which bat-

---

OFF THE BEATEN TRACK

METZABOK & NAHÁ

Situated in the Lacandón Jungle between Ocosingo and the Carretera Fronteriza town of Chancalá, the small and isolated Lacandón villages of Metzabok and Nahá straddle a network of underground rivers in a protected biodiversity zone that's home to wildlife including jaguars, tapirs, howler monkeys and ocelots. Inhabitants here still follow many Lacandón traditions and customs.

The main Lacandón settlement of Nahá contains the lodgings of **Centro Ecoturístico Nahá** (☑cell 916-1161407; www.nahaecoturismo.com; r without bathroom M$400, 1-/2-bedroom cabañas M$820/1000), with simple well-screened rooms or startlingly luxurious *cabañas* (cabins) with hot-water bathrooms. A creekside village restaurant (breakfast M$65, lunch or dinner M$100) serves Mexican and traditional Lacandón dishes. With a guide (one/two hours M$400/700), you can travel on foot or by canoe to various lagoons and learn about the area's flora and fauna.

In Metzabok, villagers offer *lancha* (motorboat) trips (up to M$730 per boat) along forest-ringed Laguna Tzibana, where you can see a moss-framed limestone wall painted with vivid red prehistoric pictograms, and hike to a lookout point above the tree canopy. Unless you want to camp (M$50 per person) and have your own transportation, Metzabok is best for a day trip, as its *cabaña* accommodations aren't well-tended, public transportation is iffy and food can be scarce.

From Palenque, **Transportes Pajchiltic** (Map p384; Av 15 de Marzo) vans leave for Metzabok (M$48, three hours) and Nahá (M$56, four hours) at 9am, 11am (sometimes) and 2pm. The solitary departure back leaves Nahá at 1am and Metzabok at 3am (ouch!). Schedules don't use daylight saving time in either direction. Note that service to Metzabok is unreliable in both directions; it will stop at the junction (6km away) if the driver decides there aren't enough passengers to bother with the detour.

From Ocosingo, trucks to Nahá (M$58, 2½ hours, 11am and noon departures) leave from a walled lot behind the market.

tled Toniná, Yaxchilán and Piedras Negras – and whose bloody defeat by Bonampak may be depicted in that site's famed murals, or perhaps it is the ancient city of Ak'e' (Turtle), where the royalty of Bonampak originated.

By car, drive 11km into Nueva Palestina from the highway; when the paved road turns left next to a clutch of lodgings signs, continue straight onto a gravel road. At about 4.5km, follow the signed left at the junction (the right turn goes to the village of Plan de Ayutla, not the ruins) and then travel another 3km to the clearly visible site. *Ejido* (common landholding) representatives, if present, may charge a small fee. Arriving by combi at the Nueva Palestina highway turnoff, you can negotiate a taxi fare with waiting time.

Bonampak

Bonampak

Bonampak's setting in dense jungle hid it from the outside world until 1946. Stories of how it was revealed are full of mystery and innuendo, but it seems that Charles Frey, a young WWII conscientious objector from the US, and John Bourne, heir to the Singer sewing-machine fortune, were the first outsiders to visit the site when Chan Bor, a Lacandón, took them there in February 1946. Later in 1946, a photographer from the US, Giles Healey, was also led to the site by Chan Bor and found the Templo de las Pinturas, with its famous murals.

The site of **Bonampak** (M\$55; ☉8am-5pm) spreads over 2.4 sq km, but all the main ruins stand around the rectangular Gran Plaza. Never a major city, Bonampak spent most of the Classic period in Yaxchilán's sphere of influence. The most impressive surviving monuments were built under Chan Muwan II, a nephew of Yaxchilán's Itzamnaaj B'alam II, who acceded to Bonampak's throne in AD 776. The 6m-high Stele 1 in the Gran Plaza depicts Chan Muwan II holding a ceremonial staff at the height of his reign. He also features in Stele 2 and Stele 3 on the Acrópolis, which rises from the south end of the plaza.

However, it's the vivid frescoes inside the modest-looking Templo de las Pinturas (Edificio 1) that have given Bonampak its fame – and its name, which means 'Painted Walls' in Yucatecan Maya. Some archaeologists theorize that the murals depict a battle between Bonampak and the city of Sak T'zi', which is believed to be Plan de Ayutla.

Diagrams outside the temple help interpret these murals, which are the finest known from pre-Hispanic America, but which have weathered badly since their discovery. (Early visitors even chucked kerosene over the walls in an attempt to bring out the colors!) Room 1, on the left as you face the temple, shows the consecration of Chan Muwan II's infant son, who is seen held in arms toward the top of the right end of the room's south wall (facing you as you enter). Witnessing the ceremony are 14 jade-toting noblemen. The central Room 2 shows tumultuous battle scenes on its east and south walls and vault, while on the north wall Chan Muwan II, in jaguar-skin battle dress, presides over the torture (by fingernail removal) and sacrifice of prisoners. A severed head lies below him, beside the foot of a sprawling captive. Recently restored and now blazing with vivid color, Room 3 shows a celebratory dance on the Acrópolis steps by lords wearing huge headdresses, and on its east wall three white-robed women puncture their tongues in a ritual bloodletting. The sacrifices, the bloodletting and the dance may all have been part of the ceremonies surrounding the new heir.

In reality, the infant prince probably never got to rule Bonampak; the place was abandoned before the murals were finished, as Classic Maya civilization evaporated.

Don't forget to look up at the intricately carved lintels when entering Edificios 1 and 6.

The Bonampak site abuts the Reserva de la Biosfera Montes Azules, and is rich in wildlife. Drinks and snacks are sold at the entrance to the Monumento Natural Bonampak protected zone, 8km before the ruins, and by the archaeological site entrance.

❶ Getting There & Away

Bonampak is 12km from San Javier, the turnoff town on the Carretera Fronteriza. If you get dropped off at San Javier instead of Crucero Bonampak (8km further in), taxis from San Javier charge M$25.

Get ready to open your wallet: the community charges M$26 per person to enter the town of Lacanjá, and private vehicles are prohibited beyond the Crucero Bonampak, where van drivers charge an exorbitant M$180 round trip per van to the ruins and back.

Lacanjá Chansayab

POP 380 / ELEV 320M

Lacanjá Chansayab, the largest Lacandón Maya village, is 6km from San Javier on the Carretera Fronteriza, and 12km from Bonampak. Its family compounds are scattered around a wide area, many of them with creeks or even the Río Lacanjá flowing past their grassy grounds. Tourism is now an important income earner, and many families run 'campamentos' with rooms, camping and hammock space. As you approach the village, you'll cross the Río Lacanjá on a bridge, from which it's about 700m to a central intersection where tracks go left (south), right (north) and straight (west).

The campamentos all offer guided walks through the surrounding forests to the 8m-high, 30m-wide Cascada Ya Toch Kusam waterfall, some partially unearthed ancient Maya Lacanjá ruins, and the 2.5km-long Laguna Lacanjá. The waterfall can actually be reached by a self-guided trail, the 2.5km **Sendero Ya Toch Kusam** (M$42), which starts 200m west from the central intersection. To continue from the fall to the ruins (a further 2km or so), you do need a guide. A typical three-hour guided walk to the fall and ruins costs M$320 to M$600 per group, plus the admission fee for the trail.

THE LACANDÓN JUNGLE

Chiapas contains swaths of wild green landscape that have nourished its inhabitants for centuries. But this rich trove of natural resources also makes it a contentious prize in the struggle for its water, lumber and oil and gas reserves.

The Selva Lacandona (Lacandón Jungle), in eastern Chiapas, occupies just 0.25% of Mexico. Yet it contains more than 4300 plant species (about 17% of the Mexican total), 450 butterfly species (42% of the national total), at least 340 bird species (32% of the total) and 163 mammal species (30% of the Mexican total). Among these are such emblematic creatures as the jaguar, red macaw, white turtle, tapir and harpy eagle.

This great fund of natural resources and genetic diversity is the southwest end of the Selva Maya, a 30,000-sq-km corridor of tropical rainforest stretching from Chiapas across northern Guatemala into Belize and the southern Yucatán. But the Lacandón Jungle is shrinking fast, under pressure from ranchers, loggers, oil prospectors, and farmers desperate for land. From around 15,000 sq km in the 1950s, an estimated 3000 to 4500 sq km of jungle remains today. Waves of land-hungry settlers deforested the northern third of the Lacandón Jungle by about 1960. Also badly deforested are the far eastern Marqués de Comillas area (settled since the 1970s) and Las Cañadas, between Ocosingo and Montes Azules. Most of what's left is in the Reserva de la Biosfera Montes Azules and the neighboring Reserva de la Biosfera Lacantún.

The Mexican government deeded a large section of the land to a small number of Lacandón families in the 1970s, creating tensions with other indigenous communities whose claims were put aside. Land within the region remains incredibly contested. Lacandones and their advocates consider themselves to be an environmentally sensitive indigenous group, defending their property against invasive settlers. Other communities within the reserve, who provide some of the Zapatista rebels' strongest support, view it as an obfuscated land grab and pretext for eviction under the guise of environmental protection. Zapatista supporters also argue that the settlers are using the forests in nonsustainable ways, and claim that the government seeks to exploit the forests for bio-prospecting (patenting) traditional plants.

The Lacandón people are amiable and welcoming, but you'll need to dig deeper to see evidence of their old way of life: the villagers here are now predominantly Presbyterian and attuned to the modern world, and only some wear the traditional long white Lacandón tunic.

🛌 Sleeping & Eating

Rates dip at least 10% outside the high season.

Cabañas Los Tulipanes CABAÑAS $
(☑community phone 55-5151-2253; d/q M$400/850) This newish place just right at the central town intersection has a cute garden, a large porch and three sunny two-queen rooms with garishly colored mosquito nets and shower curtains for bathroom doors.

Campamento Río Lacanjá CABAÑAS $$
(www.ecochiapas.com/lacanja; dm M$180, s/d/tr without bathroom M$600/700/800, restaurant mains M$75-90; P) About 2km south of the central intersection, these rustic semi-open-air wood-framed cabins with mosquito nets stand close to the jungle-shrouded Río Lacanjá and are open to the sights and sounds of the forest and river. A separate group of large rooms (room/triple/quad M$900/1000/1200) with fans, called Cabañas Ya'ax Can, have two solid wooden double beds, tile floors and a hot-water bathroom.

As well as guided walks, rafting trips on the Río Lacanjá – which has waterfalls up to 2.5m high but no rapids – are offered for a minimum of four people. A half-day outing including Lacanjá ruins and Cascada Ya Toch Kusam (both reached on foot from the river) costs M$600 per group (up to 10 people), and overnight rafting and camping trips also visiting the Bonampak ruins are around M$1400 per person. Rafting trips and tours based at Campamento Río Lacanjá can be reserved through Explora (p365) in San Cristóbal.

Campamento Topche CABAÑAS $$
(campamento-topche@hotmail.com; s/d M$355/555, r without bathroom per person M$180, cabañas M$1200; P 🐾 🛜) About 550m west of the central intersection, this *campamento* has a few options: comfortable rooms with terracotta tile floors and a vaulted and mosquito-proofed *palapa* roof; wood-cabin rooms with shared bathroom, mosquito nets and walls that don't reach the ceiling; and

detached jungly *cabañas* next to the river. All have hot water. Satellite wi-fi is available for M$30 per hour.

Signs to here also say 'Campamento Enrique Paniagua.' The owner's daughter runs a good garden restaurant (meals around M$90, open 7am–9pm) next door.

ℹ️ Getting There & Away

Combis for Lacanjá Chansayab (M$100) and other destinations along the Carretera Fronteriza leave Palenque from an outdoor *colectivo* terminal just south of the ADO bus station. The community collects M$26 per person at the town entrance. If you're traveling from Yaxchilán, combis charge M$53 between Crucero Corozal and San Javier.

Frontera Corozal

POP 5200 / ELEV 200M

This riverside frontier town (formerly Frontera Echeverría) is the stepping-stone to the beautiful ruins of Yaxchilán, and is on the main route between Chiapas and Guatemala's Petén region. Inhabited mainly by Chol Maya, who settled here in the 1970s, Frontera Corozal is 16km by paved road from Crucero Corozal junction on the Carretera Fronteriza. The broad Río Usumacinta, flowing swiftly between jungle-covered banks, forms the Mexico–Guatemala border here.

Long, fast, outboard-powered *lanchas* come and go from the river *embarcadero*. Almost everything you'll need is on the paved street leading back from the river here, including the **immigration office** (🕗8am-6pm), 400m from the *embarcadero*, where you should hand in/obtain a tourist permit if you're leaving for/arriving from Guatemala.

⊙ Sights

Museo de la Cuenca del Usumacinta MUSEUM
(Museum of the Usumacinta Basin; M$23; 🕗8am-3pm) The Museo de la Cuenca del Usumacinta, opposite the immigration office, has good examples of Chol Maya dress, and some information in Spanish on the area's postconquest history, but pride of place goes to two fine and intricately carved steles retrieved from the nearby site of Dos Caobas. If it's not open, inquire at the Restaurante Imperio Maya next door.

⎰ Sleeping & Eating

Escudo Jaguar
CABAÑAS **$$**

(🖋in Guatemala 502-5353-56-37; www.escudo jaguar.com; campsites per person M$150, s/d M$580/680; P) Often used by tour groups, Escudo Jaguar overlooks the river 300m from the *embarcadero*. Its solidly built thatched *cabañas* are kept uniformly spotless, and come equipped with fan and mosquito netting. The best are very spacious and have hot showers and terraces strung with hammocks. The restaurant serves straightforward, but well-prepared Mexican dishes (mains from M$65, breakfasts M$40 to M$75).

Nueva Alianza
CABAÑAS **$$**

(🖋in Guatemala 502-4638-24-47; www.hotel nuevaalianza.com; campsites per person M$65, s/d without bathroom M$180/340, r from M$700; P🖥) Friendly Nueva Alianza, among trees 150m along a side road from the museum, has small, plain but cheerful budget rooms with wooden walls that don't reach the ceiling, and newer stand-alone rooms with bathrooms. All have fans, good wooden furniture and hot water. There's a good on-site restaurant (mains from M$80) and the only internet access in town (M$20 per hour or M$70 per day).

❶ Getting There & Away

If you can't get a bus or combi direct to Frontera Corozal, get one to Crucero Corozal, 16km southeast of San Javier on the Carretera Fronteriza, where taxis (M$40 per person *colectivo*) run to Frontera Corozal. The *ejido* hits up visitors entering or leaving Frontera Corozal for a M$20 per person toll; keep your ticket for exiting unless you're continuing on to Guatemala.

Autotransporte Chamoán vans run hourly from Frontera Corozal *embarcadero* to Palenque (M$100, 2½ to three hours), with the last departure at 4pm or when full.

Lancha organizations have desks in a thatched building near the *embarcadero*, and all charge about the same prices for service to Bethel, Guatemala (boat for 1-3/4/5-7/8-10 people M$450/530/650/800), which is 40 minutes upstream. From Bethel, hourly buses depart to Flores (4½ hours) from 8am to 4pm. Make sure that the driver stops at the Bethel immigration office.

Yaxchilán

Jungle-shrouded Yaxchilán has a terrific setting above a horseshoe loop in the Río Usumacinta. The location gave it control over river commerce, and this in conjunction with a series of successful alliances and conquests made Yaxchilán one of the most important Classic Maya cities in the

Yaxchilán

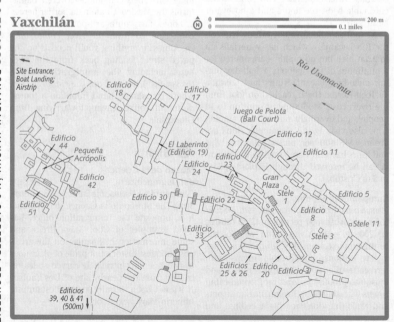

Usumacinta region. Archaeologically, Yaxchilán is famed for its ornamented facades and roofcombs, and its impressive stone lintels carved with conquest and ceremonial scenes. A flashlight is helpful for exploring parts of the site.

Howler monkeys *(saraguates)* inhabit the tall trees here, and are an evocative highlight. You'll almost certainly hear their visceral roars, and you stand a good chance of seeing some. Spider monkeys, and occasionally red macaws, can also be spotted here at times.

Yaxchilán peaked in power and splendor between AD 681 and 800 under the rulers Itzamnaaj B'alam II (Shield Jaguar II, 681–742), Pájaro Jaguar IV (Bird Jaguar IV, 752–68) and Itzamnaaj B'alam III (Shield Jaguar III, 769–800). The city was abandoned around AD 810. Inscriptions here tell more about its 'Jaguar' dynasty than is known of almost any other Maya ruling clan. The shield-and-jaguar symbol appears on many Yaxchilán buildings and steles; Pájaro Jaguar IV's hieroglyph is a small jungle cat with feathers on its back and a bird superimposed on its head.

At the site, drinks are sold at a shack near the river landing. Most of the main monuments have information boards in three languages, including English.

◉ Sights

As you walk toward the ruins (M$55; ☉8am-5pm, last entry 4pm), a signed path to the right leads up to the Pequeña Acrópolis, a group of ruins on a small hilltop – you can visit this later. Staying on the main path, you soon reach the mazelike passages of El Laberinto (Edificio 19), built between AD 742 and 752, during the interregnum between Itzamnaaj B'alam II and Pájaro Jaguar IV. Dozens of bats shelter under the structure's roof today. From this complicated two-level building you emerge at the northwest end of the extensive Gran Plaza.

Though it's difficult to imagine anyone here ever wanting to be any hotter than they already were, Edificio 17 was apparently a sweat house. About halfway along the plaza, Stele 1, flanked by weathered sculptures of a crocodile and a jaguar, shows Pájaro Jaguar IV in a ceremony that took place in AD 761. Edificio 20, from the time of Itzamnaaj B'alam III, was the last significant structure built at Yaxchilán; its lintels are now in Mexico City. Stele 11, at the northeast corner of

the Gran Plaza, was originally found in front of Edificio 40. The bigger of the two figures visible on it is Pájaro Jaguar IV.

An imposing stairway climbs from Stele 1 to Edificio 33, the best-preserved temple at Yaxchilán, with about half of its roofcomb intact. The final step in front of the building is carved with ball-game scenes, and splendid relief carvings embellish the undersides of the lintels. Inside is a statue of Pájaro Jaguar IV, minus his head, which he lost to treasure-seeking 19th-century timber cutters.

From the clearing behind Edificio 33, a path leads into the trees. About 20m along this, fork left uphill; go left at another fork after about 80m, and in some 10 minutes, mostly going uphill, you'll reach three buildings on a hilltop: Edificio 39, Edificio 40 and Edificio 41.

❶ Getting There & Away

Lanchas take 40 minutes running downstream from Frontera Corozal, and one hour to return. The boat companies are in a thatched building near the Frontera Corozal *embarcadero,* all charging about the same prices for trips (return journey with 2½ hours at the ruins for one to three/four/five to seven/eight to 10 people M$900/1050/1450/1800). *Lanchas* normally leave frequently until 1:30pm or so; try to hook up with other travelers or a tour group to share costs.

Benemérito de las Américas to Las Nubes

South of Frontera Corozal is the far eastern corner of Chiapas, known as Marqués de Comillas (for its Spanish former landowner.) After oil explorers opened tracks into this jungle region in the 1970s, settlers poured in from all over Mexico. Ranching and logging have made some rich, while others profit from smuggling drugs or immigrants. Rough-and-ready Benemérito de las Américas is the region's main town. Destinations in this area are often reached via Comitán.

REFORMA AGRARIA

The beautiful and welcoming Las Guacamayas (☑in Guatemala 502-5157-96-10; www.lasguacamayas.mx; Ejido Reforma Agraria; dm M$264, cabañas M$1350-1650, ste M$1950; ℗🐕@) ecolodge is right on the bank of the broad Río Lacantún, one of the Usumacinta's major tributaries, with the Reserva de la Biosfera Montes Azules on the opposite bank. Large, superbly comfortable thatch-roofed cabañas, with full mosquito screens, verandas and ample bathrooms with hot showers, are spread around the extensive grounds, linked by wooden walkways. Dorms are shared two-bed rooms with common bathrooms.

Las Guacamayas is the heart of an impressive community program to protect scarlet macaws (guacamayas). This spectacular and endangered member of the parrot family once ranged as far north as Veracruz, but its only Mexican home today is far eastern Chiapas. Numbers at Reforma Agraria have increased to more than 110 pairs since 1991, when the 14.5-sq-km macaw reserve was founded. The birds move in and out of the reserve in seasonal pursuit of food; the best months for observing them are December to June, when they are nesting. Ask to see the chick aviary on-site and about the possibility of accompanying staff when they monitor nests.

There's a good restaurant overlooking the river, serving Mexican meals (breakfast M$60 to M$80, mains from M$80). From March through May, the river level drops and you can swim and take advantage of a sandy beach area.

One-and-a-half-hour guided macaw-spotting walks cost M$420; they're best in the early morning or at dusk. Boat trips into the Montes Azules reserve cost M$1400 for two hours. (All activities are per tour with an eight-person maximum.) You should spot crocodiles and howler monkeys, and with luck toucans and white-tailed deer. Villagers in Reforma Agraria also rent out horses for about M$130 per hour, and charge about M$50 per person to camp and around M$120 to rent gear. In low season all prices drop around 20%; breakfast is included in September and October.

❶ Getting There & Away

The road to Reforma Agraria turns west off the Carretera Fronteriza 8km south of Benemérito. It's paved all the way through, rejoining the Carretera Fronteriza 5km south of Chajul, though large (but navigable) potholes, messy rainy-season mudslides and the occasional crumbling of the shoulder pavement will keep your eyes on the road.

From the colectivo lot near the bus terminal in Palenque, combis run to Pico de Oro (M$145, four hours) at 8am, 10am, noon and 2pm. Occasional camionetas also run between Benemérito and Pico de Oro (M$45, 30 minutes), though

you'll often have to hire a taxi (M$50 per person colectivo or M$230 private) if it's past early morning. Camionetas run from Pico de Oro to Reforma Agraria (M$30, 30 minutes), and vice versa, about hourly from 6am until early afternoon. You can also take a taxi to Reforma Agraria from Frontera Corozal (M$600), Benemérito (M$250) or Pico de Oro (M$200); prices are per carload.

From Comitán, 18 vans a day run to Reforma Agraria (M$145 to M$155, 4½ hours), passing through the Lagos de Montebello en route, though only those from Transportes Tzoyol will drop you off directly in front of Las Guacamayas. Otherwise it's a 1km walk in from the road.

LAS NUBES & AROUND

Las Nubes is 12km off the Carretera Fronteriza, 55km from Tziscao. From Transportes Tzoyol in Comitán, there are five daily combis (M$83, 3½ to four hours) between 7:30am and 4:30pm, and five daily returns.

✦ Activities

Ecoturismo Xbulanjá   RAFTING
(☑ in Guatemala 502-3137-56-91; www.xbulanja. com) From Embarcadero Jerusalén, just east of the Las Nubes highway turnoff, this Tseltal cooperative offers Class III rafting to Las Nubes for M$2200 (two to six passengers, 2½ hours), and its lodging (campsite M$50, cabañas M$800) and restaurant (mains M$60 to M$100) are a less expensive alternative to Las Nubes. Rafting-trip prices include the drive back.

🛏 Sleeping

Las Nubes   LODGE $$
(☑ in Guatemala 502-4972-02-04; www.causas verdeslasnubes.com; campsites per person M$60, cabañas M$1050) A bit of a trek but well worth it, Las Nubes is a heavenly retreat among scores of cascades and rapids on the turquoise Río Santo Domingo. Some of the river pools are great swimming spots; it's M$20 per person to swim here if you're not staying the night. A swinging bridge straddles a fierce section of water-carved canyon, making an excellent vantage point from which to swoon over the grandest waterfalls.

A 15-minute hike up to a mirador rewards you with blue-green jungle views. There's an adrenaline-pumping zip-line (M$150), and you can spelunk and rappel from February through June.

Fifteen well-built cabañas have hot water and pleasant porches, and a waterside restaurant serves meals (breakfast M$65, lunch and dinner M$90), but no alcohol, though you can bring your own. Lodging rates drop 25% in low season.

Laguna Miramar

ELEV 400M

Ringed by rainforest, pristine Laguna Miramar, 140km southeast of Ocosingo in the Reserva de la Biosfera Montes Azules (Montes Azules Biosphere Reserve), is one of Mexico's most remote and exquisite lakes. Frequently echoing with the roars of howler monkeys, the 16-sq-km lake is bathtub-warm and virtually unpolluted. Rock ledges extending from small islands make blissful wading spots, and petroglyphs and a turtle cave are reachable by canoe.

The lake is accessible thanks to a successful ecotourism project in the small Maya community of **Emiliano Zapata** (☑ community phone 200-124-88-80/81/82), near its western shore. If you arrive independently, ask for the Comité de Turismo. Through this representative you must arrange and pay for the services you need: a guide costs M$200 per day (maximum three people), a day-use fee is M$45, and rental of a *cayuco* (traditional canoe) for exploring the lake is M$100 per hour. Sleeping bags, hammocks and tents are available to rent (M$200 per person) and, for groups, local women can be hired to purchase and cook your food at the lake. Bring cash to cover your expenses.

The 7km walk from Emiliano Zapata to the lake, through *milpas* (cornfields) and forest that includes *caoba* (mahogany) and the *matapalo* (strangler fig) trees, takes about 1½ hours and can be very muddy – good closed shoes are highly recommended. At the lake, you will hear howler monkeys. Other wildlife includes spider monkeys, tapirs, macaws and toucans; butterflies are prolific. Locals fish for *mojarra* (perch), and will assure you that the lake's few crocodiles are not dangerous.

🛏 Sleeping & Eating

At the lakeshore, you can sling a hammock or camp (per person M$40) under a *palapa* shelter. But if you arrive after noon, you'll need to stay in Emiliano Zapata, as the guides want to make it home before dark. The village has a handful of simple *cabañas* (M$130 per person) with river views, all with one queen and one twin bed, a fan and shared bathrooms. A number of *comedores* make meals

---

ℹ LAS NUBES–LAGUNA MIRAMAR SHORTCUT

If you're visiting both Las Nubes and Laguna Miramar via public transit, you can avoid the east–west backtracks to the highway by walking between Las Nubes and Loma Bonita, a town about halfway in along the road to the *lanchas* for Laguna Miramar. It's approximately a 5km hike (40 minutes, with some hills) from the swinging bridge at Las Nubes to Loma Bonita, where you can catch onward combis.

---

for about M$45. You can also rent a hammock and mosquito net (M$40) and string them up in a roofed area next to the *cabañas*.

ℹ Getting There & Away

Try to visit outside the rainy season (late August to November), when land access is very difficult, and walking the muddy foot trail feels like an aerobics class in quicksand. If you're determined to go then, you can rent a pair of tall rubber boots (M$20) or a hard-working horse (M$200/400 one way/return). Some agencies in San Cristóbal de las Casas run three- or four-day trips to Miramar from San Cristóbal via the river route, with prices from M$6400 per person.

AIR

Servicios Aéreos San Cristóbal (p402) has small-plane charter flights (up to four passengers) to San Quintín from Comitán (M$5300, per plane one way).

After you land, follow the dirt road opposite a military complex beside San Quintín's airstrip. It leads to Emiliano Zapata, about a 15- to 20-minute walk; the ecotourism project is at the far end of the village.

BOAT

Take a combi from Comitán to La Democracia (across the bridge from Amatitlán) or Plan de Río Azul and hire a *lancha* (M$1250 one way, maximum eight passengers, two hours) to Emiliano Zapata via the Río Jatate. In La Democracia (by prior arrangement), **Hipólito Vásquez** (☑ community phone 55-1454-5788/89/90) is the only area *lanchero* that carries life vests. Most other boats depart from 4km on in Plan de Río Azul, where *lanchas* (M$1350 to M$2600 per boat) leave on demand until about 3pm. La Democracia and Plan de Río Azul are a rough 16km and 20km respectively from the Carretera Fronteriza highway; the first half is paved.

BUS & COLECTIVO

Transportation from Comitán and Ocosingo services San Quintín and Emiliano Zapata. The Comitán route is slightly shorter (the road is paved to Guadalupe Tepeyec, just before La Realidad; the Ocosingo road is paved to La Garrucha) and uses combis instead of trucks. Though San Quintín is technically the last stop, drivers will drop you off five minutes further in Emiliano Zapata if requested. The ecotourism project can usually organize in-town pickups for the return. Schedules are subject to change, and daylight saving time isn't used. Unpaved sections of road can be challenging in the rainy season.

From Comitán

Transportes Las Margaritas (6a Calle Sur Oriente 51, btwn 4a & 5a Av Oriente Sur) combis service Las Margaritas (M$19, 25 minutes) frequently. From Las Margaritas, **Grupo Monteflor** (cnr Av Central Sur & 1a Calle Sur Poniente) near the plaza, and **Transportes Río Euseba** (3a Av Oriente Sur btwn Calle Central & 1a Calle Oriente Sur) near the market, have daily departures to San Quintín (M$95, 4½ to six hours) from 5am to noon. The companies each depart about every two hours, but the schedules are staggered; they mostly alternate every hour. Combis return from San Quintín from 2am until noon.

From Ocosingo

Trucks leave for San Quintín (M$95, five to six hours in the dry season) from a large walled lot at the back of the market. Departures are at 9am, 10:30am, noon and 3:30pm, or when crammed full. Return trucks at midnight, 2am, 5am and noon.

Comitán

📞 963 / POP 98,000 / ELEV 1560M

With a pretty plaza of modern sculpture pieces and mature flat-topped trees where birds flock and chirp in the evening, the colonial town of Comitán has a pleasant, artsy atmosphere. Set on a high plain 90km southeast of San Cristóbal, Comitán contains some good places to stay and eat, a few interesting museums, and there are several natural and archaeological attractions less than an hour away in the verdant countryside.

◎ Sights

Iglesia de Santo Domingo CHURCH
(⊙8am-2pm & 4:30-8pm) On the plaza, the Iglesia de Santo Domingo dates back to the 16th and 17th centuries, and sports unusual and handsome blind arcading on its tower.

Its former monastic buildings next door are now the **Centro Cultural Rosario Castellanos** (1a Av Oriente; ⊙9am-9pm) FREE, which has a pretty wood-pillared patio featuring a mural on local history.

Casa Museo Dr Belisario Domínguez MUSEUM
(Av Central Sur 35; ⊙10am-6pm Mon-Sat, 9am-noon Sun) FREE Just south of the main plaza is the Casa Museo Dr Belisario Domínguez, the family home of Comitán's biggest hero and the site of his medical practice. It provides (in Spanish) fascinating insights into the state of medicine and the life of the professional classes in early-20th-century Chiapas (with a reconstruction of the onsite pharmacy), as well as the heroic tale of Domínguez' political career, ending in his assassination.

Museo Arqueológico de Comitán MUSEUM
(1a Calle Sur Oriente; ⊙9am-5pm Tue-Sun) FREE This museum, just east of the plaza, displays artifacts from the area's many archaeological sites (Spanish interpretation only). There are misshapen pre-Hispanic skulls on display – deliberately 'beautified' by squeezing infants' heads between boards.

🛏 Sleeping

Hotel del Virrey HOTEL $
(📞963-632-18-11; hotel_delvirrey@hotmail.com; Av Central Norte 13; d M$440-560, tr M$600-800; 🅿😊🛜) Resident turtles splash in a fountain at the Virrey, a 19th-century house with rooms of varying sizes radiating from a flower-draped courtyard. All have cable TV, and smaller upstairs rooms enjoy a nice view of nearby El Calvario church.

★**Hotel Nak'am Secreto** HOTEL $$
(📞963-636-73-85; www.nakan.mx; 1a Av Oriente Norte 29; r from M$861; ❄🛜) With large, modern rooms, some charming common areas and fabulously detailed service, this is Comitán's best value-for-money hotel. The super central location and views from the rooftop garden seal the deal.

Hotel Hacienda de los Ángeles LUXURY HOTEL $$
(📞963-632-00-74; www.hotelhaciendalosangeles.com; 2a Calle Norte Poniente 6; incl breakfast r M$892, ste M$1290-1620; 🅿😊❄@🛜🏊) Comitán's single luxury hotel provides complimentary welcome cocktails, professional service and spacious accommodations with

Comitán

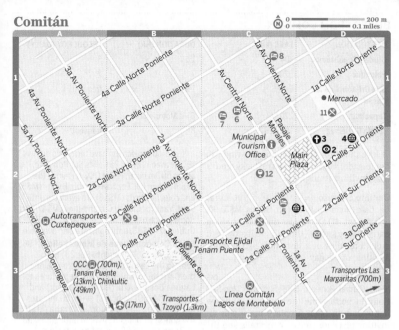

sober, classical-style decor. All rooms have at least two double beds or one king-sized bed, air-con, cable TV, bathtub and quality furnishings, and suites have two levels. There's even a dramatically lit pool with its own bar.

★ **Hotel Casa Delina**   BOUTIQUE HOTEL **$$$**
(☑ 963-101-47-93; www.hotelcasadelina.com; 1a Calle Sur Poniente 6; r M$1832; [P][☀][🛜]) Attentive restoration and the work of contemporary Mexican and international artists have transformed this 250-year-old mansion into one of the most stylish hotels in Chiapas. Set along a courtyard with original wood-pillared arches and tiling and a gorgeous garden, the eight luxurious rooms blend colonial grandeur and playful industrial chic. An on-site cafe serves excellent organic Chiapan coffees.

✗ Eating & Drinking

A handful of good typical restaurants line the west side of the plaza.

Yuli Moni Comedor   MEXICAN **$**
(Mercado; quesadillas M$20-25; ⊙ 8am-5pm; ⊖ 🔅) Come here for an inexpensive meal or snack. This mercado *comedor* has tasty and filling quesadillas; the *nopales* (cactus)

Comitán

⊙ Sights
1 Casa Museo Dr Belisario Domínguez	D2
2 Centro Cultural Rosario Castellanos	D2
3 Iglesia de Santo Domingo	D2
4 Museo Arqueológico de Comitán	D2

🛏 Sleeping
5 Hotel Casa Delina	C2
6 Hotel del Virrey	C1
7 Hotel Hacienda de los Ángeles	C1
8 Hotel Nak'am Secreto	C1

✗ Eating
9 Camino Secreto	B2
10 Pasta di Roma	C2
11 Yuli Moni Comedor	D1

🍸 Drinking & Nightlife
12 Shangri La	C2

---

and mushrooms are also good options for vegetarians.

Pasta di Roma   ITALIAN **$$**
(1a Av Poniente Sur 1; mains M$100-180; ⊙ noon-11pm Tue-Sat, to 6pm Sun) Italian can be a dodgy prospect in these parts, but this is the real deal, run by an Italian chef with plenty

BUSES FROM COMITÁN

DESTINATION	FARE (M$)	DURATION (HR)	FREQUENCY (DAILY)
Ciudad Cuauhtémoc	104	1½	3
Palenque	320	7	2
San Cristóbal de las Casas	64-86	1¾	frequent
Tapachula	270	6 via Motozintla	5
Tuxtla Gutiérrez	100-126	3	frequent

of love put into each dish, a great wine list, homemade sausages if you're lucky and a cozy, inviting atmosphere.

Camino Secreto   MEXICAN **$$**
(1a Calle Norte Poniente 48b; mains M$70-90; ⏰9am-7pm; 🐾) Don't miss the nearly hidden entry off the street – this is a great stop for a quick breakfast or a tasty home-style snack any time of the day.

Shangri La   BAR
(Calle Central Poniente 6; ⏰5pm-1am Mon-Sat) Colorful bottles line the entrance, and low lights and an open fireplace make this an inviting place for coffee or cocktails and the free snacks that come with them. Cozy up in a futon or beanbag in the toasty attic or inspect the walls plastered with photos of happy patrons.

ℹ Information

BBVA Bancomer (cnr 1a Av Oriente Sur & 1a Calle Sur Oriente; ⏰8:30am-4pm Mon-Fri) Changes euros (but not dollars) Monday through Friday; ATM.

Instituto Nacional de Migración (📞963-632-22-00; Carretera Panamericana; ⏰9am-1pm Mon-Fri) The immigration office is on the Pan-American Hwy, just past the turnoff for Tzimol, 5km south of the town center.

Municipal Tourism Office (Av Central Norte; ⏰8am-8pm Mon-Wed, to 9pm Thu-Sun)

Post Office (Av Central Sur 45; ⏰8:30am-4:30pm Mon-Fri, to noon Sat)

ℹ Getting There & Around

The Pan-American Hwy (Hwy 190), named Blvd Belisario Domínguez here but usually just called 'El Bulevar,' passes through the west of town.

Comitán's **OCC bus terminal** (📞963-632-09-80; Blvd Belisario Domínguez Sur 43) is on the Pan-American Hwy. Besides the destinations in the table, it also serves Mexico City, Villahermosa, Playa del Carmen and Cancún. Across the road from the OCC terminal, 'centro' combis (M$8) run to the main plaza; a taxi is M$32.

Numerous *colectivos* have terminals on Hwy 190 between 1a and 2a Calles Sur Poniente, about 500m north of the OCC terminal; they depart when full. For San Cristóbal, vans (M$52) and *colectivo* taxis (M$56) are available until 9pm. Vans for Ciudad Cuauhtémoc (M$47, until 8pm), which usually say 'Comalapa,' and Tuxtla Gutiérrez (M$85, until 6pm) are also available.

Línea Comitán Lagos de Montebello (📞963-632-08-75; 2a Av Poniente Sur 23) Runs vans to the Lagos de Montebello and along the Carretera Fronteriza, with departures to Laguna Bosque Azul (M$45, one hour) and Tziscao (M$50, 1¼ hours) every 20 minutes from 3am to 5pm; to Reforma Agraria (M$185, 4½ hours) 10 times from 3am until 2pm; and to Palenque (M$300, eight hours) eight times daily, 3:30am to 11am. Schedules don't use daylight saving time.

Servicios Aéreos San Cristóbal (📞963-632-46-62; www.chiapasdesdeelcielo.com; Carretera Panamericana Km 1262) Runs day trips to Bonampak and Yaxchilán with overflights of Las Nubes and Laguna Miramar (M$17,000 round trip, including site fees), plus a service that adds on a Palenque flight and overnight and a return overflight of Agua Azul (M$23,500, not including lodging or Palenque site fees). Prices are per four-passenger plane, not per person.

Transportes Tzoyol (📞963-632-77-39; 4a Av Poniente Sur 1039, at 13a Calle Sur Poniente) Runs vans to Reforma Agraria (M$152) eight times daily, 2:30am to 3pm, as well as to Plan de Río Azul (M$88, 3½ hours), the connection for boats to Laguna Miramar, four times a day between 4:30am and 2pm. It doesn't use daylight saving time.

Around Comitán

El Chiflón

These mighty waterfalls tumble off the edge of an escarpment 41km southwest of Comitán. For an up-close experience of sheer awesome power, El Chiflón is hard to beat.

One of two local *ejido* projects along the banks of the Río San Vicente, **Centro Ecoturístico Cadena de Cascadas El Chiflón** (☑963-596-97-09; www.chiflon. com.mx; M$30; ☉8:30am-5pm; 🚗) has set up a number of attractive amenities on the approach to the falls, including a dozen comfortable, well-built *cabañas* (single/double M$400/800), all with river view, bathroom and tight window netting; campsites (per person M$35); and a good open-air restaurant (mains M$80 to M$130). A small interpretive center provides information (in Spanish) on the river and wildlife in the area.

A 1km approach road heads up from Hwy 226 to the parking area, from which a well-made path leads 1.3km up alongside the forest-lined river (which has nice swimming spots) to a series of increasingly dramatic and picturesque waterfalls. Reaching the 120m Velo de Novia fall, prepare to be drenched by flying spray. You can also fly across the river on a zip-line (M$75).

In the dry season, from roughly February through July, the falls form a foamy line and the blue river water is safe enough to swim in. But during the rainy season, rapid currents turn the river a muddy brown, the falls gush with abandon and swimming is a deathly proposition.

From Comitán, **Autotransportes Cuxtepeques** (Blvd Belisario Domínguez Sur btwn 1a & 2a Calles Norte Poniente) runs hourly vans and buses to the El Chiflón turnoff on Hwy 226 (M$30, 45 minutes) from 4am to 8pm. Mototaxis (per person M$8) wait there to ferry passengers up the road. Drivers should take the Tzimol turnoff from the Pan-American Hwy, 5km south of central Comitán.

Tenam Puente

These **Maya ruins** (M$36; ☉8am-5pm) feature three ball courts, a 20m tiered pyramid and other structures rising from a terraced, wooded hillside. Like Chinkultic, Tenam Puente was one of a set of fringe Classic Maya settlements in this part of Chiapas that (unlike more famed lowland sites such as Palenque and Yaxchilán) seem to have survived in the post-Classic period, possibly as late as AD 1200. It has a pleasant rural setting and good long-distance views.

A 5km-long paved road leads west to the site from Hwy 190, 9km south of Comitán. **Transporte Ejidal Tenam Puente** (3a Av Poniente Sur 8) runs combis (M$22) every 45 minutes, 8am to 6pm. The last combi from the ruins returns at 4pm. A taxi costs about M$320 return (with an hour at the ruins).

Parador-Museo Santa María

Parador-Museo Santa María BOUTIQUE HOTEL $$$
(☑963-632-51-16; www.paradorsantamaria. com.mx; Carretera La Trinitaria-Lagos de Montebello Km 22; r M$2100, 6-8 person tents M$6800; 🅿☕🛜🏊) Evocative of a past era, this beautiful hotel-museum, 1.5km off the road to the Lagos de Montebello, is the most luxurious and atmospheric place to stay in the Comitán area. The restored 19th-century hacienda is decorated throughout with period furniture and art; some of the eight rooms have tiled bathtubs and fireplaces, and all

---

DRINKS OF CHIAPAS

Comiteco A unique variant of *mezcal*, made with a mix of *maguey* (type of *agave*) and *piloncillo* (cooked sugarcane). It's smoother and more syrupy than tequila, with a clear appearance or a greenish tint. Traditionally made in Comitán.

Tascalate A cold, sweet concoction prepared from ground cacao, pine nuts, toasted corn, cinnamon and *achiote* (annatto). Very interesting and super delicious!

Pox Inexpensive grain alcohol made from sugarcane, it's pronounced (and sometimes spelled) 'posh.' The undisputed choice for those who want to pass out cold on the street, but not so deadly when mixed with lots of fruit juice.

Pozol A thick, heavy mixture of *masa* (cornmeal dough) in water, it's often mixed with sugar and sometimes has chili or chocolate added. It's the equivalent of an energy drink, and you can see indigenous people everywhere carrying it around in reused plastic 1L bottles. Travelers often take a ball of the *masa* and make some up when there's water available.

TO/FROM GUATEMALA: CIUDAD CUAUHTÉMOC

Very frequent *colectivos* (M$48) and intermittent buses (M$62) run between Ciudad Cuautémoc and Comitán (1½ hours). From Ciudad Cuautémoc, three daily OCC buses run to San Cristóbal de las Casas (M$118, 3½ hours) and beyond from 11am to 10pm, but it's usually quicker to get to Comitán and pick up onward transportation there. Other (infrequent) destinations include Palenque, Cancún and Tapachula.

Mexican immigration (⊘8am-10pm) is across the street from the OCC terminal; *colectivos* generally assume that travelers need to be dropped off there. The Guatemalan border post is 4km south at La Mesilla, and 'Línea' combis (M$8) and taxis (M$15 *colectivo*, M$50 private) ferry people between the two sides. There are banks and money changers on both sides of the border, which closes to car traffic from 9pm to 6am.

From La Mesilla, moto taxis (M$8/Q5) can drop you at the 2nd-class bus depot. Second-class buses leave very frequently from 6am to 6pm for Huehuetenango (Q28, two hours) and Quetzaltenango (Q50, four hours), where you can find onward connections to Guatemala City. About 1km inside the border (just past the curve in the highway), first-class Línea Dorada (www.lineadorada.info) has direct daily departures to Guatemala City (Q220, eight hours) at 11pm and 8pm.

look out over expansive grassy lawns to the countryside beyond.

An odd but opulent newer lodging addition is an enormous Arabian-style tent, furnished with Oriental rugs, a bathroom with a Jacuzzi tub and animal-mouth faucets, and lavish room-dividing curtains. Gaze out over green hills from the solar-heated pool.

The chapel here is a religious art museum (M$30; ⊘9am-6pm) with an interesting array of colonial-era work from Europe and the Philippines as well as Mexico and Guatemala. The excellent Restaurant Los Geranios (mains M$150-300; ⊘8am-9pm) serves Chiapan and international dishes prepared with organic ingredients (including coffee) grown on-site.

Look for the 22km marker from La Trinitaria on the Montebello road. Prices drop 30% in the low season, but book in advance for high season.

Chinkultic

Chinkultic Ruins ARCHAEOLOGICAL SITE
(⊘8am-5pm) FREE Chinkultic was a minor Maya power during the late Classic period and, like Tenam Puente, may have survived into post-Classic times. Of 200 mounds scattered over a wide area of dramatically situated ruins, only a few have been cleared, but the site is worth a visit. Note that the site is closed periodically; it's best to check with the Comitán tourist office before heading out.

The ruins are in two groups. From the entrance, first take the path to the left, which curves around to the right below one of Chinkultic's biggest structures, E23, covered in vegetation. The path reaches a grassy plaza with several weathered steles, some carved with human figures, and a ball court on the right.

Return to the entrance, from which another path heads to the Plaza Hundida (Sunken Plaza), crosses a stream, then climbs steeply up to the Acrópolis, a partly restored temple atop a rocky escarpment, with remarkable views over the surrounding lakes and forests and down into a cenote (sinkhole) 50m below – into which the Maya used to toss offerings of pottery, beads, bones and obsidian knives.

Chinkultic is situated about 48km from Comitán, on the road to the Lagos de Montebello. Combis for the lakes can drop you at the intersection (M$45 from Comitán); the site is 2km north via a paved access road.

Lagos de Montebello

The temperate pine and oak forest along the Guatemalan border east of Chinkultic is dotted with more than 50 small lakes of varied hues, known as the Lagos (or Lagunas) de Montebello. The area is very picturesque, refreshing and peaceful. The paved road to Montebello turns east off Hwy 190 just north of La Trinitaria, 16km south of Comitán. It passes Chinkultic after 32km, and enters the Parque Nacional Lagunas de Montebello 5km beyond. A further 800m along is a ticket booth, where you must pay a M$23 park-admission fee. Here the road forks: north to the Lagunas de Colores (2km to 3km) and east to the village of Tziscao (9km), beyond which it becomes the Carretera Fronteriza, continuing east to Ixcán and ultimately circling back up to Palenque.

◉ Sights & Activities

From the park ticket booth, the northward road leads to the Lagunas de Colores, five lakes with vivid hues that range from turquoise to deep green: Laguna Agua Tinta, Laguna Esmeralda, Laguna Encantada, Laguna Ensueño and, the biggest, Laguna Bosque Azul, on the left where the paved road ends.

There's a nice 15-minute walk from here to the Grutas San Rafael del Arco, a group of caves. There's no signage, but you can hire guides for a small fee. There's an area where a river rushes through a natural rock arch, a riverside cave downstream, and a more extensive cave that turns out to be the bottom of a sinkhole.

In the Laguna Ensueño (and sometimes Bosque Azul) parking lot, *camiones* (trucks) do shared three- to five-hour lake tours for about M$600 per vehicle, though it can be harder to get a group together on weekdays. Local boys offer multilake horseback excursions that include Dos Cenotes (M$200, two to three hours), a pair of sinkholes in the forest, or to the Laguna de Montebello (about one hour away).

Along the eastward road from the park ticket booth, after 3km a track leads 200m north to the Laguna de Montebello, one of the area's larger lakes, with a flat open area along its shore, and more boys offering horseback rides to Dos Cenotes. The local *ejido* charges a M$25 entrance fee to access the lake areas along the Tziscao road; pay once and keep your receipt for the other lakes. About 3km further along the Tziscao road, another track leads left to the Cinco Lagunas (Five Lakes). Only four are visible from the road, but the second, La Cañada, on the right after about 1.5km, is one of the most beautiful Montebello lakes, nearly cut in half by two rocky outcrops.

About 1km nearer to Tziscao, another track leads 1km north to cobalt-blue Laguna Pojoj, which has an island in the middle that you can visit on simple rafts. Laguna Tziscao, on the Guatemalan border, comes into view 1km past the Pojoj junction. The turnoff to the Chuj-speaking village of Tziscao, a pretty and spread-out place stretching right down to the lakeside, is a little further on.

🛏️ Sleeping & Eating

The Laguna Ensueño and Laguna Bosque Azul parking lot have basic *comedores* that serve drinks and simple meals, and food options exist at most other lakes as well.

Villa Tziscao CABAÑAS, CAMPGROUND $
(📞in Guatemala 502-5780-27-75; www.ecotziscao.com; campsites per person M$60, 1-/2-/3-bed r or cabaña M$450/780/980; 🅿️🍽️@🛜) By the lake in Tziscao village (2km from the highway turnoff), this medium-sized lakeside complex is run by an *ejido* cooperative. Extensive, grassy grounds include a sandy beach with terrific views across the lake to the foothills of the Cuchumatanes in Guatemala. Comfortable rooms in the main hotel

Lagos de Montebello

building have new beds and bathroom tiling, plus flat-screen TVs.

More rustic wooden *cabañas* are also available, but skip the shoreside units, as they're partially submerged for weeks during the rainy season. All accommodations have a private bathroom with hot water, and campers can use the kitchen. The hotel also has a restaurant (breakfast M$70, mains from M$80).

You can rent two-person kayaks (M$60 per hour), or bicycles (M$170 for four hours) to go exploring.

La Esmeralda CABIN **$**
(☑ cell 963-1094329; cabin M$450-600) Like a cute little summer camp, these well-built two-story wood chalets have hot water, two channels of TV and a restaurant (mains M$60 to M$85). It's located 500m east off the road between Laguna Ensueño and Laguna Encantada.

ℹ Getting There & Away

Public transportation from Comitán is a snap, making it an easy day trip. Vans go to the end of the road at Laguna Bosque Azul and to Tziscao, and will drop you at the turnoffs for Museo Parador Santa María, Chinkultic and the other lakes. The last vehicles back to Comitán leave Tziscao and Laguna Bosque Azul in the early evening.

From San Cristóbal, a number of agencies offer tours that take in the lakes, throw in a visit to El Chiflón and get you back by dinnertime.

El Soconusco & Beaches

Chiapas' fertile coastal plain, 15km to 35km wide, is called the Soconusco, and is named for the Aztecs' most distant 15th-century province, called Xoconochco. It's hot and humid year-round, with serious rainfall from mid-May to mid-October. The lushly vegetated Sierra Madre de Chiapas, rising steeply from the plain, provides an excellent environment for coffee, bananas and other crops. Olive ridley and green sea turtles and the occasional leatherback nest along the coastline from June through November, and turtle preservation projects exist in Puerto Arista, Boca del Cielo, La Encrucijada and Chocohuital/Costa Azul.

The endless beach and ocean are wonderfully clean and warm here, but take care where you go in – the surf is often rough, and riptides (known as *canales*) can quickly sweep you out a long way. Bring bug repellant for overnights, as sandflies can be fierce from May through October.

OFF THE BEATEN TRACK

IGLESIA VIEJA

Believed to be the regional capital of the Zoque during the Classic period, these recently opened **ruins** (☉8am-5pm) FREE were inhabited between AD 250 and AD 400, and adventurous visitors can visit two restored groupings. The site's most prominent characteristic is its use of megalithic granite architecture, and its most impressive structure, the namesake 'Old Church,' is a 95m by 65m pyramid utilizing stone blocks weighing over a ton each. Instead of steps, the apex is reached via a ramp – look for the petroglyph cross at the south side of its base.

The other distinctive feature here is the presence of many carved anthropomorphic and zoomorphic monuments scattered throughout the site. The most well-known are the Sapodrilo (it appears to be a cross between a toad and a crocodile), and the Altar de las Cuatras Caras (Altar of the Four Faces).

An exuberant authority on regional archaeological sites, the distinguished **Ricardo López Vassallo** (☑966-663-01-05, cell 966-1042394; rilova36@hotmail.com) lives in Tonalá and can organize transportation and his services as a guide (and possibly his son for English speakers). He is paid by the government, so visitors only pay for transportation. It's worth consulting him on road conditions if you want to drive independently.

From the signed turnoff at Km 10 on the Tonalá–Arriaga highway, it's about 9km (30 minutes) east off the main road; a high-clearance vehicle is required mid-May through November because the last 2km up can be washed out, but walking a section may still be required.

Tonalá

[📞] 966 / POP 35,000

This sweaty, bustling town on Hwy 200 is the jumping-off point for the northern beaches. You can use the ATM at **Banamex** (Hidalgo 137), a block east of the plaza on the main drag. Get cash if you're heading for nearby beaches, as there aren't ATMs there.

A fine central choice fronting the east side of the plaza, the **Hotel Galilea** ([📞] 966-663-02-39; Hidalgo 138; s/d M$360/480; [P][❄][🛜]) has a convenient restaurant and clean medium-sized rooms with dark wooden furniture that give it an old-world feel. **Hotel Grajandra** ([📞] 966-663-01-44; Hidalgo 204; s/d M$560/680; [P][⊖][❄][🛜][🏊]) is a friendly place next to the OCC bus terminal, with bright, large rooms with 1970s-era decor and a breezy upstairs restaurant. One block east from the plaza (behind the Hotel Galilea), **Restaurant Nora** (Independencia 10; mains M$85-165; [🕐] 8am-6pm Mon-Fri, to 4pm Sat; [⊖]) has served ample portions in its wood-beamed dining room since 1964.

From the central plaza, the **OCC bus terminal** ([📞] 966-633-05-40; Hidalgo) is 600m west and the 2nd-class **Rápidos del Sur** (RS; Hidalgo btwn Belisario Domínguez & Iturbide) is 250m east. Both lines have frequent services to Tapachula (M$128 to M$236, three to four hours), Pijijiapan (M$66, one hour) and Tuxtla Gutiérrez (M$144 to M$216, 2½ to three hours).

Colectivo taxis for Puerto Arista (M$23, 20 minutes), Boca del Cielo (M$38, 35 minutes) and Madre Sal (M$43) run from Matamoros between 20 de Marzo and Belisario Domínguez, four blocks east of the plaza and one block downhill. Puerto Arista combis (M$20) leave from Juárez between 20 de Marzo and 5 de Mayo, one block further downhill. Combis to Madre Sal (M$33) depart from near the market on 5 de Mayo between Juárez and Allende; a private taxi costs M$240. Colectivo taxis for Pijijiapan (M$47) can be found on Hidalgo between 5 de Mayo and 20 de Mayo. Taxis and combis run until about 7pm.

Puerto Arista

[📞] 994

The state's most developed beach town is 18km southwest of Tonalá, though unless you visit during weekends, summer or holidays, when hotel prices rise and vacationing *chiapanecos* jam the place and its beach-front *palapa* seafood eateries, it's a small, ultrasleepy fishing town. There are no ATMs.

During the nesting season, a state government **turtle conservation project** ([🕐] 10am-5pm) [FREE] collects thousands of newly laid olive ridley turtle eggs from 40km of beach, incubating them and releasing the hatchlings when they emerge seven weeks later. You can stop in to see the turtle nursery, located about 3km northwest along the single street from the lighthouse (taxis charge M$30), or volunteer (M$3100 per eight days including basic food and board) with beach patrols and hatchling release by contacting San Cristóbal-based Nataté (www.natate. org). If you're in the area around the end of October, don't miss Tortufest, a festival featuring mass liberations of turtles.

For more on volunteering, see p857.

[🍴] Sleeping & Eating

José's Camping Cabañas   CABAÑAS **$**
([📞] 994-600-90-48; campsites per person M$60, RV sites M$180-200, dm M$130, s/d M$330/400, without bathroom M$200/230; [P][🏊]) Run by a long-time Canadian expat, this laid-back fruit-tree compound has simple *cabañas* with mosquito nets, fans and screens, shaded sitting areas and powerful showers. Meals (M$40 to M$120) are available and the small pool is open in season. Go 800m southeast from the lighthouse, then turn left (inland).

Garden Beach Hotel   HOTEL **$$**
([📞] 994-600-90-42; www.gardenbeach.mx; Matamoros 800; r from M$1000; [P][❄][🛜][🏊]) Across the street from the beach and 800m southeast of the lighthouse, this hotel's comfortable, pastel-shaded, air-conditioned rooms have flat-screen TVs and up to three double beds. The upper floors have great ocean views. It has a beachfront open-air restaurant (mains M$120 to M$170) and a big double pool (nonguests pay M$60 unless they eat at the restaurant).

Madre Sal

Drift to sleep pondering the ocean waves at **Madre Sal** ([📞] cell 966-1007296, cell 966-6666147; www.elmadresal.com; Manuel Ávila Camacho; hammock sites M$120, q campsites incl gear M$280, cabañas M$800; [P]), a cooperative-run ecotourism project 25km south of Puerto Arista. Named for a mangrove species, its restaurant (meals M$80 to M$150) and almost 20 thatched two-bed en suite *cabañas* (with mosquito nets) sit astride a skinny

CHIAPAS & TABASCO EL SOCONUSCO & BEACHES

RESERVA DE LA BIOSFERA EL TRIUNFO

The luxuriant cloud forests, high in the remote Reserva de la Biosfera El Triunfo (El Triunfo Biosphere Reserve) in the Sierra Madre de Chiapas, are a bird-lover's paradise and a remarkable world of trees and shrubs festooned with epiphytes, ferns, bromeliads, mosses and vines.

The Sierra Madre de Chiapas is home to almost 400 bird species, of which more than 30 are nonexistent or rare elsewhere in Mexico. This is the one place in the country where chances are good of seeing the resplendent quetzal. Visitors see hundreds of butterfly species and, often, jaguar and tapir tracks.

Visits are limited and controlled. Most visitors go in the driest months, January to May; avoid the wettest months, September and October. Make arrangements about six months in advance by contacting Claudia Virgen (☑ cell 961-1251177; www.ecobiosfera. org.mx), the visitor program coordinator. A normal six-day visit from Tuxtla (US$730 to US$900 per person, minimum eight people, maximum 12) starts with one night in a hotel in the nearest town, Jaltenango (also called Ángel Albino Corzo), followed by four nights at the basic Campamento El Triunfo, 1850m high in the reserve. The price includes meals, bilingual guides who are expert bird-spotters, transportation between Jaltenango and the coffee-growing village of Finca Prusia, and mules to carry your baggage on the 14km hike between Finca Prusia and Campamento El Triunfo (three to four hours uphill on the way in).

bar of pristine land between a lagoon and the Pacific that's reached via *lancha* (M$20 round trip) through dense mangrove forest.

Guests use candles after the 11pm power shutoff, and crabs skitter along the sand when stars fill the night sky. In season, sea turtles come ashore to lay eggs, and the night watchman can wake you if you want to watch or help collect the eggs for the Boca del Cielo hatchery.

Though the water can be rough, the beach is spotless, and there's excellent bird-watching in the mangroves, including 13 species of heron. Three-hour *lancha* trips are available (M$750 per boat, maximum 12 people), including one for bird- and crocodile-spotting.

From Tonalá, take a taxi (M$60 shared, M$250 private) or combi (M$50) to Manuel Ávila Camacho; combis charge an extra M$5 to the *embarcadero*, or you can walk five minutes.

Reserva de la Biosfera La Encrucijada

This large biosphere reserve protects a 1448-sq-km strip of coastal lagoons, sandbars, wetlands, seasonally flooded tropical forest and the country's tallest mangroves (some above 30m). The ecosystem is a vital wintering and breeding ground for migratory birds, and harbors one of Mexico's biggest populations of jaguars, plus spider monkeys, turtles, crocodiles, caimans, boa constrictors, fishing eagles and lots of waterfowl – many in danger of extinction. Bird-watching is good any time of year, but best during the November-to-March nesting season. The reserve can be visited via access points from Pijijiapan and Escuintla, and *lancha* rides take you through towering mangroves.

RIBERA COSTA AZUL

A laid-back coastal jewel, the beautiful black sandbar of Ribera Costa Azul (also called Playa Azul) is a thin strip of palm-fringed land between ocean and lagoon accessed from the Chocohuital *embarcadero,* 20km southwest of Pijijiapan. Camping is generally free, though restaurants ask that you eat your meals (seafood M$130) there to do so. Outside of the busy high season, Palapa Sinai is usually the one place open year-round for meals and simple rooms. *Lanchas* (M$15 one way) ferry passengers to the sandbar, and birding and mangrove trips (M$280 per boat per hour) can also be organized.

If you don't want to camp, head 300m north of the Chocohuital dock and pull up a pool chair at the Refugio del Sol (☑ cell 962-6252780; www.refugiodelsol.com.mx; r Mon-Thu M$1650, Fri-Sun M$1800, nonguest pool day use adult/child M$380/280; P❋🛜🛝) hotel. Spacious modern rooms feature rainforest showers, plasma TVs and great beds with comforters. Request a room with a patio or terrace. There's a M$100 pool-fee discount if you eat in the restaurant (mains M$180 to M$230, snacks M$65 to M$120).

From Pijijiapan, combis for Chocohuital (M$25, 40 minutes, 5am to 6pm) leave hourly from 1a Av Norte Poniente 27 between 2a and 3a Poniente Norte; the last one returns at 8pm.

EMBARCADERO LAS GARZAS

The Red de Ecoturismo La Encrucijada (www.ecoturismolaencrucijada.com), a network of community cooperatives, is a clearinghouse for information on tours and lodging. Private *lancha* tours (M$1100 to M$1800, up to 10 passengers) can also be organized to local beaches and bird-watching spots. *Lanchas* also serve a number of small communities where you can camp or overnight in simple *cabañas*. At the settlement of Barra de Zacapulco – which also has a sea-turtle breeding center – you can usually camp or sling a hammock for free if you eat your meals at one of its simple *comedores* (seafood plates M$95). A community cooperative there offers six basic solar-powered **cabañas** (☑918-596-25-00; r M$520) with fans, screened windows and cold-water bathrooms.

To get here, take a bus along Hwy 200 to Escuintla, then a *colectivo* taxi to Acapetahua (M$8, 10 minutes). Beside the abandoned railway in Acapetahua, take a combi 18km to Embarcadero Las Garzas (M$25, 20 minutes, every 30 minutes until 5pm). From Embarcadero Las Garzas, *colectivo lanchas* go to communities including Barra de Zacapulco (M$55, 25 minutes). The last boat back from Barra de Zacapulco may be as early as 4pm, and the last combi from Embarcadero Las Garzas to Acapetahua goes at about 5pm.

Tapachula

☑ 962 / POP 202,600 / ELEV 100M

Mexico's bustling southernmost city, the 'Pearl of the Soconusco,' doesn't quite live up to its nickname, though it does have an interesting combination of urban sophistication and tropical tempo. The city is an important commercial center, not only for the Soconusco but also for cross-border trade with Guatemala.

A hot, humid and busy place year-round, Tapachula's heart is the large, lively Parque Hidalgo, with vistas of the towering 4100m cone of Volcán Tacaná to the north on clear days. Most travelers simply pass through here on their way to or from Guatemala, but it makes a good base for a number of interesting nearby attractions.

◎ Sights

★Museo Arqueológico del Soconusco · MUSEUM

(Av 8a Norte 20; M$39; ☺9am-6pm Tue-Sun) The modern, well-displayed Museo Arqueológico del Soconusco faces Parque Hidalgo. Steles and ceramics from Izapa are prominent. On these steles, the top fringe represents the sky and gods, the middle depicts earthly life and the bottom fringe shows the underworld. There are also 5000-year-old stone heads and figurines from the coastal marshes, a collection of pre-Hispanic musical instruments (including scrapers made from human bones), and other items displaying Olmec, Teotihuacán, Maya and Aztec influences. Goths will adore the turquoise-encrusted skull.

⎙ Sleeping

Hotel Cervantino · HOTEL $

(☑962-626-16-58; 1a Calle Oriente 6; s/d from M$307/372; ❄) A block away from Parque Centenario, the location's the winner here, but rooms are clean and comfortable enough considering the price tag. Air-con costs M$100 extra.

Hotel Diamante · HOTEL $

(☑962-628-50-32; Calle 7a Poniente 43; r with fan/air-con M$310/$560; P❄🛜) A good-value hotel with modern air-conditioning, clean rooms and cable TV. Rooms 12 through 16 have dynamite views of Volcán Tacaná.

★Casa Mexicana · BOUTIQUE HOTEL $$

(☑962-626-66-05; www.casamexicanachiapas.com; Av 8a Sur 19; s/d incl breakfast M$1071/1302; P ⊖ ❄@🛜🛁) An exquisite boutique hotel paying homage to Mexican women in history. Guests can choose from sumptuous rooms named for heroines such as human rights lawyer Digna Ochoa or Zapatista commander Ramona. Antiques, lush plants and all kinds of interesting art create a soothing, creative feel. The 10 rooms on two floors surround a tropical garden-patio that even has a small pool.

With a small bar and a restaurant serving excellent homemade meals, this is a fabulous place to stay.

Tapachula

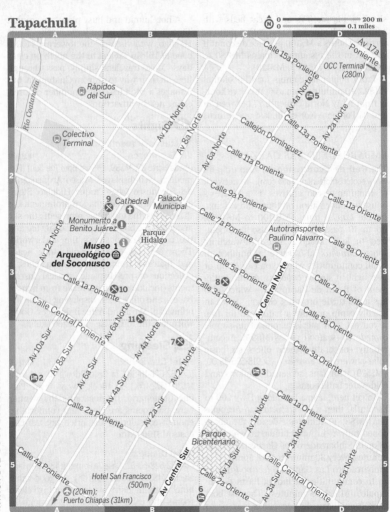

Hotel San Francisco HOTEL **$$**
(📞962-620-10-00; www.sucasaentapachula.com;
Av Central Sur 94; s/d from M$830/970; ❄️🛜🏊)
A large, business-style hotel to the south
of the center, the San Francisco offers spa-
cious, light rooms and a whole bunch of
amenities, including an inviting garden/
pool area.

Suites Ejecutivas Los Arcos HOTEL **$$**
(📞962-625-31-31; www.suitesejecutivasarcos.com;
Av 1a Sur 15; ste including small breakfast from
M$1062; ❄️🛜) Not quite as fancy as the name
implies, this is still an excellent deal in a great
downtown location. Suites are generously

sized and come equipped with kitchenette
and balconies overlooking the lush gardens.

Hotel Mo Sak HOTEL **$$**
(📞962-626-67-87; www.hotelmosak.com; Av 4a
Norte 97; s/d M$500/650; 🅿️♿❄️🛜) Helpful,
attentive staff round out this modern hotel
with minimalist furniture and free morning
coffee. King-bed rooms have kitchenettes.

✖️ Eating

Scores of clean and popular *comedores* are
hidden upstairs at the **Mercado Sebastián
Escobar** (Av 10a Norte; mains M$60-80; ⊙6am-

Tapachula

◎ **Top Sights**
1 Museo Arqueológico del
  Soconusco B3

⊜ **Sleeping**
2 Casa Mexicana.....................................A4
3 Hotel Cervantino.................................C4
4 Hotel Diamante....................................C3
5 Hotel Mo Sak.......................................D1
6 Suites Ejecutivas Los Arcos C5

⊗ **Eating**
7 Gramlich Café Terraza.......................B4
8 Long-Yin C3
9 Mercado Sebastián Escobar B2
10 Rancho Grill..B3
11 Restaurante Los Jarrones B3

5pm), dishing out mammoth plates of cooked-to-order Chinese food. Snag a bench seat at the plastic-tablecloth-covered picnic tables and come hungry!

Gramlich Café Terraza
CAFÉ $

(Calle 1a Poniente 14; coffees & snacks M$15-40, mains M$60-85; ☉9am-9:30pm) The Gramlich Café serves its delectable brew along with an extended menu of breakfasts, sandwiches and Thai salads. Seat yourself on the shaded sidewalk patio or inside with the turbo-charged air-conditioning.

Long-Yin
CHINESE $

(☑962-626-24-67; Av 2a Norte 36; mains $80-150; ☉9am-8pm; ▣) Just one portion easily feeds two ravenous diners at this excellent red-lantern-festooned place run by a fourth-generation immigrant family. Vegetarians should beeline here for the fabulous tofu dishes. Delivery available, but it's worth seeing the building across the street.

Cafetería del Parque
MEXICAN $$

(8a Calle Poniente Sur 113; breakfast M$65-80, mains M$70-155; ☉8am-10:30pm; ☻) The nice wraparound windows make this one of the better people-watching eateries around the Jardín de la Marimba, and its garish pink and blue interior is elbow to elbow with families on the weekends. With good espresso drinks, consistent food and lots of air-conditioning, it's definitely a blissful place to cool off.

Restaurante Los Jarrones
MEXICAN $$

(☑962-626-11-43; Hotel Don Miguel, Calle 1a Pte 18; breakfast M$75-100, mains M$90-170; ☉7am-11pm Mon-Sat, to 4pm Sun) Staffed by solicitous bow-tied waiters and perennially popular, Los Jarrones provides welcome air-conditioning and a big choice of Mexican and international fare. Breakfasts are particularly good, though you may want to sit near the windows to escape the painfully hokey live dinner bands.

Rancho Grill
MEXICAN $$

(8a Av Norte; mains M$80-165; ☉9am-1am) In the clutch of eateries around the central park, this one's a standout for its bustling atmosphere and great steaks. If beer's not your thing, try local favorite *horchata de cacao* (a rice and cacao drink, served cold).

❶ Information

Banorte (cnr Av 2a Norte & Calle Central Poniente; ☉8:30am-4:30pm Mon-Fri, 9am-2pm Sat) Changes dollars Monday through Friday; ATM.

Chiapas Divisas (Calle 1a Poniente 13; 8:30am-8:30pm Mon-Fri, to 6:30pm Sat, to 2:30pm Sun) Currency exchange.

Instituto Nacional de Migración (☑962-625-05-59; Vialidad 435, Fracc Las Vegas; ☉9am-1pm) Immigration office.

BUSES FROM TAPACHULA

DESTINATION	FARE (M$)	DURATION (HR)	FREQUENCY (DAILY)
Comitán	260	6hr via Motozintla	6 OCC
Escuintla	56-98	1½hr	8 OCC, very frequent RS
Mexico City	1348-1830	17-18hr	frequent OCC
Oaxaca	536	13hr	1 OCC
San Cristóbal de las Casas	346-430	7½-8hr via Motozintla	8 OCC
Tonalá	176-276	3-4hr	very frequent OCC & RS
Tuxtla Gutiérrez	394-670	4½-6hr	very frequent OCC & RS

Sanatorio Soconusco (☑ 962-626-35-66; Av 4a Norte 68, at Calle 11 Poniente) A clinic with 24-hour emergency service.

Tourist Office (www.turismochiapas.gob.mx/ sectur/tapachula; Av 8a Norte; ☺ 8am-4pm Mon-Fri) In the Antiguo Palacio Municipal.

🛈 Getting There & Away

AIR

Tapachula's modern **airport** (Carretera Tapachula-Puerto Madero Km 18.5; ☎) is 20km southwest of the city. It's a drowsy place, with just three daily flights to/from Mexico City on **Aeroméxico** (☑ 962-626-39-21; Calle Central Oriente 4).

BUS

Deluxe and 1st-class buses go from the **OCC terminal** (☑ 962-626-28-81; Calle 17a Oriente, btwn Avs 3a & 5a Norte), 1km northeast of Parque Hidalgo. The main 2nd-class services are by **Rápidos del Sur** (RS; ☑ 962-626-11-61; Calle 9a Poniente 62).

Other buses from the OCC station go to Palenque, Puerto Escondido and Villahermosa. There are also five daily buses from here to Guatemala City (five to six hours), with tickets sold at the main counter: Trans Galgos Inter (www.trans galgosinter.com.gt) at 6am, noon and 11:45pm (M$330 to M$445), Línea Dorada (www.linea dorada.com.gt) at 3pm (M$240) and Tica Bus (www.ticabus.com) at 7am (M$358).

Galgos also runs a 6am bus to San Salvador, El Salvador (M$700, nine hours), via Escuintla in Guatemala. Tica Bus continues all the way to Panama City (M$2332 to M$2951), with several long overnight stops en route.

For destinations in western Guatemala, including Quetzaltenango, it's best to get a bus from the border.

COLECTIVO

A large **colectivo terminal** (Calle 5a Poniente) houses most of the regional taxi and combi companies.

🛈 Getting Around

CAR & MOTORCYCLE

Tapachula's two rental agencies carry both automatic and manual-transmission cars.

AVC Rente un Auto (☑ cell 962-6225444) In-town pickup service available.

Europcar (☑ cell 962-1208010; www.europcar. com; Airport) Best rates online.

TAXI

Taxis within the central area (including the OCC terminal) cost M$30.

Sociedades Transportes 149 (☑ 962-625-12-87) has a booth in the airport arrivals hall, charging M$90 per person for a *colectivo* from the airport to the center; it's M$200 for a private taxi (up to three people) in either direction.

Around Tapachula

Izapa

The pre-Hispanic ruins at Izapa are important to archaeologists, and of real interest to archaeology buffs. Izapa flourished from approximately 200 BC to AD 200, and its carving style (mostly seen on tall slabs known as steles, fronted by round altars) shows descendants of Olmec deities with their upper lips unnaturally lengthened. Some Maya monuments in Guatemala are similar, and Izapa is considered an important 'bridge' be-

---

SUMMITING TACANÁ

The best months to climb Tacaná are late November to March. There are two routes up the mountain from Unión Juárez. Neither requires any technical climbing, but you need to allow two or three days for either, preferably plus time to acclimatize. Be prepared for extreme cold at the top. The less steep route is via Chiquihuites, 12km from Unión Juárez and reachable by vehicle. From there it's a three-hour walk to Papales, where you can sleep in huts for a small donation. The ascent from Papales to the summit takes about five hours. The other route is via Talquián (about two hours' walk from Unión Juárez) and Trigales (five hours from Talquián). It takes about six hours to climb from Trigales to the summit. The two routes meet a couple of hours below the summit, and on both you have access to camping areas.

Combis from Unión Juárez will carry you to the small town of Córdoba, about halfway to Talquián, also passing the turnoff for Chiquihuites (about 1½ hours' walk away). It's a good idea to get a guide for Tacaná in Unión Juárez or organize one to meet you. The Hotel Colonial Campestre (☑ 962-647-20-15; fernandao772@hotmail.com) can find guides (about M$350 per day) with three days' notice.

tween the Olmecs and the Maya. Izapa had 91 known stele-and-altar pairings, and you can see some well-preserved examples in the Tapachula museum.

Izapa is around 11km east of Tapachula on the Talismán road. There are three groups of **ruins** (Grupo A & B admission by donation, northern group free; ⊙ 9am-5pm daily, Group F closed Tue). The northern group (Grupo F) is on the left side of the road if you're arriving from Tapachula – watch for the low pyramid mounds; you'll also see a ball court and several carved steles and altars. For the other groups, go back 700m toward Tapachula and take a signposted road to the left. After 800m you'll reach a fork with signs to Izapa Grupo A and Izapa Grupo B, each about 250m further on and looked after by caretaker families that will request a small donation. Grupo A has 10 very weathered stele-and-altar pairings around a field. Grupo B is a couple of grass-covered mounds and more stone sculptures, including three curious ball-on-pillar affairs.

To get there from Tapachula, take a combi (M$16) from the *colectivo* terminal or any Talismán-bound bus.

Santo Domingo, Unión Juárez & Volcán Tacaná

📞 962

At 4100m, Volcán Tacaná's dormant cone towers over the countryside north of Tapachula. Even if you're not interested in climbing to its summit, two villages on its gorgeously verdant lower slopes make an attractive day trip, their cooler climate offering welcome relief from the Tapachula steam bath. The scenic road up is winding but well paved.

Santo Domingo lies 34km northeast of Tapachula, amid coffee plantations. The village's gorgeous three-story wooden 1920s *casa grande* (big house) has been restored. It belonged to the German immigrants who formerly owned the coffee plantation here, but it's now the **Centro Ecoturístico Santo Domingo** (📞 962-627-00-60; ⊙ 8am-8pm) and has a restaurant (mains M$60 to M$120), a small creaky-floored coffee museum (M$10) and a lovely, well-tended tropical garden and pool (M$10; free with a meal).

About 9km beyond Santo Domingo, passing some gorgeous waterfalls tucked in around tight turns, Unión Juárez (popu-

lation 2600, elevation 1300m) is the starting point for ascents of Tacaná and other, less demanding walks. Tapachula folk like to come up here on weekends and holidays to cool off and feast on *parrillada,* a cholesterol-challenging plate of grilled meat and a few vegetables.

Another local place to head for is **Pico del Loro**, a parrot-beak-shaped overhanging rock that offers fine panoramas. You can reach the rock is 5km up a drivable track that leaves the Santo Domingo–Unión Juárez road about halfway between the two villages. Ask directions to some of the various lookouts over the valley of the Río Suchiate (the international border), or to the **Cascadas Muxbal**, a natural toboggan slope, about one hour's walk from Unión Juárez.

🛏 Sleeping & Eating

There are plenty of *comedores* and restaurants around the plaza in Unión Juárez, though lodging is nothing extraordinary.

Hotel Colonial Campestre   HOTEL $
(📞 962-647-20-15; Unión Juárez; r M$380-540; 🅿🛜) Rambling and Escher-esque, this hotel has spacious rooms with bathroom, TV and good views (especially from room number 26). It also has a restaurant (mains M$65 to M$120, *parrillada* for two M$230). Look for the arch a couple of blocks below the plaza, and ask to see the tunnel and antique movie theater.

Hotel Aljoad   HOTEL $
(📞 962-647-21-06; Unión Juárez; d from M$220; 🅿♻) Just north of the plaza, the superbasic Aljoad has tidy rooms around a cluttered patio, all with hot-water bathrooms.

ℹ Getting There & Away

From Tapachula, first take a combi from the *colectivo* terminal to Cacahoatán (M$20, 30 minutes), 20km north. From where these terminate in Cacahoatán, Transportes Tacaná combis travel to Santo Domingo (M$18, 30 minutes) and Unión Juárez (M$23, 45 minutes).

Coffee Fincas

The hills north of Tapachula are home to numerous *fincas* (ranches), many of them set up by German immigrants more than a century ago. *Fincas* with tours, restaurants and overnight accommodations include the luxurious **Finca Argovia** (📞 962-626-29-66; www.argovia.

CHIAPAS & TABASCO AROUND TAPACHULA

com.mx; r M$1600-2300, ste M$2650; ⊜ 🛜 🗷) and **Finca Hamburgo** (🖍 962-626-75-78; www.finca hamburgo.com; Carr a Nueva Alemania Km 54; d/ste from M$1560/2420; P ⊜ 🛜) and the more rustic organic and biodynamic farm of **Finca Irlanda** (🖍 962-625-92-03, ext 107; www.fincairlanda. grupopeters.com; r per person M$680; ⊜) 🖌 .

Border Towns

If you're not taking a direct bus to Guatemala from the OCC station, you can go the border for connections. It's 20km from Tapachula to the international border at **Talismán**, opposite El Carmen in Guatemala. The border crossing between **Ciudad Hidalgo**, 37km from Tapachula, opposite Ciudad Tecún Umán in Guatemala, is busier and has more onward connections. Both border points have money-changing facilities and are open 24 hours – though you should get through by early afternoon for greater security and to guarantee onward transportation. Watch out for money changers passing counterfeit bills at both crossings.

🟦 Getting There & Away

From Tapachula, **Autotransportes Paulino Navarro** (🖍 962-626-11-52; Calle 7a Poniente 5) combis head to Ciudad Hidalgo (M$28, 50 minutes) every 10 minutes, 4:30am to 10pm. Across the border in Ciudad Tecún Umán, frequent buses leave until about 6pm for Guatemala City (five hours) by the Pacific slope route, through Retalhuleu and Escuintla. Buses to Quetzaltenango (three hours) depart hourly from 5am to 6pm.

Combis for Talismán (M$19, 30 minutes) leave from the Tapachula *colectivo* terminal every 10 minutes, 5am to 9pm. The majority of bus services from El Carmen, which include around 20 a day to Guatemala City (seven hours), go via Ciudad Tecún Umán, and then head along the Pacific slope route. For Quetzaltenango, you can take one of these and change at Coatepeque or Retalhuleu, but it's easier to get a *colectivo* taxi to Malacatán, on a more direct road to Quetzaltenango via San Marcos, and then look for onward transportation from there.

For Lake Atitlán or Chichicastenango, you need to get to Quetzaltenango first.

TABASCO

They say that the state of Tabasco has more water than land, and looking at all the lagoons, rivers and wetlands on the map you can certainly see why, especially during the rainy season. It's always hot and sweaty here, but marginally less so when you catch a breeze along the Gulf of Mexico or venture into the southern hills. Travelers to Villahermosa and coastal Tabasco should note the region is subject to seasonal floods, though few travelers linger in Tabasco longer than it takes to see the outstanding Olmec stone sculpture in Villahermosa's Parque-Museo La Venta. Located north of Chiapas and abutting the Gulf of Mexico, Tabasco is the site of extensive onshore and offshore oil exploitation by Mexico's state oil company (Pemex).

Villahermosa

🖍 993 / POP 350,000

This sprawling, flat, hot and humid city, with more than a quarter of Tabasco's population, was never the 'beautiful town' its name implies. It's settled on the winding Río Grijalva, but Villahermosa's most attractive attribute became its worst enemy when the river burst its banks and engulfed the city in 2007.

Oil money has pumped modernity and commerce into some of the outer districts, where you'll find glitzy malls, imposing public buildings and luxury hotels.

🟦 Sights

The central area of this expansive city is known as the Zona Luz, and extends north–south from Parque Juárez to the Plaza de Armas, and east–west from the Río Grijalva to roughly Calle 5 de Mayo. The main bus stations are between 750m and 1km north of the center.

Parque-Museo La Venta   PARK, MUSEUM
(Av Ruíz Cortines; M$47; ⊙ 8am-4pm; P 🚼) This fascinating outdoor park, zoo and museum was created in 1958, when petroleum exploration threatened the highly important ancient Olmec settlement of La Venta in western Tabasco. Archaeologists moved the site's most significant finds, including three colossal stone heads, to Villahermosa.

Plan two to three hours for your visit, and take mosquito repellent (the park is set in humid tropical woodland). Parque-Museo La Venta lies 2km northwest of the Zona Luz, beside Avenida Ruíz Cortines, the main east–west highway crossing the city. It's M$30 via *colectivo*.

Inside, you first come to a zoo devoted to animals from Tabasco and nearby regions:

cats include jaguars, ocelots and jaguarundi, and there are white-tailed deer, spider monkeys, crocodiles, boa constrictors, peccaries and plenty of colorful birds, including scarlet macaws and keel-billed toucans.

There's an informative display in English and Spanish on Olmec archaeology as you pass through to the sculpture trail, the start of which is marked by a giant ceiba (the sacred tree of the Olmec and Maya). This 1km walk is lined with finds from La Venta. Among the most impressive, in the order you come to them, are Stele 3, which depicts a bearded man with a headdress; Altar 5, depicting a figure carrying a child; Monument 77, 'El Gobernante,' a very sour-looking seated ruler; the monkey-faced Monument 56; Monument 1, the colossal head of a helmet-wearing warrior; and Stele 1, showing a young goddess (a rare Olmec representation of anything female). Animals that pose no danger (such as coatis, squirrels and black agoutis) roam freely around the park.

Museo de Historia Natural
MUSEUM

(Av Ruíz Cortines; admission M$24; ⊙8am-5pm Tue-Sun, last admission 4pm; P) Just outside the Parque-Museo La Venta entrance, the small Museo de Historia Natural has good displays on dinosaurs, space, early humanity and Tabascan ecosystems (all displays in Spanish).

Museo Regional de Antropología
MUSEUM

(http://iec.tabasco.gob.mx; Periférico Carlos Pellicer; M$60; ⊙9am-4:30pm Tue-Sun; P) Villahermosa's shiny, recently rebuilt regional anthropology museum holds some excellent exhibits on Olmec, Maya, Nahua and Zoque cultures in Tabasco – including Tortuguero #6, the infamous tablet *solely* responsible for the dire 'end of world' predictions forecast for December 21, 2012. It's in the Cicom complex, a 15-minute walk from Zona Luz and just south of the Paseo Tabasco bridge.

🛌 Sleeping

An oil town, Villahermosa has scores of comfortable midrange and top-end chain hotels, most of which offer heavily discounted online and weekend rates. Inviting budget options are scarcer.

Hotel Oriente
HOTEL $

(☑993-312-01-21; hotel-oriente@hotmail.com; Madero 425; d with fan M$270-350, with air-con

ⓘ AIRPORT BUS TO PALENQUE

The Villahermosa airport has a handy counter for ADO (www.ado.com.mx), with almost hourly minibuses departing daily to Palenque (M$278, 2¼ hours) between 7:20am and 9:20pm. Check the website for schedules to/from 'Aeropuerto Villahermosa.'

M$400-490; ❄🛜) The Oriente is a friendly and well-run downtown hotel sporting simple budget rooms, all with TV. Rooms overlooking the main street are bright, but bring earplugs for noise. It's small, so reserve two days in advance.

Hotel Provincia Express
HOTEL $$

(☑993-314-53-78; www.hotelesprovinciaexpress. infored.mx; Lerdo de Tejada 303; r incl breakfast from M$860; P🅿❄@🛜) Excellent value in a central location, this hotel has small but tidy and pleasant rooms and a homey yellow color scheme. It's on a pedestrian street, so get a window if possible; avoid the windowless rooms. There's a cafe in the lobby.

One Villahermosa Centro
HOTEL $$

(☑993-131-71-00; www.onehotels.com; Carranza 101; r incl breakfast from M$945; ❄🛜) A large, business-style hotel, this one wins points for attentive staff and a supercentral location. Rooms are what you'd expect for the price – biggish, clean and comfortable.

Hotel Olmeca Plaza
HOTEL $$$

(☑800-201-09-09, 993-358-01-02; www.hotel olmecaplaza.com; Madero 418; r Mon-Thu M$1292, Fri-Sun M$767; P🅿❄@🛜🏊) The classiest downtown hotel also has an open-air pool and a well-equipped gym. Rooms are modern and comfortable, with ample desks and good large bathrooms, and there's a quality on-site restaurant.

🍴 Eating & Drinking

A large city, Villahermosa has an eclectic collection of hotel restaurants, chain restaurants and eateries specializing in seafood and international cuisines.

La Dantesca
ITALIAN $$

(Hidalgo 406, near Parque Los Pajaritos; mains M$80-120, pizzas M$160; ⊙1-10pm; ☺) Locals flock to this lively trattoria for its fantas-

HIGHLIGHTS OF TABASCO

Tabasco has hosted as rich a procession of cultures as anywhere in Mexico. In pre-Hispanic times, Tabasco was the prosperous nexus of a far-reaching trade network extending around the Yucatán coast to Honduras, up the rivers to the jungles and mountains of Guatemala, and westward to highland central Mexico. Olmec religion, art, astronomy and architecture deeply influenced all of Mexico's later civilizations.

La Venta

Though most monuments from La Venta are at Villahermosa's Parque-Museo La Venta, this ancient Olmec ceremonial **site** (☏923-232-04-23; M$47; ⊗8am-5pm) still fascinates as the largest and most important 'capital' of Mexico's mother culture. La Venta flourished between about 800 and 400 BC on a natural plateau rising about 20m above an area of fertile, seasonally flooded lowlands. Matthew Stirling is credited with discovering, in the early 1940s, four huge Olmec heads sculpted from basalt, the largest more than 2m high.

The museum at the site entrance holds three badly weathered Olmec heads, plus replicas of some of the finest sculptures that are no longer here. The heart of the site is the 30m-high Edificio C-1, a rounded pyramid constructed out of clay and sand. Ceremonial areas and more structures stretch to the north and south.

Comalcalco

The impressive Maya ruins of ancient **Comalcalco** (M$48; ⊗8am-4pm), 50km northwest of Villahermosa, are unique because many of their buildings are constructed of bricks and/or mortar made from oyster shells. Comalcalco was at its peak between AD 600 and 1000, when it was ruled by the Chontals. It remained an important center of commerce for several more centuries, trading in a cornucopia of pre-Hispanic luxury goods.

A museum at the entrance has a fine array of sculptures and engravings of human heads, deities, glyphs and animals, such as crocodiles and pelicans.

The first building you encounter is the great brick tiered pyramid, Templo 1. At its base are the remains of large stucco sculptures, including the feet of a giant winged toad. Further temples line Plaza Norte, in front of Templo I. In the far (southeast) corner of the site rises the Gran Acrópolis, which has views from its summit over a canopy of palms to the Gulf of Mexico. The Acrópolis is fronted by Templo V, a burial pyramid that was once decorated on all sides with stucco sculptures of people, reptiles, birds and aquatic life. At Templo V's western foot is Templo IX, which has a tomb lined by nine stucco sculptures showing a Comalcalco lord with his priests and courtiers. Above Templo V is the crumbling profile of El Palacio, with its parallel 80m-long corbel-arched galleries, probably once Comalcalco's royal residence. Information is in both Spanish and English.

Hacienda La Luz (☏933-337-11-22; www.haciendalaluz.mx; Blvd Rovirosa 232; 1hr tour per person M$80; ⊗tours 9am, 11am, 1pm & 3pm Tue-Sun), one of several local plantations making chocolate from home-grown cacao, is just 300m from Comalcalco's central Parque Juárez: walk 250m west along Calle Bosada to its end at Blvd Rovirosa, turn right and you'll see the hacienda's gateposts across the road. The tour takes you round the beautiful house,

tic brick oven pizzas, house-made pastas and scrumptious desserts. Most folks come for the pizza, but the ravioli *verde* with *requesón* and *jamaica* (a ricotta-like cheese and hibiscus flowers) and other pastas are superb.

Restaurante Madan   MEXICAN **$$**
(Madero 408; mains M$60-175; ⊗7am-11pm; ☻⛭) It's not glamorous, but this very reliable and popular hotel restaurant two blocks

west of the river has good Mexican dishes and efficient, friendly service.

Rock & Roll Cocktelería   SEAFOOD **$$**
(Reforma 307; mains M$140-220; ⊗10am-10pm; ☻) A maelstrom of heat, swirling fans and blaring TVs. Everyone's here for the seafood cocktails (though it also has good ceviche and seafood stew) and cheap beer. It's on a pedestrian street across from the Miraflores Hotel, and has 60 years under its belt.

gardens and cacao plantation, shows traditional methods of turning cacao beans into chocolate, and concludes with a chocolate drink. English is spoken.

Tapijulapa

The prettiest village in Tabasco, riverside Tapijulapa sits among the lushly forested hills of far southern Tabasco, 36km from Teapa. It boasts a 17th-century church presiding over beautiful white houses with red-tiled roofs and potted flowers. The beautiful jungle park **Villa Luz** (⊙9am-5pm) is a five-minute boat ride along the Río Oxolotán from the village *embarcadero*. From the landing, it's a 1km walk to the park's **Casa Museo**, the former country villa of Tomás Garrido Canabal, the rabidly anticlerical governor of Tabasco in the 1920s and '30s (he demolished Villahermosa's 18th-century baroque cathedral, banned alcohol and gave women the vote). From here other paths lead 600m to the beautiful *cascadas* (waterfalls) tumbling into a river, with pools for a refreshing dip, and 900m to the Cueva de las Sardinas Ciegas (Cave of the Blind Sardines), named for the sightless fish that inhabit the sulfurous river inside the cave.

Mesón de la Sierra (☑932-322-40-09; mesondelasierra@hotmail.com; Francisco J Santa Maria s/n; r M$560; [P ⊖ ❋ 🛜]), is located two blocks north of the plaza on the staircase to the church. Its a very comfortable five-room inn with a light-drenched Mediterranean feel and a prime location for appreciating the spectacular forested hills beyond town. Locals also rent a variety of well-appointed rooms through the town's **Hotel Communitario** (☑932-322-41-50, cell 932-1060684; La Casa de la Turista, main plaza; r M$230-540; [❋]) network.

To reach Tapijulapa from Villahermosa, take a CAT bus to Tacotalpa and change.

Reserva de la Biosfera Pantanos de Centla

This 3030-sq-km biosphere reserve protects a good part of the wetlands around the lower reaches of two of Mexico's biggest rivers, the Usumacinta and the Grijalva. These lakes, marshes, rivers, mangroves, savannas and forests are an irreplaceable sanctuary for countless creatures, including the West Indian manatee and Morelet's crocodile (both endangered), six kinds of tortoise, tapirs, ocelots, jaguars, howler monkeys, 60 fish species and 255 bird species.

The **Centro de Interpretación Uyotot-Ja** (☑913-106-83-90; www.casadelagua.org.mx; Carretera Frontera-Jonuta Km 12.5; admission M$35, reserve fee M$28; ⊙9am-5pm Tue-Sun) visitor center, or 'Casa de Agua,' is 13km along the Jonuta road from Frontera, beside the broad, winding Río Grijalva. A 20m-high observation tower overlooks the awesome confluence of the Grijalva, the Usumacinta and a third large river, the San Pedrito – a spot known as Tres Brazos (Three Arms). Boat trips are available into the mangroves, where you should see crocodiles, iguanas, birds and, with luck, howler monkeys. March to May is the best birding season.

From Villahermosa, ADO, CAT and Cardesa buses service Frontera (near the site of conquistador Hernán Cortés' 1519 first battle against native Mexicans), from where *colectivos* run the 15-minute trip to the reserve.

Café Punta del Cielo   CAFE **$**
(Plaza de Armas; coffee M$27-45; ⊙7am-10pm; ⊖🛜) A respite from the raging heat and humidity, this small air-conditioned glass box next to the Torre del Caballero footbridge is a dream come true. Primarily a cafe, it serves premium hot and cold coffee drinks (some organic), as well as *panini* and light snacks. Go for brain freeze with an arctic frappé.

ℹ Information

There are plentiful internet cafes charging about M$10 to M$15 per hour. Most banks have ATMs and exchange dollars.

HSBC (cnr Juárez & Lerdo de Tejada; ⊙9am-5pm Mon-Fri) Bank on pedestrianized street.

Oficina de Convenciones y Visitantes de Tabasco (OCV; ☑993-316-35-54; www.visite tabasco.com; Paseo Tabasco 1504) Statewide information.

BUSES FROM VILLAHERMOSA

DESTINATION	FARE (M$)	DURATION (HR)	FREQUENCY (DAILY)
Campeche	322-472	5½-7	frequent ADO
Cancún	550-1134	12½-14½	20 ADO
Comalcalco	28-76	1-1½	very frequent Cardesa, 2 ADO
Mérida	430-960	8-9½	28 ADO
Mexico City (TAPO)	636-1232	10-12	frequent ADO
Oaxaca	736	13½	3 ADO
Palenque	85-164	2½	22 ADO, very frequent Cardesa
San Cristóbal de las Casas	402	7½	11:40pm
Tenosique	170-206	3½	11 ADO, very frequent CAT
Tuxtla Gutiérrez	336-434	4-5	16 ADO
Veracruz	540-810	6-8½	frequent ADO

Tourism Information Kiosk (⊘ 9am-6pm Mon-Sat) At the ADO bus terminal; has maps and can book hotels.

ℹ Getting There & Away

AIR

Villahermosa's **Aeropuerto Rovirosa** (☑ 993-356-01-57; Carretera Villahermosa-Macuspana Km 13) is 13km east of the center, off Hwy 186. Aeroméxico is the major airline; there are daily nonstop flights to/from Villahermosa.

Aeroméxico (www.aeromexico.com) Flys to Mérida, Mexico City and Veracruz; lots of international connections via Mexico City.

Interjet (www.interjet.com.mx) To Mexico City and Monterrey.

MAYAir (www.mayair.com.mx) To Mérida and Veracruz.

United (www.united.com) To Houston.

VivaAerobus (☑ 993-356-02-07; www.viva aerobus.com.mx) To Cancún, Monterrey and Guadalajara.

BUS & COLECTIVO

Deluxe and 1st-class buses depart from the **ADO bus station** (☑ 993-312-84-22; Mina 297), which has wi-fi, 24-hour left luggage and is located 750m north of the Zona Luz.

Transportation to most destinations within Tabasco leaves from other terminals within walking distance north of ADO, including the 2nd-class **Cardesa bus station** (cnr Hermanos Bastar Zozaya & Castillo); they run hourly between 6am and 9pm. Taxis to the center cost M$240. Alternatively, walk 500m past the airport parking lot for a colectivo (M$25) from the Dos Montes taxi stand. These terminate in the market on Carranza, about 1km north of the Zona Luz.

A system of colectivo taxis (M$25) provides the backbone of the center's public transit. Flag one down to ask if it's going your way, or join a queue at a stand outside a large store or transportation terminal, where proficient handlers ask for your destination and quickly assign you a shared taxi. There's no fee for the match-up, and no haggling necessary. Private taxis charge M$50 within the center.

ℹ Getting Around

Comfortable ADO minibuses ferry passengers between the airport and the ADO bus terminal (M$204); they run hourly between 6am and 9pm. Taxis to the center cost M$240. Alternatively, walk 500m past the airport parking lot for a colectivo (M$25) from the Dos Montes taxi stand. These terminate in the market on Carranza, about 1km north of the Zona Luz.

A system of colectivo taxis (M$25) provides the backbone of the center's public transit. Flag one down to ask if it's going your way, or join a queue at a stand outside a large store or transportation terminal, where proficient handlers ask for your destination and quickly assign you a shared taxi. There's no fee for the match-up, and no haggling necessary. Private taxis charge M$50 within the center.

Oaxaca

Includes ➡

Oaxaca City	422
Monte Albán	443
Pueblos Mancomunados	452
Puerto Escondido	456
Puerto Ángel	470
Zipolite	471
San Agustinillo	474
Mazunte	476
Bahías de Huatulco	480
Barra de la Cruz	487
Juchitán	488

Best Places to Eat

➡ Casa Oaxaca (p437)

➡ Alessandro (p478)

➡ Pascale (p464)

➡ La Providencia (p473)

➡ Restaurante Los Danzantes (p437)

Best Places to Stay

➡ Punta Placer (p475)

➡ Casa Oaxaca (p434)

➡ El Diablo y la Sandía (p434)

➡ Hotel Las Golondrinas (p433)

➡ Un Sueño (p475)

Why Go?

The state of Oaxaca (wah-*hah*-kah) has a special magic felt by Mexicans and foreigners alike. A bastion of indigenous culture, it's home to the country's most vibrant crafts and art scene, some outstandingly colorful and extroverted festivities, a uniquely savory cuisine and diverse natural riches. At the center of the state in every way stands beautiful, colonial Oaxaca city, an elegant and fascinating cultural hub. Nearby, the forested Sierra Norte is home to successful community-tourism ventures enabling visitors to hike, bike and ride horses amid delicious green mountainscapes. To the south, across rugged, remote ranges, is Oaxaca's fabulous tropical coast, with its endless sandy beaches, pumping Pacific surf, seas full of dolphins, turtles and fish, and a string of beach towns and villages that will make any traveler happy: bubbly Puerto Escondido; planned but relaxed Bahías de Huatulco; and the mellow delights of Mazunte, Zipolite and San Agustinillo.

When to Go
Oaxaca City

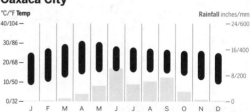

Jan–Mar Driest months: a lively coastal winter escapee scene; best hiking conditions in the Sierra Norte.

Jul & Aug Guelaguetza festival in Oaxaca city; summer-vacation fun time on the coast.

Late Oct & Nov Día de Muertos in Oaxaca City; Fiestas de Noviembre in Puerto Escondido.

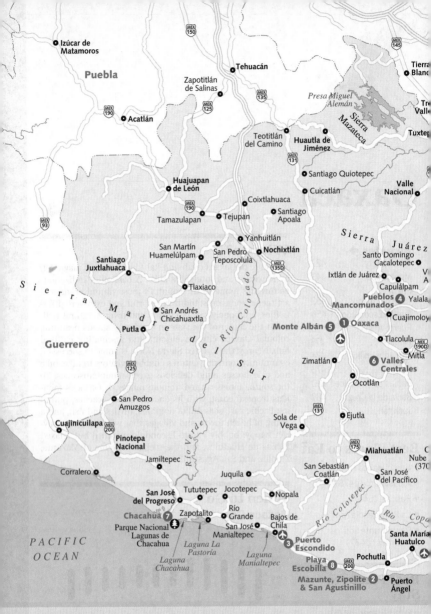

Oaxaca Highlights

1 Indulging in the culture, cuisine, color, crafts – and mezcal – of festive, colonial **Oaxaca city** (p422).

2 Chilling out for longer than you planned at the travelers' beach hangouts of **Mazunte** (p476), **Zipolite** (p471) and **San Agustinillo** (p474).

3 Riding the surf on the gorgeous beaches of **Puerto Escondido** (p456).

4 Hiking through otherworldly cloud forests between the mountain villages of the **Pueblos Mancomunados** (p452).

5 Enjoying the majestic

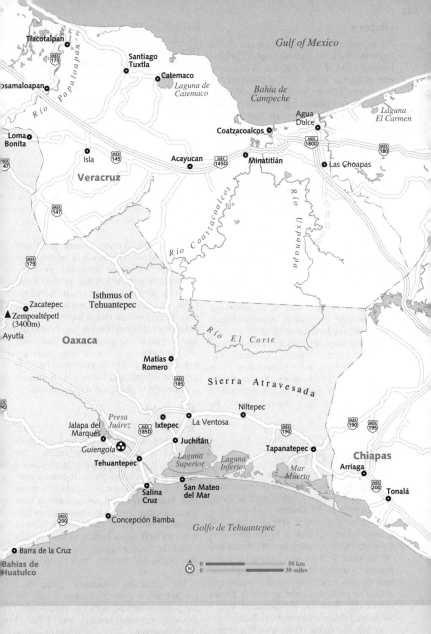

Gulf of Mexico

Tlacotalpan

Santiago
Tuxtla

Catemaco

*Laguna de
Catemaco*

*Bahía de
Campeche*

*Laguna
El Carmen*

Agua
Dulce

Coatzacoalcos

osamaloapan

Loma
Bonita

Isla

Acayucan

Minatitlán

Las Choapas

Veracruz

Río Coatzacoalcos

Río Uxpanapa

Isthmus of
Tehuantepec

Zacatepec

▲ Zempoaltépetl
(3400m)

Ayutla

Oaxaca

Río El Corte

Matías
Romero

Sierra Atravesada

Niltepec

Jalapa del
Marqués

*Presa
Juárez*

Ixtepec

La Ventosa

Guiengola

Tehuantepec

Juchitán

*Laguna
Superior*

*Laguna
Inferior*

Tapanatepec

Chiapas

Arriaga

Tonalá

*Mar
Muerto*

Salina
Cruz

San Mateo
del Mar

Concepción Bamba

Golfo de Tehuantepec

Barra de la Cruz

**Bahías de
Huatulco**

0   50 km
0   30 miles

---

setting and mysterious
architecture of **Monte Albán**
(p443).

6 Getting a feel for
indigenous village life at the
markets, fiestas and artisans'
workshops of the **Valles
Centrales** (p443).

7 Riding across bird-filled
lagoons to a stunning beach at
Chacahua (p468).

8 Seeing thousands of

turtles struggling ashore
to nest on **Playa Escobilla**
(p469).

9 Enjoying beach life with
creature comforts at **Bahías
de Huatulco** (p480).

History

Pre-Hispanic cultures in Oaxaca's Valles Centrales (Central Valleys) reached heights rivaling those of central Mexico. The hilltop city of Monte Albán became the center of the Zapotec culture, which conquered much of Oaxaca and peaked between AD 350 and 700. From about 1200 the Zapotecs came under the growing dominance of Mixtecs from Oaxaca's northwest uplands. Mixtecs and Zapotecs alike were conquered by the Aztecs in the 15th and early 16th centuries.

The Spanish had to send at least four expeditions before they felt safe enough to found the city of Oaxaca in 1529. The indigenous population declined quickly and disastrously: rebellions continued into the 20th century.

Benito Juárez, the great reforming president of mid-19th-century Mexico, was a Zapotec from the Oaxaca mountains. Another Oaxacan, Porfirio Díaz, rose to control Mexico with an iron fist from 1877 to 1910, bringing the country into the industrial age but fostering corruption, repression and, eventually, the Revolution in 1910.

Today, while tourism thrives in and around Oaxaca city and on the coast, underdevelopment still prevails in the backcountry. There is still a wide gulf between the state's rich, largely mestizo (people of mixed ancestry) elite and its poor, disempowered, heavily indigenous majority.

OAXACA CITY

✈ 951 / POP 260,000 / ELEV 1550M

A burgeoning cultural and culinary capital with a beautiful colonial core of lovely, tree-shaded streets, Oaxaca is one of Mexico's most captivating cities. Artists and artisans are inspired by the area's creative atmosphere, indigenous traditions and bright, clear light. Oaxaca has top-class museums, charming inns, fascinating markets and its own superb version of Mexican cuisine. The easygoing pace frequently breaks out into the fireworks of a fiesta, and there's some brightly colored event unfolding in the streets or the Zócalo (Oaxaca's lovely central square) almost every day.

Set at the nexus of three mountain-flanked valleys, the city is surrounded by fascinating archaeological sites and villages, many of the latter housing creative artisans and staging bustling weekly markets. The surrounding country provides abundant opportunities for hiking, biking, horseback riding and cultural trips, and good active-tourism operators make it easy to enjoy these experiences.

Despite its cultural riches, the state of Oaxaca is one of Mexico's poorest, and the city's fringe settlements and some outlying villages are as impoverished as any in Mexico. Yet the people of Oaxaca are among the most warmly hospitable in the country.

History

Oaxaca's origins are in the Aztec settlement of Huaxyácac, from which its name is derived. The Spanish laid out a new town around the Zócalo in 1529, and it quickly became the most important place in southern Mexico.

In the 18th century Oaxaca grew rich from the export of cochineal (a red dye made from insects living on the prickly pear cactus) and from textile weaving. By 1796 it was probably the third-biggest city in Nueva España, with about 20,000 people (including 600 clergy) and 800 cotton looms.

Oaxaca's major expansion has come in the past 30 years, with tourism, new businesses and rural poverty all encouraging migration from the countryside. Together with formerly separate villages and towns it now forms a conurbation of about half a million people.

◉ Sights

★ Zócalo   PLAZA

Traffic-free, shaded by tall trees and surrounded by elegant *portales* (arcades), the Zócalo is the perfect place to start soaking up the Oaxaca atmosphere. It bustles with life by day and night, as marimba ensembles, brass bands and roving buskers float their melodies among the crowds, hawkers try to offload pretty carpets and hideous balloons, and lovers parade in slow rounds under the trees, while anyone and everyone sits, drinks and watches from the sidewalk cafes.

The adjoining **Alameda** plaza, also traffic-free but without the cafes, is also ripe for people-watching with its trinket-toting vendors, gawking tourists and informal clothes market.

Palacio de Gobierno   NOTABLE BUILDING

A 19th-century wonder of marble and murals, the State Government Palace occupies the Zócalo's southern flank. The large, very detailed stairway mural (1980), by Arturo

BENITO JUÁREZ

One of the few Mexican national heroes with a truly unsullied reputation, the great reforming president Benito Juárez (1806–72) was born a humble Zapotec villager in Guelatao, 60km northeast of Oaxaca. His parents died when he was three. At the age of 12, young Benito walked to Oaxaca and found work at the house of Antonio Salanueva, a bookbinder. Salanueva saw the boy's potential and helped pay for an education he otherwise might not have received.

Juárez started training for the priesthood, but abandoned this to work as a lawyer for poor villagers. He rose to become Oaxaca's state governor from 1848 to 1852, opening schools and cutting bureaucracy, then was made justice minister in Mexico's new liberal government of 1855. His Ley Juárez (Juárez Law), which transferred the trials of soldiers and priests charged with civil crimes to ordinary civil courts, was the first of the Reform Laws, which sought to break the power of the Catholic Church. These laws provoked the War of the Reform (1858–61), in which the liberals eventually defeated the conservatives.

Juárez was elected Mexico's president in 1861 but had been in office only a few months when France invaded Mexico, forcing him into exile. In 1866–67, with US support, Juárez ousted the French and their puppet emperor, Maximilian. One of Juárez' main political achievements was to make primary education free and compulsory. He died in 1872, a year after being elected to his fourth presidential term. Oaxacans are fiercely proud of him and today countless streets, statues, schools, villages and cities all around Mexico preserve his name and memory. If the world followed his famous maxim 'Entre los individuos, como entre las naciones, el respeto al derecho ajeno es la paz' ('Between individuals as between nations, respect for the rights of others is peace'), it would be a much better place.

García Bustos, depicts famous Oaxacans and Oaxacan history, including Benito Juárez, his wife Margarita Maza, José María Morelos, Porfirio Díaz, Vicente Guerrero (being shot at Cuilapan), and the 17th-century nun and love poet Juana Inés de la Cruz.

The building also houses the interactive **Museo del Palacio** (M$25, Sun free; ⏱9:30am-5pm Mon, to 6pm Tue-Sat, to 4pm Sun). Its main displays, with a primarily educational purpose and in Spanish only, range over evolution, the pre-Hispanic ball game, biodiversity and more, with a Oaxacan handle on universal themes. Also here is what is very probably the world's largest tortilla – a 300kg *tlayuda*, decorated with the history of Mexico by Enrique Ramos.

Catedral
CATHEDRAL

Oaxaca's massive stone cathedral, begun in 1553 and finished (after several earthquakes) in the 18th century, stands just north of the Zócalo. Its main facade, facing the Alameda, features beautiful baroque carving.

Calle Alcalá
STREET

Alcalá is the dignified, mainly traffic-free street running north from the Catedral to the Templo de Santo Domingo, lined by colonial-era stone buildings which are now home to alluring shops, galleries, museums, cafes and bars, making for an always-interesting stroll and lively night life.

★Templo de Santo Domingo
CHURCH

(cnr Alcalá & Gurrión; ⏱7am-1pm & 4-8pm except during Mass) Gorgeous Santo Domingo is the most splendid of Oaxaca's churches, with a finely carved baroque facade and nearly every square centimeter inside decorated in 3D relief with intricate gilt designs swirling around a profusion of painted figures. Most elaborate of all is the 18th-century Capilla de la Virgen del Rosario (Rosary Chapel) on the south side. The whole church takes on a magically warm glow during candlelit evening Masses.

Santo Domingo was built mainly between 1570 and 1608 as part of the city's Dominican monastery, with the finest artisans from Puebla and elsewhere helping in its construction. Like other big buildings in this earthquake-prone region, it has immensely thick stone walls.

Santo Domingo de Guzmán (1172–1221), the Spanish monk who founded the Dominican order, appears as the right-hand one of the two figures holding a church in the center of the facade, and his elaborate family tree adorns the ceiling immediately inside. The Dominicans observed strict vows

Oaxaca City

400 m
0.2 miles

Calzada Niños Héroes de Chapultepec (Hwy 190)

Itanoni Antojería y Tortillería (400m)

Teotitlán del Valle (29km); Mitla (46km)

1st-class bus station

Sectur

Panteón General (300m)

Aldama

39

19

Aldama

Parque Juárez (El Llano)

20

Zárate

Cosijopii

43

Libres

83

Abasolo

Pino Suárez

25

Sectur

Ceprotur

Reforma

Jardín Conzatti

Gómez Farías

Humboldt

Maza de Juárez

Berriozábal

Juárez

Constitución

36

79

26

62

Templo de Santo Domingo

11

50

61

Murguía

24

67

5

Quintana Roo

45

21

70

Museo de las Culturas de Oaxaca

Jardín Etnobotánico

1

2

49

Plazuela Labastida

6

Alcalá

4

14

12

Municipal Tourist Information Kiosk

47

El Pochote-Xochimilco (200m)

Cosijopi

44

46

29

Quetzalcoatl

Callejón Hidalgo

Plazuela del Carmen Alto

64

54

10

13

56

72

60

52

9

78

84

71

33

García Vigil

Pérez

48

55

58

31

73

Carranza

Allende

53

23

Porfirio Díaz

74

77

Callejón del Carmen

42

37

34

Boca del Monte

40

41

Bravo

69

Tinoco y Palacios

16

Cerro del Fortín

75

La Unión

Aranda

38

28

Matamoros

Crespo

Morelos

Jardín Sócrates

Plaza de la Danza

San Agustín Etla (16km)

Independencia

A B C D E F G
1 2 3 4

Oaxaca City

◉ Top Sights

1 Museo de las Culturas de Oaxaca	D3
2 Templo de Santo Domingo	D3
3 Zócalo	C5

◉ Sights

4 Arte de Oaxaca	D4
5 Bodega Quetzalli	E4
6 Calle Alcalá	D4
7 Catedral	C5
8 Centro Cultural San Pablo	D5
9 Centro Fotográfico Álvarez Bravo	D4
Galería Quetzalli	(see 50)
10 Instituto de Artes Gráficas de Oaxaca	D3
11 Jardín Etnobotánico	E3
12 La Mano Mágica	D4
13 Museo Casa de Juárez	D3
14 Museo de Arte Contemporáneo de Oaxaca	D4
15 Museo de los Pintores Oaxaqueños	C5
Museo del Palacio	(see 18)
16 Museo Rufino Tamayo	C4
17 Museo Textil de Oaxaca	D5
18 Palacio de Gobierno	C6

◯ Activities, Courses & Tours

19 Alma de Mi Tierra	G4
20 Amigos del Sol Meeting Point	F2

Becari Language School (Bravo)	(see 23)
21 Becari Tonatzin Language School	D2
22 Bicicletas Pedro Martínez	B6
23 Expediciones Sierra Norte	C4
Fundación En Vía	(see 25)
24 Horseback Mexico	E4
25 Instituto Cultural Oaxaca	F1
26 La Casa de los Sabores	E4
27 Ollin Tlahtoalli	D8
28 Spanish Immersion School	B4
29 Tierraventura	C2
Turismo El Convento	(see 47)

◉ Sleeping

30 Azul Cielo	E7
31 Casa Ángel	C2
32 Casa de la Tía Tere	F5
Casa de las Bugambilias	(see 26)
33 Casa Oaxaca	C4
34 El Diablo y la Sandía (Boca del Monte)	C3
35 El Diablo y la Sandía (Libres)	F5
36 Hostal Casa del Sol	E3
37 Hostal Pochón	C2
38 Hotel Azucenas	B4
39 Hotel Casa Arnel	G3
40 Hotel Casa del Sótano	C3
41 Hotel Las Golondrinas	C3
42 La Betulia	C2

of poverty, chastity and obedience, and in Mexico they protected the indigenous people from other colonists' excesses.

★ Museo de las Craturas de Oaxaca   MUSEUM

(☎951-516-29-91; Alcalá; M$64, video M$45; ⊙10am-6:15pm Tue-Sun) The Museum of Oaxacan Cultures, housed in the beautiful monastery buildings adjoining the Templo de Santo Domingo, is one of Mexico's best regional museums. The rich displays take you right through the history and cultures of Oaxaca state up to the present day, emphasizing the continuity between pre-Hispanic and contemporary cultures in areas such as crafts, medicine and food.

A gorgeous stone cloister serves as antechamber to the museum proper. The greatest treasure is the Mixtec hoard from Tomb 7 at Monte Albán, in Room III (the first on the right upstairs). This dates from the 14th century, when Mixtecs reused an old Zapotec tomb at Monte Albán to bury one of their kings and his sacrificed servants, along with a stash of beautifully worked silver, turquoise, coral, jade, amber, pearls, finely carved bone, crystal goblets, a skull covered in turquoise, and a lot of gold. The treasure was discovered in 1932 by Alfonso Caso.

Halls I to IV are devoted to the pre-Hispanic period, halls V to VIII to the colonial period, halls IX to XIII to Oaxaca in the independence era and after, and the final room (XIV) to Santo Domingo Monastery itself. At the end of the long corridor past hall IX, glass doors give a view into the beautifully ornate choir of the Templo de Santo Domingo.

Surprisingly, the museum's explanatory material is in Spanish only. Also here is a good book-and-souvenir shop.

Jardín Etnobotánico   GARDENS

(EthnobotanicalGarden; ☎951-516-79-15; www.jardin oaxaca.org.mx; cnr Constitución & Reforma; 2hr tours in English or French M$100, 1hr tours in Spanish M$50; ⊙English tours 11am Tue, Thu & Sat, Spanish tours 10am, noon & 5pm Mon-Sat, French tours 5pm Tue) In former monastic grounds behind the Templo de Santo Domingo, this garden features plants from around Oaxaca state, including a staggering variety of cacti. Though it has been growing only since the 1990s, it's already a fascinating demonstration of Oax-

OAXACA

43 La Casa de Mis Recuerdos F3
44 La Casona de Tita D2
45 Ollin Bed & Breakfast D2
46 Posada Don Mario D2
47 Quinta Real Oaxaca D4
48 Un Sueño Valle de Huajes......................C1

Eating
      Cafe El Ágora................................ (see 39)
49 Café Los Cuiles.. D4
50 Casa Oaxaca...E4
51 Cenaduría Tlayudas Libres....................F5
52 Comala D3
53 Gourmand C3
54 La Biznaga D3
55 La Jícara C2
      La Olla .... (see 26)
56 La Popular.. D3
57 Mercado 20 de Noviembre................... C7
58 Mercado Sánchez Pascuas C2
59 Nimbus..F7
60 Restaurante Los Danzantes................. D4
61 Tastavins...E4
62 Vieja Lira E3
63 Xuncu Choco B5
64 Zandunga.. D3

Drinking & Nightlife
65 Café Brújula D5
66 Café del Jardín C6

67 Candela...E4
68 Cuish...B7
69 In Situ...C4
70 La Mezcalerita.......................................D2
      La Santísima Flor de
        Lúpulo .... (see 53)
71 La Tentación D4
72 Los Amantes D3
73 Piedra Lumbre C3
74 Txalaparta C4

Entertainment
75 Auditorio Guelaguetza............................A2
      Guelaguetza Show .... (see 47)
76 Guelaguetza Show C5
77 La Nueva Babel.......................................C4

Shopping
78 Amate Books..D4
      Arte Textil Indígena......................(see 60)
79 El Nahual E4
80 La Casa del Rebozo...............................D5
81 Mercado de Artesanías B7
82 Mercado Juárez......................................C6
83 Unión de Palenqueros de
        Oaxaca F4
84 Voces de Copal, Aullidos del
        Alma D4

aca's biodiversity. Visits are by guided tour only: be there five minutes before they start.

Museo Rufino Tamayo MUSEUM
(951-516-47-50; Morelos 503; M$40; 10am-2pm & 4-7pm Mon & Wed-Sat, 10am-3pm Sun) This top-class collection of pre-Hispanic art was donated to Oaxaca by its most famous artist, Rufino Tamayo (1899–1991). In a fine 17th-century building, the exhibits trace artistic developments in preconquest times and include some truly beautiful pieces.

Museo Textil de Oaxaca MUSEUM
(951-501-11-04; www.museotextildeoaxaca.org.mx; Hildago 917; 10am-8pm Mon-Sat, to 6pm Sun) FREE The textile museum promotes Oaxaca's traditional textile crafts through exhibitions, workshops, films, presentations and a library. Themed selections from its stock of around 5000 Oaxacan and international textile pieces, many of them a century or more old, are always on view. There's a top-quality crafts shop here too.

One-hour guided visits (M$10) are given at 5pm on Wednesday, in English and/or Spanish, if five or more people turn up.

Museo Casa de Juárez MUSEUM
(951-516-18-60; http://museocasajuarez.blogspot.com.es; García Vigil 609; M$47; 10am-7pm Tue-Sun) The simple house of bookbinder Antonio Salanueva, who supported the education of the great 19th-century Mexican leader Benito Juárez (p423) during his youth, is now an interesting little museum. The binding workshop is preserved, along with Benito memorabilia and period artifacts.

Centro Cultural San Pablo ARTS CENTER
(www.facebook.com/fahhosanpablo; Independencia 904; 10am-8pm) FREE Housed in the recently restored Ex-Convento de San Pablo (a 16th-century Dominican monastery), the impressive San Pablo center stages concerts, films, and exhibitions, and holds classes, presentations and conferences, with an emphasis on promoting and preserving Oaxacan culture, especially its indigenous aspects.

Its research library holds valuable anthropological archives and there's a sound library with recordings of indigenous music.

CONTEMPORARY ART IN OAXACA

Of Mexico's major art hubs, Mexico City may have the most and the fanciest galleries, and Monterrey the most impressive presentations – but only in Oaxaca will you find such a dense concentration of talent, innovation and galleries within a small, accessible area.

A delight in color and light, a dreamlike feeling and references to indigenous mythology have long been trademarks of Oaxacan art. Two artists laid the basis for today's flourishing scene: the great muralist Rufino Tamayo (1899–1991) and European-influenced Francisco Gutiérrez (1906–45). The next generation was led by three artists. The colorful art of Rodolfo Morales (1925–2001) from Ocotlán, with its childlike angel figures, has deep roots in local myths. Rodolfo Nieto (1936–85) populated his work with vivid fantasy animals and dream figures. Francisco Toledo (b 1940), from Juchitán, works in many media, often focusing on grotesque beasts. He's still an active figure in Oaxacan cultural life.

Workshops for young artists organized by Tamayo in the 1970s encouraged talents such as Abelardo López, Ariel Mendoza and Alejandro Santiago. Their work is highly varied, but indigenous roots and a dreamlike quality run through a lot of it. More or less contemporary is Sergio Hernández, whose limitless imagination melds the figurative with the abstract and fantastic. Artists who appeared around the turn of the 21st century, such as Demián Flores, Soid Pastrana and Guillermo Olguín, tend to reject representation and 'folklorism' in favor of postmodernism, video and symbol-loaded graphic compositions designed to make us ponder.

A wave of political and social protest in Oaxaca in 2006 saw an explosion of street art, which continues to fight a running battle with the authorities who are forever painting over the latest murals in the city's historic center. Oaxacan street art has reached global audiences through the work of artists such as Yescka (http://guerilla-art.mx) and especially Lapiztola (www.facebook.com/lapiztola.stencil), a small collective whose startling, brilliantly executed murals are usually based on photographically real images with creative embellishments and a strong political message. Lapiztola's work has appeared or been exhibited from Stockholm to London to São Paulo to Tijuana to the USA.

Top Galleries & Museums

Museo de Arte Contemporáneo de Oaxaca (MACO; ☑ 951-514-22-28; www.museoma co.com; Alcalá 202; M$20, Sun free; ⊙ 10:30am-8pm Wed-Mon) Changing exhibits of first-rate contemporary Mexican and international art, in a beautifully revamped colonial house.

Museo de los Pintores Oaxaqueños (MUPO, Museum of Oaxacan Painters; ☑ 951-516-56-45; museodelospintores.blogspot.co.uk; Independencia 607; M$20, Sun free; ⊙ 10am-6pm Tue-Sun) Exhibitions by artists from Oaxaca and elsewhere – often provocative contemporary work.

Arte de Oaxaca (☑ 951-514-15-32; www.artedeoaxaca.com; Murguía 105; ⊙ 11am-3pm & 5-8pm Mon-Sat) FREE A commercial gallery presenting a wide range of quality art, it includes a room devoted to Rodolfo Morales' work.

Centro Fotográfico Álvarez Bravo (☑ 951-516-98-00; www.cfmab.org; Bravo 116; ⊙ 9:30am-8pm Wed-Mon) FREE With a taste for provocative social commentary, this photo gallery displays quality work by international photographers.

Galería Quetzalli (☑ 951-514-26-06; Constitución 104; ⊙ 10am-2pm & 5-8pm Mon-Sat) FREE A leading commercial gallery, handling big names such as Francisco Toledo and Guillermo Olguín. It has a second exhibition space, **Bodega Quetzalli** (Murguía 400; ⊙ variable), a few blocks away.

Instituto de Artes Gráficas de Oaxaca (IAGO, Oaxaca Graphic Arts Institute; ☑ 951-516-69-80; www.institutodeartesgraficasdeoaxaca.blogspot.com; Alcalá 507; ⊙ 9:30am-8pm, library closed Sun) FREE Offers changing exhibitions of graphic art plus a superb arts library open to all.

La Mano Mágica (☑ 951-516-42-75; Alcalá 203; ⊙ 10:30am-3pm & 4-8pm Mon-Sat) Art by the likes of Tamayo, Morales and Hernández, plus a small but fine handicrafts selection.

🏃 Activities

⭐ Tierraventura
OUTDOORS

(☑ 951-501-21-96; www.tierraventura.com; Porfirio Díaz 719; per person day trips M$900-1300, longer trips per day M$1300-2000; ⊙ 10am-2pm & 4-6pm Mon-Fri) 🏃 Well-organized Tierraventura, run by a multilingual European and Mexican team, offers enticing trips focused on hiking, nature, meeting locals and supporting rural tourism projects. Local guides accompany travelers wherever possible.

Options include hiking in the Sierra Norte, trips to Santiago Apoala, and some truly off-the-beaten-track destinations such as Santiago Quiotepec in the dramatic La Cañada area (where you'll see a rarely visited Zapotec fort, Mexico's last military macaws and some amazing cardón cacti), or the northern village of Santo Domingo Cacalotepec, where prize-winning coffee and everything else is grown organically and you'll swim beneath waterfalls and hike through ancient high-altitude rainforest. Tierraventura also offers rare opportunities to experience Mexican traditional medicine through medicinal-herb walks, consultations or cleansings with traditional healers, or a temascal (pre-Hispanic-style therapeutic steam bath).

Expediciones Sierra Norte
OUTDOORS

(☑ 951-514-82-71; www.sierranorte.org.mx; Bravo 210A; ⊙ 9am-7:30pm Mon-Fri, 9:30am-2pm Sat) 🏃 Some of Oaxaca's most exhilarating outdoor experiences are to be had among the mountain villages of the Pueblos Mancomunados, where this community-run outfit maintains a network of good trails, comfortable *cabañas* (cabins), guide services, and horse and bike hire. This city office has copious information (including a useful guide map; M$50) and some English-speaking staff, and can make reservations for all services.

Bicicletas Pedro Martínez
CYCLING, HIKING

(☑ 951-514-59-35; www.bicicletaspedromartinez. com; Aldama 418; ⊙ 9am-8pm Mon-Sat) 🏃 This friendly team headed by Mexican Olympic cyclist Pedro Martínez offers mostly off-road rides (and some great day walks) amid some of Oaxaca state's best scenery. Van support cuts out the less interesting bits and hardest climbs. The shortest options are half-day or full-day rides in the Valle de Tlacolula (full day per person for groups of two/four M$1500/1350).

The two-day 'Cascadas y Mangos' jaunt (per person for two/four people M$3800/3400) runs from Nochixtlán to spectacular Santiago Apoala, then across the scenic Tehuacán-Cuicatlán biosphere reserve. The four-day Oaxaca–Puerto Escondido route (M$5800 to M$6500 per person) takes you right down through the mountains to the Pacific coast.

Zapotrek
HIKING, CYCLING

(☑ 951-502-59-57, cell 951-2577712; www.zapotrek. com) 🏃 Zapotrek specializes in hiking, biking and driving trips among indigenous Zapotec villages and their often-spectacular countryside with the help of local guides and experts, opening windows on Zapotec culture and eating local meals, often in local homes. It's run by English-fluent Eric Ramírez, a native of Tlacolula, 31km east of Oaxaca.

Options include hiking up a sacred mountain near San Bartolomé Quialana, visiting mezcal plantations and distilleries east of Ocotlán, and a unique approach to Hierve el Agua. Day-trips cost US$100 to US$150 per person (minimum two people).

Horseback Mexico
HORSEBACK RIDING

(☑ cell 951-1997026; www.horsebackmexico.com; Murguía 403; ⊙ 11am-6pm Sun-Fri) This experienced, enthusiastic Canadian–American-run outfit offers equestrian adventures for all levels from beginners up. Two-hour rides on Arabian and Mexican Criollo horses in the countryside around their ranch at Rojas de Cuauhtémoc, 15km east of the city, cost US$65 per person including round-trip transportation from Oaxaca.

Other options include full-day rides, overnight rides and one-week riding vacations based at the ranch's comfortable guest accommodations.

🐴 Courses

Oaxaca is a very popular place for learning some Spanish or taking classes in Mexican cooking.

Language Courses

Oaxaca has numerous good, professional language schools, all offering small-group instruction at varied levels and most emphasizing spoken language. At most schools you can start any Monday (at some you can start any day). Most also offer individual tuition if wanted, plus volunteer opportunities and optional activities like dance or cooking classes, trips and *intercambios* (meetings with locals for conversation). If you're looking for some social life with other students, the bigger schools are best. Enrollment/registration fees, textbooks and materials are extra costs at some schools.

Schools can arrange accommodations with families or in hotels, apartments or their own student houses. Homestays with a private room typically cost around US$20/25/29 a day with one/two/three meals.

Becari Language School   LANGUAGE COURSE
(15/20/30hr per week US$150/200/300; 🎯) Highly rated, medium-sized Becari has two branches – **Bravo** (📷 951-514-60-76; www.becari.com.mx; Bravo 210; 🎯) and **Tonatzin** (📷 951-516-46-34; www.becariqr.com; Quintana Roo 209; 🎯); you can study at either or both. Optional extras include salsa, folk dance, weaving and cooking, and Becari also offers special courses such as medical Spanish, Zapotec language and Spanish for volunteers and children.

Amigos del Sol   LANGUAGE COURSE
(📷 cell 951-1968039; www.oaxacanews.com/amigosdelsol.htm; Calzada San Felipe del Agua 322; 15/20hr per week US$168/224) A professional, good-value, flexible school popular with travelers. Maximum class size is three, you can start any day, and there's no minimum duration or registration charge. Contact the school up to the day before by email or call any day after 5pm.

The school is in a residential area in the north of the city, with free transportation for the short drive from its meeting point at Pino Suárez 802, facing Parque Juárez (El Llano).

Instituto Cultural Oaxaca   LANGUAGE COURSE
(ICO; 📷 951-515-34-04; www.icomexico.com; Juárez 909; 15/20/32hr per week US$140/157/178; 🎯) A large, long-established school with a professional approach and ample gardens where some of the classes take place. The 32-hour-a-week main program includes eight hours of cultural workshops (dance, cooking, arts, crafts and more) and four hours' *intercambio*. You can study for any period from one week up.

Courses in medical and business Spanish, and for children and teachers, are also offered.

Ollin Tlahtoalli   LANGUAGE COURSE
(📷 951-514-55-62; www.ollinoaxaca.org.mx; Ocampo 710; 15/20hr per week US$120/140) Ollin focuses on practical language learning with an emphasis on Mexican culture and society. Email in advance to discuss your needs.

Spanish Immersion School   LANGUAGE COURSE
(📷 cell 951-1964567; www.spanishschoolinmexico.com; Matamoros 502; classes per hour US$10) This school employs the novel method of giving one-on-one classes in cafes, parks, libraries, homestays or on the move while visiting markets, museums and galleries. They're very flexible: you can study from three to eight hours daily, for as long as you like, or even just take a teacher for a day's excursion.

Cooking Classes

Oaxaca has its own memorable take on Mexican cuisine, based on its famous seven *mole* sauces (p436), ancient culinary traditions and unforgettable flavor combinations. Numerous cooks regularly impart their secrets to visitors – in classes that are (or can be) held in English, and include market visits to buy ingredients and a meal to enjoy the fruits of your work!

La Casa de los Sabores   COOKING
(📷 951-516-66-68; www.casadelossabores.com; La Olla, Reforma 402; per person US$75) Pilar Cabrera, owner of the excellent La Olla (p436), gives classes most Wednesday and Friday mornings. Participants prepare and eat one of 17 varied lunch menus. Make inquiries and reservations at La Olla: participants meet there at 9:30am and are delivered back there around 2:30pm after a market visit and the class and lunch at Pilar's house.

Alma de Mi Tierra   COOKING
(📷 951-513-92-11; www.almademitierra.net; Aldama 205, Barrio Jalatlaco; per person US$75) Nora Valencia, from a family of celebrated Oaxacan cooks (her parents run La Casa de Mis Recuerdos, p435), conducts five-hour morning classes at her home in quaint Barrio Jalatlaco; 48 hours' notice is needed.

El Sabor Zapoteco   COOKING
(📷 951-524-46-58; www.cookingclasseselsaborzapoteco.blogspot.com; Juárez 30, Teotitlán del Valle; per person US$75) These highly recommended classes, preparing traditional village dishes by traditional methods, are given by Reyna Mendoza in her lovely open-air kitchen in the famous textile village of Teotitlán del Valle, 25km east of Oaxaca (two-way transportation included). Classes are normally held on Tuesday and Friday mornings (Teotitlán's main market days). You can reserve

in Oaxaca at the crafts shop **El Nahual**
(☑ 951-516-42-02; Reforma 412A; ☉ 10:30am-2pm
& 4-8pm Mon-Sat).

Seasons of My Heart   COOKING COURSE
(☑ cell 951-5080469; www.seasonsofmyheart.com;
group day class incl transportation per person
US$85) This well-known cooking school, at
a ranch in the Valle de Etla, is run by Oaxacan food expert and writer Susana Trilling.
It offers half-day or one-day group classes
(most Wednesdays), weeklong courses, and
culinary tours around Oaxaca state and other Mexican regions.

La Cocina Oaxaqueña   COOKING
(☑ cell 951-1562893; http://oaxacacuisine.com;
Yagul 209, San José la Noria; per person M$800)
A friendly mother-and-son team give well-
priced, five-hour morning classes in their
prettily decorated open kitchen. Normally
you'll make four typical Oaxacan dishes. Try
to reserve a day or two ahead; they'll pick
you up and drop you back at your accommodations. Vegetarian classes available.

⌕ Tours

Guided trips can save hassles, be a lot of
fun and tell you more than you might otherwise learn. A typical small-group day trip
to El Tule, Teotitlán del Valle, Mitla, Hierve
El Agua and a mezcal factory costs anywhere
between M$180 and M$330 per person; trips
to Monte Albán are M$150 to M$200. Admission fees and meals are usually extra. You
can book these and other tours at many accommodations, or direct with agencies such
as **Turismo El Convento** (☑ 951-516-18-06;
www.oaxacatours.mx; Quinta Real, 5 de Mayo 300;
☉ 9am-7pm), which is at the higher end of the
price range and provides a good service.

Fundación En Vía   VILLAGE LIFE
(☑ 951-515-24-24; www.envia.org; Instituto Cultural Oaxaca, Juárez 909; tour per person US$55;
☉ tours 1pm Thu & 9am Sat) ∅ Nonprofit organization En Vía provides interest-free
microfinance loans and other help to small
groups of village women to help them develop small businesses. The program is funded
by En Vía's unique six-hour tours, which
take you into the women's houses for lunch
and explanations of local crafts and the local
economy, providing a rare close-up look at
village life.

En Vía is staffed largely by volunteers
and there are often openings for positions
with them.

Traditions Mexico   CULTURAL, HANDICRAFTS
(☑ cell 951-2262742; www.traditionsmexico.com;
day tours per person US$85; ⚑) These expertly
guided trips yield insights into Oaxacan
crafts, food, festivals and culture that few
tours match, getting off the beaten track into
artisans' workshops and villagers' kitchens
for first-hand and hands-on encounters with
indigenous Zapotec culture. Eight-hour day
trips explore a different facet of Zapotec life
each day (Tuesday to Sunday; minimum
three people).

Longer eight-to-10-day tours (from
US$1795) delve deep into rural Oaxaca.

✯ Festivals & Events

All major national festivals are celebrated
here, and local festivals seem to happen
every week somewhere in the city. The biggest and most spectacular of Oaxacan festivals is the Guelaguetza (p432).

Oaxaca FilmFest   FILM
(http://oaxacafilmfest.mx) First held in 2010,
Oaxaca FilmFest gets bigger and better by
the year and presents a great weeklong program of independent films from Mexico and
around the world, usually in the first half of
October. All showings are free and all are
in their original language with subtitles in
Spanish, English or both.

Día de Muertos   TRADITIONAL
Oaxaca's Muertos (Day of the Dead) cel-
ebrations are among the most vibrant in
Mexico, with concerts, exhibitions and oth-

GUELAGUETZAS LARGE & SMALL

The Guelaguetza is a brilliant feast of Oaxacan folk dance staged on the first two Mondays after July 16 in the large, semi-open-air Auditorio Guelaguetza on Cerro del Fortín. Magnificently costumed dancers from the seven regions of Oaxaca state perform a succession of dignified, lively or comical traditional dances, tossing offerings of produce to the crowd as they finish.

Excitement climaxes with the incredibly colorful pineapple dance by women of the Papaloapan region, and the stately Zapotec Danza de las Plumas (Feather Dance), which symbolically re-enacts the Spanish conquest.

The auditorium holds about 11,000 people: tickets for the front sections of seating (A and B, together holding about 5000 people) for each show go on sale about two months ahead through the state tourism office, Sectur (p441), and www.ticketmaster.com.mx for M$750 to M$1050. The remaining 6000 or so seats (sections C and D) are free and first come, first served.

The event takes place at 10am and 5pm on each of the Mondays, lasting about three hours. The dates vary only when July 18, the anniversary of Benito Juárez' death, falls on a Monday. Guelaguetza then happens on July 25 and August 1.

The Guelaguetza period also sees many other colorful celebrations in Oaxaca, including concerts, exhibitions, a mezcal fair in Parque Juárez (El Llano) and fantastically festive Saturday-afternoon parades along Calle Alcalá. Thousands of people flock into the city for the festivities (including visiting pickpockets, so stay alert).

Smaller Guelaguetzas are held in outlying towns and villages, such as Zaachila, Tlacolula, Atzompa, Tlacochahuaya and San Agustín Etla, and even Tututepec down near the Oaxaca coast, usually on the same days, and can make a refreshing change from what might seem the overcommercialized hubbub of Oaxaca.

The Guelaguetza celebrations have their origins in a colonial-era fusion of indigenous festivities with Christian celebrations for the Virgen del Carmen. The current format dates back to 1932.

er special goings-on starting days beforehand. Homes, cemeteries and some public buildings are decorated with fantastically crafted *altares de muertos* (altars of the dead); streets and plazas are decked with *tapetes de arena* (colored sand patterns and sculptures); and *comparsas* (satirical fancy-dress groups) parade through the streets.

Oaxaca's main cemetery, the Panteón General, 1km east of downtown, is the scene of concerts in the evenings of October 31 and November 1. Many villages, too, stage special events, with some Oaxaca accommodations and agencies arranging visits: the candlelit graveyard vigil through the October 31–November 1 night in Santa Cruz Xoxocotlán, a few kilometers south of the city, is particularly beautiful.

Noche de los Rábanos   CULTURAL
Amazing figures carved from specially grown giant radishes are displayed in the Zócalo on December 23, the Night of the Radishes.

🛏 Sleeping

Accommodations range from bargain-price hostels to luxury hotels in historic colonial buildings – and there are many charming B&Bs and hotels. Some places (mostly mid-range and top-end) raise rates around four main festivals: Semana Santa, Guelaguetza, Día de Muertos and Christmas–New Year's.

★ **Casa Ángel**   HOSTEL $
(📞 951-514-22-24; www.casaangelhostel.com; Tinoco y Palacios 610; dm M$200-250, s/d M$700/800, without bathroom M$450/550, all incl breakfast; ⊜@🛇) Deservedly popular, Casa Ángel is run by a friendly, helpful young team and kept scrupulously clean. Rooms are thoughtfully designed and the bright common areas include a good kitchen, a plasma screen with Netflix, and a great roof terrace with a BBQ every Sunday.

Three of the six private rooms have their own little terraces, and the dorms (two of them women only) have good solid bunks with private reading lights. The new 'deluxe' dorms are capsule-style, with curtained, comfy, wood-paneled bunks equipped with their own electrical plugs and USB chargers. Plenty of bathrooms too.

Azul Cielo
HOSTEL $

(☑951-205-35-64; http://azulcielohostel.mex.tl; Arteaga 608; dm M$150-170, d/tr/q M$480/650/800, all incl breakfast; ⊖@🛜) A sunny, grassy garden is at the heart of this attractive hostel with the comfy atmosphere of a private home. A semiopen lounge area sits at one end, along with two dorms and a clean, modern kitchen. The six brightly decorated private rooms at the other end boast murals, good fans and wooden furniture.

Free bikes (two hours a day) and cooked breakfasts add to the appeal.

Hostal Casa del Sol
HOSTEL $

(☑951-514-41-10; www.hostalcasadelsol.com.mx; Constitución 301; dm M$200, d M$500-650, tr/q M$600/700, all incl breakfast; ⊖🛜) This well-run, friendly spot is as much budget hotel as hostel, and offers good value. There are five large, clean and attractive private rooms with touches of art and crafts, and one huge four-bed dorm, all around a leafy courtyard. The shared bathrooms are clean. The guest kitchen is open from 8:30am to 6pm.

Hostal Pochón
HOSTEL $

(☑951-516-13-22; www.hostalpochon.com; Callejón del Carmen 102; dm M$125-145, d without bathroom M$325-370, all incl breakfast; ⊖@🛜) Budget-friendly Pochón, on a quiet street, provides five dorms for four to eight people (one for women only) and four private rooms with decent beds. It's not *luxe* but it's well kept and well run, it has a full kitchen and good common areas, and the included breakfast is worthwhile. It also offers free drinking water and bike rentals.

★ Hotel Las Golondrinas
HOTEL $$

(☑951-514-32-98; www.lasgolondrinasoaxaca.com; Tinoco y Palacios 411; r M$750-830; ⊖@🛜) Lovingly tended by friendly owners and staff, this small hotel has about 30 rooms around three beautiful patios dripping with foliage and blooms. Rooms are tastefully decorated and immaculately clean, and good breakfasts (dishes M$45 to M$75) are served in one of the patios. It's very well run and very good value.

La Villada Inn
HOSTEL $$

(☑951-518-62-17; www.facebook.com/lavillada. hostel; Felipe Ángeles 204 , Ejido Guadalupe Victoria; dm/s/d/tr/q US$16/22/39/49/61, s/tr without bathroom US$20/43; P⊖@🛜🏊) Though it's set on the city's far northern edge, La Villada is preferred by some poeple for its good facilities, helpful English-speaking staff, spacious, relatively tranquil premises and rural views. The mostly adobe-built rooms have good wooden furniture, and there's a reasonably priced cafe, plus an excellent swimming pool, bar, yoga room and tour service (though no guest kitchen).

If you call ahead, or from the bus station, they'll send a taxi to pick you up for M$50.

Un Sueño Valle de Huajes
HOTEL $$

(☑951-514-29-64; www.unsueno.com; Faustino Olivera 203; r M$875; ⊖🛜) On a quiet street, Un Sueño's style is contemporary and uncluttered with gentle color tones, the 12 ample rooms sitting on two floors around a sunny patio. Beds are comfy, staff are exceptionally friendly and helpful, and there's a lovely roof terrace where breakfast and drinks are served with views to the hills and mountains.

Original decorative touches in the rooms include the deft murals illustrating different stages in the life cycle of the locally abundant *huaje* tree.

Hotel Azucenas
HOTEL $$

(☑951-514-79-18, 800-717-25-40, in the USA & Canada 800-882-6089; www.hotelazucenas.com; Aranda 203; r M$750; ⊖@🛜) The Azucenas is a small, friendly, very well-run Canadian-owned hotel in a beautifully restored century-old house. The 10 attractive, cool, tile-floored rooms have ample bathrooms, and a continental buffet breakfast (M$58) is served on the panoramic roof terrace. There's a three-night minimum stay at some peak periods. No children under eight.

Posada Don Mario
GUESTHOUSE $$

(☑951-514-20-12; www.posadadonmario.com; Cosijopí 219; s/d M$650/750, without bathroom M$450/650, all incl breakfast; ⊖@🛜) Cute, cheerful and friendly, this colorful courtyard guesthouse has an intimate feel, with neat, brightly decorated rooms – the five up on the roof terrace being particularly appealing. There's free drinking water, and helpful services include bookings for cooking classes, tours and transportation to the coast.

Hotel Casa del Sótano
HOTEL $$

(☑951-516-24-94; www.hoteldelsotano.com.mx; Tinoco y Palacios 404; s/d/tr/q M$760/960/1160/1260; ⊖@🛜) Offering a stunning cafe-and-terrace view of Oaxaca's rooftops and church towers, this good-value hotel has attractive, spotless rooms sporting great beds, traditional-style furniture and a spot of antique art.

Hotel Casa Arnel
HOTEL $$

(☎951-515-28-56; www.casaarnel.com.mx; Aldama 404, Barrio Jalatlaco; s M$300-900, d M$400-1100; P☎) A longtime travelers' haunt, family-run Arnel is five minutes' walk from the 1st-class bus station. Clean, well-kept, mostly smallish rooms, with attractive color schemes, surround a big, leafy courtyard.

There are bikes to rent, breakfast and helpful traveler services are offered, and the bright little **Cafe El Ágora** (cnr Aldama & Hidalgo; dishes M$30-85; ⊙7:30am-10:30pm), under the same ownership, is next door.

Casa de la Tía Tere
HOTEL $$

(☎951-501-18-45; www.casadelatiatere.com; Murguía 612; s M$770-890, d M$890-1500, bungalows M$1300-2100, all incl breakfast; P⊛@☎) One of the few midrange accommodations with a pool. Rooms are large and mostly bright, with good showers; breakfast is ample and Tía Tere also offers a large, clean kitchen and dining room, plus free coffee.

Casa Adobe
B&B $$

(☎951-517-72-68; www.casaadobe-bandb.com; Independencia 801, Tlalixtac de Cabrera; s/d incl breakfast US$59/69, apt US$50-55; ⊛☎) On a quiet lane in the village of Tlalixtac de Cabrera, 8km east of the city, this is a charming retreat full of lovely art and crafts, and a good base for visits to the city and exploring outlying areas. Breakfast is served in the verdant little patio, and there's a nice roof terrace and cozy sitting room.

The amiable owners will pick you up on arrival in Oaxaca and offer free rides to town in the mornings. They'll also tell you about good restaurants locally. Minimum stay is two nights for the three rooms, three nights for the two apartments.

★Casa Oaxaca
BOUTIQUE HOTEL $$$

(☎951-514-41-73; www.casaoaxaca.com.mx; García Vigil 407; s M$2350, d M$3100-4100, all incl breakfast; P⊛☎) The seven large rooms and suites in this converted 18th-century house are in stunning contemporary Oaxacan style with original art and *artesanías* (handicrafts). It has a lovely pool in the rear patio, art exhibits in the beautiful main courtyard, and an excellent little patio restaurant. Mezcal tastings and cooking classes with the chefs are on offer too. No kids under 12.

★El Diablo y la Sandía (Boca del Monte)
B&B $$$

(☎951-514-40-95; www.eldiabloylasandia.com; Boca del Monte 121; s US$65-85, d US$70-90, all incl breakfast; ⊛☎) The brand-new Boca del Monte branch of the established B&B El Diablo y la Sandía has eight spotless, cosy rooms around a wide courtyard with colorful plants, plus two roof terraces, contemporary-styled bathrooms using solar-heated water, and slightly more understated Oaxacan *artesanías* decor than the original Libres branch (below). But everything is still infused with the same impeccably original taste of owner María Crespo.

Boca del Monte also offers the same delicious breakfasts, welcoming atmosphere, helpful Oaxaca information and postbreakfast kitchen use as the original branch.

Casa de las Bugambilias
B&B $$$

(☎951-516-11-65, in the USA & Canada 866-829-6778; http://lasbugambilias.com; Reforma 402; s M$1120-1750, d M$1260-1820, all incl breakfast; ⊛@☎) Bugambilias' delightful rooms are decorated with inspired combinations of antiques and folk and contemporary art; some are also equipped with air-con and/or a balcony. The gourmet two-course Oaxacan breakfast is a big treat, and the big roof terrace gives superb views over the city. There's a 15% discount for cash payments.

The family also runs two smaller, similarly attractive B&Bs not far away, as well as the adjoining La Olla (p436) restaurant and the Casa de los Sabores (p430) cooking school.

Ollin Bed & Breakfast
B&B $$$

(☎951-514-91-26; www.oaxacaollin.com; Quintana Roo 213; r/ste incl breakfast US$95/125; ⊛@☎) Ollin's four rooms and four two-bedroom suites are large and appealing, with bright Mexican colors. There's a pool in the courtyard, common areas (including a big roof terrace) are spacious, and everything is decked with lovely Oaxacan handicrafts. Add the excellent Oaxacan breakfast and charmingly friendly staff and you've got pretty much all you can ask from a Oaxaca B&B!

El Diablo y la Sandía (Libres)
B&B $$$

(☎951-514-40-95; www.eldiabloylasandia.com; Libres 205; s/d incl breakfast US$80/90; ⊛☎) A tasty Oaxacan breakfast emerges daily from the big kitchen range at this B&B, which is as quaintly stylish as its name (The Devil and the Watermelon). The six rooms are spotlessly clean with comfy beds and pretty, very original Oaxacan *artesanías*. Four are set around the light-filled central courtyard; another sits upstairs beside the roof terrace.

The atmosphere is welcoming, with a cozy sitting room with drinks and snacks available, and plenty of Oaxaca information on offer. Guests can use the kitchen after breakfast.

La Casona de Tita   HERITAGE HOTEL **$$$**
(☑951-516-14-00; www.hotelcasonadetita.com; García Vigil 105; r incl breakfast M$3050-3950; ☻❄🛜) This lovely conversion of an 18th-century house is set around a wide, stone-paved courtyard, with just six large and comfortable rooms, done in a tasteful combination of antique wooden furnishings with contemporary art and crafts.

La Casa de Mis Recuerdos   B&B **$$$**
(☑951-515-56-45, in the USA & Canada 877-234-4706; www.misrecuerdos.net; Pino Suárez 508; s US$60-90, d US$90-125, all incl breakfast; ☻❄@🛜) A marvelous decorative aesthetic prevails throughout this welcoming guesthouse, with old-style tiles, mirrors, masks and all sorts of other Mexican art and crafts adorning the rooms and halls. The best rooms overlook a fragrant central patio, and the Oaxacan breakfast, a highlight, is served in a beautiful dining room. There's a three-night minimum at some peak periods.

Family member Nora Valencia gives cooking classes at her school Alma de Mi Tierra (p430).

La Betulia   B&B **$$$**
(☑951-514-00-29; www.labetulia.com; Cabrera Carrasquedo 102; s/d incl breakfast US$75/85, apt per week/month US$675/1650; 🅿☻🛜) The good-sized, uncluttered rooms here have an appealing contemporary feel with simple, harmonious color schemes and photos of Oaxaca valleys scenes. They're set around a pretty garden courtyard where your full Oaxacan breakfast is served. There's also a bright, two-bedroom apartment for longer stays.

Quinta Real Oaxaca   HISTORIC HOTEL **$$$**
(☑951-501-61-00; www.quintareal.com/oaxaca; 5 de Mayo 300; r from M$2670; ☻❄🛜🏊) This 16th-century convent was converted into a very classy hotel in the 1970s. The old chapel is a banquet hall, one of the five beautiful courtyards contains a swimming pool, and lovely thick stone walls help keep the place cool. The 91 rooms are nicely done in colonial styles, with high ceilings, though the ordinary (nonmaster) suites are modestly sized.

Call or check online for best available rates.

Eating

From fashionable restaurants dealing in creative fusion to street vendors doling out spicy banana-leaf-wrapped *tamales* (steamed corn dough with fillings), Oaxaca's food is among Mexico's most inventive and memorable. The city has far more than its fair share of talented contemporary chefs, concocting novel taste combinations based on the huge variety of locally available ingredients. Heaps of care and love are lavished on Oaxaca's traditional dishes too. Do get a good sampling of the famous *mole* sauces (p436), but the *moles* are just the beginning of Oaxaca's traditional flavors. Other specialties include *tasajo* (slices of pounded beef), *tlayudas* (big crisp tortillas with varied toppings that usually include a spread of *asiento* – pork lard – although vegetarians can ask for this to be omitted), *memelas* or *memelitas* (thick, smallish tortillas topped with cheese, beans, chili sauce, *asiento* and sometimes more), *tostadas* (small, crisped corn tortillas with assorted toppings), *quesillo* (stringy cheese) and *chapulines* (grasshoppers – usually fried or roasted with some combination of chili powder, garlic, salt or lime juice).

In the beverage department, aside from the ever-more-popular mezcal, Oaxacan favorites include steaming hot chocolate (often spiced with cinnamon) and *champurrado* and *tejate*, which combine chocolate with corn.

★**Tastavins**   MEDITERRANEAN **$**
(Murguía 309; dishes M$50-150; ⊙6pm-midnight Mon-Sat; 🛜🍽) The seven tables and three or four bar stools tend to fill up quickly, so get there earlyish. Tastavins is superpopular for its combination of tasty Spanish and Italian dishes, excellent fresh salads and good selection of well-priced Mexican, Spanish, Chilean and Argentine wines.

Café Los Cuiles   CAFE **$**
(www.cuiles.com; Plazuela Labastida 115; light dishes M$35-85; ⊙8am-10pm; ☻🛜🍽) 🌿 Los Cuiles is a nice spot for breakfast, fruit smoothies, organic coffee and good light eats (including soups, organic salads, hummus and enchiladas), with a handy central location and a relaxed lounge-gallery feel.

Xuncu Choco
OAXACAN $

(Independencia 403; breakfasts M$45-70, menú del día M$60; ⊘8am-12:30pm & 2-6pm Tue-Sat, 8am-12:30pm Sun; 🛜) Popular with locals and visitors alike, Xuncu Choco has just five tables in its little black-walled cafe room, plus three more in the pretty courtyard behind. It's a good-value spot for breakfast (with omelettes or *antojitos* such as enchiladas), the three-course set lunch, or its Isthmus of Tehuantepec specials – try the *pescadillas* (fish quesadillas) or *camarones nanixhe* (spicy sautéed shrimp).

Mercado Sánchez Pascuas
OAXACAN $

(cnr Porfirio Díaz & Callejón Hidalgo; dishes M$13-25; ⊘8am-4pm) This excellent indoor food market has a great local feel, and its *comedores* (food stalls) provide a delicious, down-to-earth eating experience. Head to the ones toward the west end (where you eat at counters right in front of the cooks), ask for a *tamal*, *memela* or empanada, and practice your Spanish in deciding what you want on or in it.

Cenaduría Tlayudas Libres
OAXACAN $

(Libres 212; tlayudas M$30-55; ⊘9pm-6am) Drivers double-park along the entire block to eat at this after-dark streetside institution. The filling, tasty *tlayudas* are large, light and crisp, and half the fun is taking in the late-night scene as motherly cooks fan the charcoal grills, raising showers of sparks.

Mercado 20 de Noviembre
MARKET $

(cnr Flores Magón & Aldama; dishes M$25-50; ⊘7am-10pm) Dozens of good, clean *comedores* inside this large market serve up tasty, traditional Oaxacan and Mexican staples. The biggest treat for carnivores is the hugely popular Pasillo de Carnes Asadas (Grilled Meat Passage) on the east side, where a dozen stands specialize in grilling *tasajo* or *cecina enchilada* (slices of chili-coated pork) over hot coals.

A half-kilogram of *tasajo* or *cecina* for M$80 to M$100, with a couple of M$15 sides of grilled onions, guacamole, radishes or *nopal* (prickly pear cactus, without the prickles) should more than satisfy two people.

★ La Olla
OAXACAN $$

(📞951-516-66-68; www.laolla.com.mx; Reforma 402; breakfasts M$100-125, mains M$90-210; ⊘8am-10pm Mon-Sat; ⊖🛜✏) This superb little restaurant and cafe produces a spectrum of marvelous Mexican (mainly Oaxacan) specialties from squash-flower soup to beef fillet in *mole amarillo* (yellow *mole*) with wild mushrooms, as well as good rye-bread

---

HOLY MOLE

Oaxaca's multicolored *moles* ('*moh*-les'; nut-, chili- and spice-based sauces) are its culinary signature. To Mexicans, the meat the *mole* is served over is secondary in importance to the *mole* itself. Oaxaca's most famous variety, *mole negro* (black *mole*), is a smoky, savory delight bearing a hint of chocolate. It's the most complex and labor-intensive to create, though its popularity ensures that it's easy to find. While in Oaxaca, seek out the other colors of the *mole* family:

Mole amarillo A savory *mole* using a base of tomatillo (a small, husked tomato-like fruit), spiced with cumin, clove, cilantro and hierba santa, and often served over beef. To the untutored eye it's more red than *amarillo* (yellow).

Mole verde A lovely, delicate sauce thickened with corn dough and including tomatillos, pumpkin seeds, the herbs *epazote* and hierba santa, and different nuts such as walnuts and almonds. Often served with chicken.

Mole colorado A forceful *mole* based on *ancho*, *pasilla* and *cascabel* chilies, black pepper and cinnamon.

Mole coloradito (or mole rojo) This tangy, tomato-based blend might remind gringos of their neighborhood Mexican joint back home; it is exported in dumbed-down form as enchilada sauce.

Mancha manteles The brick-red 'tablecloth stainer' has a deep, woody flavor, often used to complement tropical fruit.

Chíchilo negro A rare *mole* whose defining ingredients include *chilguacle negro*, *mulato* and *pasilla* chilies, avocado leaves (which give a touch of anise flavor), tomatoes and corn dough.

sandwiches, juices and salads, all with an emphasis on organic and local ingredients. And it does terrific breakfasts and a great four-course set lunch (M$115) too!

La Popular
MEXICAN $$

(García Vigil 519; dishes M$75-120; ⊙1-11pm; 🔊🖊) A little corner restaurant with a sideline as an art gallery, La Popular does a variety of excellent *antojitos* and other Oaxacan and Mexican dishes: ceviches (raw seafood marinated in citrus, chili and seasonings), wild-mushroom dishes, tacos and more. With mellow music, it's also a place where you can linger over a glass or two of good mezcal.

Nimbus
OAXACAN, EUROPEAN $$

(González Ortega 508; mains M$80-170; ⊙2-10pm Tue-Sun; 🖊) This relaxed family-run restaurant with six tile-topped tables serves large, flavorful Oaxacan and Euro dishes (including some of the best pizzas in town), imaginative salads and good desserts – a welcome surprise that's well worth the walk to its slightly out-of-the-way location.

Comala
OAXACAN, INTERNATIONAL $$

(Allende 109; dishes M$60-140; ⊙noon-midnight Mon-Sat; 🖥🔊) A neat and gently arty cafe/bar with a black-and-red theme and lively evening atmosphere, Comala serves up a successful mix of Oaxacan specialties – including a great *botana oaxaqueña* (plate of assorted Oaxacan snacks such as meats, cheeses and, of course, grasshoppers) – and international fare including what are probably the best burgers in town.

There's a wonderfully scenic roof terrace – and live jazz Monday and Thursday nights.

Zandunga
OAXACAN $$

(García Vigil 512E; mains M$85-185; ⊙2-11pm Mon-Sat; 🔊) The Isthmus of Tehuantepec has its own take on Oaxacan cuisine based on ingredients like tropical fruits and seafood, with many dishes cooked in banana leaves. Festive Zandunga brings those flavors to Oaxaca, and the M$395 *botana* (a sampler of dishes which easily serves two) is perfect for whiling away a couple of hours with some of its many mezcals.

La Jícara
MEXICAN, INTERNATIONAL $$

(www.librespaciolajicara.com; Porfirio Díaz 1105; mains M$85-170, menú del día M$90; ⊙1-11pm Mon-Sat; 🖥🔊🖊📶) La Jícara is not just a restaurant but also an alternative cultural center, with films, live music and a bookstore selling titles from independent publishers. The courtyard restaurant does well-prepared fare from pepper steak to chicken curry, carrot cake, hummus or goat-cheese salad, with many vegan dishes. Also Mexican craft beers and varied mezcals.

★ Casa Oaxaca
FUSION $$$

(☑951-516-85-31; www.casaoaxacaelrestaurante.com; Constitución 104-4; mains M$200-335; ⊙1-11pm Mon-Sat, 1-9pm Sun; 🖥) Casa Oaxaca restaurant works magic combining Oaxacan and other ingredients in original and delectable ways. You might go for the chilies stuffed with ceviche accompanied by tropical-fruit sauce, the organic turkey breast in *mole negro* (black *mole*) with fried bananas, and the chocolate rolls with chocolate-and-*guanábana* (custard apple) mousse – but anything you order is likely to be a treat!

Unlike in some other creative restaurants, servings are ample. All is enhanced by the choice of courtyard or roof-terrace dining, and the exceptional range of artisanal mezcals and beers, international wines and good fruit drinks.

★ Restaurante Los Danzantes
FUSION $$$

(☑951-501-11-84; www.losdanzantes.com; Alcalá 403; mains M$115-285; ⊙1:30-11:30pm; 🖥) Excellent Mexican fusion food in a spectacular architect-designed patio makes Los Danzantes one of Oaxaca's special dining spots. The hierba santa leaves rolled round two cheeses are a great starter, and crème brûlée with walnut crumble is a perfect dessert. In between, you could go for a fish fillet in *mole amarillo* (yellow *mole*) or a rib-eye steak with wild mushrooms. There's quality house mezcal too.

Danzantes fare on a budget is available via the M$145 set lunch, served till 4pm Wednesday and Friday.

La Biznaga
OAXACAN, FUSION $$$

(☑951-516-18-00; www.labiznaga.com.mx; García Vigil 512; mains M$100-240; ⊙1-10pm Mon-Thu, to 11pm Fri & Sat; 🖥) Locals and visitors alike jam the atmospheric courtyard for delicious nouveau-Oaxacan fusion dishes. The choices are chalked on blackboards: you might start with the *sopa del establo* (a creamy Roquefort and chipotle chili soup), follow up with turkey breast in a blackberry *mole negro*, and finish with the delectable chocolate mousse and guava.

For lighter appetites and budgets, there are baguettes, quesadillas and *tostadas*. La Biznaga has a great bar too, including draft microbrew beer and fine mezcal.

Vieja Lira
ITALIAN $$$
(www.viejalira.com; Reforma 502; mains M$120-300; ⊘1-11pm Mon-Thu, to midnight Fri & Sat, to 10pm Sun; ⊜) Vieja Lira tops Oaxaca's Italian list with its tasty food, atmospheric courtyard setting, good service and international wines. Choose from eight types of pasta and 19 sauces, or go for a good risotto or pizza.

🍷 Drinking & Nightlife

Oaxaca's drinking opportunities come in large number and great variety and have been expanded by a flood of new *mezcalerías* (bars specializing in the ever-more-fashionable spirit mezcal), of which this city is the world capital. Alcalá, García Vigil and nearby streets are quite a party zone on Friday and Saturday nights. Several restaurants double as fine places for a drink, including Comala (p437) and La Biznaga (p437).

Los Amantes
MEZCALERÍA
(www.losamantes.com; Allende 107; ⊘4-10pm Tue-Sun) Squeeze into this quirky little tasting room for the perfect mezcal primer. Friendly bar staff will explain all about the three different artisanal mezcals that they give you to taste for M$150.

La Santísima Flor de Lúpulo
BREWERY
(Allende 215; ⊘5pm-1am Mon-Sat) Santísima may well be Oaxaca's first nano-brewery (that's a brewery even smaller than a micro-brewery). The bar itself is pretty small too, and usually pretty busy. It serves a few great craft beers, plus mezcals, and the same excellent food menu as **Gourmand** (Porfirio Díaz 410; dishes M$45-90; ⊘9am-1am Mon-Sat; 🗢🖉), next door.

In Situ
MEZCALERÍA
(http://insitumezcaleria.com; Morelos 511; ⊘1-11pm Mon-Sat; 🗢) A don't-miss stop on any mezcal trail, In Situ stocks a vast variety of artisanal mezcals (from M$30) and a three-type tasting is M$200.

Café del Jardín
BAR
(☑951-514-76-16; Portal de Flores 10; ⊘8am-midnight; 🗢) The Jardín has a peerless position beneath the arches at the Zócalo's

southwest corner. In the evening you're likely to be serenaded by one of Mexico's funkiest marimba ensembles.

Café Brújula
CAFE
(www.cafebrujula.com; Alcalá 104; cakes, cookies & sandwiches M$10-70; ⊘8am-10pm Mon-Sat, 9am-9pm Sun; 🗢) Brújula has a tranquil courtyard where you can hook into the wi-fi over some of the best coffee in town (a strong, flavorsome, organic bean from cooperative growers in western Oaxaca), a fruit smoothie or home-baked banana bread.

Piedra Lumbre
MEZCALERÍA
(Tinoco y Palacios 602; ⊘6pm-1am Wed-Sat) A quaint and discreet little mezcal and cocktail bar that is also an art gallery and hosts occasional jazz nights. Tasty bites to go with your drinks too.

La Mezcalerita
MEZCALERÍA
(Alcalá 706C; ⊘2pm-2am) This is a mellow and rustic spot with a wooden terrace and a mostly 20s and 30s clientele chilling over a great selection of Oaxacan mezcals (from M$40) and craft beers sourced from all over Mexico.

Cuish
MEZCALERÍA
(Díaz Ordaz 712; ⊘10am-10pm) 🖉 Cuish is officially an *expendio* (drink retailer) rather than a bar, but it has a quaint, narrow bar anyway and will happily let you sample a glass (M$30 to M$60) or two. It's an outlet for small organic producers making mezcal from wild agaves. The upstairs gallery hosts live music, often jazz, from around 9pm Wednesday, Friday and Saturday and can be a good party scene.

Txalaparta
DANCING
(www.facebook.com/txalapartabar; Matamoros 206; ⊘1pm-2am Mon-Sat, 6pm-2am Sun) By day Txalaparta is a quietish multiroom bar with hookahs; around midnight it becomes a place to dance to assorted rhythms from Latin to jazz, world music, trip hop, reggae and more (sometimes with live bands or guest DJs). It gets a good party atmosphere going with a 20-to-35 crowd on Friday and Saturday nights.

Candela
DANCING
(☑951-514-20-10; Murguía 413; M$50; ⊘10pm-2am Thu-Sat) Candela's writhing Latin bands and beautiful colonial-house setting have kept it high on the Oaxaca nightlife lists

for years. Get there soon after opening for a good table. Latin dance classes are held here too.

La Tentación DANCING
(Matamoros 101; ⏰9:30pm-3am Mon-Sat) This den of live Latin music gets up a good head of steam on Friday and Saturday nights.

☆ Entertainment

Oaxaca has a vibrant cultural life. You'll find what's-on listings (including concerts and plenty of art-house movie showings) at Qué Pasa Oaxaca (www.quepasaoaxaca.com).

Look out for gigs by local bands La China Sonidera (pop *cumbia*; dance music originating from Colombia) and Los Molcajete

MEZCAL

When Oaxacans tell you mezcal is a *bebida espirituosa* (spirit) they're not just saying it's a distilled liquor; they're hinting at an almost-spiritual reverence for the king of Oaxacan drinks. When you sip mezcal, you're imbibing the essence of an agave plant that has taken at least seven, sometimes 70, years to reach maturity. Mezcal is a drink to be respected while being enjoyed, a drink that can put people into a kind of trance – *'Para todo mal, mezcal,'* they say, *'Para todo bien, también.'* (`For everything bad, mezcal; for everything good, too.)

In the past decade or so, this once little-trumpeted liquor has become positively fashionable, not just in Mexico but also in the USA and beyond. *Mezcalerías* (mezcal bars), from the trendy to the seriously connoisseurish, have proliferated in Oaxaca, Mexico City and elsewhere, and a mind-boggling diversity of mezcal varieties and brands has hit the market.

It's strong stuff (usually 40% to 50% alcohol content), and best sipped slowly and savored. A glass of reasonable mezcal in a bar is unlikely to cost less than M$30 and a top-class one might cost M$300.

Mezcal-type drinks are produced in many parts of Mexico but only those that meet established criteria from certain specific areas can legally be marketed as 'mezcal'. Otherwise they are known as *destilados de agave*. Around 60% of mezcal (and most of the best) is produced in and around Oaxaca's Central Valleys.

Mezcal can be made from around 20 different species of agave (or *maguey* – the words are synonymous). The majority comes from the widely cultivated *espadín*, which has a high sugar content and matures relatively quickly. Mezcals from *agaves silvestres* (wild, uncultivated agaves) are specially prized for their organic nature, unique tastes and usually small-scale production methods. Best known of these is the *tobalá*, which yields distinctive herbal notes.

The mature plant's *piña* (heart), with the leaves removed, is cooked for several days over a wood fire, typically in an oven in the ground. Thus sweetened, it is crushed to fibers which are fermented with water for up to three weeks. The resulting liquid is distilled twice to produce mezcal. It can be drunk *joven* (young) or *reposado* (aged in oak for between two months and one year) or *añejo* (aged in oak for at least a year). A *pechuga* mezcal is one with flavors imparted by a chicken or turkey breast *(pechuga)* and/or fruits and spices placed in the distillation vessel.

You can observe the mezcal-making process and sample the product at dozens of mezcal factories and *palenques* (small-scale producers) in the Oaxaca area, especially around Mitla and along the road to it, and above all at the village of Santiago Matatlán, which produces about half of all Oaxaca's mezcal. If you really want to get down to grass roots and learn about the mezcal-making process first-hand and in detail, take a trip with **Mezcal Educational Tours** (☑951-132-82-03; www.mezcaleducationaltours.com; tours per group per hour US$30).

The taste variations of different mezcals are amazingly wide, and as a general rule you get what you pay for – but the only sure way to judge a mezcal is by how much you like it!

The infamous *gusano* (worm) is actually a moth caterpillar that feeds on the agave and is found mostly in bottles of cheaper mezcal. While no harm will come from swallowing the *gusano*, there is definitely no obligation! Mezcal is, however, often served with a little plate of orangey powder, *sal de gusano*, which is a mix of salt, chili and ground-up *gusanos*. Along with slices of orange or lime, this nicely counterpoints the mezcal taste.

(*son jarocho*/rock/jazz fusion), who always whip up a great atmosphere.

La Nueva Babel   LIVE MUSIC
(Porfirio Díaz 224; ⊘9am-2am Mon-Sat, 9pm-2am Sun) There's live music at 9pm or later almost every night at this tightly squeezed little bar – it could be *son* (folk), blues, *trova* (troubadour-type folk), jazz, *cumbia*... The atmosphere varies from buzzing to gravelike depending on the night.

Guelaguetza Show   DANCE
(✉951-501-61-00; Quinta Real Oaxaca, 5 de Mayo 300; incl buffet dinner M$420; ⊘7pm Fri) If you're not in Oaxaca for the Guelaguetza dance festival itself (July), it's well worth attending one of the regular imitations. The Quinta Real's highly colorful three-hour event is the best of them.

Guelaguetza Show   DANCE
(✉951-516-27-77; Hotel Monte Albán, Alameda de León 1; M$100; ⊘8:30pm) This 1½-hour show goes ahead if at least 15 people reserve earlier in the day. It's usually with recorded music.

🛍 Shopping

The state of Oaxaca has the richest, most inventive folk-art scene in Mexico, and the city is its chief marketplace. You'll find the highest-quality crafts mostly in smart stores, but prices are lower in the markets. Some artisans have grouped together to market their products directly in their own stores.

Oaxacan artisans' techniques remain fairly traditional – back-strap and pedal looms, hand-turning of pottery – but designs, motifs and products are constantly evolving in response to the big demand for Oaxacan crafts. The ubiquitous fantasy animals carved from copal wood, known as *alebrijes*, were developed within recent decades from toys that Oaxacans had been carving for centuries.

Other special products to look for include the distinctive black pottery from San Bartolo Coyotepec; blankets, tapestries and rugs from Teotitlán del Valle; creative pottery figures made in Ocotlán and Atzompa; assorted jewelry; and *huipiles* (indigenous women's sleeveless tunics) and other colorful textiles from numerous indigenous villages. Many shops can mail things home for you.

Oaxaca's crowded commercial area, stretching over several blocks southwest of the Zócalo, can be just as fascinating as its craft markets. Oaxacans flock here, and to the big Central de Abastos market, for all their everyday needs.

Mercado Juárez   MARKET
(cnr Flores Magón & Las Casas; ⊘6am-9pm) This daily indoor market, a block south of the Zócalo, peddles a mix of flowers, hats, shoes, cheap clothes and jewelry, baskets, leather belts and bags, fancy knives, mezcal, herbs (medicinal and culinary), spices, meat, cheese, ready-made *mole*, fruit, vegetables, grasshoppers and almost every other food a Oaxacan could need – a fascinating browse.

PEOPLES OF OAXACA

Much of Oaxaca's distinctive character derives from its indigenous population, who officially comprise almost half the state's 3.8 million people – unofficial estimates put the figure higher (up to 80%). Indigenous peoples are generally at the bottom of the economic and social scale here, as they are throughout Mexico, but they are rich in culture, and are a key driving force behind Oaxaca's unique *artesanías* (handicrafts), festivities, cuisine and art scene.

Each of Oaxaca's 15 indigenous groups has its own language, customs, religious beliefs and colorful costumes (though some members now speak only Spanish and many now wear mainstream clothing). All are direct descendants of peoples who lived here well before the Spanish arrived in the 16th century. You will probably have most contact with the Zapotecs, possibly 800,000 strong, who live mainly in and around the Valles Centrales and on the Isthmus of Tehuantepec. Many of the artisans and market traders in and around Oaxaca city are Zapotec. The other largest group is the Mixtecs, numbering perhaps 750,000, who are spread around the mountainous borders of Oaxaca, Guerrero and Puebla states. The state's other large indigenous groups include 300,000 or so Mazatecs and 200,000 Chinantecs in the far north, and some 170,000 Mixes in the mountains northeast of the Valles Centrales.

La Casa del Rebozo HANDICRAFTS
(5 de Mayo 114; ⊙9:30am-9pm Mon-Sat, 10am-6pm Sun) A cooperative of 84 artisans from around Oaxaca state, La Casa del Rebozo stocks quality pottery, textiles, *alebrijes*, tinware, bowls and baskets made from pine needles, and palm-leaf bags, baskets, mats and hats.

Amate Books BOOKS
(Alcalá 307; ⊙10:30am-2pm & 3-7:30pm Mon-Sat) Probably the best English-language bookstore in the country, stocking almost every in-print English-language title related to Mexico.

El Pochote-Xochimilco FOOD, HANDICRAFTS
(Xochimilco Churchyard, Juárez, Barrio de Xochimilco; ⊙8am-3pm Fri & Sat) ⌀ A small, relaxed open-air market dealing in natural products, especially crafts, food and mezcal, nearly all sold by their makers. Stop for some *tamales* or blue-corn tortillas from one of the food stalls. Long tables are set under the trees for people to sit, eat, drink and chat.

Voces de Copal,
Aullidos del Alma HANDICRAFTS
(Alcalá 303; ⊙8am-9:30pm) A classy crafts shop with superb *alebrijes* from the workshop of Jacobo and María Ángeles in San Martín Tilcajete (p450). Check out the roomful of wooden hummingbirds!

Central de Abastos MARKET
(Periférico; ⊙6am-8pm) The enormous main market, nearly 1km west of the Zócalo, is a hive of activity all week, with Saturday the biggest day. You can find almost anything here, and it's easy to get lost among the household goods, *artesanías* and overwhelming quantities of fruit, vegetables, sugarcane, maize and other produce grown from the coast to the mountaintops.

Arte Textil Indígena CLOTHING
(Alcalá 403-2; ⊙10am-9pm Mon-Sat, noon-8pm Sun) This boutique sells attractive indigenous-made clothing, mostly in cotton, with forms and designs styled to modern taste – blouses, skirts, tops, shawls, scarves.

Mercado de Artesanías HANDICRAFTS
(cnr JP García & Zaragoza; ⊙9am-8pm Mon-Sat, to 6pm Sun) An indoor crafts market almost entirely devoted to textiles: tablecloths, bags, blouses, *huipiles,* shawls and more.

Unión de Palenqueros de Oaxaca DRINK
(☑951-513-04-85; Abasolo 510; ⊙9am-9pm) ⌀ This hole-in-the-wall is the outlet for a group of small-scale mezcal producers from Santiago Matatlán. It has excellent and very well priced (M$80 to M$600 per liter) *reposado, pechuga* and smoky *añejo* varieties.

ℹ Information

EMERGENCY
Ambulance, Fire & Police (☑066)
Ceprotur (Centro de Protección al Turista; ☑951-502-12-00, ext 1525; Juárez 703; ⊙9am-3pm Mon-Fri) Helps tourists with legal problems, complaints, lost documents and the like.

INTERNET ACCESS
Internet shops are plentiful; most charge around M$10 per hour. There is free wi-fi in some public spaces, including Parque Juárez.

MEDICAL SERVICES
Hospital Reforma (☑951-516-09-89; www.hospitalreforma.com.mx; Reforma 613) Recommended, centrally located private hospital.

MONEY
There are plenty of ATMs around the center, and several banks and *casas de cambio* (exchange houses) will change cash US dollars.
CI Banco (Armenta y López 203; ⊙8:30am-6pm Mon-Fri, 10am-2pm Sat) Exchanges cash US and Canadian dollars, euros, pounds sterling, yen and Swiss francs, and euro traveler's checks.

POST
Main Post Office (Alameda de León; ⊙8am-7pm Mon-Fri, to 3pm Sat)

TOURIST INFORMATION
Municipal Tourist Information Kiosk (Plazuela Labastida; ⊙9am-6pm)
Municipal Tourist Information Office (☑951-514-28-82; Matamoros 102; ⊙9am-8pm)
Sectur (☑951-502-12-00, ext 1506; www.oaxaca.travel; Juárez 703; ⊙9am-8pm) The Oaxaca state tourism department's main information office. Also has desks at the **1st-class bus station** (p443), Museo de los Pintores Oaxaqueños (Independencia 607; ⊙9am-8pm) and Teatro Macedonio Alcalá (Independencia 900; ⊙9am-8pm).

USEFUL WEBSITES
Lonely Planet (www.lonelyplanet.com/mexico/oaxaca-state/oaxaca) Planning advice, author recommendations, articles, images and video.
Oaxaca Tu México (www.oaxaca.travel) The official state tourism site.

Oaxaca Wiki (http://oaxaca.wikispaces.com) A mine of information and photos on what's happening in and around Oaxaca. Dig around.

Planeta.com (www.planeta.com) This conscientious travel site has good info on Oaxaca.

❶ Getting There & Away

AIR

Oaxaca Airport (☏ 951-511-50-88; www.asur.com.mx) is 6km south of the city, 500m west off Hwy 175.

Aeroméxico (☏ 951-516-10-66; www.aeromexico.com; Hidalgo 513; ☺9am-6pm Mon-Fri, to 4pm Sat) To/from Mexico City several times daily.

Aerotucán (☏ 951-502-08-40; www.aerotucan.com.mx; Emilio Carranza 303, Colonia Reforma; ☺8am-7:30pm Sat) Thirteen-seat Cessnas make half-hour hops to Puerto Escondido (M$1993) and Bahías de Huatulco (M$2042), on the Oaxaca coast, both daily – spectacular flights, but they are sometimes cancelled or rescheduled at short notice.

Interjet (☏ 951-502-57-23; www.interjet.com.mx; Plaza Mazari, Calzada Porfirio Díaz 256, Colonia Reforma; ☺9am-7pm Mon-Fri, 9am-3pm Sat, 10am-2pm Sun) Mexico City two or three times daily.

TAR Aerolíneas (in Mexico City ☏ 55-2629-5272; www.tarmexico.com) Toluca and Guadalajara daily, Huatulco four times weekly.

United (☏ 800-900-50-00; www.united.com) Houston, Texas daily.

Vivaaerobus (in Monterrey ☏ 81-8215-0150; www.vivaaerobus.com) Budget airline flying to/from Monterrey two or three times weekly.

Volaris (in Mexico City ☏ 55-1102-8000; www.volaris.com) Flights to Mexico City (three weekly), Tijuana (five), Monterrey (two).

BUS & VAN

For destinations on the Oaxaca coast, buses from the 1st-class bus station take a long and expensive route via Salina Cruz. Unless you're prone to travel sickness on winding mountain roads, it's cheaper and quicker to use one of the comfortable 12- to 18-seat van services that go directly to Puerto Escondido, Pochutla, Mazunte or Huatulco. Some hostels can arrange for these services to pick you up for an extra charge of around M$50.

New highways to Puerto Escondido and Tehuantepec, which may open in 2016, will reduce journey times to coastal destinations and are likely to affect schedules and routes of some services.

BUSES & VANS FROM OAXACA CITY

DESTINATION	FARE (M$)	DURATION (HR)	FREQUENCY (DAILY)
Bahías de Huatulco	200-368	7-8	13 Expressos Colombo, 9 Huatulco 2000, 5 from 1st-class terminal
Mazunte	200	7	11 Atlántida
Mexico City (TAPO)	560-944	6-7	27 from 1st-class terminal
Pochutla	170-388	6-10	11 Atlántida, 30 Líneas Unidas, 4 from 1st-class terminal
Puebla	370-690	4½	19 from 1st-class terminal
Puerto Escondido	200-412	7-11	15 Express Service, 18 Villa del Pacífico, 4 from 1st-class terminal
San Cristóbal de las Casas	604-726	10-11	4 from 1st-class terminal
Tapachula	536	12	7pm from 1st-class terminal
Tehuantepec	258	4½	15 from 1st-class terminal
Veracruz	590	7-8	4 from 1st-class terminal
Zipolite	190	6¾	11 Atlántida

1st-class bus station (Terminal ADO; ☑ 951-502-05-60; 5 de Mayo 900, Barrio Jalatlaco) Two kilometers northeast of the Zócalo; used by ADO Platino and ADO GL (deluxe service), ADO and OCC (1st class) and AU, Sur and Cuenca (2nd class). You can buy tickets for these lines downtown at Ticketbus (www.ticket bus.com.mx; 20 de Noviembre 103; ☺ 8am-10pm) or Boletotal (Valdivieso 2; ☺ 7am-9pm).

2nd-class bus station (Central de Autobuses de Segunda Clase; Las Casas) Mainly useful for some buses to villages around Oaxaca, it's 1km west of the Zócalo.

Atlántida (☑ 951-514-13-46; Armenta y López 621) Vans to Pochutla, Zipolite and Mazunte

Express Service (☑ 951-516-40-59; Arista 116) Vans to Puerto Escondido.

Expressos Colombo Huatulco (Trujano 600) Vans to Bahías de Huatulco.

Huatulco 2000 (Hidalgo 208) Vans to Bahías de Huatulco.

Líneas Unidas (☑ 951-187-55-11; Bustamante 601) Vans to Pochutla.

Transportes Villa del Pacífico (Galeana 322A) Vans to Puerto Escondido.

CAR & MOTORCYCLE

Hwy 135D branches off the Mexico City–Veracruz highway (150D) to make a spectacular traverse of Oaxaca's northern mountains to Oaxaca city. Automobile tolls from Mexico City to Oaxaca total M$430; the trip takes five to six hours.

The roads of Oaxaca state are mostly poorly maintained, though the major routes are being slowly improved and new highways to Puerto Escondido and Tehuantepec, which may be open in 2016, will improve matters. Away from Oaxaca city, traffic is light and the scenery is fantastic. Walk-in rental prices in Oaxaca start around M$600 a day with unlimited kilometers.

Europcar (☑ 951-143-83-40; www.europcar. com.mx; ☺ 6am-10:30pm) At the airport.

Europcar (☑ 951-516-93-05; www.europcar. com.mx; Matamoros 101; ☺ 8am-7pm) In the city center.

Only Rent-A-Car (☑ 951-514-02-55; www.only rentacar.com; 5 de Mayo 215A; ☺ 8am-8pm)

ⓘ Getting Around

TO/FROM THE AIRPORT

The Transporte Terrestre ticket-taxi desk in the airport charges M$70 per person anywhere downtown in a van, or M$285 for a whole cab. For the same service going to the airport, reserve a day ahead at **Transportación Terrestre Aeropuerto** (☑ 951-514-10-71; Alameda de León 1G; ☺ 9am-7pm Mon-Sat, 10am-2pm Sun). Other taxis to the airport generally cost M$180.

BICYCLE

Two full-service shops rent out good mountain bikes and sell bikes and equipment:

Bicicletas Pedro Martínez (www. bicicletaspedromartinez.com; Aldama 418; per 4hr M$200-250, per day M$250-350; ☺ 9am-8pm Mon-Sat)

Zona Bici (www.zonabici.com.mx; García Vigil 406; per 4hr/day M$150/200; ☺ 10am-8pm Mon-Sat)

BUS

City buses cost M$7.50. From the main road outside the 1st-class bus station, westbound 'Juárez' buses will take you down Juárez and Ocampo, three blocks east of the Zócalo; westbound 'Tinoco y Palacios' buses go down Tinoco y Palacios, two blocks west of the Zócalo. To return to the bus station, take an 'ADO' bus north up Pino Suárez or Crespo.

TAXI

Taxis anywhere within the central area, including the bus stations, cost M$40.

VALLES CENTRALES

The countryside and villages around Oaxaca are a big part of its appeal. The city stands at the meeting point of three valleys that have been a center of civilization since pre-Hispanic times: the Valle de Tlacolula, stretching 50km east from the city; the Valle de Zimatlán, running about 100km south; and the Valle de Etla, reaching about 40km north. The people of these Valles Centrales (Central Valleys) are mostly indigenous Zapotec. The area is full of fascinating archaeological sites and traditional villages and towns that stage bustling weekly markets, produce fine *artesanías,* and celebrate colorful local fiestas. All are within easy day-trip distance of Oaxaca city. Public transportation is provided by bus, van and *taxi colectivo* services from various points in the city.

Monte Albán

The city from which the ancient Zapotecs ruled Oaxaca's Valles Centrales, **Monte Albán** (☑ 951-516-12-15; adult/child M$64/free; ☺ 8am-5pm; P ♿) stands on a flattened hilltop 400m above the valley floor, just a few kilometers west of Oaxaca. This is one of Mexico's most spectacular archaeological sites, with the remains of temples, palaces, tall stepped platforms, an observatory and

Monte Albán

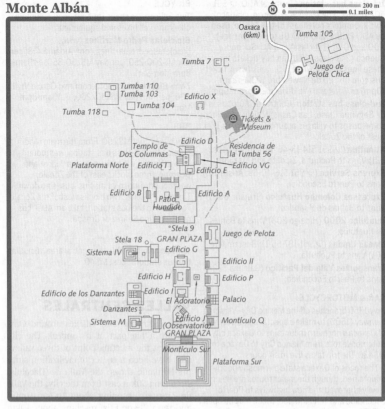

a ball court all arranged in orderly fashion, with wonderful 360-degree views over the city, valleys and distant mountains.

At the entrance to the site are a good museum (explanations in Spanish only), a cafe and a bookstore. Official guides offer their services outside the ticket office (around M$250 for a small group). The heart of the site, the Gran Plaza, is wheelchair accessible via an elevator and special walkways (ask at the ticket booth for the elevator to be activated). Explanatory signs are in Spanish, English and Zapotec.

History

Monte Albán was first occupied around 500 BC, probably by Zapotecs moving from the previous main settlement in the Valles Centrales, the less defensible San José El Mogote in the Valle de Etla. Monte Albán had early cultural connections with the Olmecs to the northeast.

The years up to about 200 BC (known as phase Monte Albán I) saw the leveling of the hilltop, the building of temples and probably palaces, and the growth of a town of 10,000 or more people on the hillsides. Hieroglyphs and dates in a dot-and-bar system carved during this era may mean that the elite of Monte Albán were the first people in Mexico to use a developed writing system and written calendar. Between 200 BC and AD 300 (phase Monte Albán II) the city came to dominate more and more of the Oaxaca region.

The city was at its peak from about AD 300 to 700 (Monte Albán III), when the main and surrounding hills were terraced for dwellings, and the population reached about 25,000. This was the center of a highly organized, priest-dominated society, controlling the extensively irrigated Valles Centrales, which held at least 200 other settlements and ceremonial centers. Many buildings here were plastered and painted red. Nearly 170 underground tombs from this period have been found, some of them elaborate and decorated with frescoes, though none of these are regularly open to visitors.

Between about 700 and 950 (Monte Albán IV) the place was abandoned and fell into ruin. Phase Monte Albán V (950–1521) saw minimal activity, although Mixtecs arriving from northwestern Oaxaca reused some old tombs here to bury their own dignitaries – notably Tumba 7, where they placed a famous treasure hoard now to be seen in the Museo de las Culturas de Oaxaca (p426).

◎ Sights

Gran Plaza   PLAZA
About 300m long and 200m wide, the Gran Plaza is the heart of Monte Albán. Some of its structures were temples, others were elite residential quarters. Many of them are now cordoned off to prevent damage by visitors' feet.

Juego de Pelota   BALL COURT
The stone terraces of the deep Ball Court, constructed about 100 BC, were probably part of the playing area, not seats for spectators. It's thought they were covered with a thick coating of lime, meaning the ball would roll down them.

Edificio P   BUILDING
Building P was topped by a small pillared temple and was probably an observatory of some sort. The sun shines directly down into a small opening near the top at the solar zenith passages (when the sun passes directly overhead at noon on May 5 and August 8).

Plataforma Sur   PLATFORM
The big South Platform, with its wide staircase, is great for a panorama of the plaza and the surrounding mountains.

Edificio J   BUILDING
Arrowhead-shaped Building J, constructed about 100 BC and riddled with tunnels and staircases (unfortunately you can't go inside), stands at an angle of 45 degrees to the other Gran Plaza structures and was an observatory. Astronomical observation enabled the ancients to track the seasons, calculate agricultural cycles and make prophesies. Figures and hieroglyphs carved on the building's walls record Monte Albán's military conquests.

Edificio de los Danzantes   BUILDING
This structure combines an early (Monte Albán I) building, which contained famous carvings known as Danzantes (Dancers), with a later structure that was built over it. There are a few original Danzantes in a short passage which you can enter, and copies of others along the wall outside. Carved between 500 and 100 BC, they depict naked men, thought to be sacrificed leaders of conquered neighboring towns.

The Danzantes generally have thick-lipped open mouths (sometimes downturned in Olmec style) and closed eyes. Some have blood flowing where they have been disemboweled.

Plataforma Norte   PLATFORM
The North Platform is almost as big as the Gran Plaza, and affords the best views overall. It was rebuilt several times over the centuries. The 12 column bases at the top of the stairs were part of a roofed hall. On top of the platform is a ceremonial complex created between AD 500 and 800, which includes the **Patio Hundido** (Sunken Patio), with an altar at its center; **Edificios D, VG** and **E**, which were topped with adobe temples; and the **Templo de Dos Columnas**.

❶ Getting There & Away

A few companies run buses to Monte Albán from Oaxaca for M$55 round trip. **Autobuses Turísticos** (Mina 501, Oaxaca) has departures hourly (half-hourly on Saturday and Sunday) from 8:30am to 3:30pm, starting back from the site between noon and 5pm.

Valle de Tlacolula

The Valle de Tlacolula, east of Oaxaca, is home to the pre-Hispanic sites of Mitla and Yagul, as well as what's claimed to be the world's biggest tree and many of the best weavings you'll see in the Oaxaca area – plus a lot of mezcal distilleries, large and small.

❶ Getting There & Away

El Tule, Teotitlán del Valle, Tlacolula and Yagul are all close to the Oaxaca–Mitla road, Hwy 190. Fletes y Pasajes (Fypsa) buses to Mitla (M$18, 1¼ hours), about every hour from Oaxaca's 2nd-class bus station, will drop you anywhere along this road. You can catch *taxis colectivos* (shared taxis) direct to El Tule (M$13, 15 minutes), Teotitlán (M$18, 30 minutes), Tlacolula (M$20, 40 minutes) or Mitla (M$25, one hour) from the corner of Hwy 190 and Derechos Humanos, 500m east of Oaxaca's 1st-class bus station, immediately past the baseball stadium.

Valles Centrales & Pueblos Mancomunados

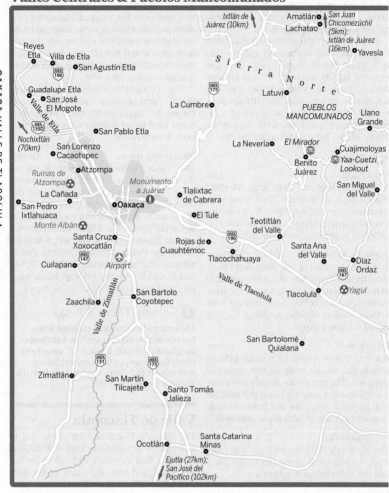

El Tule

POP 7600 / ELEV 1550M

El Tule, 10km east of Oaxaca along Hwy 190, draws crowds of visitors for one very good reason: **El Árbol del Tule** (Tree of El Tule; M$10; ☉8am-8pm), which is, by some measures, the biggest tree in the world. California's General Sherman sequoia is ahead in total volume, but at 14m in diameter, El Árbol del Tule certainly has the world's widest trunk. This vast *ahuehuete* (Montezuma cypress) dwarfs the pretty 17th-century village church beside which it towers. Much revered by Oaxacans,

the tree is reckoned to be over 2000 years old, which means it was already growing when ancient Monte Albán was in its infancy.

El Milenario (Guerrero 4A; mains M$70-130; ☉9am-8pm), one block south of the tree (past the Mercado de Artesanías), is a fine place to stop for breakfast or lunch, serving up classic Oaxacan dishes such as *tlayudas, tasajo* and *moles* with chicken, in a cheerful atmosphere.

Teotitlán del Valle

☏ 951 / POP 4400 / ELEV 1700M

This famous weaving village is 4km north of Hwy 190, about 25km from Oaxaca (*taxis*

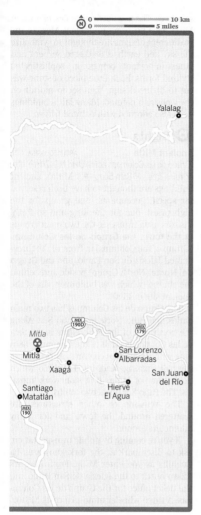

proaching the village, which tend to dominate the craft here by buying up weavers' products or employing weavers directly to weave for them. For more direct interaction head on into the village itself, where blankets and rugs wave at you from houses and workshops along the streets. Around 150 Teotitlán families specialize in weaving; they are often happy to demonstrate their techniques and methods of obtaining natural dyes. Signs point to the central **Mercado de Artesanías**, where yet more weavings are on sale.

◉ Sights

Museo Comunitario
Balaa Xtee Guech Gulal   MUSEUM
(☑ 951-524-44-63; M$10; ⊙ 10am-6pm Tue-Sun) Facing the Mercado de Artesanías on the central plaza, this interesting community-run museum displays local archaeological finds as well as exhibits on local crafts and traditions (in English as well as Spanish and Zapotec).

Templo de la Virgen de la Natividad CHURCH
(⊙ 6am-6pm) From the plaza, steps rise to this handsome 17th-century church with a fine broad churchyard and colorful 18th-century frescoes inside. It was built atop a Zapotec ceremonial site, many of the carved stones of which can be seen in the church walls; look especially in the inner patio.

Tlacolula

POP 14,000 / ELEV 1650M

Tlacolula, 31km from Oaxaca, holds one of the Valles Centrales' biggest markets every Sunday, with the area around the church becoming a packed throng. Crafts, foods and plenty of everyday goods are on sale. It's a treat for lovers of market atmosphere – and market food: there are plenty of *comedores* and the specialty here is *barbacoa* (tender, slow-cooked lamb or goat, served in a broth or tacos). Inside the church, the 16th-century **Capilla del Santo Cristo** chapel is a riot of golden, indigenous-influenced decoration comparable to the Capilla del Rosario in Oaxaca's Santo Domingo. Among the ceiling ornamentation, spot the plaster martyrs holding their own severed heads.

Yagul

Yagul ruins ARCHAEOLOGICAL SITE
(M$47; ⊙ 8am-5pm; [P]) The Yagul ruins are finely sited on a cactus-covered hill, about

colectivos shuttle between village and highway). Teotitlán weaving was already prized in pre-Hispanic times: the village had to pay tributes of cloth to the Aztecs. Quality today is high, and traditional dyes made from natural sources like indigo, cochineal and moss have been revived (though some weavers still use much cheaper synthetic dyes). The variety of designs is enormous – from Zapotec gods and Mitla-style geometric patterns to imitations of paintings by Rivera and Picasso.

Many tour groups only get as far as the larger weaving showrooms on the road ap-

1.5km north of the Oaxaca–Mitla road, 34km from Oaxaca. Unless you have a vehicle you'll have to walk the 1.5km: caution is advised on this isolated road.

Yagul was a leading Valles Centrales settlement after the decline of Monte Albán, and most of what's visible was built between AD 750 and 950. The beautiful **Juego de Pelota** (Ball Court) is the second biggest in Mesoamerica (after one at Chichén Itzá).

Patio 4, down to the left as you enter the main part of the site from the ticket office, was surrounded by four temples. On its east side is a carved-stone animal, probably a jaguar. Next to the central platform is the entrance to one of several multichambered **underground tombs**.

The labyrinthine **Palacio de los Seis Patios** (Palace of the Six Patios), above it, was probably the leader's residence. Its now creamy-yellow walls were originally plastered and painted red.

It's well worth climbing the **Fortaleza** (Fortress), the rocky hill towering above Yagul. It's topped by several ruins, and the views are marvelous.

Approaching Yagul from the main road, you can make out a large white rock painting of a person/deity/tree/sun on a cliff face on the **Caballito Blanco** rock outcrop to your right. This is the most obvious feature of a Unesco World Heritage site, the **Prehistoric Caves of Yagul and Mitla**, which stretches about 6km east from here. Caves here have yielded evidence of the earliest plant domestication in North America, about 10,000 years ago, and other valuable details about the transition from hunting and gathering to agriculture over a period of several thousand years. The Unesco-protected caves have been closed to the public to prevent vandalism and other damage; but Tierraventura (p429) runs trips to interesting caves just outside the Unesco area with paintings 10,000 years old.

Mitla

🏍 951 / POP 8200 / ELEV 1700M

The unique stone 'mosaics' of ancient Mitla, 46km southeast of Oaxaca, stand today in the midst of a modern Zapotec town. The ruins date from the final two or three centuries before the Spanish conquest in the 1520s, and comprise what was probably the most important Zapotec religious center at the time – a cult center dominated by high priests who performed literally heart-wrenching human sacrifices. The geometric 'mosaics' of ancient Mitla have no peers in ancient Mexico: the 14 different designs are thought to symbolize the sky and earth, a feathered serpent and other important beings, in sophisticated stylized forms. Each little piece of stone was cut to fit the design, then set in mortar on the walls and painted. Many Mitla buildings were also adorned with painted friezes.

◉ Sights

Ancient Mitla ARCHAEOLOGICAL SITE
(Grupo de las Columnas adult/child M$47/free, other ruins free; ⊙8am-5pm; Ⓟ) Mitla's ancient buildings are thought to have been reserved for specific occupants: one group for the high priest, one for the king and so forth. Visitors usually just see the two main groups in the town: the **Grupo de las Columnas** (Group of the Columns) in front of the three-domed Iglesia de San Pablo, and the **Grupo del Norte** (North Group) beside and behind the church (which was built over part of the ancient site in 1590).

The Grupo de las Columnas has two main patios, the Patio Norte and Patio Sur. Along the north side of the Patio Norte is the Sala de las Columnas (Hall of the Columns), 38m long with six massive columns. At one end of this hall, a passage leads into El Palacio, which holds some of Mitla's best stonework 'mosaics.' The Patio Sur holds two tombs.

The remains of other structures are scattered around the town and for many kilometers around.

If you're coming by public transportation, ask to disembark at the fork known as La Cuchilla as you enter Mitla. From here it's 1.2km north to the Iglesia de San Pablo and the ticket office for the Grupo de las Columnas. A three-wheeler moto-taxi costs M$10.

🛏 Sleeping & Eating

Hotel Don Cenobio HOTEL $$
(☎951-568-03-30; www.hoteldoncenobio.com; Av Juárez 3; r M$729-949, mains M$75-145; Ⓟ◉🅰🅰) Set on the central plaza, this is easily Mitla's best hotel, its 23 comfortable rooms sporting multicolored carved furnishings from Guadalajara. In and around the grassy central garden are a swimming pool, bar and the hotel's restaurant (open 8am to 6:30pm), serving Oaxacan fare.

Restaurante Doña Chica OAXACAN $$
(☎951-568-06-83; Av Morelos 41; mains M$75-100; ⊙7am-7pm) Less than 100m from La

Cuchilla, spotless, bright Doña Chica serves delicious Oaxacan dishes like *moles,* enchiladas and *tasajo* from an open kitchen. Good soups, *antojitos,* salads and desserts round out the careful menu.

Shopping

Mitla's streets are sprinkled with shops selling local mezcal. Many of them will invite you to taste a couple of varieties – as will many of the mezcal distilleries along the road toward Oaxaca. Many other shops, and the large Mercado de Artesanías near the ruins, sell local textiles including lots of hammocks.

Hierve El Agua

ELEV 1800M

At Hierve El Agua, 14km southeast of Mitla, bubbling **mineral springs** (M$25; ☉7:30am-7:30pm; **P**) run into natural infinity pools right on a cliff's edge with spectacular panoramas. Water dribbling over the cliff edge for millennia has created mineral formations that look like huge frozen waterfalls. Hierve El Agua means 'The Water Boils,' but the mineral-laden water is actually cool to cold, though usually swimmable. Altogether it's an utterly unique bathing experience; there are changing rooms just above the pools.

Hierve El Agua is a popular outing for *oaxaqueños* (people from Oaxaca) on their days off. Above the pools and cliffs are a number of **comedores** (antojitos M$35-50; ☉8am-6:30pm), plus community-run **cabañas** (per person M$160; **P**) providing simple but clean rooms with one bathroom per two rooms.

Hierve El Agua is on the itinerary of day tours from Oaxaca, and there's public transportation by the *camionetas* (pickup trucks) of Transportes Zapotecos del Valle Oriente (M$40 one way) from La Cuchilla in Mitla. They leave when they have enough passengers. If you're driving, 'Hierve El Agua' signs approaching Mitla will lead you on to the new Hwy 190D toll road (M$43 for cars) which bypasses Mitla: you turn off (signposted to Hierve El Agua) after 19km then go another 7km (unpaved for the last 4km). Alternatively, drive through Mitla and follow the older Hwy 179, which more or less parallels the toll road: the signed turnoff to Hierve El Agua comes up 18km from Mitla.

Valle de Zimatlán

South from Oaxaca, Hwy 175 goes through San Bartolo Coyotepec, famed for its black pottery; Ocotlán, with one of the Valles Centrales' busiest weekly markets; and San José del Pacífico, famed for its magic mushrooms, en route to Pochutla near the coast. Hwy 147 goes to Cuilapan.

Cuilapan

POP 12,000 / ELEV 1560M

Cuilapan (Cuilápam), 9km southwest of Oaxaca, is one of the few Mixtec towns in the Valles Centrales. It's the site of a historic Dominican monastery, the **Ex-Convento Dominicano** (cloister M$39; ☉9am-5pm; **P**), where in 1831 the Mexican independence hero Vicente Guerrero was executed by soldiers supporting the rebel conservative Anastasio Bustamante. Bustamante had ousted the liberal Guerrero from the presidency and Guerrero had fled by ship from Acapulco – but the ship's captain put in at Huatulco and betrayed him to the rebels, who transported him to Cuilapan to die.

A long, low, beautiful, unfinished **church** in front of the monastery has stood roofless since work on it stopped in 1560. It has stately arches and some detailed stone carving. Behind is the church that succeeded it, which contains the **tomb of Juana Donají** (daughter of Cosijoeza, the last Zapotec king of Zaachila) and is normally open only for Mass (noon and 5pm Saturday and Sunday). Behind the church is a two-story Renaissance-style **cloister**: a painting of Guerrero hangs in the small room where he was held, and outside, a **monument** marks the spot where he was shot.

Zaachila Yoo (Bustamante 601, Oaxaca) runs buses from Oaxaca to Cuilapan (M$7, 30 minutes) about every 15 minutes.

San Bartolo Coyotepec

☏951 / POP 4000 / ELEV 1550M

Barro negro, the polished, surprisingly light, black pottery that you find in hundreds of forms around Oaxaca, comes from San Bartolo Coyotepec, 11km south of the city. To head to the original source, look for the signs to the **Alfarería Doña Rosa** (☏951-551-00-11; Juárez 24; ☉9am-7pm; **P**), a short walk east off the highway. It was Rosa Real Mateo (1900–80) who invented the method of burnishing the *barro negro* with quartz stones for the distinctive shine. Her family *alfarería* (pottery) is the biggest in the village, and staff will demonstrate the process to anyone who asks. The pieces are hand-molded by an age-old technique using two saucers as a rudimentary potter's wheel. They are then fired in pit kilns and turn black from smoke and the iron oxide in the clay.

The **Museo Estatal de Arte Popular de Oaxaca** (☑951-551-00-36; www.meapo.oaxaca. gob.mx; adult/child M$20/free; ☉10am-6pm Tue-Sun), on the south side of the main plaza, features a collection of fine *barro negro* and exhibits of other quality Oaxacan folk art.

Autobuses Halcón (Bustamante 606A, Oaxaca) runs buses from Oaxaca city to San Bartolo (M$9, 20 minutes) about every 10 minutes.

San Martín Tilcajete

San Martín Tilcajete, 1km west of Hwy 175, 24km south of Oaxaca, is the source of many of the bright copal-wood *alebrijes* seen in Oaxaca. Dozens of villagers carve them, and you can see and buy them in makers' houses, many of which have '*Alebrijes*' or '*Artesanías de Madera*' (Wooden Handicrafts) signs outside. **Jacobo & María Ángeles** (☑951-524-90-47; http://tilcajete.org; Callejón del Olvido 9; ☉8am-6pm) have been making particularly wonderful *alebrijes* for over 20 years and now run a workshop employing 80 villagers. Visitors get a free tour of the workshop and can take a two-hour *alebrije*-painting class for M$180. Many of the pieces made here are based on the sacred animals of Zapotec mythology. The best sell for many thousands of pesos, and some huge and very detailed pieces can take as long as four years to make.

Good pieces are also displayed at **Azucena Zapoteca** (Hwy 175 Km 23.5; mains M$80-160; ☉8am-6pm; ☎), a popular and good lunch stop opposite the Tilcajete turnoff.

Ocotlán-bound buses from Oaxaca will drop you at the turnoff to San Martín (M$20, 35 minutes). *Taxis colectivos* run from Ocotlán itself.

Ocotlán

POP 15,000 / ELEV 1500M

Ocotlán, 31km south of Oaxaca, was the home town of artist Rodolfo Morales (1925–2001), who turned his international success to the area's benefit by setting up the Fundación Cultural Rodolfo Morales (www.fcrom.org.mx), which has done marvelous renovation work on local churches and promotes the area's arts, heritage, environment and social welfare. One major restoration was the handsome 16th-century **Templo de Santo Domingo** just off Ocotlán's main plaza, which now sports beautiful paintwork inside and out. The foundation also turned the adjoining **Ex-Convento de Santo Domingo** (M$15; ☉9:30am-5:30pm), previously a dilapidated jail, into a first-class art museum, which includes several of Morales' own canvases. Morales' ashes are here too.

Ocotlán's most renowned artisans are the four Aguilar sisters and their families, who create whimsical, colorful pottery figures of women with all sorts of unusual motifs. Their houses are together on the west side of the main road entering Ocotlán from the north, almost opposite the Hotel Real de Ocotlán. Most renowned is **Guillermina Aguilar** (Morelos 430), who turns out, among other things, miniature 3D re-creations of Frida Kahlo works.

Most visitors come to Ocotlán on Friday, when its big **weekly market** sprawls around the central plaza. The covered **Mercado Morelos** (☉6:30am-8pm), on the plaza's west side, is worth a look any day, and contains several *comedores* serving bargain Oaxacan food for M$25 to M$40 per dish. One, **La Cocina de Frida**, is presided over by a local woman who resembles Frida Kahlo – and dresses the part.

Automorsa (Bustamante 601, Oaxaca) runs buses (M$20) and vans (M$25) from Oaxaca to Ocotlán (45 minutes) about every 10 minutes, 6am to 9pm.

San José del Pacífico

📞 951 / POP 370 / ELEV 2380M

High in the misty mountains that close off the south end of the Valles Centrales, 135km from Oaxaca, San José del Pacífico is chiefly renowned for one thing – the hallucinogenic mushroom *Psilocybe mexicana*. Though their consumption is officially illegal, these *hongos mágicos* (magic mushrooms) help to make San José quite a popular travelers' stop en route between Oaxaca city and the coast. There's a significant community of alternative lifestylers here and in nearby villages. Mushrooms or no mushrooms, San José has a touch of magic anyway and is a beautiful place to break a journey. When the clouds clear, the views over pristine forested ranges and valleys are fabulous. There are good walks, a handful of surprisingly good places to stay, and several places where you can take a temascal steam bath.

🍽 Sleeping & Eating

There are several cafes and small restaurants along the main road in the village, plus a few shops selling food.

La Puesta del Sol CABAÑAS $
(📞 951-596-73-30; www.sanjosedelpacifico.com; Hwy 175 Km 131; r incl breakfast M$350-650; 🅿 🛜) Just below the highway 500m north of town, La Puesta del Sol offers cosy, clean *cabañas* with marvelous panoramas. All except the cheapest have fireplaces.

El Sueño Atrapado CABAÑAS $
(📞 951-510-92-43; www.facebook.com/trapped dream; Hidalgo 11; dm M$80, d without bathroom M$250, breakfast/dinner M$10/40; 🅿 🛜) Decent, friendly, Australian-run budget lodgings with good-value meals, 350m up the side street from Super Acuario on the main road. The well-constructed wooden buildings contain three small dorms and two double rooms, with more planned. Guests can use the kitchen. Bathrooms are outside and basic.

Refugio Terraza de la Tierra BUNGALOW $$
(http://terrazadelatierra.com; Hwy 175 Km 128; r M$500-850, breakfast/dinner M$100/150; 🅿 🛜) 🍴 A beautiful mountain retreat,

Terraza de la Tierra has six lovely big rooms in adobe, wood and tile bungalows around its large organic garden, on a 1.5-sq-km hillside property with over 20 waterfalls. Excellent vegetarian meals are served, and there are cute little glass meditation pyramids and a big-windowed yoga room.

It's 300m off the highway, 3.5km north of town.

Gringo Burger BURGERS $
(Hwy 175 Km 127; burgers M$30-100; ⊙ noon-10pm Apr-Oct, 11am-9pm Nov-Mar) This roadside hut, 4.5km north of town, is run by a New Yorker who serves up some of the best burgers you've ever had. Seriously!

❶ Getting There & Away

San José sits on Hwy 175, the Oaxaca–Pochutla road, 33km south of Miahuatlán. All the frequent van services running between Oaxaca (M$95, three hours) and Pochutla (M$95, 3½ hours), Mazunte (M$130 or M$140, 4¼ hours) or Bahías de Huatulco (M$140, four hours) stop here.

Valle de Etla

Atzompa

📞 951 / POP 22,000 / ELEV 1600M

The archaeological site of Atzompa, 6km northwest of central Oaxaca, is a fascinating complement to the larger, more famous, parent city Monte Albán. Together with Santa María Atzompa village's museum and crafts market, it provides fascinating proof of the continuity of Atzompa's pottery-making expertise from pre-Hispanic times to the present day. The village center has several straightforward *comedores* if you fancy stopping for a bite.

◉ Sights

Atzompa Ruins ARCHAEOLOGICAL SITE
(⊙ 8am-4:30pm; 🅿) **FREE** Still partly under excavation, the Atzompa ruins sit on top of Cerro El Bonete hill 2km above Atzompa village. The site flourished from AD 650 to 850 and provides spectacular views to Monte Albán, 4km south, as well of Oaxaca and of the Valle de Etla stretching away to the north.

Three ceremonial plazas, one ball court and the remains of two large residences have been exposed to view. A specially intriguing feature is the reconstructed pottery-firing oven on the north side – identical to ovens still used by potters in modern Atzompa.

Museo Comunitario   MUSEUM
(M$10; ⊙10am-5pm) Two kilometers down the road from the ruins toward Santa María Atzompa, the Community Museum exhibits some very fine pieces of pottery found at the ruins, including detailed effigies of nobility or deities and huge pots used for storing water, grain or seeds.

Shopping

Mercado de Artesanías   HANDICRAFTS
(Crafts Market; Av Libertad 303; ⊙9am-7pm) The work of over 100 contemporary Atzompa potters is on sale in the Mercado de Artesanías: items range from animal figures and lampshades to pots, plates, cups and more – some bearing Atzompa's traditional green glaze, others in more colorful, innovative styles. Prices are reasonable but much of the best work goes to shops in Oaxaca and elsewhere.

ℹ Getting There & Away

Access to the ruins is by paved road, either 3km up from Santa María Atzompa village, or 2.5km up from La Cañada village on the road from Oaxaca to San Pedro Ixtlahuaca. From Monte Albán, vehicles can drive direct to La Cañada and the ruins without returning to Oaxaca. There's no public transportation to the site. Taxis charge about M$150 round trip from Oaxaca or M$50 from Santa María Atzompa.

Taxis colectivos to Santa María Atzompa (M$8, 20 minutes) leave from Trujano on the north side of Oaxaca's 2nd-class bus station.

San Agustín Etla
🖅 951 / POP 3700 / ELEV 1800M

Pretty San Agustín sits on the Valle de Etla's eastern slopes, 18km northwest of Oaxaca. Its large, early-20th-century textile mill has been superbly restored as the **Centro de las Artes de San Agustín** (CASA; 🖅951-521-30-42; www.casa.oaxaca.gob.mx; Independencia s/n, Barrio Vistahermosa; ⊙9am-6pm) FREE, an arts center with two long, large halls used for concerts, conferences and often-wonderful craft or art exhibitions. The center also hosts many courses and workshops. Events are well publicized in Oaxaca and on the website.

The turnoff for San Agustín is on the east side of Hwy 190, 13.5km from central Oaxaca, marked by a tiny 'San Sebastián Etla' sign beside the large-ish Instituto Euro-Americano. It's 4km up to the village. *Taxis colectivos* to San Agustín (M$12, 30 minutes), from Trujano on the north side of Oaxaca's 2nd-class bus station, will take you to CASA.

SIERRA NORTE

The mountains separating the Valles Centrales from low-lying far northern Oaxaca are called the Sierra Juárez, and the more southerly parts of this range, rising from the north side of the Valle de Tlacolula, are known as the Sierra Norte. These beautiful, forested highlands are home to several successful community ecotourism ventures providing comfortable accommodations and a wonderful opportunity to get out on foot, mountain bike or horseback into pristine landscapes. Over 400 bird species, 350 butterflies, all six Mexican wild cats and nearly 4000 plants have been recorded in the Sierra Norte. Be prepared for cool temperatures: in the higher, southern villages it can snow in winter. The wettest season is from late May to September; there's little rain from January to April.

Pueblos Mancomunados

The Pueblos Mancomunados (Commonwealth of Villages) are eight remote villages (Amatlán, Benito Juárez, Cuajimoloyas, La Nevería, Lachatao, Latuvi, Llano Grande and Yavesía) with ecotourism programs that offer great wilderness escapes and an up-close communion with Zapotec village life. More than 100km of scenic tracks and trails run between the villages and to local beauty spots and places of interest, and you can easily enjoy several days exploring. Elevations in these hills range from 2200m to over 3200m, and the landscapes, with canyons, caves, waterfalls and panoramic lookouts, are spectacular.

For centuries, these villages have pooled the natural resources of their 290-sq-km territory, sharing profits from forestry and other enterprises. In recent years they have also turned to ecotourism to stave off economic difficulties and population decline. All offer a friendly welcome, comfortable, good-value *cabañas* (mostly with hot-water bathrooms and fireplaces), *comedores* serving good local meals (with vegetarian options available) from 8am to 8pm, guides, and horses and mountain bikes for rent.

Several Oaxaca agencies offer trips to the Pueblos Mancomunados, but it's not difficult to visit independently. Six of the villages (the exceptions are Lachatao and Yavesía) cooperate in an excellent combined ecotourism program, Expediciones Sierra Norte (p429), which has a helpful office in Oaxaca city where you can get information and reserve any services you want including transportation. Each participating village also has an ecotourism office open from about 9am to 8pm daily, where it's possible just to roll up and organize what you need on the spot, though Expediciones prefers people to book ahead at the city office.

Local guides, knowledgeable about the ecology, folklore and history of these sierras, are available for excursions. You don't need one for some routes, but not all trails are well signposted so a guide is recommended for them. English-speaking guides cost a little extra and should be requested one day ahead (as must horses).

One of the most attractive and interesting villages, Lachatao, runs its own separate, particularly dynamic ecotourism program, **Lachatao Expediciones** (☑ cell 951-2925419, cell 951-1810523; www.facebook.com/lachatao expediciones) ✐, with exceptionally good *cabañas* and similar services and prices to Expediciones Sierra Norte. Lachatao lies on possible routes between Expediciones Sierra Norte villages, but any reservations here have to be made separately.

◉ Sights & Activities

The easiest-to-reach villages are **Cuajimoloyas**, **Llano Grande** and **Benito Juárez**, all at the Sierra Norte's higher, southern end, nearest to Oaxaca. It's possible to base yourself in one village and take local walks or rides from there. Some superb lookout points are easily accessible from the southern villages, such as the 3200m-high **Yaa-Cuetzi** on the edge of Cuajimoloyas, or **El Mirador**, 2.5km above Benito Juárez. Yaa-Cuetzi is the starting point of a spectacular 1km-long **zip-line** (M$235) which carries you over the Cuajimoloyas rooftops at speeds reaching 65km/h. Cuajimoloyas also hosts the gastronomic **Feria de Hongos Silvestres** (Wild Mushroom Festival) in mid-July, the weekend before the first Guelaguetza (p432) in Oaxaca city. Tiny **La Nevería** is less visited but very welcoming and pretty, and additional routes from here take you through the forests to La Cumbre on Hwy 175, or right down to Tlalixtac de Cabrera in the Valle de Tlacolula.

Good day-walk routes include the Ruta Loma de Cucharilla from Cuajimoloyas to Latuvi (about six hours, nearly all downhill), and two ancient tracks leading on from Latuvi: the **Camino Real** to San Juan Chicomezúchil and Amatlán, and the beautiful **Latuvi–Lachatao canyon trail** passing through cloud forests festooned with bromeliads and hanging mosses (keep your eyes peeled for trogons on this route).

Lachatao is one of the most atmospheric villages, with a huge 17th-century church containing an extraordinary wealth of sculpture, an excellent community museum, and the spectacular pre-Hispanic site **Cerro del Jaguar** or **Cerro del Rayo** (Xia-Yetza) 2km west. From Lachatao or nearby **Amatlán** you can visit the remains of old gold mines and colonial mining haciendas, and do a spot of rappelling in the mines. Lachatao hosts some interesting arts festivals, one of which includes pre-Hispanic ceremonies on Cerro del Jaguar around the spring equinox (March 21).

❶ Getting There & Away

Check with Expediciones Sierra Norte (p429) in Oaxaca for current public-transportation details. It can also transport up to 14 people by van to any of their villages for M$2900 roundtrip; reserve at least one day before.

THE SOUTHERN VILLAGES

The Flecha del Zempoaltépetl line runs buses from Oaxaca's 2nd-class station to

---

❶ EXPEDICONES SIERRA NORTE PRICES

➡ private *cabaña*: M$540 for two people including firewood

➡ shared *cabaña*: M$180 per person

➡ meals: M$60 to M$70 each

➡ camping: M$55 per person

➡ tent rental: M$60 per night

➡ bicycle: M$120/175 per three hours/day

➡ horse: M$235/350/465 per three/four/five hours

➡ guide for up to six people: hiking M$175 to M$350, biking M$300 to M$540, horse M$410 to M$700, depending on route

➡ one-time access fee: adult/child M$60/35

Cuajimoloyas (M$42, two hours) and Llano Grande (M$45, 2½ hours), but schedules are changeable and at the time of writing there was only one departure daily (4pm). For Benito Juárez get out at the Benito Juárez turnoff ('desviación de Benito Juárez'), 3km before Cuajimoloyas, and walk 3.5km west to Benito Juárez. From Benito Juárez, La Nevería is a 9km walk west, and Latuvi 10km north.

AMATLÁN & LACHATAO

The most convenient option is taxi: from the Monumento a Juárez on Hwy 190, 4km east of Oaxaca's 1st-class bus station, 'Sitio El Punto' cabs will take you to Amatlán or Lachatao for M$300 to M$350.

You can also head to Ixtlán de Juárez on Hwy 175 (M$50, 1½ hours, 15 daily buses from Oaxaca's 1st-class bus station), then take a *camioneta* to Amatlán (M$35, 45 minutes) or Lachatao (M$35, one hour) from beside the *escuela primaria* (primary school) in central Ixtlán at 7am, noon and 3pm, Monday to Friday, or noon on Saturday (one hour later during daylight saving from April to October). A taxi from Ixtlán to Lachatao costs around M$250.

There is also a bus to Amatlán and Lachatao (both M$55, 2½ to three hours) at 4pm Monday, Tuesday, Friday and Saturday (one hour later during daylight saving) from beside the Ixcotel *gasolinera* (gas station) just off Hwy 190, 1.5km east of the 1st-class bus station in Oaxaca.

WESTERN OAXACA

Western Oaxaca is dramatic and mountainous, with a fairly sparse population and some thick forests as well as overfarmed and deforested areas. Along with adjoining parts of Puebla and Guerrero states, it is known as the Mixteca, for its Mixtec indigenous inhabitants. The region offers a chance to get well off the beaten track, enjoy hiking or biking in remote areas and see some outstanding colonial architecture. Guided trips are available from Oaxaca with operators such as Tierraventura (p429) and Bicicletas Pedro Martínez (p429).

Yanhuitlán, Coixtlahuaca & Teposcolula

The beautiful 16th-century **Dominican monasteries** in the villages of Yanhuitlán, Coixtlahuaca and San Pedro Teposcolula rank among Mexico's finest architectural treasures. Their scale – especially the enormous *capilla abierta* (open chapel) spaces

used for mass conversions of indigenous people – testifies to the size of local populations when the Spanish arrived. The monasteries' restrained stonework fuses European and indigenous styles, and all three have ornate interior decoration, including enormous gilded wooden *retablos* (altarpieces). Recent renovations have restored their grandeur. Should you want to stay overnight, the villages have a few acceptable, basic hotels and inns.

 Sights

Templo y Ex-Convento de Santo Domingo CHURCH, MONASTERY
(Yanhuitlán; church free, museum adult/child M$39/free; ⊙ church 9am-2pm & 4-6pm Mon-Sat, museum 9am-5pm Mon-Sat; P) Yanhuitlán's church towers above Hwy 190, 14km northwest of Nochixtlán. Built over an old Mixtec religious site, it has beautiful carving on its north and west facades. Inside are many gilded *retablos* full of paintings and statuary, and a fine Mudejar ceiling beneath the choir loft, which contains an impressive pipe organ. The museum, in the handsome cloister, has fairly sparse exhibits on Dominican evangelization in Oaxaca.

Templo y Ex-Convento de San Juan Bautista CHURCH, MONASTERY
(Coixtlahuaca; ⊙ 9am-6pm; P) FREE The Coixtlahuaca church's white-stone western and northern facades have wonderful detailed carving, including rose windows, and inside is a particularly magnificent main *retablo* of finely sculpted wood with gold highlights and 20 large niches holding statuary and 16th-century paintings. On one side of the church is a pretty two-story cloister; on the other, the graceful, partly ruined *capilla abierta* bears Mixtec religious symbols, notably serpents and eagles, on its main arch.

The village is 3.5km east off Hwy 135D, about 30km north of Nochixtlán.

Templo y Ex-Convento de San Pedro y San Pablo CHURCH, MONASTERY
(San Pedro Teposcolula; ⊙ variable) FREE The church dominating San Pedro Teposcolula has a particularly stately *capilla abierta* with several beautifully proportioned arches and Gothic ceiling tracery. The museum in its cloister contains unusually well-preserved murals but was closed for renovation at the time of research. The village is about 30km southwest of Yanhuitlán, on Hwy 125.

OFF THE BEATEN TRACK

SANTIAGO APOALA

This small, remote village, lying in a green, Shangri-la–like valley flanked by cliffs, is a great spot for hiking, biking and climbing. In traditional Mixtec belief, this valley was the birthplace of humanity, and the scenery around Apoala is appropriately spectacular, with the 60m waterfall **Cascada Cola de la Serpiente**, the 400m-deep **Cañón Morelos** and a number of caves and ancient rock carvings and paintings among the highlights.

The easy way to get here is with an agency from Oaxaca, but it's cheaper to make your own way and arrange things directly with the village's community-tourism unit, the **Unidad Ecoturística** (Ecotourism Unit; in Mexico City ☑ 55-51519154; cnr Pino Suárez & Independencia; ⊙ 8am-5pm) 🍴, which runs cozy cabañas (double M$350–450, family M$550, mains M$45) 🍴 with hot-water bathrooms in an appealing riverside location, and offers mountain-bike rental (M$100 per hour). The M$30 registration fee includes guide service. It's not normally necessary to book ahead (and its phone often doesn't work when it's cloudy).

Santiago Apoala is 40km north of the town of Nochixtlán, signposted along a mostly unpaved road which takes 1½ hours to drive. Nochixtlán is served by eight daily buses from Oaxaca's 1st-class bus station (M$12, one hour). A *camioneta* (pickup truck) to Apoala (M$50, two hours) leaves from opposite the church beside Nochixtlán market daily at 2pm (returning at 6am next day): a taxi is M$250.

❶ Getting There & Away

All three villages can be seen in a longish but not difficult day trip by car from Oaxaca. Public-transportation options include **Transportadora Excelencia** (Díaz Ordaz 314, Oaxaca), running comfortable vans every half-hour to Yanhuitlán (M$80, one hour) and Teposcolula (M$100, 1¾ hours). **Fletes y Pasajes** (Fypsa) runs 2nd-class buses (M$110, 1½ hours, 15 daily) from Oaxaca's 2nd-class bus station to the Caseta Coixtlahuaca tollbooth on Hwy 135D, from which it's a 3.5km walk or *taxi colectivo* ride to Coixtlahuaca village.

OAXACA COAST

Oaxaca's beautiful, little-developed Pacific coast has everything you need for a wonderful time by the ocean. With several varied, relaxed beach destinations, and the near-empty shoreline strung with long golden beaches and lagoons full of wildlife, you can't go wrong. Offshore are turtles (this is a major global sea-turtle nesting area), dolphins and whales, plus diving, snorkeling, sportfishing and some of North America's best surfing swells. In this tropical climate, the pace is never too hectic, the atmosphere is relaxed and the people are welcoming. Everywhere the scenery is spectacular and you're in direct touch with the elements wherever you go, from the endless sandy beaches to the crashing surf to the forest-clad, river-threaded

mountains rising just inland. No need to pack too many clothes!

In the center of the coast, three beach villages – Zipolite, San Agustinillo and Mazunte – are perfect for just taking it easy, with a laid-back traveler vibe but also a growing number of appealing midrange accommodations and seriously good restaurants. Further west is Puerto Escondido, a larger fishing, market and vacation town with a string of great beaches (including Playa Zicatela, home to the pumping surf of the Mexican Pipeline), which pleases everyone from backpackers to surfers to winter 'snowbirds' from Canada and the US. Toward the coast's eastern end is Bahías de Huatulco, a modern, planned resort along a string of beautiful bays with a pleasantly low-key atmosphere.

The trip down here from Oaxaca city is a spectacular experience in itself, whether you go by bus, car or light plane. There are airports at Huatulco and Puerto Escondido, both with daily flights from Oaxaca and Mexico City. Huatulco is the more convenient for the Zipolite-to-Mazunte area and also has some direct flights from the USA and Canada.

Most of the year's rain here falls between June and September, turning everything green. From November the landscape starts to dry out, though conditions can remain seriously humid. May is the hottest month.

Puerto Escondido

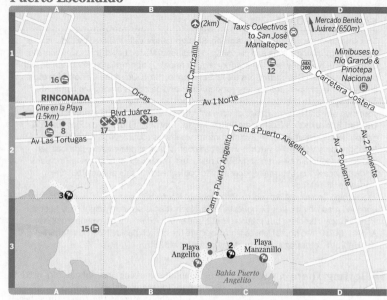

Puerto Escondido

📱 954 / POP 40,000

A magnet for surfers, would-be surfers and every other kind of beach lover, this 'Hidden Port' is one of the most enjoyable spots on Mexico's Pacific coast. By day, you can surf, snorkel, dive, swim, tan, go sportfishing or look for turtles, dolphins and whales. By night, a busy cafe, restaurant and bar scene brings live music and a freewheeling, unpretentious nightlife. Development here has happened gradually over several decades and remained on a human scale, and part of Puerto's charm is that it remains very much a fishing port and market town as well as a tourist destination.

The heart of town rises above the small Bahía Principal. The Carretera Costera (Hwy 200) runs across the hill above the bay, dividing the upper town – where buses arrive and most locals live and work – from the lower, more touristic part. The lower town's main strip, part of Av Pérez Gasga, is known as El Adoquín (Spanish for 'paving stone'). The hub of the surf and traveler scene is Playa Zicatela, stretching 3km southeast from Bahía Principal to Punta Zicatela (La Punta). Rinconada, a residential area above Playa Carrizalillo, west of the center, has further places to stay, and good restaurants and services.

⊙ Sights

★ Playa Zicatela   BEACH

(Map p463; 🅿) Three-kilometer-long Zicatela is Puerto Escondido's most happening beach, with enticing cafes, restaurants and accommodations, as well as the legendary surfing waves of the Mexican Pipeline. The heart of the action, including the Pipeline, is at Zicatela's northern end (nearest town). Nonsurfers beware: the waters here have a lethal undertow and are not safe for the boardless. Lifeguards rescue several careless people most months.

The **Punta Zicatela** area at Zicatela's far southern end also has decent surf and a mellower vibe, favored chiefly by backpackers and beginner surfers.

Bahía Principal   BEACH

(Map p456) Puerto Escondido's central bay is long enough to accommodate restaurants at its west end, a fleet of fishing boats in its center (Playa Principal), and sun worshipers and young bodyboarders at its east end (Playa Marinero), where the waters are a little cleaner. Pelicans wing in centimeters above

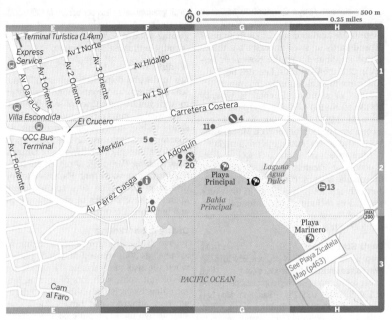

the waves, boats bob on the swell and a few hawkers wander up and down.

Playa Carrizalillo BEACH
(Map p456) Small Carrizalillo beach, west of the center, is in a cove reached by a stairway of 157 steps. It's popular for swimming, bodyboarding and beginner's surfing, and has a line of *palapa* (thatch-roofed) beach bars.

Bahía Puerto Angelito BEACH
(Map p456) The sheltered bay of Puerto Angelito has two smallish beaches with shallow, usually calm waters: the western Playa Angelito and the eastern Playa Manzanillo. Both have lots of seafood *comedores* and are very popular with Mexican families at weekends and on holidays. Manzanillo has the more relaxed vibe. You can rent snorkels for around M$40.

🏃 Activities

Surfing

Puerto Escondido has surfable waves most days of the year. The Zicatela **Pipeline** is one of the world's heaviest and scariest beach breaks, normally best with the offshore winds in the morning and late afternoon, and at its biggest between about May and August. Even when the Pipeline is flat, the point break at **Punta Zicatela** works almost

Puerto Escondido

⊙ Sights
1 Bahía Principal G2
2 Bahía Puerto Angelito C3
3 Playa Carrizalillo A2

⊕ Activities, Courses & Tours
4 Aventura Submarina G1
5 Experiencia F2
6 Gina's Tours F2
7 Lalo Ecotours F2
   Oasis Language School ....(see 8)
8 Oasis Surf School A2
9 Omar's Sportfishing C3
10 Sociedad Cooperativa Turística
   Nueva Punta Escondida F2
11 Viajes Dimar G2

🛏 Sleeping
12 Hostel Losodeli C1
13 Hotel Flor de María H2
14 Hotel Villa Mozart y Macondo............A2
15 Villas Carrizalillo A3
16 Vivo Escondido A1

🍽 Eating
17 Almoraduz...B2
18 El Nene B2
19 El Sultán B2
20 Pascale F2

day in, day out. **Playa Carrizalillo** has good beginners' waves. Several professional surf contests are held annually at Zicatela: dates depend partly on swell forecasts, but there's always an event during the November fiestas. In 2015 the World Surf League's Big Wave Tour came to Zicatela for the first time.

Long- or shortboard rental is typically M$130 to M$150 per day; bodyboards are normally M$80 to M$100. You can buy secondhand boards for between M$1800 and M$5000 at several surf shops on Zicatela.

Numerous surf shops, schools and individuals at Zicatela, Punta Zicatela and Rinconada offer surfing lessons. Lessons normally last 1½ to two hours in the water, with prices including board use and transportation to wherever the waves are most suitable (often Carrizalillo).

Oasis Surf School   SURFING
(Map p456; ☎954-582-14-45, cell 954-1016732; www.spanishandsurflessonsmexico.com; Blvd Juárez 6, Rinconada; small-group class per person US$30, 5 classes US$125; ☺9am-6pm Mon-Sat) Based near Playa Carrizalillo, Oasis offers classes with qualified, bilingual teachers and a maximum of two students per instructor. It's run by local pro surfer and board maker Roger Ramírez, and combines with Oasis Language School (p460) to offer surfing-and-Spanish packages, with attractive apartments available too.

Puerto Surf   SURFING
(☎954-122-01-72, cell 954-1096406; www.puerto surf.com.mx; Nuevo León, Punta Zicatela; 5-day/6-night surf course & accommodations package s/d from M$3800/7000, course only group/individual M$1750/2500, single class group/individual M$400/460) Run by the amiable David Salinas, the youngest of six well-known Puerto surfer brothers, Puerto Surf offers good five-day surf courses (two hours a day). Shorter courses or single classes are also available, and they have a comfortable five-room guesthouse in La Punta.

Puerto Surf Lessons   SURFING
(☎cell 954-1099329; http://puertosurflessons. com; Guerrero 4, Punta Zicatela; 1/3/5 classes M$450/1250/1850) This recommended school, based in La Punta, is run by lifeguard and highly experienced surfer Celestino Rodríguez.

Zicazteca   SURFING
(Map p463; ☎cell 954-1105853; www.zicazteca. com; Hotel Rockaway, Calle del Morro, Zicatela;

small group/private class per person M$350/600; ☺7am-7pm) A relatively young surf school gaining good reports for its teaching and friendly, enthusiastic instructors.

Wildlife Trips

Sea turtles and dolphins are plentiful in the seas off Puerto, and from around November to April you have a chance of seeing humpback whales, manta rays and even whale sharks. Three-hour small-group trips to spot the animals are usually M$500 per person; try bilingual Omar Ramírez of **Omar's Sportfishing** (Map p456; ☎cell 954-5594406; http://tomzap.com/omar.html; Playa Angelito) or dive shop Deep Blue Dive (p458). These operators have policies of not jumping in and molesting the turtles.

Diving & Snorkeling

Typical visibility is around 10m, rising to as much as 30m between May and August, when the seas are warmest. The reefs are of volcanic rock, with lots of marine life, including big schools of fish, spotted eagle rays, stingrays and turtles. Most dive sites are within a 15-minute boat ride. Both Puerto's dive outfits offer snorkeling and marine-life-spotting trips as well as dives for certified divers and a variety of courses.

Deep Blue Dive   DIVING, SNORKELING
(Map p463; ☎cell 954-1003071; www.deepblue divemexico.com; Beach Hotel Inés, Calle del Morro, Zicatela; ☺9am-2pm & 5:30-8pm) This professional, European-run outfit with Professional Association of Diving Instructors (PADI) Dive Master guides does one-tank, two-tank and night dives for certified divers (US$40, US$70 and US$50 respectively), one-morning Discover Scuba sessions (US$65) and a range of PADI diving courses. Two-hour, two-site snorkeling outings are US$25 per person.

Aventura Submarina   DIVING
(Map p456; ☎cell 954-5444862; www.facebook. com/aventurasubmarina.puertoescondido; Av Pérez Gasga 609; ☺9am-2pm & 6-9pm) PADI instructor Jorge Pérez Bravo has three decades' experience diving local waters, and offers two-tank dives for M$1200 plus a range of diving courses and snorkeling trips.

Fishing

Local fishers will take two to four people fishing for marlin, sailfish, tuna or smaller inshore fish: a four-hour trip costs M$2000 to M$2500. Contact Omar's Sportfish-

SURFING OAXACA

The monster tubes of the Mexican Pipeline off Puerto Escondido's Playa Zicatela (p456) rank among the world's top surfing waves, attracting experienced big-wave surfers from around the globe for their thrilling challenge.

But the Oaxaca coast is dotted with dozens more fine surf spots. The best swells generally roll in between March and November and are at their biggest from about May to July. Many breaks are right-hand point breaks, some of them peeling for hundreds of meters.

Toward the west end of the coast, Chacahua (p468) has a good long point break and a scattering of basic *cabaña* (cabin) accommodations. Puerto Escondido itself has a variety of breaks besides the Pipeline: the left-hand point break of Punta Zicatela (p461), at Playa Zicatela's far southern end, works almost year-round, while the gentler waves of Playa Carrizalillo (p457) are perfect for beginners. The town has numerous surf schools and instructors.

Further east, San Agustinillo (p474) has perfect bodyboarding waves. The river-mouth right-hander at La Bocana (p482) makes Bahías de Huatulco a worthwhile stop, and the very long point break at the village of Barra de la Cruz (p487), 20km further down the coast, is a popular classic.

The Salina Cruz region at the east end of the coast has a couple of dozen top-class point, beach and jetty breaks. The area has minimal tourism development but the town and nearby coast have a number of 'surf camps' catering to package clients who fly in for surfing at around US$200 a day. Some of these camps have gained a reputation for chasing off independent surfers from the best spots so that they can monopolize the waves. Concepción Bamba (p489), 40km west of Salina Cruz, has a much more economical and freewheeling surf camp and is the best place for independent surfers to head.

ing (p458) or **Sociedad Cooperativa Turística Nueva Punta Escondida** (Map p456; ☑ cell 954-1188070; Restaurante El Pescador, Marina Nacional). Catch-and-release is encouraged, but boat owners can also arrange for some of the catch to be cooked for you at one of the town's seafood restaurants.

Yoga, Massage & Therapies

Puerto has a growing yoga, massage and holistic-therapy scene. Check www. healing-haven.com for listings.

Temazcalli   SPA, MEDITATION
(☑ 954-582-10-23; www.temazcalli.com; Calle Temazcalli 3, off Av Infraganti, Colonia Lázaro Cárdenas; ⊙ 9am-6pm) The experts at Temazcalli have been practicing the healing arts in Puerto for 20 years and offer a big range of massages and beauty treatments (M$500 to M$650) and holistic medicine including temascals (M$400), plus yoga classes (9am to 10:30am Tuesday and Thursday; M$60) at their peaceful, green property on the edge of town.

 Courses

Experiencia   LANGUAGE COURSE
(Map p456; ☑ 954-582-18-18; www.spanishpuerto. com; Andador Revolución 21; programs per week

incl activities US$135-529, registration US$95, textbooks each US$20) Experiencia has a reputation for professionalism and a good atmosphere, and combines language learning with activities, excursions and volunteer projects. Tuition is in small groups or one-to-one, and programs range from 10 to 40 classes per week, with all levels catered for. There are good discounts for walk-ins.

Special programs are offered for travelers and professionals, and Experiencia recently opened a surf school in Punta Zicatela, offering surfing or Spanish-and-surfing courses. Lodging is available at both the school's spacious central premises and at Punta Zicatela.

Instituto de Lenguajes
Puerto Escondido   LANGUAGE COURSE
(Map p463; ☑ 954-582-20-55; www.puerto school.com; Carretera Costera, Zicatela; small-group/private classes per person per hour US$8/12) This small, student-centered school emphasizes both spoken and written Spanish and receives good reports for teaching quality. Excursions and activities including surfing, salsa and tai chi are available at extra cost. It's set in tropical gardens overlooking Zicatela beach, with wi-fi and student bungalows available on-site.

You can start any day, at any level, and study for as long as you like.

Oasis Language School LANGUAGE COURSE
(Map p456; ☎954-582-14-45, cell 954-1091319; www.spanishandsurflessonsmexico.com; Blvd Juárez 6, Rinconada; 1½hr private classes US$14, 10 classes US$126; ⏲9am-6pm Mon-Sat) Housed in neat premises in the Rinconada district, Oasis operates in tandem with Oasis Surf School (p458), offering Spanish-and-surfing deals if you want to learn both. Group and intensive language classes, and attractive student apartments, are available too.

Tours

★**Gina's Tours** CULTURAL, HISTORICAL
(Map p456; ☎954-582-02-76, 954-582-11-86; https://ginainpuertoescondido.wordpress.com; Tourist information kiosk, Av Pérez Gasga) Gina Machorro, Puerto's energetic and knowledgeable tourist information officer, leads a variety of personally guided tours including popular Saturday-morning visits to the Mercado Benito Juárez (p464) with an introduction to local history, food and religion (per person M$350, two hours).

She also arranges cooking classes at a local cook's home (M$1200 and you take your lunch home to eat), and leads trips to Playa Escobilla (p469) to observe nesting turtles, and to **Tututepec** village, an ancient indigenous Mixtec capital west of Puerto Escondido, which has ruins, Mixtec *artesanías* (handicrafts) and a good little archaeological museum. Tututepec trips cost M$700 per person (minimum five), including lunch and a 20-minute local dance and music performance.

Viajes Dimar TOUR
(Map p456; ☎954-582-02-59; www.viajesdimar.com; Av Pérez Gasga 905; ⏲9am-9pm Mon-Sat, to 5pm Sun) Long-established and reliable Dimar offers a good range of day and half-day trips to Manialtepec, Chacahua, waterfalls, hot springs and other places of interest in the area, with English-speaking guides, for M$400 to M$800 per person (minimum four people). It also has a branch in **Zicatela** (Map p463; ☎954-582-23-05; www.viajesdimar.com; Calle del Morro s/n, Zicatela; ⏲9am-9pm Mon-Sat, to 5pm Sun).

Festivals & Events

A busy calendar of events from surf contests and food fairs to traditional national and religious festivals keeps Puerto lively year-round. Check www.facebook.com/puertoescondidoturismo for events.

Fiestas de Noviembre CULTURAL, SPORTS
Puerto buzzes throughout November with the many events and festivities, including the Festival Costeño de la Danza (folk dance), an international sportfishing tournament (www.pescapuertoescondido.com), surfing and motocross contests, and plenty more.

Sleeping

Accommodations are scattered from the Rinconada and Bacocho areas in the west of town to the central Adoquín area and out to the southeast along Playa Zicatela.

Rates given are those that commonly apply during the main visitor seasons, roughly mid-December to Easter, and July and August. During the Christmas–New Year and Easter vacations, prices can double or even more, but in the low season many rates drop dramatically. It's worth reserving ahead in the busy seasons.

Playa Zicatela

★**Hotel Casa de Dan** HOTEL $
(Map p463; ☎954-582-27-60; http://hotelcasadan.zicatela.net; Jacarandas 14, Colonia Santa María; r M$400-670; P ⊖ ❄ 🛜 ≋) Everything here is set around verdant patios and gardens, and you can enjoy a nice long lap pool as well as a terrace with a perfect Zicatela surf view. The 15 spotlessly clean units are of varying size, but all with fully equipped kitchens, terraces and nicely tiled bathrooms, and you can walk through to the excellent Dan's Café Deluxe (p462). Reservations advised.

Hotel Las Olas HOTEL $
(Map p463; ☎954-582-09-19; www.hotel-lasolas.com; Calle del Morro s/n; r M$350-450, with air-con M$550-650; ❄ 🛜 ≋) Las Olas has good, clean, excellent-value rooms, with pretty tiling and craft details, and a recently added pool. Second-floor choices have ocean-view hammocks, and there's a small sundeck.

Aqua Luna HOTEL $
(Map p463; ☎954-582-15-05; www.hotelaqualuna.com; Vista Hermosa s/n, Colonia Santa María; r M$350-900; ⊖ ❄ 🛜 ≋) An excellent medium-sized hotel popular with surfers, Aqua Luna has a panoramic roof deck with a view of the Zicatela Pipeline. The rooms are bright, in a clean, contemporary style, and

most are without air-con and in the budget price range. All-day breakfasts and other light dishes (M$35 to M$65) are served at the poolside bar.

Big discounts for monthly stays. No under-18s allowed.

Hotel Buena Vista
HOTEL $

(Map p463; ☑954-582-14-74; www.facebook.com/hotelbuenavistapuertoescondido; Calle del Morro s/n; r with/without air-con M$500/350, with kitchen add M$50; ❄️🖥️) The 11 no-frills rooms are big and spotless, with two beds, mosquito screens, hot-water bathroom and breezy balconies. It's good value and would be even better if it had a common area where guests could socialize.

★Hotelito Swiss Oasis
HOTEL $$

(Map p463; ☑954-582-14-96; www.swissoasis.com; Andador Gaviotas; s/d/tr/q M$500/600/750/900; ⊖🖥️🖥️) This good small hotel provides a guest kitchen with free coffee, tea and purified water, and a pool in the pretty garden, in addition to eight spotless, cool rooms with good beds, mosquito screens and attractive color schemes. The well-traveled Swiss owners speak four languages and are very helpful with local information. No under-15s here.

Beach Hotel Inés
HOTEL $$

(Map p463; ☑954-582-07-92; www.hotelines.com; Calle del Morro s/n; r US$26-110; 🅿️❄️🖥️🖥️) German-run Inés has a wide variety of bright, cheerful *cabañas,* rooms, apartments and suites, around a shaded pool area with a restaurant serving good Euro/Mexican food. Most accommodations have air-con available, and some come with kitchens or Jacuzzis. You can arrange horseback riding, surf lessons, diving and other outings – and security is particularly good here.

Bungalows Puerta del Sol
HOTEL $$

(Map p463; ☑954-582-29-22; www.bungalowspuertadelsol.com; Calle del Morro s/n; r M$450-500, with air-con M$650-850; 🅿️❄️🖥️🖥️) This well-kept, family-run place has a small pool and a communal kitchen either side of a nice green courtyard. The 22 spacious rooms boast cheerful art and crafts and, in most cases, balcony and hammock. Best are the six new upper-floor rooms all with air-con and king-size beds.

Hotel Santa Fe
HOTEL $$$

(Map p463; ☑954-582-01-70; www.hotelsantafe.com.mx; Calle del Morro s/n; r from M$1800;

🅿️❄️@🖥️🖥️) This neocolonial-style hotel is set around two good pools in palm-shaded gardens. The 60-plus rooms have attractive terracotta-tile floors and wood furnishings, and the airy vegetarian-and-seafood **restaurant** (Map p463; Calle del Morro s/n; mains M$70-250; ⊗7:30am-10pm; 🖥️🍴) looks out along Zicatela beach. There's a three-night minimum in some busy periods and discounts are often available; check the website.

🛏️ Punta Zicatela

La Punta, as it's known, is the far southern end of Playa Zicatela, with a more laid-back, traveler-oriented ambience than the surfer-focused main Zicatela scene about 2km up the beach. Brisas de Zicatela is short way north of La Punta.

Hostal One Love
HOTEL, HOSTEL $

(☑cell 954-1298582; www.hostalpuertoescondido.com; Tamaulipas s/n, Brisas de Zicatela; dm US$10, r US$30-62; ⊖🖥️) Well-built circular two-storey bungalows are set in a small tropical garden, each housing three or four rooms or dorms with terraces and good wooden furnishings and all themed to different '60s rock stars. It's a good option for anyone from surfers to couples to families, and the excellent restaurant (p464) and panoramic roof terrace (with morning yoga sessions) are big pluses.

Cabañas Buena Onda
HOSTEL $

(☑954-582-16-63; buenaondazicatela@live.com; Cárdenas 777, Punta Zicatela; camping/hammock/dm per person M$70/70/120, cabañas M$290; 🖥️) Popular Buena Onda is set in a shady palm grove, with a beachfront *palapa* hangout area. The 10 rustic *cabañas* are clean and equipped with mosquito nets, fans and hammocks, and there are adequate bathrooms and kitchen.

Frutas y Verduras
CABAÑAS, ROOMS $

(☑cell 954-1230473; http://frutasyverdurasmexico.com; Cárdenas s/n, Punta Zicatela; s M$200-400, d M$300-500, camping s/d M$150/250; 🖥️) Has a range of smallish but well-kept accommodations – simple *cabañas* with mosquito nets, highly colorful mosquito-screened rooms, and one apartment – plus good shared bathrooms and kitchen, a decent restaurant, surfboards for rent and free bicycles.

Osa Mariposa
HOSTEL $

(☑cell 954-1108354; www.osamariposa.com; Privada de Cancún, Brisas de Zicatela; dm M$100-110, d M$250; 🖥️) The 'Bear Butterfly' has well-built wooden rooms and three- or four-person dorms, with mosquito nets, fans and clean shared bathrooms, in a steamy tropical garden. Vegetarian food and good juices, mezcal and beer are served in the restaurant-and-bar area (restaurant open 8am–2.30pm and dinner 8pm).

They make their own tofu, bread, hummus and soy milk, and dinner (reserve earlier in the day) is an all-vegan affair (mains M$50, dinner M$60).

Casamar SUITES $$

(☎954-582-25-93; www.casamarsuites.com; Puebla 407, Brisas de Zicatela; r US$56-147; P❋🞰🛜❄) North American–owned Casamar is a lovely, comfortable, healthy vacation retreat. The 15 spacious, air-conditioned rooms are spotless and all have well-equipped kitchens with tasteful Mexican art and crafts, much of it locally made. At the center of things is a large, green garden with a sizable pool, and from December to April there's a gourmet vegan cafe serving breakfast and lunch to guests only.

Health coaching services are offered, and there are free yoga and exercise-dance classes. The Monday-night cocktails also help bring guests together. Excellent discounts for stays of a week or more.

🛏 Playa Marinero

Hotel Flor de María HOTEL $$

(Map p456; ☎954-582-05-36; www.mexonline.com/flordemaria.htm; 1a Entrada a Playa Marinero; r US$45-65; P🞰🛜❄) A popular Canadian-owned hotel with 24 ample rooms sporting good large bathrooms, folksy Mexican decor and pretty wall and door paintings. A highlight is the expansive roof terrace with its fabulous views, bar and small pool. No under-12s here.

🛏 Rinconada

Vivo Escondido HOSTEL $

(Map p456; ☎954-1335928; www.vivoescondido.com; Barriletes 2; dm M$150, d with/without bathroom M$450/350; 🛜❄) This relaxed and spacious hostel close to all Rinconada's facilities is a great recent addition to Puerto's budget accommodations. Spacious dorms with solid wooden bunks, ample, mural-bedecked common areas, a good big kitchen and free drinking water are all part of the deal. The icing on the cake is the pool area out front with a small bar and table tennis too.

Hostel Losodeli HOSTEL $

(Map p456; ☎954-582-42-21; www.casalosodeli.com; Prolongación 2a Norte; dm M$115-130, r M$360-700; P❋🛜❄) Popular, well-run Losodeli, located between the bus stations and Rinconada, provides most things a budget traveler needs: clean accommodations with a choice between bunk dorms and private rooms (some very spacious), friendly staff, a well-equipped, well-organized kitchen, a good pool in the central garden, an eating area with bar service, breakfast available (M$35) and bookings for many outings and activities.

Hotel Villa Mozart y Macondo BUNGALOW $$

(Map p456; ☎954-104-22-95; www.hotelmozartymacondo.com; Av Las Tortugas 77; r incl breakfast M$800-1000; ☺🛜) A short walk from Playa Carrizalillo, secluded Villa Mozart offers two comfy, artistically designed and decorated bungalows (with a third on the way), giving on to a sculpture-strewn tropical garden which is another work of art in itself. Each bungalow contains one king-size bed and has a kitchen.

The welcoming owners and their aesthetic taste, with some quality original art, add to the appeal here, and the garden cafe is open all day till 9pm.

Villas Carrizalillo BOUTIQUE HOTEL $$$

(Map p456; ☎954-582-17-35; www.villascarrizalillo.com; Av Carrizalillo 125, Rinconada; apt US$184-244; P❋🞰🛜❄) Beautifully perched on the cliffs above Playa Carrizalillo, Villas Carrizalillo has spacious, stylish, air-conditioned apartments from one to three bedrooms, nearly all with kitchens and private terraces and some with great coastal views. The panoramic in-house restaurant is a great place to be at sunset. A path goes directly down to the beach, and the hotel has snorkel gear for rent, and free surfboards and bikes.

Discounts are offered for cash payments.

Eating

Puerto's large and varied eating scene ranges from solidly satisfying Mexican/international places to a growing number of enticing contemporary fusion restaurants. Seafood is plentiful and usually fresh, and there's some good vegetarian fare too.

🍴 Playa Zicatela

Dan's Café Deluxe INTERNATIONAL $

(Map p463; www.facebook.com/danscafedeluxe; Jacarandas 14, Colonia Santa María; breakfasts

Playa Zicatela

Playa Zicatela

◎ **Top Sights**
1 Playa Zicatela A3

◆ **Activities, Courses & Tours**
Deep Blue Dive .... (see 7)
2 Instituto de Lenguajes Puerto
Escondido B3
3 Manglar Birdwatching A3
4 Viajes Dimar A4
5 Zicazteca...A4

⬤ **Sleeping**
6 Aqua Luna..B5
7 Beach Hotel Inés A4
8 Bungalows Puerta del Sol...................A4
9 Hotel Buena Vista A2
10 Hotel Casa de Dan B5
11 Hotel Las Olas A2
12 Hotel Santa Fe A1
13 Hotelito Swiss Oasis B3

◆ **Eating**
14 Costeñito Cevichería............................A3
15 Dan's Café Deluxe................................B5
16 El Cafecito...A4
Hotel Santa Fe........................... (see 12)
17 La Hostería Bananas A4
18 Restaurante Los Tíos A4

◆ **Drinking & Nightlife**
19 Casa Babylon A3
20 Playa Kabbalah A3

◆ **Entertainment**
21 Atemoztli..A4
22 Split Coconut..A1

excellent grilled fresh fish and shrimp-stuffed avocados.

La Hostería Bananas ITALIAN, MEXICAN **$$**
(Map p463; ☎954-582-00-05; Calle del Morro s/n; mains M$80-220; ⊙8am-11:30pm; 🛜☑️👪) The Hostería is an Italian labor of love, from its gleaming kitchen (with computerized wood-fired pizza oven) to the Talavera-tiled bathrooms. A broad selection of tasty dishes, including many veggie and homemade pasta options, is paired with a great drinks list, good breakfast deals and strong coffee.

El Cafecito MEXICAN, INTERNATIONAL **$$**
(Map p463; Calle del Morro s/n; breakfast dishes M$25-80, mains M$60-250; ⊙6am-11:30pm; 🍽🛜👪) It sometimes seems as if half the town descends on the Cafecito for breakfast, and with good reason, as the combinations (including a 'Hungry Starving Surfer'

M$40-60, light meals M$40-70; ⊙7am-4pm; 🛜☑️) A great spot for hearty, surfer-pleasing breakfasts, great juices and *licuados* (smoothies), and healthy lunch options like salads, whole-wheat sandwiches and vegetable stir-fry.

Costeñito Cevichería SEAFOOD **$$**
(Map p463; Calle del Morro s/n; dishes M$90-150; ⊙1-11pm) Right on the edge of the sands, rustic but professional Costeñito specializes in large and delicious ceviches (a favorite Mexican coastal delicacy) but also does

offering) are tasty and filling, the service good and the coffee cups bottomless.

Restaurante Los Tíos
SEAFOOD $$

(Map p463; ☑954-582-28-79; Calle del Morro; mains M$50-160; ⊙8am-10pm Wed-Mon) 'The Uncles,' right on the sand's edge, serves great *licuados* and fresh juices to go with its tasty, well-priced egg dishes, *antojitos* and seafood. It's popular with locals and nicely relaxed.

✗ Punta Zicatela

Alaburger
INTERNATIONAL $

(Cárdenas s/n, Punta Zicatela; mains M$60-120; ⊙11am-11pm; 🛜) Alaburger satisfies the hungry at La Punta with big burgers (including fish and veggie options), tasty pizzas big enough for two, and baked potatoes with bacon and blue-cheese fillings. Seating is at a few large communal tables under the *palapa* roof. It's opposite Cabañas Buena Onda.

★Lychee
THAI $$

(www.facebook.com/lycheemex; cnr Cárdenas & Héroes Oaxaqueñas, Punta Zicatela; mains M$70-100; ⊙5pm-midnight; 🍴) Superb Thai dishes – tom yum soup, red or green curries, chicken satay – and other Southeast Asian favorites are cooked up in the middle of a large, rectangular wooden bar, with alfresco log tables and benches set on the earth around it. Save room for the dessert of caramelized banana on filo pastry with ice cream!

One Love
EUROPEAN, MEXICAN $$

(www.hostalpuertoescondido.com; Tamaulipas s/n, Brisas de Zicatela; mains M$75-150; ⊙8am-9.30pm Tue-Sun; 🛜) Excellent Euro-Mexican dishes with fresh local ingredients are served up in this restaurant run by a Mexican and French couple. You could start with the 'One Love taco' (a ceviche wrap with a mango-and-*habanero*-chili dressing) and follow up with 'Give Peace a Chance' (breaded catch of the day with tabbouleh and chili mayo), but there's plenty of choice, including good pasta and vegetarian dishes.

✗ El Adoquín & Around

★Pascale
MEXICAN, EUROPEAN $$$

(Map p456; ☑cell 954-1030668; www.pascale. mx; Av Pérez Gasga 612; mains M$110-225; ⊙6-11pm; 🛜) With romantically candlelit tables

right under the Playa Principal palms, Pascale prepares original and delicious seafood, meat, homemade pasta dishes (with a choice of tasty sauces) and French desserts with rare flair. The seafood is fresh as can be, there's a short but select wine list, and everything is served up with professional polish.

✗ Rinconada

El Sultán
MIDDLE EASTERN $

(Map p456; ☑954-582-05-12; www.el-sultan. com; Blvd Juárez; dishes M$15-60; ⊙10am-10pm Sun-Thu; 🍴) Good hummus, falafel and kebabs at excellent prices.

Almoraduz
MEXICAN $$

(Map p456; ☑954-582-31-09; www.guiapuerto escondido.com/almoraduz; Blvd Juárez 11-12; mains M$100-150; ⊙2-10pm Tue-Sun; 🍴) Almoraduz' husband-and-wife chef team creates memorable flavor combinations from market-fresh local ingredients. The menu changes frequently: their most popular offerings range from fig salad or fish in green *mole* to chocolate lava cake, but you have to see and taste to appreciate the culinary art here.

The drinks selection, including artisanal mezcals, craft beers and original fruit drinks, is top-notch too.

El Nene
MEXICAN, FUSION $$

(Map p456; Blvd Juárez; mains M$120-180; ⊙2-10pm Mon-Sat) El Nene serves up excellent and enormous tacos (three for M$50 to M$100) and Mexican- and international-style fish, shrimp and chicken mains. Fish of the day in white wine or Cajun-style is a good choice, and you could start with a flavorsome Thai or *nopal* soup. The plant-fringed patio setting adds to one of Puerto's best eating experiences.

✗ Other Areas

Mercado Benito Juárez
MARKET $

(Av 8 Norte btwn Avs 3 & 4 Poniente; mains M$40-100; ⊙8am-7pm) For tasty local flavors and local atmosphere, head up to the main market in the upper part of town, where welcoming *comedores* serve up fresh fish and shrimp, soups and *antojitos* at good prices. Wander round the flower, food and craft stalls and try out some of the unusual offerings at the line of juice stalls.

'Mercado' buses (M$7) run up Av Oaxaca.

🍷 Drinking & Entertainment

If your dream of Mexico is sitting in a palm-roofed bar, enjoying the crash of waves and an ice-cold beer, you might have to pinch yourself in Puerto Escondido. Numerous establishments along all the beaches are ideal for this purpose. Playa Zicatela has several spots open late with a party scene for its international crowd and regular DJ and live-music nights. The music scene combines the significant talents of locals, expats and visiting artists playing anything from Latin and jazz to blues and rock, and is busiest from around Christmas to March, when there's at least one gig somewhere almost every night.

★ Playa Kabbalah   BAR
(Map p463; www.playakabbalah.com; Calle del Morro 312, Zicatela; ☺8am-midnight or later; 🛜) A hip beach bar for nocturnal drinks with a Zicatela crowd clustering at the bar and on loungers on the sands, and mostly electronic dance music playing to flashing fluorescent lights. The DJ nights and the Tuesday and Thursday Ladies' Nights (free cocktails for women from 10pm to midnight) are especially popular. At weekends there's often live salsa and/or reggae too.

Casa Babylon   BAR
(Map p463; Calle del Morro s/n, Zicatela; ☺9am-2am; 🛜) Quirky Babylon has a great Mexican mask collection, a big selection of books to exchange, and varied live music or a DJ Thursday to Saturday (several nights weekly in January and February). The owner prides herself on her mojitos and mezcal margaritas.

Split Coconut   LIVE MUSIC
(Map p463; www.facebook.com/brads-split-coconut-1437993356450263; Playa Marinero; ☺2pm-midnight Wed-Mon) This beach bar hosts several live-music nights a week from about December to March, featuring talented local and visiting musicians playing rock, blues, jazz, world music and more. The rest of the year there's usually a gig on Saturday or Sunday. It does good gringo food (ribs, steaks, burgers...) too.

Atemoztli   LIVE MUSIC
(Map p463; www.facebook.com/atemoztlimusic; Calle del Morro, Zicatela; ☺1pm-3am; 🛜) Hosts different live music nightly, including jazz on Tuesdays, salsa and Latin on Thursdays, and rock and blues Saturday and Monday.

The atmosphere varies a lot depending on the night.

Cine en la Playa   CINEMA
(Cinema on the Beach; www.facebook.com/hotelvillasol; Playa Bacocho; ☺7pm or 8pm Wed, Nov-May) **FREE** An excellent program of movies, from recent feature films to art house, classics and documentaries, is shown on the sands of Playa Bacocho in front of Hotel Suites Villasol's beach club. Films are generally in Spanish with English subtitles, or vice versa.

ℹ️ Information

DANGERS & ANNOYANCES
To minimize any risk of robbery or assault, avoid isolated or empty places and stick to well-lit areas (or use taxis) at night. Don't urinate on the beach after nocturnal drinks – police have pulled people in for this.

MEDICAL SERVICES
Dr Omar López Pérez (📞954-582-04-40; Av Oaxaca 603 Altos; ☺9am-1pm & 4-7pm Mon-Fri, 9am-1pm Sat) A recommended English-speaking GP clinic.

MONEY
Playa Zicatela has a couple of ATMs but the ones in town work more reliably.

Banamex (Av Pérez Gasga 314; ☺9am-4pm Mon-Fri) Uphill from the west end of El Adoquín, Banamex has an ATM and exchanges cash US and Canadian dollars and euros (bring your passport).

Centro Cambiario Joycy (Av Pérez Gasga 905; ☺10am-9pm Mon-Sat, 3-9pm Sun) Changes Canadian dollars as well as US dollars and euros; passport not needed.

Centro Cambiario Joycy (Calle del Morro s/n; ☺10am-3pm & 5:30-8pm Mon-Sat, 10am-2pm Sun) Changes Canadian dollars as well as US dollars and euros; passport not needed.

HSBC (Av 1 Norte btwn Av 2 Poniente & Carretera Costera) Has a dependable ATM.

TOURIST INFORMATION
Tourist Information Kiosk (Map p456; 📞954-582-11-86; ginainpuerto@yahoo.com; Av Pérez Gasga; ☺10am-2pm & 4-6pm Mon-Fri, 10am-1pm Sat) Gina Machorro, the energetic, dedicated, multilingual information officer, knows everything that's happening in and around Puerto, happily answers your every question and conducts her own interesting **tours** (p460).

TRAVEL AGENCIES
You can buy air and bus tickets at Viajes Dimar's branches (p460).

Head to **Lonely Planet** (www.lonelyplanet.com/mexico/oaxaca-state/puerto-escondido) for planning advice, author recommendations, articles and more.

Getting There & Away

AIR

Airport (☎ 954-582-04-91) Three kilometers west of the center on Hwy 200.

Aeromar (☎ 954-582-09-77; www.aeromar.com.mx; Airport; ⊙ 9am-6pm) Up to three daily flights to/from Mexico City.

Aerotucán (☎ 954-582-34-61; www.aerotucan.com.mx; Airport; ⊙ 7am-3pm Mon-Sat, noon-2pm Sun) Flies 13-seat Cessnas daily to/from Oaxaca (M$1990). Flights are sometimes rescheduled at short notice.

Interjet (☎ cell 954-1079957; www.interjet.com; Airport; ⊙ 8am-7pm) To/from Mexico City four or five times weekly.

VivaAerobus (www.vivaaerobus.com) Budget airline flying daily to/from Mexico City. Flights bought in advance can cost less than M$500.

BUS & VAN

OCC Bus Terminal (Map p456; ☎ 954-582-10-73; Carretera Costera 102) Used by OCC 1st-class and Sur and AU 2nd-class services.

Terminal Turística (Central Camionera; cnr Avs Oaxaca & 4 Poniente) In the upper part of town; used by AltaMar (1st class) and Turistar (deluxe).

Oaxaca

Travel to/from Oaxaca will become quicker and easier once a new highway, joining Hwy 200 a few kilometers east of Puerto Escondido to Hwy 175 south of Ejutla, opens – possibly in 2016. This will reduce driving time from seven hours to about four hours and will undoubtedly alter bus and van services. Until then, the most convenient way of traveling to Oaxaca is in the comfortable van services via Hwy 131 (seven hours), offered by at least two companies. OCC's 1st-class buses (M$412, 11 hours, three daily) take a much longer route via Salina Cruz and Hwy 190.

Express Service (Map p456; ☎ 954-582-08-68; Hotel Luz del Ángel, cnr Avs 1 Norte & Oaxaca) Vans to Oaxaca (M$209) hourly from 4am to 5pm, and at 8pm, 10pm, 11pm and 11:30pm.

Villa Escondida (Map p456; Av Hidalgo s/n) Vans to Oaxaca (M$200) hourly from 3:30am to 9:30pm, and at 11pm.

Other Destinations

For Mexico City, the AltaMar and Turistar services from the Terminal Turística go via the outskirts of Acapulco and are much quicker than OCC, which takes a longer route via Salina Cruz.

CAR & MOTORCYCLE

To/from Oaxaca city, the winding Hwy 131 via Sola de Vega will soon (possibly by 2016) be superseded by a new highway linking Hwy 200 just east of Puerto Escondido with Hwy 175 south of Ejutla. This will reduce driving time from about seven hours to about four.

Between Puerto Escondido and Acapulco, figure on about seven hours for the 400km drive along Hwy 200, which is well enough surfaced but has a lot of speed bumps.

Los Tres Reyes (☎ 954-582-33-35; http://lostresreyescarrent.com; cnr Carretera Costera & Belmares, Colonia Santa María; ⊙ 8am-7pm) Rents saloon cars from M$700 per day. The office is on the highway above Colonia Santa María, just up from Playa Zicatela. It has an airport office too.

⊙ Getting Around

Ticket taxis from the airport will drop you in town for M$35 per person (M$70 to Punta Zicatela). You can usually find a whole cab for a similar price on the main road outside the airport. Taxi rides within town cost M$25 to M$35.

BUSES FROM PUERTO ESCONDIDO

DESTINATION	FARE (M$)	DURATION (HR)	FREQUENCY (DAILY)
Acapulco	395	8	7 AltaMar
Bahías de Huatulco	72-138	2½	23 from OCC terminal
Mexico City (Sur)	915-1170	12	Turistar 6pm & 6:45pm, AltaMar 5:45pm & 8:30pm
Pochutla	45-88	1¼	25 from OCC terminal
Salina Cruz	258-274	5	11 from OCC terminal
San Cristóbal de las Casas	668	13	OCC 6:30pm & 9:30pm

Taxis colectivos, local buses and *camionetas* marked 'Zicatela' or 'La Punta' (all M$7) run approximately every 20 minutes to Punta Zicatela from Mercado Benito Juárez up in the north of the town (near the Terminal Turística), from sunrise to about 8:30pm. They travel down 3 Poniente then east along the Carretera Costera: for El Adoquín or Playa Zicatela you can hop off and walk down in two minutes.

Around Puerto Escondido

Playa Delfines

Campamento Tortuguero
Palmarito
WILDLIFE-WATCHING

(🏕) 🏊 A few kilometers west of Puerto Escondido, the Palmarito sea-turtle camp collects tens of thousands of new-laid turtle eggs each year, and reburies them in a fenced enclosure to protect them from human and animal predators. When the baby turtles hatch after about six weeks, visitors can help release them into the sea (donations welcome).

Lalo Ecotours (p467) and other agencies take groups from town to participate for around M$250 per person: look for *'Liberación de Tortugas'* signs. The camp is down a track off Hwy 200 just after the Km 134 marker, 3km past the airport.

Laguna Manialtepec

The 6km-long Manialtepec Lagoon, beginning 14km west of Puerto Escondido along Hwy 200, is a paradise for bird enthusiasts and a fascinating place for anyone interested in nature. Ibises, roseate spoonbills, parrots, pelicans, falcons, ospreys, herons, kingfishers and several types of hawk and iguana call Manialtepec home for at least part of the year. The best bird-watching months are December to March, and the best time of day is soon after dawn. The lagoon is mainly surrounded by mangroves, but tropical flowers and palms accent the ocean side, and the channel at the west end winds through to a pristine sandbar beach.

Several operators run three-hour bird-spotting trips in motorized *lanchas* (outboard boats), with English-speaking guides, binoculars and round-trip transportation from your accommodations in Puerto Escondido. A magical Manialtepec phenomenon is the *fosforescencia*, when phosphorescent plankton appear for a few nights several times a year. At these times nocturnal boat trips are offered, and you can swim or trail your hand in the water to activate the strange phosphorescent glow. July, August, November and December are often good months for this.

🚩 Tours

Hidden Voyages Ecotours   BIRDWATCHING
(www.hiddenvoyagesecotours.com; ⊘lancha tours Mon-Wed, Fri & Sat mid-Dec–late Mar) 🏊 *Lancha* trips are led by knowledgeable Canadian ornithologist Michael Malone, costing M$650 per person (departure from Puerto Escondido 7am), with a 45-minute beach break midcruise. You can book at Viajes Dimar's El Adoquín (p460) or Zicatela (p460) branches in Puerto Escondido. Dimar itself offers year-round trips (per person M$550) with local bird guides.

La Puesta del Sol   BIRDWATCHING
(☑cell 954-5889055, cell 954-1328294; www.facebook.com/lapuestamanialtepec; Hwy 200 Km 124; ⊘restaurant 9am-6pm; 🏕) This pretty, family-run, lakeside restaurant, just off Hwy 200 about 2.5km from the eastern end of Laguna Manialtepec, is a good base if you're getting to Manialtepec under your own steam. It serves excellent food (breakfast dishes M$40 to M$65, mains M$80 to M$140), and does bird-watching boat trips for M$1200 (four to six people) or M$1000 (two or three people).

For early-morning trips, it's a good idea to call the day before: ask for English-speaking Ulíses. You can also rent one-/two-person kayaks for M$100/200 per hour.

Manglar Birdwatching   BIRDWATCHING
(Map p463; ☑cell 954-5592431, cell 954-1186713; http://manglarbirdwatch.blogspot.com; Calle del Morro, Zicatela, Puerto Escondido; ⊘office 8:30am-9pm) 🏊 Run by a Manialtepec family, Manglar does recommended lagoon trips from Las Negras village (about halfway along the lagoon's north shore) for US$40 per person, including transportation from/to Puerto Escondido.

Lalo Ecotours   BIRD-WATCHING
(Map p456; ☑954-582-16-11, cell 954-5889164; www.lalo-ecotours.com; Av Pérez Gasga, Puerto Escondido; ⊘office 10am-6pm) 🏊 Lalo's is run by an experienced, English-speaking local bird guide. *Lancha* trips cost M$600 per person.

ℹ Getting There & Away

From Puerto Escondido, take a *taxi colectivo* bound for San José Manialtepec from Av 4

Poniente (M$15 to La Puesta del Sol, 15 minutes), running from about 6am to 8pm, or a Río Grande-bound minibus (M$20) from Av Hidalgo 5, leaving about every 20 minutes from 4am to 8pm.

Atotonilco Hot Springs

These mineral-laden springs are a lovely horseback ride of one hour each way along the lushly vegetated Río Manialtepec, from the village of San José Manialtepec, 23km west of Puerto Escondido. You crisscross the river several times en route to your dip in the hot springs, so it's best to go between October and March, when the river is not too high. Viajes Dimar's offices (p460), Manglar Birdwatching (p467) and Lalo Ecotours (p467) offer trips from Puerto Escondido for M$500 to M$600 per person, or you can organize it direct with guide **Jesús 'Chucho' Villavicencio** (☑954-488-18-82; cnr Hidalgo & Porfirio Díaz, San José Manialtepec) in San José for M$400 (M$450 including a meal). *Taxis colectivos* to San José (M$18, 20 minutes) go from Av 4 Poniente in Puerto Escondido.

Parque Nacional Lagunas de Chacahua

West of Manialtepec, Hwy 200 wends its way along a coast studded with lagoons, pristine beaches and prolific bird and plant life. Settlements in this region are home to many Afro-Mexicans, descendants of slaves who escaped from the Spanish.

The area around the coastal lagoons of Chacahua and La Pastoría forms the beautiful 149-sq-km Parque Nacional Lagunas de Chacahua, which attracts many migratory birds from Alaska and Canada in winter. Mangrove-fringed islands harbor roseate spoonbills, ibises, cormorants, wood storks, herons and egrets, as well as mahogany trees, crocodiles and turtles. El Corral, a tunnel-like waterway filled with countless birds in winter, connects the two lagoons. The boat trip along the lagoons is fabulous, and at its end Chacahua village sits upon a gorgeous beach curving at least 20km eastward, inviting you to stop for a meal or a night in rustic *cabañas*.

CHACAHUA

Chacahua village straddles the channel that connects the west end of Chacahua lagoon to the ocean. The ocean side of the village, fronting a wonderful beach, is a perfect place to bliss out. The waves here (a very long right-hand point break) can be good for surfers, including beginners, but there are strong currents; check where it's safe to swim. Some of the beach *comedores* rent surfboards for around M$100 a day. You can also rent a kayak to paddle around the waterways or take a two-hour small-motorboat trip (M$300) to explore for birds and crocodiles. Some nights from October to March, turtles arrive to nest on the beach.

Local *lanchas* (M$15 per person) will whiz you across the channel to the inland half of the village, where the **Cocodrilario de Chacahua** (Chacahua Crocodile Sanctuary; Calle Chiapas; guided tour by donation; ☒8am-6pm) houses over 200 crocodiles, releasing some of them into the lagoons occasionally in a program to save the local wild croc population from extinction by poaching. The Cocodrilario offers nocturnal croc-spotting boat trips for M$500 for up to five people.

The beach has a number of simple *comedores*, serving egg dishes, pasta and *antojitos* for M$30 to M$60, and fish or seafood for around M$100 to M$120. Many of them also have basic *cabañas* costing around M$150 for two people, with shared bathrooms. You can usually sleep in a hammock or camp for free if you eat at a particular establishment. **Restaurante Siete Mares** (☑954-114-00-62, 954-132-22-63; cabañas M$250), at the beach's west end (nearest the river), has some of the better *cabañas*, each with two double beds, fans, mosquito nets, electric light and curtained-off shower.

❶ Getting There & Away

The starting point for boat trips along the lagoons to Chacahua village is the small fishing village of Zapotalito, at the eastern end of Laguna La Pastoría, 63km from Puerto Escondido.

From Puerto Escondido, take a minibus bound for Pinotepa Nacional from Av Hidalgo 5 (departures about every 20 minutes, 4am to 8pm) and get out at the Zapotalito turnoff (M$40, 1¼ hours), 58km from Puerto (and 8km past the town of Río Grande). From the turning, taxis will shuttle you the 5km to Zapotalito for M$60 (M$15 *colectivo*).

Competing boat cooperatives offer *lancha* services from Zapotalito to Chacahua village, charging M$840/1120 one way/round trip for up to 10 people. The round-trip option lasts about four hours, including about two hours at Chacahua. When there is sufficient traffic, *colec-*

PLAYA ESCOBILLA

This 15km-long beach, beginning about 30km east of Puerto Escondido, is one of the world's major nesting grounds for the olive ridley turtle (*tortuga golfina* to Mexicans). Up to a million female olive ridleys a year arrive at Escobilla to lay their eggs, with numbers peaking at night for a period of about a week around the full moons from May to February – a spectacular phenomenon known as an *arribada* or *arribazón*. The olive ridley is one of the smaller sea turtles (around 70cm long), but still an impressive animal, especially when seen emerging from the surf at a rate of several thousand per hour, as happens during Escobilla's biggest *arribadas*.

To protect the turtles, there is no general access to the beach, and this is enforced by the Mexican army. But a community ecotourism cooperative, **Santuario La Escobilla** (☑ 958-596-44-08; www.facebook.com/ecoturismo.escobilla; Hwy 200 Km 180, Escobilla; ⌖) 🍃, will take you to see the *arribadas* (per person M$130) and offers canoe trips (M$40) on the local lagoon. Before traveling to Escobilla, check first whether an *arribada* is definitely happening: they're often announced on the Facebook page. Some Puerto Escondido agencies make things easier with organized trips: a great option is Gina's Tours (p460), charging M$600 per person, which gives you the guidance of a resident biologist at Escobilla.

You can stay at Escobilla in clean, sturdy, well-kept *cabañas* (double/quad/family M$250/300/500) in a neat garden, equipped with electric light, fans, mosquito nets and hot-water bathrooms. Good local meals (M$60 to M$90) are available in the spacious restaurant.

Santuario La Escobilla is beside Hwy 200 on the west side of Escobilla village: look for the 'Restaurante La Tortuga Feliz' and 'Centro Ecoturístico La Escobilla' signs. Buses between Puerto Escondido and Pochutla will drop you here (M$24, 45 minutes).

OAXACA POCHUTLA

tivo services run for M$150/200 per person one way/round trip. All prices go up about 40% at peak holiday times such as Christmas–New Year's and Semana Santa.

For drivers, a mostly unpaved road heads 27km south to Chacahua village from San José del Progreso on Hwy 200. It's passable for normal cars except when waterlogged, which it often is between May and November.

Pochutla

☑ 958 / POP 14,000

Bustling, sweaty Pochutla is the market town and transportation hub for the central part of the Oaxaca coast, including the nearby beach spots of Puerto Ángel, Zipolite, San Agustinillo and Mazunte.

Hwy 175 from Oaxaca runs through Pochutla as Av Lázaro Cárdenas, the narrow main street, and meets the coastal Hwy 200 about 1.5km south of town. The bus and van terminals cluster toward the southern, downhill end of Cárdenas.

🛏 Sleeping & Eating

Hotel Izala (☑ 958-584-01-15; Av Cárdenas 59; s/d M$250/500, with air-con M$400/700; P❄) and **Hotel San Pedro** (☑ 958-584-11-23; Av

Cárdenas s/n; s/d M$400/500; P❄🛜), respectively 300m north and 300m south of the main bus station, are both OK for a night.

★ **Finca de Vaqueros**   PARRILLA $$
(☑ 958-100-43-31; El Colorado village; mains M$135-190; ⌖10am-9pm; ⌖) This ranch-style eatery with long tables in a large, open-sided barn is worth an expedition from anywhere on the coast for its superb grilled meats. It's 2km south of Pochutla on the Puerto Ángel road (M$40 by taxi). Order some *frijoles charros* (bean soup with bacon bits) and *queso fundido* (melted cheese) to start, followed by some tender *arrachera* (skirt steak) and *chistorra* sausage, for a feast you won't forget.

There's excellent mezcal and draft Dos Equis beer too, and the *costillas ahumadas* (smoked pork ribs) are another great option. When the moustachioed host Pedro is in the mood, he'll sing some sentimental *ranchera* (Mexico's urban 'country music') songs.

ⓘ Information

Banco Azteca (Av Cárdenas s/n; ⌖9am-9pm) Exchanges cash US dollars and euros; inside the Elektra store 75m south of the main bus station. Lines can be long.

Clínica Hospital San Carlos (☎ 958-584-06-03; Zaragoza 14, Sección 4a; ☺24hr) Recommended private hospital on the hill behind the municipality building.

Scotiabank ATM (Av Cárdenas 57) About 350m up the main street from the main bus station.

❶ Getting There & Away

OAXACA

Oaxaca is 245km away by the curvy Hwy 175 – six hours in the convenient and fairly comfortable air-conditioned van services (M$170) offered by several companies. The same services will drop you in San José del Pacífico (M$95, 3½ hours). Drivers will also usually stop when you need a bathroom break, or need to vomit, as a few people do on this route. OCC runs three daily 1st-class buses to Oaxaca (M$388, nine hours) from the Terminal de Autobuses San Pedro Pochutla, but they take a much longer and more expensive route via Salina Cruz.

Atlántida (☎ 958-584-92-39; Av Cárdenas 85) Eleven vans to Oaxaca daily, from the Rápidos de Pochutla terminal 30m north of the main bus station.

Líneas Unidas (☎ cell 958-5841322; Av Cárdenas 94) Across the street from the main bus terminal, with vans to Oaxaca every 30 to 60 minutes, 3:30am to midnight.

OTHER DESTINATIONS

Terminal de Autobuses San Pedro Pochutla (cnr Av Cárdenas & Constitución) The main bus station, entered through a white-grilled doorway toward the south end of Cárdenas. It's used by Turistar (deluxe), OCC and AltaMar (1st-class) and Sur and AU (2nd-class) services. For distant destinations with limited service, such as San Cristóbal de las Casas and Mexico City, it's advisable to get tickets a couple of days ahead.

Transportes Rápidos de Pochutla (TRP; Av Cárdenas 85) About 30m north of the main terminal; 2nd-class buses to Huatulco.

Puerto Ángel

☎ 958 / POP 2600

The small fishing port and naval town of Puerto Ángel straggles around a pretty little bay between two rocky headlands, surrounded by thickly wooded hills, 13km south of Pochutla. Once the main travelers' base on this coast, Puerto Ángel today has a somewhat down-at-heel feel and most travelers stay a few kilometers west at Zipolite, San Agustinillo or Mazunte – but Playa La Boquilla, on the eastward coast, makes a lovely outing and has an excellent small hotel. The main town beach is Playa del Panteón on the west side of the bay, with several seafood eateries.

◉ Sights & Activities

Playa La Boquilla   BEACH
(Ⓟ) The coast east of Puerto Ángel is dotted with nice small beaches, none of them very busy. Playa La Boquilla, on a scenic bay about 5km from town, is the site of the Bahía de la Luna hotel and restaurant, and is good for snorkeling. It's fun to go by boat (M$250/500 each way for two/four people): ask at Puerto Ángel pier or Playa del Panteón.

You can also get here by a 3.5km unpaved road from a turnoff 4km out of Puerto Ángel on the Pochutla road: a taxi from Puerto Ángel costs around M$90, or from Pochutla about M$160.

BUSES FROM POCHUTLA

DESTINATION	FARE (M$)	DURATION (HR)	FREQUENCY (DAILY)
Bahías de Huatulco	25-60	1	TRP every 10-15min 5:15am-8:15pm, Sur hourly 7:20am-8:20pm, 9 OCC
Mexico City (Sur)	920-1180	13½	Turistar 5pm, AltaMar 4:20pm
Puerto Escondido	45-88	1¼	Sur hourly 7am-8pm, 8 OCC, 4 AltaMar
Salina Cruz	208	4	8 OCC
San Cristóbal de las Casas	584	11-12	OCC 8pm & 10:50pm
Tapachula	656	12	OCC 6:40pm

ℹ CENTRAL COAST TRANSPORTATION

If you're coming to the beach villages of Puerto Ángel, Zipolite, San Agustinillo or Mazunte from Oaxaca, the most convenient public transportation is Atlántida (p443), as its vans from Oaxaca (via San José del Pacífico and Pochutla) run direct to these villages. If you're coming from Puerto Escondido or Huatulco, the best bet is to take a 2nd-class Sur bus as far as San Antonio, on Hwy 200 12km west of Pochutla, and switch there to a local *camioneta* (pickup truck with benches in the back; M$10) or a taxi (M$50 to Mazunte or San Agustinillo, M$100 to Zipolite).

Another option is to get yourself to Pochutla, the main transportation hub hereabouts, and take a *camioneta* or taxi from there. One route goes south from Pochutla to Puerto Ángel only; the other heads west to San Antonio on Hwy 200, then southeast to Mazunte, San Agustinillo and Zipolite. *Camionetas* and *taxis colectivos* (shared taxis) for both routes start from the Capilla del Niño Jesús chapel (250m north on Av Cárdenas from Pochutla's main bus station, then 150m west along Calle Jamaica). They operate during daylight hours, charging M$10 to M$15 to any of the villages. A private taxi is M$100 to M$150. Private taxis between one village and another cost M$50 to M$70 (plus M$10 or M$20 after dark).

A taxi to Huatulco or Puerto Escondido airports from any of the villages should cost M$400 to M$500.

Azul Profundo   WATER SPORTS

(☑ cell 958-1060420; www.hotelcordelias.com; Playa del Panteón) Azul Profundo offers many waterborne activities including sportfishing for marlin, swordfish, sailfish, tuna or mahimahi. A boat for three people, with two lines, costs M$400 per hour (minimum three hours). The company can pick you up and drop you off in Zipolite at its internet cafe Azul Profundo (p474). All guides speak at least a little English.

They can also take you diving (the drops and canyons out from Puerto Ángel are thick with fish and there's an 1870 shipwreck), and on four-hour snorkeling boat trips (M$180 per person) where you should also see turtles, dolphins and with luck (from December to April) whales.

🛏 Sleeping

Casa de Huéspedes
Gundi y Tomás   GUESTHOUSE $

(☑ cell 958-1192995; www.puertoangel-hotel.com; d M$350-420, without bathroom M$250-350; ☺🛜) A rambling establishment up steps from Blvd Uribe opposite the naval base, it offers well-kept, basic rooms with some offbeat artistic touches, and serves up fresh fish and many vegetarian options with organic vegetables (mains M$35 to M$120).

Bahía de la Luna   BUNGALOW $$

(☑ 958-589-50-20; www.bahiadelaluna.com; Playa La Boquilla; r M$875-1750, q M$2100-2500, all incl breakfast; ℗🛜) This rustic-chic hideaway sits in splendid isolation out at lovely Playa La Boquilla – a place for really escaping from the world. The bright adobe bungalows sit on tree-covered hillsides overlooking the beach. Some have kitchens but there's also an informal Mexican/international-fusion beach restaurant (lunch dishes from M$60, two-course dinner from M$300), with excellent seafood and steaks, generous margaritas and mezcal from the barrel.

Snorkel gear, kayaks and a paddleboard are free for guests, and snorkeling boat tours cost around M$250 per person.

ℹ Information

Banco Azteca (Blvd Uribe; ⊙ 8am-8pm) Changes cash US dollars and euros.

Zipolite

☑ 958 / POP 1100

The spectacular 1.5km stretch of pale sand called Zipolite, beginning about 2.5km west of Puerto Ángel, moves at a slow pace, withering in the midday heat. This coast's original budget beach-bum magnet, it attracts a bohemian international array of sun lovers, latter-day hippies and other hedonists to its wonderfully elemental surroundings of crashing surf, pounding sun, rocky headlands and tall *palapa*-roofed buildings. There are still plenty of reassuringly rustic budget lodgings and an unmistakable hippie vibe, but a number of more comfortable accommodations and classier restaurants at the west end of the beach now cater to a midrange clientele who also love the Zipolite ambience. There's a certain magic here, and you may postpone departure more than once.

Zipolite has an exaggerated fame as a nudist beach. Total nudity nowadays only happens in a couple of coves at the western end of the beach and in the small bay called Playa del Amor at the east end, which is a favorite spot for gay men.

The eastern end of Zipolite (nearest Puerto Ángel) is called Colonia Playa del Amor, the middle part is Centro, and the western end, where most of the traveler scene is, is Colonia Roca Blanca, where you'll find what amounts to the main street, Av Roca Blanca (also called El Adoquín), a block back from the beach.

🏃 Activities

The essence and glory of Zipolite is that organized activity is minimal. This is a place for hanging out and doing just as little as you like.

Azul Profundo (p471) provides free transportation for its fishing, diving and snorkeling trips from Puerto Ángel: you can reserve at its internet shop (p474) on Av Roca Blanca.

Piña Palmera   VOLUNTEERING
(📞 958-584-31-47; www.pinapalmera.org; Colonia Roca Blanca; ⊙8am-3pm Mon-Sat) 🅿 Piña Palmera, a rehabilitation and integration center for disabled people from rural communities, has a beautiful palm-grove site in Zipolite. There are long-term volunteer opportunities here (see the website) and anyone can help by doing a spot of shopping at

---

the **Tienda de Artesanías Piña Palmera** (cnr Pelícano & Carretera, Colonia Roca Blanca; ⊙9am-5pm Mon-Sat) 🅿, which sells products made here. For more on volunteering, see p857.

🛏 Sleeping

The majority of accommodations are in and around the Roca Blanca area at the west end of Zipolite. Some beach restaurants will rent you a hammock for M$40 or so, or let you sling your own or pitch a tent for around M$30 – just mind the sand flies and lock away your valuables.

Accommodation rates given are for the main season, January to Easter. In May, June, September, October and November, some places slash prices by as much as half. They may also double them during the Christmas–New Year and Semana Santa vacations.

Lo Cósmico   CABAÑAS $
(www.locosmico.com; west end Playa Zipolite; r M$400-600, without bathroom M$300; 🅿🖥) Relaxed Lo Cósmico's conical-roofed *cabañas*, dotted around a tall rock outcrop, offer among the best value on the beach. They're clean, plain and neat, all with hammocks, fans and mosquito nets; the best have balconies, views and private bathroom. The open-air restaurant (dishes M$30 to M$70; open 8am to 4pm, Tuesday to Sunday) serves excellent crepes, salads and breakfasts from an impeccably clean kitchen.

In the dry season (about November to May) you can sleep cheaply on the hammock terrace for M$70 or so.

Posada México   ROOMS $
(📞958-584-31-94; www.posadamexicozipolite.com; Av Roca Blanca; r M$400-950, without bathroom M$250-350; 🅿🖥) This Italian-run beachfront joint is on a friendly, personal scale and has smallish but clean, colorful rooms with good beds, four-poster mosquito nets, ingenious water-saving showers and sandy little hammock areas. Best are the two larger, more expensive, beach-facing rooms.

There's a fine restaurant (p474) too.

Las Casitas   BUNGALOW $
(📞cell 958-1009234; www.las-casitas.net; d M$350-600, q M$800-1100; 🅿🖥) Peaceful Las Casitas enjoys good views from its elevated position on a lane behind the west end of Playa Zipolite. The seven rooms, with tasteful Mexican color schemes and cute decorative details, are in palm-thatch-and-

---

> ### ℹ ZIPOLITE PRECAUTIONS
>
> Beware: the Zipolite surf is deadly. It's fraught with riptides, changing currents and a strong undertow. Going in deeper than your knees can be risking your life. Local voluntary lifeguards rescue many, but people still drown here every year. The shore break is one only experienced surfers should attempt. Heed the warning flags: yellow means don't go in deeper than your knees, red means don't go in period.
>
> Theft is a potential problem, so it's good to stay where you can lock your valuables in a safe, and keep your wits about you when out at night.

wood bungalows scattered around a pretty garden. All have private bathrooms, kitchens and spacious hangout areas.

A major plus is the on-site restaurant La Providencia (p473).

A Nice Place on the Beach
ROOMS **$**

(☑ 958-584-31-95; http://aniceplaceonthebeach.weebly.com; Av Roca Blanca; d M$500, d/q without bathroom M$300/500; 🕿) Subtitled 'Where people come to do nothing,' this is just what it says it is. The eight rooms are basic, with wooden walls and private bathrooms upstairs, concrete and shared bathrooms downstairs, but there's an inexpensive restaurant and bar right on the sand serving Mexican and Asian food till 4:30pm – and drinks till 2am.

Hostal El Carrizo
HOSTEL **$**

(☑ 958-584-33-38; sylvianelemetais@hotmail.com; Av Roca Blanca; dm/d M$50/120; 🕿) Run by a long-time Zipolite resident from France, El Carrizo is a classic basic backpacker joint with a friendly atmosphere. There are four very simple rooms and cabins, and a five-bed dorm, plus an open-air kitchen and sitting/hammock area.

El Jardín
APARTMENT **$**

(☑ 958-584-31-69; www.eljardinzipolitebungalows.com; Mangle s/n, Colonia Roca Blanca; d/tr/q/f US$30/35/40/45; 🕿) These five apartments, a couple of blocks back from the beach, vary in size and ventilation, but all are wood-walled, thatch-roofed and tile-floored, and most have beautiful chunky tables of recycled *guanacaste* wood.

Casa Sol
APARTMENT **$$**

(☑ cell 958-1000462; www.casasolzipolite.com; Arco Iris 6; r M$600-1000; ❄🕿🛉) Canadian-owned Casa Sol overlooks little Playa Camarón, a 10-minute walk west of Playa Zipolite, and its three spacious, spotless rooms make perfect vacation retreats. No meals are served but rooms have kitchens and there's another kitchen on the large, panoramic terrace. The beach is good for snorkeling when calm (free gear is available for guests).

Vehicle access is by a signposted 400m track off the main road about 1km west of Zipolite.

Heven
APARTMENT **$$**

(☑ cell 958-1062018; www.hevenresidence.com; Arco Iris 1; r incl breakfast M$750-900; 🕿🛉) Overlooking picturesque Playa Camarón, a 10-minute walk west from Playa Zipolite, Heven features lovely handmade Mexican furniture and crafts in its eight individually designed apartments and suites and spacious communal areas. There's a lovely panoramic pool.

El Alquimista
BUNGALOW **$$$**

(☑ 958-587-89-61; www.el-alquimista.com; west end Playa Zipolite; r M$1300-2300; P❄🕿🛉) The Alquimista's excellent accommodations range from thatch-roofed bungalows just off the beach (most with double bed, fan, hot-water bathroom and hammocked porch) to big, bright rooms set back up the luxuriant hillside with ample terraces and king-size beds. Decor is simple and tasteful.

One of Zipolite's best restaurants (p474) is here too, as are a good pool and a spa, **Espacio Shanti** (☑ 958-111-50-97; ⊙10am-7:30pm), using locally made organic materials. Daily hatha yoga sessions (M$100/300 per one/four classes) take place in a bright yoga room.

✗ Eating

Most places serve a mix of Mexican and international fare with a maritime slant.

Orale! Cafe
BREAKFAST **$**

(off west end Av Roca Blanca; breakfast dishes M$30-85; ⊙8am-3pm Nov-May) This shady tropical-garden cafe with soothing music is perfect for a relaxed and tasty breakfast.

★ La Providencia
MEXICAN, FUSION **$$**

(☑ cell 958-1009234; www.laprovidenciazipolite.com; mains M$110-160; ⊙6-10:30pm Wed-Sun Nov-Apr, Jul & Aug) Zipolite's outstanding dining option, on a lane behind the western end of the beach, combines delicious flavors, artful presentation and relaxed ambience. You can sip a cocktail in the open-air lounge while you peruse the menu. It's a contemporary Mexican treat, from cold beetroot-and-ginger soup to beef medallions with red-wine reduction or coconut-crusted prawns with mango sauce. Save room for the chocolate mousse!

Reservations advised during busy seasons.

Pacha Mama
ITALIAN, MEXICAN **$$**

(Pelícano, Colonia Roca Blanca; mains M$80-160; ⊙6-11pm Fri-Wed) The chefs are from Zipolite's sizable Italian community, and they turn out very professional steaks, seafood, homemade pasta with tasty sauces, and wood-oven pizzas, in a spacious, gardenlike setting.

Posada México   MEDITERRANEAN, MEXICAN **$$**
(Av Roca Blanca; mains M$80-160; ⊙ 8am-5:30pm
& 6:30-11pm Thu-Tue, 8am-1:30pm Wed; 🛜🍴) The
Italian-run beachside restaurant here does
fine wood-oven pizzas and good pasta, as
you might expect, but also enticing seafood
creations and salads. Cocktails are two-for-
one all day all year!

Piedra de Fuego   SEAFOOD **$$**
(Mangle, Colonia Roca Blanca; mains M$60-100;
⊙ 2-10pm) You'll get a generous serving of
fresh fish fillet or shrimp, accompanied by
rice, salad and potatoes, at this superbly
simple, very clean place run by a local family.
Good *aguas de frutas* (fruit cordials) too.

El Alquimista   INTERNATIONAL **$$$**
(📞 954-587-89-61; west end Playa Zipolite; mains
M$120-230; ⊙ 8am-11pm; 🛜🍴) The Alchemist
is delightfully sited in a sandy cove, and at-
mospherically lit by oil lamps and candles at
night. Its wide-ranging fare runs from fresh
salads to meat, seafood and pasta and tempt-
ing desserts, complemented by a full bar.

🍷 Drinking & Nightlife

Zipolite's beachfront restaurant-bars have
unbeatable locations for drinks from sunset
onward, and beach bonfires provide the fo-
cus for informal partying.

Bang Bang   BAR
(⊙ 6pm-2am Mon-Sat) There's often a good
crowd at this inexpensive beach shack with
its well-stocked bar and table-tennis table,
250m east from the end of the main Roca
Blanca strip.

ℹ Information

There are ATMs outside Azul Profundo internet
cafe and inside Hotel Nude on Av Roca Blanca,
but they sometimes run out of cash. The nearest
other ATMs are in Pochutla.
Azul Profundo (📞 958-584-34-37; Av Roca
Blanca; internet per hour M$15; ⊙ 9am-10pm)

ℹ Getting There & Away

After dark, taxis are your only option for getting
to Puerto Ángel, San Agustinillo or Mazunte
(M$50 to M$60 until around 9pm; M$70 to
M$80 after that).
    Atlántida (📞 954-584-32-14; Papelería Aby,
next to La Capilla, Centro) has comfortable vans
that depart for San José del Pacífico (M$130,
four hours) and Oaxaca (M$190, 6½ hours) 11
times daily, almost round the clock.

San Agustinillo
📞 958 / POP 290

Tiny, one-street San Agustinillo, 4km west
of Zipolite by road, centers on a curved bay
between two rock outcrops, with waves that
are perfect for bodyboarding and learning
to surf. The swimming is good as well (but
avoid the rocks). A line of attractive, low-key
places to stay fronts the sands and, along
with some good eateries, makes San Agus-
tinillo a perfect place to bliss out.

🏃 Activities

Coco Loco Surf Club   SURFING, SNORKELING
(📞 cell 958-1157737; www.cocolocosurfclub.
com; Calle Principal; ⊙ 10am-6pm; 👶) Coco
Loco's qualified French surf instructor,
David Chouard, gives excellent classes for
anyone from five years old upwards (one
hour individual/small group per person
M$350/250). It also rents surfboards, boogie
boards and snorkel gear (all per hour/half-
day/day M$50/150/200), sells surf gear, and
takes surf trips to Chacahua and Barra de la
Cruz (M$500 per day per person).

Boat Trips

Local fishers will take you on boat trips to
observe turtles, dolphins, birds, manta rays
and whales (best from November to April
for these last two). The cost for three hours
is normally M$200 per person (usually with
a minimum of four) including a snorkeling
stop. The fishers also offer sportfishing
trips, usually M$400 to M$500 per hour for
up to three people (minimum three or four
hours). Ask at your accommodations.

🛏 Sleeping & Eating

Most places to stay and eat are right on the
beach. Rooms have either mosquito-screened
windows or mosquito nets.

Recinto del Viento   GUESTHOUSE **$**
(📞 cell 958-1135236; www.recintodelviento.com;
s/d without bathroom M$280/350; 👶) This wel-
coming budget option sits 100m up steps
opposite Un Sueño accommodations, with
surf views from its hammock-slung terrace.
The guest kitchen helps create a sociable
atmosphere and there's a no-wi-fi policy to
encourage guests to interact! The five rooms
are smallish but catch the breezes: one has
its own bathroom and is a bit more expen-
sive (single/double M$450/500).

Palapa de Evelia ROOMS **$**

(r M$300) There's decent budget accommodations at several of San Agustinillo's beach *comedores*. Evelia's, near the west end of the beach, offers five plain, neat, clean upstairs rooms, each with one double bed, small private bathroom, fan and mosquito net. No phone, no website, no email, no reservations!

★**Punta Placer** CABAÑAS **$$**

(☑cell 958-1090164; www.puntaplacer.com; r M$1200; [P]🛜) The eight beautiful circular rooms and one large apartment here have a fresh, open-air feel thanks to their breezy terraces and wood-slat windows. With welcome touches like good reading lights and stone-lined hot showers with excellent water pressure, they're a grade above most other San Agustinillo accommodations.

The garden of native plants opens directly on the beach, and the little restaurant here, **Vidita Negra** (mains M$70-190; ⊙7:30am-10:30pm; 🛜), serves up well-prepared Mexican and Mediterranean dishes – the fresh fish, done in three chilies or white wine, is always a good bet.

★**Un Sueño** CABAÑAS **$$**

(☑cell 958-1138749; www.unsueno.com; r/q M$850/1150; [P]🛜) Un Sueño, toward the east end of the beach, has 17 lovely, good-sized rooms sporting touches of art and craft from around the world, and a semi-open-air feel from bamboo-slat windows and hammock-slung terraces. Also fronting the sands are a breezy hammock area and an excellent restaurant (mains M$110-140; ⊙8am-6:30pm) doing excellent breakfasts and, for lunch, *sabores del Pacífico* (flavors of the Pacific) with a touch of French flair.

The short but sweet seafood-based menu runs from a delicious foil-wrapped fish with mint to Thai-style shrimp, and you shouldn't miss the lemon pie!

México Lindo y qué Rico! ROOMS **$$**

(☑cell 958-5846271; www.facebook.com/méxico-lindo-y-que-rico-cabañas-276407532375671; s/d M$500/650; ⊙closed Sep–late Oct; [P]😀🛜) Near the west end of the beach, México Lindo has friendly owners and staff, and its five sizable rooms feature slatted windows, fans and some bright decor details. Especially good are the two breezy rooms upstairs under the tall *palapa* roof.

The restaurant (mains M$100–160; open 8am-7:30pm, closed September to late October) here serves uncomplicated food that is among the best in town. Breakfasts, shrimp tacos and quesadillas, fish fillets, chicken enchiladas, stuffed avocados and pizza are all carefully prepared and served with a smile.

Rancho Cerro Largo CABAÑAS **$$**

(http://ranchocerrolargo.wix.com/ranchocerrolargo; Playa Aragón; s M$900-1250, d M$1000-1350, all incl breakfast & dinner; [P]) 🧘 With a stunning, secluded position above Playa Aragón (which stretches east from Playa San Agustinillo), Cerro Largo offers nine comfortable ocean-view *cabañas* and rooms, most constructed of mud and wattle and some with private bathrooms. Many have open walls overlooking the crashing coast below. Top-notch, mainly vegetarian meals (vegan available) are taken by all guests together, and host Mario Corella leads morning yoga sessions for all levels (suggested donation: M$50).

Access is by a signed driveway from the Zipolite–San Agustinillo road. Book ahead by email in high season.

Bambú CABAÑAS **$$**

(www.bambuecocabanas.com; d M$700-1200, q M$900-1400; [P]😀🛜) 🧘 The half-dozen rooms here, toward the beach's east end, are large, open to as much breeze as possible, and set under high *palapa* roofs. All are cleverly constructed, mainly from bamboo, with pretty tilework, fans, good mozzie nets – and quirky details like seashell shower heads and trees growing inside a couple of rooms.

The large guest kitchen area includes a barbecue grill and long communal table.

Casa Aamori BOUTIQUE HOTEL **$$$**

(in Mexico City ☑55-5436-2538; www.aamoriboutiquehotel.com; r M$2100-2600; ❄🛜🏊) San Agustinillo's classiest accommodations, lovingly designed Casa Aamori stands toward the east end of the beach. The 12 large, attractive rooms, on themes from Copacabana to Goa to Africa, feature floor mosaics and original crafts from around the world. Four look straight out on to the ocean.

The pool-and-restaurant deck leads on to a sandy area over the beach, with hanging beds under the palms. The hotel is for adults only, with a two-night minimum stay.

La Termita ITALIAN **$$**

(☑cell 958-5893046; www.posadalatermita.com; pizzas M$90-145; ⊙8am-3pm & 6:30-11pm; 🛜📶♿) Roughly in the center of the village,

OAXACA SAN AGUSTINILLO

La Termita's flavorsome, wood-oven pizzas are the best anywhere in the area, and there are good salads to go with them and carrot or chocolate cake to follow!

Also here are four attractive, big rooms (double M$900–1500, quad M$1200–1800) with good wood furnishings – two of them directly over the beach.

Restaurante La Mora
MEXICAN, ITALIAN $$

(✆ cell 958-584-64-22; www.lamoraposada.com; mains M$80-120, r with/without kitchenette M$600/500, apt M$1200; ☉ 8am-2:30pm & 6:30-10pm Wed-Mon; ☎) Friendly La Mora makes the most of its little site toward the east end of town. The neat restaurant serves good Italian and seafood dinners, breakfasts, sandwiches and organic, fair-trade coffee. Upstairs are three cheerful rooms in blue, white and yellow, and above them is a bright, spacious apartment that's good for families.

All three floors have terraces with close-up sea views.

Mazunte

✆ 958 / POP 870

A kilometer west of San Agustinillo, Mazunte has a fine, curving, sandy beach on a scenic bay, with wonderfully beautiful natural surroundings, an interesting turtle center, and a growing variety of basic and classier places to stay and eat. This is a popular travelers' hangout with a laid-back atmosphere and something of a hippie vibe, where someone somewhere is always likely to be offering yoga, massage, meditation or tattoos. Mazunte's economic mainstays used to be turtle meat and eggs: after the turtle industry was banned in 1990, it turned to ecotourism. In 2015 it was named one of

ETHICS & TURTLE TOURS

Boat tours to observe turtles, dolphins, whales and other marine life are a popular and exciting activity in several places along the Oaxaca coast. If the passengers want, some guides may jump into the sea and take hold of turtles, so that boat passengers can get a better view, or even jump in and hold the animal too. This kind of interaction with the animals has been shown to cause them distress, so we advise not joining any trip where it may happen.

Mexico's official Pueblos Mágicos (Magical Villages), which will bring an increase in domestic tourism and might dilute the alternative vibe.

The main road running through the middle of Mazunte is called Paseo del Mazunte. Four lanes run about 500m from the road to the beach: in east-to-west order they are Andador Golfina, Andador Carey, Andador La Barrita and Calle Rinconcito – this last leading down to the part of the beach called El Rinconcito, which is the best bit for swimming and has several of the best places to eat and stay nearby. The cape Punta Cometa closes off the west end of the bay. A rough road west off Calle Rinconcito heads 750m over to Playa Mermejita, a beautiful long, wild beach with a handful of attractive accommodations and eateries – unfortunately, tricky currents and strong waves make swimming inadvisable here.

◉ Sights

★ Punta Cometa
VIEWPOINT

This rocky cape, jutting out from the west end of Mazunte beach, is the southernmost point in the state of Oaxaca and a fabulous place to be at sunset, with great long-distance views.

For a beautiful walk to the point, take the lane toward Playa Mermejita off Calle Rinconcito, and go left up the track immediately after the cemetery, to reach the community nature reserve entrance after 250m. Here take the path leading down to the right (Sendero Corral de Piedra Poniente), which leads you to the point in 20 to 30 minutes via Cometa's scenic western side. You can return more directly by the Sendero Principal path. Total round-trip walking time from Calle Rinconcito (without stops) is about one hour.

Centro Mexicano de la Tortuga
AQUARIUM

(in Mexico City ✆ 55-5449-7000, ext 19001; www.centromexicanodelatortuga.org; Paseo del Mazunte; M$30.50; ☉ 10am-4:30pm Wed-Sat, to 2:30pm Sun; P ♿) ⌖ The much-visited Mexican Turtle Center, at the east end of Mazunte, is an aquarium and research center containing specimens of all the world's eight marine-turtle species (seven of which frequent Mexico's coasts), plus some freshwater and land varieties. They're on view in fairly large tanks – it's enthralling to get a close-up view of these creatures, some of which are BIG!

Activities

★ Ola Verde Expediciones RAFTING, HIKING
([🖱] cell 958-1096751; www.olaverdeexpediciones.com.mx; Calle Rinconcito; ⊙ office 10am-2pm & 4-9pm; [♿]) This team of adventure-sports enthusiasts leads exciting river adventures including a half-day canyon hike on the Río San Francisco inland from Mazunte (year-round; adult/child M$550/400), with swimming, floating and jumping into pools – a fun outing for families and anyone else.

Its other offerings include recommended rafting trips on the San Francisco (Class II to III; late July to October or later; half-day trip per person M$600) and the Río Copalita near Huatulco (Class II to IV; July to January; day trip M$1000 to M$1200, two-day expedition M$2000). All trips take in great tropical scenery and they'll pick you up free anywhere from Puerto Ángel to Mazunte.

Boat Trips
Local fishers will take three or more people out for three-hour boat trips to snorkel, look for turtles, dolphins and whales, and check out beaches. Cost is normally M$200 per person, including snorkel equipment. You can organize trips through your accommodations.

Courses

Instituto Iguana LANGUAGE COURSE
([🖱] cell 958-1075232; http://institutoiguana.com; Camino al Aguaje; 10/20hr per week per person group courses M$900/1500, individual courses M$1500/2800) ✎ In keeping with the Mazunte vibe, this language school is a relaxed, friendly place where you can start classes any day and study as intensively as you like. Run by a Mexican-German nonprofit organization, which also gives free English classes to villagers, it has a lovely breezy hilltop site centered on a beautiful big *palapa*.

Small-group courses (for beginners) run between November and February. One-on-one classes are available any time. You can offer to teach English to villagers in exchange for your Spanish classes. The school has rooms on-site (M$125 to M$250 per person), or can put you in family-run guesthouses nearby. It's 400m inland off the main road, signposted beside the bridge in the middle of Mazunte.

Festivals & Events

Festival Internacional de Jazz MUSIC
(www.facebook.com/festivalinternacionalde jazzdemazunte) This festival brings three days

of top-quality international jazz and other music, plus workshops and exhibitions, to Mazunte mid-November. All events are free!

Sleeping

Posada del Arquitecto CABAÑAS $
(www.posadadelarquitecto.com; El Rinconcito; dm M$70, estrella s/d M$90/150, cabañas incl breakfast d M$350-1000, per extra person M$100; [P] [🛜]) Built into and around the natural features of a small hill by the beach, this popular place provides a variety of airy accommodations. Options range from hilltop open-air hanging beds known as *estrellas*, to attractive *cabañas* and casitas (bungalows) constructed with mostly natural materials. The beachfront cafe adds to the appeal.

Hostal La Isla HOSTEL $
(in Mexico City [🖱] 55-4825-8745; http://laisla mazunte.jimdo.com; off Calle Rinconcito; camping per person M$70, dm M$120, r M$300-350, all incl breakfast; [❄] [🛜]) A friendly, relaxed budget option with an international crowd, just behind the beach. There's an inexpensive cafe in its hammock-strung garden area, serving food all day except in May, June, September and October (when there's still dinner several times a week). The dorm offers mattresses on the floor and a few beds, all with mosquito nets.

Private rooms are basic, with fans and clean shared bathrooms. No kids allowed.

Hotel DF HOTEL $
(www.hoteldfplayamazunte.com; off Calle Rinconcito; r M$300-1000; [❄] [🛜]) Right on the sand toward the west end of the beach, the DF has a great spacious and airy feel. The seven large rooms, most on the upper deck, have minimal decor but good solid wood furnishings, king-size beds and large bathrooms. The two most expensive ones look straight out to the ocean.

There's also a spacious guest kitchen, and hammocks and loungers on the sand.

Cabañas Balamjuyuc CABAÑAS $
([🖱] cell 958-5837667; http://balamjuyuc.blogspot.com; Camino a Punta Cometa; camping per person M$80, tent & bedding rental M$100, dm M$150, cabañas M$400-800; [P] [🛜]) Relaxed Balamjuyuc occupies a spacious hilltop site off Calle Rinconcito, with superb coastal views. The three big, airy *cabaña* rooms have private bathrooms; dorms have clean shared bathrooms. Breakfast is available for M$40 to M$100, and guests can use the kitchen. Also

on offer are daily yoga sessions, therapeutic massages and temascal steam-bath sessions.

Hotel Arigalan
HOTEL **$$**

(☑ cell 958-1086987; http://arigalan.com; Cerrada del Museo de la Tortuga; cabañas US$40-50, r US$50-100, ste US$85-140; P☺❄☎) This small hotel commands fine coastal views from its hilltop site at the village's east end, and offers sizable, tastefully furnished rooms and suites (some with air-con and/or plunge pools), plus a few pleasant, fan-cooled *cabañas*. A path leads directly down to San Agustinillo beach. No under-18s accepted here.

Oceanomar
CABAÑAS **$$**

(☑ cell 958-5890376; www.oceanomar.com; Camino a Mermejita; s/d/tr M$1000/1200/1400; P☎☒) On a lovely and cleverly landscaped hillside site with great views over Playa Mermejita, Italian-owned Oceanomar boasts a gorgeous pool and just five spacious, well-built rooms with nice craft details, hammock-slung terraces and good bathrooms. The restaurant (mains M$100–190; open to hotel guests 8am to 10pm, to the public 7pm to 10pm) serves quality pasta, fish and meat dishes plus Mexican favorites such as *tamales* and *chiles rellenos* (chilies stuffed with meat or cheese).

El Copal
CABAÑAS **$$**

(☑ cell 55-41942167; www.elcopal.com.mx; Playa Mermejita; cabañas M$1050-1350 ; P☎) ✐ Copal's four *cabañas* of adobe, wood and palm thatch stand on a leafy hillside and all contain a double bed on the ground floor and two or three singles above. Their bathrooms are quaint open-air affairs with views. The international fusion restaurant (mains M$85–120; 7am to 10:30pm) has beautiful views along the beach.

Casa Pan de Miel
HOTEL **$$$**

(☑ cell 958-1004719; www.casapandemiel.com; r US$100-225; P☺❄☎☒) This is a place for real relaxation, boasting a lovely infinity pool in front of an inviting large *palapa* dining/lounge area. The nine bright, elegant air-conditioned rooms are adorned with varied Mexican art, and all have sea views, kitchen or kitchenette, and terraces with hammocks. The excellent breakfasts (US$9 to US$15) include organic eggs and homemade jams, breads and yogurt.

It's up a steep track from the main road at the east end of Mazunte and enjoys wonderful views. Children are not accepted because of the cliff-top position.

Celeste del Mar
ROOMS **$$$**

(☑ cell 958-1075296; www.celestedelmar.com; Playa Mermejita; r US$90-125; ☎) ✐ A few steps from Playa Mermejita, this small hotel offers eight carefully designed rooms in two-story *palapa*-roofed cottages with attractive contemporary decorative details. The four airy upstairs rooms feature loft areas with big double hammocks under their high *palapa* roofs; no under-18s.

✖ Eating

Fish Taco El Rey
MEXICAN **$**

(Calle Rinconcito; tacos M$30-35, other dishes M$70-100; ☽4-10:30pm Tue-Sun) Just back up the street from El Rinconcito beach, El Rey lives up to its name with big, tasty fish tacos, plus shrimp, veggie and *arrachera* varieties, and a very good Thai coconut-and-shrimp soup.

Comedor los Traviesos
MEXICAN **$**

(Paseo del Mazunte; mains M$40-140; ☽8:30am-10pm) A place to come for traditional Oaxacan and Mexican cooking at good prices, Los Traviesos does the best *tlayudas* in the area. It's just west of the bridge in the middle of town.

★ Alessandro
ITALIAN **$$**

(El Rinconcito; mains M$95-145; ☽6-10:30pm Wed-Mon; ✐) Tiny but brilliant, this place has a handful of tables in a corner of the Posada del Arquitecto (p477). It serves up wonderful homemade pasta (eg in arugula-and-avocado pesto), fresh fish (eg in *guajillo*-chili-and-tomatillo sauce), *filet miñón* (beef tenderloin, eg in white wine and olive oil, with parmesan) and desserts (eg mousse of Oaxacan chocolate with orange-and-rum perfume).

Good drinks include Argentine wine, Oaxacan mezcal and *aguas de frutas* (fruit cordials). Go early to avoid waiting – and if the restaurant isn't there, ask where it has gone, as it has moved around a bit over the years.

El Rincón de Mermejita
MEDITERRANEAN, INTERNATIONAL **$$**

(http://elrincondemermejita.wordpress.com; Playa Mermejita; mains M$105-150; ☽9am-9pm Tue-Sun) ✐ Tucked into a hidden corner at the south end of Mermejita beach, this little Spanish-run alfresco eatery and bar prepares great home-style dishes, mostly from fresh local produce and with a Mediterranean and South American focus – fish meunière, Peruvian ceviche, Brazilian *moqueca* (fish stew in coconut milk), Andalucian gazpacho (cold soup) and a variety of tapas.

It has a good drinks range too, plus three simple but decent *cabañas* (single occupancy M$300, double M$400 to M$500).

La Cuisine MEDITERRANEAN, MEXICAN **$$**
(cell958-1071836;www.facebook.com/la-cuisine-132010246889452; off Calle Rinconcito; 3-course comida corrida M$170; ⊘7-11pm Mon-Sat; ✚) An immediate success when it opened in 2015, La Cuisine does a delicious three-course *comida corrida gourmet* (gourmet set menu), with two options for each course. The menu changes daily, according to the market-fresh ingredients that the dedicated French cook acquires, and is posted each morning on the Facebook page. It's just off Calle Rinconcito in the first side lane back from the beach.

🍷 Drinking & Entertainment

You can have drinks in restaurants and cafes, but the only regular organized entertainment is live Latin music at Siddhartha or Estrella Fugaz, two adjacent restaurants just back from El Rinconcito beach; there's usually something on a few times a week from December to March, between about 9pm and midnight.

🛍 Shopping

Cosméticos
Naturales Mazunte HANDICRAFTS
(cell 958-5874860; www.cosmeticosmazunte.com; Paseo del Mazunte; ⊘9am-4pm Mon-Sat, 10am-2pm Sun) ✎ This very successful small cooperative, toward the west end of the village, makes and sells products such as shampoo, cosmetics, mosquito repellent, soap and herbal medicines, using natural sources like maize, coconut and essential oils. You'll find its toiletries in hotel bathrooms all over Oaxaca state! It also sells organic coffee and tahini, and you can have a look at the workshop while here.

ℹ Information

Banco Multiva ATM (Paseo del Mazunte) Opposite the church.
Tourist Information Kiosk (Paseo del Mazunte; ⊘9am-5pm Sat & Sun) By the roadside at the west end of the village.

ℹ Getting There & Away

Atlántida (☑ cell 958-1009904) Comfortable vans depart for San José del Pacífico (M$140, 4¼ hours) and Oaxaca (M$200, 6¾ hours) 11 times daily from Paseo del Mazunte, just east of the church.

La Ventanilla

Some 2.5km along the road west from Mazunte, a sign points to the tiny beach village of La Ventanilla, 1.2km down a dirt track, where you can take a fascinating boat trip on a crocodile-filled lagoon, go bird-watching or ride a horse along the beach. Somehow this tiny village manages to have two rival cooperatives offering these services: both have some English-speaking guides and do a fine job. There are a few simple *comedores* near the beach and both cooperatives offer clean, well-built *cabañas*, some with private bathroom, for M$300 to M$400 a double.

🏃 Activities

Servicios Ecoturísticos
La Ventanilla WILDLIFE-WATCHING
(☑cell 958-1087726; www.laventanilla.com.mx; 1½hr lagoon tours adult/child M$100/50; ⊘tours 8am-5pm) ✎ With its office and restaurant by the roadside as you enter the village, this cooperative (the members of which wear white shirts) runs 12-passenger boat trips on the mangrove-fringed lagoon which will show you endangered river crocodiles (there are several hundred in the local protected area), lots of water birds (most prolific from November to March) and a few deer, monkeys, eagles and coatis in enclosures on an island.

It also offers three-hour horseback rides (M$500) and bird-watching tours (per person per hour M$100; best at 6am); reserve both the day before. On certain days there's the chance to release turtle hatchlings or join night patrols to see turtles laying eggs.

Lagarto Real WILDLIFE-WATCHING
(☑cell 958-1080354; www.facebook.com/lagarto.real; 1½hr lagoon tours adult/child M$50/30; ⊘tours 8am-6pm) ✎ Lagarto Real, the members of which wear red shirts, has its office on the roadside near the beach. It offers lagoon boat trips (without an island stop), early-morning bird-watching (per person per hour M$100), and nocturnal turtle-nesting observation.

ℹ Getting There & Away

Camionetas and *taxis colectivos* on the Zipolite–Mazunte–Pochutla route pass the Ventanilla turnoff, leaving you with the 1.2km walk. A taxi from Mazunte should cost M$50.

Bahías de Huatulco

📞 958 / POP 19,000

Mexico's youngest planned coastal resort lies along a series of beautiful sandy bays *(bahías)* 50km east of Pochutla. This stretch of coast had just one small fishing village until the 1980s. The developers have trodden fairly gently here: pockets of construction are separated by tracts of unspoiled shoreline, the maximum building height is six stories and no sewage goes into the sea. Huatulco (wah-*tool*-koh) is a relaxed resort with a friendly atmosphere, and relatively uncrowded except at Mexican holiday times and when cruise ships dock in Bahía de Santa Cruz (an average of four times monthly between October and May). The cruise market has helped to spawn all sorts of ready-packaged activities for visitors here.

The Huatulco bays are strung along the coast for 15km west and 10km east from the harbor at Santa Cruz Huatulco. The 'downtown' area, 1km north of Santa Cruz, is called La Crucecita, with a street grid focused on the leafy Plaza Principal. The other main developments are at Chahué and Tangolunda to the east.

☉ Sights

Huatulco's beaches are beautiful and sandy with turquoise waters. Some have coral offshore and excellent snorkeling. As in the rest of Mexico, all beaches are under federal control, and anyone can use them, even when hotels appear to treat them as private property.

Some of the western bays and most of the eastern ones are accessible by road, but a boat ride is more fun, if more expensive, than a taxi. *Lanchas* will whisk you out to most beaches from Santa Cruz harbor any time after 8am and return to collect you by dusk. Round-trip rates for up to 10 people: Playa La Entrega M$800, Bahía Órgano M$1200, Bahía Maguey M$1200, Bahía Cacaluta M$1500, Playa La India M$2500, Bahía San Agustín M$3200. For Cacaluta and Bahía Chachacual to its west, there's a M$25 fee for entering the **Parque Nacional Huatulco**, also collected at the harbor. Use of nonbiodegradable sunscreen is prohibited within the national park.

Several operators offer a **seven-bay day tour** in larger boats for M$300 to M$350 per person. You can buy tickets at hotels, agencies and tour kiosks.

Playa Santa Cruz   BEACH
(**P**) Santa Cruz Huatulco's small beach is easily accessible but often crowded, and its looks are marred by the cruise-ship pier. It has several beach restaurants of the kind where staff stand outside with menus trying to pull people in.

Playa La Entrega   BEACH
(**P** 🛖) La Entrega lies toward the outer edge of Bahía de Santa Cruz, a five-minute *lancha* trip or 2.5km drive from Santa Cruz. This 300m beach, backed by a line of seafood *palapas,* can get busy, but it has decent (if sometimes crowded) snorkeling on a coral plate from which boats are cordoned off. Gear is available at **Renta de Snorkel Vicente** (📞 cell 958-1168197; mask & snorkel M$30, fins M$30, lifejacket M$30, all 3 M$75, underwater camera M$250; ⊙7:30am-dusk) at the beach's northern end.

'La Entrega' means 'The Delivery': in 1831 Mexican independence hero Vicente Guerrero was handed over here to his political enemies by a Genoese sea captain. Guerrero was then taken to Cuilapan near Oaxaca and shot.

Bahía Maguey   BEACH
(**P** 🛖) Two kilometers west of Santa Cruz, Maguey's fine 400m beach curves around a calm bay between forested headlands. A line of large, family-friendly *palapas* serves fish and seafood dishes for M$100-plus, and there's good snorkeling around the rocks on the east side of the bay; **Escualo** (snorkeling set M$75; ⊙8am-6pm) rents gear.

Bahía El Órgano   BEACH
Just east of Bahía Maguey, this beautiful 250m beach has calm waters good for snorkeling, and no crowds because there's no vehicle access and no *comedores.* You can come by boat, or walk to the beach during dry weather by a 1km path through the forest. The path starts about 1.3km back toward Santa Cruz from the Maguey parking lot; the entry is marked by signs telling people not to molest wildlife, light fires etc.

Bahía Cacaluta   BEACH
Cacaluta is 1km long and protected by an island, though there can be undertow. Snorkeling is best around the island. There are no services at the beach. *Lancha* is one way to get here; you can also walk by the **Sendero Zanate**, a interpretative trail of about 2km passing two lagoons with birdlife.

The start of the trail is about 700m along the 'Cacaluta' road off the road to Bahía

Bahías de Huatulco

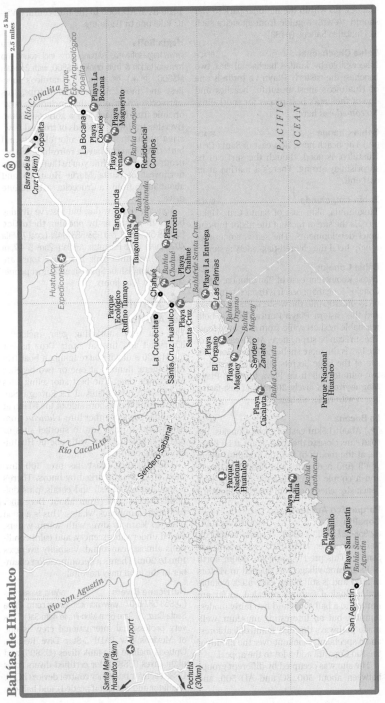

5 km
2.5 miles

PACIFIC OCEAN

Río Copalita
Parque Eco-Arqueológico Copalita
Copalita
Barra de la Cruz (14km)
La Bocana
Playa La Bocana
Playa Conejos
Playa Magueyito
Bahía Conejos
Playa Arenas
Residencial Conejos
Tangolunda
Playa Tangolunda
Bahía Tangolunda
Playa Arrocito
Bahía Chahué
Playa Chahué
Bahía de Santa Cruz
Playa La Entrega
Chahué
Las Palmas
Parque Ecológico Rufino Tamayo
La Crucecita
Bahía El Órgano
Playa Santa Cruz
Santa Cruz Huatulco
Playa El Órgano
Bahía Maguey
Playa Maguey
Sendero Zanate
Bahía Cacaluta
Huatulco Expediciones
Parque Nacional Huatulco
Playa Cacaluta
Río Cacaluta
Sendero Sabanal
Parque Nacional Huatulco
Bahía Chachacual
Playa La India
Playa Riscalillo
Playa San Agustín
Bahía San Agustín
San Agustín
Río San Agustín
Airport
Pochutla (30km)
Santa María Huatulco (9km)

Maguey. It's within the national park so you should go with a guide from agencies such as Huatulco Salvaje (p483).

Bahía Chachacual
BEACH

Inaccessible by land, Chachacual has two beaches: the easterly **Playa La India** is one of Huatulco's most beautiful beaches and one of the area's best places for snorkeling. No *comedores* here.

Bahía Chahué
BEACH

(**P**) The beach here, 1km east of Santa Cruz Huatulco, is good, though the surf can be surprisingly strong. There's a marina at its east end.

Bahía Tangolunda
BEACH

Tangolunda, 5km east of Santa Cruz Huatulco, is the site of most of the major top-end hotel developments. The sea is sometimes rough: heed the colored-flag safety system.

Bahía Conejos
BEACH

Three kilometers east of Tangolunda, Bahía Conejos' long main beach is divided by a small rocky outcrop into the western **Playa Arenas** and the eastern **Playa Punta Arenas**, both reachable by short walks from the paved road. The surf can be strong here. At the east end of the bay is the more sheltered **Playa Conejos**, site of the large Secrets Huatulco Resort. A two-minute walk from Playa Conejos, **Playa Magueyito** is a lovely, 300m-long east-facing beach with rocks offshore.

La Bocana
BEACH

(**P**) About 1.5km east of Playa Conejos, the road runs close to the coast again at La Bocana, at the mouth of the Río Copalita, where you'll find a decent right-hand surf break and a couple of restaurants. Another long beach stretches east from the river mouth.

Parque Eco-Arqueológico Copalita
ARCHAEOLOGICAL SITE

(☑958-587-15-91; Blvd Copalita-Tangolunda; Mexican/foreigner M$60/80; ⊙8am-5pm Tue-Sun; **P**) This pre-Hispanic site 600m north of La Bocana village was opened to visitors in 2010 and is still being excavated. Notable archaeological features revealed so far are limited to a ball court and two fairly modest temples, but an interesting museum, well-made pathways through semitropical forest and a spectacular lookout over the mouth of the Río Copalita add a lot to the appeal.

The site was occupied by different groups between about 500 BC and AD 500, and again from AD 1000 to the 16th century. Visits take one to 1½ hours.

Hagia Sofia
FARM

(www.hagiasofia.mx; Apanguito; incl round-trip transportation & fruit drinks M$500, with 2 meals M$600; **P**🖼) 🍃 One of Huatulco's loveliest and most interesting day trips, this 'agro-ecotourism' operation includes a large organic fruit orchard and a gorgeous 500m riverside trail with 60 kinds of tropical flowering plants that attract colorful birds and butterflies. You can have a refreshing dip beneath a waterfall while you're there. It's 9km northwest of Santa María Huatulco and about 30km from La Crucecita (a 45-minute drive).

You can visit any day, but reserve the day before in person or by phoning the **office** (☑958-587-08-71, cell 958-5837943; Local 7, Mitla 402, Santa Cruz Huatulco; ⊙9am-2pm & 4-7pm Mon-Sat) in Santa Cruz Huatulco: tours are given in English or Spanish and most people stay about four hours.

🏃 Activities

Sea Activities

You can rent snorkeling gear, including life jacket and fins, at Santa Cruz harbor for M$130 a day if you're taking a boat trip from there. Renters at one or two beaches have lower rates. The best snorkeling sites include the coral plates at La Entrega, San Agustín and the inshore side of the island at Cacaluta. You can either hire a *lancha* from Santa Cruz to take you to snorkel sites or take a snorkeling tour with one of Huatulco's diving outfits.

The Huatulco coast has over 100 dive sites, 40 of them marked by buoys. There's a good variety of fish and corals, plus dolphins, turtles and (from about December to March) humpback whales. This is a good place to learn to dive, with warm waters, varied underwater scenery, and calm conditions almost year-round. Visibility averages 10m to 20m. There's a decompression chamber in the local navy hospital.

Hurricane Divers
DIVING, SNORKELING

(☑958-587-11-07; www.hurricanedivers.com; Playa Santa Cruz; ⊙9am-6pm Mon-Fri, to 4pm Sat) This very professional international crew is one of Mexico's few PADI 5-Star Dive Resorts. Options include two-tank dives (US$95) and night dives (US$70) for certified divers (plus US$5 each for buoyancy control device (BCD), regulator and wet suit if needed), and half-day

PADI Discover Scuba courses (US$150) for beginners, which include two short dives.

The popular full-day snorkeling excursion (US$135 per person; minimum two) includes about four stops and a beach lunch. English, Spanish, Dutch and German spoken. The website is an excellent information source on Huatulco diving and snorkeling.

Buceo Sotavento DIVING, SNORKELING
(☑958-587-21-66, cell 958-1095950; www.coug. net/sotavento; Local 18, Plaza Oaxaca Mall, Plaza Principal, La Crucecita; ◉9am-9pm) A friendly local outfit offering a range of diving options from a four-hour introduction (US$90) to open-water certification (five days, US$450). One-/two-tank dives for certified divers are M$60/90. Sotavento also does four-hour snorkeling trips for U$30 per person (two to seven people), and is certified by the Federación Mexicana de Actividades Subacuáticas (Mexican Underwater Activities Federation).

Huatulco Salvaje ADVENTURE TOUR
(☑cell 958-1193886, cell 958-5874028; www.huat ulcosalvaje.com; Local 2, Mitla 402, Santa Cruz Huat ulco; ◉9am-2pm & 4:30-7:30pm Mon-Sat; ⊞) ✦ Huatulco Salvaje is a group of certified tour guides from the local community, many of them from village families displaced when the Parque Nacional Huatulco was created in the 1990s. They know their stuff when it comes to nature tours around here.

Seaborne activities include five-hour snorkeling boat trips (M$2000 to M$3500 for up to 10 people), night snorkeling (M$650 per person, minimum four), and whale-, dolphin- and turtle-watching (October to April, four hours, M$650 per person, minimum five).

Hiking & Mountain Biking

Huatulco Salvaje (p483) leads interesting guided hikes and bike trips along trails within the Parque Nacional Huatulco. Its 'Sendero al Mar' trip follows the Sendero Zanate trail to Bahía Cacaluta and then takes you on a three-bay boat trip (M$3000 for up to four people).

Rafting

Huatulco Expediciones RAFTING
(☑958-587-21-26; www.huatulcoexpediciones.com; Hwy 200 Km 256, Puente Tangolunda, Comunidad La Jabalina) Does rafting trips on the Río Copalita near Huatulco, from all-day outings on the Class III–IV Alemania section starting 800m above sea level (per person M$650 to M$700, minimum two people, generally July to December) to a gentler 2½-hour jaunt down the Copalita's final 5km to the

ocean at La Bocana (per person M$300 to M$350, minimum two people, available all year and suitable for children).

Prices include pickup at your accommodations. Rafting trips sold by agencies are very often with Huatulco Expedicones.

🛏 Sleeping

You'll find all budget and many midrange options in La Crucecita. Further midrange possibilities are in Chahué and Santa Cruz. The top-end resort hotels are at Tangolunda and beyond. Midrange and top-end places tend to raise their rates dramatically for a couple of weeks around Christmas–New Year's and Easter, and from about mid-July to mid-August.

Air-and-lodging package deals are your best bet for a good-value vacation in a top-end Huatulco hotel.

Hotel Jaroje Centro HOTEL $
(☑958-583-48-01; www.hotelhuatulco.com.mx; Bugambilia 304, La Crucecita; d/q M$350/450; ◉❀⊛) Bright Jaroje, two blocks south of the Plaza Principal, has 13 large, clean, white rooms with mosquito screens, air-con and either one king-size bed or two normal-size double beds. Good value.

Posada Leo PENSION $
(☑958-587-26-01; posadaleo_hux@hotmail.com; Bugambilia 302, La Crucecita; r with/without air-con M$350/300; ◉❀⊛) A friendly little budget spot 2½ blocks south of the Plaza Principal. Its six smallish but neat and well-kept rooms all have hot-water bathrooms and mosquito-screened windows.

★ **Misión de los Arcos** HOTEL $
(☑958-587-01-65; www.misiondelosarcos.com; Gardenia 902, La Crucecita; r M$595, ste M$714-833; ◉❀⊛) This well-run, welcoming hotel, half a block off the Plaza Principal, is embellished by a touch of colonial style and interior greenery. It has big, bright rooms with air-con, very comfortable beds and homey touches, for which you would pay a lot more in many other places. There's walk-through access to the excellent Terra-Cotta restaurant (p484), under the same ownership.

Hotel Posada Edén Costa HOTEL $$
(☑958-587-24-80; www.edencosta.com; Zapoteco 26, Chahué; r/ste incl breakfast M$600/900; ℗◉❀⊛⊞) Swiss- and Laotian-owned Edén Costa, 500m inland from Bahía Chahué, has attractive rooms with nice touches including colorful bird murals. Most rooms have two

BAHÍA SAN AGUSTÍN

The long, sandy beach here, 14km west of Santa Cruz Huatulco, is backed by a fishing village, and in contrast to Huatulco's other settlements, there's no resort-type development – just a line of rustic *comedores* (simple restaurants) stretching along the beach, serving seafood and fish dishes for M$80 to M$130 and simple *antojitos* (typical Mexican snacks) for less. Usually the waters of the bay are calm, and there is coral with very good snorkeling around the rocks in the bay and at Playa Riscalillo round the corner to the east.

San Agustín is popular with Mexicans on weekends and vacations, but quiet at other times. Some *comedores* rent snorkel gear, and most of them can arrange boats to Riscalillo or Playa La India. Many also have hammocks for rent overnight, or tent space; they may let you stay free if you eat with them. **El Tronco** (☑ cell 958-1031808; 2-person tents M$150, hammock per person M$50; ℗) toward the north end is run by a friendly family and has a tent to rent as well as hammocks.

A 13km dirt road heads south to San Agustín from a crossroads on Hwy 200, 1.7km west of the airport. Buses between Huatulco and Pochutla will drop you at the crossroads, where taxis wait to carry people to San Agustín (M$110, or M$22 per person *colectivo*).

double beds and overlook the central pool. Suites have their own kitchens. The attached restaurant, L'échalote (p485), is a big bonus.

Hotel María Mixteca
HOTEL $$

(☑ 958-587-09-90; www.mariamixtecahuatulco.com; Guamuchil 204, La Crucecita; r US$45; ℗❄⊛) María Mixteca offers 14 prettily decorated yellow-and-white rooms on two upper floors around an open patio, with supercomfy beds, air-conditioning, good bathrooms and room safes. It's half a block east of the Plaza Principal.

Las Palmas
SUITES $$$

(☑ cell 958-1091448; www.laspalmashuatulco.com; Camino a Playa La Entrega; casitas/villas US$226/893; ℗❄⊛✈) On a lovely site looking down on little Playa Violín, along the road between Santa Cruz and Playa La Entrega, Las Palmas is a marvelous discovery for couples, families or larger groups who have a vehicle and want to self-cater. The three bright, spacious four-bedroom villas boast large sitting/eating areas opening on to their own infinity pools.

The five smaller but also-attractive casitas (for up to four people) share a kitchen, pool and large *palapa* dining area. The tilework and crafts are beautiful, kayaks and mountain bikes are provided free, and the whole place has an airy feel.

Camino Real Zaashila
LUXURY HOTEL $$$

(☑ 958-583-03-00; www.caminoreal.com; Blvd Juárez 5, Tangolunda; r from M$2410; ℗⊜❄⊛✈) This beautifully landscaped, modern hacienda-style property has a fabulously enormous pool, 120m long, in lovely gardens opening straight on to the beach. There are 151 rooms, most with sea view and many with their own small pool, plus three fine restaurants.

✗ Eating

★Antojitos Los Gallos
MEXICAN $

(cnr Carrizal & Palma Real, La Crucecita; dishes M$25-70; ⊙2-10:30pm Tue-Sun; ☎) There are few better places to eat in Huatulco than this very simple little diner serving unadulterated Mexican home-style cooking. You could start with *caldo tlalpeño* (a soup of chicken, veggies, chili and herbs, called 'traditional chicken soup' on the English-language menu) followed by a *tlayuda* with *res deshebrada* (shredded beef), or maybe some enchiladas. But really, everything is good here.

It does inventive fruit drinks too, like *agua de pepino y limón* (cucumber and lemon cordial).

Casa Mayor
CAFE $

(Bugambilia 601, La Crucecita; dishes M$65-130; ⊙8am-midnight Mon-Sat, 4pm-midnight Sun) ✎ Overlooking the Plaza Principal, Casa Mayor serves good organic Oaxacan coffee and is good for breakfast, baguettes, *antojitos* and cocktails too. A smaller **branch** (cnr Gardenia & Guanacastle; coffees M$15-40; ⊙7:30am-11pm) ✎ on the far corner of the plaza does the same excellent coffee and other drinks.

Terra-Cotta
MEXICAN, INTERNATIONAL $$

(☑958-587-12-28; Gardenia 902, La Crucecita; breakfast dishes M$40-90, mains M$70-170; ⊙7:30am-

11pm; ❄ 🛜 📶) Highly popular Terra-Cotta, half a block north of the Plaza Principal, has soothing air-con, and good service complements its excellent food: breakfasts, shrimp, steaks, fish, pasta, baguettes and ice cream.

Giordanas
ITALIAN **$$**

(📋 958-583-43-24; www.giordanas-delizie.com; cnr Gardenia & Palma Real, La Crucecita; pastas M$90-130, antipasti M$120-220; ⏰ noon-10pm Tue-Sat; 🛜 📋) The talented Italian chef here makes almost everything herself, including the pasta. Delicious options include ravioli with a choice of five fillings and nine sauces, meat or vegetarian lasagne, and some pretty good antipasti including carpaccios and Parma ham with melon. And there's Italian wine from M$50/250 per glass/bottle. Giordana also does a great choice of baguettes with Italian cheeses and salamis.

★ L'échalote
EUROPEAN, MEXICAN **$$$**

(📋 958-587-24-80; www.edencosta.com; Hotel Posada Edén Costa, Zapoteco 26, Chahué; mains M$110-220; ⏰ 2-11pm Tue-Sun; ❄) The French-Swiss kitchen prepares top-notch French, Mexican and Mediterranean dishes. Specialties include snails, *osso buco* and fish of the day in a creamy leek sauce. The desserts and French and Italian wines (from M$350) aren't too shabby either, and you can round things off with a supersmooth Armagnac.

Between 2pm and 6pm it also offers 'gourmet cantina' with a choice of tempting free *botanas* (small platefuls) with each drink.

Azul Profundo
SEAFOOD **$$$**

(📋 958-583-03-00; Camino Real Zaashila, Blvd Juárez 5, Tangolunda; mains M$200-300; ⏰ 7-11pm Mon, Wed, Fri, Sun) Tangolunda's big hotels offer a choice of expensive bars, coffee shops and restaurants. For a romantic, no-expense-spared dinner you won't go wrong at the Camino Real's Azul Profundo, right by the beach, with its delicious Mexican-Thai fusion dishes. Reservations required.

🍸 Drinking & Nightlife

La Crema
BAR

(📋 958-587-07-02; www.lacremahuatulco.com; Gardenia 311, La Crucecita; ⏰ 7pm-2am; 🛜) A lively mixed crowd of locals and visitors knocks 'em back at this quirky, dark and spacious rock-and reggae-themed den overlooking the Plaza Principal. It boasts loud tunes (often with live bands on Fridays or Saturdays), the best cocktail list in town and terrific wood-oven

pizza (medium size MS$90 to M$145). The entrance is just off the plaza on Gardenia.

Palatería Zamora
JUICE BAR

(Plaza Principal, La Crucecita; drinks M$20-66; ⏰ 7:15am-11:45pm) Thirst-zapping Zamora blends up a full range of cooling fresh-fruit juices, *licuados,* ice creams and *paletas* (popsicles).

ℹ️ Information

Tourist Information Kiosk (Plaza Principal, La Crucecita; ⏰ 9am-9pm) Has helpful staff.

ℹ️ Getting There & Away

AIR

There are direct international flights to/from Houston, USA, with United (www.united.com); and from November to May (or parts of that period) to/from several Canadian airports with Air Canada (www.aircanada.com), Air Transat (www.airtransat.ca), Sunwing Airlines (www.flysunwing.com) and WestJet (www.westjet.com), and to/from Minneapolis with Sun Country Airlines (www.suncountry.com).

Huatulco Airport (📋 958-581-90-04) is located 400m north of Hwy 200, 15km west of La Crucecita.

Aeroméxico (📋 958-581-91-26; www.aeromexico.com; airport; ⏰ 9:30am-6:30pm) Mexico City twice daily.

Aerotucán (📋 958-587-24-27; www.aerotucan.com.mx; Local 104, Plaza El Madero, Guamuchil, La Crucecita; ⏰ 11:30am-4pm Mon-Sat) Flies 13-seat Cessnas daily to/from Oaxaca (M$2042). Also has an airport office (📋 958-581-90-85; Aairport; ⏰ 8am-noon). Flights are sometimes cancelled or rescheduled at short notice.

Interjet (📋 cell 958-1051336; www.interjet.com.mx; Plaza Chahué, Blvd Juárez, Chahué; ⏰ 9am-7pm Mon-Fri, to 6pm Sat & Sun) Mexico City at least twice daily. Also has an airport office (📋 958-581-91-16; airport; ⏰ 9am-5pm).

Magnicharters (📋 800-201-14-04; www.magnicharters.com) Mexico City daily except Tuesday.

TAR Aerolíneas (www.tarmexico.com) Oaxaca four times weekly, Guadalajara and Toluca twice.

Volaris (in Mexico City 📋 55-1102-8000; www.volaris.com) Mexico City at least twice weekly.

BUS, VAN & TAXI COLECTIVO

Some buses to Huatulco are marked 'Santa Cruz Huatulco,' but they still terminate in La Crucecita. Make sure your bus is not headed to Santa María Huatulco, which is some way inland.

Taxis colectivos to Pochutla (M$30, one hour) leave from the street corner beside Soriana hypermarket on Blvd Chahué, 200m west of the OCC Bus Station in La Crucecita.

Central Camionera (Carpinteros s/n, Sector V) Located 1.2km northwest of central La Crucecita; used by Turistar (deluxe), AltaMar (1st-class), Transportes Rápidos de Pochutla (TRP; 2nd-class) and Istmeños (2nd-class) buses.

Expressos Colombo (cnr Gardenia & Sabalí, La Crucecita) Passenger vans to Oaxaca; terminal is 400m north of the Plaza Principal.

Huatulco 2000 (Guamuchil, La Crucecita) Passenger vans to Oaxaca. Located 150m east of the Plaza Principal.

OCC Bus Station (Blvd Chahué, La Crucecita) Located 500m north of the Plaza Principal; used by ADO GL (deluxe), OCC (1st-class) and Sur and AU (2nd-class) buses.

CAR & MOTORCYCLE

Europcar (☑ 958-583-47-51; www.europcar. com.mx; Local 103, Plaza El Madero, Guamuchil, La Crucecita; ◷ 8am-6pm) Reasonable rates and good service. Also has an airport desk (☑ 958-581-90-94; airport; ◷ 8:30am-6:30pm).

Los Tres Reyes (☑ cell 958-1051376; http:// lostresreyescarrent.com; Lote 20, Blvd Chahué manzana 1, La Crucecita; ◷ 8am-8pm) Efficient local firm with good rates.

❶ Getting Around

TO/FROM THE AIRPORT

Taxis autorizados (authorized taxis) cost M$130 per person on a shared basis, or M$400 for a whole cab, from the airport to La Crucecita, Santa Cruz, Chahué or Tangolunda. Get tickets at airport desks. A whole cab is to Mazunte is M$983, and M$1920 to Puerto Escondido, but you can usually get one for half those prices, or less, by walking 300m down to Hwy 200, where drivers wait at the airport intersection. Or catch a bus from the same intersection to La Crucecita (M$8) or Pochutla (M$18): they pass about every 15 minutes in both directions from about 6am to 8pm.

BUS & TAXI

Blue-and-white local buses run every few minutes during daylight. To Santa Cruz Huatulco (M$4, five minutes) they go from Plaza El Madero mall on Guamuchil, two blocks east of the plaza in La Crucecita. To the Central Camionera (M$4, five minutes) they go from Guamuchil one block east of the plaza.

Taxis from central La Crucecita cost M$25 to Santa Cruz or the Central Camionera, M$38 to Tangolunda, M$54 to Playa La Entrega and M$66 to Bahía Maguey.

SCOOTER

Zipping around on a scooter can be a fun way to get around Huatulco. **Tu Moto** (☑ cell 958-1012522; Guarumbo 306, La Crucecita; ◷ 9am-2pm & 4-7pm Mon-Sat, 10am-2pm Sun) rents good Japanese bikes, with two helmets per bike, from US$35 per day (discounts for more than one day). There's generally no insurance available with scooter rental.

BUSES & VANS FROM BAHÍAS DE HUATULCO

DESTINATION	FARE (M$)	DURATION (HR)	FREQUENCY (DAILY)
Mexico City (Sur) via Puerto Escondido	956-1235	14-15	AltaMar 3:30pm, Turistar 4pm
Mexico City (TAPO) via Salina Cruz	990-1188	14-15	4 from OCC terminal
Oaxaca via San José del Pacífico	200	7	13 Expressos Colombo, 8 Huatulco 2000
Oaxaca via Salina Cruz	368-452	8	4 from OCC terminal
Pochutla	25-60	1	23 from OCC terminal, TRP every 10-15min 5:30am-8pm
Puerto Escondido	72-138	2½	23 from OCC terminal
Salina Cruz	100-188	3	Istmeños hourly 4am-6pm, 13 from OCC terminal
San Cristóbal de las Casas	549	10	OCC 9pm, 11:55pm
Tehuantepec	110-208	3½	Istmeños hourly 4am-6pm, 12 from OCC terminal

Barra de la Cruz

POP 740

This indigenous Chontal village, about 25km east of Huatulco, offers surfers the chance to catch some amazing waves and everyone the chance to get off the grid and slow right down. The right-hand point break, off the beach 1.5km from the rustic village, gets up to a double overhead and is long and fast. Good swells for experienced surfers are frequent from March to early October and generally at their best in June and July. November to February brings good waves for learners.

🏃 Activities

There's not much to do except surf and swim, but Barra's beautiful long beach has showers, toilets and a good *comedor* with hammocks and shade. The road to the beach is open from 7am to 8pm and the municipality charges M$30 per person to pass along it.

You can rent surfboards (per day M$100 to M$150) at El Chontal or Canañas Pepe accommodations. El Chontal's English-speaking owner **Pablo Narváez** (☑ cell 958-1095087; www.facebook.com/pablo.narvaez.144) also gives surf classes (three to four hours for one or two people M$450), and expertly leads bird-watching tours (three or four hours per person M$350) around the very varied local habitats.

🛏 Sleeping & Eating

A handful of simple accommodations clusters around the entrance to the beach road.

Cabañas Pepe   CABAÑAS $

(☑ cell 958-1084200; c-pepecastillo@hotmail.com; camping/cabañas per person M$50/100, mains M$50-70; ⊙ comedor 7am-9:30pm; 🅿) Pepe's has well-built wood-and-palm-thatch cabins with fans, mosquito nets and shared toilets and showers, plus a large *palapa comedor* with couches, table tennis and a good selection of dishes. Owner Pepe speaks English.

El Chontal   ROOMS $

(☑ cell 958-1095087; pablo_rafting@yahoo.com; r with/without air-con M$350/250, mains M$90-120; 🅿 ❄) El Chontal has three quite large, bright rooms with shared bathrooms, and further air-con rooms in a nearby house, and serves good chicken, seafood and other dishes under its large *palapa*.

Comedor   MEXICAN $$

(mains M$70-100; ⊙ 9am-6pm) The community-run beach *comedor* is good for breakfast and lunch. Try its excellent *sopa de mariscos* (seafood soup).

❶ Getting There & Around

The 2.5km road to Barra de la Cruz heads off Hwy 200 2km east of Puente Zimatán bridge. From the Central Camionera in Bahías de Huatulco, *taxis colectivos* run to Barra (M$25, 40 minutes) about every half-hour from 7am to 5pm (less often in the middle of the day and on Sunday). They charge an additional M$15 to carry a surfboard. A private taxi costs around M$200 from central La Crucecita or M$300 from Huatulco airport, with or without boards.

ISTHMUS OF TEHUANTEPEC

The southern half of the 200km-wide Isthmus of Tehuantepec (teh-wahn-teh-*pek*), Mexico's narrow waist, forms the flat, hot, humid eastern end of Oaxaca state. Indigenous Zapotec culture is strong here, with its own regional twists. In 1496 the isthmus Zapotecs repulsed the Aztecs from the fortress of Guiengola, near Tehuantepec, and the isthmus never became part of the Aztec empire. An independent spirit pervades the region to this day.

Few travelers linger here, but if you do you'll encounter a lively, friendly populace whose open and confident women take leading roles in business and government. Isthmus people let loose their love of music, dancing and partying in numerous *velas* (fiestas) lasting several days. If you're here for one of these, you'll see women showing off highly colorful *huipiles,* gold and silver jewelry, skirts embroidered with fantastic silk flowers, and a variety of odd headgear. Many fiestas feature the *tirada de frutas,* in which women climb on roofs and throw fruit on the men below!

Of the three main towns, isthmus culture is stronger in Tehuantepec and Juchitán than it is in Salina Cruz, which is dominated by its oil refinery. All three towns can be uncomfortable in the heat and humidity of the day, but evening breezes are deliciously refreshing.

Salina Cruz

This port city of 77,000 bustles with Mexican life, but it's not a pretty place and there's no pressing reason to come here except for transportation connections. The main bus stations are Estrella Blanca (cnr Frontera & Tampico), 500m north of the central plaza, with 1st-class AltaMar services, and ADO (Calle 1° de Mayo), 500m further north, with deluxe, 1st-class and 2nd-class services.

Tehuantepec

971 / POP 42,000

Tehuantepec, 245km from Oaxaca city, is a friendly but hot and sweaty town, and most travelers blow through here on their way to somewhere else. June and August are the main months for partying in the fiestas of Tehuantepec's 15 barrios (neighborhoods), each of which has its own colonial church, many of which are prettily painted and floodlit after dark. There's a Tourist Information Office (Hwy 185; ⊙9am-7pm Mon-Sat) beside the highway two blocks west from the central plaza.

◉ Sights

Ex-Convento Rey Cosijopí   HISTORIC BUILDING
(☑971-715-01-14; Callejón Rey Cosijopí; ⊙8am-8pm Mon-Fri, 9am-2pm Sat) FREE This former Dominican monastery, built in the 16th century, is now Tehuantepec's Casa de la Cultura, where arts and crafts workshops and activities are held. It bears traces of old frescoes, and some rooms hold modest exhibits of traditional dress, archaeological finds and historical photos. It's on a short lane off Guerrero, 400m northeast of the central plaza.

Market   MARKET
Tehuantepec's dim indoor market is open daily on the west side of the plaza, and spills out into surrounding streets.

Guiengola   ARCHAEOLOGICAL SITE
(⊙9am-6pm) FREE This panoramic old hillside Zapotec stronghold was where King Cosijoeza fought off the Aztecs in 1496. It's 7km north of Hwy 190, from a turnoff just past Puente Las Tejas bridge 11km west of Tehuantepec. The last 2km to the ruins are a sweaty uphill walk through tropical woodland from the end of the unpaved approach road.

The unrestored site includes the remains of two pyramids, a ball court, a 64-room palace-type complex, several tombs, a thick defensive wall and several caves. There may or may not be any staff in attendance: ask at Tehuantepec's tourist office before going.

🛏 Sleeping & Eating

At night the central plaza's east side is lined with tables and chairs beside carts serving tacos and other inexpensive fare.

Hostal Emilia   PENSION $
(☑971-715-00-08; h.oasis@hotmail.com; Ocampo 8; r for up to 3 with/without air-con M$420/300; ⊜@🖤) A block south of the plaza, Emilia has six reasonably comfy rooms, most with shared bathrooms. The sign just says 'Hostal Hospedaje.' You can get a good M$45 breakfast in the cafe next door.

Hotel Calli   HOTEL $$
(☑971-715-00-85; www.hotelcalli.com; Carretera Cristóbal Colón, Km 790; s/d M$750/870, restaurant mains M$75-200; 🅿🕸🖤🛋) The good-sized, bland rooms, designed primarily for bus-tour groups, offer cable TV, air-con and small balconies. Ample common areas include a reasonable restaurant and a pool in grassy gardens. It's beside Hwy 185, 1km east of the main bus station.

Restaurante Scarú   MEXICAN $$
(Callejón Leona Vicario 4; mains M$80-150; ⊙8am-9pm Mon-Sat; 🖤) Scarú occupies an 18th-century house with a courtyard and colorful murals. Sit beneath a fan, quaff a limonada and sample one of the varied dishes on offer. Seafood is the specialty and the prawns stuffed with acelga (chard) are a good choice.

To find it go 200m south from the east side of the plaza to the end of Juárez, then one block east.

ⓘ Getting There & Around

Tehuantepec's main bus station, known as La Terminal, is by Hwy 185, 1.5km northeast of the central plaza. It's shared by deluxe, 1st-class and 2nd-class services of the ADO/OCC group. Second-class Istmeños buses to Juchitán (M$27, 30 minutes) and Salina Cruz (M$20, 30 minutes) stop on the highway outside La Terminal at least every half-hour during daylight.

Juchitán

971 / POP 75,000

Isthmus culture is strong in this friendly town, where about 30 different neighborhood velas fill the calendar with music, dancing, drink-

CONCEPCIÓN BAMBA

The coast west from Salina Cruz is spectacular, with long, sweeping sandy beaches, monster dunes and forested mountains rising just inland. It has surfers in raptures for its long-peeling, sand-bottom, right-hand point breaks and several beach and jetty breaks. Concepción Bamba, or La Bamba as it's known, 40km west of Salina Cruz, sits on a 6km beach with two point breaks in the middle, and stands out because it's home to easily the area's most appealing accommodations. The surfing season is from about March to October but swells don't come every day, so check the forecasts.

There is almost no tourism infrastructure along this coast except for a number of 'surf camps' in and around Salina Cruz itself, which cater to fly-in surfers willing to spend US$150 to US$300 a night for full-board packages with daily transportation to the surf spots. Some of these 'camps' (some of which are just houses in the city) have gained a reputation for chasing off independent foreign surfers from the best spots so that their clients can have the waves to themselves.

Cocoleoco Surf Camp (☑ 322-221-56-53; www.cabanabambasurfmx.com; camping per person US$5-7, cabañas s US$15, d M$25-40, extra person US$10; 🅿🤖) at La Bamba is a different matter – a perfect laid-back base open to everybody, in spacious grounds with appealing *cabañas* (some with private bathroom), a roofed camping area, good French/Mexican/international meals from March to October (lunch mains M$50 to M$80, dinner mains M$100 to M$120), simple local meals at other times, and also a guests' cooking area. A dozen fine surf spots lie within a 30-minute drive west or east, and they can drive up to four people for a day's surfing for US$50 per person – or if you have your own vehicle, local guides will accompany you for US$50 per day. Surf classes are available, and you can also enjoy horseback riding, kayaking or a temascal. Reservations are worthwhile. There's a community turtle camp on the beach, where turtle eggs (laid between October and March) are collected and incubated in a protected enclosure, with hatchlings being released into the ocean after about six weeks.

The signposted turnoff to Concepción Bamba is at Km 352 on Hwy 200: a 2.5km unpaved road leads to the village, with Cocoleoco on its far side, then it's 800m further to the beach. Buses between Huatulco and Salina Cruz will drop you at the turnoff, where three-wheeler moto-taxis (M$10 per person) run to the village from about 7am to 6pm. There are also *taxis colectivos* (shared taxis) to the village from Salina Cruz (M$40, plus M$10 for a surfboard), leaving about hourly, 7am to 7pm, from a lot on Hwy 200 a few steps west of its intersection with Blvd Salina Cruz in the north of town.

ing, eating and fun from April to September. Juchitán is also famed for its *muxes* – openly gay, frequently cross-dressing men, who are fully accepted in local society and hold their own *vela* in November.

⊙ Sights

Jardín Juárez   PLAZA

Jardín Juárez is the lively central square. In the busy market on its east side you'll find locally made hammocks, isthmus women's costumes, and maybe iguana on the *comedor* menus.

Lidxi Guendabiaani'   ART CENTER

(Casa de la Cultura; ☑ 971-711-32-08; Belisario Domínguez; ☉ 10am-3pm & 5-8pm Mon-Fri, 10am-noon Sat) FREE Beside the San Vicente Ferrer church one block south and one west

of Jardín Juárez, Lidxi Guendabiaani' is set around a big patio. It's used mainly for arts classes but also has a gallery and a small archaeological museum.

🛏 Sleeping & Eating

In the evening, economical open-air *comedores* (food stalls) set up tables around Jardín Juárez cooking up local specialties like *garnachas* (small corn tortillas with toppings of cheese, beans or pork) or folded-over *tlayudas*.

Hotel Central   HOTEL $

(☑ 971-712-20-19; www.hotelcentral.com.mx; Av Efraín Gómez 30; s M$362, d M$420-453; 🌀❄@🤖) A good-value hotel 1½ blocks east of Jardín Juárez, offering bare, freshly painted rooms with comfy beds, good-sized bath

BUSES FROM THE ISTHMUS OF TEHUANTEPEC

From Salina Cruz

DESTINATION	FARE (M$)	DURATION (HR)	FREQUENCY (DAILY)
Bahías de Huatulco	136-188	3	13 ADO, 4 AltaMar
Juchitán	56-78	1	33 ADO
Oaxaca	278-336	5-5½	8 ADO
Pochutla	171-208	4	8 ADO, 4 AltaMar
Puerto Escondido	236-274	5	9 ADO, 4 AltaMar
San Cristóbal de las Casas	404	7	2 ADO
Tehuantepec	38-50	½	33 ADO

From Tehuantepec's main station

DESTINATION	FARE (M$)	DURATION (HR)	FREQUENCY (DAILY)
Bahías de Huatulco	152-176	3¼	6
Mexico City (TAPO or Sur)	786-1154	12	8
Oaxaca	150-260	5	24
Pochutla	224-246	4½	4
Puerto Escondido	274-288	5½	4

From Juchitán

DESTINATION	FARE (M$)	DURATION (HR)	FREQUENCY (DAILY)
Bahías de Huatulco	172-248	3½-4	8
Mexico City (TAPO or Sur)	740-1090	12	7
Oaxaca	165-282	5-5½	26
Pochutla	230-254	4½-5	6
San Cristóbal de las Casas	362	5½-6	3
Tapachula	374-414	7½	3

rooms and bottled drinking water, though some have little natural light.

Casona de Santa Cecilia HOTEL $$
(📞971-281-00-63; casonasantacecilia@hotmail.com; Hidalgo 48B; s/d M$500/650; P❄🛜) A solid choice one block north and 1½ east of Jardín Juárez, Santa Cecilia provides clean, bright rooms with photos of local life, some with king-size beds and/or balconies over the street.

La Tossta MEDITERRANEAN, MEXICAN $$
(Av 16 de Septiembre 37; mains M$90-220; ⏱7am-midnight; 🛜) With a bright, contemporary ambience and some creative recipe combinations (breaded shrimps with coco-nut, beef medallions in port sauce), this is quite a surprise in Juchitán.

ℹ Getting There & Around

The main **bus station** (Prolongación 16 de Septiembre), used by deluxe, 1st-class and 2nd-class services of ADO/OCC, is 100m south of Hwy 190 on the northern edge of town. Many buses depart inconveniently between 11pm and 7am. 'Terminal-Centro' buses run between the bus station and the central Jardín Juárez. A taxi costs M$25.

Second-class Istmeños buses to Tehuantepec (M$27, 30 minutes) and Salina Cruz (M$40, one hour) leave at least every 30 minutes during daylight, from the next corner south from the main terminal.

Central Pacific Coast

Includes ➡

Mazatlán	493
San Blas	507
Tepic	511
Sayulita	515
Puerto Vallarta	518
Bahía de Navidad	535
Manzanillo	538
Boca de Pascuales	542
Michoacán Coast	543
Troncones	546
Ixtapa	548
Zihuatanejo	550
Acapulco	562

Best Places to Eat

➡ Héctor's Bistro (p501)
➡ La Alberca (p506)
➡ Café des Artistes (p530)
➡ El Manglito (p537)
➡ Bistro del Mar (p557)

Best Places to Stay

➡ Techos de México (p513)
➡ Siete Lunas (p516)
➡ Pepe's Hideaway (p540)
➡ Troncones Point Hostel (p547)
➡ Aura del Mar (p554)

Why Go?

Gigantic aquamarine waves provide the backdrop and pulsating rhythm to any visit to Mexico's central Pacific coast, a land of stunning beaches and giant sunsets. You can indulge in all the tropical clichés here: eating sublime seafood under simple palm-frond roofs, drinking chilled coconut water while lounging in a hammock, enjoying poolside cocktails at an upmarket resort. The nightlife is great and there's a beach for everyone, whether you prefer yours backed by high-rise hotels or tumbledown cabins.

There's even more going on in the ocean, where you can surf world-class breaks and spot humpback whales breaching on the horizon, battalions of mother turtles arriving to lay their eggs, pelicans flying in formation or pods of dolphins rising from the waves.

Whether your thing is a cushy week of beachside pampering or a budget quest for the perfect wave, the Pacific coast has it covered.

When to Go
Puerto Vallarta

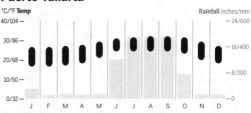

Feb Perfect beach weather. Carnaval reigns in Mazatlán.

Jun–Aug Surf's up and prices down at Pacific Mexico's prime surfing destinations.

Nov & Dec Puerto Vallarta celebrates everything from sportfishing to mariachis to gay pride.

Central Pacific Coast Highlights

1 Hanging out in the beautifully restored center of **Mazatlán** (p493), watching sunsets with a cold Pacífico beer.

2 Exploring the curious island village of **Mexcaltitán** (p506), crunching its shrimp and wondering at its history.

3 People-watching on the beautiful *malecón* (beach promenade) in **Puerto Vallarta** (p518).

4 Surfing aggressive barrel swells in **Boca de Pascuales** (p542).

5 Thrilling at the fearless finesse of **Clavadistas de la Quebrada** (cliff divers, p563) in nightlife-rich **Acapulco** (p562).

6 Soaking up the party vibe along the sands and streets of **Sayulita** (p515).

7 Enjoying the easy tempo and local hospitality in charming **Zihuatanejo** (p550).

8 Chowing down on seafood on the long beach at paradisiacal **Barra de Potosí** (p559).

9 Exploring surf beaches and traditional settlements on the **Michoacán coast** (p543).

10 Browsing the excellent collection of indigenous art at **Museo Regional de Nayarit** (p511) in Tepic.

❶ Getting There & Away

There are direct international flights from the US and Canada to resort towns such as Puerto Vallarta, Mazatlán, Acapulco and Zihuatanejo. For those traveling by car, the toll roads make for easy sailing, but are pricey. High-quality bus services connect the resort centers to inland Mexico.

Between towns, coastal Hwy 200 has had an up-and-down safety record, especially in the states of Nayarit, Michoacán and Guerrero, which still have a reputation for being unsafe at night.

❶ Getting Around

Bus travel is easy and comfortable. Second-class buses serve nearly every community, large or small, while more upmarket buses serve bigger towns.

If you're driving, note that nearly everything on coastal Hwy 200 – service stations, stores, tire shops – closes around sundown.

Mazatlán

✑ 669 / POP 440,000

Thanks to 20km of sandy beaches, Mazatlán became one of Mexico's most alluring and inviting beach destinations in the mid-20th century, before it lurched past its prime into a midmarket, package-tourist category. Recently, however, Mazatlán's historic core – referred to as 'tropical neoclassical' – has been restored and peopled by the creative class. The result is a coastal city with plenty of allure. A boldly engineered new highway from the interior means the beaches are now more accessible to Mexicans too, and the good-time vibes have returned.

To take the pulse of Mazatlán, don't linger too long in the Zona Dorada (Golden Zone), Mazatlán's traditional tourist playground. Instead head straight for the city's characterfully refurbished old town and its gloriously unrefurbished *malecón*, where you can view magic sunsets from bars and restaurants that still evoke the 1950s.

⊙ Sights

◎ Old Mazatlán

★ **Old Mazatlán** AREA
(Map p498) Mazatlán's restored old town is a picturesque compendium of noble 19th-century buildings and pretty plazas. It's set back from **Playa Olas Altas**, a small cove beach whose waterfront road strongly evokes the 1950s, with its old-fashioned bars and hotels. Though overlooked by the ugly radio masts of Cerro de la Nevería, this old quarter is delightful, with student life, and numerous art galleries, cafes, restaurants and bars.

★ **Plaza Machado** SQUARE
(Map p498; cnr Av Carnaval & Constitución) Sleepy during the day, this gorgeous tree-lined plaza comes alive in the evening, when market stalls pop up, couples stroll hand-in-hand and its numerous terrace restaurants are serenaded by musicians. It's a slightly touristy but very romantic scene.

★ **Teatro Ángela Peralta** THEATER
(Map p498; www.culturamazatlan.com; Carnaval s/n; self-guided visit M$15; ⊙ 9am-2pm & 4-6pm) Named after a 19th-century soprano and constructed between 1869 and 1874, this 1366-seat theater just off Plaza Machado was a thriving center of local cultural life for nearly a century. Fallen into decay, it was slated for demolition by the city government before dedicated local citizens came to its rescue in the late 1980s. The three-level interior has been restored to its former splendor, and all kinds of cultural events are again staged here, including the annual Festival Cultural Mazatlán.

Catedral CATHEDRAL
(Map p498; cnr Juárez & Calle 21 de Marzo; ⊙ 6am-1pm & 4-7:30pm) At the center of the old town is this striking 19th-century cathedral, with high yellow twin towers. The dramatic interior has gilt ceiling roses supporting chandeliers and blocks of stone in alternating colors. It's located on the **Plaza Principal**, which attracts legions of pigeon feeders, and local families who patronize businesses on the clogged arteries that surround it.

Casa Machado MUSEUM
(Map p498; Constitución 77; adult/student M$20/10; ⊙ 9am-6pm) Worth a peek is the Casa Machado, a 19th-century house filled with antique French and Austrian furniture, Carnaval costumes, historic photos and other items. Its 2nd-floor terrace affords a panoramic view over Plaza Machado. It was closed for restoration at the time of research.

Museo Arqueológico MUSEUM
(INAH; Map p498; ✆ 669-981-14-55; www.inah. gob.mx; Sixto Osuna 76; adult/child under 12yr

Greater Mazatlán

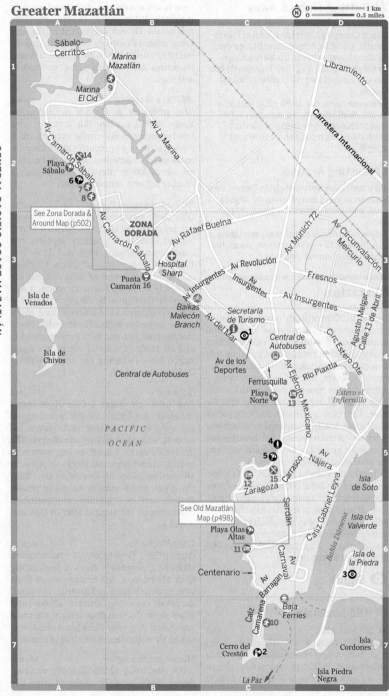

Greater Mazatlán

◎ Sights
1 Acuario Mazatlán C4
2 El Faro.. C7
3 Isla de la Piedra D6
4 Monumento al Pescador....................C5
5 Playa Norte C5
6 Playa Sábalo A2

◎ Activities, Courses & Tours
7 Aqua Sports Center............................A2
8 Aries Fleet A2
9 Flota Bibi B1
10 Flota Sábalo..C7

◎ Sleeping
11 Casa Lucila.. C6
12 Las 7 Maravillas...................................C5
13 Suitel... C4

◎ Eating
14 Carlos & Lucía's A2
15 Mercado de Mariscos Playa Norte C5

◎ Drinking & Nightlife
16 Fiesta Land B3

M$39/free, Sun free; ☉9am-6pm Tue-Fri, 10am-2pm Sat & Sun) The small but absorbing Museo Arqueológico displays pre-Hispanic archaeological finds accompanied by fascinating wall texts in Spanish and English.

Clavadistas   CLIFF DIVERS
(Map p498; Paseo Olas Altas) Although not as famous, nor as spectacular, as Acapulco's cliff divers, local *clavadistas* cast their bodies from a couple of platforms into the treacherous ocean swells for your enjoyment. Tip accordingly. They usually perform around lunchtime and in the late afternoon, but they won't risk their necks until a crowd has assembled.

Museo de Arte   MUSEUM
(Map p498; ☑669-981-55-92; www.facebook.com/museodeartedemazatlan; cnr Sixto Osuna & Carranza; ☉9am-2pm & 4-6pm Mon-Sat) FREE This is a small museum in a sprawling colonial courtyard complex, which makes a convincing case for the vitality and innovation of contemporary Mexican art with changing exhibitions of digital works, sculptures, prints and paintings.

Isla de la Piedra   ISLAND
(Map p494) A popular half-day escape from the city, this island is just southeast of Old Mazatlán and boasts a beautiful, long sandy beach bordered by coconut groves. Surfers come for the waves, and its simple *palapa* (thatched-roof) restaurants draw Mexican families, but outside weekends and high season you may have it to yourself. Though there are tours, it's easy to get here by water taxi (round trip M$30, every 10 minutes from 7am to 6pm) from the Playa Sur *embarcadero* (boat dock).

'Playa Sur' buses leave for the *embarcadero* from the corner of Serdán and Escobedo, two blocks southeast of Plaza Principal in Old Mazatlán.

El Faro   LIGHTHOUSE
(Map p494) At the Mazatlán peninsula's southern end, a prominent rocky outcrop is the base for this lighthouse, which is 135m above sea level and claimed, inaccurately, to be the second-highest in the world. You can climb up here (avoid the heat of the day) for a spectacular view of the city and coast.

◎ Zona Dorada

Onilikan   DISTILLERY
(Map p502; ☑669-668-23-70; www.onilikan.com; Av Playa Gaviotas 505; ☉8:30am-5:30pm Mon-Fri, 9am-2pm Sat) FREE This tiny distillery brews up delicious liquors from mango, agave and coffee, among other things. It's in the heart of the Zona Dorada, and you can just drop in for a friendly short explanation and free tasting.

Acuario Mazatlán   AQUARIUM
(Map p494; ☑669-981-78-15; www.acuariomazatlan.com; Av de los Deportes 111; adult/child M$110/80; ☉9:30am-6pm; ⊕) One of Mexico's largest aquariums has tanks with hundreds of species of fresh- and saltwater fish, a display of skeletons, and birds and frogs in the garden. Its sea lion shows and much-hyped shark-riding experience are the kinds of interaction with marine creatures that are a big concern to animal-welfare groups, who say that contact of this sort is harmful to the creatures and should be avoided.

Beaches
With over 20km of beaches, it's easy to find a suitable stretch of sand. The following beaches are listed in geographic order, from south to north.

In Old Mazatlán, crescent-shaped **Playa Olas Altas** (Map p498) is where tourism first flourished in the 1950s, although the pebbly beach is not ideal for swimming.

CENTRAL PACIFIC COAST MAZATLÁN

WORTH A TRIP

SINALOA'S COLONIAL GEMS

Several small, picturesque colonial towns in the Sierra Madre foothills make pleasant day trips from Mazatlán.

Concordia, founded in 1565, has an 18th-century church with a baroque facade and elaborately decorated columns. The village is known for its manufacture of high-quality pottery and hand-carved furniture. It's about a 45-minute drive east of Mazatlán; head southeast on Hwy 15 for 20km to Villa Unión, turn inland on Hwy 40 (the highway to Durango) and go another 20km.

Copala, 40km past Concordia on Hwy 40, was one of Mexico's first mining towns. It still has its colonial church (1748), period houses and cobblestone streets. It's a one-hour drive from Mazatlán.

Rosario, 76km southeast of Mazatlán on Hwy 15, is another colonial mining town. It was founded in 1655 and its most famous feature is the towering gold-leaf altar in its church, the Nuestra Señora del Rosario. You can also visit the home of beloved singer Lola Beltrán, whose long recording career made *ranchera* (Mexico's urban 'country music') popular in the mid-20th century.

In the mountains north of Mazatlán, **Cosalá** is a beautiful colonial mining village that dates from 1550. It has an 18th-century church, a mining museum in a colonial mansion on the plaza, and two simple but clean hotels. To get here, go north on Hwy 15 for 113km to the turnoff (opposite the turnoff for La Cruz de Alota on the coast) and then climb 45km into the mountains.

Backed by a promenade popular with joggers and strollers, the golden sands of **Playa Norte** (Map p494) begin just north of Old Mazatlán toward **Punta Camarón**, a rocky point dominated by the conspicuous, castle-like Fiesta Land nightclub complex.

The most luxurious hotels face pretty **Playa Las Gaviotas** (Map p502) and **Playa Sábalo** (Map p494), the latter extending north of the Zona Dorada. Sheltered by picturesque islands, here the waters are generally calm and ideal for swimming and water sports.

Further north, past **Marina El Cid** and the ever-evolving **Marina Mazatlán**, are **Playa Bruja**, a once-serene beach that has seen a flood of high-rise development in recent years, and **Playa Cerritos**. Both have a smattering of seafood restaurants and decent surf. To reach these northern beaches, catch a 'Cerritos Juárez' bus along Avenida Camarón Sábalo in the Zona Dorada.

Islands

Resembling breaching whales, the three photogenic rocks jutting from the sea offshore of the Zona Dorada offer secluded beaches and clear waters ideal for snorkeling – and great multitudes of seals and marine birds. On the left is **Isla de Chivos** (Goat Island); **Isla de Pájaros** (Bird Island) is on the right. Most visited is the one in the middle, **Isla de Venados** (Deer Island). The islands are part of a wildlife refuge designated to help protect the local birds and marine fauna. Any boat operator can take you out there, and there are also organized tours.

🏃 Activities

Mazatlán boasts some noteworthy surfing sites. There are several spots to rent boards and a handful of surf schools. Other water-sports equipment can be hired from the beaches of most large beachfront hotels.

Huana Coa Canopy   ADVENTURE SPORTS
(📞 669-990-11-00; www.huanacoamazatlan.com; per person US$75) This popular series of ziplines is set in the forested hills northeast of the city. The price includes transfers to and from your Mazatlán hotel. Book by phone, via accommodations providers or any travel agency.

Jah Surf School   SURFING
(📞 669-149-46-99; http://jahsurfschool.com; 2hr class for 1/2/3 people US$50/80/90; ⊕) Friendly, reader-recommended instructor who is happy to take on whole families. Also rents boards and equipment.

Aqua Sports Center WATER SPORTS

(Map p494; ☑669-913-04-51; www.aquasports center.com; Hotel El Cid, Av Camarón Sábalo s/n) The place to go for all sorts of water sports, including scuba diving, snorkeling rentals, Jet Skiing, banana-boat rides (for up to five passengers), parasailing, sailboat rentals and kayak rentals.

Estrella del Mar Golf Club GOLF

(☑800-727-46-53; www.estrelladelmar.com; Camino Isla de la Piedra 10; green fees Nov-Apr US$110, May-Oct US$75) Mazatlán's finest golf course is just south of the airport by the ocean.

Sportfishing

Handily located at the confluence of the Sea of Cortez and the Pacific Ocean, Mazatlán is world famous for sportfishing – especially for marlin, swordfish, sailfish, tuna and *dorado* (dolphin fish). It can be an expensive activity (US$400 to US$700 per boat per day, for boats ranging in size from 8m to 11m with four to nine people fishing); fishing from a 7m *super panga* (fiberglass skiff) is less expensive (around US$300 per day with up to four people fishing). A fishing license costs US$10 per person, and is usually organized by the operator.

The spiffiest boats leave from the marinas north of town; for lower prices, try the operators near El Faro or negotiate directly with one of the independent fishers offering half-day *panga* trips along Paseo Claussen near Playa Norte. Many operators also offer simple bottom-fishing excursions.

Flota Bibi FISHING

(Map p494; ☑669-913-10-60; www.bibifleet. com; Marina Puesta del Sol No 8, Mazatlán Marina; charters per day US$300-600) Helpful and professional set-up with three different boat options. Excursions last eight hours.

Flota Sábalo FISHING

(Map p494; ☑669-981-27-61; www.facebook. com/manuel.valdessalgado; Calz Camarena s/n; fishing trips from M$3000) This friendly set-up is run by two brothers, who offer two different boats – one an old faithful, the other sleeker and more modern – for very affordable fishing or other boating excursions. Lots of fun.

Aries Fleet FISHING

(Map p494; ☑669-916-34-68; www.elcidmarinas. com; Marina El Cid; per day from US$495) Offers fishing tours. This company supports some catch-and-release practices.

Tours

★**Onca Explorations** ECOTOUR

(Map p502; ☑669-913-40-50; www.oncaexplorations.com; Río de la Plata 409) Wildlife observation and conservation are the focus of these ecotours, led by marine ecologist Oscar Guzón. Most popular are his 'Humpback Whale Research Adventure' (adult/child US$95/65, 8am and 1pm December to April) and 'Wild Dolphin Adventure' (adult/child US$85/65, 8am year-round) tours, which offer excellent opportunities to observe marine mammals up close.

Other options include an excursion to the Las Labradas (adult/child US$75/40) beachside petroglyph site, and custom bird-watching tours to Santa María Bay, Isla Isabel National Park and the Chara Pinta Tufted Jay Preserve.

Vista Tours TOUR

(Map p502; ☑669-986-86-10; www.vistatours. com.mx; Av Camarón Sábalo 51; ⊙8am-7pm) Reliable set-up that offers a variety of tours in and around Mazatlán, including city tours (US$30), a colonial tour (US$50) to the foothill towns of Concordia and Copala, a tequila-factory tour (US$45) and all-day jaunts to Mexcaltitán (US$129).

King David BOAT TOUR

(Map p502; ☑669-914-14-44; www.kingdavid.com. mx; Av Camarón Sábalo 333; ⊙7:30am-5pm) Offers a variety of boat tours, including a 'Jungle and Beach' tour (adult/child US$45/30) into the mangrove-fringed waterways of the Isla de la Piedra wildlife refuge. You may get it cheaper by booking at its run-down office instead of via hotels. Its 'Isla de la Piedra' tour is more cheaply (and better) done by yourself.

Festivals & Events

Carnaval CARNIVAL

(www.carnavalmazatlan.net; ⊙Feb or Mar) Mazatlán has Mexico's most flamboyant Carnaval celebrations. For the week leading up to Ash Wednesday, the town goes on a nonstop partying spree. Reserve hotels in advance.

CineSeptiembre FILM

(☑669-176-46-35; www.facebook.com/cineseptiembre; ⊙Sep) An annual international film festival that has an emphasis on Spanish-language shorts and features. Screenings are free and take place in the beautiful Teatro Ángela Peralta (p504).

Old Mazatlán

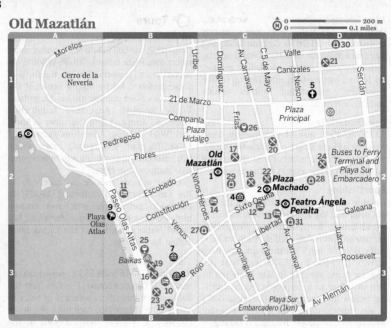

Old Mazatlán

◎ Top Sights
1 Old Mazatlán	C2
2 Plaza Machado	C2
3 Teatro Ángela Peralta	C2

◎ Sights
4 Casa Machado	C2
5 Catedral	D1
6 Clavadistas	A2
7 Museo Arqueológico	B3
8 Museo de Arte	B3
9 Playa Olas Altas	B2

⬤ Sleeping
10 Casa de Leyendas	B3
11 Hotel La Siesta	B2
12 Hotel Machado	C2
13 Jonathon	C2
14 Melville Suites	C2

⊗ Eating
15 Angelina's Kitchen	B3
16 Fonda de Chalio	B3
17 Héctor's Bistro	C2
18 La Tramoya	C2
19 Looney Bean	B3
20 Nieves de Garrafa de con Medrano	C2
21 Panamá	D1
22 Pedro & Lola	C2
23 Puerto Viejo	B3
24 Topolo	D2

◎ Drinking & Nightlife
| 25 Hotel Belmar Bar | B3 |
| 26 Vitrolas Bar | C1 |

✪ Entertainment
| Teatro Ángela Peralta | (see 3) |

⬢ Shopping
27 Casa Etnika	C3
28 Gandarva Bazar	D2
29 La Querencia	C2
30 Mercado Pino Suárez	D1
31 Nidart	C2

Festival Cultural Mazatlán PERFORMING ARTS
(www.culturamazatlan.com; ⊗ Oct-Dec) If you
love the performing arts, witness captivating
theatrical and musical performances in and
around the Teatro Ángela Peralta (p504).

Artwalk ARTS
(www.artwalkmazatlan.com; ⊗ 4-8pm 1st Fri of the
month Nov-May) Get a taste of Mazatlán's arts
scene through this self-guided art walk.

Día de Nuestra
Señora de Guadalupe RELIGIOUS
(⊙ Dec 12) The day of the Virgen de Guadalupe is celebrated at the cathedral. Children come in colorful costumes.

🛏 Sleeping

★**Funky Monkey Hostel** HOSTEL $
(Map p502; ☑ cell 669-4313421; www.facebook.com/funkymonkeyhostel; Boludo 112; dm/d M$180/450; P⊖❄@🛜🖵) Genially run in a quiet residential suburb about 1.2km from the beach, this facility-packed hostel makes a fine place to hang out, with its ample lounging space, pretty pool, two kitchens and hammock deck. Private rooms are cramped, but the fan-cooled dorms are spacious with colorful bed covers and decent mattresses. You can rent bikes and surfboards here.

Suitel GUESTHOUSE $$
(Map p494; ☑ 669-985-41-40; www.suitel522.com; Rio Presidio 522; r M$888-912; ❄🛜🖵) 🍃 Three blocks back from the beach, this is a good-value option offering darkish, spotless rooms with kitchenette and either a king-sized double or twins along a pleasant plant-filled patio. It rents bikes, bodyboards and fishing gear and has an ecologically minded policy. Turn off the coast road opposite the gold statue of a *pulmonía* taxi.

Los Girasoles APARTMENT $$
(Map p502; ☑ 669-913-52-88; losgirasoles@hotmail.com; Av Las Gaviotas 709; apt M$1200; P⊖❄🛜🖵) A leafy complex of decent, if dark, apartments and suites on a quiet neighborhood street. Expect a friendly boss, red-tiled floors, tinted windows, kitchenette, a small sitting room with a futon and a big bedroom with one or two beds. The pool area is terrific. Outside high summer, it can be one of the best-value spots in the Zona Dorada.

Hotel La Siesta HOTEL $$
(Map p498; ☑ 669-981-26-31; www.lasiesta.com.mx; Paseo Olas Altas 11; interior/ocean-view r M$952/1171; ❄@🛜🖵) Sitting pretty above Playa Olas Altas, La Siesta is a good option if you can snag one of the choice sea-view rooms. Interior rooms, while spacious and tidy, are less appealing. The pleasant central courtyard and attached restaurant are good places to meet other travelers. Books out quickly in summer.

Casa Contenta APARTMENT $$
(Map p502; ☑ 669-913-49-76; www.casacontenta.com.mx; Av Playa Gaviotas 224; apt/house M$1271/2971; P⊖❄🛜🖵) Right on the beach in the heart of Zona Dorada, these spacious apartments – each with cable TV, kitchenette, dining area, double bed and two twins – make a decent option for families. The rooms could do with a bit of modernizing, but it's friendly and pretty decent value for this great location.

Hotel Machado HOTEL $$
(Map p498; ☑ 669-669-27-30; www.hotelmachado.com; Sixto Osuna 510A; d incl breakfast M$950; ❄@🛜) Gorgeous Plaza Machado's only hotel is a mixed bag. Despite its lovely facade and the funky charm of checkerboard floors and wrought-iron beds, rooms are rather basic. The high-ceilinged 2nd-floor *salón social* (sitting room) is a delightful place to read or gaze out over the square. Rates are complex, with Wednesdays much cheaper and two-day stays recommended at weekends.

★**Casa de Leyendas** B&B $$$
(Map p498; ☑ 669-981-61-80; www.casadeleyendas.com; Venustiano Carranza 4; r incl breakfast M$1300-1900; ❄@🛜🖵) Affable expats host one of Old Mazatlán's homiest B&Bs. Six comfy rooms, all with coffeemakers, fridges, hairdryers, safes and other nice touches occupy two floors of a sprawling old house near Playa Olas Altas. Common areas include a library, a lively, well-stocked, reasonably priced bar, a central 'cocktail pool' with Jacuzzi jets, a fully equipped guest kitchen and two spacious upstairs patios.

Jonathon BOUTIQUE HOTEL $$$
(Map p498; ☑ 669-915-63-60; www.jonathonhotel.com; Av Carnaval 1205; r M$1954-3778; P⊖❄🛜🖵) On a pedestrian street just off Plaza Machado, set around a striking columnar courtyard with a modern spiral staircase. Rooms are a good size with soaker tubs, floating beds and hardwood closets and shelving. It's slightly over the top, but super-comfortable with a great location and a rooftop pool with a view. The bar is also worth visiting for cocktails and vistas.

Las 7 Maravillas B&B $$$
(Map p494; ☑ 669-136-06-46; www.las7maravillas.com; cnr Av Las Palmas & Jabonería; r incl breakfast US$140-230; ❄🛜) A block above the waterfront but in a quiet residential area, this classy place aims at the couples market

with personalized service, security detail, Jacuzzi-with-a-view and a reader-praised breakfast buffet. Each of the seven rooms is lightly themed on the country after which it is named. It's an impressive overall package that needs to be reserved in advance. No under-15s.

Casa Lucila
BOUTIQUE HOTEL $$$

(Map p494; ☑669-982-11-00; www.casalucila. com; Paseo Olas Altas 16; r M$2837-5617; ❂❋🛜🏊) This waterfront boutique hotel dazzles guests with huge walk-in closets and showers, ultracomfy king-size beds, Bose CD players, flat-screen TVs, European-style bathroom fixtures and state-of-the-art Italian doors and windows. Six of the eight rooms have private Jacuzzis, and several have balconies with brilliant sea vistas. The spa, infinity plunge pool and in-house restaurant add to the sophisticated appeal. No kids.

Hotel Playa Mazatlán
RESORT $$$

(Map p502; ☑669-989-05-55; www.hotelplaya mazatlan.com; Av Playa Gaviotas 202; r from M$2800; 🅿❂❋@🛜🏊) This large resort – the first built in the Zona Dorada – maintains impeccable standards. Half the rooms have ocean views, and all come equipped with satellite TV, private terrace and the thoughtful touches that mark a classy operation. Manicured tropical gardens and a breezy oceanside restaurant make this Mazatlán's most stylish large hotel.

Motel Marley
MOTEL $$$

(Map p502; ☑669-913-55-33; http://travelby mexico.com/sina/marley; Av Playa Gaviotas 226; 1-/2-bedroom apt M$1470/1670; 🅿❂❋@🛜🏊) The most atmospheric of the string of low-budget spots in Zona Dorada, this place offers comfortable seafront apartments set in four-unit blocks and staggered for airflow, with well-equipped kitchens, an oceanfront lawn, a pool and – best of all – privileged beach access.

Melville Suites
HOTEL $$$

(Map p498; ☑669-982-84-74; www.themelville. com; Constitución 99; r M$1200-1600; ❂❋🛜) Enormous rooms with soaringly high ceilings and thick walls surrounding a central courtyard give this perfectly located, relaxed option plenty of old Mexico character. Rooms also come with fans, air-con and kitchenette. The tired furnishings and bathrooms could do with a bit of a face-lift for this price though, and there's loads of street noise in the front chambers on weekend nights. Car park opposite.

✖ Eating

Mazatlán is famous for fresh seafood. *Pescado zarandeado* is a delicious, spiced, charcoal-broiled fish, and the shrimp served here is as sweet as you'll ever taste.

Good locations to prowl for cheap, fresh, no-frills seafood are around the Mercado de Mariscos at the southern end of Playa Norte, and the thatched kiosks on the beach opposite hotels Hacienda and Cima, a little further north.

✖ Old Mazatlán & Around

Surrounded by atmospheric eateries, elegant Plaza Machado is sublime in the evening when jazz musicians descend, kids frolic and the plaza is softly lit to create a touristy but very romantic ambience.

Looney Bean
CAFE $

(Map p498; ☑669-136-05-07; www.looneybean mzt.com; Paseo Olas Altas 166G; pastries M$20-50; ☺7:30am-10pm Mon-Thu, to 11pm Fri-Sun; ❂🛜) A terrific local coffee shop on the main seaside drag with strong coffee and espresso drinks, juices and smoothies. It also has strawberry scones bigger than your face – they're almost impossible to eat in one sitting, though you may try (they are that good).

Mercado de Mariscos Playa Norte
SEAFOOD $

(Map p494; Av del Mar s/n; fish per kg M$50-100; ☺7am-4pm; ❂) This no-frills market sells fish and seafood straight off the boats that dock on the beach opposite. Stalls here will cook up your purchases or your own catch.

Panamá
MEXICAN, BAKERY $

(Map p498; ☑669-985-18-53; www.panama.com. mx; cnr Canizales & Juárez; dishes M$48-145; ☺7am-10:30pm; ❂🛜) With a zillion different breakfast combos, ranging from North American standards to Mexican treats such as *chilaquiles* (tortilla strips drenched in salsa), this locally popular bakery and diner is a great place to start the day, or continue it. Also has a few other locations around town.

Nieves de Garrafa de con Medrano
ICE CREAM $

(Map p498; www.facebook.com/nievesdegarrafade conmedrano; cnr Flores & Calle 5 de Mayo; ice cream M$25; ⊙11am-9pm) A local tradition since 1938, this unpretentious family-run cart near Mazatlán's Plaza Principal dishes out delicious homemade ice cream to devoted crowds. Try the vanilla, prune, banana or mandarin flavors.

Angelina's Kitchen MEXICAN $$

(Map p498; ☑669-910-15-96; www.angelinaslatin kitchen.com; Venustiano Carranza 18; mains M$90-150; ⊙8am-11pm Tue-Sat, 8am-3pm Sun; ⊜☎☑) Behind an unobtrusive facade, this surprisingly capacious restaurant is something of a local favorite and it's easy to see why. A casual menu runs from burgers and salads to ceviches and *aguachile* (spicy lime-marinated shrimp) via plenty of vegetarian options. Seafood is expertly selected and prepared here, whether it's plump, sweet crustaceans or marinated fish on your plate.

Puerto Viejo SEAFOOD $$

(Map p498; ☑669-982-18-86; Paseo Olas Altas 25; mains M$60-140; ⊙10am-11pm; ⊜☎) A classic corner bar that can't be ignored for its popular sundowner location, fresh-as-morning seafood, crowd of regulars and performing *ranchera* troubadours. Locals and tourists alike can't help but be charmed. Daily specials include swordfish, marlin soup and shrimp tacos.

Fonda de Chalio MEXICAN $$

(Map p498; Paseo Olas Altas 166; mains M$45-140; ⊙7am-11pm; ⊜☎) This street-front cafe across from the *malecón* is popular with Mazatlán's middle-aged locals. Breakfasts pack out for baskets of *pan dulce* (pastries), *chilaquiles* with *machaca* (spiced, shredded dried beef) and *huevos con nopales* (scrambled eggs with cactus paddles). Evenings get lively with *aguachile*, cold beer, and streetside music and dancing.

★Héctor's Bistro FUSION $$$

(Map p498; ☑669-981-15-77; www.hectorsbistro. mx; cnr Escobedo & Frías; mains M$140-190; ⊙8am-11:30pm Mon-Sat; ⊜☎) Commodious and with willing service, this is the new venture of a popular local chef. Dishes such as seafood carpaccios, salads bursting with fresh prawns and avocado, and tasty pastas are complemented by daily blackboard specials that might feature pork fillet or T-bone steak. The interior combines modern elegance with the high, old, beamed ceiling to good effect.

Pedro & Lola FUSION $$$

(Map p498; ☑669-982-25-89; www.restaurant pedroylola.com; Av Carnaval 1303; mains M$125-235; ⊙6pm-1am; ⊜☎) This stylish eatery on Plaza Machado does outstanding small plates, including delectable shrimp and octopus dishes. The fresh fish of the day comes cooked in a variety of ways – go papillote for the most flavor – and there are always interesting new takes on traditional Sinaloa dishes. Live jazz is common and the tables on the plaza are a nice place to listen.

Topolo MEXICAN $$$

(Map p498; ☑cell 669-1360660; www.topolomaz. com; Constitución 629; mains M$220-260; ⊙3-11pm Tue-Sun, closed Sun Jun-Aug; ⊜☎) For a romantic, mariachi-free dinner, step into this softly lit courtyard in a historic central building. Though aimed at gringos, it has plenty of charm as waiters prepare fresh salsa at your table while chefs cook specialties such as tequila shrimp or fish in cilantro butter. Don't believe the 11pm closing time: they make it obvious that they like folk out the door early.

La Tramoya MEXICAN $$$

(Map p498; ☑669-985-50-33; www.facebook. com/la.tramoya.mazatlan; Constitución 509; mains M$140-235; ⊙10am-midnight Sun-Thu, to 1am Fri & Sat; ⊜☎) Diners at spacious sidewalk tables enjoy hearty Mexican meat and seafood dishes here on Mazatlán's loveliest square. Unconventional choices include *filete azteca* – a steak stuffed with *huitlacoche* (corn fungus). It also does fusion fajitas and burgers.

✗ Zona Dorada & Around

La Cocina de Ana MEXICAN $

(Map p502; ☑669-916-31-19; Laguna 49; meals around M$60; ⊙11:30am-4pm Mon-Sat; ⊜) This homey place offers well-prepared buffet-lunch fare including marlin, meatball soup, *chiles rellenos* (chilies stuffed with meat or cheese) and *pollo estofado* (stewed chicken). Everything is sold by the kilo, and the menu changes daily.

Pura Vida SALAD BAR $

(Map p502; ☑669-916-10-10; Bugambilias 18; light meals M$35-95; ⊙8am-10:30pm; ⊜☎☑) Serves salads, sandwiches, Mexican snacks and vegetarian fare, but is most sought out for its juices and smoothies. Its menu is packed with creative concoctions blended from all the tropical fruit you love, as well as

Zona Dorada & Around

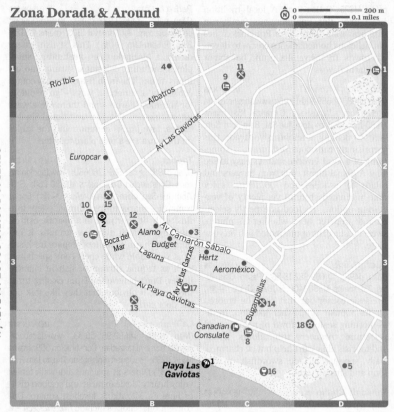

apples, dates, prunes, wheatgrass, spirulina and strawberries.

Tomates Verdes
MEXICAN $

(Map p502; ☑669-913-21-36; Laguna 42; meals M$45; ⊗8:30am-5pm Mon-Sat; ⊜) Cozy and unpretentious, this breakfast and lunch spot serves dishes such as *pechuga rellena* (stuffed chicken breast) and flavorful soups such as *nopales con chipotle* (spicy cactus). Meals come with soup, a main dish and rice and beans. The menu changes daily.

Carlos & Lucía's
CUBAN, MEXICAN $$

(Map p494; ☑669-913-56-77; Av Camarón Sábalo 2000; mains M$70-160; ⊗8:30am-10pm; ⊜⊛) What do you get when you combine the talents of a Mexican named Carlos and a Cuban-born chef named Lucía? A vibrant, colorful little restaurant serving home-style specialties from both countries. Try the *plato Carlos y Lucía,* shrimp or fish cooked in brandy, accompanied by rice, veggies and

plantains. It's opposite the Palms resort by an advertising bridge.

Pancho's Restaurant
MEXICAN $$

(Map p502; ☑669-914-09-11; www.facebook. com/panchosrestoran; Av Playa Gaviotas 408; mains M$95-220; ⊗9am-11pm; ⊜⊛) With two levels right on Playa Las Gaviotas, this place has a spectacular outlook and the food measures up. There's a big range, whether you want tasty *aguachile* or a huge seafood platter. Or just drop by for a drink: the army of waiting staff will snappily provide a monster margarita or icy-cold beer.

Todos Santos
SEAFOOD $$

(☑669-112-13-22; www.facebook.com/todosantos mariscosoficial; cnr Av Marina & Rodolfo Gaona; dishes M$110-170; ⊗noon-1am; ⊜⊛) This breezy open-air place is popular with young *mazatleco* couples for a date, offering a surf theme and cheeky, good-time vibe, though

Zona Dorada & Around

◉ Top Sights
1 Playa Las Gaviotas...............................C4

◉ Sights
2 Onilikan A3

◈ Activities, Courses & Tours
3 King David..B3
4 Onca Explorations B1
5 Vista Tours..D4

◉ Sleeping
6 Casa Contenta A3
7 Funky Monkey Hostel......................... D1
8 Hotel Playa Mazatlán..........................C4
9 Los Girasoles..C1
10 Motel Marley...A2

◈ Eating
11 Casa Loma C1
12 La Cocina de Ana B3
13 Pancho's Restaurant...........................B3
14 Pura Vida..C3
15 Tomates Verdes....................................B2

◉ Drinking & Nightlife
16 Joe's Oyster Bar....................................C4
17 Pepe Toro B3

◉ Entertainment
18 Cinemas Gaviotas................................D4

staff show plenty of attitude. The long seafood menu has lots of innovation and quality: enjoy delicious tuna, fresh oysters, a range of ceviches and some excellent fish fillet creations.

It's behind the Soriana Plus shopping center on Avenida Rafael Buelna.

Casa Loma   INTERNATIONAL **$$$**
(Map p502; ☑669-913-53-98; www.restaurant casaloma.com; Av Las Gaviotas 104; mains M$145-298; ⊙1:30-11pm; ⊖ 🛜) At this genteel eatery, enjoy roast duck *à l'orange* or poached fish *blanca rosa* (with shrimp, asparagus and mushrooms) in the swanky dining room or outdoors by the burbling fountain.

🍸 Drinking & Nightlife

Mazatlán has earned its reputation as a nightlife destination with a great selection of high-energy dance clubs frequented by visiting college students, which lends a Mexican spring-break vibe. Most clubs charge admission in the M$100 to M$200 range, generally including a free drink. The scene starts percolating around 10pm and boils over after midnight. If you're more partial to sipping and people-watching, head to Avenida Olas Altas or deeper into Old Mazatlán and you'll find a home.

Hotel Belmar Bar   BAR
(Map p498; www.hotelbelmar.com.mx; Paseo Olas Altas 166; ⊙11am-2am; 🛜) The tiled walls, old floors and wood paneling practically bead with sweat in this unrefined but popular hotel-bar on the *malecón*. So try to grab a sidewalk table where you can sip *bellenas* (1L of Pacífico) or swill buckets of beer from, gulp, plastic cups.

Vitrolas Bar   GAY
(Map p498; ☑669-985-22-21; www.vitrolasbar. com; Frías 1608; ⊙8pm-3am Fri-Sun; 🛜) This gracious gay bar in a beautifully restored building is romantically lit and, overall, more button-down than mesh muscle shirt. It's also a popular spot for karaoke and it does a decent pizza. Not at all scene-y.

Fiesta Land   CLUB
(Map p494; ☑669-989-16-00; Camarón Sábalo s/n; ⊙9pm-4am; 🛜) That ostentatious white castle on Punta Camarón at the south end of the Zona Dorada is the undisputed epicenter of Mazatlán's nightlife. Inside its walls are a half-dozen clubs, including several of the city's most popular dance spots.

Valentino's draws a mixed crowd to three dance floors throbbing with hip-hop and Latin music; **Bora Bora** is popular for its open-air dance floor and lax policy on bartop dancing; and **Sumbawa Beach Club** is the perfect after-hours spot for dancing on the sand, lounging on an oversized mattress or cooling off in the pool.

Joe's Oyster Bar   BAR
(Map p502; ☑669-983-53-33; www.joesoyster. com; Av Playa Gaviotas 100; ⊙11am-4am; 🛜) Part of the Ramada resort, this popular beachside bar with a never-ending two-for-one happy hour is a sports bar by day and morphs into a DJ-fueled disco that goes ballistic after 11pm, when it's packed with college kids dancing on tables, chairs and each other.

Pepe Toro   GAY
(Map p502; ☑669-914-41-76; www.pepetoro. com; Av de las Garzas 18; ⊙11pm-5am Thu-Sun; 🛜) This colorful club attracts a fun-loving, mostly gay crowd. It's a friendly, inclusive place with live shows on Friday and Saturday nights.

☆ Entertainment

For entertainment listings check **Pacific Pearl** (www.pacificpearl.com), available in hotel lobbies around town and online.

★ Teatro Ángela Peralta
THEATER

(Map p498; ☑ 669-982-44-46; www.culturamazatlan.com; Av Carnaval 47) To feel the pulse of Mazatlán's cultural scene, a night at the Peralta is a must. Built between 1869 and 1874, the theater was lovingly restored over five years to reopen in 1992. It has an intimate auditorium with three narrow, stacked balconies. Events of all kinds are presented – movies, concerts, opera, theater and more.

Cinemas Gaviotas
CINEMA

(Map p502; ☑ 669-984-28-48; www.cinemasgaviotas.com.mx; Av Camarón Sábalo 218; M$25-40) Six screens showing recent releases, including some in their original version with subtitles.

🛍 Shopping

The Zona Dorada is replete with tourist-oriented stores that sell clothes, jewelry, pottery and crafts. Old Mazatlán has quirkier, artier offerings.

Mercado Pino Suárez
MARKET

(Mercado Centro; Map p498; 🖋 Old Mazatlán's central market offers a classic Mexican experience, complete with vegetable stands, spice dealers, food stalls and shops selling bargain-priced crafts.

Nidart
CERAMICS, HANDICRAFTS

(Map p498; ☑ 669-985-59-91; www.nidart.com; Libertad 45; ⊙10am-2pm Mon-Sat) Sells handmade leather masks and ceramics from its in-house studio and also represents numerous other local artisans. The leathery aromas are a real treat.

Casa Etnika
HANDICRAFTS

(Map p498; ☑ 669-136-01-39; www.facebook.com/casaetnika; Sixto Osuna 50; ⊙10am-7pm Mon-Sat; 🖥) Family-run Casa Etnika offers a small, tasteful inventory of unique objects from Mexico and elsewhere and has a cafe. It can organize shipping to North America.

Gandarva Bazar
HANDICRAFTS

(Map p498; ☑ 669-136-06-65; gandarvabazar@hotmail.com; Constitución 616; ⊙10am-8pm Mon-Sat) This wonderfully atmospheric courtyard gallery is filled with drums, sculpture, masks, crosses, dolls made from gourds, hearts made from glass... It has a fair amount of mass-produced stuff, but there are some interesting reproduction Chinesco (early 1st millennium AD culture in Nayarit) ceramics too.

La Querencia
ARTS

(Map p498; ☑ 669-920-93-22; Frías 1405; ⊙10am-8pm; 🖥) This sizable gallery-shop with entrances on two streets (the main one being on Dominguez) has striking ceramics, painted wood objects, sculptures and jewelry. Some of the pieces are huge: you won't be squeezing them into your carry-on luggage.

ℹ Information

Free wi-fi is available in numerous bars, restaurants and accommodations. Banks with ATMs are common throughout the center and Zona Dorada. **Go Mazatlán** (www.gomazatlan.com) is a useful website proffering information about Mazatlán and around.

Hospital Sharp (Map p494; ☑ 669-986-56-78; www.hospitalsharp.com; Jesús Kumate s/n) Competent and modern private hospital.

Main Post Office (Map p498; www.correosdemexico.com.mx; Juárez s/n; ⊙8am-6pm Mon-Fri, 9am-2:30pm Sat) On the east side of Plaza Principal.

Secretaría de Turismo (Map p494; ☑ 669-915-66-00; http://turismo.sinaloa.gob.mx; Av del Mar 882; ⊙8am-6pm daily Jun-Aug, 9am-5pm Mon-Fri Sep-May) Gives out a mediocre free map and a few leaflets about the interior, but as far as practical information goes it is utterly useless.

ℹ Getting There & Away

AIR

Rafael Buelna International Airport (☑ 669-982-23-99; www.oma.aero; Carretera Internacional al Sur s/n) is 27km southeast of the Zona Dorada. There are direct flights to several US and Canadian destinations.

The following domestic destinations are serviced by these airlines:

➡ Guadalajara – TAR
➡ La Paz (Baja California) – TAR, VivaAerobus
➡ Mexico City – Aeroméxico, VivaAerobus, Volaris, Interjet
➡ Monterrey – VivaAerobus
➡ Tijuana – Volaris

Aeroméxico (www.aeromexico.com) Zona Dorada (Map p502; ☑ 669-914-11-11; Av Camarón Sábalo 310; ⊙9am-7:30pm Mon-Fri, 9am-2:30pm Sat); Airport (☑ 669-982-34-44)

BOAT

Baja Ferries (Map p494; ☑ 800-337-74-37; www.bajaferries.com; seat adult/child one way M$1102/551, car M$2700; ⊙ticket office 8am-4pm Mon-Fri, 8am-3pm Sat, 9am-1pm Sun) Operates ferries from the terminal at the southern end of town between Mazatlán and La Paz in Baja California Sur (actually to the port of Pichilingue, 23km from La Paz). Boats depart at 4pm (be there, ticket in hand, at 2pm) on Monday, Wednesday and Friday and take around 16 hours. They return at 5pm Tuesday, Thursday and Sunday. Winter winds may cause delays.

BUS

The full-service **Central de Autobuses** (Main Bus Station; Map p494; ☑ 669-982-83-51; Ferrusquilla s/n) is just off Avenida Ejército Mexicano, three blocks inland from the northern end of Playa Norte. All bus lines operate from separate halls in the main terminal.

Local buses to small towns nearby (such as Concordia, Copala and Rosario) operate from a smaller terminal, behind the main terminal.

CAR & MOTORCYCLE

Local all-inclusive rental rates begin at around M$600 per day during the high season.

Alamo (www.alamo.com.mx) Airport (☑ 669-981-22-66); Zona Dorada (Map p502; ☑ 669-913-10-10; Av Camarón Sábalo 410)

Budget (www.budget.com) Airport (☑ 669-982-12-20); Zona Dorada (Map p502; ☑ 669-913-20-00; Av Camarón Sábalo 413)

Europcar (www.europcar.com.mx) Airport (☑ 669-913-33-68; ⊙ 6am-10pm); Zona Dorada (Map p502; ☑ 669-913-33-68; Av Camarón Sábalo 357; ⊙7am-8pm Mon-Fri, 9am-8pm Sat, 9am-6pm Sun)

Hertz (www.hertz.com) Airport (☑ 999-118-040); Zona Dorada (Map p502; ☑ 669-913-49-55; Av Camarón Sábalo 314)

ℹ Getting Around

TO/FROM THE AIRPORT

Taxis and *colectivos* (minibuses picking up and dropping off passengers along predetermined routes) operate from the airport to town. Tickets for both can be purchased at a booth just outside the arrivals hall (*colectivo* M$100 to M$150, taxi M$340 to M$550). There is no public bus running between Mazatlán and the airport.

BIKE

Mazatlán is an easy town to navigate by bicycle, as the *malecón* leads from the town center all the way to the Zona Dorada. There are lots of bike-rental places along the coast.

Baikas (Map p498; ☑ 669-910-19-99; www.baikas.mx; Paseo Olas Altas 166; city bikes per hour/day M$70/300, hybrids M$100/400; ⊙7am-10pm) Professional set-up with city bikes and pricier hybrids. There's another branch (Map p494; ☑ 669-984-01-01; Av del Mar 1111; city bikes per hour/day M$70/300, hybrids M$100/400; ⊙7am-10pm) by the Don Pelayo hotel near the Zona Dorada.

BUS

Local buses run from 6am to 10:30pm. Regular buses cost M$7; air-con buses cost M$10.

From the **Central de Autobuses** (p505) bus terminal, go to Avenida Ejército Mexicano and catch any bus going south to the city center. Alternatively, walk 300m from the bus terminal to the beach and take a Sábalo–Centro bus heading south to the city center.

Major routes:

➡ **Playa Sur** Travels south along Avenida Ejército Mexicano, near the bus terminal and through the city center, passing the Mercado Centro, then to the ferry terminal and El Faro.

BUSES FROM MAZATLÁN

DESTINATION	FARE (M$)	DURATION (HR)	FREQUENCY (DAILY)
Culiacán	120-246	2½-3	very frequent
Durango	438-620	4	frequent
Guadalajara	405-572	7½	very frequent
Los Mochis	433-528	6	very frequent
Manzanillo	724-806	12-14	2
Mexicali	1159-1410	20-24	frequent
Mexico City (Terminal Norte)	985-1275	13-16	frequent
Monterrey	1170-1231	12-14	3
Puerto Vallarta	515-660	7-9	6
Tepic	274-400	4-5	frequent
Tijuana	1296-1582	24-26	frequent

➤ **Sábalo–Centro** Travels from the Mercado Centro to Playa Norte via Juárez, then north on Avenida del Mar to the Zona Dorada and further north on Avenida Camarón Sábalo.

TAXI

Mazatlán is renowned for its special *pulmonía* taxis, small open-air vehicles similar to a golf cart. There are also regular taxis. Rates for rides within Mazatlán range from M$40 to M$90, depending on distance, time of day and your bargaining skills.

Mexcaltitán

🏠 323 / POP 900

This shield-shaped island village is believed by some experts to be Aztlán, the ancestral homeland that the Aztecs left around AD 1091 to begin their generations-long migration to Tenochtitlán (modern Mexico City). Proponents point to the striking similarities between the cruciform design of Mexcaltitán's streets and the urban layout of early Tenochtitlán. A pre-Hispanic bas-relief in stone found in the area is also provided as evidence – it depicts a heron clutching a snake, an allusion to the sign the Aztecs hoped to find in the promised land.

These days Mexcaltitán is foremost a shrimping town. Men head out into the surrounding wetlands, which are spectacular, in the early evening in small boats, to return just before dawn with their nets bulging. All day long, shrimp are spread out to dry on any available surface in the town, making the prospect of an afternoon stroll a pungent, picturesque proposition.

It's a very laid-back, friendly place. Tourism has scarcely made a mark here. Mexcaltitán has a simple hotel, some pleasant waterside restaurants and a small museum, making it a great spot to wind down for a day or two.

⊙ Sights & Activities

Museo del Origen   MUSEUM

(Plaza s/n; M$5; ⊙10am-2pm & 4-7pm Tue-Sat, 10am-2pm Sun) This small but enchanting museum on the plaza offers info in Spanish on the history of museums, a small archaeological collection, pictures of ruins and petroglyphs. There's also a reproduction of a fascinating long scroll (the *Códice Boturini*), telling the story of the Aztec peoples' travels, with their initial departure from an island looking very much like Mexcaltitán.

Boat Trips   BOAT TOUR

You can arrange boat trips on the lagoon for bird-watching, fishing and sightseeing – every family has one or more boats. Trips start at M$50, which gets you a circuit of the island.

✦✦ Festivals & Events

Semana Santa   RELIGIOUS

(⊙Mar or Apr) Holy Week is celebrated in a big way here. On Good Friday a statue of Christ is put on a cross in the church, then taken down and carried through the streets.

Fiesta de San Pedro Apóstol   RELIGIOUS

(⊙late Jun) During this raucous festival, which celebrates the patron saint of fishing, statues of Sts Peter and Paul are taken out into the lagoon in decorated *lanchas* (motorboats).

🛏 Sleeping & Eating

Don't leave town without trying the local specialty *albóndigas de camarón* (shrimp meatballs), shrimp empanadas or perhaps a rich *jugo de camarón* (shrimp broth). The shrimp *tamales* sold in the morning from a wheelbarrow on the streets are another culinary highlight.

Hotel Ruta Azteca   HOTEL $

(🖀323-235-60-20; Venecia s/n; d M$250-400, tr M$500, q M$700; ⊛❄) The town's only hotel is run by a lovely family. Rooms are mostly dark but simple and clean; ask for one out the back that has a view of the lagoon. Air-con ones cost a little more. The street's name refers to the fact that the town is nicknamed the 'Venice of Nayarit' and regularly becomes a canal when waters are high.

★ La Alberca   SEAFOOD $

(🖀323-235-60-27; off Venecia; mains M$65-100; ⊙10am-7pm) On the east side of the island, this has a great lagoon view. It's cheerily run, despite the fact that the staff have to spend half their days peeling crustaceans. It's all about shrimp: try shrimp empanadas, shrimp ceviche and shrimp *albóndigas* (meatballs) in a delicious chili-inflected shrimp broth. Beers are cheap and the fried shrimp as a free appetizer are very moreish.

Mariscos Kika   SEAFOOD $

(🖀cell 311-1343501; mains M$70-100; ⊙9am-6pm) For fish, shrimp and octopus cooked a dozen ways, hop on a boat to this family-run place on a small island just across from Mexcaltitán's main dock. Grassy lawns and sun loungers provide a reason to linger.

❶ Getting There & Away

Catch a bus from San Blas (M$60, 1½ hours) or Tepic (M$96, 1½ hours) to Santiago Ixcuintla, 7km west of Hwy 15 and 70km northwest of Tepic. Once in Santiago, take a *colectivo* (M$30, 40 minutes, four daily) or taxi (M$200) to La Batanga, a small wharf 40km away where *lanchas* depart for Mexcaltitán. The arrival and departure times of the *lanchas* are coordinated with the *colectivo* schedule. The boat journey takes 15 minutes and costs M$25 per person. If you miss the *lancha*, you can hire a private one for M$100.

From Mazatlán, catch a Tepic-bound bus, jump off at the junction for Santiago Ixcuintla and wait for further transportation.

San Blas

📱 323 / POP 10,000

The tranquil fishing village of San Blas is a peaceful, drowsy backwater, and therein lies its charm. Visitors come to enjoy isolated beaches, fine surfing, abundant birdlife and tropical jungles reached by riverboats.

San Blas was an important Spanish port from the late 16th century to the 19th century. The Spanish built a fortress here to protect their trading galleons from marauding British and French pirates. It was also the port from which St Junípero Serra, the 'Father' of the California missions, embarked on his northward peregrination. While on either side of the main drag San Blas is just another cobblestoned backwater, on Avenida Juárez itself, the uniform whitewashed facades lend a dreamy revival quality that is immediately endearing.

❍ Sights & Activities

Life on the water is a recurring theme here, from beaches and offshore islands to boat tours through local estuaries where birds and wildlife abound. **Playa Los Cocos** and **Playa Miramar** are further down the paved road from Playa Las Islitas; they're popular for surfing and have *palapas* under which you can lounge and drink fresh coconut milk.

On the town's *zócalo* (plaza), a newer church dwarfs the cute little 18th-century one whose bells were the subject of a Longfellow poem (though the American poet never actually visited).

La Contaduría FORTRESS, RUIN
(M$10; ⊙8am-7pm) This hill is the site of the original colonial settlement, and it's well worth visiting for the views and to stroll around the sturdy ruins of the 18th-century Spanish fort, where colonial riches were once amassed and counted before being shipped off to Mexico City or the Philippines. The place is still guarded by a collection of corroded cannons. On the way up to it are the gorgeous ruins of the settlement's church, **Templo de la Virgen del Rosario**, built in 1769.

Cocodrilario ZOO
(M$30; ⊙8am-4pm) On the river and usually reached by a boat tour, but also accessible by road (8km from San Blas), this crocodile nursery rears toothy reptiles that later get released into the wild as part of a repopulation program. But there are also a few non-release crocs and other captive creatures.

Playa El Borrego BEACH
The beach closest to the town is Playa El Borrego, at the end of Azueta – look for the jet aircraft. It's a long sweep of grey sand with decent waves backed by a string of casual bar-restaurants. Swimming can be treacherous – beware of rip currents – but there are flags and a lifeguard. A handful of old gauchos offer horse rides (M$50) on the beach, which last 15 to 30 minutes.

Playa Las Islitas BEACH
The best beaches are southeast of town around Bahía de Matanchén, starting with Playa Las Islitas, 7km from San Blas. To get here, take the main road toward Tepic and turn off to the right after about 4km. This paved road goes east past the village of Matanchén, where a dirt road goes south to Playa Las Islitas and continues on to follow 8km of wonderfully isolated beach.

San Blas

Surfing

Beginner and intermediate surfers choose to hone their skills at San Blas because of its many beach and point breaks. The season starts in May, but the waves are fairly mellow until September and October when the south swell brings long rides. Surf spots include El Borrego, **La Puntilla** (by a river mouth south of Playa El Borrego), **Stoner's** (further south, between San Blas and Las Islitas) and **El Mosco** (west of San Blas on Isla del Rey).

Stoner's Surf Camp SURFING
(www.stonerssurfcamp.com; classes per person M$200, board rental per hour/day from M$60/100) At Playa El Borrego, this is the nexus of the surf scene. National longboard champion 'Pompis' Cano gives lessons and holds court under the *palapa*. You can also stay at the camp.

👉 Tours

In addition to the popular La Tovara tours, more boat trips depart from a landing on Estuario El Pozo. They include a trip to **Piedra Blanca** (M$400 for up to six people, one hour) to visit a statue of the Virgin, to **Isla del Rey** (M$15 per person, five minutes) just across from San Blas, and to **Playa del Rey**, a 20km beach on the other side of the Isla del Rey peninsula. Here you can also hire boatmen to take you on bird-watching excursions (M$400 first hour for up to six people, M$300 per hour thereafter).

Isla Isabel makes for an interesting overnight trip. It's a national park and protected ecological preserve three hours northwest of San Blas by boat. The island is a bird-watcher's paradise, but there are no facilities, so be prepared for some self-sufficient camping. You can fish your dinner, but tour operators will also help negotiate good prices with local fishers. Overnight trips generally go for M$8000 for up to six people.

La Tovara BOAT TOUR
(☑ 324-285-07-21, 323-108-41-74; www.latovara.com) A boat trip through the jungle to the freshwater spring of La Tovara is a San Blas highlight. Small boats go from the *embarcadero* at the eastern edge of town, or from the main dock 4.5km further east on the road to Matanchén. The three-hour trips go up Estuario San Cristóbal to the spring, passing thick jungle and mangroves.

There's a restaurant at La Tovara, where you can stop for lunch, or you can extend

San Blas

◎ Sights
1 La Contaduría	E1

🛏 Sleeping
2 Casa Roxanna Bungalows	B3
3 Estancia Las Flores	B2
4 Hotel Hacienda Flamingos	B2
5 Hotel Marina San Blas	B3
6 Hotelito Casa de las Cocadas	A2
7 Posada del Rey	B3

✖ Eating
8 Juan Bananas	C3
9 Mercado	B1
10 Ofro's	B2
11 Wala Wala	B2

🍸 Drinking & Nightlife
12 Billy Bob's	B2
13 Cafe Del Mar	B2

the trip to the Cocodrilario. A group of up to four people costs M$480 to go to La Tovara (two hours round trip) and M$610 to the Cocodrilario (three hours). Each additional person pays M$120 or M$150, depending on the destination.

🎉 Festivals & Events

Festival Internacional de Aves Migratorias
BIRD-WATCHING

(www.facebook.com/fiamsanblas) Bird-watchers flock to San Blas in late January or early February for the week-long International Migratory Bird Festival. Highlights include tours with English-speaking ornithologists and nightly entertainment in the plaza.

🛏 Sleeping

San Blas has plenty of very reasonably priced accommodations.

Estancia Las Flores
GUESTHOUSE $

(📞 323-285-01-20; mawesb@hotmail.com; Av Juárez 49; r M$350; ❄✳🎇) Just four rooms in a budget courtyard hotel on the main drag. The rooms are all cinder-block construction but are well-kept and spotless, with tiled floors, cable TV and artful touches. Friendly management and a shared kitchen upstairs. Good value.

Hotelito Casa de las Cocadas
HOTEL $

(📞 323-285-09-60; www.lascocadas.sanblasriviera nayarit.com/instalaciones; Av Juárez 145; d M$555; ❄✳🎇🏊) This pleasant small hotel down by the boat docks offers a genuine welcome and clean, simple yet bright rooms surrounding a central pool. It's pretty good value.

Stoner's Surf Camp
CABIN, CAMPGROUND $

(📞 323-232-22-25; www.stonerssurfcamp.com; Playa El Borrego; campsites per person M$50, cabins for 2 M$200-250, for 4 M$400-600; 🅿) The rustic *cabañas* (cabins) at this friendly traveler hangout and surf center have electricity, mosquito nets and fans. The choicest digs are the rickety, shaggy stilted *cabañas* on the beach. There's space to camp, a communal kitchen, lots of hammocks and the Playa Azul restaurant serving well-prepared fare. Guests in the *cabañas* get free use of bikes plus discounts at the surf center.

⭐ Hotel Hacienda Flamingos
HOTEL $$

(📞 323-285-09-30; www.sanblas.com.mx; Av Juárez 105; s/d from M$825/970; ste M$1440; 🅿❄✳🎇🏊) This restored orangey-red colonial gem provides the classiest accommodations in town. The spacious rooms and fountain-tinkling courtyard are evocative of old Mexico without even a whiff of kitsch. Some rooms have balconies and antique furniture; all have a filter coffeemaker. There's a very decent pool as well as a lounge serving well-crafted cocktails and *botanas* (snacks).

> **ℹ INSECT ALERT!**
>
> Take repellent to San Blas: voracious mosquitoes and sandflies are often present in large squadrons.

Casa Roxanna Bungalows
BUNGALOW $$

(☑ 323-285-05-73; www.casaroxanna.com; El Rey 1; d M$700-800, per additional person M$50; P ⊜ ❄ 🛜 🏊) This refined haven offers eight bungalows of two sizes; angle for one of the larger upstairs units (sleeping up to five) with full kitchen and screened porch overlooking the pool and manicured palmy grounds. English is spoken and discounts are offered for longer stays.

Hotel Marina San Blas
HOTEL $$

(☑ 323-285-14-37; www.sanblas.com.mx; Cuauhtemoc 197; s/d M$825/970; P ⊜ ❄ 🛜 🏊) Set near the estuary mouth, within view of the harbor, is this meticulously mantained three-star resort. The grounds are lovely, guests get a free one-hour kayak rental, and kitschy marine-themed rooms have lighthouse lamps and a strange amalgamation of cinder block and tile, but are spotless and comfy with river views and cable TV. There's a pool and small estuary swimming beach.

Posada del Rey
HOTEL $$

(☑ 323-285-01-23; www.sanblas.com.mx; Campeche 10; s/d M$595/714; ⊜ ❄ 🛜 🏊) Neat air-conditioned rooms around an appealing pool make this a worthwhile retreat from the sometimes oppressive midday humidity of San Blas. Staff are easygoing and beds and bathrooms are more than decent.

Misión de San José
GUESTHOUSE $$

(☑ 323-285-09-84; pepe-gtz@hotmail.com; Azueta 5; d/q M$800/1000; P 🛜 🏊) Handy for the beach, this motel-style set-up offers a relaxing base, with rooms along the veranda of a low-slung bungalow that faces a grassy lawn. Hammocks are strung up outside each one, original sculpture decorates the place and free coffee is available.

✕ Eating

San Blas is a town of casual restaurants and beachfront *palapas,* all serving fresh seafood at low prices. Cheaper eats, including *tortas* (sandwiches), *jugos* (juices) and *licuados* (milkshakes), can be found at the local mercado (cnr Sinaloa & Batallón de San Blas).

★ Ofro's
MEXICAN $

(☑ 323-285-07-50; Av Juárez 64; mains M$60-110; ⊙ 7am-10pm; ⊜) For honest and delicious home-cooked cuisine, head to this main-street place run by a benevolent couple. It's a simply but appealingly decorated set-up that does good breakfasts, great shrimp, chicken and potato tacos – already a substantial meal for M$60 – and plates of fish and chicken with vegetables, rice and mashed beans.

Juan Bananas
BAKERY, CAFE $

(La Tumba de Yako; www.juanbananas.mx; Batallón de San Blas 219; loaves M$50-60, snacks M$20-55; ⊙ 8am-8pm; ⊜) For four decades this little bakery has been cranking out some of the world's best banana bread; with any luck, you'll get a loaf hot from the oven. Juan himself is a terrific source of local information. There's also a cafe here doing breakfasts and tasty snacks.

Wala Wala
MEXICAN $$

(☑ 323-285-08-63; Av Juárez 183; mains M$75-140; ⊙ 7am-10pm Mon-Sat; ⊜🛜) This cheerfully decorated restaurant serves tasty home-style meals, including specialties such as lobster and *pollo con naranja* (chicken with orange).

Restaurant Alicia
SEAFOOD $$

(Playa El Borrego; mains M$70-120; ⊙ 8am-7pm; ⊜) One of the humbler yet more popular of the beachfront *comedores* (food stalls) on Playa El Borrego. The *pescado zarandeado* is delicious and it does all the fried-fish dishes as well as ceviche and *cócteles* (seafood cocktails).

Caballito del Mar
SEAFOOD $$

(☑ 323-106-80-70; Playa El Borrego; mains M$80-210; ⊙ noon-6pm) This is among the best of the seafood *enramadas* (thatch-covered, open-air restaurants) lined up along Playa El Borrego.

🍷 Drinking & Nightlife

Cafe Del Mar
BAR

(☑ 323-285-10-81; Av Juárez 5; ⊙ 6pm-midnight; 🛜) Possibly the coolest watering hole in town sits overlooking the plaza, with whitewashed walls hung with authentic indigenous masks. Jazz, salsa, reggae and rock pour from the sound system, mingling with the tropical breeze. The drinks don't live up to the atmosphere, but it's still a fine spot to sit.

Billy Bob's BAR
(Av Juárez s/n; ⊙ 10am-2am Mon-Fri, 7:30pm-2am Sat & Sun) With a sort of Texas-meets-Mexico vibe, this bar has plenty of soul and hosts a few local characters. Witticisms and worryingly named drink descriptions plaster the walls along with a few animal skulls.

ℹ️ Information

Free municipal wi-fi is available within a 150m radius of the central plaza.

Banamex ATM (Av Juárez s/n) One of a handful of ATMs in town.

Centro de Salud (☑ 323-285-12-07; cnr Azueta & Campeche; ⊙ 24hr) This central medical center is on the road that heads down to the beach.

Tourist Office (☑ 311-214-80-71; Av Juárez s/n; ⊙ 9am-3pm Mon-Fri) On the main road at the archway that marks your arrival at the center. Has maps and brochures about the area and the state of Nayarit.

ℹ️ Getting There & Around

The little **bus terminal** (Sinaloa s/n) is served by Norte de Sonora and Estrella Blanca 2nd-class buses. From/to most destinations, including Mazatlán, you'll need to change in Tepic or at the junction (*crucero de San Blas*; M$44) on Hwy 15.

Daily departures include the following:

Puerto Vallarta (M$192, three hours, four daily)

Santiago Ixcuintla (M$48, 1½ hours, four daily)

Tepic (M$66, 1½ hours, hourly 6am to 8pm)

Buses depart from the corner of Canalizo and Mercado several times a day, serving all the villages and beaches on Bahía de Matanchén.

Taxis congregate around the plaza and will take you to nearby beaches – a good option with two or more people.

Tepic

☑ 311 / POP 330,000 / ELEV 920M

Founded by the nephew of Hernán Cortés in 1524, Tepic is the capital of Nayarit state, a predominantly middle-class place with a veritable hum of provincial bustle playing out on its narrow streets. Indigenous Huicholes are often seen here, wearing their colorful traditional clothing.

The ornate **cathedral** on **Plaza Principal**, dedicated in 1804, casts a regal eye over the square. Opposite is the **Palacio Municipal** (City Hall), where you'll often find Huicholes under the arches selling handicrafts at reasonable prices.

⊙ Sights

★ **Museo Regional de Nayarit** MUSEUM
(☑ 311-212-19-00; Av México Norte 91; M$47; ⊙ 9am-6pm Mon-Fri, to 3pm Sat) Set around the courtyard of an impressive magenta *palacio* (palace), this excellent museum has a beautifully presented selection of top-quality indigenous ceramics mostly sourced from burials from around 200 BC to AD 600. Figures depicting pregnant women, houses, warriors, ball-players and musicians give a real insight into these cultures, while anthropomorphic burial urns from the local Mololoa culture (late 1st millennium AD) sport spooky faces. There's an interesting section on shells, an obsidian blade straight out of *Game of Thrones* and good information in English throughout.

🛏️ Sleeping & Eating

Hotel Real de Don Juan HOTEL $$$
(☑ 311-216-18-79; www.realdedonjuan.com; cnr Juárez & Av México Sur; r/ste M$1340/1740; 🅿️ ❄️ 🐾 🛜) This beautifully done-up old hotel overlooking Plaza Constituyentes strikes the right balance between colonial character and urbane style. Two imposing angel warrior statues keep watch over the tranquil lobby, while upstairs rooms are decked out in appealing pastel colors, with luxurious king beds and marble-accented bathrooms. A good restaurant with alcove tables over the street, classy bar and rooftop lounge add points.

El Marlin de Tepic SEAFOOD $$
(☑ 311-213-02-53; www.marlindetepic.com; Calzada del Panteón 45; mains M$120-200; ⊙ 10:30am-6pm; 🐾 🛜) Head a few blocks east of Plaza Constituyentes, then one south to find this spacious place that specializes in seafood. True to the name, smoked marlin is one of its delicious specialties, and the *pescado zarandeado* is spectacularly tasty. Most of the good stuff is only available from 1:30pm. It's within easy walking distance of the bus terminal if you have a wait between transportations.

ℹ️ Information

Banks and other services line Avenida México between the two plazas.

City Tourist Office (☑ 311-215-30-00; Plaza Principal; ⊙ 9am-7pm) In the park opposite the cathedral. Not great for information but offers city tours for M$20 per person. A nearby kiosk gives out information on Nayarit state, as does a desk at the bus terminal.

ⓘ Getting There & Around

BUS

The main bus station is on the southeastern outskirts of town; local buses (M$6) marked 'Estación' make frequent trips between the bus station and the city center. A taxi from the terminal to the center will cost M$30 to M$35.

Buses to San Blas also stop at a small terminal north of the cathedral near the Río Mololoa.

Around Tepic

Laguna Santa María del Oro

Laguna Santa María del Oro   LAKE
Surrounded by forested mountains, this idyllic lake fills a volcanic crater 2km around and is over 100m deep. The clear, clean water takes on colors ranging from turquoise to slate. It's a pleasure to walk around the lake and in the surrounding mountains, spotting birds (some 250 species) and butterflies along the way. You can also climb to an abandoned gold mine, cycle, swim, kayak or fish for black bass and perch. A number of small restaurants serve fresh lake fish.

🛏 Sleeping

Koala Bungalows   CAMPGROUND $
(🖉cell 311-1347178; www.koalabungalows.com; campsite per person M$80-100, r/bungalow M$600/800; 🅿😺😹) A peaceful park with a restaurant, campsites and some well-maintained bungalows and houses sleeping up to 10 people. Turn left at the end of the road that descends to the lake.

ⓘ Getting There & Away

If driving, take the Santa María del Oro turnoff about 40km from Tepic along the Guadalajara road; from the turnoff it's about 10km to Santa María del Oro village, then another 8km to the lake. By bus, catch a 'Santa María del Oro'

colectivo on Avenida México in Tepic, then change to a colectivo marked 'Laguna' at Santa María's town square.

Volcán Ceboruco

Volcán Ceboruco   VOLCANO
This active volcano consisting of two calderas and three cinder cones last erupted in 1870, so you'll be safe walking the short trails at the top. The 15km cobblestoned road up the volcano passes lava fields, *fumaroles* (steam vents) and lush vegetation growing on the slopes. The road begins at the village of Jala, 7km off the highway from Tepic to Guadalajara; the turnoff is 76km from Tepic, 12km before you reach Ixtlán del Río.

You can also visit as part of a tour; several Puerto Vallarta–based companies include a stop at the volcano as part of their 'tequila tour' itineraries.

Chacala

📋 327 / POP 300
Despite its charm and beauty, the tiny coastal fishing village of Chacala has somehow retained its status as a somewhat-secret paradise. Located 96km north of Puerto Vallarta and 10km west of Las Varas on Hwy 200, it sits pretty along a beautiful little cove backed by verdant green slopes and edged by rugged black-rock formations at either end. With just one main, sandy thoroughfare and a few cobbled side streets, it's an ideal place to unwind and contemplate the horizon.

There are no ATMs; the closest are in nearby Las Varas.

◉ Sights

Alta Vista Petroglyphs   ARCHAEOLOGICAL SITE
(M$20) It's a drive along a rough road, then a 1.5km walk up a riverbed to this site, but get good directions first, as it's not signposted. The site is well-stocked with petroglyphs, some geometrical, some depicting human

BUSES FROM TEPIC

DESTINATION	FARE (M$)	DURATION (HR)	FREQUENCY (DAILY)
Guadalajara	220-295	3½	frequent
Mazatlán	275-390	4-5	hourly
Mexico City (Terminal Norte)	790-960	10-11	hourly
Puerto Vallarta	215-230	3-3½	hourly

figures. A path leads you past many carvings, with Spanish-English signs explaining them. The visit ends in a glade with cascading water and rock pools for a dip.

🏄 Activities

The sea provides most of the action. For **small-boat excursions** ask at the **Capitanía del Pueblo**, a small fishing harbor located at the northern tip of the shoreline. **Whale-watching** trips cost M$250 per person, with a four-person minimum. **Fishing** trips cost around M$500 per hour, while a **surfing** expedition to the prime spot **La Caleta** – where a wicked left-breaking point break thrashes the rocky beach – runs M$500 per person, and includes round-trip service (tell the captain what time to fetch you). A couple of central spots rent mediocre surfboards. The **swimming** in Chacala's luscious bay is safe and tranquil most of the year. You can also **hike** to La Caleta; it's a challenging but rewarding two-hour effort each way.

🛏 Sleeping & Eating

Accommodations here range from the simple to the luxurious. Though there are over 50 choices, many of these need to be prebooked and cater for multiday stays only.

For self-catering, **Chacala Villas** (☏327-219-40-37; www.chacalavillas.com) offers a variety of rental housing with full kitchens, including the recommended **Casa Mágica** (two people per night US$100).

The abundance of self-catering places means that eating choices are limited.

⭐**Techos de México**   HOMESTAY, GUESTHOUSE $
(www.techosdemexico.com; r M$300-600; ☻) 🏊
Travelers interested in meeting locals should consider this organization that helps Chacala residents build good homes with adjacent guest units. Six local families offer good budget lodging through this program; check the website or look for the distinctive Techos signs as you pass through town.

Casa Aurora   GUESTHOUSE $
(☏327-219-40-27; casaaurora2@hotmail.com; Golfo de México 2; d M$500-600; ☻✳🛜) 🏊 Behind a little bungalow, friendly Aurora has five simple but smart rooms with kitchenette that make a very comfortable Chacala base. You may be able to negotiate a discount, especially if you forgo the air-conditioning.

El Palmar de Chacala   CAMPGROUND $
(Av Chacalilla s/n; campsite M$220; ℗) Right on the beach in the center of town, this campsite lacks shade, is partly used as a bus park and has basic facilities that cost a few pesos extra, but has 24-hour security and a great position. The site fee is valid for 24 hours and includes a vehicle and as many tents as you care to put up in the space allotted.

Hotel las Brisas   HOTEL $$
(☏327-219-40-15; www.lasbrisaschacala.com.mx; Av Chacalilla 4; d M$750-850; ℗☻✳🛜) This centrally located hotel is right on the beach – your room will be just a hop, skip and plunge from the water – and has a decent bar-restaurant (open 8am to 8pm) that does tasty seafood, breakfasts and cold lager. Rooms are bright, colorful and clean, with decent wi-fi and satellite TV.

Casa de Tortugas   RENTAL HOUSE $$
(☏327-219-40-72; www.casadetortugas.com; d M$1000-1200; ☻✳🛜🖼) This walled red house overlooking the north end of the beach enjoys privileged views over the bay and offers three excellent rooms, a large family suite, a roof terrace and an infinity pool. Rooms have microwave and coffee-maker, and there's a shared kitchen area. Must be prebooked: there's no reception.

Hotel Mar de Coral   HOTEL $$
(☏327-219-41-09; www.hotelmardecoral.com; Av Chacalilla s/n; d M$700-800, bungalows M$1350; ☻✳🛜🖼) Set in the center of town across the road from the beach, this incongruous modern building, with a pool in a shady courtyard lobby, offers spacious and tiled rooms with wooden beds and furnishings, and two-tone pastel paint jobs. What it calls bungalows are much larger rooms with an attached kitchen.

ℹ TAX-FREE SLEEPING

Lots of accommodations and restaurants in the beach towns along the Nayarit and Jalisco coasts don't usually charge tax on their rooms, so we've sometimes quoted tax-free prices to reflect the reality of what you'll be paying. If you want a proper invoice, though, establishments will ask you to stump up the extra 19%.

CENTRAL PACIFIC COAST CHACALA

Mar de Jade
RESORT $$$

($ 327-219-40-00, US 800-257-0532; www.marde jade.com; s/d full board from US$215/322; P ⊖ ✳ 🛜 ✷) This idyllic getaway at the far south end of Chacala's beachfront hosts regular yoga, meditation and wellness retreats, but welcomes independent travelers too. Crashing waves are audible everywhere on the property, from the spacious rooms with deep, tiled bathtubs, to the sauna, Jacuzzi and spa area, to the sprawling poolside patio where vegetarian-friendly buffet meals are served. Rates include yoga classes in winter.

Chacmool Cafe
CAFE $$

($ 327-291-40-37; www.chacmoolcafe.com; Av Chacalilla 3; mains M$115-200; ⊙ 7:30am-9:30pm; 🛜) With tables on the beach, this casual eatery is an inviting spot for coffee, breakfast or a fuller meal. Fish dishes – tuna brochettes, octopus stew and shrimp done many ways – are pretty tasty, and service is willing. The ocean view is great at any time. Accepts credit cards.

❶ Getting There & Away

For Chacala, get off a Puerto Vallarta–Tepic bus at Las Varas and take a *colectivo* (M$15) for 11km from there: these leave every half-hour or so from directly across the road from the bus stop (look for the chairs on a corner outside a locksmith). If you're driving, the Hwy 200 turnoff is 1km south of Las Varas.

San Francisco

$ 311 / POP 1500

San Francisco, aka San Pancho, is another fishing pueblo turned vacation spot, with prettier beaches and a less obvious gringo footprint than you'll find in popular Sayulita, a couple of beaches south. There's less action here too, unless you count those real-life gauchos riding horses through the riverbed and along a gorgeous blond beach, long, wild and driftwood-strewn.

Avenida Tercer Mundo leads from Hwy 200 a couple of kilometers through town to the beach, where open restaurants serve the usual fish and ceviche dishes and cold beers. There's a lone ATM here, but it's best to bring cash, unless you want to pay the extortionate fee.

🏃 Activities

Paseos a Caballo
HORSEBACK RIDING

($ 322-175-48-26) This business lives up to its name, offering horse tours on mountain trails and back down to the luscious wind-swept beach.

Las Huertas
GOLF

($ 311-258-45-21; www.lashuertasgolf.com; green fees 9 holes M$400; ⊙ 8am-4pm Tue-Sun) Las Huertas is a short but pretty nine-holer that will keep golfers happy for a couple of hours.

🍴 Sleeping & Eating

★ Refugio del Sol & Hostal San Pancho
HOSTEL, GUESTHOUSE $

($ 311-258-41-61; www.hostalsanpancho.com; Av Tercer Mundo 12; dm M$220, d with fan/air-con M$500/800, ste M$1000; ⊖ ✳ 🛜) Kitted out with travelers' needs in mind, this guesthouse-hostel is set around its surf shop near the highway. It offers superclean, simple, yet charming rooms and snazzier 'suites' (bigger rooms with an attractive design, better bathrooms and terrace). Ground-floor dorms and their outdoor bathroom are basic but comfy. The appealing upstairs area houses an excellent common kitchen and is where free breakfasts are served.

There's also free bike and skateboard use – handy to zip down to the beach, 1km away. It offers surfboard rental and classes too, as well as various tours.

★ Hotel Cielo Rojo
BOUTIQUE HOTEL $$

($ 311-258-41-55; www.hotelcielorojo.com; Asia 6; d weekday/weekend M$1100/1870; ⊖ ✳ 🛜) The most polished sleep in San Pancho is located a few blocks from the beach. Rooms are compact but comfortable and stylish, with terracotta floors, objets d'art and attractive fabrics. Rates include breakfast and, at weekends, dinner. Its restaurant, Bistro Orgánico, receives good marks.

La Chalupa
MEXICAN $

(Calle México; meals M$60-100; ⊙ 10am-8pm) It doesn't look like much from the street, but this sweet little *palapa* restaurant, owned by a fisherman and his family, does seafood dishes at nearly half the price of the beach restaurants. At lunch, *comida corrientes* (daily specials) are just 60 pesos.

La Perla
MEXICAN $$

($ 311-258-43-34; www.laperlasanpancho.com; beach at Av Tercer Mundo; mains M$140-200; ⊙ 10am-8pm, bar to 9pm) On the beach, this place offers great service, seriously cold beer and a good range of food under the decent shade of its *palapa*. The menu runs from burgers and fish sandwiches to *tostadas* piled with ceviche, octopus and shrimp, as well as roasted fish dinners and lobster (M$250).

❶ Getting There & Away

San Francisco is 7km north of Sayulita and about 49km north of Puerto Vallarta, just west of Hwy 200. There are buses around hourly from Sayulita (M$15, 10 minutes) and regular buses running between Tepic and Puerto Vallarta (M$45 to M$50, one hour). Buses drop off on the highway, from where it's an easy 1.5km stroll down the main street to the beach.

Sayulita

📞 329 / POP 2300

Once upon a time – OK, it was the late 1990s – Sayulita really *was* a tranquil fishing village. Many of the town's *norteamericano* residents still describe it that way, but the truth is that in peak season the place is full of gringos, drawn here by the beautiful (if not that clean) sandy beach, rideable waves, good restaurants and tasteful B&Bs. It's a thriving hipster-surfer scene and a very pleasant place to relax for a few days.

◉ Sights & Activities

You can arrange bicycle hire, boat trips, horseback riding, trekking or kayaking from operators on the main street.

You can also hire a boat to take you out to the uninhabited **Islas Marietas** – a protected park – for picnicking, snorkeling and swimming. Trips cost M$2500 for up to five people and include stops on two islands. It takes about 35 minutes to make the crossing.

Sayulita is a classic 'boarder' town. Medium-sized waves pour dependably from both the left and the right, so you can practice your well-honed moves or take up the sport for the first time. Several surf shops offer rentals and lessons.

Playa Los Muertos   BEACH
One popular destination near central Sayulita is Playa Los Muertos, where picnics and body-boarding top the action. It's a 15-minute walk south along the coast road, through the Villa Amor resort and the cemetery.

Sayulita Dive & Surf   SURFING, DIVING
(📞 329-298-85-32; sayulitadiveandsurf@gmail.com; Av Revolución 34; ⊙9am-8pm) Friendly, recommended set-up that offers really good, enthusiastic surf classes at a better price than many. A 2½-hour private class costs M$450, with an

❶ SAYULITA'S CHANGING TIME ZONE

Sayulita's clocks are set to Central time – unlike most of Nayarit state, which is on Mountain time. Sayulita made the switch in 2011, in order to synchronize its clocks with neighboring Puerto Vallarta and Jalisco. Why the shift? Turns out there was an epidemic of gringos arriving at Vallarta's airport an hour late and missing their homebound flights, either ignorant of the time zone difference or too blissed out by beach life to care.

hour's board rental free to practice afterward. It is also a PADI-certified dive operator, and runs excursions out to Islas Marietas.

Stand Up Sayulita   WATER SPORTS
(📞329-291-35-75; www.standupmex.com; Marlín; per hour/half-/full day M$100/300/500, lessons M$500) This is the place to learn how to captain a stand-up paddleboard and ride waves too. Lessons last an hour and include a free 45-minute paddle afterward.

🛏 Sleeping

A good selection of private villas can be browsed on the website **Sayulita Life** (www.sayulitalife.com). Low-season prices can reduce sharply.

★ Amazing Hostel Sayulita   HOSTEL **$**
(📞329-291-36-88; www.theamazinghostelsayulita.com; Pelicanos 102; dm M$220-250, d M$800; ●❄🤶) Follow the road upriver on the plaza side of the bridge to reach this excellent modern hostel, run by helpful, well-traveled folk and with tip-top facilities. Dark but cool en-suite dorms are downstairs, while upstairs is a great area with kitchen, BBQ, climbing wall, hammocks and pool. Air-con private rooms are spacious and wi-fi reliable. It rents bikes, kayaks and surfboards. Hostelling International discount.

Lush Sayulita   HOSTEL **$**
(📞329-291-37-09; www.lushsayulita.com; Pelicanos 54; dm M$250, d without/with bathroom M$600/700; ●🤶) By the bridge, this place offers a good social scene and curiously attractive dorms – there's something ship-like about them – with lockers, decent linen and proper plump mattresses. One has a balcony. There's an upstairs bar and plenty of

freebies are thrown in, including breakfast. A couple of cute dogs add character.

Hotel Sayulita Central
HOTEL **$$**

(☑329-291-38-45; www.hotelsayulitacentral.com; Delfín 7; r US$68-185; ❀❉奈) Perfectly located between the plaza and beach, this hotel has a variety of rooms named for classic rock bands. All are bright and creative, with nice touches such as water coolers, and share a sprawling lounge that is a great place to hang. Prices do reflect quality: the cheapest top-floor chambers can be furnaces in summer.

Petit Hotel Hafa
HOTEL **$$**

(☑329-291-38-06; www.hotelhafasayulita.com; Revolución 55; r US$50-85; ❀❉奈) Plenty of charm is on offer at this sweet small hotel just off the plaza, though the location means party noise can be an issue. Decor fuses North Africa and Mexico, with six individually decorated rooms offering concrete floors, fans (air-con for extra) and large baths with brass-bowl sinks. Staff are friendly though hands-off. The downstairs boutique is a gorgeous browse.

★ Siete Lunas
BOUTIQUE HOTEL **$$$**

(☑322-205-73-51; www.sietelunas.mx; Camino Playa de los Muertos 714; r US$216-248; P❀❉奈❄) Perched above jungly slopes and boasting phenomenal coastal views, these intimate bungalows make for the perfect romantic stay. Around 2km from town, past Playa de los Muertos, it's an end-of-the-road spot where a golf cart zips you up to a lodge-style retreat of real beauty. It's a honeymoon special, and no kids are allowed. Breakfast is included, but there's no restaurant service.

★ Aurinko Bungalows
BUNGALOW **$$$**

(☑329-291-31-50; www.sayulita-vacations.com; Marlín s/n; 1-/2-bedroom bungalow M$1314/2196; ❀❉奈) An exuberant thatched roof covers this enticing complex of deconstructed houses with indoor/outdoor living rooms and kitchens, and wonderful bedrooms with river-stone floors, accented by tasteful and vibrant modern art. It feels like a secluded hideaway but is actually just steps from the plaza and the beach. A yoga center was being built at our last visit.

✗ Eating

Sayulita has a beguiling selection of small, bistro-style cafes, providing an agreeable contrast to the *palapas* on the beach and the lively stands (try the seafood burritos)

that sprout every evening on the streets surrounding the plaza.

★ Naty's Cocina
TAQUERÍA **$**

(☑329-291-38-18; Marlín 13; tacos M$12-14; ⊙10am-3pm Mon-Sat; ❀) A cute and clean taco stand where tortillas are stuffed per your choice with sliced *poblano* peppers, potatos, beans and mushrooms, beef, smoked marlin, chicken with *mole* (chili sauce), or pork and cactus. Order at the counter and sit at a little drop-down wood bar or on the bench out front. Locals descend en masse for a reason.

Café El Espresso
CAFE **$**

(www.sayulitalife.com/elespresso; Av Revolución 51; dishes M$40-90; ⊙7am-10pm; ❀奈) This corner spot on the plaza – where breakfast is served until 3pm – lives up to its name. The coffee is strong and sensational, and non-dairy milk options are available. The 'Tropical Heaven' smoothie blends pineapple, yogurt, honey and papaya or strawberries with basil and coconut cream, and the Mexican breakfasts are dynamite.

Chilly Willy
SEAFOOD **$**

(☑322-127-24-38; Revolución s/n; dishes M$40-120; ⊙10am-7pm Wed-Mon; ❀) An unpretentious spot, this simple *taquería* (taco stall) makes a good stop for no-frills, tasty seafood. Munch *tostadas* piled with shrimp and octopus, seafood cocktails and fish tacos, or just stop by for a chat over a cold coconut. On Saturday and Sunday it does chicken with *mole* and *carne asada* (marinated and grilled steak). Ask about its recommended jungle-hiking, bird-watching and mountain-biking excursions.

Panino's
BAKERY, CAFE **$**

(www.facebook.com/paninossayulita; Delfín 1; light meals M$39-99; ⊙8:30am-6pm; ❀奈✎) Freshly baked, wonderfully crusty European-style bread, salads and panini (including vegetarian and vegan options). There's a range of good breakfast choices, including omelettes, French toast, fruit salad, waffles and *chilaquiles*. If there's apple strudel available, get it!

Yeikame
MEXICAN **$$**

(☑329-291-30-22; www.sayulitalife.com/yeikame; Mariscal 10; mains M$75-135; ⊙8am-10:30pm; ❀) Welcoming and reliable, this family-run place has pleasant streetside tables and produces a range of fairly traditional Mexican fare. Enchiladas, *tostadas*, tacos and more substantial plates such as chicken in *mole* or marinated pork are priced fairly and feature tasty blue-corn tortillas; finish things off with a cone from the attached ice creamery. There are delicious fruit drinks on offer, and breakfast fare is equally toothsome.

El Costeño
SEAFOOD $$

(Delfín; mains M$80-130; ☺1-8:30pm) An old-school beach bar – at over 50 years old, it's definitely the daddy of Sayulita – where tables are sunk in the sand beneath a *palapa* roof swinging with rattan lanterns. Prices are fair and the seafood fresh. If all you want is guacamole, an octopus or shrimp cocktail, or ceviche *tostadas* and a cold refreshment with a view, this place will do the trick.

Sayulita Cafe
MEXICAN $$$

(Casa del Chile Relleno; ☑329-291-37-38; Revolución 37; mains M$120-250; ☺5-11pm; ☻☎) Fake adobe lends atmosphere to this popular central restaurant, which pleases with generous portions and a few interesting dishes, such as its *molcajete de marisco*, a combination of seafood with bechamel-type sauce served in a stone dish, or tasty stuffed chili peppers, the house specialty. If you need a receipt, eat elsewhere.

Drinking & Nightlife

Friday beach parties are well-attended.

El Mezcalito
BAR

(Mariscal s/n; ☺7pm-2am) Lively Arturo runs this likable little hole-in-the-wall by the corner of the plaza and will usually have some interesting agave distillation for you to try – ask for some Jalisco *raicilla* to kick-start your evening. He often improvises some sort of live music. Great fun.

Don Pato's
BAR

(Marlín 10; ☺8pm-2am) At the rubber-duck sign and up a rickety spiral staircase, this lively bar on the main plaza pumps out live music most nights, with an open mike on Tuesdays. Don't expect a dress code: half the punters are in bathing suits. Table football is hotly contested, and the upstairs level is often where it's all at.

Shopping

Boutiques offering Mexican handicrafts of varying quality abound in Sayulita.

Tierra Huichol
HANDICRAFTS

(☑329-222-99-53; Revolución 43) While not the cheapest place to buy, this shop gives a good introduction to the Huicholes' colorful bead-work sculptures. There are some spectacular pieces here, and you can often see an artist at work.

Revolución del Sueno
CLOTHING, ACCESSORIES

(☑329-291-38-50; www.revoluciondelsueno.com; Navarrete 55; ☺10am-8pm) Specializes in silk-screened T-shirts and hipster beach bags – we love the mariachi holding a bouquet of flowers. It also has throw pillows, exquisite jewelry, and quirky stickers and decorative art pieces, including outstanding papier-mâché skulls.

❶ Information

There are several ATMs in town, but no banks, so commissions are high. The ATM in the **Oxxo convenience store** (www.oxxo.com; Av Revolución s/n) tends to have the lowest fees.

❶ Getting There & Away

Sayulita is about 35km north of Puerto Vallarta, just west of Hwy 200. Buses (M$30, one hour) operate every 20 minutes or so from the stop in front of Puerto Vallarta's Walmart. For a few more pesos, any northbound 2nd-class bus from the Puerto Vallarta bus terminal will drop you at the Sayulita turnoff, leaving you with a 1.5km walk into town.

Punta de Mita & Around

Just south of Sayulita, a stunning jungled, mountainous peninsula tumbles into the sea. Much of it has been tamed and groomed into gated resorts, and Punta Mita village is now largely a service center for these resorts. Nevertheless, it has a string of beachfront restaurants popular with Vallarta families, and its little marina is a place to jump on a boat out to sea.

The beaches that grace the coast from here to Nuevo Vallarta, a stretch known as **Riviera Nayarit**, are some of the best on the central Pacific coast. The water is almost always clear and aquamarine, the sand is white and the surf can get fun too. Laid-back fishing-ports-turned-beach-resorts worth exploring on this stretch include **La Cruz de Huanacaxtle** and **Bucerías**.

🏃 Activities

The beachfront strip has several places offering surfing rental and classes; just wander along and take your pick. After a few wipeouts, the several massage studios might look like a good idea. From the marina at the eastern end of this strip, boat trips leave for the Islas Marietas (two-hour trip M$400 plus M$30 park entrance, or M$2000 for a boat seating up to eight); the same price can see you go whale-watching (December to March). A fishing charter will cost US$300 to US$400 for a half-day, including equipment. One operator is **Punta Mita Charters** (☑ 329-291-62-98; www.puntamitacharters.com), a local cooperative.

🛏 Sleeping & Eating

Hotel Mesón de Mita   HOTEL $$

(☑ 329-291-63-30; www.hotelmesondemita.com; Av Anclote 200; d/q M$1200/1500; 🅿❄🛜🅿) On the strip, and with a more Mexican feel than most of Punta de Mita, this open-plan space behind a beachfront restaurant offers rather appealing modern rooms around a pleasant garden and pool. Try for one of the rooms with sliding doors looking onto the hammock area. Towels here get folded into birds: always a plus.

Imanta   RESORT $$$

(☑ 329-298-42-00; www.imantaresorts.com; Montenahuac s/n; d from US$500; 🅿🛏❄@🛜🅿) The domain of the rich and famous – foreign and domestic – this is one of the central Pacific coast's most upmarket resorts. Set on 100 jungled hectares that abut a natural reserve, the hotel and villas are made from stone and loom above a private rocky shore.

Even standard rooms are 175-sq-meter suites, with soaker tubs, day beds and walk-in closets, but you can also indulge in a jungle or oceanfront *casa* (from US$1040), where you'll find a private infinity pool to call your own.

Rocío   SEAFOOD $$

(☑ 329-291-51-16; Av Anclote s/n; mains M$130-250; ⊙8am-6pm) One of the best of the beachfront eateries. The ceviche is particularly fresh and tasty, and if you catch the staff cleaning fresh-caught tuna or *dorado*, order it grilled.

ℹ Getting There & Away

From Puerto Vallarta, take Hwy 200 north through Bucerías, then veer left toward La Cruz de Huanacaxtle to follow the coast toward the peninsula. Regular buses run from Puerto Vallarta (M$30, 45 minutes). To/from Sayulita, you'll need to jump off at the highway junction, cross to the other road, then flag down another bus.

Puerto Vallarta

☑322 / POP 260,000

Stretching around the sparkling blue Bahía de Banderas and backed by lush palm-covered mountains, Puerto Vallarta (or just 'Vallarta' to many) is one of Mexico's most enticing coastal destinations. Each year millions come to laze on the dazzling sandy beaches, browse in the quirky shops, nosh in the stylish restaurants and wander the picturesque central streets and enticing *malecón*. Activities aplenty include boat trips, horseback rides, diving trips and day trips to the interior, while after sunset Vallarta takes on a new identity with pumping nightlife along the *malecón* and numerous GLBT-friendly options in what is the gay beach capital of Mexico.

ℹ Orientation

The 'old' town center, called Zona Centro, is the area north of Río Cuale. Cross the river to reach the Zona Romántica, a characterful, spread-out tourist district with smaller hotels, restaurants and bars, the two most central beaches, and the hub of GLBT life. These eminently walkable downtown neighborhoods, which remain the heart and soul of Puerto Vallarta, are where most places worth visiting, staying at or eating are located.

North of the city is a strip of giant luxury hotels, the Zona Hotelera; Marina Vallarta, a large yacht marina (9km from the city center); the airport (10km); the bus station (12km); and Nuevo Vallarta, a new area of hotel and condominium developments (18km). To the south of the city is a string of winningly beautiful beaches, some backed by resort hotels.

⦿ Sights

The heart of Zona Centro is the **Plaza Principal** (Plaza de Armas), where chain-store modernism blends with the old shoeshine days of pueblo yore. The wide **malecón** stretches a little south and about 10 blocks north from here, and is dotted with bars, restaurants, nightclubs and a grand collection of public sculptures.

Or you could just go to the beach. Those on the Bahía de Banderas have many personalities. Some are buzzing with cheerful activity; others are quiet and private. Two, **Playa Olas Altas** (Map p524) and **Playa de los Muertos** (Beach of the Dead; Map p519), are handy to the city center; both are south of the Río Cuale. At the southern end of Playa de los Muertos is the stretch of sand

Greater Puerto Vallarta

Greater Puerto Vallarta

◉ Sights
1 Playa Conchas Chinas...........................A4
2 Playa de los Muertos..........................A4
3 Playa Palmares A5

⊕ Activities, Courses & Tours
4 Ecotours de México.............................A2
5 Marina Vallarta Golf Club...................A2
6 Rancho El Charro.................................B3
7 Vallarta Adventures............................A2

⊟ Sleeping
8 Blue Chairs Beach Resort...................A4

⊗ Eating
9 Benitto's..A2
10 El Barracuda...B3
11 La Leche..B3
12 Layla's Restaurante.............................B3
13 Red Cabbage Café................................B4

ⓘ Information
14 San Javier Marina Hospital.................B2

ⓘ Transport
15 Aeroméxico B3
16 Alamo B1
17 Avis A2
18 Budget...A2
19 Buses to Punta de Mita and
    Sayulita B2
20 Gustavo Díaz Ordaz International
    Airport A1
21 Long-Distance Bus Terminal..............B1
22 Sixt...A2

called **Blue Chairs**, one of Mexico's most famous gay beaches.

Northside, in the Zona Hotelera, are a string of good beaches; Nuevo Vallarta also has decent stretches of sand. But it's **southern beaches** (p520) that the most enchanting coves are found.

Los Arcos
LANDMARK

(Map p524; Plaza Morelos) Public events such as gaucho parades and mariachi festivals take place on the sea side of the plaza near an outdoor amphitheater backed by Los Arcos, a row of Romanesque-looking arches that has become a symbol of the city.

Templo de Guadalupe
CATHEDRAL

(Map p524; http://parroquiadeguadalupevallarta. com; Hidalgo s/n; ⊙7am-10pm Mon-Sat, 6am-10pm Sun) The crown-topped steeple of the Templo de Guadalupe, the town's central cathedral, is a Vallarta icon, and the hand-ringing of the bells via a long rope is a local tradition.

Isla Río Cuale
ISLAND

(Map p524) A trip to Vallarta wouldn't be complete without lingering on Isla Río Cuale, a sand island that appeared in the rivermouth in the 1920s and was then consolidated. It's very pleasant for a traffic-free stroll among the trees and to visit the Museo del Cuale.

★ **Museo del Cuale**   MUSEUM
(Map p524; Paseo Isla Río Cuale s/n; ⊙9am-2pm & 3-6pm Tue-Sat) FREE On Isla Río Cuale, this museum has a small but very well-presented collection of pre-Hispanic ceramics and gives a good archaeological overview of the various indigenous groups who lived in western Mexico. Most of the panels have been well translated into English.

Jardín Botánico de Vallarta   GARDENS
(Vallarta Botanical Garden; ☑322-223-61-82; www.vbgardens.org; Hwy 200 Km 24; adult/child M$80/20; ⊙10am-6pm Dec-Mar, closed Mon Apr-Nov) Orchids and bromeliads, agaves and wild palms line the paths of this gorgeous nature park, located 30km south of Puerto Vallarta. Follow hummingbirds through fern grottoes, or head down to bask in a chair on the warm sand and swim amid huge boulders in the river below. Take the 'El Tuito' bus (M$24) from the corner of Carranza and Aguacate in Puerto Vallarta, or hop into a taxi (about M$300).

> **DON'T MISS**
>
> ## THE SOUTHERN BEACHES
>
> A string of beautiful coves and beaches graces the bay south of central Vallarta, easily accessed by bus. Further around the southern side of the bay are three more isolated beaches – from east to west, Las Ánimas, Quimixto and Yelapa – all accessible by boat but not by road, though you can walk a trail to the first two from Boca de Tomatlán.
>
> Buses marked 'Boca' stop at both Mismaloya and Boca de Tomatlán (M$7.50); the 'Mismaloya' bus only goes as far as Mismaloya. Any of these buses work for Playa Conchas Chinas and Playa Palmares.
>
> **Playa Conchas Chinas** (Map p519) Around 3km south of downtown is the beautiful condo enclave of Playa Conchas Chinas. It's a tiny cove favored by families for the shallow and sheltered pools created by the burly rock reef further out (that's where the snorkelers and spear fishers have fun). Although the cove is small, the beach is blond and reasonably wide, with lifeguards on duty.
>
> **Playa Palmares** (Map p519) About 6km south of Zona Centro, Playa Palmares – named not for the nonexistent palms but for the condo complex of the same name – is a narrow but ample stretch of white sand. These picturesque turquoise shallows are favored by locals for swimming as the beach is far from rivers, which means clear water year-round.
>
> **Mismaloya** Mismaloya, the location for the film *The Night of the Iguana*, is about 12km south of Puerto Vallarta: you can still see the dilapidated Iguana sign by the roadside. The tiny scenic cove is dominated by a gargantuan resort and villagers are up in arms about proposals to evict them so that another resort can be built.
>
> **Boca de Tomatlán** Sixteen kilometers from Puerto Vallarta, beyond Mismaloya, southwest along the coast, is Boca de Tomatlán, a seaside village that's less commercialized than Puerto Vallarta and a good place to munch ceviche *tostadas* on the beach. You can get water taxis from here to more remote beaches further along the bay.
>
> **Playa de las Ánimas** Playa de las Ánimas is a lovely beach with a small fishing village and some *palapa* restaurants offering fresh seafood.
>
> **Playa de Quimixto** This beach, just beyond Las Ánimas, has a waterfall accessible by a half-hour hike or by hiring a pony on the beach to take you up.
>
> **Yelapa** Yelapa, the furthermost of the southern beaches from town, is one of Puerto Vallarta's most secluded and beloved bays, home to a small fishing community. Lots of day trippers turn up on organized tours, but this picturesque cove empties out when the boats leave in the late afternoon, and there are several comfortable places to stay the night. Return water taxis from Puerto Vallarta/Boca de Tomatlán cost M$280/140 per person; the trip takes 45 minutes from Vallarta and boats depart Vallarta at 11am and 4pm, returning at 8:30am and 3pm.

Activities

Restless souls need not go far to find activities such as bungee jumping, mountain biking and whale-watching. Snorkeling, scuba diving, deep-sea fishing, waterskiing, windsurfing, sailing and parasailing can be arranged on the beaches in front of any of the large hotels or through the tourist office.

Diving & Snorkeling

Below the warm, tranquil waters of Bahía de Banderas is a world of stingrays, tropical fish and garishly colored corals. Vallarta has several diving operators. Most also offer snorkeling trips, which usually means snorkelers tag along with divers. Dives typically include transportation, gear and light meals.

Banderas Scuba Republic   DIVING
(Map p524; ☑ 322-135-78-84; www.bs-republic.com; Cárdenas 230; shore/boat dives US$85/95) Maintains a high degree of professionalism with its small-group excursions to lesser-known sites.

Deep-Sea Fishing

Deep-sea fishing is popular year-round, with a major international fishing tournament held mid-November every year. Prime catches are sailfish, marlin, tuna, red snapper and sea bass. Fishing trips can be arranged dockside at Marina Vallarta or through the multitude of agencies around town. Think US$180/330 for a shared four-/eight-hour excursion, or US$300 for a half-day charter.

Horseback Riding

Vallarta's jungly mountains are wonderful to explore from a horseback perspective.

Rancho El Charro   HORSEBACK RIDING
(Map p519; ☑ 322-224-01-14; www.ranchoelcharro.com; horseback rides US$68-128) Rancho El Charro, 12km northeast of downtown Puerto Vallarta, is recommended for its healthy horses and scenic three- to eight-hour trots into the Sierra Madre. Some rides are suitable for kids. Setting it apart from competitors are its multiday tours, including the tempting 'Overnight Lost in the Jungle Ride' (US$350). Transportation is offered.

Golf

Vallarta's golf courses are north of the city. Various golf websites often offer appealing deals.

Punta Mita Golf Club   GOLF
(☑ 329-291-55-90; www.fourseasons.com/puntamita/golf; Ramal Ctra 200 Km 19, Punta Mita; green fees 9/18 holes US$155/240) At the Four Seasons resort at Punta Mita, two Jack Nicklaus–designed golf courses enjoy some spectacular ocean vistas; the **Pacífico** has a renowned optional hole with an island green and the **Bahía** lacks little by comparison.

Vista Vallarta Golf Club   GOLF
(☑ 322-290-00-30; www.clubcorp.com; Circuito Universidad 653; green fees twilight/daylight US$145/204) With Nicklaus- and Weiskopf-designed courses side by side, this is one of Mexico's premier golf resorts, and its jungle-side situation gives it a memorable appeal. It's around 9km east of the airport.

Los Flamingos Golf Club   GOLF
(☑ 329-296-50-06; www.flamingosgolf.com.mx; Hwy 200 Km 145; green fees twilight/daylight US$96/159) Affordable and just 13km north of town, handy for Puerto Vallarta. Tight fairways and plenty of bunkering make for an enjoyable challenge.

Marina Vallarta Golf Club   GOLF
(Map p519; ☑ 322-221-00-73; www.clubcorp.com; Paseo de la Marina 430; green fees twilight/daylight US$104/135) This 18-hole, par-71 course is just north of Marina Vallarta and features plenty of water wildlife including crocs. Could do with a little TLC though, at this price.

Cruises

A host of daytime, sunset and evening cruises are available in Vallarta. The most popular ones are the cruises to Yelapa and Las Ánimas beaches; others go to Islas Marietas, further out. Prices are generally negotiable, starting at M$400 for sunset cruises and beach trips; longer trips lasting four to six hours with meals and bottomless cocktails will set you back M$750 to M$1200. Leaflets advertising cruises are available throughout town.

Diana's Gay & Lesbian Cruise   CRUISE
(Map p524; ☑ 322-222-15-10; www.dianastours.com; cruise US$95; ⊙ 9:30am-5pm Thu Oct-May) On non-summer Thursdays, Diana hosts an all-day gay and lesbian cruise, with plenty of food, drink and snorkeling. It leaves from the dock at Playa los Muertos. You can book your spot via the website.

WORTH A TRIP

A DAY ON A RANCH

Hacienda El Divisadero (☑322-225-21-71; www.haciendaeldivisadero.com; Camino Tuito–Chacala Km 9, Las Guásimas) Head for the hills and immerse yourself in rural life at Hacienda El Divisadero. This vast ranch 90 minutes south of Puerto Vallarta offers a slew of fun activities in one day tour (per person US$95). You'll be picked up from Puerto Vallarta and shuttled to the ranch, where you'll enjoy a continental breakfast before your horseback excursions to local petroglyphs, a river swim and a tour of the ranch's distillery, where it produces knock-your-socks-off *raicilla* (a tequila-like distillation of wild agave).

Lunch at the on-site restaurant, where you may enjoy melt-in-the-mouth *birria* (a spicy-hot meat stew) and fabulous *mole poblano* (chili sauce from the state of Puebla), is included. You'll be dropped off at your hotel at around 5pm. The price includes everything except tips for the guides.

Without transportation, the tour costs US$75. To get here, drive south of Puerto Vallarta 45km on Hwy 200 to the town of El Tuito, then follow the signs another 10km west to the hacienda.

🎓 Courses

Centro de Estudios Para Extranjeros
LANGUAGE COURSE

(CEPE; Map p524; ☑322-223-20-82; www.cecm. udg.mx; Libertad 105-1) Language courses at this Universidad de Guadalajara–affiliated school have a range of choices, including US$450 for 50-hour intensive two-week courses.

Centro Cultural Cuale
COURSE

(Map p524; ☑322-222-95-34) An arts complex at the easternmost plaza on Isla Río Cuale, on the more local hemisphere of the island. Theater productions and battles of the bands bloom in the modest theater, and there are regular workshops where locals and tourists alike can take lessons in music, printmaking and painting.

🧭 Tours

Nature and outdoor adventure tours are one of Puerto Vallarta's strongest attributes. There's a tour agency on almost every block, some pushier than others. **Agencia Paraíso** (Map p524; ☑322-222-25-49; agencia_paraisopv@yahoo.com.mx; Morelos 236; ⊙10am-9:30pm) is a reliable central option. There are several zip-line courses, all regularly recommended.

Recorridos Turísticos
WALKING TOUR

(⊙9am & noon Tue & Wed, 9am Sat) `FREE` These free walking tours of central Puerto Vallarta are run from the tourist office, and guides can speak Spanish, English and German. A tip is appropriate at the end.

⭐Ecotours de México
WILDLIFE WATCHING

(Map p519; ☑322-223-31-30; www.ecotours vallarta.com; Proa s/n, Marina Vallarta; ⊙9am-7pm Mon-Sat, from 8am Dec-Mar, 10am-2pm Sun) 🌿 Run by enthusiastic naturalists, this outfit offers whale-watching (adult/child US$95/75), sea kayaking and snorkeling tours (US$85/75), guided hiking and snorkeling combo tours (US$67/50), dolphin-watching and perhaps swimming (US$80/70), bird-watching tours (US$85 to US$95) and multiday expeditions further afield focusing on sea turtles, monarch butterflies, whale sharks and more.

⭐Eco Ride
CYCLING

(Map p524; ☑322-222-79-12; www.ecoridemex. com; Miramar 382; tours M$600-1500) Surrounded by mountains, jungle and sea, Vallarta offers truly thrilling mountain biking. This welcoming outfit offers guided one-day tours suited for beginners and badasses alike. The all-level ride (M$600 guided, M$350 self-guided) takes you upriver to a lovely waterfall. The most challenging is a 50km expedition from El Tuito (a small town at 1100m) through Chacala and down to the beach in Yelapa.

Vallarta Adventures
ADVENTURE TOUR

(Map p519; ☑322-297-12-12; www.vallarta-adven tures.com; Mástil 13C, Marina Vallarta; ⊙8am-2pm & 4:30-7pm Mon-Fri, 8am-4pm Sat, 8am-2pm Sun) Vallarta's largest tour company has numerous agencies and hotels selling its excursions. The dizzying array of options includes seasonal whale-watching (adult/child US$89/60), Islas Marietas snorkeling and kayaking trips (US$85/55), dive sites (US$88 to US$130) and zip-lining (US$109/72). It also offers swimming with captive dolphins, which animal welfare groups say is harmful to the dolphins and should be avoided.

Canopy River TOUR
(Map p524; ☑322-223-52-57; www.canopyriver.com; Insurgentes 379; adult/child US$80/51; ⊙8am-8pm) An exhilarating, four-hour canopy tour up the Río Cuale, featuring 12 zip-lines, ranging in height from 4m to 216m and in length from 44m to a stunning 650m run: curl up like a cannonball to reach top speed. A tequila tour and mule riding are thrown in, and you can add ATV driving or get-wet river zip-lines. The price includes transportation.

★☆ Festivals & Events

Marlin & Sailfish Tournament FISHING
(www.fishvallarta.com) A major, long-standing international tournament held every November.

Festival Gourmet International FOOD
(www.festivalgourmet.com) Puerto Vallarta's culinary community has hosted this mid-November festival since 1995.

**Día de Nuestra
Señora de Guadalupe** RELIGIOUS
Puerto Vallarta honors Mexico's patron saint with two weeks of celebrations, including processions to the cathedral day and night from November 30 until December 12.

⌂ Sleeping

When it comes to accommodations in Puerto Vallarta you're spoiled for choice. Vallarta's cheapest lodgings are south of the Río Cuale. Closer to the ocean, in the Zona Romántica, you'll find several appealing midrange options. Prices are for the December to April high season; low-season rates can be as much as 20% to 50% less. Negotiate for discounts if you plan on staying a week or more; monthly rates can cut your rent by half.

Hotel Ana Liz HOTEL $
(Map p524; ☑322-779-83-81; Madero 429; s/d M$290/350; ⊛🔊) The best of a handful of budget hotels along this street, this place is welcoming and family-run. The owners take pride in their compact but neat, clean and comfortable fan-cooled rooms, some of which have a small balcony out the front. There's plenty of value on offer here.

Oasis Hostel Downtown HOSTEL $
(Map p524; ☑322-178-23-52; Juárez 386; dm/d M$200/500; ⊛🔊) Nestled in the shadow of Templo de Guadalupe, just off the plaza, are three bright dorms and one simple private room, which has two beds and a private bathroom. There's a rooftop sun deck with ocean views, free breakfast and lockers to guard your valuables. It's now no longer affiliated with the other Oasis Hostel in town, so don't confuse the two.

Hostel Central HOSTEL $
(Map p524; ☑322-113-01-23; Hidalgo 224; dm M$200; ⊛🔊) The little rooftop dorm here has both beds and bunks, and makes a compact but sweet central hideaway. This is very simple hostelling, but there's something rather nice about it and the couple that runs it are friendly and helpful.

Hotel Catedral HOTEL $$
(Map p524; ☑322-222-90-33; www.hotelcatedralvallarta.com; Hidalgo 166; d M$800-1400; ⊛❋@🔊) A charming three-star spot, steps from the waterfront and the river. The four floors of rooms surround a courtyard and have Templo de Guadalupe views from the upper reaches. Rooms are clean, if not new, with ceramic tiled floors, flat-screen TVs and a few thoughtful extras. Bathrooms are tiny, but soaps are great, service is helpful and prices very fair, especially in summer.

Hotel Yasmin HOTEL $$
(Map p524; ☑322-222-00-87; hotelyasminpv@gmail.com; Badillo 168; s/d/tr/q M$550/700/770/840; ⊛🔊❄) Something of a bargain just a block from the beach, this hotel offers cordial hospitality and an attractive courtyard area with a small pool. Some of

---

A HOLIDAY FOR WHALES

Like a fair percentage of the tourist population, during the winter months humpback whales come to the Bahía de Banderas to mate. They leave their feeding grounds in Alaskan waters and show up in Mexico from around November to the end of March. Once they have arrived, they form courtship groups or bear the calves that were conceived the year before. By the end of March the whales' attention turns to the long journey back to their feeding grounds up north. Whale-watching trips operate from December to March.

Central Puerto Vallarta

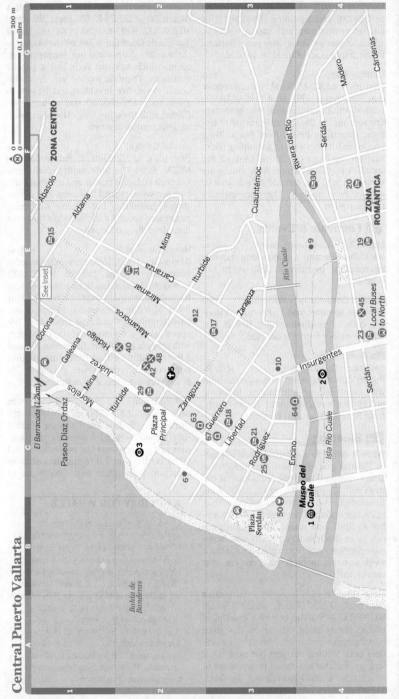

ZONA CENTRO

ZONA ROMÁNTICA

Bahía de Banderas

Río Cuale

Isla Río Cuale

El Barracuda (1.2km)

Paseo Díaz Ordaz

Plaza Principal

Plaza Serdán

1 🏛 Museo del Cuale

Local Buses to North

See Inset

200 m
0.1 miles

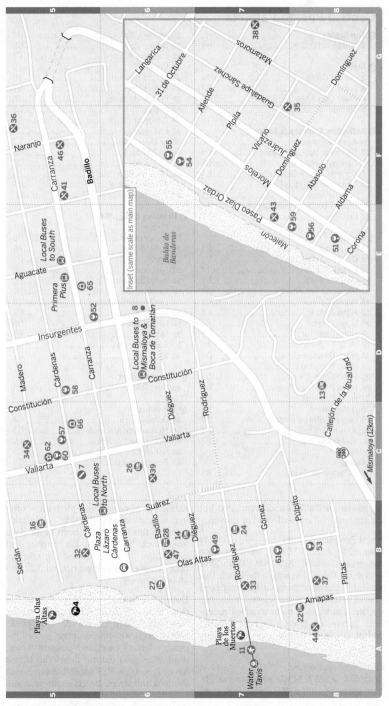

Central Puerto Vallarta

◎ **Top Sights**
1 Museo del Cuale.....................................B4

◎ **Sights**
2 Isla Río Cuale...D4
3 Los Arcos...C2
4 Playa Olas Altas......................................A5
5 Templo de Guadalupe..............................D2

⊕ **Activities, Courses & Tours**
6 Agencia Paraíso.......................................C2
7 Banderas Scuba Republic......................C5
8 Canopy River...D6
9 Centro Cultural Cuale.............................E4
10 Centro de Estudios Para
     Extranjeros..D3
11 Diana's Gay & Lesbian Cruise...............A7
12 Eco Ride...D2

⊜ **Sleeping**
13 Casa Cupula..D8
14 Casa Doña Susana...................................B6
15 Casa Dulce Vida......................................E1
16 Casa Fantasía..B5
17 Hacienda San Angel...............................D3
18 Hostel Central...C3
19 Hotel Ana Liz...E4
20 Hotel Azteca..F4
21 Hotel Catedral...C3
22 Hotel Emperador.....................................A8
23 Hotel Galería Belmar..............................D4
24 Hotel Mercurio...B7
25 Hotel Porto Allegro.................................C3
26 Hotel Posada de Roger...........................C6
27 Hotel Posada Lily....................................B6
28 Hotel Yasmin...B6
29 Oasis Hostel Downtown.........................D2
30 Rivera del Río..F4
31 Villa David...E2

⊗ **Eating**
32 A Page in the Sun....................................B5

33 Archie's Wok..B7
34 Bravos..C5
35 Café des Artistes.....................................F7
36 Chenan2...F5
37 Coco's Kitchen...B8
38 El Arrayán..G7
39 El Mole de Jovita.....................................C6
40 Gaby's..D2
41 Garlapago...F5
42 La Cigale..D2
43 La Dolce Vita...E7
44 La Palapa...A8
45 La Ronda..D4
46 Marisma Fish Taco..................................F5
47 Pancho's Takos..B6
48 Planeta Vegetariano...............................D2

◉ **Drinking & Nightlife**
49 Andale..B7
50 Antropology...B3
51 Bar Morelos..E8
52 Frida...D5
53 Garbo...B8
54 Jazz Foundation......................................F6
55 La Bodeguita del Medio..........................F6
56 La Cervecería Unión................................E8
57 La Noche..C5
58 Los Muertos...D5
59 Mandala...E8
60 Paco's Ranch...C5
61 Sama Bar..B7

⊕ **Entertainment**
62 Roxy Rock House......................................C5

⊜ **Shopping**
63 Dulcería Leal..C2
64 Mercado de Artesanías...........................C3
65 Mundo de Azulejos..................................E5
66 Olinalá...C5
67 Peyote People..C3

the rooms smell a little underventilated, but they are colorful and enlivened by artwork.

Hotel Posada de Roger   HOTEL **$$**
(Map p524; ☎322-222-08-36; www.hotelposada deroger.com; Badillo 237; s/d M$975/1050; ⊜❄🛜⊠) Three blocks from the beach, this agreeable travelers' hangout has long been one of Vallarta's most beloved midrange options and has a popular attached restaurant. Rooms are given a boost by colorful bedspreads, and there's a pool and leafy courtyard.

Hotel Galería Belmar   HOTEL **$$**
(Map p524; ☎322-223-18-72; www.belmarvallarta. com; Insurgentes 161; d M$600-850; ⊜❄@🛜)

Astute use of color and a plethora of original artwork enliven the tidy, comfortable rooms at this hotel in the heart of the Zona Romántica. Some have kitchenettes and many have balconies. Nicest are the top-floor chambers, which get natural light and an ocean breeze.

Hotel Posada Lily   HOTEL **$$**
(Map p524; ☎322-222-00-32; www.facebook. com/hotelposadalily; Badillo 109; d M$900; ⊜❄🛜) This well-priced option just off the beach offers 18 clean and pleasant rooms, most with good natural light. The largest have three beds and small balconies that overlook the street. Beach chairs and um-

brellas are available free to all guests. The only potential downside is noise. Prices drop to around M$650 in summer.

Hotel Azteca   HOTEL $$
(Map p524; ☏322-222-27-50; Madero 473; s/d M$450/650; ☏) A popular budget hotel full of brick arches. Rooms aren't huge or bright as they face an inner courtyard, but they have ceramic-tile floors, satellite TV and enough cute hand-painted touches to make them endearing. Pricier rooms come with a kitchen.

★Casa Dulce Vida   SUITES $$$
(Map p524; ☏322-222-10-08; www.dulcevida. com; Aldama 295; ste US$80-250; ☏☀✆) ✈ With the look and feel of an Italian villa, this collection of seven spacious suites offers graceful accommodations and delicious privacy. Expect a gorgeous red-bottom mosaic pool, leafy gardens and sumptuous *casas* with ceramic tiled floors, high ceilings, sunny living areas, spectacular wrought-iron doors and windows, well-stocked kitchens, whirring ceiling fans, a roof deck and bloody sunsets.

Most of the rooms have private terraces and extra beds for groups. Even when the place is fully booked, it retains a quiet and intimate atmosphere. It's a setting that begs for a cocktail, then another. Then one more.

Hacienda San Angel   BOUTIQUE HOTEL $$$
(Map p524; ☏322-222-26-92; www.hacienda sanangel.com; Miramar 336; r US$310-403; ☏☀@✆) The 20 rooms on this charming quiet backstreet, which set high above the *malecón,* are scattered through five houses, all exquisitely decorated with fine terracotta floors, antique four-poster beds, *azuelo*-tiled arches and wash basins, and knitted together by a courtyard gushing with fountains. Two resplendent pool decks offer special city and ocean views and the rooftop restaurant is good enough to earn repeat customers.

Hotel Emperador   HOTEL $$$
(Map p524; ☏322-222-17-67; www.hotelemper adorpv.com; Amapas 114; d/ste M$1262/1850; ☏☀@✆) This brilliantly located beachside complex offers cheery staff and simple but homey rooms with tiled floors, turquoise-accented walls, queen beds and flat screens on the wall. The 'suites' are large rooms that have magic views over the beach and sea and full kitchens on their spacious balconies. There are good off-season discounts. The place is gay-friendly and has a can-do attitude.

Casa Fantasía   B&B $$$
(Map p524; ☏322-223-24-44; www.casafantasia. com; Suárez 203; r incl breakfast US$144-150; ☏☀✆) A lovely B&B a block from the beach with spacious, terracotta tiled rooms sporting slanted beamed ceilings and flat-screen TVs wired with satellite. A full breakfast is served every morning in the gorgeous courtyard, gushing with fountains, where a popular bar and restaurant rocks in the high season.

Rivera del Río   BOUTIQUE HOTEL $$$
(Map p524; ☏cell 322-1089870; www.riveradel rio.com; Rivera del Río 104; r incl breakfast US$129-239; ☏☀✆) Walking along a peaceful riverside road, it's quite a surprise to come upon this place, whose sumptuous interiors are eye-popping, running from Italianate frescoes and water features to 1920s plush with not one false note. All of the rooms and suites in this vertically arranged building are strikingly different, and the overall package is very impressive. Gay-friendly.

Hotel Porto Allegro   HOTEL $$$
(Puerto Alegre; Map p524; ☏322-178-26-76; www.hotelportoallegro.com.mx; Hidalgo 119; s/d/ ste incl breakfast M$1190/1405/1620; �P☀ @☎) In an enviably central location, this hotel has spotless modern rooms that are rather nondescript but comfortable. Some are more spacious than others, and upgrading to a suite doesn't cost much extra. The rooftop terrace offers great views of the ocean and green hills, and there's a tiny pool to enjoy them from. The best feature is the cordial, genuinely welcoming staff.

Casa Doña Susana   HOTEL $$$
(Map p524; ☏322-226-71-01; www.casadona susana.com; Diéguez 171; d from M$1327; ☏☀ @✆) There's old-world elegance in the lobby, plenty of stone and brick arches, and a pretty interior courtyard. Rooms have antique wood furnishings, and the roof deck has a pool with mountain and sea views, as well as a chapel where you may count your blessings. You get full use of the nearby sister resort-hotel's facilities, including beach umbrellas and a larger pool.

✖ Eating

There's a good eating scene in Puerto Vallarta, with plenty of choice throughout the center.

✖ South of the Río Cuale

Some of the tastiest and cheapest food in town comes from the taco stands along Madero and neighboring Zona Romántica streets in the early evening.

A Page in the Sun
CAFE $

(Map p524; www.apageinthesun.com; Cárdenas 179; pastries & light meals M$20-75; ⏰7am-10pm Mon-Sat summer, to 11pm daily winter; ☕🕸) This friendly and highly recommended cafe doubles as a bookstore and social hangout, with good espresso drinks, delicious sweet treats, sandwiches, salads, beer, comfy couches and regular events.

Marisma Fish Taco
TAQUERÍA $

(Map p524; ☎322-222-13-95; www.marismafish taco.com; Naranjo 320; snacks M$22-28; ⏰9am-5pm) Delicious tacos with shrimp, smoked marlin or fried fish are served at this genial streetside taquería. Pull up a stool and watch as the servers behind the counter press fresh tortillas and fry up tasty treats from a simple menu that also offers seafood quesadillas.

Garlapago
TAQUERÍA $

(Map p524; cnr Carranza & Jacarandas; snacks M$15-30; ⏰9am-4:30pm Tue-Sat) A tiny taquería favored by locals for bacon-wrapped fish and shrimp tacos, though you can get them without bacon too. The octopus ones with zucchini flowers are also recommended. It does ceviche tostadas and octopus quesadillas too.

Pancho's Takos
TAQUERÍA $

(Map p524; Badillo 162; tacos M$13; ⏰6pm-2am Mon-Sat) Drawing a regular nighttime crowd, this spot near the beach serves delicious tacos al pastor (spit-grilled pork with diced onions, cilantro and pineapple) until the wee hours.

La Ronda
MEXICAN $$

(Map p524; ☎322-223-20-02; www.facebook. com/larondapuertovallarta; Serdán 372; mains M$105-190; ⏰1pm-midnight Tue-Sun; ☕) It may look like a standard sidewalk hole-in-the-wall eatery, but the two brothers here produce surprisingly sophisticated fare, including whole baked fish, delicious fajitas

and tasty molcajete (stew made in a traditional mortar and pestle) options. It's well worth seeking out for an authentic taste of Mexico.

Coco's Kitchen
INTERNATIONAL $$

(Map p524; ☎322-223-03-73; www.cocoskitchen pv.net; Púlpito 122; mains M$60-160; ⏰8am-11pm Mon-Sat, to 4pm Sun; ☕🕸) A preferred brunch choice south of the river. Tables are sprinkled on a ceramic-tiled patio beneath a stilted terracotta roof in a shady bar-side garden. Dishes range from carnitas (braised pulled pork) and green-chili burritos to a range of quesadillas and salads, eggs Benedict, chilaquiles, French toast and pecan waffles.

El Mole de Jovita
MEXICAN $$

(Map p524; ☎322-223-30-65; Badillo 220; mains M$80-130; ⏰3:30-10pm Mon-Sat; ☕) This family-run restaurant specializes in chicken with mole, but also serves plenty of other reasonably priced Mexican standards.

Red Cabbage Café
MEXICAN $$$

(Map p519; ☎322-223-04-11; www.redcabbage pv.com; Rivera del Río 204A; mains M$140-240; ⏰5-11pm, closed Jul-Sep; ☕🕸) Though the atmosphere is casual, with eclectic and bohemian artwork, the food is serious and features old recipes and uncommon indigenous sauces. It's a pleasant 10-minute walk from the Zona Romántica; from Cárdenas turn right on Rivera del Río, just before the Río Cuale bridge. No credit cards.

Bravos
MEXICAN, ITALIAN $$$

(Map p524; ☎322-222-03-39; www.bravospv.com; Madero 263; mains M$160-200; ⏰5-11:30pm Tue-Sun; ☕🕸) In the heart of the Zona Romántica, this low-lit bistro has a growing fan base for its refined and delicious preparations that draw on both Italy and Mexico for inspiration. Anything involving shrimp, plump and tender, is a winner, but almost everything here is tasty. Make sure you leave room for a slice of cake for dessert. Extremely welcoming service.

Archie's Wok
ASIAN $$$

(Map p524; ☎322-222-04-11; www.archieswok. com; Rodríguez 130; mains M$155-225; ⏰2-11pm Mon-Sat; ☕🕸🎵) The menu may change, but Asian fusion is always served at this elegant, urbane restaurant. Think savory fish roasted in a banana leaf, and a coconut poblano chili soup, which is a nice Thai-inflected take on tortilla soup. The noodle dishes are stellar, and the wines and margaritas tasty.

WORTH A TRIP

BITES ABOVE THE BAY

Ocean Grill (☑322-223-73-15; www.oceangrillvallarta.com; Playa Colomitos; mains M$140-280; ⊙11am-5pm Wed-Mon; ☻☎) If you like boat rides, rugged tropical shores, jungled mountains and laid-back elegance, not to mention stellar food and excellent drinks, book a lunch at this reservation-only bistro set on a rocky cliff, and a five-minute water-taxi ride from Boca de Tomatlán. Mains range from sensational seafood such as tapenade-encrusted octopus to delicious ribs; it also does burgers, chicken and steaks.

All of it is spiced, rubbed and grilled over an open flame and served in a multi-leveled dining room, its *palapa* roof supported by vine-tangled tree trunks. There are trails from here to Playa de las Ánimas or back to Boca if you want to walk off the feed. Transfers to and from Boca are included with each reservation. No under-14s.

La Palapa SEAFOOD **$$$**
(Map p524; ☑322-222-52-25; www.lapalapapv.com; Púlpito 103; mains M$180-360; ⊙8:30am-11:30pm; ☻☎) Elegant beach dining at its best. Tables are positioned to take full advantage of the sea views, making it a particularly marvelous spot for breakfast or to watch the sun set. The offering changes but always includes succulent marinated seafood and other delights. Between meals, it cuts back to a snack menu. During the day there's a fair bit of hawker and musician traffic.

✕ North of the Río Cuale

Planeta Vegetariano VEGETARIAN **$**
(Map p524; ☑322-222-30-73; www.planetavegetariano.com; Iturbide 270; buffet breakfast M$70 lunch/dinner M$95; ⊙8am-10pm Thu-Tue; ☻✐) This buffet-style place with only 10 tables eschews cheese for fresh, dairy-free dishes such as soy enchiladas, banana lasagna (yes, that's right) and a wide range of creatively conceived salads.

Gaby's MEXICAN **$$**
(Map p524; ☑322-116-22-22; www.gabysrestaurant.com.mx; Mina 252; mains M$140-260; ⊙8am-11pm; ☻☎) Since 1989, this bright and cheerful family-run place with upstairs terrace seating and a tree-shaded back patio has been serving dependably tasty Mexican classics. It's atmospheric in the evenings and great value at lunchtime, when the daily *comida corrida* (prix-fixe menu; including main dish, soup and *agua fresca*) is a steal. At night, videos are cheekily projected onto a neighboring building.

Chenan2 SEAFOOD **$$**
(Map p524; www.facebook.com/chenan2restaurant; Cárdenas 520; mains M$140-220; ⊙5:30-11pm Tue-Sun; ☻) This delightful family-run restaurant has a simple but attractive air-conditioned interior with small square tables. It excels in the kitchen, producing absolutely succulent seafood burritos as well as tasty shrimp crepes and many other dishes.

El Barracuda SEAFOOD **$$**
(Map p519; ☑322-222-40-34; www.elbarracuda.com; Paraguay 1290; dishes M$80-160; ⊙12:30-11pm Mon & Tue, 11:30am-1:30am Wed-Sat, 11:30am-11pm Sun; ☻☎) This breezy open shack on the beach makes a top venue for a seafood lunch with ocean views. Grilled-shrimp tacos are famous; the tuna sashimi is more a carpaccio but still tasty, as is *mariscos dinamita*, a shrimp, octopus and fish rice dish. Do-it-yourself smoked marlin *tostadas* are fab. Turtles still emerge here to lay eggs, and whales thrash just offshore all winter long.

Benitto's DELI **$$**
(Map p519; ☑322-209-02-87; www.benittos.com; Paseo de la Marina 21; mains M$100-165; ⊙8am-2am Mon-Sat; ☻☎) A gourmet deli in the marina area with big, bold, modern art on the walls. It's popular among upmarket locals for creative panini, mixed carpaccios, and imported beers and wines. It also does main serves of salads, soups and pastas. The kitchen is open until midnight; drinkers may linger.

La Dolce Vita ITALIAN **$$**
(Map p524; ☑322-222-38-52; www.dolcevita.com.mx; Paseo Díaz Ordaz 674; mains M$130-160; ⊙noon-2am Mon-Sat, 6pm-midnight Sun; ☻☎) A cheerful, often-crowded spot, good for wood-fired pizzas, pastas and people-watching. It's a local expat favorite. Request a table upstairs by the window for great views.

★ Café des Artistes
FUSION $$$

(Map p524; ☑ 322-222-32-28; www.cafedesar
tistes.com; Guadalupe Sánchez 740; mains M$240-
470; ☺ 6-11pm; ☺ 🛜) Many consider this to
be Vallarta's finest restaurant. You're sure to
enjoy its romantic ambience and exquisite
fusion of French and Mexican influences,
and its decor, which ranges from the candle-
lit garden to modern interior to whimsical
castle-like exterior. But the food is the thing,
with some memorable combinations on
show. Service is formal but unobtrusive, and
reservations are recommended.

El Arrayán
MEXICAN $$$

(Map p524; ☑ 322-222-71-95; www.elarrayan.
com.mx; Allende 344; mains M$190-295; ☺ 5:30-
11pm Wed-Mon; ☺ 🛜) Owner Carmen Porras
takes special pleasure in rescuing old family
recipes from obscurity, with an emphasis on
fresh local ingredients. Specialties include
crispy duck *carnitas* with orange sauce, and
rib-eye steak marinated in Mexican spices
and tequila. The restaurant, with its open
kitchen and romantic courtyard, also serves
as a venue for regular cooking classes.

La Leche
MEXICAN $$$

(Map p519; ☑ 322-293-09-00; www.laleche
restaurant.com; Medina Ascensio s/n; mains
M$200-360; ☺ 6pm-1am; ☺ 🛜) It's a dramat-
ically visual entry here, with milk being the
theme. The dairy gag continues in various
ways throughout the meal. Service is very
personal and friendly – expect pats on the
back rather than kid gloves – if a bit scatty.
The restaurant is strong on seafood and its
duck signature dish, and it makes the eating
experience lots of fun.

There's a good wine list for west coast
Mexico and a seven-course degustation
menu (M$690). Kick off your meal with a
succulent mango 'martini.' Want just a taste?
It also runs a burrito van outside (burritos
M$80). The restaurant is at the entrance to
the Fiesta Americana resort.

Layla's Restaurante
MEXICAN $$$

(Map p519; ☑ 322-222-24-36; www.laylasres
taurante.com; Venezuela 137; mains M$180-250;
☺ 9am-11pm Tue-Sat, to 9pm Sun; ☺ 🛜) Just
off the strip, but unnoticed by passers-by,
this is highly recommended for quality,
well-presented cooking without a hint of
pretension. The upstairs terrace can see you
sip a cucumber margarita before a meal of
fish, shrimp or beef, all exquisitely prepared
and served by a friendly bevy of staff. Aspar-
agus tempura was a standout when we visited, as was the minty mouth-cleanser.

Head two blocks north from where the
Ordaz waterfront strip becomes a normal
road again, then turn left.

La Cigale
FRENCH $$$

(Map p524; ☑ 322-222-79-38; www.lacigale
bistro.com; Hidalgo 398; mains M$155-295;
☺ 5pm-midnight; ☺ 🛜) In the shadow of Tem-
plo de Guadalupe, this casual-chic French
bistro with chalkboard menus and checker-
board floors serves everything from quiche
lorraine to steak tartare, accompanied by
wines from around the world.

🍷 Drinking & Nightlife

It's ridiculously easy to become inebriated in
a town where two-for-one happy hours are
as reliable as the sunset, margarita glasses
look like oversized snifters, and day drink-
ing is an obligation. Admission charges are
normally waived early in the week; on Fri-
day and Saturday nights they often include
one or two drinks.

Along the *malecón* is a bunch of places
where teen and 20-something locals and
tourists get trashed and dance on tables.

★ Bar Morelos
BAR

(Map p524; ☑ 322-111-39-40; www.facebook.
com/barmorelospuertovallarta; Morelos 589;
☺ 8pm-4am or 5am; 🛜) Stylish and with a
team of very professional staff, this makes
for a far classier drink than you can find a
block away on the *malecón*. Over 50 mez-
cals are on offer, and the staff will happily
talk you through them. Interesting midweek
DJs, a decent sound system and attractive
decor make this a standout. Don't miss a
game of table football in the toilet area.

La Cervecería Unión
BAR

(Map p524; ☑ 322-223-09-29; Paseo Díaz Ordaz
610; ☺ 8am-2am Sun-Thu, to 3am Fri & Sat; 🛜) It's
a real relief to come in here on a hot after-
noon and leave bland beer behind. There's
a fine selection of craft brews from around
Mexico and a few Belgian imports. There's
also an oyster bar, decent tacos, a long tequi-
la list and tasty *micheladas* (beer cocktails).
The bay views are great.

Jazz Foundation
BAR, CLUB

(Map p524; www.jazzpv.com; Allende 116; ☺ 6pm-
2am Mon-Sat, to midnight Sun; 🛜) This appeal-
ing upstairs venue might be constructed
out of breeze blocks, bricks and planks of
wood, but it provides plenty of class with

GAY & LESBIAN PUERTO VALLARTA

Come on out – the rainbow flag flies high over Puerto Vallarta. An ever-increasing stream of visitors descends on Vallarta annually for its formidable selection of gay bars, nightclubs, restaurants and hotels, as well as its busy annual calendar of gay- and lesbian-themed events. The **Gay Guide Vallarta** (www.gayguidevallarta.com) booklet and website has tons of information and a helpful map for finding gay-friendly businesses.

Drinking & Nightlife

Most dance clubs open from 10pm until at least 4am, and some stay open well past sunrise. For an entertaining introduction to Vallarta's gay nightlife scene, check out the **Old Town Bar Hop** (www.dianastours.com/old_town_bar_hop.php; per person US$75; ☉7:45pm-1am Fri & Sat) offered by Diana's Tours.

The Zona Romántica is teeming with cocktail bars catering to a gay and lesbian clientele.

Frida (Map p524; www.barfrida.com; Insurgentes 301A; ☉1pm-2am) Named for the artist who is on a first-name basis with the world, Frida is a sociable cantina featuring enticing drink specials. It's a top spot to kick off the evening in a relaxed, non-sceney atmosphere.

La Noche (Map p524; www.facebook.com/lanochebarpv; Cárdenas 257; ☉4pm-3am; ☎) This pre-club venue is well-loved for its convivial atmosphere and buff bartenders and go-go dancers. The soundtrack is resolutely old-school house, and there's a roof terrace.

Sama Bar (Map p524; ☎322-223-31-82; www.facebook.com/sama.martinibar; Olas Altas 510; ☉4pm-2am; ☎) This is a likable small place that draws a young crowd. Order your margarita straight up with salt. Delicious. The martinis are good and strong too.

Paco's Ranch (Map p524; ☎322-222-18-99; www.pacosranch.com; Vallarta 237; ☉10pm-5am Tue-Sun) This venerable disco-cantina stages smashing transvestite shows, with the music pumping loud. It's an amiable scene, with plenty of locals and reasonably priced drinks.

Antropology (Map p524; Morelos 101; ☉9pm-4am) It's raining men at this sizzling dance mecca and male-stripper venue with its dark, intimate rooftop patio. Women are unapologetically disallowed. There's a two-drink minimum cover.

Sleeping

Casa Cupula (Map p524; ☎322-223-24-84; www.casacupula.com; Callejón de la Igualdad 129; r US$225-404, ste US$511-701; P❄❖@☎☈) Sophisticated design and luxurious flourishes define this extremely popular resort catering to both gays and lesbians. Each room is uniquely and tastefully decorated, with amenities ranging from home-theater-sized TVs to private Jacuzzis in some suites. The beach is only a few blocks downhill, although the resort's four pools, gym, on-site restaurant and bar may encourage you to linger here all day.

Villa David (Map p524; ☎322-223-03-15; www.villadavidpv.com; Galeana 348; r US$125-160; ❄@☎☈) Reservations are essential and clothing optional at this well-loved gay retreat in a beautiful hacienda-style mansion in the characterful streets high above the *malecón*. There are great views and sunsets from here, and the tastefully appointed rooms are all different. It's a perfect choice for a romantic getaway.

Hotel Mercurio (Map p524; ☎322-222-47-93; www.hotel-mercurio.com; Rodríguez 168; s/d incl breakfast M$1366/1784; ❄@☎☈) Less than two blocks from Muertos pier, this three-story hotel features 28 pastel-brushed rooms, some of which smell mustier than others, around a pleasant courtyard with a stylish pool and bar. Rooms are simple for the price but have fridges, cable and double or king-sized beds. Buffet breakfasts, spa packages and free international phone calls are among the other perks on offer.

Blue Chairs Beach Resort (Map p519; ☎322-222-50-40; www.bluechairsresort.com; Almendro 4; r US$158-250; ❄☎☈) Overlooking one of Mexico's most famous gay beaches, this resort is a byword for gay in Vallarta. At the time of our last visit it was looking a bit down at heel, but renovations are apparently under way and the beach club scene is still worthwhile, as is the rooftop nightspot and pool. Suites are larger rooms with a kitchenette.

regular live music, jam sessions and other jazz-focused events. The ocean views are spectacular too, making it a romantic spot for a sunset drink.

La Bodeguita del Medio BAR
(Map p524; ☑ 322-223-15-85; www.labodeguita delmedio.com.mx; Paseo Díaz Ordaz 858; ◎ 9am-3am; ⓢ) The walls are scrawled with hand-written poetics and inanities in several languages, the bar is blessed with fine rums and tequilas, and the bar staff pour a mean mojito, as well as questionable variations. Loud salsa music with nightly live acts is accompanied by plenty of dancing and good cheer. The food isn't so special.

Garbo BAR
(Map p524; ☑ 322-223-57-53; Púlpito 142; ◎ 6pm-2am; ⓢ) If you enjoy jazzy stylings and an excellent martini to go with them, make your way to this concrete-floor habitat. The jazz and torch singing are decent to good, and sing-alongs may happen.

Los Muertos PUB
(Map p524; ☑ 322-222-03-08; www.losmuertos brewing.com; Cárdenas 302; ◎ noon-midnight; ⓢ) An attractive, brick-arched, concrete-floor pub and microbrewery. The beer (M$45) comes in six flavors including an IPA called 'Revenge' and a stout called 'McSanchez.' There's pizza and pub grub available (M$80 to M$100).

Mandala CLUB
(Map p524; www.mandaladisco.com; Paseo Díaz Ordaz 640; ◎ 9:30pm-late Thu-Sun) By far the best of three adjacent clubs here, this cinema-sized spot has privileged *malecón* frontage, and keeps a youngish crowd happy until late at night under a benevolent icon's gaze. Drinks are pricey, but you can buy an all-inclusive wristband if you're going to hit it hard.

Andale BAR
(Map p524; ☑ 322-222-10-54; www.andales.com; Olas Altas 425; ◎ 8am-3am; ⓢ) Party hearty with throngs of young vacationers in this dark den of drink, sports and loud rock music even during the day. This joint has old-school dive bar gravitas and is worthy of a round or two. Food is served, and there is some nice upstairs balcony seating.

⭐ Entertainment

Vallarta's main forms of nighttime entertainment revolve around dancing, drinking and dining. At night everyone and their brother strolls the *malecón*. There's often entertainment by the sea at Los Arcos (p519).

Roxy Rock House LIVE MUSIC
(Map p524; www.roxyrockhouse.com; Vallarta 217; ◎ 10pm-5am) In the heart of the Zona Romántica, this place draws an enthusiastic mixed crowd with live rock and blues cover bands nightly, and no admission charge.

🛍 Shopping

Vallarta is a haven for shoppers, with many shops and boutiques selling fashionable clothing, beachwear and crafts from all over Mexico. Tequila and Cuban cigars are also big business.

Peyote People HANDICRAFTS
(Map p524; ☑ 322-222-62-68; www.peyotepeople. com; Juárez 222; ◎ 10am-8pm Mon-Sat, to 6pm Sun) Sells some excellent Huichol beadwork, thread paintings and jewelry.

Mercado de Artesanías HANDICRAFTS
(Map p524; ☑ 322-223-09-25; Rodríguez 260) Straddling the north bank of the Río Cuale, this market sells everything from Taxco silver, *sarapes* (blankets with a head opening, worn as a cloak) and huaraches (woven leather sandals) to wool wall hangings and blown glass. Don't confuse it with the nearby market on Morelos, which, though similarly named, deals in tourist tat.

Olinalá HANDICRAFTS, ARTS & CRAFTS
(Map p524; ☑ 322-228-06-59, cell 322-1213574; www.galeriaolinala.com; Cárdenas 274; ◎ 10:30am-3:30pm Mon-Sat, closed Jul-Sep) In business since 1978, this excellent little shop displays authentic Mexican dance masks, folk art and rural antiques. You may be able to arrange a visit in the summer months by phoning ahead.

Mundo de Azulejos CERAMICS
(Map p524; www.talavera-tile.com.mx; Carranza 374; ◎ 9am-7pm Mon-Fri, to 2pm Sat) This store offers a vast array of brightly colored Talavera tiles and ceramics.

Dulcería Leal FOOD
(Map p524; Juárez 262; ◎ 10am-10pm) If you have a sweet tooth, stop by this cute *tienda* (shop) packed with temptation. It sells everything from tamarind chews to exquisite caramels to any number of dried fruit and sugary nut concoctions.

❶ Information

Although most businesses in Vallarta accept US dollars as readily as they accept pesos, rates are generally poor. Banks with ATMs and *casas de cambio* are abundant.

Main Post Office (Map p519; www.correos demexico.gob.mx; Colombia 1014)

Municipal Tourist Office (Map p524; ☑ 322-222-09-23; www.facebook.com/turismo municipalpuertovallarta; Juárez s/n; ⊙8am-8pm Mon-Fri, to 4pm Sat & Sun) Vallarta's busy but competent office, in the municipal building at the northeast corner of Plaza Principal, has free maps, multilingual tourist literature and bilingual staff.

San Javier Marina Hospital (Map p519; ☑322-226-10-00; www.sanjavier.com.mx; Ascencio 2760; ⊙24hr) Vallarta's best-equipped hospital.

❶ Getting There & Away

AIR

Gustavo Díaz Ordaz International Airport (PVR; Map p519; ☑322-221-12-98; www.aeropuertosgap.com.mx; Carretera Tepic Km 7.5; 🛜) is located 10km north of the city. There are direct flights, some seasonal, from dozens of US and Canadian cities, as well as direct charters from the UK.

The following domestic destinations are serviced by these airlines:

➡ Aguascalientes – TAR

➡ Durango – TAR

➡ Guadalajara – Aeroméxico, Interjet, TAR

➡ León – Interjet, TAR

➡ Mexico City – Aeroméxico, Interjet, VivaAerobus, Volaris

➡ Monterrey – Aeroméxico, TAR, VivaAerobus, Volaris

➡ Queretaro – TAR

➡ Tijuana – Volaris

➡ Toluca – Interjet

Aeroméxico (Map p519; ☑322-225-17-77; www.aeromexico.com; Medina Ascensio 1853; ⊙9am-7pm Mon-Fri, 10am-3pm Sat & Sun) Also has an office at the airport.

BUS

Vallarta's **long-distance bus terminal** (Map p519; Bahía de Santiago s/n) is just off Hwy 200, about 10km north of the city center and 2km northeast of the airport. Think M$120 in a cab from downtown.

Primera Plus (Map p524; Carranza 393) has a downtown office where you can buy tickets. If you're heading to Barra de Navidad, Manzanillo or other points south, you can save a trip to the bus terminal by boarding here or, for other bus lines, 50m away at the corner of Carranza and Aguacate.

CAR & MOTORCYCLE

Starting at about M$600 per day, on-the-spot car rentals are pricey during high season; you'll often do better booking online, though extra insurance charges mean online rates aren't always what they appear to be. At other times, deep discounts are offered.

A dozen car-rental agencies maintain adjacent counters in the airport arrivals hall, with offices nearby.

Alamo (Map p519; ☑322-221-30-30; www.alamomexico.com.mx; Ctra a Tepic 4690, Villa Las Flores; ⊙8am-10pm)

Avis (Map p519; ☑322-221-07-83; www.avis.mx; Medina Ascensio s/n; ⊙7am-11:30pm)

Budget (Map p519; ☑322-221-17-30; www.budget.com.mx; Medina Ascensio 141, Villa Las Flores; ⊙7am-9pm)

Sixt (Map p519; ☑322-209-06-85; www.sixt.com; Medina Ascensio 7930, Villa Las Flores; ⊙7am-10pm)

❶ Getting Around

TO/FROM THE AIRPORT

The cheapest way to get to/from the airport is on a local bus for M$7.50. 'Centro' and 'Olas Altas' buses go into town from a stop just outside the arrivals hall. Returning from town, 'Aeropuerto,' 'Juntas' and 'Ixtapa' buses stop at the airport entrance.

From the airport to the city, taxis charge fixed rates ranging from M$200 to M$340, depending on which neighborhood you're traveling to. You

BUSES FROM PUERTO VALLARTA

DESTINATION	FARE (M$)	DURATION (HR)	FREQUENCY (DAILY)
Barra de Navidad	210-300	4-5	frequent
Guadalajara	410-590	5½	very frequent
Manzanillo	276-389	5-5½	hourly
Mazatlán	515-660	7-9	6
Mexico City	962-1038	10½-12	7 (nightly)
Tepic	220-238	3½	frequent

can save money by crossing Hwy 200 via the pedestrian bridge outside the arrivals hall and taking a taxi from the opposite side of the street. A taxi back to the airport from downtown costs around M$120.

BOAT

Vallarta's water taxis serve the beautiful beaches on the southern side of the bay, some accessible only by boat. Departing from the Playa de los Muertos pier, they head south around the bay, making stops at Playa de las Ánimas (25 minutes), Quimixto (40 minutes) and Yelapa (55 minutes); the round-trip fare is M$300 for any destination. Boats depart Puerto Vallarta every hour or two between 10am and 4:30pm, returning from Yelapa (the end of the line) with the same frequency between 7:30am and 3:45pm daily.

Private yachts and *lanchas* can be hired from the southern side of the Playa de los Muertos pier, starting from around M$350 per hour. They'll take you to any secluded beach around the bay; most have gear aboard for snorkeling and fishing.

BUS

Local buses operate every five minutes from 5am to 11pm on most routes, and cost M$7.50. Plaza Lázaro Cárdenas near Playa Olas Altas is a major departure hub. Northbound local buses also stop on Insurgentes near the corner of Madero. Southbound buses either pass through the center, or loop round via a tunnel to the Zona Romántica.

Northbound buses marked 'Aeropuerto,' 'Ixtapa,' 'Mojoneras' and 'Juntas' pass through the city heading north to the airport and Marina Vallarta; the 'Mojoneras' bus also stops at Puerto Vallarta's long-distance bus terminal.

White and orange 'Boca de Tomatlán' buses (M$7.50) head south along the coastal highway through Mismaloya (20 minutes) to Boca de Tomatlán (30 minutes). They depart from the corner of Badillo and Constitución every 15 minutes.

TAXI

Cab prices are regulated by zones; the cost for a ride is determined by how many zones you cross. A typical trip from downtown to the Zona Hotelera costs M$80; to the airport or the long-distance bus terminal M$120; and to Mismaloya M$130. Always determine the price of the ride before you get in. Hailing a cab is easy in the city center along Morelos. There are several taxi stands, including one on Morelos between Corona and Galeana, one on Morelos at Rodríguez, and one on Carranza at Plaza Lázaro Cárdenas.

Costalegre Beaches

South of Puerto Vallarta, the stretch of Mexico's Pacific coast from Chamela to Barra de Navidad is blessed with fine beaches. Tourism promoters and developers refer to this shoreline as the 'Costalegre' (Happy Coast). Following are the beaches from north to south (with kilometer numbers measured from the junction of Hwys 80 and 200 just outside San Patricio-Melaque).

Fans of sea turtles (and, really, who isn't in that group?) should stop by **Campamento Majahuas** (☑329-298-12-32; www.campamentomajahuas.com; Hwy 200, Km 116; ☉turtles nesting at night Jul-Nov) 🏖, where you can camp and watch the turtles nest with local guides. There's a small hotel here too. It's become a destination for international students interested in turtles and their habitat.

Playa Pérula (turnoff Hwy 200 Km 73), a sheltered beach at the northern end of tranquil 11km-long Bahía de Chamela, is great for swimming and extended walks. There are cheap accommodations and a smattering of *palapa* restaurants. You can charter a *panga* from here to the **Islas Pajareras**, an important home of the blue-footed booby.

At Bahía de Chamela, **Playa El Negrito** (turnoff Hwy 200 Km 64) is an isolated, relaxing beach with a couple of restaurants but no hotels. The nine islands in the expansive bay are beautiful to see in silhouette at sunset.

On the palm-fringed Bahía Tenacatita, **Playa Tenacatita** (turnoff Hwy 200 Km 28) has clear snorkeling waters and a large mangrove lagoon with good bird-watching, but there is a land title in dispute here, with a development group in the process of trying to build on and partly privatize an otherwise public and undeveloped beach. You can still visit for now, but camping is no longer allowed. Bring your own food and drinks and enjoy the day.

Also on this bay are **Playa Boca de Iguanas** (turnoff Hwy 200 Km 19) and **Playa La Manzanilla** (turnoff Hwy 200 Km 13). The shorebreak on Iguanas can be steep and fast, perfect for body boarding. Manzanilla's calm water is ideal for swimming. You can spot good-sized crocs in the mangrove estuary here.

Bahía de Navidad

The tight arc of the Bahía de Navidad is practically ringed by deep, honey-colored sand with two resort towns at either end, waving amiably at each other. Situated 5km apart by road, but only a kilometer and a bit along the beach, Barra de Navidad and San Patricio-Melaque are siblings with distinct personalities. Barra is beloved for its attractive cobbled streets and aura of good living, while San Patricio-Melaque, which is larger and less quaint, draws budget-minded travelers seeking that beachfront buzz.

San Patricio-Melaque

📞 315 / POP 7600

Known by most as Melaque (meh-*lah*-keh), this kick-back beach resort is a popular vacation destination for Mexican families and a low-key winter hangout for snowbirds. The main activities are swimming, lazing on the beach, watching pelicans fish at sunrise and sunset, climbing to the *mirador* (lookout) at the bay's western end, prowling the plaza and public market, or walking the beach to Barra de Navidad.

🏃 Activities

Pacific Adventures　　　　WATER SPORTS
(📞 315-100-49-99; www.facebook.com/pacificx adventures) Enthusiastic, youthful set-up that can rent you surfboards, paddleboards and more, and also teach you to use them.

👉 Tours

★ **Experience Mex-Eco Tours**　　ECOTOUR
(📞 315-355-70-27; www.mex-ecotours.com; Gómez Farías 59-2) 🖋 Competent and friendly, this knowledgeable ecotourism company operates impressive day trips near Melaque and an array of multiday excursions throughout Mexico, all with a commitment to sustainable tourism. Highlights include visiting an indigenous women's cooperative coffee plantation (M$750), an overnight camping trip to a sea turtle biological station (M$1200), and boat trips. It also runs tours from Bucerías, near Puerto Vallarta.

🎉 Festivals & Events

Fiesta de San Patricio　　　CULTURAL
Melaque honors its patron saint with a blowout week of festivities, including all-day parties, rodeos, a carnival, music, dances and nightly fireworks, leading up to St Patrick's Day (March 17).

🛏 Sleeping

Rates rise sharply at Christmas and Semana Santa; high season is November through May. Discounts are common for longer stays.

Hotel Los Caracoles　　　GUESTHOUSE $
(📞 315-355-73-08; www.loscaracoles.com.mx; Gómez Farías 26; s/d/q M$330/440/570; 🅿🛜) Simple and superclean, this guesthouse has 13 white-tiled, fan-cooled rooms with peach walls, hand-painted bedheads and cable TV. Ground-floor rooms don't catch much natural light, but are good value nonetheless. Rooms with balconies upstairs are larger for the same price. 'Bungalows' with kitchenette are available too (M$750).

★ **Villas El Rosario
de San Andres**　　　APARTMENT $$
(📞 315-355-63-42; www.elrosariodesanandres. com; Hidalgo 10; d M$660-820, q M$760-1200; 🅿🛜❄🛜🏊) Genially family-run, this central complex offers bright studios with ceramic tiles, attractive kitchenettes, high ceilings and flat-screen TVs. Sofa-beds mean that children can be easily accommodated in most rooms. The rooftop deck is a wonderful common area with special mountain and sea views. There is also a small plunge pool.

Posada Pablo de Tarso　　　HOTEL $$
(📞 315-355-57-07; www.posadapablodetarso. com; Gómez Farías 408; d/bungalow M$700/900; 🅿🛜❄🛜🏊) This leafy, brick courtyard hotel with its luscious beachside pool area offers rooms or bungalows (with kitchenette but no air-con) that are cool and spacious with beamed ceilings and terracotta floors. Some rooms have fridges too; those overlooking the road or the beach are largest. A couple of the bungalows are across the street.

Las Arenas　　　HOTEL $$
(📞 315-355-50-97; www.lasarenas.net; Gómez Farías 11; d/tw/bungalow M$700/810/1030; 🛜❄🛜🏊) With umbrellas and chairs on a nice slice of beachfront, this property is functional rather than stylish, but has a good pool and is neat and very well maintained. Rooms have queen- or king-sized beds, tile floors and flat-screen TVs. The bungalows are simply studios with kitchenettes.

★ **La Paloma** BOUTIQUE HOTEL **$$$**
(☎ 315-355-53-45; www.lapalomamexico.com; Las Cabañas 13; studio US$165-185; P ❄ ☎ ⌨) Original artworks abound at this ocean-side boutique hotel hidden behind high walls. Singular, comfortable studios have kitchen/kitchenette plus terraces, and are vibrantly colorful, with quirky mirrors and bright ceramics. For the small price difference, consider one of the huge penthouses with sea views – we loved number 14. Plush gardens, a 25m beachside pool, library and free light breakfast; it's a fabulous retreat.

Prices plunge up to 60% off-season.

✕ Eating & Drinking

From 6pm to midnight, various food stands serve inexpensive Mexican fare a block east of the plaza along Juárez. A row of pleasant *palapa* restaurants stretches along the beach at the western end of town.

Scooby's MEXICAN **$**
(Obregón 36; snacks M$12-70; ⊙ 7-11pm; ☜ ☎) This neighborhood eatery does the tastiest *tacos al pastor* in town, and also keeps the expats coming back for the grilled ribs and prime rib steak on Sundays. The portions are generous and the owners couldn't be more welcoming. It does a fine *michelada* too.

La Flor del Café CAFE **$**
(Gordiano Guzmán, near Ramón Corona; dishes M$30-110; ⊙ 7am-1:30pm & 6:30-11pm; ☜ ☎) On a friendly, brightly hued patio, this place eschews the hottest part of the day but opens mornings for tasty smoothies, juices, coffee, sandwiches and salads. In the evenings it adds a couple of heftier dinner dishes to the menu, such as seafood fettuccine.

Papa Gallo's SEAFOOD **$$**
(☎ 315-355-58-70; Gómez Farías 27A; dishes M$80-140; ⊙ 1-9pm Mon-Sat, noon-9pm Sun; ☎) An offshoot of popular restaurant Roosters, this restaurant is reached by an alleyway opposite the bus station. There are tables on the sand, but it's cooler on the lovely raised platform above the beach. The seafood – shrimp, octopus and fish – is all decidedly tasty, the value is great and service is helpful.

☕ Drinking & Nightlife

Mamitas BAR
(Lopez Mateos 49; ⊙ 7pm-1am; ☎) The choice spot for adult beverages. It's set above the plaza and is an open, airy bar that cranks the music up pretty loud later on.

Esquina Paraíso BAR
(cnr Obregón & Corona; ⊙ 7pm-2am Wed-Mon) This curious open-air corner bar has done its decor out of driftwood, recycled packing crates and the like and is well worth a look. Don't expect luxury but enjoy the swing-seats.

ℹ Information

Banamex (www.banamex.com; Gómez Farías s/n; ⊙ 8am-4pm Mon-Fri) On the drag backing the beach. Has an ATM and will change US and Canadian dollars.

ℹ Getting There & Away

BUS

Buses stop on opposite sides of Carranza at the corner of Gómez Farías. Three companies have separate ticket offices around this intersection, with similar fares.

Local buses to Barra de Navidad (M$7, 15 minutes) leave every 15 minutes from the corner of López Mateos and Juárez at the southwest corner of the plaza, and do a slow circuit before hitting the main road. More direct white buses cost M$11.

TAXI

A taxi between Melaque and Barra costs M$60; taxis congregate at the plaza.

BUSES FROM SAN PATRICIO-MELAQUE

DESTINATION	FARE (M$)	DURATION (HR)	FREQUENCY (DAILY)
Guadalajara	305-345	5½-6	hourly
Manzanillo	61-83	1-1½	half-hourly
Mexico City (Terminal Norte)	1136-1450	12	2
Puerto Vallarta	210-300	4-5	frequent

Barra de Navidad

🖉 315 / POP 4300

Barra de Navidad greets you with mellow happiness and easy charm that seeps into your bones. It's a pueblo on a narrow isthmus between a lagoon and the beach, boasting excellent sport fishing, bird- and crocodile-watching trips, and succulent seafood. Barra first came to prominence in 1564 when its shipyards produced the galleons used by conquistador Miguel López de Legazpi and Father André de Urdaneta to deliver the Philippines to King Felipe of Spain. By 1600, however, most of the conquests were being conducted from Acapulco, and Barra slipped into sleepy obscurity.

🏃 Activities

Barra's steep and narrow beach is lovely to behold, but conditions are sometimes too rough for swimming. It's generally gentlest in the mornings.

The waters near Barra are bristling with marlin, swordfish, albacore, *dorado*, snapper and other more rarefied catches.

Sociedad Cooperativa
de Servicios Turísticos   BOAT TOUR
(Veracruz 40; ☉ 7am-sunset) Trips into the Laguna de Navidad are a Barra highlight. This boatowner's cooperative books a variety of boat tours ranging from half-hour trips around the lagoon (M$300 per boat) to all-day jungle trips to Tenacatita (M$3000 per boat).

Fishing trips on *lanchas* can also be arranged at the cooperative for M$500 per hour or M$3000 per day, including gear; many trips include snorkeling stops. Prices are posted at the open-air lagoonside office.

Grand Bay Golf Course   GOLF
(🖉 314-331-05-00; www.islanavidad.com.mx; Isla Navidad; green fees US$215 incl buggy) Grand Bay has 27 holes with excellent vistas and greens carved into ocean dunes against a backdrop of mountains. It's considered one of Mexico's finer courses. Given the geography of the area, it's appropriate that there are lots of water hazards.

🛏 Sleeping

Barra has fewer beachfront rooms than neighboring Melaque. Book well in advance for high season (between November and May). A lot of the town's options are a bit mediocre but there are some solid choices.

★ Hotel Delfín   HOTEL $
(🖉 315-355-50-68; www.hoteldelfinmx.com; Morelos 23; s/d M$495/595, with air-con M$695/795; 🅿 ⊕ ❋ 🛜 🏊) 🖋 The homey Delfín is one of Barra's best deals. It has large, pleasant rooms featuring shared balconies, a grassy pool area and a rooftop deck. Factor in excellent management and you have the kind of place you'd rather not leave. Rooms with TV and air-con cost more but are otherwise identical; fans in the others work well. Repeat customers fill the place in winter.

Hotel Sarabi   HOTEL $
(🖉 315-355-82-23; www.hotelsarabi.com; Av Veracruz 196; d/tw M$500/550; ⊕ ❋ 🛜) In the heart of things in Barra, this hotel offers three levels of excellent budget rooms with fans and air-con; the latter costs an extra M$100 if you want to turn it on. It's set around a gravel courtyard and run by a kindly woman who makes sure everything is shipshape. Something of a bargain.

Hotel Barra de Navidad   HOTEL $$
(🖉 315-355-51-22; www.hotelbarradenavidad.com.mx; Legazpi 250; d M$900-1200, ste M$1200-1750; ⊕ ❋ 🛜 🏊) Providing Barra's best beach access, this white beachside hotel looks a bit tired in parts but harbors a shaded and intimate courtyard and a small but inviting pool. The open layout means you can hear the sea nearly throughout, but best are the seaside rooms, which are modern and nondescript but boast a magnificent outlook and a little terrace to enjoy it from.

Casa Chips   HOTEL $$
(🖉 315-355-55-55; www.casachips.com; Legazpi 198; d/ste M$1050/1700; ⊕ ❋ 🛜) One of Barra's few beachfront options, Chips is most appealing for its two big ocean-facing suites with terraces, great views, nice tile- and brickwork, and kitchenettes. Less enticing are the interior and street-facing rooms, which can get a bit claustrophobic, though most have balconies.

🍴 Eating

Head to the junction with the main road for a few places doing delicious fish, including *pescado zarandeado* – **El Brody** (Hwy 200 Km 1; mains M$70-150; ☉ 11am-7pm Tue-Sun) is a favorite.

★ El Manglito   SEAFOOD $$
(🖉 315-355-81-28; Av Veracruz 17; mains M$100-170; ☉ 1-9pm) With a lovely outlook over the water and welcome breezes, this lagoon

restaurant is basically a slab of concrete and sand with a makeshift roof, plastic tables and few frills beyond plenty of greenery, but it produces some really excellent seafood – the shrimp is wonderful, fresh oysters are great, and various fish dishes also are standouts. Service is very cordial.

Nacho SEAFOOD $$
(Legazpi; mains M$50-170; ⊙10:30am-9:30pm) It doesn't look like much upon first glance, just a handful of tables under a stilted beachside *palapa* roof, but the grilled fish is the deal. Ask for some of the delicious house salsa and order one of the fine *micheladas*, elaborately made at the front bar, to wash it down.

Restaurant Ramon's MEXICAN $$
(☑315-355-64-35; Legazpi 260; mains M$80-125; ⊙8am-11pm; ⊜) This casual and friendly restaurant is justifiably popular for its excellent fish tacos, *chiles rellenos*, and local and gringo favorites such as fish and chips.

🍷 Drinking & Nightlife

Toward the pier at the foot of Legazpi, a cluster of bars keeps hopping into the wee hours.

ℹ Information

Banamex (Av Veracruz s/n) One of two ATMs just south of Barra's main plaza.
Tourist Office (☑315-355-83-83; www.costalegre.com; Av Veracruz 98; ⊙9am-5pm Mon-Fri) This regional office has maps and information about Barra and the other towns of the Costalegre.

ℹ Getting There & Around

If it's not too hot, the most pleasant way to get between Barra de Navidad and Melaque is strolling along the beach.

AIR

Barra de Navidad is served by nearby **Manzanillo International Airport** (Playa de Oro; ZLO; ☑315-333-11-19; www.aeropuertosgap.com.mx; Carretera Manzanillo-Barra de Navidad Km 42), 26km southeast of Barra on Hwy 200. To get to town from the airport, take a taxi (M$400, 30 minutes).

BOAT

Water taxis operate on demand 24 hours a day from the dock at the southern end of Veracruz, offering service to the marina, golf course and various other places. Round-trip fare to any destination is M$30.

BUS

The bus companies cluster around Avenida Veracruz just south of the marlin statue as you enter the center. There are direct buses from Barra to Manzanillo (M$56 to M$65), Puerto Vallarta (M$207 to M$259) and Guadalajara (M$369). Some services (called *coordinados*) stop at both Barra and Melaque, but most only visit Melaque. You can reach Melaque by local red buses (M$7, every 15 minutes, 6am to 9pm) that do circuits of both towns; white ones (M$11) are more direct.

TAXI

A taxi to San Patricio-Melaque costs M$60.

Manzanillo

☑314 / POP 160,000

Though it boasts miles of golden sands, Manzanillo puts bread on the table by being one of the Mexican Pacific's major seaports, and tourism takes second place. The beaches are none too clean, and the dimensions – it's 20km from the old town to the best beach at Playa Olas Altas – make it a drag to get around without a car.

That said, and though the beaches are backed by an ugly highway where mediocre hotels and chain restaurants jostle for space with car dealerships and filling stations, there are some super places to stay here, particularly on the picturesque Península de Santiago, which offers spectacular coastal views.

The old town is the most atmospheric area, and the huge blue sculpture on the waterside plaza is a nod to Manzanillo's self-proclaimed status as 'Sailfish Capital of the World.'

⊙ Sights & Activities

Beaches

Playa San Pedrito, 1km northeast of the main plaza, is the closest beach to town, and the dirtiest. Just across the harbor from the old town but quite a long way by road, spacious **Playa Las Brisas** is backed by a pleasantly quiet district of low-key hotels and restaurants. **Playa Azul** stretches northwest from Las Brisas and curves around to Las Hadas resort and the best beaches in the area: **La Audiencia, Santiago, Olas Altas** and **Miramar**. Playa La Audiencia, lining a quiet cove on the west side of the Península de Santiago, has tranquil water and is popular for motorized water sports. The scenic stretch of Miramar and Olas Altas has de-

Greater Manzanillo

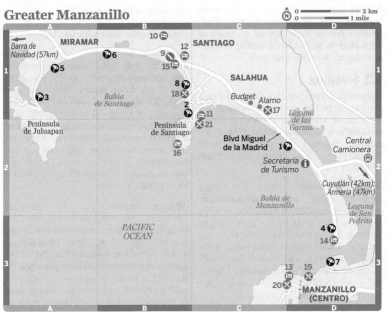

cent surfing and bodysurfing. Further west, **Playa La Boquita** is another beach with calm waters at the mouth of a lagoon where fishers lay out their nets to dry by day, and shove off by night. The beach is lined with seafood restaurants where you can hang for the day. A shipwreck just offshore makes this a popular snorkeling spot.

Diving

The scuba diving around Manzanillo can be interesting, with deep-water pinnacles luring pelagics at **Los Frailes**, and alluring swim-through arches at **Roca Elefante**.

Aquatic Sports & Adventures   DIVING
(☑314-334-63-94; www.aquaticsportsadventures.
com; Privada Los Naranjos 30; ☺9am-5pm Mon-Sat, to 2pm Sun) In the Santiago area, this is a PADI-accredited diving operator, catering for all levels of experience. Shore dives cost US$55/75 for single/two tanks, while boat dives start at US$95, with a minimum of two.

✦✦ Festivals & Events

Fiestas de Mayo   CULTURAL
These fiestas celebrate the founding of Manzanillo in 1873. Festivities involve sporting competitions and other events over two weeks from late April to early May.

Greater Manzanillo

⊚ Sights
1 Playa Azul	....	D2
2 Playa La Audiencia	....	B1
3 Playa La Boquita	....	A1
4 Playa Las Brisas	....	D3
5 Playa Miramar	....	A1
6 Playa Olas Altas	....	B1
7 Playa San Pedrito	....	D3
8 Playa Santiago	....	B1

◉ Activities, Courses & Tours
9 Aquatic Sports & Adventures	....	B1

⊜ Sleeping
10 Casa Artista	....	B1
11 Dolphin Cove Inn	....	C1
12 Hostal Manzanillo	....	B1
13 Hotel Colonial	....	D3
14 Hotel La Posada	....	D3
15 Hotel Real Posada	....	B1
16 Pepe's Hideaway	....	B2

⊗ Eating
17 El Fogón	....	C1
Los Candiles	....	(see 13)
18 Mariscos El Aliviane	....	B1
19 Mariscos El Delfín	....	D3
20 Mercado Francisco Madero	....	D3
21 Poco Pazzo	....	C2

Sailfish Tournaments FISHING
(www.deportivodepescamanzanillo.com) Manzanillo's famous international tournament takes place in November; a smaller national tournament is held in February.

🛏 Sleeping

Manzanillo's cheapest hotels are located downtown, in the blocks surrounding the main plaza, and there are several down-on-their-luck three-star habitats on Playa Santiago disguised as proper beach hotels. Top-end places can be found on the Santiago peninsula.

Hostal Manzanillo HOSTEL $
(☑ 314-334-60-26; www.hostalmanzanillo.com; Revolución 19; dm M$150, d M$350-500; ☺❋🎧) Just off a little plaza by the main road in Santiago barrio, this happy little place has cheerful private rooms, some with bathroom and air-con, and a small dorm with plenty of room to move. There's a kitchen and small common area. It's cheerily run and very welcoming.

Casa Artista B&B $$
(☑ 314-334-47-04; www.casaartistamanzanillo.com; Calle 4 No 12; apt incl breakfast M$700-1100; 🅿❄❋🎧☀) A gloriously peaceful spot up a hill on the landward side of the main road, this B&B has hummingbirds thrumming in the garden and artistically decorated apartments with kitchenette that are homey, relaxing and really attractive. It's a top spot to relax with a book. Price includes continental breakfast.

Hotel Real Posada HOTEL $$
(☑ 314-334-12-12; www.realposada.com.mx; Madrid 13801; r M$900-1000; 🅿❄❋@🎧☀) A block back from Playa Santiago, this motel-style set-up is on the main road and within walking distance to Playa Las Olas. Just as important, rooms are relatively modern with tiled floors, dark-wood furnishings, crisp sheets and cable TV. Staff are helpful, and there's a kiddie pool alongside the main one.

Hotel La Posada HOTEL $$
(☑ 314-333-18-99; www.hotel-la-posada.info; Cárdenas 201; s/d US$58/78; 🅿❄❋🎧☀) This bright, pink beachside B&B at the end of the Playa Las Brisas peninsula lures repeat guests with cool, pleasant rooms, personalized service and amenities including a library, open-air dining room and honor bar. A small pool overlooks the beach, where you can watch ships – and the occasional whale – trawling the harbor. The location can be challenging for those without a car.

Hotel Colonial HOTEL $$
(☑ 314-332-10-80; http://hotelcolonialmanzanillo.com; Bocanegra 28; s/d M$630/760; 🅿❄❋🎧) One block from Manzanillo's waterfront plaza, this atmospheric old hotel retains the character of a colonial hacienda, with tiled outdoor hallways, a spectacular exterior and a central courtyard. Big rooms are set on four floors surrounding that courtyard and have elegant drapes and wood furnishings. Downstairs rooms are darkish and suffer a lot of restaurant noise.

⭐ Pepe's Hideaway CABAÑAS $$$
(☑ 314-334-16-90; www.pepeshideaway.com; Camino Don Diego, La Punta; cabin per person incl meals & drinks US$185-225; 🅿☺🎧☀) Don't despair as you cruise the sanitized banality of the gated community wherein this place lies, for this spot is totally unexpected. It's set on a wild rocky point where noise means wind in the coconut palms and waves crashing below. A handful of utterly romantic, rustic cabins with vibrant paint jobs puts you in a sort of castaway fantasy world. Rates are all-inclusive.

Dolphin Cove Inn HOTEL $$$
(☑ 314-334-15-15; www.dolphincoveinn.com; Av Vista Hermosa s/n; d incl breakfast M$2190; 🅿☺❋@🎧☀) This cliffside hotel has awe-inspiring views and huge, spacious and bright rooms on tiered floors that cascade to a pretty bay-side swimming pool. Units range from basic doubles to two-room suites sleeping four, all with marble floors, kitchens or kitchenettes, vaulted ceilings and sea-view balconies. Bathrooms and fittings are a little disappointing for this price but the outlook is just sublime.

🍴 Eating

Down-to-earth options are near the main plaza, while chain and chain-like spots line Hwy 200 around the bay.

⭐ Mariscos El Aliviane SEAFOOD $
(Playa de Santiago; dishes M$20-120; ⏱11am-4:30pm Mon-Sat) A terrific little street stall across from Hotel Playa Santiago, where local heads crowd wooden tables for *tostadas*, *cócteles* (seafood cocktails) and platters of shrimp, octopus, scallops and ceviche. Beers are icy and the house *habanero salsa* so piquant it will leave your lips burning and

soul simmering. According to locals who know things, this is the best *cevicheria* in Manzanillo.

Mercado Francisco Madero   MARKET $
(cnr Madero & Cuauhtémoc; mains M$30-70; ⊙7am-5pm; 🚐) Manzanillo's downtown market has a number of inexpensive food stalls to choose from. It's pretty good home-style fare here, with *menudo* (tripe) a specialty in several stalls.

El Fogón   MEXICAN $$
(📞314-333-30-94; Madrid Km 9.5; mains M$115-210; ⊙1pm-midnight; 🚐📶) Under palm thatch with open-air rustic style, this meat restaurant does excellent, tender steaks from the grill house, while fresh tortillas are busily made in the hut opposite. Portions are large – even the tortilla chips come with a whole platter of sauces – and the pork tacos and *arrachera* (hanger steak) come highly recommended.

Mariscos El Delfín   SEAFOOD $$
(📞314-332-63-69; Av Niños Héroes; dishes M$15-160; ⊙10am-6pm Tue-Sun) Above the fish-market building near the center of town, this place has very soothing views over foraging pelicans and bobbing boats. It does no-frills seafood here, and very tasty it is too. The house specialty is swordfish in tamarind sauce, and there are also excellent marlin *tostadas*.

Los Candiles   MEXICAN $$
(📞314-332-10-80; http://hotelcolonialmanzanillo.com; cnr Bocanegra & Av México; mains M$60-160; ⊙6:30am-10:30pm Mon-Sat; 🚐📶) On the ground floor of the Hotel Colonial in the old town, this restaurant opens onto a pleasant patio, and has a menu of surf-and-turf fare

and a full bar with sports dominating the satellite TV.

Poco Pazzo   ITALIAN $$$
(📞314-336-85-33; Hadas Marina; mains M$130-280; ⊙5pm-midnight; 🚐📶) One of a row of restaurants on the marina within Las Hadas resort offering a romantic water-side setting. Enjoy surprisingly authentic Italian thin-crust pizza, pastas and traditional Italian steaks and seafood dishes. Try the fish, baked and piled with clams, mussels, olives and capers, and drizzled with white-wine sauce. There is a *gelateria* next door.

ℹ Information

Secretaría de Turismo (📞314-333-22-77; www.colimatienemagia.com.mx; Blvd Miguel de la Madrid 875A; ⊙8:30am-4:30pm Mon-Fri, plus 10am-6pm Sat Jul & Aug) On the main waterfront boulevard, halfway between downtown and Península de Santiago. Dispenses limited information on Manzanillo and the state of Colima.

ℹ Getting There & Away

AIR
Playa de Oro International Airport (📞314-333-11-19; www.aeropuertosgap.com.mx) lies between a long and secluded white-sand beach and tropical groves of bananas and coconuts, 35km northwest of Manzanillo's Zona Hotelera. Aeroméxico and Aeromar provide direct service to Mexico City.

BUS
Manzanillo's **Central Camionera** is 6km northeast of the city center. It's an organized place with tourist information, phones, eateries and left-luggage facilities.

BUSES FROM MANZANILLO

DESTINATION	FARE (M$)	DURATION (HR)	FREQUENCY (DAILY)
Barra de Navidad	56-65	1-1½	half-hourly
Colima	88-116	1½-2	half-hourly
Guadalajara	306-406	4¼-6	hourly
Lázaro Cárdenas	440-490	7-10	2 (nightly)
Mexico City (Terminal Norte)	902-1200	10-12	8 (nightly)
Puerto Vallarta	276-389	5-5½	hourly
San Patricio-Melaque	61-83	1-1½	half-hourly
Zihuatanejo	545-615	15	2 (nightly)

WORTH A TRIP

CUYUTLÁN

With its black-sand beaches, gentle waves and laid-back attitude, Cuyutlán feels a world away from everywhere. Located at the southeastern end of Laguna de Cuyutlán, just 40km southeast of Manzanillo, it's a quiet but attractive beach pueblo that can be popular with Mexican families on weekends.

The area's principal attraction is **El Tortugario** (☑ cell 313-1074061; www.tortugario cuyutlan.com; adult/child M$25/20; ☺9am-5pm Thu-Tue, plus Wed in school holidays) 🍃, a turtle sanctuary located 4km east of Cuyutlán along the beachside road. It has released over two million green, black and leatherback turtle hatchlings into the wild here. The center also has small iguana and crocodile sanctuaries, swimming pools and a picnic area. Don't miss the lagoon trips here on the **Palo Verde Estuary**, a nature preserve that's home to more than 100 bird species, including 257 migratory birds. *Lanchas* move through mangrove tunnels and past sunbathing crocodiles. The 45-minute ride costs M$50.

Cuyutlán is signposted just off the Manzanillo–Armería toll road (no toll if coming from Armería). Nuevo Horizonte runs two buses daily between Manzanillo's bus terminal and Cuyutlán (M$54, one hour). Alternatively, catch a bus from Manzanillo to Armería (M$56, 45 minutes, every 20 minutes), then walk two blocks north and one block east to Armería's market and transfer to a local bus to Cuyutlán (M$11, 20 minutes, half-hourly). Returning from Cuyutlán, buses leave from the main plaza.

Buses also run regularly between Cuyutlán and Tecomán (M$11, 20 minutes), where you can connect with buses heading to Colima and along Hwy 200 into Michoacán.

CAR & MOTORCYCLE

Renting a car is not only convenient for exploring the Costalegre beaches northwest of Manzanillo's airport, but recommended for getting the most out of Manzanillo in general. There are several firms at the airport; some also have downtown offices.

Alamo (☑ 314-333-24-30; www.alamo.com.mx; Madrid 1570; ☺8am-8pm)

Budget (☑ 314-333-14-45; www.budget.com.mx; Madrid Km 10)

ⓘ Getting Around

TO/FROM THE AIRPORT

There's no bus route to or from the airport, but most resorts have shuttle vans. Fixed-rate taxis from the airport charge M$440 to Península de Santiago or M$510 to downtown Manzanillo. From Manzanillo back to the airport, a taxi costs M$350 to M$400. If you jump off a bus traveling between Melaque/Barra de Navidad and Manzanillo at the airport turnoff, you'll be 5km away.

BUS

Local buses marked 'Santiago,' 'Las Brisas' and 'Miramar' head around the bay to the towns of San Pedrito, Salahua, Santiago and Miramar, and beaches along the way. Bus 8 does a circuit of the Península de Santiago. Fares are M$7.

TAXI

Taxis are plentiful in Manzanillo. From the main bus terminal, a cab fare is around M$50 to the main plaza or Playa Azul, and M$80 to Península de Santiago or Playa Miramar. But northbound buses also stop at the Santiago bus terminal, closer to the Playa Santiago area. Always agree on a price before you get into a taxi.

Boca de Pascuales

☑ 313 / POP 58

Boca de Pascuales is a legendary surf spot that attracts the best boarders from around the world, and is strictly for experienced surfers. Aggressive barrel swells range from 2m to 5m in summer and storm waves occasionally reach 10m. If you have doubt, don't go out.

🛏 Sleeping & Eating

Paco's Hotel   HOTEL $$

(☑ cell 477-3292552; www.surfpacoshotel.com; r/superior r M$600/800; P❄🛜) Family-run and plastered with autographed photos of famous surfers, Paco's offers simple but comfy rooms, each with a different theme lovingly painted by Paco's daughter Lulu. The more expensive rooms are larger, with even prettier painted decor, and look out to the back terrace and sea. The hotel also has a decent restaurant. Wi-fi costs M$60 per device per day.

★ **Las Hamacas del Mayor**   SEAFOOD $$
(☑ cell 313-3240074; www.lashamacasdelmayor.
com.mx; mains M$80-200; ⏰ 10:30am-6pm;
🚗 👪) A local fixture since 1953, this famous
seafood eatery seats 1000 and opens every
day of the year. Strolling mariachis entertain
the crowds, kids frolic in the pool, and there
are great views of surfers riding monster
waves. Dishes come in full or half-portions
and include crab and oysters as well as de-
licious specialties such as fish fillets stuffed
with octopus and shrimp.

❶ Getting There & Away

To reach Pascuales, first catch a bus from
Manzanillo to Tecomán (M$75, one hour, every
15 minutes). From here, hourly combis run the
10km to Pascuales (M$11, 20 minutes). A taxi
from Tecomán is M$80. If driving from Man-
zanillo, turn right at the enormous lime-tree
sculpture at the entrance to Tecomán, then right
again at the first major intersection.

Michoacán Coast

☑ 313 (753 FOR BARRA DE
NEXPA & CALETA DE CAMPOS)
Highway 200 hugs the shoreline most of the
way along the spectacular 250km coastline
of Michoacán, one of Mexico's most beauti-
ful states. This is one of the nation's most
memorable drives: the route passes dozens
of untouched beaches, some with wide ex-
panses of golden sand, some tucked into tiny
rocky coves, some at river mouths where
quiet estuaries harbor multitudes of birds.
Several have gentle lapping waves that are
good for swimming, while others have big
breakers suitable for surfing. Many of the
beaches are uninhabited, but some shelter
communities, many of which are largely
indigenous. Mango, coconut, papaya and
banana plantations line the highway, while
the green peaks of the Sierra Madre del Sur
form a lush backdrop inland. Blue signs
along Hwy 200 mark the turnoffs for most
beaches. Kilometer markers begin counting
down from Km 231 at the state's northern
border.

Other beaches of interest are **Ixtapilla**
(Km 180), **La Manzanillera** (Km 174), **Motín
de Oro** (Km 167), **Zapote de Tizupán** (Km
103), **Pichilinguillo** (Km 95) and **Huahua**
(Km 84). It's much easier to explore this
stretch of coast, especially the more remote
beaches, if you have your own vehicle. How-
ever, 2nd-class buses (at least half a dozen
daily) running between Temopán (easily ac-
cessed by bus from Manzanillo) and Lázaro
Cárdenas will drop off and pick up at any
town entrance along coastal Hwy 200. These
services are reasonably regularly disrupted
or cancelled by antigovernment roadblocks.

San Juan de Alima

Twenty kilometers into Michoacán is the
cobblestoned town of San Juan de Alima
(turnoff Hwy 200 Km 211). It's a pretty place
with a decent beach and seasonally popular
with surfers due to its creamy medium-sized
breakers just off the coast. There are several
beachfront restaurants and modern hotels.

Hotel Parador (☑ 313-327-90-38; www.elhotel
parador.com; d/q M$500/650;   P 🚗 ❄ 🛜 🏊)
offers a good variety of rooms, some with
balconies and views. The hotel's popular res-
taurant perches directly above the ocean on
palm-shaded terraces.

Las Brisas

The cliff-hugging road south of San Juan
de Alima climbs above the coast, offering
gorgeous views of desolate sandy beaches
below. The tiny white strand of Las Brisas
(turnoff Hwy 200 Km 205) is accented by
just a few *palapa* restaurants and the com-
fortable **Hotel Brisas de Verano** (☑ 313-
327-91-55; www.hotelbrisasdeverano.com; d/king
d M$700/1200;   P 🚗 ❄ 🛜 🏊). Rooms have a
kitschy quality with ceramic floors, built-in
concrete beds and bench seating, exposed
roughly hewn cement walls, and lots of
bright oranges and yellows.

If you're a bird-watcher, there is a nice
mangrove lagoon about 1km south of town.
This town is the southernmost point of gov-
ernment control in the area, and the hotel is
something of a base camp for federal police
and military personnel who run patrols into
the nearby cartel territory.

> ## ❶ MICHOACÁN'S BEACHFRONT PARADORES
>
> Along Hwy 200 you'll see frequent signs
> for tourist lodgings known as *paradores
> turísticos* (government-run tourist lodg-
> ings); despite mostly wearing the forlorn
> look of government projects paid for
> then not maintained, these offer reason-
> ably priced accommodations right on
> or just above the beach with killer views.
> Some are now run privately.

Playa La Ticla

A renowned surfing destination, Playa La Ticla (turnoff Hwy 200 Km 183) is 4km off the main road. It can feel like a dusty, down-at-heel town, but it's famous for its brilliant, long, left point break. The long beach is divided by a swimmable freshwater river.

On the beachfront, a few *enramadas* serve fresh seafood. Also here is the attractive, welcoming but rather unkempt **Parador Turístico La Ticla** (☏424-488-00-24, 313-327-80-86; paradorlaticla@gmail.com; d M$200, cabin for 4 upstairs/downstairs M$600/400, camping per person M$50; P☻), which has spartan rooms with minimal privacy in handsome, thatched multilevel wooden *cabañas* with hammocks on the porch and a common, circular thatched rest space.

For fine home cooking, head a few blocks inland to **Cabaña de Vicky** (☏313-328-58-23; mains M$50-120; ☻8am-11pm Mon-Sat; ☻), where daily specials are accompanied by good salsa and fresh tortillas made with corn from Vicky's own backyard.

Faro de Bucerías

Faro de Bucerías (turnoff Hwy 200 Km 173) is a sheltered crescent beach with clear, pale-blue waters and yellow sand that is perfect for sun worshipping, snorkeling or swimming. The local Nahua community operates a long line of *palapa* seafood restaurants offering plentiful, fat lobsters.

The **El Faro de Bucerías** (☏313-327-80-19; www.turismoindigena.org; d/q M$500/700; P☻☎) complex offers well-priced cabin accommodations and excellent lobster platters in its restaurant, which is open from 8am

to 7pm. Staff can arrange diving excursions and trips to see the turtles at nearby Playa Colola.

Playa Colola

An estimated 70% of the world's population of green sea turtles, along with olive ridley and leatherback turtles, lay their eggs on the long flat sands of Playa Colola (turnoff Hwy 200 Km 160), a Ramsar site. And you can see why. Here is a thick and wide slab of creamy sand that runs up against chaparral-coated hills and is framed by two picturesque headlands. Swim with caution as there can be quite an undertow.

Of course, the main draw are those turtles, and **Campamento Tortuguero Playa de Colola** (turnoff Hwy 200 Km 160; ☻Jul–early Dec) monitors the beach, protects the eggs and releases hatchlings. There are rustic camping and dormitory accommodations just by the main road, and for M$40 visitors can accompany local and international volunteers on their nightly rounds (8pm to 4am). Turtle viewing is best between September and December, when hundreds of turtles nest en masse. It's all pretty ad-hoc, with staffing variable and no system of reservations or timetable.

Playa Maruata

With clear turquoise waters and golden sandy beaches, Playa Maruata (turnoff Hwy 200 Km 150) is the most beautiful beach in Michoacán. The Nahua fishing village has a bit of a hippie reputation, attracting beach bums from all over. It's a tranquil, friendly place to hang out with your sweetie or a

---

THE CARTELS' COAST

This 150km stretch of the Michoacán Coast between Las Brisas and Caleta has traditionally been cartel-controlled, first by notorious La Familia, then by the Knights Templar. In the wake of cartel wars and government operations, these organizations have broken down, though their main business line certainly hasn't.

Various 'self-defense groups' operate here now, and they are difficult to classify. A range of issues including poverty, indigenous rights and lack of infrastructure and jobs are enmeshed with ongoing criminal activity, drug production and transportation, and battles of loyalties. There are no police or military bases here, though heavily armed patrols run up and down the highway.

What does this mean for the visitor? Very little in practical terms. Roadblocks are sometimes enforced to protest against the government, so you might be delayed for a while, but theft or violence against tourists was never tolerated by the big cartels and the region remains comparatively safe. Locals strongly recommend not driving at night along this stretch, however.

large stack of paperbacks. It's also a prime nesting site for green turtles (nightly from July to December).

Maruata actually has three beaches, each with its own unique character. The left (eastern) is the longest, a 3km pristine crescent-shaped beach with creamy yellow sand and calm waves perfect for swimming and snorkeling. The small middle arc is OK for strong swimmers. It's sheltered by a climbable rocky headland riddled with caves, tunnels and blowholes, and marked by the unusual **Dedo de Dios** (God's Finger) formation rising from the sea. The far-right (western) beach is known as **Playa de los Muertos** (Beach of the Dead), and for good reason: it has dangerous currents and ferocious waves. During low tide you can scale the rocks on the far right side of Muertos to reach a secluded cove where discreet nude sunbathing is tolerated. But don't get stuck here when the tide comes in. A crucifix on the rocks serves as a stark memorial to the people who have been swallowed by the sea.

This is an extremely poor pueblo, though a couple of recent infrastructure projects now stand in the town center. You'll find shops and simple eateries around the semi-derelict plaza. The *enramadas* on the left beach serve fresh seafood and are also your best bet for camping. Most charge from M$30 per person to pitch a tent or rent a hammock. There are rustic *cabañas* for M$300 to M$400, but the best accommodations are at the **Centro Ecoturístico Ayutl Maruata** (☑cell 555-1505110; www.turismo indigena.org; d/tr/q M$600/750/1000, hammock M$100; P☺), which has rather lovely tile-floored, *palapa*-roofed cabins on a hillside overlooking the far-right beach. There's a decent restaurant here and staff run boat trips as well as excursions to see the turtles at night (M$135 including food).

Barra de Nexpa

☑753 / POP 110

At Km 55.6, just north of Puente Nexpa bridge, and 1km from Hwy 200 down a rough cobbled road, lies the small, laid-back community of Nexpa, a hamlet misty with sea-spray. It's long been a haven for surfers, attracted to the salt-and-pepper sandbar and long left-hand break at the river mouth, which can rise to double overhead. Rides can go a half-kilometer or more here.

🍴 Sleeping & Eating

Several places along the beachfront offer camping from M$40 per person, while a half-dozen *palapas* serve local seafood.

Chicho's   GUESTHOUSE $
(☑cell 753-1309236; r M$300; ☺) One of several *enramadas* lining the beach, family-run Chicho's is a great choice for meals (dishes from M$60, open 10am to 9pm Tuesday to Sunday), thanks to gargantuan breakfast smoothies, pancakes, solid plates of shrimp and burgers, and inspiring views of wave-riding surfers. It also rents out basic and very cheap beachfront *cabañas*, featuring hammocks strung upstairs above a cement floor. No reservations.

Jorge & Helen's Place   GUESTHOUSE $$
(☑cell 753-1160570; www.surfingrionexpa.com; s/d/q M$525/600/720; P☺❋) There's a handy general store, a surf shop with board rental, and some sweet, simple digs here. Expect superclean tiled floors, pastel paint jobs, rain showers and fridge; some rooms have air-con.

Mar de Noche   CABAÑAS, HOTEL $$
(☑cell 753-1183931; www.nexpasurf.jimdo.com; r/cabaña M$600/800; ☺❋) The fan-cooled *cabañas* here have comfy beds, hammocks, kitchens and private bathrooms. There's also an adjacent six-room hotel with modern amenities including air-con (if it happens to be working, which is no guarantee). There's an attached beachfront restaurant, decorated with hand-carved wood columns. Low-season prices plummet.

Mary Jane   INTERNATIONAL $$
(mains M$70-180; ☺9:15am-9pm; ☺) Stilted above the beach, and the main gathering place for surfers. Owner Martin shoots videos of the break each morning to be screened over dinner and drinks each evening. Good pre- or post-surf breakfasts include bagels, while meals include tasty fish tacos, burgers, pastas and a handful of local delicacies. The bar is open until 11pm. And about that name...

Caleta de Campos

☑753 / POP 2000

Caleta (turnoff Hwy 200 Km 50) is a regional service center with all the essentials. It's set up on the bluffs, which taper toward an azure bay where you'll find a nice selection of seafood *enramadas* and a protected cove suited to novice surfers, if there is a swell at all.

There's a surf shop and a few hotels in the center. **Parador Turístico** (☎753-114-11-11; www.partourcaleta.com; turnoff Hwy 200 Km 51.25; cabaña M$1100-2150; [P][⊖][✱][≋]), with a fabulous outlook over the wild beach and waving palms, is on the highway 1km north of town. Its 12 comfortable ocean-view units, with terracotta floors and cable TV, surround a circular *palapa*-roofed bar and lounge area. The best suite has a kitchenette, dining room and private terrace with Jacuzzi.

Hourly buses depart Caleta's main plaza for Lázaro Cárdenas (M$55, 1¼ hours) from 5am to 7pm. A taxi between Caleta de Campos and Barra de Nexpa costs M$50 to M$60.

Lázaro Cárdenas

☑ 753 / POP 79,000

As an industrial port city, Lázaro has nothing of real tourist interest – but because it's a hub for buses up and down the coast, travelers regularly pass through. Lázaro is also a regional service center, but with excellent beaches and waves so near, there is no reason to spend the night.

❶ Getting There & Away

Lázaro has a few bus terminals, all within a few blocks of each other. From the most useful **main bus terminal** (☎753-532-30-06; Lázaro Cárdenas 1810), operators offer services to Manzanillo, Uruapan, Morelia, Colima, Guadalajara and Mexico City.

The **Estrella de Oro terminal** (☎753-532-02-75; www.estrelladeoro.com.mx; Corregidora 318) is one block north and four blocks west of Estrella Blanca and serves Zihuatanejo, Acapulco and Mexico City.

Troncones

☑ 755 / POP 600

Not long ago, Troncones was a poor, sleepy fishing and farming village, but these days expat homes and B&Bs have left the long beachfront road resembling more a California subdivision than the traditional Mexican villages at either end. The attraction is obvious: fabulous beaches, a laid-back atmosphere and world-class surfing. Troncones is a marvelous place to kick back for a few days.

The village is located about 25km northwest of Ixtapa, at the end of a 3km paved road from Hwy 200. The paved road ends at a T-intersection, from where the beachfront road continues 4.5km northwest to neighboring **Majahua** via Troncones Point and Manzanillo Bay. The majority of hotels and restaurants are along this road.

Majahua is a traditional fishing village with a few *enramadas* and a mellow beach layered with fine shells for beachcombers. From here, a dirt road (rough in the wet season) leads back out to Hwy 200.

🏃 Activities

The **swimming** in the protected cove off Playa Manzanillo is glorious, and on placid days the **snorkeling** is good here too. **Horseback riding** is quite popular; locals stroll the beach with their steeds looking for customers. Other activities that can be arranged through local inns include **mountain biking**, **fishing** and **spelunking** through the limestone cave system near Majahua.

But **surfing** rules here and Troncones has several world-class surf spots (experienced surfers only). The beach breaks can be excellent in summer, but the wave to chase is the left at **Troncones Point**. When it's small, the takeoff is right over the rocks

BUSES FROM LÁZARO CÁRDENAS

DESTINATION	FARE (M$)	DURATION (HR)	FREQUENCY (DAILY)
Acapulco	272-304	6-7	6
Guadalajara	517-541	7-8	6
Manzanillo	330-460	7	hourly
Mexico City (Terminal Norte)	705-745	8-11	frequent
Morelia	460-495	4-5	very frequent
Uruapan	296-345	3-4	frequent
Zihuatanejo	96-110	1½-2	hourly

(complete with sea urchins), but when it's big, it's beautiful and beefy and rolls halfway across the bay.

Prime Surfboards
SURFING

(☑755-103-01-80, cell 755-1143504; www.primesurfboards.com.mx; ☺7am-8pm) Around 500m north of the T-intersection, surfer Bruce Grimes offers two-hour lessons (US$60) and board repair. He also designs custom boards (short/long boards from US$500/1000) and rents out boards (per day/week M$400/US$100).

Inn at Manzanillo Bay
SURFING

(☑755-553-28-84; www.manzanillobay.com; Playa Manzanillo) Near the point, this hotel rents out an excellent selection of short and long boards (half-/full day M$240/375), body boards (M$80/120) and paddleboards/kayaks (M$380/650). It can also arrange surf lessons (US$60).

☞ Tours

Costa Nativa Ecotours
ECOTOUR

(☑755-100-74-99; www.tronconesecotours.com) This outfit organizes kayaking excursions that offer excellent wildlife-watching (M$540, three hours), guided hiking ending at a swimming hole (M$660, 5½ hours) and stand-up paddleboarding (M$750, 1½ hours), among other trips.

🛏 Sleeping

There are numerous places to stay; most are located along Troncones' main waterfront road. Reservations are advisable during the high season (November through April), when some places require multiple-night stays. During low season, prices can be 25% to 50% less, but some places close during summer.

★Troncones Point Hostel
HOSTEL $$

(☑755-553-28-86; www.tronconespointhostel.com; dm/r M$350/1000; [P]🖫🛜) 🕭 Handy for the dreamy surfing at Troncones Point, this imaginatively designed place features a variety of rooms in several very-easy-on-the-eye buildings. These range from slightly cramped but attractive dorms with bamboo beds to a curious duplex room with separate entrances. All are stylish and environmentally sound, and share a marvelous kitchen-lounge area with sea views and a telescope. Board rental available.

★Casa Delfín Sonriente
B&B $$$

(☑755-553-28-03; www.casadelfinsonriente.com; r/ste incl breakfast US$85/119; 😊🌫🛜🏊) With welcoming caretakers and a very laid-back atmosphere, this B&B makes a super place to stay about a kilometer from the T-junction. If available, grab one of the amazing upstairs suites, which have hanging beds, full kitchens, no doors (there's a lockable drawer for your valuables) and a shared rooftop patio with insane views of the wild Pacific.

There's a guest kitchen, and staff can be brought in to cook meals for you.

Tronco Bay Inn
HOTEL $$$

(☑755-103-01-10; www.tronco-bay-inn.com; d US$80-104; [P]😊🌫🛜🏊) Set at the north end of town on Manzanillo Bay is this endearing spot with terrific rooms set in six split-level duplexes. Decked out with inlaid tile floors, ceiling fans and wood furnishings, accommodations are spacious and sleep up to three. Sea-facing rooms are slightly dearer. There's a pool and a sweet slice of beachfront that lures an upmarket local crowd on weekends.

Inn at Manzanillo Bay
HOTEL $$$

(☑755-553-28-84; www.manzanillobay.com; Playa Manzanillo; bungalows US$142-194, ste US$204; [P]😊🌫🛜🏊) In a prime setting on Troncones' prettiest beach, this hotel has small but pretty thatched-roof bungalows with king-sized beds, canopied mosquito netting, ceiling fans and hammocked terraces surrounding a pool. For an extra dose of creature comforts, the suites feature air-con and tiny TVs. There's also a popular restaurant and bar, a surf shop, bike rental and easy access to the primo Troncones Point break.

A big extension was being built at our last visit.

Present Moment
RESORT $$$

(☑755-103-00-11; www.presentmomentretreat.com; s/d/tr incl breakfast & 1 class US$280/322/447; [P]😊🌫🛜🏊) 🕭 This yoga and spa resort is a rather impressive set-up on the beach, with nine thatched bungalows decorated with lovely objets d'art, including some marvelous pieces. Bungalows are breezy and romantic with open-topped walls; the upstairs suites offer more privacy, air-con and phenomenal 180-degree water views from their terrace. The centerpiece is a pretty pool and yoga platform by the ocean.

The restaurant, on an attractive sea-facing deck, is among the best, healthiest and priciest (mains M$170 to M$450, open 7am to 10pm) in town, with ample vegetarian and vegan selections available and a sociable happy hour. Though the raked paths and slightly chichi ambience of Present Moment won't appeal to everybody, it is a genuinely relaxing haven that's beloved of its many repeat customers.

✖ Eating

Café Pacífico
CAFE $

(📞 755-101-73-72; www.facebook.com/cafepacifico troncones; light meals M$40-80; ⏱ 7am-2pm & 4-10pm Dec-Aug; 🍴 🛜 🎵) This sweet, modern place does a very decent coffee and lip-smacking juices. Service is with a smile, and there are nice shady tables down the side alley to enjoy original breakfast omelettes, sandwiches and a range of well-prepared meals. Hours vary throughout the year.

Costa Brava
MEXICAN $$

(📞 755-533-28-08; dishes M$70-150; ⏱ 9am-10pm Fri-Wed; 🍴 🏠) Keeping it real amid the gringo-izing of Troncones, this likable open-air restaurant is run by a local family, does a solid selection of seafood and other dishes, and mixes a great hit-the-spot *michelada*. It's by the beach, and there's a little pool so the kids can have a paddle while you digest the fish.

Jardín del Edén
FUSION $$$

(📞 755-103-01-04; www.jardindeleden.com.mx; mains M$140-240; ⏱ 8am-10pm Nov-Apr; 🍴 🛜) Just north of Troncones Point, the French chef's fusion menu ranges from Mediterranean to Pacific Rim to traditional Mexican fare. Nightly specials such as pizza, lasagna and *cochinita pibil* (Yucatán-style slow-roasted pork) are cooked on the grill and in the wood-fired oven.

Roberto's Bistro
ARGENTINE $$$

(www.robertosbistro.com; mains M$120-260; ⏱ 8am-10pm; 🍴) Sizzling steaks and crashing waves create the stereophonic soundtrack at this Argentine-style beachfront grill, 1km south of the T-intersection. From chorizo starters to full-on feasts such as the *parrillada argentina* (T-bone, rib-eye and several other cuts grilled together with shrimp), this is a carnivore's paradise. It also does seafood. Saturdays in season are salsa night.

❶ Getting There & Away

From Zihuatanejo, take a La Unión–bound bus from the terminal near Zihua's market, or outside the bus stations. It will drop you at the turnoff (M$23). Walk down the road a little way and you'll find a stop where vans shuttle into Troncones every half-hour or so (M$12); some continue to Majahua.

Some 2nd-class buses heading northwest toward Morelia or Lázaro Cárdenas will also drop you at the turnoff.

Taxis in Troncones offer service around the area (M$70), to the airport (M$550 to M$700) or to Zihuatanejo (M$350 to M$400). A reliable air-conditioned cab is run by **Victor's Taxi Service** (📞 755-553-28-50, cell 755-1134986; victorianolopez14@hotmail.com), opposite Costa Brava restaurant.

Ixtapa

📞 755 / POP 9000

Ixtapa was nothing more than a coconut plantation until the late 1970s when Fonatur (the Mexican government's tourism development group) decided that the Pacific coast needed a Cancún-like resort. In came the developers and up went the high-rises. The result is a long string of huge hotels backing a lovely beach, but little local community. Ixtapa's appeal is best appreciated by families seeking a hassle-free all-inclusive beach getaway or those who value modern chain-hotel comforts. It's close enough to Zihuatanejo – in effect, it's a suburb of it – that you can experience that town's more authentic Mexican life easily.

⦿ Sights

Cocodrilario
WILDLIFE RESERVE

(⏱ 24hr) **FREE** Playa Linda has a small *cocodrilario* (crocodile reserve) that is also home to fat iguanas and several bird species. You can watch the hulking crocs from the safety of the well-fenced, wooden viewing platform located near the bus stop and extending toward the harbor.

Isla Ixtapa
ISLAND

Ixtapa's finest attraction is a beautiful oasis. The turquoise waters are crystal-clear, calm and great for snorkeling (gear rentals cost M$120 per day). **Playa Corales** on the back side of the island is the nicest and quietest beach, with soft white sand, and an offshore coral reef. *Enramada* seafood restaurants and massage providers dot the island. Frequent boats depart from the pier at Playa Linda (round trip M$40, five minutes.) The island gets mobbed by tourists in high season.

Beaches

Beaches are the big draw, obviously. **Playa del Palmar** is the longest (2.5km) and broadest stretch of blond sand, that's overrun by parasailing and jet-skiing concessions. The sea takes on an aquamarine sheen in the dry season when it clarifies, which makes it all the more inviting, but take care while swimming, as there can be a vicious shore break and a powerful undertow when the swell comes up. There aren't many public access points to the beach, thanks to the megaresorts lining up shoulder to shoulder, but you can always cut through a hotel lobby if need be.

Playa Escolleras, the western end of Playa del Palmar near the entrance to the marina, has a decent break and attracts surfers. Further west, past Punta Ixtapa, **Playa Quieta** and **Playa Linda** are popular with locals, though the water is murky thanks to the nearby rivers and mangroves. The latter also has some decent surf.

🏃 Activities

Cycling is a breeze along a 15km *ciclopista* (cycle path) that stretches from Playa Linda, north of Ixtapa, practically into Zihuatanejo. You can rent bikes from **Adventours** (per hour/day M$60/250).

Catcha L'Ola Surf   SURFING

(☑ 755-553-13-84; www.ixtapasurf.com; Centro Comercial Kiosco; board rental per day/week M$200/1000, 3hr lesson US$50; ☉9am-7pm, closed Sun off-season) You'll find everything you need – rentals, repairs, classes and surfing trips – here. It's next to a well-signed restaurant called Nueva Zelanda.

Mero Adventure   DIVING

(☑ cell 755-1019672; www.meroadventure.com; Hotel Pacífica; 1-/2-tank dives US$65/90; ☉9am-5pm Mon-Sat) Mero Adventure organizes diving, snorkeling, kayaking and fishing trips.

🧭 Tours

Adventours   ADVENTURE TOUR

(☑ 755-553-35-84; www.ixtapa-adventours.com; Blvd Ixtapa s/n; tours M$900-1200; ☉8am-6pm) Opposite the Park Royal hotel, Adventours offers a variety of guided cycling, kayaking,

snorkeling and bird-watching tours around Ixtapa and Zihuatanejo.

🛏 Sleeping & Eating

A couple of cheaper options are on the other side of the main road, but the beachside hotels are all top-end and best booked through package deals or from hotel websites. Several haven't had much more than a lick of paint since they were built in the 1970s. All have plentiful eating options; there are other restaurants in the shopping area across the main road, and at the down-on-its-luck marina.

★ Casa Candiles   B&B $$$

(☑ cell 755-1012744; www.casacandiles.com; Paseo de las Golondrinas 65; r US$145; ❉❀🛜🏊) Far nicer than the hulking resort hotels is this intimate little paradise a 10-minute walk back from the beach on a quiet residential street. Three stylish but homey rooms are individually decorated, one with Balinese masks, and there's a lovely pool and garden area. It backs onto jungle where you can spot birds and animals from a little path. Hospitality is very genuine.

Soleiado   INTERNATIONAL $$

(☑ 755-553-04-20; Blvd Ixtapa s/n; mains M$80-320; ☉8am-11pm; ❉🛜) Opposite the Park Royal hotel, this open-fronted restaurant has an extensive international menu, but is especially recommended for its delicious seafood and tender fish bathed in delicious sauces. It's also a fine spot for breakfast.

Deli'O   SEAFOOD $$

(☑ 755-553-22-88; www.facebook.com/restaurant bardelio; Playa del Palmar; mains M$120-200; ☉10am-7pm) One of a clutch of restaurant-bars in an accessible slice of beach between the two hotel zones (follow dolphinarium signs). This is the nicest with lower-volume music midday, zesty *micheladas,* and all the cocktails, ceviches and fish dishes you've come to expect, including a shrimp-stuffed fish fillet (M$220) big enough to share.

Captain Meuro   MEXICAN $$

(☑ 755-555-09-39; mains M$60-180; ☉8am-11pm; ❉) One of the most laid-back and reliably good restaurants in Ixtapa, this spot opposite the Barceló resort offers smoothies, *arrachera* platters, burgers, *chiles rellenos*, tacos, fajitas, tasty octopus and shrimp dishes.

🍷 Drinking & Nightlife

All the big hotels have bars and nightclubs. In the low season most of these charge less and open fewer nights.

Christine   CLUB
(📞 755-553-04-56; www.facebook.com/christine club; Hotel Krystal, Blvd Ixtapa s/n; ⊙11pm-6am Fri & Sat; 📶) Christine has the sizzling sound-and-light systems you'd expect from one of the most popular discos in town. Admission varies but is hefty (think US$20) in peak season.

ℹ️ Information

Tourist Office (📞 ext 224 755-555-07-00; www.ixtapa-zihuatanejo.com; Blvd Ixtapa s/n; ⊙8am-4pm) Provides tourist info from a little kiosk directly across from Hotel Presidente Inter-Continental.

ℹ️ Getting There & Around

Private taxis (M$440) provide transportation from the airport to Ixtapa. The return journey costs about M$200.

There are bus-ticket offices but very few long-distance buses actually stop here – for most destinations, go to Zihuatanejo.

Local buses run frequently between Ixtapa and Zihuatanejo from 5:30am to 11pm (M$10, 15 minutes). In Ixtapa, buses stop along the main street in front of all hotels. In Zihuatanejo, buses run along Morelos. Many Ixtapa-bound buses continue to Playa Linda (M$10/20 from Ixtapa/Zihuatanejo).

A taxi between Zihuatanejo and Ixtapa should be M$65 to M$85.

See also the Zihuatanejo Getting There & Away (p558) and Getting Around (p559) sections for more information about transportations to/from Ixtapa.

Zihuatanejo

📞 755 / POP 120,000

Zihuatanejo, or Zihua as it's affectionately called, is a Pacific paradise of beautiful beaches, friendly people and an easygoing lifestyle. Until the 1970s it was a sleepy fishing village but with the construction of Ixtapa next door, Zihua's tourism industry boomed practically overnight.

Parts of the city have become quite touristy, especially when cruise ships are in town, and luxury hotels are slowly replacing old family guesthouses. But for the most part, Zihua has retained its historic charm. The narrow cobblestone streets of downtown hide wonderful local restaurants, bars, boutiques and artisan studios. Fishers still meet every morning on the beach by Paseo del Pescador (Fishermen's Passage) to sell their catch of the day. At night, young lovers and families stroll carefree along the romantic waterfront sidewalk. Zihua is the best of both worlds. No wonder Andy and Red chose to live out their post-prison days here in *The Shawshank Redemption*.

◉ Sights

**Museo Arqueológico
de la Costa Grande**   MUSEUM
(📞 755-554-75-52; cnr Plaza Olof Palme & Paseo del Pescador; M$10; ⊙10am-6pm Tue-Sun) This small, rather faded museum houses exhibits on the history, archaeology and culture of the Guerrero coast. Most displays are in Spanish, but you can get by with the free English-language handout.

Beaches

Waves are gentle at all of Bahía de Zihuatanejo's beaches. If you want big ocean waves, head west toward Ixtapa. Water in the bay, particularly around the central beaches, isn't always the cleanest.

Playa Municipal, in front of town, is the least appealing beach on the bay. Shallow-watered **Playa Madera** is a pleasant five-minute walk east from Playa Municipal along a concrete walkway (popular with young couples in the evening) and around a rocky point.

Over a steep hill from Playa Madera (less than 1km) is the gorgeous broad expanse of **Playa La Ropa** (Clothes Beach), named for a Spanish galleon that was wrecked and had its cargo of silks washed ashore. Bordered by palm trees and seafood restaurants, La Ropa is great for swimming, parasailing and waterskiing; you can also rent sailboards and sailboats. It's an enjoyable 20-minute walk from Playa Madera along Carretera Escénica, which follows the clifftops and offers fine views over the water.

Isolated **Playa Las Gatas** (Cat Beach; boat tickets $35 round trip) is named – depending on whose story you believe – for the whiskered nurse sharks that once inhabited the waters or for the wildcats that lurked in the jungles onshore. It's a protected beach, crowded with sunbeds and restaurants. It's good for snorkeling (there's some coral) and as a swimming spot for children, but beware of sea urchins. Beach shacks and restaurants rent out snorkeling gear for around M$100 per day. Boats to Playa Las Gatas depart frequently from Zihuatanejo's Muelle Municipal (Pier) from 8am to 6pm. Several places sell tickets (M$40 round trip), including the **Cooperativa Zihuatanejo** (☑️755-554-85-81) booth at the foot of the pier.

About 12km south of Zihuatanejo, just before the airport, **Playa Larga** has big surf, beachfront restaurants and horseback riding. This is where Andy Dufresne and Red met up again after their lost years in Shawshank Prison together. Nearby **Playa Manzanillo**, a secluded white-sand beach reachable by boat from Zihuatanejo, offers the best snorkeling in the area. To reach Playa Larga, take a 'Coacoyul' combi from Juárez near the corner of González and get off at the turnoff to Playa Larga; another combi will take you from the turnoff to the beach.

🤸 Activities

Paty's Yoga Studio
YOGA, MASSAGE

(☑️755-554-22-13; www.zihuatanejoyoga.com; Playa La Ropa; classes M$180; ⊕8-10:45am Mon-Fri, 9-10:15am Sat & Sun Nov–mid-Apr) Few yogis can offer the kind of guaranteed enlightenment that comes from gazing through coconut palms into the sun-dappled Pacific from the upstairs terrace of this studio above Paty's restaurant on Playa La Ropa. Multi-level classes are offered daily in high season (Tuesdays and Thursdays at 9:15am off season). Massages are also available.

Water Sports

Snorkeling is good at Playa Las Gatas and even better at Playa Manzanillo. Marine life is abundant here due to a convergence of currents, and the visibility can be great – up to 35m in dry months. Migrating humpback whales pass through from December to February.

Carlo Scuba
DIVING

(☑️755-554-60-03; www.carloscuba.com; Playa Las Gatas; 1-/2-tank dives US$65/90) Carlo Scuba, run by a third-generation family operation based at Playa Las Gatas, offers dives, snorkeling trips, instruction and PADI certification. Prices include pick-up and drop-off at the Muelle Municipal.

Dive Zihua
DIVING

(☑️755-544-66-66; www.divezihuatanejo.com; Medina Ascensio 23; 1-/2-tank dives US$65/90; ⊕9:30am-8pm Mon-Sat) This outfit offers a good variety of dives, classes in underwater

---

MEXICAN COOK UP

Zihuatanejo Cooking School (☑️755-116-72-11; www.patiomexica.com; cnr Adelita & NS de los Remedios; classes M$400-450) Mónica Durán Pérez opens her home kitchen and shares her love of Mexican culinary culture in this wonderful series of classes. Start with a trip to the market (some classes only) then return to Mónica's backyard, where you grind corn, shape tortillas, pound ingredients in a *molcajete* (traditional mortar and pestle), and cook up one of several different specialties.

These might be *tamales*, fish tacos, stuffed chilis or zucchini flowers: check the website for details of different classes.

---

photography and PADI and DAN courses and certification.

Sportfishing

Sportfishing is very popular in Zihuatanejo. Sailfish are caught here year-round; seasonal fish include blue or black marlin (March to May), roosterfish (September and October), wahoo (October), mahimahi (November and December) and Spanish mackerel (December). Deep-sea fishing trips start at around US$180 for a boat holding up to four passengers. Trips run for up to seven hours and usually include equipment.

Sociedad de Servicios Turísticos Triángulo del Sol
FISHING

(☑️755-554-37-58; Paseo del Pescador 38B, near Muelle Municipal; ⊕8am-6pm) As well as fishing in a small/large boat (US$180/350 per day), this place offers snorkeling at Playa Manzanillo (M$1500 per boat including time at Playa Las Gatas) and a tour of the Zihuatanejo bay (M$350 per boat).

Sociedad Cooperativa José Azueta
FISHING

(☑️755-554-20-56; http://sociedadcooperativateni entejoseazueta.com; Muelle Municipal) Offers fishing excursions and trips to Playa Las Gatas from an office at the foot of the pier.

👉 Tours

Picante
SAILING

(☑️755-554-82-70; www.picantecruises.com; Muelle Puerto Mío) This 23m catamaran offers two enjoyable excursions. The 'Sail and Snorkel'

Zihuatanejo

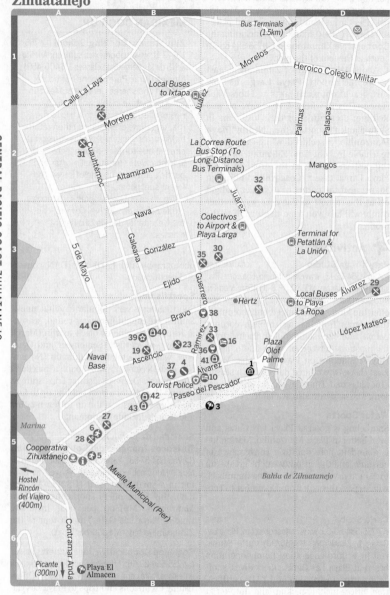

trip (adult/child US$79/55 plus US$7 for equipment rental; 10am to 2:30pm) sails south of Zihua to prime snorkeling off Playa Manzanillo. The 'Magical Sunset Cruise' (adult/child US$59/41; 6pm to 8:30pm) heads around the bay and along the coast of Ixtapa. Prices include food and open bar. Reservations are required.

🛏 Sleeping

Zihuatanejo has a huge selection for all budgets. Cheap hotels cluster around Calle

Zihuatanejo

◉ Sights
1 Museo Arqueológico de la Costa
   Grande..C4
2 Playa Madera...................................E4
3 Playa Municipal...............................C5

✛ Activities, Courses & Tours
4 Dive Zihua.......................................B4
5 Sociedad Cooperativa José Azueta ...A5
6 Sociedad de Servicios Turísticos
   Triángulo del Sol..............................A5
   Zihuatanejo Cooking School .....(see 34)

🛏 Sleeping
7 Arena Suites....................................E4
8 Aura del Mar...................................E4
9 Bungalows La Madera.....................E4
10 Hotel Ávila......................................C4
11 Hotel Irma.......................................F5
12 Hotel Villas Mercedes....................E3
13 La Casa Que Canta.........................F6
14 La Quinta de Don Andres...............F4
15 Mi Casita..F5
16 Posada Citlali..................................C4
17 Villas Naomi....................................F3

🍴 Eating
18 Bistro del Mar.................................E4
19 Chez Leo...B4
20 Coco's...F4
21 Doña Licha......................................E2
22 El Gabo...A2
23 El Murmullo.....................................B4
24 Il Mare..F6
25 Ita...E3
26 La Gula..E4
27 La Katrina..B5
28 La Sirena Gorda..............................A5
29 Las Adelitas....................................D3
30 Los Braseros...................................C3
31 Marisquería Yolanda.......................A2
32 Mercado..C2
33 Panadería Buen Gusto C4
34 Patio Mexica...................................E3
35 Restaurantes Mexicanos Any C3
   Rufo's Grill.............................(see 34)

🍷 Drinking & Nightlife
36 Andy's...C4
37 Carlo's B4
38 Temptation C4

✪ Entertainment
39 Cine Paraíso....................................B4

🛍 Shopping
40 Alberto's..B4
41 Café Caracol.................................. C4
   El Embarcadero ....(see 42)
42 El Jumil...B5
43 La Zapoteca.....................................B5
44 Mercado Turístico La Marina..........A4

Bravo in the center. High season is December through March, but even in high season, discounting of overinflated rack rates is common. Outside high season, prices drop by up to 20%. You can often negotiate lower rates, especially during slow periods or for extended stays.

Hotel Villas Mercedes
HOTEL $

(☑ 755-544-67-81; www.hotelvillasmercedes.com; Adelita 59; d/d with kitchen/d with kitchen & balcony M$350/400/500; ⊜❄🀫🕸) Nestled in the pleasant barrio behind Playa Madera, this hotel offers remarkably good value for clean, comfortable rooms surrounding a pool area. It's a friendly place with decent security measures and is popular with Mexican families.

Posada Citlali
GUESTHOUSE $

(☑ 755-554-20-43; Guerrero 4; s/d M$300/550; ⊜❄🀫) Easily the best digs in the town center, this pleasant, older, family-owned posada (inn) has simple, cozy and clean tile rooms with queen beds, cable TV, and rockers on a shared patio. There's lush garden rising through the courtyard and it's steps from the sea. It can be loud on weekends with bar noise. Air-con costs an extra M$50.

Hotel Ávila
HOTEL $

(☑ 755-554-20-10; hotelavila68@yahoo.com.mx; Álvarez 8; d M$600; 🅿⊜❄🀫🕸) Set just off the plaza and the main beach beyond, these older, sizable rooms have pastel-brushed stucco walls, air-con and a small pool, but though the price is fair and the location ideal, the property could use some love. Downstairs rooms will grab the wi-fi but are dark and suffer from traffic noise.

Hostel Rincón del Viajero
HOSTEL $

(☑ 755-103-45-66, cell 755-1308367; www.hostelzihuatanejo.com; Paseo de las Salinas 50; dm/d M$170/400; ⊜🀫) This warehouse-garden across the bridge from the center houses a friendly, original but basic hostel run by local artist and surfer Malinalli. Rooms and common areas are decorated with Mali's original artwork and Mexican handicrafts. The atmosphere is laid-back and grungy: if you like to smell the bleach, head elsewhere.

Bungalows La Madera
APARTMENT $$

(☑ 755-554-39-20; www.bungalowslamadera.com; López Mateos 25; r with kitchenette US$50-130; ⊜❄🀫🕸) This sprawling place straddles the hillside between Playa Madera and downtown. The nicest ocean-facing bungalows have two rooms and many units have sea-view terraces. In the center there's a pool and patio area. The annex across the street offers several more spacious units with spectacular balconies/living rooms with hammocks and great views over Zihua. No service at night.

Bungalows Vepao
HOTEL $$

(☑ 755-554-36-19; www.vepao.com; Playa La Ropa; d M$1000-1500; 🅿⊜❄🀫🕸) Quite a bargain for the super location right on Playa La Ropa, these cute 'bungalows' are trimmed in blue and ocher and offer plenty of space, a large pool and all the beach time you can handle. There's a variety of accommodations – ones with kitchen and/or sea view cost a little more.

Arena Suites
APARTMENT $$

(☑ 755-554-40-87; www.zihuatanejoarenasuites.com; López Mateos s/n; apt/apt with view US$70/90, ste US$115-125; 🅿⊜❄🀫) Well kept and spacious, with unbeatable views and beach access, these bungalows are simple but likable; all have thatched terraces with hammocks, room safes and kitchens or kitchenettes. There's also a suite with a Jacuzzi and a terrace overlooking Playa Madera. Steps descend directly to the sand, where the hotel has a bar-beach club.

Mi Casita
GUESTHOUSE $$

(☑ 755-554-45-10; micasita.alejandra@gmail.com; Carretera Escénica s/n; r M$800; ⊜❄🀫) This humble, welcoming, family-run place perches on the hillside between Playas Madera and La Ropa. The tidy rooms have artistic paint jobs and all open onto sweet terraces with hammocks and stirring views over the ocean far below.

★ Aura del Mar
HOTEL $$$

(☑ 755-554-21-42; www.hotelauradelmar.com; López Mateos s/n; d incl breakfast US$129-187; 🅿⊜❄@🀫🕸) A cliff-hugging, red adobe complex perched above Playa Madera, Aura del Mar is perfect for a romantic getaway. The spacious rooms and grounds are decorated with traditional Mexican furnishings, tiles and handicrafts. All have private balconies with exquisite ocean views and a hammock; some have a Jacuzzi on the balcony. Facilities are great; steep stairs lead to the beach and excellent restaurant.

★ La Villa Luz
BOUTIQUE HOTEL $$$

(☑ 755-112-18-34; www.lavillaluz.com; Carretera Escénica 97; r incl continental breakfast US$214-274; 🅿⊜❄🀫🕸) This genuinely romantic retreat climbs the hill just above Playa la Ropa (warning: plenty of stairs). The seven rooms are all sweet and characterful with artful use of inlaid wood, adobe brick and pebble mosaics; we particularly loved 'Mar', with glorious sea vistas from your comfortable bed. A couple of them are duplexes, one with a kitchen. Excellent service seals an impressive package.

La Casa Que Canta
BOUTIQUE HOTEL **$$$**

(☑ 755-555-70-30; www.lacasaquecanta.com; Carretera Escénica s/n; r US$340-630; P❄❋ 🛜🏊) The 'house that sings' is the epitome of luxury and customer service in Zihuatanejo. Perched on the cliffs between Playas Madera and La Ropa, the thatched-roof hotel features bold, striking use of interior space and shelters exquisitely decorated rooms and a raft of facilities. But perhaps the most valuable amenity is silence: there are no TVs in the rooms and kids aren't allowed to stay.

There are separate villas too.

Villas Naomi
HOTEL **$$$**

(La Casa del Árbol; ☑ 755-544-73-03; www.villasnaomi.com; Adelita 114; r/ste with kitchenette M$1350/1650; ❄❋🛜🏊) Dominated by a lovely old ceiba tree, Villas Naomi is a haven near Playa Madera. Run with quiet dignity, its little whitewashed abodes have tiled floors inlaid with river rock, built-in shelving and showers, plush linens accented with bamboo towel racks and a small flat-screen TV. With only eight rooms, it's a peaceful spot to relax around the pool.

La Quinta de Don Andres
HOTEL **$$$**

(☑ 755-554-37-94; www.laquintadedonandres.com; Adelita 11; r without/with kitchen US$125/135; P❄❋🛜🏊) This burnt-orange fauxdobe complex of modern rooms offers terracotta floors, air-con and small balconies overlooking the pool and the sea below. All rooms are large and spotless, and the ones with full sea view have kitchenettes. It's family friendly, with lots of public space and is small enough to feature excellent personal service. More than the sum of its parts.

Amuleto
BOUTIQUE HOTEL **$$$**

(☑ 755-544-62-22; www.amuleto.net; Carretera Escénica 9; r from US$400; P❄❋@🛜🏊) A boutique hotel high in the hills above Playa La Ropa, Amuleto dazzles guests with opulent, earthy rooms decorated in stone, ceramic and wood, plus suites with private swimming pools and scrumptious views. The attached restaurant is equally fabulous. A three-night minimum stay is required. No kids.

Villa Casa Luna
VILLA **$$$**

(☑ US 310-272-9022; www.villa-casa-luna.com; Playa La Ropa s/n; villa for 2/4 US$375/475; P❄❋ 🛜🏊) Within this verdant walled compound at the southern end of Playa La Ropa is a grand villa with multiple bedrooms plus a gorgeously tiled designer kitchen. It sleeps up to eight, including the delightful studio cottage. There's a nice swimming pool and the tranquillity of the garden setting.

Villa Mexicana
HOTEL **$$$**

(☑ 755-554-36-36; www.hotelvillamexicana.com.mx; Playa La Ropa s/n; r incl breakfast M$1646, with sea view M$1884; P❄❋@🛜🏊) Chain-hotel sterility won't inspire much enthusiasm, but you can't argue with the choice location right on Playa La Ropa. It's decked out in orange fauxdobe and rooms are spacious; it's worth the upgrade to the front-facing ones with direct ocean views, though the vista is partly blocked by palms. There's also a popular pool and beachside bar and restaurant.

Hotel Irma
HOTEL **$$$**

(☑ 755-554-84-72; www.hotelirma.com.mx; Adelita s/n; r M$1379-1657; P❄❋🛜🏊) Like a reliable relative, Irma attracts regulars back year after year for its family-like atmosphere and smart, professional service. Located just above Playa Madera, Irma has renovated rooms, some with great views of the bay and the huge pool and terrace below.

🍴 Eating

Guerrero state is famous for *pozole,* a hearty meat-and-veg soup that's found on most menus in town (especially on Thursday). *Tiritas* (raw fish slivers marinated with red onion, lemon or lime and chili peppers) are Zihua's specialty.

🍴 Central Zihuatanejo

Seafood here is fresh and delicious. Many popular (if touristy) fish restaurants line Paseo del Pescador, parallel to Playa Municipal; however, the quality-to-price ratio tends to improve as you move inland. A hearty and inexpensive breakfast or lunch is available in the **mercado** (Mangos s/n; meals M$30-50; ⏰7am-6pm), which has several eating zones.

★ Doña Licha
MEXICAN **$**

(☑ cell 755-1101608; Cocos 8; mains M$40-85; ⏰8am-6pm; ❄) This place near the *mercado* is renowned for its down-home Mexican cooking, casual atmosphere and excellent prices. There are always several *comidas corridas* (prix-fixe menus) to choose from, including a popular roast chicken plate; all come with rice, beans and handmade tortillas. Breakfasts are huge.

Coco's
VEGAN $
(Adelita s/n; coconuts M$20; ☺1-7pm) Our favorite coconut stop in town, this stall in a passage to a restaurant has carefully peeled fruit straight out of the fridge. You can have it *loco* in a cocktail if you're feeling that way inclined.

Panadería Buen Gusto
BAKERY $
(Guerrero 11; pastries from M$5; ☺8:30am-10pm) A good traditional Mexican bakery in the heart of downtown Zihua.

Chez Leo
SEAFOOD $$
(☎755-113-60-38; www.facebook.com/chezleo restaurant; cnr Cuauhtémoc & Medina Ascensio; mains M$80-140; ☺3:30-11pm; ☺) Though it doesn't look much from outside, the chef here takes real pride in preparing delicious seafood dishes, including great fish tartare, seared tuna and whatever's fresh that day. There are some surprising flavors, simple but handsome presentation and it's all rather good value.

El Murmullo
FUSION $$
(☎cell 755-1028790; Ascencio s/n; dishes M$100-180; ☺2-11pm Mon-Sat; ☺) An intriguing little bistro with well-dressed, candlelit wood tables spilling onto the pedestrian street. It serves everything from sashimi to Thai curries to freshly made pastas. Tuna is reliably excellent if it's on, and the bistro also does tasty sautéed shrimp in tequila. The service and atmosphere are lovely.

La Sirena Gorda
SEAFOOD $$
(☎755-554-26-87; Paseo del Pescador 90; mains M$65-220; ☺8:30am-10:30pm Thu-Tue; ☺☎) Close to the pier, this place (The Fat Mermaid) is a casual and popular open-air restaurant that's good for garlic shrimp, curry tuna and an intriguing range of fish tacos. Fresh fish fillets are done in a variety of ways, all delicious, and this is a top spot to try spicy *tiritas*.

La Katrina
MEXICAN $$
(☎755-544-85-66; www.facebook.com/lakatrina mx; Paseo del Pescador 70; mains M$120-200; ☺4pm-2am Tue-Sun; ☺☎✎) Decked out with vivid furniture and decorated on a *Catrina* (image of a skeleton in female clothing) theme, this hipster cantina offers likably casual dining with plenty of foodie flair

in dishes such as standout tuna *carnitas*, succulent pork and lip-smacking beetroot carpaccio. Some combinations didn't quite work for us, but it's all interesting. Wash your meal down with something from the long list of mezcal or mezcal-based cocktails. Service is great.

Restaurantes Mexicanos Any
MEXICAN $$
(☎755-554-73-73; www.restaurantesmexicanosany. com.mx; Ejido 18; mains M$60-160; ☺8am-11pm; ☺☎) This friendly place serves traditional Mexican cuisine under its big *palapa* roof. The decor is cheerfully and colorfully folkloric, while food highlights include to-die-for *tamales* and the sweet, corn-based hot drinks known as *atoles*.

El Gabo
SEAFOOD $$
(Morelos; mains M$70-275; ☺noon-7pm; ☺☎) A shady hideaway tucked off a major thoroughfare isn't necessarily what you'd think of as a prime seafood joint, but this open-sided place with tables scattered beneath a vaulted, tiled roof and leather saddle-bar stools delivers the goods. A menu of lobster brochettes, coconut shrimp, fresh fish done up a half-dozen ways, oysters, sashimi, seafood cocktails and ceviche attracts young lovers, happy-hour drifters and post-work professionals.

Marisquería Yolanda
SEAFOOD $$
(cnr Morelos & Cuauhtémoc; mains M$70-120; ☺10am-8pm; ☺) Staff here open oysters with a hammer, and dice and drown ceviche on the street side, where drunk boleros belly up to the sidewalk bar with the boys and sing about their unbridled, unrequited romance to one too many beers. And when the choir is breathless, the jukebox picks up the slack. It's known as the Catedral de Mariscos (cathedral of seafood) for a reason.

Los Braseros
MEXICAN $$
(☎755-554-87-36; Ejido 14; mains M$65-200; ☺8am-1am; ☺☎) Though there's a huge selection here, not all is that tasty, but what is, is well worth the visit. For a quick bite on the go, grab a few *tacos al pastor* from the street-facing counter, or sit down and linger awhile over this spot's trademark *alambres* – tasty mixes of grilled fish, meat, veggies and cheese on a big tortilla.

✖ Around the Bay

Pricey restaurants with panoramic views dominate the hilltops, while casual candlelit beachside eateries are the rule on Playa La Ropa. More affordable fare can be found in the 'gringo gastronomic ghetto' along Adelita, just inland from Playa Madera, which half shuts down from May to November.

Las Adelitas
MEXICAN $

(☑755-112-18-45; Adelita 6; mains M$40-90; ☺8am-4:30pm Wed-Mon, later Dec-Apr; ☻) This adorable breakfast and lunch cafe with serape tablecloths is on a little plaza with outdoor seating. It has a loyal local following thanks to its *chilaquiles* and omelettes in the morning and *tortas, chiles rellenos* and fried and grilled fish *comidas* at lunch. In gringo season it opens for great-value dinners too (mains M$60 to M$150).

Patio Mexica
MEXICAN $

(☑755-116-72-11; www.patiomexica.com; cnr Adelita & NS de los Remedios; mains M$50-150; ☺8am-2pm Mon-Sat Nov-Apr; ☻☎) Squash-blossom omelette and other Mexican delicacies get your day off to a sunny start at this informal breakfast place run by Mónica Durán Pérez of the Zihuatanejo Cooking School.

Ita
CAFE $

(Adelita 4; mains M$48-110; ☺7am-3pm, to 9pm Dec-Apr; ☻) An atmospheric, locally owned neighborhood cafe that steams espresso and produces fresh juices and Mexican breakfasts. In the winter high season, it also does lunch and dinner dishes with plenty of flavor and innovation. If you like what you taste, enroll in a cooking class.

Paty's
MEXICAN $$

(☑755-544-22-13; www.patys-marymar.com; Playa La Ropa; mains M$70-240; ☺7am-10pm; ☻☎) On the sand at the main access to Playa La Ropa, this place serves everything from big juices to grilled octopus and snapper to shrimp sautéed in tequila to fish fajitas, along with an array of tasty soups, salads and omelettes. Enjoy the fare under thatched and linen umbrellas in the sand with rattan lanterns dangling from the palms. Service is neither swift nor effusive.

Rufo's Grill
PARRILLA $$

(☑755-120-54-94; www.rufosgrill.com; Adelita 1; mains M$100-220; ☺4-10:30pm Mon-Sat Nov-Apr; ☻☎) Tucked onto a concrete patio under a bamboo roof fringed with Christmas lights, this unpretentious corner joint is popular among long-term gringos thanks to its fabulous barbecued meat and shrimp marinated in herbs and olive oil. Tasty grilled vegeta-

bles – red peppers, carrots, zucchini, eggplant and mushrooms – accompany every main course.

★Bistro del Mar
FUSION $$$

(☑755-554-21-42; www.hotelauradelmar.com; Playa Madera s/n; mains M$150-290; ☺8am-10:30pm; ☻☎) With its landmark sail roof over candlelit tables and its fusion of Latin, European and Asian flavors, this beachside bistro is a romantic treat. Delicious fish flavors are the mainstay, with standout *dorado* sashimi and snapper or whatever is the fish of the day done in outstandingly inventive ways. The house wines are a cut above average too. Service is outstanding.

La Gula
FUSION $$$

(☑755-554-83-96; www.restaurantelagula.com; Adelita 8; mains M$160-260; ☺5-11pm Mon-Sat Nov-Apr; ☻☎) This place wins points for its beautifully presented, creative cuisine. Dishes bear names such as *mosaico mexicano* (tequila, peppercorn and dill-marinated fish carpaccio with avocado mousse) and *eclipse de sol* (shrimp medallions with bacon and *pasilla* chili sauce). The atmosphere, on a breezy upstairs terrace, is most pleasant.

Il Mare
ITALIAN, SEAFOOD $$$

(☑755-554-90-67; www.ilmareristorante.mx; Carretera Escénica 105; mains M$145-325; ☺noon-11pm Mon-Sat, 4-11pm Sun, closed Tue May-Oct; ☻☎) A romantic Italian restaurant with a fabulous bird's-eye perspective on the bay, Il Mare is well regarded for its Mediterranean pasta and seafood specialties, including a fresh *insalata di mare* (marinated seafood salad) with squid, octopus and shrimp marinated in olive oil and lime. Pair yours with wine from Spain, Italy, France or Argentina. On Wednesday, it gets some Greek dishes going.

La Perla
SEAFOOD $$$

(☑755-554-27-00; www.laperlarestaurant.net; Playa La Ropa; mains M$150-240; ☺11am-10pm; ☻☎) Despite the beer-bucket NFL promos, this is a refined pavilion in dark wood right on Playa La Ropa. Best dishes include grilled octopus, tuna steaks seared as rare as you like, fish fillets stuffed with shrimp or whole fish grilled, and tacos piled with shrimp, lobster and chicken. Eat here and hang on the (few) beach lounges as long as you like.

🍷 Drinking & Nightlife

Downtown has a handful of bars offering two-for-one beers and margaritas, and you can find some live music and booty-shaking bass on weekends, but in its earthy soul: Zihuatanejo is all about the mellow.

Carlo's
BAR

(Álvarez s/n; ⊙5pm-1am; 🛜) With a prime balcony spot overlooking the plaza, the high tables at this open-air bar are favorites with young courting Zihua couples. It's not quite the balmy sundowner spot it seems to be, as the *banda* music is often cranked up damn loud, but it does a decent *michelada* and has plenty of character.

Andy's
CANTINA

(Guerrero s/n; ⊙7:30pm-3am Thu-Tue) Perhaps set up by Andy Dufresne himself, this two-room cantina has stone floors, a bar in the front room, and a DJ booth, dance floor and another bar in the rear. There are thick fauxdobe walls, bamboo rafters and lounges aplenty. It gets packed on weekends, though the lack of outdoor seating means it fills late on sticky nights.

Temptation
CLUB

(☑755-554-11-29; cnr Bravo & Guerrero; ⊙9pm-6am Thu-Sun; 🛜) This is built like a cruise-ship disco with a raised, lit dance floor, handsome center bar, the obligatory disco ball, and red vinyl booths and seats on the main floor and on the mezzanine above. DJs spin *cumbia* (dance music originating from Colombia), *merengue* (a ballroom dance of Dominican origin), salsa, electronica and reggae.

☆ Entertainment

Cine Paraíso
CINEMA

(☑755-554-23-18; www.ixtapayzihuatanejo.com/cartelera; cnr Cuauhtémoc & Bravo; M$40) Screens three films nightly, usually in English with Spanish subtitles.

🛍 Shopping

Zihua offers abundant Mexican handicrafts, including ceramics, clothing, leatherwork, Taxco silver, woodcarvings and masks from around the state of Guerrero. Most shops also open Sundays in high season.

Alberto's
JEWELRY

(☑755-554-21-61; www.albertos.com.mx; Cuauhtémoc 15; ⊙10am-7pm Mon-Sat) A few shops along Cuauhtémoc sell Taxco silver. Alberto's has some of the finest and most original pieces.

Café Caracol
FOOD & DRINK

(www.cafecaracol.com; cnr Álvarez & Guerrero; ⊙9:30am-7pm, plus Sun in school holidays) This shop sells delicious organic coffee from Guerrero state, as well as vanilla and honey.

La Zapoteca
HANDICRAFTS

(Paseo del Pescador; ⊙10am-8pm Mon-Sat, plus Sun Dec-Apr) If you're interested in a handwoven anything – *sarapes*, rugs or hammocks (and it has some great ones) – find this emporium, which stands out among the handicraft huddle near the fishers marina. The weaving is all from Teotitlán del Valle in Oaxaca.

El Jumil
HANDICRAFTS

(☑755-554-61-91; Álvarez s/n; ⊙10am-8pm Mon-Sat, plus Sun Dec-Apr) This shop specializes in masks – a well-known traditional handicraft of Guerrero state.

El Embarcadero
CLOTHING

(Álvarez s/n; ⊙10am-8pm Mon-Sat, plus Sun Dec-Apr) Embroidery, textiles and hand-woven clothing from Guerrero, Oaxaca, Michoacán and other neighboring states.

Mercado Turístico La Marina
MARKET

(5 de Mayo s/n; ⊙8am-9pm) Has many stalls selling clothes, bags and knickknacks.

ℹ Information

Hospital General (☑755-554-36-50; cnr Morelos & Mar Egeo) Halfway to the bus terminal.

Post Office (☑755-554-21-92; www.correos demexico.com.mx; Carteros s/n; ⊙8am-5pm Mon-Fri, 10am-2pm Sat) Behind the big yellow Coppel department store off Morelos.

Tourist Office (☑ext 224 755-555-07-00; www.ixtapa-zihuatanejo.com; Muelle Municipal; ⊙8am-4pm) This convenient office in the Terminal Marítima at the foot of Zihua's pier stocks brochures and maps even when unstaffed.

Tourist Police (☑755-554-20-40; Álvarez s/n)

ℹ Getting There & Away

AIR

The **Ixtapa/Zihuatanejo international airport** (ZIH; ☑755-554-20-70; www.oma.aero; Carretera Nacional) is 13km southeast of Zihuatanejo, a couple of kilometers off Hwy 200 heading toward Acapulco. There are direct flights from several US and Canadian destinations.

The following domestic destinations are serviced by these airlines:

➡ Acapulco – Aeromar, TAR

➡ Guadalajara – TAR

* Mexico City – Aeroméxico, Aeromar, Interjet
* Queretaro – TAR
* Toluca – Interjet

BUS

Both long-distance bus terminals are on Hwy 200 about 2km northeast of the town center (toward the airport). The main terminal, also known as Central de Autobuses, is adjacent to the smaller Estrella de Oro terminal (EDO). Buses to La Unión and Petatlán (for Troncones and Barra de Potosí respectively) leave from a small **terminal** near the market.

CAR & MOTORCYCLE

There are several car-rental companies at the airport, most with branches in Ixtapa.

Alamo (www.alamomexico.com.mx) Airport (☑755-553-02-06); Ixtapa (☑755-553-02-06; Centro Comercial Los Patios)

Europcar (☑755-553-71-58; www.europcar. com.mx) Airport (☑755-553-71-58); Ixtapa (☑755-544-82-56; Paseo Ixtapa, Local 2)

Green Motion (☑755-553-03-97; www. greenmotion.com) Airport (☑755-554-48-37); Ixtapa (☑755-553-03-97; Blvd Ixtapa s/n, Plaza Ambientes, Local 10)

Hertz (☑755-554-29-52; www.hertz.com)

❶ Getting Around

TO/FROM THE AIRPORT

The cheapest way to and from the airport is via public 'Aeropuerto' *colectivo* vans (M$10) departing from Juárez near González between 6am and 10pm and making many stops before dropping you just outside the airport gate. *Colectivo* taxis are a more direct and convenient option for incoming passengers, whisking you from the arrivals area to Ixtapa or Zihua for M$130 per person. Private taxis from the airport into either town cost M$440 (only M$120 or so from Zihuatanejo for the return journey).

BUS & COLECTIVO

To reach downtown Zihua or Ixtapa from Zihua's long-distance bus terminals, cross Hwy 200 using the pedestrian overpass directly opposite the main bus terminal. Buses for downtown

Zihua stop at the foot of the overpass. The stop for Ixtapa is a little further west.

From downtown Zihua to the bus terminals, catch 'La Correa' route buses (M$7, 10 minutes), which leave regularly from the corner of Juárez and Nava between 5:30am and 9:30pm.

'Playa La Ropa' buses go south on Juárez and out to Playa La Ropa every half-hour from 7am to 8pm (M$7).

'Coacoyul' *colectivos* heading toward Playa Larga depart from Juárez, near the corner of González, every five minutes from 5am to 10pm (M$10, 15 minutes).

TAXI

Cabs are plentiful in Zihuatanejo. Approximate fares from central Zihua include M$70 to Ixtapa, M$35 to M$50 to Playa La Ropa, M$140 to M$160 to Playa Larga, and M$30 to the bus terminals.

South of Ixtapa & Zihuatanejo

Barra de Potosí

☑755 / POP 400

About 26km southeast of Zihuatanejo is the small fishing village of Barra de Potosí, located at the far tip of Playa Larga's seemingly endless, palm-fringed, sandy-white beach and at the mouth of the brackish **Laguna de Potosí**, a saltwater lagoon about 6.5km long and home to hundreds of species of birds, including herons, kingfishers, cormorants and pelicans. It's thankfully free of any resort hotels at all and makes for a marvelous wind-down stay in a friendly Mexican community.

◉ Sights

El Refugio de Potosí   WILDLIFE RESERVE
(☑755-100-07-43; www.elrefugiodepotosi.org)
This nature center just inland from the beachfront around 3.5km north of town rehabilitates injured wildlife, breeds butterflies and

BUSES FROM ZIHUATANEJO

DESTINATION	FARE (M$)	DURATION (HR)	FREQUENCY (DAILY)
Acapulco	155-220	4-4½	6 main, 8 EDO
Lázaro Cárdenas	96-110	1½-2	10 EDO
Manzanillo	615	9	9:40pm main
Mexico City	625-735	8-10	4 EDO, 5 main
Morelia	400-530	5-6	3 main (nightly)
Puerto Vallarta	878	14	9:40pm main

parrots, and contributes to environmental education in the area. At the time of research, it was closed to the public, but guided visits were scheduled to resume: check the website.

 Tours

Nearly every *enramada* in the pueblo – all of them fishing-family owned – offers 90-minute boat tours of the lagoon, where you can glimpse crocodiles for the standard M$200 price. **Antonio Oregón** (📞755-557-22-01), based at Restaurante Rosita, is a good choice, and he also offers four-hour snorkeling and fishing trips (M$1500). Trips include a buzz out to the impressive **Morros de Potosí**, a cluster of massive guano-covered rocks about 20 minutes offshore. Boats will circle the Morros, affording views of the many seabirds that nest out here, before heading to nearby **Playa Manzanillo**, where the snorkeling is sublime. The price includes cold drinks, from young coconuts to sodas and beer.

🛏 Sleeping & Eating

A handful of guesthouses are scattered around town. Seafood is great here – *enramadas* line the beach.

★ **Casa del Encanto**   B&B **$$**
(📞 cell 755-1246122; www.lacasadelencanto.com; d incl breakfast US$70-100; ❄🛜) For bohemian charm and an intimate perspective on the local community, nothing beats this magical space of brilliantly colored open-air rooms, hammocks, fountains and candlelit stairways on a residential street about 300m inland from the beach. Owner Laura has spent years organizing international volunteers to work with neighborhood children, and she's a great resource for getting to know the town.

Rates are flexible off-season with good deals for longer stays. Adobe-baked pizzas with locally sourced ingredients might be on the menu in high season by the time you visit.

La Condesa   SEAFOOD **$$**
(mains M$80-120; ⏰9am-6pm) Northernmost of the beachfront *enramadas*, this is one of the best. Try its *pescado a la talla* (broiled fish fillets) or *tiritas*, both local specialties, or munch on some tasty *abulón* (abalone).

ℹ Getting There & Away

By car from Zihuatanejo, drive southeast on Hwy 200 toward Acapulco, turn off in Los Achotes and drive another 9km to Barra de Potosí.

By public transportation, catch a Petatlán-bound bus from outside Zihua's main terminals, or from the terminal near Zihua's market. Tell the driver to let you off at the Barra de Potosí *crucero* (turnoff; M$16, 30 minutes), where you can catch a *camioneta* (pickup truck) the rest of the way (M$12, 20 minutes).

Colectivos also run directly from the airport to Barra de Potosí (M$20, 30 minutes).

Soledad de Maciel

📞755 / POP 400

Known locally as 'La Chole,' the hamlet of Soledad de Maciel sits atop the largest, most important archaeological ruin in Guerrero state. Since excavations began in earnest in 2007, archaeologists have discovered a plaza, a ball court and three pyramids – one crowned by five temples – all left behind by pre-Hispanic cultures including Tepoztecos, Cuitlatecos and Tomiles.

Just inland from the ruins, a **museum** (www.soledaddemaciel.com; ⏰10am-5pm Tue-Sun) FREE houses three rooms full of Spanish-language displays, which place the

---

WHO PUT KETCHUP IN MY CEVICHE?

Strictly speaking, ceviche is a cold salad made with fish, which is sliced then chopped and 'cooked' in lime juice along with red onion, cilantro, chili and salt plus local additions. Up and down the Pacific coast you'll catch restaurants advertising shrimp ceviche or a mixed ceviche with scallops, octopus, shrimp and fish. Whichever way you order it, it will come on your choice of *tostada* (a snack), in a glass to be eaten with a spoon (a light meal), or on a platter served with a side stack of *tostadas* (now that's a meal).

But beware, in Guerrero, ceviche – and many *cócteles de camarón* (shrimp cocktails) – is made with a special ingredient known as industrial-grade ketchup. How this isn't seen as sacrilegious is anybody's guess, but the point is, do not order the ceviche in Guerrero. Order the *tiritas* (spicy, sliced slivers of fish marinated in citrus, chili and onions) instead.

local archaeological finds in a broader historical context. A recent find on display is a stone carved with a glyph of the name of the town in the late pre-Hispanic era: Xihuacan. The most important local artifact is the **Chole King**, a 1.5m-tall statue depicting deities of life and death, displayed in the courtyard of the village church.

Soledad de Maciel is 33km southeast of Zihuatanejo off Hwy 200. From the well-marked turnoff near Km 214, a rugged road leads 4km coastward to the museum, then continues another kilometer to the archaeological site and village. Any bus heading south to Petatlán or Acapulco will get you here; ask to be dropped at the intersection for 'La Chole,' where you can hop on a *camioneta* into town.

Pie de la Cuesta

📞744 / POP 600

Just 10km from Acapulco is the tranquil seaside suburb of Pie de la Cuesta, a rustic beach town occupied by some terrific guesthouses and seafood restaurants. But it's the odd combination of dramatic sunset views from the long beach and bloody sunrises over the lagoon that have made Pie de la Cuesta famous, for the town sits on a narrow strip of land bordered by the Pacific Ocean and the Laguna de Coyuca (where part of *Rambo: First Blood Part II* was filmed). The large freshwater lagoon contains several islands including **Isla Pájaros**, a bird sanctuary.

Pie de la Cuesta is much quieter, cheaper and closer to nature than Acapulco, but still close enough for those who want to enjoy the city's attractions and nightlife.

🏃 Activities

The rugged, steep shore break here is better for body boarders, but big swells in December get over 10ft and attract surfers. The riptide and strong waves make it sometimes dangerous for swimmers.

Waterskiing and **wakeboarding** on the lagoon are both popular pastimes; there are several waterskiing clubs along the main road, all charging around M$700 to M$800 per hour, including **Club de Ski Tres Marías** (📞744-460-00-13; www.tresmarias acapulco.com; Fuerza Aérea 375).

Several establishments offer **boat trips** on the lagoon from M$100 per person, and eager captains await your business along the main road and down by the boat launches at the lagoon's southeast corner.

Horseback riding on the beach costs about M$200 per hour. You may book through your hotel or directly from the galloping gauchos on the sand.

🛏 Sleeping

Villa Nirvana   HOTEL $$
(📞744-460-16-31; www.lavillanirvana.com; Av Fuerza Aérea 302; r M$475-1050; 🅿️🌀📶🏊) Villa Nirvana's friendly owners have lovingly landscaped this cheerful beachside property 500m from the main road turnoff. It has a variety of simple, comfortable accommodations surrounding a central garden and sizable pool. It's quite a bargain and very peaceful. The priciest rooms upstairs are larger and include sea-view terraces and large hammocks.

Hacienda Vayma Beach Club   HOTEL $$
(📞744-460-28-82; www.vayma.com.mx; Av Fuerza Aérea 378; r M$1102-1276, ste M$2320; 🅿️🌀 ❄️📶🏊) This relaxing ranch-style hotel is handsome in white and dark wood. It has a fat patch of beach with private *cabañas* and double-width lounge chairs, a big pool with swim-up bar and a choice of room types, from rustic beach-town digs to suites with hot water, air-con and Jacuzzi.

Baxar   BOUTIQUE HOTEL $$$
(📞744-460-25-02; www.baxar.com.mx; Av Fuerza Aérea 356; r M$1830-2930; 🅿️🌀❄️📶🏊) Trimmed in pink and exuding barefoot style, this is a popular and likable weekend getaway. Its range of cute rooms include sunken sitting areas, tastefully dangling rattan lampshades, mosquito nets and sweet little details. Prices drop by 30% midweek. Rates include breakfast and use of kayaks. Paddleboards are available to rent for M$150 per hour.

Quinta Erika   B&B $$$
(📞744-444-41-31; www.quintaerika.com; Carretera Barra de Coyuca Km 8.5; d incl breakfast M$1250, 4-person bungalow M$2500; 🅿️🌀📶🏊) A hidden, jungle-like retreat located 8km west of the highway junction. Six colorful rooms and one bungalow are tastefully decorated with handmade furniture and traditional handicrafts. It sits on 2 hectares of lagoon-side property, lovingly landscaped with palm and tropical fruit trees. Other perks include top breakfasts, kayaks, a whimsically decorated pool, a dock boasting spectacular

lagoon views, and upstairs lounge area with hammocks.

It's about a kilometer beyond the final bus stop in Playa Luces.

✕ Eating

A long string of beachside eateries means that finding a cold beer and shrimp cocktail presents zero difficulty.

Baxar SEAFOOD $$
(☑ 744-460-25-02; www.baxar.com.mx; Av Fuerza Aérea 356; mains M$80-180; ⊙ 8am-10pm; ☻☞) This inn and bistro on the beach, painted hot pink, serves standards such as ceviche, *cócteles* and roasted fish in coconut, and folds tasty shrimp with sautéed vegetables into grilled flour *taquitos* (crisp-fried, filled tortilla rolls). All of it is done with flair and flavor.

Restaurant Tres Marías SEAFOOD, MEXICAN $$$
(☑ 744-460-00-13; Av Fuerza Aérea s/n; mains M$150-220; ⊙ 10am-7:30pm; ☻) In an open building by the ocean, this place has cheerfully colored tablecloths and serves fantastic *huachinango al mojo de ajo* (garlicky red snapper). You can bring your own drinks if you choose a table on the beach. Its thatched extension across the road, on the lagoonside, is popular for breakfast (open from 8am).

ℹ Information

Pie de la Cuesta is strung out along the long main road (known both as Avenida Fuerza Aérea and Calzada Pie de la Cuesta) that runs between the lagoon and beach, past an air-force base and on to Playa Luces.

ℹ Getting There & Away

From Acapulco, catch a 'Pie de la Cuesta' bus on Avenida Costera across the street from the post office. Buses depart every 15 minutes from 6am until around 8pm; the trip costs M$7 and takes 30 to 90 minutes, depending on traffic – on a bad day, it can be total gridlock.

Buses marked 'Pie de la Cuesta–San Isidro' or 'Pie de la Cuesta–Pedregoso' stop at the town's arched entryway on Hwy 200, leaving you with a walk into town; more convenient 'Pie de la Cuesta–Playa Luces' buses turn off the main highway and follow Pie de la Cuesta's main street through town to Playa Luces.

Colectivo taxis to Pie de la Cuesta operate 24 hours along Avenida Costera and elsewhere in Acapulco's old town (M$14). Some start from the junction of Ocampo and Mina in the old town. A regular taxi from Acapulco costs M$100 to M$150 one way.

Acapulco

☑ 744 / POP 670,000

Acapulco was Mexico's original party town, with a stunning topography of soaring cliffs curling into a series of wide bays and intimate coves, fringed with sandy beaches and backed by jungle-green hills. It was dubbed the 'Pearl of the Pacific' during its heyday as a playground for the rich and famous, including Frank Sinatra, Elvis Presley, Elizabeth Taylor and Judy Garland. John F Kennedy and his wife Jacqueline honeymooned here, and it was immortalized in films such as Elvis' *Fun in Acapulco* and TV's *The Love Boat*.

Acapulco remains gorgeous, though overdeveloped. Worse, the city's reputation has been tarnished by years of violent battles in Mexico's ongoing drug wars. Despite the frightening homicide statistics, the violence is largely confined to internecine gang struggles for supremacy. International tourism has plummeted, but the city remains comparatively safe to visit. It still offers plenty of atmosphere and charm, with romantic cliffside restaurants, VW Beetle taxis, an impressive 17th-century fort, a world-class botanical garden, cliff divers and the old town's charming shady *zócalo*. And when you tire of the crowds, secluded beaches such as Pie de la Cuesta are just a short trip away.

ℹ Orientation

Acapulco follows the 11km shore of the Bahía de Acapulco (Acapulco Bay). Old Acapulco, centered on the cathedral and adjacent *zócalo*, is the western part of the city; Acapulco Dorado heads east around the bay from Playa Hornos to Playa Icacos; and Acapulco Diamante is a newer luxury resort area southeast of Acapulco proper, near the airport.

Acapulco's principal bayside avenue, Avenida Costera Miguel Alemán – often called 'La Costera' – hugs the shoreline all the way around the bay. Past the naval base, Avenida Costera becomes Carretera Escénica and climbs over the headland toward Diamante and the airport.

◎ Sights

Most of Acapulco's hotels, restaurants, discos and points of interest are along or near Avenida Costera, especially near its midpoint at **La Diana** (Map p570) traffic circle. From Playa Caleta on the Península de las Playas, it curves north toward the *zócalo*, then continues east along the beachfront past **Parque Papagayo** (Map p570; La Costera; ⊙ 8am-8pm) **FREE**, a large, shady park popular with Mexican families, all the way to Playa Icacos and the naval base at the bay's southeastern edge.

Beaches

Acapulco's beaches top the list of must-dos for most visitors. The beaches heading east around the bay from the *zócalo* – **Playa Hornos** (Map p570), **Playa Hornitos** (Map p570), **Playa Condesa** (Map p570) and **Playa Icacos** (Map p570) – are the most popular, though the west end of Hornos sometimes smells of fish from the morning catch. The high-rise hotel district begins on Playa Hornitos, on the east side of Parque Papagayo, and sweeps east. City buses constantly ply Avenida Costera, making it easy to get up and down the long arc of beaches.

Playas Caleta and Caletilla (Map p564) are two small, protected beaches blending into each other in a cove on the south side of Península de las Playas. They're both backed by a solid line of seafood *palapa* restaurants. The calm waters here are especially popular with families who have small children, though it is a *panga* harbor, thus isn't the cleanest. All buses marked 'Caleta' heading down Avenida Costera arrive here. A defunct aquarium sits on an islet just offshore; boats cross regularly to Isla de la Roqueta.

Playa La Angosta (Map p566) is in a tiny, protected cove on the west side of the peninsula. From the *zócalo* it takes about 20 minutes to walk here. Or you can take any 'Caleta' bus and get off near Hotel Avenida, at the corner of Las Palmas and Avenida Costera, just one short block from the beach.

The beaches on **Bahía Puerto Marqués**, about 18km southeast of the *zócalo,* are very popular, and its calm waters are good for waterskiing and sailing. You get a magnificent view of Bahía de Acapulco as the Carretera Escénica climbs south out of the city. 'Puerto Marqués' buses run here along Avenida Costera every 10 minutes from 5am to 9pm.

Beyond the Puerto Marqués turnoff and before the airport, **Playa Revolcadero** is a long, straight beach that has seen a recent explosion in luxury tourism and residential development. Waves are large and surfing is popular here, especially in summer, but a strong undertow makes swimming dangerous; heed lifeguards' instructions. Horseback riding along the beach is popular.

The two beaches closest to Old Acapulco are **Playa Tlacopanocha** (Map p566), di-

rectly across from the *zócalo,* noteworthy more as a departure point for bay cruises than as a swimming beach; and **Playa Manzanillo** (Map p566), a small crescent of sand that's popular with locals but not especially clean.

Other Sights

★ **Clavadistas de la Quebrada** CLIFF DIVERS (Map p566; ☑744-483-14-00; www.clavadistasdelaquebrada.com; Plazoleta La Quebrada; adult/child M$40/15; ◷shows 1pm, 7:30pm, 8:30pm, 9:30pm & 10:30pm) Acapulco's most famous tourist attraction, the cliff divers of La Quebrada have been dazzling audiences since 1934, plunging with fearless finesse from heights of 25m to 35m into the narrow ocean cove below. Expect around six divers; the spectacle lasts for about 20 minutes. The last show features divers holding torches. For good road karma, tip the divers on your way out. La Perla restaurant-bar provides a great but pricey view of the divers from above.

Sinfonía del Mar VIEWPOINT
(Symphony of the Sea; Map p564) The magical Sinfonía del Mar is an outdoor stepped plaza that occasionally hosts concerts, but mainly serves as an amazing place to view sunsets.

Isla de la Roqueta ISLAND
This island offers a popular (crowded) beach, and snorkeling and diving possibilities. You can rent snorkeling gear, kayaks and more. From Playa Caleta, boats make the eight-minute trip (M$60 return) regularly. Alternatively, glass-bottomed boats (by the company Yates Fondo Cristal) make a circuitous trip (M$90) from here or the *zócalo*, pointing out celebrity dwellings, sea life and the **Virgen de los Mares**, a submerged bronze Virgin statue. Visibility varies. The trip takes about 45 minutes, depending on how many times floating vendors approach your boat.

Greater Acapulco

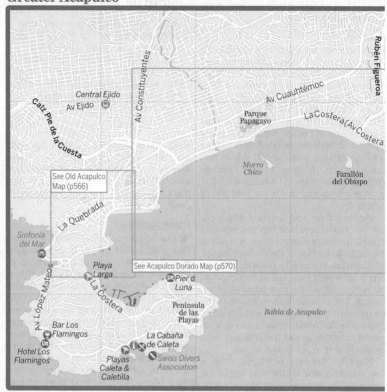

Fuerte de San Diego
FORTRESS

(Map p570; ☎744-480-09-56; Hornitos s/n) This beautifully restored pentagonal fort was built in 1616 atop a hill east of the *zócalo*. Its mission was to protect the Spanish *naos* (galleons) conducting trade between the Philippines and Mexico from marauding Dutch and English buccaneers. The fort was destroyed in a 1776 earthquake and rebuilt. It remains basically unchanged today.

The fort is home to the excellent **Museo Histórico de Acapulco** (Map p570; ☎744-482-38-28; www.inah.gob.mx; Hornitos s/n; M$52, free Sun; ⊙9am-6pm Tue-Sun) and also puts on regular evening sound-and-light shows, in Spanish and English. Call to confirm times and dates.

Zócalo
PLAZA

(Map p566) Every night Acapulco's leafy old town *zócalo* comes alive with street performers, mariachis, sidewalk cafes and occasional festivals. It's especially popular on Sunday nights with multiple generations of Mexican families. The **Nuestra Señora de la Soledad Cathedral** (Map p566; www.facebook.com/catedral.soledad; Hidalgo s/n; ⊙10am-7pm), built in 1930, dominates the square and is unusual for its blue-domed, neo-Byzantine architecture.

★ Exekatlkalli
PUBLIC ART

(Casa de los Vientos; Map p566; Inalámbrica 8) While the famed Mexican art collector Dolores 'Lola' Olmedo was away on vacation in 1956, a dying Diego Rivera decided to pep up the entrance to the villa of his friend, muse and love object with spectacular serpentine mosaic murals. They are quite an unexpected sight on this quiet hillside street. Plans are in the works to convert the house and studio into a cultural center/museum, which will give access to further Rivera mural decorations inside.

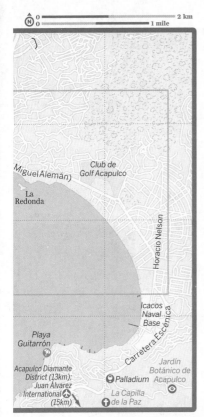

Acapulco and out to sea. The chapel's giant white cross is visible from miles across the bay. In the late afternoon, tourists jockey for positions to capture the sun setting within the sculpture of clasped hands. Access is via a gated compound: you may have to leave ID at the gate.

🏃 Activities

Acapulco's activities are largely beach-based.

Club de Golf Acapulco   GOLF
(Map p570; ☎744-484-07-81; Av Costera s/n; green fees 9/18 holes M$500/750; ⊗7am-6:30pm, last tee-off 5pm) Just back from the beach, this nine-holer is a simple but central course.

Tres Vidas   GOLF
(☎744-435-08-23; www.tresvidas.com.mx; Carretera Barra Vieja Km 7; green fees US$210; ⊗7am-7pm) Located in Barra Vieja, past the airport, this is one of Mexico's premier courses. When the wind blows, the oceanside site has a links-like feel to it. It's a spectacularly well-maintained spot, with good service and facilities. Access is for members and resort guests only, but it has reciprocal arrangements with various upmarket resorts in the area such as Banyan Tree and Las Brisas.

Paradise Bungy   ADVENTURE SPORTS
(Map p570; ☎744-484-75-29; Av Costera 107) This 50m-high bungee tower is easy to spot on Avenida Costera. For M$600 (more if you want photos etc) you can throw yourself (bungee included) from its platform, while crowds cheer you from the street and bar.

Water Sports

Just about everything that can be done on or below the water is done in Acapulco. **Waterskiing**, **boating**, **banana-boating** and **parasailing** are all popular. Outfitters, based in kiosks along the Zona Dorada beaches, charge about M$350 for a five-minute parasailing flight, M$500 for a jet-ski ride and M$800 for one hour of waterskiing or wakeboarding. The smaller Playas Caleta and Caletilla have sailboats, fishing boats, motorboats, pedal boats, canoes, snorkeling gear, inner tubes and water bicycles for rent.

Though Acapulco isn't really a scuba destination, there are some decent **dive sites** nearby.

The best **snorkeling** is off small Playa Las Palmitas on Isla de la Roqueta. Unless you pony up for an organized snorkeling trip,

Jardín Botánico de Acapulco   GARDENS
(Map p564; ☎744-446-52-52; www.acapulco botanico.org; Av Heróico Colegio Militar s/n, Cumbres de Llano Largo; adult/child M$30/free, free Sun, guided visit per person M$50; ⊗dawn-dusk) Located on the campus of a Jesuit university, these botanical gardens house an impressive collection of flora and fauna. The well-marked footpath climbs from 204m to 411m above sea level through a shaded tropical forest, with plenty of benches to stop and smell the flowers. It's 1.2km from the main road between Acapulco and Diamante; yellow shared cabs marked 'Cumbres' will drop you right outside.

La Capilla de la Paz   CHAPEL
(Chapel of Peace; Map p564; Vientos Galernos s/n, Alto Las Brisas; ⊗10am-6pm) FREE Perched on a hilltop high above Acapulco is this quiet spot for reflection, an airy '70s A-frame chapel with translucent onyx windows surrounded by beautiful views of

Old Acapulco

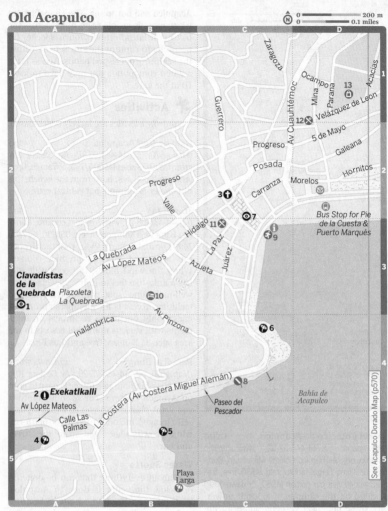

CENTRAL PACIFIC COAST ACAPULCO

you'll need to scramble over rocks to reach it. You can rent gear on the island or on Playas Caleta and Caletilla, which also have some decent spots.

Swiss Divers Association DIVING
(Map p564; ☎744-482-13-57; www.swissdivers. com; Hotel Caleta, Cerro San Martín 325; 2-tank boat dive US$75; ☺9am-5pm) This experienced set-up has a wide range of dives and PADI courses. Its office, tucked above wave-lashed rocks amid the semi-ruined splendor of the Hotel Caleta, is worth a look in itself. Snorkeling trips also available (US$38).

Acapulco Scuba Center DIVING
(Map p566; ☎744-482-94-74; www.acapulco scuba.com; Paseo del Pescador 13 & 14; 2-tank dive US$75; ☺8am-4pm Wed-Mon) One of a few diving operators that can take you out on boat dives in the bay. Offers PADI certification. Snorkeling trips also available (US$38).

Sportfishing
Sportfishing is very popular.

Blue Water Sportfishing FISHING
(☎cell 744-4282279; www.acavio.com/aventura. html; fishing charters US$250-450) Fun and friendly fishing set-up that will pick you up

Old Acapulco

◎ Top Sights
1 Clavadistas de la Quebrada.................A3
2 Exekatlkalli..A4

◎ Sights
3 Nuestra Señora de la Soledad
   Cathedral C2
4 Playa La Angosta A5
5 Playa Manzanillo B5
6 Playa Tlacopanocha C4
7 Zócalo...C2

◎ Activities, Courses & Tours
8 Acapulco Scuba Center C4
9 Acarey C3

◎ Sleeping
10 Etel Suites...B3

◎ Eating
11 El Nopalito..C3
12 Taquería Los Pioneros D1

◎ Shopping
13 Mercado de Artesanías El Parazal......D1

from the pier at the *zócalo*. Price varies according to boat size.

Cruises

Various boats and yachts offer cruises, most of which depart from around Playa Tlacopanocha or Playa Manzanillo near the *zócalo*. Cruises are available day and night. They range from glass-bottomed boats to multilevel craft (with blaring salsa music and open bars) to yachts offering quiet sunset cruises around the bay. Make reservations at the marina or through travel agencies, tour kiosks and most hotels.

Acarey   CRUISE
(Map p566; ☑744-100-36-37; www.facebook.com/acapulco.yate.acarey; La Costera s/n; adult/child under 10yr M$280/free; ◉cruises 4:30pm & 10:30pm daily, plus 7:30pm Sat) This popular boat cruise is sold by nearly every kiosk and agency in town as well as the booth by the dock. All departures offer a free bar and live music. The 4:30pm one gives a decent tour of the bay, while the night one is more of a fiesta. Trips last 2½ hours.

★ Festivals & Events

Semana Santa   RELIGIOUS
(◉Mar or Apr) Running from Palm Sunday, this is the busiest time of year for tourism in

Acapulco. There's lots of action in the discos, on the beaches and all over town.

Festival Francés   CULTURAL
(www.festivalfrances.com) The French Festival, usually held in March or April, celebrates French food, cinema, music and literature.

◎ Sleeping

Acapulco has tens of thousands of hotel rooms. Rates vary widely by season; peak season is roughly from mid-December to mid-January, Easter Week and during the July and August school holidays. You can often bargain for a better rate, especially in low season for extended stays. Package rates and online bookings can provide substantial savings.

Most of Acapulco's budget hotels are concentrated around the *zócalo*. The original high-rise zone stretches from the eastern end of Parque Papagayo and curves east around the bay; other luxury strips are southeast of town near the airport.

Hotel Márquez del Sol   HOTEL $
(Map p570; ☑744-484-77-60; Juan de la Cosa 22; r M$600; ◉❄☎⊠) This budget hotel is close to the beach but just far enough away from the main road to be peaceful at night. Decor is bland, but rooms are spacious and clean enough, though bathrooms are tight; many rooms have balconies. There's a pool in the central atrium. The hotel has little charm but offers value for its location in the heart of the zone.

Hotel Nilo   HOTEL $$
(Map p570; ☑744-484-10-99; www.hotelnilo.mx; cnr Calle 4 & Ortiz Monasterio; d/q M$800/1200; ℗◉❄☎⊠) Occupying the same price band as a whole swath of Acapulco hotels, but about 40 years newer than most of them, this likable place a block back from the strip is in the pleasant eastern end of town and amiably run. Rooms are compact but comfy and modern, and that includes the bathrooms. There's a pool on the top floor.

Hotel Acapulco Malibu   HOTEL $$
(Map p570; ☑744-484-10-70; www.acapulcomalibu.com; Av Costera 20; r M$1190-1300; ℗◉❄☎⊠) It's always nice to see a bit of originality, and the octagonal rooms here fit the bill. Compact and rather charming, they sport a small balcony, surround a creeper-draped atrium and make a fine beach base – or you could go for a dip in the pool instead, also an eight-sided job.

Hotel Los Flamingos HOTEL **$$**
(Map p564; ☎744-482-06-91; www.hotellosflamingos.com; Av López Mateos s/n; d/superior d/junior ste M$714/833/952; P⊖❄︎☎≋) The US$40-a-night hotel with the million-dollar view, once owned by Johnny 'Tarzan' Weissmuller, John Wayne and their pals, is a living, hot-pink memory of Acapulco's heyday. Perched on a cliff 135m above the ocean, this classic boasts one of the finest sunset views in town, with hammocks to enjoy them from, and a popular bar and restaurant.

Images of Hollywood's golden age grace the walls. The rooms are modest, if aged, but comfortable enough. It's well worth the upgrade to the 'junior suites,' which are significantly larger, air-conditioned and have a balcony.

Hotel Marzol HOTEL **$$**
(Map p570; ☎744-484-33-96; hotel.marzol@gmail.com; Av Francia 1A; r M$1000; ⊖❄︎☎≋) Tucked down a narrow street leading to the beach and dwarfed by huge high-rises around it, this more modest construction is a polished if unremarkable three-star choice. Rooms have high-end tile floors, high ceilings and thin, hard-ish beds. It makes a very clean, reliable base.

Etel Suites HOTEL **$$**
(Map p566; ☎744-482-22-40; www.etelsuites.com; Av Pinzona 92; r with/without terrace M$1000/800, apt M$1200; P⊖❄︎☎≋) High above Old Acapulco, with views of both the bay and the Pacific Ocean, this hotel has modest but well-kept rooms in a very quiet part of town. Management is benevolent, and midcentury modernists will love their apartments thanks to dated furnishings and terraces with outrageous city vistas.

Hotel Sands Acapulco HOTEL **$$**
(Map p570; ☎744-435-08-90; www.sands.com.mx; Av Costera 178; r M$788; P⊖❄︎☎≋) A dated but fun choice for families, Sands is located across the highway from the beach and has a huge children's playground, minigolf, pools and a waterslide. Bungalows are small but cozy (don't rely on the wi-fi reaching them); the larger rooms sleep up to four people.

Bali-Hai MOTEL **$$**
(Map p570; ☎744-485-66-22; www.balihai.com.mx; Av Costera 186; r M$952; P⊖❄︎☎≋) This Polynesian-themed motel in the heart of Bahía de Acapulco, across the street from the beach, looks a little downbeat, but has long rows of spacious rooms that are decent apart from their 1960s-vintage aquamarine toilets. They flank a pair of palm-lined pools. You'd want to bag it for 70% or less of this high-season price before it really felt like value.

★**Pier d Luna** B&B **$$$**
(Map p564; ☎744-483-97-06; www.pdluna.com; Casa No 2, Gran Vía Tropical 34; r M$1452-2083; P⊖❄︎☎≋) This tucked-away retreat has a view so good that the enormous lounge and dining room, complete with baby grand, is wholly open-sided: what a marvelous space it is. Five sweet rooms, all with individual designs, enjoy the same outlook; some have balconies to soak it all up. Hospitable hosts make this a delightful personal experience and breakfasts are abundant.

There's a pleasant pool and little Jacuzzi looking over the bay, to which you can descend via private stairs. Delicious chef-cooked French-Mexican meals are available by arrangement. Pay attention to the directions you'll be sent, as there are no signs.

★**Banyan Tree Cabo Marqués** RESORT **$$$**
(☎744-434-01-00; www.banyantree.com; Blvd Cabo Marqués, Punta Diamante; r US$450-505; P⊖❄︎@☎≋) Right over the ocean on a gated peninsula, 20km south of downtown, this gorgeous resort brings Asia to Acapulco. Accommodations are in sumptuous villas with complete privacy to enjoy your hammock deck and pool with vast vistas. They're equipped with a stylish range of robes, toiletries and thoughtful extras; in-room dining is available. Golf carts zip you around the discreet, charming facilities.

Highlights of the complex include a Thai restaurant, private massage rooms with view and a stunning infinity pool. An army of helpful staff keeps things very slick. For an utterly peaceful resort experience away from the crowds, this is hard to beat.

Hotel Elcano HOTEL **$$$**
(Map p570; ☎744-435-15-00; www.hotelelcano.com.mx; Av Costera 75; d M$1500-2000; P⊖❄︎@☎≋) Near the center of Acapulco's crescent of beaches, pleasantly retro Elcano has old-school grace, with art-deco tiles in the breezy lobby, a sumptuous pool area and a patch of beachfront. There's a maritime theme accentuated by the white-and-blue paint job. Rooms aren't huge but they are bright with marble washbasins and terraces

with a commanding view. Low-season discounts are a steal.

Eating

Lots of restaurants are dotted along the coastal strip, with a good concentration back from Playa Icacos and traditional eateries in the old town. On Thursdays *pozole* is typically served, and restaurants get lively with groups eating this and other traditional food such as *tamales*, while listening to folkloric music.

El Nopalito   CAFE $
(Map p566; La Paz; mains M$40-100; ☺8am-8pm; ☻) One of several cafes and diners strung along the streets surrounding the *zócalo*. This darkish, keep-it-real one attracts people for its daily menu including *mole* and paella on Sundays. Its plate lunches (M$55) include fruit, juice or coffee and a main such as roast chicken, beef enchilada, *carne asada* or fried fish, served with beans and tortillas.

Taquería Los Pioneros   TAQUERÍA $
(Map p566; ☎744-482-23-45; cnr Mendoza & Mina; 5 tacos M$30-55; ☺9am-1am; ☻) Still the spot for authentic *tacos al pastor*. The tacos are tiny but their fillings are tasty, plus this is one of the few *taquerías* in Mexico with a legit vegetarian option, stuffed with peppers, corn, tomato and cheese.

★ La Casa de Tere   MEXICAN $$
(Map p570; Martín 1721; mains M$60-150; ☺8am-6pm Tue-Fri & Sun; ☻☎) This homespun gem near the Estrella de Oro bus terminal is the place to go for Thursday *pozole*. Founded on doña Tere's patio in 1990 using her mother Clarita's traditional recipes, it serves a wide-ranging menu, including the sought-after Sunday special: *barbacoa de carnero* (barbecued lamb). All of it comes with house-made tortillas.

El Jacalito   MEXICAN $$
(Map p570; ☎744-486-65-12; Gonzalo de Sandoval 26; mains M$70-150; ☺8am-11pm; ☻☎) Just off the strip, and a few paces from the beach, this thatched restaurant can nevertheless have a secluded vibe. It feels very authentic, with its traditional colored-check tablecloths and cordial staff, and the food backs it up. Great rolled chicken tacos, fairly priced fish dishes and filling breakfasts make it an oasis at any time of day. The *frijoles* are delicious.

El Cabrito   MEXICAN $$
(Map p570; ☎744-484-77-11; www.elcabrito-acapulco.com; Av Costera 1480; mains M$85-255; ☺2-11pm Mon-Sat, 1:30-10:30pm Sun; ☻☎) This venerable, beloved and brightly decorated restaurant has some of the city's finest traditional Mexican food, such as Oaxaca-style black *mole* made from 32 ingredients. You'd also do quite well with *cabrito al pastor* (roast kid goat; M$255): eat it with your fingers, say the staff. The shrimp dishes are tasty, as are the house-made tortillas, and the outdoor tables offer prime people-watching opportunities.

La Cabaña de Caleta   SEAFOOD $$
(Map p564; ☎744-482-50-07; www.lacabanadecaleta.com; Playa Caleta; dishes M$80-220; ☺9am-9pm; ☻) Step back in time and into a slice of traditional Mexican beach life, c 1950, at this venerable, unpretentious seafood shack straddling the sands of Playa Caleta. Bask under a blue umbrella and gaze at the bay while savoring specialties such as *zarzuela de mariscos* (seafood stew) or *chiles rellenos* stuffed with shrimp, octopus and fish.

Pesca'o   SEAFOOD $$$
(Map p570; ☎744-481-32-07; www.pescaoacapulco.com; Maury 1A; mains M$130-270; ☺noon-7:30pm; ☻☎) Tucked down a side street off the Avenida Costera drag is this hopping seafood house with its intimate palm-leaf interior spilling out onto a pebbled sidewalk. It serves *cócteles* of shrimp, oyster, octopus, scallop and combinations of the same, flays salmon carpaccio, does seafood enchiladas, grills and fries fish a dozen different ways, and has ceviche, of course. Zesty drinks list.

El Gaucho   PARRILLA $$$
(Map p570; ☎744-484-17-00; www.elpresidente acapulco.com; Hotel Presidente, Av Costera 8; pasta M$100-140, mains M$225-375; ☺2-11:30pm Mon-Wed, 2pm-midnight Thu-Sat, 2-11pm Sun; ☻☎) This glass-box dining room leaves a little to be desired in terms of service and atmosphere – avoid the cringe-worthy faux-Argentine shows on Wednesday and Saturday nights – but it does do an excellent steak. Less carnivorous folk can choose from an assortment of pasta dishes or tasty grilled provolone cheese.

Drinking & Nightlife

The strip of huge outdoor/indoor bars around the landmark Paradise Bungy tower

CENTRAL PACIFIC COAST ACAPULCO

Acapulco Dorado

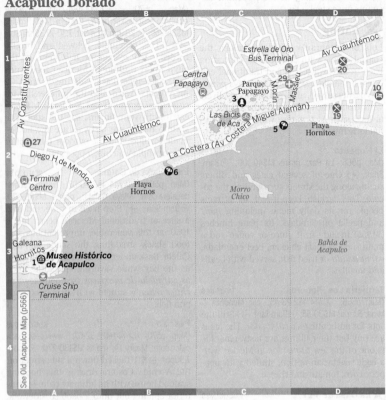

Acapulco Dorado

◎ Top Sights
1 Museo Histórico de Acapulco A3

◎ Sights
Fuerte de San Diego .... (see 1)
2 La Diana E2
3 Parque Papagayo C1
4 Playa Condesa F2
5 Playa Hornitos C2
6 Playa Hornos B2
7 Playa Icacos G3

➕ Activities, Courses & Tours
8 Club de Golf Acapulco G2
9 Paradise Bungy F2

🛏 Sleeping
10 Bali-Hai D1
11 Hotel Acapulco Malibu G2
12 Hotel Elcano G3
13 Hotel Márquez del Sol E1
14 Hotel Marzol G3
15 Hotel Nilo H4

16 Hotel Sands Acapulco E1

🍴 Eating
17 El Cabrito H3
18 El Gaucho F2
19 El Jacalito D2
20 La Casa de Tere D1
21 Pesca'o H3

🍸 Drinking & Nightlife
22 Baby'O H4
23 Barbarroja E2
24 Demás Factory G2
25 Mojito E2
26 Reinas F2

🛍 Shopping
27 Mercado Central A2

ℹ Information
28 Canadian Consulate E2
29 Hospital Magallanes D1

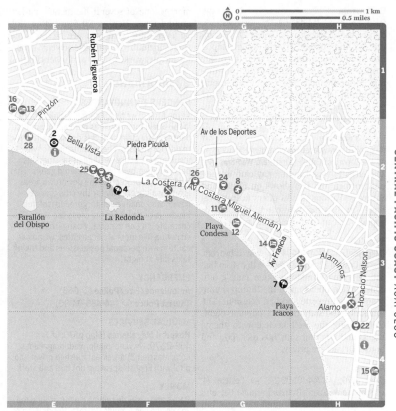

is lively from early evening until late with drinks promos, go-go dancers and other revelry.

Most clubs don't get rolling until midnight or later. Admission charges vary by season and night. Dress to impress; shorts and sneakers are frowned upon.

Acapulco has a reasonable gay scene with several bars and clubs. Its unofficial gay beach is the rocky section of Playa Condesa by the Fiesta Americana hotel.

Bar Los Flamingos
BAR

(Map p564; www.hotellosflamingos.com; Av López Mateos s/n; ⊙10am-10pm; 🖝) The clifftop bar of Hotel Los Flamingos is old-fashioned but the best sundowner spot in Acapulco, thanks to its famed menu of signature cocktails – such as *cocos locos* (made with rum, tequila, pineapple juice and coconut crème). Its restaurant also serves a tasty, traditional menu, and service is old-school impeccable.

Mojito
BAR, CLUB

(Map p570; 🕾744-484-82-74; Av Costera s/n; ⊙4pm-4am; 🖝) If you prefer dancing salsa to reggaeton or techno, this should be your go-to option on the Acapulco strip. Look for the cascading water fronting a bar that looks out over the ocean and gets lively with Cuban beats and drinks until late. There's a good range of ages too and live music on weekend nights.

Palladium
CLUB

(Map p564; 🕾744-446-54-90; www.palladium.com.mx; Carretera Escénica s/n; admission varies; ⊙11pm-6am Fri & Sat; 🖝) The best nightclub in town, Palladium attracts a young crowd, and offers fabulous bay views from floor-to-ceiling windows. An international cast of DJs pumps out hip-hop, house, trance and techno from an ultraluxe sound system. Dress up, and expect to wait in line. Usual entry is M$500 with unlimited drinks.

Barbarroja
BAR

(Map p570; ☑744-484-59-32; www.facebook.com/barbarroja.acapulco; Av Costera 107; ⊙5pm-late; 🛜) Ahoy, matey! From a design shaped like the deck of a ship to women in corsair costumes dancing on tables, this over-the-top, pirate-themed pub is one of several beachfront bars in what is the central part of the strip. It's open-air and inclusive, but doesn't have the best-quality mixed drinks.

Demás Factory
GAY

(Map p570; www.facebook.com/demasfactory; Av de los Deportes 10A; ⊙10pm-7am Wed-Sun; 🛜) The city's longest-running gay club is open only to men and has shows on Friday and Saturday. Various drinks offers keep things busy – at the time of research, M$250 gave you all-you-can-drink on Saturdays.

Baby'O
CLUB

(Map p570; ☑744-484-74-74; www.babyo.com.mx; Av Costera 22; M$100-380; ⊙11pm-6am Thu-Sat; 🛜) This Flintstone-esque faux grotto construction opens up to the thump thump of unbridled reverie and bad decisions. The fun kind. Translation: it's a popular nightclub among the well heeled, with theme nights and DJs that spin '80s rock, pop and house. Drinks are pricey.

Reinas
GAY

(Map p570; ☑744-101-02-27; Av Costera 74; ⊙8pm-late Wed-Sun) Reinas karaoke bar and nightclub is a rough-around-the-edges but popular bar serving a mostly gay clientele on Avenida Costera. Admission is free.

☆ Entertainment

Forum Mundo Imperial
CONCERT VENUE

(☑744-435-17-95; www.forumimperial.com; Av de las Naciones, Acapulco Diamante) At the airport junction in the Diamante area, this huge, striking venue attracts big-name acts for anything from comedy to rock.

🛍 Shopping

Mercado Central
MARKET

(Map p570; Hurtado de Mendoza s/n; ⊙6am-9pm) This sprawling indoor-outdoor bazaar has everything from *atoles* to *zapatos* (shoes), plus produce, hot food and souvenirs. Any westbound 'Pie de la Cuesta' or 'Pedregoso' bus will drop you here.

Mercado de Artesanías El Parazal
MARKET

(Map p566; cnr Parana & Velázquez de Leon; ⊙many shops 10am-7pm) Bargaining is the standard at this leafy and laid-back craft market, one of several handicraft markets around town. Here you'll find better deals on everything that you see in the hotel shops, including hammocks, jewelry, ceramics, lacquerwork, T-shirts and other clothing.

ℹ Information

DANGERS & ANNOYANCES

At the time of writing, Acapulco ranked third in the world for homicides per capita, but residents rightly claim that this doesn't reflect the reality for visitors. The vast majority of violent incidents are score-settling assassinations between members of drug-related gangs. That said, though protecting the downtown areas is an absolute priority for the city, tourists have occasionally been targeted in isolated incidents or caught in the cross fire. Acapulco certainly isn't an especially dangerous place to visit, but, like most Mexican cities, we advise caution with personal possessions and taking taxis late at night.

EMERGENCY

Ambulance/Fire/Police (☑066)
Tourist Police (☑744-485-04-90)

MEDICAL SERVICES

Hospital Magallanes (Map p570; ☑744-469-02-70; www.hospitalprivadomagallanes.com; Massieu 2) A well-established private hospital with English-speaking doctors and staff.

MONEY

Banks and *casas de cambio* cluster around the *zócalo* and line Avenida Costera. Hotels will also change money, but their rates are usually high.

POST

Main Post Office (Map p566; ☑744-483-24-05; www.correosdemexico.com.mx; Palacio Federal, Av Costera 315; ⊙8am-5pm Mon-Fri, 9am-1pm Sat)

TOURIST INFORMATION

CAPTA (☑744-484-98-00, 744-481-18-54) Hotline for tourist information and assistance with problems.

Municipal Tourist Kiosks (☑744-440-70-10; www.acapulco.gob.mx; ⊙9am-6pm) The city government operates several tourist information kiosks that aren't particularly helpful but are located on the marina (Map p566) across from the *zócalo*, at La Diana traffic circle (Map p570), at Playa Caleta (Map p564; Jul, Aug, Dec-Jan & Easter) and by the entrance to Walmart (Map p570) near Playa Icacos.

ℹ Getting There & Away

Acapulco is 400km south of Mexico City and 235km southeast of Zihuatanejo.

AIR

Acapulco's **Juan Álvarez International Airport** (☎744-435-20-60; www.oma.aero; Blvd de las Naciones s/n) has seen a marked decrease in international nonstop flights, although it's still easy to connect through Mexico City (a short hop from Acapulco). Airlines have offices at the airport; there are a couple of direct flights from the USA and Canada.

The following domestic destinations are serviced by these airlines:

➝ Guadalajara – TAR

➝ Ixtapa – TAR

➝ Mexico City – Aeromar, Aeroméxico, Interjet, Volaris

➝ Monterrey – VivaAerobus, Volaris

➝ Queretaro – TAR

➝ Tijuana – Interjet, Volaris

➝ Toluca – Interjet

BUS

Acapulco has four bus terminals. Fortunately, the two major ones are quite close together. There's also a bus station in the Acapulco Diamante resort area. Some luxury bus services are also called Diamante, a possible source of confusion.

Central Ejido (Map p564; ☎744-469-20-30; Av Ejido 47) This bus terminal mostly serves departures to destinations in Guerrero and Oaxaca states, run by the AltaMar/Costeños group. Estrella de Oro services to Zihuatenejo also stop here on their way north.

Central Papagayo (Map p570; ☎744-486-57-14; Av Cuauhtémoc 1605) Just north of Parque Papagayo, this modern terminal has 1st-class and luxury services all around the country run by Costa Line and its affiliates. Left luggage is available but eating options are weak.

Estrella de Oro Bus Terminal (Central Cuauhtémoc; Map p570; ☎800-900-01-05; www.estrelladeoro.com.mx; Av Cuauhtémoc 1490) All Estrella de Oro (EDO) services leave from this modern, air-conditioned terminal, which has several ATMs and left-luggage facilities.

Terminal Centro (Map p570; ☎744-482-21-84; Av Cuauhtémoc 97) Mostly 2nd-class departures to relatively nearby towns, though some services to Mexico City stop here too.

CAR & MOTORCYCLE

Several car-rental companies have offices at the airport as well as in town.

Alamo (www.alamo.com) Airport (☎744-466-94-44); Av Costera (Map p570; ☎744-484-33-05; www.alamojpsk.com.mx; Av Costera 34; ⊗8am-9pm Mon-Sat, 8am-7pm Sun)

Europcar (☎744-466-93-14; www.europcar.com; airport)

Hertz (☎744-466-91-72; www.hertz.com; airport)

Getting Around

TO/FROM THE AIRPORT

Acapulco's airport is 23km southeast of the *zócalo*. You can buy a ticket for transportation into town from the desk at the end of the domestic terminal. Fares are officially regulated: *colectivo* taxis operate whenever there's an incoming flight, charging M$120 per person to any point within Acapulco city limits. Private taxis from the airport run constantly, ranging in price depending on destination (think M$450 for central hotels).

Leaving Acapulco, taxis from the city center to the airport cost around M$250 to M$350, depending on the distance.

BUSES FROM ACAPULCO

DESTINATION	FARE (M$)	DURATION (HR)	FREQUENCY (DAILY)
Chilpancingo	64-115	1¾-3	frequent EDO, Ejido & Centro
Cuernavaca	400	4-5	5 EDO, 5 Papagayo
Mazatlán	1477-1599	23	3 Papagayo
Mexico City (Terminal Norte)	470-635	6	frequent Papagayo, some EDO
Mexico City (Terminal Sur)	470-615	5	very frequent EDO & Papagayo, some Centro
Puerto Escondido	395-415	7-8	3 Papagayo
Taxco	240	4	5 EDO
Zihuatanejo	155-220	4-5	frequent EDO, 5 Papagayo

BICYCLE

Las Bicis de Aca (Map p570; www.facebook.com/lasbicisdeaca.es; Av Costera; 1hr M$40, per hour thereafter M$30; ⊙ 4-9pm Mon-Fri, 9am-9pm Sat & Sun) Situated by the Futcenter sports complex at Parque Papagayo, almost opposite the flagpole.

BUS

At the time of research, Acapulco was preparing for the new Acabús system of (in theory) rapid-transit buses accessed via raised station platforms in the middle of the road on the main route, and via set stops on several complementary routes. Tickets will be M$7.

The major route will run from Las Cruces along Avenida Cuauhtémoc and down to the beach at La Caleta. Another key route (without platforms) will run along Avenida Costera.

Buses operate from 5am to 11pm.

CAR & MOTORCYCLE

Avoid driving in Acapulco if you can. The anarchic traffic is often horribly snarled.

TAXI

Legions of blue-and-white VW Beetle cabs scurry around Acapulco like cockroaches, maneuvering with an audacity that borders on the comical. Drivers often quote fares higher than the official ones; always agree on a price with the driver before getting in. Other blue-and-white cabs are also available. A short hop should be M$30 to M$40, while a cross-town ride will be M$80 to M$100.

Shared yellow taxis (*colectivos* or *peseros*) run along set routes and cost M$14 per journey, double if you want to sit on your own in the front and not get squashed. Their destinations are written on the windshield and they can be hailed anywhere – in fact they'll probably hail you with their horns first.

In the hotel district, Cinderella-style sparkling horse carts are a big hit with kids at night.

HURRICANE MANUEL

On September 19, 2013, what started out as a tropical storm morphed into Hurricane Manuel and hit Mexico's Pacific coast with vicious force. The storm was relatively slow-moving, gusting sustained winds of 125km/h, which meant rainfall was severe. Rivers swelled high and fast and tore through bridges. Hillsides melted, burying entire neighborhoods. The Acapulco/Costa Chica area was one of the worst affected. In total, 169 people were killed in the storm, one of the worst known Pacific cyclones to hit Mexico.

Costa Chica

Guerrero's 'Small Coast,' extending southeast from Acapulco to the Oaxaca border, is much less traveled than its bigger brother to the northwest, but it has some spectacular beaches. Afro-Mestizos (people of mixed African, indigenous and European descent) make up a large portion of the population. The region was a safe haven for Africans who escaped slavery, some from the interior, others (it's believed) from a slave ship that sank just off the coast.

From Acapulco, Hwy 200 traverses inland past small villages and farmlands. **San Marcos**, about 60km east of Acapulco, and **Cruz Grande**, about 40km further east, are the only two towns of significant size before Cuajinicuilapa near the Oaxaca border. Both provide basic services including banks, gas stations and simple hotels.

An alternative route out of Acapulco takes you along the coast past the airport to the river mouth and beach village of **Barra Vieja**, famous for its upmarket golf course (p565) and restaurants serving *pescado a la talla*. From here the road cuts inland to rejoin Hwy 200 at El Tejoruco.

Playa Ventura & Around

📋 741 / POP 400

Located 135km southeast of Acapulco, Playa Ventura (labeled Colonia Juan Álvarez on most maps) is a long, pristine beach with soft white and gold sands. Behind it is a simple, likable Mexican village, while uncomplicated beachfront accommodations and seafood restaurants line the beaches in both directions from the center of town.

Playa Ventura is an important turtle nesting site, and volunteers go out every night in the season to collect eggs and re-bury them in a little beachside compound, which looks like a tiny war cemetery with its rows of information markers, but with a more hopeful purpose.

About 13km southeast of the Playa Ventura turnoff on Hwy 200 (Km 137) is the market town of **Marquelia**. The town offers access to an immense stretch of beach backed by coconut palms, which follows the contours of the coastline for many kilometers in either direction. From Marquelia's center you can take a *camioneta* to a section of the beach known as **Playa La Bocana**, where the Río Marquelia meets the sea and forms a lagoon. La Bocana has *cabañas,* a small hotel and some *comedores* with hammocks where you can spend the night.

🛏 Sleeping & Eating

Hotel Villa Tortuga
HOTEL $

(☎741-101-30-53; www.playaventura.com.mx/villa tortuga.html; d/tr M$450/575; P🐕😊🛜🏊) Comfortable rooms, some with big windows brilliantly close to the crashing waves, are a steal at this likable, colorful place with a cavalcade of hanging shells, a decent-sized pool and a restaurant (open 10am to 6pm) in the heart of town. You can also camp here (M$80 per person).

Posada Quintomondo
CABAÑAS $$

(☎cell 741-1013018; www.posadaquintomondo.info; d M$800; P🐕😊🛜🏊) Two kilometers north of the church, this beachside retreat has romantic cabin-style rooms. There's artful use of wood throughout, including the attractive chairs on your own little terrace. The rest is sand and sea – oh, and a rather good restaurant serving Italian and Mexican dishes.

★ Los Norteñitos
MEXICAN $

(dishes M$40-120; ⊙7am–last customer) Totally authentic and genuinely welcoming, this *taquería* in the center of town is run by a local family, who call in extra members according to demand. Delicious *cecina* (cured beef) tacos are great with freshly made tomatillo salsa in a *molcajete,* while fish and prawns are reliably delicious – the whole snapper cooked in foil with a mellow chili sauce is a standout. Prices are very reasonable.

Il Giardino
ITALIAN $$

(☎741-101-30-76; meals M$80-150; ⊙noon-10pm; 😊) Two kilometers north along the beachfront road from the center, on the landward side, this simple, convivial eatery does an excellent line in genuine pizza and pasta dishes.

ℹ Getting There & Away

To get here by car, take Hwy 200 to the signposted Playa Ventura turnoff (Km 124), just east of the village of Copala, then continue 7km to the coast. By bus from Acapulco, take a southeast-bound bus to Copala (M$95 to M$120, 2¾ hours). From here, *camionetas* and microbuses depart for the turnoff to Playa Ventura (M$10, 10 minutes) from just east of the bus stop. From the turnoff, shared taxis (M$15, 10 minutes) shuttle into town. Some Cuajinicuilapa-bound buses from Acapulco will drop you directly at the turnoff.

Cuajinicuilapa
📞741 / POP 10,000

About 200km southeast of Acapulco, Cuajinicuilapa (Cuaji for short) is the nucleus of Afro-Mestizo culture on the Costa Chica. The **Museo de las Culturas Afromestizas** (Museum of Afro-Mestizo Cultures; ☎741-414-12-31; Cuauhtémoc s/n; M$10; ⊙10am-2pm & 4-7pm Tue-Sun) is a tribute to the history of African slaves in Mexico and, specifically, to local Afro-Mestizo culture. It's all in Spanish; there are some interesting stories, sweet dioramas and a model slaving ship. Behind the museum are three examples of *casas redondas,* the round houses typical of West Africa that were built around Cuaji until as late as the 1960s. The museum is just behind the basketball court on the main road in the center of town. Several hotels are strung along this road if you want to stay.

Buses to Cuajinicuilapa (M$207, 4½ hours) run by AltaMar/Costeños depart Central Ejido bus terminal in Acapulco eight times daily, and there are nine buses daily from Pinotepa Nacional (M$54, one hour) in Oaxaca state.

Western Central Highlands

Includes ➜

Guadalajara.........577
Tequila 601
Lago de Chapala.....601
Zona de Montaña... 605
Colima 607
Morelia.............612
Reserva Mariposa
Monarca............621
Angangueo 623
Zitácuaro 623
Pátzcuaro.......... 624
Uruapan............631
Angahuan 635

Best Places to Eat

➜ La Surtidora (p628)

➜ Allium (p592)

➜ Restaurante Lu (p618)

➜ Birriería las Nueve Esquinas (p591)

Best Unesco World Heritage Sites

➜ Morelia (p612)

➜ Reserva Mariposa Monarca (p621)

➜ Instituto Cultural de Cabañas (p583)

➜ Tequila (p601)

Why Go?

Welcome to the Mexico of your dreams. Many elements that define the global image of Mexico originated in the western central highlands amid snoozing volcanoes, sun-baked avocado plantations, and some of the finest pre-Hispanic ruins that no one's ever heard of. Resort escapees can sip the world's best tequila amid a sea of blue agave, listen to mariachi music in the region of its conception, or have a religious experience contemplating the magnificence of Morelia cathedral.

Less obvious (and less visited) is Lago de Pátzcuaro, where the indigenous Purépecha display dexterous craft-making skills and hold some of the most spine-tingling Day of the Dead celebrations in the nation.

Two icons stud the natural world. Volcán Paricutín is a climbable volcano that burst out of a maize field in 1943, while the Reserva Mariposa Monarca is a swath of coniferous highlands invaded annually by millions of fluttering butterflies.

When to Go
Guadalajara

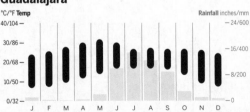

Feb Flutter with the monarch butterflies in the Reserva Mariposa Monarca.

Nov Commune with the dead on Día de Muertos in the villages around Pátzcuaro.

Mar Join the stars of cinema at Guadalajara's Festival Internacional del Cine.

History

The western central highlands were too far from the Maya and Aztecs to fall under their influence, but during the 14th to 16th centuries the Tarascos in northern Michoacán developed a robust pre-Hispanic civilization. When the Aztecs took attacked, the Tarascos were able to hold strong thanks to their copper blades. West of the Tarascos was their rival, Chimalhuacán – a confederation of four indigenous kingdoms that spread through parts of present-day Jalisco, Colima and Nayarit states. To the north were the Chichimecs.

Colima, the leading Chimalhuacán kingdom, was conquered by the Spanish in 1523. The whole region, however, was not brought under Spanish control until the notorious campaigns of Nuño de Guzmán. Between 1529 and 1536 he tortured, killed and enslaved indigenous people from Michoacán to Sinaloa. His grizzly victories made him rich and famous and won him governorship of his conquered lands, until news of his war crimes leaked out. He was sent back to Spain and imprisoned for life in 1538.

This fertile ranching and agricultural region developed gradually and Guadalajara (established in 1542 and always one of Mexico's biggest cities) became the 'capital of the west.' The church, with help from the enlightened Bishop Vasco de Quiroga, fostered small industries and handicraft traditions around the villages of Lago de Pátzcuaro in its effort to ease the continuing poverty of the indigenous people.

In the 1920s the region's two major states, Michoacán and Jalisco, were hotbeds of the Cristero rebellion by Catholics against government antichurch policies. Lázaro Cárdenas of Michoacán, as state governor (1928–32) and then as Mexican president (1934–40), instituted reforms that did much to abate antigovernment sentiments.

Today Jalisco and Michoacán hold many of Mexico's natural resources – especially timber, minerals, livestock and agriculture – and Jalisco has a thriving tech industry. In the past both states have seen large segments of their population head to the USA for work. Michoacán reportedly lost almost half its population to emigrations, and money sent home regularly exceeds US$2 billion. But with the economic slowdown in the USA, the flow north slowed and these days many have decided to return to Mexico and open up businesses on their home soil.

GUADALAJARA

📞 33 / POP 1.5 MILLION / ELEV 1550M

Mexico's second largest metropolis is actually a confederation of three cities – Zapopan, Tlaquepaque and Guadalajara proper – each with its own airs and idiosyncrasies. Together they form a culturally compelling whole, a blended cocktail not unlike one of the locally concocted margaritas – sharp, potent and remarkably well-balanced.

If you're intimidated by the size and intensity of Mexico City, Guadalajara delivers a less frenetic alternative. Many of the clichéd images recognized as Mexican have roots here: mariachi music, wide-brimmed sombreros, the Mexican hat dance and *charreadas* (rodeos). But, Guadalajara is as much a vanguard of the new Mexico as it is a guardian of the old. Chapultepec hipsters drive the cultural life forward, fusion chefs have sharpened the edges of an already legendary culinary scene (famed for its tender stews and 'drowned' sandwiches), while foresighted local planners are doing their damnedest to tackle the traffic and congestion (a bike-sharing scheme is the latest wild card).

With over four million inhabitants in its broader metro area, Guadalajara can't match the intimacy and architectural homogeneity of smaller colonial cities, though its historic core is handsome enough, anchored by the twin wonders of the cathedral and the Instituto Cultural de Cabañas, the latter a Unesco World Heritage site. Modern and spread-out, the Chapultepec neighborhood is sprinkled with fashionable restaurants, coffeehouses and nightclubs. Mellow suburbs Tlaquepaque (upscale) and Tonalá (grassroots) are a folk-art shopper's dream destinations. Zapopan has some interesting colonial sites and is known somewhat euphemistically as Guadalajara's Beverly Hills.

History

Guadalajara weathered some false starts. In 1532 Nuño de Guzmán and a few dozen Spanish families founded the first Guadalajara near Nochixtlán, naming it after Guzmán's home city in Spain. Water was scarce, the land was dry and unyielding, and the indigenous people were understandably hostile. So, in 1533 the humbled settlers moved to the village of Tonalá (today a part of Guadalajara). Guzmán disliked Tonalá, however, and two years later had the settlement moved to Tlacotán. In 1541 this site was attacked and decimated by a confederation

Western Central Highlands Highlights

1 Getting to know spectacular **Morelia** (p612), with its glowing cathedral, animated streets and grandiose architecture.

2 Exploring the excellent art museums, ancient churches and superb eating possibilities of charming **Guadalajara** (p577).

3 Absorbing the beauty of the **Reserva Mariposa Monarca** (p621), the winter retreat for millions of butterflies and an incredible natural phenomenon.

4 Peering into the mystical soul of the Purépecha people in tranquil **Pátzcuaro** (p624).

5 Bagging two volcanic peaks – the snowy and extinct **Volcán Nevado de Colima** (p610) and young, precocious **Volcán Paricutín** (p635).

6 Gazing out over Lago de Pátzcuaro from the mystical and semideserted Tarascan ruins of **Tzintzuntzan** (p631).

7 Traveling the 'Tequila Trail' to see Mexico's most famous drink being made in the distilleries of **Tequila** (p601) and other nearby towns.

Greater Guadalajara

ZAPOPAN

Basílica de Zapopan

CHAPALITA

TLAQUEPAQUE

TONALÁ

Anillo Periférico

Río Verde

Río Grande de Santiago

Av Tonaltecas

Av Giantes

San Jacinto Plutarco Elías Calles

Av Presa de Osorio

Paseo del Zoológico

Calz Obrero

Av de la Cruz

Calz Independencia

Circunvalación

Domínguez

Av Alcalde

Av Federalismo

Av 16 de Septiembre

Av Javier Mina

Calz Revolución

Blvd Barragán

Calz Gallo

Dr Michel

Calz Curiel

Calz Cárdenas

Calz Río Nilo

Av Tonalá

Autopista Guadalajara Zapotlanejo

Aeropuerto Internacional
Miguel Hidalgo (12km)

Av de Legazpi

Av 8 de Julio

Av Colón

Av Cruz del Sur

Av López Mateos Sur

Av Tepeyac

Av Guadalupe

Av de la Patria

Av Otero

Av López Mateos

Av Camacho

Av de las Américas

Av Acueducto

Av de la Patria

Av Vallarta

Av Vallarta

Anillo Periférico

Av Niños Héroes

See Central Guadalajara Map (p586)

See Chapultepec Map (p593)

See Tlaquepaque Map (p590)

Tequila (50km);
Tepic (215km)

5 km
2.5 miles

Greater Guadalajara

◉ **Top Sights**
 1 Basílica de Zapopan C1

◉ **Sights**
 2 Casa-Taller Orozco C3
 3 Museo de Arte de Zapopan C1
 4 Museo Huichol C1

⊕ **Activities, Courses & Tours**
 5 Centro de Estudios para
    Extranjeros C2

🛏 **Sleeping**
 6 Casa Pedro Loza D2

🍴 **Eating**
 7 Anita Li C3
 8 Fonda Dña Gabina Escolatica C1
    I Latina .... (see 7)
 9 Karne Garibaldi C2
 10 Lula Bistro C2

🎭 **Entertainment**
 11 Estadio Omnilife A2
 12 Teatro Diana D3

🛍 **Shopping**
 13 Centro Magno C3
 14 Galerías Guadalajara B3
 15 Plaza del Sol B3
 16 Quinta Real Guadalajara C2

ℹ **Information**
 17 Hospital México Americano C2

🚌 **Transport**
 18 Antigua Central Camionera D3
 19 Nueva Central Camionera F4

of indigenous tribes led by chief Tenamaxtli. The survivors wearily picked a new site in the valley of Atemajac beside San Juan de Dios Creek, which ran where Calzada Independencia is today. That's where the present Guadalajara was founded on February 14, 1542, near where the Teatro Degollado now stands.

Guadalajara finally prospered and in 1560 was declared the capital of Nueva Galicia province. The city, at the heart of a rich agricultural region, quickly grew into one of colonial Mexico's most important population centers. It also became the launch pad for Spanish expeditions and missions to western and northern Nueva España, and others as far away as the Philippines. Miguel Hidalgo, a leader in the fight for Mexican independence, set up a revolutionary government in Guadalajara in 1810, but was defeated near

the city in 1811, not long before his capture and execution in Chihuahua. The city was also the object of heavy fighting during the War of the Reform (1858–61) and between Constitutionalist and Villista armies in 1915.

By the late 19th century Guadalajara had overtaken Puebla as Mexico's second-biggest city. Its population has mushroomed since WWII and now the city is a huge commercial, industrial and cultural center, and the hi-tech and communications hub for the northern half of Mexico.

◉ Sights

⊙ Plaza de Armas & Around

⭐**Cathedral**   CATHEDRAL
(Map p586; Av 16 de Septiembre btwn Morelos & Av Hidalgo; ⊙ 8am-8pm, closed during Mass) FREE
Guadalajara's cathedral is the city's most beloved and conspicuous landmark with distinctive neo-Gothic towers built after an earthquake toppled the originals in the mid-19th century. Begun in 1558 and consecrated in 1618, the building is almost as old as the city itself. Time your visit right and you'll see light filter through stained-glass renderings of the Last Supper and hear a working pipe organ rumble sweetly from the rafters.

The interior includes Gothic vaults, massive Tuscan-style gold-leaf pillars and 11 richly decorated altars that were given to Guadalajara by King Fernando VII of Spain (1814–33). The glass case nearest the north entrance is an extremely popular reliquary, containing the hands and blood of the martyred Santa Inocencia. In the sacristy, which an attendant can open for you on request, is *La Asunción de la Virgen,* painted by Spanish artist Bartolomé Murillo in 1650. Of course, architectural purists may find flaws. Much like the Palacio de Gobierno, the cathedral is a bit of a stylistic hodgepodge, including Churrigueresque, baroque and neoclassical influences.

Museo Regional de Guadalajara   MUSEUM
(Map p586; ☎33-3614-9957; Liceo 60; adult/student & child M$52/free, Sun free; ⊙9am-5:30pm Tue-Sat, to 4:30pm Sun) Guadalajara's most comprehensive museum tells the story of the city and the region from prehistory to the revolution. The ground floor houses a natural history collection whose unwitting star is a mightily impressive woolly mammoth skeleton. Other crowd-pleasers include displays about indigenous life and a superb collection of pre-Hispanic ceramics

(side text, vertical) WESTERN CENTRAL HIGHLANDS GUADALAJARA

dating from 600 BC, including figurines, ceramics, and silver and gold artifacts.

The upper levels of the museum are devoted to colonial paintings depicting the Spanish conquest, as well as more austere religious allegories and a revolutionary wing where the guns and uniforms of Mexico's great rebels are on display. The building is well worth visiting for its architecture – a gorgeous tree-studded courtyard acts as its centerpiece. Many of the displays are labeled in Spanish only (although information cards in English are available).

Palacio de Gobierno
BUILDING

(Map p586; Av Corona btwn Morelos & Moreno; ⊙9am-8pm) FREE The Palacio de Gobierno, which houses state government offices, was finished in 1774. It's open to the public – just walk in – and it's well worth stopping by, mainly due to two impressive socialist realist murals by local artist José Clemente Orozco (1883–1949). The real head-turner is the 1937 mural of Miguel Hidalgo that dominates the main interior staircase. Hidalgo brandishes a torch in one fist while the masses struggle at his feet against the twin burdens of communism and fascism.

Another Orozco mural in the ex-Congreso (former Congress Hall) upstairs depicts Hidalgo, Benito Juárez and other historical luminaries. On the ground floor there's a well-curated museum about the history of Jalisco. It also includes a section on the cultivation of tequila. Labeling is in Spanish.

Museo de Arte Sacro de Guadalajara
MUSEUM

(Map p586; Av 16 de Septiembre btwn Morelos & Av Hidalgo; adult/child M$10/5; ⊙10am-5pm Tue-Sat, to 2pm Sun) A recent addition to the city's museums, this pious collection is bivouacked quite appropriately inside the cathedral (the entrance is on the eastern side). It's filled with dark and brooding 17th- to 18th-century religious art and priceless church treasures.

Teatro Degollado
BUILDING

(Map p586; Degollado; ⊙viewing noon-2pm Mon-Fri) FREE Construction on the neoclassical Teatro Degollado, home of the Guadalajara Philharmonic, was begun in 1856 and completed 30 years later. Over the Grecian columns on its front is a frieze depicting Apollo and the Nine Muses. The five-tiered interior is swathed in red velvet and gold and crowned by a Gerardo Suárez mural based on the fourth canto of Dante's *Divine Comedy*.

Plaza Guadalajara
PLAZA

(Map p586) Directly west of the cathedral, Plaza Guadalajara is shaded by dozens of lau-

---

DON'T MISS

AN EYEFUL OF OROZCO

Long before Banksy and the rebirth of politically charged street art, Mexico's muralists were making bold statements in giant public murals that doused revolutionary politics in swirls of vivid color. Guadalajara's gift to the genre was substantial. The grandfather of Mexican *muralismo* is usually held up to be Guadalajara-born artist Gerardo Murillo (1875–1964), aka Dr Atl, while one of his former pupils, José Clemente Orozco (1883–1949), came from the nearby city of Ciudad Guzmán.

Along with Diego Rivera and David Siqueiros, Orozco is considered one of the 'big three' of Mexican mural art. Some argue he was the most original of the trio, his energetic brushstrokes depicting fiery, sometimes pained figures in vivid studies of polemic symbolism. Orozco's work decorates staircases, ceilings and public spaces everywhere from New York to Mexico City, but his most personal work can be found in Guadalajara. Don't miss the following.

Casa-Taller Orozco (p584) – Contains *La Buena Vida* (1945), an uncharacteristically upbeat Orozco study of a chef holding up a fish.

Palacio de Gobierno (p582) – Glaring painting of Miguel Hidalgo (1937–38) brandishing a torch on the palace's main staircase that will literally stop you in your tracks.

Instituto Cultural de Cabañas (p583) – Orozco painted 57 murals including the kaleidoscopic *Hombre del Fuego* in this Unesco building between 1937 and 1939.

Museo de las Artes (p583) – Two pieces – *El hombre creador y rebelde* in the cupola, and *El pueblo y sus falsos líderes* on the stage backdrop (both 1937) – are encased in this museum opposite the university.

rel trees and has great cathedral views and a few fine cafes. It's a hive of human activity day and night. On its north side is the **Palacio Municipal** (City Hall ; Map p586; ⊘10am-7pm Mon-Fri) FREE, which was built between 1949 and 1952 but looks ancient. Above its interior stairway is a dark mural by Gabriel Flores depicting the founding of Guadalajara.

Rotonda de los
Jaliscenses Ilustres   MONUMENT
(Rotunda of Illustrious Jaliscans; Map p586) Welcome to Jalisco's hall of fame. The plaza on the north side of the cathedral is ringed by 20 bronze sculptures of the state's favorite writers, architects, revolutionaries and a composer. Some of them are actually buried underneath the rotunda, the round-pillared monument in the center.

Plaza de la Liberación   PLAZA
(Map p586) East of the cathedral, this plaza was a 1980s urban planner's dream project – two whole blocks of colonial buildings were eviscerated to make way for this concrete slab.

On the north side of the plaza, next to the Museo Regional de Guadalajara, is the **Palacio Legislativo** (Map p586). Distinguished by thick stone columns in its interior courtyard, this is where the state congress meets. Across the street to the east is the **Palacio de Justicia** (State Courthouse; Map p586). It was built in 1588 and began life as Guadalajara's first nunnery. Duck inside to the interior stairwell and check out the 1965 mural by Guillermo Chávez depicting legendary Mexican lawmakers, including Benito Juárez.

◎ East of Plaza de Armas

★ **Instituto Cultural de Cabañas**   MUSEUM
(Map p586; Cabañas 8; adult/child/student M$70/20/35, Tue free; ⊘10am-6pm Tue-Sun) Standing proudly at the eastern end of the brilliant Plaza Tapatía is one of Guadalajara's architectural icons – a Unesco World Heritage site, no less. Inside its enchanting neoclassical bones is a most unexpected series of modernist murals by José Clemente Orozco, which rank among the city's best sights. The complex also houses a huge collection of Orozco's other work, plus modern works by the shining lights in Mexico's current art scene.

The beautiful building, which consists of masses of hidden arched courtyards, was founded by Bishop don Juan Cruz Ruiz de Cabañas and designed by Spanish architect Manuel Tolsá, between 1805 and 1810. Its original purpose was as an orphanage and home for invalids and it remained so for 150 years, housing 500 children at once.

Between 1938 and 1939 Orozco, one of the so-called 'big three' of the Mexican muralist movement, channeled the archetypal struggle for freedom into 57 magnificent murals that now decorate the Capilla Mayor at the center of the complex. Widely regarded as Orozco's finest works, they depict pre-Hispanic Jalisco and the conquest, and seethe with dark, unnerving and distinctly modern images of fire, armor, blood and prayer. Given the issues of Orozco's era, they almost certainly serve as a warning against fascism and any institution that subverts humanity to cultivate power.

Free tours of the institute in English and Spanish are available.

Plaza Tapatía   PLAZA
(Map p586) The fabulously wide pedestrian Plaza Tapatía sprawls for more than 500m east from Teatro Degollado. Stroll the plaza on Sundays and you'll find yourself in a sea of locals who shop at low-end crafts markets, snack (from both street vendors and cafes), watch street performers and rest on the low walls of gurgling fountains. The plaza dead ends beautifully at the Instituto Cultural de Cabañas.

Plaza de los Mariachis   STREET
(Map p586) Just south of Avenida Javier Mina, this is the birthplace of mariachi music. By day it's just a narrow walking street, flanked by charming old buildings and dotted with a few plastic tables and chairs and the odd uniformed mariachi musician chatting on a cell phone. At night it can get lively, when patrons swill beer and listen to bands play requests for about M$100 per song.

◎ West of Plaza de Armas

West of the city center, where Avenidas Juárez and Federalismo meet, is the green comma of **Parque Revolución**, a haven for skaters and the grand nexus of the Vía Recreativa.

Museo de las Artes   MUSEUM
(MUSA; Map p586; ☎33-3134-1664; www.musa. udg.mx; Av Juárez 975; ⊘10am-6pm Tue-Sun) FREE To scratch your modernist itch if you've overdosed on *arte clásico*, head three blocks west of Parque Revolución to this museum housed in a French renaissance building that formerly served as the admin buildings for the University of Guadalajara. The highlight is the **Paraninfo** (auditorium), whose stage

backdrop and dome feature large, powerful murals by Orozco. The rest of the space is given over to well-curated temporary exhibitions focusing on contemporary Mexican art.

Templo Expiatorio
CHURCH

(Map p586; Madero; ⊘7am-11pm) This Gothic temple, dating from 1897, dominates the neighborhood thanks to its enormous stone columns, 15m-high mosaic stained-glass windows and kaleidoscopic steeple. At 9am, noon and 6pm, a door in the clock tower opens and the 12 apostles march out.

Casa-Taller Orozco
GALLERY

(Map p580; Aceves 27; ⊘noon-6pm Tue-Sat) FREE Facing an eponymous square named in honor of one of Mexico's greatest artists, Orozco's former studio is used today to host temporary exhibitions. On permanent display in the lobby, and worth a peep if you're in the area, is *La Buena Vida*, an unusually joyous Orozco mural the artist was commissioned to paint for Mexico City's Turf Club in 1945.

⊙ Zapopan

The fashionable, middle-class suburb of Zapopan is about 8km from the city center, on the northwestern edge of Guadalajara. There are a few interesting sights around the main plaza, which is in itself a fun place to hang out with pilgrims coming and going and all sorts of religious tack for sale. After dark the locals get the place back to themselves and the numerous bars and restaurants turn the music up and the beer flows.

To get here from the center of Guadalajara, take any bus marked 'Zapopan' heading north on Avenidas 16 de Septiembre or Alcalde and get off beside the Basílica de Zapopan. The trip takes about 40 minutes. A taxi from the city center will cost around M$110.

★ Basílica de Zapopan
CATHEDRAL

(Map p580; Eva Briseño 152) Zapopan's pride and joy, the Basílica de Zapopan, built in 1730, is home to *Nuestra Señora de Zapopan,* a petite statue of the Virgin visited by pilgrims year-round. During the Fiestas de Octubre, thousands of kneeling faithful crawl behind as the statue is carried here from Guadalajara's central cathedral. The kneeling pilgrims then make the final trek up the basílica's aisle to pray for favors at her altar.

The Virgin receives a new car each year for the procession, but the engine is never turned on (thus remaining 'virginal') – instead it's hauled by men with ropes.

Museo de Arte de Zapopan
MUSEUM

(MAZ; Map p580; ☑33-3818-2575; www.mazmuseo.com; Andador 20 de Noviembre No 166; ⊘10am-6pm Tue-Sun, to 10pm Thu) FREE One block east of the southeast corner of Plaza de las Américas in Zapopan, MAZ is dedicated to modern art. Four sleek minimalist galleries hold temporary exhibits, which have included works by Diego Rivera and Frida Kahlo as well as leading contemporary Mexican artists. Many of the exhibits are interactive and the museum acts as a nexus for numerous cultural activities.

Museo Huichol
MUSEUM

(Map p580; Eva Briseño 152; adult/child M$10/5; ⊘10am-2pm & 3-6pm Mon-Sat, 10am-3pm Sun) The Museo Huichol has a worthwhile display of artifacts from the Huichol people, an indigenous group known for their peyote rituals and bright-colored yarn art. It's just to the right of the Basílica de Zapopan (but inside the basilica grounds).

⊙ Tlaquepaque

Though just 7km southeast of downtown Guadalajara, Tlaquepaque resembles your typical *pueblo mágico* (magical village): squint and you could well be in a small colonial town miles from anywhere. But its beauty is not its sole draw: artisans live behind the pastel-colored walls of the abandoned old mansions that line Tlaquepaque's narrow cobblestone streets, and their goods, such as wood carvings, sculpture, furniture, ceramics, jewelry, leather items and candles, are sold on and around pedestrianized Calle Independencia. The shops here are fancy boutiques that contrast sharply with the more rough-and-ready feel of Tonalá.

The plaza, **Jardín Hidalgo**, is leafy and blooming with flowers, and the benches around the fountain are always packed. The eating is very good and the strolling is even better, especially at sunset when the sky behind the gorgeous, white-domed basilica burns orange and families take to the streets, enjoying the last ticks of daylight. *Voladores* ('flying men' from Papantla) give spectacular **performances** from a special 30m-high pole in the plaza most afternoons between around 3pm and 4pm.

There's a **tourist information booth** (Map p590; ⊘10am-3:30pm & 4:30-7pm) close

COLONIAL CHURCHES

Central Guadalajara has dozens of churches and cathedrals. The following are some of the city's most beautiful and interesting. Most churches are open from 8am to 8pm.

The **Santuario de Nuestra Señora del Carmen** (Map p586), facing the small plaza on the corner of Avenida Juárez and Calle 8 de Julio, is lovely with lots of gold leaf, old paintings and murals in the dome. Closer to the city center is the ornate **Templo Nuestra Señora de las Mercedes** (Map p586; cnr Loza & Av Hidalgo), which was built in 1650; inside are several large paintings, crystal chandeliers and more gold leaf. Six blocks further east is the fairly unremarkable **Templo de Santa María de Gracia** (Map p586; cnr Carranza & República), which served as the city's first cathedral (1549–1618). South of the Teatro Degollado is the baroque-style **Templo de San Agustín** (Map p586; Morelos), one of the city's oldest and loveliest churches. The sanctuary at the **Templo Santa Eduviges** (Map p586; Av Javier Mina), built in 1726, is usually packed with worshippers and, during Mass, perfumed with clouds of sandalwood smoke. It's just south of the Mercado San Juan de Dios.

The compact **Templo de Aranzazú** (Map p586; cnr Av 16 de Septiembre & Blanco) is perhaps the city's most beautiful. Built from 1749 to 1752, it has three insanely ornate Churrigueresque golden altars and lovely ceiling detail. Across the road is the larger but less impressive **Templo de San Francisco** (Map p586; cnr Sánchez & Av 16 de Septiembre), which was begun in the 1660s by the Franciscans. Come at dusk and see the stained glass glow.

to the junction of Independencia and Ejército that gives out pictorial neighborhood maps.

To get to Tlaquepaque from central Guadalajara, take bus 275 Diagonal, 275B or 647 (M$6). The turquoise TUR bus marked 'Tonalá' has air-con and is more comfortable (M$12). All these buses leave central Guadalajara from Avenida 16 de Septiembre between López Cotilla and Madero; the trip takes about 20 minutes. As you near Tlaquepaque, watch for the brick arch and then a traffic circle, after which you should get off at the next stop. Up the street on the left is Independencia, which will take you to the heart of Tlaquepaque.

Museo Pantaleón Panduro MUSEUM
(Museo Nacional de la Cerámica; Map p590; ☑ 33-3639-5646; Sánchez 191; ☉ 10am-6pm Tue-Sun) FREE This superb collection of over 500 pieces of national folk art is housed in a converted religious mission and includes miniature figurines, as well as enormous, lightly fired urns and other ceramic crafts from all over the country.

Museo Regional de la Cerámica MUSEUM
(Map p590; ☑ 33-3635-5404; Independencia 237; ☉ 10am-6pm Tue-Sat, to 4pm Sun) FREE The Museo Regional de la Cerámica is set in a great old adobe building with stone arches and mature trees in the courtyard. It has an impressive collection that exhibits the varied styles and clays used in Jalisco and

Michoacán. Explanations are in English and Spanish.

◉ Tonalá

This dusty, bustling suburb is about 13km southeast of downtown Guadalajara and home to many artisans. You can feel Tonalá beginning to take Tlaquepaque's lead with a few airy, inviting showrooms and cafes opening around town, but it remains happily rough around the edges. It's fun to roam through the dark, dusty stores and workshops, browsing glassware, ceramics, furniture, masks, toys, jewelry, handmade soap and more. Anything you can buy in Tlaquepaque you can find here for much less, which is what attracts wholesale buyers from all over the world.

Ask staff at the Tonalá tourist office (p597) about two- to three-hour **walking tours** (by donation) of Tonalá's artisan workshops. They're given in English or Spanish, but need to be reserved a couple of days in advance.

To reach Tonalá, take bus 275 Diagonal or 275D (both M$6). The turquoise TUR bus marked 'Tonalá' has air-con and is more comfortable (M$12). All these buses leave Guadalajara from the corner of Avenida 16 de Septiembre and Madero; the trip takes about 45 minutes. As you enter Tonalá, get off on the corner of Avenidas Tonalá and Tonaltecas. The Plaza Principal is three

Central Guadalajara

blocks east of Avenida Tonaltecas on Avenida Juárez.

Street Market
MARKET

On Thursday and Sunday, Tonalá bursts into a huge street market that sprouts on Avenida Tonaltecas and crawls through dozens of streets and alleys and takes hours to explore. With *torta* (sandwich), taco and *michelada* (beer and tomato juice) stands aplenty, the whole area takes on a carnival vibe. The best pieces are usually found at the workshops and warehouses, not on the street.

⮝ Courses

Guadalajara is a popular place to study Spanish, with classes available to students of all ages. Prices and curricula vary tremendously.

Centro de Estudios
para Extranjeros
LANGUAGE COURSE

(CEPE; Map p580; ☎33-3616-4399; www.udg.mx; Gómez 125) Part of the University of Guadala-

jara, CEPE offers several levels of intensive two- to five-week Spanish-language courses. Day trips, homestays and longer excursions to other parts of Mexico are available.

Instituto Mexicano-Americano
de Cultura
LANGUAGE COURSE

(IMAC; Map p586; ☎33-3613-1080; www.spanishschool.com.mx; Guerra 180; per week from US$230) Offers courses from one week upwards. Check its website for course fees and homestay options. Music and dance classes are also available.

⮞ Tours

GDL Tours
TOUR

(Map p590; ☎33-1578-0421; www.gdltours.com; Independencia 329, Tlaquepaque) Offers a full menu of English-language guided tours. Options include walking tours of Guadalajara's main sights (from M$490, four hours), trips to the town of Lago de Chapala (from

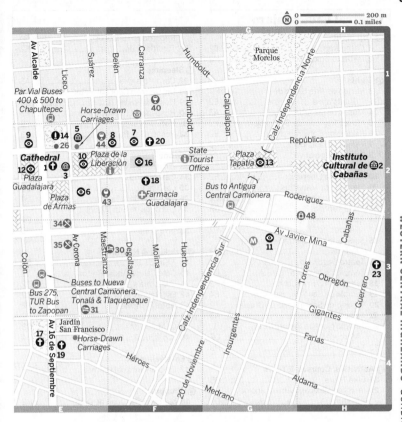

M$490, six hours) and 'Tequila Trail' tours, which include distillery visits and tastings (from M$490, nine hours). Tour prices drop when there are more participants.

Tapatío Tour BUS
(Map p586; ☎ 33-3613-0887; www.tapatiotour.com; tours adult M$120-140, child M$70-90) The ubiquitous double-decker buses of Tapatío Tour ply the city's most popular sights on a circuit track. While the prerecorded narration (in English, Spanish, French, Italian, German and Japanese) is less than inspirational, the tours allow you to hop off and on wherever you wish, making sightseeing a breeze.

Buses depart from the Rotonda de los Jaliscenses Ilustres and they operate from 10am to 8pm. Go on a weekday for cheaper rates.

Recorridos Turísticos WALKING TOUR
(Map p586; Plaza Guadalajara) FREE The city council runs free tours (in Spanish) of central Guadalajara at 9:30am and 7pm. Tours,

which leave from the Palacio Municipal, last around an hour and you need to register 15 minutes beforehand. The tourist office can provide further details.

🎭 Festivals & Events

Festival Internacional del Cine FILM
(www.ficg.mx) Mexico's most important film festival has been drawing top actors and directors to Guadalajara each March for 25 years. Sidle up to stars such as Gael García Bernal and John Malkovich at screenings and parties across the city.

Fiesta Internacional del Mariachi MUSIC
In late August and early September mariachis come to Guadalajara from everywhere to jam, battle and enjoy. Check out www.mariachi-jalisco.com.mx for more information.

Feria Internacional del Libro BOOK FAIR
(www.fil.com.mx) This book fair is one of the biggest book promotions in Latin America.

Central Guadalajara

◉ **Top Sights**
1 Cathedral..E2
2 Instituto Cultural de Cabañas..............H2

◉ **Sights**
3 Museo de Arte Sacro de
   Guadalajara...E2
4 Museo de las Artes................................A3
5 Museo Regional de Guadalajara...........E2
6 Palacio de Gobierno..............................E2
7 Palacio de Justicia.................................F2
8 Palacio Legislativo................................F2
9 Palacio Municipal..................................E2
10 Plaza de la Liberación..........................E2
11 Plaza de los Mariachis..........................G3
12 Plaza Guadalajara.................................E2
13 Plaza Tapatía..G2
14 Rotonda de los Jaliscenses
    Ilustres...E2
15 Santuario de Nuestra Señora del
    Carmen...C3
16 Teatro Degollado..................................F2
17 Templo de Aranzazú.............................E4
18 Templo de San Agustín.........................F2
19 Templo de San Francisco......................E4
20 Templo de Santa María de Gracia........F2
21 Templo Expiatorio.................................A3
22 Templo Nuestra Señora de las
    Mercedes..D2
23 Templo Santa Eduviges.........................H3

☺ **Activities, Courses & Tours**
24 Bike Tours..B3
25 Instituto Mexicano-Americano de
    Cultura...D3

Recorridos Turísticos....................(see 9)
26 Tapatío Tour..E2

⬤ **Sleeping**
27 Casa Vilasanta......................................A3
28 Del Carmen Concept Hotel...................C3
29 Home & Hostel......................................B3
30 Hospedarte Downtown..........................F3
31 Hotel Morales.......................................E3
32 Posada San Pablo.................................D3

✖ **Eating**
33 Birriería las Nueve Esquinas................D4
34 Café Madrid..E3
35 La Chata...E3
36 La Fonda de la Noche...........................B1
37 La Fonda de San Miguel
    Arcángel...D2
38 Viva Chapata..A3

◉ **Drinking & Nightlife**
39 7 Sins...D2
40 Café Galería André Breton....................F1
41 California's..C2
42 Escarabajo Scratch..............................C2
43 Hotel Francés.......................................E2
44 La Fuente..E2
45 La Mutualista.......................................C3
46 Los Caudillos..D4

◉ **Entertainment**
47 Ex-Convento del Carmen.....................C3

◉ **Shopping**
48 Mercado San Juan de Dios...................H2

It's held during the last week of November and first week of December, headlined by major Spanish-language authors, such as Gabriel García Márquez.

🛏 Sleeping

During holidays (Christmas and Easter) and festivals you *must* reserve ahead. Ask for discounts if you arrive in the low season or will be staying more than a few days.

🛏 Centro Histórico

Southeast of Mercado San Juan de Dios there's a cluster of budget hotels. This part of town is a bit rough, but you can usually find a cheap room here when other places are full. Budget digs can be found around the Antigua Central Camionera (old bus station) as well. The Centro Histórico is full of midrange options, many of which are housed in charming colonial buildings.

Casa Vilasanta　　　　　　　　HOTEL **$**
(Map p586; ☑ 33-3124-1277; www.vilasanta.com; Rayón 170; dm M$220, r M$550; ✾ ☏) The bright, pastel-colored rooms of this cheery guesthouse are scattered around a cool interior courtyard, decorated with pottery and flowers, and there's a sunny 2nd-floor terrace. The singles can feel cramped, but the doubles are large and all rooms have TV.

There's a shared kitchen and plenty of chill space on both floors. But with just 17 rooms and English-speaking management, this place books up. Reserve ahead! There are a few simple places to eat in the neighborhood.

Hospedarte Downtown　　　　　HOSTEL **$**
(Map p586; ☑ 33-3562-7520; www.hostelguada lajara.com; Maestranza 147; dm/s/d incl breakfast M$190/400/500; @ ☏) One of two Hospedarte hostels now in town, this bright-yellow downtown option is popular with a young crowd looking for a good time. The dorms are spacious four-bed rooms with lock-

ers and fans, sharing toilets and showers around a large communal area with a huge kitchen and plenty of activities laid on.

Home & Hostel
HOSTEL **$**

(Map p586; ☑ 33-1522-0834; www.homenhostel-com; Madero 720; dm M$180; ☎) This fine hostel is situated in a quiet residential area 15 minutes' walk from the city center. Rooms contain from one to four beds, there are just enough bathrooms to go around and everything is kept very shipshape. There's a sunny courtyard, plenty of travel info, a kitchen for guest use and some cheap places to eat nearby.

Posada San Pablo
HOTEL **$**

(Map p586; ☑ 33-3614-2811; www.posadasan pablo.com; Madero 429; s/d from M$380/450, without bathroom from M$300/380; ☎) This very friendly place comes complete with a grassy garden and sunny terrace. Rooms can be a little monkish, though the upstairs ones have balconies. There's a communal kitchen and you can even (hand) wash your clothes in the old-fashioned *lavandería* (laundry) out back.

★ Del Carmen Concept Hotel
BOUTIQUE HOTEL **$$**

(Map p586; ☑ 33-3614-2640; www.delcarmen. mx; Galvez 45; d/ste M$1150/1350; P ❋ ☎) The Carmen is a beautiful place to dock your suitcase for a day or three in a mansion close to the Ex-Convento del Carmen. The concept? Nine rooms individually themed around artists from Mexico's La Ruptura movement (an abstract reaction to the 20th-century muralists); hence the Tamayo room (with a curvaceous metallic bathtub) or the Friedeberg room (a trippy patchwork of blinding surrealism).

Hotel Morales
HOTEL **$$**

(Map p586; ☑ 33-3658-5232; www.hotelmorales. com.mx; Av Corona 243; r from M$965; P ❋ ☎ ☒) The darkly lit, four-tiered colonial lobby is a suitably impressive entrance to this smart, brilliant-value, central hotel. Brighter and equally brilliant is the 2nd-floor, blue-and-white-tiled, Andalucían-style courtyard. Other nooks hide fountains, bookshelves and even a rooftop pool and gym. Rooms are a good size and some have Jacuzzi-tub baths. Service is very professional and tours can be arranged.

Casa Pedro Loza
BOUTIQUE HOTEL **$$$**

(Map p580; ☑ 33-1202-2423; www.casapedroloza. com.mx; Loza 360; r incl breakfast M$1200-2300;

❋ ☎) Housed in an impressive colonial mansion in a charming part of the Centro Histórico, this hotel has been lovingly decorated. The 11 rooms are each wildly different; some are stuffed full of beautiful antiques, others are like garish love nests with circular beds and bubbly furnishings. Great for novelty value!

The retractable roof over the courtyard and the superb roof terrace are other points in the hotel's favor.

🛏 Chapultepec & Around

Top-end accommodations are generally found in Chapultepec and beyond, and are aimed at guests with their own transportation.

Hospedarte Hostel
HOSTEL **$**

(Map p593; ☑ 33-3615-4957; www.hospedarte hostel.com; Luna 2075; dm M$180, s/d M$400/450; @ ☎) On a residential side street in Chapultepec, this low-key hostel has pretty much everything a backpacker requires: clean dorms, hammock-filled garden, communal kitchen, free bikes, internet and wi-fi, bars and cheap places to eat within stumbling distance, and plenty of traveler-related services.

Discounts for IYHA card holders.

★ Villa Ganz
BOUTIQUE HOTEL **$$$**

(Map p593; ☑ 33-3120-1416; www.villaganz.com; López Cotilla 1739; ste incl breakfast from M$2500-4650; P ❋ @ ☎) Cross the threshold of Villa Ganz and behold a dazzling array of tiles, ferns, candelabras and original art. This is a boutique hotel where the word 'boutique' is taken seriously – you'll feel like you're staying in the house of a refined millionaire friend. Suites (rather than 'rooms') are luxury personified, with bathrobes, classic furniture, rich carpets and wonderful details. Even the soap holders are ornate.

The service is equally exemplary adhering to the motto 'nothing is too much': free wine in the afternoon, a real fire, evening candlelight and a fine restaurant. It's a bargain – whatever the price!

Quinta Real Guadalajara
LUXURY HOTEL **$$$**

(Map p580; ☑ 33-1105-1000; www.quintareal. com; Av México 2727; r from M$2500; P ❋ @ ☒) A sort of rural hacienda in the busy city, there is no denying the beauty of this five-star stay, with its exquisite stone and ivy-covered exterior. The lobby and bar are inviting and stylish, the grounds are impeccably manicured and the service is outstand-

Tlaquepaque

ing. But the rooms are a bit cramped and don't always live up to the price tag.

Downside: it's a bit outside Chapultepec's main hub.

Tlaquepaque

Just 15 minutes away by bus or taxi from downtown Guadalajara, Tlaquepaque is an excellent option for those who crave small-town charm but still want to visit the sights of the big city. The shopping is superb, and you won't have to lug your purchases too far.

Casa del Retoño
GUESTHOUSE $$

(Map p590; ☏ 33-3639-6510; www.lacasadelre tono.com.mx; Matamoros 182; s/d incl breakfast M$770/935; P🛜) The eight rooms in this very pleasant traditional house are all color-fully decorated, share an enormous garden, and boast TVs and good bathrooms. It's a short walk from the main square and run

by a friendly local family. Call ahead because the reception isn't always manned.

Casa Campos
GUESTHOUSE $$

(Map p590; ☏ 33-3838-5297; www.casacampos. mx; Miranda 30; s/d incl breakfast M$1000/1190; ❄@🛜) This pink and orange converted mansion has a gorgeous, flower-filled court-yard, stone columns and sleek wood furnish-ings. The 11 rooms are spacious, tasteful and well equipped (though bathrooms are noth-ing special), and it's moments from the best shopping on Independencia.

★ Casa de las Flores
B&B $$$

(Map p590; ☏ 33-3659-3186; www.casadelas flores.com; Degollado 175; r incl breakfast M$1675-1850; @🛜) Don't be deceived! This guest-house's plain street-side exterior hides *muchos secretos*. There is a ton of colorfully painted ceramics, along with a garden full of flowers and a decorative fireplace and chimney that defies belief. Rooms have an

Tlaquepaque

◎ Sights
1 Museo Pantaleón Panduro C1
2 Museo Regional de la Cerámica B2

⊕ Activities, Courses & Tours
3 GDL Tours..A2

⊜ Sleeping
4 Casa Campos B2
5 Casa de las Flores C4
6 Casa del Retoño..................................C4
7 Quinta Don José..................................C3

⊗ Eating
8 Casa Fuerte B2
9 Mariscos Progreso C3
10 Tortas Ahogadas Chimbombo's
Grill...C2

⊕ Entertainment
11 El Parián C2

⊟ Shopping
12 Antigua de México B2
13 Orígenes..B2
14 Teté, Arte y Diseño C3

engaging Mexican feel with multicolored bedcovers, tiled sinks and haunting art. You'll spend days inspecting the details.

Quinta Don José BOUTIQUE HOTEL $$$
(Map p590; ☑33-3635-7522; www.quintadonjose.com; Reforma 139; r incl breakfast from M$1670; ❉@�奈❀) From the cozy sunken lobby to the sunny, flower-filled pool terrace complete with fountains, this charming hotel is a great place to escape while remaining in the heart of Tlaquepaque. The rooms aren't as flamboyant as the gardens but that's a minor niggle.

There's a good in-house Italian restaurant (open to all) and at night you can eat out under twinkling stars and fairy lights.

Eating

Guadalajara is a gourmet's delight; many visitors find that meals here count among the highlights of their stay. A few local specialties to look out for: *birria* (a spicy goat or lamb stew), *carne en su jugo* ('meat in its juice,' a type of beef soup), *tejuino* (a fermented corn drink often sold by street vendors), and, above all, the ubiquitous *torta ahogada* (literally 'drowned sandwich'), a chili-sauce-soaked pork roll said to cure everything from hangovers to the flu.

Centro Histórico & Around

Adventurous stomachs can head to the Mercado San Juan de Dios (p596), home to endless food stalls serving the cheapest and some of the tastiest eats in town. The plaza in front of the Templo Expiatorio is a good place to snag late-night tacos, *tortas* and *elote* (grilled corn on the cob).

Viva Chapata SANDWICHES $
(Map p586; ☑33-1523-2599; Madero 795; chapatas M$50-80; ❂8am-1am Tue-Sun) Enjoy craft beers and *chapatas* (Mexican sandwiches) underneath the watchful eyes of Emiliano Zapata – a pop-art-style mural of the Mexican revolutionary adorns a wall in this bohemian new cafe near the university.

Café Madrid CAFE $
(Map p586; ☑33-3614-9504; Av Juárez 264; mains M$50-100; ❂8am-10:30pm) A 1950s-era cafe that is open all day, but best for a *huevos rancheros* breakfast (fried eggs on a corn tortilla with a tomato, chili and onion sauce served with refried beans) and *chilaquiles* (fried tortilla strips cooked with chili sauce).

It lacks the historical atmosphere of similar Mexican places, although the coffee, dispensed from a vintage silver espresso machine, has plenty of zest.

★ **Birriería las Nueve Esquinas** MEXICAN $$
(Map p586; ☑33-3613-6260; Av Colón 384; mains M$80-98; ❂8am-11pm Mon-Sat, to 9pm Sun) The village-like Nueve Esquinas (Nine Corners) neighborhood specializes in *birria,* meat stewed in its own juices until it's so tender it melts in your mouth. Birriería las Nueve Esquinas, a delightful semi-open-air restaurant covered in blue and white tiles, is renowned far and wide for being the king of *birria*.

The two main offerings here are *birria de chivo* (steamed goat) and *barbacoa de borrego* (baked lamb), although ask the staff and they won't hesitate to tell you that the *chivo* is the best of the two. Both come with a stack of fresh tortillas, pickled onions, cilantro and two salsas – wrap the meat in the tortilla, add various flavors and then dip the tortilla in the meat juice before putting it in your mouth.

La Chata MEXICAN $$
(Map p586; ☑33-3613-1315; Av Corona 126; mains M$79-128; ❂8:30am-midnight) Quality *comida típica* (home-style food), affordable prices and ample portions mean this family diner has an omnipresent queue. Fortunately, hard-working waitstaff keep the crowds

WESTERN CENTRAL HIGHLANDS GUADALAJARA

moving quickly, plus you'll be happily distracted watching the energetic chefs spin tortillas as you wait in line. The specialty is the superb *platillo jaliscense* (fried chicken with five sides); it also serves a popular *pozole* (hominy soup).

La Fonda de la Noche
MEXICAN $$

(Map p586; ✏33-3827-0917; Jesús 251; mains M$90-120; ⊙7:30pm-midnight Tue-Sun) Set in a rambling art-nouveau house, this restaurant is a stunner in every way. The cuisine is largely from the Durango region and it would be fair to say that anything that passes by your lips here will taste good, but try the *plato combinado* (combined plate; M$111) – a selection of the chef's four prize dishes.

The menu is simple, and spoken only, so you'll need to speak some Spanish to enjoy it here, although Carlos, the owner, does speak basic English. It's a little hard to find: the door is unmarked and it's in a residential area on the northwest corner of Jesús and Reforma.

La Fonda de San Miguel Arcángel
MEXICAN $$

(Map p586; ✏33-3613-0809; Guerra 25; mains M$130-200; ⊙8:30am-midnight Tue-Sat, to 9pm Sun & Mon) The courtyard of this one-time convent is so dimly lit you can barely see what you're eating, although the semidarkness has its benefits, enhancing the sounds of gurgling fountains, tinkling piano keys and twittering caged birds. Besides, who needs eye-squinting strip-lighting when you have top-drawer food?

Sample the *filete de res oro negro* – beef with *huitlacoche* (corn fungus) sauce – and the famously excellent *molcajete* (a spicy Oaxacan dish served on a sizzlingly hot stone dish with fajitas).

✕ Chapultepec & Around

Chapultepec is home to some of Guadalajara's best cuisine and to all its serious culinary experiences. To get here, catch the westbound Par Vial 400 or 500 bus from Avenidas Independencia and Alcalde. Taxis from the city center should cost around M$50.

★ Coffee Legacy
BREAKFAST, CAFE $

(Map p593; ✏33-3825-6107; Av Chapultepec Sur 155; breakfast M$50-85; ⊙8am-11pm; 🛜) This cool, hipster-ish cafe has one foot under a shaded Parisian awning and the other in a shabbily chic old house in Chapultepec and is perfect for a strong latte or late breakfast (were eggs always this good?). Passing troubadours with bruised guitars will wake you up if the home-roasted coffee fails to do so. There's an equally cool bar plugging *cervezas artesanales* (craft beer) next door.

Karne Garibaldi
MEXICAN $

(Map p580; ✏33-3826-1286; www.karnegaribaldi. com.mx; Garibaldi 1306; mains M$60-100; ⊙noon-midnight) This large, bright cantina is wildly popular with Mexican family groups and has two specialties: *carne en su jugo* and fast service (so speedy it landed in the *Guinness Book of Records* in 1996). The neighborhood is friendly and buzzes at night.

It's a 15-minute walk north of Avenida Vallarta – stroll there via the quiet backstreets and enjoy the colorful houses and little hole-in-the-wall bars on the way.

Tortas Ahogadas César
MEXICAN $

(Map p593; López Cotilla 1449; tortas M$25; ⊙9:30am-4pm) This bare-bones cafe traffics in one thing and one thing only: *tortas ahogadas,* Guadalajara's beloved hangover cure. Baguette-like rolls called *birotes* are filled with chunks of slow-roasted pork and drenched with searing *salsa picante* – ask for yours '*media ahogada*' (half-drowned) for less burn. Only die-hard chili-heads should request '*bien ahogada.*'

★ Allium
FUSION $$$

(Map p593; ✏33-3615-6401; www.allium.com. mx; López Cotilla 1752; mains M$150-250; ⊙1:30-5pm & 7-10:30pm Tue-Sat, 1:30-5pm Sun) 🍴 The sleek, new, fine-dining competitor on Guadalajara's growing gourmet circuit puts the emphasis on locally produced food: 90% of its ingredients come from the state of Jalisco. The small minimalist interior is redolent of Michelin-star restaurants in Europe, but, fear not, the prices and service are pretty down-to-earth. Try the pork belly with pear and honey.

Lula Bistro
INTERNATIONAL $$$

(Map p580; ✏33-3647-6432; www.lulabistro.com; San Gabriel 3030; mains from M$250; ⊙2-5pm & 8-11:30pm Tue-Thu, 2-5:30pm & 8pm-midnight Fri & Sat) Guadalajara's most celebrated restaurant is this superchic Chapultepec establishment. Sleek and industrial though the setting is, it's the food people come for. The long, modern menu, which could best be described as a French-Mexican fusion, is particularly strong on fish and seafood.

It's a couple of kilometers west of the Chapultepec area. Reservations are recommended.

Chapultepec

N
0 _____ 400 m
0 _____ 0.2 miles

I Latina
INTERNATIONAL $$$

(Map p580; ☑ 33-3647-7774; Av Inglaterra 3128; mains from M$250; ⊘ 7:30pm-1am Tue-Sat, 1:30-6pm Sun) This eccentrically decorated place requires a sharp double-take with its wall of ceramic pigs, a giant swordfish and lots of kitsch, fun touches. The Asian-leaning international menu is the reason to come, however, and the food is excellent. It's hugely popular with a smart and fashionable crowd, and can be loud. Tranquillity-seeking romantics might want to look elsewhere.

Next door is a lighter, brighter (and newer) sister restaurant, **Anita Li** (Map p580; ☑ 33-3647-4742; www.anitali.mx; Av Inglaterra 3100; mains from M$250; ⊘ 1:30-6:30pm Sun-Thu, 1:30pm-midnight Fri & Sat) (I Latina spelt backward) offering a similar, if slightly more casual, Thai-Mex menu.

El Cargol
SPANISH $$$

(Map p593; ☑ 33-3616-6035; López Cotilla 1513; mains M$140-240; ⊘ 2-11pm Mon, Tue & Thu, 2pm-1am Fri & Sat, 2-8pm Sun) You can pay homage to Catalonia (that Spanish collector of Michelin stars) in the unlikely environs of Chapultepec at the family-run Cargol. The Catalan-Spanish menu is billed as 'slow food' – made from scratch and worth the wait. Regulars come here for a paella fix and everyone raves about the *crema catalana* dessert.

Chapultepec

🛏 Sleeping

1 Hospedarte Hostel.................................B3
2 Villa Ganz B2

✖ Eating

3 Allium...A2
4 Coffee Legacy C2
5 El Cargol..B2
6 El Sacromonte......................................C1
7 Tortas Ahogadas César C2

🍷 Drinking & Nightlife

8 Angels Club..B2
9 El Grillo C2

El Sacromonte
MEXICAN $$$

(Map p593; ☑ 33-3825-5447; www.sacromonte.com.mx; Moreno 1398; mains M$180-300; ⊘ noon-6pm & 7pm-midnight) Guadalajara's favorite *alta cocina* (gourmet restaurant) establishment serves whimsical takes on classic dishes – think quesadillas sprinkled with rose petals and strawberry sauce, avocado-watermelon soup and giant prawns in lobster sauce with fried spinach. The decor pays homage to erstwhile matadors – someone here is clearly an aficionado of bullfighting. Reservations are recommended.

Tlaquepaque

Tlaquepaque's main plaza overflows with street-food vendors – look for *jericalla* (a flanlike custard), coconut *empanadas* and cups of lime-drenched pomegranate seeds. Just southeast of the plaza, El Parián (p596) is a block of 16 restaurant-bars with patio tables crowding a leafy inner courtyard. This is where you can sit, drink and listen to live mariachi music, especially on Saturday and Sunday, but eat elsewhere.

Casa Fuerte   MEXICAN $$
(Map p590; ☑ 33-3639-6481; Independencia 224; mains M$100-200; ⊙noon-9pm) This elegant and sprawling place leans toward fine dining, with a full cocktail bar, refreshing garden patio and a rather stately feel. It's very popular with Tlaquepaque's upper crust, although you can usually get a table with no problem.

Tortas Ahogadas
Chimbombo's Grill   MEXICAN $$
(Map p590; Madero 90B; tortas M$26, steaks M$75-110; ⊙8am-11pm) This streetside grill is where Señor Lopez prepares T-bones and skirt steaks as well as deliciously spicy *tortas ahogadas*. Steaks are rubbed with olive oil, splashed with soy sauce and served with Greek salad and garlic bread. You can eat in, or take your feast to the nearby plaza and enjoy it in the sun.

Mariscos Progreso   SEAFOOD $$
(Map p590; ☑ 33-3636-6149; Progreso 80; mains M$120-135; ⊙11am-8pm) On Saturday and Sunday afternoons it feels like all of Guadalajara has packed into this patio seafood restaurant. Dressed-up Mexican families slurp ceviche and pass around platters of pineapple shrimp and *huachinango al estilo Veracruz* (snapper with lime and tomatoes), while mariachis wander from table to table.

Oysters are a specialty – you'll recognize the place by the oyster-shucking hut out front.

Zapopan

Zapopan, right up in the far north of the city, has its own multifarious food scene, although those places that line the main road to the basilica are generally best forgotten.

Fonda Dña Gabina Escolatica   MEXICAN $
(Map p580; ☑ 33-3833-0883; Mina 237; mains M$16-62; ⊙7-11pm Tue-Sat, 2-10pm Sun) This narrow, barnlike, side-street restaurant is bedecked in sunny colored textiles and special-izes in *pozole* and a monumental *toastada de pollo*, which consists of a huge pile of chicken and salad heaped so high atop a toasted tortilla that it's virtually impossible to eat it without spilling it all down your front.

🍷 Drinking & Nightlife

The Centro Histórico gets fairly quiet at night, though there are several bright spots (if you know where to look) and a well-established gay scene. Chapultepec, however, is always jumping with international bars and clubs.

Locals dress up to go out, so when in Rome... Much of the action in the city takes place in the myriad *antros* (nightclubs). Many are gay clubs that also welcome straight people.

★ El Grillo   BAR
(Map p593; ☑ 33-3827-3090; Av Chapultepec 219; ⊙noon-2:30am) Not a brew pub, but the next best thing, this carefully undone bar stocks over 50 Mexican craft beers. Of interest are the Guadalajara-brewed Diógenes pale ale and the robust Grillo stout. The front patio is a good starting point for a Chapultepec night out – while your taste buds are still awake to the nuances of the hoppy brews.

Need to line the stomach? Order off the menu from the affiliated (and equally hip) restaurant next door, La Nacional.

★ Café Galería André Breton   BAR
(Map p586; ☑ 33-3345-2194; Manuel 175; ⊙10am-3am Tue-Sat, 2-8pm Sun) Tucked away on a side street on the eastern side of the Centro Histórico is this charming bar, cafe and live-music venue. As bohemian as its name suggests, this is one of the city's coolest hangouts. Enjoy the French menu (mains M$69) and range of artisan beers from around the world, and say *bonsoir* to live music (M$40 cover) each evening from 9pm.

La Mutualista   DANCING
(Map p586; ☑ 33-3614-2176; Madero 553; ⊙noon–around 2am Mon-Sat) With smoke-yellowed walls and antique chandeliers dangling from high ceilings, this vintage dance hall simmers with the decaying glamour of Old Havana. Thursdays and Saturdays are salsa nights, the real reason to come. A Cuban band kicks off around midnight and the all-ages crowd explodes with eye-popping moves on the dance floor. Prepare to perspire.

La Fuente   BAR
(Map p586; Suárez 78; ⊙8:30am-11pm Mon-Thu, to midnight Fri & Sat) La Fuente, set in the old

Edison boiler room, is an institution and a perfect example of what a proper Mexican cantina is supposed to be like (ie rough around the edges). It's been open since 1921 and is mostly peopled by regulars who treat newcomers like family and women like queens.

A bass, piano and violin trio sets up and jams from sunset until last call.

La Santa CLUB

(☑33-1023-9336; Av Real Acueducto 371; ⊗8pm-3am Sun & Tue-Thu, to 4am Fri & Sat) Not to be confused with the (now closed) bar of the same name that once rocked Chapultepec, this place is out in Zapopan and is a full-blown nightclub – one of the city's best (or so legend has it).

Escarabajo Scratch BAR

(Map p586; ☑33-1200-6983; Andador Coronilla 28; ⊗6pm-2:30am Mon-Thu, from 1pm Fri & Sat) This fun hipster bar in the Centro Histórico has elevated the *michelada* to a fine art, complementing it with regular music – jazz, blues and grungy rock. It's in Andador Coronilla, a purposefully shabby pedestrian street known for its nightlife.

Hotel Francés BAR

(Map p586; ☑33-3613-1190; Maestranza 35; ⊗noon-midnight) The dark marble courtyard bar at this hotel encourages you to relax back into another era, where waiters in bow ties treat you like a homecoming *amigo*, happy hour lasts until 8pm and acoustic troubadours strum gorgeous, weepy ballads.

☆ Entertainment

Guadalajara is a musical place and live performers can be heard any night of the week at one of the city's many venues (including restaurants). Discos and bars are plentiful, but ask around for the newest hot spots – *guadalajarans* love to show off their town.

Several popular venues host a range of thespian and musical pursuits. **Teatro Diana** (Map p580; ☑33-3614-7072; www.teatrodiana. com; Av 16 de Septiembre 710) is the current hippest spot. It stages traveling Broadway shows, concerts with local and international artists, and art installations. Teatro Degollado (p582) is a downtown cultural center that hosts a range of drama, dance and music performances, while Instituto Cultural de Cabañas (p583) occasionally does the same. Another downtown venue showcasing

GAY & LESBIAN GUADALAJARA

Guadalajara is one of the gayest cities in the country – some call it the San Francisco of Mexico. It's not nearly as open as San Fran, however, and has a far more dual character: despite a conservative president, mayor and local population, somehow Guadalajara becomes very openly gay after dark. In June everyone gets out and proud when the city hosts one of Latin America's largest gay pride parades.

Guadalajara's so-called 'gay ghetto' radiates out a few blocks from the corner of Ocampo and Sánchez, in the city center, but Avenida Chapultepec, just west of the city center, is starting to see upscale establishments aimed at a gay clientele. The following are some of the busiest bars and clubs in the city. You can read more listings at www. gaymexicomap.com.

7 Sins (Map p586; Moreno 532; after midnight M$50; ⊗10pm-4am Fri & Sat) The favorite hangout of the younger section of Guadalajara's gay scene. If you're over 30 you'll feel pretty out of place, but this colonial mansion has a cool staircase and ear-bleedingly loud music.

California's (Map p586; ☑33-3614-3221; Moreno 652; ⊗8pm-3am Mon-Sat) Attracts a diverse and attractive crowd – everything from cowboys to stockbrokers. It gets packed around 10pm, and Friday and Saturday nights are a madhouse, but there's no dancing – this is the place to start your night before heading to a club.

Los Caudillos (Map p586; ☑33-3613-5445; Sánchez 407; M$50; ⊗5pm-4am) A popular multistory disco, with three dance floors and endless lounges and bars full of gorgeous young things dancing.

Angels Club (Map p593; López Cotilla 1495B; ⊗9:30pm-5am Wed-Sat, 6-11pm Sun) Welcome to Guadalajara's megaclub. Sure, it's a gay venue, but straight guys and girls are just as welcome to join the party, which is spread across three dance floors where house, pop and techno reign supreme. Saturday nights get wild.

theater and art is the **Ex-Convento del Carmen** (Map p586; ☎ 33-3030-1385; Av Juárez 638).

Live Music

You can pay your respects to the mariachi tradition in its home city. The Plaza de los Mariachis, just east of the Centro Histórico, is an OK place to sit, drink beer and soak in the serenades of passionate Mexican bands. But you'll be happier at **El Parián** (Map p590; Av Juárez 84; ⏰9am-9pm Mon-Sat, to 5pm Sun), a garden complex in Tlaquepaque made up of dozens of small cantinas that all share one plaza occupied by droves of mariachis. On Saturdays and Sundays the bands battle and jockey for your ears, applause and cash.

State and municipal bands present free concerts of typical *música tapatía* (guadalajaran music) in the Plaza de Armas at 6:30pm on most Tuesdays, Thursdays and Sundays and as well during holiday seasons (especially during the Fiestas de Octubre).

Sports

Charreadas (rodeos) are held at noon most Sundays in the Lienzo Charros de Jalisco ring behind Parque Agua Azul south of the city center. *Charros* (cowboys) come from all over Jalisco and Mexico; *escaramuza* (female stunt riding) teams perform as well.

Fútbol (soccer) flows strongly through *guadalajaran* blood. The city has three local teams in Mexico's top league, the *primera división*: **Guadalajara** (www.chivasdecorazon.com.mx), the second most popular team in the country; **Atlas** (www.atlas.com.mx); and **Universidad Autónoma de Guadalajara** (www.tecos.com.mx). The seasons last from July to December and from January to June and teams play at stadiums around the city. You can get an up-to-date season schedule at www.femexfut.org.mx.

Estadio Omnilife   SPECTATOR SPORT
(Map p580; ☎ 33-3777-5700; www.estadioomnilife.com.mx; Av Circuito JVC) You'll have to trek out to Zapopan if you want to see the beloved 'Chivas' (ie Guadalajara *fútbol* team) juggle footballs and – hopefully – make their opponent's goal net ripple. The deluxe 49,850-capacity Estadio Omnilife, which opened in 2010 after six years of delays, is home to Guadalajara's most revered soccer team. As far as football epiphanies go, it's up there with Old Trafford and Camp Nou.

To get to the stadium take bus 400 run by Sistecozone from Parque Revolución.

🏠 Shopping

Guadalajara's wealthiest like to browse at big shopping centers such as **Centro Magno** (Map p580; ☎ 33-3630-1113; www.centro-magno.com/magno; Av Vallarta 2425), 2km west of the city center, and **Plaza del Sol** (Map p580; ☎ 33-3121-5750; www.plazadelsol.com; Av López Mateos Sur), 7km southwest of the city center. To reach them, take bus 258 going west from the corner of San Felipe and Avenida Alcalde, or TUR 707 going west on Avenida Juárez. The biggest and swankiest mall, **Galerías Guadalajara** (Map p580; ☎ 33-3777-7880; www.galeriasguadalajara.com; Sanzio 150), is 8km west of downtown, served by bus 25. All malls are open from approximately 10am to 9pm.

Far more appealing to travelers will be the excellent handicrafts from Jalisco, Michoacán and other Mexican states that are available in Guadalajara's many markets. Tlaquepaque and Tonalá, two suburbs less than 15km from Guadalajara's center, are both major producers of handicrafts and furniture – anyone with an interior decorating habit should plan to spend some major quality time in each. You'll find the best value (read: wholesale prices) in Tonalá.

Antigua de México   HOMEWARES
(Map p590; ☎ 33-3635-2402; www.antiguademexico.com; Independencia 255; ⏰10am-2pm & 3-6:30pm Mon-Fri, 10am-2pm Sat) Legendary Tlaquepaque boutique with gorgeous furniture showpieces, such as benches carved from a single tree, which are displayed in expansive, old-world courtyards.

Orígenes   HOMEWARES
(Map p590; ☎ 33-3563-1041; Independencia 211; ⏰10am-7pm Mon-Fri, 11am-7pm Sat, 11am-6pm Sun) Tlaquepaque-based shop with a tremendous lighting selection, elegant hammocks and even its own in-house 'Mexican gourmet' restaurant, Casa Luna (mains M$150 to M$250), with tables inside as well as outside in the shade of a tree.

Teté, Arte y Diseño   HOMEWARES
(Map p590; ☎ 33-3635-7965; www.teatearteydiseno.com; Av Juárez 173; ⏰10am-7:30pm Mon-Sat) Offers massive chandeliers, reproduction antique hardware and one-of-a-kind woodcarvings in this Tlaquepaque store.

Mercado San Juan de Dios   MARKET
(Map p586; cnr Av Javier Mina & Calz Independencia, Mercado Libertad; ⏰10am-9pm) Massive, labyrinthine market that sells pretty much everything bar the kitchen sink, but is best for

CAR-FREE GUADALAJARA

Expunge that typical Mexican image of noisy, crowded cities with snarling unapologetic traffic from your consciousness and wake up to a different Guadalajaran reality – at least on Sundays. Since 2004, Mexico's second largest city has celebrated the **Via Recreativa** (www.viarecreativa.org; ⊗8am-2pm Sun), when its arterial streets are closed to cars and given over instead to bikes, skateboards, strollers, wheelchairs and any other form of nonmotorized forward propulsion.

Adding to the convenience is an army of volunteers dispensing free bikes (ID required), offering scenic **bike tours** (Map p586; corner Av Juárez & Calle Escorzia; ⊗9:30am & 11am Sun) FREE, and organizing alfresco exercise classes. The aim of the Via Recreativa is to reduce vehicle dependence, promote health and generate social interaction. Creative artists are encouraged to take to the streets and Parque Revolución maintains a cultural pavilion with live performances. The measure – which sees an average 200,000 *tapatíos* (Guadalajara residents) take to the streets weekly – has since been adopted by other Mexican cities, including Mexico City's DF (Distrito Federal or Federal District).

Guadalajara went one step further in October 2014 when it became only the third city in Mexico to introduce a large-scale bike-sharing scheme. **Mibici** (www.mibici. net) maintains 1160 bikes at 116 stations in both the city center and the satellite city of Zapopan. Most of its users are yearly subscribers, but you can obtain a *pase temporal* (temporary pass) for M$80 per day by using your credit card in a machine at any of the docking stations. Guadalajara is still a little lacking in bike lanes, but stick to the central plazas or use Mibici during the Via Recreativa and you should be OK.

street food, in particular its *tortas ahogadas* made with a crispy sub roll 'drowned' in a spicy pork stew. Grab plenty of napkins.

ℹ️ Information

EMERGENCY
If you are a victim of crime, you may first want to contact your embassy or consulate and/or the state tourist office.
Ambulance (📞 33-3616-9616, 33-3601-3019, 33-3614-5252)
Emergency (📞 066, 080)
Fire (📞 33-1201-7700)
Police (📞 33-3668-0800, 33-3632-0330)

INTERNET ACCESS
A dwindling stash of internet cafes (M$10 to M$15 per hour) are scattered around the city but tend to change location frequently. Nearly all hotels and many restaurants, cafes and bars offer free wi-fi.

MEDICAL SERVICES
Farmacia Guadalajara (Map p586; 📞 33-3613-7509; Moreno 170; ⊗8am-10pm) Get your first aid, sundry items and prescribed meds here.
Hospital México Americano (Map p580; 📞 33-3648-3333, free call 01-800-462-2238; www.hma.com.mx; Colomos 2110) About 3km northwest of the city center; English-speaking physicians available.
US Consulate (Map p593; 📞 33-3268-2200; http://guadalajara.usconsulate.gov/medical2.

html; Progreso 175) Keeps a regularly updated online list of local English-speaking doctors, including specialists and dentists.

MONEY
Banks are plentiful in Guadalajara and most have ATMs, known as *cajeros*.

You can change cash at competitive prices around the clock at one of the eager *casas de cambio* (money changers) on López Cotilla, between Avenida 16 de Septiembre and Corona. Most will also change traveler's checks.

POST
Main Post Office (Map p586; cnr Carranza & Av Independencia; ⊗8am-7pm Mon-Fri, 9am-1pm Sat)

TOURIST INFORMATION
State Tourist Office (Map p586; 📞 33-3668-1600; Morelos 102; ⊗9am-7pm Mon-Fri) Enter from either Morelos or Paseo Degollado. English-speaking staff offer information on Guadalajara, the state of Jalisco and the upcoming week's events.
Tlaquepaque State Tourist Office (Map p590; 📞 ext 2319 33-3562-7050; www.tlaquepaque.gob.mx; Morelos 88; ⊗9am-3pm Mon-Fri) Upstairs in the Casa del Artesano. There is also a helpful tourist kiosk as you enter the main shopping area of Tlaquepaque on Ejército.
Tonalá Tourist Office (📞 33-1200-3912; Zapata 244A; ⊗9am-3pm Mon-Fri) Three blocks west of Avenida Tonaltecas on Zapata.

Tourist Information Booth (Map p586; Plaza de la Liberación; ⊙ 9:30am-2:30pm & 5-7:30pm Mon-Fri, 10am-12:30pm Sat & Sun) One of half a dozen generic booths scattered around the city, all with the same hours. You'll find others in Jardín San Francisco, Plaza de las Américas (Zapopan) and outside the Instituto Cultural de Cabañas.

USEFUL WEBSITES

Gobierno de Jalisco (www.visita.jalisco.gob. mx) Official website of Jalisco.

Vive Guadalajara (http://vive.guadalajara.gob. mx) Official website of Guadalajara.

ⓘ Getting There & Away

AIR

Guadalajara's **Aeropuerto Internacional Miguel Hidalgo** (☑ 33-3688-5248; www. aeropuertosgap.com.mx) is 17km south of downtown, just off the highway to Chapala. Inside are ATMs, money-exchange offices, cafes and car-rental companies. There's also a **tourist office** (⊙ 8am-6pm).

A multitude of airlines offer direct flights to major cities in Mexico.

Aeroméxico (☑ 800-021-40-00; www.aero mexico.com; airport)

Interjet (☑ 800-011-23-45; www.interjet.com. mx; airport)

Viva Aerobus (☑ 33-4000-0180; www.vivaaero bus.com; airport)

Volaris (☑ 55-1102-8000; www.volaris.mx; airport)

BUS

Guadalajara has two bus terminals. The long-distance bus terminal is the airport-like **Nueva Central Camionera** (New Bus Terminal; Map p580; ☑ 33-3600-0135), a large, modern, V-shaped terminal that is split into seven separate *módulos* (miniterminals). Each *módulo* has ticket desks for a number of bus lines, plus restrooms, web cafes and cafeterias. The Nueva

BUSES FROM GUADALAJARA

From Nueva Central Camionera

DESTINATION	FARE (M$)	DURATION (HR)	FREQUENCY (DAILY)
Barra de Navidad	462	5½	12
Colima	325	3	hourly
Guanajuato	495	4	13
Manzanillo	402	4	hourly
Mexico City (Terminal Norte)	685	7-8	half-hourly
Morelia	347	4	half-hourly
Pátzcuaro	386	4½	2
Puerto Vallarta	490	5	hourly
Querétaro	420	5½	half-hourly
San Miguel de Allende	645	5	every 2hr
Tepic	285	3	5
Uruapan	378	4½	hourly
Zacatecas	465	5	11
Zamora	229	2¼	half-hourly

From Antigua Central Camionera

DESTINATION	FARE (M$)	DURATION (HR)	FREQUENCY (DAILY)
Ajijic	50	1	hourly
Chapala	50	¾	very frequent
Ciudad Guzmán	173	2	hourly
Mazamitla	120	3	hourly
Tapalpa	106	3	10
Tequila	64	1	half-hourly

Central Camionera is 9km southeast of Guadalajara city center, past Tlaquepaque, just off the motorway to Mexico City.

Buses go to and from just about everywhere in western, central and northern Mexico. Destinations are served by multiple companies, based in the different *módulos,* making price comparisons difficult and time-consuming. The good news is that if you're flexible, you won't have to wait long for a bus – there are departures at least once an hour for major destinations. Fares given are for the best buses available. You can often find cheaper fares by going on slightly less plush buses.

ETN (www.etn.com.mx) and **Primera Plus** (www.primeraplus.com.mx) offer deluxe nonstop rides to many destinations. Buses have wi-fi, male-female toilets, air-con, individual TV screens, mega-comfortable seats, and free food and drink. Prices are highly reasonable.

Guadalajara's other bus terminal is the scruffier **Antigua Central Camionera** (Old Bus Terminal; Map p580; ☑ 33-3650-0479; Dr Michel & Los Ángeles), about 1.5km south of the cathedral near Parque Agua Azul. From here 2nd-class buses serve destinations within 75km of Guadalajara. There are two sides to it: Sala A is for destinations to the east and northeast; Sala B is for destinations northwest, southwest and south. There's a M$0.50 charge to enter the terminal, which offers a **left-luggage service** (Antigua Central Camionera; ⊙ 7:30am-8pm) in Sala B. Bus services run between 6am and 10pm, approximately. Buses leave multiple times an hour for nearby locations, and once an hour or so for longer trips.

CAR & MOTORCYCLE

Guadalajara is 535km northwest of Mexico City and 344km east of Puerto Vallarta. Highways 15, 15D, 23, 54, 54D, 80, 80D and 90 all converge here, combining temporarily to form the Perforce, a ring road around the city.

Guadalajara has many car-rental agencies. All the large international companies are represented, but you may get a cheaper deal from a local company, so it's worth comparing prices and availability online before you travel. Prices start at around M$350 per day for a four-door sedan; it will cost you (upward of M$3000) to leave the car in any city other than the one you rented it from.

TRAIN

The only trains serving Guadalajara are the two tourist 'tequila-tasting' trains to the nearby towns of Amatitán or Tequila.

❶ Getting Around

TO/FROM THE AIRPORT

The airport is about 17km south of central Guadalajara, just off the highway to Chapala. To get into town on public transportation, exit the airport and head to the bus stop in front of the Hotel Casa Grande, about 50m to the right. Take any bus marked 'Zapote' (M$6) or 'Atasa' (M$12) – both run every 15 minutes from about 5am to 10pm and take 40 minutes to the Antigua Central Camionera, where you can hop on a bus to the city center.

Taxis are M$300 to the city center, M$260 to the Nueva Central Camionera and M$220 to Tlaquepaque. Buy fixed-price tickets at the airport.

To get to the airport from Guadalajara's center, take bus 174 to the Antigua Central Camionera (the stop where you get off is in front of the Gran Hotel Canada) and then get on an 'Aeropuerto' bus (every 20 minutes, 6am to 9pm) at this stop. Metered taxis cost roughly M$250.

TO/FROM THE BUS TERMINALS

To reach the city center from the Nueva Central Camionera, take any bus marked 'Centro' (M$6). You can also catch the more comfortable, turquoise-colored TUR bus (M$12). They should be marked 'Zapopan.' Don't take the ones marked 'Tonalá' or you'll be headed away from Guadalajara's center. Taxis to the city center cost M$120 unless they let the meter tick (some don't use it). A direct taxi from the airport to the Nueva Central Camionera costs M$260.

To get to the Nueva Central Camionera from the city center, take any bus marked 'Nueva Central' – these are frequent and leave from the corner of Avenida 16 de Septiembre and Madero.

To reach the city center from the Antigua Central Camionera, take any bus going north on Calzada Independencia. To return to the Antigua Central Camionera from the city center, take bus 174 going south on Calzada Independencia. Taxis cost M$40.

Bus 616 (M$6) runs between the two bus terminals.

BUS

Guadalajara has a comprehensive city bus system, but be ready for crowded, rough rides. On major routes, buses run every five minutes or so from 6am to 10pm daily and cost M$6. Many buses pass through the city center, so for a suburban destination you'll have a few stops to choose from. The routes diverge as they get further from the city center and you'll need to know the bus number for the suburb you want. Some bus-route numbers are followed by an additional letter indicating which route they take through the suburbs.

The TUR buses, painted a distinctive turquoise color, are a more comfortable alternative. They have air-con and plush seats (M$12). If they roar past without stopping, they're full; this can happen several times in a row during rush hour and may drive you mad.

The tourist office has a list of the complex bus routes in Guadalajara and can help you reach

WESTERN CENTRAL HIGHLANDS GUADALAJARA

your destination. Following are some common destinations, the buses that go there and a central stop from where you can catch them.

Antigua Central Camionera Bus 174 going south on Calzada Independencia.

Chapultepec Par Vial buses 400 and 500 at Avenidas (not Calzadas!) Independencia and Alcalde.

Nueva Central Camionera Bus 275B, 275 Diagonal, TUR marked 'Tonalá' or any bus marked Nueva Central; catch them all at the corner of Avenida 16 de Septiembre and Madero.

Tlaquepaque Bus 275B, 275 Diagonal, 647 or TUR marked 'Tlaquepaque' at Avenida 16 de Septiembre between López Cotilla and Madero.

Tonalá Bus 275D, 275 Diagonal or TUR marked 'Tonalá' at Avenida 16 de Septiembre and Madero.

Zapopan Bus 275 or TUR marked 'Zapopan' going north on Avenida 16 de Septiembre or Alcalde.

HORSE-DRAWN CARRIAGE

If you fancy trotting around the city in a horse-drawn carriage, reckon on paying for M$150 per half-hour or M$200 per hour. There's a carriage stand right at Jardín San Francisco and another in front of the Museo Regional de Guadalajara.

METRO

The subway system has two lines that cross the city. Stops are marked with a 'T.' But the metro isn't tourist friendly because most stops are far

from the sights. Línea 1 stretches north–south for 15km all the way from the Periférico Norte to the Periférico Sur. It runs below Federalismo (seven blocks west of the city center) and Avenida Colón: catch it at Parque Revolución, on the corner of Avenida Juárez. Línea 2 runs east–west for 10km below Avenidas Juárez and Mina.

TAXI

Taxis are everywhere in the city center. They have meters, but not all drivers use them. Most would rather quote a flat fee for a trip, especially at night. Generally it's cheaper to go by the meter – if you're quoted a flat fee and think it's inflated, feel free to bargain. From 10pm to 6am a 'night meter' is used and fares rise 25%.

AROUND GUADALAJARA

Beyond Guadalajara's sprawling and seemingly endless suburbs, lonely mountain pueblos and lazy lakeshore towns promise an intoxicating shot of old Mexico. Lago de Chapala, just 45km south of Guadalajara, is Mexico's largest natural lake and offers spectacular scenery, traditional lakeside towns and picturesque pueblos full of retired gringos. Further south and west, Jalisco's Zona de Montaña is home to a string of mountain retreats where horses wander free through dusty streets and there's nothing to do but

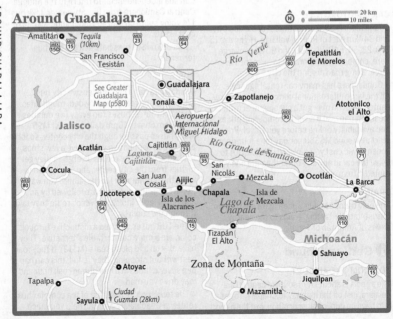

stroll through the pines and sip *rompope* (a local eggnog-like liquor) by the fire.

This region is also a major producer of tequila, and one of the most popular day trips from Guadalajara is to the town of Tequila to see how Mexico's most famous export is made.

Tequila

Surrounded by a sea of blue agave, sun-baked Tequila is a surprisingly attractive factory town that's firmly on the tour-bus circuit these days. The eponymous drink – the object of everyone's longing – is best observed in one of three local distilleries, all of which run tours.

◎ Sights & Activities

Quinta Sauza   DISTILLERY
(www.casasauza.com; Navarro 70; ☺9am-6:30pm Mon-Fri, to 2pm Sat) FREE The *Secret Garden*-invoking Sauza estate retains the refined air of a Spanish sherry bodega. The colonial-style grounds are adorned with Italianate fountains, tumbling plants and even a chapel. Indeed, 'tequila factory' are the last words that spring to mind as you recline in the sun-streaked bar. Nonetheless, tequila has been made here for eons and still is. Basic tours of the adjacent **Perseverancia Distillery** (☑374-742-41-40; www.casasauza. com; Sauza 80; tours M$100; ☺9:30am-4pm Mon-Fri, to 12:30pm Sat) last an hour.

Mundo Cuervo   DISTILLERY
(☑800-006-86-30; www.mundocuervo.com; cnr Corona & José Cuervo; tours from M$200; ☺10am-5pm Mon-Fri & Sun, to 4pm Sat) Right across from Tequila's main plaza, Mundo Cuervo, which is owned by the José Cuervo distillery, the world's oldest distillery, is a veritable tequila theme park and the biggest game in town. Hourly tours include tastings and a free margarita in a plastic cup. The hour-long tour is a bit rushed so it's worth spending a little more on one of the longer and more comprehensive tours.

La Cofradia   DISTILLERY
(☑33-1955-4800; www.tequilacofradia.com.mx; Calle La Cofradia 1297; ☺10am-6pm) Two kilometers outside the town of Tequila sits the beautiful La Cofradia estate where the 100% organic Casa Noble tequila brand is made. The elegant 'factory' is set amid mango trees and uses French oak barrels to age its spirits. Aside from factory tours, La Cofradia hosts

the **Museo de Sitio del Tequila** and an atmospherically cavernous restaurant.

For the guilty pleasure of staying in a real-life tequila distillery, reserve one of the four casitas at the on-site **Hotel Boutique Cofradia** (r from M$1650; ㋐❄🛜), furnished with exquisite only-in-Mexico designs and surrounded by fields full of agave.

Museo Nacional del Tequila   MUSEUM
(Corona 34; adult/child M$15/7; ☺9am-4pm) Set in an old colonial building just off the main plaza and spread over five rooms, this museum does a reasonable job of illustrating the history of tequila-making with photos and distillery apparatus.

❶ Getting There & Away

Buses to Tequila leave from Guadalajara's Antigua Central Camionera roughly every 30 minutes (M$85, 1¾ hours).

Amatitán

This lowlands town, 39km northwest of Guadalajara, is the biggest tequila-producing pueblo after Tequila itself. The romantic old hacienda of **Herradura** (☑33-3942-3920; www.herradura.com; Comercio 172; tours M$100; ☺9am-3pm Mon-Sat, tours 10am, 11am & 3pm Sun) is Mexico's prettiest distillery, with regularly scheduled English-language tours that most people rate as being the best of the various distillery tours. It's this distillery that the much talked about Tequila Express visits. Call ahead for Spanish-language tours at the high-end 100% agave distillery **Tres Mujeres** (☑374-745-08-40, 33-3167-9857; Carretera Guadalajara-Nogales Km 39; ☺8am-6pm) FREE.

Lago de Chapala

Lago de Chapala, Mexico's largest natural lake, lies 45km south of Guadalajara. Surrounded by mountains – some of which tumble dramatically to the shore – its beauty is deep and undeniable. This beauty combined with an addictive climate (always warm during the day and pleasantly cool at night) mean that Chapala continues to lure North American retirees to the area and, at weekends, masses of city folk out for some fresh air and a fish lunch. For foreign tourists the allure is a little less compelling, although it does still make for a fun excursion from Guadalajara.

Sadly the lake is not as healthy as it is beautiful. Water levels fluctuate due to

THE TEQUILA TRAIL

Tequila, Mexico's most famous firewater and the cause of oh-so-many regrettable late-night decisions, was born nearly half a millennium ago in the state of Jalisco. Today the countryside around Guadalajara is covered in oceans of blue agave – the gorgeous succulent from which tequila is made – and dotted with distilleries ranging from small adobe bunkers to huge *haciendas*. Many of these welcome visitors, whether or not they have official tours. The Jalisco state tourism department has created its own **Ruta del Tequila** (www.rutadeltequila.org. mx) of suggested tequila-related sights. All are accessible via day trips from Guadalajara.

When imbibing, always remember the wise words of the late comedian George Carlin: 'One tequila, two tequila, three tequila, floor.'

It Begins with Blue Agave

Spanish conquistadors first cultivated the blue agave plant *(Agave tequilana weber)* in Jalisco as early as the mid-1550s. But tequila didn't become popular until after the Mexican Revolution, when José Cuervo introduced the first bottle to the public.

Agave plants are cultivated for eight to 12 years, then the *jimadores* come calling. These tough field hands expertly strip away the spiny foliage until they've found its heart, called a *piña*. The largest, weighing up to 150kg, are hauled from the fields by *burros* (donkeys), shipped to the distillery by truck and fed into brick or clay ovens where they cook for up to 36 hours. Afterward the softened pulp is shredded and juiced and the liquid is pumped into fermentation vats where it is usually mixed with yeast.

Five Types of Tequila

Your average cantina tequila is tequila *mixto* (mixed), which can legally contain up to 49% nonagave sugars. The better stuff, which bears the '100% Agave' label, has no additives. Within these two categories, there are five main varieties of tequila.

➡ *Blanco* or *plata* (white or silver) tequila is relatively unaged, uncolored and has a distinct agave flavor. Best used as a mixer for margaritas or other cocktails.

➡ *Oro* (gold) tequila is unaged, artificially colored and best avoided.

Guadalajara's and Mexico City's water needs and intermittent drought. Commercial fertilizers washed into the lake have nourished water hyacinth, an invasive plant that clogs the lake's surface and kills aquatic life, which means few people choose to swim here.

Chapala

🎵 376 / POP 21,000 / ELEV 1550M

With a commanding location on the shores of its namesake lake, Chapala became a well-known resort destination after president Porfirio Díaz vacationed here every year from 1904 to 1909. DH Lawrence and Tennessee Williams were later visitors, sealing the town's literary pedigree, and today Chapala is a simple but charming working-class Mexican town with lovely lakeside walks and a buzzing weekend scene.

⊙ Sights

Isla de Mezcala   ISLAND

The most interesting island to visit on Lago de Chapala is Isla de Mezcala. Here you'll find ruins of a fort where Mexican independence fighters held strong from 1812 to 1816, repulsing several Spanish attacks before finally earning the respect of, and a full pardon from, their enemies. A 3½-hour round-trip boat ride costs M$1600 for up to eight people.

Isla de los Alacranes   ISLAND

A ticket booth at the pier's entrance sells boat tickets to Isla de los Alacranes (Scorpion Island), 6km from Chapala, which has some restaurants and souvenir stalls but is not very captivating. A round trip, with 30 minutes on the island, costs M$390 per boatload; for one hour on the island it's M$460.

🛏 Sleeping

★**Quinta Quetzalcóatl**   GUESTHOUSE $$$

(🎵 376-765-36-53; http://chapalabandb.com; Zaragoza 307; r incl breakfast from M$1400; ℗ @ 🛜 ☒) Behind the stone walls of this hotel are a pool, lush gardens and plenty of private outdoor space. Some of the rooms are highly

➡ Tequila *reposado* (rested) has been aged from two to nine months in oak barrels and tends to taste sharp and peppery.

➡ Tequila *añejo* (aged) is aged at least one year in oak barrels. It's sweet and smooth and works best as an after-dinner drink.

➡ Tequila *extra añejo* (vintage) is aged for at least three years. First sold in 2006, *extra añejo* is the pinnacle of the fast-growing premium tequila market. Sip it neat, of course.

In Mexico you can buy a decent bottle of tequila for M$150, though for something special you'll need to spend over M$300. Treat the good stuff like a bottle of single malt and before you sip it, sniff it a few times to prepare your palate for the heat and it won't taste so harsh.

And don't be looking for a 'special' *gusano* (worm) in each bottle. These are placed in bottles of mezcal (an agave spirit similar to tequila but distilled outside Jalisco state) as a marketing ploy – and even if you slurp the critter, you won't get any higher.

Organized Tours

GDL Tours (p586) in Guadalajara offers day trips featuring distillery tours and tastings.

Experience Tequila (☑1-55-3060-8242; www.experiencetequila.com; 4-day packages d US$1115) North American tequila aficionado Clayton Szczech offers a variety of individualized private tours departing from Guadalajara, from basic day trips to tequila country to multiday intensive tasting seminars. Book well in advance.

Tequila Express (☑33-3880-9090; www.tequilaexpress.com.mx; adult/child M$1550/1100) This popular train-trip/fiesta departs every Saturday, Sunday and on holidays from Guadalajara and includes a tour of the Herradura distillery, a mariachi show, lunch and an open bar with *mucho* tequila.

José Cuervo Express (☑US 800-523-977-377; www.josecuervoexpress.com; adult M$1700; ☺Sat & Sun) Ride in elegant train carriages on this high-class tour to the Mundo Cuervo distillery in Tequila. Prices include transportation, distillery tours, meals and a fair bit of tequila.

eccentric in style (the riding-themed Carriage House is one thing, while the pink bathroom tower in Lady Chatterley's Lover has to be seen to be believed), but the hotel nevertheless attracts many return visitors.

This is where DH Lawrence wrote *The Plumed Serpent* in 1923, and Lawrence fans can even sleep in the room where the author scribbled. The Australian owners live on site and are a good source of local information.

Lake Chapala Inn   GUESTHOUSE $$$
(☑376-765-47-86; www.chapalainn.com; Paseo Ramón Corona 23; s/d incl breakfast M$1000/1300; P ⦿ ⌑) This imposing white building right on the lakeshore is moments from the center of town and has wonderful views over the waters and off to the faraway hills. The furnishings are a little old-fashioned, but the views from two of the rooms (Rosa and Jacaranda) and the communal terrace are unbeatable.

Reductions are available for stays of more than two nights, and the traditional English breakfast is the real deal.

 Eating

Seafood joints aimed at tourists can be found all along Paseo Corona (known as the *malecón*); they all have pleasant lake views, although quality can be hit and miss.

Isla Cozumel   SEAFOOD $$
(Paseo Corona 22A; mains from M$120; ☺10am-9pm Tue-Sun) The best of the touristy lakefront restaurants, Cozumel stands at the end of the waterfront and is very popular with visitors who enjoy the complimentary margaritas as a prelude to the seafood-biased meals – everything from catfish to oysters.

Beer Garden   FISH $$
(☑376-765-36-56; Madero 200; mains from M$100; ☺noon-9pm Sun-Thu, to 10pm Fri, to 11pm Sat) This Chapala institution has drawn crowds to the lakefront since 1925. Enjoy shrimp, whitefish and, of course, beer on the rambling patio. There's regular live music.

ℹ Getting There & Away

Buses from Guadalajara (M$50, one hour) to Chapala leave from the Antigua Central Camionera multiple times an hour. Buses connect Chapala to Ajijic (M$9, 15 minutes) every 20 minutes.

Ajijic

☏ 376 / POP 10,000 / ELEV 1550M

The wonderfully named Ajijic (ah-hee-*heek*) is an outpost of North American retirees and by far the most sophisticated and energetic of the towns that line the north shore of Lago de Chapala. While the gringos may have put Ajijic on the map by opening boutiques, galleries and restaurants galore, much of the town retains its charming, colonial-era vibe, with cobblestone lanes and quiet streets of boldly painted houses. It makes a delightful place to sit back and relax awhile, although it's far from the typical Mexico here: English is almost as commonly heard on the streets as Spanish and prices are relatively high.

🏃 Activities

Ajijic has a web of sinuous trails that wrap their way around the jungle-covered hills behind the town taking in waterfalls, peekaboo lake views and some rocky scrambles. The most obvious path ascends to the **Telapo waterfall**. From town follow Encarnación Rosas, then turn right on Galeana; an interpretive sign marks the official starting point. After reaching the waterfall (20 minutes), which is only visible in the rainy season, you can carry on following the trail markers (white paint splashed on rocks). The trail will ultimately reach a clearing atop a saddle from where you can descend on another path back down to Ajijic, visible below. Allow 1½ to two hours for the circuit.

🛏 Sleeping

There is no shortage of B&Bs in Ajijic, with plenty owned by foreign retirees. Many, however, have minimum stays of several days and don't have permanently manned reception desks, which can make staying at them problematic if you're looking for a room on the run. The following are operated more like standard hotels.

Casa Mis Amores   GUESTHOUSE $$
(☏ 376-766-46-40; Hidalgo 22B; d incl breakfast M$850-1200; 🅿🛜) Arty without being precious, the town's loveliest guesthouse has a plant-filled courtyard and 12 adobe and tile rooms decorated with local art,

Moroccan-style lamps and mosaic-style bathrooms.

Casa del Sol   B&B $$$
(☏ 376-766-00-50; Mina 7; d M$1550-1800; 🅿🛜🏊) Catherine, the Texan owner of this sunny-colored B&B, has won many a fan through her warm welcome, multihued and impeccably kept rooms, easy artistic style and lush garden, home to a swimming pool that's more than just a bit inviting. A solid American-style breakfast is included.

La Nueva Posada   GUESTHOUSE $$$
(☏ 376-766-14-44; www.hotelnuevaposada.com; Guerra 9; r incl breakfast M$1250-1550; 🅿🛜) A small hotel with a certain (unpretentious) grandiosity, this lakeside retreat offers a taste of genteel, old-world Mexico. The 19 rooms are spacious, with tasteful furnishings, and some have superb lake views. The garden runs right down to the shore, giving you plenty of space to feel at ease with the world.

🍴 Eating & Drinking

Café Grano   CAFE
(☏ 376-766-56-84; Castellanos 15D; coffee from M$20; ⏱9am-9pm Sun-Thu, to 10pm Fri & Sat) This thoroughly pleasant gringo-meets-local cafe is everything a good coffee bar should be, with fine aromas, Mexican beans, chairs tailored in coffee sacking and excellent complimentary snacks. Bright murals tell the coffee story from plant to cup. It also sells high-quality beans, including Veracruz, Oaxaca and Chiapas varietals.

★ Number 4   MEDITERRANEAN $$$
(☏ 376-766-13-60; Guerra 4; mains M$190-250; ⏱dinner Mon & Fri, 2-11pm Sat, 2-8pm Sun) This upscale and highly impressive place has been generating buzz all the way to Guadalajara. Chef Greg Couillard's menu leans toward modern French and includes culinary delights such as Mombasa mussels, New York steak and jerk chicken.

The open-air dining room, with a high thatched roof, has a theatrical elegance; the attached bar is the area's hippest and there are frequent band nights and special theme evenings. Reservations are recommended.

Ajijic Tango   ARGENTINE $$$
(☏ 376-766-24-58; Morelos 5; steaks M$165-349; ⏱12:30-9pm Mon, Wed & Thu, to 10pm Fri & Sat, to 7pm Sun) Ajijic's most beloved restaurant is never less than packed with locals, tourists and expats alike, all here to enjoy the excellent steaks (it *is* an Argentinian restaurant

after all). The rest of the food, though, can be rather hit and miss. Reservations on Friday and Saturday nights are recommended.

❶ Getting There & Away

Buses from Guadalajara (M$50, one hour, hourly) to Ajijic leave from the Antigua Central Camionera and drop you on the highway at Colón next to a small ticket office. Buses connect Chapala and Ajijic every 20 minutes (M$9, 15 minutes).

Zona de Montaña

South of Lago de Chapala, Jalisco's Zona de Montaña – seemingly endless layered mountains – is an increasingly popular weekend retreat for *guadalajarans,* who come to enjoy the rangeland, pines, timeless colonial pueblos, local food and cooler climes.

Tapalpa

📞 343 / POP 18,000 / ELEV 2100M

Tapalpa, a labyrinth of white-washed walls, red-tiled roofs and cobblestoned streets surrounding two impressive 16th-century churches, is one of the most beautiful mountain towns in Mexico. This beauty hasn't gone unnoticed – at weekends flocks of people flee Guadalajara for the walking, horseback riding and generally cool and misty climate that Tapalpa offers. During the weekday calm though, when visitors are few in number, Tapalpa retains a country backwater feel; horses clip-clop down the lanes and old men in cowboy hats lounge on benches in the plaza.

◎ Sights & Activities

Perched on the slopes of the Sierra Tapalpa and ringed by a tapestry of pastureland and pine forests threaded with streams, Tapalpa offers good walking in all directions.

Las Piedrotas   LANDMARK
(🏛) Las Piedrotas are a large and impressive set of rock formations set in cow pastures 5km north of town. Most people drive there, but it's an easy, and rewarding 2½- to three-hour return walk along a quiet country lane through dark pine forests, past an abandoned old paper mill and up onto a flower-filled plateau grazed by huge horned cattle.

To get there take Hidalgo west out of town, following the signs for Chiquilistlán (and some signs for Las Piedrotas). Once you've cleared the edge of town, just follow the road straight ahead. A taxi costs around M$60.

El Salto   WATERFALL
(🏛) El Salto is a jaw-dropping, 105m-high waterfall about 18km south of town. A taxi costs around M$130.

🛏 Sleeping

There are dozens of hotels and guesthouses in town, but you should make reservations for Saturday, Sunday and holidays (when *guadalajarans* stream in).

Casa de Maty   HOTEL $$
(📞 343-432-01-89; www.lacasadematy.com.mx; Matamoros 69; r from M$850; 🖥) It can get mighty cold and damp in these hills at night, so you'll want a warm and cozy place to snuggle down. The large rooms at Casa de Maty, which overlooks the main plaza, have wood beam ceilings, wooden shutters, excellent beds and open fireplaces (and a stack of firewood) – ticking all the warm and cozy boxes.

Las Margaritas Posada   GUESTHOUSE $$
(📞 343-432-07-99; www.tapalpahotelmargaritas. com; 16 de Septiembre 81; r M$700; 🖥) Sporting bright decorations and wardrobes with carved Chinese-style dragons, this place, uphill from the plaza, offers value, comfort and eye-pleasing rooms.

🍴 Eating

Local street-food treats include *tamales de acelga* (chard-filled *tamales*) at the cheap food stalls near the church, along with *rompope* and *ponche* (pomegranate wine).

Los Girasoles   MEXICAN $$
(📞 343-432-04-58; Obregón 110; mains M$90-110) Tapalpa's classiest restaurant is just off the main plaza and offers quality dishes such as cheese- and plantain-stuffed chilis in a coriander sauce. There's a starlit outdoor patio for rare warm nights or those wrapped up well, or you can snuggle in front of the open log fire in the main dining room.

❶ Information

There's an ATM on the plaza.
Tourist Office (📞 343-432-06-50; www.tapalpa turistico.com; plaza; ⊗9am-5pm Mon-Fri, 10am-7pm Sat, 10am-3pm Sun) The tourist office has maps, info and a particularly useful website.

❶ Getting There & Away

Ten buses daily travel to Tapalpa, leaving from Guadalajara's Antigua Central Camionera (M$106, three hours); three daily go from the Nueva Central Camionera. There are also four buses a day to/from Ciudad Guzmán (M$77, two hours). Buses in Tapalpa stop at the **Sur de Jalisco bus office** (Ignacio López 10), a block off the plaza.

Mazamitla

☑ 382 / POP 8000 / ELEV 2200M

During the week Mazamitla, a simple and charming whitewashed mountain town south of Lago de Chapala and 132km by road from Guadalajara, is seldom fully awake. Shops close at 5pm, restaurants open at 6pm and *abuelas* (grandmothers) dressed in black wander haphazardly through the hilly cobbled roads, stopping traffic. But come the weekend, every man and his sombrero arrives from Guadalajara and the town is anything but sleepy: the plaza fills with music and dance, the hotels and restaurants are booked out, and the shops sell an impressive array of tourist tat, but it's all good fun.

⦿ Sights & Activities

There's a small but lively **market** (⊗ 8am-9pm) on Juárez.

Los Cazos   PARK

(adult/child M$15/10; ⊗ 9am-5pm; ⊕) About 2km south of town is the leafy park Los Cazos, with the 30m waterfall **El Salto**. You can picnic or hire a horse (M$250) and live out your John Wayne fantasies. A taxi here costs M$50 or it's an easy and pleasant walk.

⊨ Sleeping & Eating

There are masses of places to stay in Mazamitla and an equal number of places to eat. The town sports an interesting take on the Swiss alpine theme and you'll see small storefronts selling fruit preserves, cheeses, *rompope* and *cajeta* (goat's milk and sugar boiled to a paste) around the plaza.

Hostal El Leñador   GUESTHOUSE $

(☑ 382-538-01-85; www.hostalelenador.com.mx; Netzahualcóyotl 4; r from M$550; ℗ ☎) Stepping through the door of this family-run guesthouse you're likely to be greeted with *'mi casa es tu casa'* (my house is your house), and with modern and very comfortable rooms and staff that welcome, you'll probably be glad to call Hostal El Leñador home for a while.

Hotel Cabañas Colina de los Ruiseñores   CABAÑAS $

(☑ 382-538-03-80; www.mazamitlahotelcabana. com.mx; Allende 50; s/d M$250/400; ℗ ☎)

Down the hill from the plaza, the Hotel Cabañas Colina de los Ruiseñores is a pleasantly rustic place, with rambling grounds and homey rooms with open log fires.

Posada Alpina   MEXICAN $$

(☑ 382-538-01-04; Reforma 8; mains from M$100; ⊗ 8:30am-7pm Mon, Wed & Thu, to midnight Fri & Sat, to 5pm Sun; ☎) Right on the plaza, Posada Alpina is a smart hotel-restaurant that serves the best *molcajete* stew in town. It also does good breakfasts and coffee.

ⓘ Information

There's a bank on the plaza.

Tourist Office (☑ 382-538-02-30; Portal Degollado 16; ⊗ 9am-3pm Mon-Fri)

ⓘ Getting There & Away

Buses to Colima (M$142, 2¾ hours, four daily) and Morelia (M$269, five hours, one daily) leave from in front of the Pemex gas station at Galeana and Guerro.

From Guadalajara's Nueva Central Camionera (M$120, three hours) numerous buses arrive at the small bus station at the corner of 16 de Septiembre and Guerro three blocks north of Mazamitla's plaza. The many buses to Ciudad Guzmán (M$107, 2½ hours) arrive and leave from the same place.

Ciudad Guzmán

☑ 341 / POP 97,000 / ELEV 1500M

Busy Ciudad Guzmán (Zapotlán El Grande) is no tourist attraction, but it is the closest city to Volcán Nevado de Colima, a majestic volcano about 25km to its southwest.

⦿ Sights

Guzmán's crowded plaza is surrounded by market stalls and shopping arcades set around two churches: the 17th-century **Sagrado Corazón** and a neoclassical **cathedral**. In its center is a stone gazebo with a homage to famous local-boy muralist José Clemente Orozco – called *Man of Fire* – painted on its ceiling. The original is in the Instituto Cultural de Cabañas in Guadalajara.

Museo Regional de las Culturas de Occidente   MUSEUM

(Dr Ángel González 21; M$35; ⊗ 9am-6pm Tue-Sat) Some original carbon illustrations and lithographs of José Clemente Orozco – the famous Mexican muralist born in Guzmán – are displayed at the small Museo Regional de las Culturas de Occidente. It's also a good place to brush up on your history of western Jalisco.

🛏 Sleeping

There are numerous hotels surrounding the bustling plaza.

Tlayolan Hotel   HOTEL $$
(☑ 341-412-33-17; Javier Mina 35; d M$680) Tlayolan Hotel is two minutes away from the plaza. It has a gamut of rooms from plain and cheap to smart and more expensive, so take a look at both before you decide.

ℹ Information

Tourist Office (☑ 341-575-25-27; Colón 63; ⊙ 8:30am-3pm Mon-Fri) The tourist office is in the government building on Ciudad Guzmán's plaza. It can help with planning and booking an ascent of the Volcán Nevado de Colima.

ℹ Getting There & Away

Ciudad Guzmán's modern bus terminal is about 3km west of the plaza near the entrance to the city from the Guadalajara–Colima highway. Hop on bus 6 (M$5) to get there and back. Destinations include Guadalajara (M$173, two hours), Colima (M$110, one to two hours), Tapalpa (M$77, two hours), Mazamitla (M$107, 2½ hours) and Zapotitlán, which passes 2km from El Fresnito (M$12, 15 minutes), the closest village to Volcán Nevado de Colima. An alternative way to reach El Fresnito is by taking the 1C *urbano* (urban bus) from the Los Mones crossroad in Ciudad Guzmán (M$6, 20 minutes).

INLAND COLIMA STATE

The tiny but ecologically rich and diverse state of Colima (5191 sq km) connects lofty volcanoes in its arid northern highlands to idyllic turquoise lagoons near the hot and humid Pacific coast.

Inland Colima should become Mexico's next great adventure hub. The famous volcanoes in the north – the active, constantly steaming but inaccessible Volcán de Fuego (3820m) and the extinct, snowcapped Volcán Nevado de Colima (4240m) – remain the big draws, but the Reserva de la Biosfera Sierra de Manantlán is a jungle-and-limestone playground in waiting, with single-track mountain biking, exceptional hiking and canyons that see a few canyoneers abseiling, leaping into crystalline streams and bathing in the magical El Salto Falls. Tourism infra-

structure hasn't caught up to the area's potential yet, so come now.

History

Pre-Hispanic Colima was remote from the major ancient cultures of Mexico. Seaborne contacts with more distant lands might have been more important: legend says one king of Colima, Ix, had regular treasure-bearing visitors from China. Eventually, northern tribes moved in. The Otomí settled here from about AD 250 to 750, followed by the Toltecs, who flourished between 900 and 1154, and the Chichimecs from 1154 to 1428.

All of them left behind exceptional pottery, which has been found in more than 250 sites, mainly tombs, dating from about 200 BC to AD 800. The pottery includes a variety of comical and expressive figures. The most famous are the plump, hairless dogs known as xoloitzcuintles.

Two Spanish expeditions were defeated and turned back by the Chichimecs before Gonzalo de Sandoval, one of Cortés' lieutenants, conquered them in 1523. That year he founded the town of Colima, the third Spanish settlement in Nueva España, after Veracruz and Mexico City. In 1527 the town moved to its present site from its original lowland location near Tecomán.

Colima

☑ 312 / POP 140,000 / ELEV 550M

Colima is a laid-back city with blooming subtropical gardens, fine public plazas, a pleasant touch of moisture in the air and the warmest weather in the western central highlands. The city's university attracts students from around the world, while its growing tourism potential derived from nearby canyons, forests and mountains brings in a small but growing number of visitors.

The billowing volcano you see on clear days, Volcán de Fuego – visible 30km to the north – continues to rumble and shake, and the city has been hit by several major quakes over the centuries (the last in January 2003). It's no wonder that Colima has few colonial buildings, despite having been the first Spanish city in western Mexico.

◉ Sights

Cathedral   CATHEDRAL
(Reforma 21) Light floods the cathedral from the dome windows of this would-be relic on the east side of Plaza Principal. It has been

Colima

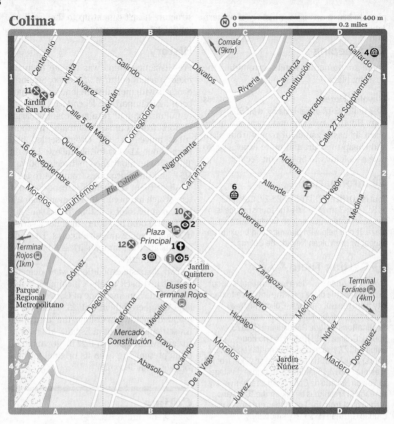

N | 0 — 400 m
0 — 0.2 miles

Comala (9km)

Gallardo **4** 🏛

Jardín de San José **11** ❌ 🍴 **9**

Río Colima

Terminal Rojos (1km)

6 🏛

7 🛏

10 ❌
8 🛏 ⊙ **2**

Plaza Principal
12 ❌ **1** ℹ
3 🏛 ℹ ⊙ **5**
Jardín Quintero

Buses to Terminal Rojos 🚌

Parque Regional Metropolitano

Mercado Constitución

Terminal Foránea (4km)

Jardín Núñez

Colima

⊙ Sights

1 Cathedral	B3
2 La Artería	B3
3 Museo Regional de Historia de Colima	B3
4 Museo Universitario de Artes Populares	D1
5 Palacio de Gobierno	B3
6 Pinacoteca Universitaria Alfonso Michel	C2

🛏 Sleeping

7 Hotel Aldama	D2
8 Hotel Ceballos	B3

❌ Eating

9 ¡Ah Qué Nanishe!	A1
10 1800	B2
11 El Charco de la Higuera	A1
12 El Trebol	B3

rebuilt several times since the Spanish first erected a cathedral here in 1527, most recently after the 1941 earthquake, so it's too new to offer old-world soul, but it remains a focal point of the community.

Palacio de Gobierno BUILDING
(Reforma; ⊙10am-6pm Tue-Sun) FREE Local artist Jorge Chávez Carrillo painted the stairway murals in the Palacio de Gobierno to celebrate the 200th birthday of independence hero Miguel Hidalgo, who was once parish priest of Colima. The murals honor freedom fighters, the indigenous roots and the land of Mexico.

There's a great collection of pottery in the museum, including some from 1500 BC.

La Artería ARTS CENTER
(☎312-312-27-06; Constitución 39; ⊙8am-3pm & 5-11pm) FREE A wonderfully disheveled art collective that showcases anything that's new, innovative and probing in Colima. The inner courtyard with its performance

space is surrounded by a small craft shop, a nano-brewery, a cafe and a gallery. Its varied calendar of events includes art exhibitions, alternative theater, indie music and even events concerned with indigenous rights. But the best events are the spontaneous ones.

Museo Regional de Historia de Colima
MUSEUM

(☎ 312-312-92-28; Portal Morelos 1; M$46; ⊙9am-6pm Tue-Sat, 5-8pm Sun) This excellent museum has an extensive collection of well-labeled artifacts spanning the region's history, from pottery to conquistadors' armor to a 19th-century horse-drawn carriage. Don't miss the ceramic xoloitzcuintles (Colima dogs) or the walk-through mock tomb excavation.

Museo Universitario de Artes Populares
MUSEUM

(cnr Barreda & Gallardo; adult/child & student M$20/10, Sun free; ⊙10am-2pm & 5-8pm Tue-Sat, 10am-1pm Sun) A pulpit for folk art including a slightly faded collection of masks, *mojigangas* (giant puppets), musical instruments, baskets, and wood and ceramic sculpture from every state in Mexico.

Pinacoteca Universitaria Alfonso Michel
GALLERY

(Guerrero 35; ⊙10am-2pm & 5-8pm Tue-Sat, 10am-1pm Sun) FREE The modern entrance to this gallery leads into a 19th-century courtyard surrounded by four halls filled with surrealist art. Included are a permanent collection of paintings by Colima's Alfonso Michel – whose work has been described as a cross between Picasso and Dalí – as well as works by José Luis Cuevas and Francisco Toledo.

La Campana
ARCHAEOLOGICAL SITE

(☎ 312-313-49-46; Av Tecnológico; M$42; ⊙9am-6pm Tue-Sun) The low, pyramid-like structures at this modest archaeological site date from as early as 1500 BC. They have been excavated and restored, along with a small tomb and a ball court (unusual in western Mexico). The structures are oriented due north toward Volcán de Fuego, which makes an impressive backdrop on clear days.

It's about 5km north of Colima city and easily accessible by buses 7 and 22; taxis cost M$45. A word of warning: wear good shoes and socks because there are lots of fire ants.

🛏 Sleeping

Hotel Aldama
HOTEL $

(☎ 312-330-73-07; Aldama 134; s/d M$350/463; ❄🐾) A five-minute walk from the central

plaza, this budget hotel kicks way above its weight with rooms that, though small, have some value-raising touches: think flowers strewn across the bed sheets, wrought-iron and heavy wooden furnishings, and desks to work at. However, there's little soundproofing.

★Casa Alvarada
B&B $$

(☎ 312-315-52-29; www.casaalvarada.com; Obregón 105; d incl breakfast M$700-850; 🅿❄🐾) Not actually in Colima at all but in the outrageously pretty whitewash village of Comala, 9km northwest of Colima, Casa Alvarada is a homey B&B run by an English-speaking husband-and-wife team. Rooms are decorated with local folk art, breakfasts are family-style, and the patio has a sumptuous hammock bed.

The owners run a whole array of highly recommended local tours, including to the volcanoes, jungle trekking, kayaking, and village and coffee-estate tours.

Hotel Ceballos
HOTEL $$

(☎ 312-316-01-00; www.hotelceballos.com; Portal Medellín 12; r from M$950; 🅿❄@🐾🏊) A typical Mexican plaza hotel with atmospheric portal-fronted communal areas (including a cafe-restaurant) backed by slightly less inspiring rooms. The property is owned by Best Western; some of the better rooms have high ceilings with crown moldings and balconies that overlook Plaza Principal. There's a small gym and tiny rooftop plunge pool, too.

🍽 Eating & Drinking

Many small restaurants around Plaza Principal offer decent fare and are good places for people-watching on weekends.

El Trebol
MEXICAN $

(☎ 312-312-29-00; Degollado 59; mains M$25-65; ⊙8am-11pm Sun-Fri) A small family restaurant that makes a great spot for breakfast. The scent of freshly squeezed orange juice perfumes the dining room, and diners devour *huevos a la mexicana* (eggs scrambled with green pepper, onion and tomatoes, representing the three colors of the Mexican flag) and scrambles with ham, bacon and chorizo.

1800
INTERNATIONAL $

(Calle 5 de Mayo No 15; mains from M$40; ⊙7pm-2am Tue-Sun) This hip restaurant lounge attracts a late-coming crowd of uni students for snacks, drinks and, on Thursday nights, live music from around the globe. The menu takes in pizza, sushi, burritos and more, but most people come here to drink and meet friends.

★ El Charco de la Higuera MEXICAN **$$**

(☑ 312-313-01-92; Jardín de San José, cnr Calle 5 de Mayo; mains M$100-150; ⊙8am-midnight) The best salt-of-the-earth restaurant in Colima doubles as a modest museum to local mask-making (check the displays of wooden masks in glass cases) and offers typical Colima cuisine. The combined *antojitos* (Mexican snacks) plate is a Colimese smorgasbord. The adventurous should try the *pepena* (cow's heart and intestines!) with hot tortillas. Slightly less exotic are the *chilaquiles*.

¡Ah Qué Nanishe! MEXICAN **$$**

(☑ 312-314-21-97; Calle 5 de Mayo 267; mains M$95-115; ⊙noon-11pm Tue-Sun) The name of this restaurant means 'How delicious!' and the rich, chocolatey, but not overwhelming *mole* (sauce) is superb. Other don't-miss Oaxacan delicacies that are available include *chiles rellenos* (stuffed chilis) or, if you're lucky, *chapulines* (crunchy fried grasshoppers). Half orders of many mains are available for 70% of the full price, making for great value.

ℹ Information

State Tourist Office (☑ 312-312-43-60; www.colimatienemagia.com.mx; Palacio de Gobierno; ⊙8am-8pm Mon-Fri, to 2pm Sat) Handily positioned in the main plaza.

ℹ Getting There & Around

Colima's **airport** (☑ 312-314-41-60; Av Lic Carlos de la Madrid Bejar) is near Cuauhtémoc, 12km northeast of the city center off the highway to Guadalajara (taxis M$140). **Aeromar** (☑ 312-313-13-40; www.aeromar.com.mx; airport) flies to Mexico City three times a day.

Colima has two bus terminals. The long-distance terminal is **Terminal Foránea** (Carretera 54), 4km east of the city center at the junction of Avenida Niños Héroes and the city's eastern bypass. There's a left-luggage facility. To reach downtown, hop on a Ruta 4 or 5 bus. For the return trip catch the same buses on Calle 5 de

Mayo or Zaragoza. There's a prepay taxi booth at the terminal and the fare to downtown is M$28.

Colima's second bus terminal (serving local towns) is **Terminal Rojos** (Bosque de Cedros), about 2km west of Plaza Principal. Ruta 4 or 6 buses run to Colima's center from this terminal. To get back here, take any bus marked 'Rojos' going north on Morelos.

Taxi fares within town cost M$10 to M$25.

Around Colima

The outlying villages and countryside around Colima are gorgeous and demand exploration. In particular don't miss **Comala** (p611), a 10-minute drive northwest of town, and a picture-perfect village. You can visit most worthy destinations on day trips or by public transportation, but a rental car is liberating.

Parque Nacional Volcán Nevado de Colima

This national park, straddling the Colima–Jalisco border, includes two dramatic volcanoes: the still-active Volcán de Fuego and the inactive Volcán Nevado de Colima. Ciudad Guzmán is the closest city but, if you have a car and set off early, Colima is a more pleasant base. Contact the state tourist office in Colima for a list of operators offering trips to climb Volcán Nevado de Colima. It can be difficult to find a guide on the fly if you only have a few days, so it's best to organize things in advance.

VOLCÁN DE FUEGO

Overlooking Colima, 30km north of the city, is steaming Volcán de Fuego (3820m), Mexico's most active volcano. It has erupted dozens of times in the past four centuries, with a big eruption about every 70 years. In June 2005 a large explosion sent ash 4.8km into the sky, all the way to Colima. To hike in the vicinity of the volcano, it is best to pre-organize through a reputable agency. Try **Corazón de**

BUSES FROM COLIMA

DESTINATION	FARE (M$)	DURATION (HR)	FREQUENCY (DAILY)
Ciudad Guzmán	110	1-2	5
Guadalajara	268	3	hourly
Manzanillo	116	2	half-hourly
Mexico City (Terminal Norte)	920	10	10
Morelia	513	2	3
Uruapan	469	6	1

COMALA

If you've made it as far as Colima, do not miss the gloriously idiosyncratic town of Comala, 10km to the north, famous for its *ponche* (liquor), *tuba* (fermented drink made from palm-tree sap), sweet bread and hand-carved wooden masks. Characterized by the kind of generic white colonial edifices that wouldn't look out of place in a *pueblos blanco* in Andalucia, Comala's centerpiece is its main plaza, one of the region's most beguiling, replete with tuba salespeople, shoe-shiners, strolling mariachis and a plethora of restaurants renowned for their free snacks (*botanas*) served when you order a drink. If you haven't got time to play eeny meeny miny moe, opt for **Don Comalón** (www.doncomalon.com; Progreso 5; drink & botana M$20; ⊙noon-7pm) and pray the staff bring you a crispy *tostada* topped with ceviche.

Comala's obligatory sight is the **Ex-Hacienda Nogueras**, the former home of Mexican artist and Renaissance man, Alejandro Rangel Hidalgo (1923–2000). The beautiful old hacienda is now owned by Colima University, which has curated a **museum** (☑312-315-60-28; M$30; ⊙10am-6pm Tue-Sun) to the man's life and art. Inside, you'll see his extensive pre-Hispanic ceramics collection and the distinctive Christmas cards for which he is remembered. The house also contains a chapel and the ruins of an old sugar factory. The grounds – including a botanical garden – are lush.

Colima Tours (☑312-314-08-96; www.corazondecolimatours.com) based out of Colima.

VOLCÁN NEVADO DE COLIMA

Nevado de Colima (4240m) is accessible on foot most of the year. Patches of pine forest cover its shoulders, while alpine desert takes over at the highest altitudes. Wildlife includes deer, wild boar, coyote and even a few pumas.

The best months for climbing are the dry months of December through May. But temperatures from December to February often dip below 0°C (32°F) and snow does regularly fall on the upper slopes – *nevado* means 'snow-covered.' Weather changes fast here and lightning strikes the peak in stormy weather, so make sure you keep an eye on the clouds. The park's October to March hours are 6am to 6pm. The summer rainy season is from July to September, when park hours are longer.

To get here on your own from Ciudad Guzmán, take the bus to El Fresnito (M$12), where you can try to hire a driver to take you the remaining 20km or so up a rough road to the trailhead at La Joya/Puerto Las Cruces (3500m). You'll pass the park entrance on the way, where you'll pay a M$30 entry fee. An alternative is to walk up from El Fresnito – a much longer and tougher proposition. If you elect to walk, stay on the bus as it covers some of the distance beyond the town.

Walkers will need camping gear and food (and some very warm clothes), because it's impossible to walk there and back in a day.

Allow six hours to get to the parking at La Joya/Puerto Las Cruces and then another two to three hours from there to the summit and about five hours all the way back down again. You can camp at La Joya/Puerto Las Cruces a few kilometers beyond the park gates. If you plan to hitchhike up, try coming on a Saturday or Sunday, when there is a steady stream of visitors; weekdays can be very quiet. Hitchhiking is never entirely safe, and we don't recommend it; know that you'll be taking a small but potentially serious risk.

The hike to the summit from La Joya is around 9km and ascends 700m. Some prefer to just hike to the *micro-ondas* (radio antennae) about 90 minutes by foot from the end of the road at La Joya/Puerto Las Cruces. If you want to bag the peak, you'll need another 90 minutes, and while the peak is easy to see, you shouldn't go alone. There are many trails up and back and it's very easy to get lost or led to areas with hazardous footing. You'll save a lot of time and bother going with a guide. Group prices start at around M$1200 per person including transportation from Ciudad Guzmán and entry fees.

The following guides are recommended:

Admire Mexico (☑312-314-54-54; www.admiremexicotours.com; Guillermo Prieto 113, Comala) A highly regarded agency based out of Casa Alvarada in Comala.

Nevado de Colima Tours (☑341-120-76-17; http://nevadodecolimatours.blogspot.mx) A reliable and experienced agency operating out of Ciudad Guzmán.

Driving up this volcano on the relatively good dirt road means that you'll be ascending to a high altitude very quickly. If you feel lightheaded or dizzy, you may be suffering from altitude sickness. Descend as quickly as possible, as this condition can be fatal.

INLAND MICHOACÁN

Pre-Hispanic traditions and colonial-era architecture meet in Michoacán to dramatic effect. The state is home to three of Mexico's coolest, most under-the-radar cities: the adobe-and-cobblestone town of Pátzcuaro, where Purépecha women sell *tamales* in the shadow of 16th-century churches; the lush agricultural city of Uruapan, gateway to the mythic Paricutín volcano; and the vibrant colonial city of Morelia, with ancient cathedrals and aqueducts built from rosy pink stone.

Michoacán is also gaining renown as a crafts capital – the Purépecha artisans of the state's Cordillera Neovolcánica highlands create wonderful masks, pottery, straw art and stringed instruments, and put on some of the country's best Día de Muertos (Day of the Dead) celebrations. Rich in natural treasures, Michoacán has one of the world's true 'life-list'-caliber sights: the annual butterfly migration to the rugged Reserva Mariposa Monarca (Monarch Butterfly Reserve), where millions of mating monarchs cover the grass and trees in a shimmering Aladdin's carpet.

Morelia

📲 443 / POP 600,000 / ELEV 1920M

The state capital of Michoacán and its most dynamic and beautiful city, Morelia is an increasingly popular destination, and rightly so: the colonial heart of the city is so well preserved that it was declared a Unesco World Heritage site in 1991, and its cathedral is not just gorgeous, it's inspirational.

Morelia, founded in 1541, was one of the first Spanish cities in Nueva España. The first viceroy, Antonio de Mendoza, named it Valladolid after the Spanish city and he encouraged Spanish nobility to move here with their families. In 1828, after Nueva España had become the Republic of Mexico, the city was renamed Morelia in honor of local hero José María Morelos y Pavón, a key figure in Mexico's independence.

Elegant 16th- and 17th-century stone buildings, baroque facades and archways line the narrow downtown streets, and are home to museums, hotels, restaurants, *chocolaterías* (chocolate shops), sidewalk cafes, a popular university and cheap-and-inviting *taquerías* (taco stalls). There are free public concerts, frequent art installations, and yet so few foreign tourists. Those who do come often extend their stay and enroll in classes to learn how to cook and speak Spanish. Word may soon leak out, but, for the moment, Morelia is like an Oaxaca waiting to happen.

◉ Sights

★ **Cathedral**　　　　　　　　　CATHEDRAL
(Plaza de Armas; ⊘ 8am-10pm) Getting bored of Mexican churches? Here's one to knock you out of your reverie! Morelia's beautiful cathedral (unforgettable when it's lit up at night) dominates the city where it sits side-on to (rather than facing) the central plaza. It took more than a century to build (1640–1744), which explains its potpourri of styles: the twin 70m-high towers, for instance, have classical Herreresque bases, baroque midsections and multicolumned neoclassical tops.

Inside, much of the baroque relief work was replaced in the 19th century with neoclassical pieces. Fortunately, one of the cathedral's interior highlights was preserved: a sculpture of the Señor de la Sacristía made from dried corn paste and topped with a gold crown from 16th-century Spanish king Felipe II. It also has a working organ with 4600 pipes. Occasional organ recitals take place – a beautiful time to be in the cathedral.

Museo del Estado　　　　　　　MUSEUM
(📲 443-313-06-29; Prieto 176; ⊘ 9am-3pm & 4-8pm Mon-Fri, 10am-6pm Sat & Sun) FREE This free museum of Michoacano history is a slightly dusty and haphazard affair, but packs in plenty of information from prehistoric times to first contact with the conquistadors. Pre-Hispanic arrowheads, ceramic figures, bone jewelry and a shimmering quartz skull can be found downstairs. Upstairs are first-person accounts of how force-fed religion coupled with systematic agricultural and economic development tamed the region's indigenous soul. Labeling is in Spanish only.

Museo Regional Michoacano　　　MUSEUM
(📲 443-312-04-07; Allende 305, cnr Abasolo; M$47, Sun free; ⊘ 9am-4:45pm Tue-Sun) Housed in a late-18th-century baroque palace and the recipient of a recent renovation, this museum keeps an impressive array of pre-Hispanic artifacts, colonial art and relics, including one

of the carved stone coyotes from Ihuatzio. There's also a spectacular scarlet Alfredo Zalce mural, *Cuauhtémoc y la Historia,* on the stairway. Labeling is in Spanish only.

Palacio Clavijero   MUSEUM
(Galeana; ⊙10am-6pm Tue-Sun) **FREE** From 1660 to 1767 the Palacio Clavijero, with its magnificently minimalist main patio, imposing colonnades and pink stonework, was home to the Jesuit school of St Francis Xavier. Today the building houses exhibition spaces showing off high-quality displays of contemporary art, photography and other creative media.

★ Museo Casa de Morelos   MUSEUM
(Morelos House Museum; ☑ 443-313-26-51; Av Morelos Sur 323; M$39, Sun free; ⊙9am-4:45pm Tue-Sun) Arguably Morelia's best museum resides in the former house of independece hero, José María Morelos y Pavón, who bought the Spanish-style mansion on the corner of Avenida Morelos and Soto y Saldaña in 1801. Well-laid-out displays have good information panels in both Spanish and English and cover Morelos' life, military campaigns and the trajectory of the independence movement thereafter. Look out for his death mask.

Fuente Las Tarascas   FOUNTAIN
The centerpiece of Plaza Villalongín, this iconic fountain erupts from a fruit tray held by three beautiful, topless Tarascan women. The original vanished mysteriously in 1940 and this reproduction was installed in the 1960s.

El Acueducto   AQUEDUCT
Morelia's impressively preserved aqueduct runs for several kilometers along Avenida Acueducto and bends around Plaza Villalongín. It was built between 1785 and 1788 to meet the city's growing water needs. Its 253 arches are memorable when illuminated at night.

Palacio de Justicia   BUILDING
(Plaza de Armas; ⊙10am-2pm & 5-7:30pm Mon-Sat) **FREE** Facing the leafy expanse of Plaza de Armas, the Palacio de Justicia was built between 1682 and 1695 to serve as the city hall. Its facade blends French and baroque styles, with stairwell art in the courtyard. An Agustín Cárdenas mural portrays Morelos in action. The on-site **museum** has revolving exhibitions; a detailed exposé of Mexico's Himno Nacional (national anthem) was showing at our last visit.

Palacio de Gobierno   BUILDING
(Av Madero Oriente) The 17th-century palace, originally a seminary and now state govern-

---

DON'T MISS

THE PERFECT LIBRARY

Town councils of the world take note: if you're going to build a public library (which you should), then please make it look like the **Biblioteca Pública de la Universidad Michoacana** (☑ 443-312-57-25; Jardín Igangio Altamirano, cnr Av Madero Poniente & Nigromante; ⊙8am-8pm Mon-Fri). Installed inside the magnificent 16th-century **Ex-Templo de la Compañía de Jesús**, the shelves of the city's breathtaking university library rise up toward the domed ceilings and are crammed from head to toe with thousands (22,901 to be exact) of dusty, antique books recounting the histories of kings and queens, Spain, Europe and the colonies.

---

ment offices, has a simple baroque facade. Its soaring historical murals inside are, arguably, the city's best. The murals were executed in 1961–62 and are the magnum opus of Pátzcuaro-born painter, Alfredo Zalce (1908–2003).

Museo Casa Natal de Morelos   MUSEUM
(Morelos Birthplace Museum; ☑ 443-312-27-93; Corregidora 113; ⊙9am-8pm Mon-Fri, to 7pm Sat & Sun) **FREE** José María Morelos y Pavón, one of the most important heroes in Mexico's struggle for independence, is king in Morelia – after all, the entire city is named after him. He was born in this house on the corner of Calles Corregidora and García Obeso, on September 30, 1765. Now home to a museum in his honor, the collection of old photos and documents is poignant, but not as comprehensive as the better-curated Museo Casa de Morelos.

An eternal torch burns next to the exact spot where he was born.

Colegio de San Nicolás   BUILDING
(cnr Av Madero Poniente & Nigromante; ⊙8am-8pm Mon-Sat) **FREE** Morelos studied here, one block west of the plaza. While not another Morelos museum, it has become a foundation for the Universidad Michoacana. Upstairs, the **Sala de Melchor Ocampo** is a memorial to another Mexican hero, a reformer-governor of Michoacán. Preserved inside is Ocampo's library and a copy of the document he signed donating it to the college, just before he was executed by a conservative firing squad on June 3, 1861.

WESTERN CENTRAL HIGHLANDS MORELIA

Morelia

Plaza Morelos
PLAZA

This irregular, conspicuously vacant plaza surrounds the **Estatua Ecuestre al Patriota Morelos**, a majestic statue of Morelos on horseback, sculpted by Italian artist Giuseppe Ingillieri between 1910 and 1913.

Running from here to the Fuente Las Tarascas is the shaded and cobbled **Calzada Fray Antonio de San Miguel**, a wide, romantic pedestrian promenade framed by exquisite old buildings. Branching off its west end, narrow **Callejón del Romance** (Romance Alley) is all pink stone, trailing vines and cavorting couples. There are a couple of good restaurants.

Santuario de Guadalupe
CHURCH

(Av Vasco) A standard baroque structure on the outside dating from 1708 to 1716, this hushed sanctuary to Mexico's patron saint is a different story within. Get ready for a glistening profusion of pink, blue and gold, gold, gold! Indeed, there's so much color inside, it feels a little like an ornate Hindu temple.

Springing out of all this elaboration are a series of huge paintings depicting the conversion of the indiginous peoples to Christianity. They show scenes such as sacrifical victims about to be beheaded before being saved by the honest, God-fearing folk of Spain. Quite.

Beside the church, the much less splashy **Ex-Convento de San Diego** (Plaza Morelos) was built in 1761 as a monastery and now houses the law school of the Universidad Michoacana.

Bosque Cuauhtémoc
PARK

Morelia's largest park is a handsome affair favored by families because of its shady trees, amusement park and museums. On its grounds are two small museums. Housed in a 19th-century building, the **Museo de Arte Contemporáneo Alfredo Zalce** (☑443-312-54-04; Av Acueducto 18; ☉10am-8pm Mon-Fri, to 6pm Sat & Sun) **FREE** has temporary exhibitions of contemporary art – some better

615

than others. The quirky **Museo de Historia Natural** (☑443-312-00-44; Ventura Puente 23; ⊙10am-6pm) **FREE**, on the east side of the park, displays stuffed, dissected and skeletal animals and human fetuses.

📚 Courses

Few foreigners and plenty of culture make Morelia an exceptional place to learn how to cook Mexican, dance salsa and speak Spanish. Ask for a discount if taking a course for more than two weeks.

Baden-Powell Institute   LANGUAGE COURSE
(☑443-312-20-02; www.baden-powell.com; Antonio Alzate 569; private lessons per hour from US$18, group lessons per week from US$180) The small, well-run and affordable Baden-Powell Institute offers courses in Spanish language, as well as Mexican politics, cooking, culture, guitar and salsa dancing. It books homestays (per day US$27) for students.

Centro Cultural de Lenguas   LANGUAGE COURSE
(☑443-312-05-89; www.ccl.com.mx; Av Madero Oriente 560; group/private lessons per week US$180/340) Offers Spanish-language classes. For those wanting more spontaneity, there is also an hourly rate of US$19. Tours and classes can also be arranged for Mexican music, dance and cooking (minimum three people).

🕵 Tours

The tourist office gives daily city tours at 10am or 4pm. For tours outside the city, ask the tourist office for recommendations.

Mexico Cooks!   CULINARY
(www.mexicocooks.typepad.com) US-born Cristina Potters, a true expert on Mexican cuisine, gives wonderful personalized foodie tours of Morelia (and Guadalajara), despite now being based in Mexico City. Contact her in advance to arrange a tour of the city.

Morelia

◉ Top Sights
1 Cathedral	C2
2 Museo Casa de Morelos	D3

◉ Sights
3 Biblioteca Pública de la Universidad Michoacana	B2
4 Bosque Cuauhtémoc	G4
5 Colegio de San Nicolás	B2
6 El Acueducto	G3
7 Estatua Ecuestre al Patriota Morelos	H3
8 Ex-Convento de San Diego	H3
9 Fuente Las Tarascas	G2
10 Museo Casa Natal de Morelos	C3
11 Museo de Arte Contemporáneo Alfredo Zalce	H3
12 Museo de Historia Natural	H4
13 Museo del Dulce	E2
14 Museo del Estado	C1
15 Museo Regional Michoacano	C2
16 Palacio Clavijero	B2
17 Palacio de Gobierno	C2
18 Palacio de Justicia	C2
19 Plaza Morelos	H3
20 Santuario de Guadalupe	H3

◔ Activities, Courses & Tours
21 Baden-Powell Institute	E3
22 Centro Cultural de Lenguas	E2

◉ Sleeping
23 Cantera Diez	C2
24 Casona Rosa	B3
25 Hotel Casa del Anticuario	B3
26 Hotel Casino	C2
27 Hotel de la Soledad	C2
28 Hotel Valladolid	F2
29 Hotel Virrey de Mendoza	C2
30 Mansión Real Morelia	D2
31 Only Backpackers Morelia	F2

◆ Eating
32 Chango Restaurante	F2
33 Fonda Las Mercedes	B2
34 Fonda Marceva	C3
35 Gaspachos La Cerrada	C3
36 La Cocina de Licha	A3
37 Los Mirasoles	B2
38 Onix	C2
39 Peltre Gastrocafé-Galería	C1
40 Plaza San Agustín	C3
41 Pulcinella	B2
Restaurante Lu	(see 26)

◉ Drinking & Nightlife
Café del Teatro	(see 47)
42 Casa de la Salsa	H3
43 Los 50s Bar	B2

◉ Entertainment
44 Casa de la Cultura	D1
45 Cinépolis	B1
46 Conservatorio de las Rosas	C1
47 Teatro Ocampo	C2

◉ Shopping
48 Casa de las Artesanías	E3
49 Mercado de Dulces	B2

✦ Festivals & Events

In addition to the usual Mexican celebrations, Morelia has many other annual festivals.

Feria de Morelia   CULTURAL
Morelia's biggest fair, running for three weeks in late April through early May, hosts exhibits of handicrafts, agriculture and livestock, plus regional dances, bullfights and fiestas. May 18 is the city's founding date (1541) and is celebrated with a fireworks show.

Festival Internacional de Cine de Morelia   FILM
(www.moreliafilmfest.com) This major international exhibition for Mexico's vibrant film industry brings a week of parties and star sightings each October.

Festival Internacional de Música   MUSIC
(www.festivalmorelia.com) The international classical-music festival occurs for two weeks in mid-November with orchestras, choirs and quartets giving concerts in churches, plazas and theaters around town.

Día de la Virgen de Guadalupe   RELIGIOUS
The Day of the Virgin of Guadalupe is celebrated on December 12 at the Ex-Convento de San Diego; in the preceding weeks a carnival erupts on Calzada Fray Antonio de San Miguel.

🛏 Sleeping

There are a lot of hotels in Morelia and not so many tourists, so competition is fierce. Except during rare busy periods, you can be almost certain that all accommodations, apart from the very cheapest hostels, will offer significant discounts of rack rates.

Only Backpackers Morelia   HOSTEL $
(☎443-425-42-09; Serdán 654; dm M$150; @ ☎) Not strictly the only backpacker hostel in Morelia, but probably the best of a mediocre bunch. This one has one private room along

with eight-bed dorms, a kitchen, and two quiet courtyards in a traditional Morelian abode. The owners are friendly and the fruit-based breakfasts fresh and filling.

Hotel Valladolid   HOTEL $

(☑ 443-312-45-62; Bartolomé de las Casas 418; s/d M$450/550; ❄ 🛜) Putting in a solid perfor-mance in Morelia's somewhat scant budget end of the market, the Valladolid delivers the basics: clean, no-frills, relatively modern rooms with flat-screen TVs and wi-fi. It lacks the embellishments of some of Morelia's more historic establishments, but if it's just a crash pad you're after, it'll do the trick.

Hotel Casino   HOTEL $$

(☑ 443-313-13-28; www.hotelcasino.com.mx; Portal Hidalgo 229; r from M$1067; P @ 🛜) Overlooking Plaza de Armas and the cathedral, the Casi-no's frontage hums with the addictive energy of Mexican street life. The rooms themselves are less interesting for a building as stately as this, but there are other bonuses: the superb location, professional service and incompara-ble Restaurante Lu, which furnishes the lobby.

Hotel Casa del Anticuario   HOTEL $$

(☑ 443-333-25-21;   www.hotelcasadelanticuario.com; Galeana 319; s/d M$650/750; 🛜) This lus-cious yellow guesthouse has rooms with ex-posed stone walls and wooden roof beams, very helpful staff, a nice central courtyard bedecked with vintage radios and grama-phones, and excellent wi-fi reception. In fact, it has everything required to give hotels twice its price a serious run for their money.

Do, however, ask for a room right at the back away from the noisy road.

Casona Rosa   GUESTHOUSE $$

(☑ 443-312-31-27; www.casonarosa.com; Galeana 274; r M$780-1500; @ 🛜) A quintessentially Mexican-flavored guesthouse with five huge rooms configured around a shared patio and dining room where you'll be served break-fast. With its Frida Kahlo meets Day of the Dead decor, the Rosa has its fans, though the profusion of knickknacks can seem a bit clutter-ridden for others.

★ Hotel de la Soledad   HISTORIC HOTEL $$$

(☑ 443-312-18-88; www.hsoledad.com; Zarago-za 90; r/ste incl breakfast from M$1770/2800; P ❄ @ 🛜) Wow! Bougainvillea flowers tumble down stone arches, fountains tinkle, classical music wafts on the breeze and palm trees reach for the skies – and that's all just in the central courtyard. The rooms them-selves all differ, but expect showers made from ancient stone arches, translucent stone basins, hand-carved wooden bedheads and a general sense of utter class.

Cantera Diez   BOUTIQUE HOTEL $$$

(☑ 443-312-54-19; www.canteradiezhotel.com; Juá-rez 63; r from M$2860; P ❄ 🛜) Facing the ca-thedral is Morelia's slickest boutique hotel. The 11 rooms are all suites, which range from spacious to palatial, all with dark-wood floors, stylish modern furnishings and sump-tuous bathrooms you could throw parties in.

Hotel Virrey de Mendoza   HISTORIC HOTEL $$$

(☑ 443-312-00-45; www.hotelvirrey.com; Av Madero Poniente 310; r from M$1600; P ❄ @ 🛜) The lob-by is drop-dead gorgeous with a spectacular stained-glass atrium that gives the stained-glass windows of the cathedral a run for their money. Rooms have an aging grace with old, wood floors and high ceilings – ask for one with plenty of windows, as some can be dark.

The restaurant does Morelia's swankiest Sunday brunch (mains average M$100), complete with made-to-order omelettes, platters of fresh tropical fruits and a dessert table with a flowing chocolate fountain.

Mansión Real Morelia   BOUTIQUE HOTEL $$$

(☑ 443-232-02-46; www.mansionrealmorelia.com; Av Madero Oriente 94; r from M$1400; ❄ @ 🛜) The rooms here might be small but they are crammed with pomp and a sense of royalty, including ceiling-scraping ornate bedheads and quality bathrooms and mattresses (with a ridiculous amount of pillows piled onto them). There's also a lovely courtyard bar and restaurant. Front-facing rooms suffer from road noise despite the soundproofing.

✖ Eating

Morelia enjoys some superb eating options to suit all budgets. Street food can be harder to find, but your searching will be well rewarded.

La Cocina de Licha   MEXICAN $

(www.facebook.com/la-cocina-de-licha-288382 117939252; Corregidora 669; set meals M$40; ⊙ 1-5pm) One of Morelia's best deals is this superfriendly place, which serves up what it undersells as *cocina económica* (literally 'economic cuisine') to a crowd of loyal locals. The daily changing set meal includes starter, main course and drink and is displayed on its Facebook page.

There's no sign and if you were to go past outside the lunchtime period you wouldn't know the place exists.

SWEETS IN MORELIA

Dulces morelianos – delicious sweets made with ingredients such as fruit, nuts, milk and sugar – are famous throughout the region. They're showcased at Morelia's Mercado de Dulces and at **Museo del Dulce** (Av Madero Oriente 440; M$20; ☉10am-8pm). This old-fashioned *chocolatería* is stacked with truffles, preserves, candied nuts and sugary chunks of candied peaches and pumpkin, and patrolled by women in starched green uniforms.

Watch for these tasty treats.

➧ *Ate de fruta* – jewel-colored squares or strips of fruit leather, commonly made from guava, mango and quince.

➧ *Cocadas* – chewy-crunchy pyramids of caramelized coconut.

➧ *Frutas cubiertas* – chunks of candied fruits such as squash, fig and pineapple.

➧ *Glorias* – cellophane-wrapped rolls of caramel studded with pecans.

➧ *Jamoncillo* – fudge-like milk sweets sold in rectangles or molded into shapes like walnuts.

➧ *Limón con coco* – candied lime halves stuffed with sweetened shredded coconut.

➧ *Obleas con cajeta* – gooey caramel sandwiched between two thin round wafers.

➧ *Ollitas de tamarindo* – tiny clay pots filled with sweet-salty-tangy tamarind paste.

Fonda Marceva MEXICAN $
(☎443-312-16-66; Abasolo 455; mains M$60-80; ☉9am-6pm Tue-Sun) Specializing in the cuisine of the *tierra caliente* (hot lands) region of Michoacán's southeast, this lovely courtyard restaurant serves a mindblowing *aporreadillo* (breakfast stew of eggs, dried beef and chili) and some of the best *frijoles de olla* (beans slow-cooked in a pot) we've ever tasted.

Plaza San Agustín MEXICAN $
(cnr Abasolo & Corregidora; snacks from M$25; ☉1-11pm) Some good cheap food stalls and lots of tables can be found under the covered arches here.

Gaspachos La Cerrada SALAD BAR $
(Hidalgo 67; gaspachos M$25; ✐) *Gaspacho* – a salad of diced mango, pineapple and jicama drowned in orange and lime juice and dashed with salt, chili sauce and cheese (optional) – is a local delicacy served all over town. But word on the street says this place is the reigning champion.

★**Restaurante Lu** MEXICAN $$
(☎443-313-13-28; www.lucocinamichoacana.mx; Portal Hidalgo 229; mains M$120-180; ☉7:30am-10pm Sun-Thu, to 11pm Fri & Sat) This unassuming restaurant inside Hotel Casino is actually Morelia's most inventive place to dine and one of the best restaurants in the whole region. Talented young chef Lucero Soto Arriaga turns pre-Hispanic ingredients into exquisite gems of *alta cocina,* all beautifully presented. Even the lowly enchilada gets a gourmet makeover.

Chango Restaurante INTERNATIONAL $$
(☎443-312-62-13; www.changorestaurante.com; Sor Juana Inés de la Cruz 129; mains M$115-210; ☉1:45pm-1:30am Wed-Mon) A lovely nook near Morelia's aqueduct, which has splendid service to back up equally splendid food. Seating is spread around various downstairs rooms and an upstairs terrace in a house that styles itself as Mexican art meets art nouveau. The menu is international and subtly experimental.

The gourmet burgers deserve a mention, as does the 'orange' risotto, and the crab and saffron ravioli. Anglophiles will enjoy the banoffee pie for dessert.

Onix INTERNATIONAL, MEXICAN $$
(☎443-317-82-90; www.onix.mx; Portal Hidalgo 261; mains M$120-200; ☉1pm-1am Sun-Thu, to 2am Fri & Sat) All the restaurants around Plaza de Armas are excellent for eavesdropping and people-watching, but some come unstuck with the food. Not Onix, locally famous for its taste-challenging menu that includes such eccentricities as scorpion served with cream cheese, and crocodile.

Less traditional than other city-center abodes, the Onix also turns heads with its seating (check out the seriously avant-garde chairs), perfectly balanced margaritas and hugely varied live music. Service is sharp.

Peltre Gastrocafé-Galería   CAFE $$

(☑ 443-312-68-09; Tapia 319; breakfast M$65-100; ⊙ 8am-11pm) Resting on your laurels in the leafy, music-filled Jardín de las Rosas is a Morelia rite of passage – the university is around the corner and the music conservatory across the road. Of the half-dozen easy-on-the-wallet cafes that line the gardens, this one is arguably the best courtesy of its coffee (home-roasted), solid breakfasts (with free fruit plate) and hip decor.

Pull up a chair and watch the plethora of music students who flop down to tune up, discuss Rachmaninoff concertos, and – occasionally – break into song.

Pulcinella   ITALIAN $$

(Allende 555; mains M$100-200; ⊙ 2-10pm Wed-Fri, 2-11pm Sat, 2-7pm Sun) This respected Italian restaurant is well worth breaking the tortilla and taco monopoly for. Housed in a simply decorated colonial house and run by a charming Italian-Mexican family, Pulcinella's specialty is its pizzas, but there's a full range of pastas too, and fantastic Caesar salads.

★ Los Mirasoles   MEXICAN $$$

(☑ 443-317-57-75; www.losmirasoles.com; Av Madero Poniente 549; mains M$120-300; ⊙ 1-11pm Mon-Sat, to 6pm Sun) Morelian and Michoacán pride oozes out of the kitchen at Los Mirasoles where you'll dine in a fine Unesco-quality house bedecked (among other quirks) with a copy of the Las Tarascas fountain. The food is doused in regional flavors.

Try the *atapakua de huachinango* (fish in a *mole*-like sauce). This was the dish served in Peru during Mexico's bid to have its cuisine listed as an Intangible Cultural Heritage by Unesco (realized in 2010). The wine cellar stocks 250 vintages.

Fonda Las Mercedes   MEXICAN $$$

(☑ 443-312-61-13; Guzmán 47; mains M$150-200; ⊙ 1:30pm-midnight Mon-Sat, noon-8pm Sun) Astonishingly decorated restaurant spread over various rooms in a colonial mansion. The rich decor could pass for a museum with paintings and mirrors in gilded frames, crucifixes, handsome columns and stone cannonball-like spheres. The food is equally upmarket with the kitchen serving four cuts of steak 10 different ways.

🍸 Drinking & Nightlife

Nightlife is more genteel than rowdy, though a few clubs keep the music pumping into the small hours. Around the Jardín de las Ro-

sas are masses of bars with terraces that fizz with life in the early evening. Another hot spot is the area around the Fuente Las Tarascas at the eastern end of the city center. The names of bars and clubs change constantly.

Café del Teatro   CAFE

(Café Galería; cnr Ocampo & Prieto; ⊙ 9am-10pm Mon-Sat, 4-10pm Sun) Even if you're not here for a play, dip into the Teatro Ocampo to visit this elegant 1st-floor cafe with a jazzy soundtrack and pictures of theater and cinema greats adorning the walls.

★ Casa de la Salsa   DANCING

(☑ 443-313-93-62; Plaza Morelos 121; ⊙ 2-9pm Mon & Tue, to 2:30am Wed-Sat) **FREE** Locals converge to shake their collective ass to a rocking four-piece salsa band (from 9:30pm Wednesday to Saturday) on a raised stage in this dark, cavernous club. Don't worry, this is not one of those high-and-mighty, show-off salsa clubs, so feel free to dance terribly when drunk. Tequila and beer are dirt cheap, which makes the atmosphere lots of fun.

Dancing isn't confined to the hours of darkness either. Fancy a whirl at 4pm on a working Tuesday? No problem! If dancing's not your thing, then there's also a bunch of pool tables.

Los 50s Bar   BAR

(Av Madero Poniente 507; cover M$30; ⊙ 5pm-late) Rock belts out of a handful of clubs on and around Av Madero Poniente after 10pm, but this is one of the best. Expect young, moody student bands reinterpreting Doors songs or blasting self-penned homages to Nirvana. There's a M$30 cover charge on music nights.

☆ Entertainment

Being a university town and the capital of one of Mexico's most interesting states, Morelia has a thriving cultural life. Stop by the tourist office or the Casa de la Cultura for *Cartelera Cultural,* a free weekly listing of films and cultural events.

For theater experiences visit the **Teatro Ocampo** (☑ 443-313-16-79; cnr Ocampo & Prieto) or **Teatro Morelos** (☑ 443-314-62-02; www.cecon expo.com; cnr Camelinas & Ventura Puente); the latter is part of the Centro de Convenciones complex, 1.5km south of the city center. **Cinépolis** (☑ 443-312-12-88; www.cinepolis.com; cnr Gómez Farías & Tapia) screens blockbusters in English with subtitles or dubbed Spanish.

The cathedral (p612) has occasional impressive organ recitals.

WESTERN CENTRAL HIGHLANDS MORELIA

DON'T MISS

MORELIA'S MUSICAL NOOKS

The tap of a dancer's shoe, the plaintive cry of a troubadour, trombonists sliding up and down their scales – follow your ears into Morelia's musical inner sanctums.

Conservatorio de las Rosas (443-312-14-69; www.conservatoriodelasrosas.edu.mx; Tapia 334) Officially verified as the oldest music conservatory in the Americas (founded in 1743), this regal building hides what you might call an 'old-school' music college. In its Alhambra-esque courtyard, you can sit and seek romantic inspiration as the sound of trumpet stabs and guitar arpeggios emanates from the surrounding classrooms. It's a beautiful experience. There are free concerts on Thursdays at 8pm.

Casa de la Cultura (443-313-12-68; Av Morelos Norte 485) After the music conservatory, this is the second pillar of Morelia's cultural life. Encased in an old Carmelite monastery dating from the 17th century, it's a blissful place to hang out and soak up the musical spirit of Mexico. The cute cafe near the entry is a good staging post, but save time for other nooks and crannies.

Guitar maestros often sit around in the cloisters quietly strumming. Magic!

Shopping

Casa de las Artesanías　MARKET
(443-317-25-81; Ex-Convento de San Francisco, Plaza Valladolid; ⏰10am-2pm & 5-7:30pm) If you don't have time to scour the Purépecha pueblos for the perfect folk-art piece, come to the House of Handicrafts, inside the Ex-Convento de San Francisco. It's a cooperative marketplace launched to benefit indigenous craftspeople; arts and handicrafts from all over Michoacán are sold here. On the upper level there's even a free **craft museum**.

Mercado de Dulces　MARKET
(Sweets Market; Gómez Farías; ⏰9am-10pm) This seductive market, on the western side of the Palacio Clavijero, deals in the region's famous sweets, including a rainbow selection of *ate de fruta* (fruit leather) in a variety of exotic flavors.

Information

DANGERS & ANNOYANCES
Violent gang warfare has scarred Michoacán for years, most recently with the Caballeros Templarios (Knights Templar) Cartel, drug-dealing Christian zealots who have killed scores of people around the state. Fortunately, bystanders are rarely affected by drug violence in Michoacán. Travelers are unlikely to face anything out of the ordinary except for a higher-than-average army and police presence in some places in the state. The Tierra Caliente region (not covered in this book) in the state's southwest is rife with civil unrest and should be avoided.

MEDICAL SERVICES
Hospital Star Médica (443-322-77-00; www.starmedica.com; Virrey de Mendoza 2000)

MONEY
Banks and ATMs are plentiful around the plaza, particularly on and near Avenida Madero.

POST
Main Post Office (Av Madero Oriente 369)

TOURIST INFORMATION
Tourist Office (443-312-04-14; Av Madero Oriente; ⏰9am-7pm) This reasonably helpful tourist office is inside the Palacio de Gobierno. There's also an info booth in Plaza de Armas (same hours).

ℹ Getting There & Around

AIR
The **Francisco J Mújica Airport** (443-317-67-80; www.aeropuertosgap.com.mx) is 27km north of Morelia, on the Morelia–Zinapécuaro Hwy. There are no public buses, but taxis to the airport cost M$200. Plenty of flights are available to cities in Mexico and limited flights serve destinations in North America.

Aeromar (443-324-67-78; www.aeromar.com.mx; Hotel Fiesta Inn, Pirindas 435)

Volaris (800-122-80-00; www.volaris.mx) Book online or at the airport desk.

BUS & COMBI
Morelia's bus terminal is about 4km northwest of the city center. It's separated into three *módulos*, which correspond to 1st-, 2nd- and 3rd-class buses. To get into town from here take a Roja 1 combi (red) from under the pedestrian bridge, or catch a taxi (M$40). First-class buses depart hourly or more frequently for most destinations.

Around town, small combis and buses operate from 6am until 10pm daily (M$7). Combi routes are designated by the color of their stripe: Ruta Roja (red), Ruta Amarilla (yellow), Ruta Rosa (pink), Ruta Azul (blue), Ruta Verde (green), Ruta Cafe (brown) and so on. Ask at the tourist office for help with bus and combi routes.

Reserva Mariposa Monarca

In the easternmost corner of Michoacán, straddling the border of México state, lies the incredible 563-sq-km **Reserva Mariposa Monarca** (Monarch Butterfly Reserve; El Rosario, Sierra Chincua & Cerro Pelón each adult/child M$45/35; ⊙6am-6pm mid-Nov–Mar). Every autumn, from late October to early November, millions of monarch butterflies flock to these forested Mexican highlands for their winter hibernation, having flown all the way from the Great Lakes region of the US and Canada, some 4500km away. As they close in on their destination they gather in gentle swarms, crossing highways and fluttering up steep mountainsides where they cling together in clusters that weigh down thick branches of the *oyenal* (fir) trees. When the sun rises and warms the forest, they take to the sky in gold and orange flurries, descending to the humid forest floor for the hottest part of the day. By midafternoon they often carpet the ground brilliantly. The best time to see them is on a warm, sunny afternoon in February – they don't fly as much in cool weather.

In the warm spring temperatures of March the butterflies reach their sexual maturity and the real fun begins – mating. When the vernal equinox strikes (March 20 or 21), pregnant females fly north to southeastern US, where they lay their eggs in milkweed and die fulfilled. Their eggs hatch into caterpillars that feed on the milkweed, then make cocoons and emerge in late May as new butterflies. These young monarchs flutter back to the Great Lakes, where they breed, so that by mid-August yet another generation is ready to start the long trip south. This is one of the most complex animal migrations on earth and scientists still have no idea how or why the butterflies do it.

Though monarch butterflies are not in danger of extinction, the migratory behavior of this particular population is threatened by insecticides and habitat destruction in both Mexico and the US. Some organizations are trying to change these patterns by offering local communities incentives to not only protect their remaining forests, but also to restore habitat via tree planting projects. For more information check out www.monarchwatch.org.

The publicly accessible part of the reserve is divided into three areas that are fully operational for visitors from roughly mid-November through March, but exact dates depend on weather, temperatures and the butterflies' arrival. El Rosario and Sierra Chincua are the most popular reserve areas. Both are accessible from Angangueo. Angangueo is the closest town to Sierra Chincua (just 8km away) and the best base for this end of the reserve. El Rosario is close to the pueblo of the same name and can be reached from Angangueo via Ocampo. Cerro Pelón is the newest reserve area and has the healthiest habitat. It's best reached from Zitácuaro.

At the beginning or end of the season ask for information on butterfly activity at the Morelia or Mexico City tourist offices before visiting, as butterfly arrival/departure dates can vary depending on the nuances of the weather. Outside butterfly season (April to October), the reserve doesn't really merit a special visit although it technically remains open. While you'll find most facilities closed, you can still stroll through the coniferous forests looking for birds and other animals.

BUSES FROM MORELIA

DESTINATION	FARE (M$)	DURATION (HR)	FREQUENCY (DAILY)
Colima	513	2	3
Guadalajara	347	4	half-hourly
Mexico City (Terminal Norte)	411	4¾	hourly
Mexico City (Terminal Poniente)	411	4½	half-hourly
Pátzcuaro	45	1	hourly
Uruapan	110	2	hourly
Zitácuaro	141	3	3

HIGH IS WHERE IT HAPPENS

Monarch butterflies like basking at altitude, so getting to them requires hiking (or horseback riding) up to 3000m. Hike slowly, remember to take plenty of breaks (and water) and be aware of the symptoms of altitude sickness.

Some people do day trips or tours from Morelia or Mexico City to see the butterflies, but this means more than eight hours of travel in one day. It's better to stay locally and fully enjoy the experience. The two local hotels, Rancho San Cayetano (p623) and JM's Butterfly B&B (p623) can arrange guided trips starting at around M$1200 per person.

The reserve areas are spread out, and most people only visit one. But even though the butterflies look the same in each spot, the changing weather does affect the butterflies' behavior and the truly interested will probably find a great deal of value in visiting all three reserves on different days.

The admission fee for each reserve area is the same and local guides are compulsory (available at entry gates). Note that the length of your hike/horseback ride will be shorter later in the season – the butterflies work their way down as the weather warms up.

El Rosario

During the height of butterfly voyeurism (February and March) El Rosario gets as many as 8000 visitors a day. It is also the most commercial area – souvenir stalls abound on the hillside and the habitat has been severely affected by illegal logging. El Rosario village and the entrance to the El Rosario reserve area are located about 12km up a good gravel road from the small village of Ocampo.

Getting to the butterflies requires a steep hike (or horseback ride), a lot of it on steps, of 2km to 4km, depending on the time of year. There are a couple of hotels in Ocampo, but it's a far more pleasant experience to stay in the village of Angangueo (just 45 minutes on foot from Ocampo). The entrance fee (M$45) includes a mandatory guide. Horses cost M$80 one-way. There's a small, free **museum** (open 9am to 5pm) worth perusing at the entrance gate with exhibits and a short film about the butterflies.

Sierra Chincua

Sierra Chincua is 8km beyond Angangueo, way up in the mountains. This area has been damaged by logging, but not as badly as El Rosario. It's a less strenuous hike; price-wise it's the same deal as El Rosario (M$45). Horses are also available. To get here from Angangueo take the 'Tlalpujahua' or Mexico City bus (M$5) and tell the driver you're going to Sierra Chincua. Taxis from Angangueo cost M$200 and up, depending on the wait.

Cerro Pelón

Cerro Pelón, which is actually located in México state, is the newest reserve area and by far the best choice. The mountains rise high (more than 3000m) here, the forest is in great shape and there is barely a trickle of tourism (on its busiest day it may get 80 visitors; you'll usually find yourself all alone on the mountain). Logging has been eliminated and local guides have replanted trees for years to restore habitat. Expect to see huge, cathedral fir trees, moss-covered trunks, wildflowers and incredible canyon views.

Be warned that the climb here is very steep and the relentless ascent takes a good mountain walker at least 1½ to two hours going at a fair pace and without stopping. People not used to mountain walking are likely to struggle. Most people choose to ascend the mountain on horseback (M$200). Camping in a natural meadow just below Cerro Pelón peak, only an hour's hike from where the butterflies gather in the early season, is a terrific option for the self-sufficient (although you will need to go with a guide). Guides will arrange *burros* to haul the heavy stuff up the mountain. Guides charge from M$200.

This reserve area is about a 40-minute drive southeast of Zitácuaro, Michoacán's third-largest city, where you can buy necessary food, water and supplies. There are a couple of access points – Macheros and El Capulín. Both are within 1.5km of each other and can be reached by public transportation from outside Zitácuaro's bus terminal (take a bus marked 'Aputzio,' for M$13, which goes as far as the border to Mexico state, then a taxi, which will cost M$20 to M$30). A taxi straight from Zitácuaro to either of the reserve areas costs M$200 to M$250.

🛏 Sleeping

JM's Butterfly B&B
B&B $$

(📞 726-596-31-17; www.jmbutterflybnb.com; Macheros; s/d incl breakfast M$850/950) This relatively new B&B in the heart of the pretty village of Macheros makes a great overnight base for the Cerro Pelón reserve. Rooms are spacious and have beautiful valley and mountain views. Meals are available and the owner, who's also a butterfly guide, speaks excellent English. It's best to phone in advance.

Angangueo

📞 715 / POP 4600 / ELEV 2980M

This drowsy old mining town is the most popular base for butterfly-watchers, because it's close to both the Sierra Chincua and El Rosario sanctuaries. The town is layered into the hills, knitted with pine forest, grazing land and cornfields. Most services can be found along a single main drag with two names (Nacional and Morelos). There are two attractive churches on Plaza de la Constitución, the center of town, from which Nacional runs down the hill.

🛏 Sleeping & Eating

Accommodations are basic. Be warned that none of the places to stay have any heating and it gets very cold up here at night. Unless you've just flown in from the Arctic tundra, you'll want several layers of thick clothing, which you'll probably sleep in as well!

Most of the half dozen or so guesthouses do food, but there are a couple of taco stands on the main plaza and a restaurant or two.

Hotel Plaza Don Gabino
GUESTHOUSE $

(📞 715-153-19-26; hotelplazagabino@hotmail.com; Morelos 147; r M$550; 🅿️🛜) By far the best of the town's guesthouses, this family-run and exceptionally welcoming place has sparkling clean rooms, hot-water showers (that work!), blankets for 'heating,' and a restaurant serving an excellent four-course dinner. It's around a kilometer downhill from the central plaza. Reserve ahead in butterfly season.

ℹ️ Information

Tourist Office (📞 715-156-00-44; Nacional 1; ⏰9am-7pm Nov-Mar, to 4pm Mon-Fri Apr-Oct) Downhill from the plaza.

ℹ️ Getting There & Away

Frequent buses from Morelia go first to Zitácuaro (M$120, three hours), where you'll catch another bus to Angangueo (M$18, 1¼ hours). From Mexico City's Terminal Poniente you can take Autobuses MTZ (M$140, four hours, two hourly) direct to Angangueo; most of the other bus lines go through Zitácuaro.

To reach the El Rosario sanctuary from Angangueo, first take a combi to Ocampo (M$10, 15 minutes, hourly), then another to El Rosario (M$18, 30 minutes, hourly), from the corner of Independencia and Ocampo. In season there are also *camionetas* (pickup trucks) that leave from the *auditorio* (auditorium) in Angangueo, or from outside hotels; these cost about M$600 for around 10 people and take 45 bumpy minutes (via a back road) to reach the sanctuary.

For Sierra Chincua take the 'Tlalpujahua' or Mexico City bus (M$5) from the bus station and tell the driver you're going to Sierra Chincua. Taxis cost M$200 and up.

Zitácuaro

📞 715 / POP 84,000 / ELEV 1940M

Zitácuaro is Michoacán's third-largest city, but it feels like a provincial working-class town. Known primarily for its baked bread and trout farms, it's no great looker, but it's a sensible base for visiting the butterflies at Cerro Pelón.

⊙ Sights

Iglesia de San Pancho
CHURCH

(⏰9am-2pm & 4-7pm) The Iglesia de San Pancho in the village of San Pancho, just south of Zitácuaro, is a restored 16th-century church that appeared in the great John Huston–Humphrey Bogart film, *The Treasure of the Sierra Madre*, and was visited by Prince Charles in 2002. Come at sunset when light streams through the stained glass. A taxi from town costs M$40.

🛏 Sleeping & Eating

⭐ Rancho San Cayetano
HOTEL $$$

(📞 715-153-19-26; www.ranchosancayetano.com; Carretera a Huetamo Km 2.3; r from M$1530; 🅿️🅰️🛜🐾) The best hotel in the entire butterfly region, the Rancho San Cayetano is owned and run by English- and French-speaking Pablo and Lisette. The grounds are huge with stands of pine and fruit trees. Rooms are rustic chic with exposed stone walls and beamed ceilings. And its multicourse, gourmet meals (reserve in advance) are superb.

Pablo is passionate about butterflies and offers detailed maps and driving directions, and shows background videos to interested guests. He can also arrange transportation to and from the sanctuaries.

Marisquería El Tejado
SEAFOOD $$

(☑715-153-43-17; Montes de Oca 4; mains M$120-190; ⊙8:30am-10pm) Something of an epiphany in workaday Zitácuaro is this fine fish restaurant hidden in the entrails of the city's unexciting suburbs. Forget the distance from the sea – the Tejado is worth finding for its exquisite seafood, including raw oysters (perfect with lime and chili sauce), crab, lobster, and prawns in garlic or breadcrumbs.

Service is exceptional and the clientele a cheery assemblage of in-the-know locals.

ℹ Getting There & Away

Zitácuaro's bus terminal is 1km from the city center. There are frequent buses to and from Morelia (M$120, three hours), Angangueo (M$18, 1¼ hours) and Mexico City Poniente (M$153 to M$179, two hours), among other destinations.

For Cerro Pelón take a bus marked 'Aputzio' (M$13; which goes as far as the border to Mexico state) from outside Zitácuaro's bus terminal, then a taxi (M$20 to M$30).

Pátzcuaro

☑434 / POP 55,000 / ELEV 2175M

Terracotta-tiled roofs, warped red-and-white adobe walls and narrow cobblestone streets give the town of Pátzcuaro the air of a large village. Unlike the Spanish-founded cities of Morelia and Guadalajara, Pátzcuaro took root in the 1320s as part of the Tarascan Empire, two centuries before the conquistadors arrived. With its tangible indigenous feel, it remains little affected by modern interference.

History whispers from the cobwebbed louvers that overlook the lively but hassle-free streets fanning out from the city's attractively landscaped Plaza Vasco de Quiroga. Adding to the atmosphere, Pátzcuaro hosts one of the most dramatic Day of the Dead celebrations in Mexico. It's also handily placed for exploring Lago de Pátzcuaro, just 3km to the north, and the craft-making Purépecha villages that cluster around its shoreline.

Make reservations during holidays and bring warm clothes from November to February – you're at altitude here and it gets frigid.

History

Pátzcuaro was the capital of the Tarasco people (now known as the Purépecha) from about AD 1325 to 1400. After the death of King Tariácuri, the Tarascan state became a three-part league. Comprising Pátzcuaro, Tzintzuntzan and Ihuatzio, the league repulsed repeated Aztec attacks, which may explain why they welcomed the Spanish, who first arrived in 1522. Bad idea. The Spanish returned in 1529 under Nuño de Guzmán, a vicious conquistador.

Guzmán's six-year reign over the indigenous people was brutal, even for those times. The colonial government recalled Guzmán to Spain, where he was arrested and locked up for life, and dispatched Bishop Vasco de Quiroga, a respected judge and cleric from Mexico City, to clean up his mess. Quiroga was an impressively enlightened man. When he arrived in 1536, he established village cooperatives based on the humanitarian ideals of Sir Thomas More's *Utopia*.

To avoid dependence on Spanish mining lords and landowners, Quiroga successfully encouraged education and agricultural self-sufficiency in the Purépecha villages around Lago de Pátzcuaro, with all villagers contributing equally to the community. He also helped each village develop its own craft specialty, from masks to pottery to guitars and violins. The utopian communities declined after his death in 1565, but the crafts traditions continue to this day. Not surprisingly, Tata Vascu, as the Tarascos called Quiroga, has not been forgotten. You'll notice that streets, plazas, restaurants and hotels all over Michoacán are named after him.

◉ Sights

★ Plaza Vasco de Quiroga
PLAZA

(Plaza Grande) Pátzcuaro's leafy main plaza is one of Mexico's best hangout spots. It is framed by the 17th-century facades of mansions that have since been converted to hotels, shops and restaurants, and watched over by a serene **statue of Vasco de Quiroga**, which rises from the fountain. The arched sides of the plaza are full of food stalls and jewelry- and folk-art sellers, and the atmosphere, particularly on the weekend when bands and street performers entertain, is wonderful.

Museo de Artes Populares
MUSEUM

(☑434-342-10-29; cnr Enseñanza & Alcantarillas; M$47; ⊙9am-5pm Tue-Sun) Highlights of this impressive folk-art museum include a room set up as a typical Michoacán kitchen, cases of gorgeous jewelry, and an entire room filled with *retablos* – crudely rendered devotional paintings offering thanks to God for saving the owner from illness or accident.

The museum is housed on the site of the Colegio de San Nicolás, arguably the Americas' first university, founded by Quiroga in 1540. The building was built on pre-Hispanic stone foundations, some of which can be seen behind the museum courtyards.

Plaza Gertrudis Bocanegra   PLAZA

(Plaza Chica) Pátzcuaro's second plaza is named after a local heroine who was shot by firing squad in 1818 for her support of the independence movement. Her statue commands the center of the plaza.

The local **market** on the west side of the plaza is where you can find everything from fruit, vegetables and fresh trout to herbal medicines, crafts and clothing – including the region's distinctive striped shawls and *sarapes* (blankets with an opening for the head). There's outstanding cheap food, too.

A tumbledown **Mercado de Artesanías** operates on the side street adjacent to the library. Wooden masks and pastel crucifixes are among the crafts sold here. The quality varies but prices are low.

Biblioteca Gertrudis Bocanegra   LIBRARY

(☑ 434-342-54-41; cnr Padre Lloreda & Titere; ☺9am-7pm Mon-Fri, 10am-1pm Sat) On the north side of Plaza Gertrudis Bocanegra is the town library. Occupying the cavernous interior of the 16th-century San Agustín church, this is the kind of library other libraries dream of imitating. There are oyster-shell skylights and a massive, colorful Juan O'Gorman mural on the rear wall that depicts the history of Michoacán from pre-Hispanic times to the 1910 revolution.

On the west side of the library, the **Teatro Emperador Caltzontzin** was a convent until it was converted into a theater in 1936; it functions today as an art-house cinema.

★Basílica de Nuestra
Señora de la Salud   CHURCH

(Plaza de la Basílica) Built on the hill atop a pre-Hispanic ceremonial site, this church and pilgrimage site was intended to be the centerpiece of Vasco de Quiroga's utopia. The building wasn't completed until the 19th century and only the central nave was faithful to his original design. Quiroga's tomb, the Mausoleo de don Vasco, is left of the main doors.

Behind the altar at the east end stands a much revered figure of the Virgin, **Nuestra Señora de la Salud** (Our Lady of Health), which 16th-century Tarascans crafted from

a corncob-and-honey paste called *tatzingue*. Soon after, people began to experience miraculous healings and Quiroga had the words 'Salus Infirmorum' (Healer of the Sick) inscribed at the figure's feet. Ever since, pilgrims have come from all over Mexico to pray for miracles. They crawl on their knees across the plaza, into the church and along its nave. Upstairs, behind the image, you'll see many tin impressions of hands, feet and legs that pilgrims have offered the mystical Virgin.

Casa de los Once Patios   MARKET

(Madrigal de las Altas Torres) This cool, rambling colonial edifice was built as a Dominican convent in the 1740s. (Before that, the site held one of Mexico's first hospitals, founded by Vasco de Quiroga.) Today it houses small *artesanías* (handicrafts) shops, each specializing in a particular regional craft. Renovations over the years mean there are now five patios rather than the previous 11 (as in the market's name – *once* is Spanish for 'eleven').

Look for copperware from Santa Clara del Cobre and instruments from Paracho, as well as lacquerware, hand-painted ceramics and vibrant textiles. Be sure to check out the **Baño Barroco**, a 16th-century bathing room.

El Estribo   VIEWPOINT

This hilltop lookout, 3.5km west of the city center, is a quintessential morning run for Pátzcuaro's more robust residents; but don't underestimate the altitude (2175m above sea level) or the terrain – a steep, cobbled, cypress-lined road. It's all worth it in the end when you emerge feeling like Mo Farah at a viewing pavilion with killer views of Lago de Pátzcuaro and its surroundings. For those with abnormal energy reserves, 422 steps lead up to the true summit.

To reach El Estribo, take Ponce de León from the southwest corner of Plaza Grande and keep walking (or running).

Churches

Built in the 16th century, the **Templo de la Compañía** (cnr Lerín & Portugal) became a Jesuit training college in the 17th century. The church is still in use and houses some Vasco de Quiroga relics. The adjacent college building fell into ruin after the expulsion of the Jesuits. It is now used for community activities and often has free temporary exhibits.

Pátzcuaro has several other old churches of interest, including the **Templo del**

Pátzcuaro

Sagrario (cnr Lerín & Portugal), **Templo San Juan de Dios** (cnr Romero & San Juan de Dios), the pink stone **Templo San Francisco** (Terán) and **Templo El Santuario** (cnr Ramos & Codallos).

🎓 Courses

Centro de Lenguas y Ecoturismo de Pátzcuaro LANGUAGE COURSE
(CELEP; ☏434-342-47-64; www.celep.com.mx; Navarrete 50; 2-week Spanish-language course US$350, language & culture program US$540) Courses here involve four to six hours of classes Monday to Friday. Cultural programs include seminars in literature and excursions to local villages. Homestays, including meals with local families, can also be arranged.

🎊 Festivals & Events

Semana Santa RELIGIOUS
(☉Mar or Apr) Easter week is full of events in Pátzcuaro and the lakeside villages, in-

cluding Palm Sunday processions; Viacrucis processions on Good Friday morning, enacting Christ's journey to Calvary and the crucifixion; candlelit processions in silence on Good Friday evening; and, on Easter Sunday evening, a ceremonial burning of Judas in Plaza Grande.

Día de Muertos RELIGIOUS
(Day of the Dead; ☉Nov 1 & 2) The villages around Pátzcuaro, most notably Tzintzuntzan and Isla Janitzio, stage the most popular (and crowded!) Día de Muertos celebrations in Mexico. Parades, crafts markets, dancing, ceremonies, exhibitions and concerts are held in and around Pátzcuaro on the days before and after Día de Muertos. Cemeteries are packed with visitors throughout the festivities.

Nuestra Señora de la Salud RELIGIOUS
(☉Dec 8) A colorful procession to the basilica honors Our Lady of Health with

Pátzcuaro

◎ Top Sights
1 Basílica de Nuestra Señora de
la Salud...D2
2 Plaza Vasco de Quiroga......................B3

◎ Sights
3 Biblioteca Gertrudis Bocanegra.........C1
4 Casa de los Once Patios....................C4
5 Market...B1
6 Mercado de Artesanías.......................C1
7 Museo de Artes Populares.................C3
8 Plaza Gertrudis Bocanegra................B2
9 Templo de la Compañía......................C3
10 Templo del Sagrario...........................C3
11 Templo El Santuario...........................A1
12 Templo San Francisco........................A3
13 Templo San Juan de Dios...................B3
14 Vasco de Quiroga Statue....................B3

◎ Activities, Courses & Tours
15 Centro de Lenguas y
Ecoturismo de Pátzcuaro................A4

◎ Sleeping
16 Hotel Casa del Refugio.......................B2
17 Hotel Casa Encantada........................B4
18 Hotel Casa Leal..................................C3
19 Hotel Misión Pátzcuaro
Centro Histórico..............................B1
20 La Mansión de los Sueños..................B2
21 Mansión Iturbe....................................B2
22 Mesón de San Antonio........................D2
23 Posada de la Basílica..........................C2
24 Posada Mandala..................................C3
25 Posada San Rafael..............................B3

◎ Eating
26 El Naranjo Restaurante.......................B3
27 El Patio..B3
28 La Surtidora...B3
29 Restaurant Lupita................................C3

traditional dance performances, including Los Reboceros, Los Moros, Los Viejitos and Los Panaderos.

Pastorelas RELIGIOUS
(☉ Dec 26–Feb 2) These dramatizations of the shepherds' journey to see the infant Jesus are staged in Plaza Grande around Christmas. *Pastorelas indígenas,* on the same theme but including mask dances, enact the struggle of angels against the devils that are trying to hinder the shepherds. These *pastorelas* are held in eight villages around Lago de Pátzcuaro, on different days between December 26 and February 2.

⌑ Sleeping

Pátzcuaro does 'pleasant colonial hotels' like Paris does refined street-side cafes. Nonetheless, it's usually worth booking ahead for Friday and Saturday nights, and months ahead for Día de Muertos, when the entire town is booked well in advance. By contrast, at all other times you need normally only raise an eyebrow at the more expensive places to see prices tumbling by up to 50% – you're on holiday so indulge in some luxury!

Posada Mandala GUESTHOUSE $
(☑ 434-342-41-76; Lerín 14; r M$300-500, without bathroom M$200; ⌘) Arty international travelers love this low-profile guesthouse, with six simple, whitewashed rooms surrounding a small plant-filled courtyard. The best rooms are those upstairs, with their own facilities and great views over the rooftops of Pátzcuaro. Weekly pizza nights are held here; make sure you're a part of one!

Posada San Rafael HOTEL $
(☑ 434-342-07-70; Portal Aldama 13; s/d M$300/420; P⌘) The love child of a colonial mission and a US motel, rooms here open onto wide verandas overlooking a driveway and parking area filled with plants. Hot water is limited to mornings and evenings, but upstairs rooms are a great deal, with plenty of beautiful details such as columns and beamed ceilings.

★ Hotel Casa Encantada B&B $$
(☑ 434-342-34-92; www.hotelcasaencantada.com; Dr Coss 15; r incl breakfast M$895-1320; P@⌘) Enchanted is the word for this American-owned B&B offering 12 elegant rooms with local rugs and beautifully tiled bathrooms in a converted 1784 mansion. Many of the rooms are enormous and some come with kitchenettes. Ask for a room at the rear of the property, as those at the front suffer from road noise.

Hotel Misión Pátzcuaro Centro Histórico HOTEL $$
(☑ 434-342-10-37; www.hotelesmision.com.mx; Obregón 10; d from M$600; P✳⌘) An impressive building once you make it past the ugly car park, the Misión has a soaring central atrium, an impressive Pátzcuaro-themed mural and a peaceful covered courtyard. The rooms are a little more institutionalized, but comfortable and kept up to date, nonetheless; many only have windows facing the indoor patio. Staff are highly responsive.

Mansión Iturbe BOUTIQUE HOTEL $$

(☑434-342-03-68; www.mansioniturbe.com; Morelos 59; r incl breakfast M$1060; ☎) Right on the main square, the rooms here are spacious, old-world in style, furnished in heavy dark woods and crammed full of antiques. Bathrooms are sumptuous. There's a wonderful terrace out the back and the feel is one of luxurious sophistication.

Hotel Casa del Refugio BOUTIQUE HOTEL $$

(☑434-342-55-05; www.casadelrefugio.com.mx; Portal Régules 9; d M$625-800; ☎) With adobe walls covered in religious motifs and portraits of saints (and possibly a few sinners), a palm-filled atrium with an enormous open fireplace and small, but immaculate rooms, this welcoming hotel might just be the best deal in town if you arrive on the right day with the right haggling skills.

Mesón de San Antonio GUESTHOUSE $$

(☑434-342-25-01; Serrato 33; s/d M$500/650; @☎) Rooms at this great-value, hacienda-style inn border a green, if unkempt, colonial courtyard. The beamed overhangs are held up by ancient timbers and the extremely cozy rooms are decorated with fine Purépecha pottery and have wood-burning fireplaces and cable TV. There's also a communal kitchen for self-caterers and a buffet restaurant.

★Hotel Casa Leal BOUTIQUE HOTEL $$$

(☑434-342-11-06; www.hotelcasaleal.com; Portugal 1; d/ste from M$1500/3000; ❇@☎) In the battle of Pátzcuaro's boutique hotels, the Leal is the clear winner. There are no real weaknesses at this neoclassical plaza-facing beauty. Examine the elegant sofas, the *Downton Abbey*–esque library, and the grand but not grandiose rooms, which maintain a delicate balance between old-world exquisiteness and modern comfort. The icing on the sponge? The refined roof terrace overlooking verdant Plaza Grande.

La Mansión de los Sueños BOUTIQUE HOTEL $$$

(☑434-342-11-03; www.mansiondelossuenos.com.mx; Ibarra 15; d/ste incl breakfast from M$1900/2900; ☎) This restored mansion built around three adjacent courtyards offers some of the most luxurious accommodations in town. There is art on every wall, coffee machines and minibars in each room, and even fireplaces and lofts in some. To be fair though, the decor in some rooms verges on being tacky, so ask to see a few before hopping into bed.

Posada de la Basílica BOUTIQUE HOTEL $$$

(☑434-342-11-08; www.posadadelabasilica.com.mx; Arciga 6; d/ste M$1500/2500; P@☎) For rustic luxury, consider this boutique hotel with a terracotta rooftop and lake views. The surprisingly bright colonial building contains 12 huge rooms with wood floors and open fireplaces. The master suites are truly special, and the entire place exudes elegance, charm and understatement. There's a restaurant with panoramic city views.

✗ Eating

Pátzcuaro has wonderful street food – look out for *corundas* (triangular *tamales* served with and without fillings), bright green *atole de grano* (an anise-flavored local variant of the popular corn-based drink), *nieve de pasta* (almond and cinnamon ice cream) and chunks of candied squash. Some of the best chow can be found at the food stalls in the open-air market on the northwest corner of Plaza Chica. If it's *corundas* you're after, head to the basilica in the morning and look for the elderly ladies with baskets.

Keep your eyes open for *sopa tarasca*, a rich tomato-based soup with cream, dried chili and bits of crisp tortilla.

Most restaurants are attached to hotels and naturally enough most cater primarily for here-today, gone-tomorrow tourists and are fussy and mediocre. There are, however, some exceptions.

★La Surtidora MEXICAN $

(☑434-342-28-35; Hidalgo 71; mains M$30-140; ☺8am-10pm; ☎) This downright heavenly place to flop down for refueling is living proof that no other country does atmospheric colonial cafes quite as well as Mexico. La Surtidora's cafe-cum-deli has been knocking out breakfasts, *comidas* and *cenas* on Plaza Grande since 1916. One wonders if the enchiladas, cakes, balletic waitstaff and – most memorably – home-roasted coffee were always this good. Probably.

Restaurant Lupita INTERNATIONAL $$

(☑434-345-06-59; Quiroga 5; mains M$95-140; ☺8am-10pm) Although the international menu clearly aims to attract gringos, the Lupita doesn't neglect its Mexican roots. In a pretty courtyard with craft-covered walls and the odd strolling troubadour, you can take a break from the Mexican kitchen (pasta anyone?), or enjoy the good old flavors of Michoacán (the local trout's pretty good).

El Naranjo Restaurante ITALIAN $$
(☑ 440-111-01-68; Plaza Vasco de Quiroga; pizza & pasta from M$100; ☺ 8am-10pm Wed-Mon) This interesting new restaurant is encased in a beautiful old coaching inn and reconfigured with chic modern adornments. El Naranjo takes on authentic Italian cuisine and the results are largely positive: the thin-crust pizza is dispatched from a wood-fired oven and the pasta's homemade and appropriately chewy. The setting's casual but comfortable, amalgamating old and new in the way that Italians are so good at.

El Patio MEXICAN $$
(Aldama 19; mains M$80-125; ☺ 8am-10pm) With much coveted seating on the Plaza Grande, this restaurant attracts as many locals as tourists and is unquestionably a pleasant place for a meal, with decent Mexican staples and some well-prepared local dishes.

❶ Information

Several banks in the city center will change currency; all have ATMs.

Municipal Tourist Office (☑ 434-344-34-86; Portal Hidalgo 1; ☺ 9am-8pm)

Post Office (Obregón 13; ☺ 9am-4pm Mon-Fri, to 1pm Sat)

❶ Getting There & Around

Pátzcuaro's **bus terminal** is a walkable 1.5km southwest of the city center. It has a cafeteria and left-luggage services.

To catch a bus heading to the city center, walk outside the terminal, turn right and at the corner take any bus marked 'Centro' (M$7). Taxis cost M$25 (with a small surcharge after 11pm).

Buses back to the terminal (marked 'Central') leave from the northeast corner of Plaza Chica. Buses to the boat pier (marked 'Lago'; M$7, five minutes) also leave from here and run from about 6am to 10pm daily.

Around Pátzcuaro

Lago de Pátzcuaro

About 3km north of central Pátzcuaro you will come over a rise to find a lake so blue that its edge blends seamlessly with the sky. Within it are a few populated islands. It is strea- fed and natural, and though pollution is a concern, it's still damn beautiful.

To get to the Muelle General, take a bus marked 'Lago' from Pátzcuaro's Plaza Chica (M$7, five minutes). The pier caters to tourists in a profoundly cheesy way – with cheap fish eateries and souvenir shops. The ticket office is about 50m down on the right-hand side. Boat tours around the lake's main islands cost around M$85.

ISLA JANITZIO
Isla Janitzio is a popular weekend and holiday destination. It's heavily devoted to tourism, with lots of low-end souvenir stalls, fish restaurants and drunk college kids on holiday. But it *is* car-free and threaded with footpaths that eventually wind their way to the top of the island, where you'll find a 40m-high **statue** of independence hero José María Morelos. You can climb up inside the statue, via the **Museo Morelos** (M$10) where an ascending series of murals depicts Morelos' life. The last part ingeniously climbs the statue's raised arm to a lookout with panoramic lake views in the see-through wrist.

Round-trip boat rides to Janitzio cost M$55 (free for children under seven years old) and take 25 minutes each way; they leave when full (about every 30 minutes, more often on Saturday and Sunday). The last one back is around 8pm.

WESTERN CENTRAL HIGHLANDS AROUND PÁTZCUARO

BUSES FROM PÁTZCUARO

DESTINATION	FARE (M$)	DURATION (HR)	FREQUENCY (DAILY)
Guadalajara	386	4½	2
Ihuatzio	10	¼	very frequent
Mexico City (Terminal Norte)	495	5½	6
Mexico City (Terminal Poniente)	495	5½	9
Morelia	60	1	hourly
Tzintzuntzan	15	$1/3$	very frequent
Uruapan	68	1	very frequent

Lago de Pátzcuaro

Map labels: San Jerónimo Purenchécuaro, Chupícuaro, Santa Fe de la Laguna, Morelia (40km), San Andrés Tziróndaro, Quiroga, Lago de Pátzcuaro, Oponguo, Tzintzuntzan, MEX 120, Isla Pacanda, Puacuaro, Isla Yunuén, Napizaro, Isla Tecuéna, Statue of José María Morelos, Cucuchucho, Erongarícuaro, San Francisco Uricho, Isla Janitzio, Ihuatzio, Sanabría, Jarácuaro, Casa Santiago, Ihuatzio, Arocutín, Isla Uranden Morelos, Muelle General (boat dock), Tzurumútaro, Tócuaro, San Pedro Pareo, Tzentzénguaro, Huecorio, MEX 14, Morelia (50km), Nocutzepo, Santa Ana Chapitiro, See Pátzcuaro Map (p626), Pátzcuaro, San Bartolo Pareo, MEX 14, Tingambato (40km); Uruapan (65km), MEX 120, Santa Clara del Cobre (15km), MEX 14D, Uruapan (Toll; 60km)

Lakeside Villages

The villages surrounding Lago de Pátzcuaro make perfect day trips from Pátzcuaro and almost all can be reached by local transportation from Pátzcuaro's bus terminal. Or, to avoid backtracking to the bus terminal, take a 'Lago' bus from Plaza Chica and get off anywhere between the Posada de don Vasco and Hwy 14; then wait by the roadside for a bus heading to your village. Buses to Ihuatzio run directly from Plaza Chica.

Frequent combis run between the villages, so you can visit several in one day. Transportation between Quiroga and Erongarícuaro is infrequent, however, so travel between the two may be quicker via Pátzcuaro.

IHUATZIO

Ihuatzio, 14km from Pátzcuaro, was capital of the Tarascan kingdom after Pátzcuaro (but before Tzintzuntzan). Today it's just a slow, dusty village where everyone knows everyone else, until *you* walk into town.

⊙ Sights

Ihuatzio Archaeological Site RUIN

(adult/child M$39/free; ⊘9am-5pm) Ihuatzio Archaeological Site is a large and partially restored set of pre-Tarascan ruins, some of which date back as far as AD 900. The site lies just over 1km up a cobbled road from the village's small plaza. The ruins' best attraction is **Plaza de Armas**, an open ceremonial space around 200m long, which features two pyramid-like structures at its west end.

Two stone coyotes were found at the site; one is in the National Anthropology Museum in Mexico City, and the other can be found at the Museo Regional Michoacano in Morelia.

🛏 Sleeping

Casa Santiago
B&B **$$**

(☑ 434-344-08-80; www.casasantiagomex.com; r incl breakfast M$720-1080; ☎) Located 1.5km west of Ihuatzio on the road to Cucuchucho, this is a great place to experience a night or two in an indigenous pueblo. Rooms are of the rustic-chic kind, and the owners, a friendly, knowledgeable US-Purépecha couple, run shopping tours and cook delectable local meals upon request (it's best to let them know in advance that you're coming).

TZINTZUNTZAN

The tiny town of Tzintzuntzan (tseen-*tsoon*-tsahn), about 15km north of Pátzcuaro, was once the Tarascan capital and served as Vasco de Quiroga's first base in the region. It has a beautiful sprawling cemetery that blooms with flowers and crepe paper during heady Día de Muertos celebrations, crumbling Tarascan ruins and some relics from the early Spanish missionary period. The town's pulse comes from its thriving Saturday and Sunday **crafts market**, saintly Quiroga's beloved olive grove and two old churches.

◉ Sights

Ex-Convento de San Francisco
CHURCH

On the lake side of Avenida Cárdenas lies the Ex-Convento de San Francisco, a compound built partly with stones from the Tarascan site up the hill that the Spanish demolished. This is where Franciscan monks began the Spanish missionary effort in Michoacán in the 16th century. The gnarled, shady olive trees in the churchyard came from seedlings planted by Vasco de Quiroga; they're believed to be the oldest olive trees in the Americas.

Museo Antiguo Convento Franciscano de Santa Ana (M$15; ☉10am-5pm) is a fascinating museum inside the crumbling, but still-functioning Templo de San Francisco (which is straight ahead as you enter the Ex-Convento de San Francisco). The museum showcases Purépecha culture and history and documents the arrival of the Spanish and the peoples' conversion to Christianity. The building includes a set of murals around the galleries and Mudejar-patterned wooden ceiling ornamentation.

Toward the right rear corner of the complex stands the church built for the Purépecha masses, the **Templo de Nuestra Señora de la Salud**. Inside is El Santo Entierro de Tzintzuntzan, a much-revered image of Christ. For most of the year it lies in a *caja de cristal* (glass coffin). During Día de Muertos celebrations it is festooned with fruit and marigolds. On Good Friday, following an elaborate costumed passion play, the image is removed from its coffin and nailed to the large cross; being a Cristo de Goznes (hinged Christ), his arms can be extended and his legs crossed. Afterward, it is paraded through town until dark, when it is returned to the church. Pilgrims descend, some in chains or carrying crosses, some crawling on their knees.

★ Tzintzuntzan Archaeological Site
RUIN

(Las Yácatas; adult/child M$52/free; ☉9am-6pm) The Tzintzuntzan archaeological site comprises an impressive group of five round, reconstructed temples known as *yácatas*. They are all that remain of the mighty Tarascan empire. The hillside location offers wonderful views of the town, lake and surrounding mountains and is rarely crowded. Recent additions include a new **museum** showcasing finds from the site and a small info point highlighting a project that's trying to entice the once abundant hummingbird back to the area.

TÓCUARO

Some of Mexico's finest mask-makers live in this cobblestoned town surrounded by cornfields, 10km west of Pátzcuaro. There are no traditional storefronts – just a sign here and there signifying entry into family courtyard compounds with workshops and showrooms.

Prepare to spend. It takes a month or more to produce a fine mask, carved from a single piece of wood. The best ones are wonderfully expressive and surreal and, thanks to a growing legion of global collectors, can cost hundreds of dollars.

Uruapan

☑ 452 / POP 260,000 / ELEV 1620M

All praise the thundering Río Cupatitzio. This impressive river begins life underground, then rises sensationally to the surface, feeding a subtropical garden of palms, orchids and massive shade trees in urban Uruapan's Parque Nacional Barranca del Cupatitzio. Without the river, the city would not exist. When Spanish monk Fray Juan de San Miguel arrived here in 1533, he was so taken with his surroundings that he gave the area the Purépecha name, Uruapan (oo-roo-*ah*-pahn), which roughly translates into 'Eternal Spring'. Fray Juan designed a large market square – still a hit with local families on weekends – built a hospital and chapel, and arranged streets into an orderly grid that survives today.

Uruapan quickly grew into a productive agricultural center renowned for macadamias and high-quality *aguacates* (avocados), and still holds the title 'Capital Mundial del Aguacate.' The Feria del Aguacate underlines that point.

Avocados may pay the bills, but the river is king. The city's nicest neighborhoods kiss the riverside. The national park, a 15-minute walk from the city center, is a rush of waterfalls and trickling streams that wind through thick vegetation.

◉ Sights

★ Parque Nacional Barranca del Cupatitzio   PARK
(☑ 452-524-01-97; Independencia; adult/child M$25/10; ⊗ 8am-6pm; ⊕) This incomparable urban park is just 1km west of the main plaza, but it's another world. Tropical and subtropical foliage is thick and broiling with birds and butterflies. The river bubbles over boulders, cascades down waterfalls and spreads into wide, crystalline pools. Cobbled paths follow the riverbanks from the river's source at the icy-clear **Rodilla del Diablo** pool, near the park's north end, and water from hidden springs peels off the surrounding hillsides before flowing into the great river.

There are a few fruit stands and *taquerías* inside the gardens and there's even a trout farm where you can net your own catch.

Museo Indígena Huatápera   MUSEUM
(Portal Mercado ; ⊗ 9:30am-6pm Tue-Sun) **FREE** Embedded in the Huatápera, an old colonial courtyard building near the northeast corner of the main plaza, this small museum has benefited from a recent makeover. Built in the 1530s by Fray Juan de San Miguel, it once housed the first hospital in the Americas. The decorations around the doors and windows were carved by Purépecha artisans in a Mudejar style. The museum showcases handsome *artesanías* from Michoacán's four main indigenous groups: Purépecha, Nahua, Mazahua and Otomí.

Fábrica San Pedro   TEXTILE FACTORY
(☑ 452-524-14-63; Treviño s/n; ⊗ tours 9am-6pm Mon-Sat) **FREE** This great old textile factory from the 19th century is essentially a living museum. Hand-loomed and hand-dyed bedspreads, tablecloths and curtains are made here from pure cotton and wool, and are avail-

able for sale. The original machines are more than 100 years old and are still used. Don't miss poking about the abandoned factory below the shop – and try not to let thoughts of ghosts scare you back up the stairs!

You can either wander about on your own or, better, call ahead for a tour and see the entire weaving process from cotton bale to finished tablecloth.

✪ Festivals & Events

Semana Santa   RELIGIOUS
(⊗ Mar or Apr) Palm Sunday is marked by a procession through the city streets. A major crafts competition takes place on this day, and two weeks after Palm Sunday a weeklong exhibition of Michoacán handicrafts fills the plaza.

Día de Muertos   CULTURAL
(⊗ Nov 1–2) Celebrated across Mexico, the famous Day of the Dead festival brings many visitors to Uruapan for the colorful local celebrations.

Feria del Aguacate   FOOD
(⊗ Nov/Dec) The Avocado Fair erupts for three weeks in November/December and is celebrated with agricultural, industrial and handicraft exhibitions. Previous years have seen record-setting attempts for the world's largest guacamole.

Festival de Coros y Danzas   DANCE
(⊗ Dec 22) A Purépecha dance and choral contest.

🛏 Sleeping

Reserve a room early for the Día de Muertos (November 1 and 2) and Semana Santa (March/April) festivities.

Hotel Regis   HOTEL $
(☑ 452-523-58-44; www.hotelregis.com.mx; Portal Carrillo 12; s/d/tr M$350/450/550; ℗ 🛜) This is the best value among the budget plaza hotels. The public areas are charming in a borderline eccentric manner and, while the rooms are small and have poky bathrooms, the hand-painted bed heads add a splash of exotic color. It's very central.

★ Mi Solar
Bed & Breakfast   BOUTIQUE HOTEL $$
(☑ 452-524-09-12; www.hotelmisolar.com; Delgado 10; r from M$913; ℗ ❄ @ 🛜) Uruapan's oldest hotel opened in the 1940s to accommodate tourists flooding in to see the newly erupted Volcán Paricutín. Today it's a wholly remod-

eled boutique place, with 17 spacious rooms on three floors surrounding an atrium bar. Rooms have luscious king beds, high ceilings and hand-carved wooden furniture.

Over the road is a newer annex with larger rooms that are very comfortable but lack the character of the main building. The rack rates shown here only apply in busy periods; expect a 30% discount at all other times. Despite the name, breakfast is not always available.

Casa Chikita GUESTHOUSE $$
(☑ 452-524-41-74; www.casachikita.com; Carranza 32; d incl breakfast M$750; P🐾🛜) This 19th-century house has just four rooms set around a garden decorated with local pottery. The rooms vary quite a bit, but the best are extremely comfortable and decorated with lovely touches, such as granite or wooden counters in the bathroom and local art on the walls.

Homemade breakfasts are sumptuous, the friendly artist owners will make you feel right at home, and you're also welcome to use the kitchen to make your own meals. The owners aren't always around so call in advance to let them know when you'll be arriving.

Hotel Plaza BUSINESS HOTEL $$
(☑ 452-523-34-88; www.hotelplazauruapan.com.mx; Av Ocampo 64; r M$1050; P❄@🛜) Something of an institution in Uruapan and perhaps a little institutionalized as a result, the Plaza nevertheless delivers the hotel basics with large rooms overlooking the town's boisterous main square. Showers and bathrooms are huge, plus there are two excellent restaurants, a small gym and a business center.

Hotel Mansión del Cupatitzio HOTEL $$$
(☑ 452-523-20-60; www.mansiondelcupatitzio.com; Calz Rodilla del Diablo 20; s/d from M$1475/1795; P@🛜🏊) Enter this beautiful property and you come face to face with mounds of flower arrangements, religious art and sparkly balls of roses. It gives off an instant air of calm. This is further enhanced by the carefully tended gardens and beautiful pool. Rooms, though, while perfectly pleasant and comfy, are a bit dowdy in comparison.

It's up by the northern entrance of the Parque Nacional Barranca del Cupatitzio.

🍴 Eating & Drinking

Café Tradicional de Uruapan CAFE $
(☑ 452-523-56-80; Carranza 5B; snacks & breakfast M$35-100; ⊙8am-10:30pm) This dark cafe

with its hand-carved wooden interior is the best place in town for breakfast. You can study the saints' faces carved below the bar as you dig into generous portions of eggs, fruit and sweet breads. It's the perfect overture to an ascent of Volcán Paricutín – and you'll probably need to come back for some cake when you've finished.

Cox-Hanal MEXICAN $
(Carranza 31A; mains M$35-95; ⊙11am-9pm) The chairs are plastic, the menu's stapled to the table, and the waiter could well roll up in a Barcelona shirt, but so what? This place is about mix-and-match *antojitos yucatecos* (small dishes from the Yucatán). There's not much to look at decor-wise, but plenty to taste in the food. Prices are very reasonable too.

La Casa PIZZA $$
(☑ 452-524-36-11; Revolución 3; mains M$50-110; ⊙2-11pm; 🍴) An understated little spot with low music, low lighting and folk art scattered within its stone walls. The specialty here is pizza, which, while not particularly great, makes a welcome change from Mexican fare. The huge steak sandwiches are also tempting.

La Mansión del Cupatitzio MEXICAN $$$
(Calz Rodilla del Diablo 20; mains M$120-250; ⊙7:30am-11pm) This indoor-outdoor restaurant in a hotel of the same name can't be equaled for setting; the alfresco part is sheltered under umbrellas in a pretty garden given extra zest by a swimming pool. It's almost heresy to come here and not order the trout from the adjacent Cupatitzio river, done various ways, but best baked with chilies and macadamia nuts.

La Lucha CAFE
(☑ 452-524-03-75; Ortiz 20; coffees M$30; ⊙8:30am-9pm) The arched interior of this charming cafe makes for a very pleasant place for a coffee and a piece of cake. There are black-and-white photos on the wall and a great little courtyard out the back. It does a brisk trade in selling its own beans. There's another smaller branch in the main plaza (same opening hours).

🛍 Shopping

Mercado de Antojitos MARKET
(Quiroga; ⊙8am-11pm) The suitably whimsical Mercado de Antojitos, on the north side of the plaza, is ideal if you're in the market for candy, DVDs, strawberries, bras, cowboy boots or a taco.

Fábrica San Pedro
CLOTHING, HOMEWARES
(Treviño ; ⊙9am-6pm) Fábrica San Pedro has exquisite handmade textiles made on site.

Mercado de Artesanías
SOUVENIRS
(Calzada de San Miguel; ⊙9am-6pm) Opposite the entrance to the Parque Nacional Barranca del Cupatitzio, the Mercado de Artesanías has local crafts, though mostly of a poor quality.

La Macadamia
FOOD
(☑452-523-82-17; Carranza 21; ⊙9am-2pm & 4-7pm Mon-Sat) La Macadamia sells – you guessed it – products made from local macadamia nuts, from delicious macadamia marzipan to macadamia moisturizer.

ⓘ Information
Several banks (with ATMs), along with a few *cambios,* are near the central plaza.

Main Post Office (Jalisco 81; ⊙9am-3pm Mon-Fri, to 1pm Sat)

ⓘ Getting There & Around
Uruapan's bus terminal is 2km northeast of central Uruapan on the highway to Pátzcuaro and Morelia. For Tingambato (M$16, 30 minutes) take the same bus as those to Pátzcuaro or Morelia.

Local buses marked 'Centro' run from just outside the bus terminal to the plaza (M$7). For taxis, buy a ticket inside the bus terminal (M$30). For the return trip catch a 'Central Camionera' bus from the south side of the plaza.

Around Uruapan

Cascada de Tzaráracua
Ten kilometers south of downtown Uruapan, the wild Río Cupatitzio makes its last act count. It pumps hard over the vine-covered, 30m-high red-rock cliffs and crashes into a misty turquoise pool. This is the **Tzaráracua waterfall** (☑452-106-04-41; adult/child M$15/5, car extra M$5; ⊙10am-6pm). A meandering hike down the 557 slippery steps leads to the foliage-framed falls, or you can mount a horse (M$100 round trip with a 30-minute wait at the falls). There are a couple of **zip-lines**. One shoots you over the forest canopy, while a separate operator offers short 'flights' over the pool in front of the falls (M$50 to M$150).

There's also a 20-minute hike upstream from Tzaráracua to the equally beautiful **Tzararacuita**, a smaller waterfall. This trail is not as well maintained, so bring waterproof sandals. To get here, follow the steep track beyond the Tzaráracua bridge and after 10 minutes turn right at the stone outcropping.

Hourly buses to Tzaráracua (M$7) depart from in front of the Hotel Regis, on the south side of Uruapan's main plaza. A round trip with a taxi will cost from M$100 to M$120 with a wait.

Tingambato
Stroll through luscious avocado groves to the beautiful **ruins** (M$47; ⊙9am-5pm) of this ceremonial site, which predates the Tarascan empire and thrived from about AD 450 to 900. Rarely visited and beautifully atmospheric as a result, they are located outside Tingambato village, about 30km from Uruapan on the road to Pátzcuaro. The ruins, which include two plazas, three altars and a ball court (rare in western Mexico), have a Teotihuacán influence. There's also an 8m-high stepped pyramid and an underground tomb where a skeleton and 32 scattered skulls were found – hinting at beheading or trophy-skull rituals.

BUSES FROM URUAPAN

DESTINATION	FARE (M$)	DURATION (HR)	FREQUENCY (DAILY)
Angahuan	21	1	half-hourly
Colima	469	6	1
Guadalajara	378	4½	hourly
Mexico City (Terminal Norte)	573	7	hourly
Morelia	110	2	hourly
Paracho	21	1	every 15min
Pátzcuaro	68	1	every 15min

Buses to Morelia leave from Uruapan's terminal every 20 minutes and stop in Tingambato (M$16, 30 minutes). The ruins are 1.4km downhill on Juárez, the first street on the right as you enter town.

Angahuan

📞 452 / POP 5700 / ELEV 2693M

Angahuan, 35km from Uruapan and the nearest town to the incredible Volcán Paricutín, is a typical Purépecha town: there are wooden houses, dusty streets, more horses than cars, women in ankle-length skirts and colorful shawls, and loudspeakers booming announcements in the Purépecha tongue.

◎ Sights

★ Volcán Paricutín VOLCANO

The young upstart of Volcán Paricutín (2800m) might be less than 80 years old, but clambering up the volcanic-scree slopes to its summit and looking out across blackened, village-engulfing lava fields is a highlight of travel in this part of Mexico.

You can trek to it on horseback or by foot (though the last part is always by foot), but whatever option you choose prepare for a long and rewarding day.

The story behind this volcano is as extraordinary as the views from its summit. On February 20, 1943, Dionisio Pulido, a Purépecha farmer, was plowing his cornfield some 35km west of Uruapan when the ground began to quake and spurt steam, sparks and hot ash. The farmer struggled to cover the blast holes, but he quickly realized his futility and ran. Good thing, because like some Hollywood B-grade movie, a growling volcano began to rise. Within a year it had reached an elevation of 410m above the rolling farmland and its lava had flooded the Purépecha villages of San Salvador Paricutín and San Juan Parangaricutiro. Thankfully, the lava flowed slowly, giving the villagers plenty of time to escape.

The volcano continued to grow until 1952. Today its large black cone whispers warm steam in a few places, but otherwise appears dormant. Near the edge of the 20-sq-km lava field, the top of the ruined **Templo San Juan Parangaricutiro**, San Juan's stone church, protrudes eerily from a sea of black lava. Its tower and altar are the only visible traces of the two buried villages. It's a one-hour (3km) walk to the church from Angahuan.

You need to be striding out of Angahuan before 9am if you want to climb Volcán Paricutín. There's no shortage of guides with horses in town offering their services to the ruined church, volcano, or both, and they will meet you at the bus from Uruapan. Horses and a guide should cost around M$700 in total per person per day. There are two standard routes up the volcano: a 14km round-trip short route and a 24km round-trip long route. Horses always go via the long route as the short route crosses a lava field. If you're going by horse allow six hours (including at least four in an unforgiving, wooden saddle).

Whichever route you take, the final scramble up the volcano – a steep syrupy grunt through warm black sand – is always on foot. Coming down is a different matter – bank on two minutes if you're brave. The standard route visits the San Juan church (3km from Angahuan) on the way back. The altar is almost always blessed with colorful offerings of candles and flowers. Close to the church are a number of food stalls serving fabulously tasty blue-corn quesadillas cooked on old, wood-burning, oil-can skillets. Bring enough water and wear decent shoes.

If wooden saddles intimidate you, or you have energy to burn, you can walk to the volcano, but you'll still need a guide (M$300 to M$500 depending on your bargaining skills) as the trail through the pine forest can be hard to find. The long route follows a sandy track for around 12km through avocado groves, agave fields and wildflowers. The short route (7km one way) starts in pine forest but then switches to difficult rock-hopping across an expansive lava field. If you're fit and want variety, ask your guide to hike out on the short route and back on the longer trek. Whichever way, set off early.

Iglesia de Santiago Apóstol CHURCH

On the main plaza is the sensational 16th-century Iglesia de Santiago Apóstol. Candles and incense burn, fresh flowers crowd the altar and the detailed doorway was carved by a Moorish stonemason who accompanied the early Spanish missionaries here.

❶ Getting There & Away

Angahuan is 35km from Uruapan. Buses leave the Uruapan bus terminal for Angahuan every 30 minutes from 5am to 7pm (M$21, one hour).

Buses return to Uruapan every 30 minutes until about 8pm (double-check on arrival) and few cabs are available in town, so don't miss that last bus!

Northern Central Highlands

Includes ➡

Querétaro	638
Tequisquiapan	645
Guanajuato	648
León	658
Dolores Hidalgo	658
San Miguel de Allende	661
Aguascalientes	673
San Luis Potosí	678
Matehuala	684
Real de Catorce	684
La Huasteca Potosina	689
Zacatecas	691
La Quemada	699

Why Go?

From cobbled lanes to pretty plazas, deserts to cloud forest, the northern central highlands region is as varied as its history, cuisine and cultures. It was here that former mineral wealth created colonial cities and revolutionary activity left ghost towns in its wake. Known as the Cuna de la Independencia (Cradle of Independence), the territory is renowned for its part in the country's fight for autonomy.

Particular jewels include silver-ridden Guanajuato and Zacatecas, arty San Miguel de Allende, the turquoise-colored Huasteca Potosina and nature-filled Sierra Gorda. And as for the cuisine... Travel a few kilometers for another take on a trusty tortilla or regional specialty. Culture vultures can feast on pre-Hispanic sites and art museums, concerts, nightlife, festivals and *callejoneadas* ("walking serenades") – the northern central highlands continue centuries of pomp and ceremony. It sure knows how to put on a good (if noisy) party.

Best Places to Eat

➡ Áperi (p669)

➡ Las Mercedes (p656)

➡ Tata (p643)

➡ Cafe Cortáo (p682)

Best Places to Stay

➡ Posada Corazón (p668)

➡ Hotel Emporio Zacatecas (p696)

➡ Villa María Cristina (p654)

➡ Casa del Atrio (p641)

When to Go
Guanajuato

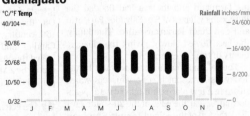

°C/°F Temp — Rainfall inches/mm

40/104 — — 24/600
30/86 — — 16/400
20/68 — — 8/200
10/50 —
0/32 — — 0
J F M A M J J A S O N D

Jul & Aug Days are mild and wildflowers bloom; it's the perfect time for do-it-yourself explorations.

Oct–Apr It's dry season in the Huasteca Potosina; great for excursions to waterfalls and rivers.

Late Mar or Apr Traditional religious festivities abound during Semana Santa (Holy Week).

Northern Central Highlands Highlights

❶ Meandering through winding cobbled alleys and marvelous museums in **Guanajuato** (p648).

❷ Feeding your soul with art, food and fiestas in popular **San Miguel de Allende** (p661).

❸ Marveling at the missions and staying in communities within in the wilderness jewel, the **Reserva de la Biosfera Sierra Gorda** (p647).

❹ Sensing the spirits of miners in the picturesque, reawakening 'ghost' town of **Real de Catorce** (p684).

❺ Plunging into the remarkable turquoise rivers of the **Huasteca Potosina** (p689).

❻ Taking a positive spin on death in **Museo Nacional de la Muerte** (p673), Aguascalientes.

History

Until the Spanish conquest, the northern central highlands were inhabited by fierce seminomadic tribes known to the Aztecs as Chichimecs. They resisted Spanish expansion longer than other Mexican peoples but were ultimately conquered in the late 16th century. The wealth subsequently amassed by the Spanish was at the cost of many Chichimecs, who were used as slave labor in the mines.

This historically volatile region sparked the criollo fight for independence from Spain, which was plotted in Querétaro and San Miguel de Allende and launched from Dolores Hidalgo in 1810. A century later Francisco Madero released his revolutionary Plan de San Luis Potosí and the 1917 signing of Mexico's constitution in Querétaro cemented the region's leading role in Mexican political affairs.

In more recent times the region has flourished economically, due in part to the boom in the motor, aerospace, manufacturing and agricultural industries, particularly around Querétaro, while San Miguel attracts many weekenders from Mexico City. The Huasteca Potosina, a subregion of San Luis Potosí, is particularly rich in culture and wilderness; this previously remote area now has a thriving tourism infrastructure.

❶ Getting There & Around

The Aeropuerto Internacional del Bajío, halfway between León and Guanajuato, is the major hub for the region's southern cities. Other airports, all with US flights (some via Mexico City), include Aguascalientes, Querétaro, San Luis Potosí and Zacatecas. Buses constantly ply the toll roads between Mexico City, Guadalajara, Querétaro and San Luis Potosí. The larger hubs, including Zacatecas, León and Aguascalientes, also host connections to northern Mexico, the US border and beyond. Frequent local buses efficiently connect the major cities and all points in between.

QUERÉTARO STATE

Querétaro state (population 1.9 million) is full of surprises. Billed primarily as an agricultural and ranching state – with the handsome Querétaro city as its capital – it is packed with diverse geography, quirky sights and historical gems. Natural phenomena, such as the world's third-largest monolith, La Peña de Bernal, pre-Hispanic ruins and the stunning Sierra Gorda Biosphere Reserve, are located within the borders of this 11,770-sq-km state. The reserve protects several mission towns, from where the local people run some excellent, community-owned tourism ventures – a must for the more intrepid traveler.

Querétaro

🎵 442 / POP 805,000 / ELEV 1800M

As far as the silver cities go, Querétaro is sometimes intimated to be the ugly sibling. Indeed, although it's believed to be one of the fastest growing cities in the northern hemisphere thanks to it being the base for international industries, including the aerospace industry, its rather frantic outskirts can give a misguided first impression. The city's large, historic heart is characterized by charming *andadores* (pedestrian streets,

and very clean ones at that), stunning plazas and interesting churches. The sophisticated restaurants serve up quality cuisine and the museums reflect Querétaro's important role in Mexican history.

History

The Otomí founded a settlement here in the 15th century that was soon absorbed by the Aztecs, then by the Spaniards in 1531. Franciscan monks used it as a missionary base not only to Mexico but also to what is now southwestern USA. In the early 19th century, Querétaro became a center of intrigue among disaffected criollos plotting to free Mexico from Spanish rule. Conspirators, including Miguel Hidalgo, met secretly at the house of doña Josefa Ortiz (La Corregidora), who was the wife of Querétaro's former *corregidor* (district administrator).

When the conspiracy was uncovered, the story goes, doña Josefa was locked in her house (now the Palacio de Gobierno) but managed to whisper through a keyhole to a co-conspirator, Ignacio Pérez, that their colleagues were in jeopardy, leading to Padre Hidalgo's call to arms.

In 1917 the Mexican constitution was drawn up by the Constitutionalist faction in Querétaro. The PNR (which later became the PRI, the Institutional Revolutionary Party) was organized in Querétaro in 1929, dominating Mexican politics for the rest of the 20th century.

◉ Sights

★ MUCAL   MUSEUM
(Museo del Calendario; www.mucal.mx; Madero 91; adult M$25; ⊙10am-6pm Tue-Sun) The first of its kind in the world, this extraordinary museum is the labor of love of its owner Señor Landin, whose family has been producing calendars in Mexico for decades. There are two parts to the museum: 19 exhibition rooms that house the original artworks (including reproductions) that featured in decades of Mexico's calendars, along with over 400 original retro-style calendars themselves. The second is the building itself, a stunningly renovated mansion, complete with beautiful garden and courtyards.

The garden, courtyards, and an excellent cafe, set on its lawns, provide a perfect oasis from the heat, and a place to reflect on the sometimes amusing (and often titillating) retro calendar depictions.

Templo de San Francisco
CHURCH

(cnr Av Corregidora & Andador 5 de Mayo; ⊗8am-9pm) This impressive church fronts Jardín Zenea. Pretty colored tiles on the dome were brought from Spain in 1540, around the time construction of the church began. Inside are some fine religious paintings from the 17th, 18th and 19th centuries.

Museo Regional
MUSEUM

(cnr Av Corregidora 3 & Jardín Zenea; M$52; ⊗9am-6pm Tue-Sun) This museum is beside the Templo de San Francisco. The ground floor holds interesting exhibits on pre-Hispanic Mexico, archaeological sites, Spanish occupation and the state's various indigenous groups. The upstairs exhibits reveal Querétaro's role in the independence movement and post-independence history (plus religious paintings). The table at which the Treaty of Guadalupe Hidalgo was signed in 1848, ending the Mexican–American War, is on display, as is the desk of the tribunal that sentenced Emperor Maximilian to death.

The museum is housed in part of what was once a huge monastery and seminary. Begun in 1540, the seminary became the seat of the Franciscan province of San Pedro y San Pablo de Michoacán by 1567. Building continued until at least 1727. Thanks to its high tower, in the 1860s the monastery was used as a fort both by imperialists supporting Maximilian and by the forces who defeated him in 1867.

Templo y Convento de la Santa Cruz
CHURCH

(Independencia 148 at Felipe Luna; M$10; ⊗9am-2pm & 4-6pm Tue-Sat, to 5:15pm Sun) Ten minutes' walk east of the center of Querétaro is one of the city's most interesting sights. The convent was built between 1654 and about 1815 on the site of a battle in which a miraculous appearance of Santiago (St James) led the Otomí to surrender to the conquistadors and Christianity. Emperor Maximilian had his headquarters here while under siege in Querétaro from March to May 1867. After his surrender and subsequent death sentence, he was jailed here while awaiting the firing squad.

Today it's used as a religious school. You must visit with a guide – you wait at the entrance until a group has formed – although tours are in Spanish. The site's main legend is the growth of the Árbol de la Cruz, an ancient tree in the convent's garden, whose thorns are in the shape of crosses. This miracle was the result of a walking stick stuck in the earth by a pious friar in 1697.

Museo de Arte de Querétaro
MUSEUM

(www.museodeartequeretaro.com; Allende Sur 14; M$30, photos M$15, Tue free; ⊗10am-6pm Tue-Sun) Querétaro's art museum, located adjacent to the Templo de San Agustín, occupies a splendid baroque monastery built between 1731 and 1748. It's worth visiting to see the building alone: angels, gargoyles, statues and other ornamental details abound, particularly around the stunning courtyard.

The ground-floor display of 16th- and 17th-century European paintings traces influences from Flemish to Spanish to Mexican art. Here, too, you'll find 19th- and 20th-century Mexican paintings. The top floor has works from 16th-century Mannerism to 18th-century baroque.

The museum has a good bookstore-cum-gift shop.

Museo de la Ciudad
MUSEUM

(www.museodelaciudadqro.org; Guerrero Norte 27; M$5; ⊗11am-7pm Tue-Sun) Inside the ex-convent and old prison that held Maximilian, the 11-room Museo de la Ciudad has some good alternating contemporary-art exhibits.

Museo de la Restauración de la República
MUSEUM

(www.queretaro.gob.mx/mrr; Guerrero Norte 23; ⊗9am-5pm Tue-Fri, from 10am Sat & Sun) FREE If you can read Spanish or are a real history buff, this museum covers Querétaro's role in Mexico's history, particularly the French occupation and the eventual ousting of Emperor Maximilian.

Teatro de la República
THEATER

(☑442-212-03-39; cnr Juárez & Peralta; ⊗10am-3pm & 5-8pm) FREE This lovely, old functioning theater, complete with impressive chandeliers, was where a tribunal met in 1867 to decide the fate of Emperor Maximilian. Mexico's constitution was also signed here on January 31, 1917. The stage backdrop lists the names of its signatories and the states they represented. In 1929, politicians met in the theater to organize Mexico's political party, the PNR (now called PRI).

Mirador
LOOKOUT

Walk east along Independencia past Convento de la Santa Cruz, then fork right along Ejército Republicano, to the mirador. There's a fine view of 'Los Arcos,' Querétaro's emblematic 1.28km-long aqueduct, with 74 towering sandstone arches built between

1726 and 1738. The aqueduct runs along the center of Avenida Zaragoza.

Mausoleo de la Corregidora   MAUSOLEUM
(Ejército Republicano s/n; ⊙9am-6pm) The Mausoleo de la Corregidora, opposite the *mirador*, is the resting place of doña Josefa Ortiz and her husband, Miguel Domínguez de Alemán.

Monumento a la Corregidora   MONUMENT
(cnr Corregidora & Andador 16 de Septiembre) FREE Plaza de la Corregidora is dominated by the Monumento a la Corregidora, a 1910 statue of doña Josefa Ortiz bearing the flame of freedom.

Templo de Santa Clara   CHURCH
(cnr Madero & Allende) The 17th-century Templo de Santa Clara has an extraordinarily ornate baroque interior. Masses are held frequently so you'll have to inquire as to the best time to enter.

Fuente de Neptuno   FOUNTAIN
(Neptune's Fountain; cnr Madero & Allende) A block west of Jardín Zenea is the Fuente de Neptuno, designed by noted Mexican neoclassical architect Eduardo Tresguerras in 1797.

Templo de Santa Rosa de Viterbos   CHURCH
(cnr Arteaga & Montes) FREE The 18th-century Templo de Santa Rosa de Viterbos is Querétaro's most splendid baroque church, with its pagoda-like bell tower, unusual exterior paintwork, curling buttresses and lavishly gilded and marbled interior. The church also boasts what some say is the earliest four-sided clock in the New World.

Cathedral   CATHEDRAL
(cnr Madero & Ocampo) FREE The 18th-century cathedral features both baroque and neoclassical styles, with an emphasis on straight lines (few curves); it's said that the first mass in the cathedral (then known as San Felipe

Neri) was lead by Padre Hidalgo, he of Independence fame.

Courses

**Olé Spanish
Language School** LANGUAGE COURSE

(442-214-40-23; www.ole.edu.mx; Escobedo 32) The Olé Spanish Language School offers a range of courses with homestay options and extracurricular programs. Prices start at around US$17.50 per hour, and week-long courses range from moderate group classes (15 hours) for US$181 to 35-hour intensive courses for $466.

Festivals & Events

Feria Internacional FAIR

Querétaro's Feria Internacional, one of Mexico's biggest state fairs, happens in the first two weeks of December. It focuses on agriculture but also hosts cultural events.

Sleeping

Casa Peti GUESTHOUSE $

(casapeti.com; Manuel Gutierrez Najera 7 Norte; r M$45) This delightful spot, with hipster-style boutique rooms and a plant-filled courtyard, is still being renovated. Though you probably wouldn't care if this industrial chic spot were a rat's nest (it's not), so friendly and hospitable is the delightful English speaking host, Ernesto. A fabulous budget choice.

Blue Bicycle House HOSTEL $

(442-455-48-13; http://bluebicyclehouse.com; Ejercito Republicano 15; dm M$175-210, d M$490-650;) Located just on the edge of the center, with a view of the aqueduct, the Blue Bicycle House (yes, there's a bicycle hanging outside) is a welcome hostel addition to Querétaro's budget scene. It's small and simple and offers dorms, including one for women only. Beds are long by Mexican standards.

Price includes a continental breakfast and one-hour bike use.

Kuku Rukú HOTEL, HOSTEL $

(442-245-87-77; www.kukuruku.mx; Vergara 12; dm from M$195; d incl breakfast M$890-1050;) When it comes to hotel-cum-hostels, usually one group of clients gets the better deal. In this funky accommodations hybrid, we think hostellers come out on top, with clean, modern dorms. The decor in the hotel rooms is pretty hip, but you'll pay substantially more for the privilege to enjoy it.

Hotel Quinta Lucca HOTEL $$

(442-340-44-44; www.hotelquintalucca.com; Juárez Norte 119A; r M$990, ste M$1200-1400;) Mexican-modern interiors in neat, clean rooms. Those in the rear are more pleasant, and surround a luscious green courtyard, where a continental breakfast is served.

Home B&B B&B $$

(442-183-91-39; www.queretarobandb.com; Calle 16 de Septiembre 104; s/d US$45/65;) Spread across two buildings, and despite the odd quirky blip, this sprawling house is in a convenient location. The rooms vary in shape and size but, true to their name, are old-style homey.

Breakfast costs US$7. Minimum two nights; prices are lower for long-term stays. Note: by reservation only.

★ La Casa del Atrio B&B $$$

(442-212-63-14; www.lacasadelatrio.com; Allende Sur 15; r incl breakfast M$1650-2450;) This gorgeous spot has morphed from its

Querétaro

◉ Top Sights
1 MUCAL A3

◎ Sights
2 Cathedral.. A3
3 Fuente de Neptuno.............................. B2
4 Mausoleo de la Corregidora F2
5 Mirador..F2
6 Monumento a la Corregidora B2
7 Museo de Arte de Querétaro B3
8 Museo de la Ciudad.............................. A2
 Museo de la Restauración
 de la República............................(see 8)
9 Museo Regional C2
10 Teatro de la República........................ B2
11 Templo de San Francisco C2
12 Templo de Santa Clara........................ B2
13 Templo de Santa Rosa de
 Viterbos... A4
14 Templo y Convento de la Santa
 Cruz..E2

🛏 Sleeping
15 Blue Bicycle House...............................F2
16 Casa Peti D1
17 Home B&B D1
18 Hotel Quinta Lucca.............................. B1

19 Kuku Rukú...C3
20 La Casa del Atrio B3
21 La Casa del Naranjo A2

✴ Eating
22 Biznarga E2
23 Breton C2
24 Brewer Gastro Pub.............................. A4
25 La Antojería C2
26 La Dolce Vita.. D1
27 La Mariposa B1
28 La Vieja Varsovia E2
29 Restaurante Bar 1810 .... C2
30 Tata E1
31 Tikua B3

🍷 Drinking & Nightlife
32 El Faro E1
33 Gracias a Dios...................................... C2

🎭 Entertainment
34 Casa de la Cultura C2
 Teatro de la República ....(see 10)

🛍 Shopping
35 Manos Queretanas............................... B3

original three-rooms-in-an-antique-store to a stunning boutique hotel, with 12 rooms, several glorious courtyard spaces and an on-site spa. The bilingual host, Antonio, will go out of his way to run a professional ship and ensure everything – from each artistic, art-filled room to the delicious breakfasts – are to your liking.

Rooms and bathrooms are spacious, though if you insist on open windows at night (all rooms feature massive doors, but not windows, that open onto courtyards), then communicate this on reservation. Otherwise it's a win-win choice.

La Casa del Naranjo BOUTIQUE HOTEL **$$$**
(☑ 442-212-76-06; www.lacasadelnaranjo.com; Hidalgo 21; r incl breakfast M$1155-1830; P🛜) The six rooms in this boutique hotel are decorated in an eclectic but stylish manner. Each room is named after a fruit and the timber from the fruit trees has been incorporated into the design. Downstairs rooms are more cramped than the airier options above, but there are several attractive outdoor lounge areas.

✖ Eating

★ **La Mariposa** CAFE **$**
(Peralta 7; snacks M$25-120; ⊘8am-9:30pm; ⊜) Unchanged since 1940 (as the photos and

coffee machine testify), this Querétaro institution is more about the quaint atmosphere than the food. Don't leave without trying the mouthwatering *volteado de piña* (a version of a pineapple cake; M$15) or the *mantecado* (egg-based ice cream; M$18 per scoop).

Breton BAKERY **$**
(Andador Libertad 82B; mains M$70-120; ⊘8am-5pm Tue-Sat; 🛜) A delightful French bakehouse with a lovely upstairs area. Serves up excellent breakfasts and lunches. Vegetarians will have a field day (and there's even vegan options).

Biznarga CAFE **$**
(Gutiérrez Najera 17; mains M$38-62; ⊘9am-2pm & 6-11pm Mon-Sat; ⊜) Their friends liked their cooking so much the owners of Biznarga opened their kitchen to the public. It serves up the grunge factor, but is a popular and fun Rasta experience with graffiti, artworks and memorabilia. Salads, homemade pizzas, juices and more.

La Antojería MEXICAN **$**
(Calle 5 de Mayo; mains M$40-85; ⊘10am-11pm; ⊜🖽) This family-friendly, fun Mexican-themed place serves up every style of

antojito (typical Mexican snacks) known in Mexico.

★ Tata
MEXICAN $$

(www.tatamezcaleria.com; 5 de Mayo 130; mains M$110-260; ⊘2pm-midnight Wed-Sat, to 6:30pm Sun) A bright funky spot that specializes in mezcal and modern Mexican using wholly Mexican and very local products. Chef Fermín Ambás' tasty and colorful creations include duck *(pato)* tacos that will have you quacking for more, a wicked chocolate mousse with *chapulines* (grasshoppers), and a wide choice of mezcals that will get you into the spirit.

The vegetable dish resembles an edible Monet painting.

Brewer Gastro Pub
INTERNATIONAL $$

(www.erlum.com.mx; Arteaga 55; mains M$95-235; ⊘1pm-2am Wed-Sat, to 8pm Sun; ⊜) 🍴 This is what happens when a local artisanal brewer joins forces with a good eatery (formerly called Erlum): a casual drinking spot that serves up fabulous brews, from honey IPAs *(miel de abeja)* to a mezcal beer mix (Agave Ale), to excellent dishes. The chef uses 'clean' food – all products are local or the provenance is known. Excellent charcuterie, pizzas and salads.

Tikua
MEXICAN $$

(www.tikua.mx; Allende Sur 13; mains M$75-180; ⊘9am-midnight Mon-Sat, 8:30am-9pm Sun) Tikua specializes in Southeastern Mexican cuisine and the dishes – from the *xi'i*, a mushroom salad, to the Oaxacan chorizo recipes – are true to their roots. The rice with *chapulines* (grasshoppers), *tasajo* (salted beef) and chocolate *mole* (a type of sauce) are especially good. Serves up a mezcal menu and mixes too.

Restaurante Bar 1810
MEXICAN $$$

(Libertad 62; mains M$140-320; ⊘8am-11pm Mon-Sat, to 10pm Sun; ⊜) Situated on the pretty plaza, this eatery has been here for a quarter of a century. It's reliable for excellent steaks and a variety of pastas and seafood dishes. Live crooners complement (or otherwise) your meal.

🍷 Drinking & Nightlife

There's a thriving bar scene in Querétaro. Bars and clubs are popping up (and sometimes down) in the historic center and beyond. Calle 5 de Mayo is the fashionable drinking strip in the center; barflies hit these places after 10pm.

El Faro
BAR

(Calle 16 de Septiembre 128) A shining light and welcome addition to the local drinking scene, The Lighthouse exudes elements of old with a recent polish (it originally opened in 1927 and is believed to be the city's oldest bar). The current owners took over in early 2015 so the interior is a little hipper for it. But the swinging cantina doors and friendly vibe are standing legacies.

Guests are addressed by their first names, free bar snacks keep you standing, and it boasts the longest happy hour in Mexico (5pm to 10pm on Monday, and 2pm to 8pm Tuesday to Friday).

Gracias a Dios
BAR

(Calle 5 de Mayo; snacks M$60-120; ⊘2pm-1:30am Tue-Sat) One of the many bars near Calle 5 de Mayo, this new place revives – *Gracias a Dios* ('Thank God') – traditions of old: a *cantina-botanero* (bar with snacks) complete with barrels and stools and a touch of grunge-and-sticky-bar-syndrome. However, it also has a touch of feminine funk and attracts a young crowd out for whiskey, tequila and brandy-fuelled fun.

☆ Entertainment

Querétaro is action-packed with cultural activities. For the latest on what's happening around town, look out for posters on bulletin boards, or pick up a copy of *Asomarte* from the tourist office. On Sunday, free concerts take place in Plaza de Armas at 1pm and in the evenings in Jardín Zenea.

Casa de la Cultura
CONCERT VENUE, PERFORMING ARTS

(🖉442-212-56-14; Calle 5 de Mayo 40; ⊘9am-2pm & 4-8pm Mon-Fri) Sponsors concerts, dance, theater and art events; stop by to view the bulletin board.

BAKERIES

Excellent contemporary bakeries abound in Queretaro. Bread and pastry lovers should definitely follow their noses to the following places, some of which double as cafes: **La Vieja Varsovia** (www.laviejavarsovia.com.mx; Plaza de los Fundadores; snacks M$50-140; ⊘8:30am-11pm Tue-Sun), **Breton** (p642) and **La Dolche Vita** (Calle 5 de Mayo).

Teatro de la República THEATER
(cnr Juárez & Peralta; tickets M$60-180) Has regular symphony concerts most Fridays.

🛍 Shopping

Manos Queretanas SOUVENIRS
(www.manosqueretanas.com; Allende Sur 20; ⏱ market 9am-8pm Tue-Sun, museum 9am-6pm Wed-Sun) FREE This community-run initiative, a project of the Centro de Desarrollo Artesanal Indígena, was established to provide a place for street sellers from around Queretaro (such as the Hnahñu, Mazahua, Purépecha, Nahua, Triquis and Wixarikas communities) to display their handicrafts and to promote their indigenous culture. It's a lovely space, with a small modern museum and a market in the rear.

ℹ Information

There are several banks with ATMs around Jardín Zenea.

Médica Tec 100 (☎ 442-477-22-22; http://hospitaltec100.com; Zaragoza 16-B) This private hospital comes recommended by expats.
Post Office (Arteaga 5)
Tourist Office (☎ 800-715-17-42, 442-238-50-67; www.queretaro.travel; Pasteur Norte 4; ⏱ 9am-7pm) Has city maps and brochures (in Spanish), plus a useful publication Asomarte with listings of what's on. Kiosks are located on the plazas (open 10am to 7pm daily). At the time of research, the new government was set to change the tourism team.

ℹ Getting There & Away

AIR

The Aeropuerto Internacional (☎ 442-192-55-00; www.aiq.com.mx), 8km northeast of the center, is around a M$300 taxi ride from the center. Primera Plus also runs from the bus terminal to Mexico City airport (M$365, three hours). United Airlines (www.united.com) has flights to various US cities from Querétaro.

BUS

Querétaro is a hub for buses in all directions; the modern Central Camionera is 5km southeast of the center. There's one building for deluxe and 1st class (labeled A), one for 2nd class (B) and another for local buses (C). Facilities include basic luggage storage.
Primera Plus (www.primeriaplus.com.mx) has regular services to Mexico City airport.

ℹ Getting Around

Once you have reached downtown, you can easily visit most sights on foot. City buses (M$8.50) run from 6am until 9pm or 10pm. They gather in an area at the end of the bus terminal; turn right from the 2nd-class terminal, or left from the 1st-class side. Several routes go to the center (the numbers change, so check.) For a taxi, get a ticket first from the bus station booth (M$50 for up to four people.)

To get to the bus station from the center, take city bus marked 'Central' (ie Central de Autobuses) from Zaragoza, or any bus labeled 'TAQ' (ie Terminal de Autobuses de Querétaro) or 'Central' heading south on the east side of the Alameda Hidalgo.

BUSES FROM QUERÉTARO

DESTINATION	FARE (M$)	DURATION (HR)	FREQUENCY (DAILY)
Ciudad Valles	570-625	7	3 daily
Guadalajara	410-620	4½-5½	frequent
Guanajuato	217	2½-3	7
Mexico City (Terminal Norte)	212-330	3-4½	every 20min 4am-11:30pm
Mexico City airport	365	3½	hourly
Morelia	185-300	3-4	frequent
San Luis Potosí	197-310	2½-2¾	frequent
San Miguel de Allende	67-115	1-1½	every 40min 6am-11pm
Tequisquiapan	50	1	every 30min 6:30am-9pm
Xilitla	326-400	5-8	1 per day with Primera Plus, 3 per day with Flecha Amarilla

BERNAL

With a population of 4000, the tiny town of Bernal is quaint, if touristy, and you can cover it in an hour or so. (Note: it comes to life during the weekends; many things are closed from Monday to Thursday.) Its drawcard is the 350m-high rock spire, **Peña de Bernal**, the third-largest monolith in the world and considered mystical by many Mexicans. During the vernal equinox thousands of pilgrims converge on the rock to take in its positive energy. Visitors can climb to the rock's halfway point (allow one hour both ways); only professional rock climbers can climb to its peak.

The town has several **churches**, and **El Castillo**, a 16th-century viceregal building. For a more in-depth explanation of the area, friendly **La Peña Tours** (☑ 441-296-73-98, cell 441-101-48-21; www.lapeniatours.com; cnr Independencia & Colon) offers an array of tours (M$150 to M$700) plus climbing sessions on the Peña. For shopping, head to **La Aurora** (Jardín Principal 1; ☺10am-8pm), an interesting *artesanías* (handicrafts) shop; request permission to see the weavers at work at their looms in the attached workshop.

Bernal is also known for its delicious *gorditas* (corn tortilla–based pocket stuffed with cheese, meat and other fillings), especially those filled with *nopales en penca* (cheese sauce with nopal cactus). Ask the way to the food market. **Casa Museo del Dulce** (Bernal; M$20; ☺10am-6pm Sat & Sun) highlights the town's former factory that produced caramelised sweets.

There are regular buses to/from Querétaro (around M$60, 45 minutes). The last return bus to Querétaro departs from the main road around 5:30pm. For connections to/from Tequisquiapan, change buses at Ezequiel Montes (M$13, 30 minutes).

Queretaro's downtown is relatively flat. For bike rental, head to **Movente** (☑ 442-212-63-65; www.movente.mx; Independencia 140; per hr from M$30; ☺11am-3pm & 6-8pm Tue-Sat), a bike shop with cool designs.

Tequisquiapan

☑ 414 / POP 30,000 / ELEV 1870M

This small town (teh-kees-kee-*ap*-an), 70km southeast of Querétaro, is a quaint weekend retreat from Mexico City or Querétaro. Tequisquiapan used to be known for its thermal springs – Mexican presidents came here to ease their aches and tensions. The town's natural pools may have long-since dried up, but its pretty, bougainvillea-lined streets, colorful colonial buildings and excellent markets make for an enjoyable browse.

⊙ Sights & Activities

Plaza Miguel Hidalgo   PLAZA
The wide and attractive Plaza Miguel Hidalgo is surrounded by *portales* (arcades), overlooked by the 19th-century neoclassical **La Parroquia de Santa María de la Asunción** (☺7:30am-8:30pm) with its pink facade and decorated tower.

Quinta Fernando Schmoll   GARDENS
(☑ 441-276-10-71; Colegio Militar 1; M$20; ☺8am-5pm Tue-Sat, 9am-5pm Sun) If you have your

own wheels, this extraordinary botanic garden, with over 4400 varieties of cactus, is on the east edge of the village of Cadereyta. It's located 38km from Tequisquiapan.

Horseback Riding   HORSEBACK RIDING
(Fray Junípero; rides per hour M$80-100; ☺10am-6pm Sat & Sun) Guided trail rides around the surrounding countryside are offered at weekends. Guides and their hacks congregate on Fray Junípero, just north of Parque La Pila.

★ Festivals & Events

Feria Nacional del Queso y del Vino   FOOD
The National Wine & Cheese Fair, from late May to early June, includes tastings and music.

Fiesta de la Asunción   RELIGIOUS
Commemorates the town's patron saint on August 15.

🍴 Sleeping & Eating

The best budget accommodations are the posadas along Moctezuma. Demand is low Monday to Thursday, when you may be able to negotiate a discount. Many restaurants around the plaza offer *comidas corridas* (prix-fixe menus). You'll find *fondas* (food stalls) at Mercado Guadalupana, a block northeast of the plaza.

Posada Tequisquiapan GUESTHOUSE $

(☑414-273-00-10; Moctezuma 6; s/d M$300/500; ℙ) A kick-back from the '50s that hasn't changed in eons. Simple but spacious rooms and a large back garden (with empty swimming pools, a legacy of the town's hot water spring days).

La Granja BOUTIQUE HOTEL $$

(☑414-273-20-04; www.hotelboutiquelagranja. com; Morelos 12; r from M$1925; ℙ❋☎☒) Located in a pretty part of town, this colonial building has been renovated into a lovely hotel, with spacious and sleek rooms and a large back garden with a pool. On-site restaurant serves breakfast.

K'puchinos MEXICAN $$

(Independencia 7; mains M$72-235; ⊗8am-10pm Sun-Thu, to midnight Sat; ☎) Handily located on the plaza, this reliable place caters to hungry souls for any Mexican meal of the day.

🛍 Shopping

Mercado de Artesanías MARKET

(Carrizal; ⊗8am-7pm) This crafts market is one of three markets, including **Mercado Artesenal** (household items) and the **Guadalupana** (for food), all found together on Carrizal, a block north of Tequisquiapan's main plaza. The main wholesale **Mercado Artesania** is opposite the bus station as you come into town (weekends only).

ℹ Information

The **tourist office** (☑414-273-08-41; Plaza Miguel Hidalgo; ⊗9am-7pm) has town maps and information on Querétaro state. On the plaza's southeast side, there's a Bancomer ATM.

ℹ Getting There & Around

Tequisquiapan is 20km northeast on Hwy 120 from the larger town of San Juan del Río. The bus terminal is around 2km north of the center in the new part of town. Local buses (M$8) from outside the bus station run to the markets on Carrizal, one block northeast of the Plaza Principal.

Flecha Azul runs half-hourly to/from Querétaro between 6:30am and 8pm (M$50, one hour). Buses also run to Ezequiel Montes (change here for Bernal; M$13, 20 minutes). ETN has deluxe buses to/from Mexico City's Terminal Norte (M$270, three hours, eight daily). Coordinados (Flecha Amarilla) and Flecha Roja have 2nd-class services to the same destination (M$195, 3½ hours, regular departures).

Northeast Querétaro State

Those with a love of nature, or a hankering to get off the beaten track, should not (again – not) miss the scenic Sierra Gorda, in northeast Querétaro. This is also home to the extraordinary Franciscan Missions that are spread out within a day's drive. But there's much more to the region besides the missions This area encompasses the incredible Reserva de la Biosfera Sierra Gorda, which, thanks to recent ecotourism projects, is becoming increasingly accessible to visitors. The only limitation is transportation: while it's possible to get to some places on the way by bus, it's much easier and less time consuming if you have your own wheels.

Jalpan

The attractive town of Jalpan centers on the **mission church**, constructed by Franciscan monks and their indigenous converts in the 1750s. It's the gateway to the five missions.

Not surprisingly, given its tropical climate, Jalpan specializes in artisanal – and very delicious – ice creams served in the many *heladerías* (ice-cream shops) around town.

🛏 Sleeping & Eating

Cabañas Centro Tierra BUNGALOW $

(☑441-296-07-00; www.sierragordaecotours.com; Centro Tierra Sierra Gorda, Av La Presa s/n, Barrio El Panteon; d M$500) The best of the budget choices, these simple, basic but comfortable rooms are run by, and situated in the gardens of, Centro Tierra Sierra Gorda (which also runs Sierra Gorda Eco Tours). It's a 15-minute walk from the center of Jalpan, near the *presa* (reservoir).

There are a few quirks, however, and be sure to check them out: gates are locked in the evening (make sure you learn how to open them as the guard is not always around); and wi-fi is not available in all the chalets.

Hotel Misión Jalpan HOTEL $$

(☑441-296-04-45; www.hotelesmision.com.mx; Fray Junípero Serra s/n; r from M$900; ℙ☺❋☒) On the west side of the plaza, Hotel Misión Jalpan has attractive gardens and a restaurant but rooms are below par for what's generally considered to be the 'top' spot in town. It often offers midweek deals.

RESERVA DE LA BIOSFERA SIERRA GORDA

Established in 1997, and now run by CONANP (Comisión Nacional de Áreas Naturales Protegidas), the Reserva de la Biosfera Sierra Gorda, in the rugged Sierra Madre Oriental mountain range, covers the northeastern third of Querétaro state (about 3836 sq km).

Known as the 'green jewel' of central Mexico, the reserve boasts 15 vegetation types, making it the most ecosystem-diverse protected area in the country. Its stunning wilderness areas encompass old-growth cloud forests, semideserts and tropical forests; jaguars, rare orchids and endemic cacti are some of the fauna and flora you might be lucky to spot.

Over the past few years, sustainable ecotourism projects have been established, to varying success. Travelers can head into villages with local guides, stay in basic cabins and camping areas, and partake in a range of activities. These include: hikes to waterfalls including El Chuveje (M$30; an easy 20-minute stroll from the main car park) and Puente de Dios (a wonderful 3½-hour return walk along the Río Escanela; M$130 with guide for one to four people,) visits to Cuatro Palos for great views (access is just before Pinal de Amoles; M$15 entrance and M$50 for guide) and a more hardcore trip to the Sótano del Barro, the world's second largest free-fall vertical cave (410m deep) to see resident macaws. (You need to leave in the middle of the night to be there for dawn. Alternatively, you can camp at the community base and head out before dawn.) Many communities have functioning workshops that produce pottery, natural remedies, dried foodstuffs, honey products and embroidery.

The reserve encompasses the municipalities of Jalpan de Serra, Pinal de Amoles, Arroyo Seco, Landa de Matamoros and Peña Miller. To get there you head on Hwy 120. It winds up to a high point of 2300m at the pretty town of Pinal de Amoles and makes dramatic ups and downs (with 360-degree hairpin turns!) before reaching Jalpan at 760m. Allow four hours to get there from Queretaro.

Several companies offer trips in the reserve. **Aventúrate** (☑ 441-296-07-14, cell 441-103-31-29; www.aventurate.mx; Benito Juárez 29) 🐾 is a professional outfit that has young, enthusiastic and experienced guides who will guide you to any number of sights and activities: the missions (M$1600 for two people including transportation and guide), Rio Escanela (to Puente de Dios), El Chuveje waterfall, Sotano de Barro and more. It is the only operator that takes trips to Gruta Jalpan, the local cave. Prices vary according to trip and number of people. It also arranges trips to 'Las Pozas', the surrealist garden of eccentric Englishman, Edward James.

Sierra Gorda Eco Tours (☑ 441-296-02-42/29; www.sierragordaecotours.com) promotes accommodations and programs within local communities. Prices start at M$1200 per person (based on two people) including transportation (if required), accommodations, meals and activities, entrance fee, plus community guide (where necessary). Around two days' notice is required.

For trips around the missions, two guides come recommended: **Arnoldo Montes Rodríguez** (☑ cell 441-108-88-24; www.sierragordaguides.com), who is based in the so-called 'tourist office' (artisan shop) next to Mision Jalpan, and **Dario Mitzli** (Jalpan Museum; ⊙10am-3pm & 5-7pm Tue-Sun) **FREE**, who works in the Jalpan museum, also on the main square.

Restaurante Carretas MEXICAN **$$**
(mains M$85-180; ⊙8am-10pm Mon-Sat, to 6pm Sun) On the main road, Restaurante Carretas serves up a reasonable Mexican feed; by far the best of a limited lot.

ℹ️ Information

Tourist Office (Plazuel Hidalgo 441; ⊙8am-3:30pm) A kiosk in the main square provides maps and information about the area. It's open daily in high season or otherwise on weekends only.

Sierra Gorda Missions

In the mid-18th century, Franciscans established five beautiful missions in this remote region, including at Jalpan. These were inscribed as a Unesco World Heritage site in 2003. Founder Fray Junípero Serra went on to found the California mission chain. The restored churches are notable for their extraordinary and colorful facades carved with symbolic figures. East from Jalpan, on Hwy 120, there are missions at **Landa de Matamoros** (1760–68); **Tilaco** (1754–62), 10km south of the highway; and **Tancoyol** (1753–60), 20km north of the highway. The mission of **Concá** (1754–58) is 35km north of Jalpan on Hwy 69. To get here, you'll need your own wheels, or head out with one of the guides.

See p647 for further information.

GUANAJUATO STATE

The rocky highland state of Guanajuato (population 5.5 million) is full of riches of every kind. In colonial times, mineral resources attracted Spanish prospectors to mine for silver, gold, iron, lead, zinc and tin. For two centuries the state produced enormous wealth, extracting up to 40% of the world's silver. Silver barons in Guanajuato city enjoyed opulent lives at the expense of indigenous people who worked the mines, first as slave labor and then as wage slaves. Eventually, resenting the dominance of Spanish-born colonists, the well-heeled criollo class of Guanajuato and Querétaro states contributed to plans for rebellion.

These days, the state's treasures are the quaint colonial towns of Guanajuato and San Miguel de Allende. Visitors to this region can enjoy its precious legacies: stunning colonial architecture, established cultural scenes and a stream of never-ending festivals...not to mention friendly, proud locals and a lively university atmosphere.

Guanajuato

📍 473 / POP 725,000 / ELEV 2045M

The extraordinary Unesco World Heritage city of Guanajuato was founded in 1559 due to the region's rich silver and gold deposits. Opulent colonial buildings, stunning tree-filled plazas and brightly colored houses are crammed onto the steep slopes of a ravine. Excellent museums, handsome theaters and a fine marketplace punctuate the cobblestone streets. The city's 'main' roads twist around the hillsides and plunge into tunnels, formerly rivers.

The city is best known internationally for its acclaimed annual international arts festival, the Festival Cervantino. Yet this colorful and lively place holds center stage all year long; much of the youthful vibrancy and prolific cultural activities – *callejoneadas*, films, theater and orchestras – can be attributed to the 20,000 students of the city's own University of Guanajuato. In short, Guanajuato is the region's slightly gritty, but very authentic, city.

The city usually boasts fine weather during the day, but beware of cold and windy nights in the winter.

History

One of the hemisphere's richest silver veins was uncovered in 1558 at La Valenciana mine; for 250 years the mine produced 20% of the world's silver. Colonial barons benefiting from this mineral treasure were infuriated when King Carlos III of Spain slashed their share of the wealth in 1765. The King's 1767 decree banishing the Jesuits from Spanish dominions further alienated both the wealthy barons and the poor miners, who held allegiance to the Jesuits.

This anger was focused in the War of Independence. In 1810 rebel leader Miguel Hidalgo set off the independence movement with his Grito de Independencia (Cry for Independence) in nearby Dolores. Guanajuato citizens joined the independence fighters and defeated the Spanish and loyalists, seizing the city in the rebellion's first military victory. When the Spaniards eventually retook the city they retaliated by conducting the infamous 'lottery of death,' in which names of Guanajuato citizens were drawn at random and the 'winners' were tortured and hanged.

Independence was eventually won, freeing the silver barons to amass further wealth. From this wealth arose many of the mansions, churches and theaters.

In the late 1990s the state prospered under its PAN (National Action Party) governor, Vicente Fox Quesada, with Mexico's lowest unemployment rate and an export rate three times the national average. Fox was chosen as the PAN candidate for the 2000 presidential election and his popularity sealed the victory (his presidential term ended in 2006).

◎ Sights

Basílica de Nuestra Señora de Guanajuato   CHURCH

(Plaza de la Paz s/n) The Basílica de Nuestra Señora de Guanajuato, a block west of Jardín de la Unión, contains a jewel-covered image of the Virgin, patron of Guanajuato. The wooden statue was supposedly hidden from the Moors in a cave in Spain for 800 years. Felipe II of Spain gave it to Guanajuato in thanks for the wealth it provided to the crown. Next door, the small Galería Mariana is dedicated to images of Mary and other Catholic relics.

Teatro Juárez   THEATER
(www.guanajuato.gob.mx; Sopeña s/n; adult M$35; ⏱10am-1:45pm & 5-7:45pm Tue-Sun) Don't leave Guanajuato without visiting the magnificent Teatro Juárez. It was built between 1873 and 1903 and inaugurated by the dictator Porfirio Díaz, whose lavish tastes are reflected in the plush red-and-gold interior. The outside is festooned with 12 columns with brass capitals, lamp posts and eight of the nine muses; inside the impression is Moorish, with the bar and lobby gleaming with carved wood, stained glass and precious metals. It's only open when no performances are scheduled; video/camera use is M$60/30.

Teatro Principal   THEATER
(☑473-732-15-23; Hidalgo s/n) It hosts a full schedule of performances during the Cervantino festival and is home to Guanajuato's impressive symphony orchestra. Performances are held most Friday nights (except October and January) at 8.30pm. Tickets cost M$80.

Teatro Cervantes   THEATER
(☑473-732-11-69; Plaza Allende s/n) It has a full schedule of performances during the Cervantino festival and less-regular shows at other times. Statues of Don Quixote and Sancho Panza grace the small Plaza Allende, in front of the theater.

Museo y Casa de Diego Rivera   MUSEUM
(Pósitos 47; adult M$20; ⏱10am-6:30pm Tue-Sat, 10am-2:30pm Sun) Diego Rivera's birthplace is now an excellent museum honoring the famous artist (the Marxist Rivera was *persona non grata* here for years). It's worth spending an hour here – longer if you're a Rivera fan.

Rivera and his twin brother were born in the house in 1886 (Carlos died at the age of two) and lived here until the family moved to Mexico City six years later. The museum's ground floor is a recreation of the Rivera family home, furnished with 19th-century antiques.

The labyrinth of upper floors exhibit a permanent collection of his original works and preliminary sketches (completed for some of his famous murals in Mexico City), plus there's a nude of Frida Kahlo. Several

COLONIAL CHURCHES

Aside from the Basílica de Nuestra Señora de Guanajuato, other fine colonial churches include **Templo de San Diego** (Jardín de la Union s/n), opposite the Jardín de la Unión; **Templo de San Francisco** (Doblado s/n); and large **Templo de la Compañía de Jesús** (Lascuraín de Retana s/n), which was completed in 1747 for the Jesuit seminary whose buildings are now occupied by the University of Guanajuato.

salas also host temporary exhibitions of work by Mexican and international artists. An intimate theater upstairs features black-and-white photographs of Kahlo and Rivera.

Monumento a El Pípila   MONUMENT
(Panoramica) The monument to El Pípila honors the hero who torched the Alhóndiga gates on September 28, 1810, enabling Hidalgo's forces to win the first victory of the independence movement. The statue shows El Pípila holding his torch high over the city. On the base is the inscription *Aún hay otras Alhóndigas por incendiar* (There are still other Alhóndigas to burn).

Two routes from the center of town go up steep, picturesque lanes. One goes east on Sopeña from Jardín de la Unión, then turns right on Callejón del Calvario (this becomes Pochote; turn right at Subida San Miguel). Another ascent, unmarked, goes uphill from the small plaza on Alonso. Alternatively, the 'Pípila-ISSSTE' bus heading west on Avenida Juárez will let you off right by the statue, or you can ride up in the funicular.

Museo Regional de Guanajuato Alhóndiga de Granaditas   MUSEUM
(☑473-732-11-12; Calle 28 de Septiembre; M$52, camera/video use M$30/60; ⏱10am-5:30pm Tue-Sat, to 2:30pm Sun) This art and history museum was the site of the first major rebel victory in Mexico's War of Independence. Built between 1798 and 1808 as a grain storehouse, the Alhóndiga became a fortress in 1810 when 300 Spanish troops and loyalist leaders barricaded themselves inside after 20,000 rebels led by Miguel Hidalgo attempted to take Guanajuato. On September 28, 1810, a miner nicknamed El Pípila tied a stone slab to his back and, protected from Spanish bullets, set the entrance ablaze. The rebels moved in and killed everyone inside.

Guanajuato

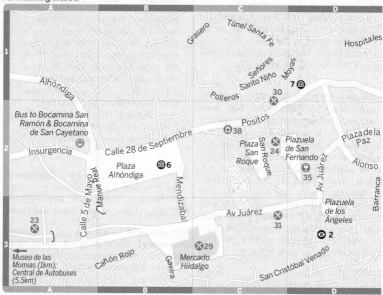

The Alhóndiga was later used as an armory, then a school, before it was a prison for 80 years (1864–1948). It became a museum in 1958. Don't miss José Chávez Morado's dramatic murals of Guanajuato's history on the staircases.

Ex-Hacienda San
Gabriel de Barrera   MUSEUM, GARDEN
(Camino Antiguo a Marfil, Km 2.5; adult M$30; ☉9am-6pm) To escape Guanajuato's bustling streets, head 2.5km west to this magnificent colonial home which is now a museum with tranquil and stunning gardens.

Built at the end of the 17th century, this was the grand hacienda of Captain Gabriel de Barrera, whose family was descended from the first Conde de Rul of the famous La Valenciana mine. Opened as a museum in 1979, the hacienda, with its opulent period European furnishings, provides an insight into the lives of the wealthy of the time.

Take one of the frequent 'Marfil' buses heading west in the subterranean tunnel under Avenida Juárez and ask the driver to drop you at Hotel Misión Guanajuato.

Museo Iconográfico del Quijote   MUSEUM
(☐473-732-33-76; Manuel Doblado 1; adult/student M$30/10; ☉9:30am-6:45pm Tue-Sun) This sur-prisingly interesting museum is worth half an hour of your time. It fronts the tiny plaza in front of the Templo de San Francisco. Every exhibit relates to Don Quixote de la Mancha, the notorious Spanish literary hero, depicted in numerous different media by different artists in different styles. Paintings, statues, tapestries, even chess sets, clocks and postage stamps, all feature the quixotic icon and his bumbling companion Sancho Panza.

Templo La Valenciana   CHURCH
(Iglesia de San Cayetano) On a hill overlooking Guanajuato, 5km north of the center, is the magnificent Templo La Valenciana. Its fa-cade is spectacular and its interior dazzles with ornate golden altars, filigree carvings and giant paintings.

One legend says that the Spaniard who started the nearby San Ramón mine prom-ised San Cayetano that if it made him rich, he would build a church to honor the saint. Another says that the silver baron of La Va-lenciana, Conde de Rul, tried to atone for ex-ploiting the miners by building the ultimate in Churrigueresque churches. Whatever the motive, ground was broken in 1765 and the church was completed in 1788.

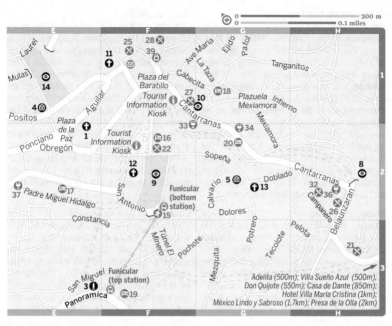

Guanajuato

◎ Sights

1 Basílica de Nuestra Señora de Guanajuato	E2
2 Callejón del Beso	D3
3 Monumento a El Pípila	E3
4 Museo del Pueblo de Guanajuato	E1
5 Museo Iconográfico del Quijote	G2
6 Museo Regional de Guanajuato Alhóndiga de Granaditas	B2
7 Museo y Casa de Diego Rivera	D1
8 Teatro Cervantes	H2
9 Teatro Juárez	F2
10 Teatro Principal	G1
11 Templo de la Compañía de Jesús	F1
12 Templo de San Diego	F2
13 Templo de San Francisco	G2
14 Universidad de Guanajuato	E1

◎ Activities, Courses & Tours

15 Funicular	F2

◎ Sleeping

16 1850 Hotel	F2
17 Alonso10 Hotel Boutique & Arte	E2
18 Casa de Pita	G1
19 Casa Zuniga	F3
20 Hostel La Casa del Tío	G2

◎ Eating

21 Café Tal	H3
22 Casa Valadez	F2
23 Central Comercio	A3
24 Delica Mitsu	C2
25 El Midi Bistró	F1
26 Habibti Falafel	H2
27 La Vie en Rose	F1
28 Los Campos	F1
29 Mercado Hidalgo	C3
30 Mestizo	C1
31 Restaurant La Carreta	C3
32 Santo Café	H2

◎ Drinking & Nightlife

33 El Incendio	F2
El Midi Bistró	(see 25)
34 Golem	G2
35 La Inundación de 1905	D2
36 Whoopees	H2
37 Why Not?	E2

◎ Shopping

38 El Viejo Zaguán	C2
39 Xocola-T	F1

Bocamina de San Ramón & Bocamina de San Cayetano
MINES

(www.bocaminasanramon.com; M$35; ⊙10am-6pm) These neighboring mines are part of the famous Valenciana mining district. Silver was discovered here in 1548. At San Ramón you can descend via steps into a mine shaft to a depth of 60m (note: not for claustrophobes). San Cayetano has an interesting museum and former miners take you on a brief tour – including a shaft visit. To reach the mines, take a 'Cristo Rey' or 'Valenciana' bus from the bus stop on the corner of Alhóndiga and Calle 28 de Septiembre. Get off at Templo La Valenciana and follow the signs behind the church.

Museo de las Momias
MUSEUM

(Museum of the Mummies; www.momiasdeguanajuato.gob.mx; Explanada del Panteón Municipal s/n; adult/student M$56/37; ⊙9am-6pm) This famous museum is one of the most bizarre (some might say distasteful) sights at the *panteón* (cemetery). The popular attraction is a quintessential example of Mexico's acceptance of, celebration of and obsession with death; visitors come from all over to see more than 100 disinterred corpses.

While technically these are mummified remains – due to the dry atmosphere in their former crypts – the bodies are not thousands of years old. The first remains were unearthed in 1865 to make room for more bodies in the cemeteries. What the authorities uncovered were not skeletons but flesh mummified (many feature grotesque forms and facial expressions).

The complex is on the western edge of town, a 10-minute ride from Avenida Juárez on any 'Momias' bus (M$5).

Museo del Pueblo de Guanajuato
MUSEUM

(Positos 7; adult M$20; ⊙10am-6:30pm Tue-Sat, to 2:30pm Sun) Located beside the university, this fascinating art museum displays an exquisite collection of Mexican miniatures, and 18th- and 19th-century art with works by Guanajuatan painters Hermenegildo Bustos and José Chávez Morado, plus temporary exhibitions. It occupies the former mansion of the Marqueses de San Juan de Rayas, who owned the San Juan de Rayas mine. The private Baroque chapel (built in 1696) upstairs in the courtyard contains an interesting three-panelled mural by José Chávez Morado depicting the Spanish colonization.

Callejón del Beso
STREET

(The Alley of the Kiss) Narrowest of the many alleyways in Guanajuato's streets is this *callejón*, where the balconies of two houses practically touch. In a local legend, a fine family once lived on this street and their daughter fell in love with a common miner. They were forbidden to see each other, but the miner rented a room opposite and the lovers exchanged furtive *besos* (kisses) from these balconies. Inevitably, the romance was discovered and the couple met a tragic end.

From the Plazuela de los Ángeles on Avenida Juárez, walk about 40m up Callejón del Patrocinio to see the tiny alley on your left.

Casa de Arte Olga Costa- José Chávez Morado
MUSEUM

(Pastita 158, Torre del Arco; adult/student M$20/5; ⊙10am-4pm Tue-Sat, to 3pm Sun) In 1966, artists José Chávez Morado and Olga Costa converted a massive old well into their home and studio; before their deaths, they donated their home and its contents for public use. On display is a small, but fascinating, collection of items from the 16th to 18th centuries, including pre-Hispanic and modern ceramics, embroidery, furniture, masks and their own artworks. It's worth heading to the 'suburb' of Pastita to experience a side of Guanajuato you might otherwise miss.

The pretty approach follows the former aqueduct that ends at their house. Take any bus marked 'Pastita' from the eastern end of town.

Universidad de Guanajuato
NOTABLE BUILDING

(UGTO; ☑473-732-00-06; www.ugto.mx; Lascuraín de Retana 5) The main building of this university, whose ramparts are visible above much of the city, is one block up the hill from the basilica. The distinctive multistory white-and-blue building with the crenelated pediment dates from the 1950s. The design was (and, some might say, continues to be) controversial as this dominating structure impedes the characteristic, historic cityscape.

Funicular
FUNICULAR

(Plaza Constancia s/n; one way/round trip M$15/30; ⊙8am-9:45pm Mon-Fri, 9am-9:45pm Sat, 10am-8:45pm Sun) This incline railway inches up (and down) the slope behind the Teatro Juárez to a terminal near the El Pípila monument. Heading up is fun, but to descend, you can save your pennies by walking down (there are two obvious, well-paved routes). Note: in 2015, the funicular had its first major incident when, after 13 years in operation, the axle broke and the funicular plummetted; two people in the carriage were injured. Because of this it was not operating at the time of research, but should be up (and down) and running by the time you read this.

Courses

Guanajuato is a university town and has an excellent atmosphere for studying Spanish. Group classes range from around US$160 to US$210 for 20 lessons (one week's worth) and private lessons average US$18 an hour. Schools can arrange homestays with meals for around US$190 per week. Additional costs may include registration and/or placement test fees, excursions and extracurricular activities. Language schools to consider include **Adelita** (☑ 473-100-49-47; www.la-adelita.org; Agua Fuerte 56), **Don Quijote** (☑ 923-277-200; www.donquijote.org; Calle Pastita 76, Barrio Pastita), and the highly recommended **Escuela Falcon** (www.escuelafalcon.com; Callejón de Gallitos; ⊙ 9am-7pm Mon-Fri, 10am-2pm Sat).

Mika Matsuishi &
Felipe Olmos Workshops   COURSE
(☑ cell 473-120-42-99; www.felipeymika.wix.com/mojigangas) Hands-on, fun art workshops for creative souls (mask-making, clay classes etc) run by talented artists and *mojiganga* (farce) specialists. Materials are included; prices vary according to activity.

Festivals & Events

Baile de las Flores   RELIGIOUS
The Flower Dance takes place on the Thursday before Semana Santa. The next day, mines are open to the public for sightseeing and celebrations. Miners decorate altars to La Virgen de los Dolores, a manifestation of the Virgin Mary who looks after miners.

Fiestas de San Juan y
Presa de la Olla   RELIGIOUS
The festivals of San Juan are celebrated at the Presa de la Olla park in late June. The 24th is the big bash for the saint's day itself, with dances, music, fireworks and picnics. Then on the first Monday in July, everyone comes back to the park for another big party celebrating the opening of the dam's floodgates.

Día de la Cueva   RELIGIOUS
Cave Day is a country fair held on different dates annually, when locals walk to a cave in the nearby hills to honor San Ignacio de Loyola and enjoy a festive picnic.

Fiesta de la Virgen
de Guanajuato   RELIGIOUS
This festival commemorates the date when Felipe II gave the people of Guanajuato the jeweled wooden Virgin that now adorns the basilica. Changing dates.

Festival Internacional Cervantino   ARTS
(www.festivalcervantino.gob.mx) Back in the 1950s, the festival merely consisted of *entremeses* (appetizers) from Miguel Cervantes' work performed by students. It has since grown to become one of Latin America's foremost arts events. Music, dance and theater groups from around the world perform diverse works (mostly non-Cervantes related) for two to three weeks in October at this arts extravaganza.

Tickets for single events range from M$30 to M$650 and should be booked in advance (www.ticketmaster.com.mx) along with hotels. In Guanajuato, tickets are available from a booth by Teatro Juarez two months before the festival.

CALLEJONEADAS – THE TRADITIONAL WAY TO PARTY

The *callejoneada* tradition is said to have come from Spain. A group of professional singers and musicians, dressed in traditional costumes, starts up in a central location such as a plaza, a crowd gathers, then the whole mob winds through the alleyways, streets and plazas playing, dancing and singing heartily. In Guanajuato they are also called *estudiantinas*. Stories and jokes (in Spanish) are told in between songs, often relating to the legends of the alleys. In Zacatecas, there are no stories, but hired bands called *tamboras* (dressed in uniform, not traditional attire) lead dancing revelers. On special occasions a burro laden with wine is brought along. Often, strangers are just expected to join the party and the crowd swells. Occasionally, the organizers foot the bill; sometimes you pay a small amount for the wine you drink (or you bring your own). In Guanajuato, the groups themselves or tour companies sell tickets (around M$100 for 1¼ hours, Tuesday through Sunday) for the *callejoneadas* and juice (not alcohol) is provided. It's great fun.

🛌 Sleeping

During the Festival Internacional Cervantino in October, Christmas, Semana Santa, and in some cases, summer vacation periods, prices may be around 25% to 50% above the regular rates given here.

Casa de Dante
HOSTEL $

(☎ 473-731-09-09; www.casadedante.com; Callejón de Zaragoza 25; dm from M$250, s/d incl breakfast from M$400/800; 🕸) 'My family is your family,' greets the owner of this ultrafriendly hostel. You can opt for a dormitory or a well-kept room (claustrophes note: one private room doesn't have a window). Some rooms have private bathrooms. In addition, there are two kitchens and an outdoor terrace barbecue available for use.

It's a little out of town on the way to La Presa and up 156-plus steps. Head up the *callejón* next to Hotel Luz de Luna on Paseo de la Presa. Prices are considerably lower outside high season and long-term stays are negotiable.

Hostel La Casa del Tío
HOSTEL $

(☎ 473-733-97-28; www.hostellacasadeltio.com.mx; Cantarranas 47; dm/r M$190/560) It's basic and hardly outstanding in any way, though its rooms are light and airy, there's a brightly painted terrace and it's central (but beware: it's on a noisy road). And it's somewhere to put your head if you're not super-fussed about fluffy towels and other trimmings.

Villa Sueño Azul
B&B $$

(☎ 473-731-01-57; www.villasuenoazul.com; San Sebastian 88; s M$790-940, d M$990-1140; 🕸🕸) Behind a blue facade is this pleasant blue-and-white themed oasis – a secure and tidy B&B with a helpful English-speaking manager, Malí, and ever-so-slightly dated rooms, a lovely sunroom and pot-plant filled terrace. It's located southeast of, but still within a 10-minute walk to, the hectic downtown area.

It's also on a bus route. (Read: possible noise in the two front rooms, which cost slightly less as a result. Buses don't run all night, however.)

Casa Zuniga
B&B $$

(☎ 473-732-85-46; www.casazunigagto.com; Callejón del Pachote 38; r incl breakfast from M$1100; 🅿🕸🕸) This sprawling B&B offers various modern rooms and receives rave reviews for its hospitality, extended by the charismatic duo Carmen and Rick, and its extra generous, carb- and protein-fuelled breakfasts. It's located on the hill near El Pípila, to the left

of the funicular (as heading uphill), or by car and bus along Panoramica.

Rates include a funicular pass (if operating) throughout your stay. It's one of the town's few places with a lap pool.

Casa de Pita
PENSION $$

(☎ 473-732-15-32; www.casadepita.com; Cabecita 26; s M$450, d M$550-800, ste incl breakfast M$1200; 🕸@🕸) A secure spot that is a literal maze of quirky guest rooms in a centrally located converted house. They vary in size and facilities: some are apartments and several verge on claustrophobic. But Spanish-speaking owner Pita is delightful and it's very secure.

Alonso10 Hotel Boutique & Arte
BOUTIQUE HOTEL $$$

(☎ 473-732-76-57; www.hotelalonso10.com.mx; Alonso 10; ste from M$2800-3100; 🕸🕸) A sleek boutique hotel located a street away from the centralized chaos. White and taupe hues rule, as do smart rooms with all the trimmings. The front two suites have fabulous balconies with quirky views of the basilica and the back of Teatro Juárez. Downstairs is an elegant restaurant (open 7:30am to 11pm; mains M$105 to M$215).

1850 Hotel
BOUTIQUE HOTEL $$$

(☎ 473-732-27-95; http://hotel1850.com/index.php/en/; Jardín de la Unión 7; r M$2750-4350; 🕸) Snappy and smart and appealing to those who go for Mexican sleek (think: converted mansion with lots of silver and designer trim and, er, contemporary dog sculptures). Each room is unique and very nice. It's in a marvellous location – right on El Jardín – and the double-glazed windows ensure you don't hear the mariachis in the adjacent plaza. The rooftop bar is unbeatable. Prices increase by 20% or so on weekends.

★ Hotel Villa María Cristina
BOUTIQUE HOTEL $$$

(☎ 473-731-21-82; www.villamariacristina.net; Paseo de la Presa de la Olla 76; ste M$4100-8000; 🕸🕸) This series of stunning converted colonial mansions, joined by a maze of patios and gardens, comes with a snob factor warning: it's definitely *the* place to be seen. The decor in the spacious rooms features neoclassical French designer furniture, original paintings by local artist Jesús Gallardo, and beds and bathrooms with all the fluffy and puffy trimmings.

It recently incorporated a neighboring mansion to tote up the luxurious rooms and suites to 33. There are fountains and wicker chairs, two swimming pools and views of La Bufa. Two on-site restaurants provide meals (7:30pm to 10pm, mains M$200 to M$350), as is a funky new bar (2pm to 9pm Monday to Saturday). It's in La Presa, a 15-minute walk from the center of Guanajuato.

✕ Eating

Eating in Guanajuato won't blow your culinary world apart; options are limited. Having said that, there are a few exceptions. For fresh produce and cheap snacks and lunches, head to the **Mercado Hidalgo** (Av Juárez), a five-minute walk west of Jardín de la Unión on Avenida Juárez. Another two blocks further down on the right is **Central Comercio** (Av Juárez), with a large supermarket.

✕ Jardín de la Unión & Around

★**La Vie en Rose**   FRENCH $
(Cantarranas 18; pastries/snacks M$30-60; ⊙10am-10pm Tue-Sat, 11am-8pm Sun) *Ooh la la!* Ok, this spot is as French as frogs legs, but forgo the Mexican *helado* (ice cream) for just one sweet break and get your mouth around some of the most genuine, mouthwatering, flavorsome French pastries and desserts around. All made by a French pastry chef.

Café Tal   CAFE $
(Temezcuitate 4; snacks M$28-40; ⊙7am-midnight Mon-Fri, 8am-midnight Sat & Sun; ☺🕾) This spot hasn't changed in the eight years we've been coming here; the grungier it gets, the more popular it is. The reason? It roasts, grinds and serves good coffee plus it's the place for wi-fi-seeking students and social expats to meet. Don't miss the *beso negro* ('black kiss'), ultra-concentrated hot chocolate (M$20).

At the time of research, the eccentric owner, Greg, was opening another branch in La Presa. If you're lucky, Tal the cat might sit on your lap.

Santo Café   CAFE $
(Puente de Campanero; mains M$55-130; ⊙10am-11pm Mon-Sat, noon-8pm Sun; ☺🕾) Stop by this casual but cozy spot on the quaint Venetian-style bridge and check the latest university vibe. It serves good salads and snacks (the soy burger is great for vegetarians; M$45). Some tables overlook the alley below.

Habibti Falafel   ARABIC $
(Sostenes Rocha 18C; falafels M$29-135; ⊙11am-11pm, to 10pm Sun) This tiny spot is one of the cheapest eats for those on a budget. It's a hole-in-the-wall with a few tables and whips up excellent and oh-so-fresh falafels. Or you can opt for plate combos of tasty morsels – hummus, tabbouleh, dahl and *hojas de parra*.

Casa Valadez   MEXICAN $$$
(🖉473-732-03-11; www.casavaladez.com; Jardín de la Unión 3; mains M$130-650; ⊙8.30am-11pm; ☺) This classic place is a smart choice in every respect and attracts a loyal crowd of well-dressed locals who like to watch. And be seen. It faces the Jardín and Teatro Juaréz so make an experience of it. Servings are Mexican (read: generous). Dishes are mainly international with a few Mexican favorites such as *pollo con enchiladas mineras* (enchiladas with chicken and the lot).

✕ Plazuela de San Fernando & Around

★**Delica Mitsu**   JAPANESE $
(Cantaritos 37; mains M$45-115; ⊙noon-6pm Mon-Sat) This tiny Japanese-run hole-in-the-wall doesn't have the most salubrious surrounds, but it serves up some of the biggest, freshest and best Japanese flavors around.

Restaurant La Carreta   GRILL $
(Av Juárez 96; mains M$60-150; ⊙10:30am-8:30pm) Follow your nose to La Carreta, a buzzing, unpretentious local eatery lined with wagon wheels, whose street-front grill 'spins' out a super-scrumptious *pollo asado con leña* (grilled chicken) and *carne asada* (grilled beef), served with large portions of rice and salad.

Mestizo   INTERNATIONAL $$
(Positos 69; mains M$90-160; ⊙1-10pm Tue-Sat, to 6:30pm Sun) *Mestizo* means 'mix'; this place used to house a restaurant and gallery (run by a famous local artist, and his son, a chef). The gallery is long gone so it now lacks a little ambience (the carpet is a little dog-eared). But look past this and enjoy fabulous cuisine; it's big on quality, especially the incredibly good value-for-money steak dishes.

✕ Plazuela del Baratillo

★**Los Campos**   TAPAS $$
(www.loscampos.mx; 4A de la Alameda, off Plaza Baratillo; mains M$65-145; ⊙1-10pm Tue-Sun) A Canadian-Mexican husband-wife team runs this small cozy, candlelit restaurant. Its seven tables fill up for dinners and late lunches. There's generous tapas plates or smaller mains (depending how you look at it) and

all pack a punch. A great Mexican wine selection too.

We love the *chile relleno* (chili stuffed with meat or cheese) on a bed of polenta, though the deconstructed mushroom lasagna is tasty, too. It's a cut above Guanajuato's eateries in terms of consistency.

El Midi Bistró MEDITERRANEAN $$
(www.elmidibistro.com; Casa Cuatro, San José 4; salads per 100g M$19; ⊘noon-11pm Wed-Mon, to 5pm Sun; 🖘) This tastefully decorated part-bistro, part-bar on the top floor serves excellent lunch-time salads (M$19 per 100g), lesser quality à la carte dinners (the menu rarely changes) and cocktail fusion fun in the evenings. Live music on Thursday evenings and looong Sunday brunches (11am to 10pm) make it one of the town's most pleasant places to kick back in.

Big magnet for expats, but not exclusively.

🍴 La Presa & Around

México Lindo y Sabroso MEXICAN $$
(Paseo de la Presa 154; mains M$80-165; ⊘9am-10pm; 🖘) Tasty Mexican dishes in tasteful and colorful surrounds, including a delightful outdoor veranda. Head up Paseo de la Presa for about 1.4km and it's on the left-hand side. The Sunday brunch buffet attracts hungry locals with big appetites.

🍴 San Javier

★**Las Mercedes** MEXICAN $$$
(☑473-732-73-75; Arriba 6, San Javier; mains M$190-310; ⊘2-10pm Tue-Sat, to 6pm Sun) In a residential area overlooking the city is Guanajuato's best restaurant. Popular with government and business officials, plus romantic diners, it serves Mexican cuisine *como la abuela* – grandmother's cooking that takes hours to prepare – such as *moles* hand ground in a *molcajete* (traditional mortar and pestle) – with a contemporary twist. Dish presentation is very stylish. Reservations recommended.

To get there, take a taxi; you'll head down the valley (in a northwesterly direction as though heading to La Valenciana), but will then turn suddenly to head west up a hill.

🍷 Drinking & Nightlife

Every evening, the Jardín de la Unión comes alive with people crowding the outdoor tables, strolling and listening to the street musicians and mariachi bands.

Given the city's immense student population (Thursday is generally their big night out), there's no lack of bars and nightclubs to choose from, though these can change at an (alcoholic) drop. Drinking and dancing establishments in Guanajuato generally start late.

El Incendio BAR
(Cantarranas 39; ⊘11am-11pm) A former old-school cantina – whose legacy is swinging doors, an open urinal (as per the old cantinas but no longer used) and mural-covered walls – that caters to a fun but rowdy student crowd.

La Inundación de 1905 BAR
(San Fernando Plaza; ⊘10am-midnight Tue-Sun) Students love this relaxed spot, named after the city's 1905 flood, for its flowing beer in the beer garden atmosphere (if a mini one at that; though it is the nearest thing you'll get to Munich's Oktoberfest). Sister bar to Foro Inundación.

Foro Inundación BAR
(⊘8am-3am Tue-Sat) Located behind Teatro Juarez, this place serves up cool cocktails, funky recycled furniture and a fun vibe. Sister bar to La Inundación de 1905.

Whoopees BAR
(Manuel Doblado 39; ⊘9pm-4am Tue-Sat) This modern, trendy gay bar is Guanajuato's hip and very happening place. And a friendly one at that.

Why Not? CLUB
(Alfonso 34) You may not be asking yourself 'why not?' after you wake up with a throbbing headache from drinking all night with the hoards of local students who head to this Guanajuato institution (especially Thursday to Saturday, when the fun gets going). Following a recent makeover, it's slightly more corporate, but is still very popular. The fun starts after midnight.

El Midi Bistró BAR
(Casa Cuatro, San Jose 4; cocktails M$50-70; ⊘noon-11pm Wed-Mon, to 5pm Sun) This pleasant place, in a refurbished mansion, offers a touch of class and culture (there's often live music) plus a fabulous old-fashioned bar. It's is a relaxing spot to head to for a pre- or post-dinner drink.

Golem BAR
(Cantarranas 38; drinks from M$25; ⊘6.30pm-3am Mon-Sat, 2pm-midnight Sun) Slightly grungy spot is the word on the lips of any

student who wants cheap drinks and cheap tapas and lots of social fun. Upstairs, a range of themed bars (gin and whiskey) keep the fun a flowin'.

☆ Entertainment

A program of events, including theater (held in one of three fine centrally located theaters), music, opera and dance, runs from March to December. A monthly program listing is available from the tourist kiosks in Jardín de la Unión.

🛍 Shopping

El Viejo Zaguán   BOOKS
(Positos 64; ⊙10:30am-3pm & 5-8pm Tue-Sat, 11am-3pm Sun) Wonderful bilingual publications, art books, gifts and a relaxing coffee stop.

Xocola-T   FOOD
(Plazuela del Baratillo 15; chocolates M$8-12; ⊙noon-8pm Mon, 9am-8pm Tue-Sat, 10am-6pm Sun) This chocoholic's nirvana sells delectable handmade chocolates of pure cocoa with natural flavors and not a trans fat in sight. Quirkier fillings include *chapulines* (grasshoppers), *gusanos* (caterpillars) and *nopal* (cactus).

❶ Information

INTERNET ACCESS

Many internet places line the streets around the university; most charge M$10 per hour. Several cafes offer wi-fi access. Public w-ifi access is also available in public places (though be careful of flaunting your hardware).

MEDICAL SERVICES

Hospital General (☑473-733-15-73, 473-733-15-76; Carretera a Silao, Km 6.5)
Centro Médico la Presa (☑473-102-31-00; Paseo de la Presa 85)

MONEY

Banks along Avenida Juárez change cash and traveler's checks (but some only until 2pm) and have ATMs.
Divisas Dimas (Av Juárez 33A; ⊙10am-8pm Mon-Sat) A *casa de cambio* that even changes traveler's checks (only American Express).

POST

Post office (Ayuntamiento 25; ⊙8am-4:30pm Mon-Fri, 8am-noon Sat)

TOURIST INFORMATION

Incredibly, the only formal information points in Guanajuato are two small tourist kiosks, located at Jardín de la Unión and an extension of this, in Calle Allende. Note: do not confuse these with official-looking booths marked 'Information Turística' that are dotted around town. The latter are private companies touting specific hotels and/or other services.

❶ Getting There & Away

AIR

Guanajuato is served by the Aeropuerto Internacional del Bajío, which is about 30km west of the city, halfway between León and Silao.

BUS

Guanajuato's Central de Autobuses is around 5km southwest of town (confusingly, to get there go northwest out of town along Tepetapa). It has card phones and luggage storage (in the cafe). Deluxe and 1st-class bus tickets (ETN and Primera Plus) can be bought in town at **Viajes Frausto** (☑473-732-35-80; Obregón 10; ⊙9am-2pm & 4:30-7:30pm Mon-Fri, 9am-1:30pm Sat). A handy **Venta de Boletos** (ticket kiosk; ⊙10am-5:30pm Mon-Sun) for Primera Plus is located in an arcade opposite Plaza Baratillo.

Ominbus de Mexico has one direct bus to San Luis Potosí (M$260 at 6.45pm); or change in León for frequent connections. Primera Plus and ETN are the main 1st class operators, while Flecha Amarilla has cheaper services to Dolores Hidalgo, León and San Miguel than those listed in the table.

BUSES FROM GUANAJUATO

DESTINATION	FARE (M$)	DURATION (HR)	FREQUENCY (DAILY)
Dolores Hidalgo	60	1½	every 30min 5:30am-10:30pm
Guadalajara	410-495	4	frequent
León	74-90	1-1¼	very frequent
Mexico City (Terminal Norte)	525-630	4½	very frequent
Querétaro	196-217	2½	frequent
San Miguel de Allende	130-155	1½-2	very frequent

ℹ️ Getting Around

A taxi to Aeropuerto Internacional del Bajío will cost about M$400 (there's a set rate of M$450 from the airport; you buy your ticket at a taxi counter inside the airport). A cheaper option from Guanajuato is one of the frequent buses to Silao (M$28; every 20 minutes) and a taxi from there (around M$120). Note: in reverse – from the airport to Silao – the taxi rates are set at M$250).

Between the bus station and downtown, 'Central de Autobuses' buses (M$6) run around the clock. From the center, you can catch them heading west on Avenida Juárez. From the bus terminal, you will enter a tunnel running east under the *centro histórico*. Alight at one of several entry/exit points: Mercado Hidalgo, Plaza de los Ángeles, Jardín de la Unión, Plaza Baratillo/Teatro Principal, Teatro Cervantes or Embajadoras (note: check the destination with the driver). A taxi to/from the bus station costs around M$50.

To get around town keep a look out – local buses display their destination. For the *centro histórico* the rule of thumb is as follows: all buses heading east go via the tunnels below Avenida Juárez (for example, if you want to go from the market to the Teatro Principal). Those heading west go along Avenida Juárez.

City buses (M$5) run from 7am to 10pm. Taxis are plentiful in the center and charge about M$35 for short trips around town (slightly more if heading uphill to El Pípila and the like).

León

Whether you like it or not, you will probably end up in the industrial city of León, 56km west of Guanajuato, thanks to its importance as a main bus hub within the state of Guanajuato. Also, it's only 20km from Aeropuerto Internacional del Bajío.

It's unlikely you'll need to stay here; bus connections are plentiful. If you want to fill an hour or two before a bus connection, it's worth wandering the streets surrounding the bus terminal, known as Zona Piel (Leather District). León has a long history of supplying goods: in the 16th century it was the center of Mexico's ranching district, providing meat for the mining towns and processing hides.

ℹ️ Getting There & Away

Aeropuerto Internacional del Bajío is 20km southeast of León on the Mexico City road. Many US airlines offer flights between US cities and here (often via Mexico City). Unfortunately, no bus service operates between Bajío airport and central León or Guanajuato (although strangely, there is one Primera Plus bus running most days at different times from León to the airport). A taxi between León and the airport costs around M$300 (M$370 from the airport using the official airport taxis).

The **Central de Autobuses** (Blvd Hilario Medina s/n), just north of Blvd López Mateos 2.5km east of downtown, has a cafeteria, left luggage, money exchange and card phones. There are regular 1st- and 2nd-class services to many places in northern and western Mexico.

Dolores Hidalgo

📞 418 / POP 59,000 / ELEV 1920M

Dolores Hidalgo is a compact town with a pretty, tree-filled plaza, a relaxed ambience and an important history. It has acquired pilgrimage status for Mexicans; the Mexican independence movement began in earnest in this small place. At 5am on September 16, 1810, Miguel Hidalgo, the parish priest, rang the bells to summon people to church earlier than usual and issued the Grito de Dolores, also known as the Grito de Independencia. His precise words have been lost to history, but their essence was 'Death to bad government and the *gachupines!*' (*Gachupines* was a derisive term for the Spanish-born overlords who ruled Mexico.)

BUSES FROM LEÓN

DESTINATION	FARE (M$)	DURATION (HR)	FREQUENCY (DAILY)
Aguascalientes	162-193	2-2½	frequent
Guadalajara	313-339	3	11
Guanajuato	67-90	¾	frequent
Mexico City (Terminal Norte)	452-580	5	very frequent (24 hours)
San Miguel de Allende	183-240	2¼	5
Zacatecas	410	4	9

MIGUEL HIDALGO: ¡VIVA MEXICO!

The balding head of the visionary priest Father Miguel Hidalgo y Costilla is familiar to anyone who has ogled Mexican statues or murals. A genuine rebel idealist, Hidalgo sacrificed his career and risked his life on September 16, 1810, when he launched the independence movement.

Born on May 8, 1753, son of a criollo (Mexican-born person of Spanish parentage) hacienda manager in Guanajuato, he earned a bachelor's degree and, in 1778, was ordained a priest. He returned to teach at his alma mater in Morelia and eventually became rector. But he was no orthodox cleric: Hidalgo questioned many Catholic traditions, read banned books, gambled, danced and had a mistress.

In 1800 he was brought before the Inquisition. Nothing was proven, but a few years later, in 1804, he found himself transferred as priest to the hick town of Dolores.

Hidalgo's years in Dolores show his growing interest in the economic and cultural welfare of the people. He started several new industries: silk was cultivated, olive groves were planted and vineyards established, all in defiance of the Spanish colonial authorities. Earthenware building products were the foundation of the ceramics industry that today produces fine glazed pots and tiles.

When Hidalgo met Ignacio Allende from San Miguel, they shared a criollo discontent with the Spanish stranglehold on Mexico. Hidalgo's standing among the mestizos (people of mixed European and indigenous ancestry) and indigenous people of his parish was vital in broadening the base of the rebellion that followed.

Shortly after his Grito de Independencia, Hidalgo was formally excommunicated for 'heresy, apostasy and sedition.' He defended his call for Mexican independence and stated furthermore that the Spanish were not truly Catholic in any religious sense of the word but only for political purposes, specifically to rape, pillage and exploit Mexico. A few days later, on October 19, Hidalgo dictated his first edict calling for the abolition of slavery in Mexico.

Hidalgo led his growing forces from Dolores to San Miguel, Celaya and Guanajuato, north to Zacatecas, south almost to Mexico City and west to Guadalajara. But then, pushed northward, their numbers dwindled and on July 30, 1811, having been captured by the Spanish, Hidalgo was shot by a firing squad in Chihuahua. His head was returned to the city of Guanajuato, where it hung in a cage for 10 years on an outer corner of the Alhóndiga de Granaditas, along with the heads of fellow independence leaders Allende, Aldama and Jiménez. Rather than intimidating the people, this lurid display kept the memory, the goal and the example of the heroic martyrs fresh in everyone's mind. After independence the cages were removed, and the skulls (and bodies) of the heroes are now in the Monumento a la Independencia in Mexico City.

Today, Hidalgo is one of Mexico's most revered heroes. Dolores was renamed in his honor in 1824. Mexicans swarm here for Independence Day (September 16), during which time the price of accommodations can more than double.

The town's *centro histórico* is worth a day visit from San Miguel de Allende, Guanajuato or Querétaro, not only for its interesting independence-themed museums (all of which are within a couple of blocks of the Plaza Principal), but also for its colored Talavera ceramics workshops (several blocks from the plaza) and ice cream (look for the carts on the plaza).

◉ Sights

Parroquia de Nuestra Señora de Dolores   CHURCH
(Plaza Principal) The Parroquia de Nuestra Señora de Dolores is the church where Hidalgo issued the Grito (a call to arms for the country's independence). It has a fine 18th-century Churrigueresque facade. Legends surround his 'cry'; some say that Hidalgo uttered his famous words from the pulpit, others claim that he spoke at the church door to the people gathered outside.

Hidalgo statue   MONUMENT
(Plaza Principal) The plaza beholds a statue of the man himself, Hidalgo (in Roman garb, on top of a tall column). Here, too, is a tree

that, according to the plaque beneath it, was a sapling of the tree of the Noche Triste (Sad Night), under which Cortés is said to have wept when his men were driven out of Tenochtitlán in 1520.

Museo Bicentenario 1810-2010   MUSEUM
(Casa del Capitán Mariano Abasolo; adult/student M$20/10, Sun free; ⏰10am-5pm Mon-Sat, to 3pm Sun) Previously the Presidencia Municipal, this museum was inaugurated in 2010 for Mexico's bicentennial celebrations. Despite its name, the majority of its seven rooms provide a cultural and historical context of the first hundred years of independence, including mementos produced for the centenary of 1910. Quirkier items include a stunning silk scarf embroidered with hair (depicting the image of Alejandro Zavala Mangas, an architect from Guanajuato city) and the original painted poster promoting the first century of independence. All explanations are in Spanish.

Museo de la Independencia Nacional   MUSEUM
(National Independence Museum; Zacatecas 6; adult/student M$15/7.50, Sun free; ⏰9am-5pm) Although this museum has few relics, it has plenty of information on the independence movement. The exhibition spans seven rooms and charts the appalling decline in Nueva España's indigenous population between 1519 (an estimated 25 million) and 1605 (1 million), and identifies 23 indigenous rebellions before 1800 as well as several criollo conspiracies in the years leading up to 1810. There are vivid paintings, quotations and details on the heroic last 10 months of Hidalgo's life.

Museo Casa de Hidalgo   MUSEUM
(cnr Hidalgo & Morelos; adult/student M$36; ⏰9am-5:30pm Tue-Sun) Miguel Hidalgo lived in this house when he was Dolores' parish priest. It was from here, in the early hours of September 16, 1810, that Hidalgo, Ignacio Allende and Juan de Aldama set off to launch the uprising against colonial rule. The house is now something of a national shrine – think: memorials, replicas of Hidalgo's furniture and independence-movement documents, including the order for Hidalgo's excommunication.

Museo José Alfredo Jiménez   MUSEUM
(www.museojosealfredojimenez.com; Guanajuato 13, cnr Nuevo León; M$35; ⏰10am-5pm Tue-Sun) If you don't know of José Alfredo Jiménez before you come to Dolores, you will by the time you leave. (Hint: he's the king of *música ranchera* and beloved by all Mexicans). Housed in a stunning space – the home where he was born – this new, modern museum cleverly depicts his life through paintings, photos, mementos and recordings (there are hi-tech ear-phones). The first room features an extraordinary painting by Octavio Ocampo, in which are hidden many figures and symbols.

Festivals & Events

Día de la Independencia   HISTORICAL
Dolores is the scene of major Día de la Independencia (September 16) celebrations, when the Mexican president may officiate – according to tradition – in his fifth year of office.

Fiestas Patrias   CULTURAL
The dates of the Fiestas Patrias festivities change annually; they run for up to two weeks and always encompass September 16.

Sleeping

Prices can double (even triple) for the independence celebrations in September, and at Easter.

Hotel Hidalgo   HOTEL $
(☎418-182-04-77; www.hotelposadahidalgo.com; Hidalgo 15; s/d/tr M$460/560/660; P❄@🐾) The reception feels a bit like a doctor's surgery, but this superclean and well-managed place offers a comfortable and '80s-modern' stay. It's conveniently located between the bus stations and the Plaza Principal.

Posada Cocomacán   HOTEL $$
(☎418-182-60-86; www.posadacocomacan.com.mx; Plaza Principal 4; s/d M$350/470; 🐾) The centrally located and absolutely apricot Cocomacán is an aged, but reliable option. Of the 37 rooms, those on the upper levels, with windows onto the street, are the best. There's also a restaurant (open 8am to 10:30pm).

Eating

Don't leave without sampling a hand-turned ice cream (around M$20) from an ice-cream vendor on the plaza or around town. You can test your taste buds on the flavors: *mole* (chili sauce), *chicharrón* (fried pork skin), avocado, corn, cheese, honey, shrimp, beer, tequila and tropical fruits. The busy market on the corner of Chihuahua and Michoacán serves up some satisfying corn-based snacks.

El Fruty CAFE $
(Hidalgo s/n; snacks M$25-55; ⊘9am-10pm) A cheap and convenient stop for filling sandwiches, natural yogurts and (just) passable coffee.

★**DaMónica** ITALIAN $$
(Nayarit 67; mains M$70-180; ⊘10:30am-10:30pm Tue-Sun) If Mexican independence started in Dolores Hidalgo, it could be claimed that Mexico's Italian culture started in the same town, in an area that is as Mexican as a fried bean. This marvel is an Italian eatery where Mónica, the Italian owner, whips up very genuine Italian delights, such as lasagna, pizza and gourmet seafood treats, Just like Mamma used to make.

🛍 Shopping

Talavera ceramics have been the signature handicraft of Dolores ever since Padre Hidalgo founded the town's first ceramics workshop in the early 19th century. Head to the Zona Artesanal, the workshops along Avenida Jiménez, five blocks west of the plaza, or (by car) to Calzada de los Héroes, the exit road to San Miguel de Allende. Some workshops here make 'antique' colonial-style furniture.

ⓘ Information

The **tourist office** (📞 418-182-11-64; www.dolores-hidalgo.com; Plaza Principal; ⊘9am-5pm Mon-Fri, 10am-2pm Sat) is on Plaza Principal's southeastern side. The helpful staff provide maps and information. Several banks with ATMs are around the plaza. The **post office** (📞418-182-08-07; cnr Puebla & Veracruz; ⊘9am-2pm Mon-Sat) is on the corner of Puebla and Veracruz.

ⓘ Getting There & Away

The **Primera Plus/Coordinados (Flecha Amarilla) bus station** (Hidalgo) is 2½ blocks south of the plaza, near the **Herradura de Plata/Autovías bus station** (📞418-182-29-37; cnr Chiapas & Yucatán).

There are regular 2nd-class connections to Querétaro (M$140), León (M$144) and San Luis Potosí (M$159).

San Miguel de Allende

📞 415 / POP 70,000 / ELEV 1900M

Many people say that San Miguel is a bit like a Mexican Disneyland for foreign (mainly American) retirees and visiting *chilangos* (those from Mexico City). While there is a certain contrived fairy tale feel to the place – and not a colonial brick out of place in its historic center – it is, nevertheless, a beautiful city, with colonial architecture, enchanting cobblestone streets and striking light (especially popular among photographers and artists). Regular festivals, fireworks and parades dominate the local scene.

The town's cosmopolitan panache is reflected in its excellent restaurants and high-class accommodations. Numerous galleries are stocked with quality Mexican *artesanías* (handicrafts) and cultural activities are on tap for residents and visitors. There are few major sights in the compact *centro histórico*: San Miguel is the sight. The city – with El Jardín, the principal plaza, and the Parroquia, the large church, at its heart – was declared a Unesco World Heritage site in 2008.

Economically speaking, this is no budget destination and is a far cry from the 1940s, when beatniks and artists shacked up here on a shoestring to pursue their creative ventures. While the foreign influence is pervasive (more than 12,000 foreigners are believed to live or have houses here), on the whole, the population coexists comfortably.

Beneath the smart B&Bs and fancy shops, another Mexico emerges. You only have to laze in the main plaza, visit the food market or interact with the local people to sense a different ambience, color and vibe.

The climate is agreeable: cool and clear in winter and warm in summer, with occasional thunderstorms and heavy rain.

BUSES FROM DOLORES HIDALGO

DESTINATION	FARE (M$)	DURATION (HR)	FREQUENCY (DAILY)
Guanajuato	73	1¼	frequent
León	144	2¼	3
Mexico City (Terminal Norte) via Querétaro	349	5-6	frequent
San Miguel de Allende	47	¾	frequent

History

The town, so the story goes, owes its founding to a few overheated dogs. These hounds were loved by a Franciscan friar, Juan de San Miguel, who started a mission in 1542 near an often-dry river 5km from the present town. One day the dogs wandered off from the mission; they were found reclining at the spring called El Chorro (p663). The mission was moved to this superior site.

San Miguel was then central Mexico's most northern Spanish settlement. Tarascan and Tlaxcalan allies of the Spanish were brought to help pacify the local Otomí and Chichimecs. San Miguel was barely surviving the fierce Chichimec resistance, until in 1555 a Spanish garrison was established to protect the new road from Mexico City to the silver center of Zacatecas. Spanish ranchers settled in the area and it grew into a thriving commercial center and home to some of Guanajuato's wealthy silver barons.

San Miguel's favorite son, Ignacio Allende, was born here in 1779. He became a fervent believer in the need for Mexican independence and was a leader of a Querétaro-based conspiracy that set December 8, 1810, as the date for an armed uprising. When the plan was discovered by the authorities in Querétaro on September 13, a messenger rushed to San Miguel and gave the news to Juan de Aldama, another conspirator. Aldama sped north to Dolores where, in the early hours of September 16, he found Allende at the house of the priest Miguel Hidalgo, also one of the coterie. A few hours later Hidalgo proclaimed rebellion from his church. After initial successes Allende, Hidalgo and other rebel leaders were captured in 1811 in Chihuahua. Allende was executed, but on independence in 1821 he was recognized as a martyr and in 1826 the town was renamed San Miguel de Allende.

The Escuela de Bellas Artes was founded in 1938 and the town started to take on its current character when David Alfaro Siqueiros began mural-painting courses that attracted artists of every persuasion. The Instituto Allende opened in 1951, also attracting foreign students. Many were US war veterans (who could settle here under the GI Bill); an influx of artists has continued ever since.

◉ Sights

Parroquia de San Miguel Arcángel CHURCH
The parish church's pink 'wedding cake' towers dominate the Jardín. These strange pinnacles were designed by indigenous stonemason Zeferino Gutiérrez in the late 19th century. He reputedly based the design on a postcard of a Belgian church and instructed builders by scratching plans in the sand with a stick. The rest of the church dates from the late 17th century. In the chapel to the left of the main altar is the much-revered image of the *Cristo de la Conquista* (Christ of the Conquest), made in Pátzcuaro from cornstalks and orchid bulbs, probably in the 16th century. The adjacent **Iglesia de San Rafael** was founded in 1742.

La Esquina: Museo del Juguete Popular Mexicano MUSEUM
(www.museolaesquina.org.mx; Núñez 40; M$30; ⊙10am-6pm Tue-Sat, to 3pm Sun) This bright, modern museum is a must-visit for all kids, big and small. To describe it as exhibiting Mexican toys (the 50-year collection of museum owner Angélica Tijerina) is to do it a disservice. It is much more. It aims to preserve and continue the tradition of toys by showcasing different pieces from the many regions of Mexico. The pieces – divided into four main themed areas – are made of a range of materials, from wheat to plastic, wood to fabric.

Kids will love the interactive games on the computer. A lovely gift shop is attached.

Jardín Botánico El Charco del Ingenio GARDENS
(☑415-154-47-15; www.elcharco.org.mx; off Antiguo Camino Real a Querétaro; M$40; ⊙9am-6pm) Northeast of town (1.5km) is the 88-hectare botanic garden, also a wildlife and bird sanctuary, plus recreational and ceremonial space. Pathways head through wetlands and magnificent areas of cacti and native plants. A canyon has an eponymous freshwater spring, the **Charco del Ingenio**. Don't miss the **Conservatory of Mexican Plants**, which houses a wonderful array of cacti and succulent species. Two-hour tours (in English) depart every Tuesday and Thursday at 10am (M$80). Monthly full-moon ceremonies also take place here.

Each Tuesday, Thursday, Saturday and Sunday a complimentary bus service leaves Calles Mesones in front of Plaza Cívica at 9:30am, returning at 1pm. Otherwise, getting to the garden can seem a slightly prickly business, thanks to urban development on the town's outskirts, which blocks the original route, but it's worth persevering. Walk uphill from Mercado El Nigromante along Homobono and Cuesta de San José. Fork left up Montitlan past a housing development (known as Los Balcones). Continue for another 15 minutes to the main gate. Be sure to keep the garden boundary fence on your left as much as possible. (Occasionally you may have to head around the new houses on sidewalks, after which you head back to the fence.)

Alternatively, a 2km vehicle track leads north from the Soriana shopping center, 2.5km southeast of the center on the Querétaro road. This can be reached on 'Soriana' buses from the bus stop from Mesones, near Plaza Cívica (10mins, M$5). A taxi to the gardens from the center costs from around M$50 to M$60.

Museo Histórico de San Miguel de Allende   MUSEUM
(Museo Casa de Allende; Cuna de Allende 1; M$47; ◷ 9:30am-4:30pm Tue-Sun) Near the Parroquia de San Miguel Arcángel is the house where Ignacio Allende was born. These days it is home to the Museo Histórico de San Miguel de Allende, which relates the interesting history of the San Miguel area. One of the floors is a reproduction of Allende's home. A Latin inscription on the facade reads *Hic natus ubique notus*, which means 'Born here, known everywhere.'

Mirador   PARK
One of the best views over the town and surrounding country is from the *mirador* southeast of town. Take Callejón del Chorro, the track leading directly downhill from here, and turn left at the bottom to reach **El Chorro**, the spring where San Miguel was founded (note the fountain and public washing tubs).

Parque Benito Juárez   PARK
A path – Paseo del Chorro – zigzags down the hill to the shady Parque Benito Juárez, a lovely place to relax and meander through.

Other Face of Mexico Gallery   MUSEUM
(www.casadelacuesta.com; Casa de la Cuesta, Cuesta de San José 32; M$50) This fascinating private collection of more than 500 masks provides an excellent context of the Mexican mask tradition. It is open by appointment only (call ☏ 415-154-43-24). The admission fee goes to charity.

Escuela de Bellas Artes   GALLERY
(School of Fine Arts | Centro Cultural Nigromante; ☏ 415-152-02-89; Hernández Macías 75; ◷ 10am-6pm Mon-Sat, to 2pm Sun) This beautiful former monastery of La Concepción church was converted into a fine-arts school in 1938. Don't miss the murals of Pedro Martínez, plus the Siqueiros Room, which features the extraordinary unfinished mural by David Alfaro Siqueiros (it plays with your mind – we won't spoil the surprise). The rest of the gallery holds temporary exhibitions.

Oratorio de San Felipe Neri   CHURCH
(Plaza Cívica) Located near the east end of Insurgentes, this multitowered and domed church dates from the 18th century. The pale-pink main facade is baroque with an indigenous influence. A passage to the right of this facade leads to the east wall, where a doorway holds the image of *Nuestra Señora de la Soledad* (Our Lady of Solitude). You can see into the cloister from this side of the church.

Inside the church are 33 oil paintings showing scenes from the life of San Felipe Neri, the 16th-century Florentine who founded the Oratorio Catholic order. In the east transept is a painting of the Virgin of Guadalupe by leading colonial painter Miguel Cabrera. In the west transept is a lavishly decorated 1735 chapel, the **Santa Casa de Loreto**, a replica of a chapel in Loreto, Italy, legendary home of the Virgin Mary. Although rarely open, the *camarín* (chapel behind the main church) has six elaborately gilded baroque altars. In one is a reclining wax figure of San Columbano; it supposedly contains the saint's bones.

Templo de San Francisco   CHURCH
(cnr San Francisco & Juárez) Adorned with an elaborate late-18th-century Churrigueresque facade, this church has an image of St Francis of Assisi at the top. Opening hours vary.

Capilla de la Tercera Orden   CHAPEL
(Chapel of the Third Order; cnr San Francisco & Juárez) Built in the early 18th century, this chapel, like the Templo de San Francisco, was part of a Franciscan monastery complex. The main facade shows St Francis and symbols of the Franciscan order.

Templo de la Salud   CHURCH
(Plaza Cívica) With its blue and yellow tiled dome and a big shell carved above its entrance, this church is just east of San Felipe Neri. The facade is early Churrigueresque. The church's paintings include one of San Javier by Miguel Cabrera. San Javier (St Francis Xavier, 1506–52) was a founding member of the Jesuits. It was once part of the Colegio de Sales.

San Miguel de Allende

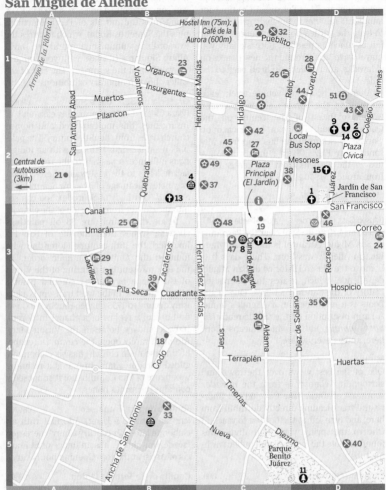

Templo de la Concepción
CHURCH

(Church of the Conception; cnr Zacateros & Canal) A splendid church with a fine altar and several magnificent old oil paintings. Painted on the interior doorway are a number of wise sayings to give pause to those entering the sanctuary. The church was begun in the mid-18th century; its dome, added in the late 19th century by the versatile Zeferino Gutiérrez, was possibly inspired by pictures of Les Invalides in Paris.

Instituto Allende
HISTORIC BUILDING

(Ancha de San Antonio 20 & 22) This large 1736 complex, the original home of the Conde Manuel de la Canal, was used as a Carmel-ite convent, eventually becoming an art and language school in 1951. These days it's split into two – one area of several patios, gardens and an old chapel is used for functions, the other for courses. Above the main entrance is a carving of the Virgin of Loreto, patron-ess of the Canal family.

Colegio de Sales
NOTABLE BUILDING

(Plaza Cívica; ⊙ 8am-2pm & 5-8pm) Once a col-lege, founded in the mid-18th century by the San Felipe Neri order, the Colegio de Sales has regained its educational status; it cur-rently houses part of the University of León.

Academia Hispano Americana
LANGUAGE COURSE

(☑415-152-03-49; www.ahaspeakspanish.com; Mesones 4) Housed in a beautiful colonial building, this place runs quality courses in the Spanish language and incorporates history classes.

The Spanish School
SPANISH

(☑415-121-25-35; www.liceodelalengua.com; Callejón del Pueblito 5) Small centrally located and extremely professional Spanish school.

Warren Hardy Spanish
LANGUAGE COURSE

(☑415-154-40-17; www.warrenhardy.com; San Rafael 6) Offers Spanish instruction. A favorite among local expats of a mature age.

Marilau – Mexican Ancestry Cooking School
COOKING COURSE

(☑415-152-43-76; http://mexican-cooking-school. com; Colonia San Antonio; course per person M$100) Marilau hails from a great line of cooks; demand for her *tamales* in San Miguel was so great in the late 1980s, locals asked her to teach them her secrets. So she did, passing on the techniques, ingredients and methods that she inherited from her family from past centuries. Minimum three to four per group.

⚑ Tours

The tourist office has promotional pamphlets of official English-speaking tour guides who offer both walking and driving tours. See *Atención San Miguel* for the weekly list of tours within San Miguel; most of these support local charities.

Bici-Burro
CYCLING

(☑415-152-15-26; www.bici-burro.com; Hospicio 1; trips US$70-120) Friendly and professional, English-speaking owner Alberto conducts excellent guided mountain-bike tours for groups of two or more. Popular trips include six- or seven-hour excursions to Atotonilco or Pozos and a wonderful 'mezcal tour' that takes in a number of haciendas, one of which produces mezcal. Bike rental also available (US$45 per day).

Bookatour
WALKING, CRAFTS

(☑415-152-01-98; www.bookatour.mx; Codo 1; ⊙9am-6:30pm Mon-Fri, to 3pm Sun) This company offers a range of tours with bilingual guides. Prices are the same for one, two or three people and include transportation. These include: walking tours around San Miguel (US$35 per hour), arts and crafts

Many of the 1810 revolutionaries were educated here. Spaniards were locked up here when the rebels took San Miguel.

🎓 Courses

Several institutions offer Spanish courses, with group or private lessons and optional classes in Mexican culture and history. Most private lessons cost around US$20 an hour; group and long-term rates are much lower. Homestays with Mexican families, including a private room and three daily meals, cost around US$33 per day.

Cooking courses are also on the rise here.

San Miguel de Allende

⊙ Sights

1 Capilla de la Tercera Orden D2
2 Colegio de Sales D2
3 El Chorro E5
4 Escuela de Bellas Artes B2
5 Instituto Allende B5
6 La Esquina: Museo del Juguete
   Popular Mexicano E2
7 Mirador E5
8 Museo Histórico de San Miguel
   de Allende C3
9 Oratorio de San Felipe Neri D2
10 Other Face of Mexico Gallery F1
11 Parque Benito Juárez D5
12 Parroquia de San Miguel
   Arcángel C3
13 Templo de la Concepción B2
14 Templo de la Salud D2
15 Templo de San Francisco D2

⊙ Activities, Courses & Tours

16 Academia Hispano Americana E2
17 Bici-Burro E3
18 Bookatour B4
19 San Miguel de Allende Walking
   Tour C3
20 The Spanish School C1
21 Warren Hardy Spanish A2

⊙ Sleeping

22 Antigua Capilla F2
23 Casa de la Noche B1
24 Casa Mia D3
25 Dos Casas B3
26 Hostal Alcatraz C1

27 Hostal Punto 79 .... C2
28 Hotel Quinta Loreto D1
29 Hotel San Borja B&B A3
30 Posada Corazón C4
31 Villa Mirasol B3

⊗ Eating

   Áperi .... (see 25)
32 Buen Día Café C1
33 Café Rama B5
34 Cumpanio D3
35 El Café de la Mancha D4
36 El Manantial E4
37 La Buena Vida C2
38 La Colmena Bakery C2
39 La Mesa Grande B3
40 La Parada D5
41 La Posadita C3
42 Los Burritos C2
43 Mercado El Nigromante D2
44 Muro D1
45 Petit Four C2
46 San Agustín D3

⊙ Drinking & Nightlife

47 La Azotea C3
   La Mezcalería .... (see 24)

⊙ Entertainment

48 El Grito C3
49 Teatro Ángela Peralta C2
50 Teatro Santa Ana C1

⊙ Shopping

51 Mercado de Artesanías D1

tours (visiting weaving and glass factories and pewter and papier maché workshops; from US$120 per hour); cantina 'crawls' (US$35 per person) and visits to Mineral de Pozos ($45 per person).

San Miguel de Allende Walking Tour   WALKING TOUR
This excellent tour (M$200) takes place every Monday, Wednesday and Friday at 10am, departing from El Jardín (tickets go on sale in El Jardín at 9:45am). The English-speaking volunteer guides provide a fascinating historical, architectural and cultural commentary on the town's sights.

Xotolar Ranch Adventures   HORSEBACK RIDING
(☑ 415-154-62-75; www.xotolarranch.com; rides from US$95) Xotolar Ranch Adventures, based on a working ranch, specializes in canyon trail rides.

★ Festivals & Events

San Miguel is well endowed with churches and patron saints (it has six) and enjoys a multitude of festivals, many imbued with strong spiritual themes. You'll probably be alerted to a festival event by firework bursts. For programs, ask at the tourist office or check out the website www.visitsanmiguel. travel.

Señor de la Conquista   RELIGIOUS
The image of Christ in the Parroquia de San Miguel Arcángel is feted on the first Friday in March, with scores of dancers in elaborate pre-Hispanic costumes and plumed headdresses.

Semana Santa   RELIGIOUS
A week of religious activities. Two Sundays before Easter, pilgrims carry an image of the Señor de la Columna from Atotonilco, 11km north, to San Miguel's church of San Juan

de Dios, departing at midnight on Saturday. During Semana Santa, the many activities include the solemn Procesión del Santo Entierro on Good Friday and the burning or exploding of Judas effigies on Easter Day.

Fiesta de la Santa Cruz HISTORICAL

This deeply spiritual spring festival has its roots in the 16th century. It happens toward the end of May at Valle del Maíz, 2km from the center of town. Oxen are dressed in lime necklaces and painted tortillas and their yokes are festooned with flowers and fruit. A mock battle between 'Indians' and 'Federales' follows. There are *mojigangas,* dancing and musicians, not to mention 96 hours' worth of fireworks.

Fiesta de los Locos RELIGIOUS

Part of the Festividad de San Antonio de Padua in mid-June, the festival of the crazies is a colorful Carnavalesque parade through town with floats, blaring music and costumed dancers throwing out candy to – sometimes at! – the crowd.

Expresión en Corto FILM

Shared with the city of Guanajuato, this short-film festival in July is internationally recognized.

Fiestas Patrias CULTURAL

Two months of cultural programs kick off toward the end of August, incorporating Independence Day. Check with the tourist office for a full event schedule.

San Miguel Arcángel RELIGIOUS

Celebrations honoring the town's chief patron saint are held around the weekend following September 29. The party is celebrated with an *alborada,* an artificial dawn created by thousands of fireworks around the cathedral, and turns into an all-night festivity with extraordinary pre-Hispanic dances.

🛏 Sleeping

Accommodations are often full during festivals and high season, so make reservations well in advance. Thanks to a couple of recent hostel additions, the city now boasts accommodations for all budgets. Midrange options are a bit light on; it's worth loosening the purse strings here. San Miguel is the mecca for good quality luxury B&Bs, boutique hotels and guesthouses. Note: a new trend for San Miguel is that hotels hike their prices on weekends. All include breakfast unless stated.

Hostal Alcatraz HOSTEL $

(☑ 415-152-85-43; www.alcatrazhostal.com; Reloj 54; dm M$150-170, s M$580, s/d without bathroom M$250/460; @) One of San Miguel's only hostels that is centrally located, with basic dorms and a shared kitchen, but a bit short on bathrooms. Associated with Hostel Inn.

Hostel Inn HOSTEL $

(www.hostelinnmx.com; Calzada de La Luz 31A; dm M$150-170, s M$580, s/d without bathroom M$250/460) Associated closely with Hostel Alcatraz, this converted house offers dorms and simple rooms, but is a bit short on bathrooms.

Hostal Punto 79 HOSTEL $

(☑ 415-121-10-34; www.punto79.com; Mesones 79; dm M$230, r with/without bathroom M$900/230; 🛜) The centrally located sprawling spot touts itself as a hotel-hostel, but the hostel rooms are far more appealing. The dorm rooms are segregated for male and female guests and are a decent place to bed down, especially if you're on a budget. There are few facilities (and no breakfast) but you're bang in the middle of town.

Hotel San Borja B&B B&B $

(☑ 415-152-53-08; www.hotelsanborja.com; Ladrillera 8; r M$950-M$1250; 🛜 ⊠) It touts itself as a B&B but breakfast is at a nearby cafe. Despite this small shortfall, this lovely midrange spot is nestled around a secluded garden. Its four rooms are plain (they lack the usual colorful Mexican decor) but they have a hotel quality with a home-style feel. Good for those seeking a bit of quiet.

Villa Mirasol HOTEL $$

(www.villamirasolhotel.com; Pila Seca 35; r from M$1320) This place is a bit like an old aunt – slightly dated, but charming and hospitable. Its bright and airy rooms face onto plant-filled patios. A reliable choice. Offers specials throughout the year.

Casa de la Noche GUESTHOUSE $$

(☑ 415-152-07-32; www.casadelanoche.com; Organos 19; s US$89-100, weekday d US$118-175, d US$135-188; 🛜) A bit like the bordello it once was, the place promises big things, especially at the beginning. The refurbished entry and living areas are superb – spacious, stylish and airy – though some of the rooms are a bit cramped and dated. To inflate your enthusiasm, numerous fun nooks and crannies are open for the taking and it's a generally satisfying experience for the price.

The friendly artist-owner 'Madame' promotes local talent; artworks prevail. Prices increase on weekends.

Hotel Quinta Loreto
HOTEL **$$**

(☑415-152-00-42; www.quintaloreto.com.mx; Loreto 15; s/d/tr M$480/610/715; P🐕🛜🏊) This dated motel-style place at the back of the artisans' market is spread around large, leafy grounds. One of the better budget to midrange options around, it is in a '60s timewarp. Some of the 28 simple rooms are pleasantly light (check first). Prices exclude breakfast. The restaurant is open for breakfast and lunch (8am to 5:30pm; mains M$45-50).

During the day, the gardens serve as a public car park, but by the evening it's tranquil.

★ Posada Corazón
B&B **$$$**

(☑415-152-01-82; www.posadacorazon.com.mx; Aldama 9; d M$1800-2200; P😊🛜) This gorgeous place of mid-century design has a heart, as the name suggests. It's set behind an inconspicuous wall in a delightfully lush plant and sculpture garden. The home's spacious open-plan living area (and library) can be shared by guests, and rooms along a deck are light, simple and stylish. Open daily to the public for breakfast (M$170).

★ Antigua Capilla
BOUTIQUE HOTEL **$$$**

(☑415-152-40-48; www.antiguacapilla.com; Callejon Chepitos 16; r US$175-200; P😊🛜) Constructed around a tiny 17th-century chapel, this utterly stylish, spick and span place is hard to fault; it boasts every mod con and service imaginable plus extraordinary breakfasts and a gorgeous plant-lined courtyard. The English- and Spanish-speaking owners are delightful. Access is up a hill but the rooftop terrace affords one of the best views in San Miguel. Excellent price-to-quality ratio.

Casa Mia
APARTMENTS **$$$**

(☑415-152-27-57; www.casamia-sanmiguel.com; Correo 61; apt per night/week from US$78/500; P🛜) Its tasteful plant-filled courtyard is lined with 13 uniquely decorated apartments, all featuring comfortable hotel-style bedrooms, cable TV, living areas and kitchens. It's better value if you plan to stay for longer than a night or two. Breakfast is not provided.

Dos Casas
BOUTIQUE HOTEL **$$$**

(☑415-154-40-73; www.doscasas.com.mx; Quebrada 101; d M$4369-6672; 😊❄🛜) This sleek sleep oozes contemporary style with its cream and black hues, fire places and private terraces. Twelve stunning rooms across two adjoining properties provide a touch of avante-garde luxury (the owner is an architect). There's a spa, plus Áperi (p669), which we predict will be one of Mexico's top restaurants, on site.

✗ Eating

San Miguel's numerous eateries serve a startling variety of quality Mexican and international fine cuisine. Thrifty travelers enjoy more traditional places catering to loyal crowds of local families. A thriving cafe society prevails.

Self-caterers should head to the supermarkets at Soriana shopping center, 2.5km southeast of the center on the Querétaro road.

For budget bites, there are several reliable food stands on the corner of Ancha de San Antonio and tree-shaded Nueva (near Instituto Allende). They alternate in the mornings and evenings, selling great-tasting juice, *gorditas* (small circles of tortilla dough, fried and topped with meat and/or cheese), burritos and tacos. Reliable juice stands front the small plaza off Insurgentes. A million miles from the gringo scene, **Mercado El Nigromante** (Colegio s/n) has basic food stalls.

Excellent traditional bakeries include **La Buena Vida** (Hernández Macías 72-14; baked goods M$20-60; ☺8am-4pm Mon-Sat) and **La Colmena Bakery** (Reloj 21; baked goods from M$8). For something more contemporary, the trendy *panaderia* (bakery) **Cumpanio** (Correo 29; baked goods M$20-150; ☺8am-9pm) is great for takeaway French pastries, as is **Petit Four** (☑415-154-40-10; Mesones 99-1; snacks M$10-45; ☺8am-6pm Tue-Sat, to 3pm Sun; 😊🛜).

★ San Agustín
CAFE **$**

(☑415-154-91-02; San Francisco 21; snacks M$40-80, mains M$70-165; ☺8am-11pm Mon-Thu, 9am-midnight Fri-Sun; 😊) A 'don't leave San Miguel without...' experience. This sweet tooth's paradise is the best place in Mexico for chocolate and *churros* (doughnut-like fritters; M$45 to M$55).

Buen Día Café
CAFE **$**

(Pueblito 3A; mains M$60-90; ☺8am-noon Tue, to 4pm Wed-Mon; 🛜) This simple, slightly more than a hole-in-the wall is located in the quaint Callejon Pueblito, opposite Calderoni B&B, and serves up great coffee (complete with latte art) and excellent breakfasts, as well as other snacks.

Café de la Aurora   CAFE $

(☑ 415-154-98-28; Calzada de la Aurora; snacks M$20-90, pizza M$95-115; ☺ 8:30am-6pm Mon-Sat, 10:30am-5pm Sun) Fittingly creative salads, soups, sandwiches and pizzas in a relaxing courtyard setting in the grounds of Fábrica La Aurora.

Los Burritos   MEXICAN $

(☑ 415-152-32-22; Hildalgo 23; snacks M$8-40; ☺ 10:30am-6pm Mon-Wed, to 10:30pm Thu-Sat, 12:30-5:30pm Sun) The place for cheap *anto-jitos* and the mouthwatering, made-to-order *guisados* (fillings) from *mole* to *chipotle* (a type of chili) and potato.

Café Rama   BAR, RESTAURANT $$

(www.cafe-rama.com; Calle Nueva 7; mains M$155-290; ☺ 8am-midnight Tue-Sun) This cool cafe-bar-restaurant comprises two separate rooms that are lovingly furnished with quirky antiques and eclectic curios, plus cozy couches near the open fireplace. It's changing menu proffers excellent international dishes and is popular with visiting Mexicans and local expats.

El Manantial   BAR, CANTINA $$

(Barranca 78; mains M$80-150; ☺ 1pm-midnight Tue-Sat, to 11pm Sun) Behind the swinging doors of a former saloon, 'The Spring' serves fabulously fresh ceviche. It's got a real buzz, also helped by *jabanero* salsa, the spiciest of chili sauces that will put hair on your chest. Tuesdays is two-for-one drinks, while Thursday offers up two-for-one nibbles.

(Warning: we suggest you don't pile the *jabanero* sauce on like the hardy locals here, a little goes a long way). Be sure to try one of their ginger margaritas (M$65).

La Parada   PERUVIAN $$

(www.laparadasma.com; Recreo 94; cerviche M$90-110; mains M$95-200; ☺ noon-10pm, Wed-Sat, to 9pm Sun & Mon) This hot spot showcases Peruvian cuisine at its best. Dish presentation is as exquisite as the names ('El Quiquiriquí', aka chicken breast and 'Chino Cochino' pork, but much fancier). And of course, the ubiquitous (and delicious) ceviche. The owners are young, hip and most importantly, trained chefs. Vegetarians can enjoy the 'veggie muncher' (M$95).

Muro   MEXICAN $$

(www.murocafe.com; Loreto 10B; M$85-130; ☺ 9am-4pm Tue-Tue) A must-stop breakfast stop. Serves up everything from *chilaquiles con ar-rachera* to french toast and pastries, plus fab-ulous freshly made juices. Local ingredients are used where possible. Ultra-professional and friendly owner Gerardo provides wi-fi access, but, as he'll tell you, he prefers that clients converse – and even has the day's weather forecast on a blackboard to get you started. It's in an inconspicuous spot with a very simple sign. Don't let that fool you.

La Posadita   MEXICAN $$

(☑ 415-154-88-62; Cuna de Allende 13; mains M$150-265; ☺ noon-10pm Thu-Tue; ☻) This enjoyable eatery gets five stars for its excellent service, Mexican fare, and location near the Parroquia de San Miguel Arcángel. Head up a steep set of stairs to the wonderful rooftop terrace for great vistas. It serves delicious margaritas, enchiladas and meat dishes.

La Mesa Grande   BAKERY $$

(www.lamesagrande.com; Zacateros 149; pastries/snacks M$45-115; ☺ 8am-5pm Mon-Wed & Fri, to 10pm Thu, 9am-5pm Sat) A contemporary *pandería*-cafe with excellent pastries, great home-baked sourdough loaves, decent snacks, and a large communal table for neighborly chats. It's open until 10pm on Thursdays for oven pizzas, and opens at 9am on Saturdays.

★**Áperi**   INTERNATIONAL $$$

(Quebrada 101; tasting menu with/without wine pairing M$1350/850, mains M$140-350; ☺ 2-10:30pm Wed-Sun) This spot is the talk of town. And for good reason. The chef at Áperi (which means 'open' in Latin) has been given the freedom to do whatever he wants. A regularly changing menu features the likes of duck, pork and seafood dishes, prepared with local San Miguelense ingredients. Think farm-to-table cuisine in a fine dining setting without unnecessary pretensions.

Vegetarian options? No problem. Ask on the spot. The Chef's Table – a 14-course tasting menu for two to five people – starts at 6:30pm (by reservation). If you want to loosen the purse strings, this is the place to do it.

🍷 **Drinking & Nightlife**

In San Miguel, drinking and entertainment are often synonymous. Many bars (and restaurants) host live music. Most of the action is on Thursday to Saturday nights, but some places have live music nightly. Calle Umarán has plenty of bar selections.

El Café de la Mancha   CAFE

(Facebook/Elcafedelamancha; Recreo 21A; ☺ 9am-6pm Mon-Fri, from 10am Sat & Sun; ☺) Just larger than a hole-in-the-wall, this is the place for coffee snobs. Need we say more. The trained owner-barista does magic with his Mexican beans and adopts every extraction method known to coffee culture (French press, chemex, aeropress, espresso).

La Azotea
BAR

(Umarán 6) Above the restaurant Pueblo Viejo, this terrace is a smart, laid-back lounge, with a smart, gay-friendly crowd; a top spot for sundowners.

La Mezcalería
BAR

(Correo 47; snacks $100; ⊙5-11pm) It's mezcal-mania time in San Miguel. This is the town's current trendy hangout, where you can get your tongue around a mighty mix of mezcals (from Oaxaca), plus good tapas plates. Don't miss the mezcal margarita!

El Grito
CLUB

(Umarán 15; ⊙10pm-4am Fri & Sat) An oversized face above the doorway of this upscale disco effectively shouts 'high prices' to the fashionable young Mexican crowd queuing outside (its name is a cheeky reference to Padre Hidalgo's call to arms).

☆ Entertainment

Performing Arts

It's one big cultural party in San Miguel; check out what's on in *Atención San Miguel*. The Escuela de Bellas Artes and the Biblioteca (in the Sala Quetzal) host a variety of cultural events, many in English; check their notice boards for schedules.

Teatro Ángela Peralta
THEATER

(☑415-152-22-00; teatro.sanmigueldeallende.gob.mx; cnr Calles Mesones & Hernández Macías) Built in 1873, this elegant venue often hosts local productions. The **ticket office** (Hernández Macías 62; ⊙8:30am-4pm Mon-Fri) is around the corner. Tickets cost between M$50 and M$500 depending on the production.

Teatro Santa Ana
THEATER

(☑415-152-02-93; Reloj 50A; tickets M$40-200) This small theater inside the Biblioteca Pública plays host to a good selection of independent and international films, as well as local plays and talks.

🔒 Shopping

Be sure to hit the Tianguis (Tuesday market), the biggest weekly outdoor extravaganza, beside the Soriana shopping center, 2.5km southeast of the center on the Querétaro road. Take a 'Soriana' or 'Placita'

bus (10 minutes, M$5) from Mesones, near Plaza Cívica.

The local market Mercado El Nigromante (p668) sells produce and assorted goods.

Part of the joy of wandering around San Miguel is to stumble upon the many galleries tucked away in streets around town; there are more commercial galleries than cafes (and perhaps, real estate agents) in San Miguel. The largest concentration of contemporary art galleries and design studios (mainly expatriates' work) is housed in the trendy **Fábrica La Aurora** (☑415-152-13-12; Aurora s/n; ⊙10am-6pm), a remodeled raw-cotton factory on the north end of town. Many galleries are promoted in local papers, but otherwise be guided by your whim.

San Miguel also has a mind-boggling number of craft shops, selling folk art and handicrafts from all over the country. Local crafts include tinware, wrought iron, silver, brass, leather, glassware, pottery and textiles. Many shops are along Canal, San Francisco, Zacateros and Pila Seca. Price and quality varies widely.

Mercado de Artesanías
HANDICRAFTS

(Colegio s/n) A decent collection of handicraft stalls appealing to different tastes (and of varying quality) in the alleyway between Colegio and Loreto.

ℹ Information

INTERNET ACCESS

Solutions (☑415-152-24-97; www.solutionssanmiguel.com; Recreo 11; per hr M$15; ⊙9am-6:30pm Mon-Fri, to 2pm Sat) Internet access as well as mail-forwarding, fax, and shipping services.

INTERNET RESOURCES

Atención San Miguel (www.atencionsanmiguel.org) Weekly bilingual newspaper that runs an excellent website.

Visit San Miguel (www.visitsanmiguel.travel) The official, government-run tourism website.

MEDICAL SERVICES

Hospital Tec100 (☑415-152-59-00; http://hospitaltec100.com/; Libramiento a Dolores Hidalgo 43) This private hospital is located around 3km west of San Miguel's town center.

MEDIA

Don't contemplate spending time in town without buying the weekly semibilingual (English-Spanish) newspaper *Atención San Miguel* (M$10). Published every Friday, it's chock-a-block with what's on for the coming week, including tours, concerts and gallery openings. It also lists yoga, Spanish, art and dance class schedules. You can buy it at the public library and many cafes or from roaming vendors.

MONEY

Most banks have their own ATMs and are located on, or within two blocks east of, El Jardín. There are also *casas de cambio* on Correo.

TOURIST INFORMATION

Tourist Office (☑ 415-152-09-00; www.visitsan miguel.travel; Plaza Principal 8; ⊙ 9am-8pm Mon-Fri, 10am-8pm Sat, to 6pm Sun) On the northern side of El Jardín. Good for maps of the town, promotional pamphlets and information on events.

TRAVEL AGENCIES

Viajes Vertiz (☑ 415-152-18-56; www.viajesver tiz.com; Hidalgo 1A; ⊙ 9am-6:30pm Mon-Fri, 10am-2pm Sat) Useful travel agency; sells domestic and international air tickets and shuttle to airport and other cities.

ⓘ Getting There & Away

AIR

The nearest airport is the Aeropuerto Internacional del Bajío, between León and Silao, around 1½ hours away by car. The obvious alternative are Queretaro Airport or Mexico City International Airport.

BUS

The Central de Autobuses is on Canal (Calzada de la Estación), 3km west of the center. Tickets can be purchased at the station. First-class tickets for Primera Plus, ETN and Ómnibus de México can also be bought at **Peradora** (☑ 415-152-80-11; Cuna de Allende 17).

Second-class services (Coordinados/Flecha Amarilla and Herradura de Plata) also leave from this station. Other 1st-class buses serve Aguascalientes, Monterrey and San Luis Potosí.

CAR & MOTORCYCLE

The only San Miguel-based agency is **San Miguel Rent-a-Car** (☑ 415-152-01-98; www. sanmiguelrentacar.com; Codo 1; ⊙ 9am-6:30pm Mon-Sat, to 3pm Sun). Prices start at about M$750 per day including insurance.

ⓘ Getting Around

TO/FROM THE AIRPORT

Many agencies provide shuttle transportation to/from Bajío airport. These include **Viajes Vertiz** (☑ 415-152-18-56; www.viajesvertiz. com; Hidalgo 1A; ⊙ 9am-6:30pm Mon-Fri, 10am-2pm Sat), **Viajes San Miguel** (☑ 415-152-25-37; www.viajessanmiguel.com; Diez de Sollano 4-Interior 3; ⊙ 9am-7pm Mon-Fri, 10am-2pm Sat), **Bajío Go** (☑ 415-152-19-99; www.bajiobo.com; Jésus 11; ⊙ 8am-8pm Mon-Sat, 10am-3pm Sun), **Bookatour** (p665) and **Peradora** (p671). Alternatively, take a bus to Silao and get a taxi from there to the airport (around M$60). For Mexico City airport, get a bus to Querétaro and a bus direct to the airport from there.

If heading from the airport to San Miguel by bus, it's easiest to go to León via taxi and take a bus from there. No bus service operates between Bajío airport and central León. A taxi to León costs around M$400 and to San Miguel M$1200 (for up to four people).

TO/FROM THE BUS STATION

Local buses (M$6) run from 7am to 9pm daily. 'Central' buses run regularly between the bus station and the town center. Coming into town these terminate at the eastern end of Insurgentes after winding through the streets. Heading out of the center, you can pick one up on Canal. A taxi between the center and the bus station costs around M$40; trips around town cost around M$35.

BUSES FROM SAN MIGUEL DE ALLENDE

DESTINATION	FARE (M$)	DURATION (HR)	FREQUENCY (DAILY)
Celaya	59-70	1¾	every 15min
Dolores Hidalgo	47-70	1	every 40min 7am-7pm
Guadalajara	500-645	5¼-5½	9
Guanajuato	98-155	1-1½	19
León	183-240	2¼-2½	11
Mexico City (Terminal Norte)	302-475	3½-4¼	8
Querétaro	67-115	1-1½	every 40min 7am-8:30pm

THERMAL SPRING POOLS

The surrounds of San Miguel are blessed with several mineral springs. Some of these have been transformed into commercial *balnearios* (swimming pools) in pretty, landscaped gardens and picnic grounds. The waters are up to 100°F (38°C). Most places are crowded with local families on weekends but *muy tranquilo* (very peaceful) during the week.

The *balnearios* are accessed via the highway north of San Miguel and all are clearly signposted. The most convenient transportation is taxis (around M$150 each way; you can ask the driver to return for you at an appointed time). Alternatively, take a Dolores Hidalgo bus from the San Miguel bus station, or a local bus marked 'Santuario' (hourly) from Calzada de la Luz. These buses will stop out front, or at the turnoffs to some of the *balnearios* from where you'll need to walk (check directions and bus connections with the tourist office). To return to town, it's best to pre-arrange a taxi pick-up, or hail a bus heading along the highway.

Balneario Xote (☑ 415-155-81-87; www.xoteparqueacuatico.com.mx; adult/child M$120/60; ☉ 9am-6pm) A family-oriented water park, 3.5km off the highway down the same cobblestone road as Taboada (without transportation this is a long, exposed trek).

Escondido Place (☑ 415-185-20-22; www.escondidoplace.com; M$120; ☉ 8am-5:30pm) Seven small outdoor pools and three connected indoor pools, each progressively hotter. Set in picturesque grounds with snack bar.

La Gruta (☑ 415-185-2162; www.lagrutaspa.com; M$110; ☉ 7am-5pm) is one of the easiest to get to – it's on the Dolores highway, just past Parador del Cortijo at Km 9.5. It's justifiably a favorite among visitors and has three small pools, a tunnel and a cave.

Around San Miguel de Allende

Cañada de la Virgen

Opened in 2011 after many years of archaeological excavation and negotiations with the owner (who donated the ruins and surrounds to the government to allow for public access), the **Cañada de la Virgen** (www.canadadelavirgen.com; ☉ 10am-4pm Tue-Sun) is an intriguing pre-Hispanic pyramid complex and former ritual and ceremonial site located around 25km southeast of San Miguel, dating from around AD 300 to 1050. Bones, believed to be from sacrificial ceremonies, and remnants were discovered here. The most interesting aspects include the alignment of the planets and the main temple and the design of the site (these reflect the surrounding landscape).

A shuttle bus is the compulsory transportation for visitors. It runs between the site office and the site (several kilometers away); these depart on the hour between 10am and 4pm and cost M$30. The tours are in Spanish (although are little more than a rote learned orientation), and you'll be walking on cobbled surfaces and steep steps.

Tours

Coyote Canyon Adventures TOUR (☑ 415-154-41-93; www.coyotecanyonadventures.com; 4 people or more per person US$50) Possibly the easiest and most rewarding visit for non-Spanish speakers is to take a tour with Coyote Canyon Adventures. The guides include archaeologists and anthropologists who discuss the site's fascinating cultural and historical context; prices include transportation from San Miguel.

Santuario de Atotonilco

The hamlet of Atotonilco, 11km north of San Miguel and 3km west of the Dolores Hidalgo highway, is dominated by an extremely important sanctuary, at least in the eyes of Mexicans. The sanctuary was founded in 1740 as a spiritual retreat, and Ignacio Allende married here in 1802. Eight years later he returned with Miguel Hidalgo and a band of independence rebels en route from Dolores to San Miguel to take the shrine's banner of the Virgin of Guadalupe as their flag.

A journey to Atotonilco is the goal of pilgrims and penitents from all over Mexico, and the starting point of an important and solemn procession two weekends before Easter. Participants carry the image of the Señor de la Columna to the church of San Juan de

Dios in San Miguel. Inside, the sanctuary has six chapels and is vibrant with statues, folk murals and paintings. Traditional dances are held here on the third Sunday in July.

From San Miguel, taxis charge around M$120 to M$150 for a one-way trip. Local buses signed 'Atotonilco' or 'Cruz del Palmar' depart from Calzada de La Luz every hour on the half hour (M$10, 45 minutes).

AGUASCALIENTES STATE

The state of Aguascalientes (population 1.2 million) is one of Mexico's smallest; its focus is the city of the same name. According to local legend, a kiss planted on the lips of dictator Santa Anna by the wife of a prominent local politician brought about the creation of a separate Aguascalientes state from Zacatecas.

Beyond the museum-rich city formal tourist sites are few, but it's a pleasant enough drive en route to or from Zacatecas, through fertile lands of corn, beans, chilies, fruit and grain.

The state's ranches produce beef cattle as well as bulls, which are sacrificed at bullfights countrywide.

Aguascalientes

📞 449 / POP 720,000 / ELEV 1880M

This prosperous industrial city is home to more than half of the state's population. Despite its messy outskirts (defined by ring roads), at its heart are a fine plaza and handsome colonial buildings. Museums are its strong point: the Museo Nacional de la Muerte justifies a visit, as do those devoted to José Guadalupe Posada and Saturnino Herrán. It's worth heading here for a day, even on the way to somewhere else.

History

Before the Spanish arrived, a labyrinth of catacombs was built here; the first Spaniards called it La Ciudad Perforada (The Perforated City). Archaeologists understand little of the tunnels (unfortunately, these are off-limits to visitors).

Conquistador Pedro de Alvarado arrived in 1522 but was driven back by the Chichimecs. A small garrison was founded here in 1575 to protect Zacatecas–Mexico City silver convoys. Eventually, as the Chichimecs were pacified, the region's hot springs sparked the growth of a town; a large tank beside the Ojo Caliente springs helped irrigate local farms that fed hungry mining districts nearby.

Today, the city's industries include textiles, wine, brandy, leather, preserved fruits and car manufacturing.

⊙ Sights & Activities

⭐ **Museo Nacional de la Muerte**   MUSEUM
(www.museonacionaldelamuerte.uaa.mx;   Jardín del Estudiante s/n; adult/student M$20/10, Tue free; ⊙10am-6pm Tue-Sun) This is one 'near death' experience not to be missed. The Museo Nacional de la Muerte exhibits all things relating to Mexico's favorite subject – death – from the skeleton La Catrina to historic artifacts. The contents – over 2500 artifacts, drawings, literature, textiles, toys and miniatures – were donated to the Universidad Autónoma de Aguascalientes by collector and engraver, Octavio Bajonero Gil. Over 1200 are on display. They span several centuries, from Mesoamerican to contemporary artistic interpretations.

In room one, look out for the miniature crystal skull. It's believed to be from Aztec times and there are only two in the world. This wonderful place is far from macabre but a colorful, humorous and insightful encounter.

Museo de Aguascalientes   MUSEUM
(www.aguascalientes.gob.mx; Zaragoza 505; adult/ student M$10/5; ⊙11am-6pm Tue-Sun) Housed in a handsome neoclassical building, this museum houses a permanent collection of work by the brilliant Aguascalientes artist Saturnino Herrán (1887–1918), and there are also temporary exhibitions. His works are some of the first to honestly depict the Mexican people. The sensual sculpture *Malgretout* on the patio is a fiberglass copy of the marble original by Jesús Fructuoso Contreras.

Teatro Morelos   HISTORIC BUILDING
(Plaza de la Patria) Teatro Morelos, scene of the 1914 Convention of Aguascalientes, was constructed during the reign of Pofirio, in which revolutionary factions led by Pancho Villa, Venustiano Carranza and Emiliano Zapata attempted unsuccessfully to mend their differences. Busts of these three, plus one of Álvaro Obregón, stand in the foyer and there are a few exhibits upstairs.

Catedral   CATHEDRAL
(Plaza de la Patria) The well-restored 18th-century baroque Cathedral, on the

Aguascalientes

Aguascalientes

◎ Top Sights
1 Museo Nacional de la Muerte C2

◎ Sights
2 Casino de la Feria B3
3 Catedral C3
4 Ex-Plaza de Toros San
   Marcos B3
5 Expoplaza A4
6 Museo de Aguascalientes D1
7 Museo de Arte
   Contemporáneo D2
8 Museo José Guadalupe
   Posada D4
9 Museo Regional de Historia C3
10 Palacio de Gobierno C3
   Teatro Morelos .... (see 3)
11 Templo de San Antonio D1
12 Templo de San Marcos A3
13 Templo del Encino D4

◎ Sleeping
14 El Giro Hostel B3
15 Fiesta Americana A4
16 Hacienda del Roble C1

✖ Eating
17 Mercado Jesús Terán C2
18 Mercado Juárez C2
19 Mercado Morelos C2
20 Restaurant Mitla D2
21 Rincón Maya D4
22 San Marcos Merendero A3

◉ Drinking & Nightlife
23 Pulquería Posada B3

✪ Entertainment
24 Casa de la Cultura C3
25 Teatro Morelos C3

◉ Shopping
26 Casa de las Artesanías C3

plaza's west side, is more magnificent inside than out. Over the altar at the east end of the south aisle is a painting of the Virgin of Guadalupe by Miguel Cabrera. There are more works by Cabrera, colonial Mexico's finest artist, in the cathedral's *pinacoteca* (picture gallery). It's open at Easter only (although if you are lucky, ask a priest and he might let you in).

Palacio de Gobierno   HISTORIC BUILDING

(Plaza de la Patria; ☉8am-8:30pm Mon-Fri, to 2pm Sat & Sun) On the south side of Plaza de la Patria, the red-and-pink stone Palacio de Gobierno is Aguascalientes' most noteworthy colonial building. Once the mansion of colonial baron Marqués de Guadalupe, it dates from 1665 and has a striking courtyard with two levels of murals. Noteworthy is the mural depicting the 1914 convention by the Chilean artist Osvaldo Barra. Barra, whose mentor was Diego Rivera, also painted the mural on the south wall, a compendium of the economic and historic forces that forged Aguascalientes.

Museo José Guadalupe Posada   MUSEUM

(☑449-915-45-56; Jardín El Encino s/n; adult/student M$10/5, Sun free; ☉11am-6pm Tue-Sun) Aguascalientes native Posada (1852–1913) was in many ways the founder of modern Mexican art. His engravings and satirical cartoons broadened the audience for art in Mexico, highlighted social problems and were a catalyst in the later mural phase, influencing artists like Diego Rivera, José Clemente Orozco and Alfaro David Siqueiros. Posada's hallmark is the *calavera* (skull or skeleton) and many of his *calavera* engravings have been widely reproduced. There's also a permanent exhibition of work by Posada's predecessor Manuel Manilla (1830–90).

Templo del Encino   CHURCH

(Jardín El Encino; ☉7am-1pm & 6-9pm) Located beside the Posada museum, this church contains a black statue of Jesus that some believe is growing. When it reaches an adjacent column, a worldwide calamity is anticipated. The huge *Way of the Cross* murals are also noteworthy.

Templo de San Antonio   CHURCH

(☉7am-1pm & 6-9pm) This church is a crazy quilt of architectural styles built around 1900 by self-taught architect Refugio Reyes. San Antonio's interior is highly ornate, with huge round paintings and intricate decoration highlighted in gold.

Museo de Arte Contemporáneo   MUSEUM

(☑449-915-79-53; cnr Morelos & Primo Verdad; adult/student M$10/5, Sun free; ☉11am-6pm Tue-Sun) A small, modern museum displaying the work of Enrique Guzmán (1952–86) as well as temporary exhibitions; it is well worth visiting.

Museo Regional de Historia   MUSEUM

(☑449-916-52-28; Av Carranza 118; adult M$47; ☉9am-6pm Tue-Sun) This history museum was designed by Refugio Reyes as a family home and features a small chapel. Its exhibits run all the way from the big bang to the colonial conquest. It also has a beautiful chapel with *ex voto* paintings and works attributed to Correa. Anyone interested in Mexican history will appreciate these displays. For others, the temporary exhibitions can be fascinating; pass by to check what's on.

Expoplaza   PLAZA

Half a kilometer southwest of Plaza de la Patria via Avenida Carranza, Expoplaza is a modern shopping and restaurant-bar strip. On the mall's south side, the wide and soulless pedestrian promenade comes alive at night and during the annual Feria de San Marcos. At its west end, the mammoth **Plaza de Toros Monumental** is notable for its modern-colonial treatment of traditional bullring architecture.

On Expoplaza's east side, the pedestrian street Pani runs two blocks north to the 18th-century **Templo de San Marcos** (Pani, Jardín de San Marcos) and the pretty, shady **Jardín de San Marcos**. The **Palenque Frederico Méndez**, in the **Casino de la Feria** building on Pani, is the city's cockfighting arena (only during the *feria*).

Ex-Plaza de Toros San Marcos   STADIUM

(Jardín de San Marcos) Near the northeast corner of Jardín de San Marcos, the Ex-Plaza de Toros San Marcos, the old bullring, is now a school for aspiring matadors. If there's someone in the office, ask and they will show you around. If not, the caretaker will happily let you in (you might want to consider tipping him).

★✩ Festivals & Events

Feria de San Marcos   FAIR

(☉mid-Apr) Mid-April sees Mexico's biggest annual three- to four- week fair, the Feria de San Marcos. It centers on Expoplaza and attracts thousands of visitors with exhibitions, bullfights, cockfights, rodeos, concerts and

MINERAL DE POZOS (POZOS)

Less than 100 years ago, Mineral de Pozos (population 3500, evelation 2200m) was a flourishing silver-mining center of 70,000 people, but with the 1910 Revolution and the flooding of the mines, the population dwindled. Empty houses, a large and unfinished church (note the dome) and discarded mine workings and shafts were the legacy of abandonment. Today, this tiny place is gradually winning back its place on the map. Visitors can explore the crumbling buildings and tour the fascinating surrounds, including several mine ruins, by mountain bike or horse. Warning: many mine shafts are unfenced and, at 150m deep, are extremely dangerous.

In Pozos, be sure to explore beyond the square Jardin Juarez and head up the hill to Plaza Zaragoza and down the hill to Plaza Mineros. As well as galleries, many craft shops are dotted around town, where community members sell their work. **Manos Creativos** (Mariscala 2) is a women's cooperative that sells lovely handmade regional doll costumes. Several workshops make pre-Hispanic musical instruments, but the best is **Casa del Venado Azul** (☑ 468-688-62-30; Calle Centenario 34), whose maker of pre-hispanic drums tours internationally.

If the tranquility is to your taste, then consider a night at the lovely **Posada de las Minas** (☑ 442-293-02-13; www.posadadelasminas.com; Doblado 1; r from M$1500; ☎), which also has a good restaurant. Those on a budget should definitely opt for **Casa del Venado Azul** (☑ 468-688-62-30, cell 468-117-03-87; azulvenado@hotmail.com; Calle Centenario 34; r per person from M$350).

If you have your own wheels, Pozos is a one-hour trip. Alternatively, the easiest way to get to Pozos is with **Bookatour** (p665). Its five-hour trips cost $45 per person (minimum three). **Bici-Burro** (p665) offers day-long bike tours to the town and mines. Unfortunately, by bus (from San Miguel de Allende or Queretaro) it will take the best part of a day: you must go first to Dolores Hidalgo, then to San Luis de la Paz (14km north of Pozos, a detour east of Hwy 57) and then take a third bus to Pozos.

cultural events. The big parade takes place on the saint's day, April 25.

Festival de las Calaveras   CULTURAL
(☉Nov) During the 10-day Festival de las Calaveras (the dates vary but always encompass November 1 and 2), Aguascalientes celebrates **Día de Muertos** (Day of the Dead) with an emphasis on the symbolism of *calavera*.

🛌 Sleeping

Prices skyrocket during the Feria de San Marcos (April) and accommodations are completely booked for the fair's final weekend; residents run a lucrative homestay service at this time.

El Giro Hostel   HOSTEL $
(☑449-917-93-93; www.elgirohostal.com.mx; Ignacio Allende Ote 41; dm from M$250) This colorful spot is a welcome newcomer to the hostel scene. It has slightly squishy bunk rooms, but positive reports of staff and it's in a good location. Take bus 31 from the bus station and disembark at the corner of Calles Elizondo and Rayon from where you can walk three blocks north along Elizondo to the hostel.

Hacienda del Roble   HOTEL $
(☑449-915-39-94; Calle 5 de Mayo 540; s/d M$350/450) This is the best of the limited midrange choices, with 33 small but modern carpeted rooms, external-facing windows and reasonable bathrooms. The downside is the grittier and noisier location – right on Calle 5 de Mayo.

Fiesta Americana   LUXURY HOTEL $$$
(☑449-910-05-00; www.fiestaamericana.com; Laureles s/n, Colonia Las Flores; r from M$1800; ⓟ⊖❄☎⡩⡭) This luxury chain hotel is a pleasant five-star experience if slightly pricey; the 192 rooms feature all the amenities and there's a fitness center and an inviting pool. Weekend packages for two cost around M$1500 and include buffet breakfast. Best to check the website for special offers.

🍴 Eating

Four blocks north of the Plaza de la Patria, fresh produce and cheap eats are available in three markets: **Mercado Juárez**, **Mercado Jesús Terán** and **Mercado Morelos**. Carranza is lined with eateries. Callejón del Codo is the place to go for small cafes and coffee.

San Marcos Merendero
MEXICAN $

(Andador Pani 144; mains M$60-200; ⊘noon-3am) This bustling, barn-like place is where everyone comes to whoop it up. There are performing mixologists who whip up good margaritas, friendly staff (some of whom have been here longer than the decor) and a blend of traditional Mexican folkloric paraphernalia, including stuffed bulls heads. Here, the idea is to chat and drink – the more you do of both, the more *botanas* (tasty snacks) are served. Live music nightly; styles vary.

Restaurant Mitla
MEXICAN $$

(Madero 220; mains M$65-200; ⊘7am-10pm, to 9pm Sun) This large, pleasant and popular restaurant is caught in a time warp: 1938, the year it started. There are white-shirted waiters and efficient service, plus a grand menu with a choice of Mexican specialties, set breakfasts (from M$90) and buffet lunches (M$130).

Rincón Maya
YUCATECAN $$

(Abasolo 113; mains M$100-180; ⊘2pm-midnight Mon-Sat, to 10:30pm Sun) Until lunchtime, this place has service at La Mestiza Yucateca (open 8am to 2pm), its alter ego next door. Both are located in a former hacienda and both serve delectable Yucatecan specialties.

Drinking

Pulquería Posada
BAR

(Nieto 445; ⊘10am-2:30pm, 5:30-11pm Tue-Sun) You might 'walk on in' to this verging-on-grungy, popular student hangout...but just 'sway on out'. It's fun. And it's cheap. A half-liter *jarra* (jug) of *pulque* (a traditional Aztec tipple made from fermented agave sap) costs M$18. There's also a good range of mezcals, flavored with everything from lime to guava. Aguascalientes used to be renowned for its *pulque,* and this place has reintroduced the tradition.

Entertainment

Pani, the pedestrian street between the Expoplaza and Jardín de San Marcos, is lively most evenings, with a good selection of bars and restaurants. Aguascalientes also has two theaters, **Teatro de Aguascalientes** (☑449-978-54-14; http://www.aguascalientes.gob.mx; cnr Calles Chávez & Aguascalientes) and **Teatro Morelos** (☑449-915-19-41; Nieto 113, Plaza de la Patria), which stage a variety of cultural events.

Casa de la Cultura
ARTS CENTER

(☑449-910-20-10; Av Carranza 101) In a fine 17th-century building, the Casa de la Cultura hosts art exhibitions, concerts, theater and dance events.

Shopping

Casa de las Artesanías
HANDICRAFTS

(Nieto 210) The recently opened Casa de Las Artesanías showcases a range of stunning handicrafts made in the region, from local sweets to leather products (using the intricate *piteado* technique).

Information

Several pharmacies in the city center are open 24 hours.

Banks with ATMs are common around Plaza de la Patria and Expoplaza. *Casas de cambio* cluster on Hospitalidad, opposite the post office.

Police (☑080, 066)

Star Médica (☑449-910-99-00; www.star medica.com; Universidad 101) Private hospital.

State Tourist Office (☑449-915-95-04; www.aguascalientes.gob.mx; Palacio de Gobierno, Plaza de la Patria; ⊘9am-8pm Mon-Sat, 10am-5pm Sun) Free city maps. Ask for *Agenda Cultural,* a monthly what's-on listing.

Getting There & Away

AIR

Aéropuerto Jesús Terán (☑449-918-28-06) is 26km south of Aguascalientes off the road to Mexico City. **Aeroméxico Connect** (☑449-918-21-27; Madero 474) has flights to Mexico City, Monterrey plus flights via Mexico City to Los Angeles and New York. **Volaris** (www.volaris.mx) serves Los Angeles. American Airlines has regular flights to Houston, Dallas and Los Angeles.

BUS

The **bus station** (Central Camionera; Av Convención) is 2km south of the center. It has card phones, a cafeteria and luggage storage.

Deluxe, and 1st- and 2nd-class buses operate to/from Aguascalientes. Deluxe and 1st-class companies include ETN, Primera Plus, Futura and Ómnibus de México. The main 2nd-class line is Coordinados (Flecha Amarilla).

As well as those outlined in the table, frequent services go to Ciudad Juárez, Monterrey, Morelia and Torreón. For Guanajuato, it's easiest to change in León.

Getting Around

Most places of interest are within easy walking distance of each other. Regular city buses (M$6) run from 6am to 10pm. Buses display route numbers; check which bus heads to the city center as these change regularly. Disembark at the first stop after you go through the town's one tunnel on Calle 5 de Mayo. This is one block from the plaza. From the city center to the bus station, several buses head to the bus station from the corner Galeana (near Insurgentes).

Taxis charge as per metered fares. Between the bus station and the center the taxi fare is from around M$25 to M$30.

SAN LUIS POTOSÍ STATE

The historic state capital city, San Luis Potosí, and the fascinating 'ghost town,' Real de Catorce, are on the high and dry expanses of the state's north and west and are the main reasons visitors come to this region. The pretty tropical, verdant eastern region, the Huasteca Potosina, with its lush green valleys and waterfalls, is popular among local tourists, but few foreign tourists venture here.

The state is steeped in history. Before the Spanish conquest, western San Luis Potosí was inhabited by Guachichiles, warlike hunters. In the 18th century the area gained a reputation for maltreatment of indigenous people, partly because the nonmonastic clergy replaced the more compassionate Franciscans.

Today, mining, agriculture, ranching and industry are the economic mainstays of this fairly prosperous state with a population of 2.6 million.

San Luis Potosí

📞 444 / POP 736,000 / ELEV 1860M

A grand old dame of colonial cities, San Luis Potosí was once a revolutionary hotbed, an important mining town and seat of government to boot. Today the city has maintained its poise as the prosperous state capital, orderly industrial center and university seat.

A great place to wander through, the city's colonial core is made up of numerous plazas and manicured parks that are linked by attractive pedestrian streets. Although not as striking as Zacatecas or Guanajuato, this lively city's cultural elegance is reflected in its delightful colonial buildings, impressive theater and numerous excellent museums.

History

Founded in 1592, San Luis is 20km west of the silver deposits in Cerro de San Pedro, and was named Potosí after the immensely rich Bolivian silver town, which the Spanish hoped it would rival. The mines began to decline in the 1620s, but the city was established enough as a ranching center to remain the major city of northeastern Mexico until overtaken by Monterrey at the start of the 20th century.

Known in the 19th century for its lavish houses and imported luxury goods, San Luis was twice the seat of President Benito Juárez's government during the 1860s French intervention. In 1910 in San Luis, the dictatorial president Porfirio Díaz jailed Francisco Madero, his liberal opponent, during the presidential campaign. Freed after the election, Madero hatched his Plan de San Luis Potosí (a strategy to depose Díaz), announcing it in San Antonio, Texas, in October 1910; he declared the election illegal, named himself provisional president and designated November 20 as the day for Mexico to rise in revolt – the start of the Mexican Revolution.

⊙ Sights

Museo Federico Silva   MUSEUM
(www.museofedericosilva.org; Obregón 80; adult/student M$30/15; ⊙10am-6pm Wed-Mon, to 2pm Sun) This museum should not be missed. The original 17th-century building on the north side of San Luis Potosí's Jardín de San Juan del Dios was once a hospital and later

BUSES FROM AGUASCALIENTES

DESTINATION	FARE (M$)	DURATION (HR)	FREQUENCY (DAILY)
Guadalajara	255-287	2¾-3	frequent
Guanajuato	225	3	2 daily
León	162-215	2-3½	frequent
Mexico City (Terminal Norte)	475-635	6	frequent
Queretaro	391-510	5	frequent
San Luis Potosí	168-226	3-3½	hourly
Zacatecas	160-210	2	hourly

a school under *el porfiriato* (the Porfiriato period). It has been exquisitely transformed into an art museum, ingeniously integrating the building's previous neoclassical finish with the monolithic sculptures of Silva. It hosts temporary exhibitions of international contemporary sculptors.

Centro de las Artes Centenario   ARTS CENTER
(Antigua Penitenciaria; Calz de Guadalupe; adult M$15; ⊙10am-2pm & 5-8pm Mon-Fri, 11am-5pm Sat & Sun) Up until 1999, the building was a prison believed to have briefly held Francisco Madero. Ten years later, it was transformed – without losing its fundamental design – into an arts and cultural center. Some of the former cells have been maintained; others have been converted into offices. It's located 12 blocks south of Alameda. A must visit for architects.

At 5pm, 6pm and 7pm there are guided tours (in Spanish; tip the guides).

Palacio de Gobierno   PALACE
(Calle 5 de Mayo) FREE The neoclassical Palacio de Gobierno was built between 1770 and 1816. Its most illustrious lodger was Benito Juárez – first in 1863 when he was fleeing from invading French forces, then in 1867 when he confirmed the death sentence on the puppet-emperor Maximilian.

◉ Plaza de Armas

Also known as Jardín Hidalgo, this pedestrianized plaza is the city's central square.

Catedral   CATHEDRAL
FREE This impressive three-nave baroque cathedral was built between 1660 and 1730. Originally it had just one tower; the northern tower was added in the 20th century. The marble apostles on the facade are replicas of statues in Rome's St Peter's Basilica. On the hour, the electronic bells, a more recent addition, ring out.

Palacio Municipal   HISTORIC BUILDING
(⊙8am-8pm) The 19th-century Palacio Municipal features powerful stone arches. Finished in 1838, it was the home of Bishop Ignacio Montes de Oca from 1892 to 1915. The city's coat of arms in stained glass overlooks a double staircase.

**Jardín de San Francisco
(Jardín Guerrero)**   PLAZA
Dominated by the bulk of the Templo de San Francisco and convent, and with a lovely fountain gracing its interior, this square is one of the city's most fetching.

Templo de San Francisco   CHURCH
(Jardín de San Francisco) The altar of the 17th- and 18th-century Templo de San Francisco was remodeled in the 20th century, but the sacristy (the priest's dressing room), reached by a door to the right of the altar, is original and has a fine dome and carved pink stone. The Sala De Profundis, through the arch at the south end of the sacristy, has more paintings and a carved stone fountain. A beautiful crystal ship hangs from the main dome.

Museo Regional Potosino   MUSEUM
(Plaza de Aranzazú s\n; M$47, Sun free; ⊙9am-6pm Tue-Sun) This fetching museum was originally part of a Franciscan monastery founded in 1590. The ground floor – part of which is housed in the small Capilla de San Antonio de Padua – has exhibits (predominantly pottery) of pre-Hispanic Mexico, especially the indigenous people of the Huasteca. Upstairs is the lavish, gold and aqua **Capilla de Aranzazú**, an elaborate private chapel constructed in the mid-18th century in Churrigueresque style. New monks were ordained here.

◉ Plaza del Carmen

Templo del Carmen   CHURCH
(⊙8am-1pm & 5-8pm) The Plaza del Carmen is dominated by San Luis's most spectacular structure, the Churrigueresque Templo del Carmen (1749–64). On the vividly carved stone facade, hovering angels show the touch of indigenous artisans. The Camarín de la Virgen, with a splendid golden altar, is to the left of the main altar inside. The entrance and roof of this chapel are a riot of small plaster figures.

Museo del Virreinato   MUSEUM
(www.museodelvirreinato.mx; Villerías 155; adult/student M$15/10, camera use M$20; ⊙10am-7pm Tue-Fri, to 9pm Sat, to 5pm Sun) Beside the Templo del Carmen, this museum has a large collection of paintings and artifacts from the Spanish vice-regency. More of interest might be its temporary exhibitions – check what's on.

Museo Nacional de la Máscara   MUSEUM
(National Mask Museum; Villerías 2; adult/student M$20/15, camera use M$10; ⊙10am-6pm Tue-Fri, to 5pm Sat, 11am-3pm Sun & Mon) Displays an interesting collection of ceremonial masks from across Mexico and around the world. There are good descriptions in English and interesting videos of dances performed during festivals in communities.

San Luis Potosí

N

0 ———————— 200 m
0 ———————— 0.1 miles

San Luis Potosí

◉ Sights
1 Catedral	B2
2 Jardín de San Francisco (Jardín Guerrero)	A3
3 Museo del Ferrocarril	D1
4 Museo del Virreinato	C2
5 Museo Federico Silva	C1
6 Museo Nacional de la Máscara	C3
7 Museo Regional Potosino	A4
8 Palacio de Gobierno	B2
9 Templo de San Francisco	A3
10 Templo del Carmen	C2

◆ Activities, Courses & Tours
11 Operatour Potosina	C2

⊟ Sleeping
12 Hotel Museo Palacio de San Agustín	B3
13 Hotel Panorama	A2
14 Hotel San Francisco	B3

⊗ Eating
15 Antojitos El Pozole	A1
16 Cafe Cortáo	A4

⊜ Drinking & Nightlife
17 Callejon 7B	A3

✪ Entertainment
Orquesta Sinfónica	(see 4)
18 Teatro de la Paz	C3

⊞ Shopping
19 Casa Grande Esencia Artesanal	B3

Plaza de los Fundadores PLAZA

The least pretty of the plazas, Plaza de los Fundadores (Founders' Plaza) is where the city was born. On the north side is a large building constructed in 1653 as a Jesuit college. Today it houses offices of the Universidad Autónoma de San Luis Potosí. It was probably on this site that Diego de la Magdalena, a Franciscan friar, started a small settlement of Guachichiles around 1585.

Templo de San José
CHURCH

(Alameda Park) Inside the Templo de San José, facing the Alameda's south side, lies the image of El Señor de los Trabajos, a Christ-like figure attracting pilgrims from near and far. Numerous *retablos* (altarpieces) around the statue testify to prayers answered in finding jobs and other miracles.

Museo del Ferrocarril
MUSEUM

(Av Othón; M$25; ⊙10am-6pm Tue-Sat, to 4pm Sun) On the north side of the Alameda, this museum is housed in the city's former train station and very cleverly brings to life its past. The existing building was designed by Manuel Ortiz Monasterio and was constructed in 1936. Exhibits include modern installations relating to train travel plus former locomotive parts. Don't miss the two murals by muralist Fernando Leal (completed in 1943) that grace the station interior.

☞ Tours

Tranvía
TOUR

(☑444-814-22-26; www.tranviasanluis.com; 1hr trip M$50) Two *tranvías,* imitations of antique trolleys, do a loop around the historic center starting from in front of the Cathedral on Plaza de Armas. The smaller blue *San Luis Rey* goes up the narrower streets making for a more interesting ride. Hours change; check with the tourist office.

Operatour Potosina
TOUR

(☑444-151-22-01; www.operatourpotosina.com.mx; Sarabia 120) If you want to do a tour, Operatour Potosina is *the* outfit to do it with. The friendly and knowledgeable English-speaking operator, Lori, offers tours around the city, as well as to *haciendas,* Real de Catorce, Zacatecas and the Huasteca Potosina (minimum two people). Custom-made tours also available. The office is located in the Hotel Napoles.

✷ Festivals & Events

Semana Santa
RELIGIOUS

Holy Week is celebrated with concerts, exhibitions and other activities; on Good Friday (March/April) at 3pm, Christ's passion is re-enacted in the barrio of San Juan de Guadalupe, followed at 8pm by the Silent Procession through the city center (one of the city's most important events).

Feria Nacional Potosina
FAIR

San Luis' National Fair, normally in the last three weeks of August, includes concerts, bullfights, rodeos, cockfights and agricultural shows.

Día de San Luis Rey de Francia
RELIGIOUS

On August 25 the city's patron saint, St Louis IX, is honored as the highlight of the Feria Nacional. Events include a parade, concerts and plays.

Festival Internacional de Danza Lila López
DANCE

(www.facebook.com/FestivalInternacionaldeDanza ContemporaneaLilaLopez) This wonderful annual national festival of contemporary dance is usually held on changing dates over two months.

🛏 Sleeping

Corazón de Xoconostle
HOSTEL $

(☑444-243-98-98; www.corazondexoconostle.com; 5 de May 1040; dm with shared bathroom M$160-180, r M$360-420; 🛜) A welcome addition to San Luis (which has always had a dearth of good budget accommodations), this delightfully renovated house is an attractive, well-run hostel. Good dorms with lockers (though beware, some rooms have large colonial doors, and this means no windows) and one female-only dorm.

Use of kitchen and laundry facilities (free), a roof terrace and lovely citrus-tree-filled courtyard make it excellent value. It even serves up a continental breakfast. The downside is the bathroom shortage – it might keep you hopping on your feet during 'peak' bathroom hours.

Hotel Panorama
BUSINESS HOTEL $$

(☑444-812-17-77, 800-480-01-00; www.hotelpano rama.com.mx; Av Carranza 315; r/ste M$920/1340; 🅿❄🛜🏊) It's the best of San Luis' rather average lot of midrange accommodations options and has position going for it – it's opposite Plaza de los Fundadores. Beyond that, it's smart(ish) and all 126 rooms have floor-to-ceiling windows; those on the south side overlook the pool. Popular with business travelers.

Hotel San Francisco
HOTEL $$

(www.sanfranciscohotel.mx; Universidad 375; r M$730; 🅿❄🛜) Run by the same crew as Panorama, this converted historic building offers modern, business-style rooms. Rooms at the front with external facing windows are susceptible to traffic noise; while interior rooms don't get the fresh air. But it's a good choice either way.

Hotel Real Plaza   HOTEL $$

(☏444-814-69-69; www.realplaza.com.mx; Carranza 890; s/d M$690/730; P❄☎) A dated '80s style hotel, though rooms here are light, clean and neat and some have decent views of the city. Popular with business travelers.

Hotel Museo Palacio de San Agustín   HISTORIC HOTEL $$$

(☏444-144-19-00; www.palaciodesanagustin.com; Galeana 240; r US$372-410; P🅿❄☎) Warning: this plush 'museum hotel' comes with a snob rating. Formerly a house for retired monks of the nearby San Agustín monastery, this extraordinary property has been restored to its original condition (think: hand-painted gold-leaf finishes, crystal chandeliers and 700 certified European antiques).

If you want to have a sneak peak without dishing out big bucks, opt instead for their cafe-restaurant, Monasterio (open 7am to 10pm daily; mains M$120 to M$255).

✕ Eating & Drinking

One local specialty is *tacos potosinos* – red, chili-impregnated tacos stuffed with cheese or chicken and topped with chopped potato, carrot, lettuce and loads of *queso blanco* (white cheese).

Antojitos El Pozole   MEXICAN $

(cnr Calles Carmona & Arista; mains M$44-82; ⊙noon-11:30pm Tue-Sun) The is the place for the local *enchiladas potosinas* – the tortilla dough is red from chili. This place was started by a woman selling *antojitos* (Mexican snacks) in her home in the 1980s. Demand for her goods was so high she opened several restaurants specializing in what she knows best – *tacos rojos, pozole* and *quesadillas de papa* (potato quesadillas)...yes, they're that good.

★ Cafe Cortáo   MEXICAN $

(Independencia 1150; snacks M$40-65; ⊙8:30am-1:30pm & 6:15-9:30pm Mon-Fri, 9:30pm-late Sat) Sí. This simple spot is our top pick. It's the perfect example of a local eatery that serves up lashings of quality Mexican meals to a local crowd – from business folk, to ladies who lunch, to those on a budget. All done with efficient service, an ultra-lively atmosphere where chatter fills the air, by a charismatic owner (who will soon learn your name). In

other words, it's as Mexican as a tortilla in every possible way.

Don't miss the *huevo abolengo* (eggs on bread with a mushroom and manchego cheese sauce; M$65).

Cielo Tinto   INTERNATIONAL $$

(www.cielotinto.com.mx; Carranza 700; mains M$90-125; ⊙8am-11:30pm Mon-Sat, to 5pm Sun) A reliable fallback in an *ex-hacienda* (former mansion) with a beautiful courtyard, and perfect for cravings of all kinds, from meats to Mexican tacos. Good set breakfasts (M$69 to M$83).

Rincon Huasteco   MEXICAN $$

(www.rinconhuasteco.com; Cuauhtémoc 232; mains M$60-180; ⊙8am-11pm Mon-Sat, to 9pm Sun) Ignore the decor – it's nothing outstanding – and concentrate on the food. Amazing and distinctly different flavors from the Huasteca Potosina. Like the interiors, the hue of the meals can be a little 'fifty shades of brown' (or cream or green), but don't let this deter you.

The likes of *zacahuil* (a massive tamale that's been cooked for 12 hours), *cabuches* (catcus flowers) and *queso de guaje* (cheese filled with, um, more cheese) will have your taste buds quite stimulated enough.

El México de Frida   MEXICAN $$

(☏444-811-46-03; www.elmexicodefrida.com; Valentín Gama 646; set meals M$180-300; ⊙1pm-midnight Mon-Sat, 1-6pm Sun) Although it's painted with Kahlo-esque colors and theme, this restaurant is not Frida-kitsch. Rather, the tasteful and tasty menu serves up scrumptious Mexican fare. Try the *chiles ventilla,* chilies with cheese and the most tantalizing creamy sauces. It's 3km along (and just south of) Avenida Carranza.

Callejon 7B   BAR

(Universidad 153) A hip bar named after the very beer it produces, Siete (7) barrios (in turn, named after the seven main regions of the city). After you've tried one of its artisanal brews, from blonde ales to robust porters, you can bar hop your way down the laneway to surrounding drinking dens.

☆ Entertainment

San Luis has an active cultural scene. Ask in the tourist office about what's on and keep your eye out for posters. The free monthly *Guiarte* booklet and posters detail cultural attractions.

Teatro de la Paz CONCERT VENUE
(☑ 444-812-52-09; Villerias 2) This neoclassical theater (1889–94) contains a concert hall with 1500 seats and exhibition gallery as well as a theater. Posters announce upcoming dance, theater and music events.

Orquesta Sinfónica MUSIC
(☑ 444-814-36-01; tickets from M$100) San Luis' own symphony orchestra plays in Teatro de la Paz and other venues; check with the tourist office.

Shopping

La Casa del Artesano HANDICRAFTS
(Jardín Colón 23; ⊙ 8am-3pm & 5-7pm Mon-Fri, 10am-5pm Sat) For local products, try this shop full of *potosino* pottery, masks, woodwork and canework.

Casa Grande
Esencia Artesanal ARTS & CRAFTS
(Facebook/Casagrande-Esencia-Artesanal; Universidad 220; ⊙ 10am-8pm Mon-Sat, 11am-6pm Sun) Great for gifts that are 100% made in the region of San Luis Potosí.

ⓘ Information

INTERNET ACCESS
Fox Ciberkafe (Escobedo 315; per hr M$15; ⊙ 9am-9pm Mon-Sat, 10am-8:30pm Sun)

MEDICAL SERVICES
Hospital Lomas de SLP (☑ 444-102-5900; www.hls.com.mx; Av. Palmira 600, Villas del Pedregal) Located on the western edge of city in suburb of Villas de Pedregal.

MONEY
Banks with ATMs are scattered around town, including the Plaza de Armas and Plaza de los Fundadores. Several *casas de cambio* are along Morelos.

POST
Post Office (Av Universidad 526; ⊙ 8am-3pm Mon-Fri)

TOURIST INFORMATION
Municipal Tourist Office (☑ 444-812-57-19; Palacio Municipal; ⊙ 8am-8pm Mon-Sat, 10am-5pm Sun) On the east side of Plaza de Armas.

Sectur (State tourist office; ☑ 444-812-99-39, 800-343-38-87; www.visitasanluispotosi.com; Av Manuel José Othón 130; ⊙ 8am-9pm Mon-Fri, 9am-3pm Sat & Sun) Has maps and good information on off-the-beaten-track attractions in San Luis Potosí state.

ⓘ Getting There & Away

AIR
Aeropuerto Ponciano Arriaga (☑ 444-822-00-95; www.oma.aero/en/) is 10km north of the city off Hwy 57. Aeroméxico Connect offers direct service to/from Mexico City and Monterrey with connecting flights to various US cities.

BUS
The **Terminal Terrestre Potosina** (TTP; ☑ 444-816-46-02; Carretera 57), 2.5km east of the center, is a busy transportation hub that has deluxe, 1st-class and some 2nd-class bus services. Its facilities include card phones, 24-hour luggage storage and snack places.

First-class companies include ETN, Primera Plus, Transportes del Norte and Futura. The main 2nd-class companies are Coordinados

BUSES FROM SAN LUIS POTOSÍ

DESTINATION	FARE (M$)	DURATION (HR)	FREQUENCY (DAILY)
Aguascalientes	168-226	2½-3	hourly
Ciudad Valles	537	4½	hourly
Guadalajara	441-605	5-6	hourly
Guanajuato	248	3	1 direct at 7am
Matehuala	213	2½	4 daily
Mexico City (Terminal Norte)	450-620	5-6½	hourly
Monterrey	590-725	6	5
Querétaro	228-310	2½-4	frequent
Rio Verde	292	2	half-hourly
Xilitla	442	6	5 daily
Zacatecas	235-255	3	frequent

(Flecha Amarilla) and Estrella Blanca. Vencedor runs east to Xilitla, Ciudad Valles and Rio Verde.

Daily buses go to Juárez, Chihuahua, Dolores Hidalgo, León, Morelia, Nuevo Laredo, Saltillo, Torreón, and many other destinations.

CAR & MOTORCYCLE

Car-rental prices cost around US$20 per day (excluding some insurances); week-long packages also available.

Sixt (444-814-3010; Obregón 670)

❶ Getting Around

Taxis charge around M$200 to M$220 for the half-hour trip to/from the airport.

To reach the center from the bus station, take any 'Centro' or bus 46. A convenient place to get off is on the Alameda, outside the former train station. A booth in the bus station sells taxi tickets (M$35 to M$70) to the center.

From the center to the bus station, take any 'Central TTP' or bus southbound on Avenida Constitución from the Alameda's west side.

City buses run from 6:30am to 10:30pm (M$8). For places along Avenida Carranza, catch a 'Morales' (bus 9) or 'Carranza' (bus 23) at the bus depot behind Museo de Ferrocaril.

Matehuala

The pleasant but unremarkable town of Matehuala (pop 80,000), between Saltillo and San Luis Potosí on Hwy 57, is the compulsory changing point for buses north to Real de Catorce.

The bus station is just west of the highway, 2km south of the center. From Matehuala, Estrella Blanca, Noreste and Transportes del Nord all have services. There are daily bus departures to Mexico City Terminal Norte (M$633 to M$675, eight hours, nine 1st class direct), Monterrey (M$356 to M$380, 4½ hours, hourly 1st class), Saltillo (M$230 to M$280, 3¼ hours, seven 1st class), San Luis Potosí (M$210 to M$250, 2½ hours, hourly 1st class), and Querétaro (M$355 to M$410 to M$406, 4½ to 5½ hours, seven 1st class).

Real de Catorce

📞 488 / POP 1300 / ELEV 2730M

Energy – in a spiritual sense – is a word commonly ascribed to the alluring village of Real de Catorce. This stark, compact and functioning 'ghost town' sits high on the

---

HUICHOL VISIONS

The remote Sierra Madre Occidental, in and around the far north of Jalisco, is the home of the Huicholes, one of Mexico's most distinctive and enduring indigenous groups. A fiercely independent people, they were one of the few indigenous groups not subjugated by the Aztecs.

The arrival of the Spanish had little immediate effect on the Huicholes and it wasn't until the 17th century that the first Catholic missionaries reached the Huichol homelands. Rather than convert to Christianity, the Huicholes incorporated various elements of Christian teachings into their traditional animist belief systems. In Huichol mythology, gods become personalized as plants, totem animal species and natural objects, while their supernatural form is explored in religious rituals.

Every year the Huicholes leave their isolated homeland and make a pilgrimage to the Sierra de Catorce, in northern San Luis Potosí state. In this harsh desert region, they seek out the *mescal* cactus (*Lophophora williamsii*), known as peyote cactus. The rounded peyote 'buttons' contain a powerful hallucinogenic drug (whose chief element is mescaline) that is central to the Huicholes' rituals and complex spiritual life.

The fact is: peyote is illegal in Mexico. Many unthinking and uncaring travelers seem intent on ignoring this fact, so we'll repeat it here – peyote is illegal. Under Mexican law, the Huicholes are permitted to use it for their spiritual purposes. For the Huicholes, indiscriminate use is regarded as offensive, even sacrilegious.

Traditionally, the main Huichol art forms were telling stories and making masks and detailed geometric embroidery, or 'yarn pictures.' In the last few decades, brightly colored beads have replaced the yarn. This is painstaking work, where the beads are pressed into a beeswax-covered substrate. This exquisite artwork is sold in craft markets, shops and galleries. Prices are usually fixed and the Huicholes don't like to haggle. To see the best work, visit one of the specialist museums or shops in Zapopan (Guadalajara), Tepic, Puerto Vallarta or Zacatecas.

fringes of the magical Sierra Madre Oriental. It was a wealthy silver-mining town of 40,000 people until early last century. Not long ago, it was nearly deserted, its streets lined with crumbling buildings, its mint a ruin and a few hundred people eking out an existence from the annual influx of pilgrims and old mine tailings.

Real has experienced a slight revival; it has attracted investors (including Europeans) who run some of the businesses and smarter hotels in town. Although no longer a 'ghost town', doors do creak in the breeze, dusty cobblestone streets end abruptly and many buildings remain in ruins.

At the time of research, a Canadia mining company had reopened mines surrounding the town. Many view it as a potential environmental nightmare – having a detrimental effect on water springs in the mountains and age-old Huichol traditions and culture. Others see it as a potential source of employment for many locals, including poorer surrounding communities.

History

Real de Catorce translates as 'Royal of 14': the '14' may have been derived from the 14 Spanish soldiers killed here by indigenous resistance fighters around 1700. The town was founded in the mid-18th century and the church built between 1790 and 1817.

The town reached its peak in the late 19th century, vying to surpass the famed Valenciana mine of Guanajuato. It had opulent houses, a bullring and shops selling European luxury goods.

Just why Real became a ghost town within three decades is a mystery. Some locals claim (as they do in many ghost towns) that during the Revolution (1910–20) *bandidos* hid out here and scared off other inhabitants. A more plausible explanation is that the price of silver slumped after 1900.

◉ Sights

Templo de la Purísima Concepción CHURCH
(⊙7am-7pm) FREE This charming *parroquia* (parish church) is an impressive neoclassical building. The attraction for thousands of Mexican pilgrims is the reputedly miraculous image of St Francis of Assisi, displayed at the front of the church. A cult has grown up around the statue, whose help is sought in solving problems and cleansing sins.

Walk through the door to the left of the altar to find a roomful of *retablos,* small pictures depicting threatening situations from which St Francis has rescued the victim, with a brief description of the incident – car accidents and medical operations, for example – and some words of gratitude. *Retablos* have become much sought after by collectors and are very occasionally seen in antique shops. Sadly, most of those on sale have been stolen from churches.

**Centro Cultural de
Real de Catorce** MUSEUM
(Casa de la Moneda; M$10; ⊙10am-6pm Wed-Sun) Opposite the church's facade, the Centro Cultural de Real de Catorce, the old mint, made coins for 14 months (1,489,405 pesos to be exact) in the mid-1860s. This classic monument has been exquisitely restored over the last few years. It now houses a cultural center-cum-gallery with several levels of temporary exhibitions. The bottom floor has a permanent exhibition depicting photos and machinery from the original mint.

Palenque de Gallos MONUMENT
(Xicotencatl s/n; ⊙9am-5pm) FREE A block northwest of Plaza Hidalgo, lies a monument to the town's heyday – the Palenque de Gallos, a cockfighting ring, built like a Roman amphitheater. It was restored in the 1970s and sometimes hosts theater or dance performances.

Capilla de Guadalupe CHURCH, CEMETERY
(⊙8am-5pm) Follow Zaragoza-Libertad north of Real de Catorce to the Capilla de Guadalupe and *panteón*. Before you go, ask for the key at the tourist office (in case it's closed). Further along this road you'll hit the remains of the former bullring, **Plaza de Toros**.

⚐ Activities

Hiking
The ambience of the desert setting makes up for the lack of major sights around town. If you're into walking or horseback riding, there's plenty to keep you occupied here for a couple of days.

If you prefer to do your own hikes, you can head out from Real in almost any direction. The hike closest to home is that up the hill to the Pueblo Fantasmo (Ghost Town), on the hill behind, and clearly visible from, the town center. Head along Lanzagorta and stay left (avoid the road that veers right to the car park). The track you follow was the former entrance to town before the tunnel existed. Allow at least one hour to get to the top – there is another section around 100m further on behind the ruins visible from the town. Beware that there are two large shafts (estimated to be hundreds of meters deep) in the ruins.

To extend this hike, head northwest along the ridge to the antennas and to the cross over the town (make sure you note this from the town before you leave, as it becomes obscured when on the ridge). Follow the path behind the cross before you weave your way down to the cemetery (allow three to four hours for the longer hike).

Another shorter hike is to Socavón de Purísima, a large chimney of a former mine. Head down Allende and veer right at its end. You are on the road to Estación de Catorce. Follow this road until you reach the chimney (about 45 minutes one way). The road passes through a cut or split rock, the Cerro Trocado. If open, you can enter the mouth of the mine (donation). To return, it's a longer and harder slog back up the hill (one hour one way; on weekends you might be able to grab a lift in a 'Jeep Willys'). Caution: be prepared – tell others where you're headed, and take water, a hat and strong footwear; it's dry and unforgiving country.

Horseback Riding

Ride 'em cowboy! Numerous trails lead out into the dry, stark and fascinating desertscapes – hilly and flat – around Real. The most popular guided trail ride is the three-hour trip to El Quemado, the sacred mountain of the Huicholes. Here you'll find expansive views of the high-desert plateau and a small shrine to the sun god.

Horse guides now belong to an association, approved by the municipality; the best of the two is **Caballerangos del Real** (2hr trip M$150-200). Rates are around M$150 to M$200 for a trip of a couple of hours. Note that no protective hats are provided; you clomp off at your own risk.

The horses and guides congregate every morning around Plaza Hidalgo.

ⓘ CASH UP BEFORE YOU COME

There's one ATM in Real de Catorce, located in the tourist office, but on busy weekends it occasionally runs out of money and is often out of order thanks to electricity cuts and the like. Try to bring cash.

Jeep Rides

Trips in 'Jeep Willys' can also be arranged to many of the same locations, mainly on weekends. Ask any of the drivers along Lanzagorta or Allende, or at the tourist office. Rates vary according to the trip and numbers; they are cheaper as 'collectives'.

Cycling

Lalo Bike   CYCLING
(☑ cell 488-105-1981; https://facebook/MTB-Bici tours-Expeditions; 1½hr rides per person M$100; ☺ Fri-Sun Nov-Sep) Cyclists of all levels can head out around Real de Catorce on some great-value rides with Lalo (he speaks Spanish only but can arrange an English speaking guide). Prices include mountain bike, helmet and guide. Spanish speakers can email or ring ahead or, if you are in Real, inquire at Mesón de la Abundancia.

✯✯ Festivals & Events

Fiesta de San Francisco   RELIGIOUS
From the end of September to the end of October, 150,000 pilgrims pay homage to the figure of St Francis of Assisi in the town's church. Many of them just come for the day, while thousands stay in the town, filling every rentable room and sleeping rough in the plazas.

The streets are lined with stalls selling religious souvenirs and food, while many of the town's more upmarket restaurants close for a month. Note: travelers who desire the tranquil 'ghost-town experience' of Real de Catorce are best staying away during this festival period to avoid disappointment.

Festival del Desierto   CULTURAL
The Festival del Desierto cultural festival features folkloric music and dance performances in towns all around the region. Dates vary annually; check before you come.

🛏 Sleeping

It can be very cold here in winter in the cheapest digs; bring a sleeping bag or request extra blankets.

Hotel Real de Álamos   PENSION $
(Hospedaje Familiar; ☑ 488-887-50-09; Constitución 21; s/d M$200/350) As basic as they come, but rooms are clean and have bathrooms.

Mesón de Abundancia   HOTEL $$
(☑ 488-887-50-44; www.mesonabundancia.com; Lanzagorta 11; d M$750-1350, f M$1350-1550; 🛜)

Real de Catorce

Real de Catorce

⊙ **Sights**
1 Centro Cultural de Real de
Catorce B2
2 Palenque de Gallos A1
3 Templo de la Purísima
Concepción C2

🛌 **Sleeping**
4 Hotel Real de Álamos B1
5 Mesón de Abundancia B2
6 Refugio Romano D1

🍴 **Eating**
7 Café Azul B2
Mesón de Abundancia .... (see 5)

🍷 **Drinking & Nightlife**
8 Amor Y Paz C1

Relive the town's bonanza era on the desert plateau in this delightful stone citadel. The 19th-century former *tesorería* (treasury) building has been renovated into a hotel and restaurant. A massive old-fashioned key lets you in to one of 11 rooms; these are simply and tastefully decorated with local crafts (minus TV) and make a cozy retreat on chilly nights. Rates are significantly lower outside of high season.

Refugio Romano GUESTHOUSE **$$**
(☎ 488-111-93-53; www.refugioromano.com; Iturbide 38; d M$800-900; 🛜) 🅿 Yes, keep going... It really is up this rickety laneway. At the end, you'll be rewarded with a true oasis. A lovely green garden of cacti and fruit trees, plus three simple – with a touch of hippy – rooms, each with its quirky idiosyncrasy, from a 'cave' to a terrace. The owners, one an Italian (and a great cook), will whip up organic meals for their clients (mains M$110 M$140). It follows sustainable practices where possible.

🍴 Eating & Drinking

Café Azul CAFE **$**
(Lanzagorta 27; snacks M$30-80; ⊙ 8.30am-5pm Thu-Tue, to 10pm Fri & Sat) Open all day, this airy, Swiss-run spot is perfect for breakfasts, freshly baked cakes and light meals, including excellent crepes. The delightful owners are very helpful with local info.

Mesón de Abundancia MEXICAN, ITALIAN **$$**
(www.mesonabundancia.com; Lanzagorta 11; mains M$90-170; 🛜🅿) There are several cozy eating areas at the restaurant in this hotel, one with a bar and fireplace. The hearty (read massive) servings of Italian and Mexican dishes are *muy rico* (delicious). It's open all day, every day, including for breakfast.

Amor Y Paz BAR
(cnr Juaréz & Iturbide; ⊙ 6pm-late Fri & Sat) Real's reputation as a ghost town may in part be due to the fact that its residents and visitors are often all hiding out here at this funky bar, hidden behind the walls of Hotel El Real. It's decked out in antiques (note the amazing wooden bar), retro seating, and quirky chandeliers, and serves a range of mezcals and alcoholic tea infusions.

ℹ️ Information

See http://realde14.net for a good overview of the town.

Tourist Office (Palacio Municipal, Constitución s/n; ☉9am-4pm) Opening hours are a little flexible; simple street maps are available.

ⓘ Getting There & Away

BUS

Sendor runs 1st-class buses from Matehuala's bus station to Real de Catorce (around M$88, 1½ to two hours) at 7:45am, 11:45am, 1:45pm and 5:45pm (with an extra one on Sundays at 9:45am). The bus can be caught 15 minutes later at the Sendor office in Matehuala, a little east of and across the street from Hotel Álamo on Méndez. Important: the ticket will show the time the bus leaves from the center, not the bus station

(ie 8am, noon, 2pm, 6pm). Don't get caught out; it leaves the main bus station 15 minutes before the time stated.

If you're coming from San Luis Potosí, you can buy a one-way (or return; valid for six months) ticket and change in Matehuala (the total cost for two tickets one-way is M$301).

On arrival in Real, buses park at the east entrance of the Ogarrio tunnel. There, in order to pass through the tunnel, you change to a smaller bus that drops off (or picks up if returning to Matehuala) at the western end of the tunnel, in Real. Confirm the return bus schedule upon arrival. At the time of research, buses from Real to Matehuala (with connections to San Luis Potosí) were at 7:45am, 11:45am, 3:45pm and 5:45pm (M$88,

---

> **WORTH A TRIP**

LAS POZAS

Take a wealthy English eccentric, an idyllic tract of Mexican jungle and an extremely hyperactive imagination, and you'd still struggle to come up with the audacious, bizarre and – frankly – madcap experiment that is **Las Pozas** (The Pools; www.xilitla.org; adult/child M$50/25; ☉9am-6pm).

Situated on the sweeping slopes of the Sierra Madre Oriental, near the small and attractive mountain town of Xilitla (he-*leet*-la), Las Pozas is a monumental sculpture garden built in thick jungle that links a series of concrete temples, pagodas, bridges, pavilions and spiral stairways with a necklace of natural waterfalls. The surreal creation stands as a memorial to the imagination and excessive wealth of Edward James (1907–84). A drop-out English aristocrat and poet, he became a patron of Salvador Dalí in the late 1930s and subsequently went on to amass the largest private collection of surrealist art in the world.

In 1945 James' adventures took him to Xilitla where he met Plutarco Gastelum, who helped build Las Pozas. It began with 40 local workers crafting giant, colored concrete flowers beside an idyllic jungle stream. Then, for 17 years, James and Gastelum created ever larger and stranger structures – many of which were never finished – at an estimated cost of US$5 million.

James died in 1984, leaving no provision to maintain his creation, which, since 2008, has been in the hands of a Mexican-run nonprofit foundation. The extravagant labyrinth of surreal sculptures and edifices with stairways leading nowhere (to heaven?) covers 36 hectares and is worth a significant diversion for anyone with the vaguest creative inclinations. If you're in fairly good shape, you could spend the whole day contemplating the lovely swimming holes and mazelike trails.

Las Pozas has a good on-site **restaurant** (open 10am to 6pm) and there are several small campsites and posadas nearby. For the true Las Pozas experience, you should stay at **Posada El Castillo** (☏489-365-00-38; www.junglegossip.com; Ocampo 105; d incl breakfast US$70-110; ☏☒), the surrealist-inspired former Gastelum home (and also James' lodgings), now transformed into a verdant Pozas-esque guesthouse run by the Gastelum family in the heart of Xilitla.

Xilitla itself rewards a day or so of exploration. It's seriously off the beaten tourist trail but a fun time can be had walking the quiet mountain roads through the forest and farmland that ring the town. Ask someone to show you the way to the big cave where masses of green parakeets roost

To get to Las Pozas you'll need to connect through Tuxpan to Tampico. From here regular connections travel to Xilitla. There are also buses from Xilitla to San Luis Potosí.

A taxi from Xilitla to the Las Pozas site is M$70, or it's an easy 2km walk. Guided tours of Las Pozas are available for M$200 (Spanish) and M$250 (English).

1½ to two hours). Tickets are purchased at the Senda ticket office, on the edge of the car park at the tunnel's western entrance in Real; if this is not open, you can buy them on board the bus.

CAR

If driving from Hwy 57 north of Matehuala, turn off toward Cedral, 20km west. After Cedral, you turn south to reach Catorce on what must be one of the world's longest cobblestone roads. It's a slow but spectacular zigzag drive up a steep mountainside. The 2.3km-long Ogarrio tunnel (M$20 per vehicle) is only wide enough for one vehicle; workers stationed at each end with telephones control traffic flow between 7am and 11pm. If it's really busy, you'll have to leave your car at the eastern tunnel entrance and continue by pick-up or cart. If you drive through, you must leave your car in the parking area to the left of the market.

Vintage 'Jeep Willys' leave Real around noon (and on demand), downhill from the plaza along Allende, for the rough but spectacular descent to the small hamlet of Estación de Catorce (around M$50 per person in a 'collective', one hour). From there, buses head to San Tiburcio, where there are connections for Saltillo and Zacatecas.

La Huasteca Potosina

The stunning, tropical Huasteca Potosina, is a lush, remote subregion of San Luis Potosí and, although part of the same region, could be worlds away.

A huge drawcard are the region's incredible waterfalls and swimming holes, the result of the rivers that flow eastward from the slopes of the Sierra Madre Oriental. They look as though they've been naturally photo-shopped, so rich is their aquamarine hue, thanks to the high calcium content in the surrounding rocks. You can swim near and take boat trips to some of these spectacular cascades.

A rich culture of the local Huastec people (Tének), plus extraordinary sinkholes and birds, make a visit here extremely rewarding.

The entire Huasteca encompasses parts of San Luis Potosí, Hidalgo, Puebla, Queretaro, Tamaulipas and Veracruz. The name 'Huasteca' refers to the place where the Huastec culture developed; the region is known for *huasteco* (or *huapango*), a style of music that combines violins and the guitar-like *jarana,* and local dishes, such as the *zacahuil,* a massive tamale.

Over the last decade in particular, Mexicans and adventurists have 'discovered' the Huasteca Potosina; as yet, few foreigners know of it. You can get to Xilitla by public

transportation; for the rest, it's easiest to have your own transportation or go with a local tour operator.

Rio Verde, east of San Luis Potosí, falls just outside the boundaries of the Huasteca Potosina but its crystalline, warm water lagoon attracts divers and families.

❶ Getting There & Away

The Huasteca Potosina can most easily be reached from San Luis Potosí, Sierra Gorda or Tampico. The best time to visit is in dry season, between November and March (wet season brings heavy rains and high, and less clear, waters).

◉ Sights

Sótano de las Golondrinas　　CAVE
(Aquismón; M$35; ⊙dusk to dawn) The extraordinary limestone sinkhole, known as Swallows' Cave (or 'Swallows Basement'), is located near Aquismón. One of the world's deepest pits at over 500m (over 370m freefall), it's known for the thousands of *vencejos* (white-collared swifts) that nest in the caves. At dawn, flocks of swifts leave the cave, spiraling their way up to the opening. At dusk, on return to the cave, they circle above the cave mouth before they break off in groups and dive-bomb into the abyss.

It's popular with rappelers and base jumpers who drop from the cave's mouth. To get there, you must walk from the car park, down hundreds of steps (and back again), which is about a 20-minute walk.

Sótano de las Huahuas　　CAVE
(San Isidro Tampaxal; M$30; ⊙dusk to dawn) This impressive sinkhole is one of two (along with Sótano de las Goldonrinas) to view swift flocks exiting and entering their cavern. A favorite for rappelling enthusiasts, the chasm itself is around 478m deep. Accessing the cave is a little trickier – from the car park you must walk for 1km through remarkable jungle – but it's worth it for its beautiful cedar and local tree and bird species. To access the cave, turn off toward San Isidro Tampaxal (around 8km).

Ciudad Valles

Ciudad Valles, while not a very attractive city, is useful for its adventure organizations plus two interesting museums that focus on the region's history of the Huastec and Nahuatl peoples.

WORTH A TRIP

THE WATERFALLS OF THE HUASTECA POTOSINA

A huge drawcard are the region's incredible waterfalls which look as though they've been naturally Photoshopped, so rich is their aquamarine hue, thanks to the high calcium content in the surrounding rocks. You can swim near, and take boat trips to, some of these spectacular cascades.

Los Micos (per person M$20; ⊗8am-5pm) is the nearest waterfall to Ciudad Valles, if also the most touristic of the Huasteca Potosina's falls. Seven waterfalls of different heights cascade down a river bed. You can do a see-and-snap boat ride (M$60 for 10 minutes, minimum four persons) or a jumping expedition down the seven waterfalls (M$150 per person; two hours; helmet and life jacket supplied). Many operators are located in the car park and offer the same activity.

Located 78km northwest of Ciudad Valles, the stunning cascades of **Minas Viejas** (M$20; ⊗7am-8pm) comprises a principal waterfall with a drop of 55m plus a stunning water pool. From here, a series of smaller cascades and pools drop over terraces. It's a popular destination for adventure groups, who jump over the terraces.

El Meco FREE, a stunning 38m-high waterfall, 105km northwest of Ciudad Valles, is the furthest of all the falls but well worth the trip. It's a view-only experience (you'll see why; it's high). However, guests of boutique hotel **Huasteca Secreta** (☑444-825-63-38; www.huastecasecreta.com; El Naranjo; d M$2700; ☀) boutique hotel enjoy breakfast overlooking the falls, in the Huasteca Secreta restaurant. The hotel – in a stunning locale – comprises delightful cabins that are set on a turquoise river and framed by a green lawn. (Note: there's no wi-fi or telephone reception but there is a wonderful infinity pool.)

Nearly 54km southwest of Ciudad Valles, near the village of Tamasopo, are the **Cascadas de Tamasopo** (Tamasopo; adult/child M$20/10, parking M$20; ⊗7:30am-7:30pm). This lovely set of three cascades and swimming holes is among the most accessible and populated of the region's water attractions.

From here, head 5km northeast along a rough road to **Puente de Dios** (M$20). This features a 600m-long wooden walkway with stunning rainforest and fabulous swimming opportunities. The main feature, 'God's Bridge' is a turquoise-colored water hole with an adjoining cave entrance (not accessible or recommended in high waters).

Southeast of Valles the fantastic **Cascada de Tamul** plunges 105m into the pristine Río Santa María. Take Hwy 70 for 24km, then turn left following signs to the waterfall for another 18km to Tanchachín; from there you can reach the waterfall by *lancha* (motorboat; around M$600 per boat). **MS Xpediciones** (p690) arranges excellent canoeing and rafting adventures (M$700, minimum two, including transportation and a delicious meal with a local family).

⊙ Sights

Museo Regional Huasteco
Joaquín Meade MUSEUM
(Rotarios 623, cnr Artes, Ciudad Valles; ⊗9am-4pm Mon-Fri) FREE Showcases over 10,000 archaeological pieces from the region, from around 600 BC until the Spanish conquest.

Museo de Cultura de la
Huasteca Tamuantzán MUSEUM
(☑481-381-26-75; Carr. México-Laredo y Libramiento Sur, Ciudad Valles; ⊗9am-4pm Mon-Fri) FREE An excellent starting point to learn more about the Huasteca region and local cultures.

🏃 Activities

Although it's a fairly rushed trip, if you are short on time, you could consider heading to the Huasteca Potosina from San Luis Potosí. An excellent outfit to do this with is Operatour Potosina (p681). Knowledgeable English-speaking owner, Lori, runs two-day trips or can arrange a customised tour.

MS Xpediciones ADVENTURE TOUR
(☑481-381-18-88; www.msxpediciones.com; Blvr México Laredo, Escontría 15-B, Interior Hotel Misión, Ciudad Valles; ⊗9am-8pm Mon-Sat, plus 9am-noon Sun Jul & Aug) The pick of the region's operators for its community-aware, friendly and professional approach. Its range of activities and adventures includes trips to Xilitla and Las Pozas, to the bird caves, and many of the region's waterfalls. Also arranges excellent canoeing adventures, including to Tamul (M$700 minimum two people, including

transportation and a meal with a local family) plus rafting expeditions.

Rio Verde

Located west of the environs of the Huasteca Potosina, Rio Verde, a scrappy agricultural town, is located 140km east of San Luis Potosí. It is a useful stopover en route to Ciudad Valles, though most head here for its phenomena – a prehistoric freshwater thermal lagoon – that is especially popular for beginner diving courses.

Activities

Laguna de la Media Luna   DIVING
(www.manantialmedialuna.com; adult/child M$40/20) Located 18km southwest of Rio Verde, this extraordinary prehistoric lagoon (860m above sea level) is fed by six thermal springs (up to between 10m and 36m). Water temperatures range between an appealing 80°F and 86°F (27°C and 30°C). Its crystal clear waters mean snorkelers and divers can view beds of water lilies, an ancient petrified forest and several fish species. Hundreds of families flock here on weekends. You can hire snorkeling gear from one of the many stalls inside the area.

Diving courses are also available. The most highly recommended is **Escuela de Buceo Media Luna** (✆ 487-872-81-89; http://buceomedialuna.com/; diving courses from M$950), run by Master Scuba Diver and oceanographer, Ossiel Martinez.

🛏 Sleeping

El Molino   GUESTHOUSE $
(www.hotelelmolino.webs.com; Porfirio Díaz 1417, Rio Verde; d M$550; 🅿 🛜) Based in the rather scrappy agricultural town of Rio Verde, 140km east of San Luis Potosí, 'The Mill' has 15 tasteful rooms (some of which are around the central living room) and a pretty garden. These were built on the ruins of an 18th-century sugarcane factory and provide sweet respite from the heat or a water-logged day.

It's a lovely place to stay if you plan to visit the region's main attraction, Laguna de la Media Luna. Breakfast costs M$70.

ZACATECAS STATE

The state of Zacatecas (za-ka-*te*-kas) is a dry, rugged, cactus-strewn expanse on the fringe of Mexico's northern semideserts. The state is best known for the wealthy silver city of the same name. Visitors can enjoy the region's historical and natural monuments including the mysterious ruins of La Quemada, a testament to centuries of cultures. The state is one of Mexico's largest in area (73,252 sq km) but smallest in population (1.5 million); it is believed that as many people again (1.5 million), who come from the state, currently live in the United States.

Zacatecas

✆ 492 / POP 138,000 / ELEV 2430M

The most northern of Mexico's fabled silver cities, fascinating Zacatecas – a Unesco World Heritage site – runs along a narrow valley. The large historic center is jam-packed with opulent colonial buildings, a stupendous cathedral (useful as a central landmark), magnificent museums and steep, winding streets and alleys. Excellent restaurants and fine hotels make it a very comfortable location for any traveler.

The city has a legacy of historical highs and lows: it was here that Pancho Villa defeated a stronghold of soldiers (today he is still much feted by the locals). Here, too, thousands of indigenous slaves were forced by the Spanish to toil in the mines under terrible conditions. Today, travelers can have their own lofty experiences in a *teleférico* (cablecar) to the Cerro de la Bufa, an impressive rock outcrop; the trip affords great views of a collage of church domes and rooftops. Alternatively, you can drop below the surface to tour the infamous Edén mine, or vibrate to the rhythms of its underground disco.

History

Indigenous Zacatecos – one of the Chichimec tribes – mined local mineral deposits for centuries before the Spanish arrived; it's said that the silver rush here was started when a Chichimec gave a piece of the fabled metal to a conquistador. The Spaniards founded a settlement in 1548 and started mining operations that sent caravan after caravan of silver off to Mexico City, creating fabulously wealthy silver barons in Zacatecas.

By the early 18th century, the mines of Zacatecas were producing 20% of Nueva España's silver and the city became an important base for Catholic missionaries.

In the 19th century political instability diminished the flow of silver. Although silver production later improved under Porfirio

Zacatecas

N 0 ——————————— 200 m
   0 ——————————— 0.1 miles

Los Dorados de Villa (200m);
Museo Rafael
Coronel (200m)

4 la del Seminario

Tirolesa 840
(650m);
Museo Toma de
Zacatecas (1km)

Bosque

Duranzo

Fortín

Juan de Tolosa

Abasolo

Moral

Triste

Paseo Díaz Ordaz

Cerro del Grillo
Teleférico Station

3

Bosque

Mante

Del Salto

Rojas

Urizar

Cerro de la
Bufa (250m)

Mante

Mercedita

De Los Bolos

Genaro Codina

Av Hidalgo

Pankhurst

Grillo

Del Auxilio

Mina Club
(50m)

De la Loma

Del Cobre

Gómez

Serdán

Lancaster

7 **13**

Plazuela
de Santo
Domingo

16 Plaza de
Armas

10 **11** **9**

1

24

32

Dr Hierro

12

30 **20**

14

Villalpando

27

28

8

6

26

Plazuela
Francisco
Goitia

17

Aguascalientes

Medina

2

Plaza
Miguel Auza

25

Auza

Del Estudiante

Callejón del Lazo

18

Parque
Alameda

Cadena

31

29

21

Jardín
Morelos

Jardín
Juárez

Plazuela
Genaro
Codina

Tenorio

Av Guerrero

Aurora

Amador

Av Juárez

33

15

23

Arroyo de la Plata

Correa

Av González Ortega

Trabajo

Bus Stop
Route 7

Jardín
Independencia

22

García de la Cadena

Salazar

Ponce

5

Estrada

Parque
Enrique
Estrada

Independencia

Plaza del
Bicentenario

Calz de la Paz

Salinas

Estrada

Rayón

Morelos

Calderón

Blvd López Mateos

Local Buses
to Guadalupe

19

Zacatecas

◎ Sights
1	Catedral	C3
2	Ex-Templo de San Agustín	B4
3	Mina El Edén	B2
4	Museo del Arte Abstracto Manuel Felguérez	C1
5	Museo Francisco Goitia	A6
6	Museo Manuel M. Ponce	C4
7	Museo Pedro Coronel	C3
8	Museo Zacatecano	C4
9	Palacio de Gobierno	D3
10	Palacio de la Mala Noche	C3
11	Plaza de Armas	D3
12	Teatro Calderón	C3
	Templo de Santo Domingo	(see 13)
13	Templo de Santo Domingo	C3

🛏 Sleeping
14	Cielito Lindo Hostal	D4
15	Hotel Condesa	C5
16	Hotel Emporio Zacatecas	C3
17	Hotel Reyna Soledad	C4
18	La Terrasse	B4
19	Quinta Real Zacatecas	B7

✶ Eating
20	Acrópolis Café	C3
21	El Recoveco	A5
22	Mercado Arroyo de la Plata	C5
23	Mercado El Laberinto	C5
24	Panificadora Santa Cruz	D3
	Restaurant La Plaza	(see 19)
25	San Patrizio Caffé	C4
26	Trattoria Il Goloso	C4

◎ Drinking & Nightlife
27	Cantina 15 Letras	B4
28	Dalí Café & Bar	B4
29	La Famosa Cantina Típica	B5

✹ Entertainment
30	Teatro Calderón	C3

🛍 Shopping
31	Casa de las Artesanías	B4
32	Centro Platero Gallery	C3
33	Fonart	B5

Díaz, the Revolution disrupted it. In 1914 in Zacatecas, Pancho Villa defeated a stronghold of 12,000 soldiers loyal to President Victoriano Huerta. After the Revolution, Zacatecas continued to thrive on silver.

◎ Sights & Activities

★ Museo Rafael Coronel · MUSEUM

(cnr Abasolo & Matamoros; adult/student M$30/15; ⊙10am-5pm Thu-Tue) The amazing Museo Rafael Coronel is not to be missed. Imaginatively housed in the ruins of the lovely 16th-century Ex-Convento de San Francisco, it houses Mexican folk art collected by the Zacatecan artist Rafael Coronel, brother of Pedro Coronel and son-in-law of Diego Rivera. Take your time to wander through the various spaces (follow the arrows; it's easy to miss sections).

The skeleton of the Capilla San Antonio is interesting, though the highlight is the astonishing display of more than 3000 masks (another 8000 are in storage) used in traditional dances and rituals. Also here are pottery, puppets, instruments, pre-Hispanic objects and sketches by Rivera. The grounds and garden are a wonderful place to come and relax.

Museo Pedro Coronel · MUSEUM

(Plaza de Santo Domingo s/n; adult/student M$30/15; ⊙10am-5pm Tue-Sun) The extraordinary Museo Pedro Coronel is housed in a 17th-century former Jesuit college and, given that it was recently remodelled, is one of provincial Mexico's best art museums. Pedro Coronel (1923–85) was an affluent Zacatecan artist who bequeathed his collection of art and artifacts from all over the world, as well as his own works. The collection includes 20th-century works by Picasso, Rouault, Dalí, Goya and Miró; and pre-Hispanic Mexican artifacts, masks and other ancient pieces.

Cerro de la Bufa · LANDMARK

The most appealing of the many explanations for the name of the hill that dominates Zacatecas is that 'bufa' is an old Basque word for wineskin, which is certainly what the rocky formation looks like. The views from the top are superb and there's an interesting group of monuments, a chapel and a museum. It is also the site of a zip line, **Tirolesa 840** (☏ cell 492-946-31-57; www.vivazacatecasadventure.com; rides M$200-250; ⊙10am-6pm), a 1km ride (840m of actual flying) across a former open-pit mine.

The small **Museo Toma de Zacatecas** (☏492-922-80-66; adult/student M$20/10; ⊙10am-4:30pm), at the top of La Bufa, was reopened in 2014, to commemorate the centenary of the 1914 battle that was fought on the hill's slopes, and in which the revolutionary División del Norte, led by Pancho Villa and Felipe Ángeles, defeated President Victoriano Huerta's forces. This gave the revolu-

NORTHERN CENTRAL HIGHLANDS ZACATECAS

tionaries control of Zacatecas, which was the gateway to Mexico City. It's a technological delight, with talking ghosts, actual footage of the battle and other delights.

La Capilla de la Virgen del Patrocinio, adjacent to the museum, is named after the patron saint of miners. Above the altar of this 18th-century chapel is an image of the Virgin, said to be capable of healing the sick. Thousands of pilgrims flock here each year on September 8, when it is carried to the cathedral.

Facing the chapel are three imposing **statues** of the victors of the battle of Zacatecas – Villa, Ángeles and Pánfilo Natera.

From the right of the statues, a paved path along the foot of the rocky hilltop leads to the **Mausoleo de los Hombres Ilustres de Zacatecas**, with the tombs of Zacatecan heroes from 1841 to the present.

A convenient way to ascend La Bufa (to the church and museum) is by *teleférico*. Alternatively, you can walk up, starting at Calle del Ángel from the cathedral's east end. To reach it by car, take Carretera a la Bufa, which begins at Avenida López Velarde, a couple of kilometers east of the center. A taxi costs around M$55. You can return to town by the *teleférico* or by a footpath leading downhill from the statues.

Mina El Edén   MINE
(www.minaeleden.com.mx; tours adult/child M$80/40; ☉tours every hour 10am-6pm) Visiting one of Mexico's richest mines (1586–1960s) provides an insight into a source of wealth and the terrible price paid for it. Digging for hoards of silver, gold, iron, copper and zinc, enslaved indigenous people worked under horrific conditions. Up to five people a day died from accidents or tuberculosis and silicosis. These days, it's a safer story. An elevator or miniature train takes you inside Cerro del Grillo. Guides lead you along floodlit walkways past shafts and over subterranean pools.

The mine has two entrances. To reach the higher one (the east entrance), walk 100m southwest from Cerro del Grillo *teleférico* station; from this entrance, tours start with an elevator descent. To reach the west entrance from the town center, walk west along Avenida Juárez and stay on it after its name changes to Avenida Torreón at the Alameda. Turn right immediately after the IMSS hospital (bus 7 from the corner of Avenida Hidalgo goes up Avenida Juárez and past the hospital) and a short walk will bring you to the mine entrance. Tours begin here with a trip on the narrow-gauge rail-

way (540m), after which you walk another 350m or so.

Museo del Arte Abstracto Manuel Felguérez   MUSEUM
(Ex-Seminario de la Purísima Concepción; adult M$30; ☉10am-5pm Wed-Mon) This art museum is worth visiting for the building alone; originally a seminary, it was later used as a prison and has been renovated to create some remarkable exhibition spaces, transforming the former dark, depressing cells and steel walkways into a beautiful site.

It has a stunning and varied collection of abstract art, particularly the work of Zacatecan artist Manuel Felguérez, and a good bookstore and gift shop.

Catedral   CATHEDRAL
(Plaza de Armas) Built between 1729 and 1752, the pink-stone cathedral is an ultimate expression of Mexican baroque.

The stupendous main facade is a wall of detailed carvings; this has been interpreted as a giant symbol of the tabernacle. A tiny figure of an angel holding a tabernacle is in the middle of the design, the keystone atop the round central window. Above this, in the third tier, is Christ and above Christ is God. The 12 Apostles are featured, as well as a smaller Virgin figure above the doorway.

The southern facade's central sculpture is of La Virgen de los Zacatecanos, the city's patroness. The north facade shows Christ crucified, attended by the Virgin Mary and St John.

Unveiled in 2010, the grand altar is the work of Mexico's famous artist, Javier Marín. It features 10 large bronze figures and the figure of Christ, arranged on a backdrop of golden blocks.

Museo Zacatecano   MUSEUM
(Dr Hierro 301; adult/student M$30/15; ☉10am-5pm Wed-Mon) Zacatecas' former mint (Mexico's second-biggest in the 19th century) now houses the wonderful Museo Zacatecano. Spread over a number of rooms, this contemporary museum exhibits a weird mix of all things *zacatecano*. Unfortunately, the first few *salas* are text-heavy information boards (in Spanish). The highlight – in the last halls – is the superb collection of Huichol art. Videos (all in Spanish) provide each *sala's* context.

Plaza de Armas   PLAZA
The plaza is the open space north of the cathedral. At the time of research, it was being remodelled to raise the ground to pavement level. Some locals claim it was originally

constructed this way, while others view the change as a waste of money. The **Palacio de Gobierno** (Plaza de Armas) on the plaza's east side was built in the 18th century for a colonial family. In the turret of its main staircase is a mural of the history of Zacatecas state, painted in 1970 by Antonio Rodríguez.

Across the road, and directly opposite the Palacio, the **Palacio de la Mala Noche** (Plaza de Armas) was built in the late 18th century for a mine owner and now houses state-government offices.

Teatro Calderón
HISTORIC BUILDING

(☉10am-8pm) **FREE** Opposite the *plazuela* on Avenida Hidalgo, the lovely, renovated 1890s Teatro Calderón dates from the Porfiriato period and holds plays, concerts, films and art exhibitions. Worth a stickybeak even if you don't plan to see a performance.

Museo Manuel M. Ponce
MUSEUM

(Dr Hierro 301; adult M$20; ☉10am-5pm Tue-Sun) This five-roomed museum is a touching tribute to the musician Manuel M. Ponce, a well-traveled, intellectual Mexican, whose best-known score includes *Estrellito*. One of Ponce's pupils, Carlos Vasquez, was bequeathed Ponce's belongings on the maestro's death and Vasquez in turn spent his life trying to promote Ponce. This included donating his collection to a museum (sadly, Vasquez died only months before the opening in 2014).

Templo de Santo Domingo
PLAZA

(Plazuela de Santo Domingo) The **Templo de Santo Domingo** in a *plazuela* of the same name, is in a baroque style, with fine gilded altars and a graceful horseshoe staircase. Built by the Jesuits in the 1740s, the church was taken over by Dominican monks when the Jesuits were expelled in 1767.

Museo Francisco Goitia
MUSEUM

(☑492-922-02-11; Estrada 101; adult M$30; ☉10am-4:45pm Tue-Sun) The Museo Francisco Goitia displays work by several 20th-century Zacatecan artists, including some evocative paintings of indigenous people by Goitia (1882–1960) himself. Other artists include Pedro Coronel, Rafael Coronel and Manuel Felguérez. The museum is in a former governor's mansion, above Parque Enrique Estrada, and is worth it for the building and manicured gardens, overlooking the acqueduct.

Ex-Templo de San Agustín
NOTABLE BUILDING

(☉10am-4.30pm Tue-Sun) The Ex-Templo de San Agustín was built for Augustinian monks in the 17th century. During the 19th-century anticlerical movement, the church became a cantina and Masonic lodge. In 1882 it was purchased by American Presbyterian missionaries who destroyed its 'too Catholic' main facade, replacing it with a blank white wall. One surviving feature is the church's plateresque carving of the conversion of St Augustine over the north doorway.

In the 20th century the church returned to the government.

Teleférico
CABLE CAR

(☑492-922-01-70; one-way ticket M$50; ☉10am-6pm) Zacatecas' most exhilarating ride, and the easiest way to Cerro de la Bufa's summit, is the Swiss-built cablecar that crosses high above the city from Cerro del Grillo. It's a short walk east from Mina El Edén (east entrance) to the *teleférico's* Cerro del Grillo station. Alternatively, huff up the steep steps of Callejón de García Rojas, which lead straight to the *teleférico* from Genaro Codina. Cars depart every 15 minutes (except when it's raining or when winds exceed 60km/h) and the trip takes seven minutes.

✪ Festivals & Events

La Morisma
RELIGIOUS

Usually held on the last weekend in August. Features a spectacular mock battle commemorating the triumph of the Christians over the Muslims in old Spain. Two rival 'armies' – around 10,000 participants from the *barrio* of Bracho – parade through the streets in the morning, then, accompanied by bands of musicians, enact two battle sequences that take place between Lomas de Bracho and Cerro de la Bufa.

Feria de Zacatecas
CULTURAL

Annual fair with a folkloric focus, held during the first three weeks in September. Renowned matadors fight famous local bulls. There are also *charreadas* (rodeos), concerts, plays, agricultural and craft shows. On September 8 the image of La Virgen del Patrocinio is carried to the cathedral from its chapel on Cerro de la Bufa.

🛌 Sleeping

Disappointingly, there are limited budget options in Zacatecas. Midrange and top-end accommodations tend to hike their rates (on those provided here) up to double during Zacatecas' high seasons – September's festivals, Christmas and Semana Santa (March/April).

Cielito Lindo Hostal   HOSTEL $

(☑ 492-921-1132; www.cielitolindohostal.com; Aguascalientes 213; dm M$200, d from M$500, f M$950) At last! Zacatecas almost-non-existent budget category has a much-welcomed addition: a delightful, funky and stylish hostel. The former home of a religious *padre,* this converted colonial mansion is blessed with an array of rooms. The dorms are especially well serviced, with shelves for recharging electronics, plus lockers, while the private rooms vary in size and shape.

Note: some of the rooms are windowless, due to the massive doors, which, once closed, create a cocoon (typical of the colonial buildings). But efficient service, use of the kitchen and tea and coffee make this a winner.

Hotel Condesa   HOTEL $

(☑ 492-922-11-60; www.hotelcondesa.com.mx; Av Juárez 102; s/d/tr M$450/550/580; ☺) The Condesa's 52 '80s-style modern rooms are a good budget option. The nicest have external-facing windows. An attached restaurant serves breakfast (open 8am to 9:30pm; M$50 to M$70) and other meals.

La Terrasse   BOUTIQUE HOTEL $$

(☑ 492-925-53-15; www.terrassehotel.com.mx; Villalpando 209; d incl breakfast M$700-880, tr incl breakfast M$1000; ☺✳☎) This small, friendly and centrally located boutique option is run by a proud owner. It has 14 contemporary and slightly sparse rooms, but is by far the best midrange option. Back rooms have internal-facing windows, which could be claustrophobic for some, quiet for others.

Hotel Reyna Soledad   HOTEL $$

(☑ 492-922-07-90; www.hostalreynasoledad.com. mx; Tacuba 170; r M$590-750; P☎) Set in a converted 17th-century convent, the colonial patios of this perfectly located place are tranquil, if very dated (think oodles of pine furniture). It's OK if your focus is the city, not the accommodations.

★ Hotel Emporio Zacatecas LUXURY HOTEL $$$

(☑ 492-925-65-00, 800-227-2272; www.hoteles emporio.com; Av Hidalgo 703; r from M$1275; P☺☎) Zacatecas' central upmarket hotel boasts a superb location, luxurious rooms and delightful terrace areas. Service is professional, and the rooms provide a quiet oasis from external noise. The downer is there's no air-conditioning. The website sometimes promotes special deals.

Quinta Real Zacatecas   LUXURY HOTEL $$$

(☑ 492-922-91-04, 800-500-40-00; www.quintare al.com; Rayón 434; ste incl breakfast from M$2850; P☺✳@☎) It's worth seeing red (in terms of your bank balance) to experience this luxury treat. Spectacularly situated around the country's oldest – now retired – bullring and near El Cubo aqueduct, the 49-room hotel is one of Mexico's most contemporary and fetching. The least expensive rooms are spacious, comfortable master suites.

An elegant restaurant, La Plaza, overlooks the ring, and the bar, El Botarel, is in the former holding pens.

✗ Eating

There are some excellent Mexican and international restaurants serving a range of fare. Local specialties feature ingredients such as nopal and pumpkin seeds.

In the morning, look around Avenida Tacuba for the *burro* (donkey) carrying pottery jugs of *aguamiel* (honey water), a nutritional drink derived from the maguey cactus. The two central produce markets are **Mercado El Laberinto** (Plazuela Genaro Codina) and **Mercado Arroyo de la Plata** (Arroyo de la Plata).

San Patrizio Caffé   CAFE $

(Av Hidalgo 403C; drinks & snacks M$22-80; ☺9am-10:30pm Mon-Sat, 11am-9pm Sun; ☎) Reasonable coffee, light snacks and Italian sodas; set in an attractive and relaxing courtyard setting.

Panificadora Santa Cruz   BAKERY $

(Tacuba 216A; snacks M$10-45; ☺7:30am-10:30pm) Almost abutting the cathedral, this reliable bakery-eatery has excellent sinful treats – *pan dulces* (pastries), pizzas and *tortas* (sandwiches). Offers set 'nothing-special-but-fills-a-hole' type breakfasts (M$58 to M$78).

Acrópolis Café   MEXICAN $

(cnr Av Hidalgo & Plazuela Candelario Huizar; mains M$95-170; ☺☎) Near the cathedral, this Greek-owned cafe has a quirky '50s-style diner feel, and is *the* place to meet for locals and visitors – perhaps more for its location than its food. It offers light meals, set breakfasts and coffees.

El Recoveco   MEXICAN $

(Torreón 513; breakfast buffet M$89, lunch buffet M$99; ☺8:30am-7pm Mon-Sat, 9am-7pm Sun) 'Cheap and good' is how the locals describe this long-standing, cafeteria-style eatery.

NORTHERN CENTRAL HIGHLANDS ZACATECAS

JEREZ

The delightful country town of Jerez (pop 43,000), 30km southwest of Zacatecas, is as Mexican as a tortilla. As such, it's is a great place to head for a day to watch the local action. Sunday – market day – is especially fun as you'll see saddle-bound *rancheros* drinking outside the saloons. Jardín Páez, the pretty main plaza, has an old-fashioned gazebo, trees and benches. Here, too, is a **tourist information kiosk** (☉10am-4pm). Banks (with ATMs) and phones are around the plaza.

Jerez is known for its lively one-week long Easter fair, featuring, among other activities, *charreadas* (Mexican rodeos) and cockfights.

The town also has some exceptionally fine buildings. The 18th-century **Parroquia de la Inmaculada Concepción** and the 19th-century **Santuario de la Soledad** have lovely stone carvings. Go one block south from Jardín Páez' southeast corner, then one block west for the shrine, or one block east for the church. Just past the shrine, on Jardín Hidalgo's north side, is the not-to-be-missed 19th-century **Teatro Hinojosa** (Reloj Esq Salvador Varela; ☉8am-7pm Mon-Fri, 11am-5pm Sat & Sun). Head inside to relive the theatrical days of the 1870s. The design and decoration reflects the wealth of the times. The **Casa Museo Ramón Lopez Velarde** (Calle de la Parroquia 33; M$20; ☉10am-5pm Tue-Sun) pays homage to one of Mexico's well-known poets who was born in the house in 1888. It provides insight into the life of a middle-class family during the era.

The best option for nosh is the colorful **Hotel Jardín** (mains M$55-120; ☉8:30am-10pm), on the plaza.

The Jerez turnoff is near Malpaso, 29km south of Zacatecas on the Zacatecas–Guadalajara road. Ómnibus de México and Estrella Blanca have regular services from Zacatecas' bus station to Jerez (M$60, one hour) as does the slower and cheaper service Linea Zacatecas Jerez (M$50). Jerez' bus station is on the east side of town, 1km from the center along Calzada La Suave Patria. From here, 'Centro' buses (M$6) run to/from the center.

This means buffet style (as much as you can eat and as many plates as you like) and tasty enough Mexican fare that holds no surprises.

★**Los Dorados de Villa**　　MEXICAN **$$**
(☏492-922-57-22; Plazuela de García 1314; mains M$80-150; ☉3pm-1am Mon-Sat, 3-11pm Sun; ☻) You may have to fight to get into this popular revolutionary-themed restaurant: knock at the door – it's always locked. Inside it's a blast of warmth and color and chock-a-block with atmosphere and relics. Plus it serves up a delicious array of everything – except Pancho Villa himself. Don't miss the *enchiladas valentinas* (M$80).

Trattoria Il Goloso　　ITALIAN **$$**
(Dr Hierro 400; mains M$120-220; ☉2-9:30pm Tue-Thu, 2-11pm Fri & Sat, 2-8pm Sun; ☻) Trade the tacos for fabulous Italian pasta and other mains in this Italian eatery. It comes complete with enthusiastic, sociable chefs. Aldo whips up wonderful Mexican-Italian fusion creations, such as *salmón Papa Beto* (delicious salmon recipe from his grandfather). It's behind San Patrizio Caffé.

Restaurant La Plaza　　INTERNATIONAL **$$$**
(Quinta Real Zacatecas, Rayón 434; mains M$180-350; ☻) The elegant hotel dining room at the Quinta Real Zacatecas is especially memorable for its outlook to the aqueduct and bullring, as well as for its refined ambience and good international cuisine with a few Mexican standards. Head here for a Sunday brunch (M$225) or an evening cocktail in the bar, opposite the restaurant on the other side of the ring. Tables in the bar area are nestled in niches, which are former bull-holding pens (6pm to 1am). Reservations are advisable.

🍷 Drinking

Zacatecas has a good late-night scene, especially after 9pm.

★**Cantina 15 Letras**　　BAR
(☏492-922-01-78; Mártires de Chicago 309; ☉1pm-3am Mon-Sat) Stop for a drink at this oft-crowded classic, filled with bohemians, drunks and poets. The art showcases some well-known local and international artists, including Pedro Coronel.

La Famosa Cantina Típica BAR

(Callejón Cuevas 110) This ultra-popular bar pumps with well-dressed young 'thangs'. Whether they slam down a few mezcals, sip more sedately on a whisky, they're all here for the same thing: fun. Like most bars, it gets going late.

Dalí Café & Bar BAR

(Plaza Miguel Auza 322; snacks M$35-100; ⊘noon-1am Mon-Sat, 5pm-1am Sun; 🛜) This sprawling cafe-bar in front of Ex-Templo de San Agustín offers a surreal mix of furniture, cocktails and post-drink munchies (plus good hot chocolate drinks).

Mina Club BAR

(Dovali s/n; cover M$50-150; ⊘4-11pm Thu-Fri, 10pm-late Sat) Strike it lucky in this unique bar-cum-club – the tunnel of the Mina El Edén. On Saturday, it morphs into a club; check opening hours as these change seasonally.

☆ Entertainment

Teatro Calderón THEATER

(☑492-922-81-20; Av Hidalgo s/n; ⊘10am-9pm) This top venue hosts a variety of cultural events including theater, dance and music performances. Check the posters or with the tourist office for current events.

🔒 Shopping

Zacatecas is known for silver and leather products and the colorful *sarape* (a blanket with an opening for a head). Try along Arroyo de la Plata (and its indoor market) and at **Casa de las Artesanías** (Plazuela Miguel Auza 312) and **Fonart** (www.fonart.gob.mx; Hidalgo 111; ⊘10am-8pm Mon-Fri, to 7pm Sat, to 5pm Sun).

Centro Platero JEWELRY

(☑492-899-09-94; www.centroplaterodezacatecas. com; ⊘10am-5pm Mon-Fri, to 2pm Sat) The Za-catecas silversmith industry lives on in workshops at the Centro Platero, a few kilometers east of town on the road to Guadalupe at the converted 18th-century Ex-Hacienda de Bernardez. Here, young artisans produce various designs, from the traditional to the funky contemporary. To get here, it's easiest to take a taxi (around M$60). Alternatively, shop in its **gallery** (☑492-925-35-50; Villalpando 406; ⊘10am-8pm Mon-Sat, to 6pm Sun) in town.

ℹ️ Information

Banks in the center have ATMs and change cash and trave'rs checks. Public telephones are at Callejón de las Cuevas, off Avenida Hidalgo. Most internet cafes charge around M$15 per hour for internet access.

Hospital Santa Elena (☑492-924-29-28; Av Guerrero 143)

Post Office (Allende 111; ⊘8am-4pm Mon-Fri, to 2pm Sat)

Tourist Office (www.zacatecastravel.com; Av Hidalgo s/n; ⊘9am-9pm Mon-Sat, to 6pm Sun) This information kiosk is run by Securz, the municipal tourist organization, and offers maps and information. Ask for a copy of Agenda Cultural, an excellent month-by-month listing.

ℹ️ Getting There & Away

AIR

Zacatecas' airport is 20km north of the city. **Volaris** (www.volaris.com) has budget flights between Zacatecas and Los Angeles, San Francisco and Chicago. **American Airlines** (www. aa.com) also offers flights to Dallas.

BUS

Zacatecas' main bus station is on the southwest edge of town, around 3km from the center. Deluxe, 1st- and 2nd-class buses operate to/from here. Deluxe and 1st-class companies include ETN, Ómnibus de México, and Futura/Chihuahuenses. The main 2nd-class company is

BUSES FROM ZACATECAS

DESTINATION	FARE (M$)	DURATION (HR)	FREQUENCY (DAILY)
Aguascalientes	180-189	2-3	hourly
Durango	350-470	4½-7	hourly
Guadalajara	465-615	4-7	hourly
León	315-410	3-4	4
Mexico City (Terminal Norte)	765-825	6-8	frequent
Monterrey	480-630	7-8	14
Querétaro	490-640	5-6¼	14
San Luis Potosí	235	3-3½	hourly

Zacatecas Jerez (the latter has frequent departures to Jerez, as does Ómnibus de México).

Some buses to nearby destinations including Villanueva (for La Quemada) leave from **Plaza del Bicentenario** (Blvd López Mateos).

See the table for daily departures from the main bus terminal. For Guanajuato, take a León bus and change there for Guanajuato.

✈ Getting Around

The easiest way to get to/from the airport is by taxi (M$350 to M$400).

Taxis from the bus station to the center of Zacatecas cost around M$45. Bus 8 from the bus station (M$5) runs directly to the cathedral. Heading out of the center, catch a 'route 8' bus heading south on Villalpando.

La Quemada

The impressive **ruins** (M$46; ⊘ 9am-5pm) of La Quemada stand on a hill overlooking a broad valley 45km south of Zacatecas, 2.5km east of the Zacatecas–Guadalajara road. The remote and scenic setting makes the ruins well worth the day trip from Zacatecas. The area is known to have rattlesnakes; keep an eye – and ear! – out.

The exact purpose of the site is extremely vague. Many suppositions surround the area – one theory is that it was where the Aztecs halted during their legendary wanderings toward the Valle de México. What is known for sure is that the constructions were destroyed by fire – and thus they came to be called La Quemada (meaning 'burned city').

The modern **site museum** (site & museum M$50; ⊘ 9am-5pm) has interesting archaeology exhibits and an excellent video (with English subtitles). It's worth heading here first to contextualize the area and view the museum's miniature site model to get your bearings for your wanderings.

La Quemada was inhabited between about AD 300 and 1200, and it is estimated to have peaked between 500 and 900 with as many as 3000 inhabitants. Around 400 it was part of a regional trade network linked to Teotihuacán, but fortifications suggest that La Quemada later tried to dominate trade in this region.

Of the main structures, the nearest to the site entrance is the **Salón de las Columnas** (Hall of the Columns), probably a ceremonial hall. Slightly further up the hill are a **ball court**, a steep **offerings pyramid** and an equally steep staircase leading toward the site's upper levels. From the upper levels of the main hill, a path leads westward for about 800m to a spur hilltop (the highest point) with the remains of a cluster of buildings called **La Ciudadela** (the Citadel). To return, follow the defensive wall and path back around to the museum. Take water and a hat; it's mighty exposed out there.

✈ Getting There & Away

From Zacatecas's Plaza del Bicentenario, board a combi bus for Villanueva (M$40) and ask beforehand to be let off at *las ruinas;* you'll be dropped at the turnoff; it's a 2.5km walk to the site entrance. Returning to Zacatecas, you may have to wait a while for a bus – don't leave the ruins too late.

AROUND ZACATECAS

Guadalupe

🕿 492 / POP 100,000 / ELEV 2272M

About 10km east of Zacatecas, Guadalupe boasts a fascinating historic former monastery, the **Convento de Guadalupe**. The Convento was established by Franciscan monks in the early 18th century as an apostolic college. It developed a strong academic tradition and was a base for missionary work in northern Nueva España until the 1850s. You'll need a couple of hours to wander through the monastery. A quaint plaza, Jardín Juárez, forms a pretty front setting to the convent.

Visitors can enter two parts of the convento: the impressive **church**, which attracts pilgrims to honor the country's beloved Virgin, and **Museo Virreinal de Guadalupe** (Jardín Juárez Oriente; M$52, Sun free; ⊘ 9am-6pm Tue-Sun) (which is integral to the convent itself), and features one of Mexico's best colonial art collections. It houses the building's original religious paintings by Miguel Cabrera, Juan Correa, Antonio Torres and Cristóbal Villalpando. Wandering through the building is a delight; note the extraordinary perspectives in the paintings in the Cloister of San Fransisco. Visitors can see part of the library and its 9000 original volumes (the oldest dates to 1529 and thousands are in storage), and step into the stunning choir on the church's upper floor, with its fine carved and painted chairs. From here, you can peer into the gilded and beautifully decorated 19th-century Capilla de Nápoles. The chapel opens for special occasions only.

The museum hosts the **Festival Barroco**, a cultural festival, at the end of September and the town holds an annual fair during the first two weeks of December, focused on the **Día de la Virgen de Guadalupe** (December 12).

Regular Transportes de Guadalupe buses run between Zacatecas and Guadalupe (M$6, 20 minutes); wait at the bus stop on Blvd López Mateos across from Plaza del Bicentenario. A taxi between Zacatecas and Guadalupe costs around M$80.

Baja California

Includes ➜

Tijuana 702
Ensenada 710
Mexicali 715
Guerrero Negro 717
San Ignacio 718
Santa Rosalía 720
La Paz 727
Cabo Pulmo 733
Cabo San Lucas 737
Todos Santos 740

Best Tours

➜ Whale Shark Mexico (p727)

➜ Red Travel Mexico (p727)

➜ Sergio's Sportfishing Center (p711)

➜ Malarrimo Eco Tours (p717)

➜ Ecoturismo Kuyimá (p720)

Best Places to Stay

➜ Bungalows Breakfast Inn (p738)

➜ La Damiana Inn (p724)

➜ Casa Natalia (p734)

➜ El Ángel Azul (p729)

➜ Palapas Ventana (p732)

Why Go?

Baja, the earth's second-longest peninsula, offers over 1200km of the mystical, ethereal, majestic and untamed. Those lucky enough to make the full Tijuana to Los Cabos trip will find that the Carretera Transpeninsular (Hwy 1) offers stunning vistas at every turn. The middle of nowhere is more beautiful than you ever imagined, and people are friendly, relaxed and helpful – even in the border towns. Side roads pass through tiny villages and wind drunkenly along the sides of mountains. Condors carve circles into an unblemished blue sky. Some people simply sip drinks and watch the sun disappear into the Pacific. Some choose to feel the rush of adrenalin as they surf that perfect wave. Others walk through sherbet-colored canyons or stare up at the night's canopy of scattered-diamond stars. Whichever way you choose to take it, you'll discover some of Baja's many joys.

When to Go
Cabo San Lucas

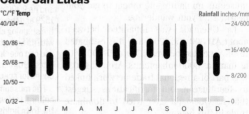

Jan–Mar Flowers bloom, things get green. Whales and whale sharks play, and big waves delight surfers.

Aug–Sep Beaches all but empty. You'll have Baja all to yourself, but it's hot – even in the shade.

Oct–Nov Party-goers, don't miss Sammy Hagar's birthday bash or the Día de Muertos fiesta.

Baja California Highlights

 **Kayaking to Espíritu Santo** (p727) as the big Baja sun drops into the bay.

 **Sipping, swilling and savoring the** bucolic delights of the **Ruta del Vino** (p706) in northern Baja's unspoiled Valle de Guadalupe.

 **Taking the plunge** at mystical **Las Sirenitas** (p733), in Cabo Pulmo, home to the Sea of Cortez' only living coral reef.

 **Marveling at the** hundreds of ancient cave paintings at the **Sierra de San Francisco** (p719).

 **Crossing the** world's most crossed border in **Tijuana** (p702) to eat, drink or shop to your heart's content.

 **Enjoying the** cosmopolitan charms of the delightful small coastal town of **Loreto** (p723).

 **Taking a sunset** cruise in **Cabo San Lucas** (p737) as the sun plunges into the Pacific.

 **Perusing the** galleries on arty Boulevard Mijares in the heart of **San José del Cabo** (p734).

History

Before Europeans arrived, an estimated 48,000 mobile hunter-gatherers were living in today's Baja; their mysterious murals still grace caves and canyon walls. European settlement failed to reach Baja until the Jesuit missions of the 17th and 18th centuries, and the missions soon collapsed as European-introduced diseases ravaged the indigenous people. Ranchers, miners and fishers were the next to arrive. During the US prohibition era of the 1920s, Baja became a popular south-of-the-border destination for gamblers, drinkers and other 'sinners'. Today, the region is growing in economic power, population and popularity, albeit with problematic ecological and environmental consequences.

🛈 Getting There & Around

There are six official border crossings from the US state of California to Baja (p764).

Mexican mainland, US and international flights leave from and arrive at La Paz, Loreto and San José del Cabo. Ferries from Santa Rosalía and Pichilingue, near La Paz, connect Baja California to the mainland by sea.

Air-conditioned, nonsmoking and reasonably priced buses operate daily between towns all along the peninsula; however, car travel is often the only way to reach isolated villages, mountains and beaches. You can rent cars in larger cities and major tourist destinations.

Highways are good and there are few toll roads. Drivers using the scenic (*cuota;* toll highway) route to Ensenada will need M$31; the Tijuana–Mexicali route costs M$170. Denominations larger than US$20 or M$200 are not accepted.

NORTHERN BAJA

Tijuana, Mexicali and Tecate form the northern border of an area known as La Frontera, which extends as far south as San Quintín on the west and San Felipe on the east. Increasingly, the Ruta del Vino (between Ensenada and Tecate) is gaining Napa Valley–like fame for its boutique wines. Though northern Baja's border cities and beaches are undeniably hedonistic, Tijuana and Mexicali are also major manufacturing centers.

Tijuana

📞 664 / POP 1.8 MILLION

Tijuana boasts the 'most crossed border in the world,' and in many ways is a typical border town with its vibrant cocktail of cultures, vigorous nightlife, great range of restaurants and bars, and sleazy red light district. In recent years high-profile murders related to drug cartels have made the headlines and scared off tourists even though, in reality, they are almost never a target. One result was that vendors on the famous souvenir strip of Avenida Revolución suffered dramatically. Although many remain, this lack of day trippers from the US has resulted in lower rents and a positive: the emergence of a dynamic urban art scene with several *pasajes* (passages) off La Revo (as it is commonly known) now home to contemporary galleries and arty cafes. Another area that is witnessing a revamp, particularly in terms of cool new restaurants, is Zona Río, the upscale commercial center that runs alongside the river.

History

At the beginning of the 20th century, TJ was literally just a mud hole. Prohibition drove US tourists here for booze, gambling, brothels, boxing and cockfights, causing Tijuana's population to balloon to 180,000 by 1960. With continued growth have come the inevitable social and environmental problems. Today the drug and illegal-immigrants trade into the US are the city's biggest concerns, although in 2015 the latter had dropped to its lowest figures in close to two decades due to enhanced border security combined with demographic changes and an overall improved economy in Mexico.

👁 Sights & Activities

⭐ **Museo de las Californias**   MUSEUM
(Museum of the Californias; ☎ from US 011-52-664-687-9600; www.cecut.gob.mx; Centro Cultural Tijuana; cnr Paseo de los Héroes & Av Independencia; adult/child under 12yr M$27/free; ⏰10am-6pm Tue-Sun; 🅿♿) The Museo de las Californias chronicles the history of Baja California from prehistoric times to the present. The exhibit kicks off with replica cave paintings, then covers important historical milestones, illustrated in many cases by realistic dioramas and scale models, including replicas of a 16th-century ship, several missions and even a freestone chapel.

Pasaje Rodríguez   ARTS CENTER
(Av Revolución, btwn Calles 3a & 4a; ⏰noon- 10pm) Once lined with souvenir shops, this atmospheric arty alley reflects TJ's growing urban

art scene. The walls are painted with vibrant graffiti style murals – the perfect backdrop to the boho style cafes, music bars, bookstores and craft shops.

Vinícola L.A. Cetto
WINERY

(L.A. Cetto Winery; 📞664-685-30-31; www.cetto wines.com; Cañón Johnson 2108; tour & tasting US$2; ⊙10am-5pm Mon-Sat) Still operated by descendants of Italian immigrants who arrived in Baja in 1926, this winery offers tours and tasting. L.A. Cetto produces a range of tasty varietals, as well as sparkling wines and a decent brandy.

⭐ Festivals & Events

Tijuana has a busy calendar of annual celebrations and events.

Expo Artesanal
ARTS

(www.expoartesanal.com.mx; Centro Cultural; cnr Paseo de los Héroes & Av Independencia; ⊙20-24 May) A superb arts and crafts festival held at the Cultural Center with handicrafts for sale from all over Mexico.

International Craft Beer Festival
BEER

(www.facebook.com/TjBeerFest; ⊙1-7 Jul) This boozy festival serves some of the best beers, both new and old. Mix with Clamato for the true Mexican experience.

Feria del Platillo Mexicano
FOOD

(Mexican Food Festival; 🍴) This one day festival has been held annually on the last Sunday of September since 1982. Head for Avenida Revolución where tables wobble under the weight of plates piled high with goodies just waiting to be gobbled down.

Expo Tequila
TEQUILA

(Tequila Festival; www.expo-tequila.com; ⊙mid-Oct) Your chance to become a tequila pro with a vast variety available for tasting and purchase.

🛏 Sleeping

The cheapest rooms in Tijuana are sometimes shared with, ahem, hourly rate clientele, so be wary. La Revo can be noisy, so try the side streets or prepare to sleep with a pillow on your head.

Hotel Baja
HOTEL $

(📞664-688-22-88; Calle 5a 8163; s/d M$390/540; 🅿🌀❄🛜) Opened in 2014, this small modern hotel, just off La Revo, has motel-style rooms set around a small astro turf garden. The decor is a dazzle of green-and-white

---

> ### BAJA SAFETY
>
> In Baja California, basic caution and awareness, such as keeping valuables (including surfboards) out of sight and doors locked, will minimize risk. Most serious crime is not aimed at tourists, and of that, most is crime of opportunity. Border towns such as Tijuana have received awful press due to drug-trade-related killings and La Paz had a spate of drug related homicides in early 2015. However, in both cases, tourists have rarely been affected, and Baja California Sur remains one of the safest states in all of Mexico.
>
> Sanitation standards in Baja are higher than in other states, and water – even tap water – is usually safe to drink.

paintwork and, while the rooms are on the small size, the bathrooms are spacious with walk-in showers.

Hotel Nelson
HISTORIC HOTEL $

(📞664-685-43-02; Av Revolución 721; s/d/tr M$450/530/645; 🅿🌀❄🛜) The friendly Nelson is a longtime favorite, with high ceilings and 1950s-era touches, such as a real live barbershop of old. The carpeted rooms are slightly scuffed but come with color TV, and some have a view of the (less-than-soothing!) Avenida Revolución.

Hotel Caesar's
HISTORIC HOTEL $$

(📞664-685-16-06; www.hotelcaesars.com.mx; Av Revolución 1079; s/d M$600/750; 🅿🌀❄🛜) If walls could talk! This is Tijuana's most famous historic hotel, dating from the 1920s prohibition era when it was popular with movie stars from over the border. Today, only the facade reflects these belle epoque days; the rooms are large, modern, carpeted and, in fairness, fairly anonymous. But the price is good and the adjacent restaurant is one of the best in town.

Hotel La Villa de Zaragoza
MOTEL $$

(📞664-685-18-32; www.hotellavilla.biz; Av Madero 1120; s/d M$680/770; 🅿🌀❄@🛜) Rooms here are set around a central courtyard and car park, typical motel-style, and the decor is predictably business-style bland with a predominantly cream-and-brown color scheme. However, the location is central yet quiet, rooms are immaculate and clean and there's a good on-site restaurant, plus room service.

Tijuana

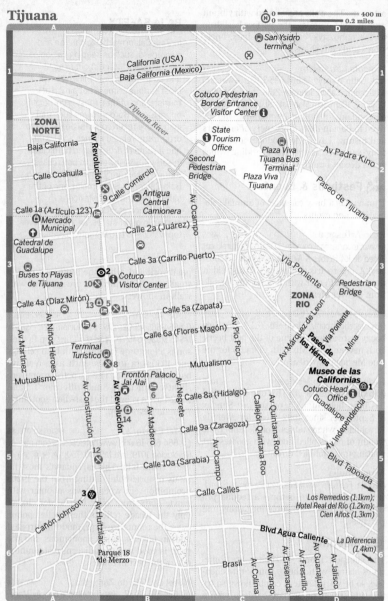

Hotel Real del Río HOTEL $$$

(☏ 664-634-31-00; www.realdelrio.com; Av Velasco 1409; r incl breakfast M$900; P❄✳☎) The contemporary building-block style exterior here sets the tone for a slick modern hotel with comfortable carpeted rooms, a gym, a rooftop sundeck for catching the rays and an excellent restaurant and bar; well known among locals for its Sunday brunch. Located in the Zona Río area.

Tijuana

⊙ Top Sights
1 Museo de las Californias D4

⊙ Sights
2 Pasaje Rodríguez B3
3 Vinícola L.A. Cetto A5

⊟ Sleeping
4 Hotel Baja A4
5 Hotel Caesar's B3
6 Hotel La Villa de Zaragoza B4
7 Hotel Nelson A2

⊗ Eating
8 Colectivo 9 .... B4
9 El Museo B2
10 Happy Vegan A3
11 Praga B3
12 Tacos El Gordo A5

⊛ Entertainment
Centro Cultural Tijuana .... (see 1)
Domo Imax .... (see 1)

⊙ Shopping
13 Emporium A3
14 Sanborns B5

✗ Eating

Avoid the places with 'free' drink offers. Head to the eateries listed here for great authentic eats.

★ Colectivo 9   INTERNATIONAL $
(Av Revolución 1265; mains M$55-80; ⊙1-8pm Tue-Thu & Sun, to midnight Fri & Sat; ⓘ) The narrow *pasaje* (passage) approach provides an appropriate taster of what's to come with its hip small boutiques and cafes; the Colectivo comprises nine small restaurants set around a central courtyard and fountain. What do you fancy? Italian, Japanese, Middle Eastern, Mexican, Italian...take your pick, the standard is superb, while the setting has a contemporary urban feel that can seem lacking in downtown TJ.

Tacos El Gordo   TAQUERÍA $
(Av Constitución 1342; tacos M$15; ⊙10am-5pm Mon-Sat) Locals in the know flock to this place (which also happens to be across from the best bakery in town – Panadería La Mejor). Tacos, including succulent grilled beef or goat, tossed with cilantro and fried onions, ensure a constant line of salivating customers.

Praga   CAFE $
(Av Revolución, btwn Calles 4a & 5a; salads M$55, crepes M$58; ⊙8am-11pm Mon-Sat, 9am-9pm Sun; ⓢ) At last! Somewhere in town that serves seriously good coffee, including cappuccinos, macchiatos and espressos. Crepes, croissants, sandwiches and some lightweight salads, like spinach with mozzarella, pear and apple, are also served for those suffering from burrito burnout. Enjoy live jazz on Wed and Sat at 9pm.

Happy Vegan   VEGAN $
(Pasaje Rodríguez, Av Revolución, btwn Calles 3a & 4a; snacks M$35-45; ⊙noon-10pm) This hip little place sells tasty vegan food, including burritos and veg burgers. Bread is homemade and ingredients are organic. There are just four tables but takeaway is available.

Caesar's   ITALIAN $$
(www.caesarstijuana.com; Av Revolución 1927; Caesar salad M$90, mains M$110-120; ⊙noon-10:30pm Mon-Wed, to midnight Thu-Sat, to 9pm Sun) Step inside and you are transported to the 1950s. Sepia pics of Hollywood movie stars line the walls, while the dark wood decor oozes elegance. The Caesar salad (M$110), prepared with panache at your table, was apparently invented here by the restaurant's founder Caesar Cardini, an Italian immigrant from the 1920s.

The owners also run an Italian-style *trattoria* across the road.

El Museo   MEXICAN $$
(Av Revolución 506; mains M$120-150) Bear in mind that this restaurant fronts the so-called mariachi square, so whispering sweet nothings to your sweetheart may be tricky. Aside from this, El Museo is a great place with good food and plenty of atmosphere. If you are here between August and October, *chiles rellenos* (stuffed peppers) are the specialty with a filling of meat, cheese or fish.

★ La Diferencia   MODERN MEXICAN $$$
(☎664-634-70-78; www.ladiferencia.com; Blvd Sánchez Taboada 10521, Zona Río; mains M$160-200; ⊙7.30am-10pm Mon-Thu, to 11pm Fri & Sat, to 6pm Sun; ⓢ) This restaurant specializes in entomophagy, particularly between April and June when there are up to nine edible insects available. If toasted grasshoppers

RUTA DEL VINO & VALLE DE GUADALUPE

You can skip Tijuana's long lines and treat yourself to some beautiful scenery by entering Mexico via Tecate. The border crossing (open 6am to 10pm) is far less congested, and south of Tecate lies the Ruta del Vino in the intoxicatingly beautiful Valle de Guadalupe (Hwy 3). Maps of the wine route (available at local hotels, tourist offices and wineries) will help you locate the vineyards.

Dedicated drinkers should designate a driver first, as 90-plus wineries and one brewery await. If you don't fancy driving, **Baja Wine & Sun** (☑ 646-177-12-50; www.baja winesun.com; Ensenada; tours US$40) is just one of several reputable tour companies that organize wine tours in the region. Start at the landmark **Cuauhtémoc Moctezuma Heineken Mexico Brewery** (☑ 665-654-94-90; www.cuamoc.com; cnr Calles Hidalgo & Obregón, Tecate; ☺ 10am-5pm Mon-Fri, to 2pm Sat) FREE, which produces Tecate, Dos Equis, Carta Blanca, Bohemia and Sol, among others, and is now under Heineken's umbrella. Tours are run by appointment only at noon and 3pm Monday to Friday, and 11am and 2pm Saturday. Alternatively, just order a brew from the bar. The best place to stay in Tecate is the **Estancia Inn Hotel** (☑ 665-521-30-66; www.estanciainn.com.mx; Blvd Benito Juárez 1450, Encanto Norte s/n; r M$950; P ☏), which has attractive, carpeted rooms with large walk-in showers, and a good restaurant.

From Tecate, the first winery you come to heading southward (albeit after around 70km) is Mexico's largest producer, **L.A. Cetto** (☑ 646-175-23-63; www.lacetto.com; Carretera Tecate-El Sauzal Km 73.5; tour & tastings M$25; ☺ 9am-5pm). It runs tours every half hour, which include the tasting of four wines, one being its highlight cabernet sauvignon. It also offers olive oil, bread and local aged cheese.

Due south of here is **Bibayoff** (☑ 646-176-10-08; www.bibayoff.net; Carretera Franciso Zarco-El Tigre Km 9.5; tastings US$5; ☺ 10am-4pm Tue-Sun), a boutique winery off the beaten path. Its small museum recounts the fascinating history of the Russians who came here in the early 1900s (the current owner is a descendant). Be sure to ask for a taste of the fruity moscatel.

Continuing toward Ensenada make a stop at **Castillo Ferrer** (☑ 646-132-03-56; www. castilloferrer.com; Carretera Ensenada-Tecate Km 86.3; tastings 2-4 wines M$50-100; ☺ noon-6pm Mon-Thu, to 7pm Fri-Sun). This small winery produces just 12,000 bottles a year: its Aurum, a blended cabernet sauvignon and tempranillo is particularly noteworthy. Taste wines on the terrace accompanied by Italian-inspired light eats that includes mouthwatering rosemary-infused *focaccia* served warm with a platter of local cheese and cold cuts. Just over the road from here **El Pinar de 3 Mujeres** (vinicola3mujeres@gmail. com; Carretera Tecate-Ensenada Km 87; set menu M$295; ☺ 1-6pm Apr-Oct), named after the three women owners and winemakers, combines a winery, restaurant and craft shop; meals are served under the trees with scenic vineyard views. Continuing on the highway, **Liceaga** (☑ 646-155-32-81; www.vinosliceaga.com; Carretera Tecate-San Antonio de las Minas Km 93.5; tastings M$150; ☺ 11am-6pm) is a well-established winery with a range of wines and the valley's only true *grappa* (a strong spirit distilled from grape skins or stems). The tasting fee includes a plate of bread and cheese.

Continuing south, make a stop at the tour center for **Santo Tomás** (☑ 646-155-31-37; www.santo-tomas.com; Carretera Tecate-El Sauzal Km 73; tour & tastings US$20; ☺ 10am-5pm). A 50ft wall of winebottles backs the sparkling tasting room, where the bar is creatively made from an unused wine press. On the tour note the fermenting tanks that double as chalkboards (listing types of grape, their leaf patterns, wine processes, etc). There's also a video presentation and wine-specific laser show.

For those ready to turn in for the night but not ready to leave the valley, **La Villa del Valle** (☑ 646-156-80-07; www.lavilladelvalle.com; Carretera Tecate-San Antonio de las Minas Km 88; r from US$245; P ☻ ✷ ☏) is a delightful boutique B&B with spectacular views of the valley...and it owns the **Corazón de Tierra** (☑ 646-156-80-30; www.corazondetierra.com; Carretera Tecate-San Antonio de las Minas Km 88; menu M$880; ☺ 1.30-4.30pm & 6.30-8.30pm Wed-Mon), perhaps the finest dining in the Ensenada area. The restaurant looks out over picturesque rolling vineyards and hillsides, and the juxtaposition of rough-hewn timbers and starched tablecloths fits the rustic vineyard motif to a T.

don't tickle your fancy, the menu has a range of superbly prepared innovative (and decorative) dishes and appetizers, like chicken broth with chilies, corn and squash blossom. Dine in a courtyard setting, complete with bubbling fountain and a canary in a cage.

Cien Años MODERN MEXICAN $$$
(☑664-634-30-39; Av Velasco 2331, Zona Río; mains M$235-250; ☺7:30am-11pm Mon-Sat, to 5pm Sun; 🐾) Enjoy delicious and innovative *alta cocina Mexicana* (contemporary Mexican cuisine) as well as traditional dishes such as *sopa Azteca* with avocado and tortilla strips, *crepes de huitlacoche* (made from a type of corn fungus) with a creamy pistachio-flavored sauce and *chiles rellenos* with shrimps and lobster bisque. Ask the waiter to prepare the classic *salsa de molcajete* (roasted salsa made with a traditional Mexican mortar and pestle) at your table.

Drinking

Drinkers in TJ may feel like hounds let loose in a fire-hydrant factory. The bars and clubs off Calle 6a are packed at weekends.

Los Remedios CANTINA
(www.losremedios.mx; Av Rivera 2479; ☺1:30pm-1:30am) Enjoy fabulous festive decor at this cavernous cantina with its bullfighting posters, classic '50s movie posters, colorful paper flags and ceiling papered with lotto tickets. You can't miss the canary yellow facade right on the roundabout in Zona Río. Live music at weekends.

☆ Entertainment

If you're in TJ you owe it to yourself to let loose, if only to pay perfectly good money for a photo of yourself on one of the zebra-painted donkeys. Tourist info will have details of current events and performances.

Centro Cultural Tijuana ARTS CENTER
(CECUT; ☑from US 011-52-664-687-9600; www.cecut.gob.mx; cnr Paseo de los Héroes & Av Independencia; ☺9am-7pm Mon-Fri, 10am-7pm Sat & Sun; 🖼) Tijuana's sophisticated arts and cultural center would make any comparably sized city north of the border proud. It houses an art gallery, the superb Museo de las Californias (p702), a theater, and the globular cinema **Domo Imax** (www.cecut.gob.mex; Centro Cultural Tijuana; cnr Paseo de los Héroes & Av Independencia; tickets from M$50; ☺1-11pm Tue-Sun), which shows predominantly arthouse movies.

🛍 Shopping

Tijuana is great for souvenirs, but be cautious when buying gold and silver as much of it is fake (at those prices it would have to be, right?). You'll note the many drugstores here; they specialize in selling discounted generic pharmaceuticals to US citizens.

Emporium JEWELRY
(☑664-685-13-24; Av Revolución 1025; ☺9am-7pm daily) This is one of the few places with fair silver prices that are already marked, plus the English-speaking owner is knowledgeable and not too pushy.

Sanborns DEPARTMENT STORE
(www.sanborns.com.mx; Av Revolución 1102; ☺7:30am-11pm Sun-Thu, to 1am Fri & Sat) This department store has a decent selection of newspapers and magazines from the USA and Mexico. Note the extended opening hours.

ℹ Information

DANGERS & ANNOYANCES

If you're street smart and not after trouble, then it is unlikely you'll have problems. Touts are sometimes irksome but they deserve a respectful 'no' – they are trying to make a living in a place that has seen a huge downturn in tourism.

Don't drink on the streets. As in any big city, being plastered late at night can invite trouble.

Coyotes and *polleros* (both mean 'people smugglers') congregate along the river west of the San Ysidro crossing. After dark, avoid this area and Colonia Libertad, east of the crossing.

EMERGENCY
Tourist Assistance Hotline (☑078)

INTERNET RESOURCES
See Tijuana (www.seetijuana.com) A Tijuana tourism site.

MEDICAL SERVICES
Hospital General (☑664-684-00-78; Av Padre Kino, Zona Río) Northwest of the junction with Avenida Rodríguez.

MONEY
Use caution when changing money, especially at night. Everyone accepts US dollars and most banks have ATMs.

TOURIST INFORMATION
Cotuco Visitor Center (☑664-685-31-17; www.descubretijuana.com; Av Revolución, btwn Calle 3a & Calle 4a; ☺9am-6pm Mon-Sat) There is also a visitor center at the border (☑664-607-30-97; www.descubretijuana.com; ☺9am-6pm Mon-Sat, 9am-3pm Sun) and a head office

(☎ 664-684-05-37; www.descubretijuana.com; ste 201, Paseo de los Héroes 9365; ☺ 9am-6pm Mon-Fri) on Paseo de los Héroes.

State Tourism Office (Secretaría de Turismo del Estado; ☎ 664-682-33-67; www.descubre bajacalifornia.com; Alarcón 1572, Zona Río; ☺ 8am-8pm Mon-Fri, 9am-1pm Sat) This is the main state tourism office in town.

ⓘ Getting There & Away

Mexican tourist permits are available 24 hours a day at the San Ysidro–Tijuana border's *Instituto Nacional de Migración* (INM) office at a cost of US$23. They can be issued for up to 180 days.

AIR

Aeroméxico (☎ 664-684-92-68, 664-683-84-44; www.aeromexico.com) Aeroméxico serves many mainland Mexican destinations, and has nonstop flights to La Paz and flights to Tucson and Phoenix in the USA.

Aeropuerto Internacional General Abelardo L Rodríguez (☎ 664-607-82-00; www.tijuana-airport.com; Carretera Aeropuerto-Otay Mesa) The airport is in Mesa de Otay, east of the city.

BUS

The main bus terminal, about 5km southeast of downtown, is the **Central Camionera** (☎ 664-621-29-82), where **Elite** (www.autobuseselite.com.mx) and **Estrella Blanca** (www.estrella blanca.com.mx) offer 1st-class buses with air-con and toilets. Destinations in mainland Mexico include Guadalajara (M$1620, 36 hours) and Mexico City (M$1759, 44 hours, 12 daily, hourly). **ABC** (www.abc.com.mx) and **Auto Transporte Águila** (www.autobusesaguila.com) operate mostly 2nd-class buses to mainland Mexico's Pacific coast and around Baja California.

Suburbaja (☎ 664-688-00-45) local buses use the handy downtown **Antigua Central Camionera** (cnr Av Madero & Calle 1a), with buses leaving for Tecate (M$50 to M$65, one hours, every 15 minutes).

For border crossings by bus, **Mexicoach** (p710) runs frequently (US$5 one way, US$8 round trip) from its **San Ysidro terminal** (☎ 619-428-62-00; 4570 Camino de la Plaza) to Tijuana's

Terminal Turístico (☎ 664-685-14-70; Av Revolución 1025) between 8am and 6pm. It also runs Playas de Rosarito–bound shuttles from San Ysidro by reservation. Returning shuttles leave from the Rosarito Beach Hotel (M$175, twice daily).

Between 5am and 11pm, buses leave from the **San Diego Greyhound terminal** (☎ 800-231-22-22, in the US 619-515-1100; www.greyhound.com; 120 West Broadway, San Diego) and stop at **San Ysidro** (☎ in the US 619-428-1194; 799 East San Ysidro Blvd) en route to Tijuana's Central Camionera bus terminal or the airport. Fares from San Diego/San Ysidro to the Central Camionera or airport are US$6.50 one way, US$12 for the round trip.

CAR & MOTORCYCLE

The San Ysidro border crossing, a 10-minute walk from downtown Tijuana, is open 24 hours, but motorists may find the Mesa de Otay crossing (also open 24 hours) less congested; it's 15km to the east of San Ysidro.

Rental agencies in San Diego are the cheapest option, but most of them only allow journeys as far as Ensenada. Renting a car in Tijuana or taking the bus may be your best option for heading further south.

TROLLEY

San Diego's popular **trolley** (www.sdmts.com) runs from downtown San Diego through to San Ysidro (US$2.25) every 15 minutes from about 5am to midnight. From San Diego's Lindbergh Field airport, city bus 992 (US$2.25) goes to the Plaza America trolley stop in downtown San Diego, across from the Amtrak depot.

ⓘ Getting Around

For about M$10, local buses go everywhere, but the slightly pricier route taxis are much quicker. To get to the Central Camionera take any 'Buena Vista,' 'Centro' or 'Central Camionera' bus from Calle 2a, east of Avenida Constitución. Alternately, take a gold-and-white 'Mesa de Otay' route taxi from Avenida Madero between Calles 2a and 3a (M$12). Regular taxis will charge about M$75 for rides in and around Avenida Revolucíon or the Zona Río. The airport is about M$200, but always double check first.

BUSES FROM TIJUANA

DESTINATION	FARE (M$)	DURATION (HR)	FREQUENCY (DAILY)
Ensenada	155	1½	frequent
Guerrero Negro	1400	12	3
La Paz	2385	24	3
Loreto	2195	18	3
Mexicali	260	2¾	frequent
Santa Rosalia	1810	16½	2

Playas de Rosarito

[☑] 661 / POP 91,000

Once a deserted, sandy beach and then a Hollywood film location, Playas de Rosarito is finally coming into its own. Developments and condos are everywhere, but despite the construction clamor, Rosarito is a quieter place to party and is an easy day trip (or overnight trip) from Tijuana or San Diego. **Hotel Rosarito** (now the landmark Rosarito Beach Hotel) and its long, sandy beach pioneered local tourism in the late 1920s. **Fox Studios Baja**, built in 1996 for the filming of *Titanic*, is still a popular filming location.

Boulevard Juárez, Rosarito's only major street (and part of the Transpeninsular) has many restaurants, clubs and hotels where the prices balloon to the outrageous during spring break. Don't miss having an amble on the sand and a cold beer at one of the many seafront bars.

[⌷] Sleeping

Hotel del Sol Inn   HOTEL $$

([☑] 661-612-25-52; www.del-sol-inn.com; Blvd Juárez 32; s/d M$800/960; [P][⊖][❄]) The Sol is a motel-style lodging right on the main drag with clean, carpeted rooms with TV, bottled water and simple furniture. Note that prices triple during the short spring-break holiday.

Casa Farolito   B&B $$$

([☑] 619-786-80-00; www.casafarolito.com; San Antonio del Mar; s/d incl breakfast from US$90/135;

[P][⊖][❄][🛜]) Located beachside around 5km north of Playas de Rosarito, this place has bucketfulls of charm. Rooms are all different with just enough colorful Mexican pizzazz to avoid a headache coming on. Perks include a welcome margarita, free use of boogie boards, complimentary beach chairs and parasols, and a slap-up breakfast with *huevos rancheros* the specialty.

[✕] Eating

Tacos El Yaqui   TAQUERÍA $

(cnr Palma & Mar del Norte; tacos M$25; ☉8am-5pm Mon, Tue & Thu, 9am-9:30pm Fri-Sun) This delicious taco stand is so popular that it often closes early when the ingredients run out. Get in line before 4pm if you don't want to risk missing out.

[★]**Susanna's**   NORTH AMERICAN $$

(Blvd Juárez 4356; mains US$15-24; ☉1-9:30pm Wed-Mon; [🛜]) Owner Susanna dishes up delightful plates of tasty fare based on fresh seasonal produce spiked with Californian pizzazz. Light salads with innovative dressings, pasta, meat and fish dishes can be enjoyed in a courtyard setting or homey dining room with chintzy furniture and olive green walls. The wines are from Valle de Guadalupe.

El Nido   STEAK $$

(www.elnidorosarito.net; Blvd Juárez 67; mains M$120-160; ☉8am-9:30pm; [🛜][♿]) You can't miss the vast rustic frontage of this steakhouse in the center of town. And the atmos-

PUERTO NUEVO

If fresh lobster is your thing, the fishing village of Puerto Nuevo, located just 5km south of Playas de Rosarito, is the dining destination of your dreams. Over 70 no-frills restaurants vigorously compete for punters with prices as low as US$18 for a medium lobster (fried and served in melted butter), plus tortillas, *frijoles* (refried beans), Mexican rice, guacamole and even a margarita for good measure. For the best deals, go to the smaller places on the southern edge of the village, which get less foot traffic and often outdo each other with amazing specials.

phere continues with exposed brick, beams, strings of garlic and a foliage-filled back terrace, complete with aviary. Tortillas are made fresh to order and the menu includes venison, rabbit and chicken, plus the star billing: steak.

❶ Getting There & Around

From downtown Tijuana, *colectivos* (shared cars) for Playas de Rosarito (M$18) leave from Avenida Madero between Calles 3a and 4a. Look for a yellow station wagon with a white triangle on the door. You can catch a **Mexicoach** (☎ 619-428-95-17; www.mexicoach.com) shuttle (M$175) to Tijuana from the parking lot of the Rosarito Beach Hotel twice daily.

Ensenada

☎ 646 / POP 460,000

Ensenada, 108km south of the border, is hedonistic Tijuana's cosmopolitan sister. The city has a quirky mix of just-off-the-boat cruise shippers, drive-by tourists from California, visitors from mainland Mexico and seen-it-all locals. In case you've forgotten you're in Mexico (what with all those US dollars and English menus), just look up: a Mexican flag, so large it's probably visible from space, flutters proudly over the tourist zone. Wander Avenida López Mateos (Calle 1a) and you'll find almost anything ranging from tasteful ceramics to tasteless T-shirts.

Ensenada was the capital of Baja territory from 1882 to 1915, but the capital shifted to Mexicali during the revolution. The city subsequently catered to 'sin' industries until the federal government outlawed gambling in the 1930s. Today, the town is a tourist resort and weekend retreat for more than four million visitors annually.

◉ Sights

★ Riviera del Pacífico   HISTORIC BUILDING

(☎ 646-177-05-94; Blvd Costero; ℗) Opened in the early 1930s as Hotel Playa Ensenada, the extravagant Riviera del Pacífico, a Spanish-style former casino, is rumored to have been a regular haunt of Al Capone. It now houses the small **Museo de Historia de Ensenada** (☎ 646-177-05-94; Blvd Costero; M$10; ⊗ 10am-5pm Mon-Sat, noon-5pm Sun) while the **Casa de Cultura** offers classes, retrospective film screenings and art exhibitions.

Museo del Instituto Nacional de Antropología e Historia   MUSEUM

(Museo del INAH; ☎ 646-178-25-31; Av Ryerson 99; adult/child under 12yr M$10/free; ⊗ 9am-4pm Mon-Fri) Built in 1886 and once the Aduana Marítima de Ensenada, the city's oldest public building now houses this historical and cultural museum. It has a relatively small but comprehensive collection of artifacts, and discusses (mainly in Spanish) the area's history from prehistoric times.

El Mirador   LOOKOUT

Atop the Colinas de Chapultepec, El Mirador offers panoramic views of the city and Bahía de Todos Santos. Climb or drive (note: there's no off-street parking) to this highest point in town, up Avenida Alemán from the western end of Calle 2a in central Ensenada.

☆ Activities

Surfing

Isla de Todos Santos   SURFING

This island off Ensenada's coast (not to be confused with the town near Los Cabos) is where one of the world's top big-wave surfing contests is held each year. **El Martillo** (The Hammer) is legendary, with swells commonly double or triple overhead, even bigger when conditions are right. Boats can be chartered out from the harbor. Prices start at about M$800 per person, four people minimum.

San Miguel   SURFING

(parking M$75) There's not much here but a few campers, a parking lot, and a wonderful point break just offshore. When the waves are big it's an awesome ride.

Fishing & Whale-Watching

Ensenada is known the world over for its excellent sport fishing, though you must have a valid Mexican fishing license (available online at www.bestbajafishing.org) if you want to reel in a live one. Most charter companies also offer whale-watching tours from mid-December to mid-April.

Sergio's Sportfishing Center　　　FISHING

(☑646-178-21-85; www.sergiosfishing.com; day trips from M\$1200; ☺8am-6pm) Well regarded, Sergio's can be found on the sport fishing pier off Ensenada's Malecón. Fishing trips include the necessary gear. Day trips are available as well as private charter trips.

Courses

Spanish School Baja　　　LANGUAGE

(☑646-190-60-49; www.spanishschoolbaja.com; Calle 10, btwn Avs Ruiz & Obregón) Costs start at US\$270 for a week.

Festivals & Events

The events listed here constitute a tiny sample of the 70-plus annual sporting, tourist and cultural happenings. Dates change, so contact tourist offices for details.

Carnaval　　　CARNIVAL

(☺) A Mardi Gras–type celebration 40 days before Ash Wednesday in February when the streets flood with floats and dancers.

Fiesta de la Vendimia　　　WINE

(Grape Harvest Festival; ☺early Aug) Mid-summer wine harvest. Cheers!

International Seafood Fair　　　FOOD

(☺Sep) Sample scrumptious seafood.

Baja 1000　　　RACING

(☺mid-Nov; ☺) Baja's biggest off-road race. See 'truggies' (truck-buggies) tear up the desert to the cheers of just about everyone. The Baja 500 is in June.

Sleeping

Hotel demand can exceed supply at times, particularly at weekends and in summer.

Hotel Cortez　　　HOTEL \$\$

(☑646-178-23-07; www.bajainn.com; Av López Mateos1089; r from M\$1200; 🅿☺✳@🛜🏊) This is a solid choice in a good location with facilities that include a small gym. The (heated) pool is surrounded by lofty trees. Some of the rooms are a tad dark. If you can, go for the premi-

um rooms, with their chic and contemporary look: all earth colors and plush fabrics.

Hotel Santo Tomás　　　HOTEL \$\$

(☑646-178-33-11; hst@bajainn.com; Blvd Costero 609; s/d M\$870/1100; 🅿☺✳🛜) Although the furnishings are a little tired, this vast hotel with its questionable pea-green-and-purple exterior is still a great choice. The quirky lobby has a grand sweeping staircase, an elevator with disco mirrors and a cage of cuddly chinchillas. Rates increase on Friday and Saturday (along with the noise levels outside).

Hotel Bahía　　　HOTEL \$\$

(☑646-178-21-01; www.hotelbahia.com.mx; Av López Mateos 980; r M\$975; 🅿✳🛜🏊) Despite the Stalinist drab exterior, this hotel offers pleasant and spacious carpeted rooms. An attractive pool area with adjacent bar and service direct to your sunbed, is another perk.

Best Western Hotel El Cid　　　HOTEL \$\$\$

(☑646-178-24-01; www.hotelelcid.com.mx; Av López Mateos 993; s/d M\$1123/1504; 🅿☺✳@🛜🏊) This four-star hotel has comfortable rooms with firm beds, a respected restaurant and a lively bar. The bilingual staff are particularly gracious and friendly and the situation is central, in the more upmarket end of town.

Eating

Ensenada's dining options range from corner taco stands to places serving excellent Mexican and international cuisine.

★La Guerrerense　　　TAQUERÍA \$

(www.laguerrerense.com; cnr Avs Alvarado & López Mateos; tacos US\$4.50; ☺10.30am-5pm Wed-Mon) Sabina Bandera's award-winning seafood stand dates from the 1960s and attracts long lines with its outstanding seafood tacos, juicy ceviche (seafood marinated in lime juice) and *tostadas* (tortilla fried in deep fat). It also produces its own salsa line (US\$5) and there's usually some streetside guitar strumming to add to the atmosphere.

Mariscos El Norteño　　　SEAFOOD \$

(Local 4, mercado de mariscos; tacos M\$30; ☺8am-9pm Mon-Sat, from 7am Sun) You can't go wrong at any of the seafood stalls across from the *mercado de marisco*s (fish market), but this one has plenty of seating and a superb range of salsas including roasted jalapeños and red chili. Try an original Baja-style taco, which is a deep-fried fish or shrimp taco with shredded cabbage in a creamy white sauce.

Ensenada

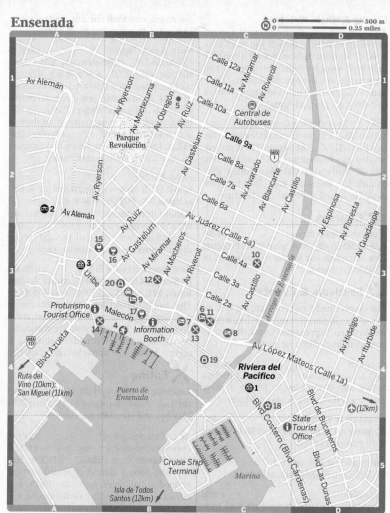

El Parián

MEXICAN **$**

(☎ 646-128-82-32; cnr Calle 4a & Av Castillo; mains M$80-95; ⊗ 7:30am-11:30pm; 🖐) Paper streamers, murals and sherbert-colored furniture give a festive atmosphere to enjoying great enchiladas, quesadillas, burritos, *agua de jamaica* (hibiscus water) and friendly service. Flat-screen TVs in every corner mean you (or the wait staff) never have to miss a moment of that cheesy Mexican soap.

La Guadalajara

MEXICAN **$$**

(Av Macheros 154; mains M$80-110; ⊗ 7am-10pm; 🖐) A great barn of a place famous for its *birria de chivo* (goat stew), but also serves excellent tacos and charcoal grilled meats. Popular with families, the atmosphere is boisterous and noisy with a large open plan kitchen, four TVs, strolling mariachis and decor that has changed little since the opening in 1972.

El Rey Sol

FRENCH **$$$**

(Av López Mateos 1000; mains M$175-250; ⊗ 7am-10:30pm; 🖥) Set within an elegant building's sumptuous interior, replete with flocked wallpaper, chandeliers and stained glass, this landmark restaurant dates from 1947. The cuisine is predominantly French (in-

Ensenada

⊙ Top Sights
1 Riviera del Pacífico C4

⊙ Sights
2 El Mirador... A2
Museo de Historia de
Ensenada......................................(see 1)
3 Museo del Instituto Nacional de
Antropología e Historia A3

⊕ Activities, Courses & Tours
4 Sergio's Sportfishing Center B4
5 Spanish School Baja.............................. B1

⊟ Sleeping
6 Best Western Hotel El Cid.................... C3
7 Hotel Bahía.. B4
8 Hotel Cortez... C4
9 Hotel Santo Tomás................................ B3

✖ Eating
10 El Parián C3
11 El Rey Sol C4
12 La Guadalajara B3
13 La Guerrerense....................................... B4
14 Mariscos El Norteño A4

⊖ Drinking & Nightlife
15 Hussong's Cantina A3
16 Ojos Negros B3
17 Wendlandt B3

⊕ Entertainment
18 Centro Estatal de las Artes...................C4

⊟ Shopping
19 Galería Pérez Meillon C4
20 Tequila Room B3

cluding *escargot)*, but also includes Mexican favorites and pasta. This is a dress-for-dinner kind of place – don't arrive in flipflops.

🍷 Drinking

On weekends most bars and cantinas along Avenida Ruiz are packed from noon to early morning. If that's not your scene, head for one of the many quality hotels and fine restaurants where you're likely to find a laidback spot to sip a margarita (said to have been invented here) or sample a top-shelf tequila.

★**Hussong's Cantina**   CANTINA
(www.cantinahussongs.com; Av Ruiz 113; ⊙11am-2am Tue-Sun) The oldest and perhaps liveliest cantina in the Californias has been serving tequila since 1892. A Friday or Saturday night will be packed with locals, a sprinkling of tourists and touting mariachis. The history is fascinating, so request the leaflet (in English and Spanish).

Wendlandt   BEER HALL
(www.wendlandt.com.mx; Diez 385; ⊙6pm-midnight Tue-Sat) Enjoy craft beers made by the owners, as well as from national and international small breweries; five samplers will cost you just 50 pesos. The surroundings have an urban chic vibe with chunky wood furniture, exposed brick walls and clever quirky lighting incorporating beer bottles.

Ojos Negros   WINE BAR
(Av Ruiz 105; ⊙11am-midnight Tue-Sat, 2-10pm Sun; 🛜) Suffering from margarita melt-down? Then head to this relaxed wine bar for a glass of fruity Passion Meritage, an award-winning red from the owners' vineyards: Bodegas San Rafael. Lounge-like seating, chill-out music and burgundy-washed walls set the scene nicely. Nibbles include gourmet flatbread pizzas.

☆ Entertainment

Centro Estatal de las Artes   ARTS CENTER
(☑646-173-43-07; www.cearte.info; cnr Av Riviera & Blvd Costero; ⊙8am-8pm Mon-Sat, noon-7pm Sun, plus event hours in evening) The Centro Estatal de las Artes has shows and exhibits throughout the year.

🛍 Shopping

Tequila Room   DRINK
(Av López Mateos; ⊙10am-6pm Tue-Thu, to midnight Fri & Sat) The Irish-Mexican owner is passionate about tequila but you won't find any of the more commercial brands here; these are sourced from all over Mexico. Even if you don't fancy a tipple (tastings are free), you can admire the bottles, many of which are art-works in themselves.

Galería Pérez Meillon   HANDICRAFTS
(☑646-175-78-48; Blvd Costero 1094; ⊙9am-5pm) In the Centro Artesanal de Ensenada, this gallery sells authenticated pottery from the Paipai (one of Baja California's indigenous peoples known for fine craftwork, particularly pottery and baskets) and Mata Ortiz (a major pottery center in central north Mexico), and Kumiai weaving.

BAJA CALIFORNIA ENSENADA

❶ Information

EMERGENCY
Municipal Police (☎ 646-176-43-43, 066)
State Police (☎ 066, 646-172-35-30)
Tourist Assistance (☎ 078)

INTERNET RESOURCES
Discover Baja California (www.discoverbaja california.com) The state's tourism site.
Enjoy Ensenada (www.enjoyensenada.com) Ensenada's tourism site.

MEDICAL SERVICES
Sanatorio del Carmen (☎ 646-178-34-77; cnr Av Obregón & Calle 11a)

TOURIST INFORMATION
Proturismo Tourist Office (☎ 646-178-24-11; www.proturismoensenada.org.mx; Blvd Costero 540; ☺ 8am-8pm Mon-Fri, 9am-5pm Sat & Sun) Dispenses maps, brochures and current hotel information. There's an information booth (☎ 646-178-30-70; Plaza Cívica; ☺ Tue-Sun) in the Plaza Cívica.
State Tourist Office (☎ 646-172-54-44; www. descubrebajacalifornia.com; Blvd Costero 1477; ☺ 8am-6pm Mon-Fri, 9am-1pm Sat & Sun) Carries similar information to the Proturismo office.

❶ Getting There & Away

Immigration Office (☎ 646-174-01-64; Blvd Azueta 101; ☺ document delivery 8am-6pm Mon-Fri, document pickup 1-3pm Mon-Fri) The immigration office sells tourist permits for those arriving into the country by boat.

BUS
Central de Autobuses (Av Riveroll 1075) Ten blocks north of Avenida López Mateos, serving far-flung destinations like Guadalajara (M$1400, 36 hours) and Mexico City (M$1800, 48 hours) as well as local Baja destinations.

CAR & MOTORCYCLE
The drive from Tijuana to Ensenada on the scenic (cuota) route has three tolls (total M$95), and a military checkpoint.

❶ Getting Around

The main **taxi stand** (cnr Avenidas López Mateos & Miramar) is at the corner of Avenidas López Mateos and Miramar; taxis also congregate along Avenida Juárez. Most fares within the city cost from M$50 to M$100.

La Bufadora

La Bufadora is a popular 'blowhole' (really a notch in the rock that sprays waves upwards) 40km south of Ensenada. If conditions are right it sends a jet of water up to 30m into the sky, drenching cheering onlookers. Conditions aren't always ideal, but if you're up for a gamble you can catch a taxi (M$175 per person round-trip, minimum four persons) or a shuttle tour (M$190), or drive south on the Transpeninsular to the 'Bufadora' sign, then follow the road all the way around to the Pacific side. Parking costs M$20 and the approach is flanked by souvenir stalls (and touts).

Parque Nacional Constitución de 1857

At the end of a challenging unpaved 43km road out of Ojos Negros (east of Ensenada at Km 39 on Hwy 3), Parque Nacional Constitución de 1857 has beautiful conifers, fields of wildflowers and a sometimes-dry lake, **Laguna Hanson** (Laguna Juárez; ☎ 686-554-44-04, ☺ 8am-3pm) at an altitude of 1200m. *Cabañas* (cabins M$650) or campsites (M$150) are available, but the water may be contaminated by livestock, so bring your own.

BUSES FROM ENSENADA

DESTINATION	FARE (M$)	DURATION (HR)	FREQUENCY (DAILY)
Guerrero Negro	1210	10	3
La Paz	2230	22	3
Mexicali	415	4	12
Playas de Rosarito	125	1	frequent
Tecate	175	2	frequent
Tijuana	155	1½	frequent
Tijuana Airport	280	1¾	frequent

PARQUE NACIONAL SIERRA SAN PEDRO MÁRTIR

Bobcats, deer and bighorn sheep await visitors to San Pedro Mártir national park, but its real claim to fame isn't what's on the ground but what's in the air: this park is one of only six places in the world where the almost-extinct California condor has been successfully reintroduced into the wild. At the time of writing around 38 of these majestic birds call this area home and several chicks have been hatched over the past few years, showing promise for a future recovery.

Even if one of the world's largest birds doesn't soar over your head, there are lots of other reasons to make the detour. Conifers scrape the sky, the air is pine scented and clean, and the (tortuously winding) drive passes through boulder-studded, ethereal landscapes that seem more Martian than something here on earth.

To reach the park, turn left at the sign at approximately Km 140 on the Transpeninsular, south of Colonet. A 100km paved road climbs to the east through an ever-changing desert landscape, affording satisfying vistas all along the way. Camping is possible (no toilets, bring water) in designated areas, but there are no other facilities.

Observatorio Astronómico Nacional (☑646-174-45-80; www.astrossp.unam.mx; ☉10am-1pm) is the country's national observatory, from where it's possible to observe both the Pacific Ocean and the Sea of Cortez. On clear days you can see all the way to the Mexican mainland.

It's a sublime spot for mountain biking, hiking or just getting away from it all, as long as everyone else isn't getting away at the same time – in peak holiday times it can be busy, but it's a beautiful spot any time of year. The park is also accessible by a steeper road east of Km 55.2, 16km southeast of the Ojos Negros junction.

Mexicali

☑686 / POP 690,000

Mexicali is what Tijuana must have been before the tourist boom – gritty, even scary – and most tourists just head southward. The city offers some decent restaurants and some fun nightlife, but be particularly careful around the border areas after dark.

The Zona Hotelera, far safer at night than the border, is on the east side, along Calzada Juárez from Plaza Azteca to Independencia and beyond. In summer, Mexicali is one of the hottest places on earth – stay away, if possible.

◎ Sights

Plaza Constitución is a good place to hear *banda* (big-band music) groups rehearse in the late afternoon – hence its nickname, Plaza del Mariachi. Most of Mexicali's historic buildings are northeast of Calzada López Mateos.

Catedral de la Virgen de Guadalupe   CATHEDRAL
(cnr Av Reforma & Morelos) This cathedral is the city's major religious landmark.

🛏 Sleeping

If you don't fancy sleeping in a hotel that has hourly rate customers, you're best off in the pricier Zona Hotelera.

Araiza   LUXURY HOTEL $$$
(☑686-564-11-00; www.araizahoteles.com; Calz Juárez 2220, Zona Hotelera; d/ste incl breakfast US$125/150; P 🐾 🌐 @ 🛜 🏊) This family-friendly hotel has well-appointed spacious rooms, two excellent restaurants (including Japanese), a bar, tennis courts, a gym and a convention center. For a quieter stay, request a room in the executive wing away from the road and pool area.

🍴 Eating

Atico Cafe   CAFE $
(Zaragoza 1690; snacks from M$45; ☉10am-11pm; 🦖) Escape the big-city frenzy at this chill-out cafe, with its sink-into sofas, board games, moody lighting and vintage-cum-pop culture decor. Light snacks include salads, crepes and comfortingly homemade-style cakes and desserts. Exotic cocktails are another agreeable specialty.

Asadero Acatlan de Juarez MEXICAN $

(cnr Indepencia & Villa Hermosa; tacos M$30-45; ⊙noon-10pm) This real-deal place services the best tacos and *sincronizada* (tortilla-based sandwich) in town; the latter filled with grilled Oaxaca cheese, salty ham and refried beans. Best washed down with a glass of refreshing rice water.

Los Arcos SEAFOOD $$

(☑686-556-09-03; Calafia 454; mains M$126-290; ⊙11am-10pm) Dating from 1977, this is Mexicali's most popular seafood restaurant. The *shrimp culichi* (shrimp in a creamy green chili sauce) is spectacular. Live music brightens the night on Thursday and Friday. Reservations recommended.

ℹ Information

Bancomer (cnr Azueta & Madero; ⊙8:30am-4pm Mon-Fri)

Hospital Hispano-Americano (☑686-552-23-00; Reforma 1000)

State Tourist Office (☑686-566-12-77; www.descubrebajacalifornia.com; Blvd Juárez 1; ⊙8am-6pm Mon-Fri, 9am-1pm Sat) Patient, bilingual staff and plenty of information about regional attractions and events.

Tourist Assistance (☑078)

ℹ Getting There & Away

Mexican tourist permits are available at the main Calexico–Mexicali border crossing 24 hours a day. A second border complex east of downtown is open from 6am to 10pm.

AIR

Aeroméxico (☑686-555-70-47; www.aeromexico.com) Aeroméxico flies to La Paz, Cabo San Lucas and Tijuana.

Aeropuerto Internacional General Rodolfo Sánchez Taboada (☑686-552-23-17; www.aeropuertosgap.com.mx/es/mexicali; Carretera Mesa de Andrade Km 23.5) The airport is 18km east of town.

BUS

Long-distance and mainland bus companies leave from the **Central de Autobuses** (☑686-556-19-03; Calz Independencia 1244; ⊙24hr), near Calzada López Mateos, and Baja-bound buses leave from the **Terminal Turística** (☑686-552-51-00; Av Mexico 343; ⊙24hr), closer to the border. Autotransportes del Pacífico, Norte de Sonora and Elite serve mainland-Mexican destinations, while ABC serves the Baja peninsula.

Greyhound (p859) has offices in Mexicali and directly across the border in Calexico. There are several departures daily from Mexicali to Los Angeles (one way from US$33, round-trip US$65) and 12 to San Diego (one way from US$24, round-trip US$46), as well as other destinations in the US.

CAR & MOTORCYCLE

Vehicle permits are available at the border. The main Calexico–Mexicali border crossing is open 24 hours, while the new crossing east of downtown (built to ease congestion) is open from 6am to 10pm.

ℹ Getting Around

Taxis to the airport cost M$175 to M$200, but may be shared. Agree on the price first.

Most city buses start from Avenida Reforma, just west of Calzada López Mateos; check the placard for the destination. Local fares cost around M$10.

A taxi to the Centro Cívico-Comercial or Zona Hotelera from the border is usually around M$75.

SOUTHERN BAJA

Parts of the state Baja California Sur (southern Baja) look like a Dr Seuss illustration: no plant more so than the funky boojum tree *(cirio)*, which looks like a giant inverted parsnip with some yellow fluff at the top. You can't help but smile. Cardón cacti, ocotillo, cholla and other desert marvels thrive in areas that sometimes don't

BUSES FROM MEXICALI

DESTINATION	FARE (M$)	DURATION (HR)	FREQUENCY (DAILY)
Ensenada	415	4	12
Guerrero Negro	1710	15	2
La Paz	2645	26	2
Loreto	1842	20	3
Mexico City	1950	42	11
Tijuana	260	2¾	frequent

receive any rain for a decade. Look out for crumbling missions, leafy date palms, coconuts and mangrove swamps as you meander southward.

The 25,000-sq-km **Reserva de la Biosfera El Vizcaíno** is one of Latin America's largest single protected areas. It sprawls from the Península Vizcaíno across to the Sea of Cortez and includes the major gray-whale calving areas of Laguna San Ignacio and Laguna Ojo de Liebre, and the Sierra de San Francisco with its stunning pre-Hispanic rock art – more than 60 sites, many of which only archaeologists can view.

The southernmost part of the peninsula contains the cosmopolitan city of La Paz, small seaside towns and villages, and the popular resorts of San José del Cabo and Cabo San Lucas, aka 'Los Cabos.' After the quiet isolation of the state's north, Los Cabos will either be a jarring shock or a welcome relief.

Remember that Baja California Sur state uses mountain time, so it is an hour ahead of Pacific time, used in northern Baja (Baja California state).

Guerrero Negro

☑ 615 / POP 13,000

After the crowds and clamor of the touristy border towns, unassuming Guerrero Negro – a town that sprang up to service the lone salt factory – is a welcome relief. Though the main tourist draw is the proximity to the seasonal migrations of gray whales, there's also excellent bird-watching in the shallow marshes, and the salt factory's odd white crystalline plains are quite beautiful.

🏃 Activities

Guerrero Negro can surprise you. If whales aren't around, try cave-painting viewing in the Sierra de San Francisco, bird-watching or touring the **salt factory**. On the east side of the inlet is a mini Sahara of 3m-to-6m sand dunes made of powdery white sand.

Bird-Watching

Head to the **Old Pier** and *faro* (lighthouse) if you're a bird-watcher, as there is a pleasant 11km drive through salt flats and marshland; prime territory for ducks, coots, eagles, curlews, terns, herons and other birds.

Whale-Watching

During whale-watching season agencies arrange trips on the shallow waters of **Laguna Ojo de Liebre**, where visitors are virtually

BEST CLAMS IN BAJA

Tiny San Quintín is the pismo clam capital, and these mouthwatering morsels are well worth stopping for. Look for 'Almeja Ahumada' signs as you drive southwards and, if time and itinerary permits, stop at one of the roadside stalls for a fire-roasted plate of clams. If you're really a do-it-yourselfer, sharpen your clam rake, get a fishing license (available online at www.bestbajafishing.org) and stay a while.

guaranteed a view of whales in their natural habitat.

Malarrimo Eco Tours   WILDLIFE-WATCHING
(☑ 615-157-01-00; www.malarrimo.com; Blvd Zapata 42; adult/child M$800/650; 🚐) Located beside the hotel of the same name, Malarrimo is one of the most respected and longest standing operators in town and offers four-hour whale-watching tours.

Other Activities

Salt Factory   TOUR
(1-2hr tour per person M$200) Tours of the salt factory can be arranged via any hotel or tour agency in Guerrero Negro.

🛏 Sleeping

The whale-watching season can strain local accommodations; reservations are advisable from January through March.

Hotel Malarrimo   HOTEL $
(☑ 615-157-01-00; www.malarrimo.com; Blvd Zapata 42; s/d M$400/500, campsites M$150, RV sites M$130-200; P🐕❄@🛜) Hot, strong showers and a lot more ambience than the other options in town. Whale headboards and a general whale theme make it impossible to forget why you've come here. There is also a small gift shop, an excellent restaurant, plus whale-watching tours can be arranged. Campsites and RV hookups available.

Terra Sal   MOTEL $$
(615-157-01-33; Emiliano Zapata s/n; s/d incl breakfast M$550/620; P🛜) Located on the approach to town, this place looks like a run-of-the-mill motel, but the rooms are definitely in the classier hotel category with earth colors, chunky wood furniture, mosaic tiling and a choice of either Jacuzzi tubs or walk-in showers. There's a decent restaurant, as well.

Los Caracoles
HOTEL **$$**

(☎615-157-10-88; www.hotelloscaracoles.com.mx; Calz de la República s/n; r M$650; P☻❄@☎) This attractive sand-colored hotel blends well with its desert surroundings, as do the modern rooms and, come to that, the bathrooms – all are decorated in tones of yellow and gold. There's a souvenir shop and several computer terminals for the use of guests.

✕ Eating

Malarrimo
MEXICAN **$$**

(www.malarrimo.com; Blvd Zapata 42; mains M$80-100; ⊙7.30am-10.30pm; ☎) A solid dining choice at this longstanding hotel, serving primarily seafood dishes; the fish soup comes highly recommended. Vegetarian meals are available on request and the adjacent bar and pool table could equal an evening's entertainment in this somewhat sleepy town.

Santo Remedio
MEXICAN **$$$**

(☎615-157-29-09; Carballo Félix; mains M$150-200; ⊙8am-10pm) One of the fancier Guerrero Negro options, with soft lighting, folk art, ocher-washed walls, a pretty patio and a variety of meat and seafood dishes, ranging from T-bone steak to Galician-style octopus.

ℹ Information

Nearly all hotels, restaurants and other services are along Blvd Zapata, including an ATM at Banamex.

Clínica Hospital IMSS (☎615-157-03-33; Blvd Zapata) Guerrero Negro's main medical facility.

ℹ Getting There & Away

Guerrero Negro's tiny airport is 2km north of the state border, west of the Transpeninsular.

Aéreo Calafia (☎615-157-29-99; www.aereo calafia.com.mx; Blvd Zapata; ⊙8am-7pm Mon-Fri, to 4pm Sat) Runs flights to Hermosillo and Isla Cedros, and offers charters.

Bus Station (Blvd Marcello Rubio; ⊙24hr) Offers wide range of bus services throughout Baja.

San Ignacio
☎615 / POP 720

With its lush, leafy date palms and pretty tranquil lagoon, sleepy San Ignacio is a welcome oasis after the endless Desierto de Vizcaíno. Jesuits located the **Misión San Ignacio de Kadakaamán** here, but Dominicans supervised construction of the striking church (finished in 1786) that still dominates the picturesque, laurel-shaded plaza. With lava-block walls nearly 1.2m thick, and surrounded by bougainvillea, this is one of Baja's most beautiful churches. A small self-guided **museum** (Misión San Ignacio de Kadakaamán; ⊙8am-5pm Mon-Fri) **FREE** offers a glimpse of the area's natural history and also recreates the famous cave drawings found in the Sierra de San Francisco; however was closed for restoration at the time of research due to a recent fire.

◉ Sights & Activities

Casa Leree
MUSEUM

(☎615-154-01-58; www.casaleree.com; Morelos 20; ⊙10am-5pm Mon-Sat) Part museum and part bookstore, this beautiful old building sits around a verdant garden with magnificent trees, including a soaring (and shady) *ficus indiga*. The US owner is a wealth of information about the area and has one of the best collections of books on Baja anywhere.

Ecoturismo Kuyima
ADVENTURE SPORTS

(☎615-154-00-70; www.kuyima.com; Plaza Benito Juaréz 9; whale-watching per person US$50; ⊙8am-8pm) This local cooperative on the plaza arranges whale-watching trips to the beautiful Laguna San Ignacio, a protected site, as well as visits to rock-art sites in the surrounding area.

⌂ Sleeping & Eating

San Ignacio has excellent accommodations tucked away beneath its swaying palms.

BUSES FROM GUERRERO NEGRO

DESTINATION	FARE (M$)	DURATION (HR)	FREQUENCY (DAILY)
Ensenada	1210	10	3
La Paz	1385	11	4
Loreto	745	5-6	4
Mexicali	1710	15	2
Mulegé	500	4	4
Tijuana	1400	12	3

BAJA'S BEST BITES...

(...and we don't mean restaurant reviews.) Some of Baja's coolest creatures are well worth getting to know, but don't get too close – these critters are sporting nature's meanest defenses and an encounter could send you to hospital.

Black Widow Spider This pea-sized black spider packs a potent (though rarely fatal) punch. Look for the crimson hourglass on the underside of the abdomen for positive ID.

Portuguese Man O' War Also known as *agua mala* (bad water), these jellyfish are stunningly pretty, but their bright-blue tentacles can sting long after the animal is dead. Don't pick one up on the beach, and minimize risk when participating in water sports by wearing a full-body rash guard or wetsuit.

Scorpion Glowing under UV light, Baja's scorpions sting, especially if stepped on. Shake your shoes in the morning, use netting at night and look before you sleep.

Stingrays Painfully common in the shallows of many popular beaches, the stingray usually flicks its tail and stabs heels or ankles with a poisonous barb. Minimize risk at beaches by wearing surf booties.

Whether you think they're cool or creepy, these are creatures that will rarely cause you harm if they are left alone. For more information, track down a copy of Steven Foster's book *A Field Guide to Venomous Animals and Poisonous Plants*.

The modest cafe-restaurants and kiosks around the plaza are your best best for a quick snack. If you need some energy for the road, dates from the palms cost M$10 to M$30 per bag.

★ **Ignacio Springs**　　　　　　　B&B **$$**
(☑ 615-154-03-33; www.ignaciosprings.com; San Ignacio; d from US$87; P ※) This Canadian-owned B&B comprises eight yurts and three *cabañas*. Idyllically situated fronting the lagoon, the decor ranges from conventional US-style to Aztec ethnic, with brightly colored rugs and ceramics. Breakfast includes homemade breads, preserves and (even) sausages. Kayaks available.

Hotel Desert Inn　　　　　　　HOTEL **$$**
(☑ 615-154-03-00; mmabarca@fonatur.gob.mx; Camino a San Ignacio Km 72; d M$960; P ⊡ ⊛) A modern mission-style hotel with spacious airy rooms decorated in a soothing paint palette of creams, browns and ocher, plus plenty of wardrobe space and large walk-in showers. Rooms are set around a central pool area landscaped with lofty palms and dazzling bougainvillea bushes.

★ **Tootsie's Bar & Grill**　　INTERNATIONAL **$$**
(Francisco y Madera 11; mains US$8-13; ⊙1-9pm Tue-Sun, 3-9pm Mon Dec-May; ☑ ⊞) ⚲ Just not what you expect to find tucked away on a back street near the plaza. The Canadian owner-cum-chef is inventive and accomplished. Ask for her recommendations,

which could be anything from pasta with homemade pesto to Indian dhal with steaming hot chapatis. An organic herb (and soon to be veg) garden contributes to the fresh-from-the-farm flavors.

❶ Getting There & Away

The **Bus Station** (☑ 615 154-04-68) is near the San Lino junction outside of town. Buses pick up passengers here, arriving about every four hours from 5am to 11pm, both north- and southbound to locations such as Tijuana (M$1670), Mexicali (M$1980), La Paz (M$1340) and Cabo San Lucas (M$1625).

Around San Ignacio

Sierra de San Francisco

The sheer quantity of beautiful petroglyphs in this region is impressive, and the ocher, red, black and white paintings remain shrouded in mystery. In recognition of its cultural importance, the Sierra de San Francisco has been declared a Unesco World Heritage site. It is also part of the **Reserva de la Biosfera El Vizcaíno**.

Cueva del Ratón, a cave named for an image of what inhabitants once thought was a rat (or mouse) but is more likely a deer, is the most easily accessible site. Drivers can get there on their own after registering and paying the park entry (M$42) and additional guide fee (M$80 for two people) at the office

CALIFORNIA GRAY WHALES

The migration of gray whales from Siberian and Alaskan waters to the lagoons of Baja is an amazing animal event. In the calving grounds of Laguna Ojo de Liebre and Laguna San Ignacio, 700kg calves will draw their first breaths and begin learning the lessons of the sea from their ever-watchful mothers. The season is long but varies due to the fact that some whales arrive early in the Pacific lagoons, while others take weeks or months to round Land's End and find their favorite bays in the Sea of Cortez.

Peak months to see mothers and calves in the lagoons are February to early April, but the official whale-watching season begins December 15 and lasts until April 15.

If you've got *ballena* (whale) fever, one of these destinations will provide a cure:

➡ Laguna Ojo de Liebre (Scammon's Lagoon)

➡ Laguna San Ignacio

➡ Puerto López Mateos

➡ Puerto San Carlos

of the **Instituto Nacional de Antropología e Historia** (INAH; ☑ 615-154-02-22; ⊗ 8am-5pm Mon-Sat Apr-Oct, daily Nov-Mar), adjacent to the Misión San Ignacio on the plaza in San Ignacio, then picking up their guide in the pueblo closest to the paintings. Bringing a camera costs M$50 per day. INAH fees for guides for other trips start at M$250 per day, and each pack animal adds M$175. These are INAH fees only, and guides themselves charge additional fees.

Those with time should visit the dramatic and well-preserved **Cañón San Pablo**. At **Cueva Pintada**, Cochimí painters decorated 150m of high rock overhangs with vivid red-and-black representations of human figures, bighorn sheep, pumas and deer, as well as more abstract designs. **Cueva de las Flechas**, across Cañón San Pablo, has similar paintings.

The beautiful mule-back descent of Cañón San Pablo requires at least two days, preferably three, and is best done through a tour operator like **Ecoturismo Kuyimá** (☑ 615-154-00-70; www.kuyima.com; Morelos 23; ⊗ 9am-3pm Mon-Sat), which can arrange three-day trips for US$537 per person (four-person minimum). Longer tours are also available.

Santa Rosalía

☑ 615 / POP 12,000

Southbound travelers will welcome their first sight of the Sea of Cortez after crossing the Desierto de Vizcaíno. Though the town was badly damaged in by Hurricane Jimena in 2009, and by the subsequent Hurricane Odile in 2014 , it has repaired and rebounded. Brightly painted clapboard-sided houses, the

Iglesia Santa Bábara, the port, the *malecón* (seaside promenade) and the mining museum are prime attractions, although they are rivaled by the black-sand beaches, pelicans and great views from the surrounding hills.

The town has become a prosperous mining center once again, with the reopening of the historic El Boleo copper and cobalt opencast mine in 2013 adding around 3800 jobs to the local economy.

⊙ Sights

Central Santa Rosalía is a cluster of densely packed houses, restaurants, inns and stores. Plaza Benito Juárez, four blocks west of the highway, is the town center.

Museo el Boleo   MUSEUM
(☑ 615-152-29-99; Cousteau 1; M$20; ⊗ 8am-3pm Mon-Fri, 9am-1pm Sat) Built in 1885 by the French to house the offices of the Boleo Company, this mining museum watches over town and the copperworks from its perch on the hill near the Hotel Francés. It's surrounded by cool abandoned locomotives and other pieces of machinery.

Iglesia Santa Bárbara   CHURCH
Designed and erected for Paris' 1889 World's Fair, then disassembled and stored in Brussels for shipping to West Africa, Gustave Eiffel's (yes, of Eiffel Tower fame) prefabricated Iglesia Santa Bárbara was, instead, shipped here when a Boleo Company director signed for its delivery to the town in 1895.

🛏 Sleeping

Santa Rosalía has a handful of well-priced accommodations.

Hotel Las Casitas de
Santa Rosalía
BOUTIQUE HOTEL **$$**

(☑615-152-30-23; Carretera Sur Km 195; s M$650, d M$750-900; P🐾📶) US-owned Las Casitas has a real five-star holiday-in-the-sun look with large rooms that have balconies, seamless Sea of Cortez views, exquisite tilework and tasteful artwork. The less expensive doubles share the views, but are considerably smaller; there is a small communal space with some cooking facilities plus a state-of-the art exercise bike for the use of guests.

Hotel Francés
HISTORIC HOTEL **$$**

(☑615-152-20-52; Av Cousteau 15; r M$890; P📶🏊) Overlooking the Sea of Cortez and rusting hulks of mine machinery, Hotel Francés is charming and historic. Built in 1886 and originally the dormitory for the 'working girls' of a brothel near the mine, the hotel features beautiful rooms with high ceilings, cloth-covered walls and charming stained-wood details.

✖ Eating

For cheap eats, hit one of the taco stands along Avenida Obregón.

Panadería El Boleo
BAKERY **$**

(☑615-152-03-10; Av Obregón 30; baked goods M$5-20; ⏰8am-9.30pm Mon-Sat, 9am-2pm Sun) Since 1901, this has been an obligatory stop for those in search of delicious Mexican pastries and, more unusually, authentic French baguettes. Baking begins at 4am daily, but they usually run out by midday.

El Muelle
MEXICAN **$$**

(☑615-152-09-31; cnr Av Constitución & Calle Plaza; mains M$120-150; ⏰8am-11pm; 📶) Easy to find in the center of town, the walls here sport everything that is, well, sporty, including cricket bats, ice skates, skis, golf clubs and baseball bats. The menu is less surprising, specializing in sound Mexican fare. Push the boat out with Veracruz-style fish (M$135) accompanied by an ice-cold Corona.

Tonka's Grill
STEAK **$$**

(Montoya; mains M$90-120; ⏰6-11pm Tue-Sun) Join the loyal regulars and dine al fresco in a pretty courtyard on succulent grilled steaks and burgers swished down by a beer or two; note that cocktails are not served.

❶ Getting There & Away

BOAT

The passenger/auto ferry *Santa Rosalía* sails to Guaymas at 9am on Tuesday, Wednesday, Friday and Saturday, and 8pm on Sunday, arriving 10 hours later. Double check as timings may change.

The ticket office is at the **ferry terminal** (☑615-152-12-46; www.ferrysantarosalia.com; ⏰9am-1pm & 3-6pm Mon-Sat, 9am-1pm & 3-8pm Sun) on the highway. Passenger fares are around M$900 (children's tickets are half price). Vehicle rates vary with vehicle length.

BUS

The **Bus Terminal** (☑615-152-14-08; ⏰24hr) is found just south of the entrance to town, in the same building as the ferry terminal.

Mulegé

☑615 / POP 3300

The palm- and mangrove-lined Río Mulegé, with its delta, birds, wildlife and snorkeling and diving opportunities, makes Mulegé a great stop for the outdoorsy or those with kids. Set down in a narrow *arroyo,* Mulegé is prone to flooding in major storms – it was pummeled by hurricanes in 2009, 2012 and 2014. The 18th-century mission and town

BUSES FROM SANTA ROSALÍA

DESTINATION	FARE (M$)	DURATION (HR)	FREQUENCY (DAILY)
Ensenada	1365	13	3
Guerrero Negro	390	3	4
La Paz	1180	8	6
Loreto	360	3	6
Mexicali	1785	16	2
Mulegé	115	1	5
San Ignacio	135	1	4
San José del Cabo	1260	12	1
Tijuana	1810	16½	2

square give the town a quiet charm that is fast disappearing in other parts of Baja.

◎ Sights

Misión Santa Rosalía de Mulegé MISSION
Come to the hilltop Misión Santa Rosalía de Mulegé (founded in 1705, completed in 1766 and abandoned in 1828) for great photos of the site and river valley.

Museo Mulegé MUSEUM
(Barrio Canenea; adult/child under 12yr M$10/free; ☉9am-2pm Mon-Sat; ⊕) The former territorial prison was famed for allowing prisoners to roam free in town during the day. Now the Museo Mulegé, its eclectic collection ranges from fairly mundane prison artifacts to a section of a rocket that plummeted from the sky in the year 2000! Note the blackened cell where a prisoner apparently set fire to himself after hearing his wife was having an affair.

⚡ Activities

Diving
Mulegé's best diving spots can be found around the Santa Inés Islands (north of town) and just north of Punta Concepción (south of town). Diving tour operators come and go; check at La Tienda (p723) if you want to hire gear or organize a dive; they should be able to help.

Kayaking
The beautiful river, the estuary delta and the southern beaches make Mulegé a prime spot for kayaking.

NOLS Mexico KAYAKING
(☑in the US 307-332-5300, in the US toll-free 800-710-6657; www.nols.edu/courses/locations/mexico/) ✦ Runs sea-kayaking, sailing and backpacking courses, and trips out of its sustainable, ecofriendly facility on Coyote Bay, south of Mulegé.

🛏 Sleeping

Hotel Las Casitas HOTEL $
(☑615-153-00-19; javieraguiarz51@hotmail.com; Madero 50; s/d/tr M$395/495/595; ▣⊛❄ি) Perhaps inspired by its very pretty courtyard, fountains, statues and shady garden of tropical plants, beloved Mexican poet Alán Gorosave once inhabited this hotel. The restaurant serves decent food and has an open-fire grill. The rooms are simple and somewhat threadbare, but are decorated with traditional fabrics and artwork.

Hotel Mulegé HOTEL $
(☑615-153-00-90; Moctezuma s/n; s/d/tr M$400/500/550; ▣❄@ি) Located just beyond the arch at the entrance to town; despite the dated decor and brown carpeting, the rooms here are well maintained and spotless.

ON A MISSION FROM GOD

Baja's missions have a dubious history – built by Jesuits and Dominicans intent on bringing salvation, they instead brought death through introduced European diseases. Many missions were abandoned as populations dropped below sustainable levels. Today, however, these beautiful buildings, whether in use or out in the middle of nowhere, make for great photos and fun day trips, and they're an undeniable part of Baja's checkered past. You should not need a 4WD to visit any of those listed here, though the roads can be impressively bad (or impassable) at times.

Misión Nuestra Señora de Loreto (p724) The oldest mission, an impressive monument still in use today.

Misión San Borja (btwn Rosarito/Bahía de los Ángeles; ☉8am-6pm) Out in the middle of nowhere but well worth the drive. Its treasures include a hot spring and a secret tunnel (now walled up). José Gerardo, a descendant of the original preconquest inhabitants, will show you around.

Misión San Francisco Javier de Viggé-Biaundó (p725) Remote and beautifully preserved, it feels like stepping back in time. The drive here offers awesome vistas and even some cave paintings along the way.

Misión Santa Rosalía de Mulegé (p722) Extremely photogenic. Don't miss the view from behind looking out over the palm-edged river.

Resources for further reading include *Las Misiones Antiguas,* by Edward W Vernon, and www.vivabaja.com/bajamissions; both feature beautiful photos.

Hotel Serenidad HOTEL **$$**
(☑ 615-153-05-30; www.serenidad.com.mx; Mulegé; d M$1065, cabañas M$2125; ℙ⊜❀🛜🏊) Dating back to the 1960s, this hotel is an institution. Plenty of famous folk have flown in here (it has its own 4000-ft paved airstrip!), including John Wayne. The rambling property has carafes of character, with a vast restaurant, rustic double rooms and small *cabañas*. There's a pig roast every Saturday with live music and a Mexican fiesta theme on Wednesdays.

The hotel is located approximately 3.8km south of town, signposted off the Carretera Transpeninsular.

🍴 Eating & Drinking

The sidewalks are rolled up pretty early in Mulegé, so dine earlier than usual.

Ana's SEAFOOD **$$**
(Playa Santispac; mains M$140-160) In the mood for seafood? Then it is well worth the 10km drive southwest of town to this lovely beachside restaurant where you can dine on a succulent seafood platter comprising shrimp, clams and whatever has been caught that day. Popular with families at weekends, there are a couple of cheap rooms to rent if you fancy a sunrise shore side (M$200).

Doney Mely's MEXICAN **$$**
(☑ 615-153-00-95; Moctezuma s/n; mains M$90-125, menú M$285; ⊙ 7:30am-10pm Wed-Mon; 🛜🍴) A colorfully decorated restaurant with a special weekend menu for two that includes a gut-busting choice of local favorites like *chiles rellenos* and *enchiladas verdes*. Breakfasts come plumply recommended as well.

Los Equipales INTERNATIONAL **$$$**
(☑ 615-153-03-30; Moctezuma s/n; mains M$190-220; ⊙ 8am-10pm; 🛜) Just west of Zaragoza, this restaurant and bar has gargantuan meals and breezy balcony seating that's perfect for an evening margarita with friends. Lobster salad, T-bone steak and pork ribs are a sampling of the surf turf fare.

🛍 Shopping

La Tienda SPORTS
(Martínez s/n; ⊙ 9am-1pm & 4-6pm Mon-Sat) Sells fishing and diving gear and can also advise on local diving instruction.

ℹ Getting There & Away

Bus Terminal (Transpeninsular Km 132; ⊙ 8am-11pm) Located near the large entry arch, northbound buses include Santa Rosalía (M$120, one hour) and Tijuana (M$1330, 14 hours) stop six times daily. Southbound buses pass to destinations including Loreto (M$225, two hours) and La Paz (M$815, six hours) five times daily.

Around Mulegé

Cañón La Trinidad

Trinity Canyon is great for bird-watchers, with the chance to see vermilion flycatchers, gila woodpeckers and a host of raptors and buteos. The narrow, sherbet-colored canyon walls and shimmering pools of water are stunning, as are the pre-Hispanic cave paintings. Rendered in shades of ocher and rust, the paintings feature shamans, manta rays, whales and the famous Trinity Deer, leaping gracefully from the walls of the cave as arrows pass harmlessly over its head. You're not allowed to enter by yourself, but Mulegé native Salvador Castro Drew of **Mulegé Tours** (☑ 615-161-49-85; mulegetours@hotmail.com; day excursions per person M$500) knows just about everything about the site you'd want to know, including how to avoid the two nasty beehives that 'guard' the paintings. He also does taxi runs to other area sites.

Beaches

As you wind your way south you'll pass some of Baja's most pristine *playas* (beaches). You can string up a hammock, pop the top on something frosty and watch the pelicans dive-bomb for fish. Some beaches have bars, restaurants or *cabañas*. **Bahía Concepción** (Km 11.5), with its pelican colonies, funky rock formations and milky, blue-green water, remains a top stop for kayakers. **Playa Escondido** (Km 112) and **Playa Perla** (Km 91) are just a few of the possible stops along the Transpeninsular on the way. Be extremely cautious about weather alerts – the glassy water here and in Loreto can quickly become dangerous during storms.

Loreto

☑ 613 / POP 17,000

Loreto has a lot going for it. It's a very pretty small town with an excellent choice of hotels and restaurants, and it's a water-sports paradise. It's also home to the magnificent Parque Nacional Bahía de Loreto, where the shoreline, ocean and offshore islands are protected from pollution and uncontrolled fishing.

The Loreto area is also considered by anthropologists to be the oldest human settlement on the Baja Peninsula. Indigenous cultures thrived here due to plentiful water and food. In 1697 Jesuit Juan María Salvatierra established the peninsula's first permanent mission at this modest port some 135km south of Mulegé.

Most hotels and services are near the landmark mission church on Salvatierra, while the attractive *malecón* is ideal for evening strolls.

◉ Sights & Activities

Misión Nuestra Señora de Loreto   MISSION
Dating from 1697, this was the first permanent mission in the Californias and was the base for the expansion of Jesuit missions up and down the Baja peninsula. Alongside the church, the **Museo de las Misiones** (☑613-135-04-41; Salvatierra 16; M$40; ◉9am-1pm & 1:45-6pm Tue-Sun) chronicles the settlement of Baja California.

★Parque Marine
Nacional Bahía de Loreto   PARK
This park makes Loreto a world-class destination for all types of outdoor activities; a number of outfitters offer everything from kayaking and diving along the reefs around Islas del Carmen and Coronado to horseback riding, hiking and mountain biking in the Sierra de la Giganta. Pay the M$50 per person entrance fee at the park's office in the marina. Staff can advise on water activities.

Loreto Sea and Land Tours   WATER SPORTS
(☑613-135-06-80; www.toursloreto.com; Madero s/n; diving/snorkeling/kayaking from US$100/65/95; 🖋) 🖋 Loreto is awash with companies offering outdoor sports. This recommended eco-friendly place covers a wide range of activities, including diving, kayaking and snorkeling.

🛏 Sleeping

Most of Loreto's accommodations are on or near the *malecón*.

Hostal Casas Loreto   HOTEL $
(☑613-116-70-14; Misioneros 14; s/d M$450/600) Rooms here are set around a long covered courtyard so can seem a tad dark. On the plus side they are tastefully decorated with rustic furniture and stone walls. There is a well-equipped kitchen for the use of guests.

★La Damiana Inn   HISTORIC HOTEL $$
(☑613-135-03-56; www.ladamianainn.com; Madero 8; r US$75, casitas US$90; ◉❄🖥) This historical posada has spacious, individually furnished rooms with decor ranging from brightly colored Baja fabrics, ceramics and artwork to mellow earth tones and native American pieces. There's a communal kitchen and gorgeous mature garden with fruit trees and hammocks.

There is also a charming casita (small house) that sleeps up to four people, with its own kitchen and secluded terrace.

Posada del Cortes   BOUTIQUE HOTEL $$
(☑613-135-02-58; www.posadadelcortes.com; Callejon Pipila 4; r M$1100; ◉❄🖥) This elegant small hotel exudes a chic atmosphere with ocher-and-cream paintwork, forest-green tilework, dark-wood furniture and lashings of white linen. There's a small terrace with wrought-iron furniture and a trickling fountain. Rooms include coffeemakers.

Posada de las Flores   LUXURY HOTEL $$
(☑613-135-11-62; www.posadadelasflores.com; Plaza Cívica; r incl breakfast M$928; ◉❄🖥🏊) Sitting majestically on the main plaza in town, the interior has a palatial feel due to its stone columns and arches, trickling fountains and an earthy color palette. Rooms are surprisingly small and dark, with curious textured paintwork. Not to worry, the stunning public spaces extend to a rooftop pool, bar and terrace that has views stretching to the mission.

🍴 Eating & Drinking

Enjoy the regional standards: excellent seafood with plenty of tasty lime and cilantro, potent margaritas and fruity *aguas frescas* (ice drinks).

Café Olé   CAFE, MEXICAN $
(☑613-135-04-96; Madero 14; mains M$35-70; ◉7am-9:45pm Mon-Sat, to 1pm Sun; 🖥) This inexpensive cafe near the main square has good, basic fare, including great Mexican breakfasts.

Tacos del Rey   MEXICAN $
(cnr Benito Juárez & Misionero; tacos M$30; ◉9am-2pm) Way and beyond the best tacos in town are sold at this simple taco kiosk-cum-restaurant, which is clinical in its cleanliness (there is a tap plus sign reminding patrons to wash their hands before they eat). The *carne asado* (roasted meat) variety are particularly stand out and there is plenty of topping choice to custom design your taco.

★ Orlando's MEXICAN $$

(Madero Norte; mains M$80-110; ☺7.30am-9pm Tue-Sat) Colorful tablecloths, plastic furniture, a *palapa* (thatch made from dried palm leaves) roof; this place has a no-frills setting but serves superb food. Try the coconut shrimp with mango salsa for a real tastebud treat. The service is gracious and efficient, the soundtrack is unobtrusive and the margaritas hit the spot.

1697 Restaurant Pub MEXICAN, ITALIAN $$

(Davies 18; mains M$99-160; ☺6-10pm Tue-Sun) Owned by a Mexican-Irish couple (ask how they met, now there's a story!), this restaurant and micro brewery has cuisine that is fittingly diverse, ranging from creamy pastas to fillet steak and chicken fajitas. Its decor and terrace under the stars make it a good choice for a romantic dinner.

🛍 Shopping

The pedestrian mall between Madero and Independencia is best for shopping.

El Caballo Blanco BOOKS

(Hidalgo 19; ☺10am-5pm Mon-Sat) Probably the most comprehensive collection of books on Baja in the region, plus maps, art materials, pottery and a bottomless coffee pot for browsers.

Silver Desert SILVER

(📞613-135-06-84; Salvatierra 36; ☺9am-2pm & 3-8pm Mon-Sat, 9am-2pm Sun) Sells good quality Taxco sterling-silver jewelry. There's a second outlet at **Magdalena de Kino 4** (📞613-135-06-84; Magdalena de Kino 4; ☺9am-2pm & 3-8pm Mon-Sat, 9am-2pm Sun).

❶ Information

Municipal Department of Tourism (📞613-135-04-11; Plaza Cívica; ☺8am-3pm Mon-Fri) Has a good selection of brochures.

❶ Getting There & Away

Aeropuerto Internacional de Loreto (📞613-135-04-99; Carretera Transpeninsular Km 7) Served by several airlines, including Aéreo Calafia and Aereoservicio Guerrero.

Bus Station (☺24hr) Near the convergence of Salvatierra, Paseo de Ugarte and Paseo Tamaral, a 15-minute walk from the town center.

❶ Getting Around

Taxis from the airport, 4km south of Loreto, cost M$160. Groups start at M$70 per person.

Around Loreto

Misión San Francisco Javier de Viggé-Biaundó MISSION

(btwn Loreto & La Paz) Whale-watching tours are the main tourist draw between Loreto and La Paz, but this wonderful mission is well worth a daytime detour. The windy road passes minor cliff paintings and some beautiful *arroyos* (streams) before arriving at the mission. Be sure to wander to the back garden to see the 300-year-old olive tree with rope-like bark that looks like something out of a Tolkien fantasy. The mission itself is almost unchanged from its look of three centuries ago.

Head south on the Transpeninsular for around 35km and look for the sign to the right shortly after you leave Loreto.

Ciudad Constitución
📞 613 / POP 43,000

Landlocked, and primarily a farming and industrial city, Ciudad Constitución offers little for tourists other than hotels for whale-watching day trips. Transportation to the port cities of López Mateos and San Carlos is infrequent – it's far better to have your own set of wheels.

BAJA CALIFORNIA AROUND LORETO

BUSES FROM LORETO

DESTINATION	FARE (M$)	DURATION (HR)	FREQUENCY (DAILY)
Guerrero Negro	745	5-6	4
La Paz	760	5	6
Mexicali	1842	20	3
San José del Cabo	1080	8	6
Santa Rosalía	360	3	6
Tijuana	2195	18	3

🛏 Sleeping & Eating

Ciudad Constitución's lodgings are limited.

Hotel Oasis   HOTEL $

(☑ 613-132-44-58; www.hoteloasis.mx; Vicente Guerrero 284; s/d M$450/550; [P][🛜]) Located at the entrance to town, coming from Loreto, this is one of the latest hotels in town and offers pleasant spacious rooms decorated in cool cream marble contrasting with the hot orange paintwork of the modular designed exterior.

Posadas del Ryal   MOTEL $

(☑ 613-132-48-00; www.posadasdelryal.blogspot. com; Victoria s/n; s/d/ste M$450/500/720; [P][♿][❄][🛜]) This two-story motel has rooms decorated in appropriate desert-colored hue, set around a palm-filled courtyard. Bathrooms are small, unless you opt for the spacious 'La Mexicana suite,' which also sports a small terrace.

Asadero 'Tribi'   MEXICAN $$

(☑ 613-132-73-53; Olachea, btwn Madero & Pino Suárez; mains M$140-165; ⊙ 8am-midnight Mon-Sat; [🛜][♿]) Surround yourself in rustic brick-and-wood decor and enjoy specials like barbecued ribs, T-bone steak and meat or fish tacos – it's the best restaurant in town.

❶ Getting There & Away

Bus Terminal (☑ 613-132-03-76; cnr Juárez & Pino Suárez; ⊙ 24hr) There are two daily departures for Puerto López Mateos (M$115, 1pm and 8:15pm) and Puerto San Carlos (M$98, 11am and 6pm).

Puerto López Mateos

☑ 613 / POP 2200

Located 58km northwest of Ciudad Constitución, shielded by the offshore barrier of Isla Magdalena, Puerto López Mateos is one of Baja's best whale-watching sites. During the season, the narrow waterway that passes by town becomes a veritable *ballena* cruising strip. Curva del Diablo (Devil's Bend), 27km south of town, is reported to be the best viewing spot. Three-hour *panga* (skiff) excursions from Puerto López Mateos (M$750 per hour for six to eight people, from 7am to 6pm in season) are easy to arrange.

Free camping (bring water), with pit toilets only, is possible at tidy **Playa Boca de la Soledad**, which is near Playa El Faro, 1.6km east of town (turn left at the water tower). Accommodations in Puerto López Mateos are basically left to various locals who hang out signs advertising rooms to rent during the whale-watching season. **Baja Mar** (☑ 613-131-51-96; breakfast M$55, mains M$100; ⊙ 8am-8pm; [🛜]) offers family-style Mexican dishes.

The bus service to Ciudad Constitución (M$115) leaves at 6am and 4pm from a small ticket office across from the school.

Puerto San Carlos

☑ 613 / POP 7000

Puerto San Carlos is a deep-water port and fishing town located 57km west of Ciudad Constitución on Bahía Magdalena. The town turns its attention to whales and travelers when the *ballenas* arrive in January to calve in the warm lagoon. From then until March *pangueros* (boatmen) take passengers for whale-watching excursions (about M$750 per hour for six people).

🏃 Activities

Ecotours Villas Mar y Arena   ADVENTURE TOURS

(☑ 613-136-00-76; www.villasmaryarena.com; Carretera Federal Km 57; whale-watching per person M$900, fishing trip per person M$650; ⊙ Oct-Jun; [♿]) 🍃 Whale-watching and fishing trips run from the ecofriendly Hotel Mar y Arena, which is located at the entrance to town.

🛏 Sleeping & Eating

Accommodations can be tough to find when the whales are in town.

Hotel Alcatraz   HOTEL $

(☑ 613-136-00-17; www.hotelalcatraz.mx; Calle San Jose del Cabo s/n; s/d M$450/550; [P][❄][🛜]) This rambling hotel has rooms set around a mature leafy courtyard, complete with sunbeds under the trees. Attractive pale-blue tilework gives the decor a sunny seaside feel. There is a bar and restaurant (mains M$100 to M$250).

★ Hotel Mar y Arena   CABAÑAS $$

(☑ 613-136-00-76; www.villasmaryarena.com; Carretera Federal Km 56; r US$80-90; [P][♿][❄][🛜]) 🍃 These *palapa*-style *cabañas* have chic earth-toned interiors and luxurious bathrooms. Solar power, desalinated water and a sensitivity to feng shui principles are all part of the local owner's eco-vision.

Los Arcos   SEAFOOD $$

(Puerto La Paz 170; mains M$80-145; ⊙ 10am-9pm) A simple place with tables set under the palm fronds, but the seafood dishes are the town's best. Go for one of the nine shrimp dishes or a simple *pescado de la plancha* (grilled fish). Note that the taco stand across the road from here is the best in town.

ℹ Getting There & Away

Autotransportes Águila (📞613-136-04-53; Calle Puerto Morelos; ⏰7am-7:30am, 11:30am-1:45pm & 6:30-7:30pm) Runs buses at 7:30am and 1:45pm daily to Ciudad Constitución (M$98) and La Paz (M$453), Cabo San Lucas (M$645) and San José del Cabo (M$680). This is the only public transportation from Puerto San Carlos.

La Paz

📞612 / POP 250,000

Cosmopolitan La Paz is a mix of laid-back, old-world beauty and chichi upscale trends. It's surprisingly international – you're as likely to hear French, Portuguese or Italian here as English or Spanish, and yet paradoxically it's the most 'Mexican' city in all of Baja. Its quirky history includes American occupation and even being temporarily declared its own republic. Hernán Cortés established Baja's first European outpost near La Paz, but permanent settlement waited until 1811.

The beachside *malecón,* superb restaurants and funky stores make it a great place to meander, and you can shop uninterrupted by touts' invitations. The city makes a good base for day trips to Cabo Pulmo and Todos Santos, and there's a lively, long-term expat community in and around the marina.

The port of Pichilingue receives ferries from the mainland ports of Topolobampo and Mazatlán, and the airport is served by several US carriers. La Paz' grid street pattern makes basic orientation relatively easy.

◉ Sights

★ Espíritu Santo   ISLAND

A treasure of shallow azure inlets and sorbet-pink cliffs, Espíritu Santo is one of La Paz' gems. It's part of a Unesco World Heritage site comprising 244 Sea of Cortez islands and coastal areas, and a worthy day trip. A number of operators run activities here, including kayaking and snorkeling.

★ Museo de la Ballena   MUSEUM

(www.museodelaballena.org; Paseo Obregón; adult/child US$10/7; ⏰9am-6pm Tue-Sun) Opened in February 2016, the museum comprises five exhibition spaces with models, audiovisual displays and multilingual explanations concerning all aspects of the grey whales

that live and breed in the local waters. A soundtrack of whales in the wild adds to the atmosphere, as well as the well lit and airy gallery spaces. Together with the exhibitions and audiovisual displays, the museum's foundation promotes the study and conservation of whales.

There is also a section dedicated to local turtles covering the seven different species native to Mexico, plus a cafeteria and gift shop.

Museo Regional de
Antropología e Historia   MUSEUM

(cnr Calles 5 de Mayo & Altamirano; adult/child under 12yr M$30/free; ⏰9am-6pm; 🖐) This is a large, well-organized museum chronicling the peninsula's history (in Spanish) from prehistory to the revolution of 1910 and its aftermath.

Unidad Cultural Profesor
Jesús Castro Agúndez   CULTURAL CENTER

(📞612-125-02-07; cnr Gómez Farías & Legaspi; ⏰Cultural Center 8am-2pm & 4-6pm Mon-Fri) The **Teatro de la Ciudad** (📞612-125-00-04; Altamirano; ⏰hours vary), part of this large cultural center, is the main performance venue in La Paz.

Santuario de la Virgen de
Guadalupe   MONUMENT

(cnr Calles 5 de Febrero & Aquiles Serdán; ⏰7am-6pm) The Santuario de la Virgen de Guadalupe is La Paz' largest religious monument. Its 12m-tall altar is grandiose.

🏃 Activities

Whale Shark Mexico   WILDLIFE-WATCHING

(📞612-154-98-59; www.whalesharkmexico.com) 🌿 From October to March you can help researchers study juvenile whale sharks, which congregate in the placid waters of La Paz bay. Duties vary each trip: you can assist with tagging and even get a chance to name one. These researchers do not rent or provide any gear, and trips must be arranged in advance and only when the weather conditions are right. The cost is currently M$975 per person, which goes directly toward the costs of radio tags and other research expenses.

Red Travel Mexico   ECOTOUR

(📞612-122-60-57;www.redtravelmexico.com;Salvatierra 740, Colina de la Cruz; ⏰9am-6pm; 🖐) Finances major conservation projects throughout Baja like endangered sea-turtle monitoring. Other activities include educational activities for children and deep sea diving in Cabo Pulmo.

La Paz

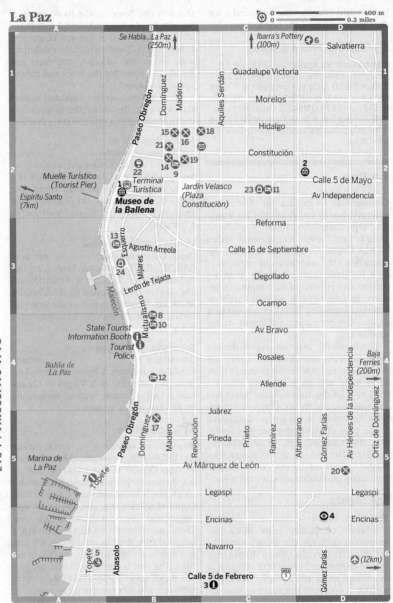

Snorkeling Carey DIVING, SNORKELING
(612-128-40-48; www.buceocarey.com; cnr Topete & Legaspi; snorkeling US$100, diving US$150;
) A family-run establishment that offers
snorkeling, diving, whale-watching, trips to
see a sea lion colony and other tours.

Mar y Aventuras KAYAKING
(612-122-70-39; www.kayakbaja.com; Topete
564; 7/10 days US$1050/1400) Book an eight-
or nine-day kayak expedition, or outfit your
self-guided trip.

La Paz

⊚ **Top Sights**
1 Museo de la Ballena.............................. B2

⊚ **Sights**
2 Museo Regional de Antropología
   e Historia D2
3 Santuario de la Virgen de
   Guadalupe C6
4 Unidad Cultural Profesor Jesús
   Castro Agúndez D6

🟢 **Activities, Courses & Tours**
5 Mar y Aventuras A6
6 Red Travel Mexico D1
7 Snorkeling Carey A5

🛏 **Sleeping**
8 Baja Backpackers B4
9 Baja Bed & Breakfast B2
10 Casa Tuscany B4
11 El Ángel Azul C2
12 Hotel Mediterrane B4

13 Hotel Perla B3

⊗ **Eating**
14 Bagel Shop.. B2
15 Buffalo BBQ B2
16 Las Tres Virgenes.................................. B2
17 Maria California B5
18 Nim C2
19 Organic Market..................................... B2
20 Taco Fish La Paz D5
21 Tio Bencho.. B2

🍷 **Drinking & Nightlife**
22 Harker Board B2

🎭 **Entertainment**
   Teatro de la Ciudad....................... (see 4)

🛍 **Shopping**
23 Allende Books.......................................C2
24 Antigua California................................. B3

📖 Courses

Se Habla...La Paz
LANGUAGE COURSE

(📞612-122-77-63; www.sehablalapaz.com; Madero 540) All levels of Spanish classes, plus an introduction to the culture and cuisine of the country and homestays arranged, if necessary. Walk-ins welcome, space permitting. Courses cost US$275 per week plus US$75 registration with a maximum of five students in a class.

🎉 Festivals & Events

Festivals and other seasonal events often take place at Plaza Constitución, between Revolución and Madero at Calle 5 de Mayo.

Carnaval
CARNIVAL

(☺early May) The annual carnival here is considered to be one of the country's best with parades, concerts and plenty of partying in the streets.

🛏 Sleeping

Accommodations in La Paz run the gamut from budget digs to swanky hotels.

Baja Backpackers
HOSTEL $

(www.bajabackpackers.com; Mutualismo 330; 4-bed dm M$300, d M$500; ✳🛜) Separate men's and women's dorms, plus a community kitchen, a sitting room, a sea-view terrace, and complimentary coffee make this a good choice if you are peso-pinching. It's run by a friendly American-Mexican couple who also rent snorkeling equipment.

Hotel Mediterrane
HOTEL $$

(📞612-125-11-95; www.hotelmed.com; Allende 36; r M$889-1299; P➔✳@🛜) Greek-inspired hotel with cool rooms, delicious cafe menu and a rooftop terrace with bay views. Go for the Mykonos room if you can – it has a private terrace and domed roof.

Baja Bed & Breakfast
B&B $$

(📞612-123-13-70; www.bajabedandbreakfast.com; Madero 354; s/d inc breakfast US$60/70; 🛜✢) Located in the trendiest part of town with its organic stores, and coffee shops, this homey B&B has rooms set around a free-form pool and leafy patio with sunbeds and outdoor kitchen for the use of guests. Terracotta tiles, pastel paintwork and tasteful art on the walls contribute to the welcoming feel of the place.

Hotel Perla
HOTEL $$

(📞612-122-07-77; www.hotelperlabaja.com; Paseo Obregón 1570; r incl breakfast M$1190; P➔✳@🛜) Pacific-blue fabrics, pine furniture, mosaic-tiled bathrooms and scenic sea-view terraces make this family friendly hotel a good central choice. There are also two Jacuzzis.

★El Ángel Azul
BOUTIQUE HOTEL $$$

(📞612-125-51-30; Av Independencia 518; r incl breakfast US$100-120; P➔✳🛜) Possibly the loveliest of La Paz' lodging options, the Blue Angel offers simply furnished, pastel-washed rooms, which surround a beautiful courtyard that is filled with palms, cacti, birdsong and

BAJA CALIFORNIA LA PAZ

bougainvillea. There is a colorfully cluttered bar and sitting room, plus a kitchen for the use of guests.

Casa Tuscany
B&B $$$

(☎612-128-81-03; www.tuscanybaja.com; Av Bravo 110; d incl breakfast from US$87; ❀✲🛜) Situated a seagull's swoop from the *malecón,* this picturesque B&B has homely rooms decorated with bright paintwork, local rugs and traditional ceramics. Set around a tranquil central courtyard, the rooms vary in size; the most expansive, 'Romeo & Juliet,' has three terraces on several levels with sea views. Breakfast includes *aebleskiver* (Danish pancakes).

✗ Eating

La Paz' restaurant scene has become increasingly sophisticated – you'll find most of the top choices on Calles Domínguez and Madero, north of Calle 5 de Mayo. There's also an **organic market** (Madero s/n; ◷9am-2.30pm Sat).

Taco Fish La Paz
SEAFOOD $

(cnr Avs Márques de León & Héroes de la Independencia; tacos M$35; ◷8am-4pm Tue-Sun) Largely undiscovered by tourists, locals have been coming here in shoals since 1992. Expect pristine stainless-steel surfaces, the obligatory TV turned to the football channel and the best fish tacos and ceviche in town.

Bagel Shop
BAGELS $

(Domínguez 291; bagels from M$40; ◷8am-3pm Tue-Sun) Owner Fabrizio learned the art of bagel making in the US, and he makes a steaming batch daily. Fillings range from classic lox and cream cheese to smoked marlin with German sausage.

★ Maria California
MEXICAN $$

(www.mariacaliforniarestaurant.com; Juárez 105; breakfast mains M$90-100; ◷7:30am-2pm Mon-Sat) Great for breakfast with live music and a fabulous atmosphere throughout the cozy cluttered dining rooms and terraces. Local artwork, photos and brilliant colored paintwork adorn the walls.

Tio Bencho
MEXICAN $$

(cnr Domínguez & Constitución; mains M$100-120; ◷8am-12am Tue-Sun) Sit under the red umbrellas on the leafy terrace at this hip local place where the specialty is green, white or red *pozole* (savoury stew) and *enmoladas* (enchiladas with *mole,* typical of Guerrero) and Oaxaca-style tamales. Smaller appetites can opt for tasty appetizers like grilled *panela* cheese.

Buffalo BBQ
STEAK $$

(Madero 1145; mains M$140-160; ◷2-11pm) Under the mighty mounted buffalo head, eat a carnivorous feast that includes hamburgers, rib eye steak and grills. Lightweights can opt for the fish of the day. Post dusk, head to the courtyard with its twinkling lights and homespun feel.

★ Las Tres Virgenes
INTERNATIONAL $$$

(☎612-165-62-65; Madero 1130; mains M$140-185; ◷1-11pm) An elegant oasis of a restaurant where you can dine in an atmospheric courtyard surrounded by leafy trees and statues. The menu includes both traditional and innovative dishes like seafood risotto, roasted bone marrow, spicy sea snails and a classic Caesar salad made with suitable flourish at your table. Reservations recommended.

TOP SPOTS FOR FANTASTIC FISH TACOS

Simple and versatile, the humble fish taco is Baja's comfort food. Done right they're magical. These spots are all worth seeking out for a taste of this sublimely delicious snack.

La Guerrerense (p711), Ensenada. Good enough to win an international street food competition. Enough said.

El Caballero (p734), Cabo Pulmo. These come with a homemade salsa that's *picante* (spicy) without being smolderingly hot. Perfect after a long, invigorating snorkel.

Los Arcos (☎661-612-04-91; Blvd Juárez 29; mains M$65-90; ◷8am-7pm Mon, Tue, Thu & Fri, to 10pm Sat & Sun), Playas de Rosarito. Casual family-run place with guacamole, sour cream and *pico de gallo* (fresh chopped salsa).

Venado (p739), Cabo San Lucas. Flaky, moist morsels of fish on corn or flour. Shrimp tacos are just as good.

Taco Fish La Paz (p730), La Paz. Superb seafood tacos at this, one of the longest standing places in town.

Nim INTERNATIONAL $$$
(www.nimrestaurante.com; Revolución 1110; mains M$180-295; ⊙1-10.30pm; 🐾) Situated in a sumptuous historic house with art deco floor tiles and a chic pale-gray painted interior, organic produce is used in dishes that span the continents, like Moroccan *tagines,* Italian pastas, clam chowder and locally sourced sauteed oysters. Hugely popular with the resident expat population.

🍷 Drinking & Nightlife

The highest concentration of bars is between Calles 16 de Septiembre and Agustín Arreola, across from the *malecón* .

Harker Board BAR
(cnr Constutución & Paseo Obregón; ⊙7am-2am Wed-Mon; 🐾) Head upstairs to the terrace for views over the bay and a *cerveza* (beer). The local Baja Brewery beer is on tap, and there are 17 more bottled varieties. Pizza also available. This great place doubles as a rental place for paddleboards (MS$100 per hour).

Club Marlin BAR
(El Centenario; ⊙noon-10pm Tue-Sat, 10am-8pm Sun; 🐾) Located in El Centenario, around 5km north of the center, this hotel, bar and restaurant dates from the 1980s and has long served as the resident expat haunt. The views of the bay are sublime and the place (and patrons) have plenty of sun-kissed warmth and character. Regular live music.

🛍 Shopping

Local stores that cater to tourists have plenty of junk but a smattering of good stuff.

Ibarra's Pottery CERAMICS
(www.ibarraspottery.com; Prieto 625; ⊙9am-3pm Mon-Fri, to 2pm Sat) See potters at work at this ceramics workshop and store that dates back to 1958 – it is famed throughout Baja.

Antigua California CRAFTS
(Paseo Obregón 220; ⊙9:30am-8:30pm) Features a wide selection of crafts from throughout the country.

Allende Books BOOKS
(📱612-125-91-14; www.allendebooks.com; Av Independencia 518; ⊙10am-6pm Mon-Sat) English-language bookstore with a good selection of books on Baja California and mainland Mexico.

ℹ Information

The majority of banks (most with ATMs) and *casas de cambio* are on or around Calle 16 de Septiembre.

Hospital Salvatierra (📱612-178-05-01; Av Paseo de los Deportistas 5115; ⊙24hr) The largest hospital in southern Baja, located 4.6km southwest of the center, via calles 5 de Febrero and Forjadores de Sudcalifornia.

State Tourist Information Booth (📱612-122-59-39; cnr Paseo Obregón & Av Bravo; ⊙8am-10pm) Brochures and pamphlets in English.

Tourist Police (📱612-122-59-39, 078; ⊙8am-10pm) Small booth on Paseo Obregón; hours may vary.

Viva La Paz (www.vivalapaz.com) La Paz' official tourism site.

ℹ Getting There & Away

AIR
Aeroméxico (📱612-122-00-91; www.aeromex ico.com; Paseo Obregón) Has flights every day but Sunday between La Paz and Los Angeles, and daily flights to Tijuana and mainland Mexican cities.

Aeropuerto General Manuel Márquez de León (📱612-124-63-36; www.aeropuertosgap.com. mx; Transpeninsular Km 9) About 9km southwest of the city, it is served by Aeroméxico, Aéreo Calafia and others. The airport has an immigration office (📱612-124-63-49; ⊙7am-11pm).

BOAT
Ferries to Mazatlán and Topolobampo leave the ferry terminal at Pichilingue, 23km north of La Paz. Baja Ferries has flights every day (📱612-125-63-24; Port) at the port and a **larger office** (📱612-123-66-00; www.bajaferries.com; Allende 1025; ⊙8am-5pm Mon-Fri, to 2pm Sat) in town.

Ferries to Mazatlán depart at 5pm Tuesday and Thursday and arriving 16 to 18 hours later; return ferries leave Mazatlán at 4pm Monday, Wednesday and Friday. Passenger fares in *salón*

FERRIES FROM LA PAZ

DESTINATION	VEHICLE	FARE (M$)
Mazatlán	car 5.4m or less/motorcycle/motorhome	2354/2006/15,469
Topolobampo	car 5.4m or less/motorcycle/motorhome	2004/1728/7963

(numbered seats) are M$1102 per adult and M$551 per child.

Topolobampo services depart at 2:30pm Monday to Friday and 11pm on Saturday. The return ferry from Topolobampo to La Paz leaves at 11pm Sunday to Friday, arriving in Pichilingue six to seven hours later. Passenger fares in *salón* are M$897 per adult and M$448 per child.

Ensure that you arrive at the pier two hours before departure. Vehicle rates vary with vehicle length and destination.

Before shipping any vehicle to the mainland, officials require a vehicle permit. You can obtain one at **Banjército** (www.banjercito.com.mx; ⊙7am-3pm Mon, Wed & Fri-Sun, to 7pm Tue & Thu) at the ferry terminal, or from its vehicle permit modules in Mexicali or Tijuana.

There's an **immigration office** (☑ 612-122-04-29; Paseo Obregón; ⊙ 8am-8pm Mon-Fri, 9am-3pm Sat) near the center of town.

BUS

Terminal Turística (☑ 612-122-78-98; cnr malecón & Av Independencia) The Terminal Turística is centrally located on the *malecón*. Convenient local services include five daily buses to Playa Tecolote (M$85, 30 minutes) and six to Playa Pichilingue (M$61, 20 minutes) between 10am and 5pm.

ⓘ Getting Around

Car-rental rates start around M$600 per day.
Budget (☑ 612-122-60-40; www.budget.com; cnr Paseo Obregón & Manuel Pineda) One of several agencies with locations both on the *malecón* and at the airport.

Around La Paz

On Península Pichilingue, the beaches nearest to La Paz are **Playa Palmira** (with the Hotel Palmira and a marina), **Playa Coromuel** and **Playa Caimancito**, both with bar-restaurants, toilets and *palapas* (open-sided huts). **Playa Tesoro**, the next beach north, has a restaurant. Some 100m north of the ferry terminal is **Playa Pichilingue**, with camping, restaurants, a bar, toilets and shade. **Playa Balandra** is a beautiful enclosed cove with shallow azure water, great for paddling toddlers. **Playa Tecolote** has plenty of spots where those with cars could camp, and launches leave from here for Espíritu Santo.

La Ventana

☑ 612 / POP 180

Come to this strip of seaside to watch whale sharks, sea lions, whales, sea turtles and a myriad of fish – without the crowds. Diving is best in the summer when the water visibility reaches 25m or 30m (80ft or 100ft). The same winds that made Los Barriles a wind-and-kite surfing mecca also blow here.

🛏 Sleeping

Baja Joe's   HOTEL $$

(☑ 612-114-00-01; www.bajajoe.com; La Ventana; s/d US$40/50; P 🢅) This place is excellent value with tidy small rooms fronting a communal terrace. The property encompasses a kitesurfing school, two kitchens and Joe's Garage, a popular bar with 10 frothy ales on tap. There are also *cabañas* (US$105 to US$115).

★Palapas Ventana   CABAÑAS $$$

(☑ 612-114-01-98; www.palapasventana.com; La Ventana; cabañas incl breakfast & lunch M$1430-2015; P 🢅 ❄ @ 🢅 🢅) Stay in a delightful *palapa*-style *cabaña* right on the water. Accommodations include a hearty, home-style

BUSES FROM LA PAZ

DESTINATION	FARE (M$)	DURATION (HR)	FREQUENCY (DAILY)
Cabo San Lucas	300	3	frequent
Ciudad Constitución	385	3	12
Ensenada	2230	22	3
Guerrero Negro	1385	11	4
Loreto	760	5	6
Mulegé	1050	6	5
San Ignacio	1340	9	4
San José del Cabo	320	3½	frequent
Tijuana	2385	24	3
Todos Santos	140	1½	frequent

breakfast and lunch. The more expensive rooms are spacious and have en suite bathrooms. US-owned, Palapas Ventana outfits for diving, snorkeling, windsurfing, kitesurfing, sportfishing, petroglyph hikes and more. It also organizes adventure tours to the Reserva de la Biosfera Sierra de la Laguna (and elsewhere).

Eating

Las Palmas
MEXICAN $

(El Sargento; mains from M$70; ⊙8am-10pm) Find this restaurant in El Sargento, a couple of kilometers north of La Ventana, in a sublime spot overlooking the water and Isla Cerralvo. The Mexican dishes are definitely a notch above the norm; try the *chilis rellenos* or stuffed clams.

Playa Central
PIZZA $$

(www.playacentralkiteboarding.com; La Ventana; pizza M$115-185; ⊙9am-10pm; 🕿) Located beachside in the center of town, this cavernous former shrimp factory not only serves terrific thin-crust pizza but also has regular live music, a popular bar, a weekly organic farmers' market and kitesurfing rental and instruction.

Los Barriles

📍624 / POP 1200

South of La Paz, the Transpeninsular brushes the gulf at this attractive small town. It is a spectacular spot for wind- and kitesurfing thanks to brisk winter westerlies that average 20 to 25 knots.

🏃 Activities

Vela Windsurf
WINDSURFING

(www.velawindsurf.com; Hotel Playa del Sol; kitesurfing from US$90; ⊙9am-5pm) One of the longer-established water-sports companies with centers worldwide. The winds die down considerably between April and August, so that is not a good time to take out a board.

🛏 Sleeping & Eating

Hotel Los Barriles
HOTEL $$

(📞624-141-00-24; www.losbarrileshotel.com; 20 de Noviembre s/n; s/d US$65/80; 🅿❄🕿❄) This hotel has a comfortable laid-back feel. Rooms are set around a pretty lagoon-style pool area, complete with outside bar and hot tub. The owner prides himself on his superior German mattresses and regularly updates the rooms; all have fridges.

⭐El Viejo
MEXICAN $

(20 de Noviembre s/n; mains M$65-80; ⊙8am-3pm; 🍴) Join the locals under the giant *palapa* and order shrimp tacos or any seafood dish (in particular); this is one of the best budget dining spots in Baja.

Caleb's Cafe
CAFE $$

(20 de Noviembre s/n; mains M$60-120; ⊙7.30am-3pm Tue-Sat; 🕿) This delightful, American-run cafe is famed for its gooey, buttery sticky buns. Other favorites include zucchini bread and carrot cake, while breakfasts are healthy and hearty (think broccoli scrambled eggs and feta-cheese omelette).

🛍 Shopping

Plum Loco
CRAFTS

(20 de Noviembre s/n; ⊙9am-5pm) The US owner imports crafts from all over Mexico, as well as further afield. He also has free books and coffee for browsers and, as an amiable long-term resident, is a great source of information.

ℹ Getting There & Away

Fairly good dirt roads follow the coast south to San José del Cabo. Beyond Cabo Pulmo and Bahía Los Frailes, are sandy but passable for most vehicles, but they are impassable for RVs and may be difficult for any vehicles after rainstorms. This road offers awesome glimpses of the coast, Shipwreck Point and the 'green' desertscape. Seven daily buses run to Los Barriles from San José del Cabo (M$90, 1½ hours), en route to La Paz.

Cabo Pulmo

📍624 / POP 50

If you're looking for snorkeling or diving without the crowds, come to Cabo Pulmo, a small town and a 17,571-acre Marine Protected Area (MPA), one of the most successful national marine parks in the world. Cabo Pulmo is also home to the only Pacific coral reef in the Sea of Cortez. You don't need a 4WD to enjoy the drive out here along the spectacular Eastern Cape (from the south) coastal road or through the Sierra de la Laguna (to the west).

🏃 Activities

For some of the best snorkeling, head for the beach at **Los Arbolitos**, or follow the shoreline hiking trail to **Las Sirenitas**, where wind and wave erosion has made the rocks look like melting wax sculptures. Eerie and beautiful, they're accessible by boat as well.

Offshore snorkeling, diving and sea-lion colony trips can be booked via companies that operate out of kiosks down by the water.

🛏 Sleeping & Eating

Eco Bungalows
CABAÑAS $$
(☎624-158-97-31; www.tourscabopulmo.com; Cabo Pulmo; cabañas with/without bathroom M$600/500; ℗) 🏊 These two solar-powered *palapa*-style *cabañas* near the water are plain but pleasantly furnished. The owners organize water sports and whale-watching tours from their Eco Adventures kiosk on the waterfront.

El Caballero
MEXICAN $
(Cabo Pulmo; mains M$80; ⊙7am-10pm Fri-Wed) This place serves huge dishes of traditional Mexican cuisine, including superb fish tacos.

Nancy's
MEXICAN $$
(☎in the US 617-524-4440; Cabo Pulmo; mains US$10-15) Hailing from Illinois and now in her 80s, Nancy gave up her B&B to concentrate on her restaurant (she was fed up with making beds). Sit under the trees on the terrace and try her crab-cake tacos or vegetable enchiladas. There's also a book exchange.

Palapa Cabo Pulmo
SEAFOOD $$
(Cabo Pulmo; mains M$100-120; ⊙noon-9pm) With its unbeatable position right on the beach, this friendly place with its terrace seating serves superb seafood dishes, like coconut shrimp. Some readers have complained of slow service but, heck, what's to fuss about when the mango margaritas taste this good.

Reserva de la Biosfera Sierra de la Laguna

Hardcore backpackers can strap on their hiking boots, fill their water bottles and head into the uninterrupted wilds of the lush and rugged Sierra de la Laguna biosphere reserve, south of the intersection of the Transpeninsular and Hwy 19. This is not a place for inexperienced hikers, or for anyone unfamiliar with the unique challenges presented by desert trails, but the rewards are great: stunning vistas, close encounters with wildlife, and a unique meadow that was once a lake bed (the feature from which the area gets its name). Baja Sierra Adventures (☎624-166-87-06; www.bajasierra dventures.com; Reserva de la Biosfera Sierra de la Laguna; day trips from US$60), in a tiny ranch called El Chorro, offers a variety of day and overnight trips, biking and trekking through

this unique region. Palapas Ventana (p732) is another option for tours to this region.

San José del Cabo
☑624 / POP 70,000
San José del Cabo is like the 'mild' sister of 'wild' Cabo San Lucas, offering quiet shopping, an attractive plaza, a beautiful church and excellent dining opportunities.

The Fiesta de San José, on March 19, celebrates the town's patron saint.

◉ Sights & Activities

San José del Cabo consists of San José proper, about 1.5km inland, and a Zona Hotelera with large beachfront hotels, condos and eyesores, er, timeshares. Linking the two areas, Blvd Mijares is a tourist zone of restaurants and galleries.

The best beaches for swimming are along the road to Cabo San Lucas and include Playa Santa María at Km 13.

★Iglesia San José
CHURCH
(Plaza Mijaras; ⊙sporadic) The colonial-style Iglesia San José, built to replace the 1730 Misión San José del Cabo, faces the spacious Plaza Mijares.

🛏 Sleeping

Reserve ahead during peak winter months.

Hotel Colli
HOTEL $$
(☎624-142-07-25; www.hotelcolli.com; Hidalgo s/n; d/tr M$750/900; ℗🅿❋🛜) Friendly and family-owned for three generations, the Colli has sunny yellow paintwork in the rooms and is in a great position, only steps away from the plaza and next to the best bakery in town.

Posada Terranova
HOTEL $$
(☎624-142-05-34; www.hterranova.com.mx; Degollado s/n; r M$750; ℗🅿❋@🛜) There are views of the pueblo from some of the contemporary look rooms at this long-standing popular choice. Plus there's a good restaurant and helpful English-speaking staff.

★Casa Natalia
BOUTIQUE HOTEL $$$
(☎624-146-71-00; www.casanatalia.com; Blvd Mijares 4; d/ste with spa from US$165/295; ❋🛜❄) The fabulous Natalia opens onto San José's plaza and has rooms overlooking a luxurious pool and meandering water feature. The whole place has a sophisticated big city feel with contemporary furnishings

San José del Cabo

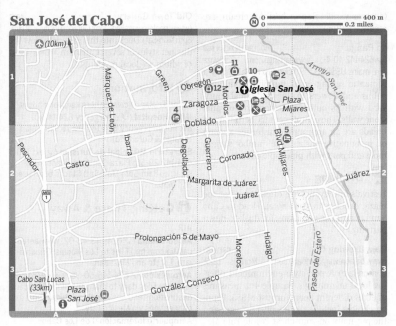

and walk-in bathrooms. The restaurant is superb.

Tropicana Inn
HOTEL **$$$**

(☑624-142-15-80; www.tropicanainn.com.mx; Blvd Mijares 30; s/d incl breakfast US$104/113; ❄☞☒) The spacious rooms are decked out with terracotta tiles and pretty floral-tiled bathrooms. Perks include satellite TV, a fridge and coffeemaker, while the bucolic courtyard has a huge, partially *palapa*-shaded pool and the squawking parrot 'Paco'.

🍴 Eating

French Riviera
BAKERY, CAFE **$$**

(www.frenchrivieraloscabos.com; cnr Hidalgo & Doblado; pastries M$35, mains M$120; ⏱7am-11pm) A French-inspired spot with tasty breads, croissants and pastries, gelati that hits the spot on a hot day, and excellent dinners. The Med-inspired decor is tasteful and contemporary.

La Ostería
MEDITERRANEAN **$$**

(Obregón 1907; tapas M$90-110, mains from M$140; ⏱11am-9pm) The leafy courtyard setting combined with live music make this an atmospheric venue in which to eat, drink and be merry. Share a tapas plate with 14 choices for just M$220 or go for a grilling with steak, chicken or fish.

San José del Cabo

◎ Top Sights

1 Iglesia San José	C1

🛏 Sleeping

2 Casa Natalia	C1
3 Hotel Colli	C1
4 Posada Terranova	B1
5 Tropicana Inn	C2

🍴 Eating

6 French Riviera	C1
7 La Ostería	C1
8 La Panga	C1
Mi Cocina	(see 2)

🍷 Drinking & Nightlife

9 Baja Brewing Co	C1

🛍 Shopping

10 La Sacristia	C1
11 Necri	C1
12 Old Town Gallery	C1

★ Mi Cocina
MEXICAN, FUSION **$$$**

(☑624-146-71-00; Blvd Mijares 4; dinner mains M$190-260; ⏱3:30-10:30pm Wed-Mon; ☎) Set inside the Casa Natalia hotel, Mi Cocina is as classy as dining in San José gets. The decor is artistic, the mains sublime, and desserts (such as vanilla flan or basil ice cream) are creative culinary masterpieces.

La Panga MODERN MEXICAN $$$
(☑ 624-142-40-41; www.lapanga.com; Zaragoza s/n; mains US$20-37; ☺ noon-10pm; 🖥) Enjoy a romantic setting amid tumbling fountains, palms and flowers in this traditional courtyard with its outdoor kitchen and original stone walls. The complimentary herb-infused breads are an appropriate taster for a menu of imaginative dishes like jumbo shrimp mole and pork with pineapple chutney.

🍷 Drinking

Festivals and events are often staged at the plaza; check with your hotel. Head to Cabo San Lucas if you're looking for dusk-to-dawn partying.

Baja Brewing Co BREWERY
(www.bajabrewingcompany.com; Morelos 1227; ☺ noon-1am) A pub-style environment offering local microbrews. Sample 4oz measures of eight different beers for just M$85. Popular choices include the Raspberry Lager and the put-hairs-on-your-chest Peyote Pale Ale.

🛍 Shopping

Boulevard Mijares is the self-proclaimed art district and boasts numerous galleries, studios and stores. The district has an Art Walk on Thursdays from 5pm to 9pm, with open studios, wine tasting and more.

La Sacristia CRAFTS
(Hidalgo 9; ☺ 10am-8pm) This multigallery space showcases art and crafts from throughout Mexico. Don't miss the rainbow-colored beaded animal sculptures made by the mainland Mexican Huichol tribe.

Necri CERAMICS
(www.necri.com.mx; Obregón 17; ☺ 10.30am-8pm) One of the longest-established ceramic stores in town, Necri also sells pewter pieces, original Talavera jewelry and mainland crafts.

Old Town Gallery ARTS
(www.theoldtowngallery.com; Obregón 1505; ☺ 10am-6pm Mon-Sat) Duck into this gallery to view the distinct styles of seven Canadian artists, most of whom are local residents.

ℹ Information

Several *casas de cambio* here keep long hours.
IMSS Hospital (☑ emergency 624-142-01-80, nonemergency 624-142-00-76; cnr Calles Hidalgo & Coronado)
Secretaria Municipal de Turismo (☑ ext 150 624-142-29-60; Plaza San José, Transpeninsular; ☺ 8am-5pm Mon-Sat) Stocks brochures and maps.

ℹ Getting There & Away

AIR

Aéreo Calafia (☑ 624-143-43-02; www.aereo calafia.com.mx) Flies to Los Mochis, Guadalajara, Loreto and Mazatlán.
Aeroméxico (☑ 624-146-50-98; www.aeromex ico.com) Flies daily to many mainland Mexican destinations and Los Angeles. International connections via Mexico City.
Aeropuerto Internacional de Los Cabos (☑ 624-146-51-11; www.aeropuertosgap.com.mx; Carretera Transpeninsular Km 43.5) The airport, north of San José del Cabo, also serves Cabo San Lucas. All airline offices are found here.

BUS

Main Bus Terminal (☑ 624-130-73-39; González Conseco s/n) East of the Transpeninsular.

CAR & MOTORCYCLE

The usual agencies rent from the airport. Rates start at about M$600 per day.

ℹ Getting Around

The official government-run company runs bright-yellow taxis and minibuses to the airport for about M$250. Local buses from the main bus terminal to the airport junction cost around M$25, but taking one means a half-hour walk to the air terminal. The toll road from the Transpeninsular to the airport costs M$32.

BUSES FROM SAN JOSÉ DEL CABO

DESTINATION	FARE (M$)	DURATION (HR)	FREQUENCY (DAILY)
Cabo San Lucas	35	1	frequent
Ensenada	2520	24	2
La Paz	320	3½	frequent
Los Barriles	115	1½	6
Tijuana	2680	28	2

Los Cabos Corridor

Nowhere in Baja is the desert disappearing faster than in the Los Cabos 'Corridor,' the once-spectacular coastline between San José del Cabo and Cabo San Lucas. In its place: cookie-cutter resorts, American chain stores, aquifer-depleting golf courses and all-inclusive hotels.

Experienced surfers claim that summer reef and point breaks at **Costa Azul** (aka Zippers) match Hawaii's best. The reefs off **Playa Chileno** are excellent for diving. **Playa Santa María**, at Km 13, is one of the best for swimming.

Cabo San Lucas

☎ 624 / POP 68,500

Come to Cabo expecting to toss your inhibitions to the wind – everyone else does. And speaking of wind, this town took a real hammering from Hurricane Odile in 2014. You wouldn't know it now though. Where else do clubs round up conga lines so that waiters can pour tequila down dancers' throats? Those moments of absurdity and abandon notwithstanding, Cabo San Lucas has a curious charm. The beaches are protected by beautiful Land's End, and the activities are endless: jet-skiing, banana-boating, parasailing, snorkeling, kitesurfing, diving and horseback-riding opportunities can all be found just by walking down to the beach. If you rent a car and get outside the city limits, you'll be surrounded by majestic scenery: cardón cacti, caracara birds and mystical *arroyos* that will impress you just as much as that crazy club you partied at the night before.

◉ Sights

★ **Land's End**   LANDMARK
Land's End is by far the most impressive attraction Cabo has to offer. Hop on a *panga* (M$175) and head to **El Arco** (the Arch), a jagged natural feature that partially fills with the tide. Pelicans, sea lions, sea, sky – this is what brought people to Cabo in the first place, and it's still magical, despite the backdrop of cruise ships.

Beaches
For sunbathing and calm waters **Playa Médano**, on the Bahía de Cabo San Lucas, is ideal. **Playa Solmar**, on the Pacific, is pretty but has a reputation for dangerous breakers and rip tides. Nearly unspoiled **Playa del Amor** (Lover's Beach; water taxi from Playa Médano or Plaza Las Glorias docks) shouldn't be missed; near Land's End, it is accessible by boat (M$175 round trip). Appropriately, **Playa del Divorcio** (Divorce Beach) is nearby, across the point on the Pacific side.

🏃 Activities

The best diving areas are **Roca Pelícano**, the sea-lion colony off Land's End, and the reef off **Playa Chileno**, at Bahía Chileno east of town. Two-tank dives cost around M$1200 and full-certification courses are M$4000 or more. **Tio Sports** (☎ 624-143-33-99; www.tiosports.com; Playa Médano; scuba diving per hr from US$60) at Playa Médano, is one of the largest water-sports outfitters, but there are numerous alternatives.

Surprisingly good snorkeling can be done right from Playa del Amor, swimming left, toward the marina. A mask, a snorkel and fins should run about M$150 per day. *Panga* rides cost about M$150 for a round trip if you bargain directly with a captain. Tipping is expected.

🧭 Tours

Ecocat   BOAT
(☎ 624-157-46-85; www.caboecotours.com; dock N-12; tours per person from US$40; 🚹) Offers two-hour sunset sailing tours, snorkeling and whale-watching trips, and also plays host to a variety of other options off its giant catamaran.

🎊 Festivals & Events

Sammy Hagar's Birthday Party   DANCE
(Cabo Wabo; ⊙ early Oct) This is a major Cabo event with lots of drinking and dancing. Invitations (free) are required – try concierges at the larger hotels or look out for giveaways.

Día de San Lucas   RELIGIOUS
(⊙ 18 Oct) A local celebration honoring the town's patron saint, with fireworks, food stalls and a fiesta spirit.

Fishing Tournaments   FISHING
(⊙ Oct-Nov) Cabo San Lucas is a popular staging ground for fishing tournaments in the autumn. The main events are the **Gold Cup**, **Bisbee's Black & Blue Marlin Jackpot** and the **Cabo Tuna Jackpot**.

Cabo San Lucas

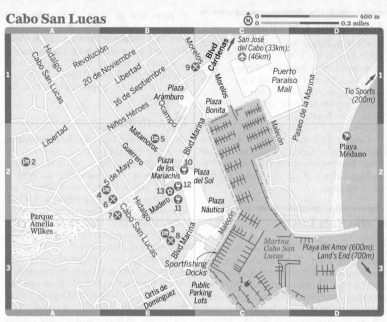

Cabo San Lucas

🔵 Activities, Courses & Tours
1 Ecocat...C3

🛏 Sleeping
2 Bungalows Breakfast Inn......................A2
3 Casa Bella...B3
4 Hotel Baja Cabo...................................B2
5 Hotel Los Milagros..............................B2

✴ Eating
Invita Bistro.....................................(see 3)
6 Jo's Garden..B2
7 Mi Casa..B2

8 Pancho's...B3
9 Venado..C1

🍷 Drinking & Nightlife
10 Canela..B2
11 J&J..B2
12 Slim's Elbow Room.............................B2

🎭 Entertainment
13 Cabo Wabo...B2

🛍 Shopping
Mercado Mexicano.........................(see 8)

🛏 Sleeping

Cabo has plenty of accommodations.

Hotel Baja Cabo   HOTEL **$$**
(📞624-105-07-11; bajacabo-hotel@hotmail.com; cnr Cabo San Lucas & Calle 5 de Mayo; r M$750; 🅿✴🛜) This former hostel still offers good value rooms with tiled floors, en suite bathrooms and air-conditioning. There's a large terrace with barbecue and hammocks and the current owner is making improvements all the time.

Hotel Los Milagros   HOTEL **$$**
(📞624-143-45-66, in USA 718-928-6647; www.losmilagros.com.mx; Matamoros 116; d from US$75;

🅿✴🛜🏊) The tranquil courtyard and 12 unique rooms provide a perfect escape from Cabo's excesses. A desert garden (complete with resident iguanas), beautiful deep-blue pool, and friendly, courteous service make a stay here unforgettable.

★ Bungalows Breakfast Inn   B&B **$$$**
(📞624-143-05-85; www.thebungalowshotel.com; cnr Libertad & Herrera; bungalows incl breakfast US$185-215; ste incl breakfast US$165-215; 🅿✖ ✴🛜🏊) Extremely attentive service, delicious breakfasts, tastefully furnished rooms, fragrant palm-thatched *palapas,* hammocks and an expansive swimming pool set this B&B apart. Fresh-fruit smoothies, fruit juic-

es, excellent coffee and warm, welcoming bilingual staff make the bungalows feel like home. Beautiful handmade soaps are one of the many tiny details that makes this *the* place to splurge.

Casa Bella   HOTEL **$$$**
(☑624-143-64-00; www.casabellahotel.com; Hidalgo 10; d from US$160; 🌐❄🛜🛏) Set amid the bustle of terrace restaurants and souvenir shops, this hacienda-style hotel has a real away-from-it-all feel thanks to the juxtaposition of its mature trees and tropical garden to its sunbaked ocher facade. Individually decorated with antiques, rooms have stunning oversized bathrooms.

🍴 Eating

Cabo's culinary scene ranges from humble taco stands to gourmet restaurants.

Venado   TAQUERÍA **$**
(☑624-147-69-21; Niños Héroes, btwn Zaragoza & Morelos; dinner mains M$50-90; ⊘11am-7am) Open all night and packed from 3am until dawn, Venado has delicious fish tacos, fresh salsas and other *antojitos* (Mexican snacks). If it's slow, the friendly waitresses might drop a coin in the jukebox and invite you to dance.

Jo's Garden   ITALIAN **$**
(☑624-157-51-18; cnr Cárdenas & Cabo San Lucas; pizzas M$80-150; ⊘5-10pm Tue-Sun) A rare find in these parts; authentic Italian-style thin-based pizza made in a traditional wood-fired oven. This simple place also sells wonderful rustic pots and decor items. There are a few outside tables and chairs on the terrace. Or opt for takeway.

Mi Casa   MEXICAN **$$$**
(www.micasarestaurant.com.mx; cnr Cárdenas & Cabo San Lucas; mains M$230-250; ⊘10am-11pm) This place has real wow factor. The courtyard-style interior has rooms on several levels and feels like something out of a 1950s Mexican musical – plants, statues, folksy murals, wicker lights, painted furniture, Día de Muertos figurines and wandering mariachis all set the stage. Try one of the traditional dishes, like *el mole poblano* (chicken with mole sauce).

Invita Bistro   MEDITERRANEAN **$$$**
(www.invitabistro.com; Hidalgo 3; mains M$220-330; ⊘5pm-midnight) Plenty of Italian-inspired dishes here, plus Spanish favorites like ice-cold Spanish gazpacho (so refreshing on a sizzling-hot day!) and French-style souffles. The portions are huge: come hungry. The decor could be a touch fancier at these prices, but few patrons seem to care.

Pancho's   MEXICAN **$$$**
(☑624-143-28-91; www.panchos.com; cnr Hidalgo & Zapata; mains M$220-300, tequila tasting M$650) Full of festive atmosphere, mariachi band tunes, good food and aromas from the open grill, Pancho's also offers 'all you want to know about tequila'. The tasting is like an intensive tequila class, with inebriation in place of a graduation certificate.

🍷 Drinking & Nightlife

Cabo is a proud party town, and alcoholic revelry is encouraged all day long. You have been warned.

J&J   BAR
(www.jnjcabo.com; Madero s/n; mojitos US$10; ⊘10am-10.30pm Mon-Sat, to 6pm Sun; 🛜) Buy your big puffer from the shelves of Cuban cigars then step next door for a real deal mojito served in a giant jam jar with plenty of fresh mint (but no tadpoles).

Canela   BAR
(Plaza del Sol; ⊘8am-11pm) A classier option than most for a Corona or cocktail. Moody lighting, rustic furniture and a curious (and entertaining) *Día de Muertos* theme.

Slim's Elbow Room   BAR
(Blvd Marina s/n; ⊘10am-midnight) In the shadow of Cabo Wabo, this teeny, easy-to-miss watering hole, wallpapered in dollar bills and clients' signatures, claims to be the world's smallest bar. With four seats inside and two standing spaces, it's a contender for sure.

Cabo Wabo   CLUB
(☑624-143-11-88; www.cabowabo.com; cnr Calles Guerrero & Madero; ⊘9am-2am; 🛜) The most famous bar and club in town, established by legendary rocker Sammy Hagar of Van Halen fame. Come here for live music and the legendary margaritas made with Hagar's own-label tequila.

🛍 Shopping

Mercado Mexicano   MARKET
(cnr Hidalgo & Zapata) This sprawling market, which contains dozens of stalls with crafts from around the country, is Cabo's most comprehensive shopping area.

ℹ Information

It's an indication of who calls the shots here that Cabo has no government-sanctioned tourist offices. The 'info' booths you'll see are owned by timeshares, condos and hotels. The staff are friendly and can offer maps and info, but their only pay comes from commissions from selling timeshare visits: expect a firm, sometimes desperate, pitch for you to visit model homes. Be warned – the promised freebies are rarely worth wasting precious vacation time on.

Internet cafes abound and many hotels have lobby computers the public can use. Rates are, not surprisingly, cheaper as you go further away from the water.

All About Cabo (www.allaboutcabo.com) A useful site for visitors.

Amerimed American Hospital (☑ 624-143-96-70; Blvd Cárdenas) Near Paseo de la Marina.

Tourist Assistance (☑ 078)

ℹ Getting There & Away

Immigration Office (☑ 624-143-01-35; cnr Blvd Cárdenas & Farías; ⊙ 9am-1pm Mon-Sat) Near the center of Cabo San Lucas.

AIR

The closest **airport** (p736) is at San José del Cabo.

BUS

Buses depart from either the **Águila** (www. autotransportesaguila.net; Hwy 19; ⊙ 24hr) company, located at the Todos Santos crossroad, north of downtown, or the bus station, a 40-minute walk northwest from the tourist zone and waterfront.

CAR & MOTORCYCLE

Numerous car-rental agencies have booths along Paseo de la Marina and elsewhere in town with prices starting at around M$70 per day.

ℹ Getting Around

The **airport shuttle bus** (☑ 624-146-53-93; per person M$150) leaves every two hours (10am to 4pm) from Plaza Bonita or Plaza Náutica. Cab van fares within town range from M$75

to M$100, and a taxi to the airport is around M$800. The airport shuttle vans (M$175) can drop you off at your hotel. Avoid rides offered by the timeshare touts.

Todos Santos

☑ 612 / POP 5200

Todos Santos is one of the most appealing towns in all of Baja, maybe even all of Mexico. A quirky mix of locals, fishers, surfers and New Age spiritualists, the town of 'All Saints' has thus far escaped the rampant tourism of the other Cape towns, but still has all kinds of things to see and do. Think Taos, New Mexico, before Ansel Adams and Georgia O'Keefe brought the world there. Be prepared for high prices, however.

Todos Santos' newfound prosperity does not reflect its history. Founded in 1723, but nearly destroyed by the Pericú rebellion in 1734, Misión Santa Rosa de Todos los Santos limped along until its abandonment in 1840. In the late 19th century Todos Santos became a prosperous sugar town with several brick *trapiches* (mills), but depleted aquifers have nearly eliminated this thirsty industry. The crumbling, photo-worthy brick structures still remain in several parts of town.

Like many other parts of Baja, Todos Santos is changing and local development is rampant. So come here now before it changes forever.

◉ Sights & Activities

Centro Cultural   MUSEUM

(☑ 612-145-00-41; Juárez; ⊙ 8am-8pm Mon-Fri, 9am-4pm Sat & Sun; 🖶) FREE Housed in a former schoolhouse, the Centro Cultural is home to some interesting nationalist and revolutionary murals dating from 1933. Also on display is an uneven collection of regional artifacts, fascinating old photos and a replica ranch house. Take note of the cradle 'cage' hanging from the ceiling.

BUSES FROM CABO SAN LUCAS

DESTINATION	FARE (M$)	DURATION (HR)	FREQUENCY (DAILY)
La Paz	300	3	frequent
Loreto	1045	8¾	5
San José del Cabo	35	1	frequent
Tijuana	2630	27	2
Todos Santos	145	1	frequent

SURF'S UP

Baja is a prime surfer's paradise with swells coming in off the Pacific that, even on bad days, are challenging and fun. Boards can be rented from surf shops (rental costs around M$250), but use extreme care at all times, as rips, undertow and behemoth waves are dangerous even for experienced surfers. If you're looking for good breaks, check out the following:

Costa Azul Needs southerly swell, but this intermediate break is a whole lot of fun and it's close to either of the Cabos.

Los Cerritos Beautiful sand, good waves, mellow vibe – this is a great beginner beach with a powerful Pacific swell…and eagle rays below.

San Miguel (p710) Rocky point break that offers awesome rides when the waves are big. Isla de Todos Santos is another option for the serious.

For more info on surfing, check out the no-nonsense *Surfer's Guide to Baja* by Mike Parise. For surf lessons, contact **Mario Surf School** (p741).

Trapiches

Scattered around town are several former *trapiches*, many of which have been repurposed over the years. The restored **Teatro Cine General Manuel Márquez de León** is one – it's on Legaspi, facing the plaza. **Molino El Progreso**, the ruin of what was formerly El Molino restaurant, is another. On Juárez, opposite the hospital, is **Molino de los Santana**.

Surfing

Surfers come here for some of the nicest swells in all of Baja. **San Pedrito** offers Hawaii-like tubes (and Hawaii-like sea urchins if you wipe out). Catch that perfect wave as eagle rays glide below you, or just hang out with the mellow crowd on **Los Cerritos** and watch the coral sun plunge into the Pacific. Boards can be rented for M$150 per day at Pescadero Surf Camp (p741), near the beaches.

Mario Surf School   SURFING
(☑612-142-61-56; www.mariosurfschool.com; Hwy 19 Km 64; 1hr surf lessons from US$60; 🚐) Offers excellent lessons for all levels in the Todos Santos and Pescadero area.

✹ Festivals & Events

Todos Santos' two-day **Festival de Artes** is held in early February. At other times it's possible to visit local artists in their home studios, and there are galleries galore.

🛏 Sleeping

Pescadero Surf Camp   CABAÑAS $
(☑612-130-30-32; www.pescaderosurf.com; Hwy 19 Km 64; casita M$450-600, penthouse M$775, campsites per person M$125; P@) Located in dusty El Pescadero, 13km south of town, Pescadero Surf Camp has everything a surfer could need – rentals, lessons, advice, a community kitchen and even a BYO swim-up bar.

★ Posada La Poza   SUITES $$$
(☑612-145-04-00; www.lapoza.com; Camino a la Poza 282; ste incl breakfast US$210-520; P 🖱 ❄ 🛜 🏊) Boasting 'Mexican hospitality combined with Swiss quality,' this beautiful boutique retreat is right on the Pacific. A saltwater swimming pool, freshwater lagoon, lush garden and superb restaurant with excellent Mexican wines set it apart. A Mexican sweat lodge and saltwater Jacuzzi offer alternate ways to let stress slip away. No TVs.

Hotel California   HOTEL $$$
(☑612-145-05-25; www.hotelcaliforniabaja.com; Juárez s/n; r M$1585; ❄ 🛜 🏊) Although this is the Hotel California that has capitalized on the legendary Eagles song the most, it is more classy sophistication than raucous rock and roll. The public spaces, in particular, are gorgeous, especially around the pool, which is surrounded by lush foliage, blood-red hibiscus and lofty palms. There is tasteful artwork throughout and the rooms are traditionally and attractively furnished.

Guaycura   BOUTIQUE HOTEL $$$
(☑612-175-08-00; www.guaycura.com; cnr Legaspi & Topete; s/d US$195/266; ❄ 🛜) All soothing colors, restful lighting and tasteful traditional furniture and artwork, the Guaycura also offers guests the free use of their beach club with its celebrated restaurant, plus a skydeck bar and small book-lined library,

WORTH A TRIP

PUNTA LOBOS

This point in Todos Santos, named for its sea-lion colony, is where the fishers launch *pangas* (skiffs). It's just a sandy beach and a bit out of the way, but anytime from 1pm to about 3pm you can come and bargain for just-off-the-boat fish to cook at home. Pelicans joust for scraps, and a hiking trail winds up the point to an unparalleled lookout spot.

complete with sink-into sofas for kickback reading time, old-fashioned style.

Todos Santos Inn BOUTIQUE HOTEL **$$$**
(☑612-145-00-40; www.todossantosinn.com; Legaspi 33; d US$125-225; ☻☎☀) Fashioned from a restored 19th-century brick building, American-owned Todos Santos Inn has only eight intimate rooms, each with a four-poster bed and a luxurious atmosphere. A tiny swimming pool sits within a verdant tropical courtyard.

✕ Eating & Drinking

Taco stands along Heróico Colegio Militar offer cheap eats.

Fonda El Zaguán MODERN MEXICAN **$$**
(Juaréz; mains M$125-165; ☺noon-9pm Mon-Sat; ☎🍴) Good value prices and creative Mexican cuisine make this one of the most popular places on the main street. Opt for a daily special such as fillet of fish sauteed in a mango *beurre blanc* or organic salad with grilled tofu. And step outside the box with a bitter orange margarita (M$70). Delicious!

Ristorante Tre Galline ITALIAN **$$**
(☑612-145-02-74; cnr Topete & Juaréz; dinner mains from M$140; ☺noon-10pm Mon-Sat) This attractive Italian-owned restaurant has tables arranged on descending terraces, which give everyone a little more privacy (candlelight adds to the atmosphere). The seafood platters are particularly scrumptious and the pasta is made fresh daily.

★ Café Santa Fe ITALIAN **$$$**
(☑612-145-03-40; Centenario 4; dinner mains M$310-500; ☺noon-9pm Wed-Mon) The *insalata Mediterranea* (steamed seafood drizzled in lemon juice and oil) will make even seafood haters change their ways. The open-air kitchen, designed by the owner himself, allows you to see the food as it's being prepped. Anything on the menu will delight, surprise and tantalize.

If you need suggestions, however, go for the mussels in wine or any one of the various handmade raviolis: lobster, meat, or spinach and ricotta cheese.

Los Adobes de Todos Santos MODERN MEXICAN **$$$**
(www.losadobesdetodossantos.com; Av Hidalgo; mains M$210-255; ☺11am-9pm; ☎) Check out the stunning desert garden at the back of this popular restaurant with its *alta cocina* menu of creatively prepared traditional dishes like *caldo pepita:* a homespun chicken broth with dumplings and cilantro spiked with guajillo chili peppers and sprinkled with pumpkin seeds.

Cafe Felix CAFE
(Juaréz; frappé M$55; ☺8am-9pm Wed-Mon; ☎) This arty cafe is always packed with the local expats here for great coffee and gut-busting breakfasts. On hot days, go for one of its dozen-plus frappés or a creamy mango smoothie.

🛍 Shopping

There are numerous galleries to wander through, especially around the plaza.

Faces of Mexico CRAFTS
(Morelos; ☺11am-6pm Wed-Mon) Duck into the warren of dark rooms here to discover an extraordinary collection of masks, sculpture, ethnic art, antique baubles and plenty of somber Día de Muertos beaded and painted decorative skulls. This is not your usual souvenir shop – check it out.

Agua y Sol Joyeria JEWELRY
(cnr Centenario & Analia Gutiérrez; ☺10am-5pm) The silver jewelry here is made by local artisans and well priced with some stunning, unusual designs.

ℹ Information

El Tecolote (☑612-145-02-95; cnr Juárez & Av Hidalgo) The town lacks an official tourist office, but this English-language bookstore has magazines with town maps and a sketch map of nearby beach areas.

ℹ Getting There & Away

Hourly between 6:30am and 10:30pm, buses head to La Paz (M$140, 1½ hours) and to Cabo San Lucas (M$145, one hour) from the **bus stop** (☑612-148-02-89; Heróico Colegio Militar; ☺7am-10pm) between Zaragoza and Morelos.

Copper Canyon & Northern Mexico

Includes ➡

Ferrocarril Chihuahua
Pacífico 749
Urique. 753
Creel 757
Batopilas 761
Puerto Peñasco 765
San Carlos. 770
Álamos. 771
Los Mochis 775
Chihuahua. 777
Durango 786
Parras. 791
Monterrey 794

Best Places to Eat

➡ Teresitas (p774)

➡ Madre Oaxaca (p799)

➡ La Galería Café (p798)

➡ Cremería Wallander (p788)

➡ Bonifacio's (p771)

Best Places to Stay

➡ Riverside Lodge (p763)

➡ Hotel San Felipe El Real (p781)

➡ Hotel Luz del Sol (p773)

➡ Hacienda de los Santos (p773)

➡ Méson Verde Obscuro (p792)

Why Go?

Northern Mexico is the ultimate frontier land: vast cactus-strewn deserts, craggy mountains and breathtaking canyons define this most iconic of regions, familiar to almost anyone from its role in countless Wild West movies. If the landscape is diverse, then the people of the north are equally so: cowboys, revolutionaries and bandits have, over the centuries, left their mark on the region, while the varied and still deeply traditional indigenous peoples of this part of the country remain some of Mexico's least westernized.

Though the narco wars have impacted the north terribly in recent years, it remains a safe place to visit for anyone taking a few sensible precautions, and these days you'll find you have it pretty much to yourself. The Farrocarril Chihuahua Pacifico (Copper Canyon Railway), Mexico's only remaining long-distance passenger train ride, is the region's most outstanding sight, but its colonial towns, superb beaches and diverse wildlife are other strong lures.

When to Go
Chihuahua

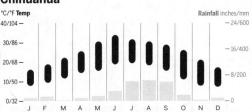

Jun & Jul Heavy rainfall. Key festivals like Las Jornadas Villistas in Hidalgo del Parral.

Late Sep–Oct Pleasantly hot during the day. Good time to visit the coming-into-bloom Copper Canyon.

Dec & Jan Balmy, dry weather on the Pacific coast makes for a popular winter escape.

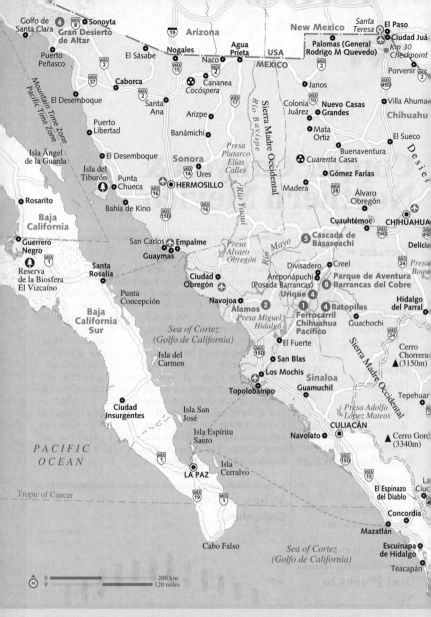

Copper Canyon & Northern Mexico Highlights

1 Riding Mexico's last passenger train through mesmerizing canyon scenery on the **Ferrocarril Chihuahua Pacífico** (p749).

2 Checking into a colonial hotel and taking in the beauty of the exquisite old silver town of **Álamos** (p771).

3 Being shocked and awed by Monterrey's **Horno3** (p797) museum, a monument to the city's heavy metal heritage.

4 Exploring the canyon's floor and visiting the delightful towns of **Urique** (p753) and **Batopilas** (p761).

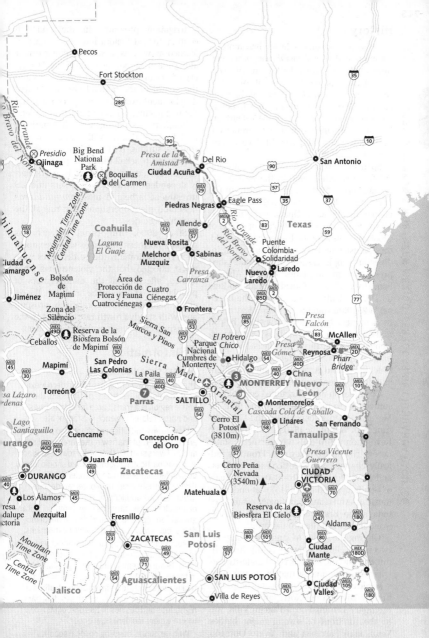

5 Chilling in the plunge pool of Mexico's highest full-time waterfall, **Cascada de Basaseachi** (p761).

6 Experiencing the lunar landscapes and silence of the desert in the remote **Gran Desierto de Altar** (p767).

7 Drinking local wines in the tranquil and unpretentious surrounds of colonial **Parras** (p791).

8 Soaring over the incredible Copper Canyon on a series of zip-lines at the adrenaline-pumping **Parque de Aventura Barrancas del Cobre** (p756).

History

Pre-Hispanic northern Mexico had more in common with the Anasazi and other cultures of the southwest USA than with central Mexico. The most important town here was Paquimé, a vital trading link between central Mexico and the dry north before its destruction around AD 1340. Outlying Paquimé settlements such as Cuarenta Casas built their dwellings on cliffsides for protection against attack.

Spanish slavers and explorers, arriving chiefly in search of gold in the 16th century, had mixed fortunes in the north. In the northwest they encountered indigenous peoples including the Opata, Seri, Yaqui and Mayo. Rather than the fabled province of Cíbola with its supposed seven cities of gold, the Spanish found silver and, conscripting indigenous people as slave miners, established prosperous mining cities such as Álamos. Spaniards also soon forged the Camino Real de Tierra Adentro (Royal Road of the Interior), a 2560km trade route from Mexico City to Santa Fe, New Mexico, wwhich helped make towns en route such as Durango extremely wealthy. In the northeast, however, harsh conditions and attacks by indigenous Chichimecs and Apaches meant settlement and development came more slowly.

The Spanish never tightened control here sufficiently to quell revolts. In the fight for Mexican Independence (1810), the Mexican–American War of the 1840s and the Mexican Revolution (1910–20) the northern states necessarily played a key role. Frontiers radically changed with Mexico's loss of Texas and New Mexico (1830s–1850s): the Treaty of Guadalupe Hidalgo (1848) that ended the Mexican–American War finally established today's Río Bravo del Norte (Rio Grande) frontier between the two nations.

Glaring inequities of land ownership between the elite – grown wealthy from the mines – and the impoverished majority contributed to the unrest that made the north a Mexican Revolution hot spot. The revolutionary División del Norte, an army led by legendary Durango-born Pancho Villa, was in the forefront of several major battles. Venustiano Carranza and Álvaro Obregón, other main revolutionary figures, were, respectively, from the northern states of Coahuila and Sonora. All three were initially allies and subsequently enemies in the Revolution, which meant the split of allegiances in the north was acute.

Irrigation programs in the mid-20th century turned Sonora into the granary of Mexico as well as a cattle-ranching center alongside neighboring Chihuahua. Discovery of petroleum, coal and natural gas and the arrival of the railroad also accelerated development from the late 19th century, and the region emerged as an industrial leader.

Today this is the most North Americanized part of Mexico, with money and resources surging back-and-forth across the border and baseball the main sport in many towns. The Texan economy is particularly dependent on Mexican workers and US investment is behind most *maquiladoras* (assembly-plant operations) that ring all the region's big cities.

Since 2006, drug cartel violence has plagued northern Mexico as gangs compete for territory. Initially the border cities were worst affected, but the violence has since spread, affecting all the main centers of population. Yet despite the headlines, the region's economy remains relatively prosperous, with steady growth rates (except in the tourism sector, which continues to suffer).

ℹ Information

DANGERS & ANNOYANCES

The vast majority of visitors to northern Mexico enjoy a safe, trouble-free trip. That said, the entire region is a transit area for illegal drugs, and narco-related violence is a fact of life.

Most towns and cities are affected to a degree, and trouble erupts as new routes are established and turf wars shift. Of the border towns, Ciudad Juárez is particularly notorious and should ideally be avoided, although many travelers still pass through without incident. Monterrey, despite having serious problems as recently as 2011, has been calm for several years now. Tampico, Durango and Torreón have also had their share of incidents, but remain perfectly viable destinations.

Most violence is gang-on-gang or between the cartels and the security forces, and foreign tourists are extremely unlikely to get caught up in these skirmishes: indeed, tourists are statistically more likely to be involved in a traffic accident than a shoot-out. It's worth avoiding bars, nightclubs and casinos in this part of Mexico, where violent incidents can occur.

Web resources advising on local security situations are rarely that useful. Insight Crime (www.insightcrime.org) provides regular reports on drug violence in Mexico as does Borderland Beat (www.borderlandbeat.com). Your best bet is asking hotel or travel agency staff for the latest safety situation in any given area.

If driving, lock up when on the road to guard against carjackings. Try to avoid driving after dark, avoid isolated roads and use safer toll roads whenever possible.

Particular care should be taken on roads heading from/to border towns. Hwys 101 and 180 in Tamaulipas are notorious for carjackings and armed robberies.

The region is also a cultivation zone for marijuana and – in the Sierra Madre Occidental, which spans parts of northwest Mexico, the Copper Canyon and parts of central north Mexico – opium poppies. It is unwise to travel anywhere off the beaten path here without a trusted local guide.

❶ Getting There & Around

There are international airports in Monterrey, Chihuahua, Hermosillo and Torreón. Monterrey has the most international connections, including flights to the US cities of Chicago, Dallas, Detroit and Los Angeles. Los Mochis and Durango airports also have good national connections. A new airport serving the Copper Canyon was scheduled to open in Creel in 2016.

Two ferry crossings link Baja California with northwest Mexico.

Once inside northern Mexico, connections are excellent, with good, frequent bus services and highways heading south. Better roads are usually toll roads, and the tolls add up fast: expect to pay almost M$1000 for the journey between Durango and Los Mochis on the impressive new highway through the mountains. It's often remote country, so if you're driving, don't set out beyond major highways without a full tank of gas.

THE COPPER CANYON & FERROCARRIL CHIHUAHUA PACÍFICO

The simply breathtaking highland scenery in the Copper Canyon (Barranca del Cobre) region is nature on a very grand scale indeed. Of everything there is to see in northern Mexico, nothing comes close to the Copper Canyon, with its astonishing vistas at every turn, towering pine-clad mountains and the fascinating culture of the native Tarahumara people.

A labyrinth of seven main canyons covers an area four times larger than Arizona's Grand Canyon, and the canyons are, in several places, considerably deeper (over 1800m) than the Grand Canyon's. The canyons have been gouged out of the sierra's 25-million-year-old volcanic rock by tectonic movements and rivers. Tropical fruits grow in the canyon bottoms while the high ground is covered in alpine vegetation and, often, winter snows. Dress accordingly, and be prepared year round for both chilly and warm days.

The name Copper Canyon, coined by the Spanish when they mistook the greenish glow of lichen for copper, refers specifically to the chasm carved by the upper course of the Río Urique. Apart from the Barranca del Cobre, its other major canyons are the Barrancas de Urique, Sinforosa, Batopilas, Oteros, Chinipas and Candameña. All seven plunge to depths of 1300m or more.

It's perfectly possible to visit the region by car, though most prefer to take the 'Chepe' railway (the Ferrocarril Chihuahua Pacífico), perhaps Mexico's greatest feat of engineering. This epic railroad meanders over 656km between Los Mochis near Mexico's Pacific coast and Chihuahua on its central high plains.

You *can* ride the train all the way through, or even make an overnight stop before heading back the way you came. But the spectacular canyon deserves much more exploration. The highland village of Creel makes an excellent base near some outrageously scenic spots. For similar cusp-of-the-canyon experiences you can also stay in the smaller villages of Cerocahui, Areponápuchi or Divisadero, all near the railway. But to get a real feel for the canyons, venture right down into them and stay in either Urique or Batopilas, the two most charming and remote towns on the canyon bottom. All manner of natural wonders – cliffs, towering rock massifs, rivers, waterfalls, lakes, forests – as well as fascinating indigenous culture, are accessible from all these places by foot, horse and in many cases mountain bike or motor vehicle.

For the ultimate buzz, head to the Parque de Aventura Barrancas del Cobre, where you can soar over death-defying drops on a series of Mexico's most hair-raising zip-lines almost to the canyon floor, before returning by cable car to the canyon top. It's a touristy place popular with groups, but nevertheless well worth visiting overnight to explore the canyon in such an exciting and immersive way.

Good seasons to visit are spring or autumn, when temperatures are not too hot at the bottom of the canyons nor too cold

Copper Canyon

0   20 km
0   12 miles

Adolfo López
Mateos (La Junta)

Presa Abraham
Gonzalez

Cuauhtémoc (40km);
Chihuahua (150km)

Vallecillo

MEX 16

Yepáchi

Hermosillo
(420km)

Pinos Altos

San
Miguel

Sigoyna

MEX 16

Basaseachi

Parque Nacional
Cascada de
Basaseachi

Ocampo

Huajumar

Cascada de
Basaseachi

Río Tomochi

Río Terrero

Treviño   Ataros

Río Agua Caliente

Barranca de Candameña

Talayotes

San Juanito

Ferrocarril Chihuahua Pacífico
(Copper Canyon Railway)

Río
Mayo

Sierra Monterde

Uruachi

Río Oteros

Maguarichi

Bocoyna

Valle de las Ranas
y los Hongos

Sisoguichi

Valle de los
Monjes

Barranca de Oteros

San José
Guacayvo

Creel

Lago
Arareko

Panalachi

Chihuahua

Aguas
Termales
Rekowata

Cascada Cusárare

El Lazo

Pitorreal

Barranca de Tararecua

Cusárare

Areponápuchi
(Posada Barrancas)

Divisadero

Parque de Aventuras
Barrancas del Cobre

San Rafael

Wakajípare

Barranca del Cobre

Basihuare

Tejabán

Río Mochomo

Barranca de Chinipas

Chinipas

Bahuichivo

Cuiteco

Guaguachique

Rejogochi

Humirá

Parajes

Chúro

Parque Natural
Barranca del Cobre

Samachique

Río Chinipas

Témoris

Cerocahui

Cerro del
Gallego

Guadalupe
Coronado

Napuchi

Basigochi

Témoris
Station

Álamos
(50km)

Mesa de
Arturo

Urique

Mirador
La Bufa

Quírare

Guamuchil

Guapalaina

Pie de la
Cuesta

La Bufa

Río Septentrión

Piedras
Verdes

Barranca de Batopilas

Sonora

Sinaloa

Cerro
Colorado

Batopilas

Yoquivo

Tubares

Satevó

El Fuerte (60km);
Los Mochis (135km)

Choix
(80km)

Río Fuerte

Barranca de Urique

Río Urique

---

at the top. A particularly good time to come is between mid-September and November, when vegetation is green after the summer rains (which fall from around late June to late August). Hiking and riding down in the canyons is only really practicable from October to March. May and June are near-unbearably hot at the bottom of the canyons but far milder at the top.

The isolated recesses of this region harbor marijuana and opium plantations, which occasionally provoke bloody incidents involving rival groups and/or the Mexican army. While these narcos do not target tourists, it's advisable to sound out the situation before venturing to remote areas, and take a trusted local guide if you go anywhere really off the beaten track.

Ferrocarril Chihuahua Pacífico

Ferrocarril Chihuahua Pacífico   TRAIN RIDE
(Copper Canyon Railway; ✆ 614-439-72-12, from the US 888-484-1623; www.chepe.com.mx; full journey 1st/2nd class M$2482/1767) The stats say everything: 656km of track, 37 bridges, 86 tunnels and more than 60 years in the making. The Ferrocarril Chihuahua Pacífico is one of the world's most incredible rail journeys, and northern Mexico's biggest single attraction. Completed in 1961, it is as phenomenal in its engineering prowess as in the canyon views it yields. Nicknamed 'El Chepe' (using the Spanish initials of 'Chihuahua' and 'Pacífico'), the railway operates one daily train in each direction, taking a full day.

The line is the major link between Chihuahua and the coast, heavily used for freight as well as passengers. It connects the Pacific coast with the mountainous, arid interior of northern Mexico via tricky canyon gradients that force it to rise up over 2400m.

Between Los Mochis and El Fuerte, the train trundles through flat farmland, then begins to climb through hills speckled with dark pillars of cacti. It passes over the long Río Fuerte bridge and through the first of the 86 tunnels about four hours after leaving Los Mochis. The train hugs the sides of deepening canyons and makes a spectacular zigzag ascent into a tunnel above Témoris, after which pine trees appear on the hillsides. By the next station, Bahuichivo, you are in the Sierra Madre uplands, with flower-dotted meadows bisecting an entrancing alpine landscape. The biggest highlight of the train ride is stopping at Divisadero, where you get your only glimpse of the actual Copper Canyon. The train circles back over itself in a complete loop to gain height at the suitably named El Lazo (the Lasso), before chugging on to Creel and Chihuahua.

There's not that much difference between *primera* and *económica* carriages – the former has a dining room, the latter a canteen. Snacks cost M$20, meals around M$100. Coffee is instant in both classes. All carriages are rather showing their age (dating

from the 1980s), and Chepe ticket prices are overpriced given the moderate comfort levels. Both classes have air-conditioning, heating and reclining seats with ample leg room. The *clase económica* is certainly nice enough for most travelers, although often you'll have no choice but *primera*.

Note that you're not allowed to consume alcohol on any Chepe train, but that smoking is tolerated in the open-air gap between carriages. All trains are staffed with machine-gun-toting police.

ℹ️ Information

TICKETS

You can board the train at any station without a ticket if there are free seats, and pay the conductor. Outside the peak seasons (Semana Santa, July/August and Christmas/New Year), you will almost always be able to do this. However it's advisable to reserve/buy tickets a month or more ahead for peak-season travel, and a day ahead at other times, although in practice most of the time you'll have no problem buying tickets on the day of travel.

Tickets are sold at Los Mochis station and Chihuahua station for trips starting at any station. *Primera express* tickets are sold up to a month in advance, and *clase económica* tickets a day in advance. Tickets can be made up to a year in advance by telephone (English speakers available) and email. On the *primera express*, you can make stopovers (usually up to three) at no extra cost, if you specify places and dates when you make the booking.

For same-day tickets, you should be at Los Mochis or Chihuahua station an hour ahead of departure. Only Los Mochis, Creel, Cuauhtémoc and Chihuahua stations have ticket offices.

Agencies such as **Viajes Flamingo** (p777) in Los Mochis and **Rojo y Casavantes** (p783) in Chihuahua sell *primera express* tickets at least one day in advance. Any of the area's many **Balderrama Hotels** (www.mexicoscoppercanyon.com), which command a virtual monopoly on tour groups in the region, will also assist their clients in making reservations.

El Fuerte

☑️ 698 / POP 13,000 / ELEV 180M
Clustered around a striking plaza and with a center packed full of brightly painted colonial houses, El Fuerte oozes historic character. For many centuries the most important commercial center in northwestern Mexico due to its proximity to the silver mines in the canyons, this is now a picturesque little town surrounded by one

RAILWAY SCHEDULE – FERROCARRIL CHIHUAHUA PACÍFICO

There's one daily train in each direction. *Primera express* (1st-class only, and with fewer stops) trains run on Monday, Wednesday, Thursday and Saturday from Los Mochis. From Chihuahua they run on Sunday, Tuesday, Wednesday and Friday. On other days, the train has both *primera* and *clase económica* carriages, meaning it travels rather slower and makes more stops, which impacts the timetable and means that the entire journey takes around an hour longer (13½ hours in total) to run the whole route.

Schedules change and both trains tend to run a little late (by an hour or two), so timetables comprise just a rough guideline. If you are heading to Los Mochis with hopes of catching the Baja ferry from Topolobampo the same day, don't count on it; you'll find it far easier to schedule an overnight stop in Los Mochis.

There is no time change between Los Mochis and Chihuahua.

Eastbound – Los Mochis to Chihuahua

STATION	PRIMERA EXPRESS ARRIVES	FARE FROM LOS MOCHIS (M$)	CLASE ECONÓMICA ARRIVES (TUE, FRI, SUN)	FARE FROM LOS MOCHIS (M$)
Los Mochis	6am (departs Los Mochis)	–	6am (departs Los Mochis)	–
El Fuerte	8:16am	456	9:24am	325
Témoris	11:20am	809	11:47am	579
Bahuichivo	12:20pm	958	12:42pm	685
San Rafael	1:27pm	1083	1:52pm	771
Posada Barrancas (Areponápuchi)	1:47pm	1121	2:16pm	798
Divisadero	2:20pm	1136	2:58pm	809
Creel	3:44pm	1357	4:12pm	966
Cuauhtémoc	6:37pm	1976	8:26pm	1407
Chihuahua	8:54pm	2482	9:28pm	1767

Westbound – Chihuahua to Los Mochis

STATION	PRIMERA EXPRESS ARRIVES	FARE FROM CHIHUAHUA (M$)	CLASE ECONÓMICA ARRIVES (MON, THU, SAT)	FARE FROM CHIHUAHUA (M$)
Chihuahua	6am (departs Chihuahua)	–	6am (departs Chihuahua)	–
Cuauhtémoc	8:25am	505	8:25am	360
Creel	11:20am	1125	11:47am	804
Divisadero	1:04pm	1269	1:41pm	961
Posada Barrancas (Areponápuchi)	1:11pm	1345	1:52pm	972
San Rafael	1:37pm	1398	2:16pm	999
Bahuichivo	2:28pm	1524	3:12pm	1085
Témoris	3:25pm	1672	4:12pm	1191
El Fuerte	6:23pm	2170	7:19pm	1548
Los Mochis	8:30pm	2482	9:28pm	1767

of Latin America's last-standing dry tropical forests. Far preferable to Los Mochis as a place to start or end a trip on the Ferrocarril Chihuahua Pacífico, it's worth a stay of more than just a night to take a trip on the Río Fuerte and explore the unique subtropical countryside.

El Fuerte was founded in 1564, and is named for a 17th-century fort built on its distinctive high point of Cerro de las Pilas to protect settlers from indigenous attacks.

◉ Sights & Activities

Bosque Secreto FOREST
(Secret Forest) 🖉 Five hundred years ago, over 550,000 sq km of dry tropical forest stretched down the coast from northern Mexico to Panama. Much of the remaining 10% is around El Fuerte, an area known as Bosque Secreto. The delightful Río Fuerte, which is incredibly rich in birdlife (including herons, osprey, kingfishers and flycatchers), winds through much of the forest. Expert bird-watching guide Chal Gámez at the Hotel Río Vista organizes kayak or boat trips (M$250 per person) along the river, taking in some 2000-year-old petroglyphs.

Museo Mirador El Fuerte MUSEUM
(☑ 698-893-15-01; Montes Claros; adult/student M$10/5; ⊙7am-7pm; P) This curiously designed museum, built to look like the town's original fort, has a moderate collection of exhibits including ceramics, Mayo handicrafts and information about the Bosque Secreto. There are some splendid views over the river from here.

🛌 Sleeping

Hotel Guerrero HOTEL $
(☑698-893-05-24; www.hotelyhostelguerrero.jimdo.com; Juárez 106; r M$350; ⊝❄🛜) This excellent budget hotel in the center of El Fuerte has charming staff who go the extra mile to look after their guests. The rooms, set around a shady pillared patio, are colorful and comfortable. Avoid the cell-like rooms on the left, and try for one of the older but roomier ones on the right.

Hotel Río Vista HOTEL $
(☑698-104-26-47, 698-893-04-13; hotelriovista@hotmail.com; Junto Al Museo Mirador; r M$500; P❄🛜🛁) This quirky place tucked behind the town's hilltop museum has been hosting travelers for years. Stylistically it's a bit of a shock to the senses with murals, garish colors and an excess of Mexicana and oth-

er bizarre curios (plus maintenance could be better). But hey, the superb river views compensate. Chal Gámez, the bird-watching owner, offers highly recommended, guided boat tours.

Hotel La Choza HOTEL $$
(☑698-893-12-74; www.hotellachoza.com; 5 de Mayo 101; r M$850; P⊝❄🛜🛁) This deceptively large hotel has a colonial facade, but becomes rather more modern as you enter its enormous courtyard. It boasts very inviting rooms, all with quaint touches such as hand-painted sinks, enormous crucifixes over the beds and high, brick-vaulted ceilings. It's excellent value, and the in-house Diligencias restaurant is a good bet too.

★Torres del Fuerte BOUTIQUE HOTEL $$$
(☑698-893-19-74; www.hotelestorres.com; Robles 102; r from M$1200; P⊝❄🛜) A 400-year-old hacienda that fuses colonial class, rustic elegance and contemporary art, set around gorgeous gardens. All rooms are uniquely themed, many with slate bathrooms and exposed adobe walls. Giant cacti frame the rooms, while high ceilings with wooden beams soar overhead. There's also a gourmet restaurant, **Bonifacio's** (mains M$70-300; ⊙7am-10pm).

Posada del Hidalgo HERITAGE HOTEL $$$
(☑698-893-02-42; www.hotelposadadelhidalgo.com; Hidalgo 101; s/d/tr M$1525/1625/1850; P❄@🛜🛁) This highly atmospheric hotel inside a rusty red colonial hacienda offers bundles of classic charm with spacious, elegant rooms grouped around shady garden courtyards and jaw-dropping public areas. There's a spa, a beautiful open-air restaurant, a Jacuzzi and a popular bar for socializing. Hummingbirds join guests for breakfast.

🍴 Eating

The wealth of fresh water around El Fuerte produces must-have local specialties such as *cauques* or *langostinos* (freshwater crayfish) and *lobina* (black bass). That said, restaurant choices are very limited in town.

Restaurante Chayita MEXICAN $
(cnr Juárez & Independencia; meals M$40-80; ⊙7:30am-7pm Mon-Sat) Head here for cheap breakfasts, *carne asada* (marinated grilled beef), *tostadas* (crispy corn snack with topping) and *chiles rellenos* (stuffed peppers) in very humble, plastic-chair-fantastic surrounds.

El Mesón del General   FISH $$

(☑698-893-02-60; Juárez 202; mains M$95-250; ⊙11am-9:30pm; ☻) Traditional, formal restaurant that specializes in fish and seafood, with several styles of *pulpo* (octopus) and combo plates of various river delicacies. You'll find it on El Fuerte's main drag, an oasis from the bustle of the nearby market.

Restaurante Diligencias   MEXICAN $$

(☑698-893-12-74; 5 de Mayo 101; mains M$68-200; ⊙7am-11pm; ☻☎) This restaurant inside Hotel La Choza is a good choice for breakfasts (around M$50), with typical Mexican choices and free coffee refills served up under soaring vaulted ceilings, tribal masks and a mounted bull's head. Later on, you'll find good steaks and seafood, including shrimp tacos.

❶ Getting There & Around

Buses to Los Mochis (M$80, two hours) depart about every half-hour, 5am to 7:30pm, from Juárez near Calle 16 de Septiembre, right in the center of town. From Los Mochis it's easy to connect to elsewhere in northern Mexico.

The train station is 6km south of town (M$100 by taxi). Many hotels offer station pickup and drop-off for clients, for which they may or may not charge (up to the taxi rate). If you arrive by train in the evening, waiting shared taxis charge M$50 a person for a run into the town center.

The dirt road to Álamos from here requires 4WD and takes five hours: it's actually quicker heading to Los Mochis and taking the highway.

Cerocahui

☑635 / POP 1600 / ELEV 1600M

The tiny, attractive village of Cerocahui, dedicated mainly to forestry, sits in the middle of a verdant, vista-laden valley, and is easily reached from the Chepe stop Bahuichivo, 16km away. The canyon country around here sees far fewer tourists than the region near Creel, and the enticing canyon-bottom village of Urique is within striking range.

On the central plaza, Cerocahui's pretty yellow-domed church, San Francisco Javier de Cerocahui, was founded in 1680.

There's good hiking around Cerocahui, and excursions (offered by all accommodations) to Cerro del Gallego, a spectacular lookout over the Barranca de Urique, 25km on along the Urique road, are well worth it.

🛏 Sleeping & Eating

★ Hotel & Restaurante Jade   MEXICAN $$

(☑635-456-52-75; Parque Central; r incl Bahuichivo transfers M$600; ⊙7am-9:30pm; Ⓟ☻✿) This simple place has 10 clean and comfortable rooms (each with twin beds and balconies) that are the best value in town. The warm welcome from hosts Alberto and Francia and the outstanding cooking (including homemade bread, fish dishes and veggie options; meals M$60 to M$90) in the adjacent restaurant really make this place stand out though. A range of tours is offered.

Hotel Paraíso del Oso   HOTEL $$$

(☑in Chihuahua 614-421-33-72, in the US 800-884-3107; www.mexicohorse.com; s/d incl full board & Bahuichivo transfers US$120/185; Ⓟ☻@✿) This excellent family-owned rural lodge is a great base for bird-watching, hikes (from M$40), horseback rides (M$130 per hour) and community tourism (the owners have good Tarahumara contacts). The set-up includes spacious, ranch-style rooms overlooking a garden courtyard and a fascinating book collection to browse. It's located 2km north of Cerocahui, on the road to Bahuichivo.

Cabañas San Isidro   CABAÑAS $$$

(☑635-293-75-02, 635-456-52-57; www.copper canyonamigos.com; Carretera a Urique Km 24; s/d/tr incl 3 meals & Bahuichivo transfers US$85/115/140; Ⓟ) ✎ High in the hills above Cerocahui, 8km along the road to Urique, this working farm makes a perfect (if isolated) rural base for all kinds of hikes, horseback riding and trips in canyon country. Owners Mario and Tito have excellent links to the Tarahumara community's runner-guides. The cozy adobe-and-wood cabins have wood-burning stoves and the cooking is tasty and plentiful.

Hotel Misión   HOTEL $$$

(☑635-456-52-94; www.hotelmision.com; Parque Central; r incl full board & Bahuichivo transfers M$2850; Ⓟ☻@✉) This delightful former hacienda on the town's central plaza offers grand if somewhat rustic accommodations complete with *chimeneas* (fireplaces), an evocative bar-restaurant, a games room with a pool table and lovely gardens planted with vines. It's popular with tour groups 'doing' the canyon, but discounts are often available to independent travelers. Wi-fi is planned for the near future.

WORTH A TRIP

CUAUHTÉMOC

The small city of Cuauhtémoc, 103km west of Chihuahua, is chief center for Mexico's Mennonites. Often blonde-haired and blue-eyed, with men wearing baggy overalls and women wearing long dark dresses and headscarves, Mennonites speak in a dialect of Low German and trace their origins to Dutchman Menno Simons who founded the sect in the 16th century. Mennonite beliefs (including an extreme pacifism and a refusal to swear oaths of loyalty other than to God) put them at odds with many governments, and thus communities have from time to time moved en masse from one country to another. In the 1920s around 6000 Mennonites left Canada for northern Mexico and the largest numbers of Mexican Mennonites are today living around Cuauhtémoc.

Indeed, most travelers come to this orderly town, standing in a lush vale of country-side producing most of Mexico's apples, solely to see the Mennonite *campos* (villages). The widely acclaimed movie *Luz silenciosa* (Silent Light), directed by Mexico's Carlos Reygadas – a story of adulterous love in a Mennonite community – was filmed here in 2007. It gave the town unprecedented publicity.

Mennonite *campos* are best visited on a tour (around M$500 per person, if there's a minimum of five people), which can be set up in Creel, as you will learn far more (and visiting the *campos* independently is not always possible). If you haven't pre-arranged a tour, ask at the Museo y Centro Cultural Menonita. It's best to visit during the week (on Saturdays and Sundays Mennonite businesses are partially or fully closed).

Museo y Centro Cultural Menonita (☑625-583-18-95; www.museomenonita.com; Carretera Cuauhtémoc-Álvaro Obregón Km 10.5; adult/child M$25/15; ☺9am-6pm Mon-Fri) is a large museum out in Mennonite country just north of town holding tools and other paraphernalia from the early years of Mennonite settlement here. A variety of crafts, cheeses and fruit preserves are sold. On the road out, **Campo 2B** (Carretera Cuauhtémoc-Álvaro Obregón Km 7.5) purportedly has the best *quesería* (cheese factory/shop). A taxi to both the museum and cheese factory from downtown and back will cost you about M$350.

The train station northeast of the central square is the last/first stop on the Ferrocarril Chihuahua Pacífico, with daily trains to Chihuahua, and Los Mochis via Creel.

Estrella Blanca (☑625-582-10-18; cnr Allende & Calle 13), at the east end of town, has buses to Chihuahua (M$124, 1½ hours) every 45 minutes and over a dozen daily to Creel (M$195, three hours).

❶ Getting There & Away

Cerocahui hotels will pick you up at Bahuichivo station if you have reserved. If you haven't, you can often catch a ride with one of their vans anyway, though they'll be expecting you to check in on arrival.

Alternatively a local bus leaves Bahuichivo station for Cerocahui (M$40, 40 minutes) and Urique (M$180, 3½ hours or more) daily after the last train of the day arrives. Returning, it leaves Urique at 7am, passes through Cerocahui at around 10am, and aims to connect with the bus leaving Bahuichivo for San Rafael (M$80, about one hour) at around 11am. From San Rafael there are five daily buses to Areponápuchi (M$20, 15 minutes), Divisadero (M$20, 20 minutes), Creel (M$60, 1½ hours) and Chihuahua (M$300, six to seven hours). A bus back to Bahuichivo leaves San Rafael at 1pm.

There are several intriguing back roads from Cerocahui that look temptingly direct on maps but should not be attempted without expert local advice. These roads have tough 4WD-only stretches, traverse isolated lands harboring drug plantations and parts can be washed out after heavy rains. A track connects Cerocahui to Choix (from where there's a paved road to El Fuerte), and another links Bahuichivo with Álamos via Témoris. Consult the owners of Hotel Paraíso del Oso or Cabañas San Isidro about security and road conditions.

Urique

☑635 / POP 1100 / ELEV 550M

This starry-skied ex-mining village lies at the bottom of the deepest of all the canyons, the spectacular Barranca de Urique (measuring 1870m from rim to river), yet it's the easiest canyon-bottom village to access, and the trip to do so is nothing short of spectacular. The village could not be more dramatically situated, scattered along the west bank of the turquoise Río Urique and surrounded on all sides by towering

URIQUE'S ULTRAMARATHONS

Normally held in Urique in early March, the **Ultra Caballo Blanco** (www.ultracb.com) is an 82km ultramarathon on tough canyon trails and at altitude. It was established by Micah True, a legendary American runner known locally as Caballo Blanco (The White Horse) who lived for years in the Copper Canyon region, and gained international attention when featured in Christopher McDougall's book *Born to Run*.

The ultramarathon pays homage to the native Tarahumara, who have a centuries-old tradition of long-distance running and whose very name means 'the running people.' Their huaraches (sandals with a thin sole usually made from recycled tires) are said to have inspired the barefoot running method (which tests have shown also reduces energy use) that has now gone global.

Another event, **Carrera de los Pies Ligeros** ('Race of the Light Feet'), held each December, is a *rarajipari,* a long-distance Tarahumara relay-style running race with two teams kicking a ball along a course. *Rarajipari* are actually much truer to Tarahumara traditions than pure running races. There are two races, one for each sex, each involving two teams (who run with torches at night) over a distance of more than 100km. This race lasts between 12 and 24 hours, and is only open to Tarahumara people.

In a dark twist, the ultramarathons were cancelled in 2015 and 2016 due to safety concerns. The ultramarathon route took runners through territories used by drug cartels for the cultivation of marijuana and poppies, and several threats were received. The organizers hope that the event will return in the future, but for now it appears to be another victim of Mexico's multifaceted battle with the narco-trade.

cliffs. It's a natural hiking base and is one of the friendliest and most welcoming places in northern Mexico. Getting there is part of the fun: the unpaved road (a mere 40km trip from Cerocahui, but one with more hairpin bends than straight sections) makes for an extraordinarily scenic descent to the village.

While Urique is a charming place, it certainly has its dangers too: in 2015 its annual ultramarathon, the famous Ultra Caballo Blanco, was cancelled just 24 hours before it was due to begin due to violent clashes with local drug cartels. Indeed, marijuana fuels the local economy, so be a little wary about town.

🏃 Activities

For day hikes you can go up the Río Urique to **Guadalupe Coronado** village (7km) or downriver to **Guapalaina** (4km), both wonderful walks along the riverside dirt roads. The two- to three-day trek to Batopilas is a bigger challenge. As robberies have occurred on the route via Cerro Colorado, a more southerly route via Pie de la Cuesta is an alternative. Local guides charge around M$4000 for this trip. As ever in northern Mexico, check the safety situation carefully on the ground before setting out.

🛏 Sleeping & Eating

★ **Entre Amigos** CABAÑAS, CAMPGROUND $
(☎635-105-23-71; www.amongamigos.com; campsites per person M$140, dm/r M$225/750; 🅿😊@🐾) 🌿 This beautifully designed place has been hosting travelers since 1975. Homey stone cabins, dorms and wonderful campsites are dotted around gorgeous grounds that are dominated by an unbelievably gigantic cactus. No meals are offered but there's a good guests' kitchen. Entre Amigos can hook you up with dependable local guides for hiking, camping or fishing and there's an impressive library.

It's located near the riverbank, a short walk beyond the town center. If arriving by bus, the driver will normally be happy to drop you off.

Hotel Barrancas de Urique HOTEL $
(☎635-456-60-76; Principal 201; r M$250-300) Turn right onto the main street when you reach the bottom of the hill to find this hotel, the only one in Urique with its own restaurant. Simple and clean rooms over two stories line a drive-in courtyard. All rooms have cable TV and hot water to boot.

Hotel El Paraíso Escondido HOTEL $
(☎635-456-60-34; escondidodeurique@hotmail.com; Principal s/n; r M$250; ❄) Simple, clean,

friendly and cheap, this 13-room motel-style hotel is right in the center of town. To get here turn right when you get to the bottom of the hill as you enter the town; the hotel will be located on your right-hand side. There's no sign.

Restaurante del Centro MEXICAN $
(Plaza; mains M$60-80, steaks M$160-180; ⊙7:30am-9:30pm) This friendly place may boast the least comfortable chairs in Mexico, but it's otherwise welcoming and even has an English menu (of sorts). There's a breakfast menu, a buffet lunch option and plenty of choice at dinner, including several well-prepared steaks. You'll find it just off the main plaza.

Restaurant Plaza MEXICAN $$
(☑635-456-60-03; Principal s/n; meals M$90; ⊙6am-9pm) The excellent family-run Restaurant Plaza offers fine food with a real home-cooked flavor. The specialty, *aguachile* (M$80), is a soupy, spicy shrimp cocktail full of onions and tomatoes served in a *molcajete* (traditional mortar and pestle). Sadly the small dining room is dominated by an enormous television that is on all day long. Also, the menu is spoken: non-Spanish speakers beware!

❶ Information

Tourist Office (☑635-456-60-42; turismo.urique@gmail.com; ⊙8am-3pm) The town hall on the main street has a small, efficient tourist office.

❶ Getting There & Away

A bus leaves Bahuichivo train station daily for Urique (M$180, 3½ hours or more) after the last train of the day arrives. The bus back from Urique leaves from outside Restaurant Plaza at 7am each morning, and travels via Cerocahui to Bahuichivo. Hotels in Urique can arrange transfers from Bahuichivo for about M$1000. Cerocahui hotels also offer transportation: Cabañas San Isidro and Hotel & Restaurante Jade both charge M$1500 for a return day trip to Urique with a guide.

Areponápuchi (Posada Barrancas)

☑635 / POP 240 / ELEV 2220M

Right on the lip of the canyon, the tiny settlement of Areponápuchi or 'Arepo' is just a couple of dozen houses, a church and a few hotels, the pricier of which are right on the canyon edge with mind-blowing views. This is the most touristy bit of the Copper Canyon, with its superb adventure park, which allows you to take a series of 12 zip-lines almost to the canyon bottom before soaring back up to the rim by cable car – a must-do half-day out.

The village itself is unremarkable, with most people just spending a night or two to visit the adventure park before continuing on the Chepe. An easy path with several good viewpoints runs along the canyon edge to the left (north) of Hotel Mirador, and several lookouts (as well as the adventure park) lie short distances off the road between here and Divisadero. Local accommodations can organize canyon trips, from hikes along the rim to horseback rides or overnight camping treks right down to the river.

🛏 Sleeping & Eating

Cabañas La Esmeralda GUESTHOUSE $
(☑635-111-47-80, 635-589-40-88; r M$500; P❋) The best value in town, this neat row of spotless rooms is simple, well cared for and shares a communal terrace. There are no views, but the owners are friendly and helpful. It's located on the main road, 600m or so from the Posada Barrancas station.

Cabañas Díaz CABAÑAS $
(☑635-578-30-08; s with/without bathroom M$300/200, d with/without bathroom M$500/400; P) Family-run lodge known for its rustic cabins, which all come with fireplaces but are also fairly dark and cobbled together. The Díaz family also offers tasty home-cooked meals (M$70 to M$80), and is the only place in the village to eat if you're not staying at one of the big hotels. Go into the village and look for the sign on the right.

Excellent guided hikes and horseback rides (four-hour outing for two by foot/horse M$300/600) are offered too.

Hotel Mansión Tarahumara HOTEL $$$
(☑800-777-46-68, 635-578-30-30; www.hotelmansiontarahumara.com.mx; s incl 3 meals M$1400-1800, d incl 3 meals M$2000-2600; P❋☼) This castle-like hotel (complete with turrets and battlements) offers a variety of accommodations just a few minutes up the hill from the station. Rooms on the canyon rim (commanding the highest prices) are the showstoppers, with plush beds and balconies. There's a huge and gothic restaurant (meals M$200) and a pool and Jacuzzi. It's also the only place in town with wi-fi.

THE CHANGING FACE OF THE CANYONS

The Parque de Aventura Barrancas del Cobre is the beginning of the redevelopment project known as Megaproyecto Barrancas del Cobre, which, depending on your viewpoint, will either revitalize tourism locally or forever tarnish one of nature's greatest wonders. Overall opinion seems to sway toward the former, and the new canyon attractions are far from the mar on the majestic landscape that was feared. Locals generally welcome the prospect of more money and jobs, though two Tarahumara villages have fought attempts to replace them with hotels. There are also tentative plans for more luxury hotels, an amusement park with canyon-lip roller-coaster and even a canyon-top golf course. But with Copper Canyon tourism in decline, it's uncertain how many of these projects will see the light of day. One project that is nearing completion (due to open in late 2016) is Creel's new international airport.

Hotel Mirador HOTEL $$$
(☎ 800-816-81-96, 635-578-30-20; www.mexicos coppercanyon.com; s/d incl 3 meals M$2100/3250; 🅿) Suspended over the canyon, this hotel's 75 rooms (each with private balcony, beamed ceilings and attractive furnishings) enjoy unbeatable views, as does the restaurant where buffet meals are served at communal tables. It's popular with tour groups and is a bit overpriced, but it's just about worth it overnight for the extraordinary canyon panorama.

ⓘ Getting There & Away

Most visitors arrive at the Posada Barrancas station on the train, which is within easy walking distance of the Arepo and the canyon-edge hotels.

Five daily buses operated by Autotranspotes Turísticos Noroeste connect Areponápuchi with Creel (M$50, one hour) and San Rafael (M$50, 15 minutes) to the south. Buses drop you at the entrance to the main highway just outside the village.

Parque de Aventura Barrancas del Cobre

Parque de Aventura Barrancas del Cobre CABLE CAR
(Copper Canyon Adventure Park; ☎ 01-800-887-47-66; www.parquebarrancas.com; M$20, zip-lining M$650; ⊙ 9:30am-4:30pm) The astonishing Parque de Aventura Barrancas del Cobre on the canyon rim between Areponápuchi and Divisadero includes Mexico's longest series of *tirolesas* (zip-lines), suspended over some of the world's most profound canyon scenery. The park's seven lines take you from a height of 2400m to over halfway to the canyon floor and they include one single line

that is an extraordinary 2.5km in length, the world's longest.

A couple of heart-in-mouth wobbly bridges help you complete the cross-canyon odyssey. Safety standards are excellent: you're always accompanied by a team of experienced zip-liners and all participants are decked out in full safety gear. Allow at least 2½ hours to descend to the spectacular viewpoint of Mesón de Bacajípare, as you have to travel in a group of around 15 people, meaning that there's some waiting time as each person takes each line. Mesón de Bacajípare doubles as the lower station for the **teleférico** (Cable Car; adult/child under 12yr return M$300/150; ⊙ 9am-4:30pm), which you will have to take back up (included in the zip-lining price). If zip-lining isn't your thing, you can head straight down from the canyon edge on the cable car (10 minutes each way, plus a 20-minute stop) for some equally breathtaking views.

The **park center** (☎ 689-589-68-05; Piedra Volada; ⊙ 9:30am-4:30pm), built over a gob-smacking fissure in the canyon walls, has a restaurant (meals M$70 to M$100) and souvenir shop. Rappelling and rock climbing, both M$550 per person, can be arranged here. You can also organize hiking (M$50 to M$200) and spectacular downhill mountain biking (M$400) with Tarahumara guides.

ⓘ Getting There & Away

The nearest public transportation is at Arepo or Divisadero, both an easy 1.5km walk away via a great canyon-lip-hugging trail. If you're coming by train, get off at the Posada Barrancas station on the Chepe, cross the train line, and head up the hill around to the left.

Five direct daily buses from Chihuahua to Areponápuchi pass the park entrance courtesy of **Autotranspotes Turísticos Noroeste** (www.turisticsnoroeste.com). Returning, it's not always easy to flag a bus down but it's a pleasant and short walk to either Divisadero or Areponápuchi.

Divisadero

ELEV 2240M

Divisadero, a train stop without a village, is your only chance to see into the miraculous canyon if you're just doing the train ride. All trains halt here for 20 minutes, giving you enough time to jump out, gawp, snap some photos at the viewpoint over the road and hop back on. You can just discern a tiny fragment of the Río Urique at the bottom of the actual Copper Canyon. Ration your time carefully, as the station is also a souvenir market and spectacular food court. *Gorditas* (masa cakes, some made with blue corn), burritos and *chiles rellenos,* cooked up in makeshift oil-drum stoves, are worth the stop alone. Gobble your food up quickly – the conductors aren't supposed to allow food back onto the train.

All this, together with the nearby adventure park 1.5km south, means a stay of longer than 20 minutes is a great idea. There's a good choice of places in the nearby village of Areponápuchi, or you'll find **Hotel Divisadero Barrancas** (☑ in Chihuahua 614-415-11-99, in the US 888-232-4219; www.hoteldivisadero.com; r incl 3 meals from M$1415; P ➔) right by the canyon viewpoint; here, standard rooms lack views but the newer ones (Nos 35 to 52) have astonishing vistas.

Buses serving Areponápuchi, San Rafael and ultimately Bahuichivo also run through Divisadero, stopping below the train station – quicker and cheaper than continuing by train.

Creel

☑ 635 / POP 5000 / ELEV 2330M

The Copper Canyon's main tourism center, Creel is actually no more than a low-key highland town strung out along the railway line. It's a very likable place, surrounded by pine forests and interesting rock formations and it boasts several good hotels and restaurants. The Tarahumara, in their multihued dress, are commonly seen about town, and there's a consistent tourist presence here, mainly in the form of tour groups.

Creel can be very cold in winter, even snowy, and it's none too warm at night in

autumn either. In summer, the alpine air is a welcome relief from Mexico's coastal lowland and desert heat.

⊙ Sights

Museo Casa de las Artesanías del Estado de Chihuahua   MUSEUM
(☑ 635-456-00-80; Av Vías del Ferrocarril 178; M$10; ⊙ 9am-5:30pm Mon-Sat, to 1pm Sun; P) Offers excellent exhibits with text in English on local history and Tarahumara culture and crafts. Here you'll see gorgeous woven baskets, traditional clothing, photos and more.

⊂⊐ Tours

As soon as you check into a hotel (or even before that), you'll be approached to sign up for a tour. Standard minivan tours tend to be rushed, ticking off a roster of nearby sights in a short time frame (most are half-day trips), such as canyons, waterfalls, Tarahumara settlements, hot springs and other places. Themed excursions tend to be more rewarding. Most tours require a minimum number of people, typically four. One popular trip of around five hours covers Cusárare village and waterfall, Lago Arareko and the Valley of the Frogs and Mushrooms. Typical prices are M$250 per person for half-day trips and up to M$500 for full-day trips. Other good half- or full-day destinations include Divisadero, the Cascada de Basaseachi and Rekowata hot springs.

Seriously consider exploring the region yourself. This is prime riding country, and many attractions near Creel can be enjoyed on horseback, bicycle or scooter. This is particularly attractive as you can cover terrain the minivans can't manage, and with significantly more peace and quiet. The whole area is a mountain-bike playground: you could just rent a bike and take in all the area's attractions independently.

★ **3 Amigos**   TOUR
(☑ 635-456-00-36; www.amigos3.com; Av López Mateos 46) A very passionate and well-run English-speaking agency, 3 Amigos has built its reputation on helping you 'be your own guide in the Copper Canyon'; to do this it provides maps to help you negotiate the region's trails, rents Rockhopper mountain bikes (per four hours/day M$150/250) and scooters (per day M$800), and offers multiple day trips in 4WDs with drivers (per day M$1400).

COPPER CANYON & NORTHERN MEXICO CREEL

Creel

N 0 — 100 m
0 — 0.05 miles

Creel

◎ **Sights**
1 Museo Casa de las Artesanías del
   Estado de Chihuahua A2

✈ **Activities, Courses & Tours**
2 3 Amigos A4
3 El Aventurero Ecopaseos A5
4 Tarahumara Tours................................B2
5 Umarike Expediciones B4

🛏 **Sleeping**
6 Best Western The Lodge at Creel.......A4
7 Casa Margarita.....................................B2
8 Cascada Inn B4
9 Hotel Plaza Mexicana..........................B3
10 Quinta Mision A5
11 Real de Chapultepec Hotel.................B3

🍴 **Eating**
12 La Cabaña...B3
13 Lupita..A3
   Restaurant Sierra Madre ....(see 6)
14 Restaurant Verónica B3
   Rico's ....(see 6)

🛍 **Shopping**
15 Artesanías Misión A2

Mon-Fri, 9am-3pm Sat) Superb horseback riding excursions run by Norberto and Susan, a Mexican-US couple who own the ranch. Thrifty backpackers should ask them about their 'bare-bones' riding rates. Rides cost from around M$100 per hour (minimum two hours and three riders), and there's a comprehensive list of routes, including Rekowata hot springs and Lago Arareko. Accommodations and Spanish lessons are also offered.

Umarike Expediciones ADVENTURE TOUR
(☑ 635-456-06-32, cell 614-4065464; www.umarike.com.mx; Av López Mateos) Mountain-biking specialist offering guided bike and hiking adventure trips from one to eight days. Rental bikes (M$400 per day), maps and information are also available.

Tarahumara Tours GUIDED TOUR
(☑ info 635-199-61-64; creeltour@hotmail.com; plaza; ⊙ 9am-7pm) Local driver-guides offering escorted trips, from two hours to two days, at competitive rates. Prices range from M$150 per person for a two-hour tour taking in five local beauty spots to M$800 for a two-day trip to Batopilas, not including food or accommodations.

The full-day self-guided mountain bike route to the Rekowata hot springs and full-day scooter ride to the canyon bottom by the Humira bridge pass through simply mind-blowing scenery and are highly recommended. The agency is also the best source of information in town, and its website is a great place to start planning your Copper Canyon adventure.

★ **El Aventurero
Ecopaseos** HORSEBACK RIDING
(☑ 635-294-45-85; www.ridemexico.com; Av López Mateos 68; rides per hr from M$100; ⊙ 9am-6pm

🛏 Sleeping

Casa Margarita
HOSTEL, HOTEL $

(☑635-456-00-45; www.casamargaritacreel.com.
mx; Av López Mateos 11; dm/s/d incl breakfast
& dinner from M$100/300/400; P❀🛇) This
deceptively large establishment contains
both hostel- and hotel-style rooms and is a
long-running backpackers and tour-group
stronghold. Accommodations are provided
in simple, clean, brightly colored rooms,
while bathrooms have Creel's hottest, fastest
showers. Buffet meals are served up in the
downstairs restaurant.

Real de Chapultepec Hotel
HOTEL $

(☑635-456-08-94; realdechapultepec@hotmail.
com; Flores 260; r from M$250; P🛇) A passa-
ble budget place with the cheapest rooms in
town, the Real de Chapultepec is definitely
no oil painting and there was construction
work ongoing when we last visited. The
units are grouped around a parking lot and
divide into truly ancient rooms with thread-
bare furnishings and recently added rooms
that are far better, though still some way
from charming.

★ Hotel Plaza Mexicana
HOTEL $$

(☑635-456-02-45; www.casamargaritacreel.com.
mx; Batista s/n; s/d/tr/q incl breakfast & dinner
M$600/700/800/900; P❀🛇) This second
hotel from the family that runs the Casa
Margarita is a step up from the bustling
original; friendly staff welcome guests and
comfortable rooms are grouped around a
pretty yellow painted courtyard. Rates in-
clude good breakfasts (with eggs cooked to
order), though evening meals are usually
taken at Casa Margarita, a short walk up the
road.

Cascada Inn
HOTEL $$

(☑635-456-01-51; www.motelcascadainn.com; Av
López Mateos 49; r incl breakfast M$650-900;
P❀🛇) This long-standing family-run spot
has recently been taken over by the younger
generation and significant renovations have
begun. The rooms that have been redone are
excellent, with marble bathrooms and vast
flat-screen TVs. The older, cheaper rooms
are all a good size and have cable TV and
terracotta floors.

Quinta Mision
HOTEL $$

(☑635-456-00-21; www.quintamision.com; Av
López Mateos; r M$1180; P❀✻🛇) 🖉 Perhaps
Mexico's most ecologically senstive hotel,
this intriguing place recycles water and uses

wind and solar power. Twenty suite-sized
rooms have been created from the shell of
an old furniture factory, all with fridge and
enough space for a small family.

Best Western The Lodge at Creel
LODGE $$$

(☑635-456-07-07, in the US 800-716-3562; www.
thelodgeatcreel.com; Av López Mateos 61; s/d/ste
M$1563/1785/2100; P❀@🛇) Utterly fas-
cinating in its determination to be a Wild
West hotel catering to traveler fantasies,
this Best Western boasts antler chandeliers
and cow skins on the wall. Its 41 rooms are
spacious and smart though, with fireplaces,
exposed stone, sitting nooks and swing seats
on their verandas. There's a small fitness
center and spa, plus numerous eating and
drinking options.

🍴 Eating

Creel has a limited choice of restaurants,
though by the standards of smaller villages on the canyon floor, quality is high. For
a packed lunch, grocery stores on the main
drag sell tasty *queso menonita* (Menonite
cheese) and bread.

Lupita
MEXICAN $

(Av López Mateos 44; mains M$50-90; ⊙7am-9pm;
🛇) This brightly decorated thee-room space
with plastic coverings on the tablecloths is
run by a team of friendly locals who are well
used to travelers killing time between bus
and train rides. The menu includes a range
of breakfasts, the full spectrum of Mexican
dishes and several seafood options as well.

La Cabaña
MEXICAN, INTERNATIONAL $$

(Av López Mateos 36; mains M$75-150; ⊙7:30am-
9:30pm; ❀🛇) This orderly Catalan-owned
restaurant is one of the fancier places in
town. As well as good breakfasts (M$50 to
M$90), La Cabaña does a mean *tampiqueña*
(steak accompanied by several side orders),
not to mention tasty salads, grills and
changing daily specials such as local trout
stuffed with shrimp.

Restaurant Verónica
MEXICAN $$

(☑635-456-06-31; Av López Mateos 33; mains
M$50-130; ⊙7:30am-10:30pm; ❀🛇) Famous
for its huge portions, the signature dish here
is *el norteño,* a cheesy, beefy mess served in
a cast-iron skillet that you eat with tortillas.

Rico's
CAFE, PIZZA $$

(Av López Mateos 61; pizzas M$100; ⊙2-10pm;
❀🛇) Located within the Best Western,
this likable place is the only spot in Creel to

get a decent espresso (the house coffee is a blend of three high-altitude Chiapas beans). It's also a good bet for a panini, homemade cakes, or pizza (try the three-cheese *menonita*) from a wood-fired oven.

Restaurant Sierra Madre
MEXICAN, INTERNATIONAL $$

(☑635-456-00-71; Av López Mateos 61; mains M$75-200; ☉noon-9pm; ☕🐕) The Best Western's restaurant is a ranch-style set-up, complete with stone walls, wood beams and plenty of taxidermy. It offers steaks, seafood, pasta and pizza, and less expensive *antojitos* (snacks).

Shopping

Shops in Creel sell Tarahumara handicrafts as well as distinctive Mata Ortiz pottery.

Artesanías Misión
HANDICRAFTS

(☑635-456-00-97; Parroquia 64; ☉9am-1pm & 3-6pm Mon-Sat) Traditional selection of handicrafts. All the store's earnings go to support Creel's Catholic mission hospital, which provides free medical care for the Tarahumara.

ℹ Information

Clínica Santa Teresita (☑635-456-01-05; Parroquia; ☉24hr) Behind Casa Margarita. Offers basic health-care services.

Police Station (☑635-456-04-50) Just off the plaza.

Post Office (☉8am-4:30pm Mon-Fri, 8am-noon Sat) On the plaza.

Santander (Av López Mateos 17; ☉9am-4pm Mon-Fri) Has the only two ATMs in town.

ℹ Getting There & Around

BUS

If speed and convenience is the name of the game, then bus is actually the most efficient way to travel between Creel and Chihuahua, not to mention between Creel, Divisadero and Areponápuchi: trips are shorter, far cheaper and more frequent.

Autotransportes Noroeste (www.turisticos noroeste.com; Villa) Runs buses to Cuauhtémoc (M$160, three hours) and Chihuahua (M$315, 4½ hours) eight times daily at 1½ hourly intervals from 6:30am until 5pm. Noroeste also offers buses to Divisadero (M$90, one hour), Areponápuchi (M$90, one hour) and San Rafael (M$90, 1¼ hours) every two hours between 10:30am and 6:30pm. The first bus to San Rafael connects with the 1pm departure from there to Bahuichivo.

Estrella Blanca/Rápidos Cuauhtémoc (☑635-456-00-73) Has eight daily buses to Chihuahua (M$420, 4½ hours) via Cuauhtémoc (M$195, 2½ hours); these leave at roughly hourly intervals between 6:30am and 4:45pm.

Transportes Turísticos (Av López Mateos) Runs a minibus to Batopilas (M$300, four hours) that leaves daily except Sunday from outside its offices on Avenida López Mateos. The bus departs at 9:30am on Monday, Wednesday and Friday, while on Tuesday, Thursday and Saturday it departs at 7:30am.

CAR & MOTORCYCLE

There are paved roads all the way from Chihuahua to Creel and on to Divisadero, Batopilas and Bahuichivo. Motorbikes and 4WDs (with drivers, only) can be rented from 3 Amigos. If you want to self-drive in the region, bring a rental car from Los Mochis or Chihuahua, but proceed with caution: some areas around Creel are controlled by drug cartels, so always check your planned route with someone who has plenty of up-to-date local knowledge before setting off.

TRAIN

Tickets for the Chepe are sold at **Creel station** (☑635-456-00-15; Av Tarahumara) from one hour before trains depart.

Around Creel

The area around Creel is rich in natural wonders, from waterfalls and hot springs to surreal rock formations and expansive parklands, all within a day's hike, ride or drive from town. Local guides offer various tours, or you can go solo on a rented bicycle, scooter or 4WD. There are some lodging options if you want to stay overnight.

One kilometer southeast of town you enter the Tarahumara *ejido* (communal farming district) of San Ignacio (admission M$25), which spreads over some 200 sq km and is home to about 4000 people living in caves and small houses among farmlands, small canyons and pine forests. The road leads into the **Valle de las Ranas y los Hongos** (Valley of the Frogs and Mushrooms), 2km from the edge of town and named for its respectively fat-and-squashed and thin-but-big-headed rocks. Here you'll find the photogenic, 18th-century **San Ignacio Mission Church** and **Cueva de Sebastián**, a cave inhabited by 14 Tarahumara and regularly visited by tourists (donations or craft purchases welcome).

Around 7km further east is the **Valle de los Monjes** (Valley of the Monks), a spectacular outcrop of vertical rock formations that inspire its Tarahumara name Bisabíra-chi, meaning 'Valley of the Erect Penises.' If you've an hour or so to spare, the countryside around Valle de los Monjes is well worth exploring and less visited than the area around the 'frogs' and 'mushrooms.'

Lago Arareko, a twisting, bluish-green lake whose waters reflect the surrounding pines and rocks, sits beside the Cusárare road 8km from Creel. It can be linked with the frogs, mushrooms and monks in a half- to full-day circuit. Rowboats can be rented out for M$50 by the lakeshore.

About 14km on down the road past Arareko is the turning to the Tarahumara village of **Cusárare** (2km), where the 18th-century mission church was restored in the 1970s with striking Tarahumara patterned murals. On Sundays the village is full of life. The **Museo Loyola** (M$20) here holds an exceptional collection of colonial religious paintings, but it's closed unless pre-booked, so ask your guide to arrange for it to be opened if you're visiting on a tour. About 400m past the Cusárare turning, at Km 111 on the highway, a right turn marked 'Cascada de Cusárare' marks the start of a trail that follows a bubbling stream, then passes through a sweeping highland valley to the lovely 30m waterfall **Cascada Cusárare** (M$20; ⊙8am-5pm), 3km from the road. If you want to do a little hiking, this section from the road to the falls is shady and very beautiful, offering the chance of a dip along the way.

The lovely **Aguas Termales Rekowata** (Rekowata Hot Springs; M$25) are approached from the Divisadero road 7km south of Creel. To get to these hot springs you need to follow a signposted dirt road for 11km from the highway to the parking lot. It's then a 3km hike down a rough cobblestone track to the blissfully warm bathing pools into which the springs are channeled. Local Tarahumara offer transportation (M$60 return) in 4WDs from the parking lot. There's also a superb mountain bike trail from Creel to Rekowata. This route initially takes the Cusárare road but then heads off road down tracks to the right (south) just beyond the outskirts of Creel. You pass through a scenic river valley then an utterly astonishing canyon viewpoint before beginning a steep descent to Rekowata. It's a full-day return-trip ride; 3 Amigos (p757) can provide a map.

With a scooter or car, you've the chance to reach the bottom of the Copper Canyon with your own wheels. Grab a packed lunch

WORTH A TRIP

MEXICO'S HIGHEST FULL-TIME WATERFALL

Cascada de Basaseachi Few natural sites in Mexico boast the exquisitely pristine beauty of the country's highest full-time waterfalls, Cascada de Basaseachi, where a plume of water tumbles 246m to pools below, where you can swim. Basaseachi is 140km northwest of Creel and takes a full day to visit from there (including three hours to walk down to the falls and back). The waterfall is part of the homonymous national park, south of which is the old mining town of Maguarachi, where there are delightful **hot springs**.

Both sites are accessible via San Juanito, 35km north of Creel. To visit you'll really need your own wheels or a tour with a Creel agency.

in Creel first. The route is very simple: you follow the excellent paved highway southeast of town toward Guachochi. The scenery is staggering; the best section between Km 133 and Km 150 winds around the great ocher walls of the Copper Canyon itself then descends to the Humira bridge beside the foaming waters of the Urique river. It's the same route back, via Cusárare and Lago Arareko. This is another full-day return trip.

Batopilas
🖉 649 / POP 1500 / ELEV 460M

The most charming of the towns on the bottom of the Copper Canyon, the former silver-mining village of Batopilas is a sleepy place where everybody knows everyone else and whose warm and laid-back air works a gentle magic on all who visit. After years of work, a newly surfaced road into the jaw-dropping Barranca de Batopilas brings you to the town with relative ease and it has more twists, turns and heart-in-mouth vertical drops than any amusement ride.

Batopilas was founded in 1708, and peaked in prominence in the late-19th century when silver mining boomed. The climate is subtropical here year-round, which means scorching in the summer months and pleasantly warm the rest of the year.

Batopilas can be slightly rough around the edges, with marijuana fueling the local economy, but while the odd robbery has

THE TARAHUMARA

A fascinating part of canyon life is the presence of one of Mexico's most distinctive indigenous groups, the Tarahumara, who live in caves and small houses across the countryside here. Most easily identifiable are the women, dressed in colorful skirts and blouses and often carrying infants on their backs. They sell beautiful hand-woven baskets and carved wooden dolls and animals at ridiculously low prices at tourist sites around the sierra. Most men now wear modern clothes like jeans instead of the traditional loincloth, but both sexes still often walk in *huaraches* – sandals hewn from tire tread and strips of leather.

The Tarahumara remain largely an enigma. Even their name is debated (Tarahumara, or Rarámuri?). Many believe it was originally 'ralamuli', which was Hispanicized to 'Rarámuri' and evolved to 'Tarahumara,' the term by which they usually refer to themselves. Contrary to popular belief, the Spanish incursion did not force the Tarahumara into the canyons: they were here when the first Jesuits arrived in 1608.

There are two main Tarahumara groups: the Alta (high) and the Baja (low) with whom outside contact was made by Jesuit priests from higher-altitude Hidalgo del Parral and lower-altitude El Fuerte respectively. Culture and language are radically different between the Altas and Bajas, and because of long-term isolation, every community has a slightly different culture and language. No one even knows how many Tarahumara exist. Estimates vary between 50,000 and 120,000.

Rarámuri means 'those who run fast' – and these people are most famous for running long distances swiftly, sometimes up to 20 hours without stopping. They used their aptitude for running to hunt deer by bow and arrow as little as a generation ago. The Copper Canyon area now has its own annual ultramarathon (p754) at Urique.

But a better cultural insight into the Tarahumara is their sense of fairness. 'Korima' is a custom where someone who has a good crop is 'blessed' and obliged to share his good fortune with others. Another tradition is the *tesgüinada,* a raucous social gathering at which Tarahumara relax their natural reserve and celebrate communal work and festivals with plenty of *tesgüino,* a potent corn beer.

Even these traditionally isolated people have been influenced by incomers, and many have adopted a type of Catholicism. However, their take on Christianity and Christian festivals is often idiosyncratic – regularly accompanied by drumming and lots of *tesgüino*.

But the Tarahumara have maintained their lifestyle despite incursions of conquistadors, missionaries, railways, drug gangs and tourism. They have one word to refer to all non-Tarahumara people: *chabochi,* which means 'with spider-webbing on the face,' a reference to bearded Spanish colonists. The majority continue to live a subsistence life in the remote Sierra Madre Occidental countryside.

The Tarahumara are also generally materially poor, and their communities have some serious health problems: there are high rates of infant mortality, malnutrition and teenage pregnancy, with some of the little relief coming from Catholic missions.

occurred, foreign tourists aren't usually targeted, though it's important to take local advice about out-of-town excursions.

Things shut up early here, save for some makeshift bars selling beer from back rooms. However, there are great excursions locally, and for many the journey here from Creel alone makes this trip worthwhile.

Be aware that there are no banks or ATMs in town, and that the internet has yet to reach the canyon floor.

◉ Sights & Activities

Hacienda San Miguel　　　RUIN
(M$20; ☺8am-5pm; Ⓟ) The monumental, castle-like ruins of the Hacienda San Miguel were built on a very grand scale indeed. They're highly evocative, with bougainvillea tumbling over towers and roots and shoots reclaiming a once-grand stone structure. It's at the entrance to the town, just by the bridge you cross when your first enter Batopilas.

Museo de Batopilas   MUSEUM
(plaza; ⊙11am-6pm Mon-Sat) **FREE** Offers a good overview of the town's history with a mock-up of a silver mine and some interesting photos and artifacts. English-speaking director Rafael will likely embellish proceedings with his own anecdotes. Tourist information is available here.

Satevó Mission Church Hike   HIKING
One of the most popular hikes from Batopilas is to the 18th-century Satevó Mission Church, in a remote spot 8km down Copper Canyon. Simply follow the river downstream (the mission suddenly appears, framed in a forested river gorge); it's also possible to drive there.

Ruta de Plata   HIKING
(Silver Trail) One of northern Mexico's best treks or horseback rides, the Ruta de Plata follows the ancient mule route between Batopilas and Chihuahua. However, be sure to check the local safety situation before setting out on this route.

🛏 Sleeping

Casa Monse   HOMESTAY $
(Plaza Principal; r per person M$150; ⊕) There's no sign, but you'll not find a cheaper bed in Batopilas, nor such a local welcome. The entire place is chaotic, but undeniably has its own (very) rustic charm, with its back garden, shared kitchen and various Tarahumara handicrafts on sale. The owner will fix you Tarahumara cuisine and can help organize tours with local guides.

Hotel Juanita's   HOTEL $
(☑cell 614-1205652; Plaza Principal; s/d M$250/400; ⊕✳) Charming, well-kept rooms each get their own crucifix plus a shared river-facing courtyard complete with gurgling fountain. Some rooms have air-con, but all have a fan. There's no food on offer, so you'll have to eat out.

Casa Real de Minas   HOTEL $$
(☑649-456-90-45; www.coppercanyonlodges.com; Guerra 1; d/tr/q US$55/65/75; P⊕✳) Just beyond the Plaza Principal, this gorgeous converted townhouse has 10 brightly decorated rooms, two courtyards and several communal areas stuffed with antiques and historical photos. You're immersed in silver mining history here, and there are few such atmospheric midrange hotels in Mexico. Rooms are enormous, comfortable and all individually decorated.

★ Riverside Lodge   HOTEL $$$
(☑635-456-00-36, cell 614-2208632; www.copper canyonlodges.com; ⊙r incl breakfast US$130; P⊕✳) For the ultimate hacienda experience, check in to this stunning colonial mansion, expertly and sympathetically renovated and decorated with lavish murals, oil paintings, rugs and oak furniture. All 14 rooms are individually furnished and boast vast bathrooms with claw-foot tubs. Look out for its blue domes just by the church: there's no sign otherwise. Enter through the gate under an anchor.

🍴 Eating

Doña Mica   MEXICAN $
(Plaza de la Constitución; meals M$60-90; ⊙7am-9pm; ⊕🍴) Run by Velia and her husband, this place hits the spot for hearty home-cooked meals. There's usually no menu, just a few choices daily delivered in rapid-fire Spanish.

Restaurant Carolina   MEXICAN $$
(☑649-456-90-96; Plaza de la Constitución 10; dishes M$70-135; ⊙8am-8pm) Rifles on the walls, pickles in jars and local scenes captured in paintings sum up this family-run restaurant a block beyond Batopilas' main plaza. Choose between filling breakfasts (M$40 to M$80), delicious tacos (ask for the mango salsa) or more elaborate dishes such as freshwater trout. The whole place is inside Carolina's home, and there are always several generations at work in the kitchen.

Los Mangos   MEXICAN $$
(mains M$100-145; ⊙9am-8pm) A five-minute walk beyond the village, this slightly out-of-the-way spot is nestled amid a mango orchard by the river, from where trout and shrimp are fished. Breakfasts are served, and steaks are also on offer. To get here, follow the direction of the river out of town past the basketball courts, and when the road splits, keep left.

❶ Getting There & Away

The newly paved road to Batopilas from Creel is one of Mexico's most scenic drives, and most drivers will stop at the incredible Mirador La Bufa for some mind-blowing views.

Minibuses (M$300, four hours) run by **Transportes Turísticos** (p760) leave from Creel every morning except Sunday for Batopilas. They depart at 9:30am on Monday, Wednesday and Friday, while on Tuesday, Thursday and Saturday they depart at 7:30am. Buses back to

ℹ CROSSING THE BORDER

There are more than 40 official US–Mexico border crossing points, many open 24 hours daily. **US Customs & Border Protection** (www.cbp.gov) provides opening hours and estimated waiting times for drivers.

Tourists visiting Mexico must carry a passport or (for Americans entering and leaving by land or sea) a US passport card. All tourists must also obtain a Mexican **tourist permit** (*forma migratoria para turista*, FMT, or *forma migratoria múltiple*, FMM) on arrival, unless they are staying within the border zone and not staying over 72 hours. The border zone generally extends 20km to 30km south from the border but also stretches as far as Puerto Peñasco in Sonora and Ensenada and San Felipe in Baja California. For more information on tourist permits and visas, see p856.

Travelers taking a vehicle must purchase Mexican insurance (available at borders, p860). If you're heading beyond the border zone deeper into Mexico (except in Baja California), you must obtain a temporary vehicle importation permit for US$51, or a Sólo Sonora permit for US$49.50. Both permits can be obtained for less if ordered way in advance and either delivered by mail or picked up at outlets around the border.

To organise the vehicle permit in advance use the **Banjército** website (www.banjercito.com.mx) or simply apply at one of Mexico's 38 **IITV** (Importación e Internación de Vehículos) offices at northern borders and some locations past the border, including in Sonora at Agua Zarca (21km south of Nogales), in Chihuahua state 30km south of Ciudad Juárez, and in Baja California at Pichilingue (near La Paz) and Ensenada. All IITV locations are given at www.banjercito.com.mx (click on 'Red de Módulos IITV').

If you're only traveling in Sonora, the **Sólo Sonora** program is worth considering. This allows North Americans to bring a vehicle into northwest Sonora with less hassle (reduced paperwork and no bond to deposit) and is also available from Banjército or at IITV offices. Sólo Sonora is limited to Hwy 2 between Agua Prieta and Imuris and Hwy 15D between Imuris and the checkpoint at Km 98 east of Empalme near Guaymas. To travel beyond these points, you must get a full vehicle permit; staff at the Km 98 checkpoint can authorize one pretty rapidly if you have the paperwork, and are friendly, efficient and speak English.

If you take a vehicle into Baja California, and then ship it to mainland Mexico by ferry from Pichilingue, you must get a vehicle permit before embarking your vehicle.

The main border crossings (ordered west to east) are:

San Diego (California)–Tijuana (Baja California) The three border crossings here include San Ysidro–El Chaparral (24 hours), the world's busiest border crossing. Others include the cross-border terminal at Tijuana's international airport (24 hours, for ticketed passengers only) and the Otay Mesa crossing (24 hours).

Calexico (California)–Mexicali (Baja California) The two border crossings here are Calexico West (24 hours) and Calexico East (6am to midnight).

Lukeville (Arizona)–Sonoyta (Sonora) Best for Puerto Peñasco (6am to midnight).

Creel leave from outside the church in Batopilas every morning except Sunday at 5am sharp.

Two-day van tours from Creel (normally four-person minimum) cost from M$4000 to M$5000. If you have your own wheels, it's simple to visit Batopilas independently – now that the new road is complete you don't even need a 4WD.

A back road (high-clearance 4WD needed), affording canyon-lip views, runs from Batopilas to Urique, fording the Río Urique (passable November to April). Check the security situation before heading out on this route, which is also perfect for mountain biking.

NORTHWEST MEXICO

The magnets for visitors to Mexico's northwest are the inviting beaches of the Sea of Cortez, and the abundant marine life, including some 40 sea lion colonies and 27 species of whale and dolphin. Tourism here originates largely from Arizona (some towns are so easily reachable from there that they're fast becoming Mexican-American communities), but the region, encompassing Sonora (by far the safest of Mexico's border states) and northern Sinaloa, still bursts

Deconcini crossing From Nogales (Arizona) to Nogales (Sonora, 24 hours). Hwy 15/15D is the main highway south.

Santa Teresa crossing Some 20km west of Juárez in Chihuahua state; good for avoiding security risks near Juárez (6am to 10pm).

El Paso (Texas)–Ciudad Juárez (Chihuahua) Bridge of the Americas (24 hours); El Paso St–Avenida Juárez (24 hours); Stanton St–Avenida Lerdo (24 hours). Pedestrian crossings are via the bridges of Stanton St–Avenida Lerdo or El Paso St–Avenida Juárez. To return on foot you must use Avenida Juárez. Access for vehicles is via the Bridge of the Americas (Puente Córdova). Tourist permits are available at the end of the Stanton St–Avenida Lerdo bridge and Bridge of the Americas. Hwy 45D from Juárez is the principal southbound route.

Presidio (Texas)–Ojinaga (Chihuahua) From Ojinaga, it's 225km along Hwy 16 direct to Chihuahua (24 hours).

Del Rio (Texas)–Ciudad Acuña (Coahuila) Open 24 hours.

Eagle Pass (Texas)–Piedras Negras (Coahuila) Open 24 hours.

Laredo (Texas)–Nuevo Laredo (Tamaulipas) Two main crossings: Puente Internacional No 1 and Puente Internacional No 2. The latter bypasses the city and is the safer option, connecting with Hwy 85D from Nuevo Laredo to Monterrey, from where there are good connections to elsewhere in Mexico (24 hours).

McAllen (Texas)–Reynosa (Tamaulipas) Open 24 hours.

Brownsville (Texas)–Matamoros (Tamaulipas) Puente Nuevo (24 hours); Puente Zaragoza (6am to midnight).

There are plenty of cross-border bus services into the region from US cities, most involving a change of buses in a city on the US or Mexican side of the border. Given the time it can take to get through the border, it is often quicker to disembark before the border, make the crossing on foot, and pick up further transportation on the other side.

If you want to avoid staying long in Mexico's border towns, some services will take you directly deeper into Mexico, including Phoenix–Puerto Peñasco via Sonoyta with **Transportes Supremo** (p768), El Paso–Chihuahua via Juárez with **Autobuses Americanos** (☑ in the US 915-532-1748; www.autobusesamericanos.us; 1007 S Santa Fe St, El Paso), which has many offices across Texas, and Tufesa (www.tufesa.com.mx), which operates many cross-border buses to California and Arizona.

Many border towns rank among Mexico's most dangerous places. The security situation can change quickly. Ciudad Juárez and Nuevo Laredo have been notorious for years and are best avoided, or at least transited during daylight hours, but you should be careful anywhere. The Sonoran border crossings were deemed pretty *tranquillo* at the time of research. All border cities mentioned in this chapter have good sleeping and eating facilities if you do choose to spend the night.

with homespun character. The strains of *norteña* (country) music and the inviting smell of the trademark regional snack, *carne asada* (marinated grilled beef), waft past cowboy-hatted ranchers on the streets.

The perfunctory towns and cities won't detain you long: Los Mochis harbors little of interest except as a jumping-off point for the spectacular train ride up the Copper Canyon or for a boat to Baja. The state capital, Hermosillo, is a vast and faceless place with little cultural interest. The glorious exception is delightful Álamos, a colonial jewel surrounded by peaks of the Sierra Madre Occidental, that's replete with atmospheric restaurants and cafes and is well worth a diversion off Hwy 15.

Puerto Peñasco

☑ 638 / POP 57,000

Until the 1920s, 'Rocky Point,' as US citizens affectionately call this Sea of Cortez coastal resort, was just that: a landmark on naval/military maps and no more. Its location alongside one of the driest parts of the Desierto Sonorense (Sonoran Desert) deterred all would-be settlers bar intrepid fishers until Prohibition gave the fledgling community an unexpected boost. When the global economy nosedived in the 1930s, Peñasco enjoyed a (very) lengthy siesta, until state investment and a desalination plant kick-started the local economy in the early 1990s. The result has been a boom in both development and population, and now this beach town is home to so many non-natives it has become the seaside destination Arizona never had.

The historic core hugs the rocky point itself while its main waterfront stretch, Sandy Beach, is a sprawling stretch of massive condo-hotel resorts, golf courses carved out of the desert, expensive restaurants and minimal Mexican culture.

Travelers without a car, beware: there is no reliable local public transportation around town. Note that Spring Break is a big deal in Peñasco, and in March the resort is rammed with margarita-chugging US college students.

◉ Sights & Activities

Fishing, snorkeling, diving, kayaking, parasailing and sunset cruises are all popular. There are extensive rock pools to explore at low tide, and trips around the estuary and beyond to the remarkable Reserva El Pinacate y Gran Desierto de Altar can be set up by the likes of the Intercultural Center for the Study of Desert & Oceans (CEDO).

Isla San Jorge   ISLAND
Also known as Bird Island, Isla San Jorge is one of the best boat excursions in northern Mexico. This rocky island 40km southeast of Peñasco is home to nesting sea birds and also a large community of sea lions (which are curious by nature and will swim alongside boats). Dolphins are often spotted en route, while whales (fin, grey, killer and pilot) are sometimes encountered between October and April. Full-day cruises are offered by Del Mar Charters (🗷 520-407-60-54, 638-383-28-02; www.delmarcharters.com; adult/child incl lunch US$85/55).

★CEDO   WILDLIFE-WATCHING
(Intercultural Center for the Study of Desert & Oceans; 🗷 638-382-01-13, in the US 520-320-5473; www.cedointercultural.org; Blvd Las Conchas; ⊙9am-5pm Mon-Sat, 10am-2pm Sun) 🖋 **FREE** CEDO is a wonderful place to learn about

Rocky Point's fascinating desert-meets-sea ecosystem. Dedicated to the conservation of the upper Gulf of California and surrounding Desierto Sonorense, CEDO has an 'Earthship' visitor center with a good store. There are free natural-history talks in English at 2pm Tuesdays and 4pm Saturdays. CEDO also runs a fascinating program of nature tours, some in collaboration with local cooperatives.

These include tidepool walks (US$15 per person), kayaking on Morúa estuary (US$50), boat trips to Isla San Jorge (US$100) and excursions to El Pinacate Biosphere Reserve with an English-speaking naturalist (US$60).

Tequila Factory   DISTILLERY
(🗷 638-388-06-06; www.tequilafactory.mx; cnr Blvd Benito Juárez & Calle 12; ⊙10am-6pm) **FREE** This family owned, small-scale operation brews artisan tequilas and offers presentations on tequila production as well as tastings. You can also try-before-you-buy in the shop. The oak-aged Añejo and triple-distilled are recommended. It's downstairs from the tourist office.

⌷ Sleeping

The Old Port has agreeable down-to-earth options (though it's slim pickings for tight budgets, unless you're in the market for an RV park). All the mega-hotel complexes are at Sandy Beach, to the northwest.

★Posada La Roca   HISTORIC HOTEL $
(🗷 638-383-31-99; www.hotelposadalaroca.blog spot.com; Av Primero de Junio 2; M$415-580; 🅿😀❄🛜) An atmospheric stone structure (built in 1927) in the Old Port, this curious place was once a casino-hotel-brothel for US mobsters, including, by all accounts, Al Capone, during Prohibition. The 20 simple, homey rooms are inviting, there's a patio and living room for socializing, and the location is convenient. These are easily the best value accommodations in town.

Hospedaje Mulege   GUESTHOUSE $$
(🗷 638-383-29-85; www.hospedajemulege.com; cnr Av Circunvalación & Calle 16 de Septiembre; r incl breakfast US$60-75; 😀❄🛜) It's all about hospitality and the personal touch here at one of Puerto Peñasco's most popular guesthouses. Lupita and Israel preside over guests with real pride and love to show them the flip side to the town's megaresorts in this friendly and unpretentious Old Port vil-

GRAN DESIERTO DE ALTAR

Northeast of Puerto Peñasco are the lunar landscapes of the **Reserva de la Biosfera El Pinacate y Gran Desierto de Altar** (El Pinacate Biosphere Reserve; ☑ 638-105-80-16, 638-108-00-11; M$40; ☉9am-5pm), one of the driest places on earth. This remote, spectacular 7145-sq-km reserve is a Unesco World Heritage site and contains ancient eroded volcanoes, 10 giant craters, 400-plus ash cones and petrified lava flows. Wildlife includes pronghorn antelope (the fastest land mammal in the Americas), bighorn sheep, pumas, amphibians, reptiles and bountiful birdlife. There's an excellent, highly informative solar-powered visitor center, interpretive hiking trails and two campgrounds.

The extraordinary landscapes here are so unusual that Neil Armstrong and Buzz Aldrin used this region in the 1960s to prepare themselves for their Apollo 11 moon landing.

Today over 70km of dirt roads (4WD only in parts) penetrate the reserve. Visitors must register to climb the 1190m **Cerro del Pinacate** volcano.

The visitor center is about 8km west of Km 72 on Hwy 8 (27km from Puerto Peñasco). The craters are accessed by a separate turnoff further north at Km 52 on Hwy 8. CEDO (p766) in Puerto Peñasco organizes excellent tours to the reserve: good walking shoes are recommended, and note that there's no water or electricity available anywhere in the reserve, except at the visitor center.

la. The seven rooms are comfortable and homey, and guests quickly feel part of the family.

Dream Weaver Inn APARTMENT $$
(☑638-383-48-05; www.dreamweaverinn.com; Calle Pescadores 3; apt US$50-80; P❄️✳️🛜) Operated by Óscar and Lupita, a welcoming couple who run a tight ship, this well-cared-for place has a selection of apartment-style units that are individually decorated with local handicrafts and in true Mexican style. Each unit has basic cooking facilities and some have sea views. It's very close to the Old Port, shops and restaurants.

Eating & Drinking

★ Chef Mickey's Place INTERNATIONAL $$
(☑638-388-95-00; Plaza del Sol 4, Blvd Freemont; mains M$120-250; ☉1-10pm) Eponymous chef Mickey has been cooking up a storm here for years, and you'll be hard pressed to find better quality and innovation elsewhere in town. Steak, seafood and fresh fish dominate the eclectic menu, with some Mexican dishes as well. Mickey's is beloved by the local expat community and so reservations are a good idea.

Kaffee Haus CAFE, EUROPEAN $$
(☑638-388-10-65; www.coffeeshaus.com; Blvr Benito Juarez 216B; breakfasts M$85, lunches M$80-135; ☉7:30am-4pm Mon-Sat, 7:30am-2pm Sun; 🍴🛜) A long-standing favorite, this local institution remains an excellent choice, with its enormous breakfast served daily until

2pm, great house burger and superb apple strudel, to name just a few menu highlights. It's fearsomely popular, however, and you may have to line up to get a table at peak times. Portions are huge, so consider sharing a plate.

La Curva MEXICAN $$
(☑638-383-34-70; Blvd Kino 100; mains M$80-180; ☉7:30am-9:30pm Sun-Thu, to 10:30pm Fri & Sat) A good place to remind yourself you're in Mexico rather than north of the border, this restaurant is the opposite of the glitzy beach restaurant, and you'll barely see a wristband in the whole place. Huge plates of traditional Mexican cooking are served up in a simple and unfussy environment; try the amazing *mariscada* (seafood platter) or the *carne asada*.

JJ's Cantina BAR
(www.jjscantina.com; Cholla Bay; ☉10am-2am; 🛜) There are spectacular views over Cholla Bay, particularly at sunset, from this popular bar-restaurant, an expat favorite, which has live music and pool tables. Skip the food and just enjoy a few sundowners in a Mexican village atmosphere away from the frenetic pace of the resorts in town.

ℹ️ Information

Convention & Visitors Bureau (☑638-388-04-44; www.cometorockypoint.com; Plaza Pelícanos, Av Coahuila 444; ☉9am-5pm Mon-Fri) This helpful tourist office has English-speaking staff and can assist with booking accommodations and tours. The excellent website has lots of useful information about the town and surrounding areas.

❶ Getting There & Around

Puerto Peñasco International Airport (Aeropuerto Mar de Cortés; ☑638-383-60-97; www.aeropuertomardecortes.com; Libramiento Caborca-Sonoita 71) is 3km north of town. At the time of writing there were only infrequent chartered flights, though Aeroméxico (www.aeromexico.com) normally offers flights to Las Vegas and Hermosillo.

Several shuttle-van services operate between Puerto Peñasco and Arizona, including **Transportes Supremo** (☑638-383-36-40; www.transportesupremo.com; Calle Lázaro Cárdenas), which runs to/from Phoenix four times daily (US$52, four hours).

Albatros (☑0800-624-66-18, 638-388-08-88; www.albatrosautobuses.com; Blvd Juárez btwn Calles 29 & 30) runs 11 daily buses to Hermosillo (M$325, 5½ hours) and five to Nogales (M$338, six hours). **ABC** (☑800-025-02-22; www.abc.com.mx; cnr Constitución & Bravo), one block north of Blvd Juárez, heads to Tijuana (M$600, nine hours) five times daily.

Taxis cost around M$30 for short rides, but around M$60 from the Old Port to Las Conchas or the Sandy Beach resorts – and can be double that or more coming back.

Bahía de Kino

☑662 / POP 7000

Laid-back Bahía de Kino is a gorgeous stretch of beach paradise named after Padre Eusebio Kino, who established a small mission here for the indigenous Seri people in the 17th century. The old part, Kino Viejo, is a rough and ready Mexican fishing village that fans out along the lengthy main beach. By contrast Kino Nuevo, a couple of kilometers to the north, is a far smarter place full of American-style bars and restaurants, and is the destination of choice for many 'snowbirds' (retired North American citizens who head south for winter). It also boasts the best strip of beach, a seemingly endless swath of pristine golden sand. High season is from November to March; at other times, you may find yourself blissfully alone by the water.

◉ Sights & Activities

Punta Chueca   INDIGENOUS CULTURE
This village is home to the Seri people, one of Mexico's smallest indigenous groups (less than 1000 people). The Seri are famous for their handicrafts, including their highly re-garded baskets and carvings from ironwood. You'll need a 4WD with high clearance to make the journey along the dirt road to the settlement. Punta Chueca is situated 34km north of Bahía de Kino.

Isla del Tiburón   ISLAND
(3km offshore from Punta Chueca) Mountainous Isla del Tiburón, Mexico's largest island, was once a Seri homeland, but it was depopulated when the island was declared a nature reserve in 1963. Today it's administered by the Seri tribal authorities. An intact desert ecosystem, Tiburón is home to bighorn sheep and large colonies of sea birds. There's good snorkeling around its coast. You need a permit to visit the island – speak to guides Alfredo López or Ernesto Molina in Punta Chueca who can set up tours.

Museo de los Seris   MUSEUM
(☑662-212-64-19; cnr Av Mar de Cortez & Progreso, Kino Nuevo; admission M$10; ⊙9am-6pm Wed-Sun) This small but well-curated museum displays an interesting collection of artifacts and handicrafts and panels about Seri culture and history, though signage is in Spanish only.

🛏 Sleeping & Eating

The Kino Nuevo strip has abundant RV parks and eating options. Other than the odd low-key bar, there's no nightlife: locals call 9pm 'Kino midnight.' Take care in Kino Viejo after dark.

Eco Bay Hotel   HOTEL $
(☑662-242-04-91; www.ecobayhotel.com; cnr Guaymas & Tampico, Kino Viejo; r incl breakfast from M$590; P❄❋🞋❄) Spotless and spacious rooms surround a small pool and parking lot at this good-value and friendly option a few blocks from the beach. There are good bathrooms, a social atmosphere in the bar area (though music can be loud if your room is nearby) and a decent cooked breakfast is included.

**Apartments Alcatraz
Kino Bay**   APARTMENT $$
(☑662-242-06-93; www.kinoalcatraz.com; cnr Av Miramar & Bahía Adahir; apt M$500-750; P❋🞋❄) As the name suggests, this place, one block back from the beach in Kino Viejo, is very secure, with a high fence all around it. The good-value apartments inside are the best inexpensive lodgings in Kino, however, and each has cooking facilities, fridge and

RÍO DE SONORA VALLEY

The north and east of Sonora is pure frontier country: the region's mountains and prairies convey what life would have been like for Spanish settlers centuries ago. This area is best known for its well-preserved Jesuit missions, many of which were established by Mexico's famed missionary, Padre Eusebio Kino. Dreamy time-warped colonial towns here also boast beautiful architecture, thermal baths and interesting accommodations. You'll need your own vehicle: public transportation is scarce.

Following Hwy 14 northwest from Hermosillo, it's 80km up to mellow **Ures** with its shady Plaza Zaragoza and shops selling the Sonoran version of tequila, *bacanora*. After another 30km, Hwy 118 branches north to reach **Baviácora**, with one of Sonora's finest cathedrals. **Aconchi**, 15km on, has wonderful thermal baths. A further 22km north is the laid-back colonial town of **Banámichi**, close to good bird-watching and hot springs.

The landscape becomes increasingly eroded with interesting rock formations as you near **Arizpe**, once capital of Nueva España's Provincias Internas (including California, New Mexico and Texas) in the 18th and 19th centuries. You can loop back to Hermosillo via **Magdalena de Kino**. Padre Kino is buried in the town's mission here, and Magdalena is a great base for visiting surrounding missions such as **Pitiquito** (with outstanding indigenous art on the walls) on the Caborca road, **Tubutama** and the dramatic ruins of **Cocóspera**.

One of the best hotels in the area, friendly **La Posada de Río Sonora** (🗗 623-231-02-59; www.mexicoecoresort.com; main plaza; r M$980-1500; ❄🐾🛜) offers home-cooked meals and horseback riding, and is a good place to base yourself when exploring the Río de Sonora Valley. Rooms are a striking (and sometimes garish) blaze of Mexican colors and folk art.

TV. The tiny pool is great for cooling off. Rates drop the longer you stay.

Casa Tortuga
APARTMENT $$$

(🗗 662-242-01-22; rentcasatortuga@aol.com; Av Mar de Cortez 2645; apt US$85-105; 🅿🐾❄🛜) Beachfront Casa Tortuga has two atmospheric, very comfortable apartments: Pelican, with its stunning ocean-facing, *palapa*-roofed terrace (complete with sunbeds, BBQ and table for outdoor dining) is particularly recommended. There are complimentary kayaks, and the owners sometimes take guests out in a boat to Isla Pelícano for bird-watching. Prices increase slightly in the summer months, but every seventh night is free.

Casablanca Inn
HOTEL $$$

(🗗 662-242-07-77; www.casablancakinobay.com; cnr Cádiz & Av Mar de Cortez; r incl breakfast M$1200; 🅿🐾❄🛜) This beautifully cared-for hotel and restaurant is a real find. With rain showers, tiled floors, white painted walls and attractive wooden furniture, the rooms are both stylishly minimalist and high quality.

The busy restaurant here (mains M$80 to M$160; open 8am to 3pm Monday to Thursday, to 9:30pm Friday to Sunday) is something of a local expat hub, with the famous eggs Benedict always doing a brisk trade at breakfast time.

Marlin
SEAFOOD $

(Av Tastiota btwn Guaymas & Bahía Adair, Kino Viejo; mains M$40-80; ⏱9am-10pm) This unassuming-looking place in the middle of Kino Viejo does superb marlin tacos, has a selection of cold beers by the bottle, including dark beer, and offers a full menu of other seafood delights in the midst of a kitschy venue you won't quickly forget.

El Pargo Rojo
SEAFOOD $$

(🗗 662-242-02-05; Av Mar de Cortez 1426; mains M$100-220; ⏱noon-8pm Mon-Fri, 10am-10pm Sat & Sun) This thatch-roof shack is the most popular place in Kino Nuevo and is often full of regulars enjoying delicious fish dishes and hearty Mexican breakfasts. The *camarones rellenos* (stuffed shrimp) are a real treat.

ℹ Information

Casa del Mar (🗗 662-242-02-21; cnr Bilbao & Esqueda; ⏱9am-4pm Wed-Sun) This visitor center services the 900-island Área de Protección de Flora y Fauna Islas del Golfo de California, a biodiverse protected area of islands in the Sea of Cortez. It has very informative displays in Spanish and English, and issues permits for visiting the islands (M$50 per person per island per day).

❶ Getting There & Around

Buses to Hermosillo (M$85 to M$100, two hours) run roughly hourly from the bus station about halfway along the strip. You can use these services to get around (local rides cost M$10) as there's no other public transportation. Taxis cost M$50 for a ride of up to 5km, more after dark.

San Carlos

☑ 622 / POP 7000

With its striking desert-and-bay landscape, the low-key beach retreat of San Carlos feels a universe apart from its gritty port neighbors. It's presided over by some dramatic hills – notably the majestic twin peaks of Cerro Tetakawi – that glow an impressive red-earthed hue as the sun descends.

San Carlos' beaches are a mix of dark sand and pebbles. Head beyond the busy and built-up central strip to remoter and quieter **Playa Algodones** (famed for its role in the movie *Catch-22*) and you'll find white sands and turquoise water on one of the best beaches in northern Mexico.

❶ Orientation

San Carlos is not pedestrian friendly, spread over some 8km. Most amenities are on the 2.5km stretch of Blvd Beltrones. Head right at the intersection by the Oxxo store after the Beltrones strip to get out to Playa Algodones (6km northwest), or straight on for Marina San Carlos (500m west).

❊ Activities

For many, sportfishing tops the list here: April to September are best for big fish and there are seven main annual tournaments. There are coves for diving and snorkeling, as well as some wrecks offshore. At **Isla San Pedro Nolasco**, 35km out to sea, you can snorkel or dive with a sea-lion colony.

★ Gary's Dive Shop   DIVING

(☑ 622-226-00-49; www.garysdiveshop.com; Blvd Beltrones Km 10; ☉ 7am-5pm) This professional, long-established dive shop and adventure-sports center offers fishing excursions and scenic cruises from its premises on the main drag. Dive trips to Isla San Pedro Nolasco (Seal Island) cost US$95 (excluding gear rental), while snorkeling trips to Aquarium Cove cost US$65 (including gear). Gary's also rents good-quality snorkeling gear for US$11 a day.

Hattie Sunset Cruises   BOAT TOUR

(☑ 622-197-13-51; Marina San Carlos; 2hr cruise US$30) Based at the Marina San Carlos, these two-hour sunset cruises offer the possibility of dolphin and whale encounters and guarantee spectacular views (and margaritas on tap).

⌖ Sleeping

San Carlos is mainly geared to visitors from over the US border, and there are few inexpensive places to stay.

Hotel Creston   MOTEL $$

(☑ 622-226-00-20; www.hotelcreston.com.mx; Blvd Beltrones Km 10; d/tr M$600/900; ⓟ❄☎☲) The beach idyll is somewhat diminished by the location on busy Blvd Beltrones, but these clean spacious rooms (with satellite TV and good air-con) arranged around a nice pool are great value for downtown San Carlos. Look for the huge cacti either side of the entrance on the main road.

Posada Condominiums
& Resort Hotel   APARTMENT $$$

(☑ 622-226-10-31; www.posadacondominiums. com; Blvd Beltrones Km 11.5; apt from US$156; ⓟ⊜❄☎☲) Right on the beach (you can hear the waves lapping on the shore at night), these attractive condos all enjoy fine sea vistas from their generous balconies. All boast fully equipped kitchens, attractive living rooms and all mod cons. They're a short walk from the Marina San Carlos and its restaurants. Rates can drop below US$100 at quiet times of year.

✕ Eating & Drinking

Soggy Peso Bar & Grill   SEAFOOD $$

(☑ 622-226-17-16; www.soggypeso.net; Playa Algodones; mains M$100-190; ☉ 11am-sunset; ☎♨) With its sand floor and families dining in their swimsuits, this lively and popular seafood restaurant makes for a fun and informal lunch where fresh fish and seafood are king. It's on the north end of San Carlos' best beach and also functions as a popular bar, serving up some of Mexico's best margaritas.

La Palapa Griega   MEXICAN, GREEK $$

(Blvd Beltrones Km 11.5; mains M$150-200; ☉ 11am-9pm Mon-Sat, 10am-8pm Sun) Right on the beach, this long-standing Greek-owned restaurant offers a memorable setting for a meal. Try a sampler (hummus, taramasalata, baba ghanoush), a Greek salad or some freshly caught local seafood.

★ Bonifacio's
FUSION $$$

(☑ 622-227-05-15; www.bonifacios.com; Playa Algodones; mains M$100-300; ⊙11am-11pm Mon-Thu, to 3am Fri & Sat, to 10:30pm Sun; 🛜 📶) Perfectly poised on the sands of lovely Playa Algodones, this excellent place exudes sophistication, from the spacious chandelier-lit, antique-furnished interior to the imaginative Mexican fusion cuisine. Try the *mariscada* (thin slices of raw fish cured in lime) with *governador* (shrimp) tacos and *chicharrón* (fried pork rinds) or just a plate of sublime sashimi.

ℹ️ Information

Banamex (Blvd Beltrones) With two ATMs.

ℹ️ Getting There & Around

Buses from Guaymas run as far as Marina San Carlos; local rides within San Carlos cost around M$8. Taxis charge M$50 to M$100 in the San Carlos area.

Long-distance buses will likely drop you at either the **Grupo Estrella Blanca** (Calle 14 No 96, Guaymas) or **Tufesa** (Blvd García López 927, Guaymas) terminals in Guaymas. From Grupo Estrella Blanca, walk north on Calle 14 to Blvd García López and catch the white San Carlos bus (M$12, every 30 minutes). From Tufesa, cross the road to catch the same bus. A taxi from either terminal to San Carlos is M$180.

The nearest **airport** (☑ 622-221-05-11; www.asa.gob.mx) is 10km north of Guaymas. **Aéreo Calafia** (www.aereocalafia.com.mx) has flights to Baja California cities including La Paz and Los Cabos.

Álamos

☑ 647 / POP 9400 / ELEV 432M

The most civilized, architecturally rich town in northwest Mexico, Álamos is a cultural oasis and culinary capital. Sheltered in the forested foothills of the Sierra Madre Occidental, its hushed cobblestone streets and imposing colonial buildings hint at a fascinating history, much of it to do with Álamos' role as Mexico's northernmost silver mining town. The town is both a national historical monument and one of Mexico's *pueblos mágicos* (magical villages).

Álamos' charms have proven irresistible to many US retirees and creative types who, since the '50s, have snapped up decaying colonial buildings to renovate into second homes and hotels. These well-heeled expats comprise a small but influential segment of Álamos' population, and their establishments dominate the colonial center of town.

The town's lush surroundings include tropical deciduous forest and mountains covered in pine and oak. The 929-sq-km **Sierra de Álamos–Río Cuchujaqui Flora & Fauna Protection Area**, which almost encircles Álamos has great birding and wonderful walks.

More bizarrely, Álamos and vicinity is where most of the world's jumping beans – beans that 'jump' due to the presence of a larva inside, sold as a novelty – originate.

The nicest time to come is between mid-October and mid-April, when the climate is cooler. The biggest number of Mexican tourists come in the rainy months (July to September); at other times, it's far quieter.

History

The area's silver mines were discovered around La Aduana (4km west of Álamos) in the 16th century. Álamos itself was founded in the 1680s, probably as a dormitory suburb for La Aduana's wealthy colonists. Despite hostilities from the indigenous Yaqui and Mayo, Álamos boomed into one of Mexico's principal 18th-century mining centers.

During Mexico's 19th-century turmoils, Álamos was attacked repeatedly, by French invaders, by factions seeking its silver wealth and by the fiercely independent Yaqui. The Mexican Revolution took a further toll, and by the 1920s most mines were abandoned and Álamos was practically a ghost town.

In 1948, Álamos was reawakened by William Levant Alcorn, a Pennsylvania dairy farmer who bought the Almada mansion on Plaza de Armas and converted it into Hotel Los Portales. Other *norteamericanos* followed, restoring crumbling mansions to their former glory. Recently they've been joined by wealthy Mexicans, seduced by the relaxed ambience and benign winter climate, creating something of a real estate boom, which is still visible in the multiple realtor signs you see around town today.

◉ Sights

Álamos is ideal for sauntering around and soaking up one of Mexico's most idyllic colonial centers with perhaps a break at one of its atmospheric restaurants.

Parroquia de la Purísima Concepción
CHURCH

(Plaza de Armas) FREE Álamos' parish church is the tallest building in town. It was built between 1786 and 1804 and its altar rail, lamps, censers and candelabra were all originally fashioned from silver, but were melted down in 1866 on the orders of General Ángel Martínez after he booted French troops out of Álamos. Seven or so subterranean passageways between the church and Álamos mansions – probably escape routes for rich families in times of attack – were blocked off in the 1950s.

El Mirador
VIEWPOINT

This magnificent lookout tops a hill on Álamos' southeastern edge, affording sweeping views of the town and its mountainous surroundings. It's accessible by steps from the Arroyo Agua Escondida, two blocks down Obregón from Victoria, and is best climbed first thing in the morning or late in the afternoon, when the light is better and the heat not so fierce.

Museo Costumbrista de Sonora
MUSEUM

(☑647-428-00-53; Victoria s/n; M$10; ⊗9am-6pm Wed-Sun) This well-done museum of Sonoran customs has extensive exhibits (all in Spanish) on the history and traditions of the state. Special attention is paid to the influence of mining on Álamos and the fleeting prosperity it created for the town's well-off, including rooms filled with antiques, period furniture and even a few vintage carriages.

Museo de María Félix
MUSEUM

(Linda Vista 6; M$10; ⊗10am-4pm Thu-Sun; P) Movie star María Félix (known simply as 'La Doña,' and often dubbed Mexico's Marilyn Monroe) is the town's most famous daughter, and this museum is dedicated to her. Inside are paintings, photographs and personal effects and an illustration by Diego Rivera. It's on the main road out of town toward Navojoa, a 15-minute walk from the plaza.

☞ Tours

For highly informative tours around town, English-speaking **Emiliano Graseda** (☑647-101-48-75), who can be found at the Álamos tourist office most weekends, charges M$250 per person. Tours take in Álamos' landmarks and private homes and continue in the nearby village of La Aduana to visit a brickworks, *artesanías* workshops and a mission.

Amigos de la Educación de Álamos (www.amigosdealamos.typepad.com; per person M$10) runs tours of Álamos' most famous houses and gardens every Saturday at 10am; groups meet in front of the Museo Costumbrista de Sonora on the Plaza de Armas.

★Solipaso
ADVENTURE TOUR

(☑647-428-15-09; www.solipaso.com; El Pedregal, Privada s/n, Barrio el Chalatón) Runs expert bird-watching trips (half-day M$1050) and

---

FERRIES TO BAJA

Two ferry services link mainland northwest Mexico with Baja California. From Topolobampo near Los Mochis, **Baja Ferries** (p776) leaves at 2:30pm Monday to Friday and 11pm on Saturday for La Paz in Baja; the trip takes around seven hours. In the other direction there is a ferry leaving La Paz at 11pm nightly, except on Saturday. For travel around Semana Santa and Christmas/New Year and in June and July reserving a month ahead is recommended. You can buy tickets in Los Mochis or, on departure day, at the Topolobampo terminal. Vehicles can also be transported on this route.

The ferry **Santa Rosalía** (☑01-800-505-50-18; www.ferrysantarosalia.com; seating saloon-class M$840, motorcycle/car M$1420/3200) sails from Guaymas for Santa Rosalía, Baja California, at 8pm Tuesday, Thursday and Saturday, arriving the next morning around 6am. From mid-November to mid-March, strong winds may cause delays, and Tuesday sailings are occasionally canceled in low season. The ferry returns from Santa Rosalía on Wednesday and Friday at 8:30am and on Sunday at 8pm. The **ticket office** (☑622-222-02-04; Recinto Portuario Zona Franca s/n, Terminal de Transbordadores, Colonia Punta Arena; ⊗8am-2pm & 3:30-8pm Mon-Sat) is 2km east of Guaymas city center, though reservations are only necessary if you want a cabin or are taking a vehicle (three days in advance is sufficient). All passengers and vehicles should be at the terminal by 6:30pm.

also superb floating river excursions (per person M$1440, four to 12 people; November to March) on the Río Mayo northwest of Álamos. You visit ancient petroglyphs, a stone aqueduct and a Mayo village, and there's guaranteed to be spectacular coastal and tropical birdlife; river otters and coatimundis are also encountered. Guides are highly knowledgeable. There are no regular office hours; call directly to book.

Pronatura BIRDWATCHING
(☑ 647-428-00-04; www.pronatura-noroeste.org; Juárez 20; 2hr town tour per person M$200; ⊙ 7:30am-7:30pm Mon-Fri) This environmental group is the main contact point for the local guides of bird-watching group Alas de Álamos (Wings of Álamos). It also offers day trips further afield.

★✿ Festivals & Events

Festival Alfonso Ortíz Tirado MUSIC
(www.festivalortiztirado.gob.mx) One of northern Mexico's premier cultural events, Álamos' 10-day late-January festival features top-class classical and chamber music, blues, bossa nova and trova performed by artists from across the globe. There are also events for kids.

⌨ Sleeping

Álamos has some of the most atmospheric and attractive accommodations in all of Mexico, many in converted colonial mansions featuring gorgeous interior design. However, peso-watchers should be aware that budget options are limited.

Such is the summer heat, the cooler months (October to April) are high season in Álamos, although year-round it's largely a weekend town, with Mexican weekenders coming from nearby cities to get away from it all. Midweek discounts are often available year-round.

Casa de los Tesoros BOUTIQUE HOTEL $$
(☑ 647-428-00-10; www.tesoros-hotel.com; Obregón 10; r M$1100; ⊜❄🢅🏊) This former convent oozes atmosphere and screams potential: the bones of a great hotel are here with two gorgeous courtyards hung with religious art, a fantastic pool, an atmospheric old-world bar famous for its margaritas and large rooms full of individual details, but the management is rather asleep at the wheel at present and could do much better.

That said, it's still a good option, even if you do have trouble finding a staff member at the front desk and even if the restaurant is rarely open.

Casa de las Siete Columnas B&B $$
(☑ 647-428-01-64; www.lassietecolumnas.com; Juárez 36; r incl breakfast M$850-950; ⊙ 15 Oct-15 Apr; ⊜❄🢅🏊) An inviting Canadian-owned hotel in an imposing centuries-old building – look out for the stunning seven-columned front portico. Rooms surround a pretty, plant-filled courtyard and small heated pool and feature beamed ceilings, fireplaces and tasteful decor. There's a guests' lounge with a TV and pool table.

Posada de Don Andrés HOTEL $$
(☑ 647-428-11-10; posadadedonandres@hotmail.com; Rosales; s/d/tr/q M$500/708/826/924; 🅿❄🢅) This decent-value hotel overlooks Plaza Alameda and features two floors of spacious rooms that are comfortable enough but a little on the dark side. Jorge, the owner, is a friendly, welcoming character who makes coffee for his guests each morning in the strangely charming lounge packed full of dark woodwork sculptures.

Hotel Juan HOTEL $$
(☑ 647-428-62-52; hotel-sanjuan@hotmail.com; Juárez 40B; s/d M$590/708; ⊜❄🢅) One of the cheaper options in Álamos, this simple 14-room place, a short wander from the heart of the colonial town, is on the basic side, but rooms have hot water and TV, if few windows.

★ Hotel Luz del Sol BOUTIQUE HOTEL $$$
(☑ 647-428-04-66; www.luzdelsolalamos.com; Obregón 3; s/d incl breakfast M$1050/1250; ⊜❄🢅🏊) This high-end but excellent-value hotel has a warm ambience thanks to welcoming staff and the presence of one of the town's best cafes. There are only three rooms, each very spacious with sultan-sized beds, sumptuous furnishings, high ceilings and vast adjoining bathrooms with vintage tiling and tubs. The charming courtyard and roof terrace plus the intimate atmosphere make this a superb choice.

★ Hacienda de los Santos LUXURY HOTEL $$$
(☑ 647-428-02-22; www.haciendadelossantos.com; Molina 8; r/ste incl breakfast from M$3100/7880; 🅿⊝❄@🢅🏊) By far Álamos' most exclusive place to stay, this hacienda encompasses five restored colonial houses, three pools,

three restaurants, a movie theater, a spa, a gym, landscaped grounds and a bar (with a 520-strong tequila collection!). Accommodations are astounding, luxurious and highly atmospheric, while the sheer size of the place and its incredible gardens is simply mind-blowing.

Rates plummet in the hot months. If you're curious to peek inside without decimating your budget, M$50 tours of the property are given most days at 2pm.

Hotel Colonial
HOTEL $$$

(☑647-428-13-71; www.alamoshotelcolonial.com; Obregón 4; r incl breakfast M$2170-2644; P☀❋⚛) The attention to detail at this incredibly classy historic mansion is highly impressive: it feels more like you are stepping into an Edwardian period drama than it does a Mexican hotel. That said, the 10 rooms don't quite live up to the promise made by the sumptuous public areas, though they do feature tapestries, oil paintings, antiques and stately fireplaces.

El Pedregal
LODGE $$$

(☑647-428-15-09; www.elpedregalmexico.com; Privada s/n, Barrio el Chalatón; d/q incl breakfast M$1500/2000; P☀❋@⚛) 🌿 There are just five lovely adobe and straw-bale cabins here, all with stylish artistic furnishings and luxury bedding scattered around 8 hectares of tropical deciduous forest on the edge of Álamos, 2km from the plaza. The welcoming owners are expert birders and lead tours. A good-sized pool, a yoga studio and a massage parlor complete the scene.

✖ Eating

Cenaduría Dõna Lola
MEXICAN $

(☑647-428-11-09; Volantín s/n; mains M$50-100; ☺7am-10pm; ☀) This fan-cooled, family-run place is both simple and welcoming. The soups are crammed with ingredients (try the excellent *sopa de tortillas*) and there's a huge menu of delicious *antojitos* and breakfasts as well. It can be found on a small side street south of the Plaza de Armas, off Juárez. There's a covered terrace at the rear. It's also known as Koky's.

Terracotta
MEXICAN $

(Juárez, Plaza de Armas; mains M$50-130; ☺7am-10pm) Simple and cheap but very tasty Mexican dishes are served up in the peaceful courtyard of an old colonial mansion on the main square.

★ Teresitas
INTERNATIONAL, BAKERY $$

(www.teresitasalamos.com; Allende 41; mains M$150-280, breakfasts M$60-70, sandwiches M$75-100; ☺8am-9pm Tue-Sat, 9am-6pm Sun; ❋⚛) It's quite amazing that somewhere as small and remote as Álamos boasts this simply outstanding bakery-cum-bistro. There's an open kitchen and a changing menu that features excellent salads, pastas, steaks and paninis, as well as offerings less usual in rural Mexico: *arancini*, spicy chicken wings and Thai noodle soup. Desserts are fully catered for with sublime cakes and pastries.

Either eat in the fountain-flanked garden or enjoy the comfort of a royal-blue banquette inside.

Café Luz del Sol
CAFE $$

(☑647-428-04-66; Obregón 3; mains M$65-140; ☺7:30am-6:30pm; ❋⚛) In a region cruelly deprived of decent coffee shops, this colonial cafe is a better find for caffeine-starved travelers than any silver mine. Devour beautifully prepared breakfasts, Mexican and North American lunches, homemade cakes and good coffee. There's an elegant interior hung with locally produced art, and a small patio.

ℹ Information

Banorte (Madero 37; ☺9am-4pm Mon-Fri) ATM; money exchange.

Hospital General de Álamos (☑647-428-02-25; Madero s/n; ☺8am-8pm) Basic local hospital with no emergency services.

Tourist Office (☑647-428-04-50; Victoria 5; ☺8am-3pm Mon-Fri, 9am-6pm Sat & Sun) A helpful information office right on the Plaza de Armas. On weekends it's usually staffed by local independent guide **Emiliano Graseda** (p772).

ℹ Getting There & Away

Álamos is 53km east of Navojoa and 156km north of Los Mochis. Its **Transportes Baldomero Corral** (☑647-428-00-96; Morelos 7) terminal is on Plaza Alameda. Second-class buses run by **Albatros** (☑647-428-00-96; www.albatrosautobuses.com; cnr Guerrero & No Reelección, Navojoa) run between Navojoa and Álamos (M$35, one hour) every 30 minutes from 6:30am to 6:30pm; there's also a late bus at 9pm. Over 20 daily 1st-class Albatros and **Tufesa** (☑642-421-32-10; www.tufesa.com.mx; cnr Hidalgo & No Reelección, Navojoa) buses connect Navojoa with Guaymas and Hermosillo.

If you're coming by car from Los Mochis, stick to the longer paved road via Navojoa, as the shorter back road is unpaved and rather wild for much of the journey.

Los Mochis

Los Mochis

📞 668 / POP 260,000

There is nothing much to detain you in Los Mochis, a giant urban sprawl mainly notable for being the first or last stop on the Chepe (Ferrocarril Chihuahua Pacífico), and within an easy hop of ferries that link the mainland to Baja California. The climate here is perpetually humid and there are no real sights to savor unless you count an excess of sleazy bars. However, if you're venturing to Baja by boat or to the Copper Canyon by train, you may well find yourself staying overnight, and in that case you'll actually find decent eating and sleeping options available, including what is said to be northern Mexico's best seafood.

🛏 Sleeping

Hotel Fénix　　　　HOTEL $
(📞668-812-26-23; hotelfenix@email.com; Flores 365 Sur; s/d/tr M$495/595/615; 🅿🌬🛜) This is the best moderately priced hotel in town, with welcoming staff, a sparkling lobby, an excellent restaurant and renovated rooms that represent good value. Accommodations can be on the small side, and some lack natural light, but as an overnight stop it's a great choice.

Los Mochis

🛏 **Sleeping**
1 Best Western Los Mochis B1
2 Hotel del Valle D1
3 Hotel Fénix C1

🍴 **Eating**
4 Alma Mia C1
5 El Farallón C2
6 La Cabaña de Doña Chayo D3
7 La Medusa B1

Hotel del Valle　　　　HOTEL $
(📞668-812-01-05; www.hoteldelvalle.hostel.com; Prieto 302 Sur; s/d/tr M$300/400/450; 🌬🛜) This is a central and clean budget option, which, while lacking much charm, makes for a cheap place to spend the night. The rooms are all rather small, but have clean sheets and their own bathrooms.

Best Western Los Mochis　　　　HOTEL $$$
(📞668-816-30-00; www.bestwestern.com; Obregón 691 Poniente; r/ste M$1665/2713; 🅿♿🌬@🛜♨) Enjoying a prime spot overlooking the central plaza, this business-class hotel offers professional staff and service and very comfortable, carpeted rooms with modern bathrooms. It may be a big leap in price, but it's definitely the best place in town.

✕ Eating

Alma Mia CAFE **$**
(Guerrero 401 Sur, Plazuela 27 de Septiembre; breakfasts M$40-80; ⏱7am-11pm; 🛜) Excellent coffee, friendly staff and even valet parking at this coffee shop on the main square. Good breakfasts are served too.

La Cabaña de Doña Chayo TAQUERÍA **$**
(📞668-818-54-98; Obregón 99 Poniente; tacos & quesadillas M$33-45; ⏱8am-1am; 🍴) A simple yet enjoyable place with delectable quesadillas, burritos and tacos with *carne asada* or *machaca* (spiced, shredded, dried beef). It's fearsomely popular, and yet even at busy times the welcome is warm.

La Medusa SEAFOOD **$$**
(📞668-176-61-64; Obregón 878A Poniente; mains M$100-180; ⏱1pm-1am; 🛜) This sophisticated and thoroughly contemporary self-described 'fish kitchen' is a real find. The menu includes an excellent tuna burger, salmon teriyaki and *dorado* (dolphin fish) tacos, and you'll even find a selection of excellent local-brewed artisanal beers. There's an attached deli selling all manner of local culinary goodies that make for excellent souvenirs.

El Farallón SEAFOOD **$$**
(📞668-812-12-73; www.farallon.com.mx; Obregón 499 Poniente; mains M$150-200; ⏱8am-11pm Sun-Thu, to midnight Fri & Sat; 🍴🛜) Furiously air-conditioned, upmarket seafood restaurant with a far-ranging selection of dishes: stick to the tried-and-tested Mexican and Sinaloan dishes (rather than fusion-style sushi rolls and the like) and you won't go wrong. The ceviche and *pescado a la plancha* (grilled fish) are particularly recommended,

though for something more adventurous try the *fiesta de mariscos*, an enormously varied seafood platter.

🛈 Getting There & Away

AIR

Los Mochis Airport (📞668-818-68-70; www.aeropuertosgap.com.mx; Carretera Los Mochis-Topolobampo Km 12.5) Los Mochis Airport has daily flights to Mexico City, Hermosillo, Tijuana, Mazatlán and Guadalajara with airlines including Aeroméxico Connect (📞668-812-02-16; www.aeromexico.com.mx; Obregón 1104 Poniente), **Aéreo Calafia** (www.aereocalafia.com.mx) and **Volaris** (www.volaris.com). Several small airlines fly to Baja California destinations.

BOAT

Baja Ferries (📞01-800-337-74-37, 668-817-37-52; www.bajaferries.com; Local 5, cnr Blvds Rosales & Centenario; adult/under 12yr M$970/485; ⏱8am-6pm Mon-Fri, 9am-3pm Sat) This company offers tickets for ferries to Pichilingue, near La Paz in Baja California Sur, leaving from Topolobampo, 24km southwest of Los Mochis. Tickets can be purchased up to two months ahead. Cars (M$2200) can also be transported.

BUS

Despite being a big transportation hub, Los Mochis lacks a central bus station, meaning that each bus company operates from its own depot in the city. Particularly useful lines are Grupo Estrella Blanca (GEB), Transportes y Autobuses Pacífico (TAP) and Tufesa. The main intercity bus stations all have round-the-clock departures.

Azules del Noroeste (📞668-812-34-91; Tenochtitlán 399 Poniente) Second-class buses to El Fuerte (M$80, two hours, every 30 minutes).

Grupo Estrella Blanca/Transportes y Autobuses Pacífico (GEB/TAP; 📞01-800-507-55-

BUSES FROM LOS MOCHIS

DESTINATION	FARE (M$)	DURATION (HR)	FREQUENCY (DAILY)
Guadalajara	741-886	13-15	half-hourly TAP, 13 Tufesa
Guaymas	286	5-6	25 Tufesa
Hermosillo	352-430	6-7	half-hourly 1st-class GEB, half-hourly Tufesa
Mazatlán	372-428	6-7	frequent GEB/TAP, 11 Tufesa
Navojoa	118-146	2	frequent 1st-class GEB, 32 Tufesa
Nogales	610-731	10-12	17 Tufesa
Phoenix	1137-1493	14-16	10 Tufesa

00; www.estrellablanca.com.mx; Blvd Castro btwn Constitución & Domínguez) Deluxe and 1st-class buses to Mexico City, Nogales and Tijuana.

Tufesa (☑ 668-818-22-22; www.tufesa.com. mx; Blvd Antonio Rosales 2300) First-class buses to Navojoa (for Álamos), Nogales, Phoenix, Mazatlán and Guadalajara. The terminal is 3km northeast of the center of Los Mochis (M$60 in a taxi).

TRAIN

Los Mochis Train Station (☑ 668-824-11-51; ◷ 5am-5:30pm Mon-Fri, 5-9am & 10:30am-1pm Sat & Sun) The ticket office at Los Mochis train station sells railway tickets up to a month ahead of travel. Opening hours are notoriously unreliable, however, so be warned. In town, Viajes Flamingo (☑ 1-800-896-8196; www. mexicoscoppercanyon.com; Hotel Santa Anita cnr Calles Leyva & Hidalgo) also books tickets in advance.

The station is located 4km southeast of the town center at the end of Bienestar; a taxi from downtown is M$80.

ⓘ Getting Around

Buses 72 'Castro-Chamizal' and 118 'DIF Castro Estación' (M$6) do the 15-minute run to the train station from Blvd Castro, between Zaragoza and Prieto (5:30am to 9pm). They drop you one block before the station. However, as the morning train leaves at 6am, the bus is only useful for reaching the ticket office; you'll need to take a taxi if you want to make the train on time.

Buses to Topolobampo (M$20, every 20 minutes until 7:30pm) leave from the corner of Cuauhtémoc and Prieto for the Baja ferry.

Taxis in town cost M$50, and to the airport/ Topolobampo approximately M$160 to M$200. They line up on Obregón, by the Best Western.

CHIHUAHUA & CENTRAL NORTH MEXICO

Alluringly off the tourist radar, and with an affable frontier feel, central north Mexico is barely known except as a starting or ending point for Copper Canyon excursions (Chihuahua is the eastern terminus for the canyon-traversing Ferrocarril Chihuahua Pacífico train ride). Yet this region offers some of Mexico's most important historic sights across a triptych of colonial cities (Chihuahua, Hidalgo del Parral and Durango) and some fantastic scenery. The landscape is classic cowboy flick, typified by the starkly beautiful Desierto Chihuahuense (Chihuahuan Desert), which covers most of Mexico's largest state, Chihuahua – and while it rises in the west into the fertile folds of the Sierra Madre Occidental, you'll be forgiven wherever you go for thinking you've wandered into a B-grade western (Durango, incidentally, is where many famous westerns *were* filmed).

Just as Chihuahua state license plates proclaim, this is very much the 'Tierra del Encuentro' (Land of Discovery). History buffs will delight in compelling museums commemorating famous revolutionaries such as Pancho Villa, while there are also some fascinating archaeological sites.

The tourism industry has been ravaged by recent upsurges in drug-gang violence, so do not venture anywhere off the beaten track without a guide. The 'Golden Triangle' area – where southern Chihuahua, northwest Durango and northeast Sinaloa converge – is noted for its opium production and particularly high levels of violence. There's some danger of being caught in the wrong place at the wrong time, but perpetrators have not targeted tourists and there have been few incidents involving visitors.

Tourism has been ravaged by recent upsurges in drug-gang violence, so do not venture anywhere off the beaten track without a guide. The 'Golden Triangle' area – where southern Chihuahua, northwest Durango and northeast Sinaloa converge – is noted for its opium production and particularly high levels of violence. While there is some danger of being caught in the wrong place at the wrong time, as was horribly illustrated by the murder of two Australian surfers who resisted a robbery attempt on a highway south of Topolobampo in Sinaloa in 2015, in general perpetrators have not targeted tourists and there have been few incidents involving visitors.

Chihuahua

☑ 614 / POP 810,000 / ELEV 1440M

Chihuahua, capital of Mexico's biggest state, is a quirky but pleasant combination of *norteño* character, revolutionary history and bohemian studenty hangouts. Many travelers use it only as an overnight stop before or after riding the Ferrocarril Chihuahua Pacífico, but Chihuahua is worth more of your time. The city center combines grand colonial

Chihuahua

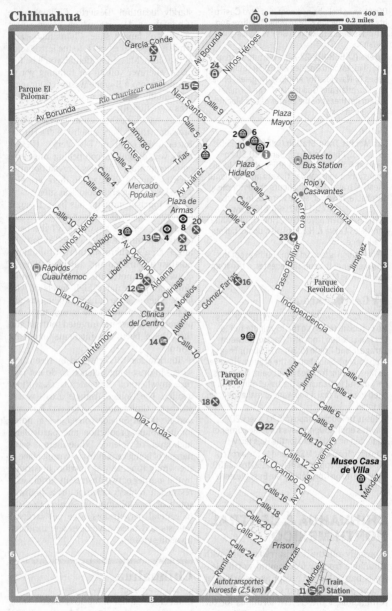

buildings, several beautiful plazas, pedestrianized lanes and a crop of restaurants, cafes and bars. Its museums bear witness to the key episodes of Mexican history that unfolded here. In short, you'll find it an intriguing city with a strong sense of identity.

History

Founded in 1709, Chihuahua soon became the key city of the Nueva España's Provincias Internas (stretching from California to Texas and Sinaloa to Coahuila). The Spanish brought pro-independence rebels, in-

Chihuahua

◉ Top Sights
1 Museo Casa de Villa D5

◉ Sights
2 Casa Chihuahua.................................C2
3 Casa Sebastián B3
4 Cathedral B3
Galería de Armas ....(see 6)
5 Museo Casa de Juárez......................C2
6 Museo de Hidalgo C2
7 Palacio de Gobierno C2
8 Plaza de Armas B3
9 Quinta Gameros.................................C4

✪ Activities, Courses & Tours
10 Chihuahua Bárbaro C2

🛏 Sleeping
11 Hostal El Chepe.................................D6
12 Hotel Jardín del Centro......................B3
13 Hotel Plaza.......................................B3
14 Hotel San Felipe El Real B4
15 Motel María Dolores B1

🍴 Eating
16 Cafe Cortez.......................................C3
17 El Papalote B1
18 Encantada...C4
19 La Casa de los Milagros B3
20 La Fábrica de Pan y Cafe B3
21 Mesón de Catedral B3

🍷 Drinking & Nightlife
22 La Antigua Paz C5
23 Momposina...C3

🛍 Shopping
24 Casa de las Artesanías del
Estado de Chihuahua C1

cluding Miguel Hidalgo, to be condemned and shot here in 1811. The Porfirio Díaz regime brought railways and helped consolidate the wealth of the area's huge cattle fiefdoms. Luis Terrazas, one-time Chihuahua state governor, held lands nearly the size of Belgium: 'I am not from Chihuahua, Chihuahua is mine,' he is reported to have said.

After Pancho Villa's forces took Chihuahua in 1913 during the Mexican Revolution, Villa established his headquarters here, arranged various civic projects and soon acquired the status of local hero. Today, the city has one of Mexico's highest living standards, with *maquiladora* (parts factory) jobs contributing significantly to this.

◉ Sights

★ Museo Casa de Villa　　　　　　MUSEUM
(Calle 10 No 3010; adult/student M$10/5; ☉9am-7pm Tue-Sat, 10am-4pm Sun) Housed in Quinta Luz, Pancho Villa's 48-room former mansion, this museum is a must-see for anyone who appreciates a made-for-Hollywood story of crime, stakeouts and riches. The interior is loaded with Villa's personal effects and photographs, and in the back courtyard you'll find the bullet-riddled black Dodge that Villa was driving when he was murdered. Information is in Spanish and English.

After his assassination in 1923, 25 of Villa's 'wives' filed claims for his estate. Government investigations determined that Luz Corral de Villa was the *generalísimo*'s legal spouse; the mansion was awarded to her and became known as Quinta Luz. She opened the museum and the army acquired it after her death in 1981.

The rear of the museum concentrates on Mexican revolutionary history.

Casa Chihuahua　　　　　　　　MUSEUM
(☎614-429-33-00; www.casachihuahua.org.mx; Libertad 901; M$50, Sun free; ☉10am-6pm Wed-Mon) Chihuahua's former Palacio Federal (built 1908–10) has been used as a mint, a Jesuit monastery, a military hospital and a post office, but is now a cultural center full of good-quality exhibits, with most explanations in English and Spanish. Modern displays concentrate on the culture and history of Chihuahua state with features on Mormons, Mennonites and the Tarahumara. The most famous gallery is **Calabozo de Hidalgo**, the subterranean dungeon where Miguel Hidalgo was held prior to his execution.

The historic dungeon and the church towering above it were preserved within the later buildings erected on the site. A short audiovisual heightens the mournful atmosphere of the dungeon, which contains Hidalgo's bible and crucifix. A plaque outside recalls the verses the revolutionary priest wrote in charcoal on his cell wall in his final hours thanking his captors for their kindness.

Quinta Gameros　　　　　　　　GALLERY
(☎614-416-66-84; Paseo Bolívar 401; adult/child & student M$20/10, Sun free; ☉11am-2pm & 4-7pm Tue-Sun) Built in an incredibly elaborate belle epoque architectural style by a wealthy mine owner, this museum is filled with a mix of period furnishings and art. Every room is

PANCHO VILLA: BANDIT TURNED REVOLUTIONARY

Macho womanizer, revolutionary, cattle rustler, lover of education, a man of impulsive violence who detested alcohol. No hero in Mexico's history is as colorful or contradictory as Francisco 'Pancho' Villa.

Villa is best known as a leader of the Mexican Revolution but as much of his adulthood was given over to robbing and chasing women as to any noble cause. Born Doroteo Arango to hacienda workers in northern Durango state in 1878, he turned to banditry by the age of 16, taking the name Francisco Villa, possibly in honor of his grandfather. The story goes that Villa became an outlaw after shooting one of the hacienda-owning family who tried to rape his sister. Between 1894 and 1910, Villa's life veered between spells of banditry and attempts to lead a legitimate existence.

In 1910, amid intensifying opposition to the dictatorial regime of President Porfirio Díaz, Villa was lobbied for support by Abraham González, leader in Chihuahua state of the revolutionary movement headed by Francisco Madero. González knew he needed natural fighting leaders and encouraged Villa to return to marauding. Villa soon raised a fighting force to join the Revolution, which began on November 20, 1910.

When Villa's rebels took Ciudad Juárez in May 1911, Díaz resigned. Madero was elected president, but in 1913 he was toppled from power by one of his own commanders, General Victoriano Huerta, and executed. Villa fled across the US border to El Paso, but within a couple of months he was back as one of four revolutionary leaders opposed to Huerta. He quickly raised an army of thousands, the famed División del Norte, and by the end of 1913, with the help of US-supplied guns, he had taken Ciudad Juárez (again) and Chihuahua, installing himself as state governor for the next two years. He expropriated property and money from rich *hacendados* (landowners), lowered prices of basic necessities and established schools, but favored his troops over noncombatants and tolerated no dissent. His victory over a pro-Huerta army at Zacatecas in June 1914 signaled the end for Huerta. But the four revolutionary forces soon split into two camps, with liberal leaders Venustiano Carranza and Álvaro Obregón on one side, and the more radical Villa and Emiliano Zapata on the other. Villa was routed by Obregón in the Battle of Celaya (1915) and never recovered his influence.

After the USA recognized Carranza's government in October 1915, Villa decided to simultaneously discredit Carranza and seek revenge on US president Wilson. On March 9, 1916, Villa's men sacked the US town of Columbus, New Mexico, which was home to both a US cavalry garrison and Sam Ravel, who had once cheated Villa on an arms deal. Though as many as half of Villa's 500 militiamen may have died that day (there were 18 US deaths) and Ravel wasn't found (he was at the dentist in El Paso), the attack ended up a success for Villa because it drew a US Army punitive expedition into Mexico in pursuit of him, and boosted his legend. Villa carried on fighting the Carranza regime, raiding cities and haciendas, but now had to maintain his fighting force by conscription, and sometimes allowed his men to pillage and slaughter.

In 1920 Carranza was deposed by his former ally Obregón, and Villa signed a peace treaty with provisional president Adolfo de la Huerta. Villa pledged to lay down his arms and retire to a hacienda in Canutillo, for which the Huerta government paid M$636,000. Villa was given money to cover wages owed to his troops and help the widows and orphans of the División del Norte. He settled 759 of his former troops at Canutillo, setting up a school for them and their children.

For the next three years, Villa led a relatively quiet life. He bought a hotel in Hidalgo del Parral and regularly attended cockfights. He installed one of his many 'wives,' Soledad Seañez, in a Parral apartment, and kept another at Canutillo. Then, one day while he was leaving Parral in his Dodge touring car, a volley of shots rang out and the legendary revolutionary was killed. The light prison sentences the eight-man assassin team received led many to conclude that the order for the killing came from President Obregón, though with all the enemies Villa made over the years, there are many suspects.

unique and, while the quality of the stained glass, carved wood and moldings is no doubt high, the overall impression is of the most criminal bad taste. It's definitely worth a look around though, as it is certainly one of Chihuahua's most unforgettable buildings.

Manuel Gameros started building Quinta Gameros in 1907 as a wedding present for his much younger fiancée, Elisa Muller. By the time it was finished three years later, she had died, and soon afterward the Revolution began and the Gameros family fled Mexico. To add yet more color to the story, some guides tell that Elisa fell for Colombian architect Julio Corredor and ran off with him instead.

Plaza de Armas   PLAZA
Chihuahua's historic heart, with its mass of pigeons, shoe-shiners and cowboy-hatted characters, is a simple but pretty place. Its majestic baroque **cathedral** (☑614-410-38-77; Plaza de Armas; ⊙6am-9pm Tue-Sun), built between 1725 and 1826, presides over the bustle, still containing the original organ installed in 1796.

Palacio de Gobierno   HISTORIC BUILDING
(☑614-429-35-96; Aldama 901; ⊙8am-8pm) FREE The courtyard of this handsome, 19th-century, state-government building features striking 1950s murals by Aarón Piña Mora showing Chihuahua's highly eventful history. You can get a free booklet on the murals at the tourist office.

Hidalgo and the Mexican independence are the subjects of two small museums in the *palacio*: **Museo de Hidalgo** (⊙9am-5pm Tue-Sun) FREE and **Galería de Armas** (⊙9am-5pm Tue-Sun) FREE.

Museo Casa de Juárez   MUSEUM
(Juárez House Museum; ☑614-410-42-58; Av Juárez 321; adult/child & student M$10/5; ⊙9am-7pm Tue-Sun) President Benito Juárez' residence in this house during the French occupation made Chihuahua the capital of the Mexican republic from 1864 to 1866. Now a museum with the 1860s feel still intact, it includes documents signed by the great reformer, as well as period exhibits, including replicas of his furniture. It's also called the Museo de la Lealtad Republicana (Museum of Republican Loyalty).

Casa Sebastián   GALLERY
(☑614-410-75-06; Av Juárez 601; ⊙8am-6pm Mon-Fri) FREE The main draws of this restored 1880s gallery's are the small-scale models of the massive metal sculptures by renowned Chihuahuan artist Sebastián, whose work is seen in cities worldwide. There are several real Sebastianes around Chihuahua, including one just above Parque El Palomar.

👉 Tours

Chihuahua Bárbaro   TOUR
(www.chihuahuabarbaro.com; 3hr city tour adult/child M$120/85) This trolleybus offers tours of Chihuahua's main historic sights (narrated in Spanish) and beyond. Its three-hour city tour departs from the Plaza de Armas (where there's a ticket booth) four times daily, and includes the Pancho Villa museum and Quinta Gameros.

🛏 Sleeping

Motel María Dolores   MOTEL $
(☑614-416-74-20; motelmadol@hotmail.com; Calle 9A No 304; s/d/tw/tr M$345/369/419/464; P🅿❄@🛜) Just down from Plaza Mayor, this impeccably run motel's basic but modern rooms are a very good deal given the excellent location. It's particularly handy for drivers, with its big, secure parking lot.

Hostal El Chepe   HOSTEL $
(☑614-345-14-64; Méndez 2005; r M$300; 🖥❄🛜) This simple place enjoys a location directly in front of the train station, and so is perfect for early starts and late arrivals. Rooms are basic and rather dark but clean. The hotel is run by a friendly woman, who also runs a shop selling marble in the entrance to the hotel.

Hotel Jardín del Centro   HOTEL $$
(☑614-415-18-32; hoteljardindelcentro@hotmail.com; Victoria 818; s/d M$560/650; 🖥❄🛜) Offering fine value, this pleasant, inviting little hotel has cozy, attractive rooms around a pretty plant-filled courtyard, plus a good little restaurant. Twins in the back are not as atmospheric as the doubles with high ceilings at the front. Staff are sweet and its location is conveniently close to the center, though its loud caged birds will not thrill some.

★**Hotel San Felipe El Real**   BOUTIQUE HOTEL $$$
(☑614-437-20-37; www.hotelsanfelipeelreal.com; Allende 1005; r/ste incl breakfast M$1370/1650; P🅿❄@🛜) Unassuming it may be from the outside, but inside this gorgeous 1880s house you'll find a courtyard with a burbling

fountain and six uniquely furnished rooms, all replete with antiques and period furniture. The owners spoil guests, and serve breakfast on one long table in the homey kitchen. Airport and train station pickups are offered.

Hotel Plaza HOTEL $$$
(614-415-12-12; www.hotelplazachihuahua.com; Cuarta 204; r incl breakfast M$1428; P❄✿🌐) Clean, modern and spacious rooms with wooden floors, modish furniture and quality bed linen await you here, just a stone's throw from the cathedral. The roof terrace where breakfast is served boasts fine city views and service is friendly and attentive.

✖ Eating

★ Cafe Cortez CAFE $
(Gómez Farías 8; mains M$35-80; ⊙9am-11pm Mon-Fri, 10am-11pm Sat, 4-11pm Sun; 🌐) Chihuahua hardly does hipster, but this hangar-like place painted black outside and a riot of colors inside is probably the most likely environment to find the nearest local equivalent. The real reason to come here though is the excellent coffee, as well as the tasty and enormous paninis, salads and sandwiches, which make it a great lunch stop.

La Casa de los Milagros MEXICAN $
(614-437-06-93; Victoria 812; dishes M$65-100; ⊙11am-11:30pm Sun-Thu, to 1:30am Fri & Sat; ❄🌐) Legend has it that Pancho Villa and his pals hung out in this atmospheric 110-year-old mansion featuring tiled floors, lots of snug little rooms and an airy covered courtyard. The menu is enormous and rather confusing, as typical Mexican dishes are all humorously renamed, but the food is excellent. There's live music in the evenings.

El Papalote MEXICAN $
(cnr García Conde & Calle 9; mains M$30-150; ⊙7:30am-10:30pm; ❄🌐) Breakfast heartily among Chihuahua's Mennonite residents in this American-style diner that has been hard at work since 1982. You'll find a good selection of egg combinations, as well as abundant *antojitos* and full-on Mexican meals as well.

La Fábrica de Pan y Cafe CAFE $$
(Independencia 408; mains M$100-170; ⊙8:30am-10pm Sun-Thu, to midnight Fri & Sat; ❄🌐) A centrally located coffee shop and breakfast place that does a full menu of pizza, pasta, burgers and sashimi from 1pm. The coffee isn't actually very good, but the tasty muffins, baguettes, pancakes and breakfasts (try

the *huevos franciscanos* – poached eggs and bacon) make up for that.

Encantado STEAK $$
(Av Ocampo 1810; dishes M$50-140; ⊙8am-8pm; 🌐) A stylish restaurant in a historic building with tables in rooms dotted around a covered patio. The menu is pretty straightforward, with Mexican favorites, salads, filling sandwiches, steaks, burgers and breakfasts.

Mesón de Catedral INTERNATIONAL $$$
(Plaza de Armas; mains M$100-200; ⊙8am-midnight Mon-Wed, to 2am Thu-Sat, to 10pm Sun; ❄🌐) Go to the 2nd floor of this modern building to find the best vista in Chihuahua. With a terrace overlooking the city's cathedral, this upmarket place is worth spending a little extra on: try the fish fillet stuffed with peppers or the beefsteak with giant shrimp in red wine dressing. There's live music on Thursday, Friday and Saturday evenings.

🍷 Drinking

★ Momposina BAR
(614-410-09-75; Coronado 508; ⊙4pm-1am Mon-Sat; 🌐) A bohemian bar where a crowd of creative types gather during the day to lounge on mismatched seats, snack on paninis and sip espressos. Later on, it morphs into a bar and there's often live music featuring Mulata, the Colombian-Mexican owners' band. Beers are inexpensive and the vibe is cool.

La Antigua Paz CANTINA
(Calle 12 No 2203; ⊙noon-1am) This classic Mexican cantina has revolutionary memorabilia on the walls and a good mix of students, 30-somethings and cowboys. It has live music most nights.

🛍 Shopping

Chihuahua is a big city with little to recommend it for shoppers. However, the strong cowboy culture here means there are plenty of cowboy-related items to be found for those on the prowl. Cowboy-boot shoppers should make a beeline to Libertad between Independencia and Avenida Ocampo, where lots of boot shops line the street.

Casa de las Artesanías
del Estado de Chihuahua HANDICRAFTS
(614-410-60-73; Niños Héroes 1101; ⊙9am-5pm Mon-Fri, 10am-5pm Sat) Good selection of *chihuahuense* crafts (including Mata Ortiz pottery) and Mexican foodstuffs such as pecans, oregano oil and *sotol*, a local spirit made from desert spoon plants.

❶ Information

Clínica del Centro (🖉 614-439-81-00; www.clinicadelcentro.com.mx; Ojinaga 816; ⊙24hr) Has a 24-hour emergency department.

Post Office (Libertad 1700; ⊙8am-4:30pm Mon-Fri, 8am-noon Sat)

Rojo y Casavantes (🖉 614-439-58-58; www.rojoycasavantes.com; Guerrero 1207) For bus, train and plane tickets.

State Tourist Office (🖉 800-508-01-11, 614-429-35-96; www.ah-chihuahua.com; Palacio de Gobierno, Aldama; ⊙9am-5pm Mon-Sat) Helpful office that can hook you up with guides for city tours and more.

❶ Getting There & Away

AIR

Chihuahua's **airport** (🖉 614-478-70-00; www.oma.aero; Blvd Juan Pablo II Km 14) is 17km from the city center and has daily international flights to Houston and Dallas. Aeroméxico, Interjet, VivaAerobus and Volaris provide domestic service, with daily flights (often two or more) to Guadalajara, Hermosillo, Mexico City, Monterrey and Tijuana.

BUS

Chihuahua's busy main **bus station** (🖉 614-420-53-98; Blvd Juan Pablo II No 4107) is 7km east of the center.

Buses to the US also leave from the main bus station, with destinations including Dallas (M$1324, 17 to 19 hours, one daily) and Los Angeles (M$1464, 22 hours, three daily).

For Cuauhtémoc (M$124, 1½ hours) and Creel (M$315, 4½ hours) there are regular departures from both **Rápidos Cuauhtémoc** (🖉 614-416-48-40; Av Borunda) and **Autotransportes Noroeste** (🖉 614-411-57-83; www.turisticosnoroeste.com; Av Terrazas 7027). The latter also has five daily departures (6am to 4pm) to the Copper Canyon hot spots of Creel, Divisadero (5½ hours) and San Rafael (six hours) via Parque de Aventura Barrancas del Cobre.

TRAIN

Chihuahua is the northeastern terminus for the Ferrocarril Chihuahua Pacífico, with departures at 6am daily. All trains have 1st-class carriages, while on Monday, Thursday and Saturday, *clase económica* carriages are coupled on the back. The **station** (🖉 614-439-72-12; Méndez s/n; ⊙5am-5:30pm Mon-Fri, 9am-12:30pm Sat) is 1.5km south of Plaza de Armas; there are no amenities nearby, just a ticket office. You can nearly always buy tickets on the day of travel.

❶ Getting Around

To get to the main bus station, catch a 'Circunvalación Sur' bus (M$7, 30 to 50 minutes) heading northwest on Carranza, almost opposite Plaza Hidalgo.

Chihuahua recently rolled out a fancy new public transportation network called Vivebús, with air-conditioned, wheelchair-friendly buses that run on designated busways (5:30am to 10pm). No cash is accepted: you need a card (M$20) and journeys cost M$7.

From the center, there are taxis to the train station (M$50), bus station (M$100) and airport (M$200). Airport taxis back to town are pricey (around M$300).

Nuevo Casas Grandes & Casas Grandes

🖉 636 / POP 61,000 / ELEV 1463M

Nuevo Casas Grandes, 320km northwest of Chihuahua, is a prosperous but unremarkable country town, with small communities of Mormon and Mennonite settlers. Tourism-wise, it's a decent base for the

BUSES FROM CHIHUAHUA

DESTINATION	FARE (M$)	DURATION (HR)	FREQUENCY (DAILY)
Ciudad Juárez	535	5-6	hourly
Durango	985	10-13	10
Guadalajara	1315-1590	13	2
Hidalgo del Parral	315	3-5	hourly
Mexico City (Terminal Norte)	1485-1605	19-22	16
Monterrey	805-865	11-12	8
Nuevo Casas Grandes	435	4½	hourly
Saltillo	714	10	7
Zacatecas	940	8	6

prettier village of Casas Grandes by the pre-Hispanic ruins of Paquimé (7km south) and the pottery center of Mata Ortiz (27km south).

◎ Sights

Paquimé
ARCHAEOLOGICAL SITE

(☑636-692-41-40; www.centroculturalpaquime. mex.tl; adult M$52, child under 13yr & Sun free; ☺10am-5pm Tue-Sun) The ruins of Paquimé, in a broad valley with panoramas to distant mountains, contain the mazelike adobe remnants of northern Mexico's most important trading settlement. Paquimé was the center of the Mogollón or Casas Grandes culture, which extended north into New Mexico and Arizona and over most of Chihuahua. The site's impressive, meticulously detailed **Museo de las Culturas del Norte** (included in the admission cost) has displays about Paquimé and the linked indigenous cultures of northern Mexico and the southwest USA.

The site was sacked, perhaps by Apaches, around 1340. Excavation and restoration began in the 1950s; Unesco declared it a World Heritage site in 1998. Plaques, in Spanish and English, discuss Paquimé culture: don't miss the clay macaw cages and the distinctive T-shaped door openings. The Paquimé people revered the scarlet macaw and some structures here represent this beautiful bird, which has never been native to northern Mexico and is evidence of Paquimé's far-reaching trade network.

The Paquimé people were great potters and produced striking cream-colored earthenware with red, brown or black geometric designs; some amazing original examples are on display in the museum, and modern reproductions are for sale.

🛏 Sleeping & Eating

Las Guacamayas B&B
B&B $$

(☑636-692-41-44; www.mataortizollas.com; Av 20 de Noviembre, Casas Grandes; s/d incl breakfast US$50/70; [P][⊜][❄][📶]) 🐾 This adobe-walled place has charming rooms with beamed roofs, all built using recycled materials, and a lovely garden area. Owner Mayte Lujan has a world-class collection of Mata Ortiz pottery and is extremely knowledgeable about the region. It is located just a stone's throw from the entrance to the ruins of Paquimé.

Pompeii
MEXICAN $$

(☑636-661-46-03; Av Juárez 2601, Nuevo Casas Grandes; mains M$120-180; ☺11am-midnight; ☻) This friendly and smart spot is favored by groups visiting Mata Ortiz. It serves up scrumptious modern Mexican dishes with an emphasis on the area's specialty, *pavo* (turkey).

❶ Getting There & Around

In Nuevo Casas Grandes, **Ómnibus de México** (☑636-694-05-02; www.odm.com.mx; Obregón 312) and **Estrella Blanca/Chihuahuenses** (☑636-694-07-80; www.estrellablanca.com. mx; Obregón 308) offer 1st-class buses to Chihuahua (M$435, 4½ hours, hourly), the border at Nogales (M$545, seven hours, seven daily) and Ciudad Juárez (four hours, M$357, 15 daily).

To get to Paquimé from Nuevo Casas Grandes, 'Casas Grandes' buses (M$10, 20 minutes) depart every 40 minutes, northbound from Constitución, just north of Calle 16 de Septiembre. Get off in Casas Grandes' plaza and walk 800m south on Constitución to the ruins. A taxi from Nuevo Casas Grandes to Paquimé is around M$100.

Mata Ortiz

Twenty-seven kilometers south of Casas Grandes, Mata Ortiz, a tiny town of dusty, unpaved streets, loose chickens and unfinished adobe houses, is a major pottery center. Artisans here use materials, techniques and decorative styles inspired by those of the ancient Paquimé culture, and their best pieces of work now sell worldwide for big, big bucks (though you can pick up a nice small one for about M$250).

The well-marked workshop-showroom of Juan Quezada, who revived the tradition in the 1970s, is across from the old train station at the village entrance. Strolling through the village, you'll pass numerous other potteries and will be able to see people working.

Mata Ortiz has no bus service. A taxi from Nuevo Casas Grandes, including a one-hour wait, costs about M$500.

Hidalgo del Parral

☑627 / POP 110,000 / ELEV 1652M

Easy-going Parral has a big place in Mexican history and some good museums. Its chief claim to fame is that it's where Pancho Villa was murdered on July 20, 1923, and buried – with 30,000 attending his funeral at Parral's Panteón de Dolores cemetery. Three years after his burial, his corpse was dug up and beheaded by persons unknown, and in 1976, his remains were moved to Mexico City.

Founded as a mining settlement in 1631, Parral grew rich on the slave labor of the indigenous people who mined the rich veins of silver and other minerals from Parral's La Prieta mine throughout the 17th century.

If you're anywhere near Parral in mid-July, don't miss the spectacular celebrations to mark Villa's death.

⊙ Sights

Museo Francisco Villa MUSEUM
(627-525-32-92; cnr Juárez & Barreda; M$10; ⊙10am-5pm Tue-Sun) The building from which Pancho Villa was shot and killed in 1923 houses the Museo Francisco Villa. It has two floors of interesting photos of Villa the man (fording a river in his beloved Dodge, posing with his gun in midconflict etc), guns and memorabilia. Guided tours (by donation) are available in Spanish (and sometimes English).

Mina La Prieta MINE
(Cerro de la Cruz; adult/child M$30/15; ⊙10am-5pm Tue-Sun; P) This mine was the basis of Parral's economy for centuries after it opened in 1629, producing mainly silver but also gold, copper, zinc and lead. Today, it's one of the world's oldest mines still in operation. You can drop down 87m in an original elevator to the second of its 25 levels (the 23 below are now flooded) and walk 250m along a tunnel hand-cut around 1820, with historical displays on mining methods used throughout La Prieta's history.

⚑ Festivals & Events

Las Jornadas Villistas HISTORICAL
For a week leading up to the anniversary of Pancho Villa's death (July 20), Parral goes wild. Thousands of bikers show up and horseback riders make a six-day journey from the north, recalling Villa's epic journeys. A reenactment of the assassination itself concludes proceedings.

⛉ Sleeping

Note that hotels are booked far in advance for the Las Jornadas Villistas festival in mid-July.

Hotel Acosta HOTEL $
(627-522-02-21; Barbachano 3; s/d/tr M$350/420/500; @☎) A quirky time warp of a place, which appears little-changed since the 1950s, with a fantastic old lobby, original furniture and welcoming staff. Rooms are a bit creaky but comfortable enough and certainly cheap; some have fine city views.

Nueva Vizcaya Suites SUITES $$
(627-525-56-36; Flores Magón 17; s/d M$495/680; P✿❀@☎) A great deal, this efficiently run and central suite-hotel has lovely views of the Cerro de la Cruz hill from some rooms. All accommodations have modern bathrooms and cable TV, and the suites have kitchens. There's an attractive on-site bar-restaurant and helpful staff.

✗ Eating & Drinking

Disfruta HEALTH FOOD $
(Domingo Sarmiento 311; snacks & meals M$25-55; ⊙8am-6:30pm; ❀☎) Yes, northern Mexico is a carnivore's paradise but if you're in need of a fruity pick-me-up head to hip, healthy Disfruta for wonderful fruit cocktails, juices and *licuados* (smoothies), as well as baguettes, salads and crepes.

Al Gusto Restaurante MEXICAN $$
(627-103-19-24; Calle 20 de Noviembre No 5; dishes M$60-140; ⊙8am-10pm; ❀) 🖉 Air-conditioned Al Gusto offers great burgers, salads and filling fajitas.

Micro Cafe BAR
(Independencia 198; ⊙6:30pm-midnight Mon-Sat; ☎) Quite a find in a cowboy town like Parral, this intimate bar has a decidedly boho, artistic vibe with DJs (electronic dance music and techno) and live music (indie, acoustic) on Fridays and Saturdays. There's draft beer and a cool, friendly crowd.

ⓘ Information

The helpful **tourist office** (627-525-44-00; ⊙10am-4pm) is at Mina La Prieta. Banks with ATMs are around Plaza Principal. Many cafes and restaurants have wi-fi.

ⓘ Getting There & Around

The **Central de Autobuses** (627-523-02-43; Calle de Lille 5) is 2km east of the center along Independencia. The easiest way to get there is by taxi (M$30). Buses run to Chihuahua (M$315, three to four hours, hourly), Torreón (M$378, three to four hours, seven daily) and Durango (M$435, five to six hours, 10 daily).

Durango

📞 618 / POP 560,000 / ELEV 1912M

Durango, capital of the eponymous desert state, is an immensely likable place, with an attractive, beautifully kept and laid-back city center and a friendly local populace. It is also one of Mexico's most isolated cities: you have to travel hours through the desert or the Sierra Madre mountains from here before you hit another significant settlement. Yet isolation has fostered unique regional traits, such as the distinctive local cuisine and wry humor.

Founded in 1563, Durango's early importance was due to nearby iron-ore deposits, along with gold and silver from the Sierra Madre. Today hundreds of *maquiladoras* (assembly plants) dominate the economy. For visitors, the city's striking colonial center commands attention, while good accommodations and restaurants are plentiful.

Note: Durango state's time zone is one hour ahead of Chihuahua and Sinaloa.

⊙ Sights

Constitución, pedestrianized between Jardín Hidalgo past the Plaza de Armas to Plazuela Baca Ortiz, is among Mexico's most likable traffic-free streets, lined with restaurants and cafes and lively day and night.

Plaza de Armas   PLAZA

Flower- and fountain-filled Plaza de Armas is graced by the handsome baroque **Catedral del Basílica Menor** (⊙ 8am-9pm). In the plaza's center, you can descend the **Tunel de Minera** (Tunnel of Mining; Plaza de Armas; M$20; ⊙ 10am-4pm Tue-Sun), an underground space with displays and audiovisual presentations devoted to the history of mining in Durango.

★ Museo de la Ciudad 450   MUSEUM

(cnr Av 20 de Noviembre & Victoria; M$22; ⊙ 9am-8pm Tue-Sat, 11am-8pm Sun) This impressive museum dedicated to Durango city is housed in a structure that dates back to 1901. The museum's 14 rooms feature an interesting permanent collection of interactive exhibits, from pre-Hispanic times through colonization to the present day, and deal with Durango's economy, mining, traditions and culture.

Museo Regional de Durango   MUSEUM

(📞 618-813-10-94; www.museo.ujed.mx; Victoria 100 Sur; adult/child M$12/3, Sun free; ⊙ 8am-3pm Mon-Fri) In a palatial French-style, 19th-century mansion, this museum has thorough displays on Durango state's history and culture. Pancho Villa and the area's impressive array of minerals get special attention, and there are paintings by Miguel Cabrera. Most explanations are in English and Spanish.

Museo de las Culturas Populares   MUSEUM

(📞 618-825-88-27; Av 5 de Febrero 1107 Poniente; M$10; ⊙ 9am-6pm Tue-Fri, 10am-6pm Sat, noon-6pm Sun) Exhibits craftwork from Durango state's indigenous Tepehuanes and Huicholes and other artisans, including some hauntingly beautiful masks.

☞ Tours

★ Aventura Pantera   ADVENTURE TOUR

(📞 618-813-98-75; www.aventurapantera.com.mx; Pino Suarez 436 Oriente, 2nd fl) Aventura Pantera is run by English-speaking Walter Bishop Velarde, one of the pioneers of Mexican ecotourism. He organizes exciting trekking, bird-watching, mountain-biking and camping trips into the Sierra Madre Occidental, Piaxtla Canyon and wildlife-rich Reserva de la Biosfera Bolsón de Mapimí north of Durango.

✯ Festivals

Feria Nacional   FAIR

(www.ferianacionaldurango.gob.mx) For three weeks between late June and mid-July, Durango's big annual party remembers its agricultural roots with *charreada* (Mexican rodeos) plus a *duranguense* music and culture fest.

🛏 Sleeping

Hotel Plaza Catedral   HOTEL $

(📞 618-813-24-80; Constitución 216 Sur; r M$330; P 🛜) This hotel has tons of history, but unfortunately that extends to the room furnishings and bed linen. Indeed, it's rather dark and dingy, but also doable for a cheap overnight stay right in the center of the city. The views are unmatched, so try to score a room with a balcony facing the cathedral.

Hotel Posada San Jorge   HOTEL $$

(📞 618-813-32-57; www.hotelposadasanjorge.com.mx; Constitución 102 Sur; s/d incl breakfast M$590/660; P 🚗 ❄ 🛜) In an imposing ex-convent with accommodations upstairs around a courtyard, the San Jorge has spacious rooms, each with two beds and some with sofas and small balconies. Pampas, a

Durango

Brazilian restaurant in the countyard below, serves up breakfast each day, and also offers other meals.

★ **Hostal de la Monja** HOTEL $$$
(☑ 618-837-17-19; www.hostaldelamonja.com.mx; Constitución 214 Sur; r incl breakfast from M$1693; ▣☺✳@☎) This 19th-century mansion facing the cathedral has been tastefully converted into an atmospheric 20-room hotel and is by far the best address in central Durango. The luxurious rooms manage to combine tradition and modern amenities well and there's a good restaurant too. Do request a room at the back if you're noise sensitive, however, as sound from the restaurant carries.

✖ Eating & Drinking

Specialties in Durango include *caldillo duranguense* (Durango stew), made with *machaca* (dried shredded meat) and *ate*

Durango

◎ **Top Sights**
1 Museo de la Ciudad 450 ....C3

◎ **Sights**
2 Catedral del Basílica Menor C3
3 Museo de las Culturas Populares.......A4
4 Museo Regional de Durango C2
5 Plaza de Armas C3
6 Tunel de Minera C3

🛏 **Sleeping**
7 Hostal de la Monja C3
8 Hotel Plaza Catedral.............................C3
9 Hotel Posada San Jorge......................C2

✖ **Eating**
10 Cremería Wallander A2
11 Fonda de la Tía Chona........................A3
12 Los Equipales C2

🍷 **Drinking & Nightlife**
13 Wirikuta...A3
14 Wirikuta Cafe......................................C1

(pronounced 'ah-tay' – a quince paste enjoyed with cheese).

★**Cremería Wallander** DELI **$**
(☑618-811-77-05; Independencia 128 Norte; pizzas M$65-90; ☺8:30am-9pm Mon-Sat, 9am-3:30pm Sun; ☻) An incredible find in Durango, this wonderful deli sells the fabulous products of the Wallander family farm, as well as regional delicacies, fresh bread and amazing cakes. Outside in the back courtyard you can enjoy healthy breakfasts, extraordinary *tortas* (sandwiches) and sublime pizzas. Foodies will love the selection here, while for everyone else it'll be a welcome break from standard Mexican dishes.

Los Equipales TAQUERÍA **$$**
(cnr Constitución & Serdán; mains M$75-150; ☺1pm-midnight Sun-Thu, 1pm-1:30am Fri & Sat; ☻) Los Equipales serves up satisfying meals, including huge plates of tacos in various guises, the *mega-gringa* (a large tortilla topped with avocado, cheese and Durango beef or lamb) and steaks in a convivial, sports-bar atmosphere. There are also tables outside for taking in the crowds walking down Constitución.

Fonda de la Tía Chona MEXICAN **$$**
(☑618-812-77-48; Nogal 110; mains M$80-180; ☺5-11:30pm Mon-Sat, 1-6pm Sun; ☻) A Durango institution, this richly atmospheric, venerable place is dedicated to *durangueño* cuisine such as *caldillos* (beef stews) and delicious *chiles en nogadas* (peppers in walnut sauce).

★**La Fogata Steak House** STEAK **$$$**
(☑618-817-03-47; Cuauhtémoc 200; mains M$215-400; ☺1-11pm; ☻☎) Tuxedo-sporting waiters will fuss over you inside this formal and pleasingly bizarre steak house that's well worth the short M$50 trip by taxi from the center for a blow-out meal. Choice cuts of meat are served on sizzling hot plates and accompanied by various side dishes, and there's even a small garden for eating outside.

★**Wirikuta Cafe** CAFE
(Coronado 600; ☺8am-10pm; ☎) Mind-blowingly good coffee is dispensed here, one of the few places in northern Mexico where coffee culture is taken seriously. The friendly and passionate baristas also sell excellent pastries and fresh bread, making Wirikuta a great spot for breakfast. There's a second hole-in-the-wall location on Florida (cnr Florida & Nogal; ☺8am-10pm).

❶ Information

Durango State Tourist Office (☑618-811-11-07; www.durango.gob.mx; Florida 1106; ☺9am-7:30pm Mon-Fri, 10am-5:30pm Sat & Sun) Friendly and enthusiastic English-speaking staff and lots of brochures.

Hospital General (☑618-813-00-11; cnr Av 5 de Febrero & Fuentes; ☺24hr) For emergencies or walk-in medical care.

Post Office (Av 20 de Noviembre 1016 Oriente; ☺8am-4pm Mon-Fri, 9am-1pm Sat) Durango's main post office.

❶ Getting There & Away

Aeropuerto Guadalupe Victoria (☑618-817-88-98; www.oma.aero; Autopista Gómez Palacios Km 15.5), 15km northeast of town on Hwy 40D, is a relatively quiet regional airport. It has flights to Houston, Los Angeles, Mexico City and Tijuana. A taxi here from central Durango is about M$180.

The **Central de Autobuses** (☑618-818-36-63; Blvd Villa 101), 4km east of the center, has frequent bus departures, including several 1st-class options.

FIRST-CLASS BUSES FROM DURANGO

DESTINATION	FARE (M$)	DURATION (HR)	FREQUENCY (DAILY)
Chihuahua	795	8½-11	12
Hidalgo del Parral	435	6	10
Los Mochis	925	6	3
Mazatlán	620	3	11
Mexico City (Terminal Norte)	1215	11-13	14
Monterrey (via Saltillo)	635-875	7	8
Zacatecas	355	4-5	hourly

MOVIE LOCATIONS

From the 1950s to the 1990s, both Hollywood and the Mexican film industry made hundreds of movies in Durango's unspoiled deserts and mountains. John Wayne, Clark Gable and Steve McQueen spent many hours filming here. *Bandidas* (2006), starring Salma Hayek and Penélope Cruz, was made in the state.

Villa del Oeste (☑ 618-112-28-82; Hwy 45; adult/child M$30/20; ⊙ 11am-7pm) Many of the big-screen cowboys have swaggered through this film set. Today, the set is a souvenir-drenched theme park with gunslingers shooting it out at weekends (2:30pm and 4:30pm on Saturday, 1:30pm, 3:30pm and 5:30pm Sunday), while the rest of the week it's empty. Either way, it's kind of fun.

On weekends, a bus (adult/child M$40/30 including admission) leaves from Durango's Plaza de Armas a half-hour before each show. To get there on weekdays, take any northbound bus (M$10, about every 30 minutes) and remind the driver to drop you there. To get back you'll have to flag down a bus, so expect to stand in the sun for a while.

Chupaderos (www.setchupaderos.com.mx; adult/child M$30/15; ⊙ 10am-6pm) The unfazed residents of Chupaderos have moved right into this former film set. Big-screen-ready cowboys still ride past the village saloon here, but they aren't actors. Big guns battle it out on Saturdays and Sundays (2:30pm and 4:30pm).

❶ Getting Around

'ISSSTE' or 'Centro' buses (M$7) from the Central de Autobuses parking lot get you to the Plaza de Armas. Metered taxis cost about M$40 to the center.

To reach the Central de Autobuses from downtown, catch 'Camionera' buses along Avenida 20 de Noviembre anywhere near the plaza. Get off before the major intersection with the Pancho Villa equestrian monument and a McDonald's, and walk a short way northeast.

Around Durango

La Ferrería   PYRAMID
(⊙ 9am-5pm) **FREE** These are the most northerly ancient pyramids in the Americas, though in truth the site requires a large amount of both enthusiasm and imagination, as very little survives. There's a well-kept **museum** explaining the culture of the Chalchihuites people who built the pyramids. Taxis cost about M$300 for a return trip from Durango, including waiting time.

Puente Baluarte   BRIDGE
(Autopista Durango-Mazatlán) Soaring an incredible 402m above the Río Baluarte, this incredible feat of engineering is the highest bridge in the Americas. It's one of many incredible bridges on the newly opened Durango–Mazatlán Hwy, a magnificent toll road that boasts some of Mexico's most incredible scenery, with epic tunnels through mountains, hairpin bends and jaw-dropping views all the way. If you only drive one road in Mexico, this certainly wouldn't be a bad choice.

NORTHEAST MEXICO

The northeast gets almost totally shunned by tourists these days, which is a mistake. Close to the US, the foreign visitors are mostly North Americans heading south but the appealing towns and cities here make convenient journey-breakers, and when you do stop, you'll be very glad you did. Colonial centers such as Saltillo, modern, culturally vibrant megalopolises like Monterrey, and the idyllic wine mecca of Parras are highlights. The northeast also does nature like nowhere else. There's the chance to explore unique desert ecosystems at Cuatro Ciénegas, and to hike or watch wildlife in desert scrub or cloud forest at the Reserva de la Biosfera El Cielo, one of Mexico's most biologically diverse corners.

The region is not without dangers, and has seen some of Mexico's biggest increases in drug violence over recent years. In the main border towns (particularly Nuevo 'narco' Laredo, but also Matamoros, Reynosa and Piedras Negras), as well as Monterrey and Torreón, the security situation is tense. Outside Torreón, Coahuila state is far safer and Parras and Cuatro Ciénegas are *tranquilo* (safe and relaxed).

It's important to stress that tourists are rarely affected by narco-related violence, and the vast majority of visitors experience no trouble and enjoy their time in the northeast.

Saltillo

📞 844 / POP 760,000 / ELEV 1600M

Set high in the arid Sierra Madre Oriental, Saltillo is a large and fast-growing place with the normal endless sprawl of any big Mexican city, but the center maintains a relaxed small-town feel. Founded in 1577, it's the northeast's oldest town, boasting fine colonial buildings and cracking cultural surprises (some leading art galleries and museums). Most attractions are conveniently central, and a burgeoning student population adds energy. It's also on the main routes between the northeast border and central Mexico, making it a decent spot to break a journey.

◉ Sights

Saltillo's cultural core around the handsome, expansive Plaza de Armas is replete with historic buildings and ideal for exploring on foot. **Alameda Zaragoza**, Saltillo's green lung, is six blocks northwest of the plaza.

★ Museo del Desierto
MUSEUM

(📞 844-986-90-00; www.museodeldesierto.org; Pérez Treviño 3745; adult/child & student M$90/50; ⊙ 10am-5pm Tue-Sun; 🚼) Saltillo's top attraction, this no-expense-spared museum is highly enjoyable and informative (even if you don't speak Spanish). Exhibits reveal why sea currents can create deserts and how sand dunes are formed. Children will love the dinosaurs, particularly the Tyrannosaurus rex. There's also a reptile house, prairie dogs and a botanical garden with more than 400 cactus species.

Museo de Sarape
MUSEUM

(📞 844-481-69-00; www.museodelsarape.com.mx; Allende 160 Sur; ⊙ 9am-1pm & 3-7pm Mon-Sat) **FREE** An excellent museum devoted to the Mexican *sarapes* (blankets with an opening for the head) that Coahuila is renowned for. There's a priceless collection to admire, and lots of fascinating background information about weaving techniques, looms, natural dyes and regional variations. You'll find very detailed English in-

formation in each room and there's a store next door for purchases.

Catedral de Saltillo
CHURCH

(Plaza de Armas; ⊙ 9am-1pm & 4-7:30pm) Built between 1745 and 1800, Saltillo's cathedral has one of Mexico's finest Churrigueresque facades, with columns of elaborately carved pale-gray stone. In an unusual touch, given the Catholic church's traditionally poor view of indigenous religions, the central dome features carvings of Quetzalcóatl, the Aztec rain god.

Museo de las Aves de México
MUSEUM

(Museum of Mexican Birds; 📞 info 844-414-01-67; www.museodelasaves.org; cnr Hidalgo & Bolívar; adult/child & student M$10/5; ⊙ 10am-6pm Tue-Sat, 11am-7pm Sun) Mexico ranks 10th in the world in terms of avian diversity, and this museum displays more than 800 stuffed and mounted species, some in convincing dioramas of their natural habitat. There are special sections on feathers, beaks, migration and similar subjects. Information is only in Spanish.

🛏 Sleeping

★ Hotel Rancho el Morillo
HISTORIC HOTEL $$

(📞 844-414-40-78; www.ranchoelmorillo.com; Colonia Landín; s/d/tr/q US$60/65/70/75; 🅿 😊 🛜 ❄) Founded in 1934, this highly atmospheric hacienda on the edge of Saltillo is set in very extensive grounds with trails that take in a pine forest, orchard and semi-desert. The family owners are very welcoming and good meals are prepared – after which the homemade *licor de membrillo* (quince liquor) is the perfect digestif.

Hotel San Jorge
HOTEL $$

(📞 844-412-22-22; Acuña 240; s/d M$720/840; 🅿 😊 ✳ 🛜 ❄) This slightly bland business-style hotel has neutral, but generously proportioned rooms. It has a (tiny) rooftop pool and a 6th-floor restaurant with panoramic vistas that's great for hearty breakfasts.

🍴 Eating & Drinking

Superb *fondas* (family-run eateries) occupy the 2nd floor of Mercado Juárez, by Plaza Acuña.

★ Flor y Canela
CAFE $$

(📞 844-414-31-43; Juárez 257; meals M$70-120; ⊙ 8:30am-10pm Mon-Fri, 9am-10pm Sat & Sun; 😊 🛜 ❄) A welcoming cafe with a bohemian ambience that's perfect for breakfast (M$60 to M$80), a good-value set lunch, paninis or a salad. There's an espresso machine (and organic Chiapas coffee for sale), and lots of *postre* (dessert) action on the menu. Wine and daiquiris are available.

El Tapanco   INTERNATIONAL, MEXICAN **$$$**
(Allende 225; mains M$180-350; ⊙noon-11pm Tue-Sun; ⊛) The most elegant restaurant in town, this classy family-run place has an atmospheric interior and courtyard seating. The menu includes seafood and fish dishes, as well as a long list of meat grills. Try the *cabrería azteca* (beef with black mushrooms), the duck tacos or the house specialty, *perejil frito* (fried parsley).

🛍 Shopping

El Sarape de Saltillo   CLOTHING
(📞844-414-96-34; Hidalgo 305; ⊙9:30am-6pm Mon-Sat) This shop sells fine quality, colorful *sarapes* and other Mexican *artesanías*; see wool being dyed and woven on looms inside.

ℹ Information

Hospital Universitario de Saltillo (📞844-411-30-00; www.hus.uadec.mx; Madero 1291; ⊙24hr)

Post Office (Victoria 203; ⊙9am-5pm Mon-Fri, 9am-1pm Sat)

ℹ Getting There & Away

AIR
Saltillo's **Plan de Guadalupe Airport** (📞844-488-17-70; Carretera Saltillo-Monterrey Km 13.5) is 15km northeast of town and has regular flights to Mexico City. There are buses between Saltillo's bus terminal and Monterrey's airport, which has many more flights.

BUS
The **bus station** (Periférico Echeverría) is on the south side of town, 2.5km from the center (a 10-minute bus ride).

Direct departures to many destinations leave at least hourly, with the exceptions of Durango (it's often quicker to change in Torreón) and Cuatro Ciénegas.

Autobuses Americanos (📞844-417-04-96; www.autobusesamericanos.com.mx) has services to Dallas (US$65, 14 hours) and Houston (US$58, 13 hours).

ℹ Getting Around

Saltillo's airport lies 15km northeast on Hwy 40 and is best reached by taxi (M$140) along Xicoténcatl. To reach the city center from the bus station, take minibus 9 (M$7) from in front of the station. To reach the bus station from the center, catch the returning bus 9 on Aldama, between Zaragoza and Hidalgo. Taxis around town cost M$50.

Parras

📞842 / POP 35,000 / ELEV 1520M

A graceful and historic oasis town in the heart of the Coahuilan desert some 160km west of Saltillo, Parras has a beautifully cared-for center of real colonial character and a delightfully temperate climate, both of which have contributed to its reputation for being one of northern Mexico's next big things.

However, Parras is most famous for its wine: the *parras* (grapevines) that give the town its name have grown here since the late 16th century, and its most famous

BUSES FROM SALTILLO

DESTINATION	FARE (M$)	DURATION (HR)	FREQUENCY (DAILY)
Cuatro Ciénegas	265	5	1
Durango	434	6½	5
Mexico City (Terminal Norte)	860-978	10	12
Monterrey	86-96	1¾	every 45min
Nuevo Laredo	355	4-5	every 45min
Parras	130	2½	8
San Luis Potosí	448-496	5	hourly
Torreón	295-340	3	hourly
Zacatecas	334	4½-5½	hourly

vineyard, Casa Madero, is the oldest winery in the Americas.

With great places to stay, several enticing natural bathing pools and all that vino, this is a place where you can easily linger for days.

⊙ Sights & Activities

The biggest attractions in Parras are the town's wineries, located on the outskirts.

Iglesia del Santo Madero   CHURCH
(⊙10am-6pm Thu-Tue) This deeply striking and rather iconic church perched precariously on the rocky outcrop on the south edge of town has, once you've undergone the steep-but-rewarding climb up, some wonderful, expansive views over the town and its vineyards. It's a 30-minute walk from the center, east along Madero then up Aguirre Benavides.

★Estanque La Luz   SWIMMING
(Aguirre Benavides; adult/child M$15/10; ⊙7am-7pm) Estanque La Luz is the cleanest and most attractive of the three *estanques* (natural spring-water-fed pools) around town. It's an ideal place to cool off on a hot day, with a kid's pool and a vast 3m-deep main pool that comes complete with lots of small fish in it. To get here from the Plaza de Armas, take Madero west four blocks and then turn left and walk uphill along Aguirre Benavides.

🛏 Sleeping & Eating

Parras is packed with *dulcerías* (candy stores) selling the region's famous *queso de higo* (fudgy candy with figs), but sadly its eating options beyond that still have a long way to go to catch up with its excellent array of hotels.

Hotel Posada Santa Isabel   HOTEL $
(☑842-422-04-00; www.posadasantaisabel.com. mx; Madero 514; r M$500-700; P⊖❄🐾🏊) Just off the main square, this wonderful former convent has been converted into an inviting hotel that offers excellent value for money. The rooms are clean and comfortable, though they become more cramped the further back through the garden you go. The main attraction here is the lovely garden and fruit-tree-filled courtyard. Give the restaurant a miss, however. Midweek means discounts.

Hostal El Farol   HOTEL $$
(☑842-422-11-13; www.hostalelfarol.com; Arizpe 301; d/q/ste M$940/1135/1700; P⊖🐾🏊) This colonial hotel has a lovely central courtyard and oozes charm. The 25 spacious rooms have some period character, including terracotta floor tiles and wooden furniture, though they're rather on the dark side and don't quite live up to the promises made by the lobby. Rates drop from Sunday to Thursday.

★Méson Verde Obscuro   BOUTIQUE HOTEL $$$
(☑842-422-38-88; m-verdeobscuro@outlook.es; Orilla del Agua 16; s/d incl breakfast M$1000/1300; P⊖❄🐾) This recently opened hotel inside a rustic colonial mansion is a pleasantly relaxed and unfussy choice, with its atmospheric bar area, charming garden and terrace. The 12 rooms, all of which are individually decorated with antiques and folk art, enjoy enormous bathrooms and lots of atmosphere. There's one six-bed room at the back perfectly suited for families (M$1500).

Casona del Banco   BOUTIQUE HOTEL $$$
(☑842-422-19-54; lacasonadelbanco@gmail.com; Arizpe 285; r incl breakfast M$2800; P⊖❄🐾) For a proper splurge, opt for colonial luxury on a grand and impressive scale at this wonderful – if definitely overpriced – conversion of a bank. The 12 rooms surround a grassy courtyard, and the public areas, including the enormous communal kitchen and lounge, are breathtaking. There's a dark and stylish downstairs bar as well, and a swimming pool is promised.

La Noria   MEXICAN $$
(☑842-422-05-47; Arizpe 301, Hostal El Farol; mains M$100-200; ⊙7:30am-11pm; 🐾) This restaurant has tables both in its smart dining room and outside in a lovely colonial courtyard. It's pleasingly formal, with white tablecloths and smart waiters, and serves up memorable food from a large menu heaving with steaks and seafood.

El Méson de Don Evaristo   MEXICAN $$
(cnr Madero & Cayuso; mains M$65-195; ⊙7am-11pm) In the middle of town, this friendly courtyard restaurant serves up meals on tables surrounding a small fountain. The mood is colonial splendor, but the food is pretty standard Mexican fare, including a good selection of breakfasts (M$35 to M$60) and even espresso when the machine is working.

FINE WINE TIME

Parras claims an important place in the history of Mexican wine. A warm climate, together with the region's natural irrigation (underground streams from the sierra, which surface hereabouts), meant this part of Coahuila became a principal wine-growing area of Nueva España (New Spain).

Parras valley wines are mostly gutsy, full-bodied reds, although Casa Madero produces a great cabernet sauvignon rosé and whites made from chenin blanc, chardonnay and semillon grapes. These, along with local varieties such as San Lorenzo (a white), are available for trying and buying in Parras restaurants and shops, and there's even a **Feria de la Uva** (Grape Fair) every August with its somewhat cacophonous climax at Casa Madero.

Casa Madero (📞 842-422-00-55; www.madero.com.mx; Carretera 102 Paila-Parras Km 18.5; wine tour M$15; ⊙ 9am-5pm) This, the first winery in the Americas, was established at Parras in 1597, a year before the town itself sprang up. It's now an industrial-sized operation exporting wine all over the world, although it's still housed on pleasingly old-fashioned premises. Casa Madero offers half-hour tours through the history of wine-making, discovering equipment old and new.

You can buy quality wine and brandy on-site too. From near the main plaza in Parras, catch one of the regular buses (M$20) that pass the winery; just tell your driver where you want to get off. Or take a taxi (M$100); the winery is 7km north of Parras.

El Vesubio (Madero 36; ⊙ 9am-1pm & 2-7pm Mon-Fri, 9am-7pm Sat & Sun) Founded in 1891, this quaint winery consists of a few dozen wooden wine barrels and a little shop in front of the family home. It's well worth a visit just to look around and soak up the wonderful atmosphere, as much to purchase wine.

ⓘ Information

Parras Tourist Office (📞 842-422-02-59; www.parrascoahuila.com.mx; Arizpe 122; ⊙ 10am-3pm Mon-Fri) Helpful staff at the main tourist office give out free town maps. Some English is spoken. There's a small information kiosk on the Plaza del Reloj as well.

ⓘ Getting There & Away

Only 2nd-class buses serve Parras from the small but modern **bus station** (📞 842-422-08-70; cnr Allende & 16 de Septiembre), but most are perfectly comfortable and air-conditioned. There are eight daily to/from Saltillo (M$130, 2½ hours) and four daily to/from Monterrey (M$200, 3½ hours). If you want to head to Cuatro Ciénegas without backtracking to Saltillo, catch a bus to San Pedro Las Colonias (M$90, 1½ hours, four daily) and then a bus from there to Cuatro Ciénegas (M$145, two hours, nine daily).

Cuatro Ciénegas

📞 869 / POP 13,000 / ELEV 747M

The serene and remote frontier town of Cuatro Ciénegas is bespeckled with adobe and colonial buildings and a handful of hotels and restaurants. It's a pleasantly out-of-the-way spot to enjoy the natural world of northern Mexico, and the perfect base for exploring the Área de Protección de Flora y Fauna Cuatrociénegas.

◉ Sights & Activities

★ **Área de Protección de Flora y Fauna Cuatrociénegas** NATURE RESERVE
(M$30) With hundreds of shimmering cerulean *pozas* (pools) and streams in the middle of the Desierto Chihuahuense (Chihuahuan Desert), this 843-sq-km nature reserve is a surreal sight. Fed by a network of more than 500 underground springs, it's a desert habitat of extraordinary biological diversity. Cuatrociénegas is home to over 75 endemic species, including three kinds of turtles and 11 kinds of fish, as well as primative organisms called *estromatolitos* (stromatolites).

Some pools and the nearby river have been set aside for recreational activities, including swimming.

Even if you don't have your own transportation, exploring the area alone is tricky, as the desert tracks are not always signposted. Using the services of a guide is wise. Though it is theoretically possible to visit the park without a car (buses to Torreón will drop you at the entrances to sites around the park, but usually won't stop to pick people up), it's not advisable: distances are long, tracks are poorly marked and there is little shade.

Poza Azul
Visitors Center   INFORMATION CENTER
(⊙10am-6pm Tue-Sun; P) This center has illustrated displays about the Cuatrociénegas nature reserve's ecology in Spanish and English. The little **Poza Las Tortugas**, a good turtle-spotting pool, is right behind here, while 1.5km further back is the aptly named **Poza Azul** (Blue Pond), one of the reserve's most photographed sites.

Dunas de Yeso   DESERT
(Las Arenales; M$30; ⊙10:30am-6pm) These blinding-white gypsum sand dunes contrast superbly with the six mountain ranges that ring the valley. To visit you'll need your own transportation and to stop by the Poza Azul Visitors Center to pay and get the key that opens the gate at the beginning of the track out.

Casa de Cultura   MUSEUM
(☑869-696-05-56; Hidalgo 401 Poniente; adult/ child & student M$10/5; ⊙9am-1pm & 3-7pm Mon-Fri, 10am-6pm Sat & Sun) Located in the former home of Venustiano Carranza, a revolutionary leader involved in the overthrow of Porfirio Díaz, this museum has a small but interesting display of ancient objects unearthed in the area.

Río Los Mezquites   SWIMMING
(☑869-696-04-08; M$50; ⊙9am-7pm) Swimming with the fish and turtles in this sublime stretch of slow-flowing blue water amid the desert landscape of the Cuatrociénegas nature reserve is a surreal, revitalizing experience. There are *palapas* (thatched shelters) for shade.

👣 Tours

Two- or three-day excursions can be organized with guides for about M$1500 per person. Contact them through the travel agency on the plaza (corner of Juárez and Carranza) or the tourist office. These include trips to **Valle Hundidos**, a magnificent spot to experience the diverse desert ecosystem. Rates include car transportation.

Tours organised by the Hotel Misión Marielena and Hotel Plaza are also recommended, with four different options that include the Turtle and Blue ponds.

🛏 Sleeping & Eating

Hotel Plaza   HOTEL $$
(☑869-696-00-66; www.plazahotel.com.mx; Hidalgo 202 Oriente; s/d incl breakfast M$595/760; P❄✱🤖❄) Right on the main square in the heart of Cuatro Ciénegas, this great-value hotel has spacious, comfortable, attractively furnished rooms that all face a shaded patio and that all-important heat-busting pool. There's an on-site restaurant and tours of the area can be arranged.

Hotel Misión Marielena   HOTEL $$
(☑869-696-11-51; www.hotelmisionmarielena.com. mx; Hidalgo 200 Oriente; s/d from M$543/840; P❄✱🤖❄) This historic hotel has large, well-maintained and well-furnished rooms, all of which are set around two rear courtyards with a pool and mountain views. The hotel's restaurant, La Mision, is also recommended, with good breakfasts, grilled meats and local wines available.

La Esquina del Marisco   SEAFOOD, MEXICAN $$
(Hidalgo 242; meals M$60-150; ⊙9am-7pm) Seafood in the desert? You'll find just that at this inexpensive and informal place in the center of town. The menu includes a delicious *cokteles de camarón* (spicy shrimp cocktails served with salty crackers), along with grilled fish and squid. Look out for the garishly painted green building.

ℹ Information

Tourist Office (☑869-696-09-02; www.sede turcoahuila.gob.mx; Carranza 100; ⊙9:30am-5pm Mon-Fri) The tiny but helpful tourist office is in the Presidencia Municipal building.

ℹ Getting There & Away

The bus terminal occupies the southwest corner of the plaza. First-class buses run to Torreón (M$276, 3½ hours, eight daily), Saltillo (M$265, five hours, one each morning) and the border at Piedras Negras (M$345, six hours, four daily).

Monterrey

☑81 / POP 4.6 MILLION / ELEV 530M

Cosmopolitan Monterrey is Mexico's third-largest city, second-largest industrial center and *número uno* in per-capita income. This economic powerhouse has a strong entrepreneurial ethos, humming cultural scene, vibrant universities and the best nightlife in northern Mexico.

With sprawling suburbs of gargantuan air-conditioned malls and manicured housing estates, this is also one of Mexico's most Americanized cities. Boasting world-class museums and a jagged mountain backdrop that offers terrific outdoor adventure sports, the city's attractions are diverse and myriad.

All of this makes Monterrey fiercely independent and very different to any other Mexican metropolis you'll encounter, and its long-running rivalry with Mexico City is the stuff of legend. The city experienced the drug wars up close and personal as recently as 2012, but by 2016 cultural life was once again back with aplomb in the heart of the city, with boutiques, restaurants and bars thriving in the newly safe Barrio Antiguo.

If you stay in the center, this historic core is very accessible. Most of Monterrey's main cultural attractions are clustered close by and you'll have the Barrio Antiguo on your doorstep. Away from the center, the city is dominated by thundering highways, so a car becomes essential.

History

Dating from 1596, it wasn't until after Mexican independence that the city began to prosper as proximity to the US gave it advantages in trade and smuggling.

In 1900, the first heavy industry in Latin America, a vast iron and steel works (now the site of the Parque Fundidora), rose to dominate the cityscape. Monterrey was soon dubbed the 'Pittsburgh of Mexico,' and still produces about 25% of Mexico's raw steel. The city also churns out around 60% of the nation's cement and half of its beer.

◉ Sights & Activities

Most major sights are concentrated around the extraordinary Gran Plaza in the center. East of here is the atmospheric Barrio Antiguo quarter, with low-slung colonial buildings, cobbled streets and lots of boho cafes, bars and restaurants.

From the Gran Plaza you can jump aboard a metro or catch a boat along a beautiful urban river, the Paseo Santa Lucía, to the city's other main cultural hub: the Parque Fundidora.

★ **Gran Plaza**   PLAZA
(Macroplaza; Ⓜ Zaragoza) A monument to Monterrey's late-20th-century ambition, this city-block-wide series of interconnected squares, also known as the **Macroplaza**,

was created in the 1980s by the demolition of a prime chunk of city-center real estate. A controversial, but ultimately successful piece of redevelopment, its charm has increased over the years as the once-naked urban space – said to form the largest public square in the world – has been softened by parks, trees, fountains and pools.

Vistas of the surrounding mountains open up between the roster of iconic edifices – classically designed municipal buildings and incongruously modern structures housing some of Mexico's finest museums – that line the Gran Plaza. For visitors, it's a delight to explore on foot, as most traffic is directed away from the area by underpasses.

At the southern end of the Gran Plaza, the 70m concrete tower **Faro del Comercio** (Lighthouse of Commerce) soars above the city, its green lasers piercing the night sky. The Faro abuts the baroque form of the **Catedral Metropolitano de Monterrey**, capped by a neon cross. North of here is a shady park, **Plaza Zaragoza** (Gran Plaza), popular with snacking families and smooching lovers, and also the venue for open-air concerts and old-school Latin dancing every Sunday.

Continuing north, the rest of the Gran Plaza is lined with a succession of concrete municipal structures. If you're a fan of brutalism, you'll love the **Teatro de la Ciudad** and its architectural cousin, the lofty **Congreso del Estado**. Then down some steps is the **Explanada de los Héroes** (Esplanade of the Heroes; Gran Plaza) lined with statues, and finally the 1908 neoclassical **Palacio de Gobierno**.

Museo de Arte Contemporáneo   MUSEUM
(Marco; ☑81-8262-4500; www.marco.org.mx; cnr Zuazua & Jardón; adult/child & student M$80/60, Wed free; ⊙10am-6pm Tue & Thu-Sun, 10am-8pm Wed; Ⓜ Zaragoza) Don't miss the terrific Museo de Arte Contemporáneo, its entrance marked by Juan Soriano's gigantic black dove sculpture. Inside, its idiosyncratic spaces are filled with water and light and major exhibitions (all temporary, there's no permanent collection) of work by contemporary Mexican and Latin American artists. Call in advance to get a tour in English. Marco also has a fine bookstore and a gourmet restaurant.

Plaza 400 Años   PLAZA
(boat ride adult/child round-trip M$50/30; Ⓜ Zaragoza) This plaza, graced with fountains

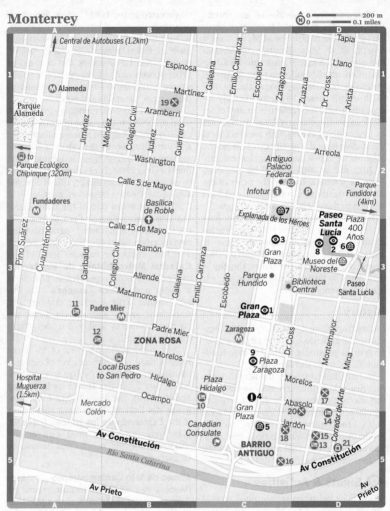

and pools, forms an impressive approach to the sleek, modernist Museo de Historia Mexicana and the Museo del Noreste. It is the terminus of the lovely Paseo Santa Lucía promenade.

Museo de Historia Mexicana MUSEUM
(☎81-8345-9898; www.museohistoriamexicana.org.mx; Plaza 400 Años; adult/child M$40/20, Tue & Sun free; ☺10am-8pm Tue & Sun, 10am-6pm Wed-Sat) This sleek modernist museum presents an extensive but easily manageable chronology of Mexican history. There's also an Earth section, full of mounted animals

and realistic-looking plants at its heart. All explanations are in Spanish only, but English tours can be arranged by phoning in advance.

Museo del Noreste MUSEUM
(www.3museos.com; Plaza 400 Años; adult/child M$40/20, Tue & Sun free; ☺10am-8pm Tue & Sun, 10am-6pm Wed-Sat) Technically this is a separate institution to the Museo de Historia Mexicana, but, practically speaking, its galleries on the culture and history of Nuevo León, Tamaulipas, Coahuila and Texas, packed with video screens and artifacts,

Monterrey

◎ **Top Sights**
- 1 Gran Plaza...C3
- 2 Paseo Santa Lucía D3

◎ **Sights**
- 3 Explanada de los Héroes C3
- 4 Faro del Comercio C4
- 5 Museo de Arte Contemporáneo........C5
- 6 Museo de Historia Mexicana..............D3
- 7 Palacio de Gobierno C2
- 8 Plaza 400 Años.....................................D3
- 9 Plaza Zaragoza.....................................C4

🛌 **Sleeping**
- 10 Gran Hotel Ancira C4
- 11 Hotel Misión.......................................A3
- 12 iStay..A4
- 13 La Casa del Barrio.............................D5
- 14 Yeccan D5

🍴 **Eating**
- 15 El Infinito D5
- 16 El Rey del Cabrito.............................C5
- 17 La Galería Café D4
- 18 Madre Oaxaca....................................C5
- 19 Mercado Juárez B1
- 20 Trece Lunas D5

🛍 **Shopping**
- 21 Corredor del Arte..............................D5

function as a new wing of the history museum with one ticket working for both. Begin on the bottom floor to follow the displays chronologically.

★ **Paseo Santa Lucía**   RIVER, GARDENS
(☉24hr) The stunning promenade of Paseo Santa Lucía, which stretches 2.4km, is a world-class example of urban regeneration. This (artificial) river forms a turquoise ribbon through the heart of industrial Monterrey, offering a natural corridor between the Gran Plaza and Parque Fundidora. Take a stroll down this delightful pathway, lined with tropical greenery, or hop in one of the regular boats (M$60 return). The landscaping is amazing, with lighting illuminating the water at night and striking modernist bridges spanning the river.

There's 24-hour security, a few bars and restaurants at its western end and the whole promenade has free public wi-fi. Every city should have one.

★ **Parque Fundidora**   PARK
(☎81-8126-8500; www.parquefundidora.org; ☉6am-10pm; ℙ 🚻; Ⓜ Parque Fundidora) **FREE**
Formerly a vast steel-factory complex, this once-blighted industrial zone has been transformed into a huge urban park. Designers cleverly retained the iconic smoke stacks and industrial relics to give a surreal and at times apocalyptic feel, but also a vibe very much in keeping with Monterrey's heritage. You can rent bikes, jog the trails, take in a film or browse the photography on display here. Bring the kids. And above all, visit the Horno3 museum, the undoubted star of the show.

Three other disemboweled redbrick factories comprise the **Centro de las Artes** (☎81-8479-0015; www.conarte.org.mx; film screenings M$45; ☉10am-9:30pm Tue-Sun) **FREE**, an arts center with high-class rotating exhibitions that also screens independent and foreign films.

The metro stops within a 10-minute walk of the park, but the most enjoyable way to get here is to walk along Paseo Santa Lucía from Plaza 400 Años.

★ **Horno3**   MUSEUM
(Museum of Steel; ☎81-8126-1100; www.horno3.org; adult/child & student M$90/55, nocturnal climbs M$40; ☉10am-6pm Tue-Thu, 11am-7pm Fri-Sun, nocturnal climbs 6-10pm Tue-Thu & Sun, 7-10pm Fri & Sat) Blast Furnace No 3 in the former industrial site of the Parque Fundidora has been converted into Horno3, an exceptionally impressive high-tech, hands-on museum devoted to Mexico's steel industry. No expense has been spared here, from the steaming rocks at the entrance to the metal staircase that climbs to the summit. The entire process of steel-making is explained (with some English translations) and its vital relevance to Monterrey and Mexico.

Don't miss the dramatic furnace show, beamed from the bulk of Horno3 itself, and ask about nocturnal climbs of the metal tower. Last tickets are sold one hour before closing. There's a good cafe-restaurant, El Lingote (p799), here too.

🎉 Festivals & Events

Festival Internacional de Cine en Monterrey   FILM
(www.monterreyfilmfestival.com/es) This impressive festival held in late August showcases Mexican and international art-house films.

Aniversario de Independencia   CULTURAL
Monterrey's biggest celebrations are held on Mexico's Independence Day, September 16, with fireworks, *musica norteña* (country ballads) and a parade.

🛏 Sleeping

Monterrey has few stand-out accommodations in the center of the city.

★ Yeccan
HOSTEL $

(☎81-8340-6165, 81-8344-5265; www.yeccan.hostel.com; Abasolo 916A; dm/r M$230/460; ❄🛜; Ⓜ Zaragoza) This outstanding hostel in the heart of the Barrio Antiguo is owned by an artistic crew who have created a very contemporary look with whitewashed walls and stylish modern furniture. Accommodations are in clean and inviting dorms (with lockers and fans) and neat private rooms. There's also a lovely common area with TV and sofas, a pool room, a guests' kitchen and a patio.

La Casa del Barrio
HOSTEL $

(☎81-8344-1800; www.lacasadelbarrio.com; Montemayor 1227 Sur; dm M$200, s/d M$350/500; ❄@🛜; Ⓜ Zaragoza) A popular and good-value hostel in the middle of the Barrio Antiguo, this place doubles as a Spanish school and also has its own restaurant, Waffles & More, for deliciously calorific breakfasts. The two private rooms are a little cramped and can be hot, as there's no air-conditioning, making the dorms a better option.

Hotel Misión
HOTEL $$

(☎81-8150-6500; www.hotelesmision.com; Padre Mier 201 Poniente; r/ste from M$828/1278; Ⓟ❄❉🛜; Ⓜ Padre Mier) This large hotel on Monterrey's main shopping street won't win any architecture awards, but its rooms offer good value: all are spacious and have desks and commodious bathrooms (although the air-conditioning is ancient). The restaurant downstairs serves surprisingly good buffet breakfasts.

iStay
HOTEL $$

(☎81-8228-5100; www.istaymty.istay.com.mx; Morelos 191 Poniente; r from M$675; Ⓟ❄❉🛜❄; Ⓜ Padre Mier) A huge concrete hotel that enjoys a great location, facing pedestrianized Morelos and close to Monterrey's Gran Plaza. The branding screams 'hip hotel' but iStay's carpeted rooms are actually very standard fare, though comfortable enough and fair value. Rates vary enormously: try booking online to access the best offers.

Gran Hotel Ancira
HOTEL $$$

(☎81-8150-7000; www.gammahoteles.com; Ocampo 443 Oriente; r/ste incl breakfast from M$944/1932; Ⓟ❄❉@🛜❄; Ⓜ Zaragoza)

Monterrey's smartest and most atmospheric hotel is this grand dame, which dates from 1912 and was built in a French art nouveau style. The mirror-ceilinged, gingham-tiled reception and restaurant area is quite something, and how many hotels have a live classical pianist at breakfast? Rooms are spacious and comfortable, but nothing extraordinary. The best rates can be found on the website.

🍴 Eating & Drinking

Monterrey's signature dish is *cabrito al pastor* (roast kid goat). Barrio Antiguo has a good selection of places to eat (and drink), though it's still recovering from the recent years of violence, and the restaurant scene hasn't quite caught up with the renewed safety or the renewed appetite locals have to dine out.

Mercado Juárez (Av Juárez; ⊙8am-7pm Mon-Sat, to 3pm Sun; Ⓜ Alameda) has *fondas* selling tasty, cheap grub.

★ La Galería Café
ITALIAN $$

(Morelos 902; mains M$80-120; ⊙5pm-1am; ❄🛜; Ⓜ Zaragoza) Popular with a young and affluent crowd, this hip and contemporary restaurant-bar is a very popular pre-clubbing dinner and cocktail spot. It serves superb pasta (choose from 11 classic sauces), crepes and rightly popular *pizzettas* (mini pizzas) with electronic mixes in the background. On weekend nights the groovy upstairs terrace comes into its own for nightscape gazing and cocktail sipping.

Trece Lunas
INTERNATIONAL $$

(Abasolo 870; mains M$70-200; ⊙8am-10pm; 🍴) If you like your decor eclectic, your spaces multicultural and your food slow, this unusual and innovative Barrio Antiguo place may just be for you. There's a huge menu that is focused on sharing plates called *botanas*, which are piled high with food. Throw into the mix vegetarian options, crepes, salads, sandwiches and good coffee, and you have a winner.

El Infinito
CAFE $$

(☎81-8989-5252; Jardón 904; mains M$70-150; ⊙6pm-12.30am; ❄🛜🍴; Ⓜ Zaragoza) Highly enjoyable culture cafe set inside colonial premises with books to browse and occasional art-house movies and live music. Offers filling soups, sandwiches, cheese plates, fruit frappés, mango martinis and properly made espresso.

El Rey del Cabrito
MEXICAN $$

(☑ 81-8345-3352, 81-8345-3292; www.elreydel cabrito.com.mx; cnr Dr Coss & Av Constitución; mains M$100-250; ⊗ 11am-midnight; ☺; Ⓜ Zaragoza) This local institution is synonymous with Monterrey and serves up its most famous dish: goat. It's a masterwork of kitsch with an extraordinary neon interior complete with deer and lions hung on the wall. The signature *cabritos* are slow-roasting over charcoal in the window as you arrive, and dishes come still sizzling on a bed of onions, with salad and tortillas.

★ Madre Oaxaca
MEXICAN $$$

(Jardón 814; mains M$140-260; ⊗ 1-11pm Mon-Sat; ☺ �〉; Ⓜ Zaragoza) One of Monterrey's best restaurants, this real charmer is set in a historic building and decked out with an extraordinary collection of handicrafts and folk art over its several intimate dining rooms. The menu is loaded with authentic Oaxacan dishes using rich *moles* – try a mixed *tlayuda oaxaqueña* (huge flat bread with toppings), and do not miss the sublime desserts.

El Lingote
MEXICAN, INTERNATIONAL $$$

(www.ellingoterestaurante.com; Horno3, Parque Fundidora; mains M$170-300; ⊗ 1pm-midnight Tue-Sun; ☺ 🔊) This expensive but amazing-looking restaurant inside the Horno3 museum is well worth a splurge while you explore the wonderful Parque Fundidora. The cooking puts a modern twist on Mexican classics with fare such as goatling tacos, *achiote*-marinated sea bass and tuna sashimi. The evocative and beautifully crafted setting is superb.

🛍 Shopping

Try the main downtown market, Mercado Juárez (p798), for everyday items, though keep your wits about you.

★ Corredor del Arte
ARTS & CRAFTS, MARKET

(Art Corridor; Mina; ⊗ 10am-6pm Sun; Ⓜ Zaragoza) On Sundays, Calle Mina in the Barrio Antiguo becomes the Corredor del Arte, a wonderful combination of antiques, arts and crafts, and flea market. The whole area comes out to play and you can find one-off items amid the piles of junk. Bands play too.

ℹ Information

DANGERS & ANNOYANCES

The Zona Rosa area on the west side of Gran Plaza and Barrio Antiguo on the east, are both largely considered safe by day and night, but it's always advisable to avoid walking alone after dark and to stick to the main roads. Across the Río Santa Catarina, the crime-plagued barrio of Colonia Independencia is still affected by narco gangs and should not be entered day or night.

MEDICAL SERVICES

Hospital Muguerza (☑ 81-8399-3400; www.christusmuguerza.com.mx; Hidalgo 2525 Poniente; ⊗ 24hr; Ⓜ Hospital) Monterrey's main hospital.

POST

Post Office (Washington 648 Oriente; ⊗ 8am-4:30 Mon-Fri, 8am-12:30pm Sat; Ⓜ Zaragoza)

TOURIST INFORMATION

Infotur (☑ 81-2020-6789; Antiguo Palacio Federal, Washington 648; ⊗ 9am-6pm Mon-Fri, to 5pm Sat & Sun) Friendly, English-speaking staff at this info center have plentiful information about sights and events across Nuevo León. There's a kiosk at the bus station too.

ℹ Getting There & Away

AIR

Monterrey's busy **airport** (☑ 81-8288-7700; www.oma.aero; Carretera Miguel Alemán Km 24, Apodaca) has direct flights to all of Mexico's major cities, plus direct international flights to Atlanta, Dallas, Havana, Houston, Los Angeles, Las Vegas, Miami and New York. The airport is located 27km from the city center, in the suburb of Apodaca.

BUS

Monterrey's colossal bus station, **Central de Autobuses** (Av Colón; Ⓜ Cuauhtémoc), is busy 24/7 with departures and arrivals from across Mexico. Use the official taxi desk inside the station; the fare is M$50 to most central locations.

ℹ Getting Around

TO/FROM THE AIRPORT

Noreste (www.noreste.com.mx) runs hourly buses (M$75, 45 minutes) from the airport to the main bus terminal. A taxi to/from the center is around M$275.

BUS

Frequent buses (M$8 to M$10) get you most places you can't reach by metro.

METRO

Monterrey's modern, efficient metro system **Metrorrey** (single trip M$4.50; ⊗ 5am-midnight) currently consists of two lines. Elevated Línea 1 runs from the northwest of the city to the eastern suburbs, passing the Parque Fundidora. Línea 2 begins underground at the

BUSES FROM MONTERREY

Prices are for first-class buses.

DESTINATION	FARE (M$)	DURATION (HR)	FREQUENCY (DAILY)
Chihuahua	865	9-11	12
Dallas, US	925-1033	12	3
Durango	635	8-9	14
Houston, US	962	11	4
Mazatlán	973	16	1
Mexico City (Terminal Norte)	930-1015	11	half-hourly
Nuevo Laredo	300	3	every 20min
Piedras Negras	620	5-7	9
Reynosa	300	3	half-hourly
Saltillo	86-96	1¾	every 45min
San Luis Potosí	545-590	6½	every 45min
Zacatecas	480	7	every 45min

Gran Plaza and runs north past Parque Niños Héroes up into the northern suburbs. The two lines cross right by the bus station at Cuauhtémoc station.

Several metro stations are connected with metrobuses (specialized buses with set stops) to outlying areas. Construction has also started on Línea 3, which will connect Zaragoza station by the Gran Plaza to the northeastern suburbs. Work is expected to be completed in 2016.

TAXI

Taxis (all have meters) are ubiquitous in Monterrey and reasonably priced. From the Zona Rosa to the bus terminal or Parque Fundidora is usually about M$35. Call ☑ 81-8372-8800 or ☑ 81-8130-0600 for radio-taxi service.

Around Monterrey

Part of Monterrey's charm has always been the awe-inspiring natural scenery nearby, although be sure to check the local security situation before embarking on a trip outside the city.

Right outside town is a stunning mountainside section of the Parque Nacional Cumbres de Monterrey, **Parque Ecológico Chipinque** (☑ 81-8303-5575; www.chipinque.org.mx; pedestrian/cyclist/vehicle M$20/35/35; ☺ 6am-8pm). It's incredible that such a wild locale can exist so close to such a large city. There's great hiking and mountain biking on trails through dense forest, and up to rocky peaks including high point **Copete de Águilas** (2200m). Maps, snacks, trail advice and permits for those heading into the park are available at the **visitor center** (☑ 81-8303-2190; www.chipinque.org.mx; San Pedro; ☺ 9am-6pm Mon-Fri) located near the entrance, a 15-minute drive southwest of central Monterrey via Avenida Gómez Morín in the San Pedro neighborhood.

Free Saturday, Sunday and holiday buses to Chipinque leave from the southwest corner of Parque Alameda at 8am, 10am and noon; be sure to ask when the last bus returns. Alternatively use bus 130 from the San Pedro Garza García area (from the junction of Vasconcelos and Gómez).

Understand Mexico

MEXICO TODAY 802

President Peña Nieto is trying to rouse a slumbering economy – but the people are angrier than ever with government.

HISTORY 804

A truly epic story – the Maya, the Aztecs and the Spanish conquistadors, plus rebellions, revolution and democracy.

THE MEXICAN WAY OF LIFE.................. 817

A window on what makes Mexicans tick, from the Virgin of Guadalupe to *lucha libre* (Mexican wrestling.)

THE ARTS 821

From Frida Kahlo and New Mexican Cinema to its countless artisans, musicians and street artists, Mexico bubbles with creativity.

THE MEXICAN KITCHEN......................830

An inside track on Mexico's delectable flavors: know your *sopes* from your *sopas,* and the best way to drink tequila. Written by expert author Mauricio Velázquez de León.

LANDSCAPES & WILDLIFE....................836

Jungles and oceans, volcanoes and deserts; whale sharks, howler monkeys and scarlet macaws – Mexico is one of the world's most dramatic and biologically diverse countries.

Mexico Today

The Partido Revolucionario Institucional (PRI), Mexico's longtime ruling party of the 20th century, got a new shot at governing when its candidate Enrique Peña Nieto was elected president in 2012, on hopes he could spark a long-awaited economic takeoff and tackle some of the country's dire social and security problems. But by the midpoint of his term in 2015, Mexico was in the grips of an unprecedented wave of public rage at its entire governmental class, to which no obvious remedy was apparent.

Best on Film

Amores Perros (Love's a Bitch; 2000) Gritty groundbreaker that set director Alejandro González Iñárritu and actor Gael García Bernal on the path to stardom.

Y Tu Mamá También (And Your Mother Too; 2001) Classic 'growing up' road movie about two privileged Mexico City teenagers (Gael García Bernal and Diego Luna).

Heli (2013) Amat Escalante won Cannes' best-director garland for this tale of a young couple caught up in the drug war.

600 Miles (2015) Tim Roth plays a kidnapped US law-enforcement agent in Gabriel Ripstein's arms-smuggling thriller.

Best in Print

God's Middle Finger Richard Grant investigates the narco-riddled Sierra Madre Occidental (called *Bandit Roads* in the UK.)

Pedro Páramo The ultimate Mexican novel, by Juan Rulfo.

El Narco Ioan Grillo spent more than a decade covering the drug war in some of the most dangerous territories.

Sliced Iguana Travel writer Isabella Tree's warm, perceptive account of Mexico and its indigenous cultures.

The 43

On September 26, 2014, three trainee teachers from Ayotzinapa in Guerrero state were killed by municipal police in the city of Iguala, and another 43 disappeared. The event sparked months of protests around the country in an outpouring of Mexicans' anger and grief about the insecurity of their country and the perceived corruption, criminality and impunity of so many in authority. Many believed high levels of government and/or the security forces were somehow behind the students' disappearance. A repeated slogan among the protesters was *'Fue el estado'* (It was the state).

Iguala's mayor and his wife were among over 70 people arrested in the weeks following the disappearance. Six weeks after the disappearance, Mexico's attorney general announced that investigators had determined the 43 had been kidnapped by police on the mayor's orders and then handed over to drug gangsters, who murdered them, burned the bodies at a garbage tip and threw the ashes into a stream.

Why? One theory is that the buses which the students had commandeered to go to Iguala were, unknown to them, being used for drug shipments. Another is that the drug gang to which the students were handed over mistook them for a rival gang. Another is that the mayor and his wife thought they had come to disrupt a rally they were holding.

But many people were unconvinced by the official version of events, and parents of the victims requested a separate investigation by the Inter-American Commission on Human Rights (IACHR). In September 2015 the IACHR team reported that it was 'scientifically impossible' for all the bodies to have been incinerated at the tip, and voiced suggestions there may have been a cover-up of some evidence. The government then reopened its investigation into the case. The affair clearly still had far to run.

Insecurity

The Iguala affair happened against a background of three decades of increasingly violent activity by Mexico's drug gangs, who have corrupted many government officials, politicians and members of the security forces along the way. President Peña Nieto came to power with the stated intention of trying to tackle the root causes of cartel violence at a local level. But according to Mexico's Citizens' Council for Public Security, organized-crime-related killings were still happening at a rate of about 9000 a year in late 2015. The government scored a much-needed triumph when Mexico's most wanted man, Joaquín 'El Chapo' Guzmán, leader of the powerful Sinaloa cartel, was captured in 2014 – and suffered a desperate disaster when he escaped from his high-security jail through a 1.5km-long tunnel the following year. The government regained some credibility when he was recaptured in early 2016.

The drug gangs don't just ship drugs to the USA. They traffic people too, and kidnap people for ransom, and practice extortion. Mexico has one of the world's highest kidnapping rates, estimated by the country's Human Rights Commission at around 10 per day. The common perception that the authorities are often in league with the cartels is what unleashed the wave of disgust after the Iguala incident.

On the Brighter Side

Nevertheless, most Mexicans are not directly affected by organized crime and their disillusionment with the governmental class seems to make many people more determined to create a better Mexico on a small-scale, personal level. Tourists, for their part, have very rarely been among the victims of drug-related violence, and the gangs' activities are mostly away from tourist destinations (Acapulco is an unfortunate exception.) International tourist arrivals in Mexico reached a record 29.3 million in 2014, and the numbers were heading even higher in 2015. Visitors are highly unlikely to see any sign of trouble or even unease, except perhaps the odd graffiti with a political protest message.

Meanwhile economic takeoff might not be *so* far away. Laws passed in 2014 finally allowed more competition into telecoms and broadcasting and ended state-owned Pemex' monopoly on Mexico's oil industry. It's hoped these changes will bring a flood of foreign investment, better services and lower prices for some key products. But takeoff or no takeoff, Mexico is likely to remain one of the world's most economically unequal countries: the richest 10% earn 30 times as much as the poorest 10%.

POPULATION: **122 MILLION**

AREA: **1.9 MILLION SQ KM**

GDP PER CAPITA: **US$11,321**

POPULATION BELOW POVERTY LINE: **52%**

RECOGNIZED NATIONAL LANGUAGES: **69**

if Mexico were 100 people

30 would have predominantly indigenous ancestry
9 would have predominantly European ancestry
61 would have mixed ancestry

belief systems
(% of population)

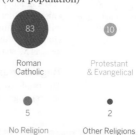

83 Roman Catholic

10 Protestant & Evangelical

5 No Religion

2 Other Religions

population per sq km

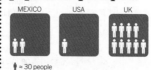

MEXICO   USA   UK

👤 ≈ 30 people

History

Mexico's story is always extraordinary and at times barely credible. How could a 2700-year tradition of sophisticated indigenous civilization crumble in two short years at the hands of a few hundred adventurers from Spain? How could Mexico's 11-year war for independence from Spain lead to three decades of dictatorship by Porfirio Díaz? How could the people's revolution that ended that dictatorship yield 80 years of one-party rule? Mexico's past is present everywhere you go, and is key to any understanding of Mexico today.

The Ancient Civilizations

Ancient Cultures

Mexico: From the Olmecs to the Aztecs (Michael D Coe)

The Aztecs (Richard F Townsend)

The Maya (Michael Coe)

Chronicle of the Maya Kings & Queens (Simon Martin and Nikolai Grube)

The political map of ancient Mexico shifted constantly as cities, towns or states sought domination over one another, and a sequence of powerful states rose and fell through invasion, internal conflict or environmental disaster. These diverse cultures had much in common. Human sacrifice, to appease ferocious gods, was practiced by many of them; they observed the heavens to predict the future and determine propitious times for important events like harvests; society was heavily stratified and dominated by priestly male ruling classes. Versions of a ritual ball game were played almost everywhere and seem to have always involved two teams trying to keep a rubber ball off the ground by flicking it with various parts of the body. The game sometimes served as an oracle, and could also involve the sacrifice of some players.

A common framework divides the pre-Hispanic era into three main periods: pre-Classic (before AD 250); Classic (AD 250–900); and post-Classic (AD 900–1521). The most advanced cultures in Mexico emerged chiefly in the center, south and east of the country. Together with Maya lands in what are now Guatemala, Belize and a small part of Honduras, this zone is collectively known to historians and archaeologists as Mesoamerica.

Beginnings

The pre-Hispanic inhabitants of the Americas arrived from Siberia in several migrations during the last Ice Age, between perhaps 60,000 and

TIMELINE	8000–3000 BC	1200–400 BC	AD 0–150
	Agriculture develops in places such as the Tehuacán valley and Yagul. Chili seeds and squashes are planted, then corn and beans are cultivated, enabling people to live semi-permanently in villages.	Mexico's 'mother culture', the Olmecs, flourishes on the Gulf coast at San Lorenzo and La Venta. Jade, a favorite pre-Hispanic material, appears in a tomb at La Venta.	A huge planned city, including the 70m-high Pyramid of the Sun, is laid out in a grid arrangement at Teotihuacán in central Mexico.

8000 BC, crossing land now submerged beneath the Bering Strait. Early Mexicans hunted big animal herds in the grasslands of the highland valleys. When temperatures rose at the end of the last Ice Age, the valleys became drier, ceasing to support such animal life and forcing the people to derive more food from plants. In central Mexico's Tehuacán Valley and at Yagul near Oaxaca, archaeologists have traced the slow beginnings of agriculture between about 8000 and 3000 BC.

The Olmecs

Mexico's 'mother culture' was the mysterious Olmec civilization, which appeared in the humid lowlands of Veracruz and Tabasco. The evidence of the masterly stone sculptures they left behind indicates that Olmec civilization was well organized and able to support talented artisans, but lived in thrall to fearsome deities. Its best-known artifacts are the awe-inspiring 'Olmec heads,' stone sculptures up to 3m high with grim, pug-nosed faces and wearing curious helmets. Far-flung Olmec sites in central and western Mexico may have been trading posts or garrisons to ensure the supply of jade, obsidian and other luxuries for the Olmec elite.

Olmec art, religion and society had a profound influence on later Mexican civilizations. Olmec gods, such as the feathered serpent, persisted right through the pre-Hispanic era.

Teotihuacán

The first great civilization in central Mexico arose in a valley about 50km northeast of the middle of modern Mexico City. The grid plan of the magnificent city of Teotihuacán was laid out in the 1st century AD. It was the basis for the famous Pyramids of the Sun and Moon as well as avenues, palaces and temples that were added during the next 600 years. The city grew to a population of about 125,000 and became the center of the biggest pre-Hispanic Mexican empire, stretching as far south as modern El Salvador. It may have had some hegemony over the Zapotecs of Oaxaca, whose capital, Monte Albán, grew into a magnificent city in its own right between AD 300 and 600, with architecture displaying clear Teotihuacán influence. Teotihuacán's advanced civilization – including writing, and a calendar system with a 260-day 'sacred year' composed of 13 periods of 20 days – spread far from its original heartland.

Teotihuacán was eventually burned, plundered and abandoned in the 8th century. But many Teotihuacán gods, such as the feathered serpent Quetzalcóatl (an all-important symbol of fertility and life) and Tláloc (the rain and water deity), were still being worshipped by the Aztecs a millennium later.

HISTORY THE ANCIENT CIVILIZATIONS

Virtual Visits

Colecciones Especiales Street View (Google Street View for 27 archaeological sites; www. inah.gob.mx/es/ inah/322-colecciones-especiales-street-view)

Museo Nacional de Antropología (Mexico City; www. inah.gob.mx/ paseos/mna)

Teotihuacán (www.inah.gob. mx/paseos/ sitioteotihuacan)

Templo Mayor (Mexico City; www.inah.gob. mx/paseos/ templomayor)

250–600	250–900	695	750–900
Teotihuacán's Pyramid of the Moon is built; the city grows to an estimated 125,000 people and comes to control the biggest of Mexico's pre-Hispanic empires.	The brilliant Classic Maya civilization flowers in southeast Mexico, Guatemala, Belize and parts of Honduras and El Salvador.	The great Maya city of Tikal (in modern-day Guatemala) conquers Maya rival Calakmul (in Mexico), but is unable to exert unified control over Calakmul's subjects.	Maya civilization in the central Maya heartland – Chiapas (southeast Mexico), El Petén (northern Guatemala) and Belize – collapses, probably because of prolonged severe droughts.

Maya Websites

Mesoweb (www.mesoweb.com)

Maya Exploration Center (www.mayaexploration.org)

Mundo Maya Online (www.maya discovery.com)

The Classic Maya

Maya civilization during the Classic period (AD 250–900), in the view of many experts the most brilliant civilization of pre-Hispanic America, flowered over a large area stretching from the Yucatán Peninsula into Belize, Guatemala, Honduras and the lowlands of Chiapas (Mexico). The Maya attained heights of artistic and architectural expression, and of learning in fields like astronomy, mathematics and astrology, that were not surpassed by any other pre-Hispanic civilization.

Politically, the Classic Maya were divided among many independent city-states, often at war with each other. A typical Maya city functioned as the religious, political and market hub for surrounding farming hamlets. Its ceremonial center focused on plazas surrounded by tall temple

ANCIENT RELIGION & BELIEF

The Maya developed a complex writing system, partly pictorial, partly phonetic, with 300 to 500 symbols. They also refined a calendar used by other pre-Hispanic peoples into a tool for the exact recording and forecasting of earthly and heavenly events. Temples were aligned to enhance observation of the heavens, helping the Maya predict solar eclipses and movements of the moon and Venus. The Maya measured time in various interlocking cycles, ranging from 13-day 'weeks' to the 1,872,000-day 'Great Cycle.' They believed the current world to be just one of a succession of worlds, and this cyclical nature of things enabled the future to be predicted by looking at the past.

To win the gods' favors they carried out elaborate rituals involving dances, feasts, sacrifices, consumption of the alcoholic drink *balche,* and bloodletting from ears, tongues or penises. The Classic Maya seem to have practiced human sacrifice on a small scale, the post-Classic Maya on a larger scale.

The Maya universe had a center and four directions, each with a color: the center was green; east was red; north, white; west, black; and south, yellow. The heavens had 13 layers, and Xibalbá, the underworld to which the dead descended, had nine. The earth was the back of a giant reptile floating on a pond.

The later Aztecs similarly observed the heavens for astrological purposes and also saw the world as having four directions, 13 heavens and nine hells. Those who died by drowning, leprosy, lightning, gout, dropsy or lung disease went to the paradisaical gardens of Tláloc, the rain god, who had killed them. Warriors who were sacrificed or died in battle, merchants killed while traveling far away, and women who died giving birth to their first child all went to heaven as companions of the sun. Everyone else traveled for four years under the northern deserts in the abode of the death god Mictlantecuhtli, before reaching the ninth hell, where – perhaps a blessed relief – they vanished altogether.

The Aztecs believed they lived in the 'fifth world,' whose four predecessors had each been destroyed by the death of the sun and of humanity. Aztec human sacrifices were designed to keep the sun, and themselves, alive.

c 1000	1325	1487	1519–20
Chichén Itzá, an abandoned Maya city on the Yucatán Peninsula, is reoccupied, developing into one of Mexico's most magnificent ancient cities, in a fusion of Maya and central Mexican styles.	The Aztecs settle at Tenochtitlán, on the site of present-day Mexico City. Over the next two centuries they come to rule an empire extending over nearly all of central Mexico.	Twenty thousand human captives are sacrificed in four days for the rededication of Tenochtitlán's Great Temple after a major reconstruction.	A Spanish expedition from Cuba, under Hernán Cortés, reaches Tenochtitlán. Initially well received, the Spaniards are attacked and driven out on the Noche Triste (Sad Night), June 30, 1520.

pyramids (usually the tombs of rulers, who were believed to be gods). Stone causeways called *sacbeob*, probably for ceremonial use, led out from the plazas, sometimes for many kilometers. In the first part of the Classic period most of these appear to have been grouped into two loose military alliances, centered on Tikal (Guatemala) and Calakmul (in the south of the Yucatán Peninsula).

Classic Maya Zones

Within Mexico, there were four main zones of Classic Maya concentration. Calakmul lies in a now-remote area known as the Río Bec zone, where Maya remains are typically long, low buildings decorated with serpent or monster masks and with towers at their corners. A second zone was the Chenes area in northeastern Campeche state, with similar architecture except for the towers. A third area was the Puuc zone, south of Mérida, characterized by buildings with intricate stone mosaics, often incorporating faces of the hook-nosed rain god Chaac. The most important Puuc city was Uxmal. The fourth zone was lowland Chiapas, with the cities of Palenque (for many people the most beautiful of all Maya sites), Yaxchilán and Toniná.

The Classic Maya Collapse

In the second half of the 8th century, conflict between Maya city-states started to increase, and by the early 10th century, the several million inhabitants of the flourishing central Maya heartland (Chiapas, Guatemala's Petén region and Belize) had virtually disappeared. The Classic era was at an end. A series of droughts combined with population pressure is thought to have brought about this cataclysm. Many Maya probably migrated to the Yucatán Peninsula or the highlands of Chiapas, where their descendants live on today. The jungle grew back up around the ancient lowland cities.

The Toltecs

In central Mexico, for centuries after the fall of Teotihuacán, power was divided between varying locally important cities, including Xochicalco, south of Mexico City; Cacaxtla and Cantona to the east; and Tula to the north. The cult of Quetzalcóatl remained widespread, society in at least some places became more militarized, and mass human sacrifice may have started here in this period. The Quetzalcóatl cult and large-scale human sacrifice were both exported to the Yucatán Peninsula, where they're most evident at the city of Chichén Itzá.

Central Mexican culture in the early post-Classic period is often given the name Toltec (Artificers), a name coined by the later Aztecs, who looked back to the Toltec rulers with awe.

Find out all about Maya time, what your birth day signifies, and what you should do each day of the 20-day week with the iPhone app Maya Calendar (www.mayan-calendar.com).

HISTORY THE ANCIENT CIVILIZATIONS

The Mel Gibson–directed *Apocalypto* (2006), a violent tale of a young man trying to escape becoming a human sacrifice, gives some idea of what ancient Maya life might sometimes have been like.

1521	1524	1534–92	1540s
The Spanish, with 100,000 native Mexican allies, capture Tenochtitlán, razing it building by building. They rename it 'México' and go on to rebuild it as the capital of Nueva España (New Spain).	Virtually all the Aztec empire, plus other Mexican regions such as Colima, the Huasteca and the Isthmus of Tehuantepec, have been brought under Spanish control.	The Spanish find huge lodes of silver at Pachuca, Zacatecas, Guanajuato and San Luis Potosí, north of Mexico City.	The Yucatán Peninsula is brought under Spanish control by three (related) conquistadors all named Francisco de Montejo. Nueva España's northern border runs roughly from modern Tampico to Guadalajara.

The Aztecs

The Aztecs' legends related that they were the chosen people of the hummingbird deity Huizilopochtli. Originally nomads from somewhere in western or northern Mexico, they were led by their priests to the Valle de México, the site of modern Mexico City, where they settled on islands in the valley's lakes. By the 15th century the Aztecs (also known as the Mexica) had fought their way up to become the most powerful group in the valley, with their capital at Tenochtitlán, where downtown Mexico City stands today.

The Aztecs formed the Triple Alliance with two other valley states, Texcoco and Tlacopan, to wage war against Tlaxcala and Huejotzingo, east of the valley. The prisoners they took became the diet of sacrificed warriors that voracious Huizilopochtli (no sweet hummingbird himself) demanded to keep the sun rising every day.

The Triple Alliance brought most of central Mexico, from the Gulf coast to the Pacific, under its control. This was an empire of 38 provinces and about five million people, geared to extracting tribute (tax in kind) of resources absent from the heartland – items like jade, turquoise, cotton, tobacco, rubber, fruits, vegetables, cacao and precious feathers, all needed for the glorification of the Aztec elite and to support their war-oriented state.

Aztec Society

Tenochtitlán and the adjoining Aztec city of Tlatelolco grew to house more than 200,000 people. The Valle de México as a whole had more than a million people. They were supported by intensive farming based on irrigation, terracing and swamp reclamation.

The Aztec emperor held absolute power. Celibate priests performed cycles of great ceremonies, typically including sacrifices and masked dances or processions enacting myths. Military leaders were usually elite professional soldiers known as *tecuhtli*. Another special group was the *pochteca* – militarized merchants who helped extend the empire, brought goods to the capital and organized large daily markets in big towns. At the bottom of society were pawns (paupers who could sell themselves for a specified period), serfs and slaves.

Other Post-Classic Civilizations

On the eve of the Spanish conquest, most Mexican civilizations shared deep similarities. Each was politically centralized and divided into classes, with many people occupied in specialist tasks, including professional priests. Agriculture was productive, despite the lack of draft animals, metal tools and the wheel. Corn tortillas, *pozol* (corn gruel) and beans were staple foods, and many other crops, such as squash, tomatoes, chilies, avocados, peanuts, papayas and pineapples, were grown in

Legend tells that the Aztecs built their capital at Tenochtitlán because there they witnessed an eagle on a cactus, devouring a snake – a sign, their prophecies told, that they should stop their wanderings. The temple they built on the spot (the Templo Mayor) was considered the center of the universe. Today the Aztecs' eagle-snake-cactus emblem sits in the center of the Mexican flag.

1605	1767	1810	1811
Mexico's indigenous population has declined from an estimated 25 million at the time of the Spanish conquest to little over a million, mainly because of new diseases from Europe.	The Jesuits, important missionaries and educators in Nueva España and many of them criollos (Mexican-born people of Spanish ancestry), are expelled from all Spanish dominions, unsettling criollos in the colony.	On September 16 priest Miguel Hidalgo launches Mexico's War of Independence with his Grito de Dolores (Cry of Dolores), a call to rebellion in the town of Dolores.	After initial victories, the rebels' numbers shrink and their leaders, including Hidalgo, are captured and executed in Chihuahua. José María Morelos y Pavón, another priest, assumes the rebel leadership.

various regions. Luxury foods for the elite included turkey, domesticated hairless dog, game and chocolate drinks. War was widespread, and often connected with the need for prisoners to sacrifice to a variety of gods.

Several important regional cultures arose in the post-Classic period:

Michoacán
The Tarascos, who were skilled artisans and jewelers, ruled Michoacán from their base around the Lago de Pátzcuaro. They were one group that managed to avoid conquest by the Aztecs.

Oaxaca
After 1200 the Zapotecs were increasingly dominated by the Mixtecs, skilled metalsmiths and potters from the uplands around the Oaxaca–Puebla border. Much of Oaxaca fell to the Aztecs in the 15th and 16th centuries.

Yucatán Peninsula
The abandoned Maya city of Chichén Itzá was reoccupied around AD 1000 and developed into one of ancient Mexico's most magnificent cities, in a fusion of Maya and central Mexican (Toltec) styles. The city of Mayapán dominated most of the Yucatán after Chichén Itzá declined around 1200. Mayapán's hold dissolved from about 1440, and the Yucatán became a quarreling ground for many city-states.

The Spanish Arrive
Ancient Mexican civilization, nearly 3000 years old, was shattered in two short years by a tiny group of invaders who destroyed the Aztec empire, brought a new religion, and reduced the native people to second-class citizens and slaves. Rarely in history has a thriving society undergone such a transformation so fast. So alien to each other were the newcomers and the indigenous Mexicans that each doubted whether the other was human (Pope Paul III declared indigenous Mexicans to be human in 1537). From this traumatic encounter arose modern Mexico. Most Mexicans today are mestizo, of mixed indigenous and European blood, and thus descendants of both cultures.

The Spanish Background
In 1492, the year Christopher Columbus arrived in the Caribbean, Spain was an aggressively expanding state, fresh from completing the 700-year Reconquista (Reconquest), in which Christian armies had gradually recovered the Spanish mainland from Islamic rule. With their mix of brutality and bravery, gold lust and piety, the Spanish conquistadors of the Americas were the natural successors to the crusading knights of the Reconquista.

General History Resources

A Brief History of Mexico (Lynn V Foster)

Mexico Online (www.mexonline.com)

Mexconnect (www.mexconnect.com)

1813	1821	1821–22	1824
Morelos' forces blockade Mexico City for several months. A congress at Chilpancingo adopts principles for the independence movement, but Morelos is captured and executed two years later.	Rebel leaders Vicente Guerrero and Agustín de Iturbide devise the Plan de Iguala, for an independent Mexico with constitutional monarchy and Catholic religious supremacy.	The Plan de Iguala wins over all influential sections of society, and the Spanish viceroy agrees to Mexican independence. Iturbide takes the new Mexican throne as Emperor Agustín I.	A new constitution establishes a federal Mexican republic of 19 states and four territories. Guadalupe Victoria, a former independence fighter, becomes its first president.

Spanish Conquest: First-Hand Accounts

The Broken Spears: The Aztec Account of the Conquest of Mexico (Miguel Leon-Portilla)

History of the Conquest of New Spain (Bernal Díaz del Castillo)

Seeking new westward trade routes to the spice-rich Orient, Spanish explorers and soldiers landed first in the Caribbean, establishing colonies on the islands of Hispaniola and Cuba. They then began seeking a passage through the land mass to the west, and soon became distracted by tales of gold, silver and a rich empire there. Spain's governor on Cuba, Diego Velázquez, asked a colonist named Hernán Cortés to lead one such expedition westward. As Cortés gathered ships and men, Velázquez became uneasy about the costs and Cortés' loyalty, and tried to cancel the expedition. But Cortés, perhaps sensing a once-in-history opportunity, ignored him and set sail on February 15, 1519, with 11 ships, 550 men and 16 horses.

The Conquest

The Cortés expedition landed first at Cozumel island, then sailed around the coast to Tabasco, defeating inhospitable locals in the Battle of Centla near modern-day Frontera, where the enemy fled in terror from Spanish horsemen, thinking horse and rider to be a single fearsome beast. Afterward the locals gave Cortés 20 young women, among them Doña Marina (La Malinche), who became his indispensable interpreter, aide and lover.

Unhappy Aztec subject towns on the Gulf coast, such as Zempoala, welcomed the Spaniards. And as the Spaniards moved inland toward Tenochtitlán, they made allies of the Aztecs' longtime enemies, the Tlaxcalans.

Aztec legends and superstitions and the indecision of Emperor Moctezuma II Xocoyotzin also worked to the Spaniards' advantage. According to the Aztec calendar, 1519 would see the legendary Toltec god-king Quetzalcóatl return from banishment in the east. Was Cortés actually Quetzalcóatl? Omens proliferated: lightning struck a temple, a comet sailed through the night skies and a bird 'with a mirror in its head' was brought to Moctezuma, who saw warriors in it.

The Taking of Tenochtitlán

The Spaniards, with 6000 indigenous allies, were invited to enter Tenochtitlán, a city bigger than any in Spain, on November 8, 1519. Aztec nobles carried Moctezuma out to meet Cortés on a litter with a canopy of feathers and gold, and the Spaniards were lodged, as befitted gods, in the palace of Moctezuma's father, Axayácatl.

Anna Lanyon's The New World of Martin Cortes tells the fascinating and poignant story of the first mestizo, the son of Hernán Cortés and La Malinche.

Though entertained in luxury, the Spaniards were trapped. Unsure of Moctezuma's intentions, they took him hostage. Believing Cortés a god, Moctezuma told his people he went willingly, but tensions rose in the city. Eventually, after six or seven months, some of the Spaniards killed about 200 Aztec nobles in an intended pre-emptive strike. Cortés persuaded Moctezuma to try to pacify his people. According to one version of events, the emperor tried to address the crowds from the roof of Ax-

1836	1845–48	1847–48	1858–61
US settlers in the Mexican territory of Texas declare independence. Mexican forces under President Santa Anna wipe out the defenders of the Alamo mission, but are then routed on the San Jacinto River.	US Congress votes to annex Texas, setting off the Mexican–American War (1846–48). US troops occupy Mexico City. Mexico cedes Texas, California, Utah, Colorado and most of New Mexico and Arizona.	The Maya people of the Yucatán Peninsula rise up against their criollo overlords in the 'War of the Castes' and narrowly fail to drive them off the peninsula.	Liberal government laws requiring the church to sell property spark the War of the Reform: Mexico's liberals (with their 'capital' at Veracruz) defeat the conservatives (based in Mexico City).

ayácatl's palace, but was killed by missiles; other versions say it was the Spaniards who killed him.

The Spaniards fled, losing several hundred of their own and thousands of indigenous allies, on what's known as the Noche Triste (Sad Night). They retreated to Tlaxcala, where they built boats in sections, then carried them across the mountains to attack Tenochtitlán from its surrounding lakes. When the 900 Spaniards re-entered the Valle de México in May 1521, they were accompanied by some 100,000 native allies. The defenders resisted fiercely, but after three months the city had been razed to the ground and the new emperor, Cuauhtémoc, was captured. Cuauhtémoc asked Cortés to kill him, but he was kept alive until 1525 as a hostage, undergoing occasional foot-burning as the Spanish tried to make him reveal the whereabouts of Aztec treasure.

Mexico as a Colony

The Spanish crown saw Mexico and its other American conquests as a silver cow to be milked to finance its endless wars in Europe, a life of luxury for its nobility, and a deluge of new churches, palaces and monasteries that were erected around Spain. The crown was entitled to one-fifth of all bullion sent back from the New World (the *quinto real,* or royal fifth).

SOME WE LOVE, SOME WE LOVE TO HATE

Mexicans have strong opinions about some of their historical characters. Some are immortalized by statues and street names all over the country. Others, just as influential, are considered objects of shame and ridicule.

Heroes

Cuauhtémoc Aztec leader who resisted the Spanish invaders.

Benito Juárez Reforming indigenous president who fought off French occupiers.

Miguel Hidalgo Priest who launched the War for Independence.

Pancho Villa Larger-than-life revolutionary.

Villains

Hernán Cortés The original evil Spanish conqueror.

Carlos Salinas de Gortari President from 1988 to 1994, blamed for the drugs trade, corruption, peso crisis, the North American Free Trade Agreement (Nafta), you name it...

Santa Anna Winner at the Alamo, but loser of Texas, California, Arizona, Utah, Colorado and New Mexico.

La Malinche Doña Marina, Hernán Cortés' indigenous translator and lover.

1861–63	1864–67	1876–1911	1910–11
Liberal Benito Juárez becomes Mexico's first indigenous president, but Mexico suffers the French Intervention: France invades Mexico, taking Mexico City in 1863 despite a defeat at Puebla on May 5, 1862.	Napoleon III sends Maximilian of Hapsburg over as emperor in 1864, but starts to withdraw his troops in 1866. Maximilian is executed by Juárez' forces in 1867.	The Porfiriato: Mexico is ruled by conservative Porfirio Díaz, who brings stability but curbs civil liberties and democratic rights, and concentrates wealth in the hands of a small minority.	The Mexican Revolution starts when the country rises against the Díaz regime on November 20, 1910. Díaz resigns in May 1911; reformist Francisco Madero is elected president in November.

Conquistadors and colonists, too, saw the American empire as a chance to get rich. Cortés granted his soldiers *encomiendas,* which were rights to the labor or tribute of groups of indigenous people. Spain asserted its authority through viceroys, the crown's personal representatives in Mexico.

The populations of the conquered peoples of Nueva España (New Spain), as the Spanish named their Mexican colony, declined disastrously, mainly from new diseases introduced by the invaders. The indigenous peoples' only real allies were some of the monks who started arriving in 1523. The monks' missionary work helped extend Spanish control over Mexico – by 1560 they had converted millions of people and built more than 100 monasteries – but many of them also protected local people from the colonists' worst excesses.

Northern Mexico remained beyond Spanish control until big finds of silver at Zacatecas, Guanajuato and elsewhere spurred efforts to subdue it. The northern borders were slowly extended by missionaries and a few settlers, and by the early 19th century Nueva España included (albeit loosely) most of the modern US states of Texas, New Mexico, Arizona, California, Utah and Colorado.

Colonial Society

A person's place in colonial Mexican society was determined by skin color, parentage and birthplace. At the top of the tree, however humble their origins in Spain, were Spanish-born colonists. Known as *peninsulares,* they were a minuscule part of the population, but were considered nobility in Nueva España.

Next on the ladder were the criollos, people of Spanish ancestry born in the colony. As the decades passed, the criollos began to develop a distinct identity, and some of them came to possess enormous estates (haciendas) and amass huge fortunes from mining, commerce or agriculture. Not surprisingly, criollos sought political power commensurate with their wealth and grew to resent Spanish authority.

Below the criollos were the mestizos, and at the bottom of the pile were the indigenous people and African slaves. Though the poor were paid for their labor by the 18th century, they were paid very little. Many were *peones* (bonded laborers tied by debt to their employers), and indigenous people still had to pay tribute to the crown.

Social stratification follows similar patterns in Mexico today with, broadly speaking, the 'pure-blood' descendants of Spaniards at the top of the tree, the mestizos in the middle and the indigenous people at the bottom.

Freedom from Spain: Key Sites

Alhóndiga de Granaditas (Guanajuato)

Dolores Hidalgo

Calabozo de Hidalgo, Casa Chihuahua (Chihuahua)

Ex-Hotel Zevallos (Córdoba)

Museo Casa de Morelos (Morelia)

1913–14	1917	1920–24	1926
Madero is deposed and executed by conservative Victoriano Huerta. Northern revolutionary leaders unite against Huerta. Huerta's troops terrorize the countryside, but he is forced to resign in July 1914.	Reformists emerge victorious over radicals in the revolutionary conflict, and a new reformist constitution, still largely in force today, is enacted at Querétaro.	President Álvaro Obregón turns to post-Revolution reconstruction. More than a thousand rural schools are built; some land is redistributed from big landowners to peasants.	President Plutarco Elías Calles closes monasteries, outlaws religious orders and bans religious processions, precipitating the Cristero Rebellion by Catholics (until 1929).

Mexico as a Republic

Criollo discontent with Spanish rule really began to stir following the expulsion of the Jesuits (many of whom were criollos) from the Spanish empire in 1767. The catalyst for rebellion came in 1808 when Napoleon Bonaparte occupied Spain, and direct Spanish control over Nueva España evaporated. The city of Querétaro became a hotbed of intrigue among criollos plotting rebellion against Spanish rule. The rebellion was launched on September 16, 1810 by Padre Miguel Hidalgo in his parish of Dolores (now Dolores Hidalgo). The path to independence was a hard one, involving almost 11 years of fighting between rebels and loyalist forces, and the deaths of Hidalgo and several other rebel leaders. But eventually rebel general Agustín de Iturbide sat down with Spanish viceroy Juan O'Donojú in Córdoba in 1821 and agreed on terms for Mexico's independence.

Mexico's first century as a free nation started with a period of chronic political instability and wound up with a period of stability so repressive that it triggered a revolution. A consistent thread throughout was the opposition between liberals, who favored a measure of social reform, and conservatives, who didn't. Between 1821 and the mid-1860s, the young Mexican nation was invaded by three different countries (Spain, the USA and France), lost large chunks of its territory to the US and underwent nearly 50 changes of head of state.

Santa Anna had a leg amputated after being wounded by French forces in 1838. He later had the leg buried with military honors in Mexico City. Its whereabouts are now unknown but its prosthetic replacement was captured by Americans in 1847 and now resides in the Illinois State Military Museum.

HISTORY MEXICO AS A REPUBLIC

Juárez & Díaz

It was an indigenous Zapotec from Oaxaca who played the lead role in Mexican affairs for two tumultuous decades after the midpoint of the century. Lawyer Benito Juárez was a key member of the new liberal government in 1855, which ushered in the era known as the Reform, in which the liberals set about dismantling the conservative state that had developed in Mexico. Juárez became president in 1861. With the French Intervention soon afterward, his government was forced into exile in

THE TRAGICOMEDY OF SANTA ANNA

Intervention in politics by ambitious soldiers plagued Mexico throughout the 19th century. Antonio López de Santa Anna first hit the limelight by deposing Emperor Agustín I in 1823. He also overthrew President Anastasio Bustamante in 1831, then was himself elected president in 1833, the first of 11 terms in 22 chaotic years. Above all, Mexicans remember Santa Anna for losing large chunks of Mexican territory to the US. After his 1836 post-Alamo defeat in Texas and his disastrous territorial losses in the Mexican–American War of 1846–48, a Santa Anna government sold Mexico's last remaining areas of New Mexico and Arizona to the US for US$10 million in 1853.

1929	1934–40	1940s & '50s	1964–70
Elías Calles founds the Partido Nacional Revolucionario: it and its later mutations, the Partido de la Revolución Mexicana and the Partido Revolucionario Institucional (PRI), will rule Mexico until 2000.	President Lázaro Cárdenas redistributes 200,000 sq km of land and expropriates foreign oil operations, forming the state oil company Petróleos Mexicanos (Pemex). Foreign investors avoid Mexico.	The Mexican economy expands, helped by growth during WWII, major infrastructure projects and tourism development. The population almost doubles in two decades, and millions migrate to urban areas.	President Gustavo Díaz Ordaz resists democratizing the PRI. During demonstrations against one-party rule before the 1968 Olympics, an estimated 400 protesters are massacred at Tlatelolco, Mexico City.

Modern Maya

The Caste War of Yucatán (Nelson Reed)

Time Among the Maya (Ronald Wright)

provincial Mexico, eventually to regain control in 1866. Juárez set an agenda of economic and social reform. Schooling was made mandatory, a railway was built between Mexico City and Veracruz, and a rural police force, the *rurales*, was organized to secure the transportation of cargo through Mexico. Juárez died in 1872 and remains one of the few Mexican historical figures with a completely unsullied reputation.

A rather different Oaxacan, Porfirio Díaz, ruled as president for 31 of the following 39 years, a period known as the Porfiriato. Díaz brought Mexico into the industrial age, stringing telephone, telegraph and railway lines and launching public works projects. He kept Mexico free of civil wars – but political opposition, free elections and a free press were banned. Peasants were cheated out of their land by new laws, workers suffered appalling conditions, and land and wealth became concentrated in the hands of a small minority. All this led, in 1910, to the Mexican Revolution.

The Mexican Revolution

The Revolution was a tortured 10-year period of shifting conflicts and allegiances between forces and leaders of all political stripes. The conservatives were pushed aside fairly early on, but the reformers and revolutionaries who had lined up against them could not agree among themselves. Successive attempts to create stable governments were wrecked by new outbreaks of devastating fighting. All told, one in eight Mexicans lost their lives.

Francisco Madero, a wealthy liberal from Coahuila, would probably have won the presidential election in 1910 if Porfirio Díaz hadn't jailed him. On his release, Madero called successfully on the nation to revolt, which spread quickly across the country. Díaz resigned in May 1911, and Madero was elected president six months later. But Madero could not contain the diverse factions now struggling for power throughout the country. The basic divide was between liberal reformers like Madero and more radical leaders such as Emiliano Zapata, who was fighting for the transfer of hacienda land to the peasants, with the cry '*¡Tierra y libertad!*' (Land and freedom!).

In 1913 Madero was deposed and executed by one of his own generals, Victoriano Huerta, who had defected to conservative rebels. The liberals and radicals united (temporarily) to defeat Huerta. Three main leaders in the north banded together under the Plan de Guadalupe: Venustiano Carranza, a Madero supporter, in Coahuila; Francisco 'Pancho' Villa in Chihuahua; and Álvaro Obregón in Sonora. Zapata also fought against Huerta.

But fighting then broke out again between the victorious factions, with Carranza and Obregón (the 'Constitutionalists,' with their capital at Veracruz) pitted against the radical Zapata and the populist Villa. Zapata and Villa never formed a serious alliance, and it was Carranza who emerged the victor. He had Zapata assassinated in 1919, only to be

In the 1920s outstanding Mexican artists such as Diego Rivera were commissioned to decorate important public buildings with large, vivid murals on historical and social themes. Many of these can be seen in Mexico City.

1970s	1980s	1985	1988–94
Mexico enjoys an economic boom thanks to a jump in world oil prices. On the strength of the country's vast oil reserves, international institutions begin lending Mexico billions of dollars.	Oil prices plunge and Mexico suffers its worst recession in decades. Amid economic helplessness and rampant corruption, dissent and protests increase, even inside the PRI.	On September 19 a massive earthquake, with a magnitude of 8.1 on the Richter scale, strikes Mexico City. At least 10,000 people are killed.	The PRI's Carlos Salinas de Gortari narrowly defeats left-of-center Cuauhtémoc Cárdenas in a disputed presidential election. Salinas reforms Mexico's economy toward private enterprise and free trade.

liquidated himself the following year on the orders of his former ally Obregón. Pancho Villa was killed in 1923.

Mexico as a One-Party Democracy

From 1920 to 2000, Mexico was ruled by the reformists who emerged victorious from the Revolution and their successors in the political party they set up, which since the 1940s has borne the name Partido Revolucionario Institucional (Institutional Revolutionary Party), or PRI as it's universally known. Starting out with some genuinely radical social policies, these governments became steadily more conservative, corrupt, repressive and self-interested as the 20th century wore on. Mexico ended the century with a bigger middle class but still with a yawning wealth gap between the prosperous few and the many poor.

Between the 1920s and '60s more than 400,000 sq km of land was redistributed from large estates to peasants and small farmers. Nearly half the population received land, mainly in the form of *ejidos* (communal landholdings). Meanwhile, Mexico developed a worrying economic dependence on its large oil reserves in the Gulf of Mexico. The 1970s and '80s saw the country veer from oil-engendered boom to oil-engendered slump as world oil prices swung rapidly up then just as suddenly down. The huge government-owned oil company Pemex was just one face of a massive state-controlled economic behemoth that developed as the PRI sought control over all important facets of Mexican life.

Decline of the PRI

The PRI was discredited forever in the minds of many Mexicans by the Tlatelolco Massacre of 1968, in which an estimated 400 civil-liberties protesters were shot dead. The PRI came to depend increasingly on strong-arm tactics and fraud to win elections.

Mexicans' cynicism about their leaders reached a crescendo with the 1988–94 presidency of Carlos Salinas de Gortari, who won the presidential election only after a mysterious computer failure had halted vote-tallying at a crucial stage. During Salinas' term, drug trafficking through Mexico – on the rise since the early '80s when traffickers from Colombia began shifting their routes from the Caribbean to Mexico – grew into a huge business, and mysterious high-profile murders proliferated. Salinas did take steps to liberalize the monolithic state-dominated economy. The apex of his program, the North American Free Trade Agreement (Nafta), boosted exports and industry, but was unpopular with food growers and small businesses threatened by imports from the US. The last year of his presidency, 1994, began with the left-wing Zapatista uprising in Mexico's southernmost state, Chiapas, and shortly before Salinas left office he spent nearly all of Mexico's

The best movie about the Mexican Revolution is Elia Kazan's *Viva Zapata!* (1952), starring Marlon Brando. John Steinbeck's script is historically sound up to the 1914 meeting between Pancho Villa and Emiliano Zapata in Mexico City. Beyond that point it flounders until Zapata is assassinated.

Revolution Sites

Museo Casa de Villa (Chihuahua)

Museo Francisco Villa (Hidalgo del Parral)

Cuartel General de Zapata (Tlaltizapán, Morelos)

Museo de la Revolución (Puebla)

1994	1994–2000	2000	2006
The North American Free Trade Agreement (Nafta) takes effect. The Zapatista uprising in Chiapas begins. Luis Donaldo Colosio, Salinas' chosen successor as PRI presidential candidate, is assassinated.	Under President Ernesto Zedillo, Mexico emerges from a recession triggered by a currency collapse days after he took office. Crime and migration to the US increase.	Vicente Fox of the right-of-center Partido Acción Nacional (PAN) wins the presidential election under a new, transparent electoral system, ending eight decades of rule by the PRI and its predecessors.	The PAN's Felipe Calderón narrowly defeats Andrés Manuel López Obrador of the left-of-center Party of the Democratic Revolution (PRD) in the presidential election, and declares war on Mexico's drug mobs.

foreign-exchange reserves in a futile attempt to support the peso, engendering a slump that he left his successor, Ernesto Zedillo, to deal with.

It was also left to Zedillo to respond to the rising clamor for democratic change in Mexico. He established a new, independently supervised electoral system that opened the way for his own party to lose power when Vicente Fox of the business-oriented Partido Acción Nacional (PAN) won the presidential election in 2000.

In 1970 the average Mexican woman gave birth seven times in her lifetime. Today the figure is just 2.27. Publicity campaigns, education and family-planning clinics have all helped to slow the birth rate.

PAN Rule

Vicente Fox's election itself – a non-PRI president after 80 years of rule by that party and its predecessors – was really the biggest news about his six-year term. He entered office backed by much goodwill. In the end, his presidency was considered a disappointment by most. Lacking a majority in Mexico's Congress, Fox was unable to push through reforms that he believed were key to stirring Mexico's slumbering economy.

Fox was succeeded in 2006 by another PAN president, Felipe Calderón. During Calderón's term Mexico's economy sprang back surprisingly fast after the recession of 2009, and Mexico became something of a global environmental champion when it enshrined its carbon-emissions targets in law in 2012. But his presidency will be remembered far more for its war on drugs.

The Drug Wars

Mexican migration to the USA fell from 2.94 million people between 1995 and 2000 (with 670,000 returning), to 870,000 between 2009 and 2014, with onr million coming back home, according to the Pew Research Center (www. pewhispanic.org). About 12 million Mexican citizens still live (legally or illegally) in the US.

Presidents Zedillo and Fox had already deployed the armed forces against the violent mobs running the multi-billion-dollar business of shipping illegal drugs into the USA, but had failed to rein in their violence or their power to corrupt. By 2006 over 2000 people a year were already dying in violence engendered chiefly by brutal turf wars between rival gangs.

Calderón declared war on the drug mobs and mobilized 50,000 troops plus naval and police forces against them, predominantly in cities along the US border. Some top gang leaders were killed or arrested, and drug seizures reached record levels, but so did the killings – an estimated 60,000 in the six years of Calderón's presidency. The gangs' methods grew ever more shocking, with street gun-battles, gruesome beheadings and torture. The northern city of Ciudad Juárez, with over 3100 killings in 2010, became the world's murder capital. Cities such as Monterrey, Nuevo Laredo, Acapulco and Veracruz saw violence spike when local turf wars erupted. When the numbers of killings finally started to fall at the end of Calderón's presidency, many people believed this was simply because the two strongest mobs – the Sinaloa cartel in the northwest of Mexico and Los Zetas in the northeast – had effectively wiped out their weaker rivals.

2006–12	2012	Jul & Aug 2014	26 Sep 2014
In the six years of Calderón's war on drugs, 50,000 troops are deployed around the country and some 60,000 people are killed, most of them in intergang turf wars.	The PRI returns to power as Enrique Peña Nieto wins the presidential election, promising reforms to propel the economy forward. López Obrador of the PRD again comes a close second.	Mexico's Congress passes new laws ending Pemex's monopoly in the oil industry and increasing competition in telecoms and broadcasting, intended to spark an economic takeoff.	Forty-three students from Ayotzinapa, Guerrero state, disappear after clashing with police in Iguala, sparking outrage at perceived corruption and criminality in Mexico's governing and security apparatus.

The Mexican Way of Life

Travels in Mexico quickly reveal that Mexicans are a vastly diverse bunch, from the industrial workers of Monterrey to the rich sophisticates and bohemian counterculture of Mexico City and indigenous villagers eking out subsistence in the southern mountains. But certain common threads run through almost everyone here – among them a deep vein of spirituality, the importance of family, and a simultaneous pride and frustration about Mexico itself.

Life, Death & the Family

One thing you can never do with Mexicans is encapsulate them in simple formulas. They're hospitable, warm and courteous to guests, yet are most truly themselves within their family group. They will laugh at death, but have a profound vein of spirituality. They embrace modernity while remaining traditional in essence.

Many Mexicans, however contemporary and globalized they may appear, still inhabit a world in which omens, coincidences and curious resemblances take on great importance. When sick, some people still prefer to visit a traditional *curandero* – a kind of cross between a naturopath and a witch doctor – rather than resort to a modern *médico*.

While most Mexicans are chiefly concerned with earning a living for themselves and their strongly knit families, they also take their leisure time very seriously, be it partying at clubs or fiestas, or relaxing over an extended-family Sunday lunch at a restaurant. Holidays for religious festivals and patriotic anniversaries are essential to the rhythm of life, ensuring that people get a break every few weeks.

Mexicans may despair of their country ever being governed well, but at the same time they are fiercely proud of it. They naturally absorb a certain amount of US culture and consciousness, but they also strongly value what's different about Mexican life – its more humane pace, its strong sense of community and family, its unique food and drinks, and the thriving, multifaceted national culture.

Nobel Prize–winning Mexican writer Octavio Paz argues in *The Labyrinth of Solitude* that Mexicans' love of noise, music and crowds is just a temporary escape from personal isolation and gloom. Make your own judgment.

The Great Divides

Fly into Mexico City and you'll get a bird's-eye view of just how little space is not occupied by buildings or roads. Around the edges of the city, streets climb the steep slopes of extinct volcanoes, while the city's fringes are ringed with shacks made from a few concrete blocks or sheets of tin that 'house' the poorest. In the most affluent neighborhoods, imposing detached houses with well-tended gardens sit behind high walls with strong security gates.

One in every two Mexicans now lives in a city or conurbation of more than a million people. A quarter of them live in smaller cities and towns, and another quarter in villages. The number of urban dwellers continues to rise as rural folk are sucked into cities.

Out in the villages and small towns, people still work the land and members of an extended family often live in yards with separate small buildings of adobe, wood or concrete, often with earth floors. Inside these homes are few possessions – beds, a cooking area, a table with a few chairs and a few family photos. Few villagers own cars.

Mexico's eternal wealth gap yawns as wide as ever. The world's second richest man, entrepreneur Carlos Slim Helú, is a Mexican. His net worth was estimated at US$77 billion by *Forbes* magazine in 2015. At the other extreme, the poorest city dwellers barely scrape an existence as street hawkers, buskers or home workers in the 'informal economy,' rarely earning more than M$70 (US$5) a day.

While rich kids go clubbing in flashy cars and attend private schools (often in the US), and the bohemian urban counterculture enjoys its mezcal bars, state-funded universities and underground dance clubs, poor villagers may dance only at local fiestas and often leave school well before they reach 15.

The secrets of physical and spiritual health of a Nahua *curandera* (literally 'curer') are revealed in *Woman Who Glows in the Dark* by Elena Ávila.

Land of Many Peoples

Mexico's ethnic diversity is one of its most fascinating aspects. The major distinction is between mestizos – people of mixed ancestry (mostly Spanish and indigenous) – and the *indígenas*, the indigenous descendants of Mexico's pre-Hispanic inhabitants. Mestizos are the majority that holds most positions of power and influence, but the *indígenas*, while mostly materially poor, are often culturally rich. Approximately 60 Mexican indigenous peoples survive, each with their own language and, often, unique costumes, and their way of life is still imbued with communal customs, beliefs and rituals bound up with nature. By official figures almost 16 million people in Mexico (14% of the population) are indigenous. The biggest group is the Nahua, descendants of the ancient Aztecs, over three million of whom are spread around central Mexico. The approximately two million Maya on the Yucatán Peninsula are direct descendants of the ancient Maya, as (probably) are the Tzotziles and Tzeltales of Chiapas (totaling just over one million). Also directly descended from well-known pre-Hispanic peoples are the estimated one million Zapotecs and over 800,000 Mixtecs, mainly in Oaxaca; over 400,000 Totonacs in Veracruz; and over 200,000 Purépecha (Tarascos) in Michoacán.

Around 10% of Mexicans adhere to non-Catholic varieties of Christianity. Some are members of Protestant churches set up by US missionaries in the 19th century. Millions of indigenous rural poor of southeast Mexico have been converted in recent years by a wave of American Pentecostal, Evangelical, Mormon, Seventh-Day Adventist and Jehovah's Witness missionaries.

The Spiritual Dimension

Yoga, the temascal (pre-Hispanic steam bath) and New Age cosmic energies may mean more to some Mexicans today than traditional Roman Catholicism, but a spiritual dimension of some kind or other remains important in most Mexicans' lives.

Roman Catholicism

About 85% of Mexicans profess Roman Catholicism, making this the world's second-biggest Catholic country after Brazil. Almost half of Mexican Catholics attend church weekly and Catholicism remains very much part of the nation's established fabric. Most Mexican fiestas are built around local saints' days, and pilgrimages to important shrines are a big feature of the calendar.

The church's most binding symbol is Nuestra Señora de Guadalupe, the dark-skinned manifestation of the Virgin Mary who appeared to an Aztec potter, Juan Diego, on Cerro del Tepeyac hill in what's now northern Mexico City in 1531. A crucial link between Catholic and indigenous spirituality, the Virgin of Guadalupe is now the country's religious patron, an archetypal mother whose blue-cloaked image is ubiquitous and whose name is invoked in political speeches and literature as well as

COMMUNING WITH DEPARTED SOULS

Few festivals reveal more about Mexican spirituality than Día de Muertos (Day of the Dead), the remembrance of departed loved ones at the beginning of November. Muertos originated in colonial times, when the Catholic Church fused indigenous rites honoring and communing with the dead with its own celebrations of All Saints' Day (November 1) and All Souls' Day (November 2).

Today Muertos is a national phenomenon, with people everywhere cleaning graves and decorating them with flowers, holding graveyard vigils, sprinkling the graves with liquor (the dead also like to party!) and building elaborate altars to welcome back their loved ones with their favorite dishes. For the mestizo (mixed ancestry) majority, it's a popular folk festival and family occasion. The Catholics believe that departed souls are in heaven or in purgatory, not actually back on a visit to earth. Nevertheless, many find comfort in a sense that lost loved ones are somehow more present at this time. Among many indigenous communities, Muertos is still very much a religious and spiritual event. For them, the observance might more appropriately be called Noche de Muertos (Night of the Dead), because families actually spend whole nights at the graveyard communing with the dear departed.

Sugar skulls, chocolate coffins and toy skeletons are sold in markets everywhere, both as Muertos gifts for children and graveyard decorations; this tradition derives in great measure from the work of artist José Guadalupe Posada (1852–1913), renowned for his satirical figures of a skeletal Death cheerfully engaging in everyday life, working, dancing, courting, drinking and riding horses into battle.

religious ceremonies. December 12, her feast day, sees large-scale celebrations and pilgrimages all over the country, biggest of all in Mexico City.

Though some church figures have supported causes such as indigenous rights, the Mexican Catholic Church is a socially conservative body. It has alienated some sectors of the population by its strong opposition to the legalization of abortion and to the gay marriages or civil unions in Mexico City and the states of Colima, Quintana Roo and Coahuila. On June 19, 2015, Mexico's Supreme Court ruled that laws restricting marriage to a man and a woman were unconstitutional and more states may follow suit.

Indigenous Religion

The Spanish missionaries of the 16th and 17th centuries won indigenous Mexicans over to Catholicism by grafting it onto pre-Hispanic religions. Old gods were renamed as Christian saints, old festivals were melded with Christian feast days. Indigenous Christianity is still fused with ancient beliefs today. Jalisco's Huichol people have two Christs, but Nakawé, the fertility goddess, is a more important deity. In the church at the Tzotzil Maya village of San Juan Chamula, you may see chanting *curanderos* (healers) carrying out shamanistic rites. In the traditional indigenous world almost everything has a spiritual dimension – trees, rivers, hills, wind, rain and sun have their own gods or spirits, and illness may be seen as a 'loss of soul' resulting from wrongdoing or from the malign influence of someone with magical powers.

Letting off Steam

Mexicans have many ways of releasing their emotional and physical energy. Religion, artistic expression and the countless fiestas are among them. So are sports.

Fútbol

No sport ignites Mexicans' passions more than *fútbol* (soccer). Games in the 18-team Liga MX, the national First Division, are played at weekends

The 2008 film *Rudo y Cursi* tells the (fictional) tale of two brothers from a poor Mexican village rising to professional playing success in a corrupt Mexican *fútbol* (soccer) world. It's a comical and lovable movie that stars two of the country's top actors, Gael García Bernal and Diego Luna.

SANTA MUERTE

A challenge to mainstream religion comes from the cult of Santa Muerte (Saint Death) – condemned as blasphemous by the Vatican in 2013 it has, by some estimates, over eight million followers in Mexico. Mexicans disillusioned with the traditional Catholic Trinity and saints now pray and make offerings to a cloaked, scythe-wielding female skeleton, the goddess of death whose origins date to pre-Hispanic Mexico. Criminal gangs are notoriously among the cult's most loyal followers, and there have even been reports of alleged human sacrifices to Santa Muerte, though she is also seen as a protector of LGBT communities and of outcasts from society. The best known **Santa Muerte altar** (p101) is in Mexico City's crime-ridden Tepito neighborhood.

almost year-round before crowds averaging 25,000 and followed by millions on TV. Attending a game is fun, and rivalry between opposing fans is generally good-humored. Tickets are sold at the entrance for anything from M$70 to M$1600, depending on the stadium, game and seat. For *fútbol* fixtures and results, check www.espnfc.com.

The two most popular teams with large followings everywhere are América, of Mexico City, known as the Águilas (Eagles), and Guadalajara, called Chivas (Goats). Matches between the two, known as Los Clásicos, are the biggest games of the year. Other leading clubs include Cruz Azul and UNAM (Pumas) of Mexico City, Monterrey and UANL (Los Tigres) from Monterrey, Santos Laguna from Torreón, and Toluca.

Bullfights

Bullfighting arouses strong passions in many Mexicans. While it has many fans, there is also a strong antibullfighting movement spearheaded by groups such as Mexican Animal Rights Association (AMEDEA) and AnimaNaturalis. Bullfights are now banned in the states of Sonora, Guerrero and Coahuila.

Bullfights usually take place on Sunday afternoons or during local festivals, chiefly in the larger cities. In northern Mexico the season generally runs from March or April to August or September. In central and southern Mexico, including Mexico City's Monumental Plaza México, one of the world's biggest bullrings, the main season is from October to February.

Other Sports

The highly popular *lucha libre* (wrestling) is more showbiz than sport. Participants give themselves names like Último Guerrero (Last Warrior), Rey Escorpión (Scorpion King) and Blue Panther, then clown around in Day-Glo tights and lurid masks. Mexico City's 17,000-seat Arena México (p127) is the big temple of this activity.

Charreadas (rodeos) are popular events, particularly in the northern half of Mexico, during fiestas and at regular venues often called *lienzos charros* – www.decharros.com has plenty of information.

Mexico has produced many world champions in boxing. The legendary Julio César Chávez won five world titles at three different weights, and achieved an amazing 87 consecutive wins (or 90 unbeaten) after turning pro in 1980.

The Arts

Mexicans are an obsessively creative people. Wherever you go in their country, you'll be impressed by the marvelous artistic expression on display. Colorful painting, stunning architecture and beautiful crafts are everywhere; Aztec dancers vibrate in the very heart of Mexico City and musicians strike up on the streets and in bars and buses. This is a country that has given the world some of its finest painting, music, movies and writing.

Architecture

Mexico's priceless architectural heritage from pre-Hispanic and colonial times is one of its greatest treasures.

Pre-Hispanic

At places like Teotihuacán, Monte Albán, Chichén Itzá, Uxmal and Palenque you can still see fairly intact, spectacular pre-Hispanic cities. Their grand ceremonial centers were designed to impress, with great stone pyramids (topped by shrines), palaces and ritual ball courts – all built without metal tools, pack animals or wheels. While the architecture of Teotihuacán, Monte Albán and the Aztecs was intended to awe with its grand scale, the Maya of Chichén Itzá, Uxmal, Palenque and countless other sites paid more attention to aesthetics, with intricately patterned facades, delicate stone 'combs' on temple roofs, and sinuous carvings, producing some of the most beautiful human creations in the Americas.

The technical hallmark of Maya buildings is the corbeled vault, a version of the arch: two stone walls leaning toward one another, nearly meeting at the top and surmounted by a capstone. Teotihuacán architecture is characterized by the *talud-tablero* style of stepped buildings, in which height is achieved by alternating upright *(tablero)* sections with sloping *(talud)* ones.

Colonial Period

The Spaniards destroyed indigenous temples and built churches and monasteries in their place, and laid out new towns with handsome plazas and grids of streets lined by fine stone edifices – contributing much to Mexico's beauty today. Building was in Spanish styles, with some unique local variations. Renaissance style, based on ancient Greek and Roman ideals of harmony and proportion, with shapes such as the square and the circle, dominated in the 16th and early 17th centuries. Mérida's cathedral and Casa de Montejo are outstanding Renaissance buildings, while Mexico City and Puebla cathedrals mingle Renaissance and baroque styles.

Baroque, which reached Mexico in the early 17th century, layered new dramatic effects – curves, color and increasingly elaborate decoration – onto a Renaissance base. Painting and sculpture were integrated with architecture, notably in ornate, enormous *retablos* (altarpieces) in churches. Mexico's finest baroque buildings include Zacatecas cathedral and the churches of Santo Domingo in Mexico City and Oaxaca. Between

The 2012 documentary *Hecho en México* is a fascinating, colorful look at contemporary Mexican life and arts, with participation of many of the country's top musicians, actors and writers. It's directed by Duncan Bridgeman.

Mexico's Biggest Pyramids

Pirámide Tepanapa (Cholula)

Pirámide del Sol (Pyramid of the Sun; Teotihuacán)

Pirámide de la Luna (Pyramid of the Moon; Teotihuacán)

1730 and 1780 Mexican baroque reached its final, spectacularly out-of-control form known as Churrigueresque, with riotous ornamentation.

Indigenous artisans added profuse sculpture in stone and colored stucco to many baroque buildings, such as the Rosary Chapels in the Templos de Santo Domingo at Puebla and Oaxaca. Spanish Islamic influence showed in the popularity of *azulejos* (colored tiles) on the outside of buildings, notably on Mexico City's Casa de Azulejos and many buildings in Puebla.

Neoclassical style, another return to sober Greek and Roman ideals, dominated from about 1780 to 1830. Outstanding buildings include the Palacio de Minería in Mexico City, designed by Mexico's leading architect of the time, Manuel Tolsá.

Check out the latest (and the future) in Mexico City architecture and planning at www.dezeen.com/tag/mexico-city.

19th to 21st Centuries

Independent Mexico in the 19th and early 20th centuries saw revivals of colonial styles and imitations of contemporary French or Italian styles. Mexico City's semi-art nouveau Palacio de Bellas Artes is one of the most spectacular buildings from this era.

After the 1910–20 Revolution came 'Toltecism,' an effort to return to pre-Hispanic roots in the search for a national identity. This culminated in the 1950s with the Ciudad Universitaria campus in Mexico City, where many buildings are covered with colorful murals.

The great icon of more recent architecture is Luis Barragán (1902–88), who exhibited a strong Mexican strain in bringing vivid colors and plays of space and light to the typical geometric concrete shapes of the International Modern Movement. His strong influence on Mexican architecture and design is ongoing today. His oeuvre includes a set of wacky colored skyscraper sculptures in Ciudad Satélite, a Mexico City suburb, and his own house in Mexico City, which is on the Unesco World Heritage list. Another modernist, Pedro Ramírez Vázquez (1919–2013), designed three vast public buildings in Mexico City: the Estadio Azteca and Museo Nacional de Antropología in the 1960s and the Basílica de Guadalupe in the '70s. The capital has seen its share of eye-catching prestige structures popping up in the last decade or so: undoubtedly the top conversation piece is the Museo Soumaya Plaza Carso which opened in 2011 to house part of the art collection of multi-multi-billionaire Carlos Slim. Designed by Slim's son-in-law Fernando Romero, it's a love-it-or-hate-it six-story construction that resembles a giant, twisted blacksmith's anvil covered in 16,000 honeycomb-shaped aluminium plates.

Painting & Sculpture

Since the earliest times Mexicans have exhibited a love of color and form, and an exciting talent for painting and sculpture. The wealth of art in mural form and in Mexico's many galleries is a highlight of the country.

Top Ancient Mural Sites

Palacio de Tepantitla (*Teotihuacán*)

Cacaxtla

Bonampak

Pre-Hispanic

Mexico's first civilization, the Olmecs of the Gulf coast, produced remarkable stone sculptures depicting deities, animals and wonderfully lifelike human forms. Most awesome are the huge Olmec heads, which combine the features of human babies and jaguars.

The Classic Maya of southeast Mexico between about AD 250 and 800 were perhaps ancient Mexico's most artistically gifted people. They left countless beautiful stone sculptures, complicated in design but possessing great delicacy of touch.

Colonial & Independence Eras

Mexican art during Spanish rule was heavily Spanish-influenced and chiefly religious in subject, though portraiture advanced under wealthy patrons. Miguel Cabrera (1695–1768), from Oaxaca, is widely considered the most talented painter of the era.

The years before the 1910 Revolution finally saw a break from European traditions. Mexican slums, brothels and indigenous poverty began to appear on canvases. José Guadalupe Posada (1852–1913), with his characteristic *calavera* (skull) motif, satirized the injustices of the Porfiriato period, launching a tradition of political and social subversion in Mexican art.

The Muralists

In the 1920s, immediately following the Mexican Revolution, education minister José Vasconcelos commissioned young artists to paint a series of public murals to spread a sense of Mexican history and culture and of the need for social and technological change. The trio of great muralists – all great painters in smaller scales, too – were Diego Rivera (1886–1957), José Clemente Orozco (1883–1949) and David Alfaro Siqueiros (1896–1974).

Rivera's work carried a left-wing message, emphasizing past oppression of indigenous people and peasants. His art, found in many locations in and around Mexico City, pulled Mexico's indigenous and Spanish roots together in colorful, crowded tableaus depicting historical people and events, with a simple moral message.

Siqueiros, who fought in the Revolution on the Constitutionalist (liberal) side, remained a political activist afterward and his murals convey a clear Marxist message through dramatic, symbolic depictions of the oppressed and grotesque caricatures of the oppressors. Some of his best works are at the Palacio de Bellas Artes, Castillo de Chapultepec and Ciudad Universitaria, all in Mexico City.

Orozco, from Jalisco, focused more on the universal human condition than on historical specifics. He conveyed emotion, character and atmosphere. His work was at its peak in Guadalajara between 1936 and 1939, particularly in the 50-odd frescoes in the Instituto Cultural de Cabañas.

Other 20th-Century Artists

Frida Kahlo (1907–54), physically crippled by a road accident and mentally tormented in her tempestuous marriage to Diego Rivera, painted anguished self-portraits and grotesque, surreal images that expressed her left-wing views and externalized her inner tumult. Kahlo's work suddenly seemed to strike an international chord in the 1980s and '90s. She's now better known worldwide than any other Mexican artist, and her Mexico City home, the Museo Frida Kahlo (p95), is a don't-miss for any art lover.

Rufino Tamayo (1899–1991) from Oaxaca is sometimes thought of as the fourth major muralist, but he was a great artist at other scales too, absorbed by abstract and mythological images and effects of color. After WWII, the young artists of La Ruptura (the Rupture), led by José Luis Cuevas (b 1934), reacted against the muralist movement, which they saw as too obsessed with *mexicanidad* (Mexicanness). They opened Mexico up to world trends such as abstract expressionism and pop art. Sculptor Sebastián (b 1947), from Chihuahua, is famed for his large, mathematics-inspired sculptures that adorn cities around the world.

Contemporary Art

Today, thanks to dynamic artists, galleries and patrons and the globalization of the world art scene, contemporary Mexican art is reaching galleries the world over, and Mexico City has become an international art hot spot, while other cities such as Monterrey, Oaxaca, Mazatlán and Guadalajara also have thriving art scenes. Mexican artists attempt to interpret

Modern Art Websites

Kurimanzutto (www.kuriman zutto.com)

LatinAmericanArt (www.latinameri canart.com)

Museo Colección Andrés Blaisten (www.museo blaisten.com)

Fundación Jumex (http://fundacion jumex.org)

THE ARTS PAINTING & SCULPTURE

Mexico City's annual contemporary art fair, Zona Maco, held over five days every February, pulls in galleries, dealers and cognoscenti from around the world.

the uncertainties of the 21st century in diverse ways. The pendulum has swung away from abstraction to hyper-representation, photorealism, installations, video and street art. Rocío Maldonado (b 1951), Rafael Cauduro (b 1950) and Roberto Cortázar (b 1962) all paint classically depicted figures against amorphous, bleak backgrounds. Check out Cauduro's murals on state-sponsored crime in Mexico City's Suprema Corte de Justicia. Leading contemporary lights such as Miguel Calderón (b 1971) and Gabriel Orozco (b 1962) spread their talents across many media, always challenging the spectator's preconceptions.

For shots of street art all around the country, check out Fatcap's Mexico pages – www.fatcap.com/country/mexico.html.

Street Art – the New Muralists

The contemporary art that is having most public impact in Mexico – and which you are most likely to set eyes on – is street art, whose direct popular appeal provides a powerful channel for Mexicans to express themselves and reach an audience. Mexico City, Oaxaca and Guadalajara lead the way in truly accomplished street art, often with a powerful political-protest message – check out Street Art Chilango (www.streetartchilango.com) for Mexico City, and Lapiztola (www.facebook.com/lapiztola.stencil) and Guerilla-art.mx (http://guerilla-art.mx) for Oaxaca.

Today's street artists follow in the footsteps of the 20th-century muralists, with the difference that they tend to be independent and rebellious and do not serve governments. Some do, however, use their art for specific positive social projects – none more so than the Mexico City-based Germen Crew (www.facebook.com/muralismogermen), who in 2015 turned the entire Las Palmitas neighborhood in the city of Pachuca into one big rainbow-colored mural – a remarkable work, sponsored by the local city hall, which by all accounts has restored pride and smiles to a formerly sketchy area.

Music

Music is everywhere in Mexico. It comes booming out of sound systems in markets and passing automobiles, and live musicians may start up at any time, on plazas, in buses or the Mexico City metro. These performers are playing for a living and range from marimba (wooden xylophone) teams and mariachi bands (trumpeters, violinists, guitarists and a singer, all dressed in smart Wild West–style costumes) to ragged lone buskers with out-of-tune guitars. Mariachi music, perhaps the most 'typical' Mexican music, originated in the Guadalajara area but is played nationwide. Marimbas are particularly popular in the southeast and on the Gulf coast.

Art Books

The Art of Mesoamerica by Mary Ellen Miller

Mexican Muralists by Desmond Rochfort

Mexicolor by Tony Cohan & Masako Takahashi

Rock & Hip-Hop

Mexico can claim to be the most important hub of *rock en español*. Talented Mexico City bands such as Café Tacuba and Maldita Vecindad emerged in the 1990s and took the genre to new heights and new audiences (well beyond Mexico), mixing influences from rock, hip-hop and ska to traditional Mexican folk music. They're still popular and active today, as is the Monterrey rap-metal band Molotov, who upsets just about everyone with their expletive-laced lyrics. Mexico's 21st-century indie rock wave threw up successful bands such as Zoé from Mexico City, who are popular throughout the Spanish-speaking world, and Monterrey's Kinky. The Mexico City five-piece Little Jesus are on the rise with their catchy, dancey brand of pop-rock; their first album was *Norte* (2013).

Mexican rap is the true sound of the streets, and top homegrown talents include Eptos One (or Eptos Uno), from Ciudad Obregón (Sonora), C Kan from Guadalajara, and Monterrey's Cartel de Santa.

Powerful, colorful Alejandra Guzmán is known as La Reina del Rock (Queen of Rock) and has sold 10 million albums in a two-decade career.

The Mexican rock band most famous outside Mexico is undoubtedly Guadalajara's unashamedly commercial Maná.

Pop

Paulina Rubio is Mexico's answer to Shakira. She has also starred in several Mexican films and TV series, and lately turned to judging for TV talent shows. Natalia Lafourcade, a talented singer-songwriter who mixes pop and bossa nova rhythms, won Record of the Year and several other 2015 Latin Grammies with her album *Hasta La Raíz*. Another versatile singer-songwriter and diva of the pop world is Julieta Venegas from Tijuana, best known for her 2007 album, *Limón y Sal*.

Balladeer Luis Miguel is Mexico's Julio Iglesias and incredibly popular, as is Juan Gabriel, who has sold millions of his own albums and written dozens of hit songs for others.

Ranchera & Norteño – Mexico's 'Country Music'

Ranchera is Mexico's urban 'country music' – mostly melodramatic stuff with a nostalgia for rural roots, sometimes with a mariachi backing. The hugely popular Vicente Fernández, Juan Gabriel and Alejandro Fernández (Vicente's son) are leading artists.

Norteño or *norteña* is country ballad and dance music, originating in northern Mexico over a century ago and now nationwide in popularity. Its roots are in *corridos,* heroic ballads with the rhythms of European dances such as waltz or polka. Originally the songs were tales of Latino-Anglo strife in the borderlands or themes from the Mexican Revolution. Modern *narcocorridos* tell of the adventures and exploits of people involved in the drugs trade. Some gangs even commission *narcocorridos* about themselves.

Norteño groups *(conjuntos)* go for 10-gallon hats, with instruments centered on the accordion and the *bajo sexto* (a 12-string guitar), along with bass and drums. *Norteño's* superstars are Los Tigres del Norte, originally from Sinaloa but now based in California. They play to huge audiences on both sides of the frontier, with some *narcocorridos* in their repertoire. Other top stars include Los Huracanes del Norte, Los Tucanes de Tijuana and accordionist/vocalist Ramón Ayala.

Also very popular, especially in the northwest and along the Pacific coast, is *banda* – Mexican big-band music, with large brass sections replacing *norteño* guitars and accordion, and playing a range of styles from *ranchera* and *corridos* to tropical *cumbia* and Mexican pop. Sinaloa's Banda El Recodo have been at the top of the *banda* tree for decades.

Son – Mexico's Folk Roots

Son (literally 'sound') is a broad term covering Mexican country styles that grew out of the fusion of Spanish, indigenous and African music. Guitars or similar instruments (such as the small *jarana*) lay down a strong rhythm, with harp or violin providing the melody. *Son* is often played for a foot-stomping dance audience, with witty, sometimes improvised, lyrics. There are several regional variants. The exciting *son jarocho,* from the Veracruz area, is particularly African-influenced: Grupo Mono Blanco have led a revival of the genre with contemporary lyrics. The famous 'La

THE ARTS MUSIC

Vive Latino (www. vivelatino.com. mx), a festival held over a weekend in March or April at Mexico City's Foro Sol, is one of the world's major annual *rock en español* events. Big electronica events with top Mexican or international DJs are frequent in or around the big cities: www.facebook. com/kinetik. tv and http:// trance-it.net/ proximos-eventos have details.

LILA DOWNS

Singer Lila Downs is rapidly gaining international popularity with her passionate and original versions of Mexican folk songs, often with a jazz influence. If you saw the 2002 movie *Frida*, you heard Lila on the soundtrack. Her best albums include *La sandunga* (1997), *Border* (*La línea*; 2001) and *Pecados y milagros* (2011).

Bamba' is a *son jarocho*. *Son huasteco* (or *huapango*), from the Huasteca area in northeastern Mexico, features falsetto vocals between soaring violin passages. Listen out for top group Los Camperos de Valles.

Trova

Mexconnect (www.mexconnect.com) features a wealth of articles and links on Mexican arts.

This popular genre of troubadour-type folk music, typically performed by solo singer-songwriters *(cantautores)* with a guitar, has roots in 1960s and '70s folk and protest songs. Many *trova* singers are strongly inspired by Cuban political musician Silvio Rodríguez.

Cinema

The historical golden age of Mexican movie-making was the 1940s, when the country was creating up to 200 films a year – typically epic, melodramatic productions. The four big stars were Dolores del Río, María Félix, Mario Moreno ('Cantinflas') and Pedro Infante. Then Hollywood reasserted itself, and Mexican filmmakers struggled for funding for decades. Today Mexico has the world's fifth-biggest cinema audience, but the great majority of box-office takings are still for US-made films.

The good news is that Mexican cinema has made quite a comeback since the start of the 21st century. A clutch of fine, gritty movies by young Mexican directors has won commercial success as well as critical acclaim; government support for the film industry has climbed; the number of Mexican productions has risen to over 100 a year; and several places including Morelia, Guadalajara, Oaxaca, Monterrey, Los Cabos and the Riviera Maya now stage successful annual film festivals.

Nuevo Cine Mexicano (New Mexican Cinema) confronts the ugly, tragic and absurd in Mexican life, as well as the beautiful and comical. The first to really catch the world's eye was *Amores perros* (Love's a Bitch; 2000), directed by Alejandro González Iñárritu and starring Gael García Bernal, who have since both become international celebrities. Set in contemporary Mexico City, with three plots connected by one traffic accident, it's a raw, honest movie with its quota of blood, violence and sex as well as ironic humor.

Y tu mamá también (And Your Mother Too), Alfonso Cuarón's 2001 'growing up' road movie about two privileged Mexico City teenagers (Gael García Bernal and Diego Luna), was at the time the biggest grossing Mexican film ever, netting more than US$25 million. Carlos Carrera's

MÚSICA TROPICAL

Although their origins lie in the Caribbean and South America, several brands of percussion-heavy, infectiously rhythmic *música tropical* are highly popular throughout the country. Mexico City, in particular, has clubs and large dance halls devoted to this scene, often hosting international bands.

Two kinds of dance music – *danzón,* originally from Cuba, and *cumbia,* from Colombia – both took deeper root in Mexico than in their original homelands. The elegant, old-fashioned *danzón* is strongly associated with the port city of Veracruz but is currently enjoying quite a revival in Mexico City and elsewhere too. The livelier, more flirtatious *cumbia* has its adopted home in Mexico City. It rests on thumping bass lines with brass, guitars, mandolins and sometimes marimbas. *Cumbia* has spawned its own subvarieties: *cumbia sonidera* is basically electronic *cumbia* played by DJs, while 'psychedelic *cumbia*' harks back to Peruvian *cumbia* of the 1970s.

Almost every town in Mexico has some place where you can dance (and often learn) salsa, which originated in New York when jazz met *son,* cha-cha and rumba from Cuba and Puerto Rico. Musically, salsa boils down to brass (with trumpet solos), piano, percussion, singer and chorus – the dance is a hot one with a lot of exciting turns. *Merengue,* mainly from the Dominican Republic, is a blend of *cumbia* and salsa.

El crimen del Padre Amaro (The Crime of Father Amaro; 2003), again starring Gael García Bernal, painted an ugly picture of church corruption in a small town.

Success has spirited some of these talents away from Mexico. González Iñárritu moved to Hollywood to direct two more great movies with interconnected multiple plots and a theme of death – *21 Grams* (2003) and *Babel* (2006). He followed up with *Biutiful* (2010), a stunning Mexican-Spanish production starring Javier Bardem in a harrowing 'down and out in Barcelona' tale, then scooped four Oscars, including Best Picture and Best Director, with *Birdman* (2014), the brilliantly crafted story of an aging Hollywood superhero (Michael Keaton) trying to revive his career on Broadway. Alfonso Cuarón moved on to *Harry Potter and the Prisoner of Azkaban* (2004) and the multi-Oscar-winning (including Best Director) science-fiction epic *Gravity* (2013). It was little surprise that the cinematographer behind both *Birdman* and *Gravity* – winning Oscars for both – was another Mexican, Emmanuel Lubezki. Meanwhile González Iñárritu's and Cuarón's friend Guillermo del Toro (the three are known as the Three Amigos) has scored success with varied films including the triple-Oscar *Pan's Labyrinth* (2006) and the 2013 sci-fi monster movie *Pacific Rim*.

Meanwhile, homegrown Mexican films have been raking in awards at Cannes and other festivals. Carlos Reygadas took Cannes' 2012 Best Director award for *Post tenebras lux*, a confusing mix of fantasy and reality about a middle-class family living in the countryside. Amat Escalante was Cannes' 2013 best director with *Heli*, the story of a young couple caught in Mexico's violent drug wars. Another acclaimed 2013 movie was Diego Quemada-Diez's *La jaula de oro* (The Golden Cage), about young Central American migrants trying to get to the USA through Mexico. Migrants, this time Mexican, also take center stage in the 2015 thriller *Desierto*, starring Gael García Bernal and directed by Alfonso Cuarón's son Jonas.

Also in the 2015 crop, Gabriel Ripstein's arms-smuggling thriller *600 Miles*, starring Tim Roth as a kidnapped US law-enforcement agent, was garlanded at the Berlin and Guadalajara festivals, and became Mexico's candidate for the 2016 Best Foreign Language Film Oscar. Tim Roth featured again, now as a male nurse for terminally ill patients, in the moving *Chronic*, directed and written by Mexican Michel Franco and named best screenplay at Cannes in 2015. Another 2015 release, *Los jefes*, digs into the brutal reality of the narco world in Monterrey, an added curiosity being that its lead roles are played by rap musicians Cartel de Santa.

On a more commercial note, Gary Alazraki's comical 2013 film addressing Mexican class divisions, *Nosotros los nobles* (We the Nobles), became the all-time biggest-grossing Mexican film in Mexican cinemas, with 3.3 million viewers. The first Mexican 3D horror movie, *Más negro que la noche* (Darker than the Night) directed by Henry Bedwell (2014), also did well, both at the box office and with critics.

Literature

Mexicans such as Carlos Fuentes, Juan Rulfo and Octavio Paz have written some of the great Spanish-language literature.

Fuentes (1928–2012), a prolific novelist and commentator, is probably Mexico's best-known writer internationally. His most famous novel, *The Death of Artemio Cruz* (1962), takes a critical look at Mexico's post-revolutionary era through the eyes of a dying, corrupted press baron and landowner. Less known is the magical-realist *Aura* (1962), with a truly stunning ending.

In Mexico, Juan Rulfo (1918–86) is widely regarded as the supreme novelist, even though he only ever published one full-length novel: *Pedro*

Frida & Diego Books

Frida Kahlo and Diego Rivera by Isabel Alcántara and Sandra Egnolff

The Diary of Frida Kahlo (with introduction by Carlos Fuentes)

Frida by Hayden Herrera

Rivera by Andrea Kettenmann

Mexico in Others' Words

The Power and the Glory by Graham Greene

Under the Volcano by Malcolm Lowry

The Treasure of the Sierra Madre and *The Rebellion of the Hanged* by B Traven

Queer by William Burroughs

On the Road by Jack Kerouac

All the Pretty Horses by Cormac McCarthy

Páramo (1955), about a young man's search for his lost father among ghostlike villages in western Mexico. It's a scary, desolate work with confusing shifts of time – a kind of Mexican *Wuthering Heights* with a spooky, magical-realist twist.

Octavio Paz (1914–98), poet, essayist and winner of the 1990 Nobel Prize for Literature, wrote a probing, intellectually acrobatic analysis of Mexico's myths and the national character in *The Labyrinth of Solitude* (1950).

The 1960s-born novelists of the *movimiento crack* take their name from the sound of a limb falling off a tree, representing their desire to break with the past and move on from magical realism. Their work tends to adopt global themes and international settings. Best known is Jorge Volpi, whose *In Search of Klingsor* (1999) and *Season of Ash* (2009) weave complicated but exciting plots involving science, love, murder, mysteries and more, with a strong relevance to the state of the world today.

The *crack* seemed to open the way for a new generation of novelists who are right now putting Mexico back in the vanguard of world literature. These are typically superimaginative, impossible-to-classify writers whose multilayered works leap around between different times, places, voices and perspectives. Valeria Luiselli's *Faces in the Crowd* (2012) and *The Story of My Teeth* (2015) are, on the surface, respectively about a woman writing a novel and a man who replaces his own teeth with (supposedly) Marilyn Monroe's. Then there's Álvaro Enrigue with *Sudden Death* (2013), a novel of vast scope set among the many world-changing events of the 16th century in Europe and the Americas, and Yuri Herrera, whose *Signs Preceding the End of the World* (2009) illluminates small-town and big-city Mexico, the Mexico–US border and the US itself through a young woman sent to retrieve her brother from across the border. Carmen Boullosa's 17 novels range from *They're Cows, We're Pigs* (1991), examining the world of 17th-century Caribbean pirates, to *Texas, the Great Theft* (2014), a reimagining of the Tex-Mex borderlands in the 19th century.

The 'yarn paintings' of the indigenous Huichol people – created by pressing strands of yarn onto a wax-covered board – depict scenes resembling visions experienced under the influence of the drug *peyote,* which is central to Huichol culture.

Folk Art

Mexicans' skill with their hands and their love of color, fun and tradition find expression everywhere in their wonderful *artesanías* (handicrafts). Crafts such as weaving, pottery, leatherwork, copperwork, hat-making and basketry still fulfill key functions in daily life as well as yielding souvenirs and collectibles. Many craft techniques and designs in use today have pre-Hispanic origins, and it's Mexico's indigenous peoples, the direct inheritors of pre-Hispanic culture, who lead the way in *artesanías* production.

Traditional Textiles

In some of Mexico's indigenous villages you'll be stunned by the variety of colorful, intricately decorated attire, differing from area to area and often from village to village. Traditional costume – more widely worn by women than men – serves as a mark of the community to which a person belongs. The woven or embroidered patterns of some garments can take months to complete.

Three main types of women's garments have been in use since long before the Spanish conquest:

Huipil A long, sleeveless tunic, found mainly in the southern half of the country.
Quechquémitl A shoulder cape with an opening for the head, found mainly in central and northern Mexico.
Enredo A wraparound skirt.

Spanish missionaries introduced blouses, now often also embroidered with great care and detail.

The primary materials of indigenous weaving are cotton and wool, though synthetic fibers are also common. Natural dyes have been revived – deep blues from the indigo plant, reds and browns from various woods, and reds and purples from the cochineal insect.

The basic indigenous weavers' tool, used only by women, is the backstrap loom *(telar de cintura)* on which the warp (long) threads are stretched between two horizontal bars, one of which is fixed to a post or tree, while the other is attached to a strap around the weaver's lower back; the weft (cross) threads are then intricately woven in, producing some amazing patterns. Backstrap-loom *huipiles* from the southern states of Oaxaca and Chiapas are among Mexico's most eye-catching garments.

Treadle looms, operated by foot pedals (usually by men) can weave wider cloth than the backstrap loom and tend to be used for rugs, *rebozos* (shawls), *sarapes* (blankets with an opening for the head) and skirt material. Mexico's most famous rug-weaving village is Teotitlán del Valle, Oaxaca.

Ceramics

Many small-scale potters' workshops turn out everything from plain cooking pots to elaborate works of art. One highly attractive pottery variety is Talavera, made chiefly in Puebla and Dolores Hidalgo and characterized by bright colors (blue and yellow are prominent) and floral designs. The Guadalajara suburbs of Tonalá and Tlaquepaque produce a wide variety of ceramics. In northern Mexico, the villagers of Mata Ortiz make a range of beautiful earthenware, drawing on the techniques and designs of pre-Hispanic Paquimé, similar to some native American pottery in the US southwest. Another distinctive Mexican ceramic form is the *árbol de la vida* (tree of life). These elaborate, candelabra-like objects are molded by hand and decorated with numerous tiny figures of people, animals, plants and so on. Some of the best are made in Metepec in the state of México, which is also the source of colorful clay suns.

Masks

For millennia Mexicans have worn masks in dances, ceremonies and shamanistic rites: the wearer temporarily becomes the creature, person or deity represented by the mask. You can admire mask artistry at museums in cities such as San Luis Potosí, Zacatecas and Colima, and at shops and markets around the country. The southern state of Guerrero makes probably the broadest range of fine masks.

Wood is the basic material of most masks, but papier-mâché, clay, wax and leather are also used. Mask-makers often paint or embellish their masks with real teeth, hair, feathers or other adornments. Common masks include animals, birds, Christ, devils, and Europeans with comically pale, wide-eyed features.

Lacquerware & Woodwork

Gourds, the hard shells of certain squash-type fruits, have been used in Mexico since antiquity as bowls, cups and small storage vessels. The most eye-catching decoration technique is lacquering, in which the gourd is coated with paste or paint and then varnished, producing a nonporous and, to some extent, heat-resistant, vessel. Lacquering is also used to decorate wooden boxes, trays and furniture, with a lot of the most appealing ware coming from remote Olinalá in Guerrero, where artisans create patterns using the *rayado* method of scraping off part of the top coat of paint to expose a different-colored layer below.

The Seri people of Sonora work hard ironwood into dramatic human, animal and sea-creature shapes. Villagers around Oaxaca city produce brightly painted imaginary beasts carved from copal wood, known as *alebrijes*.

THE ARTS FOLK ART

Crafts Books

The Crafts of Mexico by Margarita de Orellana and Alberto Ruy Sánchez

Arts and Crafts of Mexico by Chloë Sayer

Mexican Textiles by Masako Takahashi

Diamond shapes on some *huipiles* from San Andrés Larrainzar, in Chiapas, represent the universe of the villagers' Maya ancestors, who believed the earth was a cube and the sky had four corners.

The Mexican Kitchen

In Mexico, we love food, especially our own. Ask a group of Mexicans where to find, say, the best *carnitas* (braised pork) in Mexico City, and you're launching a passionate, well-informed, lengthy debate. Visiting Mexico, you'll find out why. The food will be fresh, often locally grown, and enormously varied from one place to another, a far cry from the 'Mexican' fare served in restaurants outside the country. If you want to know Mexico and its people, you must try our food.

This chapter was written by Mauricio Velázquez de León. Born in Mexico City, his food writing has been published in Mexico and the US. He is the author (under the name Puck) of *My Foodie ABC: A Little Gourmet's Guide* (duopress, 2010). Additional research by Kate Armstrong.

What's on the Menu?

A Mexican menu will vary with the region you are visiting, but in most cases you can find food that is made with a few staples: corn, dry and fresh chilies, and beans. Contrary to popular belief, not all food in Mexico is spicy. Chilies are used as a flavoring for ingredients and to provide intensity in sauces, *moles* and *pipiáns,* and many appreciate their depth over their piquancy. But beware, some dishes do indeed have a kick, sometimes reaching daredevil levels. The *habanero* chili in the Yucatán is the world's spiciest pepper, and the *chile de árbol* can be fierce. A good rule of thumb is that when chilies are cooked and incorporated into the dishes as sauces they tend to be on the mild side, but when they are prepared for salsas (relishes or sauces) they can be really hot.

There are other staples that give Mexican food its classic flavoring. Among them are spices such as cinnamon, clove and cumin, and herbs such as thyme, oregano and, most importantly, cilantro (coriander) and *epazote.* A pungent-smelling herb (called pigweed or Jerusalem oak in the US), *epazote* may be the unsung hero of Mexican cooking and used for flavoring beans, soups, stews and certain *moles.*

Eating as a Whim

Antojitos are at the center of Mexican cooking. The word *antojo* translates as 'a whim, a sudden craving,' so an *antojito* is a little whim, but as any Mexican will quickly point out, it is not merely a snack. An *antojito* can be an entire meal, an appetizer, or a *tentempíe* (quick bite).

Markets are perfect places to munch on some really good *antojitos.* In the gargantuan **Mercado de la Merced in Mexico City** (cnr Anillo de Circunvalación & General Anaya; ⊙8am-7pm; ⓊMerced) the best *antojito* may be the *huarache,* a 30cm-long tortilla shaped like the shoe for which it is named, grilled and topped with salsa, onions, cheese and a choice of *chorizo* sausage, steak, squash blossoms and more. A competitor to the *huarache* can be found in the markets of Oaxaca city, where large flat tortillas called *tlayudas* are spread with refried beans and topped with Oaxacan string cheese, salsa and pork strips.

American award-winning chef and Mexican food expert Rick Bayless has a great way to define *antojitos* by grouping them according to the one component present in all: corn *masa* (dough). There are eight types of *antojitos*:

➡ **Tacos** The quintessential culinary fare in Mexico can be made of any cooked meat, fish or vegetable wrapped in a tortilla, with a dash of salsa and garnished with onion and cilantro. Soft corn tortillas are used to wrap grilled meats in *tacos al carbón*, an array of stews in *tacos de guisado*, or with griddle-cooked meats and vegetables in *tacos a la plancha*. When tacos are lightly fried they are called *tacos dorados*. If you are in northern Mexico, chances are you will find tacos with flour tortillas *(tortillas de harina)* and the fillings will be more meat-based than vegetarian.

➡ **Quesadillas** Fold a tortilla with cheese, heat it on a griddle and you have a quesadilla. (*Queso* means cheese, hence the name.) But real quesadillas are much more than that. In restaurants and street stalls quesadillas are stuffed pockets made with raw corn *masa* that is lightly fried or griddled until crisp. They can be stuffed with *chorizo* and cheese, squash blossoms, mushrooms with garlic, *chicharrón* (fried pork fat), beans, stewed chicken or meat.

➡ **Enchiladas** In Spanish 'enchilar' means to put chili over something, so enchiladas are a group of three or four lightly fried tortillas filled with chicken, cheese or eggs and covered with a cooked salsa. Enchiladas are usually a main dish, and can also be baked, like the famous *enchiladas suizas* (Swiss-style enchiladas).

➡ **Tostadas** Tortillas that have been baked or fried until they get crisp and are then cooled. In this state they can hold a variety of toppings. *Tostadas de pollo* are a beautiful layering of beans, chicken, cream, shredded lettuce, onion, avocado and *queso fresco* (a fresh cheese).

➡ **Sopes** Small *masa* shells, 5cm to 7.5cm in diameter, that are shaped by hand and cooked on a griddle with a thin layer of beans, salsa and cheese. *Chorizo* is also a common topping for *sopes*.

➡ **Gorditas** Round *masa* cakes that are baked until they puff. Sometimes *gorditas* are filled with a thin layer of fried black or pinto beans, or even fava beans.

➡ **Chilaquiles** Typically served as breakfast. Corn tortillas are cut in triangles and fried until crispy. At this point they are indeed tortilla chips *(totopos)*. When cooked in a tomatillo sauce (for *chilaquiles verdes*) or tomato sauce *(chilaquiles rojos)* they become soft and then are topped with shredded cheese, sliced onions and Mexican crema.

➡ **Tamales** Made with *masa* mixed with lard, stuffed with stewed meat, fish or vegetables, wrapped and steamed. Every Mexican region has its own, the most famous being the Oaxacan-style *tamales* with *mole* and wrapped in banana leaves, the Mexico City *tamales* with chicken and green tomatillo sauce wrapped in corn husks, and the Yucatecan style, made with chicken marinated in *achiote* (annatto paste) and wrapped in banana leaves.

Top Mexican Cookbooks

Authentic Mexican, 20th Anniversary Edition: Regional Cooking from the Heart of Mexico by Rick Bayless

The Essential Cuisines of Mexico by Diana Kennedy

The Food and Life of Oaxaca: Traditional Recipes from Mexico's Heart by Zarela Martínez

THE MEXICAN KITCHEN EATING AS A WHIM

MULLI (MOLE)

Mexican chef and author Zarela Martínez once told me that in *mole* the sauce is the dish. What she meant was that when we eat *mole* we eat it because we want the sauce. The meat – whether it be chicken, turkey or pork – plays a secondary role. A complex sauce made with nuts, chilies and spices, *mole* defines Mexican cuisine. Although *mole* is often called chocolate sauce, only a very small percentage of *moles* include this ingredient. The confusion is understandable since the recipe for *mole poblano* (*mole* from the state of Puebla), the most widely known *mole* in the country, includes a small amount of chocolate. But most Mexicans would agree that when it comes to *mole*, Oaxaca is the place to go. It's known as 'The Land of Seven Moles' (p436).

832

THE MEXICAN KITCHEN A DAY OF EATING: FROM SUNRISE TO SUNSET & BEYOND!

A Day of Eating:
From Sunrise to Sunset & Beyond!

It's easy to find a place to eat in Mexico. From an early *antojito* at a small *puesto* (street or market stall) to a lavish late dinner at a fine restaurant, food is always available.

→ Desayuno (breakfast) Usually served in restaurants and *cafeterías* from 8:30am to 11am; it tends to be on the heavy side. Egg dishes are popular morning fare. *Huevos rancheros*, two fried eggs atop lightly fried tortillas with a layer of black beans and topped with a tomato, onion and chili salsa, are widely served. In the Yucatán region, you will find *huevos motuleños*, a similar preparation that also includes diced ham, peas and plantains. Many *cafeterías* offer an array of *pan de dulce* (sweet breads) with amusing names such as *bigotes* (mustaches), *conchas* (shells), *besos* (kisses) and *orejas* (ears).

→ Almuerzo Those who have a light breakfast or skip it altogether can have an *almuerzo* (a mid-morning snack) or an *antojito* or other quick bite. *Taquerías* (places specializing in tacos), *torterías* (small establishments selling *tortas*) and *loncherías* (places that serve light meals) are good options for *almuerzo*.

→ Comida This is the main meal in Mexico. It is usually served from 2pm to 4:30pm in homes, restaurants and cafes. Places called *fondas* are small, family-run eateries that serve *comida corrida,* an inexpensive fixed-price menu that includes soup, rice, a main dish, beverage and dessert. In many big cities it's common to see people enjoying long business lunches or friend gatherings where food, conversation and drinks mingle for a couple of hours. Popular *comida* fares are soups, such as *sopa de fideo* (vermicelli noodles in a soupy tomato broth), or *sopa de frijol* (bean soup), while main dishes include *guisados* (stews), such as slowed-braised meats and vegetables in cooked chipotle, tomatillo or tomato salsas.

→ Cena Frequently dinner is not served until 9pm and it is usually light when eaten at home. In restaurants, however, dinner is often a social gathering where eaters share a complete meal that can last until midnight.

→ And... When people go to a bar, a club or a late movie, they often stop off for a quick taco before returning home. Many famous *taquerías* cater to hungry insomniacs and don't close until the wee hours. On Fridays and Saturdays so many customers visit these places that sometimes you have to wait for a table at 3am!

Under the Jaguar Sun by Italian writer Italo Calvino is a compelling account of a husband and wife discovering Mexico and its cuisine. The couple in the story becomes so enamored of the cuisine that their passion is transferred from the bedroom to the dining table.

THE NEW BREED OF CHEFS

The typical Mexican kitchen is very much a matriarchal place, where the country's culinary traditions are preserved and practiced year in, year out. But it's mostly males who are garnering celebrity status from the new wave of creative contemporary restaurants that meld the traditional and the innovative in ingredients and recipes with a flair for presentation. Mexico City is the epicenter of this movement and Enrique Olvera of the famed **Pujol** (p115) is often considered the father of new Mexican cuisine. He has been mentor to other leading lights in the capital like Eduardo García of **Maximo Bistrot Local** (p115). Ricardo Muñoz is famed for his reinventions of traditional recipes at **Azul y Oro** (p116), while Monica Patiño of **Taberna del León** (p116) and Elena Reygadas of Rosetta (Mexico City) keep the flag flying for women. Benito Molina of Manzanilla in Baja California and Pablo Salas of Amaranta (Toluca) are known for their progressive cuisine. Chefs such as Alejandro Ruiz at **Casa Oaxaca** (p437) and Diego Hernández Baquedano at **Corazón de Tierra** (p706) in Baja California's Valle de Guadalupe wine region, are spreading the word to the regions.

VEGETARIANS & VEGANS

In many parts of Mexico, 'vegetarian' is not a word in the local lexicon. Many Mexicans think of a vegetarian as a person who doesn't eat meat, but by 'meat' they mean red meat, not chicken or fish. Many more have never even heard the word *veganista* (vegan). The good news is that almost every city, large or small, has real vegetarian restaurants, and their popularity is increasing. Also, many traditional Mexican dishes are vegetarian: *ensalada de nopales* (cactus-leaf salad); quesadillas made with mushrooms, cheeses and even flowers such as zucchini flowers; *chiles rellenos de queso* (cheese-stuffed poblano chilies); and *arroz a la mexicana* (Mexican-style rice). Be warned, however, that many dishes are prepared using chicken or beef broth, or some kind of animal fat, such as *manteca* (lard).

Have You Heard the Word 'Fiesta'?

Food and fiestas go hand-to-hand in Mexico. They can be national holidays, religious festivals, local fiestas or personal celebrations, but chances are you will get caught in one of them during your visit. During national holidays food's always present, but toasting with tequila is a prerequisite, especially during Día de la Independencia (September 16), which celebrates independence from Spain. The largest religious festivity is the Día de Nuestra Señora de Guadalupe (December 12), where *tamales, mole* and an array of *antojitos* are traditional fare. During Lent, meatless dishes such as *romeritos* (a wild plant that resembles rosemary served with dried shrimp, potatoes and *mole*) show up on most menus. On the Día de los Santos Reyes (Three Kings Day; January 6) we celebrate by eating *rosca de reyes,* a large oval sweetbread decorated with candied fruit. The *rosca* is served with corn *tamales* and hot chocolate. During Christmas, a traditional Mexican menu includes turkey, *bacalao* (dry codfish cooked with olives, capers, onions and tomatoes) and *romeritos.*

There is no celebration in Mexico with more mystique than Día de Muertos (Day of the Dead; November 2). Its origins date to pre-Hispanic times and it commemorates lost relatives and loved ones. By celebrating death we salute life and we do it the way we celebrate everything else, with food, drinks and music. An altar to death is set up in a house, or, as some families prefer, in the graveyard. It is decorated with bright *cempasuchil* (marigold) flowers, plates of *tamales,* sugar-shaped skulls and *pan de muerto* (bread of the dead; a loaf made with egg yolks, mezcal and dried fruits), and the favorite foods of the deceased are laid out so that they feel welcomed upon their return.

¡Salud!

Tequila

In Mexico we love tequila. We drink it on large and small national holidays, at funerals and anniversaries, at casual lunches, and at dinner and in bars with friends. Legally, tequila is our champagne. All tequila has to come from the state of Jalisco and is protected with a Designation of Origin (DO) by the Consejo Regulador del Tequila (Tequila Regulatory Council). This organization ensures that all tequila sold throughout the world comes from this state in western Mexico. This arid area with highland soil creates the perfect conditions for the blue agave, the plant from which tequila is distilled, to grow. No tequila made in China (or elsewhere), *por favor*. We drink it because we are proud of its Mexican provenance, and because we really like its taste.

Taste is a key word when it comes to tequila. Tequila has become more and more sophisticated and today is considered a refined drink that

English sailors coined the term 'cocktail' upon discovering that their drinks in the Yucatán port of Campeche were stirred with the thin, dried roots of a plant called *cola de gallo,* which translates as 'cock's tail.'

Josefina Velázquez de León is considered the mother of Mexican cuisine. She ran a successful culinary school and wrote more than 140 cookbooks, the most ambitious being *Platillos regionales de la República Mexicana*, considered to be the first book to collect Mexico's regional cuisine in one volume.

rivals an imported single-malt whiskey or a quality cognac, and not only in price but in its smooth, warm taste. Today's finest tequilas are meant to be enjoyed in a small glass, with pleasure, in tiny sips.

The process of making tequila starts by removing the *piña* (heart) of the blue agave plant. This *piña* is then steamed for up to 36 hours, a process that softens the fibers and releases the *aguamiel* (honey water). This liquid is funneled into large tanks where it is fermented. Fermentation determines whether the final product will be 100% agave or *mixto* (mixed). The highest-quality tequila is made from fermenting and then distilling only *aguamiel* mixed with some water. In tequilas *mixtos*, the *aguamiel* is mixed with other sugars, usually cane sugar with water. When tequila is 100% agave it will say so on the label. If it doesn't say 100%, it is a *mixto*.

The next step in the tequila-making process is to distill the *aguamiel* and store it in barrels for aging. The aging is important, especially for today's fancier tequilas, because it determines the color, taste, quality and price. Silver or *blanco* (white) is clear and is aged for no more than 60 days. Tequila *blanco* is used primarily for mixing and blends particularly well into fruit-based drinks. Tequila *reposado* (rested) is aged from two to nine months. It has a smooth taste and light gold color. Tequila *añejo* (old) is aged in wooden barrels for a minimum of 12 months. The best-quality *añejos* are aged up to four years. Tequila *añejo* has a velvety flavor and a deep, dark color. These three kinds of tequilas are equally popular in Mexico, and it is entirely a matter of personal taste that determines which one to drink.

Mezcal

Mezcal is tequila's brother and it is currently experiencing a boom with people who believe tequila has gone too mainstream (and expensive!). *Mezcalerías* (bars specializing in mezcal) are a recent trend, especially in cities. Like tequila, mezcal is distilled from agave plants, but mezcal doesn't have to come from blue agave, or from the tequila-producing areas of Jalisco. In other words, all tequila is mezcal, but not all mezcal is tequila. Since mezcal can be made with any type of agave plant, it can also be produced throughout the country, where it's sometimes known by other names, such as *bacanora* in Sonora state or *sotol* in Chihuahua.

Pulque

If tequila and mezcal are brothers, then *pulque* would be the father of Mexican spirits. Two thousand years ago ancient Mexicans started to extract the juice of agave plants to produce a milky, slightly alcoholic drink that the Aztecs called *octli poliqhui*. When the Spanish arrived in Mexico they started to call the drink *pulque*. Even though *pulque* has a lower alcohol content than tequila or mezcal, it is much harder on the palate. Because it is not distilled, it retains an earthy, vegetal taste and has a thick, foamy consistency that some people find unpleasant. In some places it is mixed with fruit juices, such as mango or strawberry, to make it more palatable. When *pulque* is mixed with juices it is called *curado*.

Micheladas are prepared chilled beers ranging from simple drinks to complex cocktails. The basic *michelada* is a mix of the juice of one or two key limes in a chilled mug, a few ice cubes, a dash of salt and a Mexican cold beer. They are often served with a few drops of hot sauce, Worcestershire sauce and Maggi seasoning.

Beer

For some visitors, '*Una cerveza, por favor*' is their most commonly used Spanish phrase while in Mexico. This makes sense. Mexican *cerveza* is big, and it's a great match with, well, Mexican food! Most Mexican brands are light and quench beautifully the spiciness of a plate of enchiladas. Beers are also a great companion for the thousands of *fútbol* matches that we follow in this country with religious zeal.

Two major breweries dominate the Mexican market. Grupo Modelo, now owned by Belgium-based AB InBev, makes around 18 brands,

CANTINAS

Cantinas are the traditional Mexican watering holes. Until not long ago, women, military personnel and children were not allowed in cantinas, and some cantinas still have a rusted sign stating this rule. Today, everybody is allowed, although the more traditional establishments retain a macho edge. Beer, tequila and *cubas* (rum and coke) are served at square tables where patrons play dominos and watch *fútbol* (soccer) games on large TV screens. Cantinas are famous for serving *botanas* (appetizers) such as *quesadillas de papa con guacamole* (potato quesadillas with guacamole) or snails in chipotle sauce.

among them Corona, Victoria, Modelo Especial, Pacífico, Montejo and Negra Modelo. Although Corona is one of the world's best-selling beers, beer aficionados regard Negra Modelo, a darker beer, as the brewery's jewel. In the industrial city of Monterrey, Cervecería Cuauhtémoc Moctezuma (now a subsidiary of Heineken International) produces Sol, Carta Blanca, Dos Equis, Superior, Tecate and Bohemia, among others. The original early-20th-century version of Dos Equis, the darker and fuller-bodied Dos Equis Ámbar, is enjoying a resurgence in popularity today. Recently, however, microbrews *(cervezas artesanales)*, have hit the beer scene; many are increasingly offered in the better restaurants and **bars** (p24). The array of Mexican beer allows for drinking them in many different environments. A day on the beach calls for a Corona, a Superior or a Pacífico. Victoria and Montejo are good matches for seafood; Modelo Especial and Carta Blanca go really well with meat; and a Bohemia or Negra Modelo would pair perfectly with a very good, decadent dinner.

Wine

Now may be the right time to expand your Spanish vocabulary to include *'Una copa de vino, por favor.'* Although the wine industry is still much smaller than that of tequila or beer, Mexican wines are leaping forward at a great rate. Since the 1990s, challenged in part by the success of Californian, Chilean and Argentinean wines, Mexican producers began yielding good wines in nine regions, from Querétaro to Sonora, with the best coming from Valle de Guadalupe, in the north of Baja California (the area even boasts a wine route). The two larger wineries in Mexico, Pedro Domecq and LA Cetto, offer solid table wines and some premium labels such as Chateau Domecq and Private Reserve Nebbiolo. 'Boutique wineries' with names such as Monte Xanic, Casa de Piedra and Casa Valmar are also producing great wine in smaller quantities.

Nonalcoholic Drinks

The great variety of fruits, plants and herbs that grow in this country are a perfect fit for the kind of nonalcoholic drinks Mexicans love. All over the country you will find classic *juguerías,* street stalls or small establishments selling fresh-squeezed orange, tangerine, strawberry, papaya or carrot juices. These places also sell *licuados,* a Mexican version of a milkshake that normally includes banana, milk, honey and fruit. There are some creative combinations too, with ingredients such as *nopal* (cactus leaves), pineapple, lemon and orange, or vanilla, banana and avocado.

In *taquerías* and *fondas* you will find *aguas frescas,* juices diluted with water and sugar. Some of them resemble iced teas. In *agua de tamarindo*, the tamarind pods are boiled and then mixed with sugar before being chilled, while *agua de jamaica* is made with dried hibiscus leaves. Others such as *horchata* are made with melon seeds and/or rice.

In Tenochtitlán (present-day Mexico City), chocolate was considered the 'drink of the gods' and it was called *tlaquetzalli* (precious thing) in the Náhuatl language. Chocolate was so valued by the Aztecs that the cacao bean, from which chocolate is derived, was also used as a form of currency.

Landscapes & Wildlife

One of the thrills of travel in Mexico is the incredible, ever-changing natural scenery. From the cactus-strewn northern deserts and the snowcapped volcanoes of central Mexico to the tropical forests and wildlife-rich lagoons of the south, there's rarely a dull moment for the eye. Nature lovers will revel in this country which, thanks to its location straddling temperate and tropical regions, is one of the most biologically diverse on earth.

The Land

Nearly two million sq km in area, Mexico is the world's 14th-biggest country. With 10,000km of coastline and half its land above 1000m in elevation, the country has a spectacularly diverse and rugged topography. Almost anywhere you go, except the Yucatán Peninsula, there'll be a range of mountains in sight, close or distant.

In all its 1400km length, the Sierra Madre Occidental is crossed by only one railway and three paved roads: the Ferrocarril Chihuahua Pacífico (Copper Canyon Railway) from Los Mochis to Chihuahua, Hwy 16 (Hermosillo to Chihuahua), and Hwys 40 and 40D (Mazatlán to Durango).

Central Volcanic Belt

The Cordillera Neovolcánica, the spectacular volcanic belt running east–west across the middle of Mexico, includes the classic active cones of Popocatépetl (5452m), 70km southeast of Mexico City, and Volcán de Fuego de Colima (3820m), 30km north of Colima. Some 30 million people live within the area that could be directly affected should smoking 'Popo' erupt in a big way. Also in the volcanic belt, but dormant, are Mexico's highest peak, Pico de Orizaba (5611m; pictured right), and the third-highest peak, Popo's 'sister' Iztaccíhuatl (5220m). Mexico's youngest volcano, and the easiest to get to the top of, is Paricutín (2800m), which popped up in 1943 near the Michoacán village of Angahuan.

The upland valleys between the volcanoes have always been among the most habitable areas of Mexico. It's in one of these – the Valle de México (a 60km-wide basin at 2200m elevation) – that Mexico City, with its 20 million people, sits ringed by volcanic ranges.

Northern Plains & Sierras

A string of broad plateaus, the Altiplano Central, runs down the middle of the northern half of Mexico, fringed by two long mountain chains – the Sierra Madre Occidental in the west and Sierra Madre Oriental in the east. The *altiplano* and the two *sierras madre* end where they run into the Cordillera Neovolcánica.

The *altiplano* is criss-crossed by minor mountain ranges, and rises from an average elevation of about 1000m in the north to more than 2000m toward the center of the country. The sparsely vegetated Desierto Chihuahuense (Chihuahuan Desert) covers most of the northern *altiplano* and extends north into the US states of Texas and New Mexico. The landscape here is one of long-distance vistas across dusty brown plains to distant mountains, with eagles and vultures circling the skies. The southern *altiplano* is mostly rolling hills and broad valleys, and includes some of the best Mexican farming and ranching land in the area known as El Bajío, between the cities of Querétaro, Guanajuato and Morelia.

The extremely rugged Sierra Madre Occidental is fissured by many spectacularly deep canyons, including the famous Barranca del Cobre (Copper Canyon) and its 1870m-deep continuation, the Barranca de Urique.

The Sierra Madre Oriental includes peaks as high as 3700m, but has semitropical zones on its lower, eastern slopes.

Baja California

Baja California, one of the world's longest peninsulas, runs down Mexico's northwest coast. It is believed to have been separated from the 'mainland' about five million years ago by tectonic forces, with the Sea of Cortez (Golfo de California) filling the gap. Baja is 1300km of starkly beautiful deserts, plains and beaches, with a mountainous spine that reaches up to 3100m in the Sierra San Pedro Mártir.

Coastal Plains

Coastal plains stretch all along Mexico's Pacific coast and as far south as the Tabasco lowlands on the Gulf coast. Both coasts are strung with hundreds of lagoons, estuaries and wetlands, making them important wildlife habitats.

On the Pacific side, a dry, wide plain stretches south from the US border almost to Tepic, in Nayarit state. As they continue south to the Guatemalan border, the lowlands narrow to a thin strip and become increasingly tropical.

The Gulf coast plain, an extension of a similar plain in Texas, is crossed by many rivers flowing down from the Sierra Madre Oriental. In the northeast, the plain is wide, with good ranchland, but is semi-marshy near the coast. It narrows as it nears Veracruz.

The South

Yet another rugged, complicated mountain chain, the Sierra Madre del Sur stretches across the states of Guerrero and Oaxaca, roughly paralleling the Cordillera Neovolcánica, from which it's divided by the broiling hot Río Balsas basin. The Sierra Madre del Sur ends at the

Volcano Watch

Monitoreo Volcánico Popocatépetl (www.cenapred. unam.mx:8080/ monitoreo Popocatepetl)

Volcán Colima y Más Volcanes (www.facebook. com/volcancolima)

Webcams de México (www. webcamsdemexico. com)

LANDSCAPES & WILDLIFE THE LAND

Pico de Orizaba (p235)

low-lying, hot and humid Isthmus of Tehuantepec, Mexico's narrow 'waist', which is just 220km wide.

In the southernmost state of Chiapas, the Pacific lowlands are backed by the Sierra Madre de Chiapas. Dormant Volcán Tacaná, whose 4110m cone rises on the Mexico–Guatemala border, is the westernmost of a string of volcanoes that stretch across Guatemala. Behind the Chiapas highlands, the land sinks to the lowlands of the Lacandón Jungle and the flat expanses of the huge limestone shelf that is the Yucatán Peninsula. The Yucatán's soft, easily eroded limestone has led to the formation of many underground rivers and more than 6000 sinkholes, known as cenotes, many of which make fantastic swimming holes. Off the Yucatán's Caribbean coast is the world's second largest barrier reef, known variously as the Great Maya, Mesoamerican or Belize Barrier Reef and home to a fantastic variety of colorful marine life that makes it one of the world's top diving and snorkeling destinations.

Wildlife

From the whales, sea lions and giant cacti of Baja California to the big cats, howler monkeys and cloud forests of the southeast, Mexico's fauna and flora are exotic and fascinating. Getting out among it all is becoming steadily easier as growing numbers of local outfits offer trips to see birds, butterflies, whales, dolphins, sea turtles and more.

Those That Walk

The surviving tropical forests of the southeast are still home to five species of large cat (jaguar, puma, ocelot, jaguarundi and margay) in isolated pockets, plus spider and howler monkeys, tapirs, anteaters and some mean reptiles, including a few boa constrictors. Small jaguar populations are scattered as far north as the northern Sierra Madre Occidental, just 200km from the US border, and the Sierra Gorda in the Sierra Madre Oriental. You may well see howler monkeys – or at least hear their eerie growls – near the Maya ruins at Palenque and Yaxchilán.

In the north, urban growth, ranching and agriculture have pushed the larger wild beasts – such as the puma (mountain lion), wolf, bobcat, bighorn sheep, pronghorn and coyote – into isolated, often mountainous pockets. Raccoons, armadillos and skunks are still fairly common – the last two in much of the rest of Mexico too.

In all warm parts of Mexico you'll encounter two harmless, though sometimes surprising, reptiles: the iguana, a lizard that can grow a meter or so long and comes in many different colors; and the gecko, a tiny, usually green lizard that may shoot out from behind a curtain or cupboard when disturbed. Geckos might make you jump, but they're good news – they eat mosquitoes.

Top Turtle Camps

Cuyutlán

Isla Mujeres

Madre Sal, Chiapas

Majahua Biological Station, Costalegre, Jalisco

Playa Colola, Michoacán

Playa Escobilla, Oaxaca

Puerto Arista

Tecolutla

GREAT DIVERSITY

One of the top-five most biologically diverse countries on earth, Mexico is home to about 1100 bird species, more than 500 mammals, over 1200 amphibians and reptiles, over 5000 crustaceans, about 2000 butterflies and over 25,000 plants – for each of these groups, that's about 10% of the total number of species on the planet, on just 1.4% of the earth's land. The southern state of Chiapas alone, thanks largely to its Lacandón Jungle, has some 10,000 plant species, more than 600 bird species (twice as many as the USA) and 1200 species of butterflies.

Those That Swim

Baja California is famous for whale-watching in the early months of the year. Gray whales swim 10,000km from the Arctic to calve in its coastal waters. Between Baja and the mainland, the Sea of Cortez hosts more than a third of all the world's marine mammal species, including sea lions, fur and elephant seals, and four types of whale. Humpback whales follow plankton-bearing currents all the way down Mexico's Pacific coast between December and March, and, like dolphins and sea turtles, are commonly seen on boat trips from coastal towns.

Mexico's coasts, from Baja to Chiapas and from the northeast to the Yucatán Peninsula, are among the world's chief nesting grounds for sea turtles. Seven of the world's eight species frequent Mexican waters. Some female turtles swim unbelievable distances (right across the Pacific Ocean in the case of some loggerhead turtles) to lay eggs on the beaches where they were born. Killing sea turtles or taking their eggs is illegal in Mexico, and there are more than 100 protected nesting beaches – at many of which it's possible to observe the phenomenon known as an *arribada*, when turtles come ashore in large numbers to nest, and to assist in the release of hatchlings.

Dolphins play along the Pacific and Gulf coasts, while many coastal wetlands, especially in the south of the country, harbor crocodiles. Underwater life is richest of all on the coral reefs off the Yucatán Peninsula's Caribbean coast, where there's world-class diving and snorkeling. Near Isla Contoy, off the Yucatán's northeast tip, you can snorkel with whale sharks, the world's biggest fishes.

Those That Fly

All of coastal Mexico is a fantastic bird habitat, especially its estuaries, lagoons and islands. An estimated three billion migrating birds pass by or over the Yucatán Peninsula each year, and Veracruz state is a route of passage for a 'river of raptors' over 4 million strong every fall. Inland Mexico abounds with eagles, hawks and buzzards, and innumerable ducks and geese winter in the northern Sierra Madre Occidental. Tropical species such as trogons, hummingbirds, parrots and tanagers start to appear south of Tampico in the east of the country and from around Mazatlán in the west. The southeastern jungles and cloud forests are home to colorful macaws, toucans, guans and even a few quetzals. Yucatán has spectacular flamingo colonies at Celestún and Río Lagartos. Dozens of local operators around the country, especially along the coasts, offer bird-watching trips.

Mexico's most unforgettable insect marvel is Michoacán's Reserva Mariposa Monarca (p621), where the trees and earth turn orange when millions of monarch butterflies arrive every winter.

Endangered Species

By most counts over 200 animal species are in danger of disappearing from Mexico. Many of these are endemic to Mexico – they exist nowhere else. The endangered list includes such wonderful creatures as the jaguar, ocelot, northern tamandua (an anteater), pronghorn, Central American (Baird's) tapir, harpy eagle, resplendent quetzal, scarlet macaw, Cozumel curassow, loggerhead turtle, sea otter, Guadalupe fur seal, four types of parrot, and both spider and howler monkeys. The beautiful little vaquita (harbor porpoise), found only in the northern Sea of Cortez, was down to an estimated 100 individuals by 2015, despite recent efforts by government and conservationists to save it. The Margarita Island kangaroo rat and Hubbs freshwater snail may be less glamorous, but their disappearance too will forever affect the other plants and animals around them. Additionally, they're endemic to

Bird Books

Mexican Birds by Roger Tory Peterson and Edward L Chalif

Birds of Mexico and Central America by Ber van Perlo

Mexico Birds by James Kavanagh

Spectacular Birds

Scarlet macaw (Reforma Agraria)

Resplendent quetzal (Reserva de la Biosfera El Triunfo)

California condor (Parque Nacional Sierra San Pedro Mártir)

Flamingo (Celestún & Río Lagartos)

LANDSCAPES & WILDLIFE WILDLIFE

Mexico, so once gone from here, they're gone from the universe. A host of factors contribute to these creatures' endangered status, including deforestation, the spread of agriculture and urban areas, species trafficking and poaching.

Mexico's main tools for saving endangered species are its network of protected areas such as national parks and biosphere reserves, which covers 13% of the national territory, and a range of specific schemes aimed at conserving certain habitats or species. Government programs are supplemented by the work of local and international conservation groups, but progress is slowed by large gaps in the protected areas network, patchy enforcement and limited funding.

WWF's Wildfinder (worldwildlife. org/science/ wildfinder) is a database of over 26,000 animal species, searchable by species or place. For each of 23 Mexican eco-regions, it will give a list of hundreds of species with their names in English and Latin, their threatened status, and often pictures.

Plants

Northern Mexico's deserts, though sparsely vegetated with cacti, agaves, yucca, scrub and short grasses, are the world's most biodiverse deserts. Most of the planet's 1000 or so cactus species are found in Mexico, including more than 400 in the Desierto Chihuahuense alone. Isolated Baja California has a rather specialized and diverse flora, from the 20m-high cardón (the world's tallest cactus) to the bizarre boojum tree, which looks like an inverted carrot with fluff at the top.

Mexico's great mountain chains have big expanses of pine (with half the world's pine species) and, at lower elevations, oak (135 types). In the southern half of the country, mountain pine forests are often covered in clouds, turning them into cloud forests with lush, damp vegetation, many colorful wildflowers, and epiphytes growing on tree branches.

The natural vegetation of the low-lying southeast is predominantly evergreen tropical forest (rainforest in parts). This is dense and diverse, with ferns, epiphytes, palms, tropical hardwoods such as mahogany, and fruit trees such as the mamey and the chicozapote (sapodilla), which yields chicle (natural chewing gum). Despite ongoing destruction, the Selva Lacandona (Lacandón Jungle) in Chiapas is Mexico's largest remaining tropical forest, containing a significant number of Chiapas' 10,000 plant species.

The Yucatán Peninsula changes from rainforest in the south to tropical dry forest and savanna in the north, with thorny bushes and small trees (including many acacias).

Parks & Reserves

Mexico has spectacular national parks and other protected areas – nearly 13% of its territory (256,000 sq km) is under some kind of federal environmental protection. Governments have never had enough money for fully effective protection of these areas, but gradually, with some help from conservation organizations, more 'paper parks' are becoming real ones.

Parks & Reserves Websites

Comisión Nacional de Áreas Naturales Protegidas (www. conanp.gob.mx)

Unesco (biosphere reserves; www.unesco. org/new/en/ natural-sciences/ environment)

National Parks

Mexico's 66 *parques nacionales* (national parks) cover 14,113 sq km of territory. Many are tiny (smaller than 10 sq km), and around half of them were created in the 1930s, often for their archaeological, historical or recreational value rather than for ecological reasons. Several recently created parks protect coastal areas, offshore islands or coral reefs. Despite illegal logging, hunting and grazing, national parks have succeeded in protecting big tracts of forest, especially the high, coniferous forests of central Mexico.

Biosphere Reserves

Reservas de la biosfera (biosphere reserves) are based on the recognition that it is impracticable to put a complete stop to human exploitation of many ecologically important areas. Instead, these reserves encourage sustainable local economic activities within their territory. Today Mexico has over 50 Unesco-protected and/or national biosphere reserves, covering some 142,000 sq km. They protect some of the country's most beautiful and biologically fascinating areas, focusing on whole ecosystems with genuine biodiversity. Sustainable,

TOP PARKS & RESERVES

PARK/RESERVE	FEATURES	ACTIVITIES	BEST TIME TO VISIT
Parque Nacional Archipiélago Espíritu Santo (p841)	Waters around Espíritu Santo & neighboring islands in Sea of Cortez	Kayaking with whale sharks; snorkeling with sea lions; sailing	year-round
Parque Nacional Bahía de Loreto (p841)	Islands, shores & waters of the Sea of Cortez	Snorkeling; kayaking; diving	year-round
Parque Nacional Iztaccíhuatl-Popocatépetl (p841)	Live & extinct volcanic giants on rim of Valle de México	Hiking; climbing	Nov-Feb
Parque Nacional Lagunas de Chacahua (p841)	Oaxacan coastal lagoons; beach	Boat trips; bird-watching; surfing	year-round
Parque Nacional Volcán Nevado de Colima (p841)	Live & inactive volcanoes; pumas; coyotes; pine forests	Volcano hiking	Dec-May
Reserva de la Biosfera Banco Chinchorro (p841)	Largest coral atoll in northern hemisphere	Diving; snorkeling	Dec-May
Reserva de la Biosfera Calakmul (p841)	Rainforest with major Maya ruins including Calakmul, Hormiguero and Chicanná	Visiting ruins; wildlife-spotting	year-round
Reserva de la Biosfera El Vizcaíno (p841)	Coastal lagoons where gray whales calve; deserts	Whale-watching; hikes to ancient rock art	Dec-Apr
Reserva de la Biosfera Mariposa Monarca (p841)	Forests festooned with millions of monarch butterflies	Butterfly observation; hiking	Nov-Mar
Reserva de la Biosfera Montes Azules (p841)	Tropical jungle; lakes; rivers	Jungle hikes; canoeing; rafting; bird-watching; boat trips; wildlife-watching	Dec-Aug
Reserva de la Biosfera Ría Celestún (p841)	Estuary & mangroves with plentiful birdlife, incl flamingos	Bird-watching; boat trips	Nov-Mar
Reserva de la Biosfera Ría Lagartos (p841)	Mangrove-lined estuary full of birdlife, including flamingos	Bird-, crocodile- and turtle-watching	Apr-Sep
Reserva de la Biosfera Sian Ka'an (p841)	Caribbean coastal jungle, wetlands & islands with incredibly diverse wildlife	Bird-watching; snorkeling & nature tours, mostly by boat	year-round
Reserva de la Biosfera Sierra Gorda (p841)	Transition zone from semidesert to cloud forest	Hiking; bird-watching; colonial missions	year-round

community-based tourism is an important source of support for several of them, and successful visitor programs are in place in reserves like Calakmul, Sierra Gorda, Montes Azules, Mariposa Monarca, La Encrucijada and Sian Ka'an.

Ramsar Sites

Nearly 90,000 sq km of Mexican landmass and coastal waters are protected as Wetlands of International Importance, known as Ramsar sites for the Iranian town where the 1971 Convention on Wetlands of International Importance was signed. Mexico's 142 separate sites include whale calving grounds, turtle nesting beaches, coral reefs, and coastal lagoons and mangrove forests that are of crucial importance for birds and many marine creatures.

The Nature Conservancy (www.nature.org), Conservation International (www.conservation.org) and WWF (wwf.panda.org; www.wwf.org.mx; www.worldwildlife.org) all provide lots of information on the Mexican environment, including on their programs in the country.

Environmental Issues

Mexico achieved the status of a global standard-bearer on climate change in 2012 when it became only the second country (after the UK) to enshrine carbon-emission commitments into law. The climate change law committed Mexico, currently the world's 13th biggest carbon emitter, to be producing 35% of its electricity from renewable and nuclear energy by 2024, and to cut its carbon emissions by 50% from previously expected levels by 2050.

In 2015 it became the first non-European country to formally submit its climate-change commitments to the United Nations, with a minimum 25% cut in greenhouse-gas emissions from previously expected levels by 2030. Mexico also set a target of zero deforestation by 2030.

Air pollution and deforestation are among Mexico's own biggest environmental problems, and while the country is one of the world's major exporters of crude oil, it has had to import half of its gasoline because it is short on refineries. Replacing costly imports with homegrown renewable energy makes much sense. Sunny Mexico has plenty of potential for solar power, and already at least 13% of its electricity comes from hydro sources and 3% from wind and geothermal.

How the country can meet its targets is another matter. Reforms in the oil sector passed by Enrique Peña Nieto's government in 2014 are intended to boost Mexico's oil output, leading critics to argue that prospects of reducing the country's oil dependency are slim. Wind power is the only renewable energy source that has generated significantly increased amounts of electricity in recent years.

Water & Forests

President Peña Nieto's six-year national development plan, announced in 2013, prioritized the crucial issue of water sustainability – a key question in a nation where the south has 70% of the water, but the north and center have 75% of the people, and around 5% of the population still lacks access to clean drinking water.

The country's water supplies are often badly polluted (which is why Mexicans are the world's leading consumers of bottled water), and sewerage systems are seriously inadequate in many areas. The plan that the government eventually came up with, in 2015, was to privatize the water system, or parts of it, on the theory that private companies could provide water cheaper, cleaner and more efficiently than the state. This brought protests across the country from many people who feared the opposite would happen, leading to a postponement of the legislation.

On another key issue – forest conservation – Mexico has achieved some success. The country has lost about three-quarters of the forests it had in pre-Hispanic times, as all types of forest from cool pine-clad highlands to tropical jungles have been cleared for grazing, logging and farming. Today only about 17% of the land is covered in primary forest, though a further 16% has regenerated or replanted forest. The good news is that, on government figures at least, deforestation rates declined from about 3500 sq km a year in the 1990s to under 1600 sq km a year today. Part of the success story is that around 70% of forests are controlled by local communities, who tend to manage them in a sustainable way.

Urban Problems

Mexico City is a high-altitude megalopolis surrounded by a ring of mountains that traps polluted air in the city. The capital consumes over half of Mexico's electricity and has to pump up about a quarter of its water needs from lowlands far below, then evacuate its waste water back to the lowlands via 11,000km of sewers. Efforts to improve air quality are intensifying. For years, most vehicles have been banned from the roads one day every week. The city's climate action plan for 2014–2020 aims to cut CO_2 emissions by 30% through such means as

COMMUNITY ECOTOURISM

Environmental awareness has made big bounds in Mexico. The country has no large-scale environmental party or movement, but it does have many smaller organizations working on local issues. One of the highest-profile sectors of grass-roots environmentalism is the community ecotourism movement, which has made huge strides since its beginnings in the 1990s. The theory behind it is that rural communities can gain income and stem population drain by conserving, rather than depleting, their natural resources, and welcoming tourism – a win, win, win situation for the communities, their visitors and the environment. It is working handsomely in many places all around Mexico, especially in the south.

Successful community ecotourism schemes provide comfortable *cabaña* accommodations and good local meals, and supply information, guides and infrastructure (such as maintained trails, bikes, horses or boats to rent, and even zip-lines) to enable visitors to enjoy their unspoiled natural surroundings. Urban Mexicans flock to the fresh air and open space, and foreign visitors get a genuine experience of rural Mexico that they might otherwise miss.

Ecotourism projects that meet government guidelines for good environmental practices are listed at www.ecoturismocertificado.mx.

Community Ecotourism Top 12

➡ Pueblos Mancomunados (p452)
➡ Laguna Miramar (p399)
➡ Community Tours Sian Ka'an (p288)
➡ Las Guacamayas (p397)
➡ Servidores Turísticos Calakmul (p345)
➡ Playa Escobilla (p469)
➡ Santiago Apoala (p455)
➡ Síijil Noh Há (p293)
➡ La Ventanilla (p479)
➡ Reserva de la Biosfera Sierra Gorda (p647)
➡ Ecoguías La Mancha (p244)
➡ Madre Sal (p407)

energy-efficient buses, electric-powered taxis, more bicycle use, and a switch to energy-saving light bulbs.

The capital's problems of water supply, sewage treatment, overcrowding and air pollution are mirrored on a smaller scale in most of Mexico's faster-growing cities.

Tourism, a key sector of Mexico's economy, can bring its own environmental problems when development is on a large scale. In 2012, the then President Felipe Calderón canceled plans for the large-scale Cabo Cortés tourism development in Baja California, because its developers had failed to show that it would be environmentally sustainable. This delighted campaigners who had argued for years that the project would seriously damage the Cabo Pulmo Marine National Park.

On the Caribbean coast's Riviera Maya, organizations such as Centro Ecológico Akumal (p285) and Mexiconservación (http://mexiconservacion.org) work to limit damage from reckless tourism development to coral reefs, turtle-nesting beaches, mangrove systems and even the water in the area's famed cenotes (limestone sinkholes). A slowly growing number of hotels and resorts in the region are adopting green policies.

Mexico's largest and probably most influential environmental group is Pronatura (www.pronatura.org.mx), which has numerous programs around the country working to protect species, combat climate change, preserve ecosystems, and promote ecotourism, environmental education and sustainable development.

Survival Guide

DIRECTORY A–Z . . . 846

Accommodations 846

Activities 847

Customs Regulations . . . 848

Discount Cards 848

Electricity 848

Embassies
& Consulates 848

Food 849

Gay & Lesbian Travelers . . 849

Health 849

Insurance 850

Internet Access 851

Language Courses 851

Legal Matters 851

Maps 852

Money 852

Opening Hours 852

Photography 852

Post 853

Public Holidays 853

Safe Travel 853

Telephone 854

Time 855

Tourist Information 856

Travelers
with Disabilities 856

Visas
& Tourist Permits 856

Volunteering 857

Women Travelers 857

TRANSPORTATION . . 858

GETTING
THERE & AWAY 858

Entering the Country 858

Land 858

Sea 860

GETTING AROUND 860

Air 860

Bicycle 861

Boat 861

Bus 861

Car & Motorcycle 862

Local
Transportation 864

Train 864

LANGUAGE 865

Glossary 871

Food Glossary 874

Directory A–Z

Accommodations

Accommodations in Mexico range from hammocks and huts to hotels of every standard, including super-luxury resorts. In popular destinations at busy times, reserve a room in advance.

'Single' (abbreviated to 's') means a room for one person; 'double' ('d') means a room for two people. Mexicans sometimes use the phrase *cuarto sencillo* (single room) to mean a room with one bed, which may be a *cama matrimonial* (double bed). A *cuarto doble* often means a room with two beds, which may both be *camas matrimoniales*.

The air-con icon and non-smoking icon mean that the establishment offers some air-conditioned and non-smoking rooms, respectively.

Price Categories

Many midrange and top-end establishments in tourist destinations raise their rates during the Semana Santa (Easter) and Christmas–New Year holiday periods or local festival times. Budget accommodations are more likely to keep the same rates all year.

Budget ($) Most cities popular with international budget travelers have hostels, as well as cheap hotels. Budget accommodations also include campgrounds, hammocks, *cabañas* (cabins) and guesthouses.

Airbnb (www.airbnb.com) is also gaining popularity in Mexico.

Midrange ($$) Many midrange places have a restaurant and a bar, almost all have wi-fi and many have swimming pools. Many are atmospheric old mansions and inns turned into hotels. You'll also find some B&Bs, apartments, bungalows and more comfortable *cabañas* that are midrange.

Top end ($$$) Accommodations in this category offer the expected levels of luxury – pools, gyms, bars, restaurants, design, professional service – at prices that are sometimes agreeably modest. They range in style from converted haciendas or small, chic boutique hotels to expansive modern resorts and spas. To save money, look for deals on hotel websites. Triple or family rooms tend to be a bargain for groups.

Taxes

The price of accommodations in Mexico is subject to two taxes:

IVA (value-added tax; 16%)

ISH (lodging tax; 2% or 3% depending on the state)

Many of the less-expensive establishments only charge you these taxes if you require a receipt, and they quote room rates accordingly (ie not including taxes).

Types of Accommodations

Apartments In some resort towns you can find tourist apartments with fully equipped kitchens. They're good value for three or four people, especially if you're staying more than a few days.

B&Bs Mexican B&Bs are usually small, comfortable, midrange or top-end guesthouses, often beautifully designed and offering friendly, personal attention. Many of them are effectively boutique hotels.

Cabañas Cabins or huts (of wood, brick, adobe or stone), often with a palm-thatched roof, most often found at beach destinations. The most basic *cabañas* have dirt floors and a bed, and you provide the padlock for the door. Other *cabañas* are positively deluxe, with electric lights, mosquito nets, large comfy beds, bathrooms, hammock-strung decks and even air-con and a kitchen. The most expensive *cabañas* are on the Caribbean, where some luxury units can cost over M$2000.

BOOK YOUR STAY ONLINE

For more accommodations reviews by Lonely Planet authors, check out http://lonelyplanet.com/hotels/. You'll find independent reviews, as well as recommendations on the best places to stay. Best of all, you can book online.

SLEEPING PRICE RANGES

The following price ranges refer to accommodations for two people in high season, including any taxes charged.

$ less than M$600

$$ M$600–1200

$$$ more than M$1200

Campgrounds & Trailer Parks
Most organized campgrounds are actually trailer parks set up for RVs (recreational vehicles, campers) and trailers (caravans) that are also open to tent campers at lower rates. Some restaurants and guesthouses in beach spots or country areas will let you pitch a tent on their patch for around M$50 per person.

Hammocks Hammock space is available in many of the more low-key beach spots. A hammock can be a very comfortable and cheap place to sleep in hot areas (keep mosquito repellent handy). Some places have hammocks to rent for anywhere between M$50 and M$100. It's easy to buy hammocks in Mexico, especially in Oaxaca and Chiapas states and on the Yucatán Peninsula.

Hostels Hostels provide dormitory accommodations typically from M$150 to M$200 per person, plus communal kitchens, bathrooms, living space, nearly always wi-fi and often private double rooms for a bit more than the price of two dorm beds. The best hostels have pools, bars, gardens and sundecks. Cleanliness and security vary, but popular hostels are great places for meeting fellow travelers. International hostel websites such as **Hostelworld** (www.hostelworld.com) provide plentiful listings and online reservations.

Posadas & Casas de Huéspedes Posadas are inns, meaning anything from basic budget hotels to tastefully designed, small, midrange places. A *casa*

de huéspedes is a guesthouse, a home converted into simple, inexpensive guest lodgings, usually family-run.

Activities

If you're planning to fly to Mexico with a surfboard, check with the airline first. Most of them charge US$50 or more (each way), and some won't carry them to some destinations, or at some times of the year. Interjet is the most surfer-friendly.

Resources

AMTAVE (www.amtave.org) The Mexican Adventure Tourism & Ecotourism Association, with over 90 member organizations.

Magic Seaweed (www.magic-seaweed.com) Webcams, surfing forecasts, surf-spot info and more.

Planeta.com (www.planeta.com) Good resource on active and responsible tourism.

Mexiconline.com (www.mex-online.com) Includes listings of activity providers.

SAFETY GUIDELINES FOR DIVING

Before embarking on a scuba-diving, free-diving or snorkeling trip, consider the following to ensure a safe and enjoyable experience:

➡ Possess a current diving-certification card from a recognized scuba-diving instruction agency (if diving).

➡ Be sure you are healthy and feel comfortable diving.

➡ If you don't have your own equipment, ask to see the dive shop's before you commit. Make sure you feel comfortable with your dive master: after all, it's your life.

➡ Obtain reliable information about physical and environmental conditions at the dive site from a reputable local dive operation, and ask how local trained divers deal with these considerations.

➡ Be aware of local laws, regulations and etiquette about marine life and the environment.

➡ Dive only at sites within your level of experience. Engage the services of a competent, professionally trained dive instructor or dive master.

➡ Find out if your dive shop has up-to-date certification from **PADI** (www.padi.com), **NAUI** (ww.naui.org) or the internationally recognized Mexican diving organization **FMAS** (www.fmas.com.mx).

➡ Know the locations of the nearest decompression chambers and the emergency telephone numbers.

➡ Avoid diving less than 18 hours before a high-altitude flight.

Customs Regulations

You may bring the following into Mexico duty-free:

➡ two cameras

➡ three cell phones

➡ one laptop or notebook

➡ three surfboards

➡ two musical instruments

➡ medicine for personal use, with prescription in the case of psychotropic drugs.

See www.aduanas.gob.mx for further details.

Discount Cards

For reduced air tickets at student- and youth-oriented travel agencies, use:

➡ ISIC student card

➡ IYTC (under 26 years) card

➡ ITIC card for teachers

Reduced prices on Mexican buses, at museums and at archaeological sites are usually only for Mexican residents, but these cards will sometimes get you a reduction.

Electricity

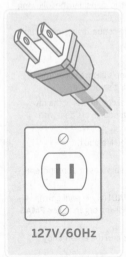

127V/60Hz

127V/60Hz

Embassies & Consulates

The website of Mexico's foreign ministry, the **Secretaría de Relaciones Exteriores** (www.sre.gob.mx), links to the websites of all Mexican diplomatic missions worldwide.

Australian Embassy (☑55-1101-2200; www.mexico.embassy.gov.au; Rubén Darío 55, Mexico City)

Belizean Embassy (☑55-5520-1274; www.mfa.gov.bz; Bernardo de Gálvez 215, Lomas de Chapultepec, Mexico City); Chetumal Consulate (☑983-129-3328; conbelizeqroo@gmail.com; Av Juárez 226B, btwn Avs Primo de Verdad & Carranza, Chetumal; ⊙9am-noon Mon-Fri)

Canadian Embassy (☑55-5724-7900; Schiller 529, Polanco, Mexico City); Acapulco Consulate (Map p570; ☑744-484-13-05; Pasaje Diana, La Costera 121, L-16, Fraccionamiento Magallanes, Acapulco); Cabo San Lucas Consulate (☑624-142-43-33; Local 82, Plaza San Lucas, Carretera Transpeninsular Km 0.5, Local 82, Colonia El Tezal, Cabo San Lucas); Cancún Consulate (☑998-883-33-60; Oficina E7, Centro Empresarial, Blvd Kukulcán Km 12, Zona Hotelera, Cancún); Guadalajara Consulate (☑33-3671-4740; Piso 8, Torre Pacífico, World Trade Center, Av Otero 1249, Colonia Rinconada del Bosque, Guadalajara); Mazatlán Consulate (Map p502; ☑669-913-73-20; Office 41, Centro Comercial La Marina Business Life, Blvd Marina Mazatlán 2302, Colonia Marina Mazatlán, Mazatlán); Monterrey Consulate (Map p796; ☑81-8378-0240; Ste 404, Torre Gómez Morín 955, Av Gómez Morín 955, San Pedro Garza García, Monterrey); Oaxaca Consulate (☑951-513-37-77; Local 11B, Pino Suárez 700, Oaxaca); Puerto Vallarta Consulate (☑322-293-00-98; Local Sub F, Plaza Península, Blvd Medina Ascencio 2485, Zona Hotelera Norte, Puerto Vallarta); Tijuana Consulate (☑664-684-04-61; Condominio del Parque, Gedovius 10411-101, Zona Río, Tijuana)

French Embassy (☑55-9171-9700; www.ambafrance-mx.org; Campos Elíseos 339, Polanco, Mexico City); Guadalajara Consulate (☑33-3616-5516; López Mateos Norte 484, Colonia Ladrón de Guevara, Guadalajara); Mérida Consulate (☑999-930-15-00; Calle 60 No 385, Mérida; ⊙9am-5pm Mon-Fri); Mexico City Consulate (☑55-9171-9700; Lafontaine 32, Polanco, Mexico City); Oaxaca Consulate (☑951-515-21-84; Planta Baja, 3a Privada de J López Alavez 5, San Felipe del Agua, Oaxaca); Playa del Carmen Consulate (☑984-112-34-72; Bureau 23, Plaza Antigua, 10 Av, Playa del Carmen)

German Embassy (☑55-5283-2200; www.mexiko.diplo.de; Horacio 1506, Los Morales, Mexico City); Cancún Consulate (☑998-884-15-98; Punta Conoca 36, SM24, Cancún); Guadalajara Honorary Consulate (☑33-3810-2146; Calle 7 No 319, Colonia Ferrocarril, Guadalajara); Mérida Honorary Consulate (☑999-944-32-52; Calle 49 No 212, Mérida)

Guatemalan Embassy (☑55-5520-6680; http://embajadaguatemalamx.mex.tl; Av Explanada 1025, Lomas de Chapultepec, Mexico City); Comitán Consulate (☎963-110-68-16; www.minex.gob.gt; 1a Calle Sur Poniente 35, Int.3 4th fl, Comitán; ⊗9am-1pm & 2-5pm Mon-Fri); Tapachula Consulate (☎962-626-12-52; www.minex.gob.gt; Quinta Norte No 3, 3rd fl; ⊗9am-5pm Mon-Fri)

Irish Embassy (☎55-5520-5803; www.irishembassy.com.mx; Cerrada Blvd Ávila Camacho 76-3, Lomas de Chapultepec, Mexico City); Cancún Honorary Consulate (☎998-112-54-36; Av Coba 15, MZ 8, SM 22, Cancún)

Netherlands Embassy (☎55-5258-9921; http://mexico.nlambassade.org; 7th fl, Edificio Calakmul, Av Vasco de Quiroga 3000, Mexico City); Cancún Consulate (☎998-884-86-72; Pabellón Caribe, Av Nichupté, Lote 22, MZ 2, SM 19, Cancún); Guadalajara Consulate (☎33-1655-0269; Condominio Santa Anita, Paseo del Bosque 203, Tlajomulco de Zuñiga, Guadalajara); Mérida Consulate (☎999-924-31-22; Calle 64 No 418, Mérida)

New Zealand Embassy (☎55-5283-9460; www.nzembassy.com/mexico; Level 4, Jaime Balmes 8, Mexico City)

UK Embassy (☎55-1670-3200; http://ukinmexico.fco.gov.uk; Río Lerma 71, Colonia Cuauhtémoc, Mexico City; ⊗8am-4pm Mon-Thu, to 1:30pm Fri); Cancún Consulate (☎998-881-01-00; Royal Sands, Blvd Kukulcán Km 13.5, Cancún; ⊗9am-2pm Mon-Fri); Mexico City Consulate (☎55-1670-3200; Río Usumacinta 30, Mexico City); Tijuana Consulate (☎664-686-53-20; Blvd Salinas 1500, Fraccionamiento Aviación, Tijuana)

US Embassy (☎55-5080-2000; http://mexico.us embassy.gov; Paseo de la Reforma 305, Mexico City; ⊗8:30am-5:30pm Mon-Fri); Cancún Consular Agency (☎998-883-02-72; mexico.usembassy.gov; Despacho 301, Torre La Europea, Blvd Kukulcán Km 13, Cancún; ⊗8am-1pm Mon-Fri); Ciudad Juárez Consulate (☎656-227-30-00; http://

ciudadjuarez.usconsulate.gov; Paseo de la Victoria 3650, Fraccionamiento Partido Senecú, Ciudad Juárez); Guadalajara Consulate (☎33-3268-2100; Progreso 175, Colonia Americana, Guadalajara); Mazatlán Consular Agency (☎669-916-58-89; Playa Gaviotas 202, Local 10, Zona Dorada, Mazatlán); Mérida Consulate (☎999-942-57-77; http://merida.usconsulate.gov; Calle 60 No 338K, Mérida; ⊗9am-1pm Mon-Fri); Oaxaca Consular Agency (☎951-514-30-54; Office 20, Plaza Santo Domingo, Alcalá 407, Oaxaca); Puerto Vallarta Consular Agency (☎322-222-00-69; Paradise Plaza, Paseo de los Cocoteros 85 Sur, Nuevo Vallarta); San Miguel de Allende Consular Agency (☎415-152-23-57; Locales 4 & 5, Plaza La Luciérnaga, Libramiento Zavala 165, Colonia La Luciérnaga, San Miguel de Allende); Tijuana Consulate (☎664-977-20-00; http://tijuana.usconsulate.gov; Paseo de las Culturas s/n, Mesa de Otay, Tijuana)

Food

There is a 16% value-added tax (IVA) on restaurant prices, nearly always included in the menu prices.

Gay & Lesbian Travelers

Mexico is increasingly broad-minded about sexuality, although the conservative influence of the Catholic Church remains strong. Gays and lesbians don't generally adopt a high profile, but rarely attract open discrimination or violence. The legalization of gay marriages in Mexico

City has energized gay life in the capital, which has a hip, international bar and club scene. Puerto Vallarta is the gay beach capital of Mexico. There are also lively scenes in places such as Guadalajara, Veracruz, Cancún, Mazatlán, Mérida and Acapulco. Gay marriages or civil unions are also legal in the states of Colima, Quintana Roo and Coahuila and are likely to extend to other states following the 2015 Supreme Court ruling.

The website www.gaymexico.com.mx has a clickable map linking to gay guides for many cities, while www.gaymexicomap.com also has listings of accommodations, bars and clubs in many cities, and www.gaycities.com is good for Mexico City, Guadalajara, Puerto Vallarta and Cancún. Also well worth checking out are the **International Gay & Lesbian Travel Association** (www.iglta.org), with worldwide information on travel providers in the gay sector, and www.outtraveler.com.

The **Cliníca Condesa** (www.condesadf.mx; Gral Benjamín Hill 24, Condesa) is the first of its kind in the country. A flagship health center specializing in sexual health, especially (but not only) LGBT issues, with treatment at no charge, even for foreigners.

Health

Travelers to Mexico need to guard chiefly against food- and mosquito-borne diseases. Besides getting the proper vaccinations, carry a good insect repellent and exercise care in what you eat and drink.

EATING PRICE RANGES

The following price ranges refer to prices of typical main dishes, including value-added tax (IVA).

$ less than M$80

$$ M$80–160

$$$ more than M$160

Private hospitals generally provide better care than public ones, but are more expensive: the best are in Mexico City. Your country's embassy or consulates in Mexico and the national tourism secretariat, **Sectur** (☑078, 55-5250-0151, 800-903-92-00, in the US 800-482-9832; www.visitmexico.com), can usually give information on local hospitals. You should have travel insurance that covers the cost of air evacuation to another country should you develop a life-threatening condition.

Recommended Vaccinations

Make sure all routine vaccinations are up to date and check whether all vaccines are suitable for children and pregnant women. See the Centers for Disease Control & Prevention website (www.cdc.gov/travel) for more details.

Hepatitis A All travelers (except children less than a year of age).

Hepatitis B Long-term travelers in close contact with local population (requires three doses over a six-month period).

Rabies For those who may have contact with animals and may not have access to medical care.

Typhoid All travelers.

Yellow Fever Mexico requires proof of a yellow-fever vaccination if you're arriving from a country with risk of yellow fever.

Health Hazards in Mexico

Altitude Sickness May develop in travelers who ascend rapidly to altitudes greater than 2500m. Symptoms may include headache, nausea, vomiting, dizziness, malaise, insomnia and loss of appetite. Severe cases can lead to death. To lessen the chance of altitude sickness, ascend gradually to higher altitudes, avoid overexertion, eat light meals and avoid alcohol. People showing any symptoms of altitude sickness should not ascend higher until the symptoms have cleared. If the symptoms become worse, or if someone shows signs of fluid in the lungs (high-altitude pulmonary edema) or swelling of the brain (high-altitude cerebral edema), descend immediately to a lower altitude. Descent of 500m to 1000m is generally adequate except in cases of cerebral edema.

Dengue Fever A viral infection transmitted by aedes mosquitoes, which usually bite during the day. Usually causes flu-like symptoms. There is no vaccine and no treatment except analgesics.

Malaria Transmitted by mosquito bites, usually between dusk and dawn. The main symptom is high spiking fevers. Malaria pills are recommended when visiting Chiapas or rural areas in Oaxaca, Sinaloa, Nayarit and parts of Sonora, Chihuahua and Durango states. The first-choice malaria pill is chloroquine. Protecting yourself against mosquito bites is just as important as taking malaria pills.

Snake & Scorpion Bites In the event of a venomous snake bite or scorpion bite, keep the bitten area immobilized and move the victim immediately to the nearest medical facility. For scorpion stings, immediately apply ice or cold packs.

Chikungunya A viral disease transmitted to humans by infected aedes mosquitoes, causing fever and severe joint pain. A growing number of cases have been reported throughout Mexico since October 2014, mostly in Guerrero, Oaxaca, Chiapas and Michoacán, with isolated cases in 12 other states. There is no vaccine or treatment.

Precautions

Mosquito Bites Wear long sleeves, long pants, hats and shoes. Don't sleep with windows open unless there is a screen. Use a good insect repellent, preferably one containing DEET, but don't use DEET-containing compounds on children under the age of two. If sleeping outdoors or in accommodations that allow entry of mosquitoes, use a bed net, ideally treated with permethrin.

Sun Stay out of the midday sun, wear sunglasses, a wide-brimmed hat and apply sunscreen with SPF 15 or higher. Drink plenty of fluids and avoid strenuous exercise when temperatures are high.

Water Tap water in Mexico is mostly not safe to drink. Purified water in plastic bottles is sold everywhere and is also available from large dispensers in some accommodations. The most effective means of water purification is vigorous boiling for one minute (three minutes at altitudes over 2000m). Another option is a SteriPen (www.steripen.com), which kills bacteria and viruses with ultraviolet light. Pregnant women and those with a history of thyroid disease should not drink iodinated water.

Insurance

A travel-insurance policy to cover theft, loss and medical problems is a very good idea. Some policies specifically exclude dangerous activities

---

PRACTICALITIES

➡ Mexico uses the metric system for weights and measures.

➡ Mexican law does not allow smoking in indoor public spaces, except in specially designated smoking areas. It also requires at least 75% of a hotel's rooms to be nonsmoking. Enforcement, however, is very patchy.

➡ Mexico's only English-language daily newspaper (actually, Monday to Friday) is the News (www.thenews.com.mx). Distribution is very patchy outside Mexico City. The best and most independent-minded Spanish-language national newspapers include Reforma and the left-wing La Jornada.

such as scuba diving, motorcycling and even trekking.

You may prefer a policy that pays doctors or hospitals directly rather than you having to pay on the spot and claim later. If you have to claim later, ensure that you keep all documentation. Check that the policy covers ambulances or an emergency flight home.

Worldwide travel insurance is available at www.lonelyplanet.com/bookings. You can buy, extend and claim online anytime, even if you're already on the road.

Internet Access

Wi-fi (internet inalámbrico) is common in Mexican accommodations and also available in some cafes, bars, airports and city plazas. Our wi-fi icon means that wi-fi is available on the premises. The internet icon means that the establishment has internet-enabled computers for guests to use. Some of these services are free of charge.

The number of internet cafes in Mexican cities is declining due to the proliferation of wi-fi elsewhere and travelers using mobile data on their smartphones instead.

Language Courses

Mexico has many professional, experienced Spanish schools, offering everything from short courses for beginners, with emphasis on the spoken language, to longer courses for serious students. Many schools are located in Mexico's most attractive and interesting cities, such as Oaxaca, Guanajuato, San Cristóbal de las Casas, Mérida, Cuernavaca, Morelia and Guadalajara, as well as Puerto Morelos and Playa del Carmen. They present a great opportunity to get an inside experience of Mexican life, with plenty of extracurricular activities such as dance, cooking, music, excursions and volunteering usually available.

Some courses are geared mainly to college students wanting credits for courses back home, while other schools focus on travelers or independent language students. Some Mexican universities have special departments with tailor-made courses for foreigners (usually lasting between one month and one semester). Private schools typically offer shorter courses, from a few days to three months, with more flexible schedules and, often, smaller classes.

The website **123 Teach Me** (www.123teachme.com) offers listings of over 70 language schools in Mexico.

The **National Registration Center for Study Abroad** (www.nrcsa.com), **CIEE** (www.ciee.org), **AmeriSpan** (www.amerispan.com) and **Spanish Abroad** (spanishabroad.com) are among US-based organizations offering a range of study programs in Mexico.

Costs

➡ A typical rate for group classes in private schools is around US$10 per hour.

➡ Most schools offer a choice of living options, including homestays, apartments and their own student accommodations. Homestays are often the cheapest option (typically around US$100 to US$125 per week for your own room in a family's home and two meals a day).

➡ All up, 25 hours of classes per week, plus homestay accommodations and meals, averages US$350 to US$375.

➡ Some schools charge extra for enrollment and registration and/or materials.

Legal Matters

Mexican Law

Mexican law is based on the Roman and Napoleonic codes, presuming an accused person guilty until proven innocent.

A law passed in 2009 determined that possession of small amounts of certain drugs for personal use – including cocaine (500mg), heroin (50mg) and methamphetamine (40mg) – would not incur legal proceedings against first-time offenders. But those found in possession of small amounts may still have to appear before a prosecutor to determine whether it is for personal use. The easiest way to avoid any drug-related problems is not to use them.

A November 2015 ruling by the Mexican Supreme Court stated that individuals should have the right to grow marijuana for personal use, paving the way for de facto legalization, though the president denies that this is the case.

It's against Mexican law to take any firearm or ammunition into the country (even unintentionally).

Useful warnings on Mexican law are found on the website of the **US State Department** (http://travel.state.gov).

Getting Legal Help

If a foreigner is arrested in Mexico, the Mexican authorities, according to international law, are supposed to promptly contact the person's consulate or embassy if asked to do so. They may not. If they do, consular officials can tell you your rights, provide lists of lawyers, monitor your case, try to make sure you are treated humanely and notify your relatives or friends – but they can't get you out of jail. By Mexican law, the longest a person can be detained without a specific accusation after arrest is 48 hours (though official arrest may not take place until after a period of initial questioning).

Tourist offices in Mexico, especially those run by state governments, can often help you with legal problems such as complaints and reporting crimes or lost articles. The national tourism ministry, **Sectur** (Map p88; ☎55-5250-

0151, US 800-482-9832; www.sectur.gob.mx; Av Masaryk 172, Bosques de Chapultepec), has a toll-free number for 24-hour telephone advice.

If you are the victim of a crime, your embassy or consulate, or Sectur or state tourist offices, can give advice. In some cases, there may be little to gain by going to the police, unless you need a statement to present to your insurance company. If you go to the police, take your passport and tourist permit, if you still have them. If you want to report a theft for insurance purposes, say you want to 'poner una acta de un robo' (make a record of a robbery). This should make it clear that you merely want a piece of paper, and you should get it without too much trouble.

Maps

Nelles, ITM and Michelin all produce good country maps of Mexico that are suitable for travel planning. ITM also publishes good larger-scale maps of many Mexican regions.

Tourist offices in Mexico provide free city, town and regional maps of varying quality. Bookstores and newsstands sell commercially published ones, including Guía Roji's recommended all-Mexico road atlas, Por Las Carreteras de México.

Inegi (Instituto Nacional de Estadística, Geografía e Informática; www.inegi.org.mx) Sells large-scale 1:50,000 and 1:250,000 topographical maps at its Centros de Información in every Mexican state capital (detailed on the website), subject to availability.

Money

ATMs and exchange offices are widely available. Credit cards accepted in many midrange and top-end hotels.

ATMs

ATMs (cajero automático) are plentiful. You can use ma-

jor credit cards and Maestro, Cirrus and Plus bank cards to withdraw pesos. The exchange rate you'll get is normally better than the 'tourist rate' for currency exchange at banks and casas de cambio (exchange offices), though that may be negated by the M$30 to M$70 fee the ATM company charges and any foreign-transaction fees levied by your card company.

For maximum security, use ATMs during daylight hours and in secure indoor locations.

Banks & Casas de Cambio

You can exchange cash at casas de cambio and some banks. Casas de cambio exist in just about every large town and many smaller ones. They are often open evenings or weekends and usually offer similar exchange rates to banks. Banks go through more time-consuming procedures, and usually have shorter exchange hours (typically 9am to 4pm Monday to Friday and 9am to 1pm Saturday).

Taxes

Mexico's impuesto al valor agregado (IVA; value-added tax) is 16%. By law the tax must be included in virtually any price quoted to you, and should not be added afterward. Notices in stores and on restaurant menus often state 'IVA incluido.'

Hotel rooms are also subject to the impuesto sobre hospedaje (ISH; lodging tax) of 2% or 3%, depending on which Mexican state they're in.

Tipping & Bargaining

Tourism and hospitality workers often depend on tips to supplement miserable basic wages. Normal tips:

Restaurants About 10% to 15%, unless service is included in the check.

Hotels Around 5% of your room costs for the staff, especially if you stay a few days.

Taxis No tip expected unless some special, extra service is provided.

Airport & hotel porters From M$50 to M$100.

Gas-station & car-parking attendants Tip M$5 or M$10.

For information on bargaining, see p23.

Opening Hours

Typical hours are as follows, though variations exist:

Banks 9am to 4pm Monday to Friday, 9am to 1pm Saturday. Banks in smaller towns may close earlier and not open Saturday.

Bars 1pm to midnight

Cafes 8am to 10pm

Restaurants 9am to 11pm

Stores & Shops 9am to 8pm Monday to Saturday; in the south, some close from 2pm to 4pm. Supermarkets and department stores usually open from 9am or 10am to 10pm daily.

Photography

It's polite to ask before taking photos of people. Some indigenous people can be especially sensitive about this matter.

Lonely Planet's Travel Photography is a comprehensive guide to getting the best shots from your travels.

Special permits are required for any photography or filming with 'special or professional equipment' (which includes all tripods but not amateur video cameras) at any of the 187 archaeological sites or 129 museums administered by INAH, the National Archaeology and History Institute. Permits cost M$4843 per day for still photography and M$9686 per day for movie or video filming, and must be applied for at least two weeks in advance. You can apply by email; details are given in Spanish at www.tramites.inah.gob.mx.

Post

Mail to the US or Canada typically takes between four and 10 days to arrive. Mail to Europe averages one to two weeks.

If you're sending a package internationally from Mexico, be prepared to open it for customs inspection at the post office; it's better to take packing materials with you, or not seal it until you get there. For assured and speedy delivery, you can use one of the more expensive international courier services, such as **UPS** (www.ups.com), **FedEx** (www.fedex.com) or Mexico's **Estafeta** (www.estafeta.com). A 1kg package typically costs around US$39 to US$43 to the US or Canada, or from US$49 to Europe.

Public Holidays

On official national holidays, banks, post offices, government offices and many other offices and shops close throughout Mexico.

Año Nuevo (New Year's Day) January 1

Día de la Constitución (Constitution Day) February 5 (observed on first Monday of February)

Día de Nacimiento de Benito Juárez (anniversary of Benito Juárez's birth) March 21 (observed on third Monday of March)

Día del Trabajo (Labor Day) May 1

Día de la Independencia (Independence Day) September 16

Día de la Revolución (Revolution Day) November 20 (observed on third Monday of November)

Día de Navidad (Christmas Day) December 25

National holidays that fall on Saturday or Sunday are often switched to the nearest Friday or Monday.

In addition, many offices and businesses close on the following optional holidays:

Día de los Santos Reyes (Three Kings' Day, Epiphany) January 6

Día de la Bandera (Day of the National Flag) February 24

Viernes Santo (Good Friday) Two days before Easter Sunday; March or April

Cinco de Mayo (anniversary of Mexico's victory over the French at Puebla) May 5

Día de la Madre (Mother's Day) May 10

Día de la Raza (commemoration of Columbus' arrival in the New World) October 12

Día de Muertos (Day of the Dead) November 2

Día de Nuestra Señora de Guadalupe (Day of Our Lady of Guadalupe) December 12

Safe Travel

Mexico's drug war is undeniably horrific and frightening, but the violence is almost exclusively an internal matter between the drug gangs and people involved with them, or between gangs and Mexican security forces. Tourists have rarely been victims. Before you go, consult sources such as the US State Department and UK Foreign Office. Keep your eye on the news, travel by day and on toll highways where possible, and don't go into neighborhoods unfrequented by tourists after dark.

Mexico's main visitor destinations are by and large pretty safe places, and sensible precautions apply. Enjoy yourself along the coasts, but beware of undertows and riptides on ocean beaches, and don't leave your belongings unattended while you swim.

Theft & Robbery

Pickpocketing and bag snatching are risks on crowded buses and subway trains, at bus stops, bus terminals, airports, markets and in packed streets and plazas, especially in large cities. Pickpockets often work in teams, crowding their victims and trying to distract them.

Mugging is less common but more serious. These robbers may force you to remove your money belt, watch, rings etc. Do not resist, as resistance may be met with violence, and assailants may be armed. There are occasional victims of 'express kidnappings', with people forced to go to an ATM and withdraw money, but this rarely happens to foreign visitors.

The following precautions will minimize risks:

➡ Avoid semideserted places, such as empty streets and empty metro cars at night, pedestrian underpasses and isolated beaches.

➡ Use taxis instead of walking in potentially dodgy areas. In Mexico City, make sure you take the right kind of cab.

➡ Be alert to the people around you.

➡ Leave valuables in a safe at your accommodations unless you have immediate need of them. If no safe is available, divide valuables into different stashes secreted in your room or a locker.

GOVERNMENT TRAVEL ADVICE

These government websites have information on potential danger areas and general safety tips:

Australia (www.smartraveller.gov.au)

Canada (http://travel.gc.ca)

Germany (www.auswaertiges-amt.de)

Netherlands (www.rijksoverheid.nl)

New Zealand (www.safetravel.govt.nz)

UK (www.fco.gov.uk)

USA (http://travel.state.gov)

THE DRUG WARS

By most estimates, since 2007 an average of about 8000 people a year have died in violence in Mexico involving the gangs who traffic some US$19 to US$27 billion worth of illegal drugs to US drug users each year, with a rise in drug-related executions during the presidency of Peña Nieto. But the great majority of the violence happens in a relatively small number of areas.

➡ Cities along the US border (from Tijuana to Matamoros) and areas south from the border as far as Culiacán, Torreón and Tampico, have always been among the worst hit in intergang turf wars.

➡ Further south, the states of Michoacán and Guerrero have seen some of the highest organized-crime-related murder rates. Within each of these regions, violence occurs mostly in certain specific areas.

➡ Mexico's most visited regions, the Yucatán Peninsula and Baja California Sur, as well as parts of Oaxaca, Chiapas, Guanajuato, Querétaro and Puebla states, see minimal drug-related violence.

➡ Major coastal tourism destinations generally see little violence. Acapulco is the exception, but the vast majority of violent incidents take place between drug gang members and don't target visitors (though tourists have occasionally been caught in the crossfire).

➡ Durango state and northern Chihuahua are considered unsafe in parts, though Monterrey and Durango cities (particularly Monterrey) are now generally considered safe. It's essential to take local advice before trekking in remote parts of the Copper Canyon.

➡ Currently the US government advises against all travel in Michoacán outside Morelia. Most of the violence is confined to the Tierra Caliente.

➡ The stretch of the Michoacán coast between Las Brisas and Caleta has traditionally been cartel-controlled, though the cartels have never tolerated violence aimed at tourists. Roadblocks are sometimes set up to protest against the government and driving at night is not recommended.

Government foreign affairs departments and websites of embassies and consulates in Mexico offer information on drug-violence blackspots, though they tend to be over-cautious and some of the information is outdated, such as the age-old warning on the US government website regarding San Luis Potosi. Since the drug wars are a shifting phenomenon, it's a good idea to keep an eye on the media and ask local advice as you travel. Two well-informed websites are **InSight Crime** (www.insightcrime.org) and **Justice in Mexico Project** (http://justiceinmexico.org).

Kidnapping and extortion, including 'virtual kidnapping', in which the villains attempt to convince victims by telephone that they are under threat and must pay ransoms, are practiced by the drug gangs. Again, tourists are rarely victims.

➡ Carry just enough cash for your immediate needs in a pocket. If you have to carry valuables, use a money belt, shoulder wallet or pouch underneath your clothing.

➡ Don't keep cash, credit cards, purses, cameras and electronics in open view any longer than necessary. At ticket counters in bus terminals and airports, keep your bag between your feet.

➡ Go easy on alcohol – drunkenness makes you an easier victim.

If you do become a victim, report the incident to a tourist office, the police or your country's nearest consulate.

Telephone

Cell (Mobile) Phones & Smartphones

Mexico's main cell-phone (*teléfono celular*) companies include **Telcel** (www.telcel. com), **Movistar** (www.movistar.com.mx), **Virgin Mobile México** (www.virginmobile. mx) and **IUSACell** (www.iusa cell.com.mx). Telcel has the most widespread coverage, while Virgin Mobile SIMs have 30 days of free Whatsapp use.

➡ Roaming in Mexico with your own phone from home is possible if you have a GSM, 3G or 4G phone, but can be extremely expensive. **Roaming Zone** (www. roamingzone.com) is a useful source on roaming arrangements.

➡ Much cheaper is to put a Mexican SIM card ('chip') into your phone, but it will need to be unlocked for international use. Many Mexican cell-phone stores can unlock it for M$200 to M$300.

➡ SIMs are available from countless phone stores, often for M$50 or less.

➡ For around M$300 you can buy a new, no-frills Mexican cell phone with a chip and some call credit included. New smartphones start around M$1500, plus M$300 to M$500 a month for calling and data credit. Take your passport for ID when you go to buy a chip or phone; you may also have to provide a local address and postcode.

➡ You can buy new credit at convenience stores, newsstands, pharmacies and department stores.

CALLING CODES & COSTS

Like Mexican landlines, every Mexican SIM card has an area code. The area code and the phone's number total 10 digits.

➡ From cell phone to cell phone, just dial the 10-digit number.

➡ From cell phone to landline, dial the landline's area code and number (also a total of 10 digits).

➡ Landline to cell phone, dial ☑044 before the 10 digits if the cell phone's area code is the same as the area code you are dialing from, or ☑045 if the cell phone has a different area code.

➡ From another country to a Mexican cell phone, dial your international access code, then the Mexican country code (☑52), then 1, then the 10-digit number.
At the time of buying your chip you can choose your area code; calls are cheaper within your phone's area code.

Collect Calls

A *llamada por cobrar* (collect call) can cost the receiver more than if they call you, so you may prefer to arrange for the other party to call you. You can make collect calls from public card phones without a card. Call an operator on ☑020 for domestic calls; ☑090 for international calls.

Landlines

Mexican landlines *(teléfonos fijos)* have two- or three-digit area codes.

➡ From a landline to another landline in the same town, just dial the local number (seven or eight digits).

➡ From a landline to a landline in a different Mexican town, dial the long-distance prefix ☑01 then the area code then the local number.

➡ To make an international call, dial the international prefix ☑00 then the country code (☑1 for the US or Canada, ☑44 for the UK etc), area code and local number.

➡ To call a Mexican landline from another country, dial your international access code then the Mexico country code ☑52 then the area code and number.

Operator & Toll-Free Numbers

In 2016 the emergency phone number for Mexico is due to switch to ☑911, replacing numbers for the Red Cross, fire and police. The ☑911 number will be a free call, even from public phones and cell phones without credit.

Domestic operator ☑020

Emergency ☑066, ☑086

International operator ☑090

Mexican toll-free numbers
800 followed by seven digits; they always require the ☑01 long-distance prefix

Public Card Phones

You'll usually find some at airports and bus terminals and around town. Most are run by **Telmex** (www.telmex. com). To use a Telmex card phone you need a *tarjeta Ladatel* (phone card), sold at kiosks and shops every-where in denominations of M$30, M$50 and M$100. Insert it into the phone to make the call. Calls cost M$3 for unlimited time for local calls (M$1.50 per minute to local cell phones); M$2.50 per minute long distance within Mexico (M$3 to cells); M$5 per minute to the US (except Alaska and Hawaii), Canada and Central Amer-ica; and M$10 per minute anywhere else.

Time

Time Zones

Hora del Centro The same as CST (US Central Time; GMT minus six hours in winter, and GMT minus five hours during daylight saving), this time zone applies to most of Mexico, including Campeche, Chiapas, Tabasco and Yucatán.

Hora de las Montañas The same as MST (US Mountain Time; GMT minus seven hours in winter, GMT minus six hours during daylight saving), this time zone applies to five northern and western states in Mexico – Chihuahua, Nayarit, Sinaloa, Son-ora and Baja California Sur.

Hora del Pacífico The same as PST (US Pacific Time; GMT minus eight hours in winter, GMT minus seven hours during

---

SMARTPHONE TIPS

➡ Turn off mobile data in the phone's settings to avoid background apps swallowing up your phone credit.

➡ Make sure your phone is properly unlocked before signing up for a data package. All unlocked smartphones should be compatible with Mexican data systems.

➡ Free instant-messaging apps such as Whatsapp and Viber are widely used. When adding a phone contact, be sure to add 521 before the Mexican cell-phone number.

daylight saving), this time zone applies to Baja California Norte.

The state of Quintana Roo observes US Eastern Standard Time (GMT minus five hours during daylight saving).

Daylight Saving

Daylight saving time (*horario de verano;* summer time) in nearly all of Mexico runs from the first Sunday in April to the last Sunday in October. Clocks go forward one hour in April and back one hour in October. Exceptions to the general rule:

➡ The northwestern state of Sonora ignores daylight saving (like its US neighbor Arizona), so remains on MST all year.

➡ Ten cities on or near the US border – Ciudad Acuña, Ciudad Anahuac, Ciudad Juárez, Matamoros, Mexicali, Nuevo Laredo, Ojinaga, Piedras Negras, Reynosa and Tijuana – change their clocks on the second Sunday in March and the first Sunday in November to synchronize with US daylight-saving periods.

Tourist Information

Most towns of interest to tourists have a state or municipal tourist office. These are helpful with maps and brochures, and some staff members usually speak English.

You can call the Mexico City office of the national tourism secretariat, **Sectur** (✆078, 55-5250-0151, 800-903-92-00, in the US 800-482-9832; www.visitmexico.com), 24 hours a day, seven days a week, for information or help in English or Spanish. You'll find links to tourism websites of each Mexican state at www.sectur.gob.mx.

Travelers with Disabilities

A gradually growing number of hotels, restaurants, public buildings and archaeological sites provide wheelchair access, but sidewalks with wheelchair ramps are still uncommon. Mobility is easiest in major tourist resorts and more expensive hotels. Bus transportation can be difficult; flying or taking a taxi is easier. The absence of formal facilities is partly compensated by Mexicans' helpful attitudes, and special arrangements are gladly improvised. **Mobility International USA** (www.miusa.org) offers useful info.

Lonely Planet's free Accessible Travel guide can be downloaded here: http://lptravel.to/Accessible Travel

Visas & Tourist Permits

Every tourist must have a Mexican-government tourist permit, easily obtained on arrival. Citizens of the US, Canada, EU countries, Argentina, Australia, Brazil, Israel, Japan, New Zealand, Norway and Switzerland are among those who do not need visas to enter as tourists. Chinese, Indians, Russians and South Africans are among those who do need a visa. But Mexican visas are not required for people of any nationality who hold a valid visa for the USA.

If the purpose of your visit is to work (even as a volunteer), report, study or participate in humanitarian aid or human-rights observation, you may need a visa whatever your nationality. Visa procedures may take a few weeks and you may be required to apply in your country of residence or citizenship.

The websites of some Mexican consulates, including the **London consulate** (http://consulmex.sre.gob.mx/reinounido) and **Washington consulate** (http://consulmex.sre.gob.mx/washington), give information on visa regulations and similar matters. The rules are also summarized on the website of Mexico's **Instituto Nacional de Migración** (www.inm.gob.mx).

Non-US citizens passing (even in transit) through the USA on the way to or from Mexico should check well in advance on the US's complicated visa rules. Consult a US consulate or the **US State Department** (http://travel.state.gov) or **Customs and Border Protection** (www.cbp.gov) websites.

Tourist Permits & Fees

You must fill out the Mexican *Forma migratoria múltiple* (FMM; tourist permit) and get it stamped by Mexican immigration when you enter Mexico, and keep it till you leave. It's available at official border crossings, international airports and ports. At land borders you have to ask for the tourist permit.

The length of your permitted stay in Mexico is written on the card by the immigration officer. The maximum is 180 days, but they may sometimes put a lower number unless you tell them specifically what you need.

The fee for the tourist permit is around M$360, but it's free for people entering by land who stay less than seven days. If you enter Mexico by air, the fee is included in your airfare. If you enter Mexico by land, you must pay the fee once you arrive or at a bank in Mexico at any time before you re-enter the border zone to leave Mexico (or before you check-in at an airport to fly out of Mexico). The border zone is the territory between the border itself and the INM's control points on highways leading into the Mexican interior (usually 20km to 30km from the border).

Most Mexican border posts have on-the-spot bank offices where you can pay the DNR fee immediately on arrival in Mexico. Your tourist permit will be stamped to prove that you have paid.

Look after your tourist permit because you need to hand it in when leaving the country. Tourist permits (and fees) are not necessary for visits shorter than 72 hours within the border zones.

EXTENSIONS & LOST PERMITS

If the number of days given on your tourist permit is fewer than 180, its validity may be extended up to this maximum. To get a permit extended, apply to the INM, which has offices in many towns and cities: they're listed on the **INM website** (www.inm.gob.mx). Click 'Contact Us' then select 'Oficinas y Horarios' from the 'Contacto' box. The procedure costs the same as the tourist permit and should only take half an hour or so. You'll need your passport, tourist permit, photocopies of them and, at some offices, evidence of 'sufficient funds' (a major credit card is usually OK). Most INM offices will not extend a permit until a few days before it's due to expire.

If you lose your permit, contact your nearest tourist office, which should be able to give you an official note to take to your local INM office, which will issue a replacement for about M$500.

Volunteering

A good way to engage with and contribute to Mexican communities is to do some volunteer work. Many organizations can use your services for periods from a few hours to a year or more. Work ranges from protecting sea turtles to helping disadvantaged children. Some organizations are looking for people with relevant experience and/or Spanish-language skills, while others can use almost any willing hand.

Many language schools offer part-time local volunteering opportunities to complement the classes you take.

Volunteer Directories

Go Abroad (www.goabroad.com)

Go Overseas (www.gooverseas.com)

Idealist.org (www.idealist.org)

The Mexico Report (http://themexicoreport.com/non-profits-in-mexico)

Transitions Abroad (www.transitionsabroad.com)

Volunteer Oaxaca (http://volunteer-oaxaca.com)

Mexico-Based Programs
SOCIAL PROGRAMS

Casa de los Amigos (www.casadelosamigos.org) Mexico City–based, with volunteer programs to assist refugees and migrants.

Fundación En Vía (Map p424; www.envia.org) Oaxaca-based nonprofit organization providing micro-finance loans to help village women develop small businesses.

Junax (www.junax.org.mx) Offers information and lodging in San Cristóbal de las Casas for people volunteering with indigenous communities in Chiapas; Spanish-language skills needed.

Piña Palmera (www.pina palmera.org) Work with physically and intellectually disabled people at Zipolite on the Oaxaca coast.

ENVIRONMENTAL PROGRAMS

Centro Ecológico Akumal (www.ceakumal.org) Environmental work, including coastal management and turtle protection.

Grupo Ecologista Vida Milenaria (www.vidamilenaria.org.mx) Excellent turtle project at Tecolutla.

Natat é (www.natate.org) Turtle conservation and other projects in Chiapas and elsewhere.

Nomad Republic (www.nomadrepublic.net) Assisting with local cooperatives throughout Mexico in agriculture, education, tourism, health, water, energy and other fields.

Flora, Fauna y Cultura de México (984-871-52-44; www.florafaunaycultura.org) Conservation volunteering with turtles on the Caribbean coast.

Pronatura (www.pronaturappy.org.mx) Marine conservation and other projects in the Yucatán.

WWOOF Mexico (www.wwoofmexico.org) Volunteering on organic farms around Mexico.

Organizations Based Outside Mexico

Global Vision International (www.gviusa.com) Anything from marine conservation projects to volunteering with disadvantaged children.

Los Médicos Voladores (www.flyingdocs.org) Lend your medical skills to communities throughout Mexico and Central America.

Projects Abroad (www.projects-abroad.org) Volunteer projects involving teaching, conservation, agriculture and more.

Women Travelers

Gender equality has come a fair way, and Mexicans are generally a very polite people, but machismo is still a fact of life and lone female travelers may still be subject to some whistles, loud comments and attempts to chat them up.

Follow the examples of local women and avoid drinking alone in a cantina, hitchhiking, walking alone through empty streets at night, or going alone to isolated places. Keep a clear head. Excessive alcohol will make you vulnerable. For moral support, head for accommodations such as hostels and popular hotels where you're likely to meet other travelers, or join group excursions and activities.

On the streets of cities and towns and on local transportation, Mexican women cover up and don't display too much skin.

Transportation

GETTING THERE & AWAY

As well as flying in, you can enter Mexico by car or bus from the USA, Guatemala or Belize. Flights, tours and rail tickets can be booked online at www.lonelyplanet.com/bookings.

Entering the Country

US citizens traveling by land or sea can enter Mexico and return to the US with a passport card, but if traveling by air will need a passport. Citizens of other countries need their passport to enter. Some nationalities also need a visa.

Land

Belize

Frequent buses run from Chetumal's Nuevo Mercado Lázaro Cárdenas to the Belizean towns of Corozal (M$40 to M$50, one hour) and Orange Walk (M$75, two hours). Some continue on to Belize City (M$150, four hours).

Each person leaving Belize for Mexico needs to pay a US$15 exit fee for visits of less than 24 hours and US$19 for longer stays. All fees must be paid in cash, in Belizean or US currency; officials usually won't have change for US currency.

Guatemala

The road borders at Ciudad Cuauhtémoc–La Mesilla, Ciudad Hidalgo–Ciudad Tecún Umán and Talismán–El Carmen are all linked to Guatemala City and nearby cities within Guatemala and Mexico by buses and/or combis. The Ciudad Hidalgo–Ciudad Tecún Umán border is famous for shakedowns on the Guatemalan side; Talismán–El Carmen is definitely the border crossing to go for.

These companies run daily buses between Tapachula, Chiapas and Guatemala City (five to six hours):

Línea Dorada (www.lineadorada.com.gt) Fare M$240, departure 3pm.

Tica Bus (www.ticabus.com) Fare M$358; departure 7am.

Trans Galgos Inter (www.transgalgosinter.com.gt) Fare M$330-445; departures at 6am, noon and 11.45pm.

Between Chetumal and Flores, Línea Dorada runs one daily bus each way (M$450 or Q206, eight hours) via Belize City.

For the Río Usumacinta route between Palenque, Mexico, and Flores, there are vans between Palenque and Frontera Corozal (M$130, 2½ to three hours), from where it's a 40-minute boat trip to Bethel, Guatemala (M$80 to M$450 per person, depending on numbers). From Bethel hourly 2nd-class buses run to Flores (4½ hours) until 4pm.

Travel agencies in Palenque and Flores offer bus-boat-bus packages between the two places for M$450 to M$600, but if you're traveling this

---

CLIMATE CHANGE & TRAVEL

Every form of transportation that relies on carbon-based fuel generates CO_2, the main cause of human-induced climate change. Modern travel is dependent on airplanes, which might use less fuel per kilometer per person than most cars but travel much greater distances. The altitude at which aircraft emit gases (including CO_2) and particles also contributes to their climate change impact. Many websites offer 'carbon calculators' that allow people to estimate the carbon emissions generated by their journey and, for those who wish to do so, to offset the impact of the greenhouse gases emitted with contributions to portfolios of climate-friendly initiatives throughout the world. Lonely Planet offsets the carbon footprint of all staff and author travel.

route it's well worth taking the time to visit the outstanding Maya ruins at Yaxchilán, near Frontera Corozal.

Another possible route between Mexico and Flores is via the border at El Ceibo, near Tenosique, Tabasco. Vans, buses and taxis run between Tenosique and El Ceibo, and there are vans between the border and Flores.

USA

There are more than 40 official crossing points on the US–Mexico border. Some Mexican cities on the border and elsewhere in northern Mexico are affected by drug-gang violence, so check travel warnings if you are thinking of crossing this border. Ciudad Juárez is best passed through as quickly as possible. The road between Matamoros and Tampico was one to avoid at the time of writing.

A pedestrian-only crossing opened between the US and Mexico at Boquillas del Carmen–Big Bend National Park in 2014.

BUS

Cross-border bus services link many US and Mexican cities. On most trips you will transfer between a US and a Mexican bus on the US or Mexican side of the border, although you can usually buy a ticket right through to your final destination thanks to affiliations between different bus lines.

Autobuses Americanos (www.autobusesamericanos.com.mx) From Chicago and cities across the southern half of the USA to northeast, central north and central Mexico.

Greyhound (☑760-357-18-95, 558-79-95; www.greyhound.com; Calexico 123 East 1st St; Mexicali

1244 Centro Cívico-Comercial; ⏰5.30am-11.30pm) From California, Arizona and Texas to border cities, with onward transfers into northwest Mexico.

Ómnibus Mexicanos (www.omnibusmexicanos.com.mx) From Texas to northeast, central north and central Mexico.

Transporte Supremo (www.transportesupremo.com) Shuttle-van service between Phoenix, Sonoyta, Nogales, Yuma, Agua Prieta and Puerto Peñasco.

Tufesa (www.tufesa.com.mx) From many cities in the US southwest and California to northwest Mexico, Mazatlán and Guadalajara.

Turimex Internacional (www.turimex.com.mx) From Chicago, Texas and southeastern USA to northeast, central north and central Mexico.

Most routes are covered by several buses daily.

You can (often as quickly) go to the border on one bus (or train – see www.amtrak.com), cross it on foot or by local bus then catch an onward bus on the other side.

CAR & MOTORCYCLE

The rules for taking a vehicle into Mexico change from time to time. Check with a Mexican consulate, **Sanborn's** (www.sanborns insurance.com) or, in the US, the free **Mexican tourist information number** (☑800-482-9832).

Driving into Mexico is most useful for travelers who have plenty of time, like independence, have surfboards, diving equipment or other cumbersome luggage and/or will be traveling with at least one companion. Drivers should know at least a little Spanish and have basic mechanical knowledge. A sedan

with a trunk (boot) provides safer storage than a station wagon or hatchback.

Mexican mechanics are resourceful, but take as many spare parts as you can manage (spare fuel filters are very useful). Tires (including spare), shock absorbers and suspension should be in good condition. For security, have something to immobilize the steering wheel and consider getting a kill switch installed.

Motorcycling in Mexico is not for the fainthearted. Roads can be rough, and parts and mechanics hard to come by. Parts you'll find most easily will be for Kawasaki, Honda and Suzuki bikes.

VEHICLE PERMIT

You will need a *permiso de importación temporal de vehículo* (temporary vehicle import permit), costing US$44 (not including IVA tax), to take a vehicle into Mexico beyond the border zone that extends 20km to 30km into Mexico along the US frontier and up to 70km from the Guatemalan and Belizean frontiers. The only exceptions to this are the Baja California peninsula, where the permit is not needed, and Sonora state as far south as Guaymas, which offers a cheaper, simplified procedure – but you will need a permit if you embark a vehicle at Pichilingue (La Paz) in Baja California, on a ferry to 'mainland' Mexico.

The vehicle permits are issued by offices at border crossings, or at posts a few kilometers into Mexico, and also at Ensenada port and Pichilingue ferry terminal in Baja California. Details of all these locations, including their opening hours,

SAMPLE CROSS-BORDER BUS SERVICES

ROUTE	FARE (US$)	DURATION (HR)
Dallas–Monterrey	62	12
Houston–Mexico City	115	24
LA–Guadalajara	167	36

are given on the website of Banjército (www.banjercito.com.mx), the bank that deals with vehicle-import procedures – click on 'Red de Módulos IITV.' US and Canadian residents can also apply for the permit (at least a couple of weeks before your trip) on Banjército's website ('Application for Temporary Import Permit for Vehicles'), in which case it will be delivered to you by courier. The online procedure also involves obtaining electronic pre-authorization for your Mexican tourist permit.

The person importing the vehicle will need to carry the original and one or two photocopies of each of the following documents, which must all be in their own name (except that you can bring in your spouse's, parent's or child's vehicle if you can show a marriage or birth certificate proving your relationship):

➡ tourist permit (FMM); at the border go to *migración* before you process your vehicle permit

➡ certificate of title, or registration certificate, for the vehicle (you should have both of these if you plan to drive through Mexico into either Guatemala or Belize)

➡ a Visa or MasterCard credit or debit card issued outside Mexico, or a cash deposit of between US$200 and US$400 (depending on how old the car is). Your card details or deposit serve as a guarantee that you'll take the car out of Mexico before your FMM expires

➡ passport or US passport card

➡ if the vehicle is not fully paid for, a credit contract, or invoice letter not more than three months old, from the financing institution

➡ for a leased or rented vehicle, the contract, in the name of the person importing the vehicle

➡ for a company car, proof of employment by the company as well as proof of the company's ownership of the vehicle

With the permit you will be given a hologram sticker to display on your windshield.

When you leave Mexico, you must have the import permit canceled by the Mexican authorities. An official may do this as you enter the border zone, usually 20km to 30km before the border itself. If not, find the right official at the border crossing. If you leave Mexico without having the permit canceled, the authorities may assume you've left the vehicle in the country illegally and decide to keep your deposit, charge a fine to your credit card, or deny you permission to bring a vehicle into the country next time.

INSURANCE

It is essential to have Mexican liability insurance. If you are involved in an accident in Mexico, you can be jailed and have your vehicle impounded while responsibility is assessed. If you are to blame for an accident causing injury or death, you may be detained until you guarantee

restitution to the victims and payment of any fines. Adequate Mexican insurance coverage is the only real protection: it is regarded as a guarantee that restitution will be paid.

Mexican law recognizes only Mexican motor insurance *(seguro)*, so a US or Canadian policy, even if it provides coverage, is not acceptable to Mexican officialdom. You can buy Mexican motor insurance online through the long-established **Sanborn's** (www.sanbornsinsurance.com) and other companies. Mexican insurance is also sold in border towns in the US and at some border points. At the busiest border crossings there are insurance offices open 24 hours a day.

Short-term insurance is about US$15 a day for full coverage on a car worth under US$10,000. For longer than two weeks, it's often cheaper to get a semi-annual or annual policy. Liability-only insurance costs around half the full coverage cost.

Sea

Daily boats sail between Chetumal and San Pedro (US$60) and Caye Caulker (US$65) in Belize.

GETTING AROUND

Air

More than 60 Mexican cities have airports with scheduled passenger services. Flying can be good value on longer journeys, especially considering the long bus trip that is probably the alternative.

Aeroméxico (including its subsidiary, Aeroméxico Connect) has the biggest network, but Interjet, TAR Aerolíneas, Volaris and VivaAerobus serve many cities often with lower fares. VivaAerobus offers some

---

DEPARTURE TAX

The airport departure tax Tarifa de Uso de Aeropuerto (TUA) is almost always included in your ticket cost, but if it isn't, you must pay in cash during airport check-in. It varies from airport to airport and costs approximately US$25 for international flights and a little less for domestic flights. This tax is separate from the fee for your tourist permit, which is always included in airfares.

particularly low fares, but its website does not accept all foreign credit or bank cards.

Bicycle

Cycling is not a common way to tour Mexico. The size of the country, poor road surfaces, careless motorists and other road hazards are deterrents. If you're up for the challenge, take the mountainous topography and hot climate into account when planning. All cities have bicycle stores: a decent mountain bike suitable for a few weeks' touring costs around M$5000.

Consider the bring-your-own-bike tours of southern Mexico and the central volcano country offered by the fun and friendly **iEl Tour** (www.bikemexico.com).

Boat

Vehicle and passenger ferries connecting Baja California and the Mexican mainland sail Santa Rosalía–Guaymas; La Paz–Mazatlán; and La Paz–Topolobampo. One-way passenger seat fares cost M$897 to M$1102, depending on the route. A car up to 5.4m long costs M$2004 to M$2354.

Bus

Mexico has a good road network and comfortable, frequent, reasonably priced bus services connect all cities. Most cities and towns have one main bus terminal from which all long-distance buses operate. It may be called the Terminal de Autobuses, Central de Autobuses, Central Camionera or La Central (not to be confused with *el centro*, the city center!).

Bus stations in major cities tend to be generally clean, safe and highly functional.

Classes

Mexico's buses (called *camiones*, unlike in other Spanish-speaking countries) offer the following classes.

DELUXE & EXECUTIVE

De lujo services, *primera plus* and the even more comfortable *ejecutivo* (executive) buses run mainly on the busier intercity routes. They are swift and comfortable, with reclining seats, plenty of legroom, air-conditioning, movies on (individual) video screens, few or no stops, toilets on board (sometimes separate ones for men and

women) and often drinks, snacks and even wi-fi. They use toll roads wherever available.

FIRST CLASS

Primera (1a) clase buses have a comfortable numbered seat for each passenger. All sizable towns are served by 1st-class buses. Standards of comfort are adequate at the very least. The buses have air-conditioning and a toilet, and they stop infrequently. They show movies on TV screens. They also use toll roads where possible.

SECOND CLASS

Segunda (2a) clase or *'económico'* buses serve small towns and villages and provide cheaper, slower travel on some intercity routes. A few are almost as quick, comfortable and direct as 1st-class buses. Others are old, slow and shabby. Few have toilets. These buses tend to take non-toll roads and will stop anywhere to pick up passengers, so if you board midroute you might make some of the trip standing. In remoter areas, they are often the only buses available.

MEXICAN DOMESTIC AIRLINES

AIRLINE	WEBSITE	AREAS SERVED
Aéreo Calafia	www.aereocalafia.com.mx	Baja California, northwest and central Mexico, Puerto Vallarta
Aeromar	www.aeromar.com.mx	central Mexico, west Mexico, northeast Mexico, Gulf coast, Pacific coast
Aeroméxico	www.aeromexico.com	46 cities nationwide
Interjet	www.interjet.com.mx	34 cities nationwide
Ka'an Air	www.kaanair.com.mx	Tuxtla Gutierrez to Palenque, Villahermosa and Tapachula
Magnicharters	www.magnicharters.com	Mexico City, Guadalajara, León, Mérida, coastal resorts
Mayair	www.mayair.com.mx	Yucatán Peninsula, Veracruz
TAR Aerolíneas	www.tarmexico.com	16 cities nationwide, excluding the north
VivaAerobus	www.vivaaerobus.com	24 cities nationwide
Volaris	www.volaris.com	39 cities nationwide

TRANSPORTATION GETTING AROUND

Companies

Mexico has hundreds of bus companies. Many of the major ones belong to large groups that dominate bus transportation in different parts of the country. Their websites have schedule information.

ETN Turistar (www.etn.com.mx) Comprises two good executive lines, ETN and Turistar, covering the center, north and west of Mexico and down the Pacific coast to Puerto Escondido.

Grupo ADO (www.ado.com.mx) Connects Mexico City and the east, south and southeast of the country. Companies include ADO Plátino (deluxe), ADO GL (deluxe/1st class) and ADO and OCC (1st class).

Grupo Estrella Blanca (www.estrellablanca.com.mx) Focuses on Mexico City and the center, north and west of Mexico. Includes Futura Select (deluxe) and Futura, Elite, Oriente and Transportes Chihuahuenses (1st class).

Primera Plus (www.primeraplus.com.mx) This 1st-class company provides frequent service in the center of the country.

Costs

First-class bus fares cost around M$1.25 per kilometer and travel 70km to 80km in an hour. Deluxe buses cost about 20% more than 1st class; executive services can be 50% more. Second-class buses cost about 20% less than 1st class.

Reservations

For 1st-class, deluxe and executive buses, buy your ticket in the bus terminal before the trip. For trips of up to four or five hours on routes with frequent service, you can usually just go to the bus terminal, buy a ticket and leave without much delay. For longer trips, or routes with infrequent service, or for any trip at holiday times, it's best to buy a ticket a day or more in advance. You can usually select your seat when you buy your ticket. Try to avoid the back of the bus, which is where the toilets are located and also tends to give a bumpier ride.

Many 2nd-class services have no ticket office; you pay your fare to the conductor.

In some cities you can buy bus tickets from downtown agencies to avoid a trip to the bus terminal. **Mi Escape** (www.miescape.mx) has dozens of ticket offices for Grupo ADO buses, in around 20 cities.

Car & Motorcycle

Having a vehicle in Mexico gives you a whole lot of flexibility and freedom, and with a little adaptation to local road conditions is no more difficult than in most other countries.

Driver's License

To drive a motor vehicle in Mexico, you need a valid driver's license from your home country.

Fuel

All *gasolina* (gasoline) and diesel fuel in Mexico is sold by the government's monopoly, Pemex (Petróleos Mexicanos). Most towns, even small ones, have a Pemex station, and stations are pretty common on most major roads. In remote areas, fill up whenever you can. Gasoline is all *sin plomo* (unleaded). There are two varieties:

Magna (87 octane) Roughly equivalent to US regular unleaded, costing about M$13.57 per liter (US$3.10 per US gallon).

Premium (91 octane and lower in sulfur content) Roughly equivalent to US super unleaded, costing about M$14.38. Diesel fuel is widely available at around M$14.20 per liter. Regular Mexican diesel has a higher sulfur content than US diesel, but a *bajo azufre* (low sulfur) variety has started to become available in Mexico City and some nearby areas. Gas stations have pump attendants (who appreciate a tip of around M$5).

HOW MANY STOPS?

It's useful to understand the difference between the types of bus service on offer.

Sin escalas Nonstop

Directo Very few stops

Ordinario Stops wherever passengers want to get on or off the bus; deluxe and 1st-class buses are never *ordinario*

Express Nonstop on short- to medium-length trips; very few stops on long trips

Local Bus that starts its journey at the bus station you're in and usually leaves on time; *local* service is preferable to *de paso*.

De paso Bus that started its journey somewhere else; you may have to wait until it arrives before any tickets are sold, and if it's full you have to wait for the next one

Vía corta Short route

Vía cuota By toll road

Viaje redondo Round trip

Rental

Auto rental in Mexico can be expensive by US or European standards, but is not hard to organize. Many major international rental firms have offices throughout the country.

Renters must provide a valid driver's license (your home license is OK), passport and major credit card, and are usually required to be at least 21 years of age (sometimes 25, or if you're aged 21 to 24 you may have to pay a surcharge). Read the small print of the rental agreement. In addition to the basic rental rate, there will be tax and insurance costs. Comprehensive insurance can more than double the basic cost quoted in some online bookings – you'll usually have the option of liability-only insurance at a lower rate. Ask exactly what insurance options cover: theft and damage insurance may only cover a percentage of costs, or the insurance might not be valid for travel on country tracks. It's best to have plenty of liability coverage.

Rental rates typically start around M$500 to M$600 a day, including unlimited kilometers, basic insurance and tax. In some beach resorts you may pay as little as M$400. If you rent by the week or month, per-day costs come down. The extra charge for drop-off in another city, when available, is usually about M$5 per kilometer.

Motorbikes or scooters can be rented in a few tourist centers. You're usually required to have a driver's license and a credit card. Many renters do not offer any insurance, however.

Road Conditions & Hazards

➡ Highways are serviceable and fairly fast when traffic is not heavy. There are more than 6000km of toll highways (*autopistas*), which are generally good, four-lane roads. Tolls vary from M$1 to M$2 per kilometer.

THE GREEN ANGELS

The Mexican tourism secretariat, Sectur, maintains a network of Ángeles Verdes (Green Angels) – bilingual mechanics in green uniforms and green trucks who patrol 60,000km of major highways throughout the country daily from 8am to 6pm looking for tourists in trouble. They can give you directions, make minor repairs, change tires, provide fuel and oil and arrange towing and other assistance if necessary. Service is free, and parts, gasoline and oil are provided at cost. If you have access to a telephone, you can call the **hotline** (🗗078).

➡ Driving at night is best avoided, since unlit vehicles, hard-to-see speed bumps, rocks, pedestrians and animals on the roads are common and drunken drivers are more numerous – and general highway security is better by day.

➡ Some hijackings, holdups and illegal roadblocks connected with drug-gang activities occur, mainly in the north. The northeastern states of Tamaulipas and Nuevo León are especially notorious – above all, the Tampico–Matamoros road. In this part of the country especially, it is best to stick to toll highways, drive only by day and keep doors locked and windows closed when driving through cities. Check travel warnings and seek local advice. If you do become a victim, do not try to resist.

➡ There are also some perfectly genuine military and police roadblocks, which are generally looking for illegal weapons, drugs, migrants or contraband. They are unlikely to give tourists a hard time and are no cause for alarm.

➡ It's best to leave vehicles in secure lock-up parking lots overnight. These are fairly common in cities, and hotels can tell you where they are if they don't have their own secure parking.

➡ About 14 of every 100,000 Mexicans die in road accidents each year – more than double the rate of most Western countries. Driving under the influence of alcohol and non-use of seat belts are more prevalent here, but otherwise Mexicans seem to drive as cautiously and sensibly as people anywhere. Traffic density, poor surfaces, speed bumps, animals, bicycles and pedestrians all help to keep speeds down.

➡ Be wary of Alto (Stop) signs, *topes* (speed bumps) and holes in the road. They are often not where you'd expect them and missing one can cost you in traffic fines or car damage. 'Tope' or 'Vibradores' signs warn you of many speed bumps – the deadly ones are the ones with no warning signs!

➡ There is always the chance that you will be pulled over by traffic police. If this happens, stay calm and polite. If you don't think you have committed an infraction, you don't have to pay a bribe, and acting dumb may eventually make the cop give up. You can also ask to see the officer's identification, the documentation about the law you have supposedly broken, ask to speak to a superior, and note the officer's name, badge number, vehicle number and department (federal, state or municipal). Make clear that you want to pay any fines at a police station and get a receipt. If you then wish to make a complaint, head for a state tourist office.

Road Rules

➡ Drive on the right-hand side of the road.

➡ Speed limits range between 80km/h and 120km/h on open highways (less when highways pass through built-up areas), and between 30km/h and 50km/h in towns and cities.

➡ One-way streets are the rule in cities.

➡ Legal blood-alcohol limits for drivers range from 0.5g/L to 0.8g/L – roughly two or three beers or tequilas.

➡ Antipollution rules in Mexico City ban most vehicles from the city's roads on one day each week.

Local Transportation

Bicycle

Bicycle culture is on the up in Mexican cities. Most of them are flat enough to make cycling an option and some city authorities are starting to accommodate cyclists. Mexico City offers free bike rental and at least three dedicated bike routes. In December 2014 Guadalajara introduced Mibici (www.mibici.net), Mexico's third bike-sharing scheme after Mexico City and Puebla. They work in the same way as other global bike-shares. You can hire decent road and mountain bikes in several other towns for M$250 to M$650 per day. Seek out less traffic-infested routes and you should enjoy it. Mass Sunday rides are a growing phenomenon.

Bus

Generally known as *camiones*, local buses are usually the cheapest way to get around cities and out to near-by towns and villages. They run frequently, and fares in cities are a few pesos. In many cities, fleets of small, modern *microbuses* have replaced the noisy, dirty older buses.

Buses usually halt only at fixed *paradas* (bus stops),

PRACTICAL TIPS

➡ Buses do occasionally get held up and robbed. Traveling by day and on deluxe or 1st-class buses, which use toll highways where possible, minimizes any risk.

➡ Baggage is safe if stowed in the baggage hold – get a receipt for it when you hand it over. Keep your most valuable possessions in the cabin with you.

➡ Air-conditioned buses can get cold, so wear long pants or a skirt and take a sweater or jacket and maybe a blanket on board. Eye-pads can be handy if you don't want to watch videos the entire trip!

though in some places you can hold your hand out to stop one at any street corner.

Colectivo, Combi, Minibus & Pesero

In some areas a variety of small vehicles provide alternatives to buses. *Taxis colectivos* (shared taxis, usually carrying four passengers who each pay a quarter of the full cab fare), Volkswagen minibuses (combis) and more comfortable passenger carrying vans, such as Chevrolet Suburbans or Nissan Urvans, operate services between some towns. Fares are typically a little less than 1st-class buses. *Microbuses* or 'micros' are small, typically fairly new, 2nd-class buses with around 25 seats, usually running short routes between nearby towns. More primitive are passenger-carrying *camionetas* (pickups) and *camiones* (trucks), with fares similar to 2nd-class bus fares. Standing in the back of a lurching truck full of *campesinos* (land workers) and their machetes and animals is always an experience to remember!

Metro

Mexico City, Guadalajara and Monterrey all have metro (subway, underground railway) systems. Mexico City's, in particular, is a quick, cheap and useful way of getting around. With 195 stations and over four million passengers every weekday, it's the world's third-busiest subway, so avoid using it in rush hour.

Taxi

Taxis are common in towns and cities, and surprisingly economical. City rides cost around M$15 to M$20 per kilometer. If a taxi has a meter, you can ask the driver if it's working ('¿Funciona el taxímetro?'). If the taxi doesn't have a functioning meter, establish the price of the ride before getting in (this may involve a bit of haggling).

Many airports and some big bus terminals have a system of authorized ticket-taxis – you buy a fixed-price ticket to your destination from a special *taquilla* (ticket window) and then hand it to the driver instead of paying cash. This saves haggling and major rip-offs, but fares are usually higher than you could get on the street.

Renting a taxi for a day-long out-of-town jaunt generally costs similar to a cheap rental car – around M$600.

Train

The spectacular **Ferrocarril Chihuahua Pacífico** (Copper Canyon Railway; ☑ 614-439-72-12, from the US 888-484-1623; www.chepe.com.mx; full journey 1st/2nd class M$2482/1767), running through the Sierra Madre Occidental between Los Mochis and Chihuahua, is one of the highlights of travel in Mexico. The rest of Mexico's regular passenger-train system died after the railroads were privatized in the 1990s.

Language

Mexican Spanish pronunciation is easy, as most sounds have equivalents in English. Also, Spanish spelling is phonetically consistent, meaning that there's a clear and consistent relationship between what you see in writing and how it's pronounced. Note that kh is a throaty sound (like the 'ch' in the Scottish *loch*), v and b are like a soft English 'v' (between a 'v' and a 'b'), and r is strongly rolled. There are also some variations in spoken Spanish across Latin America, the most notable being the pronunciation of the letters *ll* and *y*. In some parts of Mexico they are pronounced like the 'll' in 'million', but in most areas they are pronounced like the 'y' in 'yes', and this is how they are represented in our pronunciation guides. In other Latin American countries you might also hear them pronounced like the 's' in 'measure', the 'sh' in 'shut' or the 'dg' in 'judge'. The stressed syllables are indicated with italics in our pronunciation guides. Bearing these few things in mind and reading our colored pronunciation guides as if they were English, you should be understood just fine.

The polite form is used in this chapter; where both polite and informal options are given, they are indicated by the abbreviations 'pol' and 'inf'. Where necessary, both masculine and feminine forms of words are included, separated by a slash and with the masculine form first, eg *perdido/a* (m/f).

BASICS

Hello.	*Hola.*	o·la
Goodbye.	*Adiós.*	a·dyos

WANT MORE?

For in-depth language information and handy phrases, check out Lonely Planet's *Mexican Spanish Phrasebook*. You'll find it at **shop.lonelyplanet.com**, or you can buy Lonely Planet's iPhone phrasebooks at the Apple App Store.

How are you?	*¿Qué tal?*	ke tal
Fine, thanks.	*Bien, gracias.*	byen gra·syas
Excuse me.	*Perdón.*	per·don
Sorry.	*Lo siento.*	lo syen·to
Please.	*Por favor.*	por fa·vor
Thank you.	*Gracias.*	gra·syas
You're welcome.	*De nada.*	de na·da
Yes.	*Sí.*	see
No.	*No.*	no

My name is ...
Me llamo ...   me ya·mo ...

What's your name?
¿Cómo se llama Usted?   ko·mo se ya·ma oo·ste (pol)
¿Cómo te llamas?   ko·mo te ya·mas (inf)

Do you speak English?
¿Habla inglés?   a·bla een·gles (pol)
¿Hablas inglés?   a·blas een·gles (inf)

I don't understand.
Yo no entiendo.   yo no en·tyen·do

ACCOMMODATIONS

I'd like a room.	*Quisiera una habitación ...*	kee·sye·ra oo·na a·bee·ta·syon ...
single	*individual*	een·dee·vee·dwal
double	*doble*	do·ble

How much is it per night/person?
¿Cuánto cuesta por noche/persona?   kwan·to kwes·ta por no·che/per·so·na

Does it include breakfast?
¿Incluye el desayuno?   een·kloo·ye el de·sa·yoo·no

campsite	*terreno de cámping*	te·re·no de kam·peeng
hotel	*hotel*	o·tel
guesthouse	*pensión*	pen·syon

KEY PATTERNS

To get by in Spanish, mix and match these simple patterns with words of your choice:

When's (the next flight)?
¿Cuándo sale   kwan·do sa·le
(el próximo vuelo)?   (el prok·see·mo vwe·lo)

Where's (the station)?
¿Dónde está   don·de es·ta
(la estación)?   (la es·ta·syon)

Where can I (buy a ticket)?
¿Dónde puedo   don·de pwe·do
(comprar un billete)? (kom·prar oon bee·ye·te)

Do you have (a map)?
¿Tiene (un mapa)?   tye·ne (oon ma·pa)

Is there (a toilet)?
¿Hay (servicios)?   ai (ser·vee·syos)

I'd like (a coffee).
Quisiera (un café).   kee·sye·ra (oon ka·fe)

I'd like (to hire a car).
Quisiera (alquilar   kee·sye·ra (al·kee·lar
un coche).   oon ko·che)

Can I (enter)?
¿Se puede (entrar)?   se pwe·de (en·trar)

Could you please (help me)?
¿Puede (ayudarme),   pwe·de (a·yoo·dar·me)
por favor?   por fa·vor

Do I have to (get a visa)?
¿Necesito   ne·se·see·to
(obtener   (ob·te·ner
un visado)?   oon vee·sa·do)

youth hostel	albergue	al·ber·ge
	juvenil	khoo·ve·neel
air-con	aire acondi-	ai·re a·kon·dee-
	cionado	syo·na·do
bathroom	baño	ba·nyo
bed	cama	ka·ma
window	ventana	ven·ta·na

DIRECTIONS

Where's ...?
¿Dónde está ...?   don·de es·ta ...

What's the address?
¿Cuál es la dirección? kwal es la dee·rek·syon

Could you please write it down?
¿Puede escribirlo,   pwe·de es·kree·beer·lo
por favor?   por fa·vor

Can you show me (on the map)?
¿Me lo puede indicar me lo pwe·de een·dee·kar
(en el mapa)?   (en el ma·pa)

| at the corner | en la esquina | en la es·kee·na |

at the traffic lights	en el semáforo	en el se·ma·fo·ro
behind ...	detrás de ...	de·tras de ...
far	lejos	le·khos
in front of ...	enfrente de ...	en·fren·te de ...
left	izquierda	ees·kyer·da
near	cerca	ser·ka
next to ...	al lado de ...	al la·do de ...
opposite ...	frente a ...	fren·te a ...
right	derecha	de·re·cha
straight ahead	todo recto	to·do rek·to

EATING & DRINKING

Can I see the menu, please?
¿Puedo ver el menú,   pwe·do ver el me·noo
por favor?   por fa·vor

What would you recommend?
¿Qué recomienda?   ke re·ko·myen·da

Do you have vegetarian food?
¿Tienen comida   tye·nen ko·mee·da
vegetariana?   ve·khe·ta·rya·na

I don't eat (meat).
No como (carne).   no ko·mo (kar·ne)

That was delicious!
¡Estaba buenísimo!   es·ta·ba bwe·nee·see·mo

Cheers!
¡Salud!   sa·loo

The bill, please.
La cuenta, por favor. la kwen·ta por fa·vor

I'd like a table for ...	Quisiera una mesa para ...	kee·sye·ra oo·na me·sa pa·ra ...
(eight) o'clock	las (ocho)	las (o·cho)
(two) people	(dos) personas	(dos) per·so·nas

Key Words

bottle	botella	bo·te·ya
breakfast	desayuno	de·sa·yoo·no
cold	frío	free·o
dessert	postre	pos·tre
dinner	cena	se·na
fork	tenedor	te·ne·dor
glass	vaso	va·so
hot (warm)	caliente	kal·yen·te
knife	cuchillo	koo·chee·yo
lunch	comida	ko·mee·da
plate	plato	pla·to
restaurant	restaurante	res·tow·ran·te
spoon	cuchara	koo·cha·ra

Meat & Fish

bacon	*tocino*	to·*see*·no
beef	*carne de vaca*	*kar*·ne de *va*·ka
chicken	*pollo*	*po*·yo
crab	*cangrejo*	kan·*gre*·kho
duck	*pato*	*pa*·to
goat	*cabra*	*ka*·bra
ham	*jamón*	kha·*mon*
lamb	*cordero*	kor·*de*·ro
lobster	*langosta*	lan·*gos*·ta
mutton	*carnero*	kar·*ne*·ro
octopus	*pulpo*	*pool*·po
oysters	*ostras*	*os*·tras
pork	*cerdo*	*ser*·do
shrimp	*camarones*	ka·ma·*ro*·nes
squid	*calamar*	ka·la·*mar*
turkey	*pavo*	*pa*·vo
veal	*ternera*	ter·*ne*·ra
venison	*venado*	ve·*na*·do

Fruit & Vegetables

apple	*manzana*	man·*sa*·na
apricot	*albaricoque*	al·ba·ree·*ko*·ke
banana	*plátano*	*pla*·ta·no
beans	*frijoles*	free·*kho*·les
cabbage	*col*	kol
cactus fruit	*tuna*	*too*·na
carrot	*zanahoria*	sa·na·o·*rya*
cherry	*cereza*	se·*re*·sa
corn	*maíz*	ma·*ees*
corn (fresh)	*elote*	e·*lo*·te
cucumber	*pepino*	pe·*pee*·no
grape	*uvas*	*oo*·vas
grapefruit	*toronja*	to·*ron*·kha
lentils	*lentejas*	len·*te*·khas
lettuce	*lechuga*	le·*choo*·ga
mushroom	*champiñón*	cham·pee·*nyon*
nuts	*nueces*	*nwe*·ses
onion	*cebolla*	se·*bo*·ya
orange	*naranja*	na·*ran*·kha
peach	*melocotón*	me·lo·ko·*ton*
peas	*guisantes*	gee·*san*·tes
pepper	*pimiento*	pee·*myen*·to
pineapple	*piña*	*pee*·nya
plantain	*plátano macho*	*pla*·ta·no *ma*·cho
plum	*ciruela*	seer·*we*·la
potato	*patata*	pa·*ta*·ta

pumpkin	*calabaza*	ka·la·*ba*·sa
spinach	*espinacas*	es·pee·*na*·kas
strawberry	*fresa*	*fre*·sa
(red) tomato	*(ji)tomate*	(khee·)to·*ma*·te
watermelon	*sandía*	san·*dee*·a

Other

bread	*pan*	pan
butter	*mantequilla*	man·te·*kee*·ya
cake	*pastel*	pas·*tel*
cheese	*queso*	*ke*·so
cookie	*galleta*	ga·*ye*·ta
(fried) eggs	*huevos (fritos)*	*we*·vos (*free*·tos)
French fries	*papas fritas*	*pa*·pas *free*·tas
honey	*miel*	myel
ice cream	*helado*	e·*la*·do
jam	*mermelada*	mer·me·*la*·da
pepper	*pimienta*	pee·*myen*·ta
rice	*arroz*	a·*ros*
salad	*ensalada*	en·sa·*la*·da
salt	*sal*	sal
soup	*caldo/sopa*	*kal*·do/*so*·pa
sugar	*azúcar*	a·*soo*·kar

Drinks

beer	*cerveza*	ser·*ve*·sa
coffee	*café*	ka·*fe*
juice	*zumo*	*soo*·mo
milk	*leche*	*le*·che
smoothie	*licuado*	lee·*kwa*·do
sorbet	*nieve*	*nye*·ve
(black) tea	*té (negro)*	te (*ne*·gro)
(mineral) water	*agua (mineral)*	*a*·gwa (mee·ne·*ral*)
(red/white) wine	*vino (tinto/ blanco)*	*vee*·no (*teen*·to/ *blan*·ko)

QUESTION WORDS

How?	*¿Cómo?*	*ko*·mo
What?	*¿Qué?*	ke
When?	*¿Cuándo?*	*kwan*·do
Where?	*¿Dónde?*	*don*·de
Who?	*¿Quién?*	kyen
Why?	*¿Por qué?*	por *ke*

EMERGENCIES

Help!	*¡Socorro!*	so·ko·ro
Go away!	*¡Vete!*	ve·te
Call ...!	*¡Llame a ...!*	ya·me a ...
a doctor	*un médico*	oon me·dee·ko
the police	*la policía*	la po·lee·see·a

I'm lost.
Estoy perdido/a. es·toy per·dee·do/a (m/f)

I'm ill.
Estoy enfermo/a. es·toy en·fer·mo/a (m/f)

It hurts here.
Me duele aquí. me dwe·le a·kee

I'm allergic to (antibiotics).
Soy alérgico/a a soy a·ler·khee·ko/a a
(los antibióticos). (los an·tee·byo·tee·kos) (m/f)

Where are the toilets?
¿Dónde están los don·de es·tan los
baños? ba·nyos

SHOPPING & SERVICES

I'd like to buy ...
Quisiera comprar ... kee·sye·ra kom·prar ...

I'm just looking.
Sólo estoy mirando. so·lo es·toy mee·ran·do

Can I look at it?
¿Puedo verlo? pwe·do ver·lo

I don't like it.

NUMBERS

1	*uno*	oo·no
2	*dos*	dos
3	*tres*	tres
4	*cuatro*	kwa·tro
5	*cinco*	seen·ko
6	*seis*	seys
7	*siete*	sye·te
8	*ocho*	o·cho
9	*nueve*	nwe·ve
10	*diez*	dyes
20	*veinte*	veyn·te
30	*treinta*	treyn·ta
40	*cuarenta*	kwa·ren·ta
50	*cincuenta*	seen·kwen·ta
60	*sesenta*	se·sen·ta
70	*setenta*	se·ten·ta
80	*ochenta*	o·chen·ta
90	*noventa*	no·ven·ta
100	*cien*	syen
1000	*mil*	meel

No me gusta. no me goos·ta

How much is it?
¿Cuánto cuesta? kwan·to kwes·ta

That's too expensive.
Es muy caro. es mooy ka·ro

Can you lower the price?
¿Podría bajar un po·dree·a ba·khar oon
poco el precio? po·ko el pre·syo

There's a mistake in the bill.
Hay un error ai oon e·ror
en la cuenta. en la kwen·ta

ATM	*cajero automático*	ka·khe·ro ow·to·ma·tee·ko
credit card	*tarjeta de crédito*	tar·khe·ta de kre·dee·to
internet cafe	*cibercafé*	see·ber·ka·fe
market	*mercado*	mer·ka·do
post office	*correos*	ko·re·os
tourist office	*oficina de turismo*	o·fee·see·na de too·rees·mo

TIME & DATES

What time is it? *¿Qué hora es?* ke o·ra es

It's (10) o'clock. *Son (las diez).* son (las dyes)

It's half past (one). *Es (la una) y media.* es (la oo·na) ee me·dya

morning	*mañana*	ma·nya·na
afternoon	*tarde*	tar·de
evening	*noche*	no·che
yesterday	*ayer*	a·yer
today	*hoy*	oy
tomorrow	*mañana*	ma·nya·na

Monday	*lunes*	loo·nes
Tuesday	*martes*	mar·tes
Wednesday	*miércoles*	myer·ko·les
Thursday	*jueves*	khwe·ves
Friday	*viernes*	vyer·nes
Saturday	*sábado*	sa·ba·do
Sunday	*domingo*	do·meen·go

January	*enero*	e·ne·ro
February	*febrero*	fe·bre·ro
March	*marzo*	mar·so
April	*abril*	a·breel
May	*mayo*	ma·yo
June	*junio*	khoon·yo
July	*julio*	khool·yo
August	*agosto*	a·gos·to

September	*septiembre*	sep·*tyem*·bre
October	*octubre*	ok·*too*·bre
November	*noviembre*	no·*vyem*·bre
December	*diciembre*	dee·*syem*·bre

TRANSPORTATION

boat	*barco*	*bar*·ko
bus	*autobús*	ow·to·*boos*
plane	*avión*	a·*vyon*
train	*tren*	tren
first	*primero*	pree·*me*·ro
last	*último*	*ool*·tee·mo
next	*próximo*	*prok*·see·mo
A ... ticket, please.	*Un billete de ..., por favor.*	oon bee·*ye*·te de ... por fa·*vor*
1st-class	*primera clase*	pree·*me*·ra *kla*·se
2nd-class	*segunda clase*	se·*goon*·da *kla*·se
one-way	*ida*	*ee*·da
return	*ida y vuelta*	*ee*·da ee *vwel*·ta

I want to go to ...
Quisiera ir a ...   kee·*sye*·ra eer a ...

Does it stop at ...?
¿Para en ...?   *pa*·ra en ...

What stop is this?
¿Cuál es esta parada?   kwal es *es*·ta pa·*ra*·da

What time does it arrive/leave?
¿A qué hora llega/sale?   a ke o·ra ye·ga/*sa*·le

Please tell me when we get to ...
¿Puede avisarme cuando lleguemos a ...?   *pwe*·de a·vee·*sar*·me *kwan*·do ye·*ge*·mos a ...

I want to get off here.
Quiero bajarme aquí.   *kye*·ro ba·*khar*·me a·*kee*

airport	*aeropuerto*	a·e·ro·*pwer*·to
aisle seat	*asiento de pasillo*	a·*syen*·to de pa·*see*·yo
bus stop	*parada de autobuses*	pa·*ra*·da de ow·to·*boo*·ses
cancelled	*cancelado*	kan·se·*la*·do
delayed	*retrasado*	re·tra·*sa*·do
platform	*plataforma*	pla·ta·*for*·ma
ticket office	*taquilla*	ta·*kee*·ya
timetable	*horario*	o·*ra*·ryo
train station	*estación de trenes*	es·ta·*syon* de *tre*·nes

SIGNS

Abierto	Open
Cerrado	Closed
Entrada	Entrance
Hombres/Varones	Men
Mujeres/Damas	Women
Prohibido	Prohibited
Salida	Exit
Servicios/Baños	Toilets

window seat	*asiento junto a la ventana*	a·*syen*·to *khoon*·to a la ven·*ta*·na
I'd like to hire a ...	*Quisiera alquilar ...*	kee·*sye*·ra al·kee·*lar* ...
4WD	*un todo-terreno*	oon to·do·te·*re*·no
bicycle	*una bicicleta*	*oo*·na bee·see·*kle*·ta
car	*un coche*	oon *ko*·che
motorcycle	*una moto*	*oo*·na *mo*·to
child seat	*asiento de seguridad para niños*	a·*syen*·to de se·goo·ree·*da* pa·ra *nee*·nyos
diesel	*petróleo*	pet·*ro*·le·o
helmet	*casco*	*kas*·ko
hitchhike	*hacer botella*	a·ser bo·*te*·ya
mechanic	*mecánico*	me·*ka*·nee·ko
petrol/gas	*gasolina*	ga·so·*lee*·na
service station	*gasolinera*	ga·so·lee·*ne*·ra
truck	*camion*	ka·*myon*

Is this the road to ...?
¿Se va a ... por esta carretera?   se va a ... por es·ta ka·re·*te*·ra

(How long) Can I park here?
¿(Cuánto tiempo) Puedo aparcar aquí?   (*kwan*·to *tyem*·po) *pwe*·do a·par·*kar* a·*kee*

The car has broken down (at ...).
El coche se ha averiado (en ...).   el *ko*·che se a a·ve·*rya*·do (en ...)

I had an accident.
He tenido un accidente.   e te·*nee*·do oon ak·see·*den*·te

I've run out of petrol.
Me he quedado sin gasolina.   me e ke·*da*·do seen ga·so·*lee*·na

I have a flat tyre.
Tengo un pinchazo.   *ten*·go oon peen·*cha*·so

MEXICAN SLANG

Pepper your conversations with a few slang expressions! You'll hear many of the following expressions all around Mexico, but some are particular to Mexico City.

¿Qué onda?
What's up?/What's happening?

¿Qué pasión? (Mexico City)
What's up?/What's going on?

¡Qué padre!
How cool!

fregón
really good at something/way cool/awesome

Este club está fregón.
This club is way cool.

El cantante es un fregón.
The singer is really awesome.

ser muy buena onda
to be really cool/nice

Mi novio es muy buena onda.
My boyfriend is really cool.

Eres muy buena onda.
You're really cool.

pisto (in the north)
booze

alipús
booze

echarse un alipús/trago
to go get a drink

Echamos un alipús/trago.
Let's go have a drink.

tirar la onda
try to pick someone up/flirt

ligar
to flirt

irse de reventón
go partying

¡Vámonos de reventón!
Let's go party!

reven
a 'rave' (huge party with loud music and a wild atmosphere)

un desmadre
a mess

Simón.
Yes.

Nel.
No.

No hay tos.
No problem. (literally: 'there's no cough')

¡Órale! (positive)
Sounds great! (when responding to an invitation)

¡Órale! (negative)
What the ...? (taunting exclamation)

¡Caray!
Shit!

¿Te cae?
Are you serious?

Me late.
Sounds really good to me.

Me vale.
I don't care./Whatever.

Sale y vale.
I agree./Sounds good.

¡Paso sin ver!
I can't stand it!/No, thank you!

¡Guácatelas!/¡Guácala!
How gross!/That's disgusting!

¡Bájale!
Don't exaggerate!/Come on!

¡¿Chale?! (Mexico City)
No way!?

¡Te pasas!
That's it! You've gone too far!

¡No manches!
Get outta here!/You must be kidding!

un resto
a lot

lana
money/dough

carnal
brother

cuate/cuaderno
buddy

chavo
guy/dude

chava
girl/gal

jefe
father

jefa
mother

la tira/julia
the police

la chota (Mexico City)
the police

GLOSSARY

(m) indicates masculine gender, (f) feminine gender, (sg) singular and (pl) plural

adobe – sun-dried mud brick used for building

agave – family of plants with thick, fleshy, usually pointed leaves, from which tequila, mezcal and *pulque* are produced (see also *maguey*)

Alameda – name of formal parks in some Mexican cities

alebrije – colorful wooden animal figure

Ángeles Verdes – Green Angels; government-funded mechanics who patrol Mexico's major highways in green vehicles; they help stranded motorists with fuel and spare parts

arroyo – brook, stream

artesanías – handicrafts, folk arts

atlas (sg), atlantes (pl) – sculpted male figure(s) used instead of a pillar to support a roof or frieze; a telamon

autopista – expressway, dual carriageway

azulejo – painted ceramic tile

bahía – bay

balneario – bathing place; often a natural hot spring

baluarte – bulwark, defensive wall

barrio – neighborhood of a town or city

boleto – ticket

brujo/a (m/f) – witch doctor, shaman; similar to *curandero/a*

burro – donkey

cabaña – cabin, simple shelter

cabina – Baja Californian term for a public telephone call station

cacique – regional warlord; political strongman

calle – street

callejón – alley

calzada – grand boulevard or avenue

camioneta – pickup truck

campesino/a (m/f) – country person, peasant

capilla abierta – open chapel; used in early Mexican monasteries for preaching to large crowds of indigenous people

casa de cambio – exchange house, place where currency is exchanged; faster to use than a bank

casa de huéspedes – cheap and congenial accommodations; often a home converted into simple guest lodgings

caseta de teléfono, caseta telefónica – public telephone call station

cenote – a limestone sinkhole filled with rainwater; often used in Yucatán as a reservoir

central camionera – bus terminal

cerro – hill

Chaac – Maya rain god

chac-mool – pre-Hispanic stone sculpture of a hunched-up figure; the stomach may have been used as a sacrificial altar

charreada – Mexican rodeo

charro – Mexican cowboy

chilango/a (m/f) – person from Mexico City

chinampa – Aztec garden built from lake mud and vegetation; versions still exist at Xochimilco, Mexico City

chultún – cistern found in the Chenes region, in the Puuc hills south of Mérida

Churrigueresque – Spanish late-baroque architectural style; found on many Mexican churches

clavadistas – cliff divers of Acapulco and Mazatlán

colectivo – minibus or car that picks up and drops off passengers along a predetermined route; can also refer to other types of transportation, such as boats, where passengers share the total fare

colonia – neighborhood of a city, often a wealthy residential area

combi – minibus

comedor – food stall

comida corrida – set lunch

completo – no vacancy (literally 'full up'); a sign you may see at hotel desks

conde – count (nobleman)

conquistador – early Spanish explorer-conqueror

cordillera – mountain range

criollo – Mexican-born person of Spanish parentage; in colonial times considered inferior by *peninsulares*

cuota – toll; a *vía cuota* is a toll road

curandero/a (m/f) – literally 'curer'; a medicine man or woman who uses herbal and/or magical methods and often emphasizes spiritual aspects of disease

de paso – a bus that began its route somewhere else, but stops to let passengers on or off at various points

DF – Distrito Federal (Federal District); about half of Mexico City lies in DF

edificio – building

ejido – communal landholding

embarcadero – jetty, boat landing

entremeses – hors d'oeuvres; also theatrical sketches such as those performed during the Cervantino festival in Guanajuato

escuela – school

esq – abbreviation of *esquina* (corner) in addresses

ex-convento – former convent or monastery

feria – fair or carnival, typically occurring during a religious holiday

ferrocarril – railway

fonda – inn; small, family-run eatery

fraccionamiento – subdivision, housing development; similar to a *colonia*, often modern

gringo/a (m/f) – US or Canadian (or other Western) visitor to Latin America; can be used derogatorily

grito – literally 'shout'; the Grito de Dolores was the 1810 call to independence by priest Miguel Hidalgo, sparking the struggle for independence from Spain

gruta – cave, grotto

guayabera – man's shirt with pockets and appliquéd designs up the front, over the shoulders and down the back; worn in hot regions in place of a jacket and tie

hacha – ax; in archaeological contexts, a flat, carved-stone object connected with the ritual ball game

hacienda – estate; Hacienda (capitalized) is the Treasury Department

henequén – *agave* fiber used to make sisal rope; grown particularly around Mérida

hostal – small hotel or budget hostel

huarache – woven leather sandal, often with tire tread as the sole

huevos – eggs; also slang for testicles

huipil (sg), huipiles (pl) – indigenous woman's sleeveless tunic(s), usually highly decorated; can be thigh-length or reach the ankles

Huizilopochtli – Aztec tribal god

iglesia – church

INAH – Instituto Nacional de Antropología e Historia; the body in charge of most ancient sites and some museums

indigena – indigenous, pertaining to the original inhabitants of Latin America; can also refer to the people themselves

isla – island

IVA – *impuesto de valor agregado,* or 'ee-vah'; a sales tax added to the price of many items (16% on hotel rooms)

jai alai – the Basque game *pelota,* brought to Mexico by the Spanish; a bit like squash, played on a long court with curved baskets attached to the arm

jardín – garden

Kukulcán – Maya name for the plumed serpent god *Quetzalcóatl*

lancha – fast, open, outboard boat

larga distancia – long-distance; usually refers to telephone calls

local – refers to premises, such as a numbered shop or office; a *local* bus is one whose route starts from the bus station you are in

maguey – *agave;* sometimes refers specifically to *Agave americana,* from which *pulque* is made

malecón – waterfront boulevard or promenade

maquiladora – assembly-plant operation importing equipment, raw materials and parts for assembly or processing in Mexico, then exporting the products

mariachi – small ensemble of street musicians playing traditional ballads on guitars and trumpets

marimba – wooden xylophone-like instrument popular in southeastern Mexico

mercado – market; often a building near the center of a town, with shops and open-air stalls in the surrounding streets

Mesoamerica – historical and archaeological name for central, southern, eastern and southeastern Mexico, Guatemala, Belize and the small ancient Maya area in Honduras

mestizo – person of mixed (usually indigenous and Spanish) ancestry

Mexican Revolution – 1910 revolution that ended the *Porfiriato*

milpa – peasant's small cornfield, often cultivated using the slash-and-burn method

mirador (sg), miradores (pl) – lookout point(s)

Mudejar – Moorish architectural style imported to Mexico by the Spanish

municipio – small local government area; Mexico is divided into 2394 of them

Nafta – North American Free Trade Agreement

Náhuatl – language of the Nahua people, descendants of the Aztecs

nao – Spanish trading galleon

norteamericano – North American; someone from north of the US–Mexican border

Nte – abbreviation for *norte* (north); used in street names

Ote – abbreviation for *oriente* (east); used in street names

palacio de gobierno – state capitol, state government headquarters

palacio municipal – town or city hall, headquarters of the municipal corporation

palapa – thatched-roof shelter, usually on a beach

PAN – Partido Acción Nacional (National Action Party); the political party of Felipe Calderón and his predecessor Vicente Fox

panga – fiberglass skiff for fishing or whale-watching in Baja California

parada – bus stop, usually for city buses

parque nacional – national park; an environmentally protected area in which human exploitation is banned or restricted

parroquia – parish church

paseo – boulevard, walkway or pedestrian street; the tradition of strolling around the plaza in the evening, men and women moving in opposite directions

Pemex – government-owned petroleum extraction, refining and retailing monopoly

peninsulares – those born in Spain and sent by the Spanish government to rule the colony in Mexico

periférico – ring road

pesero – Mexico City's word for *colectivo;* can mean 'bus' in the northeast

peyote – a hallucinogenic cactus

pinacoteca – art gallery

piñata – clay pot or papier-mâché mold decorated to resemble an animal, pineapple, star, etc and filled with sweets and gifts, then smashed open at fiestas

pirata – literally 'pirate'; used to describe passenger-carrying pickup trucks in some parts of Mexico

playa – beach

plaza de toros – bullring

plazuela – small plaza

poblano/a (m/f) – person from Puebla; something in the style of Puebla

Porfiriato – reign of Porfirio Díaz as president-dictator of Mexico for 30 years until the 1910 *Mexican Revolution*

portales – arcades

posada – inn

PRI – Partido Revolucionario Institucional (Institutional Revolutionary Party); the political party that ruled Mexico for most of the 20th century

Pte – abbreviation for *poniente* (west), used in street names

puerto – port

pulque – milky, low-alcohol brew made from the *maguey* plant

quetzal – crested bird with brilliant green, red and white plumage native to southern Mexico, Central America and northern South America; quetzal feathers were highly prized in pre-Hispanic Mexico

Quetzalcóatl – plumed serpent god of pre-Hispanic Mexico

rebozo – long woolen or linen shawl covering women's head or shoulders

refugio – a very basic cabin for shelter in the mountains

reserva de la biosfera – biosphere reserve; an environmentally protected area where human exploitation is steered toward sustainable activities

retablo – altarpiece, or small painting placed in a church as thanks for miracles, answered prayers etc

río – river

s/n – *sin número* (without number); used in addresses

sacbé (sg), sacbeob (pl) – ceremonial avenue(s) between great Maya cities

sanatorio – hospital, particularly a small private one

sarape – blanket with opening for the head; worn as a cloak

Semana Santa – Holy Week – the week from Palm Sunday to Easter Sunday; Mexico's major holiday period when accommodations and transportation get very busy

sierra – mountain range

sitio – taxi service

stela/stele (sg), stelae/steles (pl) – standing stone monument, usually carved

sur – south; often seen in street names

taller – shop or workshop; a *taller mecánico* is a mechanic's shop, usually for cars; a *taller de llantas* is a tire-repair shop

talud-tablero – stepped building style typical of Teotihuacán, with alternating vertical (*tablero*) and sloping (*talud*) sections

taquilla – ticket window

telamon – statue of a male figure, used instead of a pillar to hold up the roof of a temple; an *atlas*

teleférico – cable car

teléfono (celular) – (cell/mobile) telephone

temascal – pre-Hispanic–style steam bath, often used for curative purposes; sometimes spelt *temazcal*

templo – church; anything from a chapel to a cathedral

teocalli – Aztec sacred precinct

Tezcatlipoca – multifaceted pre-Hispanic god; lord of life and death and protector of warriors; as a smoking mirror he could see into hearts; as the sun god he needed the blood of sacrificed warriors to ensure he would rise again

tezontle – light red, porous volcanic rock used for buildings by the Aztecs and *conquistadores*

tianguis – indigenous people's market

tienda – store

típico/a (m/f) – characteristic of a region; used to describe food in particular

Tláloc – pre-Hispanic rain and water god

tope – speed bump; found on the outskirts of towns and villages; they are only sometimes marked by signs

trapiche – mill; in Baja California usually a sugar mill

UNAM – Universidad Nacional Autónoma de México (National Autonomous University of Mexico)

universidad – university

voladores – literally 'fliers'; Totonac ritual in which men, suspended by their ankles, whirl around a tall pole

War of Independence – war for Mexican independence from Spain (from 1810 to 1821), ending three centuries of Spanish rule

War of the Castes – 19th-century Maya uprising in the Yucatán Peninsula

zócalo – literally 'plinth'; used in some Mexican towns for the main plaza or square

FOOD GLOSSARY

For basic food terms, see p863
For basic menu terms, see p47

adobada – marinated with adobo (chili sauce)

al albañil – 'bricklayer style' ie served with a hot chili sauce

al mojo de ajo – with garlic sauce

al pastor – cooked on a pit, shepherd's style

albóndigas – meatballs

antojitos – 'little whims': tortilla-based snacks like tacos and enchiladas

arroz mexicana – pilaf-style rice with a tomato base

atole – gruel made with ground corn

avena – oatmeal

barbacoa – pit-smoked barbecue

bolillo – French-style roll

brocheta – shishkabob

burrito – filling in a large flour tortilla

cajeta – goat's milk and sugar boiled to a paste

calabacita – squash

carnitas – pork simmered in lard

cecina – thin cut of meat, flavored with chili and sautéed or grilled

chicharrones – fried pork skins

chile relleno – chili stuffed with meat or cheese, usually fried in egg batter

chiles en nogada – mild green chilies stuffed with meat and fruit, fried in batter and served with a sauce of cream, ground walnuts and cheese

chorizo – Mexican-style bulk sausage made with chili and vinegar

chuleta de puerco – pork chop

churros – doughnut-like fritters

cochinita pibil – pork, marinated in chilies, wrapped in banana leaves, and pit-cooked or baked

coctel de frutas – fruit cocktail

costillas de res – beef ribs

crepas – crepes or thin pancakes

empanada – pastry turnover filled with meat, cheese or fruits

filete a la tampiqueña – Tampico-style steak: a thin tenderloin, grilled and served with chili strips and onion, a quesadilla and enchilada

flor de calabaza – squash blossom

frijoles a la charra – beans cooked with tomatoes, chilies and onions (also called *frijoles rancheros*)

guacamole – mashed avocado, often with lime juice, onion, tomato and chili

horchata – soft drink made with melon seeds

huachinango veracruzana – Veracruz-style red snapper with a sauce of tomatoes, olives, vinegar and capers

huevos motuleños – fried eggs sandwiched between corn tortillas, and topped with peas, tomato, ham and cheese

huevos rancheros – fried eggs served on a corn tortilla, topped with a sauce of tomato, chilies, and onions, and served with refried beans

huevos revueltos – scrambled eggs

huitlacoche – a much esteemed fungus that grows on corn

lomo de cerdo – pork loin

machacado – pulverized jerky, often scrambled with eggs

menudo – tripe stew

milanesa – thin slices of beef or pork, breaded and fried

mixiote – chili-seasoned lamb steamed in agave membranes or parchment

mole negro – chicken or pork in a very dark sauce of chilies, fruits, nuts, spices and chocolate

mole poblano – chicken or turkey in a sauce of chilies, fruits, nuts, spices and chocolate

nopalitos – sliced cactus paddles, sautéed or grilled

picadillo – ground beef filling that often includes fruit and nuts

pipián verde – stew of chicken, with ground squash seeds, chilies and tomatillos

pozole – soup or thin stew of hominy, meat, vegetables and chilies

queso fundido – cheese melted, often with chorizo or mushrooms, and served as an appetizer with tortillas

rajas – strips of mild green chili, often fried with onions

tinga poblana – stew of pork, vegetables and chilies

Behind the Scenes

SEND US YOUR FEEDBACK

We love to hear from travelers – your comments keep us on our toes and help make our books better. Our well-traveled team reads every word on what you loved or loathed about this book. Although we cannot reply individually to your submissions, we always guarantee that your feedback goes straight to the appropriate authors, in time for the next edition. Each person who sends us information is thanked in the next edition – the most useful submissions are rewarded with a selection of digital PDF chapters.

Visit **lonelyplanet.com/contact** to submit your updates and suggestions or to ask for help. Our award-winning website also features inspirational travel stories, news and discussions.

Note: We may edit, reproduce and incorporate your comments in Lonely Planet products such as guidebooks, websites and digital products, so let us know if you don't want your comments reproduced or your name acknowledged. For a copy of our privacy policy visit lonelyplanet.com/privacy.

OUR READERS

Many thanks to the travelers who used the last edition and wrote to us with helpful hints, useful advice and interesting anecdotes:

A Alan Forbes, Albert Ambrosio, Anna Abdelnoor, Antonie Vervenne **B** Barbara Swain **C** Carol Dyer, Casper Jensen, Celia Kawai **D** Daniel Druce, Danny Walden, David Hixson, Dorothy Melander-Dayton **E** Erwan Lamberoy, Esteban Balderrama, Ester de Koning, Evana Stanonik, Evelyne Berne **F** Fernando Garcia, Fernando Garcia Lopez, Fernando Romero, Freek De Smedt **G** Grant Murfett, Guillermo Moreno **I** Irving Levinson **J** Jacqueline Garcia, Jeff Jones, Jerry Peek, Jose Lassalle, Joseph Porter, Juliana Secchi **K** Kathy Bowman **L** Luigi Zeccardo **M** Manuela Arigoni, Marcos Arbesu, Marianne Eberhardt, Marissa Castro, Megan Norris **P** Patricia Kubala, Pedro Gamez, Peter Straus, Phil Gillette, Philip Brunelle **R** Rachel Van Ness, Ramon Antonijoan, Ricardo Abuauad, Ricardo Balderrama, Richard Tamkin, Roland Bourque, Romey Glenn, Ruben Lelivelt **S** Shane Malyon, Simon Barr, Stephan Hipp, Steve Anderson, Steve Douglas **T** Thomas Shearer **V** Veronica Ciambra, Virginia Ferguson-Sharp **Y** Yossi Margoninsky

AUTHOR THANKS

John Noble

Extra special thanks to Julien Pardinilla, Gina Machorro, Fausto Jasso, Alvin Starkman, los Velasco and Rebecca Bailey.

Kate Armstrong

Muchas gracias to enthusiastic travelers, and generous folks who share their passion of Mexico with me, especially Lori Jones in San Luis Potosí and Sally Wilson and Ernesto de la Vega in Queretaro. My love, as always, to Chris Nelson, this time for sharing the driving and watery adventures. A big thanks to Clifton Wilkinson for the fabulous opportunity, fellow authors and the in-house team.

Stuart Butler

First and foremost I must, once again, thank my wife, Heather, for putting up with my extended periods away whilst working on this project and coping so admirably with two small children on her own. And, thank you to Jake and Grace for also putting up with their daddy disappearing off again. In Mexico thank you to the many hoteliers, other travelers, restaurant owners and random people on the bus who knowingly, or unknowingly, helped out.

John Hecht

Thanks to the countless number of good people in the Yucatán who helped make this wonderful journey so precious. Special gratitude goes out to commissioning editor Cliff Wilkinson, LP co-author Lucas Vidgen, the book's previous authors, Yurij Gabassi, Indira Gallegos and my wife, Lau, for looking after La Milanesa.

Anna Kaminski

I would like to thank Cliff for entrusting me with these chapters, and my fellow scribes – John Noble, Josephine Quintero, Andy Symington, John Hecht, Brendan Sainsbury, Lucas Vidgen, Phillip Tang, Tom Masters, Kate Armstrong and Stuart Butler – for their detailed and well-thought-out input when I was putting my chapters together. From past travels in Mexico, I'd like to thank E.C. Bell in San Miguel, Ricardo in Sayulita, Chey in Tijuana, John and Christina in Nayarit, Enrique on the Copper Canyon train, Gustavo in Mexico City, Sophie and Pete in Guadalajara, Cristian in Palenque and many more who introduced me to the many facets of this remarkable country.

Tom Masters

Many thanks to Rosemary Masters, who joined me for much of my research trip and was always great company, patient, uncomplaining and unfazed, even when required to go zip-lining down a canyon at rather short notice. Thanks also to the hoteliers and restaurateurs who were so generous with time and information, especially to Alberto & Francia at the Hotel & Restaurant Jade in Cerocahui, who were so kind to us when illness unexpectedly joined us on the road.

Josephine Quintero

I would like to thank all the helpful folk at the various tourist information offices, as well as Sally Harrison, who provided a valuable base in La Paz, as well as invaluable company. Thanks too to destination editor Cliff Wilkinson and to all those involved in the title from the Lonely Planet offices, as well as to all my Mexican Quintero family, particularly Linda Sinclair who joined me on the road trip.

Brendan Sainsbury

Thanks to all the untold bus drivers, taxi drivers, tourist info volunteers, tortilla-makers, mariachis and *voladores* who helped me and/or answered copious questions during my research. Special thanks to Eusebio for his guiding skills on Volcán Paricutín and Florencio for showing me the wonders of Comala and Volcán de Fuego.

Andy Symington

Various random bus and taxi drivers provided invaluable company and information. Thanks are also owed for various helpful acts to Luis Gutiérrez, Eugenia Michel Gómez, Yazmin Casillas, Verónica Bello Damián, Flor Anaya and Ginna Abud. It would be difficult to be away so much without the help of people like Eduardo Cuadrado Diago and José Eliseo Vázquez González; my family also offers constant support. Particular thanks go to Jorge Villarroel and José Vicente Revilla García for a great dossier on the Jalisco and Nayarit coasts.

Phillip Tang

Gracias to the Mexicans who shared their knowledge. *Merci* to Géraldine Galvaing, Fiona Ross, Wendy Risteska, Alberto Ramírez Romero, Jocsan L Alfaro, and Armando Palma for DF; thanks to Monica Gomez in Pachuca; *gracias* Ernesto A Alanís for Valle de Bravo and Cuernavaca; *salud* Manuel Aveleyra García for DF and Cuernavaca. Thanks for virtual support from Lisa N'paisan, Vek Lewis, Jack Kennerley, Anna Glayzer, Waimei Lee, and Venus Vamp. In loving memory of Cecelia Cataño Carrillo.

Lucas Vidgen

Thanks first and foremost to the Mexicans for making such an enjoyable country to travel and work in. Specifically, Andres and Sylvia were a huge help in San Cristóbal and the Campeche section wouldn't have been the same without Alonso Escobar and his compadre César. And as always, thanks to América, Sofía and Teresa for being there, and being there when I got back.

ACKNOWLEDGEMENTS

Climate map data adapted from Peel MC, Finlayson BL & McMahon TA (2007) 'Updated World Map of the Köppen-Geiger Climate Classification', Hydrology and Earth System Sciences, 11, 163344.

Cover photograph: Folk art for sale in San Miguel de Allende; Macduff Everton/Corbis ©

Chichén Itzá illustration pp324–5 by Michael Weldon.

THIS BOOK

This 15th edition of Lonely Planet's *Mexico* guidebook was researched and written by John Noble, Kate Armstrong, Stuart Butler, John Hecht, Anna Kaminski, Tom Masters, Josephine Quintero, Brendan Sainsbury, Andy Symington, Phillip Tang and Lucas Vidgen. The essay 'The Mexican Kitchen' was written by Mauricio Velázquez de León. This guidebook was produced by the following:

Destination Editor Clifton Wilkinson

Product Editors Vicky Smith, Bruce Evans

Senior Cartographer Mark Griffiths

Book Designer Wendy Wright

Assisting Editors Andrew Bain, Michelle Bennett, Bridget Blair, Carly Hall, Victoria Harrison, Kellie Langdon, Anne Mulvaney, Charlotte Orr, Ross Taylor, Jeanette Wall

Assisting Cartographers Corey Hutchison, David Kemp, Valentina Kremenchutskaya

Cover Researcher Naomi Parker

Thanks to Paul Harding, Elizabeth Jones, Kate Mathews, Jenna Myers, Kirsten Rawlings, Alison Ridgway, Angela Tinson, Tony Wheeler

Index

A

Acapulco 562-74, **564-5**, **566**, **570-1**, 19
  accommodations 567-9
  activities 565-7
  drinking 569, 571-2
  emergencies 572
  entertainment 572
  events 567
  festivals & events 567
  food 569
  medical services 572
  nightlife 569, 571-2
  shopping 572
  sights 562-5
  tourist information 572
  travel to/from 572-3
  travel within 573-4
accommodations 846-7, see also individual locations
  language 865-6
Aconchi 769
activities 847, see also individual activities
Acuario Inbursa 24
adventure parks
  Areponápuchi 755
  Parque de Aventura Barrancas del Cobre 756
adventure tours
  Álamos 772
  Creel 758
  Durango 786
Aguascalientes 673, 675-8, **674**
Aguascalientes state 673-678
air travel 860-1
Ajijic 604-5
Akumal 284-6
Álamos 771-4

Map Pages **000**
Photo Pages **000**

altitude sickness 850
Amatenango del Valle 373
Amatitán 601
amusement parks
  All Ritmo 259
  La Feria 91
  Yucatán Peninsula 274
Angahuan 635
Angangueo 623
Angel of Independence 84, **11**
animals 838-40
anthropological museums
  Museo de Antropología (Córdoba) 228
  Museo de Antropología (Xalapa) 218
  Museo de Antropología e História (Toluca) 196
  Museo del Instituto Nacional de Antropología e Historia (Ensenada) 710
  Museo Nacional de Antropología (Mexico City) 86-7
  Museo Regional de Antropología (Villahermosa) 415
  Museo Regional de Antropología e Historia (La Paz) 727
  Museo Regional Huasteco Joaquín Meade 690
antojitos 830-1
aquariums
  Acuario de Veracruz 208
  Acuario Inbursa 24, 91
  Acuario Mazatlán 495
  Centro Mexicano de la Tortuga 476
archaeological museums
  Gran Museo del Mundo Maya 301
  Museo Arqueológico (Mazatlán) 493-5
  Museo Arqueológico de Campeche 336-7

Museo Arqueológico de Comitán 400
Museo Arqueológico de la Costa Grande 550
Museo Arqueológico del Soconusco 409
Museo de Arte Prehispánico Carlos Pellicer 177-8
Museo de la Cultura Maya 298
Museo de las Culturas de Oaxaca 426
Museo del Sitio 149
Museo Maya de Cancún 255-8
Santa Elena Museum 314
archaeological sites 48-53, **51**
  Alta Vista Petroglyphs 512-13
  Atzompa 451-2
  Aztec Temples (Malinalco) 201
  Balamkú 343
  Becán 344-5, **340**
  Bonampak 390-1, 393-4, **393**
  Cacaxtla 171-3
  Calakmul 343-4
  Cañada de la Virgen 672
  Cantona 174
  Chiapa de Corzo 356
  Chicanná 344
  Chichén Itzá 15, 322-8, 324-5, **362**, **15**, **48**, **324**, **325**
  Chinkultic 404
  Chula Zona Arqueológica 163-4
  Cobá Ruins 291-2
  Comalcalco 416
  Dzibanché 300
  Dzibilchaltún 318-19
  Edzná 339-42
  Ek' Balam 331-2
  El Caracol 324, 327, **324**, **324**

El Cedral 280-1
El Tajín 240-2, **241**
Grutas de Loltún 316
Guiengola 488
Hormiguero 346
Iglesia Vieja 406
Izapa 412-13
Kabah 314-15
Kinich-Kakmó 321
Kinichná 300
Kohunlich 300
La Campana 609
La Quemada 699
La Venta 416
Labná 315-16
Mitla 448-9
Monte Albán 443-5
Oxkintok 320
La Venta 416
Palenque 381-4, **382**, **36-7**
Paquimé 784
Parque Eco-Arqueológico Copalita 482
Plan de Ayutla 392-3
Quiahuiztlán 244
Río Bec 346
Ruinas de Mayapán 316-17
San Gervasio Ruins 281
San Miguelito 258-9
Sayil 315
Sierra de San Francisco 719-20
Soledad de Maciel 560-1
Templo Mayor 67
Tenam Puente 403
Teotihuacán 146-50
Tingambato 634-5
Toniná 378-9
Tula 144-6
Tulum 286-8, **287**, **288-9**, **35**, **50**
Tzintzuntzan 631
Uxmal 310-13, **312**, **26**
Xlapak 315
Xochicalco 186
Xochitécatl 171-3

Xpuhil 345
Yagul 447-8
Yaxchilán 390-1, 396-7, **396**
Yohualichán 176
Zempoala 216
Zona Arqueológica Cuicuilco 97
Zona Arqueológica El Rey 259
architecture 649, 821-2
area codes 855
Areponápuchi 755-6
Arizpe 769
art 428
art galleries, 27-8, *see also* anthropological museums, archaeological museums, cultural centers, museums
Arte de Oaxaca 428
Casa Sebastián 781
Casa-Taller Orozco 584
Centro de la Imagen 80
Centro de las Artes Centenario 679
Centro Fotográfico Álvarez Bravo 428
Escuela de Bellas Artes 663
Fototeca 208
Galería de Arte Contemporáneo 220
Galería López Quiroga 91-2
Galería Quetzalli 428
Instituto Cultural de Cabañas 583
Instituto de Artes Gráficas de Oaxaca 428
La Mano Mágica 428
Laboratorio de Arte Alameda 79
MUCA Roma 86
Museo Casa del Risco 93
Museo Casa Estudio Diego Rivera y Frida Kahlo 93
Museo de Aguascalientes 673
Museo de Arte (Mazatlán) 495
Museo de Arte Carrillo Gil 93
Museo de Arte Contemporáneo (Aguascalientes) 675
Museo de Arte Contemporáneo (Mérida) 304
Museo de Arte Contemporáneo (Monterrey) 795

Museo de Arte Contemporáneo de Oaxaca 428
Museo de Arte de Querétaro 639
Museo de Arte de Tlaxcala 168
Museo de Arte de Zapopan 584
Museo de Arte del Estado 233
Museo de Arte Moderno 87, 90, 197
Museo de Arte Popular 79
Museo de Arte Popular de Yucatán 304
Museo de Arte Virreinal 191
Museo de Bellas Artes 197
Museo de la Ciudad (Querétaro) 639
Museo de las Artes 583-4
Museo de los Pintores Oaxaqueños 428
Museo del Pueblo de Guanajuato 652
Museo Dolores Olmedo 92
Museo José Guadalupe Posada 675
Museo Jumex 91
Museo Nacional de Arte 73
Museo Nacional de la Estampa 79
Museo Nacional de San Carlos 81
Museo Pedro Coronel 693
Museo Soumaya Plaza Carso 91
Museo Tamayo 90
Museo Universitario Arte Contemporáneo 95
Museo Universitario del Chopo 81
Oaxaca City 428
Palacio Clavijero 613
Palacio de Bellas Artes 77
Paseo Cimentación 81
Pinacoteca Diego Rivera 219
Pinacoteca Universitaria Alfonso Michel 609
Quinta Gameros 779
artesanías, see handicrafts, textiles
arts 821-9
books 824, 827

contemporary 428, 823-4
internet resources 823, 826
street art 824
ATMs 852
Atotonilco Hot Springs 468
Atzompa 451-2
Aztecs 64-5, 808
religion 806

B

Bahía de Kino 768-70
Bahía de Navidad 535-8
Bahía San Agustín 484
Bahías de Huatulco 480-6, **481**
Bahías de Punta Solimán 284
Baja California 60, 700-42, **701**
accommodations 700
climate 700
highlights 701, **701**
history 702
tours 700
travel to/from 702, 772
travel within 702
Balamkú 343
ball courts 804
Banámichi 769
banks 852
bargaining 23, 852
Barra de la Cruz 487
Barra de Navidad 537-8
Barra de Nexpa 545
Barra de Potosí 559-60
Batopilas 761-5
Baviácora 769
beach resorts 25
beaches 25
Acapulco 19, 563, **19**
Bahías de Huatulco 480-2
Cancún 259-60
Costalegre 534
El Soconusco 406-9
Isla Cozumel 281
Isla Mujeres 267
Ixtapa 549
Jicacal 253
La Paz 732
Los Cabos Corridor 737
Mahahual 294
Manzanillo 538-9
Mazatlán 495-6
Mulegé 723
Paamul 284

Península Pichilingue 732
Playa del Carmen 275
Playa Maruata 544-5
Playa Ventura 574-5
Puerto Ángel 470
Puerto Escondido 456-7
Puerto Vallarta 520
Ribera Costa Azul 408-9
San Blas 507
Sayulita 515
Tuxpan 237
Veracruz City 210
Xpu-Há 284
Zihuatanejo 550-1
Becán 344-5, **340**
beer 834-5
Bernal 645
bicycle travel, *see* cycling
biodiversity 838
birds 839, *see also* individual species
bird-watching
Álamos 771, 773
Barra de Potosí 559-60
Calakmul 343-4
Cañón La Trinidad 723
El Feurte 751
Guerrero Negro 717
Isla Mujeres 267-8
Laguna Manialtepec 467-8
Parque Nacional Isla Contoy 271
Parque Nacional Lagunas de Chacahua 468-9
Parque Nacional Sierra San Pedro Mártir 715
Reserva de la Biosfera El Triunfo 408
Reserva de la Biosfera Ría Celestún 317
Río Lagartos 332
Saltillo 790
San Blas 509
Xalapa 220
boat travel 772, 860, 861
boat trips
Acapulco 567
Barra de Navidad 537
Barra de Potosí 560
Bosque Secreto 751
Los Cabos Corridor 737
Mazunte 477
Puerto Peñasco 766
Puerto Vallarta 521
Río Lagartos 332
San Agustinillo 474

boat trips *continued*
San Blas 508-9
Tlacotalpan 246
Boca de Pascuales 542-3
Bolonchén de Rejón 342-3
Bonampak 390-1, 393-4, **393**
books 802, 817, 818, 827, 839
art 824, 827
crafts 829
food 831, 832, 834
history 804, 809, 810
Maya 814
border crossings 858-60
USA 764-5
boxing 820
breweries 24
Baja Brewing Co 736
Cuauhtémoc Moctezuma
Heineken Mexico Brewery 706
La Santísima Flor de Lúpulo 438
brujos 250
budget 21
bullfighting 820
Mexico City 127
bus travel 859, 861-2
language 862
to/from Belize 858
to/from Guatemala 858
to/from Mexico 859
to/from the USA 859
within Mexico 861-2
business hours 852
butterflies 18, 621-2, **18**

C
cabaret 126
cable cars
Teleférico (Taxco) 191-2
Teleférico (Zacatecas) 695
Teleférico de Orizaba 233
Cabo Pulmo 17, 733-4, **17**
Cabo San Lucas 737-40, **738**
Cacaxtla 171-3
Calakmul 343-4
Caleta de Campos 545-6
California graywhales 720
callejoneada 653

calling codes 855
Campeche 333-9, **334-5**
Campeche state 333-9
Cancún 255-66, **258**, **262**, **37**
Cañón del Sumidero 357
Cañón La Trinidad 723
cantinas 835
Cantona 174
car travel 859, 862
insurance 860
rental 863
vehicle permits 859-60
Carnaval 30
Carretera Fronteriza 390-1
Carretera Transpeninsular 709
cartels 544
casas de cambio 852
Casas Grandes 783-4
Catemaco 250-2, **251**
cathedrals, see churches & cathedrals
caves
Cueva de Sebastián 760
Grutas de Balankanché 322
Grutas de Calcehtok 320
Grutas de Loltún 316
Grutas de San Cristóbal 376
Parque Nacional Grutas de Cacahuamilpa 195-6
Sótano de las Golondrinas 689
Sótano de las Huahuas 689
Xtacumbilxunaan 342-3
celebrity chefs 832
Celestún 317-33
cell phones 20, 854-5
cenotes 315, **340**, **341**
Cenote Azul 296
Cenote Sagrado 15, 325, 326, **15**, **325**
Cenotes de Cuzamá 320
Cenote X'Kekén 330
Cenote Zací 330
Choo-Ha 292
Cristalino Cenote 278
Gran Cenote 290
Ik Kil Parque Eco-Arqueológico 322
Multún-Ha 292
Sacred Cenote 15, 325, 326, **15**, **325**
Tamcach-Ha 292
Valladolid region **341**

Central Pacific Coast 59, 491-575, **492**
accommodations 491
climate 491
food 491
highlights 492, **492**
travel seasons 491
ceramics 829
Cerocahui 752-3
Cerro Pelón 622-3
ceviche 560, **46**
Chacahua 468-9
Chacala 512-14
Chapala 602-4
charreadas 596, 820
Chepe railway 747-50
Chetumal 297-300, **297**
Chiapa de Corzo 355-7
Chiapas 58, 347-416, **348-9**
accommodations 347
climate 347
highlights 348, **348-9**
history 350
travel seasons 347
Chicanná 344
Chichén Itzá 15, 322-8, **324-5**, **326**, **15**, **48**, **324**, **325**
Chicxulub 319
Chihuahua 777-83, **778**
chikungunya 850
children, travel with 54-6
Mexico City 67
Riviera Mayo 274
chilies, 830, **44**
Chinkultic 404
chocolate 835
Cholula 163-6, **164**
Chupaderos 789
churches & cathedrals
Augustinian Convent 201
Basílica de Guadalupe 99-100
Basílica de Nuestra Señora de Guanajuato 648
Basílica de Nuestra Señora de la Salud 625
Basílica de Zapopan 584
Basílica del Carmen 250
Capilla de las Capuchinas Sacramentarias 98
Catedral (Aguascalientes) 673-5
Catedral (Colima) 607-8
Catedral (Guadalajara) 581
Catedral (Oaxaca City) 423

Catedral (Mazatlán) 493
Catedral (Morelia) 612
Catedral (Puebla) 155
Catedral (Querétaro) 640
Catedral (San Cristóbal) 363
Catedral (San Luis Potosí) 679
Catedral (Zacatecas) 694
Catedral de Guadalupe 709
Catedral de la Inmaculada Concepción 228
Catedral de la Virgen de Guadalupe 715
Catedral de Nuestra Señora de la Purísima Concepción 335
Catedral de Saltillo 790
Catedral de San Ildefonso 304
Catedral de San José 145
Catedral Metropolitana (Mexico City) 71-3
Catedral Metropolitana (Xalapa) 219
Ex-Convento de San Francisco 631
Ex-Convento Dominico de la Natividad 177
Iglesia de Jesús 304-5
Iglesia de la Compañía 156
Iglesia de Nuestra Señora de la Asunción 238
Iglesia de San Pancho 623
Iglesia de Santiago Apóstol 635
Iglesia de Santo Domingo 400
Iglesia del Santo Madero 792
Iglesia San José 734
Iglesia Santa Bárbara 720
La Capilla de la Paz 565
Oratorio de San Felipe Neri 663
Parroquia de la Purísima Concepción 772
Parroquia de Nuestra Señora de Dolores 659
Parroquia de San José 220
Parroquia de San Juan Bautista 96
Parroquia de San Miguel Arcángel 662, **7**

Recinto de la Catedral 183

San Ignacio Mission Church 760

Santuario de Guadalupe 614

Santuario de la Virgen de Ocotlán 169

Templo & Ex-Convento de Santo Domingo de Guzmán 363

Templo de Guadalupe 519

Templo de la Concepción 664

Templo de la Purísima Concepción 685

Templo de la Salud 663

Templo de la Santísima Trinidad 75

Templo de la Virgen de la Natividad 447

Templo de San Bernardino 330

Templo de San Antonio 675

Templo de San Francisco (Puebla) 157

Templo de San Francisco (Querétaro) 639

Templo de San Francisco (San Luis Potosí) 679

Templo de San Fran-cisco (San Miguel de Allende) 663

Templo de San José 681

Templo de San Juan 375

Templo de Santa Clara 640

Templo de Santa Prisca 191

Templo de Santa Rosa de Viterbos 640

Templo de Santo Domingo (Oaxaca City) 423-6

Templo de Santo Do-mingo (Puebla) 155

Templo de Santo Domingo de Guzmán 356

Templo del Carmen 679

Templo del Encino 675

Templo Expiatorio 584

Templo La Valenciana 650

Templo y Convento de la Santa Cruz 639

Templo y Ex-Convento de San Juan Bautist 454

Templo y Ex-Convento de San Pedro y San Pablo 454

Templo y Ex-Convento de Santo Domingo 454

cinema 826-7

Ciudad Constitución 725-6

Ciudad Guzmán 606-7

Ciudad Hidalgo 414

Ciudad Universitaria 93-5

Ciudad Valles 689-691

Clavadistas 495

cliff diving 563

climate 20, 30-3, **20** see also individual regions

climate change 858

Coatepec 224-6

Cobá 290-2

Cocóspera 769

Coixtlahuaca 454-5

colectivos 864

Colima 607-10, **608**

Colima state 607-12

colonial towns 26-7

Comala 611

combis 864

Comitán 400-2, **401**

Concepción Bamba 489

Concordia 496

consulates 848-9

cooking courses 44

Mérida 305

Mexico City 102

Oaxaca City 430-1

Puerto Morelos 273

San Miguel de Allende 665

Tepoztlán 178

Tlaxcala 170

Copala 496

Copper Canyon 60, 743, 747-64, **744**, **748**, **28**

accommodations 743

climate 743

food 743

highlights 744, **744**

safe travel 746-7

travel seasons 743

travel to/from 747

Copper Canyon Railway 13, 747-50, **13**

Córdoba 228-30

Cortés, Hernán 810-11

Cosalá 496

Coscomatepec 232

Costa Chica 574-5

Costa Esmeralda 243-4

Costa Maya 16, 266

Costalegre 534

courses, see cooking courses, language courses

Creel 757-60, **758**

Cuajinicuilapa 575

Cuarón, Alfonso 826-7

Cuatro Ciénegas 793-4

Cuauhtémoc 753, 811

Cuautla 180-1

Cuernavaca 182-90, **184**

Cuetzalan 174-6

Cuevas, José Luis 823

Cuilapan 449

cultural centers

Casa Frisaac 98

Centro Cultural (Todos Santos) 740

Centro Cultural Casa Número 6 334

Centro Cultural de España 73

Centro Cultural El Carmen 363

Centro Cultural Jesús Reyes Heroles 97

Centro Cultural San Pablo 427-9

Centro Cultural Universitario Tlatelolco 99

Centro de Cultura Casa Lamm 86

Centro de Cultura Digital 85

Cuartel del Arte 151

La Ciudadela 79

Unidad Cultural Profesor Jesús Castro Agúndez 727

culture 817-20

currency 20

customs regulations 848

Cuyutlán 542

cycling 861

Ixtapa 549

Mexico City 100

Oaxaca City 429

Puerto Vallarta 522

Real de Catorce 686

Tulum 288

D

dance

danzón 214

Mexico City 124

dangers, see safety

Day of the Dead, see Día de Muertos

de Santa Anna, Antonio López 813

dengue fever 850

Día de la Independencia 33

Día de Muertos 33, 819, 833, **31**

Mexico City 102

Pátzcuaro 626

Uruapan 632

Díaz, Porfirio 814

disabilities, travelers with 856

discount cards 848

distilleries

Onilikan 495

tequila 601, 766

diving & snorkeling 28, 285, 847, **340**

Acapulco 566

Akumal 285

Bahías de Huatulco 482-3

Banco Chinchorro 294

Cabo Pulmo 17, 733-4, **17**

Cancún 260

Isla Cozumel 281

Isla Mujeres 267-8

Ixtapa 549

Laguna de la Media Luna 691

Laz Paz 728

Los Cabos Corridor 737

Mahahual 294

Manzanillo 539

Mulegé 722

Parque Marine Nacional Bahía de Loreto 724

Playa del Carmen 275

Puerto Escondido 458

Puerto Morelos 273

Puerto Vallarta 521

safety 847

San Agustinillo 474

San Carlos 770

Sayulita 515

Tulum 288

Tuxpan 237

Veracruz City 209-10

Xcalak 295

Zihuatanejo 551

Divisadero 757

Dolores Hidalgo 658-61

Downs, Lila 825

drinks 403, 833-5, see also distilleries

mezcal 29, 118, 439, 834

tequila 29, 602-3, 833-4

driving, see car travel

drug wars 802-3, 816, 854

drugs 854

Dunas de Yeso 794

Durango 786-9, **787**

Dzibilchaltún 318-19

E

economy 803, 815, 816
ecotourism 843
Ek' Balam 331-2
El Ángel 84, **11**
El Árbol del Tule 446
El Caracol 324, 327, **324**, **324**
El Castillo 323, 325, **325**, **325**
El Chiflón 402-3
El Fuerte 749, 751-2
El Rosario 622
El Soconusco 406-9
El Tajín 240-2, **241**
El Tule 446
electricity 848
Embarcadero Las Garzas 409
embassies 848-9
emergencies 855
    language 868
Ensenada 710-14, **712**
environmental issues 285, 842-4
Espíritu Santo 18, 727, **18**
ethnicity 818
etiquette 23
events, see festivals & events
exchange rates 21
Exekatlkalli 564

F

Faro de Bucerías 544
fauna 838
Ferrocarril Chihuahua Pacífico 13, 747-50, **13**
ferry travel 772
Festival Alfonso Ortíz Tirado 773
Festival Internacional de Cine en Monterrey 797
festivals & events 30-3, **31**, see also Día de Muertos, fiestas
    Acapulco 567
    Aguascalientes 675-6
    Chula 165
    Cuernavaca 185-6
    Cuetzalan 175
    Dolores Hidalgo 660
    Ensenada 711
    Guanajuato 653
    La Paz 729

Map Pages **000**
Photo Pages **000**

Los Cabos Corridor 737
Manzanillo 539-40
Mazatlán 497-9
Mazunte 477
Mérida 305
Mexico City 102-3
Mexcaltitán 506
Museo Nacional del Virreinato 141
Oaxaca City 431-2
Puebla 158
Puerto Escondido 460
Puerto Vallarta 523
Real de Catorce 686
San Blas 509
San Luis Potosí 681
San Miguel de Allende 666-7
Taxco 193
Tepoztlán 178
Tijuana 703
Tlaxcala 170
Todos Santos 741
Zacatecas 695
fiestas 833
films 789, 802, 807, 815, 819, 821
fincas 413-14
fishing
    Acapulco 566-7
    Chacala 513
    Ensenada 711
    Mazatlán 497
    Puerto Ángel 471
    Puerto Escondido 458-9
    Puerto Peñasco 766
    Puerto Vallarta 521
    San Agustinillo 474
    San Carlos 770
    Zihuatanejo 551
flag 808
folk art 828-9
food 14, 27, 42-7, 830-5, 849, see also individual locations
    antojitos 830-1
    books 831, 832, 834
    cantinas 835
    ceviche 560, **46**
    chilies 830, **44**
    fish tacos 730
    glossary 874
    language 866-7
    mole 436, 831, **47**
    Oaxacan desserts **42**
    tortillas 831, **14**
    vegans 833
    vegetarians 833
football, see fútbol

forests, see also national parks & reserves
    Bosque Secreto 751
Fortín de las Flores 230-1
fortresses
    Baluarte de Santiago 207
    Castillo de Chapultepec 87
    Fuerte de San Diego 564
    Fuerte Museo San José del Alto 336
    Laguna Bacalar 296
    San Juan de Ulúa 207
Frontera Corozal 395-6
Fuentes, Carlos 827-8
fútbol 819-20
    Guadalajara 596
    Mexico City 127

G

galleries, see art galleries
gardens, see parks & gardens
gay travelers 126, 531, 849
    Guadalajara 595
geography 836-8
golf
    Acapulco 565
    Barra de Navidad 537
    Mazatlán 497
    Puerto Vallarta 521
    San Francisco 514
Gran Juego de Pelota 323, 325, **325**
Gran Desierto de Altar 767
Green Angels 863
Grupo de las Mil Columnas 324, 327, **324**
Grutas de Loltún 316
Guadalajara 18, 577-600, **580**, **586-7**, **590**, **593**, **18**, **26**
    accommodations 588-91
    courses 586
    drinking & nightlife 594-5
    emergencies 597
    entertainment 595-6
    festivals & events 587-8
    food 591-4
    internet access 597
    shopping 596
    sights 581-6
    tourist information 597-8
    tours 586-7
    travel to/from 598-9
    travel within 599-600

Guadalajara region 600-7, **600**
Guanajuato 19, 648-58, **650-1**, **19**
Guanajuato state 648-73
Guelaguetza 32, 432
Guerrero Negro 717-18

H

Hacienda El Lencero 224
handicrafts 14, **14**
    Amatenango del Valle 373
    Bahía de Kino 768
    Chihuahua 782
    Creel 760
    Mérida 308
    Puebla 162
    Puerto Vallarta 532
    San Cristóbal de las Casas 371
    Teotitlán del Valle 446-7
health 849-50
Hidalgo, Miguel 659, 813
Hidalgo del Parral 784-5
Hierve El Agua 449
hiking 29, **28**
    Bahías de Huatulco 483
    Barranca de Metlac 230
    Batopilas 763
    Cerro Pelón 622
    Copper Canyon 29, **28**
    Iztaccíhuatl 167
    Mazunte 477
    Nevado de Toluca 199
    Oaxaca City 429
    Real de Catorce 685-6
    Reserva de la Biosfera Sierra de la Laguna 734
    Urique 754
    Volcán Tacaná 412
    Volcán Paricutín 17, 635, **17**
historic buildings
    Casa de Cortés 96
    Casa de los Azulejos 74
    Ex-Convento de Churubusco 97
    Ex-Hotel Zevallos 228
    La Jalisciense 98
    Na Bolom 359
    Palacio de Gobierno 582, 781
    Palacio Postal 73
    Teatro Degollado 582
history 804-16
    Aztecs 808
    books 804, 809, 810

Classic Maya 806-7
drug wars 816
films 807, 815
internet resources 805, 806, 809
Mexican independence 813-14
Mexican Revolution 780, 814-15
Olmecs 805
PAN (Partido Acción Nacional) 816
PRI (Partido Revolucionario Institucional) 815-16
Spanish colonization 811-12
Spanish conquest 809-11
Teotihuacán 805
Toltecs 807
history museums
Museo de Historia de Tlalpán 98
Museo de la Restauración de la República 639
Museo del Estado 612
Museo Nacional de Historia 87
Museo Nacional de las Intervenciones 97
Museo Regional de Historia de Colima 609
holidays 853
Hormiguero 346
horseback riding 29
Creel 758
Oaxaca City 429
Pie de la Cuesta 561
Puerto Vallarta 521
Real de Catorce 686
San Francisco 514
Tequisquiapan 645
hot springs, see thermal baths
Huamantla 173-4
Huasteca Potosina 16, 689, **16**
Huichol people 684

I
ice-skating 101
Ihuatzio 630-1
immigration 816
Iñárritu, Alejandro González 826-7
indigenous peoples 220, 376
Aztecs 64-5
Classic Veracruz

civilization 220
Huastecs 220
Huichol 684
Lacandones 376
Oaxaca 440
Olmecs 220
Seri 768
Tarahumara 762
textiles 371
Totonacs 220
insurance 850-1, 860
internet access 851
internet resources 21
Isla Contoy 271
Isla Cozumel 279-84, **280**, **282**
Isla de la Piedra 495
Isla de la Roqueta 563
Isla de los Alacranes 602
Isla de Mezcala 602
Isla de Todos Santos 710
Isla del Tiburón 768
Isla Holbox 271-3
Isla Ixtapa 548-9
Isla Janitzio 629
Isla Mujeres 266-71, **267**, **268**
Isla Río Cuale 519
Isla San Jorge 766
Isthmus of Tehuantepec 487-90
itineraries 34-41, **34**, **36**, **39**, **40-1**
Ixtapa 548-50
Ixtapan de la Sal 202
Izamal 320-1
Iztaccíhuatl 166-7

J
Jalcomulco 226
Jalpan 646-7
Jerez 697
Jicacal 253
Juárez, Benito 423, 427, 813-14
Juchitán 488-90

K
Kabah 314-15
Kahlo, Frida 80, 92, 93, 95-6, 168, 823
kayaking 29
La Paz 728
Mexico City 100
Mulegé 722
Parque Marine Nacional Bahía de Loreto 724
kidnapping 803

kitesurfing
La Ventana 732-3
Los Barriles 733

L
La Antigua 217
La Barra 253
La Bufadora 714
La Huasteca Potosina 16, 689, **16**
La Malinche 173
La Paz 727-32, **728**
La Quemada 699
La Ruptura 823
La Ventana 732-3
La Ventanilla 479
Lacandón Jungle 392, 394
Lacanjá Chansayab 394-5
Lago de Chapala 601-5
Lago de Pátzcuaro 629-31, **630**
Lagos de Montebello 404-6, **405**
Laguna Bacalar 296, **16**
Laguna Catemaco 252
Laguna de Sontecomapan 252-3
Laguna Manialtepec 467-8
Laguna Miramar 399-400
Laguna Santa María del Oro 512
lakes, see rivers & lakes
language 20, 23, 865-74
bus travel 862
courses 851
Mexican Spanish slang 870
language courses 851
Ensenada 711
Guadalajara 586
Guanajuato 653
Laz Paz 729
Mazunte 477
Mérida 305
Mexico City 101
Morelia 615
Oaxaca City 429-30
Pátzcuaro 626
Playa del Carmen 275
Puerto Escondido 459-60
Puerto Morelos 273
Puerto Vallarta 522
Querétaro 641
San Cristóbal de las Casas 364
San Miguel de Allende 665
Taxco 192-3

Veracruz City 210
Xalapa 221
Las Brisas 543
Las Islas Marías 507
Las Nubes 398
Las Palmitas 24
Las Pozas 688
Lázaro Cárdenas 546
legal matters 851-2
legends 806
León 658
lesbian travelers 126, 531, 849
Guadalajara 595
LGBTI travelers 126
libraries
Biblioteca Gertrudis Bocanegra 625
Biblioteca Pública de la Universidad Michoacana 613
literature 827-8, see also books
Loreto 723-5
Los Cabos Corridor 737, **738**
Los Mochis 775-7, **775**
Los Tuxtlas 252-3, **253**
lucha libre 820
luxury hotels 25

M
Madre Sal 407-8
Magdalena de Kino 769
Mahahual 294-5
malaria 850
Malinalco 201-2
Manzanillo 538-42, **539**
maps 852
marathons 754
markets **44**, **46**
Acapulco 572
Cancún 264
Cuernavaca 189
Guadalajara 586, **46**
Mercado Roma 24
Mercado San Juan de Dios 596-7, **26**
Mexico City 81, 85, 92, 101, 128-30
Oaxaca City 440
Pátzcuaro 625
Tehuantepec 488
Tepoztlán 179
Tequisquiapan 646
Tlacolula 447
Uruapan 633
Valles Centrales 450

masks 829
massages 459
Mata Ortiz 784
Matehuala 684
Maya 806-7, 418
Maya calendar 806, 807
Mazamitla 606
Mazatlán 493-506, **494**, **498**, **502**
Mazatlán-Durango Highway 24
Mazunte 476-9
measures 850
Mennonites 753
Mercado Roma 24
Mercado San Juan de Dios 596-7, **26**
Mérida 13, 301, 304-10, **302-3**, **311**, **13**, **31**, **340**
Mérida region 310-17, 320, **311**
metro 864
Metzabok 392
Mexcaltitán 506-7
Mexicali 715-16
Mexican jumping beans 771
Mexican Revolution 780, 814-15
Mexico City 11, 57, 62-139, **63**, **68-9**, **76-7**, **82-3**, **88-9**, **94**, **106-7**, **122**, **11**
accommodations 62, 103-9
activities 100
children, travel with 67
climate 62
courses 100-2
drinking 117-23
emergencies 130
entertainment 123-7
events 102-3
festival & events 102-3
food 62, 109-17
highlights 63
history 64-6
internet access 130-1
itineraries 64
medical services 131
nightlife 117-23
safe travel 130
shopping 127-30
sights 66-100
tourist information 132

tours 102
travel seasons 62
travel to/from 132-4, 136-7
travel within 134-9
walking tour 72, **72**
Mexico City region 140-202, **142-3**
mezcal 29, 118, 439, 834
Michoacán 612-35
Michoacán Coast 543-6
Mineral de Pozos 676
Mineral del Chico 152-4
mines
  Bocamina de San Ramón & Bocamina de San Cayetano 652
  Mina La Prieta 785
missions
  Baja 722
  Misión Nuestra Señora de Loreto 724
  Misión San Francisco Javier de Viggé-Biaundó 725
  Misión Santa Rosalía de Mulegé 722
Mitla 448-9
mobile phones 20, 854-5
Moctezuma 810
mole 436, 831, **47**
monarch butterflies 18, 30, 621-2, **18**
monasteries
  Convento de San Antonio de Padua 320
  Ex-Convento del Santo Desierto de Nuestra Señora del Carmen 99
  Templo de San Francisco 74-5
  Templo y Ex-Convento de San Juan Bautist 454
  Templo y Ex-Convento de San Pedro y San Pablo 454
  Templo y Ex-Convento de Santo Domingo 454
money 20, 21, 23, 852
  discount cards 848
monkeys **4**
Monte Albán 443-5, **444**
Monterrey 794-800 , **796**
accommodations 798
activities 795-7
drinking 798-9
events 797
festivals & events 797
food 798-9
history 795

medical services 799
safe travel 799
shopping 799-800
sights 795-7
tourist information 799
travel to/from 799
travel within 799-800
Monumento a la Independencia 84, **11**
monuments
  Monumento a El Pípila 649
  Monumento a la Corregidora 640
  Monumento a la Independencia 84, **11**
  Monumento a la Revolución 80-1
  Monumento a Los Niños Héroes 90
  Olmec Head 247
  Rotonda de los Jaliscenses Ilustres 583
  Volador Monument 238
Morelia 612-21, **614-15**
motorcycle travel 859
mountain biking 29
  Bahías de Huatulco 483
  Monterrey 800
  Parque de Aventura Barrancas del Cobre 756
mountaineering 167
movimiento crack 828-9
Mulegé 721-3
muralists 814, 823
murals
  Las Palmitas 24
  Museo Jardín del Agua 91
  Museo Mural Diego Rivera 78
  Pasaje Rodríguez 24
  Secretaría de Educación Pública 76
  Suprema Corte de Justicia 75
museums 27-8, 50, *see also* anthropological museums, archaeological museums, art galleries, history museums
  Anahuacalli 96
  Antiguo Colegio de San Ildefonso 77
  Café Museo Café 363
  Casa Chihuahua 779
  Casa de Arte Olga Costa-José Chávez Morado 652
  Casa de Cultura (Monterrey) 794

Casa de los Venados 329
Casa de Montejo 301-4
Casa Lereé 718
Casa Machado 493
Casa Museo Agustín Lara 246
Casa Museo Dr Belisario Domínguez 400
Casa-Museo Totomoxtle 227
Centro Cultural de Real de Catorce 685
Centro Cultural Mexiquense 197
Centro Ecológico Akumal 285
Ex-Hacienda San Gabriel de Barrera 650
Ex Teresa Arte Actual 74
Galería y Museo de Arte Popular 336
Horno3 797
La Esquina: Museo del Juguete Popular Mexicano 662
Mini-Zoológico Museo 246
MMAPO 183-4
MUCAL 638
Museo Agustín Lara 208
Museo Amparo 155
Museo Antiguo Convento Franciscano de Santa Ana 631
Museo Archivo de la Fotografía 73
Museo Bicentenario 1810-2010 660
Museo Bichos e Insectos 363
Museo Capitán Dulché 267
Museo Casa de Hidalgo 660
Museo Casa de Juárez (Chihuahua) 781
Museo Casa de Juárez (Oaxaca City) 427
Museo Casa de las Artesanías del Estado de Chihuahua 757
Museo Casa de León Trotsky 96
Museo Casa de Morelos 613
Museo Casa de Villa 779
Museo Casa de Xalapa 219
Museo Casa del Alfeñique 158
Museo Casa Natal de Morelos 613

Museo Comunitario 452

Museo Comunitario Balaa Xtee Guech Gulal 447

Museo Costumbrista de Sonora 772

Museo de Arte Sacro de Guadalajara 582

Museo de Artes Populares (Pátzcuaro) 624-5

Museo de Batopilas 763

Museo de Cultura de la Huasteca Tamuantzán 690

Museo de Culturas Populares 197

Museo de El Carmen 93

Museo de Historia Mexicana 796

Museo de Historia Natural 415

Museo de la Amistad México-Cuba 236

Museo de la Arquitectura Maya 335

Museo de la Ballena 24, 727

Museo de la Basílica de Guadalupe 100

Museo de la Ciudad 450 786

Museo de la Ciudad (Campeche) 335

Museo de la Ciudad (Chetumal) 298

Museo de la Ciudad (Querétaro) 639

Museo de la Ciudad de Cholula 164

Museo de la Ciudad de México 75

Museo de la Ciudad de Veracruz 207

Museo de la Ciudad Teodoro Cano 238

Museo de la Cuenca del Usumacinta 395

Museo de la Independencia Nacional 660

Museo de la Isla de Cozumel 279

Museo de la Marimba 351

Museo de la Medicina Maya 359

Museo de la Memoria 169

Museo de la Pintura Mural Teotihuacana 149

Museo de la Restauración de la República 639

Museo de la Revolución 157-8

Museo de la Secretaría de Hacienda y Crédito Público 74

Museo de la Tortura 74

Museo de las Aves de México 790

Museo de las Californias 702

Museo de las Culturas Afromestizas 575

Museo de las Culturas Populares 786

Museo de las Momias 652

Museo de los Altos de Chiapas 363

Museo de los Seris 768

Museo de María Félix 772

Museo de Minería 151

Museo de Sarape 790

Museo de Sitio (Palenque) 384

Museo de Títere 173

Museo del Ámbar de Chiapas 363

Museo del Arte Abstracto Manuel Felguérez 694

Museo del Café 351

Museo del Calendario 638

Museo del Calzado El Borceguí 101

Museo del Cuale 520

Museo del Desierto 790

Museo del Estanquillo 74

Museo del Ferrocarril (Puebla) 156

Museo del Ferrocarril (San Luis Potosí) 681

Museo del Juguete Antiguo México 101

Museo del Noreste 796

Museo del Objeto del Objeto 86

Museo del Origen 506

Museo del Tequila y el Mezcal 74

Museo del Vestido 227

Museo del Virreinato 679

Museo el Boleo 720

Museo El Cafétal Apan 225

Museo Ex-Hacienda El Lencero 224

Museo Federico Silva 678-9

Museo Francisco Goitia 695

Museo Francisco Villa 785

Museo Franz Mayer 79

Museo Frida Kahlo 95-6

Museo Guillermo Spratling 191

Museo Histórico de San Miguel de Allende 663

Museo Histórico del Oriente 180

Museo Histórico Naval 206

Museo Huichol 584

Museo Iconográfico del Quijote 650

Museo Indígena Huatápera 632

Museo Interactivo de Economía (MIDE) 73

Museo José Alfredo Jiménez 660

Museo José Luis Bello y González 158

Museo José Luis Cuevas 77

Museo Loyola 761

Museo Manuel M. Ponce 695

Museo Memoria y Tolerancia 79

Museo Mirador El Fuerte 751

Museo Morelense de Arte Popular 183-4

Museo Mulegé 722

Museo Nacional de Arquitectura 78

Museo Nacional de Culturas Populares 96

Museo Nacional de la Máscara 679

Museo Nacional de la Muerte 673

Museo Nacional de la Revolución 81

Museo Nacional de las Culturas 75

Museo Nacional del Virreinato 141

Museo Pantaleón Panduro 585

Museo Rafael Coronel 693

Museo Regional de Durango 786

Museo Regional de Guadalajara 581-2

Museo Regional de Guanajuato Alhóndiga de Granaditas 649-50

Museo Regional de Historia 675

Museo Regional de la Cerámica 585

Museo Regional de las Culturas de Occidente 606

Museo Regional de Nayarit 511

Museo Regional de Tlaxcala 169

Museo Regional Michoacano 612

Museo Regional Potosino 679

Museo Regional (Querétaro) 639

Museo Robert Brady 183

Museo Rufino Tamayo 427

Museo Salvador Ferrando 246

Museo Textil de Oaxaca 427

Museo Tuxteco 247

Museo Universitario de Artes Populares 609

Museo Universitario de Ciencias 95

Museo Vivo de Artes y Tradiciones Populares 169

Museo y Casa de Diego Rivera (Guanajuato) 649

Museo y Centro Cultural Menonita 753

Museo Zacatecano 694

Other Face of Mexico Gallery 663

Palacio de Gobierno 608

Palacio de Hierro 233

Papalote Museo del Niño 90-1, 185

Parque-Museo La Venta 416

Postal Museum 73

music 620, 824-6

cumbia 826

danzón 826

festivals 773, 825

música tropical 826

norteño 825

ranchera 825

N

Nahá 392

national parks & reserves 840-2, *see also* parks & gardens, wildlife reserves

Área de Protección de Flora y Fauna Cuatrociénegas 793

national parks &
reserves *continued*
Cerro de Venado 249
Parque de Aventura
Barrancas del Cobre
756-7
Parque Ecológico
Chipinque 800
Parque Marine Nacional
Bahía de Loreto 724
Parque Nacional
Constitución de 1857
714-15
Parque Nacional Desi-
erto de los Leones 99
Parque Nacional El Chico
152-4
Parque Nacional
Grutas de
Cacahuamilpa 195-6
Parque Nacional Isla
Contoy 271
Parque Nacional
Lagunas de Chacahua
468-9
Parque Nacional Sierra
San Pedro Mártir 715
Parque Nacional Volcán
Nevado de Colima
610-12
Parque Punta Sur 279-80
Reserva de la Biosfera
El Pinacate y Gran
Desierto de Altar 767
Reserva de la Biosfera El
Triunfo 408
Reserva de la Biosfera La
Encrucijada 408-9
Reserva de la Biosfera
Los Tuxtlas 252-3, **253**
Reserva de la Biosfera
Pantanos de Centla
417
Reserva de la Biosfera
Ría Celestún 317
Reserva de la Biosfera
Sian Ka'an 292-3
Reserva de la Biosfera
Sierra de la Laguna 734
Reserva de la Biosfera
Sierra Gorda 647
Reserva Ecológica de
Nanciyaga 252
Reserva Mariposa
Monarca 18, 621-3, **18**
Sierra de Álamos-Río
Cuchujaqui Flora &
Fauna Protection
Area 771

Nevado de Toluca 199
newspapers 850
Northern Central Highlands
60, 636-99, **637**
accommodations 636
climate 636
food 636
highlights 637, **637**
history 637-8
travel seasons 636
travel to/from 638
travel within 638
Northern Mexico 60, 743,
744-5
accommodations 743
climate 743
food 743
highlights 744-5, **744-5**
safe travel 746-7
travel seasons 743
travel to/from 747
Nuevo Casas Grandes
783-4
Nuevo Cine Mexicano 826

O
Oaxaca state 12, 59, 419-
90, **420-1**, **14**
accommodations 419
art 428
climate 419
food 419, **42**
highlights 420-1, **420-1**
history 422
travel seasons 419
Oaxaca City 12, 422-43,
424-5, **13**
accommodations 432-5
activities 429
courses 429-31
drinking 438-9
emergencies 441
entertainment 439-40
events 431-2
festivals 431-2
food 435-8
internet access 441
medical services 441
nightlife 438-9
shopping 440-1
sights 422-7
tourist information 441
tours 431
travel to/from 442-3
travel within 443
Ocosingo 377-8
Ocotlán 450-1

olive ridley turtles 407, 469,
544, *see also* turtles
Olmecs 805
opening hours 852
organized crime 802-3
Orizaba 232-5
Orozco, José Clemente
582, 823
Oxkintok 320

P
Pachuca 150-2
painting 822-4
palaces
Palacio de Atetelco 149
Palacio de Bellas
Artes 77
Palacio de Cortés 182-3
Palacio de Gobierno
(Aguascalientes) 675
Palacio de Gobierno
(Mérida) 304
Palacio de Gobierno
(Morelia) 613
Palacio de Gobierno
(Oaxaca City) 422-3
Palacio de Gobierno
(San Luis Potosí) 679
Palacio de Iturbide 74
Palacio de Justicia 613
Palacio de Minería 73
Palacio de
Quetzalpapálotl 148-9
Palacio de Tepantitla 149
Palacio de Tetitla 149
Palacio Municipal
(Mérida) 304
Palacio Nacional 70
Palacio Postal 73
Palenque 11, 380-90, **382**,
384-5, **10-11**, **36-7**
PAN 816
Papantla 238-40
parks & gardens
Alameda Central 78
Bosque Cuauhtémoc
614
Bosque de Chapultepec
86-7, 90-1
Cosmovitral Jardín
Botánico 196-7
Ex-Hacienda San Gabriel
de Barrera 650
Jardín Botánico
(Mexico City) 90
Jardín Botánico Claviejro
220
Jardín Botánico de
Acapulco 565
Jardín Botánico de
Vallarta 520

Jardín Botánico Dr
Alfredo Barrera Marín
273
Jardín Botánico El
Charco del Ingenio
662
Jardín de la Bombilla 93
Jardín Etnobotánico
426-7
Jardín Juárez
(Cuernavaca) 182
Los Cazos 606
Museo y Jardín de
Orquideas 225
Parque Alameda 233
Parque Ecológico
Macuiltépetl 219
Parque Ecológico Paso
Coyol 228
Parque España 85
Parque Fundidora 797
Parque Madero 351
Parque México 85
Parque Miguel Hidalgo
225
Parque-Museo La Venta
416
Parque Nacional Barranca
del Cupatitzio 632
Parque Paseo de los
Lagos 219
Parque Revolución 583
Parque Santa Lucía 304
Paseo Santa Lucía 797
Quinta Fernando Schmoll
645
Villa Luz 417
Viveros de Coyoacán 97
Parque de Aventura
Barrancas del Cobre
756-7
Parque Marine Nacional
Bahía de Loreto 724
Parque Nacional Con-
stitución de 1857 714-15
Parque Nacional Grutas de
Cacahuamilpa 195-6
Parque Nacional Sierra San
Pedro Mártir 715
Parras 791-3
Parroquia de San Miguel
Arcángel 662, **7**
Partido Acción Nacional
816
Partido Revolucionario
Institucional
Pasaje Rodríguez 24
Pátzcuaro 624-9, **626**
Paz, Octavio 827-8
photography 852
Pico de Orizaba 17, 235-6,
17, **837**

Pie de la Cuesta 561-2
Pirámide de la Luna 12, 147
Pirámide del Sol 12, 147, **12**
Pitiquito 769
planning 22-3, *see also individual regions*
  calendar of events 30-3
  children 54-6
  food 42-7
  highlights 8-9, **8-9**
  itineraries 34-41
  Mexico's regions 57-60
  repeat visitors 24
  travel to/from Mexico 858-60
  travel within Mexico 860-4
  visiting ruins 48-53
plants 840
Playa Colola 544
Playa del Carmen 275-9, **276**
Playa Delfines 467
Playa Escobilla 469
Playa La Ticla 544
Playa Maruata 544-5
Playa Ventura 574-5
Playa Zicatela **463**
Playas de Rosarito 709-10
plazas
  Gran Plaza (Monterrey) 795
  Jardín de la Marimba 351
  Parque Castillo 233
  Parque de 21 de Mayo 228
  Parque Juárez 218
  Plaza 31 de Marzo 362
  Plaza 400 Años 795-6
  Plaza (Chiapa de Corzo) 356
  Plaza Cívica 351
  Plaza de Armas (Chihuahua) 781
  Plaza de Armas (Durango) 786
  Plaza de Armas (Guadalajara) 581-3
  Plaza de la Liberación 583
  Plaza de las Tres Culturas 98
  Plaza de los Mariachis 583
  Plaza de Santa Veracruz 79
  Plaza Garibaldi 74
  Plaza Gertrudis Bocanegra 625
  Plaza Guadalajara 582

Plaza Hidalgo & Jardín Centenario 96
Plaza Juárez (Mexico City) 79
Plaza Miguel Hidalgo 645
Plaza Morelos 614
Plaza San Jacinto 93
Plaza Santa Catarina 97
Plaza Santo Domingo 75
Plaza Tapatía 583
Plaza Tolsá 73
Plaza Vasco de Quiroga 624
Zócalo (Mexico City) 66-7
Zócalo (Papantla) 238
Zócalo (Veracruz City) 206
Pochutla 469-70
Popocatépetl 166-7
population 803
Posada Barrancas 755-6
Posada, José Guadalupe 819
postal services 853
pre-Hispanic sites 48-53, **51**, **48-9**, **50**
PRI 815-16
Progreso 319-20
public holidays 853
public transportation 864
Puebla 154-63, **156-7**
Pueblos Mancomunados 452-4, **446-7**
Puerto Ángel 470-1
Puerto Arista 407
Puerto Escondido 456-67, **456-7**, **463**, **14**
Puerto López Mateos 726
Puerto Morelos 273-5
Puerto Nuevo 710
Puerto Peñasco 765-8
Puerto San Carlos 726-7
Puerto Vallarta 518-34, **519**, **524-5**
  accommodations 523-7
  activities 521
  courses 522
  drinking 530-2
  entertainment 532
  events 523
  festivals 523
  food 528-30
  medical services 533
  nightlife 530-2
  shopping 532
  sights 518-20
  tourist information 533
  tours 522-3

  travel to/from 533
  travel within 533-4
pulque 834
Punta Allen 293
Punta de Mita 517-18
Punta Lobos 742
Punta Villa Rica 244-5
pyramids 25-6, 821, *see also* archaeological sites
  Chula Zona Arqueológica 163-4
  El Castillo 323, 325, **325**, **325**
  La Ferrería 789
  Pirámide de la Luna 12, 147
  Pirámide de los Nichos 241-2
  Pirámide de Quetzalcóatl 186
  Pirámide de Tepozteco 177
  Pirámide del Sol 12, 147, **12**

Q
Querétaro 638-45, **640-1**
Querétaro state 638-48
Quiahuiztlán 244
Quintana Roo 255-300

R
rabies 850
rafting 29
  Bahías de Huatulco 483
  Jalcomulco 226
  Las Nubes 398
  Mazunte 477
railways 747-50, *see also* Ferrocarril Chihuahua Pacífico
Real de Catorce 684-9, **687**
Real del Monte 153
Reforma Agraria 397-8
religion 803, 818-19
Reserva de la Biosfera El Pinacate y Gran Desierto de Altar 767
Reserva de la Biosfera Sierra de la Laguna 734
Reserva de la Biosfera Los Tuxtlas 252-3, **253**
reserves, *see* national parks & reserves
Ribera Costa Azul 408-9
Río Bec 346
Río de Sonora Valley 769
Río Lagartos 332-3
Rio Verde 691

Rivera, Diego 80, 823
  collections 92, 233
  frescoes 76
  murals 70, 77, 91, 96, 183
  museums 78-9, 93, 219, 649
rivers & lakes
  Lago Arareko 761
  Lago de Chapala 601-5
  Lago de Pátzcuaro 629
  Lagos de Montebello 404-6
  Laguna Catemaco 250, 252
  Laguna de Sontecomapan 252-3
  Laguna Encantada 249
  Laguna Manialtepec 467-8
  Laguna Miramar 399-402
robbery 853
rock climbing
  Cerro de Metates 244
  Parque de Aventura Barrancas del Cobre 756
rodeos 596, 820
Rosario 496
Rulfo, Juan 827-8
Ruta del Vino 706
Ruta Puuc 315-16

S
Sacred Cenote 15, 325, 326, **15**, **325**
safety 746-7, 765, 850, 853-4
Salina Cruz 488
Saltillo 790-1
San Agustín Etla 452
San Agustinillo 474-6
San Andrés Tuxtla 248-50
San Bartolo Coyotepec 449-50
San Blas 507-11, **508-9**
San Carlos 770-1
San Cristóbal de las Casas 15, 358-73, **360-1**, **374**, **15**
  accommodations 365-8
  courses 364
  drinking 370
  entertainment 370-1
  events 365
  festivals 365
  food 368-9
  medical services 372
  nightlife 370
  shopping 371-2

San Cristóbal de las Casas
continued
  sights 359-63
  tourist information 372
  tours 364-5, 374
  travel to/from 372-3
  travel within 373
San Francisco 514-15
San Ignacio 718-19
San José del Cabo 734-6,
  735
San José del Pacífico 451
San Juan Chamula 374-5
San Juan de Alima 543
San Lorenzo Zinacantán
  375
San Luis Potosí 678-84,
  680
San Luis Potosí State
  678-91
San Martín Tilcajete 450
San Miguel de Allende 661-
  71, **664-5**, **2-3**
San Miguel de Cozumel
  279, 281-2, 283, **282**
San Patricio-Melaque 535-6
Santa Anna 813
Santa Elena 313-14
Santa Muerte 820
Santa Rosalía 720-1
Santiago Apoala 455
Santiago Tuxtla 247-8
Santo Domingo 413
Santuario de Atotonilco
  672-3
Santuario de la Cruz
  Parlante 293
Sayulita 515-17
scorpion bites 850
sculpture 822-4
Selva Lacandona 392, 394
shaman 250
shopping 27, *see also
  individual regions*
  language 868
Sierra de San Francisco
  719-20
Sierra Gorda Missions
  647-8
Sierra Norte 452-4
Siijil Noh Há 24
Sima de las Cotorras 355
sinkholes, *see* cenotes
Siqueiros, David Alfaro 823
slang (Mexican Spanish)
  870

smoking 850
snake bites 850
snorkeling, *see* diving &
  snorkeling
soccer, *see* fútbol
Soledad de Maciel 560-1
Spanish language 865-74
spas 25
spider monkeys **4**
sportfishing 497, 551, 566-7
stand-up paddleboarding
  515, 547, **38**
Sumidero Canyon 357
surfing 28-9
  Baja 741
  Barra de la Cruz 487
  Barra de Nexpa 545
  Boca de Pascuales 542-3
  Chacala 513
  Concepción Bamba 489
  Ensenada 710
  Isla Cozumel 281
  Isla de Todos Santos 710
  Ixtapa 549
  Mazatlán 496
  Oaxaca 459
  Pie de la Cuesta 561
  Playa La Ticla 544
  Puerto Escondido 457-8
  San Agustinillo 474
  San Blas 508
  Sayulita 515
  Todos Santos 741
  Troncones 546-8
swimming
  Akumel 285
  Cuatro Ciénegas 794
  Laguna Bacalar 296, **16**
  Monterrey 794
  Parras 792
  Progreso 319
  Puerto Morelos 273
  Tulum 290, 292
  Valladolid 330
  Yucatán Peninsula 254

T
Tabasco 58, 414-18, **348-9**
  climate 347
  highlights 348, 416-17,
    348-9
  travel seasons 347
Talismán 414
Talking Cross, Shrine to
  the 293
tamales 831, **45**
Tamayo, Rufino 823
Tankah 284

Tapachula 409-12, **410**
Tapalpa 605-6
Tapijulapa 417
Tarahumara people 754,
  762
Taxco 190-5, **192**
taxes 846, 852
taxis 864
Tecolutla 242-3
Tehuantepec 488
Telapo 604
telephone services 20, 21,
  854-5
temples 25-6
  Templo de las
    Inscripciones 382,
    10-11
  Templo de los Guerreros
    325, 327, **325**
Tenochtitlán 808
Teotihuacán 12, 146-50,
  805, **148**, **12**
Teotitlán del Valle 446-7
Tepic 511-12
Teposcolula 454-5
Tepotzotlán 141-4
Tepoztlán 176-80, **177**
tequila 29, 602-3, 833-4
  distilleries 601, 766
Tequila 601
Tequisquiapan 645-6
textiles 371, 632, 828-9
theft 853
thermal baths
  Aconchi 769
  Aguas Termales Reko-
    wata (Creel) 761
  Cuautla 180
  Ixtapan de la Sal 202
  Maguarachi 761
  San Miguel de Allende
    672
Tijuana 702-8, **704**, **38-9**
time 20, 855-6
Tingambato 634-5
tipping 23, 852
Tlacolula 447
Tlacotalpan 245-7
Tlaxcala 167-71, **168**
tlayudas 831, **14**
Tócuaro 631
Todos Santos 740-2
Toltecs 807
Toluca 196-9
Tonalá 406-7
Toniná 378-9
tortillas 831, **14**
tourist information 856
tourist permits 856-7

tours
  Álamos 772-3
  Bonampak 391
  Campeche 337
  Cañada de la Virgen 672
  Cancún 260
  Celestún 317
  Creel 757-8
  Ixtapa 549
  Laguna de la Media
    Luna 691
  Los Cabos Corridor 737
  Malinalco 201
  Mazatlán 497
  Mérida 305
  Mexico City 102
  Oaxaca City 431
  Pachuca 151
  Palenque 386
  Playa del Carmen 277
  Puebla 158
  Puerto Escondido 460
  Puerto Vallarta 522-3
  San Blas 508-9
  San Luis Potosí 681
  San Miguel de Allende
    665-6
  San Patricio-Melaque
    535
  Tlaxcala 170
  Toluca 197
  Troncones 547
  Tulum 288
  Xpuhil 345
  Zihuatanejo 551-2
towers
  Estela de Luz 85
  Torre BBVA Bancomer 85
  Torre Latinoameri-
    cana 75
  Torre Mayor 84-5
train travel 864
transportation
  language 862
travel to/from Mexico
  858-60
travel within Mexico
  860-4
Tres Zapotes 248
Troncones 546-8
Tubutama 769
Tula 144-6
Tulum 286-90, **287**, **288-
  9**, **35**, **50**
turtles 242, 407, 408, 469,
  544, 838
Tuxpan 236-8
Tuxtla Gutiérrez 350-5,
  352-3

typhoid 850
Tzintzuntzan 631

U
ultramarathons 754
Unión Juárez 413
universities
    Ciudad Universitaria
        93-5
    Universidad de
        Guanajuato 652
urbanization 817-18, 843
Ures 769
Urique 753-5
Uruapan 631-4
Uxmal 310-13, **312**, **26**

V
vacations 853
vaccinations 850
Valladolid 328-31, **329**
Valle de Bravo 199-201
Valle de Etla 451-2
Valle de Guadalupe 706
Valle de las Ranas y los
    Hongos 760
Valle de los Monjes 760
Valle de Tlacolula 445-9
Valle de Zimatlán 449-51
Valles Centrales 443-52,
    446-7
vegans 833
vegetarians 833
Velázquez de León,
    Josefina 834
Veracruz 58, 203-53
    accommodations 203
    climate 203
    food 203
    highlights 204, **204**
    history 205
    travel seasons 203
Veracruz City 205-16,
    208-9
Villa del Oeste 789
Villa, Francisco 'Pancho'
    780, 814-15
Villahermosa 414-18
Villa Rica 244
Vive Latino 825
visas 20, 856-7, 858
voladores 239, 242, 584
volcanoes 767, 836
    Cerro del Pinacate 767
    Iztaccíhuatl 166-7
    La Malinche 173
    Popocatépetl 166-7
    Volcán Ceboruco 512

Volcán de Fuego 610
Volcán Nevado de
    Colima 611
Volcán Paricutín 17,
    635, **17**
Volcán Tacaná 413
Volcán Paricutín 17, 635, **17**
volunteering 242, 431,
    472, 857

W
water 850
waterfalls
    Agua Azul 379
    Cascada Bola de Oro
        225
    Cascada Cola de la
        Serpiente 455
    Cascada Cusárare
        (Creel) 761
    Cascada de Basaseachi
        761
    Cascada de las
        Golondrinas 392
    Cascada de Texolo 227
    Cascada de Tamul
        690, **16**
    Cascada de Tzaráracua
        634
    Cascada del Salto 174
    Cascada Wejlib-Já
        391-2
    El Aguacero 355
    El Chiflón 402-3
    El Salto 605
    Huasteca Potosina 690
    Las Brisas 174
    Misol-Ha 379
    Salto de Eyipantla 249
weather 20, 30-3, see
    also individual regions
weights 850
Western Central Highlands
    59, 576-635, **578-9**
    climate 576
    food 576
    highlights 578, **578-9**
    history 577
    travel seasons 576
whales 720, 839
whale-watching
    Ensenada 711
    Guerrero Negro 717
    Isla Holbox 272
    La Paz 727-8
    Parque Nacional Isla
        Contoy 271
    Puerto Escondido 458
    Puerto López Mateos 726
    Puerto San Carlos 726-7

wildlife 838-40
wildlife reserves, see
    also national parks
    & reserves, parks &
    gardens
    Cocodrilario 548
    El Refugio de Potosí
        559-60
wildlife-watching 29
    Guerrero Negro 717
    La Paz 727-8
    La Ventana 732-3
    La Ventanilla 479
    Parque Nacional Sierra
        San Pedro Mártir 715
    Playa Colola 544
    Playa Delfines 467
    Playa Escobilla 469
    Playa Ventura 574-5
    Puerto Escondido 458
    Puerto Peñasco 766
    Puerto Vallarta 522
    Punta Lobos 742
    Reserva Mariposa
        Monarca 18, 621-3, **18**
    San Agustinillo 474
    Xcacel-Xcacelito 284
windsurfing 733
wine 793, 835
wineries
    Parras 793
    Ruta del Vino 706
    Valle de Guadalupe 706
    Vinícola L.A. Cetto 703
women travelers 857
woodwork 829
World Heritage sites
    Campeche 333-9
    Guanajuato 648-58
    Instituto Cultural de
        Cabañas 583
    Morelia 612-21
    Paquimé 784
    Reserva de la Biosfera
        El Pinacate y Gran
        Desierto de Altar 767
    Reserva Mariposa
        Monarca 18, 621-3, **18**
    Sierra de San Francisco
        719-20
    Sierra Gorda Missions
        647-8
    Teotihuacán 12, 146-50,
        805, **148**, **12**
    Tequila 601
    Tlacotalpan 245-7
    Xochicalco 186
    Xochimilco 92
    Yagul 447-8
    Zacatecas 691-9, **692**
wrestling 820

X
Xalapa 217-24, **218-9**
Xcacel-Xcacelito 284
Xcalak 295
Xico 226-42
Xochicalco 186
Xochimilco 92
Xochitécatl 171-3
Xpujil 345-6
Xtacumbilxunaan 342-3

Y
Yagul 447-8
Yanhuitlán 454-5
Yaxchilán 390-1, 396-7,
    396
yellow fever 850
yoga
    Puerto Escondido 459
    San Cristóbal de las
        Casas 364
    Zihuatanejo 551
Yohualichán 176
Yucatán Peninsula 58, 254-
    335, **256-7**
    climate 254
    food 254
    highlights 256-7
    history 255
Yucatán state 300-33

Z
Zacatecas 691-9, **692**
Zacatecas state 691-699
Zapata, Emiliano 181, 814
Zapatistas 364
Zempoala 216-17
Zihuatanejo 550-9, **552-3**
zip-lining
    El Chiflón 403
    Las Nubes 398
    Parque de Aventura
        Barrancas del Cobre
        756
    Urique 755
Zipolite 471-4
Zitácuaro 623-4
Zócalo (Mexico City) 66-7
Zona de Montaña 605-7
Zona Maco 823
zoos
    Cocodrilario 507
    Parque-Museo La Venta
        414
    Zoológico de
        Chapultepec 90
    Zoológico Miguel Álvarez
        del Toro 350

NOTES

CLAARTJE SCHOUTEN

South America
on a shoestring

lonely planet

#1 best seller

LONELY PLANET IN THE WILD

Send your 'Lonely Planet in the Wild' photos to social@lonelyplanet.com
We share the best on our Facebook page every week!

Map Legend

Sights

- Beach
- Bird Sanctuary
- Buddhist
- Castle/Palace
- Christian
- Confucian
- Hindu
- Islamic
- Jain
- Jewish
- Monument
- Museum/Gallery/Historic Building
- Ruin
- Shinto
- Sikh
- Taoist
- Winery/Vineyard
- Zoo/Wildlife Sanctuary
- Other Sight

Activities, Courses & Tours

- Bodysurfing
- Diving
- Canoeing/Kayaking
- Course/Tour
- Sento Hot Baths/Onsen
- Skiing
- Snorkeling
- Surfing
- Swimming/Pool
- Walking
- Windsurfing
- Other Activity

Sleeping

- Sleeping
- Camping

Eating

- Eating

Drinking & Nightlife

- Drinking & Nightlife
- Cafe

Entertainment

- Entertainment

Shopping

- Shopping

Information

- Bank
- Embassy/Consulate
- Hospital/Medical
- Internet
- Police
- Post Office
- Telephone
- Toilet
- Tourist Information
- Other Information

Geographic

- Beach
- Gate
- Hut/Shelter
- Lighthouse
- Lookout
- Mountain/Volcano
- Oasis
- Park
- Pass
- Picnic Area
- Waterfall

Population

- Capital (National)
- Capital (State/Province)
- City/Large Town
- Town/Village

Transport

- Airport
- Border crossing
- Bus
- Cable car/Funicular
- Cycling
- Ferry
- Metro station
- Monorail
- Parking
- Petrol station
- Subway/Subte station
- Taxi
- Train station/Railway
- Tram
- Underground station
- Other Transport

Note: Not all symbols displayed above appear on the maps in this book

Routes

- Tollway
- Freeway
- Primary
- Secondary
- Tertiary
- Lane
- Unsealed road
- Road under construction
- Plaza/Mall
- Steps
- Tunnel
- Pedestrian overpass
- Walking Tour
- Walking Tour detour
- Path/Walking Trail

Boundaries

- International
- State/Province
- Disputed
- Regional/Suburb
- Marine Park
- Cliff
- Wall

Hydrography

- River, Creek
- Intermittent River
- Canal
- Water
- Dry/Salt/Intermittent Lake
- Reef

Areas

- Airport/Runway
- Beach/Desert
- Cemetery (Christian)
- Cemetery (Other)
- Glacier
- Mudflat
- Park/Forest
- Sight (Building)
- Sportsground
- Swamp/Mangrove

Anna Kaminski

The Mexican Way of Life, Directory, Transportation Anna's love affair with Mexico began in 1999, when she crossed the land border to Tijuana; she liked the merry chaos so much that she ended up backpacking all the way down to Cabo San Lucas. Since then, she's put her university background in Latin American history and culture to good use, coming back on many occasions to teach English in Oaxaca, visit every major ancient ruin in the country, learn to surf in Sayulita, criss-cross the country by bus, ride the country's only train and travel far and wide in search of the perfect fish taco. Anna tweets at @ACKaminski. Anna also contributed to the Plan Your Trip chapters of this edition.

Tom Masters

Copper Canyon & Northern Mexico Tom has had an extended love affair with Mexico ever since working in the jungle of Chiapas as a documentary producer in 2005. Since then he has lived in Mexico City and written widely about many different parts of the country for Lonely Planet. In writing the monster Copper Canyon & Northern Mexico chapter, Tom particularly found himself loving Álamos, Parras and Monterrey's reinvigorated Barrio Antiguo, as well as finally getting to do the Copper Canyon Railway. You can find Tom online at www.tommasters.net.

Josephine Quintero

Baja California Josephine was married for many years to a Mexican American with a large extended family, leading to a healthy exposure to mariachi music and margaritas. She made frequent trips over the border from her home in San Diego and continues to be enthralled by the heady mix of vibrant culture, wonderful people, fabulous food and all that history. Josephine now lives in Andalucía, Spain. A highlight of this trip was discovering the fabulous urban art in downtown Tijuana.

Read more about Josephine at lonelyplanet.com/members/josephinequintero

Brendan Sainsbury

Western Central Highlands An expat Brit now living near Vancouver, Canada, Brendan first went to Mexico in the 1990s on an ill-conceived long-distance bike ride from Veracruz to Mexico City. Having survived manic driving, thin air and a minor earthquake, he went back in 2004 to get married on a Pacific beach. This book is his second Mexican sojourn for Lonely Planet, although he has also researched and written guides to Cuba, Spain, Peru and Jamaica. When not climbing youthful volcanoes or searching for enlightenment in pre-Hispanic ruins, Brendan likes relaxing with his flamenco guitar, watching *Dr Who* and following the exploits of Southampton Football Club.

Andy Symington

Central Pacific Coast Australian and based in Spain, Andy is a widely experienced guidebook author who has written or co-written more than 100 titles with Lonely Planet and other publishers. Latin America is one of his life passions: on this trip he revelled in the superb Pacific coast seafood and tried to catch as many sunsets as possible from just beyond the breakers.

Phillip Tang

Mexico City, Around Mexico City A degree in Latin American studies brought Phillip Tang to these shores, and over a decade later he calls Mexico City home, between stints living in Sydney and London. He writes about travel on his two loves, Asia and Latin America, and has contributed to Lonely Planet's guides to China, Japan, Korea, Peru and Mexico. Find his Mexico Insta-photos from this visit through philliptang.co.uk.

Lucas Vidgen

Chiapas & Tabasco, Yucatán Peninsula Lucas first visited Mexico back in 2002, breezing through the Yucatán long enough to be captivated by the lush scenery and irresistible food. Later he moved to Guatemala, which served as a good base for exploring Chiapas and the rest of the Mundo Maya. Lucas has contributed to a variety of Lonely Planet titles, mostly in Central and South America. Back home he publishes – and very occasionally works on – Quetzaltenango's leading nightlife magazine, *XelaWho* (www.xelawho.com).

OUR STORY

A beat-up old car, a few dollars in the pocket and a sense of adventure. In 1972 that's all Tony and Maureen Wheeler needed for the trip of a lifetime – across Europe and Asia overland to Australia. It took several months, and at the end – broke but inspired – they sat at their kitchen table writing and stapling together their first travel guide, *Across Asia on the Cheap*. Within a week they'd sold 1500 copies. Lonely Planet was born.

Today, Lonely Planet has offices in Dublin, Franklin, London, Melbourne, Oakland, Beijing and Delhi, with more than 600 staff and writers. We share Tony's belief that 'a great guidebook should do three things: inform, educate and amuse'.

OUR WRITERS

John Noble

Oaxaca John has been making extended trips to Mexico for over three decades and has had a big hand in every edition of this guide since edition 3, wandering from Tijuana to Chetumal and many, many places in between. He's climbed volcanoes, boated down jungle rivers, explored the barrios of Mexico City and understood why Oaxacans revere mezcal, and he's already looking forward to the next trip. Originally from England's Ribble Valley, John has lived for 20 years in the land of Mexico's old colonial masters, Spain. John also wrote Mexico Today, History, The Arts, Landscapes & Wildlife, Exploring Mexico's Ancient Ruins and several other Plan Your Trip chapters.

Kate Armstrong

Northern Central Highlands As Australian as a kangaroo, but a Latina (she believes) in a former life, Kate visits Mexico regularly. Covering the silver cities for the fifth time for Lonely Planet, she headed to festivals, hiked gorges in Sierra Gorda, and ate kilos of gorditas (filled dough pockets). She plunged over, in and under every waterfall in the Huasteca Potosina, and talked, danced and ate her way through the magic of Mexico. She is a freelance travel writer; see www.katearmstrongtravelwriter.com and twitter @nomaditis. Kate also contributed to The Mexican Kitchen chapter and several Plan Your Trip chapters.

Stuart Butler

Veracruz Stuart first traveled to Mexico in the late 1990s as part of a longer trip through Latin America. Mexico stood out for him thanks to its heady mix of beaches, wildlife, surf, mountains and a rich culture, and he has since made a number of repeat visits. Hailing from southwest England Stuart now lives on the beautiful beaches of southwest France, close to the Spanish border, with his wife and young son and daughter. He is also the co-author of many Spain-based Lonely Planet books.

John Hecht

Yucatán Peninsula John has spent more than 20 years down Mexico way, during which time he has contributed to numerous editions of Lonely Planet's Mexico and Central America books. Among the most recent titles, he has worked on the past two editions of LP's *Cancún, Cozumel & the Yucatán*. He also wrote and produced a series of short-form videos in the Yucatán for Lonely Planet TV. Mom is starting to give up hope that he'll ever return to the good ol' USA.

OVER PAGE | MORE WRITERS

Published by Lonely Planet Publications Pty Ltd
ABN 36 005 607 983
15th edition – September 2016
ISBN 978 1 78657 0239
© Lonely Planet 2016   Photographs © as indicated 2016
10 9 8 7 6 5 4 3 2 1
Printed in Singapore

Although the authors and Lonely Planet have taken all reasonable care in preparing this book, we make no warranty about the accuracy or completeness of its content and, to the maximum extent permitted, disclaim all liability arising from its use.